World Resources 1988-89

World Resources 1988-89

A Report by
The World Resources Institute

and

The International Institute for
Environment and Development

In Collaboration with

The United Nations
Environment Programme

Basic Books, Inc., New York

The cover is a Landsat 5 satellite Thematic Mapper image of China's Huang He (Yellow River) delta and the Bo Hai Sea. Various agricultural and industrial facilities are clearly visible.

This image, collected on November 19, 1986, was one of the first transmitted to and processed by the new Landsat receiving station in Beijing, which began distribution of Landsat data in January 1987.

It was provided courtesy of Earth Observation Satellite Company of Lanham, Maryland.

The World Resources Institute and the International Institute for Environment and Development gratefully acknowledge permission to reprint from the following sources:

Part II: Table 2.1, Population Reference Bureau; Table 2.3, Allan Guttmacher Institute; Tables 2.4 and 2.5, The Population Council; Tables 2.10 and 2.12, Springer-Verlag; Table 2.11, Macmillan Publishing; Figures 2.1 and 2.2, Population Reference Bureau; Box 2.1, Table 1, University of California Press; Box 2.1, Figure 1, David Seckler and R.K. Sampath; Tables 3.1, 3.2, and 3.3, Oxford University Press; Table 3.4, Robert Fox; Table 3.6, International Statistical Institute; Table 4.4, Technology Management Group; Table 4.5, Resources for the Future; Figure 4.2, Harwood Academic Publishers; Box 4.1, Table 1, Consultative Group on International Agricultural Research; Figure 5.1, Smithsonian Institution; Figure 5.2, University of Washington, College of Forest Resources; Tables 6.1, 6.2, 6.4, 6.5, and 6.6, International Union for Conservation of Nature and Natural Resources; Table 6.7, World Wildlife Fund; Tables 7.1 and 7.2, British Petroleum International; Box 7.1, Table 2, World Energy Conference; Table 8.1, American Geophysical Union; Table 8.5, *Nature*; Figure 8.1, Oxford University Press; Figure 8.3, *Ambio*; Figure 8.4, Association of State and Interstate Water Pollution Control Administra-

tors; Table 9.1, International Union for the Conservation of Nature and Natural Resources, Conservation Monitoring Center; Table 9.2, Organization of American States; Figure 9.3, University of California Press, the Regents of the University of California; Figure 9.4, Australian Government Publishing Service; Figure 10.1, Pergamon Press Ltd.; Figure 10.2 and Figure 11.2, National Academy Press; Figure 11.3, American Geophysical Union; Figure 11.4, University of Chicago Press; Figure 11.5, *Nature*; Box 11.3, Figure 1, University of Hamburg; Tables 12.5 and 12.6, Cambridge University Press.

Part III: Tables 13.1 and 13.2, National Botanical Research Institute (India).

Part IV: Table 20.5, World Bureau of Metal Statistics; Table 22.4, Tanker Advisory Center; Figure 23.1, Macmillan Journals Ltd., International Glaciological Society, and Pergamon Press Ltd.

World Map, Rand McNally & Co.

Library of Congress International Standard Serial Number:
0887-0403
ISBN 0-465-09240-3 Cloth
ISBN 0-465-09241-1 Paper
Printed in the United States of America

Graphic design and production assistance provided by
The Forte Group, Alexandria, Virginia
88 89 MPC 9 8 7 6 5 4 3 2 1

Contents

The red tabs along the sides of pages connect Part II chapters with the corresponding data tables in Part IV.

Preface

The publication of *World Resources 1988–89* brings a number of new dimensions to the *World Resources* series. Most importantly, it marks the joining of forces of the United Nations Environment Programme (UNEP) with those of the World Resources Institute (WRI) and the International Institute for Environment and Development (IIED) in our ongoing efforts to provide the most objective and up-to-date report of conditions and trends in the world's natural resources, to a global audience.

UNEP serves a central catalytic role in bringing together the nations of the world to seek solutions to such vital issues as protecting the global environment and achieving sustainable economic growth. UNEP's collaboration in *World Resources* will help ensure that the series has access to the best available data sources, including the Global Environment Monitoring System networks. In addition, its links to both governmental and nongovernmental organizations will help the Report identify critical issues and reach the broadest possible audience around the world.

WRI, IIED, and UNEP share the conviction that the *World Resources* series can best contribute to management of the world's natural resources by providing an independent, nongovernmental perspective on these critical global issues. Therefore, final responsibility for substance and editorial content of the series remain with WRI and IIED.

World Resources 1988–89 also marks the shift of the series from an annual to a biennial cycle. This decision reflects our view that the analyses contained in each volume remain timely for more than one year and the data do not change rapidly enough to make an annual report essential. At the same time, the longer cycle enables us to make greater efforts to ensure a more complete distribution of *World Resources* to its intended audience.

Within one year of publication, *World Resources 1986*, the first volume in the series, had reached about 16,000 users in one language: English. Since then, substantial progress has been made in reaching a much wider audience. About 60,000 copies of *World Resources* in English, Chinese, and Arabic are now in the hands of policymakers, resource managers, teachers, students, the media, and other concerned individuals. A Spanish edition of *World Resources 1987* will be published shortly. The enthusiasm with which each new language edition has been received encourages us in our efforts to make *World Resources* even more widely available.

In our desire to keep the series fresh and to have each volume bring new insights to the issues of natural resources and the environment, *World Resources 1988–89* also marks the introduction of a new regional focus to the publication. While the overall report will remain strongly global, each volume in the series will devote extra attention to the problems faced by a particular region of the world and the solutions being found in that area. *World Resources 1988–89* places this focus on Asia.

The effort required to put together *World Resources 1988–89* was enormous. The *World Resources* staff have again succeeded in assembling and analyzing a massive and unique collection of information on conditions and trends in global natural resources and the environment. We commend them for their accomplishment. The Editorial Advisory Board, chaired by Dr. M.S. Swaminathan, continued to provide active advice and support at all stages of the project.

We wish to thank the many other organizations that have joined with us in supporting this endeavor: The World Bank; the United Nations Development Programme; the Inter-American Development Bank; the Asian Development Bank; the Canadian International Development Agency; the John D. and Catherine T. MacArthur Foundation; the United States Environmental Protection Agency; the National Geographic Society; the Swedish International Development Authority; the United Kingdom Overseas Development Administration; and the Finnish International Development Agency. Their financial commitment to the continuation of the *World Resources* series and its distribution throughout the developing world help to make this all possible.

James Gustave Speth
President
World Resources Institute

Brian W. Walker,
President
International Institute
for Environment and
Development

Mostafa K. Tolba
Executive Director
United Nations Environment Programme

Acknowledgments

World Resources 1988–89 is a product of the commitment and dedication of many people, without whose support and hard work this volume could not have been produced. First, we wish to thank those who provided the necessary support for both the production and distribution of *World Resources*: The World Bank; the United Nations Development Programme; the Inter-American Development Bank; the Asian Development Bank; the Canadian International Development Agency; the John D. and Catherine T. MacArthur Foundation; the United States Environmental Protection Agency; the National Geographic Society; the Swedish International Development Authority; the United Kingdom Overseas Development Administration; and the Finnish International Development Agency.

The advice and assistance of our many colleagues at the World Resources Institute, the International Institute for Environment and Development, and the United Nations Environment Programme, have been invaluable at every stage of the planning and production of *World Resources 1988–89*. Their unfailing willingness to take the time to review innumerable drafts and suggest improvements has made a major contribution to this project. We are grateful to them all.

Many of the chapters were drafted (partly or entirely) by outside writers and technical experts. Final responsibility for the chapters as they now appear rests with the *World Resources* staff, but the expertise and considerable talents of these outside individuals are reflected throughout the book. They are: John Ross, Raisa Scriabine Smith, and Catherine Karr (Population and Health); Dennis Rondinelli (Human Settlements); Sharif Elmusa, Michael Dover, and Robert Livernash (Food and Agriculture); Alan Grainger, Maryam Niamir, and Dean Treadwell (Forests and Rangelands); David Harmon (Wildlife and Habitat); Lawrence Mosher and David Zoellner (Freshwater); Vaclav Smil and Wil Lepkowski (Global Systems and Cycles); and David Harmon and Mohan Wali (Rehabilitating and Restoring Degraded Lands).

Scores of people in international organizations, governments, universities, nongovernmental organizations and elsewhere provided data, research material, and advice, and reviewed drafts of chapters. We are grateful for their generous support and assistance. They are: Richard Ackerman, William Alonso, Kathryn H. Anderson, Lief Andren, Arthur J. Askew, Christian Averous, William Bagby, Patricia Baldi, Robert F. Barnes, Jonathan Barzdo, Stephen Batt, Charles M. Becker, K. Becker, Avrom Bendavid-Val, Nora Berwick, Ulrich Bick, Clark Binkley, Thomas A. Boden, L. Brader, Mary Brandt, David J. Brooks, David Brower, Robert Bruck, E.F. Bruenig, M.A.S. Burton, John Cairns, Jr., Joseph Chamie, D.V. Chapman, Eric Chetwynd, David Cieslikowski, Maureen Clifford, William Clive, Susan H. Cochrane, M.J. Cockerell, R. Caron Cooper, Pierre Crossen, Clif Curtis, Dana Dalrymple, Raymond Dasmann, Guilliamo Davila, Ruth DeFries, H.W. de Koning, Shanta Devarajan, Roger Diedrich, James Dobbin, Ian Douglas, Betty Dow, Harold Dregne, Siegfried Dyck, Steve Edwards, Daniel Elder, Hari Eswaran, E. Gardner Evans, Julian Evans, H. Ezekiel, Malin Falkenmark, Louise Fallon, John Firor, Robert Fox, Pietro Garau, John Gladwell, Peter Gleick, José Goldemberg, Leo Goldstone, Elizabeth F. Gormley, Vivien Gornitz, Jean Gorse, Jeffrey Gritzner, Hans Groot, Gian Carlo Guarda, John Gulland, Robert J. Gurney, Andrew Hamer, James G. Hanson, Jeremy Harrison, Alberto Harth, Carl Haub, Harold Heady, Don Heisel, Ginette Hemley, John Henry, Bernard Heusch, Arthur Heyman, P. Hiernaux, Graham Higgins, Howard W. Hjort, Hart Hodges, John Hoffman, Robert Hofman, Polly Hoppin, R.A. Houghton, Norman Hudson, Maynard Hufschmidt, Ishrat Husain, Nurul Islam, Peter V. Jackson, Larry Jahn, Graeme Kelleher, Mick Kelly, M.A.K. Khalil, Lee Kimball, Alan Knesse, Mark Kosmo, Gunnar Kullenberg, J. Labrousse, J.P. Lanley, Ronal Larson, Christine Leon, Per Ljung, Lars P. Ludvigsen, H. Gyde Lund, Jack Mabbutt, Gordon MacDonald, Judy Maguire, Dennis Mahar, M. Jean Margat, Dave Mathis, David McCauley, Mike McCloskey, Arthur McKenzie, Jerry Melillo, Thomas W. Merrick, Donald Messerschmidt, Michel Meybeck, Volker Mohnen, David Moody, Paul Mudroch, Norman Myers, Virginia Fox-Norse, Anthony R. Olsen, Dale Pahl, Theodore Panayotou, K. Panzer, Francis Paraboni, Walter Parham, David W. Pearce, Rob Peters, Tim Phipps, Bruce Piasecki, Phyllis T. Piotrow, Debbie Pressman, W. Robert Rangeley, R.A. Rassmussen, Manny Ratafia, Amulya K. N. Reddy, John F. Richards, F. Riveros, G. Philip Robertson, Mike Robinson, Peter Rogers, Allan G. Rosenfield, Thomas Rosswall, Matthew Sagers, Fred T. Sai, Eneas

(continued on next page)

Salati, Rigoberto Sandoval, Stephen Sanford, Hernan Sanhueza, J.S. Sarma, M. Satin, Mark Schaeffer, Jan Schaug, Roger Sedjo, Cynthia Pollock Shea, Kenneth Sherman, K.D. Singh, John Skinner, David M. Smith, Ethan T. Smith, Mark Smith, Wim Sombroeck, Joseph Speidel, Thomas Spence, Walter Spofford, Bevan B. Stein, John Sutton, Richard Tabor, Jane Thornback, Steven Tibbitt, Michael Tillman, Sylvia Tognetti, Jan Troensegaard, Dennis Trout, Jeff Tschirley, Arthur C. Upton, John Vallentyne, Hassan Virji, R. Vollenweider, Alejo Von Der Pahlen, H.J. von Maydell, Vijay Vyas, Philip Wardle, Greg Watters, Michael Weber, Harold Weeks, Mary Beth Weinberger, Gary Wetterberg, Alan T. White, Gilbert White, Diane Wickland, David Wilcove, Richard Wiles, John C. Wilkerson, Dean Wilkinson, Michael Williams, Phyllis Windle, John P. Wise, Douglas A. Wolfe, T. Woodhead, Daniel Yergin, Garth Youngberg, Alfredo Sfeir-Younis, Montague Yudelman, Bernard Zahuranic, William Zajack, Sami Zarqa, Zhongping Zhu.

The production of this volume was an enormous task that involved a talented team of copy editors, fact checkers, proofreaders and other staff. We thank them all for their dedication, skills, hard work, and high professional standards. This team included Terry Stutzman (production assistant); Sheila Mulvihill, Ruth Williams, and Elizabeth Kraft (copy editors); Susan P. Walker, Susan Garbini, and Douglas Fuller (fact checkers); and Bart Brown (indexer). Paulette M.E. Stevens performed an outstanding job as manuscript production supervisor, overseeing the team of production typists including: Richard W. Schooley, II, Lisa Burden Yancy, Edward W. Parks, and Barbara A. Sistrunk. Once again, Maurice Allen entered the data for Part IV with unfailing accuracy.

Finally, we wish to acknowledge the excellent design and production work of The Forte Group of Alexandria, Virginia.

J.A.B.

1. Executive Summary

The issues of natural resource management and human impacts on the environment have begun to emerge at the forefront of international and national concerns. Since publication of *World Resources 1987*, several important events have signaled this growing awareness and concern:

■ The release of the report by the World Commission on Environment and Development, *Our Common Future*, calling for a concerted effort by all nations "to begin managing environmental resources to ensure both sustainable human progress and human survival."

■ The signing by 30 nations and the European Community of the Montreal Protocol to the Convention for Protection of the Ozone Layer, which calls for a 50 percent reduction in the production of ozone-depleting chlorofluorocarbons by 1999.

■ The entry into force of the protocol to the 1979 Convention on Long-Range Transboundary Air Pollution, which requires participating nations to reduce by 1993 either national sulfur emissions or their transboundary flows by 30 percent from 1980 levels.

■ The growing recognition by the development community of the important relationship between the environment and development, exemplified by the President of the World Bank's statement that "sound ecology is good economics . . . . [T]he objectives of sustainable economic growth, poverty alleviation, and environmental protection are often mutually reinforcing."

Providing impetus for these positive actions, however, are the continuing signs of degradation and destruction of our world environment and their effects on people:

■ In 1988, scientists found the first strong evidence that depletion of the protective ozone layer has already occurred over the Northern Hemisphere, not just over uninhabited Antarctica.

■ Deforestation of life-supporting tropical forests and woodlands continues at the rate of 11 million hectares per year.

■ Over 60 percent of the world's productive drylands (rangelands, rainfed croplands, and irrigated drylands) are believed to have suffered moderate to severe degradation of biological productivity, which can lead to desert-like conditions.

■ Since 1980, the number of malnourished people in developing countries has increased 30 percent, and each year the world population grows by another 84 million people.

In this setting, *World Resources 1988-89* brings together up-to-date data and new analyses of conditions and trends in the world's natural resources. As in prior years, this volume has four main sections. Part I, Perspectives, is an executive summary. Part II, World Resources Reviews, is devoted to individual resource areas such as food and agriculture, energy, freshwater, and atmosphere and climate. Part II also includes two chapters that cut across these individual resource areas: global systems and cycles, and policies and institutions. This year, the chapter on policies and institutions examines economic policies and natural resource management in developing countries.

1 Executive Summary

Part III, World Resources Issues, focuses on the critical issue of rehabilitating and restoring degraded lands. Ten chapters in Part IV, World Resources Data Tables, correspond to each of the Part II chapters except the one on global systems and cycles. Part IV has an additional chapter on basic economic indicators. This executive summary discusses the Parts II and IV chapters on the same topic together.

Beginning with *World Resources 1988–89*, each volume of *World Resources* will devote special attention to a particular region. This volume focuses on Asia. At the end of the summary, a special section describes this Asian focus.

POPULATION AND HEALTH
(Chapters 2 and 15)

Population

The world population is growing rapidly, fueled by high growth rates in developing countries. The global population doubled between 1950 and 1987, reaching 5 billion. Another billion will likely be added by 1998, and the United Nations projects that the population in 2025 will exceed 8.2 billion. Ninety percent of the growth will occur in the developing world. Although many developing countries' growth rates have been falling for more than a decade, these countries still have relatively high fertility rates and large proportions of their populations are in the reproductive years. In many African countries, population growth is *accelerating*, and by 2025, Africa's projected population will about equal the combined populations of Europe and North and South America.

Some countries emphasize fertility reduction as a national policy; others ignore it or give it low priority. Political attention, however, can be critical to whether fertility reduction efforts actually increase acceptance of contraceptives. A 1985 study found that, at a given level of national socioeconomic development, contraceptive use and declining birth rates are related to the strength of a government's fertility reduction program.

China and Sri Lanka have particularly strong government fertility-reduction programs, and contraceptive prevalence rates exceed 55 percent in both countries. Contraceptive prevalence rates in Africa are generally lower than in other regions, due, in part, to very weak fertility reduction programs.

The connection between rapid population growth and environmental degradation is complex on the *global* scale, but it appears clearer on national and subnational scales. In overcrowded Java, for example, the population has increased from 5 to 95 million in this century, forcing landless people to clear upland forests for new cropland. Yields are low on these steep slopes, and soil erosion rates are high; more than 1 million hectares of uplands have been so degraded that they can no longer support even subsistence agriculture.

Health

Health conditions have improved worldwide over the past 20 years, but wide disparities remain between developed and developing countries. Maternal mortality (500,000 women die from pregnancy-related causes each year, 99 percent of them in developing countries) and child mortality (15 million children under the age of five each year, worldwide) are much higher in developing countries, and the prevalence of low birth-weight infants and of children suffering from malnutrition speaks of a tragic ongoing situation.

Water-related diseases (e.g., cholera, malaria, dysentery, and river blindness) exact a heavy toll in developing countries, although some are being successfully attacked by drugs and public health measures. The provision of safe drinking water supplies and sanitation facilities can be an effective tool in combating water-related diseases, but service rates have improved only slightly despite the declaration of the International Drinking Water Supply and Sanitation Decade in 1980. Sanitation services cover less than half the rural population in most developing countries. Immunization coverage, however, is improving; 50 percent of the world's children were immunized against six major childhood killers by 1987, up from 5 percent a decade before.

Since it was first identified in 1981, acquired immune deficiency syndrome (AIDS) has spread rapidly. More than 73,000 cases had been reported worldwide by the end of 1987, and 5–10 million people are believed to be carrying the virus that causes AIDS. Although the pandemic is serious, AIDS still affects far fewer people than many other deadly diseases. For example, 5 million children die of diarrheal diseases every year.

Acute human exposure to pesticides (such as that experienced by unprotected farmworkers) is frequently fatal: 3,000–20,000 people die from pesticide poisoning annually, and another million people suffer less severe symptoms of acute pesticide poisoning. Chronic exposure through contaminated foodstuffs, water, soil, and air may cause neurological damage, cancers, and reproductive problems. Pesticide use has grown rapidly; sales increased from $2.7 billion in 1970 to $11.6 billion in 1980, and they are expected to reach $18.5 billion by 1990. To reduce the risks of pesticide damage to human health, governments need to regulate pesticides more carefully than they do in many countries. Lower-toxicity approaches to pest control—such as integrated pest management (IPM)—should be implemented; IPM can cut pesticide requirements by half or more while providing adequate protection for crops.

HUMAN SETTLEMENTS
(Chapters 3 and 16)

Human settlements are centers of trade, public services, and the transformation of raw materials into finished goods. They alter local and regional environments by concentrating the consumption of goods and the generation of wastes. Urban areas are growing rapidly in most regions.

The urban population is growing more rapidly than the rural population in all countries; the difference is especially striking in developing countries, where the total population is also growing rapidly. The urban populations of developed and developing regions were approximately equal in 1970, but by 2000 the urban population of developing regions will be twice the size of the developed world's urban population. About half the world population will live in urban areas by the year 2000, compared with 30 percent in 1950.

Urban areas dominate the economies of many developing countries; in extreme cases, a single city can provide most of a country's economic output. Abidjan, with 15 percent of the Cote d'Ivoire population, accounts for 70 percent of all economic and commercial transactions in the country. São Paulo, with 10 percent of Brazil's population, contributes one quarter of the net national product and 40 percent of the value added to agricultural goods and raw materials through processing and manufacturing. Large cities also affect the pattern of resource use in rural areas; farmers and food processors often find it profitable to invest in new crops and technologies that will satisfy the demands of the large urban market.

Cities provide numerous services and economic advantages that are often unavailable to rural dwellers. Urban dwellers are more likely to have access to sanitation services than rural dwellers in all 26 African countries for which data are available. (See Chapter 15, "Population and Health," Table 15.4.) Cities can also supply the critical mass of workers and consumers necessary to support diversified commercial and industrial development. A large city is often the center of the national food-marketing system, providing distribution services for the country and a gateway for international trade.

Cities are potent generators of waste products, but many developing-country cities are ill-equipped to handle rapidly increasing volumes of sewage, industrial wastewaters, and household trash. (See Chapter 20, "Energy, Materials, and Wastes," Table 20.7.) Improperly disposed of solid wastes, for example, can provide a breeding ground for disease-carrying vermin and pollute surface and groundwater. Cities attempt to manage these environmental hazards by establishing landfills, composting, and recycling.

Recycling is becoming increasingly popular in developed and developing countries. Paper, metals, and glass are now being recovered in large quantities from municipal wastes in countries as diverse as Austria, Belgium, China, and Egypt. Organic materials are frequently recycled after composting, providing animal feed and fertilizer at low cost. Recycling offers a number of benefits beyond the obvious one of waste disposal: employment (often for poor or disadvantaged members of society), cheap materials for industry (recycled scrap can cost 70–90 percent less than new materials), and various secondary products that can be sold for additional income.

Many governments recognize the environmental, social, and political pressures engendered by megacities, and they have taken steps to divert some urban growth to so-called secondary cities. A variety of policy tools can promote decentralization of the urban population. First, governments designate smaller cities and towns as regional centers for government, education, commerce, industry, health care, and transportation. In addition, tax

and other financial incentives can be directed toward secondary cities, their facilities can be upgraded, and the transportation network can be expanded to link secondary cities to larger cities and to outlying rural areas.

FOOD AND AGRICULTURE
(Chapters 4 and 17)

Enormous gains have been made in increasing global food production over the past few decades. But, because of rapid population growth and inequitable distribution of food, hunger still threatens millions throughout the developing world.

Food Production

Over the past 20 years, per capita food production has increased in every region except sub-Saharan Africa. There it fell 13 percent, largely because of rapid population growth coupled with unfavorable environmental conditions and ineffective agricultural policies. By contrast, over the same period, food production per person rose 23 percent in Asia as a whole and over 45 percent in China, Indonesia, and Malaysia.

Despite success in increasing global food production, the number of hungry people is growing. It is now thought to be 950 million—almost one fifth the world population. Poverty is the cause. Although more than enough food is produced to feed the world's 5 billion people, inequitable distribution of land and wealth causes widespread hunger. Nations with a per capita income of $400 or less account for about 80 percent of the undernourished. Most of them live in South Asia and Africa, where high population growth rates ensure that hunger will continue in coming years.

Building on the Green Revolution

Agricultural research has long been a weapon in the fight against hunger. Twenty years ago, the Green Revolution brought high-yielding crops and new techniques to farmers in many parts of the developing world, especially Asia. New inputs and technologies boosted agricultural production; they are largely responsible for the agricultural successes achieved by many Asian countries.

These successes have not been without a price. In recent years, mass production of high-yielding varieties created a cereal glut and depressed prices. Several environmental problems are also associated with Green Revolution technology. Monocultures of high-yielding varieties allowed high production and increased mechanization of agriculture. But these varieties often required heavy applications of chemical fertilizers and pesticides. In Indonesia, for example, where 83 percent of the area planted in rice is sown with high-yielding varieties, fertilizer use per hectare has tripled over the past decade. As a result of increased inputs, areas face problems of pesticide-resistant pests, decreased soil fertility, and contaminated water supplies. Some farms have returned to raising several types of crops with complementary needs for sunlight and nutrients on the same plot. This system can yield several benefits: it produces mulch for fertilizer and additional biomass for fodder, and the risk of crop failure is lower.

A limitation of the Green Revolution is its focus on irrigated croplands, neglecting rainfed drylands where many poor farmers live. Rainfed drylands covering 224 million hectares of the Earth's surface support 850 million people. Low productivity and land degradation are chronic problems. Techniques to maximize scarce water resources and drought-resistant crops are needed. Traditional practices, such as mulching and terracing slopes, substantially increase the amount of water absorbed by the soil. Researchers are now experimenting with several promising crops, such as jojoba and amaranth, that thrive in semiarid regions.

Agricultural research has changed its perspective since the days of the Green Revolution. Although production-oriented research, which was responsible for development of high-yielding varieties, is still at the forefront, some researchers are now increasing emphasis on the needs of poor farmers and on ecologically sustainable agriculture.

FORESTS AND RANGELANDS
(Chapters 5 and 18)

Forests and rangelands, which cover more than four fifths of the world's land surface, encompass a variety of ecologically and economically important ecosystems. Forests provide timber, fuel, food, and other products for human consumption. Of equal importance are forests' ecological functions. They provide habitat for millions of species, protect soils from erosion, and help regulate climate. Rangelands support livestock that produce meat, milk, hides, and other products, and they support more than 200 million pastoralists who depend on them for their livelihood.

Both forests and rangelands face increasing pressures from human activities. Every year, about 11 million hectares of tropical forests and woodlands are lost—primarily from clearing for agriculture or fuelwood harvesting. In the temperate north, forest damage linked to air pollutants affects an estimated 15 percent of the total timber volume in 17 European countries. In most regions, the area of land in permanent pasture is shrinking because of conversion to cropland.

Forests

Temperate forests account for about 57 percent of the world's total closed forest area, and they are expanding slowly with establishment of plantations. By contrast, closed forests in the tropics are being rapidly destroyed. In addition to the 7.3 million hectares of tropical closed forests cleared each year for agriculture, another 4.4 million hectares are selectively logged—a practice that frequently degrades the forest ecosystem and can lead to subsequent deforestation.

The major concern over deforestation is with tropical moist closed forests. This level of concern reflects both the high rates of loss of tropical moist forests and the value of these forests in terms of their biological diversity, wealth of timber and other products, and their

environmental functions. More species of plants and animals are believed to live in tropical moist forests than live in all the rest of the world. (See Chapter 6, "Wildlife and Habitat.")

The most important commercial product of forests is wood, nearly half of which is used for industrial purposes, and the rest for fuel. Despite the low value of wood relative to its bulk, wood products are the third most valuable commodity in world trade, after petroleum and natural gas. World trade in wood and wood products is projected to grow for the next 50 years. However, recent projections of trade in tropical hardwoods suggest that these timber resources will become depleted by deforestation and slow regeneration of logged forests. The limited numbers of high-quality hardwood plantations will not be able to keep pace with demand. As a result, global trade in tropical hardwoods is expected to peak just after the turn of the century and then drop significantly.

Two international efforts are underway to attempt to reverse these downward trends in tropical forests. The Tropical Forestry Action Plan is intended to slow tropical deforestation and promote sustainable use of the world's forests. Under the plan, national forestry reviews are being conducted in 50 developing countries to assess the extent of deforestation and to target areas for remedial actions.

The International Tropical Timber Organization (ITTO) is a new organization made up of both consuming and producing countries. With the establishment of its headquarters in Japan in 1987, ITTO has begun a series of projects designed to improve reforestation and forest management techniques.

Rangelands

Rangelands are threatened both by degradation and by the loss of land area through conversion to croplands. Although quantitative data on world rangeland conditions are limited, information from the early 1980s suggests that over 60 percent of all rangelands in dry regions suffer moderate to severe desertification. In sub-Saharan Africa, over 80 percent of dry rangelands are desertified. A qualitative review of rangeland conditions in selected Asian countries reveals substantial overgrazing and other signs of degradation.

By attempting to transplant range management techniques used in the ranching and economic systems of developed countries, most international efforts to improve the productivity of rangelands in sub-Saharan Africa have been unsuccessful. As a result, most multilateral and bilateral aid agencies reduced or withdrew their support for range projects in the late 1970s and early 1980s. Since then, planners have come to recognize that traditional systems for managing rangelands often embody knowledge and understanding of the ecological requirements of rangeland use. Although traditional systems must be adapted to encompass increased population pressure and other changes, recent projects have attempted to incorporate them into range management programs. In addition, efforts are being made to increase the participation of the people in planning and implementation.

WILDLIFE AND HABITAT
(Chapters 6 and 19)

Extent and Losses of Wildlife and Habitat

The total number of existing species of plants and animals is not known. Estimates vary from 5 million to more than 30 million, but scientists have identified only 1.4–1.7 million species. Yet species losses are growing with the destruction of large areas of wildlife habitat, and much of the Earth's biological richness may be lost before it is even identified.

The largest storehouse of biodiversity is the tropical forest. Although tropical closed forests cover only about 6 percent of the world's land surface, they contain 50–90 percent of all the Earth's species. For example, a single tree in Peru was found to be inhabited by as many different species of ants as are found in the entire United Kingdom.

Habitat loss of all types is the greatest threat to maintaining species diversity. The global loss of habitat is not known, but two recent studies in areas exceptionally rich in wildlife have shown widespread loss. In Southeast Asia, 68 percent of the original habitat for wildlife has been lost, and in sub-Saharan Africa the figure is 65 percent.

Island habitats and species are particularly vulnerable to disturbance. The isolation of islands creates delicately balanced ecosystems whose species are not able to adapt quickly to human settlements and nonnative species. About 75 percent of all recent mammal and bird extinctions were island-dwelling species.

Illegal Trade

Hunting and trapping for trade can also endanger individual species, especially those that are rare and endangered. The estimated annual value of trade in wildlife and wildlife products is at least $5 billion. One quarter to one third of this trade ($1.25–1.67 billion) is thought to be illegal.

The primary control on international trade in endangered wildlife is the Convention on International Trade in Endangered Species of Wild Fauna and Flora (CITES). Ratified by 96 nations, CITES—through a system of import, export, and reexport permits—forbids trade in listed endangered species and restricts trade in species at risk of becoming endangered.

Although one of the most successful international treaties affecting wildlife, CITES' major problems include the behavior of nonparticipating nations, lax enforcement in some areas, and "reservations" (exceptions) that participating countries can take with respect to individual species at the time they sign the treaty. And illegal trade continues to take its toll. Eighty-four percent of the world's rhinos have disappeared since 1970, and the number of African elephants has dropped 36 percent just since 1981, declining from about 1.2 million to only 764,000 by 1987.

New Approaches

Parks and protected areas have long been important tools for conserving natural areas and species. In 1988, 15 countries had designated over 10 percent of their land as protected areas, although the effectiveness of protection systems varies widely among countries. However, there is growing recognition that when conservation has to compete with development, conservation usually loses, but that if development continues its rapid destruction of the natural resource base of developing countries, economic development itself will be undermined.

The need to provide economic benefits compatible with conservation objectives has led to projects designed to encourage sustainable development alongside protected areas. One approach is the creation of biosphere reserves to protect unique biological areas. Ideally, a biosphere reserve establishes a core zone(s) to protect wildlife, habitat, and biodiversity, and various multiple-use buffer zones to provide economic benefits to the local population.

Another innovative example of this trend is the debt-for-nature swap, in which part of a developing country's debt is traded for land to be protected. The first such agreement, between Bolivia and Conservation International, created nearly 1 million hectares of protected areas in the foothills of the Andes.

ENERGY
(Chapters 7 and 20)

Economic growth has historically been linked to growth of energy use, implying the need for large prospective increases in energy consumption, especially in the developing world. Yet gains in energy efficiency focused on the end uses of energy illustrate the potential for achieving economic growth with little or no increase in energy consumption. Several developed countries have already begun to tap this potential, and a few developing nations are investigating ways to do so.

Energy Use

Understanding energy use patterns is essential for promoting efficiency and ameliorating energy-related environmental problems. Oil accounts for 43 percent of global commercial energy production, solid fuels 31 percent, natural gas 21 percent, and primary electricity 5 percent. About half the world's population, however, relies on noncommercial fuelwood as its sole energy source. A shortage of fuelwood is the most important energy-related problem for many developing countries.

Energy Efficiency

Increased energy efficiency can bring political, economic, and environmental benefits in reduced reliance on energy imports and lower emissions of carbon dioxide and other pollutants. A country can measure efficiency by the energy intensity of its economy: the amount of energy required to produce a unit of gross national product (GNP). Declining energy-to-GNP ratios indicate increasing energy efficiency and/or a structural shift toward a less energy-intensive economy. Reflecting both trends, energy intensity declined while GNP grew in 14 European countries, the United States, Canada, and Japan between 1970 and 1986.

Over the past decade, high energy prices and technological advances spurred gains in efficiency in developed countries and some oil-importing developing countries. Energy intensity increased, on the other hand, in Nigeria, Indonesia, Venezuela, and other developing countries with plentiful energy supplies.

Strategies for improving energy efficiency must be tailored to the user. Between 1973 and 1983, improved efficiency of automobiles and commercial vehicles was largely responsible for a 20 percent reduction in energy consumption per passenger. In the industrial sector—the primary consumer of commercial energy in most middle- to high-income countries—new production technologies, better design, and recycling processed materials all save energy. Die-cast parts, for example, require 95 percent less energy when made from recycled aluminum than when they are made from primary metal. Residential and commercial uses account for 20–50 percent of commercial energy consumption in most countries. Many simple technologies such as fluorescent light bulbs, improved architectural designs, and insulation can provide large household energy savings. New refrigerators, for example, require 30–70 percent less energy than 15-year-old models.

Superconductivity—a phenomenon that allows certain materials to conduct electricity without energy loss—could effect dramatic increases in energy efficiency. Although not yet commercially viable, superconductors could cut electricity losses substantially, making alternative and remote electricity sources more practical and providing better electricity storage.

Energy in the USSR and Eastern Europe

Soviet energy abundance and energy policies have tended to isolate the USSR and Eastern Europe from concerns that dominate other developed countries: price fluctuations, energy-related environmental problems, and the need for increased efficiency. The USSR, with the world's largest energy reserves, is the world's leading producer of oil and gas. These commodities are vital to the Soviet economy: energy accounts for 52 percent of all export earnings and petroleum alone for 60 percent of hard currency earnings. The Soviets hope to increase their energy earnings by increasing production and expanding oil exports outside Eastern Europe.

Most of the Eastern European countries lack oil and gas supplies, relying on indigenous coal and Soviet oil and gas. However, high Soviet oil prices and growing environmental problems have led several Eastern European countries to rethink their energy options. Energy efficiency and environmental considerations are now gaining increasing attention. Public opposition to the choking air pollution caused by coal-fired power plants and the need for a domestic energy source have led several countries to examine nuclear power as a "clean"

alternative. The world's worst nuclear power accident two years ago at Chernobyl appears not to have slowed plans for nuclear power in the Soviet Union and Eastern Europe.

FRESHWATER
(Chapters 8 and 21)

Freshwater is necessary for human survival and development. Yet global water supplies are unevenly distributed and many countries face water shortages. With growing populations and mounting demands, countries are becoming more aware of the need to manage and protect their water resources.

Water Availability

Water resources vary widely among countries. Wet, sparsely populated countries, such as Canada, Iceland, and New Zealand theoretically have access to more than 100,000 cubic meters of freshwater per person. By contrast, most arid countries in North Africa and the Middle East have less than 1 percent of that amount. But water supplies also vary widely within countries and from year to year; even well-endowed countries may face short-term or local shortages. Although freshwater supplies are critical to agriculture (the largest user) and other activities, national data on freshwater resources are difficult to compare because countries handle groundwater and river flows from other countries differently. River flows originating in another country are a major source of freshwater for many countries. In Egypt, for example, the Nile supplies more than 50 times the water provided by domestic rainfall. But rivers become an unreliable source when an upstream country diverts or pollutes its river water.

Water Management

Because most countries face occasional water shortages either nationally or locally, they are increasing management of their water resources. Building dams to capture flood runoff and drilling wells to tap groundwater are the traditional engineering means of increasing the available water supplies. These techniques are still common, especially in the developing world. In many countries, policymakers are also turning toward increasing efficiency, water reuse, and reallocation of water to stretch their supplies. Improving the efficiency of irrigation alone, which accounts for about 70 percent of global water use, would not only save large volumes of water but would prevent the salinization and waterlogging of poorly drained lands. If irrigation water losses were cut only 10 percent in the Indus region of Pakistan, for example, an additional 2 million hectares could be irrigated. Eliminating excessive irrigation subsidies and encouraging water reuse would also improve efficiency. Israel reused 35 percent of its wastewater in 1986, mostly for irrigation. By the year 2000, Israel expects to reuse 80 percent, expanding its renewable water supply 25 percent.

Water Pollution

Water supplies are also depleted by pollution. Twenty years ago, river water in many developed countries was so bad that it was unusable for industrial, agricultural, or recreational activities. Since then, several countries have installed sewage treatment plants and are regulating industrial discharges.

Pollution from diffuse sources—nonpoint pollution—is more difficult to control. Agricultural and urban runoff, which washes pesticides, nitrates, phosphates, and other pollutants into the water supply, is a problem throughout the developed world. In developing countries, much of the industrial and sewage waste is still not treated, and it remains a pressing environmental problem. Nonpoint pollution is likely to worsen with growth in urbanization, industrialization and the use of chemical inputs in agriculture.

Small Dams

The building of small dams is an ancient technology that has found renewed acceptance as a development tool. Dams are used worldwide for water supply, irrigation, flood control, and electric power. Small dams are attractive because they are less likely to cause major environmental problems than large dams. They can work in many locations, can be built with local materials and labor, and can bring electric power and other benefits to remote rural areas. Between 1950 and 1980, 6 million small dams were constructed in China.

OCEANS AND COASTS
(Chapters 9 and 22)

Ocean Currents and Fisheries

Currents and vertical circulation affect oceans' biological productivity and their interactions with the land and the atmosphere. The proximity of a warm surface current tempers the climate of otherwise inhospitable regions, as the Gulf Stream does for Northern Europe. Upwellings, like those off Peru, bring nutrient-rich bottom waters to the surface. They are especially important to fisheries because they support the phytoplankton that are the base of the oceanic food web. Changes in upwellings and surface currents can influence the abundance of fish. Some fishery managers are beginning to consider this variability in developing management plans.

The world marine fish catch has increased steadily, reaching 90 million metric tons in 1986, up from about 30 million metric tons in 1958. But some experts believe that continued large increases in world fish catch are unlikely because the annual catch is approaching the maximum sustainable yield and has exceeded it in specific fisheries. Regionally, several fisheries have been either overfished or reduced by a combination of overfishing and environmental factors, with substantial harvest declines.

Marine Protected Areas

Sustainable management of marine resources is promoted by the designation of coastal and marine protected areas. These areas protect natural ecosystems and provide a secure breeding area for marine life that is harvested elsewhere.

Japan has established 57 small marine parks, used mainly for tourism. Australia's Great Barrier Reef Marine Park, the world's largest at 350,000 square kilometers, allows multiple uses. For example, some areas are restricted to scientific research, others permit fishing, and cruise ships are permitted in other areas.

The marine protected areas of the Caribbean illustrate the promise and problems of this management strategy in developing countries. Several studies have shown that Caribbean marine protected areas are good investments because they provide income from tourism and support artisanal fisheries. Although Caribbean governments have designated 112 marine protected areas, only 25 percent have both a management budget and staff. Many are threatened by industrial and agricultural development, sediment loading, tourist damage, and overfishing. Funding is the major obstacle to managing these areas.

East Asian Regional Seas

The seas of East Asia support intense economic and ecological activity: shipping, oil production, offshore mining, commercial fishing, tourism, and the habitat of a diverse marine biota. Marine pollution, especially from petroleum, is severe in some areas. Five littoral countries, supported by the United Nations Environment Programme (UNEP), have developed a Regional Action Plan, which, it is hoped, will promote sustainable development of the area's marine resources. Implementation has been slow, partly because of funding problems.

Marine Mammals

Several mammal groups—whales, dolphins, seals, sea lions, walruses, manatees, and dugongs—depend partly or wholly on the sea for food, shelter, and/or breeding areas. In the past two centuries the hunting of marine mammals has accelerated to the point that some species face extinction. The International Whaling Commission (IWC) has regulated hunting of the great whales since 1946; more recently, the IWC declared a temporary moratorium on commercial whaling. Japan, Norway, Iceland, and South Korea continue whaling for "research" purposes. Marine mammals are also threatened by pollution, habitat destruction, accidental capture in fisheries, and entanglement in abandoned fishing gear. Piecemeal national legislation protects some marine mammals and UNEP is attempting to establish a Global Plan of Action for Marine Mammals to stimulate research and protection.

Marine Pollution

Monitoring pollution in open water, sediments, and marine organisms indicates local trends in pollution, but monitoring is not yet global. Data on ocean dumping, oil spills, land runoff, and atmospheric deposition in the oceans are somewhat better. Oil spills, for example, have been declining in frequency and volume for 15 years.

ATMOSPHERE AND CLIMATE
(Chapters 10 and 23)

Human damage to the atmosphere, seen at the local, regional, and global levels, is growing worse in many parts of the world. Pollution contributes to unhealthy air in cities and damages crops and natural ecosystems. Burning fossil fuels and clearing tropical forests is altering the global climate, and is likely to cause severe disruptions through regional climate changes, sea level rise, and unpredictable weather patterns. Depletion of the Earth's protective ozone layer, already well advanced over the South Pole, may harm both human health and delicately balanced natural systems.

Air Pollution

Air pollution exacts enormous health and environmental costs. One common pollutant, sulfur dioxide (SO_2), causes respiratory illnesses and is a precursor to acidic deposition. Overall, urban air quality has improved over the past decade in many developed countries. For example, urban SO_2 levels fell by 19–64 percent in eight countries in Europe and North America. With the exception of Milan, the world's most polluted cities are now in developing countries. Half the monitoring stations in the developing world report SO_2 levels considered unsafe by the World Health Organization; worldwide, 625 million people live in areas where the air is unhealthy.

Perhaps the biggest air pollution success story in recent years is the rapid decline of lead in the air. Lead is toxic to humans, damaging the neurological system and causing kidney disease. Because of restrictions on leaded gasoline, monitoring stations in the United States, Canada, France, and the United Kingdom reported declines in lead levels of over 50 percent between 1975 and 1986.

Nations are less successful in controlling other air pollutants. Ozone in the lower atmosphere (a component of smog) damages lung and respiratory tissue and is thought to decrease U.S. crop yields by 5–10 percent, for an annual loss of $1–2 billion. Acidic deposition and oxidants contribute to the destruction of forests in Europe and North America. In 1986, six European countries reported visible damage to more than one third of their forests.

Global Warming

Rising concentrations of carbon dioxide, nitrous oxide, methane, and other greenhouse gases are expected to cause an unprecedented global warming. Although national and regional impacts of this warming are still uncertain, scientists believe that the average global temperature will rise by 1.5–4.5°C by 2030. A warmer climate will change temperature and precipitation patterns, with implications critical to agriculture and natural ecosystems. Rising temperatures are expected to raise sea levels because sea water expands when warmed and because the polar ice caps may melt. A sea level rise of

50 centimeters—well within the range expected from a 1.5–4.5°C temperature increase—would flood many low-lying regions, displacing 16 percent of Egypt's population, for example.

Ozone Depletion

Spurred by the loss in stratospheric ozone over Antarctica each spring, delegates from 30 countries and the European Community signed the Montreal Protocol in 1987 to prevent further ozone depletion. The protocol aims to halve consumption of ozone-depleting chlorofluorocarbons by the year 2000. Stratospheric ozone prevents harmful ultraviolet-B (UV-B) radiation from reaching the Earth; a depleted ozone layer would allow more of this radiation to reach the Earth's surface. Exposure to UV-B radiation increases the incidence of skin cancers and cataracts. UV-B is also thought to suppress human immune systems and increase the occurrence of some infectious diseases. Increased UV-B radiation could harm some plant species, including major agricultural crops and aquatic plants that are food for most fish.

Although an encouraging example of international cooperation, the Montreal Protocol may not prevent further losses in the ozone layer. In 1988, a U.S. National Aeronautics and Space Administration (NASA) study found the first detailed evidence that stratopheric ozone in the Northern Hemisphere has already been depleted up to 3 percent over the past 20 years. NASA's findings sparked new debate about the adequacy of the Protocol.

Pollutant Interactions

Simple cause-and-effect relationships like that between CFCs and ozone are the exception rather than the rule with air pollutants. Pollutants interact in the atmosphere to produce a bewildering array of direct and indirect effects. Moreover, controlling one pollutant may have unintended effects on another. Although SO_2 emissions from power plants, for example, can be reduced by installing scrubbers, these devices reduce plant efficiency, increasing carbon dioxide emissions and the greenhouse effect. Solutions to such complex air pollution problems demand an understanding of pollutant interactions and the integration of energy policy with pollution control.

GLOBAL SYSTEMS AND CYCLES
(Chapter 11)

Despite our imperfect understanding of the biogeochemical cycle of nitrogen and the global water cycle, human interventions in these cycles may have reached the global scale. The impacts of these interventions often cannot be predicted precisely, but an examination of the Earth's history can help distinguish human impacts from natural variations and further our understanding of global life support systems.

The Global Nitrogen Cycle

Nitrogen is an indispensable element in all life. Almost 98 percent of the Earth's store of nitrogen is contained in rocks, beyond the reach of the biosphere. Most of the remaining 2 percent is in the atmosphere, where stable nitrogen gas (N_2) constitutes 78 percent of the total volume. Because N_2 is unusable by almost all plants and animals, an essential process in the natural nitrogen cycle is nitrogen fixation. Carried out by a small number of algae and bacteria, fixation converts nitrogen gas to forms that can be used by plants.

Industrial conversion of atmospheric nitrogen fixes 90 million metric tons of nitrogen annually, 80 percent of it for fertilizer. This effective doubling of the natural nitrogen fixation rate, although crucial for increasing agricultural production, also increases water and air pollution. The levels of nitrogen compounds in surface and groundwater have been rising in Europe and North America. Nitrate pollution in almost all rivers in the Netherlands, Spain, and the United Kingdom steadily and substantially increased from 1970 to 1980. (See Chapter 21, "Freshwater," Table 21.2.) Nitrate pollution from agricultural runoff is also growing in developing countries. Nitrates in drinking water and food are a health threat, especially to infants, and nitrogen loading of surface waters contributes to eutrophication.

Fuel combustion at high temperatures produces various nitrogen compounds that pollute urban air, help form acidic precipitation, and add to the greenhouse effect. Annual atmospheric emissions of nitric oxide (NO) have now reached more than 20 million metric tons per year, roughly equal to the natural formation of this compound. NO contributes to urban smog and acidic deposition. Nitrous oxide (N_2O), an important contributor to the greenhouse effect, is also emitted in fuel combustion as well as through use of nitrogen fertilizers.

Technologies to control air and water pollution from nitrogen compounds are often expensive. Reducing water pollution from nitrogen requires advanced sewage treatment and more efficient use of fertilizers to minimize nutrient runoff. Controlling NO and N_2O emissions requires technical modifications to automobiles and power plants and the political will to develop and enforce emissions regulations.

The Global Water Cycle

Life depends on water. Humans routinely intervene in the water cycle at the local or regional level and may soon affect the water cycle on a global scale.

The surface freshwater that sustains terrestrial life is a minute fraction of the planet's water. It bears the brunt of human impacts. Our most significant impact is withdrawal and the largest user is agriculture. Other interventions include the construction of reservoirs to control flooding and increase water supplies, the destruction of forests and draining of wetlands that alter natural runoff and modify evaporation, and the alteration of the global climate, which is certain to affect every aspect of the water cycle.

Human activities also affect the links between water and land and between water and biota. Some major effects include altering sediment flows in rivers by dams that trap sediment and by deforestation, which increases soil erosion and sediment transport. Similarly, altering

natural vegetation changes the balance between evaporation, surface runoff, and groundwater recharge. Loss of vegetation accelerates drying of the land and contributes to desertification.

Environmental History

Environmental history is a key to understanding how the Earth's systems work. It enables us to see how the world has evolved, to put recent trends in a historical context, and to see the magnitude of human impacts on natural systems and the global environment.

Several methods are used to read the Earth's natural records. Isotopic analysis enables scientists to date samples, trace the movement of materials through the environment, and obtain clues to past environmental conditions. Other methods examine substances that form in layers regularly—sediments, polar ice, peat deposits, and tree rings, for example. Analyses of seabed and lake bottom sediments reveal information on past water temperature, acidity and salinity, species diversity, and pollutant levels. Ice cores are records of temperature trends and the composition of the atmosphere. Tree rings reflect precipitation, pollution, and other environmental factors.

Environmental history describes the range of natural variability, a baseline for measuring human impacts. Using an Antarctic ice core going back 160,000 years, researchers constructed a continuous record of temperature and atmospheric levels of carbon dioxide (CO_2) extending beyond the last ice age. It shows a definite link between CO_2 levels and temperature, although whether CO_2 causes or follows rising temperatures is not clear. During the last interglacial period, the highest levels of atmospheric CO_2 were 260–280 parts per million. Today, as a result of fossil fuel combustion and deforestation, CO_2 levels are nearly 350 parts per million.

POLICIES AND INSTITUTIONS (Chapters 12 and 24)

Government policies are important in determining how natural resources are exploited and to what degree the environment is protected.

The economic policies of developing countries often promote expansion of agricultural production, timber harvests, or other sectors dependent on natural resources by altering the incentives faced by producers. By distorting normal production decisions, these policies can lead to inefficient and unsustainable use of natural resources, and environmental damage.

Agriculture

Governments of developing countries subsidize the price of agricultural inputs—pesticides, fertilizers, and irrigation water—to encourage farmers to try new technologies and, in many countries, to compensate farmers for the reduction in their earnings caused by government-controlled prices for their products. Both the subsidies and the suppressed agricultural prices cause unintentional damage to the environment, and they can cost the public millions of dollars.

In Egypt, Senegal, and Indonesia, government subsidies have covered more than 80 percent of the full retail price of pesticides, at a heavy cost to the national treasury. When pesticides are so cheap, farmers have little incentive to use them efficiently. If pesticide prices are artificially low, farmers use more pesticides, even when the additional crop output is quite small.

The overuse of pesticides carries a high price for human health and the environment. Each year thousands of people die from acute pesticide poisoning, and another million more suffer non-fatal pesticide poisoning. In addition, more than 400 insect, tick, and mite pests have developed resistance to pesticides, frequently causing farmers to use newer and more toxic pesticides.

Forestry and Livestock

Governments often underestimate the sustainable value of forest services (e.g., watershed protection and habitat) and products (e.g., wood, nuts, rattan, and medicinals) and overestimate the value of short-term exploitation and conversion to agriculture. Indonesia, for example, seeking to use its vast forests as fuel for economic development, leased large forest areas to logging concessionaires for very low fees on a noncompetitive basis.

The resulting high profit potential for the concessionaires, combined with relatively short-term leases, encouraged rapid removal of the most valuable trees with little or no concern for damage to the remaining forest. The low government revenues generated by the concession fees failed to cover the costs of long-term management of the forests for sustained use. The results were rapid forest disturbance (damage to remaining trees during felling and transport) and deforestation (settlers moved into disturbed areas to clear agricultural land).

In the mid-1960s, Brazil adopted policies to foster development of the Amazon Basin, promoting conversion of forests to alternative uses, especially livestock projects. Among the inducements were an investment tax credit, a federal income tax exemption, and subsidized loans.

Between 1965 and 1983, 469 cattle ranches averaging 23,000 hectares were established in Amazonia; these ranches were responsible for 30 percent of the rapid deforestation in Amazonia. Initially, the land could support one animal per hectare, but without investment in weed control and soil fertility, this stocking rate fell to 4 hectares per animal within five years. Given the structure of the incentives, the rancher would then abandon the land and clear new land.

Between 1965 and 1983, Brazil spent $600 million on tax credits to subsidize the development of Amazonian cattle ranches. For a typical 20,000-hectare ranch, these subsidies provided the margin between economic loss and a handsome profit. With an initial investment of $740,000 and a government subsidy of $5.1 million, an investor can expect to earn $1.9 million (in net present value terms) over the 15-year life of the project. The government recoups only a fraction of its investment.

Recognition of the environmental and economic costs of these policies is causing some developing countries to begin to reduce subsidies and reexamine other economic policies that clearly cause environmental and fiscal damages.

REHABILITATING AND RESTORING DEGRADED LANDS (Chapter 13)

Although it is far preferable to prevent degradation of land through good management, decades and sometimes centuries of misuse have left scars that must be repaired if the lands are to become productive again. With the world population expected to grow by another 3 billion people by the year 2025, land is needed more urgently than ever for food and energy production.

Land degradation is not a new phenomenon: poor irrigation in ancient Mesopotamia salinized huge areas. Until recently, little thought was given to restoring degraded lands. Low population densities enabled people simply to move on. In addition, people often lacked the technology to undo the damage they had done. This situation is changing. Global population growth and the rapid pace of modern technology are accelerating land degradation. With increasing demands for land, many developing countries will soon be forced to confront the problem of degraded lands in order to meet the growing needs of their people.

Damaged lands can be repaired in several ways. Traditionally, such lands were allowed to lie fallow to regenerate naturally. Previously sustainable practices, like slash-and-burn agriculture, were based on temporary periods of abandonment. However, these practices required plentiful land. As population densities have increased, fallow periods have grown shorter, until lands once able to regenerate naturally can no longer do so.

Human intervention to repair degraded lands takes two forms: restoration and rehabilitation. Restoration, the more ambitious of the two, aims to return a site to its natural state, complete with all the species that existed there before human disturbances. Rehabilitation is much more utilitarian. Its goal is to make the land productive for human use, employing whatever species and techniques are most effective, regardless of whether they are indigenous. In the developing world, rehabilitation is likely to have a more prominent role than restoration, because of the needs of growing populations.

Mountain Lands

Many different types of lands are under increasing stress worldwide, but mountainous regions face particular problems. Fighting gravity, mountain dwellers must find ways to preserve the vegetation and the soil. When vegetation and soil are degraded, agricultural production can decline rapidly, and the threat of flooding in nearby lowlands increases.

Engineering solutions, such as check dams and terraces, bring some stability to steep regions, but they are labor intensive and require maintenance. Sowing additional ground cover protects the soil and provides fodder for grazing animals. Local people must be shown the direct benefits of adopting more sustainable practices—for example, stall-feeding their livestock. They may need alternative income until they are able to realize the benefits of their rehabilitated land.

Drylands

Desertification—used here to describe the degradation of drylands—is an increasing problem in many developing countries. Efforts to slow or reverse this trend have been ineffective so far. Drylands comprise 18 percent of the land area in developing countries, supporting more than 300 million people. Fuelwood gathering, overgrazing, and the cultivation of lands unsuitable for agriculture threaten many of these areas. Techniques for rehabilitating these lands include prohibiting agriculture and grazing, making furrows to conserve and absorb water, reseeding, and planting shelterbelts. In addition, increased cookstove efficiency and alternative energy sources are important in reducing demands for fuelwood.

Irrigated Cropland

Loss of irrigated cropland to salinization, waterlogging, and alkalinization has vast economic costs for many countries. In India, Indonesia, Chile, and Peru, more than half the total food production is from irrigated lands; in China, the figure is 70 percent. Degradation of irrigated areas is usually due to poor water management. One solution is to drain the soils, often an expensive proposition. A more cost-effective solution in some areas is to plant crops, such as rice, that are tolerant of alkaline and waterlogged soils and that improve the soil for less tolerant crops.

Rehabilitation is a political as well as an economic issue. People living on degraded lands are often poor and have nowhere else to go. Although these powerless people may not be a government's top priority, enabling them to make a living from the land can prevent some of the problems associated with high rates of rural-to-urban migration.

Several general guidelines emerge from case studies on rehabilitating and restoring degraded lands. Local people must have a stake in improving the land, and they must be able to survive economically if sacrifices, such as reducing grazing, are required. The people must be involved in the planning and execution of projects if they are to work. Small-scale projects are often more successful because they can meet these requirements and can be tailored to local needs more easily. In addition, local materials, labor, and technology should be used whenever possible. This approach not only reduces costs but enables inhabitants to participate more fully and better maintain the project.

ASIAN FOCUS

World Resources 1988–89 inaugurates a regional feature of the series—each volume will pay special attention to resource and environmental conditions and trends in one region of the world. To highlight this volume's focus on Asia, the remainder of this section is an overview of conditions and trends throughout Asia (excluding the Asian portion of the USSR).

Asia stretches from the Mediterranean Sea to the Pacific Ocean. Its many nations are diverse in every dimension, from natural resource endowment to economic development level to political and cultural setting. Take economic development as an example. Japan and some of the oil-producing nations of western Asia (the Middle East) have per capita gross national products (GNPs) above $10,000. But many Asian countries rank among the poorest in the world. China, India, Bangladesh, and Pakistan—where 71 percent of Asia's population and 42 percent of the world population live—have per capita GNPs at or below $350. (See Chapter 14, "Basic Economic Indicators.")

Although the economically advanced countries of Asia face air and water pollution and other environmental problems stemming from industrial development, the less-developed countries are often more concerned with pressures on the natural resource base (e.g., land, forests, and water) from growing populations and the need for development.

On the whole, Asia's progress over the past two decades has been remarkable; yet large unresolved problems remain in the face of a large and growing population. In fact, population growth touches all aspects of natural resource management and economic development. Compared to other regions, Asia is less able to turn to untouched natural resources. In the coming decades, Asian nations will have to continue to find ways to increase the productivity of their natural resources to meet the growing demands of still larger populations. This effort will require sustainable management of land, water, forests, and other natural resources; substantial economic development; and continued advances in education, health care, and other human services. Asia's success in meeting these challenges may provide valuable lessons for the rest of the world.

Population Trends

Asia is the most crowded continent in the world. Two and six-tenths billion people—more than twice the count 35 years ago—compete for limited land and natural resources in the quest for food, water, and energy. Yet per capita food production has risen almost 25 percent since 1965, and population growth rates in the region are generally declining. Still, the sheer numbers added each year mean that Asia's problems are far from solved.

About every two seconds, five people are added to the global population. Three are Asian. This large contribution is due, not to a higher-than-average growth rate but to Asia's large population base. In fact, Asia's annual population growth rate matches the global average—1.63 percent, and it has slowly decreased since the late 1960s. Nonetheless, Asia's annual additions to the global population continue to outnumber those of all other continents combined.

Total fertility rates, the average number of children born to women during their reproductive years, are also declining across the continent. In the late 1960s, the average woman bore almost six children. Today, this figure is just over three. Much of the decline in fertility rates in Asia is attributable to China, where total fertility fell from 6 to 2.1 children per woman over the past 20 years. Although Asia's reduction is the most notable of the continents, fertility rates need to fall significantly further before the population stops growing. (See Chapters 2 and 15, "Population and Health.")

The success in lowering fertility rates is attributed largely to gains in health care, education, and contraceptive use. Over the past 20 years, infant mortality rates throughout Asia dropped 33 percent, and life expectancy rose from 53.3 years to 61.1 years. Many Asian countries have also implemented effective family planning programs. In a ranking of the family planning programs of 100 developing countries, 7 of the 10 countries with "strong" programs were in Asia. China, at the top of the list, has made marked progress to stem the growth of the world's largest population. Other Asian countries with strong programs were the Republic of Korea, Taiwan, Singapore, Indonesia, Hong Kong, and Sri Lanka. On the other hand, several Asian countries, Iraq and Kampuchea, for example, have weak programs or no programs at all. (See Chapter 2, "Population and Health," Trends in Fertility Reduction Efforts.)

Because almost one third of the Asian population is less than 15 years old, even if fertility rates continue their gradual descent, the number of reproductive-age women will cause the population to continue to grow. This population momentum will raise the Asian population to an estimated 4.5 billion by 2025, increasing demands on scarce natural resources.

The general downward trend in Asian population growth rates is countered by steady high or even rising rates in some countries. In Jordan, Syria, and Yemen, the annual population growth is on an upswing. Bhutan and Kampuchea have also realized modest increases. Although India's fertility rate fell throughout the late 1960s and 1970s, it seems to have leveled off since 1980, and India now surpasses China as the largest annual contributor to the global population. (See Chapters 2 and 15, "Population and Health.")

Demand for Food, Land, and Natural Resources

The most immediate implication of rapid population growth is the need for more food. This need can be met in two ways domestically: by expanding the agricultural land base and making better use of cultivated land. Historically, overcrowding and low productivity were remedied by people moving onto less populated, more fertile land. Today, most arable land is already heavily farmed, and in some countries, poor management and deteriorating environmental conditions are reducing the amount of productive farmland.

Asian cropland has grown more than two-and-one-half times since the mid-1800s. Almost four fifths of it was in forests and wooded areas. In Northern India, where the population has almost doubled over the past 30 years, agricultural land expanded over 50 percent, at the expense of most other land uses. One third of the forests have disappeared since then, and grasslands and wetlands have also succumbed to human encroachment. Similarly, in Pakistan, as population more than doubled, 3 million hectares of closed and open forests were cleared. Only two thirds of the stands from 1950 remain. (See Chapter 2, "Population and Health," and Chapter 16, "Land Cover and Settlements.")

Since the mid-1960s, however, expansion of croplands has slowed. While total food production in Asia has risen 85 percent over the past 20 years, this was accomplished with only a 4.2 percent rise in cropland. The amount of food produced per capita rose 22 percent during this period—more than twice the global average. This was accomplished by very large increases in cereal and root crop yields, although in absolute productivity Asia still trails Europe and North America. These gains resulted largely from the use of high-yielding crop varieties, fertilizers, pesticides, and irrigation. Since 1975, Asia has more than doubled the amount of fertilizer it applies annually to its soil. Irrigated lands account for 30 percent of the total arable land in Asia, twice the global average. The use of high-yield crop varieties also continues to climb. Improved wheat strains account for much of the wheat planted in Bangladesh, India, Nepal, Oman, and Pakistan. Similarly, improved rice and maize varieties are planted in about one third of Asian countries. (See Chapter 17, "Food and Agriculture.")

The successes of Asian nations in feeding their growing populations are not without costs. Most gains in agricultural productivity were part of the Green Revolution of the 1960s and 1970s. But this era of agricultural intensification had some unintended side effects that may well thwart continued progress. In some areas, for example, overuse of chemical fertilizers and irrigation water reduced land productivity.

The indiscriminate use of fertilizers, pesticides, and irrigation leads to human health hazards and land degradation. Overreliance on chemicals, to the exclusion of organic fertilizers, crop rotation, and extended fallow periods, can diminish soil fertility and water-holding capacity. The resulting water runoff carries sediment and hazardous chemicals into rivers and aquifers, causing pollution and human health problems. Excessive irrigation and insufficient drainage can waterlog the soil, raise salinity levels, and reduce productivity. In India and Pakistan, for example, more than 17 million hectares of arable land have been lost due to waterlogging. (See Chapter 12, "Policies and Institutions.")

Another outcome of the Green Revolution is widespread monocropping which presents environmental and economic trade-offs and risks. Planting only one crop season after season gradually drains soil nutrients and then requires increased applications of chemical fertilizers. Outbreaks of disease and pests, especially those resistant to commonly used pesticides, are more severe with monocropping, resulting in greater economic and ecological damage.

On a national scale, diversification is an economic buffer against fluctuating agricultural markets. World market prices for rice fell sharply during the 1980s, for example, and Thailand, where rice is grown on over 80 percent of the planted area and is a major export crop, is seeking ways to diversify. At the farm level, multicropping can increase sustained yields, help control plant diseases and pests, enrich soil fertility, and reduce erosion. (See Chapter 4, "Food and Agriculture.")

Rehabilitating Degraded Lands

Misuse and neglect have led to significant degradation of land in Asia, as in other parts of the world. Unlike many other regions, Asia has few areas with an abundance of land where the people can go when they deplete previously productive lands. Although extensive quantitative data on land degradation in Asia are lacking, the limited information available suggests that it is fairly widespread. Three types of land are of particular concern: mountain lands, drylands, and irrigated croplands.

Anecdotal information on mountain areas suggests major problems. In the Himalayas, most forests in accessible areas have been destroyed and good quality forests now cover only 4.4 percent of the region. This loss of forests often causes extreme soil loss and erosion, reducing productivity in the mountains and increasing sedimentation in lowland areas. On the island of Java, population densities in the mountain areas have led to unsustainable farming practices, leaving more than 1 million hectares of steep farmland severely eroded. (See Chapter 13, "Rehabilitating and Restoring Degraded Lands.")

Drylands are naturally somewhat fragile and are quickly degraded under the stress of intensive use for crops or livestock. Limited data from the early 1980s indicated that over 75 percent of productive drylands in Asia being used for croplands or rainfed agriculture were moderately to severely desertified. That is, they had suffered moderate to severe loss of productivity, which could lead to desert-like conditions. Desertification of drylands is most extensive in Western Asia. A qualitative assessment of Asian rangelands suggests that they are overgrazed and degraded and are facing continued pressure from both people and livestock. (See Chapter 5, "Forests and Rangelands.")

Irrigated drylands, although far smaller in area than other drylands, are of special concern because of their high productivity and the level of investments in them. In the early 1980s, an estimated 35 percent of such lands were moderately to severely desertified in Asia. (See Chapter 18, "Forests and Rangelands.")

Few countries have tried large-scale rehabilitation of degraded lands. But several relatively small-scale efforts in Asia offer some lessons.

In mountain areas, loss of vegetative cover frees water to erode soils. The key to rehabilitation is capturing the water through revegetation and engineering plus adopt-ing land use practices that reduce excessive pressures on the land while providing near- and long-term benefits to those who depend upon the land. In Nepal, overgrazing and compaction of vegetation and soils around Lake Phewa Tal caused significant erosion of surrounding watersheds. A combination of constructing small dams to catch water above the lake, stall-feeding the cattle, and planting fodder grasses in gullies was effective in reducing erosion, restoring the land, and also increasing productivity. The grass not only slowed water runoff but became a surplus crop for sale as fodder to neighboring areas. Stall-feeding reduced compaction and grazing pressure on the land and made cattle tending and manure collecting for fertilizer and fuel much easier and more efficient for the women.

Substitution of productive fruit tress—olives, peaches, almonds, and pomegranates—for traditional cereal crops in hilly areas of Jordan helped stabilize soils and reduce erosion. Important here was transitional support to the local farmers in the form of jobs and food until the fruit trees were productive. China has launched a labor-intensive program to build windbreaks and shelterbelts and recapture desertified drylands for agriculture and human settlements.

The loss of productive irrigated lands to waterlogging and salinization entails large economic and social losses. The investment costs of irrigation are high, and many Asian nations depend on irrigated land for their food supply. Half the food produced in India and Indonesia is grown on irrigated lands; in China, it is 70 percent. Reversing excessive use of water is a necessary step in rehabilitation. Pumping and draining waterlogged soils and removing built-up salt are also needed. These steps can be very costly. In India, a small-scale alternative involved planting saline-tolerant trees that effectively pump water through their roots and leaves, thereby lowering the water table. In the Indian states of Haryana, Punjab, and Uttar Pradesh, scientists and villagers dug wells and applied green manure to reverse alkalinization from overirrigation.

These generally small-scale projects demonstrate the potential rehabilitation of degraded lands. Extending these efforts and tailoring them to local conditions are necessary to return once-productive lands to productive use. Stopping unsustainable practices that led to degradation of the land is equally, if not more important for meeting the needs of Asia's growing population. (See Chapter 13, "Rehabilitating and Restoring Degraded Lands.")

Forests

Deforestation is primarily caused by conversion of forests to other uses, generally agriculture. Deforestation rates continue to be significant in Asia, although they are not so high as in Africa and Latin America. The most extensive deforestation is occurring in Indonesia, where 600,000 hectares of closed forests are lost each year. The highest *rates* of deforestation are in Nepal, Sri Lanka, and Thailand. Reforestation is growing in Asia, but it has not kept pace with deforestation in most countries. China has the world's largest reforestation program, planting new forests at the rate of more than 4.5

million hectares per year, surpassing all the rest of the developing world.

Asian wood production is the largest in the world at more than 9 million cubic meters annually; Asia dominates the world export of tropical hardwoods. But recent projections suggest that Asia's share of the world market in tropical hardwoods will fall from 80 percent to only 10 percent by the year 2000. This change will result from depleted timber reserves and increased domestic consumption. Current logging practices are inefficient and they substantially damage remaining trees. This situation often leads to further deforestation when people follow the loggers into an area to clear the remaining forests for agriculture. (See Chapters 5 and 18, "Forests and Rangelands.")

Wildlife and Habitat

The loss of tropical forests in Asia also deprives wildlife of extensive habitat. A recent study of habitat loss in Southeast Asia shows that 68 percent of original wildlife habitat has been lost. Bangladesh has lost all but 6 percent of its wildlife habitat. (See Chapter 6, "Wildlife and Habitat.")

Oceans

Asia depends more heavily than any other region on ocean fishing to supply its daily protein needs. Japan has the largest harvest in the world—more than 11 million metric tons. Fish catches in regional fisheries nearest Asia have risen continuously since about 1970, but they are approaching, or have even exceeded, the United Nations Food and Agriculture Organization's estimated maximum sustainable yields.

In the face of environmental damage from marine pollution, especially oil, five countries have joined formally to adopt an action plan for the East Asian seas as part of UNEP's Regional Seas Programme. In 1979, Indonesia, Malaysia, Thailand, Singapore, and the Philippines agreed to assess the marine environment, manage coastal activity, and coordinate national plans. Specifically, the plan seeks to study the effects of pollution on marine life—primarily from oil drilling but also from metals, sewage, sediments, and chemical wastes from on- and off-shore activity. The program has made slow progress, and is hampered by funding problems. (See Chapters 9 and 22, "Oceans and Coasts.")

Air Pollution

The monitoring of air quality is still limited in most of Asia. With the major exception of Japan, air quality in Asia has generally worsened with industrialization and the lack of effective pollution controls. Not one Global Environmental Monitoring System air quality monitoring site in Asia fully complied with World Health Organization standards for suspended particulates, and only half the stations met sulfur dioxide standards between 1979 and 1985. Overall, Asia shows no definitive trends regarding air quality; progress made in some cities to decrease certain pollutants is offset by setbacks in others. But compared to the developed countries, Asia lags far behind in controlling most air pollutants. Hong Kong and Teheran show sharp rises in ambient sulfur dioxide levels from 1974 to 1984. Particulate levels in Calcutta and Manila increased over 20 percent during the same period. (See Chapters 10 and 23, "Atmosphere and Climate.")

2. Population and Health

The world's population continues to grow rapidly, driven by very high growth rates in many developing countries. Between 1950 and 1987, the global population doubled from 2.5 to 5 billion people, and another billion people will be added before the end of the next decade. Although growth rates have dropped sharply in developed countries from their post-World War II peaks, they are just beginning to decline in many parts of the developing world and continue unabated in Africa (1).

The least developed countries and countries already facing significant depletion of their natural resources often have the highest growth rates. The effects of rapid population growth on natural resources and the environment are a critical concern, but the issue is complex. With an expanding economy, population growth can often be accommodated reasonably. On the other hand, in the absence of economic development, the needs of a rapidly growing population can contribute to the destruction or degradation of the very resource base upon which a country's development depends.

To slow population growth, many developing countries have adopted family planning programs to reduce total fertility rates (the number of children the average woman bears in her lifetime). Numerous socioeconomic and cultural factors affect fertility rates (see *World Resources 1986*, pp. 15–23), but government programs are also effective when implemented vigorously. Significant declines in fertility and population growth have been achieved by encouraging smaller families and wider spacing of children in some developing countries, especially those in Asia.

Worldwide health conditions have improved markedly during the past 20 years. Important gains in life expectancy and infant mortality have been achieved in most developing countries. However, a large gap remains between the developed and developing worlds, with developing countries' health problems closely related to the environment, natural resources, and development. Primary concerns are the lack of food, clean water, and adequate health care. Many of the most severe problems affect the children. Diarrheal diseases (related primarily to malnutrition and unclean water) cause 25 percent of the estimated 14 million childhood deaths each year. Another 25 percent are attributable to infectious diseases. These conditions (and deaths) are preventable. Various international and national programs are in place to prevent these deaths, some with notable success.

One health problem shared by industrialized and developing countries is acquired immune deficiency syndrome (AIDS). Still a far smaller health problem than such major killers as diarrheal diseases and malaria, AIDS is spreading rapidly. With no known vaccine or cure, AIDS imposes high medical care costs and premature death mainly on adults in their prime.

The health effects of pesticides are also felt in both developing and developed countries. Stemming from the pressures of growing populations for increased food production and protection from vector-borne diseases, chemical pesticide sales more than quadrupled between 1970 and 1980; they continue to rise. The most apparent health effects are the acute poisonings of workers who handle pesticides and of others who are affected by accidents. Less obvious is the contamination of soils, water, and crops and the long-term health risk for the general population.

CONDITIONS AND TRENDS

POPULATION TRENDS

Rapid growth in world population is a distinguishing characteristic of the second half of the 20th Century. (See Figure 2.1.) After millennia of low growth rates, with deaths largely offsetting births, rapidly declining death rates combined with continuing high birth rates in the developing world for a dramatically increased population growth beginning around 1950. After taking more than 100 years to double from 1.25 to 2.5 billion in 1950, the world population doubled again in only 37 years—from 2.5 to 5 billion people by 1987 (2).

Growth rates, which rose significantly in developed countries following World War II, exceeded 2 percent per year in developing countries from 1950 to 1985. (See Figure 2.2.) By comparison, the world population grew only about 0.8 percent during the first half of this century and at lower rates before then (3). Although population growth rates fell below 1 percent in the developed world by the mid-1960s, they continued to rise in developing countries until the late 1960s, peaking at over 2.5 percent per year (4).

These differences have resulted in a shift in the distribution of global population toward the developing countries. (See Table 2.1.) The developed countries contained about one third the world population from 1900 to 1950

Table 2.1 Population Trends, 1900–2100
(millions)

Region	1900	1950	1985	2000	2025	2100
Developing Regions	1,070	1,681	3,657	4,837	6,799	8,748
Africa	133	224	555	872	1,617	2,591
Asia[a]	867	1,292	2,697	3,419	4,403	4,919
Latin America	70	165	405	546	779	1,238
Developed Regions	560	835	1,181	1,284	1,407	1,437
Europe, USSR, Japan, and Oceania[b]	478	669	917	987	1,062	1,055
Canada and the United States	82	166	264	297	345	382
World Total	**1,630**	**2,516**	**4,837**	**6,122**	**8,206**	**10,185**

Source: Thomas W. Merrick, "World Population in Transition," *Population Bulletin*, Vol. 42, No. 2 (1986).
Notes:
a. Excludes Japan.
b. Oceania includes Australia and New Zealand.

but less than one quarter by 1985. Between 1950 and 1985, the largest numerical increase—more than 1.4 billion—was in Asian developing countries. However, the fastest rates of growth were experienced in Africa and Latin America where populations grew to almost two and a half times their 1950 levels (5).

Population growth rates are falling everywhere except in Africa, where they continue to exceed 3 percent per year and are not expected to decline until near the end of the century (6). Although regional statistics often mask substantial differences among countries, population growth rates in African nations are consistently high. Among the 37 nations with annual growth rates exceeding 3 percent, 22 are in Africa, 10 are Middle Eastern Arab nations, and 3 are in Central America. (See Chapter 15, "Population and Health," Table 15.1.)

Figure 2.1 Population Growth, 1750–2100

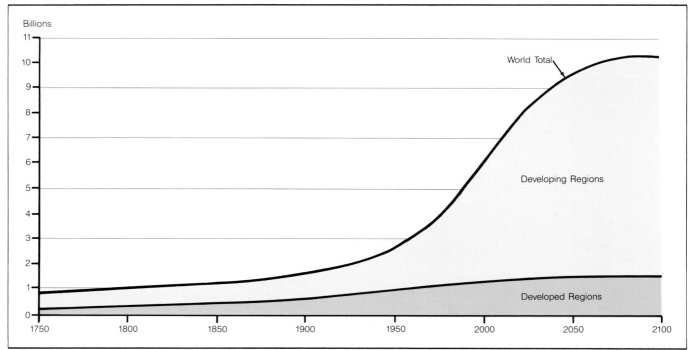

Source: Thomas W. Merrick, *et al.*, "World Population in Transition," *Population Bulletin,* Vol. 42, No. 2 (1986), Figure 1, p. 4.

Figure 2.2 Average Annual Rate of Population Growth for the World, More Developed Regions, and Less Developed Regions 1950–2025[a]

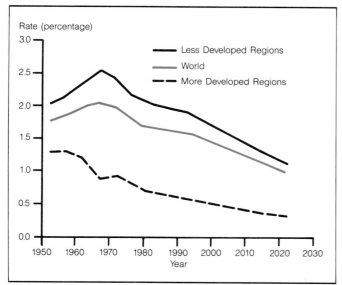

Source: United Nations (U.N.), *World Population Projects: Estimation and Projections as Assessed in 1984* (U.N., New York, 1986), p. 25.
Note: a. Growth rates are based on United Nations medium variant projection of population. See Technical Note for Chapter 15, "Population and Health," Table 15.1, "Size and Growth of Population, 1960-2025."

The United Nations projects continuing slow declines in annual population growth rates in all parts of the world. (See Figure 2.2.) This reflects declining total fertility rates (TFRs) (the number of children an average woman bears in her lifetime) in countries with high fertility rates and continuing low TFRs in the developed countries (7). Even if these assumed declines in fertility rates do occur, world population will continue to grow rapidly. The U.N. medium projection is for the world population to reach 6 billion people before the year 2000 and more than 8 billion by 2025, before stabilizing at about 10 billion, roughly twice the current world population, toward the end of the next century (8). (See Figure 2.1 and Table 2.1.) The slow decline in fertility rates is based upon recent trends, but it is an assumption. If fertility rates do not decline as rapidly as assumed, the growth of the world population will be even greater. Conversely, effective efforts to lower fertility rates more rapidly could substantially reduce the ultimate size of the population.

The Momentum of Population Growth

Continuing high growth rates result not only from continuing high fertility rates and increases in life expectancy, but also from the current demographic profile or age composition of the population. Figure 2.3 shows the current (1985) and projected (2025) age composition for the developing and developed countries. The contrasts are stark. In developing countries, 37 percent of the population is under 15 years of age and only 4 percent is 65 or older. In Africa, the figures are 45 percent under

15 and 3 percent 65 or older. By contrast, the developed countries' under-15 population is only 22 percent of the total and 11 percent is 65 or older (9).

In developing countries, the relative size of the young (under 15) population means growing demands for food, shelter, education, health care, and employment. All these basic needs increase pressure on limited natural resources and make economic development even more critical. Equally important, this age composition assures a continued large population growth in developing countries, even if total fertility rates dropped suddenly to replacement levels (an average of just over two children per woman) in the next few years, as increasing numbers of young women enter their childbearing years (10).

Because the countries with large percentages of young people are frequently the same ones that have high fertility rates, the built-in momentum of this age structure compounds the problem of high population growth. In spite of declining birth rates since about 1970, the annual increments to total population continue to rise, and they are not expected to peak until the end of this century. About 85 million people are added to the world population each year, and the figure will rise to 89 million by the year 2000 (11).

THE IMPLICATIONS OF RAPID POPULATION GROWTH FOR NATURAL RESOURCES

Increasing numbers of people increase demands on natural resources. Clearly, more people require more food, fuel, clothing, and the other necessities of life. All of them must ultimately be supplied from the planet's resources and from the sun's energy. These facts raise difficult questions about the implications of continuing rapid population growth (and very large numerical increases in world population) for the sustainability of natural resources and quality of the environment.

Can the world's natural resources support the growing world population, or will human demands overwhelm the capacity of natural systems? Can the Earth's finite resources of soil, water, and its biological processes continue to meet the demands of 5–10 billion people without collapsing and bringing on the Malthusian specter of increasing poverty and starvation?

The answers to these global-scale questions are not clear cut and depend upon numerous assumptions about economic development, technological progress, and human behavior. On a local or national scale and at current levels of economic development, however, there is substantial evidence that growing populations are pressing (or have already exceeded) the capacity of local natural resources in some areas. They cannot produce enough food and otherwise meet the needs of rapidly increasing numbers of people. Over 90 percent of the projected addition of roughly 3 billion people living in the year 2025 will live in what are now low-income African, Asian, and Latin American countries (12). Many of these countries already face agricultural land shortages, limited water supplies, depleted forest resources, and/or degraded soils. Without rapid economic development, can these countries meet the needs of almost twice as many people within the next 40 years (13)?

Figure 2.3 Population Age Pyramids, Developing and Developed Countries, 1985 and 2025

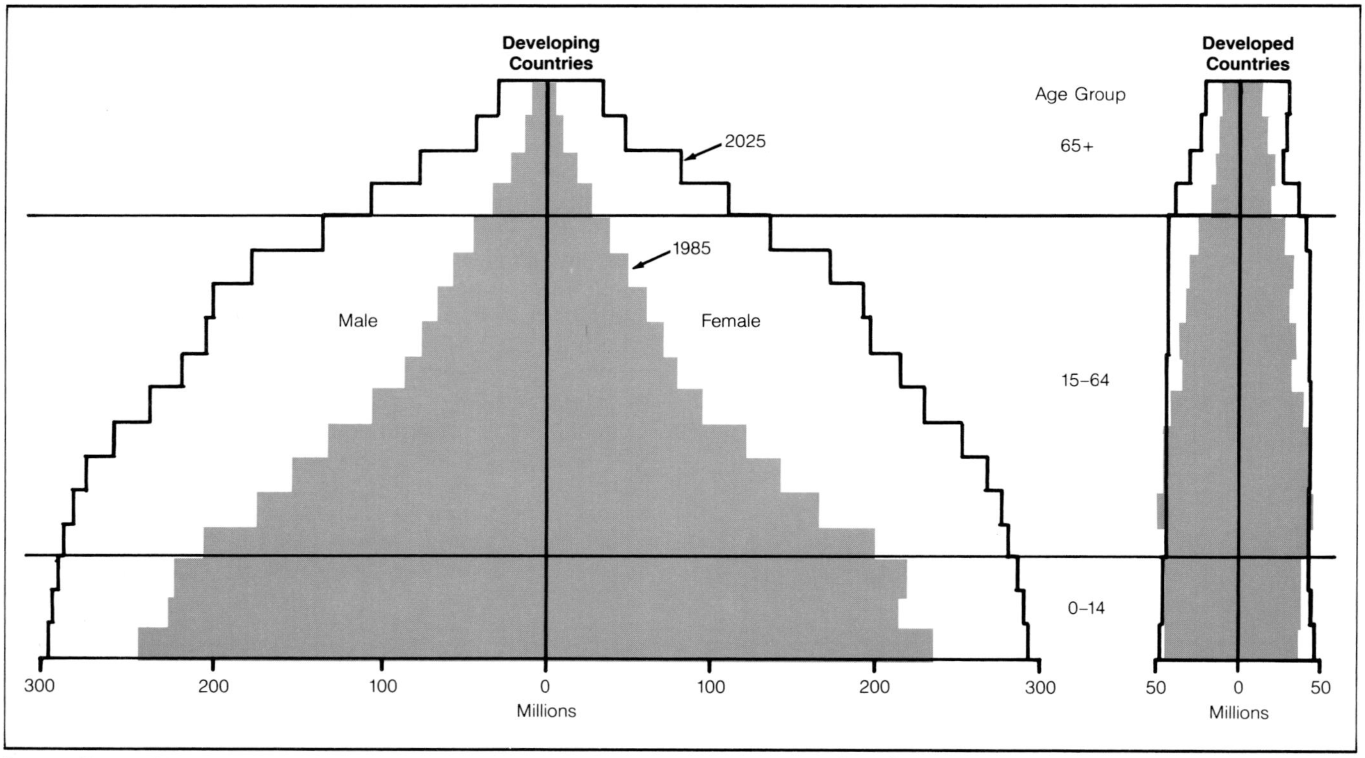

Source: Thomas W. Merrick, "World Population in Transition," *Population Bulletin,* Vol. 42, No. 2 (1986), p. 19.

Food Production and Land Use

Historically, increased food demands were met by enlarging the cultivated area. Although increasing yields has become more important since 1950, croplands continue to expand (14). Between 1850 and 1950, total croplands are estimated to have grown from 538 million hectares to almost 1.2 billion hectares. By 1980, total croplands had increased another 332 million hectares to 1.5 billion hectares. (See *World Resources 1987,* Table 18.3, p. 272.)

This increase in cropland was at the expense of rangelands, wetlands, and other ecosystems, particularly forests. Since 1950, when population has been growing the fastest in developing countries, deforestation has been concentrated in the tropics. Current estimates are that more than 6 million hectares of closed moist tropical forests are lost each year, primarily through conversion to agricultural land (15). The extent of remaining forests varies widely. Brazil, Indonesia, and Zaire still retain large forest areas, but others have substantially depleted their forest resources. Cote d'Ivoire, with the world's highest deforestation rate (5.2 percent per year), has lost over 56 percent of its forest cover since about 1965. (See Chapter 18, "Forests and Rangelands," Table 18.1.)

In addition to the direct loss of forests and associated loss of biological diversity (see Chapter 6, "Wildlife and Habitat"), the conversion to agricultural lands often increases soil erosion and depletion of soil nutrients. An example of agriculture's increasing stress on relatively fragile lands is the island of Java in Indonesia.

Java's population rose from about 5 million at the end of the 18th Century to 25 million at the beginning of the 20th Century and to 95 million in 1986 (16). Despite migration to Jakarta, the capital city, and government programs encouraging transmigration to other islands, the population of rural Java continued to grow rapidly (17).

Indonesia's economy is unable to provide sufficient nonfarm opportunities for the rapidly expanding labor force despite an annual gross domestic product (GDP) growth rate of 7.7 percent between 1970 and 1982 (18). On Java, labor requirements for growing rice have also been steadily declining over the long term. Labor hours per hectare declined from 1,523 per season in 1924–30 to 1,152 in 1977–80 (19). The resulting labor surplus reinforced the effects of population growth, forcing more and more people to cultivate marginal land. In Java's upland regions, there are 700–900 people per square kilometer of farmland, with densities as high as 2,000 per square kilometer in some locales (20). Although the average landholdings are 0.7 hectares, most households own less than 0.4 hectares and many are landless (21).

As a result of the growing pressure to eke out a subsistence on the land, most of Java's upland watersheds have been cleared of forest cover and planted with maize, cassava, and other crops. Yields are low and little effort is made to control erosion. The most severe erosion occurs on subsistence holdings of 0.4 hectares or less, often on steep inaccessible hillsides far from the villages. Over 1 million hectares of such lands (almost one quarter of Java's 4.4 million hectares of cultivated uplands) can no longer sustain even subsistence farming, and such areas of degraded land are increasing by 200,000 hectares per year (22).

In addition to threatening the subsistence of some 12 million Javanese and driving increasing numbers into abject poverty, persistent land degradation and erosion reduce water retention in the uplands and increase downstream siltation, thereby worsening floods during the rainy seasons and damaging both urban and agricultural areas downstream (23).

The increased need for agricultural land leads not only to deforestation but also to cultivation of land that is only marginally suitable for crops. Without irrigation and other artificial inputs, many arid and semiarid areas of the world are not suited to continuous cropping (24). Farmlands created by clearing forests in the moist tropics can often sustain only one or two years of crops before productivity drops significantly. When such areas were used in the past, traditional farming systems relied upon long periods of fallow for the soil to recover (25).

The demand for cropland exceeds the availability of highly productive agricultural lands. This problem is often compounded by inequitable landholding systems wherein the best agricultural land is owned by relatively few, leaving many subsistence farmers to depend on small plots of less productive land (26).

India's Rajasthan State is an example of population pressures on marginal land. Sixty percent of Rajasthan is arid. Between 1900 and 1972, its population tripled (27). To meet the subsistence needs of this burgeoning population, the cultivated area doubled from about 30 percent in 1951 to nearly 60 percent in 1971, even though the United Nations Food and Agriculture Organization (FAO) considers only 20 percent of Rajasthan's arid land suitable for rainfed agriculture (28). As cultivators moved into marginal lands (previously often left for livestock), they reduced or completely eliminated long fallow periods. The soil, stripped of its cover most of the time, was rapidly impoverished. Between 1954 and 1970, both the overall production and average yield per hectare of three of the four major crop groups (jowar, sesame, and kharif) declined consistently, even though the acreage under sesame and kharif increased (29).

By 1972, 88 percent of Rajasthan was under cultivation, and the population density had reached 48 per square kilometer—considered high for arid lands (30). Natural vegetation survived on only 13 percent of the land used by livestock, tree and shrub cover was sparse, wells yielded less water and a growing number became saline, and about one third the area was covered by a sheet of sand (31).

Similar pressures degrade rangelands. As human populations increase, more livestock is put out to graze on rangelands with limited forage. (See Chapter 5, "Forests and Rangelands.")

In Kenya and Tanzania, for example, livestock are the basis of the Maasai culture and economy. Prior to colonial rule in the 1880s, about 45,000 Maasai occupied more than 200,000 square kilometers of land. They moved their livestock between the hilly wooded areas with permanent water holes in the dry season and the

open plains with green pasture and rainfed surface water in the wet seasons (32). With the colonial administration came health and veterinary services, some water development, protection against natural predators, and the discouragement of cattle raiding and warfare. The Maasai population grew rapidly, but their nomadic life was restricted. By 1961, about 117,000 Maasai were limited to 93,000 square kilometers of rangeland. Their population density had increased more than fivefold in 80 years. Because their existence required a certain number of domestic animals, the Maasai increased their livestock proportionately (33).

Overgrazing in parts of these rangelands was a result of these rapid increases in human and livestock populations. It, in turn, contributed to the severe impacts of the series of dry years preceding the record-setting 1961 drought that was followed by heavy floods. About 3,000 Maasai and 75 percent of the total livestock in the Kajiado District (Kenya) died. Other overgrazed rangelands in Kenya and parts of Tanzania also suffered some losses (34). Between 1969 and 1979 in the Kajiado and Narok Districts, population again doubled and the livestock population increased proportionately. The effects of continued overgrazing and resulting desertification were felt during the droughts of 1972–74 and 1983–84 in Kajiado. In the famine resulting from the 1972–74 drought, the Maasai lost 90 percent of their livestock (35).

More Intensive Use of Agricultural Land

These examples focus on subsistence or low-input agriculture, upon which a high proportion of the growing Third World population depends. But increased food production need not come from increasing the amount of land under cultivation. Instead, productivity can be increased. FAO has argued that only by shifting to high-input agriculture can many countries meet the food needs of their projected populations by the year 2000 (36). In fact, the largest increases in developing countries' food production during the past two decades were due to increased yields and higher productivity rather than to expanded cropland. (See Table 2.2.) Per capita food production rose over the past 10 years in all developing regions except Africa, despite declining per capita land area for agricul-

Table 2.2 World Increases in Crop Area and Yields, by Region, 1964–85

Region	Percentage Change in Cropland 1964–66 to 1982–84	Percentage Change in Yields 1964–66 to 1983–85	
		Cereals	Roots and Tubers
World	**8.9**	**58**	**21**
Africa	13.5	13	22
Asia	4.1	77	58
North and Central America	7.8	44	23
South America	34.6	42	–1
Europe	10.5	76	19
USSR	1.3	35	13
Oceania[a]	23.5	25	13

Source: International Institute for Environment and Development and World Resources Institute, *World Resources 1987* (Basic Books, New York, 1987), Tables 18.1, pp. 268–269 and Table 19.1, pp. 276–277.
Note: a. Includes Australia and New Zealand.

ture. (See Chapter 17, "Food and Agriculture," Tables 17.1 and 17.2.) These gains were achieved through a combination of increased irrigation, fertilizer, pesticides, and use of high-yielding seed varieties (37).

For increased yields to meet the continual needs of a rapidly growing population, two conditions must be met. The higher yields must be sustainable over the long term, and the food must reach the intended recipients. The first condition depends upon financial, institutional, and technological factors. Continued high productivity requires the application of water, fertilizer, and other inputs at appropriate times and levels. This requires not only financial resources but also the institutional capacity to assure continuing supplies and the technological sophistication to make certain that the inputs are used correctly.

Unfortunately, there is substantial evidence that inappropriate use of inputs is threatening to offset recent gains in productivity. Inefficient use of irrigation water, especially where drainage is inadequate, can cause salinization and waterlogging of soil. Salinization is estimated to affect productivity seriously on 20–30 million hectares (7 percent) of the world's irrigated land (38). In India and Pakistan alone, for example, salinization may be affecting

up to 16 million hectares of irrigated land. (See Chapter 13, "Rehabilitating and Restoring Degraded Lands," and *World Resources 1987*, Table 19.3, p. 280.)

Heavy reliance upon artificial fertilizers, to the exclusion of natural methods of soil enhancement, can lead to reduced water retention, fertility loss, and runoff pollution of streams and rivers. (See Chapter 4, "Food and Agriculture," for a discussion of the environmental and sustainability problems associated with high-input agriculture.) Extensive and often inappropriate use of synthetic pesticides pose human health risks, and lead to the development of new strains of pests that are resistant to these chemicals. (See "Focus On: Pesticide Use and Health," below.) The long-term environmental effects of raising food production through the use of high levels of chemical inputs are cause for concern.

Producing more food does not necessarily mean more food consumption by the growing numbers of poor people. In fact, the growth of high-input agriculture tends to concentrate highly productive land in the hands of relatively few landholders, further increasing the number of people forced onto marginal land. (See Box 2.1.)

The issue of rapid population growth and natural resources is complex. Clearly, economic development and

Box 2.1 Long-Term Agricultural and Land Use Trends in India

India, where there are data going back nearly a century, illustrates the interplay between population growth, agricultural production, and land use. In this century, the Indian population has more than tripled, from 240 million in 1900 to 800 million in 1987, an average growth rate of 1.38 percent per year. The agricultural response has been equally dramatic.

In the first half of the century, there was a massive expansion of cropland. Data for 183 districts in the northern Indian subcontinent, including parts of present-day Bangladesh and Pakistan, show that the arable area expanded more than 25 million hectares or 45 percent between 1890 and 1970 (1). Other terrestrial ecosystems—forests, woods, grassland, and scrub—were reduced by 30 to 40 percent. (See Table 1.)

At the same time, because of population growth the land resource base diminished sharply in per capita terms. The availability of arable land declined from 0.39 to 0.23 hectares per capita and that of forests, woods, grasslands, and scrub shrank even more from 0.49 to 0.13 hectares per capita.

Offsetting the growing scarcity of arable land was a substantial intensification of land use. Irrigated acreage expanded almost ninefold, from 2.6 million hectares in 1890 (4.4 percent of the arable area) to 22.3 million hectares in 1970 (26 percent of the arable area). The colonial government invested significantly in irrigation before independence in 1947, but the irrigated area doubled after 1950, in large part from private investments in tubewells.

Cropping intensity rose sharply on this irrigated acreage. The area left fallow fell

from 17 to 10 percent between 1930 and 1970. The use of chemical fertilizers, largely in conjunction with high-yielding seed varieties, grew from a negligible amount to 8.6 million tons of nutrient used overall in India in 1985 160 kilograms per hectare of irrigated area (2). After 1950 there was no further expansion of gross cropped area, but production rose due to significant improvements in crop yields.

The figure illustrates one result of this process. Independent India has succeeded in raising foodgrain production per capita by a modest amount since 1951. Its agricultural growth rate, while not exemplary, has equaled that of developing countries as a whole. Yet current per capita output remains well below the

averages that prevailed in India in the early decades of this century.

Another result is increased pressure on the remaining nonarable land. Livestock, fed overwhelmingly on crop residues and natural forage rather than on fodder crops, increased in numbers proportionally with the expansion of cropped area. However, the ratio of livestock to people fell from 98:100 to 59:100 between 1900 and 1972 as pasturage provided by woods, grassland, and wastelands disappeared.

The transformation of these resources to cropland has affected the rural poor disproportionately, because for the most part it was a transformation from common property on which poor households depended to pri-

Table 1 Land Use in 183 Districts of Northern India, 1890–1970
(millions of hectares)

Land Type	1890	1950	1970
Total Area	155.6	155.6	155.6
Percent of total	100.0	100.0	100.0
Arable	59.1	73.1	86.1
Percent of total	38.0	47.0	55.3
Settled	2.8	4.2	6.6
Percent of total	1.8	2.7	4.2
Forest and woods	13.6	10.2	9.2
Percent of total	8.7	6.5	5.9
Interrupted woods	19.8	15.6	12.2
Percent of total	12.7	10.1	7.8
Grassland	22.3	18.5	14.2
Percent of total	14.3	11.9	9.1
Wetlands	4.9	3.6	3.2
Percent of total	3.1	2.3	2.1
Scrub and wasteland	28.7	25.8	19.6
Percent of total	18.5	16.6	12.6
Surface water	4.5	4.5	4.5
Percent of total	2.9	2.9	2.9

Source: John F. Richards, Edward S. Haynes, and James R. Hagen, "Changes in the Land and Human Productivity in Northern India, 1890-1970," in *Agricultural History*, Vol. 59, No. 4 (October 1985), Table 2, p. 530.

technological advances can increase the capacity of natural resources to support a given number of people. However, where economic development is not proceeding rapidly enough to accommodate a growing population, agriculture and natural resources are likely to continue to suffer.

TRENDS IN FERTILITY REDUCTION EFFORTS

In the developing world, fertility reduction has two aspects. On the one hand is the remarkable fall in fertility in numerous countries, particularly China (39). Declines in certain Asian and Latin American countries are impressive. Yet they are matched by the absence of appreciable declines in other large countries, especially in Africa, the Middle East, and Central America. Figure 2.4 shows trends in fertility rates for selected developing countries in all regions. (See also Chapter 15, "Population and Health," Table 15.2.)

Government Strategies to Reduce Fertility

For governments that choose to adopt them, a variety of policy measures are available to reduce fertility rates. Twelve measures ranging from the immediate and concrete to the long term and general have been identified. (See Table 2.3.)

All these measures are used by at least a few countries, some quite widely. The basic family planning program (No. 1) is used by virtually every country with a formal policy to reduce fertility, although program strength varies (see below). Under this heading come such variations as community-based distribution and integration with health programs. Many programs add sterilization (No. 2), a few add abortion (No. 3), and several are offering new contraceptive methods (No. 4), such as Norplant, the new five-year implant. Private sector distribution of contraceptives (No. 5) can be encouraged either by direct subsidy of commercial sales or by easing taxes and regulations on commercial sale of contraceptives and on services by private doctors, nurses, and midwives.

Almost every family planning program provides information and education (No. 6) to the population, usually stressing the advantages of contraceptive use for spacing pregnancies or for having fewer children. Several countries have established incentives and disincentives for fertility behavior (No. 7), most of them quite mild; they are applied to relatively small portions of the population. The chief exceptions are China, with a comprehensive set of

Box 2.1

vate property from which they were largely excluded. A study in seven Indian states, reported in 1986, found that poor households graze their animals on the commons from 70 to 90 percent of the time, compared to 20 to 40 percent for better-off rural households.

Poor households obtain 60 to 90 percent of their fuel from the common lands, compared to 10 to 20 percent for other households. The rural poor also rely much more heavily on common land for gathering food, raw materials for handcrafts, and other subsistence

(3). The loss of natural ecosystems decreased living standards most for poor households with least control over the expanding cultivated area.

In the study areas of the seven states, 26 to 63 percent of common woods, grassland, wetlands, and wasteland had disappeared in the previous three decades, mostly through conversion to private cropland. Although some conversion programs were designed to alleviate rural poverty, most of the converted land ended up in the hands of better-off households. For India's rural poor a valuable and accessible resource disappeared, and thus the transformation has had less favorable long-term implications than suggested by trends in per capita foodgrain production.

This article by Robert Repetto is reprinted with permission. It originally appeared as *Population, Resources, Environment: An Uncertain Future* in *Population Bulletin*, Vol. 42, No. 2 (1987), p. 19.

References and Notes

1. John F. Richards, Edward S. Haynes, and James R. Hagen, "Changes in the Land and Human Productivity in Northern India, 1890–1970," paper presented at the American Historical Association annual meeting, Chicago, December 29, 1984.
2. David Seckler and R.K. Sampath, "Production and Poverty in Indian Agriculture," Colorado State University, International School for Agricultural and Resource Development, Fort Collins, Colorado, November 1985.
3. N.S. Jodha, "Common Property Resources and Rural Poor in Dry Regions of India," *Economic and Political Weekly*, Vol. 21, No. 27 (1986) pp. 1169–1181.

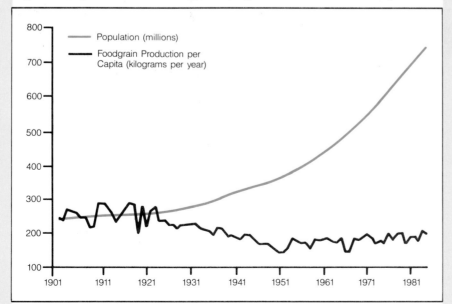

Figure 1 Population and Per Capita Foodgrain Production in India, 1901–85

Population (millions)

Foodgrain Production per Capita (kilograms per year)

Source: David Seckler and R.K. Sampath, "Production and Poverty in Indian Agriculture," Colorado State University, International School for Agricultural and Resources Development, Fort Collins, Colorado, 1985.

Figure 2.4 Trends in Total Fertility Rates for Selected Developing Countries, 1952–87

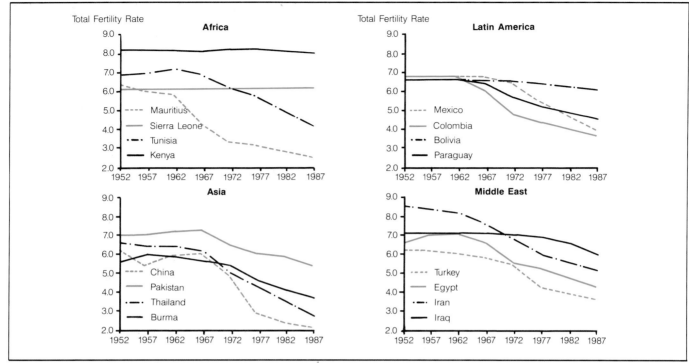

Source: United Nations Department of Economic and Social Affairs, *World Population Prospects; Estimates and Projections as Assessed in 1984,* (U.N., New York, 1986), Table A-12, pp. 102–107.

measures, and Singapore. Direct payments to acceptors (No. 8) are used in a few Asian countries for sterilization and in some cases for use of the IUD (e.g., to offset costs of travel, work lost) and sometimes, to encourage acceptance. These measures are important in India, Bangladesh, Sri Lanka, and Korea. Community pressures (No. 9) operate most notably in the two dissimilar cultures of China and Indonesia. Changes in the legal age of marriage (No. 10) have been made over the years in many countries (40), and the mean age at marriage has risen. But efforts to control internal migration are generally useless, although again China is a significant exception. Limits on family size (No. 11) are imposed probably only in China, with its one-child rule (recently relaxed in rural areas), although numerous other countries such as India, Indonesia, and Bangladesh encourage two- or three-child families.

All countries devote resources to social and economic development (No. 12), as do the various donor agencies, but their main justification is not directly related to fertility.

No country uses all 12 measures. Experience shows that different combinations fit different countries and that fertility reduction can be advanced many ways. The most common approaches and the simplest to implement are the basic family planning programs, which vary greatly in both their intensity of effort and effectiveness.

The Strength of Fertility Reduction Efforts

Some countries make essentially no effort to reduce fertility and others give it the highest priority. The strength of government program efforts to reduce fertility has been rated for 100 developing countries. The ratings cover 30 aspects of these efforts, including official policies, budgets, services provided, and availability and

Table 2.3 Strategies for Fertility Reduction

1. Improve public-sector access to current contraceptive methods, i.e., "family planning programs"
2. . . . plus sterilization
3. . . . plus abortion
4. . . . plus new and improved methods of contraception with better acceptability, continuity and/or effectiveness
5. Improve private-sector distribution of current means of fertility control
6. Promote information, education, propaganda on fertility control
7. Manipulate incentives and disincentives affecting fertility behavior (e.g., maternity cost, child assistance, housing, social security, social services)
8. . . . through direct payment of money or gifts for desired fertility performance
9. Manage community "pressure" for an antinatalist consensus
10. Impose legal sanctions on age at marriage, internal migration
11. . . . limits on family size
12. Advance socioeconomic determinants of fertility singly or collectively; e.g., general development, popular education, infant/child mortality, income, industrialization, women's status, urbanization

Source: Bernard Berelson and Robert Haveman, "On the Efficient Allocation of Resources for Fertility Reduction," *International Family Planning Perspectives,* Vol. 5, No. 4 (1979), p. 134.

accessibility of birth control methods. Each aspect was rated on a scale from 0 to 4, yielding a maximum possible score of 120. As of 1982, only China exceeded 100 (41).

Table 2.4 shows aggregate scores for all 100 countries. Seven of the 10 with strong program efforts are in Asia; most African and Middle Eastern countries appear in the "weak" and "very weak" groups. The regional mean scores reflect this picture. The average program effort score for all Asian countries is 83; by contrast, the average score for Latin America is 56, 31 for the Middle East and North Africa, and only 17 for sub-Saharan Africa (42).

Within a region, programs vary widely. Asia contains a number of countries with low program effort scores, among them Burma, Laos, and Mongolia. Asian countries with moderate scores include Bangladesh, which is struggling hard to lower its fertility under difficult conditions, and the Philippines, with a much lower density and with vastly greater per capita resources but with a fragmented program and ambivalent leadership.

The contrasts in Latin America run from the nearly nonexistent efforts in Bolivia and Paraguay to effective ones in Colombia and Mexico. Brazil's program, although concentrated in the private sector, nevertheless has a high acceptance level of contraceptive use.

Effects of Program Efforts on Contraceptive Use and Fertility

Based upon the developing countries' program ratings, fertility declines can be compared with program efforts. Have family planning programs made a difference? The chief difficulty here is the fact that the programs operated during a historical period with other strong influences on fertility. Separating their effects is difficult. (For an extensive discussion of other factors affecting fertility, see *World Resources 1986*, pp. 15–22, and *World Resources 1987*, pp. 9–10.)

Table 2.5 shows the relationship between the level of a country's program effort and the percentage of couples using contraception. Countries are grouped by their program effort scores and their socioeconomic settings (SES) (43). The SES rank is intended to capture a number of other factors affecting fertility. In general, a higher SES is associated with lower fertility rates. Within any SES category, the percentage of couples using contraception falls steadily as program efforts weaken. This pattern of marked decline is true regardless of socioeconomic level. Overall, the mean percentage of couples using contraception declines from 59 percent to only 7 percent across the four categories of program strength.

Equally significant is the fact that the percentage of couples using contraception falls steadily as the socioeconomic setting worsens. Under moderate program effort, for example, the percentage declines from 58 percent to 19 percent; under very weak or no programs, it falls from 36 percent to 3 percent. For all countries, the range is 55–4 percent. Similar patterns (not shown) are apparent in the effects of program strength and socioeconomic setting on birth rates and the rate of decline in birth rates.

More sophisticated analyses (which are able to take account of numerous influences at once and to show the proportion of fertility decline associated with each) support the same conclusions. Both program strength and SES factors matter, but regardless of the socioeconomic setting, vigorous fertility reduction programs have an important effect on lowering fertility rates (44).

Table 2.4 Family Planning Program Effort Scores for 100 Countries, 1982

Country	Score[a]	Country	Score[a]	Country	Score[a]	Country	Score[a]
Strong		**Weak**		**Very weak or none**		**Very weak or none (cont.)**	
China	101.1	Chile	52.3	Nicaragua	23.8	Bolivia	9.0
Korea, Rep.	94.8	Brazil	51.1	Ghana	21.3	Chad	8.3
Taiwan	94.3	Pakistan	48.5	Uganda	20.5	Ethiopia	7.4
Singapore	93.4	Egypt	47.6	Yemen, Dem.	20.3	Malawi	6.9
Indonesia	89.9	Nepal	44.7	Mozambique	19.7	Cote d'Ivoire	6.6
Colombia	85.3	Morocco	43.3	Sierra Leone	19.3	Kuwait	6.1
Hong Kong	82.8	Haiti	42.9	Jordan	19.0	Niger	5.5
Mauritius	82.0	Ecuador	42.2	Zambia	18.7	Guinea	5.4
Sri Lanka	80.4	Costa Rica	40.0	Congo	18.4	Burkina Faso	5.2
Mexico	79.9	Lebanon	39.8	Lesotho	16.7	Burma	5.1
		Venezuela	37.5	Togo	16.7	Mauritania	4.2
		Turkey	35.0	Guinea-Bissau	16.3	Iraq	3.7
		Guatemala	34.0	Zaire	15.5	Oman	1.7
Moderate		Western Samoa	33.8	Nigeria	15.4	United Arab	
India	75.6	Kenya	33.7	Benin	13.7	Emirates	1.5
El Salvador	75.5	Zimbabwe	32.7	Mali	13.6	Saudi Arabia	1.4
Thailand	72.9	Botswana	31.8	Afghanistan	13.5	Equatorial Guinea	0.5
Tunisia	70.2	Guyana	31.7	Iran	13.3	Libya	0.0
Bangladesh	68.5	Gambia	31.2	Syria	12.9	Kampuchea	0.0
Dominican		Cyprus	30.4	Burundi	12.6	Laos	0.0
Republic	66.3	Honduras	30.3	Central African		Mongolia	0.0
Jamaica	66.0	Algeria	30.0	Republic	12.4		
Philippines	65.2	Papua New Guinea	29.7	Somalia	11.5	Mean for all countries	69.5
Vietnam	64.0	Rwanda	27.6	Madagascar	10.3		
Malaysia	61.1	Senegal	27.2	Cameroon	10.1	Maximum possible	
Panama	60.8	Tanzania	26.8	Paraguay	9.4	source	120
Fiji	59.8	Peru	26.3	Yemen	9.2		
Korea, Dem. Peoples Rep.	59.8	Liberia	25.9	Sudan	9.0		
Cuba	59.2						
Trinidad/Tobago	55.9						

Source: Robert J. Lapham and W. Parker Mauldin, "Contraceptive Prevalence: The Influence of Organized Family Planning Programs," *Studies in Family Planning*, Vol. 16, No. 3 (1985), pp. 123-124.

Note: a. Scores indicate the strength of government efforts to reduce fertility including official policies, budgets, services, and availability of birth control methods. The maximum possible score is 120.

Table 2.5 Contraceptive Prevalence Rates in 73 Developing Countries by 1970 Socioeconomic Setting Index and 1982 Program Effort Index

1970 Socio-economic Setting	1982 Program Effort								Contraceptive Prevalence Mean (percent)
	Strong		Moderate		Weak		Very weak or none		
	Country	Percent	Country	Percent	Country	Percent	Country	Percent	
High	Hong Kong	80	Cuba	79	Costa Rica	66	Paraguay	36	
	Singapore	71	Panama	63	Brazil	50			
	Taiwan	70	Jamaica	55	Venezuela	49			
	Korea	58	Trinidad/Tobago	54	Peru	43			
	Colombia	51	Fiji	38	Chile	43			
	Mauritius	51							
	Mexico	40							
		60[a]		58[a]		50[a]		36[a]	55
Upper Middle	China	69	Thailand	58	Ecuador	40	Iran	23	
	Sri Lanka	57	Philippines	45	Turkey	40	Syria	20	
			Dominican Republic	43	Honduras	27	Ghana	10	
			Malaysia	42	Egypt	24	Nicaragua	9	
			El Salvador	34	Morocco	19	Zaire	3	
			Tunisia	31	Guatemala	18	Zambia	1	
					Algeria	7			
		63[a]		42[a]		25[a]		11[a]	30
Lower Middle	Indonesia	48	India	32	Haiti	19	Bolivia	24	
			Vietnam	21	Zimbabwe	14	Nigeria	6	
					Kenya	7	Lesotho	6	
					Pakistan	6	Burma	7	
					Papua New Guinea	5	Cameroon	2	
					Senegal	4	Uganda	1	
					Liberia	1	Kampuchea	0	
		48[a]		27[a]		8[a]		6[a]	12
Low			Bangladesh	19	Nepal	7	Benin	18	
					Tanzania	1	Sudan	5	
							Sierra Leone	4	
							Ethiopia	2	
							Somalia	2	
							Yemen, Dem.	1	
							Burundi	1	
							Chad	1	
							Guinea	1	
							Malawi	1	
							Mali	1	
							Niger	1	
							Burkina Faso	1	
							Mauritania	1	
				19[a]		4[a]		3[a]	4
Contraceptive Prevalence Mean (percent)		59		44		23		7	26

Source: Robert J. Lapham and W. Parker Mauldin, "Contraceptive Prevalence: The Influence of Organized Family Planning Programs," *Studies in Family Planning*, Vol. 16, No. 3 (1985), p. 128.
Note: a. Mean prevalence at each level of program effort and socioeconomic setting.

THE STATE OF WORLD HEALTH

Substantial progress has been made in improving health conditions throughout the world since the Global Health for All by the Year 2000 strategy was adopted by the Thirty-Fourth World Health Assembly in 1981. However, a large gap continues to exist between the developed and developing countries. Both the progress and the remaining differences are reflected in global and regional rates of life expectancy and infant mortality. (See Table 2.6.)

Life expectancy at birth now exceeds 70 years throughout Europe and North America as well as in 10 Latin American nations, 7 countries in Asia and the Near East, Australia, and New Zealand. (See Chapter 15, "Population and Health," Table 15.3 for detailed country data and trends.) By contrast, the average life expectancy in Africa is still below 50 years in 21 countries and above 60 in only 7 nations.

As minimum health objectives for the year 2000, the World Health Organization (WHO) adopted a life expectancy at birth of 60 years and infant mortality rates of fewer than 50 deaths per 1,000 births. Ninety-eight of 161

countries have achieved levels of 60 or more years (45). Life expectancy at birth ranges from a high of 77.2 years in Japan to a low of 36 years in Sierra Leone. Most countries show a higher life expectancy for women; the few exceptions are mainly in South Asia (46).

Table 2.6 Global Health Indicators

Region	Life Expectancy at Birth (years)		Infant Mortality (deaths/1,000)	
	1965–70	1985–90	1965–70	1985–90
Africa	43.9	51.3	158	101
North and Central America	67.5	72.0	39	24
South America	58.7	65.5	91	57
Asia	53.3	61.1	110	74
Europe	70.6	74.0	30	13
USSR	69.6	72.1	26	22
Oceania	64.2	69.1	48	26
World	**54.8**	**61.1**	**103**	**71**

Sources:
1. United Nations (U.N.) Population Division, *World Population Prospects: Estimates and Projections as Assessed in 1984* (U.N., New York, 1986), Table A-15, pp. 114-132 and Table A-16, pp. 134-139.
2. For continental aggregates see Chapter 15, "Population and Health," Table 15.3.

Infant mortality rates have fallen in nearly 150 countries in the last decade (47). Finland, Iceland, Sweden, and Japan have the lowest infant mortality rates—6 per 1,000 live births. In developing countries, particularly those in Africa and Asia, childhood deaths remain high (48). Of 159 nations reporting infant mortality rates, only 80 reported levels of below 50 per thousand (49). In more than a quarter of the nations, representing 29 percent of the world's population, infant mortality rates still exceed 100 per 1,000 live births (50).

Maternal mortality rates follow a similar pattern. In the United States, nine women die from pregnancy related causes for every 100,000 live births. In Scandinavia, the rate is even lower—four per 100,000 (51). In many developing nations, the rate continues to be 100–200 times that of the industrialized world. Five African countries have maternal mortality rates in excess of 1,000 per 100,000 births (52). (See Chapter 15, "Population and Health," Table 15.5.)

Maternal mortality accounts for the highest proportion of deaths among women of reproductive age in developing countries (53). Of the estimated 500,000 women dying each year of largely preventable pregnancy-related causes, 99 percent live in developing countries. Some 300,000 women die every year in South and West Asia alone compared to 6,000 in all developed countries (54). For every maternal death in developing countries, 10–15 more women suffer long-term health damage related to pregnancy (55).

The leading causes of death provide a sharp contrast between the developing and developed countries. (See Table 2.7.) In the developing world, infectious and parasitic diseases cause 40 percent of all deaths. By contrast, cardiovascular diseases account for half the deaths in industrialized countries—twice as many as cancers, the second major cause of death (56). Cardiovascular diseases, more often associated with affluent nations, are now also

the third leading cause of death (16 percent, after infectious and parasitic diseases) in developing countries (57). Cervical cancer is growing more common in the Third World (58) and lung cancers are likely to increase as tobacco use grows (59).

Health Problems of the Developing World

For millions, good health is an elusive goal. Despite adequate food supplies at the global level, hunger and malnutrition are a leading health problem in the developing world. (See Chapter 4, "Food and Agriculture," for a discussion of the problem of access to food.) An estimated 950 million people—nearly 20 percent of the world population—do not consume enough calories for an active working life (60). Although calorie and protein supplies are improving in Latin America, the Middle East, North Africa, and East Asia, they are on a downward trend in sub-Saharan Africa and Southern Asia (61). In Africa, 150 million people suffer food shortages (62); every day 40,000 children die from hunger-related diseases (63). Undernourishment also produces chronic ill health and debility, lowers resistance to infectious diseases, and increases their severity.

Waterborne and Airborne Diseases

The most common tropical diseases are water related—caused by the absence of potable water and adequate sanitation or transmitted through insects, parasites, and other water-related disease vectors. In the developing world, 80 percent of all illness is attributed to unsafe and inadequate water supplies and sanitation, and half the hospital beds are occupied by patients with water-related diseases (64). (See Chapter 15 "Population and Health," Table 15.4.)

In 27 of 149 countries, less than 20 percent of the rural population and, in 28 countries, less than 60 percent of the urban population, have access to safe water. In many African countries, access to potable water has diminished with the recent droughts and some countries report less than 1 percent coverage with adequate sanitary facilities in rural areas (65).

Cholera continues to threaten life and is still endemic to many developing countries. Although Asia had fewer cases of cholera in the past three years, the number reported in Africa has increased (66). Dracunculiasis (guinea worm disease), contracted by drinking contaminated water, affects some 10 million people a year (67). Diarrheal disease is the leading cause of infant and childhood deaths in developing countries, claiming the lives of an estimated 5 million children under five years of age each year (68).

Measures to reduce these diseases, as well as dysentery, typhoid fever, and other water and sanitation diseases are obvious. They include improvement of water quality and quantity, sanitation and excreta disposal practices, and protecting water sources from contamination. According to WHO, over 1 billion people need adequate and safe water, and over 1.5 billion need adequate sanitation (69).

Malaria, spread by the water-breeding *Anopheles* mosquito, kills some 5 million people a year. More than half of the world population lives at some risk of the dis-

Table 2.7 Leading Causes of Death, 1980

Causes	Developed Countries Number (thousands)	Developed Countries Percent	Developing Countries Number (thousands)	Developing Countries Percent	Total Number (thousands)	Total Percent
Infectious and Parasitic Diseases a	810	8	16,020	40	16,830	33
Cancers	2,050	19	2,200	5	4,250	8
Circulatory diseases and certain degenerative disorders b	5,710	54	7,620	19	13,330	26
Conditions originating in the perinatal period	170	2	3,080	8	3,250	6
Injury and poisoning	690	6	1,980	5	2,670	5
All other and unknown causes	1,240	12	9,240	23	10,480	21
All Causes	**10,670**	**100**	**40,140**	**100**	**50,810**	**100**

Source: World Health Organization (WHO), *Evaluation of the Strategy for Health for All by the Year 2000* (WHO, Geneva, 1987), Table 19, p. 72.
Notes:
a. Includes influenza, pneumonia, bronchitis, emphysema, and asthma.
b. Includes diabetes mellitus; ulcer of stomach and duodenum; chronic liver disease and cirrhosis; and nephritis, nephrotic syndrome, and nephrosis.

ease (70). With 200–400 million new cases annually, malaria is a major economic and social threat in many tropical and subtropical countries (71). Southeast Asia accounts for half the cases reported (72).

The number of cases decreased in India and China between 1976 and 1983. In Latin America in the past decade, the steady growth in cases is due in part to the introduction of malaria into newly populated areas. The Near East also experienced a resurgence of the disease in the latter half of the 1970s. Sub-Saharan Africa, where 372 million of 421 million inhabitants live in malaria-endemic areas, remains a disease center (73).

Onchocerciasis and schistosomiasis are waterborne parasitic diseases for which new drugs may facilitate control. Onchocerciasis, or river blindness, is transmitted by the bite of the blackfly; it has blinded hundreds of thousands in parts of West Africa, Central Africa, the Middle East, and Central America. According to WHO, some 18 million people are affected, and an estimated 85 million are at risk (74).

Onchocerciasis control programs began in 1974 in the Volta River Basin Africa. As a result of aerial insecticide spraying of 764,000 square kilometers, incidence of the disease in 90 percent of the program area dropped considerably. Fertile farm lands abandoned because of the disease are now being resettled (75).

Schistosomiasis (bilharzia), commonly called snail fever, infects approximately 200 million people in 74 tropical nations in Asia, Africa, and Latin America (76). Some 500–600 million are threatened by this chronic and debilitating disease (77). It is carried by parasitic blood flukes that begin their lifecycle in snails and penetrate the skin of people who wash, bathe, or play in water harboring snails (78).

Pneumonia, bronchitis, and other respiratory diseases are transmitted by airborne carriers. Transmission is facilitated by limited and overcrowded housing. Respiratory infections contribute to nearly one third of deaths among children under five in developing countries (79). Children from poor countries have a 30–70 percent higher risk of death from these diseases than do children in industrialized nations (80).

Tuberculosis is also a major public health problem in the poorest parts of the world. There are an estimated 8–10 million cases and about 3 million deaths annually. In some developing countries, tuberculosis rates appear to be declining at 1—3 percent a year, but other countries show no appreciable change (81).

Child Health Programs in Developing Countries

In developing nations, 14–15 million children under the age of five die every year from diarrhea, measles, and other diseases frequently associated with poverty, overcrowding, and malnutrition (82). (Table 2.8 shows the leading causes of childhood death.)

About 60 percent of childhood diarrheal deaths result from acute dehydration that can be prevented with good nutrition and oral rehydration therapy (ORT), ingestion of a simple solution of water, salts, and carbohydrates (e.g., sugar, rice powder) (83) (84). International and national efforts to make available the rehydration salts and

Table 2.8 Annual Deaths from Leading Causes of Childhood Mortality in Developing Countries [a]

Disease	Annual Deaths
Diarrheal disease	5,000,000
Acute respiratory infections [b]	4,000,000
Measles	2,000,000
Tetanus	1,000,000
Malaria	1,000,000
Neonatal tetanus	800,000
Pertussis	600,000
Tuberculosis	30,000
Poliomyelitis	27,000
Diphtheria	5,000
Total	**14,462,000**

Sources:
1. Institute for Resource Development/Westinghouse, *Child Survival: Risks on the Road to Good Health* (Institute for Resource Development/Westinghouse, Washington, D.C., 1987).
2. United Nations Children's Fund (UNICEF), *The State of the World's Children 1988* (UNICEF, Oxford University Press, New York, 1988).
3. "Undoing the Cursed Neo-Natal Tetanus," *Child Survival Action News,* Supplement to *International Health News* (April 1988).

Notes:
a. Undernutrition is a contributing cause in over 4 million childhood deaths a year.
b. Mainly pneumonia.

instruction on ORT use are on the rise. By the end of 1987, more than 100 countries had begun national programs. WHO estimates that ORT saves half a million children from fatal dehydration each year (85). However, the therapy is still not in widespread use. Only 8 percent of children in Africa and only 23 percent in Asia have access to centers dispensing ORT, for example (86).

WHO and the United Nations Children's Fund (UNICEF) have begun a global campaign to immunize all children against six target diseases by 1990: tetanus, measles, polio, diphtheria, pertussis, and tuberculosis. Immunization programs have largely eliminated these diseases in industrialized countries, but in developing countries, they continue to claim an estimated 3.5 million children's lives and leave an equal number blind, crippled, or mentally retarded (87).

Despite a host of challenges, including failure of children to return for needed second and third doses and loss of vaccine potency because of breaks in the "cold chain" (continuous refrigeration during transport), progress against the target diseases is significant. WHO estimates that immunization programs saved more than 1 million lives in 1987 (88). Africa, where fewer than 40 percent of infants are fully immunized before they are one year old, still lags behind other regions in overall immunization coverage (89).

International public health agencies widely promote breast-feeding for ideal nutritional balance and protection against infection. According to WHO, infants under six months of age who are not breast-fed have a 3.5–4.9 times higher risk of diarrhea than those infants who are breast-fed (90). For example, in a Costa Rican hospital where breast-feeding was actively encouraged, neonatal mortality dropped 78 percent in five years, mostly from fewer diarrheal deaths (91).

Specific dietary deficiencies create a range of chronic health problems in developing countries. More than half a million preschool-age children are blinded every year from deficiency in vitamin A. One high-dosage capsule costing as little as 2 cents can protect a child against blindness for six months. Recent studies also link improved vitamin A nutrition with a reduced childhood death rate from pneumonia, diarrhea, measles, and other infections (92).

Health Problems of Developed Countries

The major causes of death in developed countries are diseases of the circulatory system (in particular, ischemic heart disease and cerebrovascular disease), followed by cancers and respiratory diseases.

Some decline in cardiovascular disease has been reported from Australia, Finland, Japan, and the United States. The rate is stable in Austria, Ireland, and Sweden but is rising in Bulgaria, Hungary, and Poland (93). The highest mortality rates for circulatory diseases are reported in Eastern European nations—762 per 100,000 for Romania, for example (94). Coronary disease is rising in the USSR, thereby raising overall mortality rates (95). Ischemic heart disease in adults is on the rise in most European countries, but the number of deaths from cerebrovascular disease is declining markedly (96).

Lung cancer is the leading cause of cancer deaths among men, as is breast cancer among women in most industrialized countries. In the United States, lung cancer deaths among women have increased fivefold since 1945; lung cancer now rivals breast cancer as a major cause of death. Tobacco smoking is thought to be responsible for at least 80 percent of lung cancer deaths in U.S. men and 75 percent in women (97). Similarly, in Australia, mortality from lung cancer has fallen among men but is increasing rapidly among women (98).

Suicide ranks high as a cause of death in industrialized countries, and it has been rising in most European countries since the 1960s. The United Kingdom and Greece are exceptions (99). With 44 deaths per 100,000, Hungary has the highest suicide rate in Europe; compared to Greece with a low of 4 per 100,000 (100).

Progressive aging of developed country populations is increasing the incidence of chronic degenerative illnesses such as Alzheimer's and Parkinson's diseases. The growing prevalence of dementia resulting from senility and other mental disorders is a challenge to health services, and more resources will need to be allocated to psychogeriatric problems (101).

THE AIDS PANDEMIC

Since it was first identified in 1981, AIDS—acquired immune deficiency syndrome—has spread rapidly through the world. By the end of 1987, 129 nations had reported a cumulative total of 73,601 cases to WHO (102). (See Table 2.9.) Seventy-five percent of reported AIDS cases were in North and South America, almost two thirds of them in the United States. Europe and Africa each account for 12 percent of reported AIDS cases. Asia and the Western Pacific together comprise 1 percent (103).

Because AIDS cases are underreported in many parts of the world, particularly Africa and Latin America,

WHO estimates that about 150,000 cases may have occurred since the beginning of the worldwide epidemic or pandemic (104). For each AIDS case, there are also three to five cases of AIDS-related complex, a term used to describe conditions and immunological abnormalities similar to but less severe than those observed in AIDS patients.

AIDS and AIDS-related complex are caused by a retrovirus—the human immunodeficiency virus (HIV). An estimated 5–10 million people are carriers of HIV, although most will not develop symptoms of the disease for six or more years from the time of infection (105). However, recent studies suggest that virtually all individuals infected with HIV will eventually develop AIDS (106). Estimates of the number of infected individuals are very uncertain because no country has surveyed its population for the disease.

Although the AIDS pandemic is surely serious, the disease must be viewed in the context of other major health problems. The estimated total of 150,000 AIDS cases and the 5–10 million infected individuals must be compared with the annual 5 million deaths of children from diarrheal disease, the estimated 200–400 million new cases of malaria (of whom more than 5 million die), and the estimated 598,000 deaths from lung cancers. (See also Table 2.7.)

HIV destroys the body's defenses against disease, rendering the infected individual susceptible to opportunistic infections. The virus is spread through sexual contact, intravenous drug use, and transfusions of blood and blood products as well as from an infected mother to her

Table 2.9 The AIDS Pandemic

Region	Reported AIDS Cases 1987 (Cumulative)	Estimated Number of Persons Infected with HIV, 1987	Projected New[a] Cases by 1992
North America	49,473	1,530,000	382,500[2]
Latin America and the Caribbean	5,792	500,000	125,000[3]
Europe	8,773	500,000	125,000[4]
Africa	8,640	2,000,000	500,000[4]
Asia	215	10,000	2,500[5]
Oceania	708		2,000[6]
Total	**73,601**	**4,540,000**	**1,137,500**

Sources:
Reported AIDS cases, 1987:
1. World Health Organization (WHO), "Cases Reported as of December 23, 1987" (WHO, Geneva).
Estimated Number of Persons Infected with HIV, 1987:
2. North America: Public Health Service, "Codfort Report: APHS Plan for Prevention and Control of the AIDS Virus," Public Health Reports, July-August 1986, Vol. 101, No. 4, and Laboratory Center for Disease Control, Ottawa, Canada (personal communication).
3. Latin America and the Caribbean: Pan American Health Organization, March 1987 (personal communication).
4. Europe and Africa: Jonathan Mann, Speech given at Pan American Health Organization, March 1987.
5. Asia (Japan only): World Health Organization (WHO), Weekly Epidemiological Record, No. 7, February 13, 1987 (WHO, Geneva).
Projected New Cases by 1992:
6. Oceania (Australia only): Bruce Whyte, et al., "Epidemiology of the Acquired Immunodeficiency Syndrome in Australia," The Medical Journal of Australia, Vol. 146, No. 2 (January 19, 1987), p. 65.
Note: a. Projected cases in 1992 are calculated at 25 percent of those infected in 1987, based upon estimates by the World Health Organization and the U.S. National Academy of Sciences. WHO estimated that between 10 percent and 30 percent of those infected will develop AIDS within 5-7 years. (WHO, Special Program on AIDS, Strategies and Structure, Projected Needs [WHO, Geneva, March 1987], Annex I, p. I-1.) The U.S. National Academy of Sciences estimates that between 25 percent and 50 percent of infected individuals will develop the disease in 5-10 years. (National Academy of Sciences, Confronting AIDS, Directions for Public Health, Health Care, and Research, Summary and Recommendations [National Academy Press, Washington, D.C., 1986].)

infant in utero or during birth. There is no evidence that casual contact or insect vectors spread the virus.

Homosexual and bisexual men and intravenous drug abusers are the major groups affected in most areas. In sub-Saharan Africa and in some parts of the Caribbean, AIDS is largely transmitted heterosexually. In Africa, men and women are stricken in equal numbers, and in Haiti, over 36 percent of AIDS patients are female. In addition, contaminated blood supplies and the use of unsterile skin piercing equipment may continue to spread HIV infection in these areas. In Central Africa, AIDS has been a serious problem at least since the early 1980s. Surveillance studies there suggest an annual incidence of AIDS of 550–1,000 cases per million adults in 1985 (107). Assessing the extent of infection in Africa is difficult because of limited diagnostic and surveillance capabilities (108), but an estimated 2 million or more Africans presently carry the AIDS virus (109). Rates of infection are highest in urban areas, where 4–30 percent of the individuals studied are HIV carriers, and along major transportation routes. In Uganda and Tanzania, some rural areas are also heavily affected.

Studies of HIV infection in Africa focus on hospital workers, blood donors, and other select groups that may not represent the general population (110). Infection rates among these groups, therefore, may not reflect those of the general population which are, nevertheless, thought to be high and growing. AIDS is spreading from Central Africa, and increasing numbers of cases are reported in Western Africa. Based on current trends, a minimum of 10,000 new cases are expected in Africa annually (111).

In Brazil, the rapid growth of AIDS from six cases in 1982 to 2,325 in 1987, the third highest cumulative number reported worldwide, shows the explosive potential of AIDS. Sixty-five percent of Brazil's cases are male homosexuals. In the Caribbean, rates of infection among some groups are alarming—in Haiti, 6 percent of urban adults and hotel and factory workers in Port-au-Prince were carriers of the AIDS virus in 1986 (112). Pregnant women screened at health clinics in a poor area of Port-au-Prince had a 7.5 percent HIV infection rate (113).

In Western Europe, although new infection among homosexuals appears to be declining, the growth of AIDS cases among intravenous drug abusers, particularly in Italy and Spain, is a cause for concern. In 1987, addicts comprised 52 percent of AIDS cases in Spain and 59 percent in Italy (114). It is now believed that almost all those infected with HIV will develop AIDS (115). Between 500,000 and 3 million new AIDS cases are expected in the next five years among those already infected (116).

Impacts of AIDS

The personal, social, and economic costs of AIDS are inestimable, and in many developing countries the disease may affect economic growth. Unlike many diseases that favor the old or the young, AIDS primarily strikes young and middle-aged adults, 20–49 years old, the most vital segment of the population. Many individuals with AIDS, particularly in Africa, are urban elites in business, industry, and government. The potential loss of a sizable share of this population raises the potential for social, economic, and political destabilization.

Few studies assessing the economic, social and political impacts of AIDS have been conducted, largely because data on the prevalence of AIDS and HIV infection are lacking. However, the Harvard Institute for International Development projected the cost of AIDS owing to premature deaths among working age adults in Zaire. By 1995 AIDS could cost 8 percent of the gross national product (GNP)—$350 million—higher than the $314 million Zaire received from all sources of development assistance in 1984 (117).

The impact of medical expenditures for AIDS patients will be particularly severe where health care resources are already limited. In Zaire, the direct cost for health care for a person with symptoms of AIDS is estimated to range from $132–1,585 and in Tanzania from $104–631, depending on the type of health care facility (118). In Brazil, the direct cost per patient year is the equivalent of $21,500, and about 95 percent of AIDS patients receive free care. Brazil's health authorities estimate that hospitalization for AIDS patients in 1988 will cost more than $25 million (119).

Prevention is the only known way to stop the spread of AIDS. WHO has created the Special Programme on AIDS to provide technical and financial support to strengthen the 150 national AIDS committees. By October 1987, more than 50 countries had prepared short-term plans for AIDS prevention and control programs, and 26 had completed three- to five-year plans.

There is no satisfactory treatment for HIV infection, and a vaccine is not expected until the mid-1990s at the earliest (120) (121). Because of the large numbers of infected individuals, AIDS is likely to increase precipitously in the next five years despite public health efforts. New infections will continue to occur among individuals who have not been touched by educational efforts that, to date, are only selectively effective.

FOCUS ON: PESTICIDE USE AND HEALTH

The pressures of a growing population needing food and protection from vector-borne diseases have led to the growing global use of pesticides. Worldwide sales increased from $2.7 billion in 1970 to $11.6 billion in 1980; they are anticipated to reach $18.5 billion in 1990. (See Table 2.10.) Chemical pesticides battle insect pests, noxious weeds, rodents, and fungi, with the heaviest use (68 percent) in agriculture (122).

Table 2.10 World Agrochemical Market
(percent)

	1970	1980	1990
Total Expenditures ($U.S. billion)	**2.7**	**11.6**	**18.5**
Insecticides	37	35	33
Herbicides	35	41	39
Fungicides	22	19	21
Other	6	5	7

Source: Marcello Lotti, "Production and Use of Pesticides," in *Toxicology of Pesticides: Experimental, Clinical, and Regulatory Perspectives,* Lucio G. Costa, Corrado W. Galli, and Sheldon D. Murphy, eds. (Springer-Verlag, Berlin, 1987).

Table 2.11 Major Types of Insecticides and Their Effects on Human Health

Insecticides	Effects on Human Body	Symptoms of Human Poisoning
Organophosphates Parathion Malathion TEPP Mevinphos	Interfere with normal action of the enzyme acetylcholinesterase, which is involved in neurotransmission.	Anorexia, nausea, vomiting, abdominal cramps, diarrhea, involuntary defecation, increased salivation, eyes watering, pupil constriction, blurred vision, muscle twitching, weakness, hypertension, anxiety, irritability, altered sleep patterns, headache, impaired cognition, seizures, coma.
Organochlorines DDT Dieldrin Aldrin Chlordane Lindane BHC Heptachlor Endrin	Interact with ion channels in the central nervous system.	Tremors, headache, nausea, dizziness, irritability, ataxia, stomach pains, diarrhea, confusion, convulsions.
Carbamates Aldicarb Carbaryl Baygon	Same as organo-phosphates except that inhibition of acetylcholinesterase is readily reversible.	Indistinguishable from organophosphates, except the onset is more rapid.
Pyrethroids Permethrin Decamethrin	Can interfere with the electrical aspects of nerve transmission. In mammals they are rapidly detoxified.	Tremor, salivation, seizures, irritability, other central nervous system symptoms.[a]

Source: Sheldon D. Murphy, "Toxic Effects of Pesticides," in *Toxicology,* C. Klaassen, *et al.,* eds. (Macmillan Publishing, New York, 1986).
Note: a. Documented in rodent studies.

Insecticides, which account for approximately one third the world agrochemical market, have a history of environmental damage and toxic effects in humans. Table 2.11 lists some common insecticides and the symptoms of poisonings. Three main classes of compounds are used to control insect pests: organochlorines, organophosphates, and carbamates. Synthetic pyrethroids, a fourth class that shows promise of lower toxicity to humans, are becoming more common (123). Herbicide use has grown substantially and it now occupies the largest share of the world agrochemical market (40 percent) (124).

Patterns of pesticide use reflect geography, technology, and target crop differences throughout the world. Western Europe and North America use 70 percent of the herbicides produced, while 62 percent of the insecticides are applied in developing countries. Western Europe alone consumes 43 percent of the fungicides produced (125).

In developing countries, many with agriculturally based economies, growing populations, and tropical locations conducive to insect pests, the need to expand agricultural production and control vector-borne diseases led to increased consumption of insecticides despite their potential hazards. Public health programs alone used 66,000 metric tons of pesticides in 1984, up from 50,000 metric tons in 1980 (126).

In developed countries, demand is leveling off or decreasing as pesticides with more specific activity and therefore lower required dosages are developed and applied. Consumption of pesticides in the United States declined 20 percent between 1973 and 1983 to 500,000 metric tons (127).

Mortality and Morbidity from Pesticides

Pesticides are nonspecific poisons: they are poisonous to all life, not just a target pest. Human poisonings and deaths from pesticides are numerous. Most health problems are acute, the result of one or a few exposures. Chronic health effects may develop in response to limited exposure accumulated over a long period, but they are not as well understood and are not well documented. Chronic exposures may lead to cancers, neurobehavioral effects, and reproductive problems. Comprehensive information on exposure to pesticides is lacking, and only recently has an assessment of global mortality and morbidity caused by pesticide use been attempted. (See Table 2.12.)

WHO estimates that approximately 1 million people are poisoned by pesticides each year. Mortality estimates range from 3,000 to 20,000 deaths per year, depending upon reporting criteria (128). It is generally believed that most pesticide poisonings are not reported. Particularly in developing countries, governments have limited resources to monitor health effects; in addition, the symptoms of pesticide poisoning can be similar to those of other diseases (129).

The differences in the extent of pesticide-related mortality and morbidity among different countries are marked. Despite the fact that 80 percent of all agrochemicals are used in developed countries, these nations report under 1 percent of all deaths from acute pesticide poisoning (130).

Although most industrialized countries closely control pesticide registration and application in agriculture, FAO determined in 1976 that 40 percent of Third World countries had no specific control legislation. Many countries have developed legislation since then, but enforcement is a problem (131). The problem is exacerbated by the unavailability of information and lack of awareness of pesticide risks.

Direct contact with pesticides through accidents, misuse, and occupational exposure poses the most significant risks for humans. Mass poisonings from contaminated foods because of spillage during transport or storage, accidental ingestion (especially by children), and improper use are documented throughout the world (132) (133).

Agricultural workers, workers in pesticide formulation factories, and public health workers involved in pest eradication face significantly increased risks. For example, agricultural fieldworkers in California suffer the highest rates of occupationally related illness in the state, twice

Table 2.12 Alternative Estimates of Pesticide-Related Poisonings and Deaths, Worldwide

Number of Cases	Number of Deaths	Basis for Estimates
1,111,000	20,000	Area mortality reports
873,000	16,000	Area morbidity surveys
1,057,000	20,000	National mortality data from all accidental poisonings
834,000	3,000	Mortality statistics from acute pesticide poisoning

Source: Marcello Lotti, "Production and Use of Pesticides," in *Toxicology of Pesticides: Experimental, Clinical, and Regulatory Perspectives,* Lucio G. Costa, Corrado L. Galli, and Sheldon D. Murphy, eds. (Springer-Verlag, Berlin, 1987), p. 15.

that of other workers (134). In the cotton-growing regions of Central America, heavy dependence on pesticides is reflected in elevated morbidity and mortality rates. Pesticide poisoning is the leading cause of death in the Pacific coast cotton-growing region of Nicaragua although progress has been made in reducing this problem (135).

Apart from these acute and directly relatable health effects, concern is rising over possible adverse health effects from chronic exposure to low levels of pesticides. Over 90 percent of the pesticides used do not reach their target (136). They may drift far, especially when applied by aircraft, contaminating water and soil. In the United States, 65 percent of the pesticides used are applied from the air (137), as are 90 percent of pesticides used on cotton in Central America (138).

Pesticides that enter potable water supplies may poison humans and livestock. Chemical contaminants are not as easy to detect and remove from water supplies as biological pathogens. Aldicarb, a highly toxic carbamate, was found in excess of allowable limits in 13.5 percent of 6,500 drinking water wells sampled in New York State in 1979 (139). A 1980–81 study of freshwater in West Java, Indonesia, found all sources with detectable amounts of the four organophosphates and one carbamate analyzed (140).

Persistent chemicals like the organochlorines linger in soil and water for many years, and become concentrated in animals that feed on other contaminated plants or animals. Food crops are also directly contaminated through application—in fact, 90 percent of human pesticide intake is through the food chain (141). In El Salvador, dangerously high levels of DDT and other persistent chemicals have been detected in fish, shrimp, meat, and milk, including human milk (142). A study of 1,436 nursing U.S. women found traces of dieldrin, chlordane, and heptachlor in breast milk of 80 percent, 74 percent, and 63 percent, respectively (143). DDT is still used in Malaysia and levels of DDT measured in blood are five times higher than in the United States (144).

As stated earlier, the health risks of chronic exposure to pesticides are not well understood. Cancers are a major public concern. Experimental studies indicate that some pesticides may be carcinogenic (145). Knowledge of the mechanisms of carcinogenesis is not nearly as advanced as our understanding of acute injury (146). Extrapolation of animal data to humans is difficult, and there is very little solid documentation of an association between excess human cancers and pesticides (147).

The adverse reproductive effects of a number of pesticides have been extensively studied, although of all toxic hazards, the least is known about risks of and effects on mammalian reproduction (148). Animal studies have demonstrated reproductive effects of the pesticide DBCP. More important, among workers in a DBCP factory were numerous cases of male infertility and a change in the sex ratio of their offspring (149). Dioxins, byproducts, and contaminants in 2,4,5-T, a widely used herbicide and component of Agent Orange, are suspected to increase the number of miscarriages and birth defects in humans (150). Other organochlorines and organophosphates have

shown reproductive effects in animal studies, but human epidemiological data are lacking (151).

Neurobehavioral effects resulting from chronic exposure to organophosphates have also been reported. There are many anecdotal cases of exposed agricultural workers with complaints of impaired memory, concentration, alertness, and vision. However, neuropsychological tests have yielded inconsistent results, and difficulties with methods remain in this developing investigation (152).

Reducing the Risks

Unleashing toxic compounds into the environment introduces both human health and environmental risks. Complete eradication of risk is not possible, but risk identification and measurement makes reduction and control of the risk possible. Risk assessment is a rational response to the fact that chemical pesticides will continue to pollute the environment and therefore its inhabitants.

Assessments of the net risks of pesticides must take into account their benefits as well as their hazards. Six hundred fifty million people suffer from malaria, filariasis, and schistosomiasis each year (153). Thirty percent of all crops are lost to pests, weeds, and disease—without pesticides, 30 percent more would be at risk (154).

To assess the costs and benefits of pesticide use adequately, the risks must be better investigated and measured. The commitment of resources to the problems of pesticides is small compared to the multimillion-dollar pesticide market and to other disease control programs (155).

Health effects information is basic to risk reduction efforts. Because almost all acute poisonings can be traced to ignorance of pesticide toxicity and inappropriate use, education can form the first line of defense against pesticide hazards (156). Educational programs should extend to the general public, government officials, health professionals, and agricultural workers. Educating health care workers on recognition and treatment of pesticide poisoning is an urgent need. Immediate benefits of education are a reduction in the high mortality of pesticide poisonings as a result of poor diagnosis and an increase in the accuracy of reporting mortality and morbidity (157).

Training and biological monitoring are successful in reducing the hazards faced by agricultural workers. Training may cover application techniques, protective clothing, worktime duration, meteorological conditions, toxicity, and general hygiene. Safety training combined with biological monitoring in Nigeria, Kenya, and Indonesia demonstrated the fact that adverse health effects can be avoided if precautions are taken (158) (159). After implementation of educational and regulatory measures in a rural area of China, the incidence of poisoning decreased from 4.5 percent to 0.1 percent within two years despite a thirteenfold increase in pesticide use (160).

Even more fundamental than education is a strategy to reduce risk by reducing pesticide use. Integrated pest management (IPM) is an approach to agricultural pest control that relies more on natural methods and less on chemical pesticides. Its effectiveness has been proven.

IPM is actively encouraged by FAO and WHO because it can reduce human exposure to pesticides. One estimate suggests that if IPM were universally adopted in the United States, agricultural pesticide use would drop 75 percent (161). In India, the use of IPM techniques to control insect pests on rice in the state of Orissa cut the use of chemical pesticides in half. In southern China, an elaborate IPM program reduced the dollar cost of pesticide use two thirds (162).

Political action by both farmworkers and the general public in some developing countries has begun to have an effect on pesticide use. In Costa Rica, banana workers are fighting the use of DBCP through a lawsuit, and in the Philippines agricultural workers are organizing around pesticide issues (163). Citizens' groups in three South American countries launched internationally coordinated "Dirty Dozen" campaigns against 12 toxic pesticides, and as a result, since 1985 Ecuador has banned 12 pesticides, Colombia, 10; and Guatemala, 8 (164).

RECENT DEVELOPMENTS

WORLD POPULATION GROWING FASTER THAN EXPECTED

In mid-1988, stabilization of the world's burgeoning population appears even further off than population experts had previously projected. According to data recently compiled and published by the Population Reference Bureau (PRB) of Washington, D.C., the world population growth rate, which had been declining since the late 1960s, hit a plateau. The United Nations projected a growth rate that would continue to fall slowly throughout the 1980s, but instead it has remained stable. The current growth rate of 1.7 percent brings the estimated world population to 5.13 billion (165).

The basis of this revised estimate comes from news about total fertility rates in several of the most populous nations, particularly China and India. In China, the total fertility rate (TFR) rose unexpectedly in 1986 to an estimated 2.4 children per woman (up from 2.1 in 1985),

where it remains. In India, the TFR declined from 4.5 in 1984 to only about 4.3 today, less than previously anticipated (166). Because these two countries contain 37 percent of the total world population, these higher than anticipated TFRs affect the global projection significantly.

Based on these recent trends in fertility, PRB estimates a world population of 6 billion in 1998, and by the year 2020, there will be 200 million more people on Earth than the United Nations forecast in its most recent assessment (167) (168).

PROGRESS BEING MADE IN TROPICAL DISEASE PREVENTION AND TREATMENT

In 1987, medical science made important progress against two age-old debilitating diseases of the tropics—malaria and onchocerciasis (river blindness). Clinical tests of a new malaria vaccine were begun with human volunteers. The vaccine is designed to fight the malarial parasite in its sporozoite stage when a mosquito injects it. Other vaccines being tested battle the parasite after it has matured in the blood (169).

Development of a malaria vaccine is becoming increasingly important because the *Anopheles* mosquito is showing widespread and growing resistance to many insecticides. In addition, the malarial parasite has shown increasing resistance to the most frequently used antimalarial drugs. Resistance to chloroquine is frequently reported, and resistance to the more powerful fansidar drugs has been noted in both Southeast Asia and South America (170). An effective vaccine could end the scourge of this dread disease.

Control of onchocerciasis also took a major step forward in 1987 when the pharmaceutical manufacturer Merck and Co., began field tests of the drug Mectizan (ivermectin). Taken orally once a year, ivermectin destroys the larva that cause river blindness. Large-scale trial distribution of the drug began during 1988 in a dozen countries in West and Central Africa and Central America. Merck is supplying the drug free. This program complements aerial spraying of biodegradable larvicides (171) (172).

References and Notes

1. United Nations (U.N.), *World Population Prospects: Estimates and Projections Assessed in 1984* (U.N., New York, 1986), pp. 19–20.
2. Based on Thomas W. Merrick, "World Population in Transition," *Population Bulletin*, Vol. 41, No. 2 (Population Reference Bureau, Washington, D.C., 1986), p. 10.
3. United Nations (U.N.), *World Population Prospects: Estimates and Projections as Assessed in 1982* (U.N., New York, 1985), p. 11.
4. *Op. cit.* 1, p. 54.
5. *Op. cit.* 1, pp. 12–13.
6. *Op. cit.* 1, pp. 46–47.
7. *Op. cit.* 1, p. 10.
8. United Nations (U.N.), *The World Population Situation in 1983* (U.N., New York,

1984), p. 50.
9. *Op. cit.* 1, pp. 141–142.
10. International Union for Conservation of Nature and Natural Resources (IUCN), *Population and Sustainable Development* (IUCN, Gland, Switzerland, 1987), p. 21.
11. *Ibid.*, pp. 21–22.
12. Population Reference Bureau (PRB), *Human Needs and Nature's Balance: Population, Resources and the Environment* (PRB, Washington, D.C., 1987), p. 2.
13. *Ibid.*
14. Robert Repetto, "Population, Resources, Environment: An Uncertain Future," *Population Bulletin*, Vol. 42, No. 2 (1987), p. 14.
15. Alan Grainger, "Quantifying Changes in Forest Cover in the Humid Tropics: Overcoming Current Limitations," *Journal of*

World Forest Resource Management, Vol. 1, No. 1 (1984), pp. 21–22.
16. Terrence Hull, "Workshop on Java's Population Growth," *Research Note 10* (Australian National University, Department of Demography, 1983), cited in Robert Repetto, "Soil Loss and Population Pressure on Java," *Ambio*, Vol. 15, No. 1 (1986), p. 14.
17. Robert Repetto, "Soil Loss and Population Pressure on Java," *Ambio*, Vol. 15, No. 1 (1986), p. 15.
18. *Ibid.*, p. 17.
19. W. Collier, *et al.*, in *Labor Absorption in Rice-Based Agriculture*, Wilbert Gooneratne, ed. (United Nations, International Labor Office, Geneva, 1982), cited in Robert Repetto, "Soil Loss and Population

Pressure on Java," *Ambio*, Vol. 15, No. 1 (1986), p. 17.

20. U.S. Agency for International Development (U.S. AID), *Republic of Indonesia: Upland Agriculture and Conservation Project* (U.S. AID, Washington, D.C., 1984), cited in Robert Repetto, "Soil Loss and Population Pressure on Java," *Ambio*, Vol. 15, No. 1 (1986), p. 14.

21. The World Bank, *Indonesia: Selected Aspects of Spatial Development* (The World Bank, Washington, D.C., 1984), cited in Robert Repetto, "Soil Loss and Population Pressure on Java," *Ambio*, Vol. 15, No. 1 (1986), p. 14.

22. Government of Indonesia U.S. Agency for International Development (U.S. AID), *Composite Report of the Watershed Assessment Team 1* (U.S. AID, Java, Indonesia, 1983), cited in Robert Repetto, "Soil Loss and Population Pressure on Java," *Ambio*, Vol. 15, No. 1 (1986), pp. 14–18.

23. *Op. cit.* 17, p. 14.

24. Alan Grainger, *Desertification: How People Make Deserts, How People Can Stop and Why They Don't* (International Institute for Environment and Development, London, 1982), pp. 10–11.

25. Nicholas Guppy, "Tropical Deforestation: A Global View," *Foreign Affairs* (spring 1984), pp. 934–937.

26. *Op. cit.* 14, p. 13.

27. *Op. cit.* 24, p. 14.

28. *Op. cit.* 24, p. 14.

29. *Op. cit.* 24, p. 14.

30. *Op. cit.* 24, p. 14.

31. *Op. cit.* 24, p. 14.

32. Lee M. Talbott, "Rangeland Degradation in East Africa," *Population and Development Review*, Vol. 12, No. 3 (1986), p. 445.

33. *Ibid.*

34. *Ibid.*

35. *Ibid.*, p. 446.

36. United Nations Food and Agriculture Organization (FAO), *Land, Food and People* (FAO, Rome, 1984), p. xiii.

37. *Op. cit.* 14, p. 21.

38. V.A. Konda, "Loss of Productive Land Due to Salinization," *Ambio*, Vol. 12, No. 2 (1983), p. 92.

39. *Op. cit.* 1, pp. 36–37.

40. United Nations (U.N.), *First Marriage: Patterns and Determinants* (U.N., New York, 1988).

41. Robert J. Lapham and W. Parker Mauldin, "Contraceptive Prevalence: The Influence of Organized Family Planning Programs," *Studies in Family Planning*, Vol. 16, No. 3 (1985), p. 123.

42. *Ibid.*

43. The socioeconomic setting is based on measurements of adult literacy, primary and secondary school enrollment, life expectancy at birth, infant mortality rate, GNP per capita, proportion of males aged 15–64 employed outside agriculture, and proportion of the total population living in cities of 100,000 or more. Exact procedures are presented in W. Parker Mauldin and B. Berelson, "Conditions of Fertility Decline in Developing Countries, 1965–1975," *Studies in Family Planning*, Vol. 9, No. 5 (1978), pp. 6–10.

44. W. Parker Mauldin and Robert J. Lapham,

"Conditions of Fertility Decline in LDCs: 1965–1980," paper presented at the Population Association of America Annual Meeting, Minneapolis, Minnesota, May 3–5, 1984, p. 25. (Cited with Permission.)

45. World Health Organization (WHO), *Evaluation of the Strategy for Health for All by the Year 2000* (WHO, Geneva, 1987), p. 113.

46. *Op. cit.* 1, pp. 114–133.

47. *Op. cit.* 45, p. 73.

48. *Op. cit.* 1, Table A-16, pp. 134–139.

49. *Op. cit.* 45.

50. *Op. cit.* 45, p. 73.

51. United Nations Children's Fund (UNICEF), *The State of the World's Children 1988* (UNICEF, New York, 1988), p. 77.

52. *Ibid.*, p. 76.

53. *Op. cit.* 45, p. 74.

54. "Safer Motherhood," *Child Survival Action News* (November-December 1987), p. 2.

55. *Ibid.*, p. 1.

56. *Op. cit.* 45, p. 81.

57. *Op. cit.* 45, p. 81.

58. *Op. cit.* 45, p. 83.

59. William U. Chandler, "Banishing Tobacco," in *State of the World* (W.W. Norton, New York, 1986), p. 140.

60. Robert W. Kates, *et al.*, *The Hunger Report: 1988* (Preliminary) (The Alan Shawn Feinstein World Hunger Program, Brown University, Providence, Rhode Island, 1988), p. 7.

61. *Op. cit.* 45, p. 22.

62. *Op. cit.* 45, p. 22.

63. "Waging War against Hunger," *International Health News* (September 1987), p. 4.

64. "Accent on Health: Living Proof of Progress," *Horizons* (U.S. Agency for International Development, spring, 1987), p. 60.

65. *Op. cit.* 45, p. 38.

66. "Cholera in 1986," *World Epidemiological Record* (May 15, 1987).

67. "Disease Targeted for Global Eradication," *International Health News*, Vol. 9, No. 1 (1988), p. 1.

68. Institute for Resource Development/Westinghouse, *Child Survival: Risks and the Road to Health* (Institute for Resource Development/Westinghouse, Washington, D.C., 1987), p. 10.

69. *Op. cit.* 45, pp. 38–39.

70. *Op. cit.* 68, p. 25 and p. 28.

71. *Op. cit.* 68, p. 25.

72. *Op. cit.* 45, p. 78.

73. *Op. cit.* 68, pp. 28–29.

74. Martin W.G. King, "New Drugs to Fight River Blindness," *International Health News* (November 1987), p. 1 and p. 10.

75. *Op. cit.* 64, p. 59.

76. *Op. cit.* 64, pp. 59–60.

77. *Op. cit.* 45, p. 78.

78. *Op. cit.* 64, pp. 59–60.

79. U.S. Agency for International Development (U.S. AID), *Child Survival: A Third Report to Congress on the U.S. AID Program* (U.S. AID, Washington, D.C., 1988), p. 27.

80. *Op. cit.* 45, p. 76.

81. Gary Slutkin, J. Leowski, and J. Mann, "The Effects of the AIDS Epidemic on the Tuberculosis Programmes," paper presented at the First International Con-

ference on the Global Impact of AIDS, London, 1988, pp. 1–20.

82. *Op. cit.* 79, p. 3.

83. United Nation's Children's Fund (UNICEF), *The State of the World's Children 1987* (UNICEF, New York, 1987), p. 39.

84. *Op. cit.* 68.

85. *Op. cit.* 79, p. 15.

86. *Op. cit.* 68, p. 14.

87. *Op. cit.* 68, p. 16.

88. *Op. cit.* 79, p. 11.

89. *Op. cit.* 68, p. 20.

90. "Breastfeeding for Child Survival," *Child Survival Action News*, No. 6 (1987), p. 1.

91. *Op. cit.* 68, p. 36.

92. Raisa Scriabine Smith and Michael Favin, "Vitamin A: A Key to Child Survival?" *International Health News* (January 1988), p. 7.

93. *Op. cit.* 45, p. 81.

94. World Health Organization (WHO), *1987 World Health Statistics Annual* (WHO, Geneva, 1987), Table 7, pp. 342–349.

95. Richard Cooper, "Rising Death Rates in the Soviet Union: The Impact of Coronary Heart Disease," *New England Journal of Medicine*, Vol. 304, No. 21 (1981), p. 1259.

96. *Op. cit.* 45, p. 114.

97. *Health United States 1987* (U.S. Department of Health and Human Services, National Center for Health Statistics, Washington, D.C., 1987), p. 12.

98. Anthony W. Ireland and James S. Lawson, "The Changing Face of Death: Recent Trends in Australian Mortality," *Medical Journal of Australia*, Vol. 1, No. 12 (1980), p. 587.

99. *Op. cit.* 45, p. 84.

100. *Op. cit.* 94.

101. *Op. cit.* 45, p. 85.

102. World Health Organization (WHO), *AIDS Cases Reported to WHO by Region and Country as of December 23, 1987* (WHO, Geneva, 1987).

103. *Ibid.*

104. Jonathan Mann, "Focus on AIDS," *WHO Features*, No. 114 (1987), p. 2.

105. World Health Organization (WHO), *Special Programme on AIDS, Strategies, Structure, Projected Needs* (WHO, Geneva, 1987), p. 2.

106. Michael Specter, "450,000 AIDS Cases Seen by '93," *Washington Post* (June 5, 1988), p. 1.

107. Thomas Quinn, *et al.*, "AIDS in Africa: An Epidemiologic Paradigm," *Science* (November 21, 1986), p. 955.

108. U.S. General Accounting Office (GAO), *AIDS Information on Global Dimensions and Possible Impacts* (GAO, 1987), Appendix I, p. 9.

109. Jonathan Mann, "AIDS in Africa," *New Scientist* (March 26, 1987) p. 43.

110. U.S. General Accounting Office (GAO), *AIDS Information on Global Dimensions and Possible Impacts* (GAO, 1987), Appendix I, p. 9.

111. Fakhry Assad and Jonathan Mann, "AIDS—An International Perspective," *WHO Features*, No. 103 (November 1986), p. 2.

112. Jean Pape, *et al.*, "Pattern of HIV Infection in Haiti 1977–1986," paper presented at the Third International Con-

ference on AIDS, Washington, D.C., June 1987.

113. John Hopkins Medical Institutions, "High Rate of AIDS Infection Found among Poor Haitian Women," Baltimore, Maryland, June 4, 1987 (press release).

114. WHO Collaborating Centre on AIDS, *AIDS Surveillance in Europe*, No. 13 (Paris, 1987), p. 7.

115. *Op. cit.* 106.

116. *Op. cit.* 105, pp. 1–3.

117. Charles Myers, remarks at the Third International Conference on AIDS, Washington, D.C., June 1987.

118. M. Over, *et al.*, "The Direct and Indirect Cost of HIV Infection in Developing Countries: The Cases of Zaire and Tanzania," paper presented at the First International Conference on the Global Impact of AIDS, March 1988, London, p. 3.

119. Hesio Cordeiro, "Medical Costs of HIV and AIDS in Brazil," First International Conference on the Global Impact of AIDS, London, March 1988.

120. *Op. cit.* 105, p. 3.

121. *Op. cit.* 105, pp. 1–3.

122. W.J. Storck, "Pesticides Head for Recovery," *C & EN* (April 9, 1984), pp. 35–37, cited in Marcello Lotti, "Production and Use of Pesticides," in *Toxicology of Pesticides: Experimental, Clinical, and Regulatory Perspectives*, Lucio Costa, Corrado L. Galli, and Sheldon D. Murphy, eds. (Springer-Verlag, Berlin, 1987), p. 13.

123. Sheldon D. Murphy, "Toxic Effects of Pesticides," in *Toxicology*, C. Klassen, *et al.*, eds. (Macmillan Publishing, New York, 1986), p. 553.

124. *Op. cit.* 122.

125. Wood, Mackenzie, and Co. Agrochemical Service, Edinburgh and London, 1984, cited in Marcello Lotti, "Production and Use of Pesticides," in *Toxicology of Pesticides: Experimental, Clinical, and Regulatory Perspectives*, Lucio Costa, *et al.*, eds. (Springer-Verlag, Berlin, 1987) p. 14.

126. World Health Organization (WHO), *Safe Use of Pesticides* (WHO, Geneva, 1985), p. 12.

127. *Op. cit.* 122, p. 11.

128. World Health Organization, "Global Estimates of the Extent of Unintentional Acute Pesticide Poisoning," cited in Marcello Lotti, "Production and Use of Pesticides," in *Toxicology of Pesticides: Experimental, Clinical, and Regulatory Perspectives*, Lucio Costa, Corrado L. Galli and Sheldon D. Murphy, eds. (Springer-Verlag, Berlin, 1987), p. 15.

129. Foo Gaik Sim, *The Pesticide Poisoning Report: A Survey of Some Asian Countries* (International Organization of Consumers Union, Penang, Malaysia, 1985), p. 17 and p. 33.

130. J. Jeyaratnam, "Health Problems of Pesticide Usage in the Third World," *British Journal of Industrial Medicine*, Vol. 42 (1985), p. 505.

131. *Op. cit.* 129, p. 2.

132. L.W. Knapp, "Safety of Pesticide Applicators," in *Toxicology of Pesticides*, F. Kaloyanova and S. Tarkowski, eds. (World

Health Organization, Copenhagen, 1982), p. 259.

133. *Op. cit.* 123, p. 523.

134. Robert F. Wasserstrom and Richard Wiles, *Field Duty: U.S. Farmworkers and Pesticide Safety* (World Resources Institute, Washington, D.C., 1985), p. 41.

135. Douglas L. Murray, "Pesticides, Politics, and the Nicaraguan Revolution," paper presented at the XII International Congress of the Latin American Studies Association, Albuquerque, New Mexico, April 18–20, 1988.

136. Ladislav Rosival, "Pesticides," *Scandinavian Journal of Worker and Environmental Health*, Vol. 11 (1985), p. 190.

137. *Op. cit.* 134, p. 40.

138. Fernando Mazariegos, "The Use of Pesticides in the Cultivation of Cotton in Central America," *UNEP Industry and Environment* (July/August/September 1985), p. 5.

139. M.J. Coye, "Health Effects of Agricultural Production: II Health of the Community," *Journal of Public Health Policy*, Vol. 7, No. 3 (1980), pp. 340–354.

140. *Op. cit.* 129, p. 10.

141. L. Ivanova-Chemishanska, "Long Term Effects of Pesticides," in *Toxicology of Pesticides*, F. Kaloyanova and S. Tarkowski, eds. (World Health Organization, Copenhagen, 1982), p. 55.

142. Joaquin Alonso Guevera Moran, *et al.*, *El Salvador Perfil Ambiental, Estudio de Campo* (U.S. Agency for International Development, Washington, D.C., 1985), p. 153 and p. 155.

143. E.P. Savage *et al.*, "National Study of Chlorinated Hydrocarbon Insecticide Residues in Human Milk, USA," *American Journal of Epidemiology*, Vol. 113 (1981), pp. 413–422, cited in M.J. Coye, "Health Effects of Agricultural Production: II Health of the Community," *Journal of Public Health Policy*, Vol. 7, No. 3 (1986), p. 350.

144. *Op. cit.* 129, p. 15.

145. World Health Organization (WHO), International Agency for Research on Cancer, *IARC Monographs on the Evaluation of the Carcinogenic Risk of Chemicals to Humans*. Vol. 30, *Miscellaneous Pesticides* (WHO, Geneva, 1983), p. 33.

146. Gaston Vettorazzi, *International Regulatory Aspects for Pesticide Chemicals*. Vol. 1, *Toxicity Profiles*, preface (CRC Press, Boca Raton, Florida, 1979).

147. Xue Shou-zhen, "Health Effects of Pesticides: A Review of Epidemiologic Research from the Perspective of Developing Nations," *American Journal of Industrial Medicine*, Vol. 12 (1987) pp. 273–276.

148. A. Bainova, "Dermal Absorption of Pesticides," in *Toxicology of Pesticides*, F. Kaloyanova and S. Tarkowski, eds. (World Health Organization, Copenhagen, 1982), p. 55.

149. Dan S. Sharp, *et al.*, "Delayed Health Hazards of Pesticide Exposure," *Annual Review of Public Health*, Vol. 7 (1986) p. 453.

150. A.H. Smith, *et al.*, "Soft-Tissue Sarcoma

and Exposure to Phenoxyacetic Herbicides and Chlorophenols in the New Zealand," *Journal of the National Cancer Institute*, Vol. 73 (1984), pp. 1111–1117, *Op. cit.* 147, p. 276.

151. T. Vergieva, "Embryotoxicity and Teratogenicity of Pesticides," in *Toxicology of Pesticides*, F. Kaloyanova and S. Tarkowski, eds. (World Health Organization, Copenhagen, 1982), pp. 71–72.

152. *Op. cit.* 149, pp. 461–462.

153. J. Jeyaratnam, "Health Problems of Pesticide Usage in the Third World," *British Journal of Industrial Medicine*, Vol. 42 (1985), pp. 505–506.

154. World Health Organization (WHO), *Planning Strategy for the Prevention of Pesticide Poisoning* (WHO, 1986), cited in Marcello Lotti, "Production and Use of Pesticides," in *Toxicology of Pesticides: Experimental, Clinical, and Regulatory Perspectives*, Lucio G. Costa, Corrado L. Galli, and Sheldon D. Murphy, eds. (Springer-Verlag, Berlin, 1987), p. 12.

155. *Op. cit.* 129, p. 42.

156. *Op. cit.* 136, p. 191.

157. *Op. cit.* 129, p. 45.

158. World Health Organization (WHO), *Recommended Health-Based Limits of Occupational Exposure to Pesticides* (WHO, Geneva, 1982), p. 49.

159. World Health Organization (WHO), *Technical Report Series No. 634*, "Safe Use of Pesticides" (WHO, Geneva, 1979), p. 13.

160. J.H. Shih, *et al.*, "Prevention of Acute Parathion and Demton Poisoning in Farmers around Shanghai," *Scandinavian Journal of Work, Environment, and Health*, Vol. 2, Supp. 4 (1985), pp. 49–54, *Op. cit.* 147, p. 271.

161. Cited in U.S. Office of Technology Assessment, Robert F. Wasserstrom and Richard Wiles, *Field Duty: U.S. Farmworkers and Pesticide Safety* (World Resources Institute, Washington, D.C., 1985), p. 51.

162. Michael J. Dover, *A Better Mousetrap: Improving Pest Management for Agriculture* (World Resources Institute, Washington, D.C., 1985), pp. 47–48.

163. Monica Moore, Executive Director, Pesticide Education and Action Project, San Francisco, California, 1988 (personal communication).

164. *Ibid.*

165. Mary Kent and Arthur Haupt, "A Billion More People per Decade?" *Population Today*, Vol. 16, No. 5 (1988), p. 3.

166. Carl Haub, Demographer, Population Reference Bureau, Washington, D.C., 1988 (personal communication).

167. Population Reference Bureau (PRB), *1988 World Population Data Sheet* (PRB, Washington, D.C., 1988).

168. United Nations (U.N.), *World Population Prospects, Estimates and Projections as Assessed in 1984* (U.N., New York, 1986), p. 140.

169. *Op. cit.* 79.

170. *Op. cit.* 68, p. 29.

171. *Op. cit.* 64, p. 59.

172. *Op. cit.* 74.

3. Human Settlements

Cities and towns in western industrial countries have long been recognized as centers of civilization, foci of the arts and culture, and places that support important industrial and commercial activities. In the less developed countries, they are often condemned as parasitic. Critics argue that these cities, especially the largest metropolitan areas, drain economic resources from the countryside to feed their voracious growth and that they are insatiable users of natural resources and despoilers of the environment. Attempts to control their size and pace of growth generate heated debates over cities' advantages and liabilities and the means of guiding urban development.

That rapid urbanization inevitably accompanies economic development has been a fact of life in industrialized countries for a century. But as urbanization in industrial nations slows, urban populations in the less developed countries—where three quarters of the world population lives—are vigorously increasing (1). Many questions need to be answered more fully. How do urban settlements use resources? How does the growth of cities and towns affect resource use? How do settlements produce new resources for economic development? What are the effects of urbanization on natural resources and the environment in both urban and rural areas? These questions must be considered in terms of a world in which the population will be largely urban by the end of this century.

In more developed countries, the differences between urban and rural areas are less meaningful as their economies become more interdependent. In less developed countries, the relationships among agriculture, industry, and services are more apparent. Cities in an increasing number of less developed countries are important markets for agricultural goods. Their growth affects land use in surrounding rural areas and creates a need for more efficient food production and distribution. Rural towns also accommodate many small-scale industries, commercial services, and other nonagricultural activities. The terms of trade—the relative prices of goods exchanged between the agricultural sector in rural areas and the industrial and commercial sectors in towns and cities—strongly affect population and income distribution, migration from rural areas, and the growth rates of cities and towns.

The transformation of resources in cities and towns contributes significantly to economic growth in more developed countries and is quickly becoming a major source of national production in less developed countries. Economic growth and social progress depend primarily on the efficiency with which cities transform agricultural products and natural resources into finished goods to replace imports and generate exports over long periods (2).

But cities often transform resources inefficiently, and they produce vast amounts of waste that pollute the environment and degrade land, water, and other natural resources—on which people depend. The means are now available to make the transformation of resources more efficient, effective, and productive in much of the world if the growth of cities is seen in an ecological context.

CONDITIONS AND TRENDS

THE URBANIZATION OF HUMAN SETTLEMENTS

The single most important change in human settlements during the 20th Century is their rapid urbanization. (See

3 Human Settlements

Box 3.1.) Six trends are important for understanding the problems, challenges, and opportunities of human settlements:

■ The percentage of population living in urban areas is increasing.

■ Urban population is increasing at high rates in less developed countries and at declining rates in more developed countries.

■ Large increases are expected in the absolute numbers of urban residents over the next two decades, especially in less developed countries.

■ The number of cities in all size categories is growing in less developed countries.

■ The number and size of megacities are growing in less developed countries while the growth rate in major metropolitan areas in more developed countries is declining.

■ The distribution of people living in absolute poverty is shifting from rural to urban settlements at an increasing rate.

Demographic Changes in Human Settlements

The pace of urbanization during the 20th Century has been extremely rapid. Although urban population growth in more developed countries is now slowing down because of their high urbanization levels, high urban growth rates will continue in less developed countries well beyond the year 2000. In more developed countries, urban population grew an average of 2 percent a year from the 1920s to the 1960s (3); it will grow only about 0.8 percent during the 1990s and will decrease to about 0.5 percent during the first quarter of the next century (4).

But in less developed countries, urban populations in this century have been growing more than 3 percent a year, nearly double the total population growth rate and more than twice that of industrial countries. Urban population growth will be highest in Africa, where the projected annual growth is 4.8 percent to the year 2000. Because of its high level of urbanization, temperate South America's urban population will grow only about 1.5 percent a year for the rest of the century, but average annual urban population growth rates will remain at or higher than 2.2 percent a year in the Caribbean, Central America, East Asia, and South Asia.

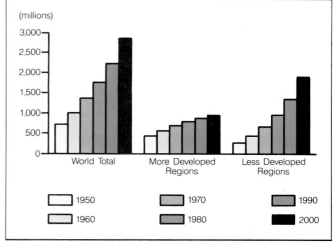

Figure 3.1 Urban Population Growth 1950–2000

Sources:
1. United Nations (U.N.), *Patterns of Urban and Rural Population Growth* (U.N., New York, 1987), Table 4, p. 11.
2. United Nations (U.N.), *The Prospects of World Urbanization, Revised as of 1984–85* (U.N., New York, 1987), Table 2, p. 8.

Only about 360 million of the world population was urban in 1920 (5); by the end of the century, the number will increase to about 2.9 billion. From 1950 to 1980, the urban population in more developed countries increased from 447 million to about 798 million. Although in 1950, only about 287 million people were living in urban settlements in less developed countries, the number more than doubled to 673 million by 1970, increased to about 966 million in 1980, and is expected to reach 1.9 billion by the year 2000. (See Figure 3.1.)

The net addition of more than 1 billion people to urban areas in developing countries between 1980 and 2000 will about equal the total urban population in more developed countries at the end of the century. By then, the less developed countries will have twice as many people living in cities and towns as industrialized countries.

In Africa, the urban population will more than double from 129 million to about 340 million between 1980 and

Box 3.1 Data and Projections on Urban Population

Most statistics on urban population and growth projections used here are taken from United Nations (U.N.) population studies. The United Nations Population Division points out the complexities of compiling and reporting international comparative data on urban areas or "agglomerations." The U.N. uses country definitions rather than one internationally standardized definition and the 205 countries from which data are collected use diverse criteria for population size, population density, physical facilities, and economic characteristics to define urban places. A U.N. urban ag-

glomeration is an area that includes a central city and surrounding urbanized localities. Metropolitan areas may contain several cities and towns and their suburban fringes.

References to urbanization and urban agglomeration for years beyond 1980 are based on U.N. projections. To project levels of urbanization, the U.N. uses a simple mathematical model based on observed differences between urban and rural population growth rates. Urban agglomeration projections are also based on a simple model using the

urban agglomeration growth rate. These statistics and projections are therefore more useful in determining orders of magnitude and directions of change in urban population than in forecasting precise urban population levels and urban agglomeration sizes (1).

References and Notes
1. United Nations (U.N.), *The Prospects of World Urbanization: Revised as of 1984–85* (U.N., New York, 1987), p. 2 and pp. 35–40.

Table 3.1 Urban Population Growth 1950–2000

	Urban Population (millions)								Projected Average Rate of Urban Population Growth		
	1950	1960	1970	1980	1990	2000	2010	2025	1990–2000	2000–10	2010–25
World Total	734	1,032	1,371	1,764	2,234	2,854	3,623	4,932	2.5	2.4	2.2
More Developed Regions	447	571	698	798	877	950	1,011	1,087	0.8	0.6	0.5
Less Developed Regions	287	460	673	966	1,357	1,904	2,612	3,845	3.4	3.2	2.8
Africa	35	53	81	129	210	340	528	894	4.8	4.4	3.9
Caribbean	6	8	11	16	21	27	33	43	2.5	2.1	2.0
Central America	15	23	37	56	79	105	134	178	2.9	2.4	2.1
Temperate South America	17	22	28	35	42	49	56	64	1.5	1.3	1.1
Tropical South America	31	54	86	130	184	239	293	370	2.6	2.0	1.7
East Asia (excl. Japan)	70	139	191	242	296	384	513	743	2.2[a]	2.4[a]	2.3[a]
South Asia	113	161	237	358	524	757	1,052	1,548	3.7	3.3	2.9

Source: United Nations Centre for Human Settlements (Habitat), *Global Report on Human Settlements 1986* (Oxford University Press, New York, 1987), Table 1.
Note: a. Includes projected urban growth rates for Japan.

Figure 3.2 Percent Population Living in Urban Areas in Less Developed Regions, 1960–2000

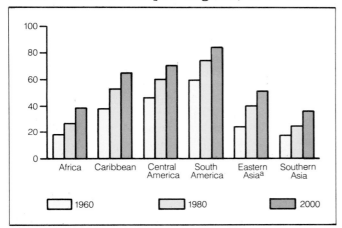

Sources:
1. United Nations (U.N.), *Patterns of Urban and Rural Population Growth*, Population Studies No. 68 (U.N., New York, 1980), Table 8, p. 16.
2. United Nations (U.N.), *The Prospects of World Urbanization, Revised as of 1984–85* (U.N., New York, 1987), Table 3, p. 11.
Note: a. Excludes Japan

2000. In South Asia, it will increase 111 percent; in South America, East Asia (excluding Japan), Central America, and the Caribbean, it will increase more than 55 percent. More than 1.1 billion people will live in urban settlements in the less developed countries of East and South Asia alone by the turn of the century. (See Table 3.1.) China will add 96 million to its urban population between 1985 and 2000; India will add 136 million; and Bangladesh, Pakistan, and Indonesia combined will add nearly 73 million to their urban settlements (6).

Thus, by the year 2000, 47 percent of the world population will be urban. In more developed countries, nearly 75 percent of the population will be urbanized. In countries now considered less developed, more than half the population will live in cities and towns. By the end of this century, only in Africa and South Asia will less than half the population reside in urban areas. (See Figure 3.2.)

These demographic changes will profoundly affect cities in less developed countries both economically and

socially. An estimated 40 percent of the urban population in less developed countries lives in slum and squatter areas with minimal housing and services. In many Third World cities, many families are squatters. More than 2 million of Calcutta's population, for example, lived in slums in 1980. Rio de Janeiro, Jakarta, Manila, Bogota, Lima, Casablanca, and Istanbul each had more than 1 million living in slum and squatter settlements (7).

By the end of this century, more than half the households in absolute poverty—that is, at or near subsistence—in developing countries will be concentrated in urban areas. The World Bank estimates that by the end of the 1990s, 90 percent of the absolute poor in Latin America and the Caribbean will be in cities, as will be about 40 percent of the poorest in Africa and 45 percent of those in Asia. The number of urban households living in poverty is expected to increase 122 percent from the 1975 level of 33.5 million to about 74.3 million at the end of the century (8).

Growth in Number and Size of Cities

Urban population growth remains high among all city size categories, driven by very high growth rates in developing countries. Worldwide, the number of cities with 100,000 or more residents grew from 946 in 1950 to 1,886 by 1980. Their population increased 677 million. (See Table 3.2.) About two thirds of the world's urban population lives in cities and towns of less than 1 million. But compared to the 1950s, the distribution of urban population has shifted from smaller cities and towns to larger ones. Table 3.3 indicates that the percentage of people living in towns smaller than 100,000 declined from 42.5 to 38.1 between 1950 and 1980, and the percentage of people in cities with 100,000–999,999 residents also declined. On the other hand, the population in cities of 1 million or more increased from about 27 percent in 1950 to about 34 percent in 1980. In less developed countries, this shift was slightly greater.

The pace of growth and the distribution of urban population among cities of various sizes, of course, differ substantially throughout the world. In Latin America, where urbanization has been rapid during the past half century, the number of cities of 5,000–50,000 increased from 1,269 in 1950 to 3,325 in 1980, and the number of people living there increased from nearly 15.5 to about

Table 3.2 Estimated Populations of Urban Areas[a] with 100,000 or More Residents 1950–80

City Size Category	1950 Number of Urban Areas	1950 Population (thousands)	1960 Number of Urban Areas	1960 Population (thousands)	1970 Number of Urban Areas	1970 Population (thousands)	1980 Number of Urban Areas	1980 Population (thousands)
4,000,000 +	13	87,825	19	136,262	23	186,922	35	281,389
3,999,999–2,000,000	17	46,955	26	66,966	39	109,242	51	140,890
1,999,999–1,000,000	48	65,470	69	95,930	98	136,070	136	182,337
999,999–500,000	101	69,551	136	94,764	173	120,049	258	176,331
499,999–250,000	192	66,050	263	90,210	384	133,148	496	170,731
249,000–100,000	575	86,716	749	115,350	930	145,548	910	148,142
Total	**946**	**422,567**	**1,262**	**599,482**	**1,647**	**830,979**	**1,886**	**1,099,820**

Source: United Nations Centre for Human Settlements (Habitat), *Global Report on Human Settlements 1986* (Oxford University Press, New York, 1987), Table 5.
Note: a. The United Nations defines an urban area or "agglomeration" as a populated area falling within the contours of a cluster of dense, contiguous settlements. The boundaries of an agglomeration frequently extend beyond the administrative boundaries of the corresponding city but may also be more restricted.

Table 3.3 Population Distribution in Four Urban Area Categories, 1950–80
(percent)

	Under 100,000	100,000–999,999	1 Million–3,999,999	4 Million or More
World Total				
1980	38.1	27.9	18.2	15.8
1970	38.9	29.3	18.0	13.7
1960	40.8	29.6	16.1	13.4
1950	42.5	30.2	15.3	11.9
More Developed Regions				
1980	36.8	29.8	19.3	14.1
1970	37.1	30.3	18.3	14.2
1960	39.6	30.0	16.2	14.2
1950	42.3	29.5	15.7	12.5
Less Developed Regions				
1980	39.1	26.3	17.3	17.3
1970	40.8	28.2	17.8	13.2
1960	42.4	29.2	15.9	12.5
1950	42.9	31.4	14.7	11.1

Source: United Nations Centre for Human Settlements (Habitat), *Global Report on Human Settlements, 1986* (Oxford University Press, New York, 1987), Table 5.

44 million over the 30 years. The number of cities with 100,000–500,000 increased from 55 to 174, and their populations rose from nearly 12 million to about 36 million. Cities of 1 million or more increased from 7 to 25, and their populations increased 70 million between 1950 and 1980. (See Table 3.4.)

Average annual growth rates in all city size categories in Latin America have been extremely high since the 1950s, for the most part exceeding 4 percent. The growth of the largest cities in Latin America, as in many more developed countries, has slowed down since the 1950s. But unlike the largest cities in more developed countries that are growing at rates below 1 percent a year (9), the population growth of Latin American cities of 500,000 and more remains above 5 percent a year.

This growth results from the graduation effect of smaller towns moving up in the city size classification because of population growth or boundary changes that incorporate surrounding areas rather than from movement of population from smaller to larger cities. Thus, the population and number of cities in any particular city size category in one census period may show growth in the next census period because smaller settlements graduate into it, even though cities originally in the category may be stagnant or even declining in population. When the graduation effect is controlled, it becomes clear that many small cities and towns in Latin America have been growing faster than the largest cities, although

urban population growth rates in all cities continue to be high (10).

Of particular concern to many governments is the continuing rapid growth in the number and size of megacities (cities with populations of more than 5 million) and large metropolitan areas. In 1980, about one third the world's urban population was in cities of 1 million or more. (See Table 3.3.) In North America, about 47 percent and in Europe about 30 percent of the urban population lived in "million cities." In less developed countries, more than one third the urban population was concentrated in cities of 1 million or more in all regions except Africa. Nearly 40 percent of the urban population in Latin America was living in million cities, as was almost 37 percent in Asia (11).

In 1970, there were 62 cities with populations of 2 million or more (see Table 3.2.); their number increased to 99 in 1985. By the end of the century, large cities in less developed countries will be more numerous and much larger than those in more developed countries. In 1950, there were 31 cities with a population of 1 million or more in less developed countries; by 1970, the number more than doubled to 77. By the year 2000, their number will triple again to 279 (12).

Megacities in more developed countries are growing far more slowly than those in less developed countries. But by the end of the century, the Tokyo-Yokohama agglomeration will reach 20 million people, and the New York, London, Los Angeles, Osaka-Kobe, and Moscow metropolitan areas will grow to more than 10 million residents each (13).

In less developed countries, megacities are growing rapidly in both number and size. The United Nations estimates that by the year 2000, more than two thirds of the 30 largest cities in the world will be in developing countries (14). Mexico City is expected to reach nearly 26 million and São Paulo about 24 million. Bombay and Calcutta are each expected to grow to 16 million or more. Seoul, Rio de Janeiro, Jakarta, Tehran, Delhi, and Shanghai are projected to exceed 13 million. (See Figure 3.3.) Cairo, Manila, Bangkok, Karachi, and Beijing will grow beyond 10 million. Madras, Lima, and Lagos are likely to exceed 8 million. The 19 cities in less developed countries with more than 5 million population in 1985 had a total population of about 163 million. The number of cities in less developed countries with more than 5 million residents will increase to 30 by the year 2000,

Table 3.4 Size Distribution and Populations of Cities in Latin America 1950–80

City Size Category	Number of Cities				Population (thousands)				Average Annual Population Growth Rate (percent)		
	1950	1960	1970	1980	1950	1960	1970	1980	1950–60	1960–70	1970–80
5,000–20,000	1,087	1,517	1,966	2,719	9,917	14,270	18,714	25,502	4.4	3.1	3.6
20,000–50,000	182	279	410	606	5,538	8,694	12,399	18,555	5.7	4.3	5.0
50,000–100,000	57	94	139	191	3,929	6,470	9,535	12,920	6.5	4.7	3.6
100,000–500,000	55	78	120	174	11,810	17,083	24,482	35,950	4.5	4.3	4.7
500,000–1,000,000	5	10	18	26	3,526	6,878	12,626	19,704	9.5	8.4	5.6
1,000,000+	7	11	17	25	17,810	31,872	55,758	88,599	7.9	7.5	5.9
Total	**1,393**	**1,989**	**2,670**	**3,741**	**52,530**	**85,267**	**133,514**	**201,230**			

Source: Robert W. Fox, consultant, unpublished data (Washington, D.C., 1987).

and their populations will total nearly 331 million (15).

One or two large cities dominate the settlement system in many developing countries. In 34 countries, more than 40 percent of the urban population is concentrated in the largest city. More than 65 percent of the urban population is concentrated in the largest cities in Senegal, Jamaica, Panama, Guinea, Lebanon, and Mozambique. Most countries with high concentrations of urban population in the largest city are either poor or geographically small or both. Fifteen of the 23 countries with more than half their urban populations in the largest city had a per capita gross national product of $1,000 or less. (See Table 3.5.)

CHANGING MIGRATION AND URBAN FERTILITY PATTERNS

The increased urban population in both more developed and less developed countries resulted largely from rural to urban migration. In poor, predominantly rural countries, except those in Asia, this migration will continue for the rest of the century.

In North America and Europe, however, lower fertility rates in metropolitan areas and relatively low levels of rural to urban migration explain overall declines in population growth rates in large metropolises. Studies in seven

Table 3.5 Countries with More Than 40 Percent of Their Urban Population Living in Largest Cities, 1985

Per Capita Gross National Product	Urban Population Living in Largest City (percent)		
	40–49	50–59	60 or More
< $400	Burkina Faso Sierra Leone Laos	Tanzania Kenya Haiti Uganda	Mozambique Benin Senegal Guinea Togo Angola
$400–$1,000	Bolivia Peoples Dem. Rep. of Yemen Paraguay	Zimbabwe Dominican Republic Mongolia	Thailand Jamaica
> $1,000	Chile Portugal Argentina South Korea Ireland	Congo Uruguay Greece Iraq	Lebanon Costa Rica Panama Libya

Source: Compiled from The World Bank, *World Development Report 1987* (The World Bank, Washington, D.C., 1987), pp. 266-267 and pp. 202-203.

European countries indicate lower gross birth rates and levels of fertility in large metropolitan areas than in rural areas or elsewhere. The in-migration of young adults is still strong. But out-migration to the suburbs and the relatively low fertility rates of those remaining in the large cities led to the relatively low levels of overall population growth in the areas studied (16).

Similar patterns of change are taking place in large cities in the United States and Germany. In both countries, the movement of middle and upper income residents to the suburbs continues. In many central cities, they are being replaced by lower income racial minorities and foreign workers (17). Migration and fertility rates are also changing in less developed countries. In an increasing number of Asian countries, urban settlements are growing more as a result of natural increase than as a consequence of migration from rural areas. Rural to urban migration now contributes less than 35 percent of urban population growth in Thailand, the Philippines, Malaysia, Pakistan, India, and Indonesia. In Pakistan, for example, rural to urban migration accounted for only about 22 percent of the population growth in urban areas in the late 1970s. About 70 percent of the urban population growth was due to natural increases in towns and cities (18).

In much of the world, urban areas are associated with lower fertility rates. Recent World Fertility Surveys for 22 less developed countries in which fertility levels could be distinguished by three categories of residence—major urban, other urban, and rural—found that urban fertility rates were lower than rural fertility rates in all 22 countries. In 13 of them fertility rates in major urban areas (a city with 1 million or more or the largest city in the country) were lowest, followed by other urban areas, then by rural areas. In three other countries, other urban and rural rates were about equal, but still much higher than in major urban areas (19).

Women living in urban areas tend to have lower fertility rates than their rural counterparts because of the differences in availability of health and contraceptive services, opportunities for schooling (the level of education is a strong factor), the costs of food and housing, the economic costs of raising a child, and the social milieu supporting family planning (20).

Studies of 19 Asian and Latin American countries indicate that contraceptive use by women is highest in the largest cities and is higher in both large and small cities than in rural areas. (Indonesia is an exception where the

Figure 3.3 Growth of Largest Cities 1970–2000
(All cities with population greater than 10 million in 2000)

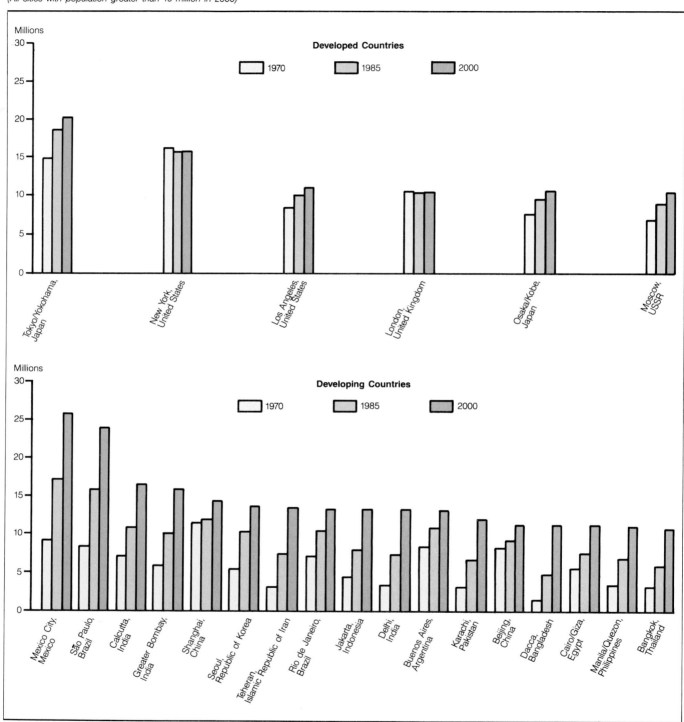

Source: United Nations (U.N.), *The Prospects for World Urbanization, Revised as of 1984-85* (U.N., New York, 1987), pp. 25-27.

two are about equal.) For all the countries, about 55 percent of the women in the principal city and 47 percent in smaller cities used contraception, but only about 33 percent of rural women used contraception. Urban women of all age groups also continue to use contraception longer than rural women (21). (See Table 3.6.)

Table 3.6 Percentage of Women Currently Using Any Method of Contraception[a]

Country	Principal City (1)	Other Urban (2)	Rural (3)	Principal City versus Rural Gap (1)-(3)
Asia and Pacific[b]				
Bangladesh	41	21	10	31
Fiji	57	61	49	8
Indonesia	40	42	42	-2
Jordan	53	42	14	39
Korea, Republic of	46	42	37	9
Malaysia	59	52	36	23
Nepal	39	16	3	36
Pakistan	26	17	4	22
Philippines	61	58	42	19
Sri Lanka	52	39	35	17
Thailand	62	59	44	18
Group Average	**49**	**41**	**29**	**20**
Caribbean and Latin America				
Colombia	70	61	36	34
Costa Rica	83	79	75	8
Dominican Republic	57	51	33	24
Guyana	45	32	37	8
Jamaica	56	46	43	13
Mexico	62	53	21	41
Panama	72	75	56	16
Peru	63	49	17	46
Group Average	**64**	**56**	**40**	**24**
All Countries Average	**55**	**47**	**33**	**22**

Source: R.E. Lightbourne, "Urban-Rural Differentials in Contraceptive Use," Comparative Studies No. 10 (World Fertility Survey, London, 1980), p. 16.
Notes:
a. To improve international comparability, the populations of women surveyed were adjusted to a standard age structure, thereby controlling for age-dependent patterns of contraceptive use.
b. Includes West Asia.

CITIES AS TRANSFORMERS OF NATURAL RESOURCES

Over the next decade, the impact of urbanization on natural resources and the environment is likely to be strongest in less developed countries because of the high levels of concentration and rapid growth of population in megacities. For this and other reasons, the growth of large cities is often considered socially and economically adverse. Large cities are often thought of as economic parasites, growing and living off surpluses generated by agriculture.

Cities are increasingly more important in transforming resources into productive goods and services that contribute strongly to national economic production. Although agriculture is still the major employer in many developing countries, it contributes more than half the gross domestic product (GDP) in relatively few countries, even the poorest. Agriculture contributed more than 50 percent of GDP in only seven countries in 1985—Bangladesh, Nepal, Bhutan, Burundi, Somalia, and Tanzania, which were among the poorest in Asia and Africa (22).

In much of the world, the largest cities have a larger share of economic activities than their share of national population. Cities contribute to economic growth by providing economies of scale and proximity that allow industry and commerce to flourish; by supporting modern social services and production facilities that generate employment; and by offering a wide variety of commercial and personal services essential to meeting human needs and supporting productive activities. Cities offer locations for facilities and services that require high

population thresholds and large markets to operate efficiently. Cities are often the centers of innovation and innovation diffusion, and they facilitate the economic and social transformation of developing countries from agrarian to manufacturing and commercial economies (23).

Modern productive activities in most developing countries tend to be concentrated in the largest urban centers at a level much higher than these cities' share of the nations' population. In Côte d'Ivoire, for example, Abidjan, with 15 percent of the population, accounts for more than 70 percent of all economic and commercial transactions in the country. The Bangkok metropolitan area accounts for 86 percent of GNP in banking, insurance, and real estate and 74 percent of manufacturing, but it has only 10 percent of Thailand's population. Lagos, with 5 percent of Nigeria's population, accounts for 57 percent of total value added in manufacturing and has 40 percent of the nation's highly skilled manpower. São Paulo, with about 10 percent of Brazil's population, contributes over 40 percent of industrial value added and one quarter of net national product (24).

Cities in less developed countries now contribute heavily to GNP. For example, 43–46 percent of Pakistan's GNP originated in urban areas over the past few years, and gross urban product grew twice as fast as gross rural product since 1977. Per capita GNP in urban areas was double that of rural areas (25). In the People's Republic of China, 300 cities containing about 10 percent of the national population produced 87 percent of national industrial output and generated 86 percent of national tax income. In Thailand, more than half of all national economic growth during the past decade is attributed to urban economic activities. Nearly half of Bangladesh's manufacturing jobs are in Dhaka. The city accounts for nearly all the country's employment in rubber products, 97 percent of the jobs in the furniture industry, 84 percent in footwear production, 82 percent in leather goods, and more than half in electrical machinery production and textiles (26).

One of the strongest impacts of urbanization on natural resources and rural land use is the fact that large cities are important markets for agricultural goods in many less developed countries (27). More than 9,000 metric tons of vegetables are brought daily to Shanghai from surrounding rural production areas. Fruit supplies to the city increased from about 148,000 metric tons in 1980 to more than 360,000 metric tons in 1986 (28). In Mexico City, nearly 8,000 metric tons of fruits and vegetables are sold each day in the principal wholesale market alone (29).

Large cities also organize the marketing system for both domestically consumed and exported commodities as well as for the distribution of imported foods. About one fourth of India's population is urban, for example. Yet the public food distribution system sends more than half the food grains that it distributes to five states that contain about 60 percent of the country's total urban population (30). Bangkok serves as the central clearing point for the pricing, bulking, distribution, and export of food grown in the large central plains surrounding the city (31). In Tanzania, the major wholesale market in the city of

Dar es Salaam is supplied by farmers from the hinterlands of Dar es Salaam, Morogoro and the coast region, Mbeya, Arusha, and Lushoto (32). Food is bulked at assembly points in smaller towns and villages by middlemen, truckers, and small-scale wholesalers and brought to the city's Kariakoo market, from which it is distributed to stores, vendors, and market stalls.

The continued growth of large cities intensifies rural land use in surrounding areas, increasing pressure to change crop mixes and characteristics and promoting more intensive agriculture. For example, the rapid growth of population in Bangkok changed farming in the rural areas nearby from semisubsistence to commercial production, increasing the use of modern inputs. As the demand for rice increased in Bangkok, broadcasting rice was replaced by transplanting, which is more productive and labor intensive. Traditional transplanted varieties were rapidly displaced by higher yielding varieties and those with shorter maturation periods, allowing double cropping (33). With double cropping and land consolidation, machines for land preparation, rice transport, and threshing were more attractive to farmers. The increasing demand for food both created opportunities for new agricultural activities in the Central Plain and allowed many farmers to diversify. Farms close to Bangkok produce three to four times the amount of poultry and much higher amounts of pork and fruit than other regions of the country. (See Chapter 4, "Food and Agriculture.")

Many of these changes brought by urban growth increase agricultural productivity and raise the incomes of farmers living on the periphery of cities. But as the FAO points out, "[u]rban growth feeds on many of the same inputs and resources that are essential to agriculture," and it is especially competitive with agriculture for the use of arable land (34). Between 1980 and 2000, urban areas in less developed countries are expected to double in area from about 8 million hectares to more than 17 million hectares. More than 476,000 hectares of land a year will be built up in less developed countries over the 20 years (35).

The expansion of cities often invades rich agricultural lands surrounding them. The growth of New Delhi, for example, appropriated more than 14,000 hectares between 1941 and 1971. The FAO estimates that worldwide, about 1.4 billion hectares of arable land will be removed from agricultural use between 1980 and 2000 because of city growth (36).

SECONDARY CITIES AND SMALL TOWNS

Although large cities are increasingly important in resource transformation in developing countries, many governments are seeking to create a more balanced distribution of urban population in secondary cities and towns dispersed broadly throughout the country (37).

The rapid growth of megacities has created serious social, economic, and physical problems in some developing countries. Among the most serious is the fact that large metropolises in many developing countries have economic bases too weak to absorb the vast numbers of workers who will be added by population growth and migration to their labor forces over the next 20 years. Some are already experiencing diseconomies because of congestion and high density. Physical disamenities of dense urban living are manifested in increasing air and water pollution and in physical deterioration. The continued growth of large metropolitan areas increases demands for limited services, facilities, infrastructure, energy, shelter, and even food in countries where municipal governments have limited financial and managerial capabilities to deal with urban problems (38).

At the other extreme, not only is the urban population in most of the poorest countries concentrated in one or two large cities, but the rural population is scattered widely in villages and hamlets of a few hundred to a few thousand people. These communities are too small to support basic health and educational services, marketing facilities, physical infrastructure, and productive activities capable of generating employment. Moreover, the towns and cities in many predominantly rural regions are not well-linked physically or economically to their hinterlands or to the larger cities. Thus, much of the rural population has little or no access to the services, facilities, and infrastructure that is concentrated in a few large cities (39).

An increasing number of governments in less developed countries are using a secondary cities development strategy to achieve a more balanced distribution of urban population and to diffuse the economic benefits of urbanization more evenly throughout the country. The strategies are based on the recognition that secondary cities and towns, like large cities, are important to economic development (40). Secondary cities and towns provide convenient and efficient locations for field offices of national government agencies, provincial and district administrative offices, as well as local government offices that can extend public services and facilities to local populations. Secondary cities and towns offer economies of scale that allow efficient provision of basic health, education, social, and municipal services. By attracting people from rural areas and towns nearby, they serve as regional or provincial centers for a variety of social services and recreational activities.

Secondary cities and towns offer a variety of basic household and consumer goods, commercial and personal services, and opportunities for off-farm employment. Their population growth and economic diversification increase the demand for cash crops and commercial agricultural goods from surrounding rural areas, stimulate the commercialization of agriculture, and increase productivity in nearby rural regions. They provide services, facilities, utilities, and raw materials as well as access to markets that accomodate small- and medium-scale manufacturing and artisan and cottage industries.

Secondary cities are also important to agricultural and rural development in accommodating agroprocessing industries and commercial facilities for supplying fertilizers, seeds, pesticides, cultivating and harvesting tools, irrigation equipment, and other supplies used to increase farm output. They are also hubs for transportation, communication, and distribution, linking their residents and those of nearby rural areas to other cities and regions.

Box 3.2 Secondary and Intermediate Cities in Colombia

Colombia is unusual among developing countries for having a large network of intermediate and secondary cities. An examination of these cities reveals the variety of economic and social roles filled by such cities.

The 1985 census showed that the secondary and intermediate cities of Colombia had absorbed a significant portion of the urban population growth over the previous two decades, although at unequal rates (1). (Definitions of secondary and intermediate cities vary by country. For this discussion, secondary cities have 500,000 people or more and intermediate cities have populations between 100,000 and 500,000.)

The more dynamic intermediate cities tend to be service centers for a cluster of smaller towns; they provide agricultural markets, government and commercial services, and agricultural materials to a population far larger than their own. For example, Armenia—which is in the heart of the Quindio coffee area and has a population of about 200,000—is the service and market center for a cluster of communities within 17 kilometers, including Calarca, Circasia, La Tebaida, and Montenegro, as well as more distant hill towns

that have a combined population of nearly 150,000. The smaller towns are specialized centers for handicrafts, coffee processing, and local services. In fact, Armenia provides services to all 12 municipalities in the Department of Quindio; it is the central hub of both the electrical and potable water networks and is the linking point for roads that extend to most other municipalities in the department (2).

Periera, a major marketing center for coffee in the Risaralda region, is a center for both services and transportation. It operates an international airport at a profit and is the hub of the road system linking it with Manizales, Armenia, and other coffee-producing cities of the region.

The other intermediate cities have also grown because they perform important regional and national economic functions. Buenaventura is the major Colombian port on the Pacific, Santa Marta is an important inland port on the Magdalena River, Barrancabermeja supports a large oil processing and refining operation, and Sogomosa's growth results from construction of the steel-producing complex of Paz de Rio. Bucaramanga and Cucuta are major trading centers near the Venezuelan fron-

tier. The network of intermediate cities in the Cauca Valley—Tulua, Cartago, Buga, and Palmira—are strongly linked to regional agriculture. As market and agroprocessing centers, bulking and distribution points, and supply centers for agricultural materials, all are joined by roads to the regional center of Cali. Villavicenio is a major agricultural market, distribution point, and service center for the Llanos frontier region in the northeast, as is Popayan for the southern Cauca Valley, Pasto for the Narino area, and Tunja for Boyaca.

References and Notes

1. Republica de Colombia, *Avance de Rusultados Preliminares: Censo 1985* (Departamento Administativo Nacional de Estadistica, Bogota, 1986), pp. 73–75.
2. Francisco Uribe-Echevarria and Edgar Forero, "The Role of Informal Activities in the Process of Urbanization: Small-Scale Industries in Peripheral Regions in Colombia" (German Foundation for International Development, Bogota, 1985).

Colombia, for example, has a relatively well-developed system of secondary cities and towns that provides an important physical structure on which to base regional economic growth in much of the Andean and Caribbean coastal areas of the country.

About 70 percent of Colombia's 27 million people are now urban. Rural areas have generally been losing population because of migration and slowed population growth. Although Bogota's population has nearly tripled over the past 20 years, the 1985 census shows that Colombia now has four cities with populations of 500,000–2 million: Medellin, Cali, Barranquilla, and Bucaramanga. These secondary cities absorbed many of the migrants who would otherwise have moved to the capital. Between 1951 and 1985, their combined populations increased from 660,000 to nearly 5 million. With about 27 percent of Colombia's urban population, these secondary cities are increasingly important to Colombia's economy as manufacturing, service, and commercial centers and are well established as economic capitals of their regions. Almost two thirds of Colombia's industrial value added is accounted for by production in Bogota, Medellin, Cali, and Barranquilla (41).

Colombia also has 17 intermediate cities with populations of 100,000–500,000. Their combined populations have more than tripled from about 1 million in 1951 to nearly 3.5 million in 1985, and they now contain slightly more than 20 percent of the urban population. Recent studies indicate that the growth of most intermediate cities in Colombia is closely related to the agricultural sector because of their agricultural markets, food distribution points, and agroprocessing and agricultural supply centers. During periods of rapid agricultural development, the urbanization rate has increased but the urban concentration rate has decreased. (See Box 3.2.)

As Colombia reached higher levels of urbanization, the annual urban population growth rate declined from an average of 5.4 percent during the 1950s to about 3 percent during the last decade. Bogota's population growth rate declined from an average of 6 percent a year in 1964–73 to about 2.9 percent in 1973–85, although in absolute terms metropolitan Bogota's population increased more than 1 million over the past decade. The four secondary cities' populations grew at a slightly lower rate than Bogota's, but increased about 1.3 million since 1973. The intermediate cities have had the highest growth rates over the past decade, averaging about 3.4 percent a year. About 13 percent of the urban population—2.5 million people—lives in small cities of 20,000–100,000. Colombia also has more than 900 towns with populations of less than 20,000, but they have been growing more slowly than other urban settlements.

Stimulating the Growth of Secondary Cities and Towns

The number of people living in secondary or intermediate cities is increasing in much of the world. According to United Nations estimates, the number of cities in less developed countries that have a population of more than 100,000 but are smaller than the largest city increased from 301 in 1950 to 644 in 1980; in Africa, the Middle East, and South America, the number of these secondary cities more than tripled. Between 1970 and 1980, the number of people living in cities of more than 100,000 outside the largest metropolis has increased from 225 million to 327 million. (See Table 3.7.)

Many developing country governments are exploring ways of stimulating growth of secondary cities to take pressure off the largest cities, to increase the access of

Table 3.7 Number, Population, and Growth Rates of Secondary Cities in Less Developed Regions, 1950, 1970, and 1980

Region	Number			Secondary Cities Population (thousands)		Percent Increase in Population 1970–80
	1950	1970	1980[a]	1970	1980	
Africa	22	74	81	18,203	30,024	64.9
Middle East	19	56	66	14,068	24,617	74.9
Central America	13	36	37	10,153	16,847	65.9
South America	34	105	110	32,263	51,988	61.1
East and Southeast Asia	213	335	350	150,397	204,079	35.7
All Regions	**301**	**606**	**644**	**225,084**	**327,555**	**45.5**

Source: Compiled from United Nations (U.N.), *Patterns of Urban and Rural Population Growth* (U.N., New York, 1980), Table 48.
Note: a. Projected on the basis of the number and population of cities of 100,000 or more, excluding the largest city in the country in 1970.

rural people to urban-based services and facilities, and to create growth centers in economically lagging rural regions.

National governments can enhance the endowments and attractiveness of intermediate and small cities through spatial distribution of investments in services and infrastructure, pricing policies, financial incentives, administrative decentralization, tax benefits, and other policies. In its report on intermediate and small cities, the United Nations Centre for Human Settlements noted that "[s]mall and intermediate settlements can provide a useful tool to help achieve social equity. . . . Small and intermediate settlements can play a role in increasing the proportion of national populations reached with services" (42).

Government actions to promote the growth and proliferation of secondary cities include the following:
■ Brazil, China, Thailand, and South Korea are extending support services for economic development by improving basic social services, upgrading municipal facilities, and providing financial resources for residents of secondary and small settlements to meet their housing needs;
■ Colombia, Brazil, Kenya, and Mexico are improving schools, hospitals, transport and market facilities, and public utilities essential to support productive activities;
■ Nepal, Colombia, India, Kenya, and Côte d'Ivoire are strengthening the planning and administrative capacity of municipal governments in intermediate and small cities;
■ Malaysia, Indonesia, and Senegal are creating financial incentives to expand the economic bases of intermediate and small cities, especially in commercial, small-scale manufacturing, agroprocessing, and marketing functions;
■ Brazil, Thailand, and Colombia are building roads and highways linking small and intermediate cities to each other and to larger urban centers that can supply them with raw materials and serve as markets for their goods (43).

Because of the growing need to provide more efficient infrastructure and services in secondary cities and towns, many developing countries are decentralizing responsibility for service and infrastructure provision to municipal and local governments and private organizations (44). Many governments are establishing programs that help municipalities raise additional revenues locally.

Colombia is attempting to strengthen municipal financial and managerial capacity; the central government will transfer up to 50 percent of the national sales tax to municipalities by 1992. By 1990, revenues from the national sales tax will exceed 500 billion pesos, and municipalities are expected to receive the equivalent of $125 billion. Part of the municipalities' share of these revenues will be distributed equally among them, and the remainder will be allocated by size, revenue collection effort, and other criteria. About 13 percent of the revenues are expected to be distributed to municipalities with populations of less than 100,000, thereby strengthening their financial base (45).

The Nigerian government has devolved a wide range of functions to locally elected governments. They are now responsible for construction and maintenance of local public roads and bridges; provision of health services, water, housing and other local services, sanitary inspection, refuse and human waste disposal; and collection of property and other local taxes. Nigeria's constitution requires both the federal and state governments to assist local authorities in carrying out these functions through grants (46).

Improvements in the quality of life in human settlements also depend on rural villages and towns performing residential, service, market, processing, and distribution functions that support primary production. Recognizing the strategic value of rural settlements in agricultural production and marketing, China is providing for delivery of these basic public services more efficiently and effectively. The People's Republic of China restricts migration from rural areas to large cities and controls population growth through a one-child-per-family policy. China's large-scale program of agricultural pricing and wage controls is trying to create parity in the costs of goods exchanged between urban and rural areas and in the individuals' and households' ability to pay for them. The government is also investing more heavily in services and facilities that improve living conditions and economic opportunities in small towns and cities (47).

These policies have had a strong impact on slowing the growth of the largest cities in China and on retaining the population of secondary cities and small towns. Shanghai, China's largest city, grew only 0.3 percent a year between 1970 and 1985. Other large cities, with the exception of Chengdu, Taibei, and Zibo, have grown less than 2 percent a year since 1970, in marked contrast to the growth rates of metropolitan areas in other less developed countries (48).

ADVERSE ENVIRONMENTAL IMPACTS OF RAPID URBANIZATION

Although cities transform resources in ways that contribute strongly to economic development and social welfare, they also generate wastes that pollute air and water and degrade renewable natural resources.

Both increasing urbanization and the continued growth of megacities have serious adverse effects on air and water quality in less developed countries. Large-scale urbanization near rivers and bays seriously affects aquatic biota. Untreated domestic sewage reduces oxygen levels, killing finfish and contaminating shellfish. Sediments and toxic materials seeping into rivers and estuaries from unsanitary landfills increase sedimentation rates and turbidity, smothering fish eggs, larvae, invertebrates, and microorganisms. Processed urban industrial wastes increase toxicity and ambient temperatures of both river and sea water and reduce oxygen solubility (49).

The sewage system in Dhaka, Bangladesh, for example, serves one fifth or less of the city. Recurrent flooding in the city, which is located in a low-lying delta, exacerbates drainage and sewage disposal problems; serious pollution and human health hazards result (50). Between 75 and 95 percent of all waterborne pollution in Indonesia's cities is caused by untreated human waste. Less than one third of the urban population in Indonesia has access to safe disposal of human waste (51).

Wastewater from the textile, brewing, slaughtering and rendering, chemical, sugar refining, and pulp and paper industries concentrated in the Lagos, Nigeria, metropolitan area is discharged directly into rivers or to open drains. Untreated organic discharges from human and industrial activities in Asian cities are wiping out local fisheries and jeopardizing water supplies from the Tjiliwung River in Jakarta, the Han River in Seoul, and the Pasig River in Manila.

Rapid urban growth on ecologically fragile land creates serious physical problems. Because of the overuse of groundwater in Bangkok, for example, much of the land in the southern and eastern parts of the city that is at or near sea level is sinking 5–10 centimeters a year—much faster than the rate at which Venice was sinking during its worst time (52).

About 80 percent of the nearly 2,500 metric tons of solid waste generated each day in Bangkok is collected, but more than half the waste collected is simply left to decompose (53). In Madras, a city with more than 4 million residents, solid waste is dumped untreated, creating serious groundwater pollution around the dump sites (54). In Delhi, 242 million liters of liquid waste are generated daily; less than half receives even partial treatment before entering the Yamuna River, which is now highly polluted (55).

Air quality standards in most large cities of developing countries are far below those of Western Europe and North America—and they are well below internationally accepted standards for good health. In cities of India that are industrializing and that depend on coal and wood for fuel, air quality is poor. Automobiles in most Indian cities generate 2–3 times the amount of air pollutants as vehicles in more developed countries. High carbon monoxide and sulfur dioxide levels are found in the air in Calcutta and Bombay (56).

The urban concentration of industries has caused serious air pollution problems in Latin America. Mexico City has one of the highest levels of suspended particulates of any Latin American city. Foundries, metal processing, paint manufacturing, cement production, and smelting operations in and around Mexico City generate the particulate matter (57). In the Sao Paulo metropolitan area, air pollution discharges total about 8,000 tons a day; almost 65 percent is carbon monoxide. Vehicle emissions and stationary fuel combustion, in addition to industrial processes, are the primary sources of air pollution in Latin American cities (58).

With increasing urbanization and the growth of large cities, household waste disposal is becoming a more serious problem. Finding effective ways of disposing of solid wastes and conserving resources in cities is a challenge to governments in both developed and less developed countries.

FOCUS ON: URBAN SOLID WASTE DISPOSAL

When solid waste is not collected and disposed of efficiently and effectively, it pollutes and degrades land and water resources essential to economic growth. Uncollected or untreated garbage creates serious human health hazards by attracting disease carrying vermin and insects, and polluting rivers, lakes, ponds, and groundwater as it decomposes.

Urban refuse generation tends to increase with the economic levels of countries and cities. (See Table 3.8.) Large cities in low income countries—such as Calcutta, Karachi, and Jakarta, for example—generate 0.5–0.6 kilograms of waste per person a day, and cities in middle income countries—Cairo, Manila, Tunis, and Hong Kong, for example—generate from 0.5–0.85 kilograms. In a city of 1 million, this rate produces 500–850 metric tons of waste each day.

Solid waste disposal in growing secondary cities can also be a serious problem. In Morocco, for example, the urban solid waste collected ranges from 107 metric tons a day in Marrakech to more than 963 metric tons in Casablanca (59). But generally, smaller cities in both more developed and less developed countries have lower per capita waste generation rates primarily because they have fewer commercial activities than larger cities (60).

Solid waste disposal is a large expenditure for cities of all sizes, and the costs increase with city size. Costs also vary with the type of disposal used. For example, littering and dumping cost a municipality virtually nothing, and engineered filling of small depressions and channels and burning of open dumps are relatively inexpensive. But these options pollute the environment and create human health hazards. Sanitary landfills with daily cover are more costly, and environmentally safe incineration is an expensive means of disposing of urban solid waste. Disposing of solid waste in landfills with daily cover and leachate control, for example, costs $20–60 per metric ton and incineration $150–200 per metric ton in developing countries. Many cities in less developed

Table 3.8 Urban Waste Generation Rates[a]

City or Country	kg/person/day
Industrialized Countries	
New York City, United States	1.80
Hamburg, Germany	0.85
Rome, Italy	0.69
Middle-Income Countries	
Singapore	0.87
Hong Kong	0.85
Tunis, Tunisia	0.56
Medellin, Colombia	0.54
Kano, Nigeria	0.46
Manila, Philippines	0.50
Cairo, Egypt	0.50
Low-Income Countries	
Jakarta, Indonesia	0.60
Surabaya, Indonesia	0.52
Bandung, Indonesia	0.55
Lahore, Pakistan	0.60
Karachi, Pakistan	0.50
Calcutta, India	0.51
Kanpur, India	0.50

Source: Sandra J. Cointreau, *Environmental Management of Urban Solid Wastes in Developing Countries* (The World Bank, Washington, D.C. 1982), Table 1, p. 10.
Note: a. For cities in developing countries where the total refuse mix was divided into major categories of waste, data indicate that the residential portion of the total refuse was 60-80 percent.

countries now spend over 30 percent of their budgets on refuse collection and disposal (61).

Although the problems and costs of urban waste disposal are increasing, solutions are evolving. Solid wastes are being recycled and reused. New technologies to reduce environmental pollution and generate new energy sources are being tested. Among the most important approaches that recycle wastes and generate energy are:

■ inorganic materials recovery in which usable refuse is sorted and classified manually or mechanically for repair or remanufacturing;

■ processing of ferrous and nonferrous metals, plastics, and polymers for reuse in manufacturing;

■ protein, humus, and fertilizer reclamation for animal feeding, fertilization and aquaculture;

■ waste water reclamation for sewage farming, effluent irrigation, and aquaculture;

■ waste disposal for land reclamation;

■ energy recovery through direct combustion, production of biogas, or recovery of energy equivalents in inorganic material.

Recycling Solid Wastes

Recycling urban solid waste offers many economic advantages. It conserves energy that would be used to incinerate garbage, reduces environmental degradation and dependence on chemical fertilizers that further pollute water resources, generates jobs and opportunities for small-scale enterprise, reduces dependence on foreign imports of metals and inorganic materials, and conserves water. The World Bank points out that using scrap ferrous metal instead of iron ore to make new steel can result in a 74 percent energy savings, using recovered rubber results in a 70 percent energy savings over production from virgin materials, and recycling aluminum results in a 96 percent energy savings over new production (62).

Solid waste is now being recycled in many European cities. Cities in industrialized countries tend to generate low density wastes with little organic material, a low water content, and a high percentage of paper, plastics, glass, and metals. This type of waste is most effectively recovered for remanufacturing or reprocessing or is incinerated. Plants in Madrid, Rome, and Vienna produce ferrous metals, paper, plastics, fibers, and compost. Significant amounts of refuse-derived fuels are also produced in Stockholm, Zoetermeer in the Netherlands, Herten in Germany, and Doncaster and Westbury in England (63).

Glass recycling is becoming a major means of waste treatment in Europe. Between 1979 and 1984, the amount of recovered glass more than doubled from 1.3 to nearly 2.7 million metric tons a year. In the Netherlands, more than half the glass used each year is made from recycled material, and recycling accounted for more than 25 percent of the glass used in Austria, Belgium, France, West Germany, and Switzerland (64). In West Germany, glass recyclers were used to salvage and reuse about 580,000 metric tons of glass bottles and containers collected from households in 1983 (65). Reprocessing in Austrian cities resulted in the recovery of about 70,000 metric tons of glass in 1986, or nearly 40 percent of the number of bottles and jars used. This return reduced the solid waste to be disposed of by about 254,000 cubic meters and saved 62.5 million kilowatt hours that would otherwise have been used to produce equal amounts of glass (66).

In less developed countries, the composition of urban household waste lends itself to other forms of disposal. Composting is a particularly promising means of disposing of household wastes in Third World cities because of the large amounts of water and vegetable and putrescible materials, including human feces. In low- and middle-income countries, vegetative and putrescible materials are a large part of urban waste. (See Table 3.9.) This high density, high moisture material is especially suitable for composting to produce methane gas, combustible pellets, and fertilizers. Composted vegetative material can also be used for pig and other animal feed and in fish farming. Compost for fertilizer is now being made in a plant in Port-au-Prince, Haiti, for example, by mixing preheated shredded refuse and pit latrine waste (67). Studies of 33 cities in India indicate that more than one third the wastes collected in nearly all the urban areas is being composted and that the cities are able to sell all the compost that they produce (68).

The People's Republic of China is experimenting with multiple waste recovery and reuse systems. Shanghai, a city of about 12 million people, produces about 13 million metric tons of solid waste each year. The Shanghai Resource Recovery and Utilization Company (SRRUC) has been able to recover about 1.5 million metric tons of reusable waste a year and to process and resell materials for enough money to cover the costs of collection and disposal, and to pay nearly 29,000 employees. In Shanghai, organic wastes are shipped to rural areas around the city for biogas production in 60,000 households and 1,200 village plants. The material is also used for composting and manuring fields. Inorganic materials are used

Table 3.9 Urban Waste Composition
(percentage by weight)

Material Type	Industrialized Cities					Middle-Income Cities				Low-Income Cities				
	Brooklyn, New York, United States	London, England	Rome, Italy	Singapore	Hong Kong	Medellin, Colombia	Lagos, Nigeria	Kano, Nigeria	Manila, Philippines	Jakarta, Indonesia	Lahore, Pakistan	Karachi, Pakistan	Luknow, India	Calcutta, India
Paper	35	37	18	43	32	22	14	17	17	2	4	<1	2	3
Glass and ceramics	9	8	4	1	10	2	3	2	5	<1	3	<1	6	8
Metals	13	8	3	3	2	1	4	5	2	4	4	<1	3	1
Plastics	10	2	4	6	6	5	X	4	4	3	2	X	4	1
Leather and rubber	X	X	X	X	X	X	X	X	2	X	7	<1	X	X
Textiles	4	2	X	9	10	4	X	7	4	1	5	1	3	4
Wood, bones, straw	4	X	X	X	X	X	X	X	6	4	2	1	<1	5
Nonfood total	74	57	29	63	60	34	21	35	40	15	27	4	18	22
Vegetative and putrescible	22	28	50	5	9	56	60	43	43	82	49	56	80	36
Miscellaneous inerts	4	15	21	32	31	10	19	22	17	3	24	40	2	42
Compostable total	26	38	71	37	40	66	79	65	60	85	73	96	82	78

Source: Sandra J. Cointreau, *Environmental Management of Urban Solid Waste in Developing Countries: A Project Guide* (The World Bank, Washington, D.C., 1982), Table 3, p. 14.
Notes: Figures may not total due to rounding.
X = not available.

for landfill and land reclamation. Slag and ash are used in brick and cement making. SRRUC sells reclaimed products at 121 retail shops in the city and additional shops in 10 suburban districts. SRRUC also reprocesses more than 1,000 materials, including ferrous and nonferrous metals, rubber, plastics, paper, rags, cotton, chemical fiber, animal bones, human hair, glass, chemicals, old machine parts, and waste oil. SRRUC extracts gold, silver, platinum, and other precious metals from solid waste at 99.9 percent purity (69).

A major problem with recycling in most countries is the lack of incentives for households to sort and segregate recyclable material. Innovative experiments are being tried in some less developed countries to segregate solid waste for reuse or recycling. In less developed countries, most reusable material is sorted by scavengers either during collection or at urban dumps. Collection and disposal of solid waste in urban areas in less developed countries provide employment or livelihood for large numbers of the poor who are employed by municipal governments or private contractors or who are simply scavengers. About 4,000 people earn their living exclusively from scavenging and recycling household wastes in Medellin, Colombia, for example. In India, 1–3 individuals per thousand collect and dispose of refuse (70). In Cairo, the religious sect Zabbaleen was granted the right to collect and reuse wastes after negotiating with owners of large buildings. Zabbaleen families collect, sort, and segregate wastes (71). Edible portions are used to feed farm animals, and inorganic materials are sold to dealers. In Bangkok, garbage collection crews supplement their incomes by sorting recoverable materials and selling them to dealers (72).

Experiments in intermediate cities in less developed countries sponsored by the U.S. Agency for International Development's Project Managing Energy and Resource Efficient Cities (MEREC) have shown that waste from urban activities can be converted inexpensively into new resources and low-cost energy (73).

Another approach to disposing of urban solid waste more effectively, especially in secondary cities and towns, involves public-private partnerships. Private organizations provide services that local governments cannot offer efficiently and effectively on their own, or private firms supplement local government services. In the central region of eastern Sudan, for example, the Regional Ministry of Health contracts with private organizations employing sweepers with donkey carts to collect dry refuse and garbage house to house in small towns. This system is more efficient and less costly than buying expensive imported garbage trucks. The costs were only 10 percent of those for truck service, and about 26 percent of them could be recovered through household charges (74).

In transforming resources for economic growth and social progress, cities and towns inevitably generate wastes that can threaten human health and the natural resource base on which their economies depend. Technological solutions to safe and efficient waste disposal and resource conservation exist. The challenge is to mobilize the commitment and financial resources to use them.

RECENT DEVELOPMENTS

HABITAT ADOPTS ENABLING STRATEGIES

The United Nations Centre for Human Settlements (Habitat) argues that less developed country governments must stop trying to provide all public services to burgeoning cities. Instead, governments should create the conditions that allow for community self-help. In its second decade, Habitat is adopting an enabling strategy for improving conditions in human settlements.

According to Habitat such a strategy must deal with two challenges. How can it handle the many problems of large numbers of poor people concentrating in cities and towns? And how can it provide autonomy for community groups to initiate and carry out development activities? Meeting these challenges requires creating and strengthening community and neighborhood groups that can identify their needs and initiate local actions to meet them, increasing local government funds, and providing materials to local communities at affordable costs. The role of nongovernmental organizations in assisting local communities will grow.

Over the next decade, Habitat will promote a new division of responsibility between governments and community self-help groups. Governments must provide the large-scale infrastructure—the streets, highways, and utilities—that are beyond the capacity of community groups to provide for themselves. The new, crucial role for community and neighborhood groups is to undertake community improvement programs that are self-determined, self-organized, and self-managed. Habitat strategies provide greater decentralization of authority and assistance to local communities in generating new sources of funds (75).

LOW-INCOME HOUSING BOUNCES BACK IN MEXICO CITY

The earthquake that devastated the center of Mexico City in September 1985 also resulted in an unprecedented mobilization of human and financial resources to rebuild damaged and destroyed low-income housing. Now, three years after the disaster, planners, architects, and multilateral development agencies are calling the reconstruction effort "an unqualified success."

In spite of this praise, the World Bank admits that the reconstruction efforts provided homes for only one out of seven families in a 25-square-kilometer area in the old section of the city, most of which was damaged by the earthquake (76).

Nonetheless, the project has received recognition as "the largest urban reconstruction effort since World War II," with 70 low-income neighborhoods in the damaged area rebuilt and about 48,000 families now living in new structures designed to preserve the social and physical integrity of historic Mexico City.

Each of the units consists of roughly 40 square meters of living space with two bedrooms, a kitchen, living room, toilet and bathing facilities as well as a balcony, water, electricity, and sewerage. Moreover, each unit is built of reinforced concrete with a box frame construction and is designed to withstand earthquakes up to 9.0 on the Richter scale. The 1985 earthquake registered 8.1 (77).

The speed and efficacy with which the reconstruction effort took place can be attributed to a combination of factors. First, Renovacion Habitacional Popular (Popular Housing Renewal or RHP), the agency specially created to provide temporary shelter and to reconstruct low-income housing after the earthquake, consulted community members throughout the planning process and implemented many of their recommendations. Second, the Mexican government immediately expropriated land for all the new housing in the damaged areas, thereby removing the largest obstacle to reconstruction. Third, the World Bank made available a large amount of money for reconstruction. And finally, RHP headquarters was set up in the midst of the damaged area so that decisions could be made rapidly and funds transferred directly to contractors without costly bureaucratic delays (78).

By most measures, the costs of reconstruction were low. The World Bank reports that the cost per housing unit averaged $3,400 for materials and labor. Administrative, design, and supervision costs added an additional indirect cost of about $600 per unit. In part, the surprisingly low total cost per unit resulted from the high productivity of RHP staff and the economic incentives that RHP gave to contractors to complete building early (79).

These low building costs were reflected in the price of the new housing. Under the system set up by RHP, the new dwellings are condominiums, with each family owning an apartment and sharing ownership of communal areas such as courtyards, stairways, and patios. To qualify as owners, former tenement residents had to have lived in the damaged areas and to have an income at or below 2.5 times the minimum wage of $90 per month (80).

References and Notes

1. The World Bank, *World Development Report 1986* (The World Bank, New York, 1986), Table A.1, p. 154.
2. Jane Jacobs, *Cities and the Wealth of Nations: Principles of Economic Life* (Random House, New York, 1984), p. 171.
3. United Nations (U.N.), *Growth of the World's Urban & Rural Population 1920–2000* (U.N., New York, 1969), Table 1.2.
4. United Nations (U.N.), *The Prospects of World Urbanization: Revised as of 1984–85* (U.N., New York, 1987), p. 14.
5. *Op. cit.* 3, Table 1.1.
6. *Op. cit.* 4, Table A-3, pp. 70–85.
7. U.S. Agency for International Development (U.S. AID), *Urbanization and Urban Growth as Development Indicators in AID-Assisted Countries* (U.S. AID, Washington, D.C., 1983), p. iv–39.
8. The World Bank, *Shelter, Poverty, and Basic Needs Series* (The World Bank, Washington, D.C., 1980), Table 1, p. 3.

9. *Op. cit.* 4, Table 6, p. 25.
10. Robert Fox, "Urban Growth in Latin America," *Populi*, Vol. 12, No. 3 (1985), pp. 5–13.
11. United Nations (U.N.), *Estimates and Projections of Urban, Rural and City Populations, 1950–2025; The 1982 Assessment* (U.N., New York, 1985), Table A-9, pp. 116–17, and pp. 118–30.
12. *Ibid.* pp. 116–130.
13. *Op. cit.* 4, p. 25.
14. *Op. cit.* 4, pp. 25–26.
15. *Op. cit.* 4, pp. 25–26.
16. Piotr Korcelli and Peer Just, "Metropolitan Growth and Population Development at the National Level," *Regional Development Dialogue*, Vol. 4, No. 1 (1983), pp. 4–10.
17. John D. Kasarda and Jurgen Friedrichs, "Comparative Demographic Employment Mismatches in U.S. and West German Cities," *Research in the Sociology of Work*, Vol. 3 (1985), pp. 1–30.

18. Asian Development Bank, *Bank Assistance for Urban Development and Housing Sector* (Asian Development Bank, Manila, 1985), p. 34.
19. United Nations (U.N.), Department of International Economic and Social Affairs, *World Population Trends, Population and Development Interrelations and Population Policies, 1983 Monitoring Report*, Vol. I (U.N., New York, 1985), pp. 61–62.
20. Susan H. Cochrane, "Effects of Education and Urbanization on Fertility," in *Determinants of Fertility in Developing Countries*, Vol. 2, R.A. Bulatao and R.D. Lee, eds. (Academic Press, New York, 1983), pp. 587–626.
21. Robert E. Lightbourne, "Urban-Rural Differentials in Contraceptive Use," Comparative Studies No. 10 (World Fertility Survey, London, 1980), pp. 15–16.
22. The World Bank, *World Development Report 1987* (The World Bank, Washington, D.C., 1987), pp. 206–207.

23. Dennis A. Rondinelli, *Secondary Cities in Developing Countries: Policies for Diffusing Urbanization* (Sage Publications, Beverly Hills, California, 1983).
24. Jorge Hardoy and David Satterthwaite, *Small and Intermediate Urban Centers* (Hoddler and Stoughton, London, 1986), Table 8.3, pp. 363–364.
25. Asian Development Bank, *Pakistan Urban Sector Profile* (Asian Development Bank, Manila, 1986), p. 36.
26. United Nations (U.N.), *Population Growth and Policies in Mega Cities: Dhaka* (U.N., New York, 1987), p. 12.
27. Dennis A. Rondinelli, "Cities as Agricultural Markets," *Geographical Review*, Vol. 77, No. 4 (1987), pp. 408–420.
28. Colin Mackenzie, "The Supply Lines to Shanghai," *Ceres*, Vol. 20, No. 5 (1987), pp. 18–19.
29. Gustavo Ponce Melendez, "Markets for the Mexican Megalopolis," *Ceres*, Vol. 20, No. 5 (1987), p. 22.
30. A. Ahmed and A.K. Singh, "Food for the City: The Role of the Informal Sector," *Geojournal*, Supplementary Issue 4 (1982), pp. 27–47.
31. Savit Bhotiwihok, "Agricultural Development Sector Study of Rural-Urban Relations in Thailand," in *Rural-Urban Relations in the Bangkok Metropolitan Dominance Subregion*, P. Pakkesem, ed. (United Nations Centre for Regional Development, Nagoya, Japan, 1978), p. 124.
32. Anders Sporrek, *Food Marketing and Urban Growth in Dar es Saalam* (Royal University of Lund, Sweden, 1985), p. 80.
33. Phisit Pakkesem, "The Spahal-Sector Transformation: Certain Creative Dimensions," in *Rural-Urban Relations in the Bangkok Metropolitan Dominance Subregion*, P. Pakkesem, ed. (United Nations Centre for Regional Development, Nagoya, Japan, 1978), pp. 26–27 and p. 35.
34. "Feeding the Cities of the Future," *Ceres*, Vol. 20, No. 5 (1987), p. 15.
35. United Nations Centre for Human Settlements (Habitat), *Global Report on Human Settlements, 1986* (Oxford University Press, New York, 1987), p. 130.
36. *Op. cit.* 33, pp. 15–16.
37. United Nations (U.N.), *World Population Trends and Policies: 1979 Monitoring Report*, Vol. 2 (U.N., New York, 1980), pp. 40–41.
38. Lester R. Brown and Jodi L. Jacobson, *The Future of Urbanization: Facing the Ecological and Economic Constraints* (Worldwatch Institute, Washington, D.C., 1987), pp. 10–28.
39. Dennis A. Rondinelli and K. Ruddle, *Urbanization and Rural Development: A Spatial Policy for Equitable Growth* (Praeger, New York, 1978).
40. *Op. cit.* 22, pp. 115–175.
41. Republica de Colombia, *Avance de Resultados Preliminares: Censo 1985* (Departamento Administrativo Nacional de Estadistica, Bogota, 1986), pp. 73–75.
42. United Nations Centre for Human Settlements (Habitat) (UNCHS), *The Role of Small and Intermediate Settlements in National Development* (UNCHS, Nairobi, 1985), p. 71.
43. *Op. cit.* 22.
44. Dennis A. Rondinelli and John R. Nellis, "Assessing Decentralization Policies in Developing Countries: The Case for Cautious Optimism," *Development Policy Review*, Vol. 4 (1986), pp. 3–23.
45. Jaime Castro, "Reforma Politica, 1982–1986," *Economia Colombiana*, No. 182 (June 1986), pp. 16–20.
46. Alex Gboyega, "Local Government Reform in Nigeria," in *Local Government in the Third World*, P. Mawhood, ed. (John Wiley & Sons, New York, 1983), pp. 225–247.
47. Yu Qingkang and Gu Wenxuan, "In Search of an Approach to Rural-Urban Integration," *Third World Planning Review*, Vol. 6, No. 1 (1984), pp. 37–46.
48. *Op. cit.* 4, pp. 168–169.
49. K. Ruddle and W. Manshard, *Renewable Natural Resources and the Environment* (Tycooly, Dublin, 1981), Table 15, pp. 258–259.
50. *Op. cit.* 25, p. 25.
51. The World Bank, *Indonesia: Urban Services Sector Report* (The World Bank, Washington, D.C., l984), p. 57.
52. H. Detlef Kammeier, "A Review of the Development and Land Use Problems in Bangkok," Working Paper No. 13 (Asian Institute of Technology, Human Settlements Division, Bangkok, 1984), cited in United Nations (U.N.), *Population Growth and Policies in Mega-Cities: Bangkok* (U.N., New York, 1987), p. 30.
53. United Nations (U.N.), *Population Growth and Policies in Mega-Cities: Bangkok* (U.N., New York, 1987), p. 31.
54. United Nations (U.N.), *Population Growth and Policies in Mega-Cities: Madras* (U.N., New York, 1987), p. 23.
55. United Nations (U.N.), *Population Growth and Policies in Mega-Cities: Delhi* (U.N., New York, 1986), p. 28.
56. U.S. Agency for International Development (U.S. AID), *Environmental and Natural Resources Management in Developing Countries: A Report to Congress*, Vol. I (U.S. AID, Washington, D.C., 1979), p. 81.
57. *Ibid.*, p. 109.
58. Vinod Thomas, "Evaluating Pollution Control: The Case of São Paulo," in *The Economics of Urbanization and Urban Policies in Developing Countries*, G.S. Tolley and V. Thomas, eds. (The World Bank, Washington, D.C., 1987), pp. 156–157.
59. R. Razouani and W. Martin, *Study of Options to Treat Municipal Solid Waste in Morocco* (U.S. Agency for International Development, Washington, D.C., 1984), pp. 2–3.
60. Sandra J. Cointreau, *Environmental Management of Urban Solid Wastes in Developing Countries: A Project Guide* (The World Bank, Washington, D.C., 1982), p. 11.
61. C.G. Gunnerson and D.C. Jones, "Costing and Cost Recovery for Waste Disposal and Recycling," paper presented at the United Nations Environment Programme/ Bundesministerium fur Forschung und Technologie, International Symposium on Solid Waste Management, Karlsruhe, Federal Republic of Germany, 1983, p. 1 and p. 3.
62. Sandra J. Cointreau, *Solid Waste Recycling: Case Studies in Developing Countries* (The World Bank, Washington, D.C., 1987), p. 3.
63. J.G. Abert, *Municipal Waste Processing in Europe: A Status Report* (The World Bank, Washington, D.C., 1985), pp. 1–9.
64. United Nations (U.N.) Environment Programme, *Environmental Data Report* (U.N., New York, 1987), Table 8.14, p. 298.
65. "Glass Is Renewable Resource in Germany," *Urban Innovation Abroad*, Vol. 8, No. 10 (1984), p. 3.
66. "Austrian Aim: 50% Glass Recycling," *Public Innovation Abroad*, Vol. 11, No. 11 (1987), p. 6.
67. L.A. Obeng and F.W. Wright, *The Composting of Domestic Solid and Human Wastes* (The World Bank, Washington, D.C., 1987), pp. 17–22.
68. Sandra J. Cointreau, *et al.*, *Recycling from Municipal Refuse: A State of the Art Review and Annotated Bibliography* (The World Bank, Washington, D.C., 1985).
69. Shanghai Resource Recovery and Utilization Company, "Resource Recovery and Utilization in Shanghai," paper presented at International Resource Recovery and Utilization Seminar, Shanghai, 1984, pp. 2–4.
70. *Op. cit.* 68, p. 42 and p. 76.
71. M.A. Lewis and T.R. Miller, *Public-Private Partnership in African Urban Development* (U.S. Agency for International Development, Washington, D.C., 1986), p. 22.
72. *Op. cit.* 60, pp. 29–35.
73. A. Bendavid-Val, *More with Less: Managing Energy and Resource Efficient Cities* (U.S. Agency for International Development, Washington, D.C., l987).
74. *Op. cit.* 71, pp. 21–22.
75. *Op. cit.* 35, pp. 197–198.
76. World Bank, "Mexico City: A Remarkable Recovery," *The Urban Edge*, Vol. 11, No. 8 (The World Bank, Washington, D.C., 1987), p. 1.
77. *Ibid.*
78. *Ibid.*
79. *Ibid.*, p. 3.
80. *Ibid.*, p. 3.

4. Food and Agriculture

Global production of all major foods—cereals, rootcrops, pulses, vegetables, melons, meat, and milk—rose again in 1987 by a healthy percentage, and the developing countries outpaced the developed countries in production of several major foods. Per capita food production continued to increase everywhere except sub-Saharan Africa.

Yet hunger persists because food is distributed unevenly. If the amount of food produced in 1985 were distributed evenly throughout the world, it could provide an adequate diet for 6 billion people—1 billion more than the Earth's population (1). But 950 million people still consume too few calories each day to support an active working life. Access to food is correlated with income. Eighty percent of these people live in the world's low-income nations (nations with a per capita income of $400 or less) (2).

The Green Revolution of the 1960s alleviated hunger in many Third World nations, especially in Asia, where high-yielding varieties of rice increased rice production many times over. Through a network of international research institutes, research continues in high-yielding cereals that respond favorably to fertilizers and pesticides. Recently, both researchers and agriculturists began to look beyond the Green Revolution to its side effects and the areas that it failed to touch.

The environmental effects of the Green Revolution include the well-known degradation that overuse of pesticides and fertilizers can cause a watershed and its surroundings. Another effect was the formation of huge areas of monoculture rice farming in Asia. Eventually an oversupply of rice led to reduced prices. Now some Asian farmers are reexamining traditional crop diversification as a sounder approach economically and environmentally. Two new research methods—farming systems research and agroecosystems research—eschew the top-down laboratory approach in favor of tailoring research to the needs of each farm and, in the case of agroecosystems research, to the environmental and economic setting.

The Green Revolution concentrated on areas of adequate rainfall and irrigated areas; it did not provide high-yielding crops for farmers on arid lands with no irrigation. Because many of the world's poor and hungry live on arid marginal lands, research and development of new crops and techniques to increase food output in these areas is urgently needed.

CONDITIONS AND TRENDS

FOOD PRODUCTION

Over the past two decades, total world food output expanded, outpacing demand. As a result, in recent years, prices of major food staples in international markets declined in real terms (3). The expansion, however, was not uniform among commodity groups or geographic regions; nor has it been steady over time.

Cereals provide about half the caloric intake worldwide. Between 1965 and 1986, cereal production increased at an impressive annual rate of 3 percent. (See Table 4.1.) However, global production fell below consumption in the 1987–88 marketing season. Largely as a result of government-sponsored programs to reduce planted acreage in the United States, cereal output in North America dropped 16 percent between 1985 and 1987. In Africa and Asia, weather conditions caused a decline in cereal production (4) (5). It is interesting to note that cereal production in developing countries now exceeds that of developed countries, as it has since 1983.

Global output of root crops, the world's other principal staple, climbed more slowly at 0.8 percent per year from 1965 to 1986. Root crops are central to the diet in Africa, where the annual growth rate reached 2.7 percent in the same period. (See Table 4.1.)

Respectable production increases also occurred in non-staple foods. Meat, milk, and fish output rose 2 percent annually over the past 21 years. The corresponding rate for other food crops—oil crops, pulses, vegetables, and melons—was 2.5 percent. For both types of commodities, growth rates were markedly higher in the developing than the developed countries. This fact reflects the low initial production and consumption levels of these commodities in the developing world and the increasing

Table 4.1 Production of Selected Food Crops, 1965–86

(thousand metric tons)

Cereals

	1965	1970	1975	1980	1982	1983	1984	1985	1986
World	1,005,926	1,205,128	1,372,727	1,567,472	1,701,537	1,643,156	1,803,902	1,847,436	1,870,109
Developing Countries	470,248	587,418	683,263	770,799	831,546	889,742	920,264	928,135	949,654
Africa	37,877	43,087	47,679	49,957	51,244	45,229	46,094	60,528	62,966
Far East	157,652	212,254	239,075	273,652	275,965	316,348	318,692	325,197	328,949
Latin America	57,640	71,307	80,545	88,498	105,318	98,593	106,667	109,441	108,678
Near East	37,821	39,962	51,689	55,536	58,541	56,746	53,829	62,785	67,078
Asian Centrally Planned Economies	179,240	220,779	264,245	303,114	340,434	372,788	394,946	370,142	381,938
Developed Countries	535,678	617,710	689,463	796,673	869,991	753,414	883,637	919,301	920,455
North America	215,893	215,389	286,543	311,336	386,618	255,065	358,183	396,617	375,677
Western Europe	116,285	128,230	146,628	177,513	181,187	173,647	211,443	196,283	190,503
Oceania	10,106	13,482	18,422	17,159	15,045	32,793	29,717	26,385	26,444
Eastern Europe & USSR	168,412	234,742	208,405	264,130	261,663	271,116	260,614	273,596	300,736

Root Crops

	1965	1970	1975	1980	1982	1983	1984	1985	1986
World	489,283	561,774	553,230	538,214	552,862	555,425	591,820	587,336	582,802
Developing Countries	246,432	302,483	330,014	353,652	347,151	351,444	365,632	370,625	366,731
Africa	58,502	68,228	79,713	84,779	86,716	82,790	91,442	101,637	102,638
Far East	33,261	36,713	45,684	58,011	59,276	58,078	65,497	64,967	58,997
Latin America	42,089	49,184	45,743	44,047	45,600	41,756	43,472	44,730	47,622
Near East	3,417	3,869	4,901	7,234	7,820	7,800	7,944	9,051	9,130
Asian Centrally Planned Economies	107,952	143,173	152,601	158,121	146,110	159,382	155,699	148,640	146,720
Developed Countries	242,851	259,290	223,216	184,563	205,711	203,980	226,188	216,712	216,071
North America	16,004	17,886	17,398	16,715	19,408	18,252	19,838	22,153	19,509
Western Europe	63,637	63,254	47,519	49,186	48,446	42,138	50,514	51,418	47,688
Oceania	812	1,068	977	1,091	1,168	1,119	1,327	1,277	1,319
Eastern Europe & USSR	152,143	169,291	151,145	111,251	129,664	135,710	147,334	134,604	140,261

Meat, Milk and Fish

	1965	1970	1975	1980	1982	1983	1984	1985	1986[a]
World	501,748	557,500	606,277	673,377	689,944	711,890	731,581	748,013	759,654
Developing Countries	114,547	136,140	152,288	183,957	194,126	197,540	211,236	224,422	231,211
Africa	10,389	12,435	13,190	15,105	16,110	16,934	15,990	16,201	16,521
Far East	37,162	42,188	51,442	61,860	66,628	68,724	74,709	78,844	81,471
Latin America	39,731	51,606	50,870	60,147	61,579	59,728	64,370	68,036	69,450
Near East	12,890	14,291	16,530	20,294	20,028	20,817	21,729	22,998	23,123
Asian Centrally Planned Economies	14,208	15,215	19,817	25,960	29,444	30,983	34,084	37,925	40,228
Developed Countries	387,200	421,362	453,988	489,421	495,819	514,352	520,346	523,591	528,443
North America	88,497	88,811	87,802	98,056	102,053	104,789	103,625	107,898	108,860
Western Europe	143,113	150,917	162,914	182,459	186,239	191,177	191,701	189,016	190,440
Oceania	15,756	16,997	16,471	16,334	16,243	16,746	17,751	18,274	18,416
Eastern Europe & USSR	124,178	143,932	164,168	167,188	165,316	174,769	179,400	180,556	182,705

Oil Crops, Pulses, Vegetables, Melons, and Fruits

	1965	1970	1975	1980	1982	1983	1984	1985	1986
World	514,161	584,298	653,611	738,782	787,263	785,018	816,331	821,659	859,567
Developing Countries	284,179	322,986	373,709	435,070	461,248	471,446	492,899	505,428	530,998
Africa	36,700	44,237	51,176	51,232	54,097	54,457	53,235	54,858	59,960
Far East	84,073	95,380	110,279	130,854	139,372	145,040	149,546	150,311	158,453
Latin America	53,435	60,534	70,841	85,392	89,148	86,997	95,833	95,079	97,475
Near East	32,584	37,859	45,714	55,521	60,164	60,959	61,510	64,129	67,245
Asian Centrally Planned Economies	76,014	83,483	94,041	110,246	116,537	122,111	130,812	139,032	145,764
Developed Countries	229,982	261,313	279,903	303,713	326,014	313,569	323,434	316,231	328,571
North America	46,734	52,368	62,953	69,765	70,937	65,955	68,096	69,054	67,655
Western Europe	99,210	110,172	111,183	118,437	124,668	121,285	121,558	119,151	125,678
Oceania	3,201	3,794	3,813	4,334	4,554	4,629	5,161	5,949	5,894
Eastern Europe & USSR	58,631	68,798	73,319	81,621	95,237	92,109	99,719	92,357	99,754

Sources: For vegetables, melons, and fruits: United Nations Food and Agriculture Organization (FAO), 1986 FAO Production Yearbook (FAO, Rome, 1987), Table 49. For 1965-80 and 1984-86 data, FAO, 1987 Country Tables: Basic Data on the Agricultural Sector (FAO, Rome, 1987), pp. 310-336. For 1982-83 data, 1985 Country Tables: Basic Data on the Agricultural Sector (FAO, Rome, 1986), pp. 352-378.
Note: a. 1986 fish catch data unavailable; 1985 repeated in their place.

demand for nonstaple foods as incomes rise. Meat, milk, and fish production in developed countries remains much higher than in the developing world.

Figures on total production tell only part of the story. To describe the adequacy of food supply, output per capita is a better indicator. Overall, food production has outpaced demand. Output per capita has increased tangibly since 1965 in all regions but Africa. (See Figure 4.1.) Asian centrally planned economies had the most significant increase in per capita food production, largely as a result of China's recent strides in improving its agriculture. Africa's food output per capita has declined in the past 20 years. (See Figure 4.1.) To some extent, the gap between supply and demand has been filled through

Figure 4.1 Index of Per Capita Food Production

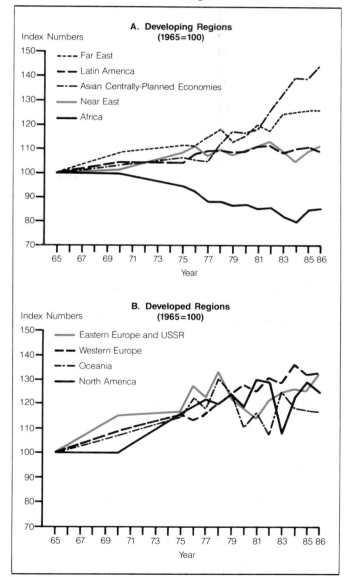

Sources: For 1965, 1970: United Nations Food and Agriculture Organization (FAO), *1987 Country Tables*, (FAO, Rome, 1987), pp. 312–336. For 1975–86: FAO, *1986 Production Yearbook* (FAO, Rome, 1987), p. 48.

increased imports and foreign aid. Even so, per capita consumption has dropped in Africa because of population growth, poverty, and ineffective agricultural policies (6).

ACCESS TO FOOD

Does the increase in per capita production mean that people have enough to eat? The answer depends in part on the dietary standards used to define "enough." Assume for a moment that all available food is distributed equally among all people. If a U.N.-recommended basic diet of 2,350 calories (principally from grains) per person per day is the yardstick, there would be enough food for 6 billion people, about 20 percent more than the world population. However, if the standard is marginally improved to include 10 percent of dietary calories from animal products (akin to the average South American diet), only 4 billion people could be fed. And if 30 percent of the calories are from animal products, only 2.5 billion people could be sustained. Hence, assuming equal distribution, the world could be said to have crossed a threshold to minimal food self-sufficiency and to be approaching a second phase marked by improved diets, but far from rich and varied ones (7).

Differences in Food Access Among Countries

But distribution is far from equal. If production levels and human needs are compared nation by nation, a different picture emerges. In 1985, average caloric consumption levels were below those needed for health, growth, and productive work in 46 countries. Of the 46, 29 are in sub-Saharan Africa, 8 are in Asia, and 6 are in Latin America and the Caribbean (8). In the crop year 1987–88, 37 countries, most of them in Africa, were projected to be unable to meet even their present inadequate food consumption rates based on existing production, stored food stocks, and ability to import. Unless food aid is forthcoming, these countries face national food shortages of crisis proportions (9).

Of course, not everybody consumes at the national average. Some are better off; many are far worse off. The World Bank estimated that, in 1980, in 87 developing countries excluding China, the diets of 730 million people (34 percent of their total population) did not contain enough calories for an active working life. Even more disturbing, 340 million of them (16 percent) did not consume enough calories to prevent stunted growth and serious disease. (See Table 4.2.) A 1988 update of this study estimated the number of people with deficient diets in the developing world at 950 million—about 20 percent of the world population (10).

In developing countries, hungry people are concentrated in the low-income countries (per capita income of $400 or less in 1983). In 1980, these nations accounted for about 80 percent of the total number of people with insufficient caloric intake to support an active working life and about the same percentage of those consuming too few calories to prevent stunted growth (11). South Asia and Africa fare worst in both relative and absolute terms. Moreover, the proportions of the inadequately fed in both

4 Food and Agriculture

Table 4.2 Prevalence of Energy-Deficient Diets in 87 Developing Countries, 1980

Country group or region[a]	Not Enough Calories for an Active Working Life[b]		Not Enough Calories to Prevent Stunted Growth and Serious Health Risks[c]	
	Percent of Population	Population (millions)	Percent of Population	Population (millions)
Developing countries (87)	34	730	16	340
Low-income (30)[d]	51	590	23	270
Middle-income (57)[e]	14	140	7	70
Sub-Saharan Africa (37)	44	150	25	90
East Asia and Pacific (8)	14	40	7	20
South Asia (7)	50	470	21	200
Middle East & North Africa (11)	10	20	4	10
Latin America & the Caribbean (24)	13	50	6	20

Source: The World Bank, *Poverty and Hunger: Issues and Options for Food Security in Developing Countries* (The World Bank, Washington, D.C., 1986), Table 2.3, p. 17.
Notes: a. The numbers in parenthesis are the number of countries in the sample. b. Below 90 percent of FAO/WHO requirements. c. Below 80 percent of FAO/WO requirements. d. Low-income countries had a per capita income below $400 in 1983. e. Middle-income countries had a per capita income above $400 in 1983.

regions rose somewhat during the 1970s, despite a general worldwide trend to the contrary (12).

A 1987 U.N. study ranks the food and nutrition problems in South Asia as "one of the world's most serious issues of human welfare" (13). The coincidence of large populations, low income levels, and skewed income distribution all abet this situation. In Africa, the nutrition situation worsened further during the early 1980s; repeated droughts and armed conflicts drastically reduced food production while the continent was experiencing some of the highest birth rates in the world (14).

Most of the advances in food consumption during the 1970s in countries with market economies occurred in East Asia, the Middle East, and North Africa. These improvements were associated with increased incomes deriving from rapid industrialization in East Asia and from the oil boom in the other two regions. This new wealth enabled countries in these three areas to finance large volumes of food imports and price subsidies. Nonetheless, 40 million people—14 percent of the population—in East Asia and the Pacific suffered from the lack of enough food in 1980. In the Middle East and North Africa, 20 million (10 percent) remained underfed. Comparable proportions were found in Latin America and the Caribbean. (See Table 4.2.)

Differences in Food Access within Countries

The evidence on disparities in access to food within countries is still sketchy and at times is contradictory. A survey of 13 countries, including India, Brazil, and Egypt, indicated that per capita caloric consumption was higher in rural than in urban areas. But another survey of eight countries suggested that malnutrition was more prevalent among rural children (15).

This inconsistency may stem partly from the failure of some surveys to account for the food that urbanites consume outside the home. Less access to adequate medical services may also help explain the higher incidence of malnutrition among rural children (16).

Rural or urban, the poorest members of society bear the brunt of hunger. In cities, they are the unemployed and recent migrants who live in slums and shantytowns. For example, low birth weight was five times more frequent in the slums than in the planned residential quarters of Manila, infant mortality was three times higher, and severe and moderate malnutrition and anemia (caused by iron deficiency) were twice as high (17).

Among rural inhabitants, the landless are probably the worst off. In Bangladesh, for example, caloric intake in landless and near-landless households was 1,925 calories per person per day on the average, compared to 2,375 in households owning more than 7 hectares. The landless comprise a large proportion of the poor in the countryside—43 percent of the total rural population in India and 32 percent in Bangladesh in 1975 (18).

Eradication of hunger is possible. The world food supply is more than sufficient to provide everyone with a basic diet but it is not equitably distributed. Even without a drastic change, the proportion of hungry people is steadily, though slowly, declining.

Efforts to combat hunger made moderate progress during the 1970s. An average increase of 100 calories in daily consumption was recorded. The proportion of the population with insufficient calories for an active working life declined 6 percent. The proportion of people whose caloric intake was inadequate to prevent stunted growth decreased a modest 2 percent.

Unfortunately, these declines are relative, not absolute, numbers. Because of population growth (especially among the poor), the total number of hungry people has increased. In 1980, there were 170 million more people in low-income countries than in 1970 with insufficient calories to prevent stunted growth and 90 million more who consumed too few calories to support active work (19).

AGRICULTURAL RESEARCH

On balance, agriculture has at least been able to keep up with population growth, and it may have made some modest gains against hunger. Much of the credit belongs to agricultural research, which helped increase productivity in both the developed and developing areas of the world. Research has provided farmers with a seemingly endless stream of products (improved seed, fertilizers, pesticides, and equipment) and techniques (reduced tillage, pest management, and irrigation). When used in the right way and in the right places, they have helped increase production dramatically. (See Box 4.1.)

But the direction and priorities of the agricultural research establishment have also been criticized. Environmental degradation, pollution, social dislocation, and income disparities are among the undesirable effects charged against the researchers. They have simply overlooked the needs of poor farmers on dry nonirrigated land. Clearly, research alone cannot eradicate hunger or reduce the inequities that are at least part of the cause of hunger. Nonetheless, a strong socially and environmentally responsible research capability will continue to be vital to maintaining an adequate food supply, enhancing economic development (especially for small farmers), and protecting valuable natural resources.

Investment in Research

The amount and placement of funding largely determine the type of research done. Global expenditures on

agricultural research for both food and nonfood commodities have grown substantially over the past three decades, increasing 258 percent in real terms. (See Table 4.3.) Research efforts remain concentrated in the developed countries, but investments increased 256 percent in Africa, 482 percent in Latin America, and 589 percent in Asia from 1959 to 1980. Asia's higher growth rate in

Box 4.1 International Agricultural Research Centers

The International Agricultural Research Centers (IARCs), of which there are 13, are part of an international agricultural system. This network of internationally funded centers originated with a joint program begun in 1941 by the Rockefeller Foundation and the government of Mexico to raise crop productivity. The effort soon centered on breeding a short stiff-strawed wheat variety, known as semidwarf, that did not topple under the grain-heavy heads. The new strain responded well to fertilizers and irrigation, and its yield was triple that of the traditional varieties. Soon the semidwarf variety was disseminated internationally (1).

This breakthrough and other developments encouraged the Rockefeller and Ford Foundations to establish the first international agricultural research center, the International Rice Research Institute in 1960 at Los Banos in the Philippines (2).

The stated purpose of IARC research is to improve the quality and quantity of food production and to raise the standard of living for the poor people in developing countries. The IARCs work on crops, livestock, and farming systems that represent about three fourths of the Third World's food supply (3).

The IARCs, often commodity specific, focus on applied research. Basic and adaptive research are seen by IARCs as more appropriate for national institutions (4). About 50 percent of IARC research outlays are spent on developing improved crop varieties (5). The

centers spent a modest $10–15 million, 6–8 percent of their total 1986 operating expenditures, on farming systems research (6).

Although the IARCs' share of global crop research expenditures is small, their effect on world agriculture is perhaps more significant than their budgets might suggest. The IARCs were the first to develop the high-yielding varieties of rice and wheat and thus usher in the Green Revolution (7). Additionally, research funds spent in the IARCs encourage increased national research outlays in developing countries (8). The overall effects of the IARCs cannot be fully separated from the accomplishments of other research organizations, but they are inextricably linked with the successes and failures of agricultural research in general and the Green Revolution in particular.

The IARCs are supported through the Consultative Group on International Agricultural Research (CGIAR), founded in 1971 as an informal association of governments, international and regional organizations, and private foundations. CGIAR government members are the donor countries (about 40 in 1985) and 10 developing countries elected by the FAO regional caucuses (9).

Table 1 lists the IARCs, their mandates and their 1986 operating expenditures.

References and Notes

1. Consultative Group on International Agricultural Research (CGIAR) *Consultative Group*

on International Agricultural Research (CGIAR, Washington, D.C., 1980) p. v, and p. 3.
2. *Ibid.*, p. 3.
3. *Ibid.*, p. v, and p. 1.
4. Hans E. Jahnke, *et al.*, "The Impact of Agricultural Research," in *Tropical Africa: A Study of the Collaboration between the International and National Research Systems* (The World Bank, Washington, D.C., 1987), p. 27.
5. Norman W. Simmonds, *Farming Systems Research: A Review* (The World Bank, Washington, D.C., 1987), p. 28.
6. Susan Poats, *et al.*, "Farming Systems Research and Extension: Status and Potential in Low-Resource Agriculture," *Enhancing Agriculture in Africa*, Vol. II, Part C-2, No. 11 (National Technical Information Service, Springfield, Virginia, 1987), p. 16.
7. Alain de Janvry and Jean-Jacques Dethier, "Technological Innovation in Agriculture: The Political Economy of its Rate and Bias", CGIAR Study Paper No. 1, The World Bank, Washington, D.C., 1987, p. 16.
8. Robert E. Evenson, Carl E. Pray, and Grant M. Scobie, "The Influence of International Research on the Size of National Research Systems," *American Journal of Agricultural Economy* (December 1985), pp. 1074–1079.
9. *Op. cit.* 7, p. 17.

Table 1 International Agricultural Research Centers

Center	Year Established	Location	Mandate	1986 Expenditures (millions)
Centro Internacional de Agricultura Tropical	1966	Cali, Colombia	Improve production of beans, cassava, rice, and beef in the Tropics of the Western Hemisphere	$21.3 12.4
Centro Internacional de la Papa	1971	Lima, Peru	Improve the potato in the Andes and develop new varieties for lower tropics	
Centro Internacional de Mejoramiento de Maiz y Trigo	1943 1966	Mexico City	Improve maize, wheat, barley, and triticale	21.4
International Board for Plant Genetic Resources	1974	Rome, Italy	Promote an international network of genetic-resources (germplasm) centers	4.8
International Center for Agricultural Research in the Dry Areas	1977	Aleppo, Syria	Focus on rainfed agriculture in arid and semiarid regions in North Africa and West Asia	18.0
International Crops Research Institute for the Semi-Arid Tropics	1972	Andhra Pradesh, India	Improve quantity and reliability of food production in the semiarid tropics	20.6
International Food Policy Research Institute	1974	Washington, D.C.	Address issues arising from governmental and international agency intervention in national, regional, and global food problems	4.5
International Institute of Tropical Agriculture	1967	Ibadan, Nigeria	Be responsible for improvement of worldwide cowpea, yam, cocoyam, and sweet potato, and for cassava, rice, maize, beans, among others	17.5
International Laboratory for Research on Animal Disease	1974	Nairobi, Kenya	Help develop controls for trypanosomiasis (transmitted by the tsetse fly) and theileriosis (transmitted by ticks)	9.3
International Livestock Centre for Africa	1974	Addis Ababa, Ethiopia	Conduct research and development on improved livestock production and marketing systems, train livestock specialists, and gather documentation for livestock industry	17.3
International Rice Research Institute	1960	Los Banos, Philippines	Select and breed improved rice varieties, maintain a germplasm collection bank	23.6
International Service for National Agricultural Research	1980	The Hague, The Netherlands	Strengthen national agricultural research systems	4.4
West Africa Development Association	1971	Monrovia, Liberia	Promote self-sufficiency in rice in West Africa and improve varieties suitable for the area's agroclimate and socioeconomic conditions	3.7

Source: Consultative Group on International Agricultural Research (CGIAR), *Consultative Group on International Agricultural Research* (CGIAR, Washington, D.C., 1980).

4 Food and Agriculture

Table 4.3 Global Agricultural Research Expenditures

(in thousands of US$, 1980)

Region	1959	1970	1980	Percent Changes 1959–80
Western Europe	274,984	918,634	1,489,588	+442
Eastern Europe and the USSR	568,284	1,282,212	1,492,783	+163
North America and Oceania	760,466	1,485,043	1,722,390	+124
Latin America	79,556	216,018	462,631	+482
Africa	119,149	251,572	424,757	+256
Asia	261,114	1,205,116	1,797,894	+589
World	**2,063,553**	**5,358,595**	**7,390,043**	**+258**

Sources: J.K. Boyce and R.E. Evenson, *National and International Agricultural Research and Extension Programs* (The Agricultural Development Council, 1975, New York); and M. Ann Judd, *et al.,* "Investing in Agricultural Supply" (Discussion Paper No. 442, Yale University Press, Economic Growth Center, 1983) quoted in Robert E. Evenson, *The International Research Centers: Their Impact on Spending for National Agricultural Research and Extension* (Consultative Group on International Agricultural Research, The World Bank, Washington, D.C., 1987), p. 2.

research occurred mainly in Japan and China. The latter's research expenditures jumped more than elevenfold in the same period [20].

Much of this research money has been spent for export crops rather than local food crops. Expenditures differ widely by commodity; most developing regions favor such export crops as coffee and cocoa over such domestically important crops as cassava or beans. Part of the reason is that levies are often imposed on export crops to fund research. However, the emphasis on export crops in research programs also reflects political and economic realities. Developing countries are often in desperate need of the hard currency gained from exports. Further, subsistence farmers usually have little influence on national decisions, including those concerned with research priorities [21].

Research Approaches

Funding levels show only part of the picture. The philosophies and strategies underlying the definition of research questions determine to a large extent the kinds of agricultural technologies and production systems that will emerge from research efforts as farming practices in the next century. Several approaches to future agricultural research exist today; sometimes they compete for resources and sometimes they complement each other. When the future of agricultural research is being considered, the paradigms most often discussed are the conventional, commodity-centered approach, farming systems research, agroecosystems research or agroecology, and biotechnology. Decisions made in the next few years on research policies and strategies will determine whether the next generation of farmers will have the tools they need to meet the world's needs without destroying their children's and grandchildren's ability to do the same.

Conventional Research

The oldest and most established type of research is variously known as conventional, commodity, or production research. Critics sometimes use a more value-laden term: industrial research [22]. Focusing on specific crops or livestock commodities, it emphasizes development of technologies that raise productivity, defined as the output per unit of input, usually land, labor, or capital. As the production data presented above testify, this approach has been spectacular in meeting its objectives. Global cereal yields rose about 90 percent between 1950 and 1982. In the developing countries, adoption of these technologies increased cereal yields significantly on about 30 percent of the harvested area [23].

Success depends heavily on development of high-yielding crop strains that respond well to chemical fertilizers, irrigation, and other inputs. For example, rice and wheat semidwarf varieties are the mainstay of the Green Revolution. These varieties show substantially greater yield gains when irrigated and fertilized than traditional varieties exhibit under the same conditions [24]. Clearly, this type of research has proved its worth, and it is likely to remain essential in meeting food needs into the foreseeable future.

Despite these important accomplishments, conventional research has had little effect on most poor farmers in the developing countries. Small farmers who benefited from Green Revolution technologies are usually in irrigated areas; the vast majority of farmers on marginal lands have not been touched by it. For example, despite years of encouraging adoption of Green Revolution technologies, studies in Bangladesh show that they are more likely to be adopted on large farms than on small ones. A comprehensive study of India found that, between 1967 and 1970, small farmers did adopt some new methods, but much more slowly than large farm owners did. Similar results have been found in other countries [25].

On marginal lands, where most of the poorest farmers are, about 90 percent of the farmers were essentially bypassed by research using the conventional approach [26]. The success of the Green Revolution relied on the existence of suitable land, water, climate, and other resources. As a strategy for increasing global food production, it was not aimed at marginal areas.

Environmental concerns have dampened enthusiasm about the conventional approach to agricultural research. The use and abuse of pesticides are high on the list of these concerns. Pests damage about 20–40 percent of crops annually worldwide; the losses are probably higher in developing countries [27]. Excessive and inappropriate chemical applications to control these pests (see Chapter 17, "Food and Agriculture," Table 17.2) have poisoned people and livestock, contaminated land and water, and led to the evolution of pesticide-resistant pest species. Conventional research has also contributed to solving the pesticide problem by developing nonchemical pest controls through breeding pest-resistant varieties and using beneficial predators and biological control agents. For example, since the mid-1970s, integrated pest management, which combines natural controls with judicious use of chemicals, has sparked considerable environmentally oriented research [28].

Soil damage has also occurred in many parts of the world, partly through the inappropriate application of chemical fertilizers and pesticides. Heavy use of these chemicals appears to be associated with reduction of such essential soil micronutrients as zinc and boron (29). One study found that chemically treated fields had 16 centimeters less topsoil and soil with less water-storage capacity than organically treated fields. Soil erosion is occurring in developed and developing countries alike. In much of Asia and Latin America, erosion has many interacting causes, including (but by no means limited to) the misapplication of lowland farming methods to upland areas. Overpopulation, lack of effective land tenure, and other social factors have contributed to the settlement and cultivation of marginally productive uplands, some of which might best be left forested (30).

Conventional research did not *cause* the uplands' problems; but technologies that contributed to the accumulation of wealth from lowland farming could be considered indirect factors leading to poor farmers moving into unsuitable upland areas. Continued attempts to eke out a living using lowland methods in these areas can only further degrade the land on which the farmers depend. Technologies applicable to the specific conditions of the uplands are desperately needed. A dual-track strategy to improve productivity while enhancing the sustainability of the area's agriculture and its soil and water resources would be the most effective (31).

Farming Systems Research

Farming systems research seeks to develop technologies that improve the lot of small, resource-poor farmers by building on their existing practices (32). Research focus goes beyond the conventional emphasis on individual commodities. Multidisciplinary teams of agronomists, biologists, economists, and sociologists conduct on-farm research and attempt to analyze all relevant aspects of entire farming systems. The researchers try to understand the farmers' goals, rather than impose their own assumptions and values, and to characterize the social and environmental constraints and opportunities in relation to those goals. Based on their analysis of these circumstances, researchers can then develop specific improvements to help farmers achieve their objectives, which may include more stable subsistence crops, diversification of crops for sale, or maximum profits (33).

Farming systems research has been receiving increased attention and support from the United Nations Food and Agriculture Organization (FAO), the World Bank, and the International Agricultural Research Centers (IARCs) because these institutions have increasingly turned to the needs of small farmers. In 1986, the IARCs spent $10–15 million a year for farming systems research, about 6–8 percent of their operating budgets. As shown by the involvement of the Green Revolution institutions, farming systems research is not considered an alternative to the conventional approach that succeeded so well in the lowland areas. Instead, farming systems research complements and extends that approach so that more farmers can benefit.

According to some of its advocates, farming systems research faces two major problems—conceptual and operational. Conceptually, it is more of an approach than a clearly defined area of research. Because it is location specific and time consuming and requires many kinds of specialists, farming systems research can be extremely costly (34). Even if it can be justified on a small scale, it may not be replicable for the millions of small farmers in the world.

Critics of farming systems research fault its emphasis on economic analysis and increasing production and maintain that it does not pay sufficient attention to environmental concerns (35) (36). Others criticize what they see as a top-down approach with no effective participation from the farmers (37).

Agroecosystems Research

Some advocates consider agroecosystems research—agroecology—an alternative to farming systems research (38) or a refinement and component of it (39). This strategy is relatively untried. Its basic principle is to understand traditional farming systems and not to introduce innovations unless a thorough analysis makes clear what needs to be altered and why and how change can be accomplished. For farming systems research, productivity is the main indicator of system performance; agroecosystems research considers a multiplicity of agronomic, economic, and environmental criteria. Farming systems research is limited to the boundaries of the farm; agroecosystems research encompasses wider environmental systems and marketing systems.

In workshops using a modeling technique called agroecosystem analysis (primarily conducted in Asia to design and evaluate research programs there), agricultural systems are characterized by four indicators: productivity, stability, sustainability, and equitability (40). The challenge of agroecosystems research is to optimize these measures to increase farmers' and farming communities' welfare while maintaining or improving environmental quality and the sustainability of the entire system. Although the application of this approach has been limited, agroecologists are offering some useful new perspectives on how to look at agriculture and how to seek improvements. Now that sustainability is gaining currency as a concern among agricultural researchers and policymakers, the theories and approaches of agroecosystems research bear scrutiny.

Biotechnology Research

Biotechnology research is opening dramatically new and often controversial frontiers in agricultural research. The term biotechnology is defined in numerous, sometimes inconsistent ways (41). In its definition, the U.S. Office of Technology Assessment includes any technique that uses living organisms to make or modify products, improve plants or animals, or develop microorganisms for specific uses (42). Others focus more narrowly on advanced cell and tissue culture techniques, monoclonal antibodies, genetic engineering, and other innovations. Of all the developments under the rubric of biotechnology, none is as far-reaching in its implications—or as controversial—as genetic engineering.

In conventional breeding, transferring single genes from one organism to another is seldom possible without backcrossing for several generations to eliminate unwanted genes associated with the one carrying a desired trait, a process that can take years. Using genetic engineering, a single gene can be identified, isolated, cloned, and then spliced into target organisms in relatively short order. These techniques also allow scientists for the first time to transfer genes between unrelated species, raising the possibility of creating entirely new crops or animals (43). (See Recent Developments, below.)

Biotechnology in plant and animal agriculture offers the possibility of better protection from pests and diseases, higher productivity, uniform characteristics, prescribed traits, and wholly new products.

For plant agriculture, biotechnology companies are developing products that they hope will inhibit frost formation in crops, protect maize from the European corn borer without chemical insecticides, and enhance the availability of nitrogen to plants without adding chemical fertilizer. Earlier research altered the genes of plant-colonizing microbes; some current research alters the genes of the plants. Scientists are also trying to engineer crop plants to "fix" nitrogen (change nitrogen to usable nitrates) from the soil and air—something only certain microbes can now do (44).

One of the more controversial strategies in plant genetic engineering is to develop herbicide-resistant crop plants. Proponents point out that such plants would allow better weed control; critics argue that the use of herbicides, with all their attendant health and environmental risks, would increase (45).

Biotechnology developments in animal agriculture include growth hormones (46), pharmaceuticals (disease-diagnostic aids, vaccines, and medications) (47), and improved artificial insemination techniques. Animal health and productivity are likely to improve significantly without genetic manipulation of the animals. At least one improvement is not without its critics. The bovine growth hormone, produced by genetically engineered bacteria, can increase milk production from treated cows as much as 40 percent. Because the dairy industry is plagued with overproduction in many developed countries, introduction of the bovine growth hormone is seen by some as exacerbating an already critical economic situation, especially for small farmers.

Two contentious issues are likely to surround biotechnology research for years to come. One—environmental risk—is being disputed in developed countries, especially the United States and Europe (48) (49). The second issue relates to the distribution of biotechnology's benefits and control of genetic resources; it is being debated internationally, with developing countries against developed countries and multinational corporations (50) (51).

Environmental critics focus on the risks of releasing new life forms, especially genetically engineered microbes, into the environment (52) and the development of herbicide-resistant crops and other products that require the use of agricultural chemicals. On the first point, they argue that little is known about the organisms being released—growth factors, dispersal, and the capability to transfer genes to other species—or about the ecology of the environments into which they are being dis-

Table 4.4 Firms and Public[a] Institutions Involved in Agricultural Biotechnology Research

Country or Region	Animal Agriculture				Plant Agriculture			
	Firms	Public Institu- tions	Total	Percent	Firms	Public Institu- tions	Total	Percent
United States	451	62	513	64	727	111	838	62
Europe[b]	121	12	133	17	180	26	206	15
United Kingdom	50	2	52	7	98	21	119	8
Japan	36	0	36	5	52	4	56	4
Canada	22	4	26	3	49	12	61	4
Australia	15	3	18	2	24	6	30	2
Other	14	12	26	2	46	16	62	4
Total	**709**	**95**	**804**	**100**	**1,176**	**196**	**1,378**	**100**

Sources:
1. Technology Management Group (TMG), "The Impact of Biotechnology on Animal Care," Biotechnology Markets in Animal Care Report, New Haven, Connecticut, December 4, 1986, Table 5, p. 9, cited in TMG, *The Impact of Biotechnology on Animal Care—An Assessment of Worldwide Opportunities in Diagnostics, Vaccines, Drugs, Growth Enhancers, and Other Products* (TMG, New Haven, Connecticut, 1986).
2. Manny Ratafia and Terry Purrington, "Biotechnology in Crop Agriculture: The Third Revolution," *Chemical Marketing & Management* (Fall 1987), Table 4, p. 47, cited in TMG, *The Impact of Biotechnology on Plant Agriculture—An Assessment of Worldwide Market Opportunities in the Grain, Fruit, Vegetable, Sugar, Oilseed, and Animal Feed Industries* (TMG, New Haven, Connecticut, 1987).

Notes:
a. Government and university research organizations.
b. Excluding the United Kingdom.

seminated (53). This argument focuses on regulatory policies and procedures (54).

The second environmental issue involves what kinds of products should be developed and questions about corporate versus societal benefits. Corporations and environmentalists alike envision a time when agribusinesses will develop complementary packages of seeds and agrochemicals; critics fear increased dependence on chemicals (55). Supporters of biotechnology research point to the possibility of engineering pest-resistant crops, thus reducing the need for pesticides. A U.S. firm plans to field-test a genetically altered bacterium that could protect corn plants from the corn borer, a caterpillar that causes $400 million damage to U.S. agriculture every year (56).

What is at issue here is who controls the biotechnology research agenda and who will benefit. Regulatory responsibility is clearly defined in most developed countries, making the debate on environmental release of genetically engineered organisms relatively straightforward. But research policy—especially the division between public and private research and the related question of how priorities are established—involves a variety of institutions and interests. Arguments about how biotechnology priorities are set and who will set them are likely to continue.

Research in agricultural biotechnology is concentrated in the developed countries. Of 804 private companies and public research organizations engaged in research on genetically engineered animal health care products worldwide, almost 90 percent are located in the United States, Europe, the United Kingdom, or Japan. So too for plant biotechnology products. (See Table 4.4.) Although several developing countries conduct research in this area, their effort is modest. Biotechnology research and development is dominated by private corporations rather than public institutions. These companies see their profit potential enhanced by favorable patent environments and governmental research subsidies (57) (58).

For plant genetics in particular, patenting is becoming a sore point in North-South relations. As private firms increase their penetration of developing countries' seed markets, the granting of patents for plant varieties may profoundly affect Third World farmers and researchers. Because most crops grown in developed countries originated in the tropics, breeders have depended on plant genetic material from the Third World as the feedstock for crop improvement. For the most part, developing countries are not compensated for transferring this resource. In 1983, an FAO conference approved a resolution calling for all plant genetic material (including that held by private companies) to be available without restriction. Opposition from the industrialized countries is likely to render this resolution meaningless. One alternative is to establish a global network of gene banks and an international plant gene fund. Developed countries'

contributions to the fund would depend on the size of their seed industry, their agricultural output, or their use of the gene banks. The money would then be used to conserve global plant resources and agricultural development in the Third World. (59)

Biotechnology as an area of research is most closely tied to the conventional commodity-oriented approach discussed above. Unlike farming systems research and agroecosystems research, it is far more oriented toward breaking problems into components than toward understanding the whole. Because it promises rapid rewards, biotechnology research attracts vast financial resources, both public and private. As a result, the need to understand agriculture as a system—of interacting biological, physical, social, and economic factors—is in danger of being lost in the rush to develop new, saleable products. In the process, the emerging effort to promote sustainability and equity in world agriculture may be forgotten.

Box 4.2 The Home Gardens of Java

Home gardens dot the landscape in rural and urban areas alike. One of the most complex and productive is the Javanese household garden, the *pekarangen*. It is one among many agroecosystems in Asia that remain largely undocumented (1). The gardens, which are in fact intensively cultivated agroforestry systems, constitute about one fifth the agricultural land in Java.

An array of plant species is grown in these gardens, including trees, perennials, and annuals of varying heights. The vertical structure of a typical home garden consists of a series of tiers, with coconut trees at the highest level. At the next lower level are mangoes, guavas, and fruit trees followed by starchy food plants. At the lowest level are vegetables, including eggplants and chili peppers. The resulting multilayered plant structure makes maximum use of light and nutrients, moderates soil temperature, and provides a plethora of edible and saleable plant products. In addition to growing crops, many Javanese raise fish, goats, and chickens in and around these gardens (2).

The gardens provide much-needed supplements to the Javanese diet, supply up to 18 percent of their caloric consumption, and 14 percent of protein (3). They also generate income, especially for poor families. In the village of Cihampelas, West Java, gardens accounted for an estimated 9 percent of the income of prosperous people and about 24 percent for the poor. As an additional benefit, income is spread over the year, because some crop is almost always ready for harvesting (4).

Researchers have found that home gardens have little soil erosion, even though land in the area is highly susceptible. Soil erosion in the home gardens is believed to be less than in the other agroforestry system in Java, *kebun-talun*, which is a long-term rotation of field crops and trees (5). In Western Java, one observer noted how the villages surrounded by a belt of gardens stood out like lush green

islands in a sea of eroding paddy land (6). The combination of trees with plants grown close to the ground effectively intercepts rainfall and shields the soil against the action of run-off water. The mix also creates a dense mat of roots at the soil surface that holds soil particles and encourages development of an erosion-resistant soil crumb structure (7).

The number of plant species in Java's home gardens is extremely high by any agricultural standard. About 230 species and 39,800 plants were found in 36 home gardens, marking these systems as invaluable living gene banks. The day may soon come when the numerous varieties found in these gardens will be drawn upon for breeding programs to improve the amount and quality of crop production elsewhere (8).

This system, however, faces challenges. Increasing demand for cash crops is leading some gardeners to use new varieties and to switch to monoculture. More families are concentrating on crops with higher economic returns—such as cloves or oranges—and phasing out others. An example of the changes a new variety can wreak is a type of coconut, the *kelapa genjah*, that has a higher yield potential but a shorter trunk than traditional trees. When this new variety replaces the traditional coconut, it occupies not the high tier that the old type did but the middle layer, where fruit trees are usually grown. The change can lead to overcrowding, followed by removal of the less valuable fruit trees (9). Hence, one varietal change may drastically alter the ecology and economy of the entire home garden complex.

The Javanese home garden is often cited as an example of the inherent ecological wisdom contained in traditional agriculture (10). But Java is not isolated from the world; new ideas, new plant varieties, and economic necessity bring changes there as elsewhere. The challenge to researchers and policymakers alike is to understand the knowl-

edge as well as the genetic material of traditional agriculture. With understanding and planning can come preservation of these irreplaceable resources along with positive economic development.

References and Notes

1. Jeff Tschirley, Environment and Energy Programmes Coordinator, United Nations Food and Agriculture Organization (FAO), Rome, 1988 (personal communication). FAO is currently documenting about 100 of 500 such systems in East China.
2. Linda Christanty, et al., "Traditional Agroforestry in West Java: The *Pekarangan* (Home garden) and *Kebun-Talun* (Annual-Perennial Rotation) Cropping Systems," in *Traditional Agriculture in Southeast Asia: A Human Ecology Perspective*, Gerald G. Marten, ed. (Westview Press, Boulder, Colorado, and London, 1986), p. 140.
3. *Ibid.*, p. 143.
4. *Ibid.*, p. 154.
5. *Ibid.*, p. 154.
6. Vera K. Ninez, *Household Gardens: Theoretical Considerations on an Old Survival Strategy* (International Potato Center, Lima, 1984), p. 23.
7. *Op. cit.* 2, p. 152 and p. 154.
8. Otto Soemarwoto, "Interrelations among Population, Resources, Environment and Development," in *Environment and Development in Asia and the Pacific: Experience and Prospects* (United Nations Environment Programme, Nairobi, 1982), p. 82.
9. *Op. cit.* 2, p. 155.
10. See Michael J. Dover and Lee M. Talbot, *To Feed the Earth: Agroecology for Sustainable Development* (Washington, D.C., World Resources Institute, 1987), p. 32.

FOCUS ON: BUILDING ON THE GREEN REVOLUTION

The Green Revolution truly changed world agriculture, as shown by the statistics presented at the beginning of this chapter. Nations that once depended on food aid to avert starvation are now net exporters. Yields of staple crops have increased many times over as improved plant varieties combined with modern agronomic practices to transform farming in parts of the developing countries. But the Green Revolution did not reach everyone everywhere, nor were its effects uniformly positive. As with any research program, however successful, it is important to reexamine priorities and needs from time to time and, if necessary, redirect thinking and resources to take new developments into account. In this section, diversification in Asian agriculture and meeting the needs of farmers in the rainfed drylands are discussed. These two subjects could occupy researchers' time and energies well into the next century.

Agricultural Diversification in Asia

Cereals, particularly rice and wheat, are the main staples in the Asian diet and the main crops sown in the region (60). Rice is grown on over 80 percent of the planted area in Bangladesh, Thailand, and Malaysia and on over 50 percent in six other Asian countries. In China and India,

the two most populous countries in the world, half of all cropland is planted with rice and wheat.

Recent rice prices on the world market fell to their lowest levels when production exceeded demand in many parts of the world. Monocropping of rice and wheat and the dependence on agricultural chemicals also engendered resistant pests, soil degradation, and other environmental problems. With low returns on their investments in such grain-specific programs as irrigation projects, governments now face the dilemma of how to diversify their agricultural base while ensuring the supply of their countries' main staples (61). Recent research suggests that diversification—particularly in the form of multiple cropping—offers several economic and ecological advantages over monocropping that may help resolve some dilemmas facing developing countries. In a way, diversification is a return to traditional agriculture. (See Box 4.2.)

Multiple cropping often produces higher and more stable yields than monocropping. The yield superiority of multiple cropping is especially evident when total biomass is considered; nonharvested portions of plants can contribute to animal production, soil fertility, and protection against soil erosion (62). A study of traditional corn, bean, and squash systems in Tabasco, Mexico, showed that the biomass yields of crop mixes averaged 1.78 times those of comparable monocrop systems (63). A survey of 574 published experiments found that in about 20 percent of the studies, crop mixes yielded more than

Figure 4.2 Drylands of the World

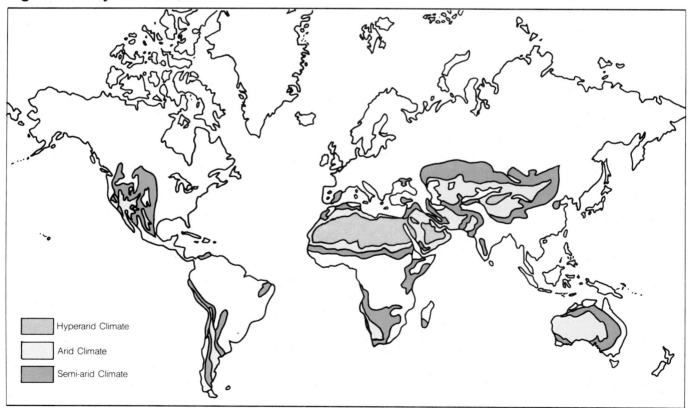

Hyperarid Climate

Arid Climate

Semi-arid Climate

Source: Harold E. Dregne, *Desertification of Arid Lands*, (Harwood Academic Publishers, New York, 1983), Figure 1.1.

single crops, indicating that differences in productivity stem from the particular mix used rather than mixes per se. Some mixes complement each other more than others in how they share light, water, soil nutrients, and other resources and how they contribute to pest control (64).

The risk of crop failure appears lower in multicropping than in monocropping. Experiments on sorghum/pigeon pea intercropping indicated that yield variability in the intercrop was less than when the same crops were planted separately. Intercropping also allowed farmers to earn more than they could with monocropping (65). Multiple cropping may also allow farmers added flexibility in using equipment and labor more efficiently by taking advantage of potential market opportunities, changing crop mixes to adjust quickly to shifts in demand (66) (67).

Some mixes resist plant pests and diseases better than monocrops do. One plant may produce chemicals that protect another from infestation. For example, experimental planting of an herb in sequence with corn or beans reduced the population of a soil-borne nematode that attacks the food crops by secreting a substance into the soil that is toxic to the nematodes. In addition, one plant species may act as a barrier to organisms that cause disease on other plants. In one study, a mixture of beans and corn was attacked less by bean rust compared to beans alone, perhaps because the tall corn prevented the airborne fungal spores from spreading (68). Further, in a review of 150 studies of plant insects, insect pest populations were reduced in crop mixes in the majority of cases, in part because the insects had more difficulty locating their host plants (69).

Multiple cropping also contributes to soil fertility and protects against erosion. For example, studying an intercrop of rubber and tea, Chinese researchers found that the litter falling on the soil provided substantial amounts of nitrogen, potassium, and phosphate and that soil erosion was reduced about 70 percent (70).

The multicropping and intercropping systems are more complex and less studied than monocultures, and statistical designs for experiments are difficult. Although overall yields may be higher than for monocrops, specific high-value crop yields may be lower, so short-term income may suffer (71). Multiple crops can be difficult to mechanize at harvest time, a problem where labor is in short supply. For multiple cropping to become a viable alternative in Asia's commercial farming, considerably more research is needed to overcome some of these drawbacks. Understanding the physical, biological, and socioeconomic factors can lead to successful adoption of improved multiple-cropping techniques. The research can also be used to develop new policies and institutions, including changes in extension services, subsidy policies, and marketing systems.

Rainfed Cropland in Dry Areas

The rainfed drylands, with their 224 million hectares of cropland and 850 million people (72), were largely left out of the Green Revolution. The drive to fend off looming food shortages in the developing countries led to a strategy that focused on the irrigated and fertile lands. The Green Revolution's technical package suited more advanced farming areas and favored farmers who could afford to pay for improved seed, irrigation water, and chemical inputs. But conditions in drylands vary more widely than in irrigated areas—both from one area to another and over time. Most important, they lack sufficient and reliable water supplies. Consequently, successful farming in these areas requires more location-specific technologies that include resource conservation and risk management as well as increased productivity.

Drylands make up about one third the Earth's land surface (73). Not only is rainfall relatively low; it is also unpredictable. It fluctuates sharply both seasonally and annually. Dry areas rarely experience "average" climatic conditions (74). Droughts are common. The entire annual rainfall of a dryland area may be concentrated in a few downpours, leaving the rest of the season dry. Most of these lands are in developing countries. (See Figure 4.2.) Drylands can be classified as hyperarid, arid, and semiarid, according to the annual amount of net rainfall (moisture remaining after evaporation). It is possible to raise crops in the semiarid zones. Much of the hyperarid and arid zones are used as rangeland. Agriculture in the drylands consists of two regimes: irrigated (126 million hectares) and rainfed (224 million hectares) (75). The rainfed areas are in particularly desperate condition and have remained largely underdeveloped. Rainfed drylands are the backbone of agriculture in North and sub-Saharan Africa and the Middle East. Latin America also has large dryland areas; in Mexico and Argentina, they comprise about half of all cropland.

The drylands suffer from a vicious cycle of low investment, low productivity, severe land degradation, and poverty. Investment in the drylands, apart from those that have been irrigated, is relatively low. For example, in World Bank-assisted projects in eastern and southern Africa, rainfed areas with less than 900 millimeters of rainfall received only 15 percent of a total of $374 million in loans. The irrigated areas received 26 percent, and those with more than 900 millimeters of rainfall received 42 percent (76). Private investment by farmers in the rainfed drylands is also minimal because of the higher risk associated with erratic rainfall. Lack of investment in the drylands has exacerbated the yield gap between them and the wetter rainfed and irrigated areas. Rice yields in Asia's rainfed drylands during the 1980s were about half those in wetter areas, where traditional farming is still practiced, about one third the yields where farming is in a transitional stage toward modern agriculture, and only one fifth the yields obtained in the modern sector that uses high-yielding varieties and chemical inputs. (See Table 4.5.)

Rainfed drylands have suffered serious desertification—deterioration of soil, severely reduced productivity of desirable plants, and declining diversity of flora and fauna—because of the activities of both people and livestock. Although desertification is not limited to the rainfed areas, they are more vulnerable because of their thin vegetative cover. About 77 percent of the rainfed drylands are believed to have experienced some degree

Table 4.5 Rice Yields under Different Production Systems in Asia, 1980s

(metric tons per hectare)

Production System	Rice Yield
Dryland Production	0.8
Wetland Production Systems	
Traditional	1.5
Transitional labor-using	> 2.5
Transitional capital-using	> 2.5
Modern labor-using	> 4.0
Modern capital-using	> 4.0

Source: Randolph Barker and Robert W. Herdt, *The Rice Economy of Asia* (Resources for the Future, Washington, D.C., 1985), Table 3.2, p. 28.

of desertification, compared to 21 percent of the irrigated dryland areas. The one encouraging note is that this process is not irreversible: about 70 percent of the currently desertified area can be restored to productive use if it is improved (77). (See Chapter 13, "Restoring Degraded Lands.")

Low investment and productivity and land degradation in the nonirrigated areas are responsible for regional poverty and income disparities. The poverty and hunger prevalent in sub-Saharan Africa may be the most poignant example. But critical conditions also exist elsewhere in the rainfed drylands. A recent survey of six Indian villages in the semiarid tropics found that the per capita income there was less than half the national average (78). Thailand's arid northeast region— "the handicapped region" where one third the country's population lives—is where more than one half the nation's poor live (79). This area's average per capita income is 57 percent of that of the north, 43 percent of the south, 28 percent of the central, and 42 percent of the national average (80).

Improving Dryland Agriculture

Improving agriculture in these areas requires solving a host of technical and institutional problems. Chief among them are the need to devise and implement good water and soil management practices, develop and disseminate crop varieties that can survive drought, design strategies for risk management, and implement programs for equitable land distribution and tenure.

Since antiquity, farmers have built embankments and levees, terraced dry riverbeds and farmlands, and channeled water to them from special catchment areas, all to conserve water and allow maximum moisture retention by the soil. Modern research has devised other techniques such as off-season tillage, leveling, mulching, and intercropping that do not depend on construction. Mulches, for example, are especially useful for water conservation when precipitation is poor, and they can take advantage of straw, stalks, and other local material (81).

The effort to restore degraded soils is meager compared with extensive erosion occurring in the dryland tropics. But there are encouraging examples. One of the most impressive is from Kenya, which has been waging a successful campaign to reduce soil erosion in its semiarid zones with the help of the Swedish International Development Authority and other international aid organizations (82). Hundreds of thousands of farmers have built terraces on over 1.5 million hilly farms. One terracing technique is based on a terrace called *fanya-juu*,

"work up." A trench is dug along the contour of the hillside, and soil and rocks are thrown from the uphill side of the trench to form a ridge. As soil is washed downhill it gradually accumulates against the ridge, leveling off the terrace, at the same time supplying extra nutrition and moisture to crops. The ridge can be used for planting grass to feed cattle and the trench for banana and other fruit trees, which also help to retain topsoil. In one area, bean and corn production has more than doubled on terraced farms. The success of this effort is attributed to three elements: simple and inexpensive methods that the small farmers can easily use, research that has carefully considered specific ecological and social conditions of the area, and a strong government commitment to soil conservation. (See *World Resources 1987*, p. 233.)

Drought-tolerant crops are another response to scarcity and irregular water supplies. Research to develop such varieties has been underway for more than two decades, principally for cereal crops, but it has yet to develop the rich plant heritage of the drylands, with the exception of some legumes and such oil seed crops as jojoba (83) (84) (85).

Numerous other plant species are suitable for dryland cultivation. Farmers in India's arid and semiarid regions grow many specialized crops, including guar for gum arabic, euphorbia for wax, sesame for oil, and isabagal for stomach disorders (86). India earns about $30 million annually from exports of guar and isabagal. A crop plant that researchers would like to revive and improve is amaranth, which is rich in protein and grows well in many ecological zones, including the drylands of Asia and Latin America (87).

Reducing Risk

Because of the uncertainty of rainfall, dryland farmers are understandably reluctant to use costly inputs (improved seed, fertilizers, and pesticides) to increase production. Studies in India's semiarid tropics demonstrated that the farmers faced a high level of risk mainly because of variations in production levels of crops rather than because of changing market prices. Thus, because crop production was so uncertain, there was a general underinvestment in the region's agriculture (88).

Risk reduction and management are vital to dryland development. Obviously, improved farming practices, drought-tolerant crops, water and soil conservation, and multiple cropping will all help to lower the risk level farmers face. But managing risk is not limited to technical changes. Inevitably, crops still fail. Farmers can manage their risk in two ways. Sometimes they can arrange with family members or others in the community to help them through hard years. Alternatively, they can turn to the government to provide credit, improve the marketing system, and establish appropriate pricing policies. Providing timely, accurate weather information can also help reduce risk by allowing farmers to time their planting, harvesting, and other activities for maximum benefit.

The Green Revolution has accomplished much since the Rockefeller Foundation first sent Norman Borlaug to Mexico in the 1940s. Many people have been fed who might otherwise have gone hungry. Many countries that might have depended on food imports are now self-sufficient in staples. But much more remains to be done. As one problem appears to be solved, many more become apparent. Environmental quality and sustainability are terms that were not in the lexicon of development planners two decades ago; today they are as important as productivity. Equity—between rich and poor and between women and men—is slowly becoming an explicit goal of many agricultural development efforts, which believe development will not succeed without it. So too, diversification of Asian agriculture and the myriad problems of the dryland tropics are issues that can be successfully met once the need is recognized and a commitment is made.

RECENT DEVELOPMENTS

GLOBAL FOOD PRIZES

Efforts to avert world hunger are gaining increasing public recognition. There are now at least five major awards for work related to increasing food supplies, reducing hunger, or for media coverage of the issue. The awards include:

■ *The World Food Prize*, a $200,000 annual award begun in 1986 by General Foods Fund, Inc., of the United States. The prize seeks to stimulate work in every discipline that affects the global food chain, from the agricultural sciences to transportation, from processing and packaging to economic policy and education. According to the fund Chairman, Philip L. Smith, the firm's decision to establish the prize was spurred by Norman E. Borlaug, who is widely regarded as the father of the Green Revolution. The two prize recipients so far were major figures in the Green Revolution, and their work has significantly reduced hunger in Asia. The World Food Prize was first awarded in 1987 to Dr. M.S. Swaminathan, an internationally renowned agricultural scientist who is considered the architect of the Green Revolution in India (89).

The 1988 recipient is Dr. Robert F. Chandler, Jr., founder of the International Rice Research Institute (IRRI) in the Philippines. Under his guidance, IRRI developed 27 new rice varieties that are grown on nearly 50 million hectares in Asia today. The new varieties increased rice production 66 percent, which has been a major factor in helping to avert famine in Asia. Dr. Chandler's success with IRRI also stimulated the creation of 12 other agricultural research centers (90). The centers are supported by the Consultative Group on International Agricultural Research. (See Box 4.1.)

■ *The Africa Prize for Leadership*, a $100,000 award of the Hunger Project, a global nonprofit organization based in New York City. The prize is for a distinguished African who has exhibited leadership in contributing to a "sustainable end of persistence of hunger" at a national, regional or continentwide level. The prize was first awarded in 1987 and was shared by Abdou Diouf, president of the Republic of Senegal, and Thomas R. Odhiambo, director of the Nairobi-based International Centre for Insect Physiology and Ecology (91).

■ *The Alan Shawn Feinstein World Hunger Awards for the Prevention and Reduction of World Hunger*. The awards were first initiated in 1986–87 and are presented annually at Brown University in Providence, Rhode Island. The Alan Shawn Feinstein Award is a single award of $25,000; in addition, up to two merit awards of $10,000 each may be awarded. In 1987–88 the main award was given to the communal farmers of Zimbabwe (in their entirety) represented by Robinson Lysias Gapare, president of the National Farmers Association of Zimbabwe (92).

■ *The Presidential End Hunger Awards*, sponsored by the U.S. Agency for International Development, honor efforts toward ending world hunger. Eleven individuals or organizations were honored in 1987, including: the *Christian Science Monitor*, for its reporting on hunger issues in Africa; John W. Mellor, director of the International Food Policy Research Institute; and Jean-Pierre Hallet, who introduced wing beans into rural Zaire (93).

■ *The World Hunger Media Awards*, which were begun in 1982 by singer-songwriter Kenny Rogers, his wife Marianne, and the late singer-songwriter Harry Chapin. A total of $100,000 is awarded annually to honor journalists who bring public attention to the issue of world hunger (94).

FAMINE EARLY WARNING SYSTEMS

After being caught unaware by the 1985 famine in Ethiopia, many international aid organizations are turning to early warning systems to spot potential food shortages at the earliest possible stage. One such system—the Global Information and Early Warning System (GIEWS), which operates under the aegis of the FAO—raised an early alarm about the 1987–88 famine in Ethiopia.

Based on forecasts of crop failures because of insufficient early rains, GIEWS sent out a "special alert" in August 1987. FAO evaluation teams then went to the field to corroborate the initial information, and in September 1987, GIEWS issued a second alert confirming a possible crop failure, especially in Eritrea and Tigre Provinces. As harvest time approached in November 1987, another team went to Ethiopia to assess the crop failure. GIEWS subsequently estimated that Ethiopia would need 1.3 million metric tons of cereal in 1988. By early February 1988, as the first clear signs of famine emerged, 1.1 million metric tons of cereal had already been pledged by donors (95).

GIEWS was prompted by the 1972–73 world food crisis. In 1974, the World Food Conference agreed that such a system was needed, and the following year, FAO began formulating its plans. The key field person in most developing countries is the FAO representative, who obtains information from government sources and independently monitors the food situation. GIEWS also receives information from satellites and a variety of other sources (96).

About 95 developing and developed countries participate in GIEWS (97). In addition to identifying countries or regions where serious food shortages are imminent, GIEWS continuously monitors world food supply and demand conditions.

Many other international, regional, and national early warning systems have been created in recent years, most of them in drought-prone, poor countries in Africa and Asia. The U.S. Agency for International Development established a famine early warning system (FEWS) during the 1985 drought in Ethiopia. FEWS monitors most drought-prone countries in Africa (98). The AGRHYMET Regional Center in Niger, run by the Permanent Interstate Committee for Drought Control in the Sahel and the World Meteorological Organization, also issues early warning system reports for West Africa (99). There are now about 25 national early warning systems (100). In time, GIEWS and FEWS may become principal international centers that work with numerous national and regional programs.

The international systems generally use a combination of ground and satellite data. Indicators gathered in the field include rainfall and temperature, crop projections, crop yields and production, market conditions, nutritional status of residents, aerial photography, and other observations (101).

The geostationary METEOSAT satellite is used to produce simple maps of cloud distributions over large areas and identify clouds that might be precipitating. From this information and ground data, precipitation estimates are developed. Another useful satellite instrument is the advanced very high resolution radiometer (AVHRR), operated by the U.S. National Oceanic and Atmospheric Administration, to produce data on the amount and condition of vegetation. The Landsat and SPOT satellites are also used to map crop areas (102).

In 1988, GIEWS is expected to implement a comprehensive satellite remote-sensing system to monitor precipitation and vegetation on a continental scale. The system, known as ARTEMIS (Africa real time environmental monitoring using imaging satellites), will make use of automated data bases of geographic features, agroclimatology, METEOSAT rainfall estimates, AVHRR vegetation indexes, and desert locust habitats (103). ARTEMIS will gather a great deal of scattered information into a single package that should be more convenient for policymakers.

Although the use of satellite data is increasing, experts agree that early warning system forecasts should depend on both ground-based and satellite information. Many of the programs began as temporary projects and have a tenuous life expectancy. In some African countries with several early warning systems programs, some duplication of effort is apparent (104).

The success of early warning systems is mixed. Credibility is often a problem, partly because users are skeptical about the validity of the reports. Users have a variety of needs, and so far program officials have done little to understand these needs. Further, there is no agreement about the relative value of ground-based and satellite data and their interrelationships (105) (106).

Several complaints are being lodged about the reports. Many say that the reports come too late. (The planned satellite data transmission system, DIANA, should speed the information flow from FAO headquarters in Rome to its correspondents in Africa (107).) The quality of ground-based data is a source of widespread unhappiness, especially those data describing market conditions, nutritional and health status, and food stocks.

As the early warning systems matured, understanding how famines occur changed significantly. More attention is now being paid to the erosion of socioeconomic support systems, reduced access to food and employment of the rural poor, disincentive farm prices, policies that lead to environmental deterioration and misuse of the land, inadequate incentives for the food marketing system, and the impact of civil strife or civil war in exacerbating these problems. Famines are increasingly seen as a relatively long process that may not be noticed by international agencies until people's ability to cope with the stress of the famine begins to break down (108).

Despite the problems, the need for the information is clear and users are interested. In the next few years, some systems may fail, the remaining systems will specialize, greater cooperation will aid development of an accepted methodology, and the causes of famines will be more fully understood.

FIRST PATENT ISSUED FOR GENETICALLY ALTERED ANIMALS: IMPLICATIONS FOR FARMS

An April 1988 decision by the U.S. Patent and Trademark Office to grant a patent for a genetically altered vertebrate—the first such patent in the world—could have an important impact on the dissemination of genetically altered animals to farmers in the developing world.

The granting of this patent—for genetically altered mice that could be used for laboratory testing of carcinogenicity—is controversial in the United States, partly because of the economic and ethical implications of private ownership of genetic traits. The U.S. Congress is considering a 2-year moratorium on further patents for higher animals (109). A U.S. patent precludes others from using or selling a technology for 17 years. The patent also covers any offspring of the mice (110).

As of June 1988, 21 patents for genetically altered animals were pending before the U.S. Patent Office. Pending U.S. patents are kept confidential until the Patent Office makes a decision; most are believed to be in the biomedical area (111).

Ten other countries (Japan, Australia, Canada, Switzerland, New Zealand, the Netherlands, Greece, Turkey, Hungary, and Argentina) allow (or do not exclude) patents for genetically altered animals. Japan has announced that it will allow animals to be patented, and Australia reportedly is considering a patent for a genetically altered pig (112).

Genetic engineering of animals is advancing rapidly. Work is underway to alter the size of livestock, increase their resistance to disease, speed up their production cycle, and develop animals that are leaner and require less feed (113).

If patents are allowed, the effect could be to consolidate control of such animals in a few corporations, with farmers paying royalties—at whatever price the market will bear—to the patent owners. Granting patents could slow or stop the dissemination of these animals to farmers in developing countries (114).

The Industrial Biotechnology Association, which represents U.S. biotechnology companies, argues for patents. It believes that patents are needed to stimulate companies to invest in biotechnology research, that the protection patents afford will encourage technology transfer because patent holders face less risk, and that the requirement that patent holders disclose the science behind their discoveries will stimulate other companies to devise new applications (115).

The association expects that companies generally will charge a slightly higher price for the initial animal but will not require royalty payments for offspring (116). These animals will not be sterile, but the characteristics of offspring may not always be the same. Periodically, farmers may have to buy new animals to refresh their stock (117).

Genetically altered farm animals are several years from development, and the initial market is expected to be largely in the United States. The development of animals such as disease-resistant cattle may ultimately prove beneficial to farmers in developing countries.

References and Notes

1. Robert W. Kates, *et al.*, *The Hunger Report: 1988* (preliminary) (The Alan Shawn Feinstein World Hunger Program, Brown University, Providence, Rhode Island, 1988), Table 1, p. 3 and note 2, p. 33.
2. The World Bank, *Poverty and Hunger: Issues and Options for Food Security in Developing Countries* (The World Bank, Washington, D.C., 1986), Table 2-3, p. 17.
3. *World Resources 1987* (Basic Books, New York, 1987), Table 4.5, p. 46.
4. *Ibid.*, p. 40.
5. Howard Hjort, Director, Policy Analysis Division, United Nations Food and Agriculture Organization, Rome, 1988 (personal communication).
6. *Op. cit.* 3, p. 42.
7. *Op. cit.* 1, p. 2 and notes 1–4, p. 33. Population estimates are for 1985.
8. *Op. cit.* 1, p. 4.
9. *Op. cit.* 1, p. 4.
10. *Op. cit.* 1, p. 7.
11. Calculated from figures in Table 4.2.
12. *Op. cit.* 2, Table 2–4, p. 18.
13. United Nations (U.N.), *First Report on the World Nutrition Situation* (U.N., Rome, 1987), p. 16.
14. *Ibid.*, p. 10.
15. United Nations Food and Agriculture Organization (FAO), *The Fifth World Food Survey* (FAO, Rome, 1985), pp. 29–30.
16. *Ibid.*, p. 30.
17. *Ibid.*, p. 29.
18. *Ibid.*, p. 29.
19. *Op. cit.* 2, p. 18.
20. Robert E. Evenson, *The International Agricultural Research Centers: Their Impact on Spending for National Agricultural Research and Extension* (The World Bank, Washington, D.C., 1987), p. 2.
21. Alain de Janvry and Jean-Jacques Dethier, "Technological Innovation in Agriculture: The Political Economy of Its Rate and Bias," CGIAR Study Paper No. 1, The World Bank, Washington, D.C., 1985, pp. 66–70.
22. Michael J. Dover and Lee M. Talbot, *To Feed the Earth: Agro-Ecology for Sustainable Development* (World Resources Institute, Washington, D.C., 1987).
23. Susan Poats, *et al.*, *Farming Systems Research and Extension: Status and Potential in Low-Resource Agriculture*, in *Enhancing Agriculture in Africa*, Vol. II, Part C-2, No. 11 (National Technical Information Service, Springfield, Virginia, 1987), p. 8.
24. Norman W. Simmonds, *Farming Systems Research: A Review* (The World Bank, Washington, D.C., 1985) p. 1.
25. Michael J. Lipton, "Modern Varieties, International Agricultural Research, and the Poor," CGIAR Study Paper No. 2, The World Bank, Washington, D.C., 1985, p. 27.
26. *Op. cit.* 23, p. 8.
27. United Nations Food and Agriculture Organization (FAO), *FAO and the Environment* (FAO, Rome, 1986), p. 62.
28. See Michael J. Dover, *A Better Mousetrap: Improving Pest Management for Agriculture* (World Resources Institute, Washington, D.C., 1985).
29. "The Price of the Green Revolution," *International Agricultural Development* (July/August 1983), p. 17.
30. John P. Reganold, *et al.*, "Long-Term Effects of Organic and Conventional Farming on Soil Erosion," *Nature*, Vol. 330 (November 26, 1987), pp. 370–372.
31. *Op. cit.* 22, pp. 11–12.
32. John S. Caldwell, "An Overview of Farming Systems Research and Development: Origins, Applications, and Issues," in *Food Policy: Integrating Supply, Distribution, and Consumption*, J. Price Gittinger, Joanne Leslie, and Caroline Hoisington, eds. (The Johns Hopkins University Press, Baltimore, 1987), p. 169.
33. Christopher J.N. Gibbs, "Agricultural Systems Research in Asia: A Comparative Discussion of Human Ecology, Agroecosystems Research, Farming Systems Research, and Cropping Systems Research," in *Agrosystem Research in Rural Resource Management and Development*, Percy E. Sajise, A. Terry Rambo, and Carmelita Rebancos, eds. (East-West Center, Honolulu, 1985), p. 81.
34. D.L. Plucknett, *et al.*, "Review of Concepts of Farming Systems Research: The What, Why, and How," in *Proceedings of the Workshop on Farming Systems Research: International Agricultural Research Centers* (International Crops Research Institute for the Semi-Arid Tropics, Andhra Pradesh, India, 1987), p. 3.
35. Miguel A. Altieri and M. Kat Anderson, "An Ecological Basis for the Development of Alternative Agricultural Systems for Small Farmers in the Third World," *American Journal of Alternative Agriculture*, Vol. I, No. 1 (1986), p. 30.
36. *Op. cit.* 22, p. 57.
37. David Runalls, Vice President, International Institute for Environment and Development-North America, Washington, D.C., 1988 (personal communication).
38. *Op. cit.* 22, p. 58.
39. Gordon R. Conway, *Agroecosystem Analysis for Research and Development* (Winrock International Institute for Agricultural Development, Bangkok, 1986), p. 17.
40. Gordon R. Conway (see above) defines these concepts as follows:
    ■ Productivity is the net increase in valued product per unit of resource (land, labor, energy, or capital),
    ■ Stability is the capacity of the system to minimize short-term fluctuations in output,
    ■ Sustainability is the capacity of the system to maintain its productivity when subject to stress (e.g., increasing soil salinity) or shock (a rare flood or drought), and
    ■ Equitability is the degree of evenness of the system's productivity among human beneficiaries.
41. Henry I. Miller and Frank E. Young, "Biotechnology: A 'Scientific' Term in Name Only," *Wall Street Journal* (January 13, 1987).
42. U.S. Office of Technology Assessment (OTA), *Technology, Public Policy, and the Changing Structure of American Agriculture* (OTA, Washington, D.C., 1986), p. 4.
43. William L. Brown, "The Character and Future Direction of Biotechnology," in *Biotechnology in Agriculture: Implications for Sustainability* (Institute for Alternative Agriculture, Greenbelt, Maryland, 1986), p. 2.
44. Gordon Graff, *et al*, "Biotechnology Growing Greener at Last," *Chemical Week* (September 30, 1987), pp. 26–27.
45. Jack Doyle, *Altered Harvest: Agriculture, Genetics, and the Fate of the World's Food Supply* (Viking Penguin, New York and Middlesex, U.K., 1985), pp. 214–220.
46. National Research Council, *Agricultural*

Biotechnology: Strategies for National Competitiveness (National Academy Press, Washington, D.C., 1987), pp. 34–35.

47. *Op. cit.* 42, p. 36.

48. Frederick Buttel, "Biotechnology and Alternative Agriculture: An Overview of the Major Issues and Concerns," in *Biotechnology in Agriculture: Implications for Sustainability* (Institute for Alternative Agriculture, Washington, D.C., 1986), p. 16.

49. David Dickson, "Europe Splits over Gene Regulation," *Science*, Vol. 238 (October 2, 1987), pp. 18–19.

50. Jack Kloppenburg, Jr., and Daniel Lee Kleinman, "Seeds of Struggle: The Geopolitics of Genetic Resources," *Technology Review* (February/March 1987), p. 47.

51. Frederick H. Buttel and Randolph Barker, "Emerging Agricultural Technologies, Public Policy, and Implications for Third World Agriculture: The Case of Biotechnology," *American Journal of Agricultural Economics* (December 1985), p. 1172.

52. Jack Doyle, "Biotechnology: Regulating the Risks, Data Gaps, and Needed Research," in *Biotechnology in Agriculture: Implications for Sustainability* (Institute for Alternative Agriculture, Washington, D.C., 1986), pp. 40–44.

53. *Op. cit.* 45, p. 42–43.

54. David F. Bezdicek, "Biotechnology and Farming Systems: On-Farm Applications and Consequences," in *Biotechnology in Agriculture: Implications for Sustainability* (Institute for Alternative Agriculture, Washington, D.C., 1986), p. 52.

55. *Op. cit.* 48, pp. 9–10.

56. Malcolm Gladwell, "Maryland Firm Plowing New Biotech Field," *Washington Post* (December 13, 1987), p. H-1.

57. *Op. cit.* 51, p. 1172.

58. Jack Doyle, "DNA—It's Changing the Whole Economy," *Christian Science Monitor* (September 30, 1987), p. 13.

59. *Op. cit.* 50, p. 47–53.

60. In Southeast Asia, permanently cropped land, the land that is planted to perennials, is significant. In Malaysia, rubber, not rice, is the dominant crop.

61. The World Bank, "Diversification Out of Rice in Africa" (preliminary), The World Bank, Washington, D.C., 1987, p. 7.

62. Grenville L. Lucas and Gerald E. Wickens, "Arid Land Plants: The Data Crisis," *Arid Land Newsletter* (December 1985), p. 10.

63. M.F. Amador, "Comportamiento de tres Especies (Maiz, Frijol, Calabaza) en Policultivos en la Chontalpa, Tabasco, Mexico," professional thesis, Colegio Superior de Agricultura Tropical, Tabasco, Mexico, 1980, cited in Stephen R. Gliessman, "Multiple Cropping Systems: A Basis for Developing an Alternative Agriculture," in U.S. Office of Technology Assessment (OTA), *Innovative Biological Technologies for Lesser Developing Countries: Workshop Proceedings* (OTA, Washington, D.C., 1985), p. 74.

64. Gerald G. Marten and Daniel M. Saltman, "The Human Ecology Perspective," *Traditional Agriculture in Southeast Asia: A Human Ecology Perspective*, Gerald G. Marten, ed. (Westview Press, Boulder, Colorado, and London, 1986), pp. 39–40.

65. M.R. Rao and R.W. Willey, "Stability of Performance of a Pigeonpea/Sorghum Intercrop System," in *International Workshop on Intercropping* (International Crops Research Institute for the Semi-Arid Tropics, Hyderabad, India, 1979), p. 306.

66. Peter Hazell, "Economic Policy for Diversification," in *Sustainability Issues in Agricultural Development*, Ted J. Davis and Isabelle A. Schirmer, eds. (The World Bank, Washington, D.C., 1987) p. 361.

67. *Ibid.*, p. 123.

68. R. Pellew, "The Production and Consumption of *Acacia* Browse for Protein Production," in *Browse in Africa*, H.N. Le Houerou, ed. (Addis Ababa, Ethiopia, 1980), cited in Stephen R. Gliessman, "Multiple Cropping Systems: A Basis for Developing an Alternative Agriculture," in U.S. Office of Technology Assessment (OTA), *Innovative Biological Technologies for Lesser Developing Countries: Workshop Proceedings* (OTA, Washington, D.C., 1985), p. 78.

69. Stephen J. Risch, *et al.*, "Agroecosystem Diversity and Pest Control: Data, Tentative Conclusions, and New Research Directions," in *Environmentally Sound Agriculture* (Praeger, New York, 1983), pp. 91–115, cited in Michael J. Dover and Lee M. Talbot, *To Feed the Earth: Agro-Ecology for Sustainable Development* (World Resources Institute, Washington, D.C., 1987), p. 37.

70. Long Yiming and Zhang Jiahe, "Ecological Effects and Economic Results of the Artificial Plant Community," paper presented at the Workshop on Ecosystem Models for Development, Kumming and Guangzhou, China, September 27–October 9, 1982, cited in Michael J. Dover and Lee M. Talbot, *To Feed the Earth: Agro-Ecology for Sustainable Development* (World Resources Institute, Washington, D.C., 1987), p. 35.

71. Stephen R. Gliessman, "Multiple Cropping Systems: A Basis for Developing an Alternative Agriculture," in U.S. Office of Technology Assessment (OTA), *Innovative Biological Technologies for Lesser Developing Countries: Workshop Proceedings* (OTA, Washington, D.C., 1985), Table 3, p. 72, and Table 4, p. 73.

72. World Commission on Environment and Development, Advisory Panel on Food Security, Agriculture, Forestry and Environment, *Food Security* (Zed Books, London, 1987), cited in World Commission on Environment and Development, *Our Common Future* (Oxford University Press, Oxford, U.K., and New York, 1987), p. 127.

73. H.E. Dregne, *Desertification in Arid Lands* (Harwood Academic Publishers, New York, 1983), p. 19.

74. L. Bowden, "Development of Present Dryland Farming Systems," in A.E. Hall, *Agriculture in Semi-Arid Environments* (Springer-Verlag, Berlin and New York, 1979), p. 65.

75. *Op. cit.* 73, Table 1.3, p. 19.

76. Stuart Marples, "Production and Investment in Marginal Areas," in *Development of Rainfed Agriculture under Arid and Semiarid Conditions*, Ted J. Davis, ed. (The World Bank, Washington, D.C., 1986), p. 87.

77. *Op. cit.* 73, p. 5; Table 1.3, p. 19; and p. 24.

78. R.P. Singh, *et al.*, *Size, Composition, and Other Aspects of Rural Income in the Semi-Arid Tropics of India* (International Crops Research Institute for the Semi-Arid Tropics, Andhra Pradesh, India, 1982), p. 3.

79. Choeng-Hoy Chung, "Risk and Rainfed Cropping Constraints: The Case of Northeast Thailand," in *Development of Rainfed Agriculture under Arid and Semiarid Conditions*, Ted J. Davis, ed. (The World Bank, Washington, D.C., 1986), p. 44.

80. *Ibid.*, p. 58.

81. K. Vijayalakshmi, "Rain Water Management in Drylands," in *Technological Advances in Dryland Agriculture*, S.P. Singh, *et al.*, eds. (Central Research Institute for Dryland Agriculture, Hyderabad, India, 1987), pp. 19–45.

82. Robert M. Press, "Kenyans Shore Up Hopes—and Topsoil— with Terraces," *Christian Science Monitor* (May 9, 1988), p. 11.

83. John Doolette, "The Diversity of Technology Needs in Rainfed Agriculture: The Case of North Africa," in *Development of Rainfed Agriculture under Arid and Semiarid Conditions*, Ted J. Davis, ed. (The World Bank, Washington, D.C., 1986), p. 26.

84. Consultative Group on International Agricultural Research (CGIAR), *CGIAR Annual Report* (CGIAR, Washington, D.C., 1985), p. 33.

85. Peter Felker, "Development of Low Water and Low Nitrogen Requiring Plant Ecosystems for Arid Land Developing Countries," in U.S. Office of Technology Assessment (OTA), *Innovative Biological Technologies for Lesser Developed Countries* (OTA, Washington, D.C., 1985), p. 90.

86. R.S. Paroda, "Resources of Indian Arid Zones for Industrial Uses," in Joe R. Goodin, *Plant Resources of Arid and Semi-arid Lands* (Academic Press, Orlando, Florida, 1979), pp. 261–267.

87. Edward C. Wolf, *Beyond the Green Revolution: New Approaches for Third World Agriculture* (Worldwatch Institute, Washington, D.C., 1986), p. 22.

88. Hans P. Binsanger, *et al.*, "Nature and Significance of Risk in the Semi-Arid Tropics," in *International Workshop on Intercropping* (International Crops Research Institute for the Semi-Arid Tropics, Hyderabad, India, 1979), p. 303.

89. General Foods World Food Prize, "The World Food Prize: Exemplifying Agricultural Leadership," press release (n.d.), p. 2.

90. General Foods World Food Prize, "Biography: Dr. Robert F. Chandler, Jr.," press release (n.d.), p. 2.

91. Kathleen Teltsch, "Donation Helps Create Housing for the Elderly: Toward Ending Hunger," *New York Times* (September 20,

1987), p. 76.

92. Howard R. Swearer, President, Brown University, Providence, Rhode Island, 1988 (personal communication).

93. David Briscoe, "11 Receive Awards for Fighting World Hunger," The Associated Press Wire Service (October 16, 1987).

94. Clarke Taylor, "World Hunger Media Awards: Shift in Focus," Los Angeles Times (November 26, 1986), Part 6, p. 4.

95. Maryam Niamir, Consultant, United Nations Food and Agriculture Organization, Rome, 1988 (personal communication).

96. United Nations Food and Agriculture Organization (FAO), "Review of the Purposes and Operational Modalities of the Global Information and Early Warning System on Food and Agriculture" (FAO, Rome, 1985).

97. Barbara Huddleston, Chief of Food Security and Information Service, United Nations Food and Agriculture Organization, Rome, 1988 (personal communication).

98. U.S. Agency for International Development (U.S. AID), A Report on the Problems and Approaches to Improved Management of Drought-Famine (U.S. AID, Washington, D.C., 1987), p. 2.

99. Charles F. Hutchinson, "Early Warning Systems for Determining Drought Conditions in Sub-Saharan Africa," The World Bank, Washington, D.C., 1987, p. 7.

100. Op. cit. 95.

101. Op. cit. 99, p. 4–5.

102. Op. cit. 99, p. 4–7.

103. J.U. Hielkema, et al., "The FAO/NASA/NLR/Artemis System: An Integrated Concept for Environmental Monitoring by Satellite in Support of Food/Feed Security and Desert Locust Surveillance," paper presented at the Twentieth International Symposium on Remote Sensing of Environment, Nairobi, December 4–10, 1986, p. 1.

104. Energy/Development International, "Assessment of the Famine Early Warning System," Washington, D.C., 1987, p. 24.

105. Op. cit. 99, p. 11.

106. United Nations Food and Agriculture Organization, "Proposal for the Development and Implementation of a Satellite Telecommunications System to Support FAO Data/Information Dissemination Requirements," Rome, 1988, p. 10.

107. Op. cit. 104, pp. 30–31.

108. Op. cit. 104, p. 24.

109. R. Weiss, "Animal Patent Report Lacks Support," Science News (April 9, 1988), p. 231.

110. R. Weiss, "First Patent Issued for Engineered Animal," Science News (April 16, 1980), p. 244.

111. Lisa Raines, Director of Government Relations, Industrial Biotechnology Association, Washington, D.C., 1988 (personal communication).

112. Animal Pharm, Vol. 1, No. 55 (1988), p. 22.

113. Marjorie Sun, "Designing Food by Engineering Animals," Science (April 18, 1988), p. 136.

114. Howard Lyman, Consultant, National Farmers Union, Washington, D.C., 1988 (personal communication).

115. Lisa Raines, Director of Government Relations, Industrial Biotechnology Association, Washington, D.C., 1988 (personal communication).

116. Ibid.

117. John Elkington, Director, Sustainability, Ltd., London (personal communication).

5. Forests and Rangelands

Forests and rangelands, which together cover about 84 percent of the Earth's land surface, supply humans with the basic products of wood, meat, and milk. Managing them sustainably is one of our greatest challenges.

A prerequisite to sound management is a thorough knowledge of the resource base. Accurate long-term monitoring studies are badly needed for both forests and rangelands. Our knowledge of deforestation rates in tropical countries remains limited because available satellite technology has not been applied, partly because of its high cost. Sophisticated monitoring of rangelands could identify degraded areas and areas with high forage potential to help managers determine use policies.

Wood from forests and woodlands has three main uses: fuelwood, wood products, and paper. Fuelwood supplies domestic energy for billions of people and is discussed at length in *World Resources 1986* (pp. 67–69). Wood for products and paper, which is often traded internationally, makes an important contribution to the economies of many tropical and temperate countries. Accurately projecting the supply and demand of wood production is a valuable service. Recently, several computer models have been developed that attempt to forecast future timber availability and prices. One model, which deals strictly with tropical timber, projects a shift in supply from Asia to Latin America and Africa after 1990 as Asian forests are logged over and no longer able to meet demand.

The story of rangeland management in developing countries is one of good intentions and unsatisfactory results. Time and again development agencies have tried techniques—boreholes, marketing schemes, herding plans—that failed because of inadequate funding, inappropriate technical solutions, inadequate research, misunderstanding of the ecosystem, and lack of adequate participation by local people. Recently some development specialists have called for integrating the traditional knowledge of pastoralists in rangeland management projects and in emphasizing local participation in planning.

The grasslands of China, Mongolia, India, Pakistan, and Afghanistan are vast and legendary, but they are overgrazed in many areas and some are in danger of severe erosion. Other volumes of *World Resources* have discussed rangeland conditions in West Asia and Africa. This volume discusses rangelands in selected Asian countries.

CONDITIONS AND TRENDS

FOREST RESOURCES

Types of Forests

The Earth is covered by a number of major types of forests and woodlands. (See *World Resources 1986*, Figure 5.1, p. 63.) The upper part of the northern hemisphere is dominated by a vast band of evergreen coniferous forest stretching over parts of Canada, the United States, Scandinavia, the USSR, and China. Further south, as the climate gets warmer, the needleleaved conifers like spruce and pine give way to broadleaved trees like oak and beech. Large areas of the United States, Europe, the

USSR, and China are covered by deciduous broadleaved forests, whose trees shed their leaves with the onset of the colder seasons.

Temperate coniferous and deciduous forests are distributed as a complex mosaic rather than as two distinct bands. Because high altitudes have vegetation similar to high latitudes, temperate conifers grow in hilly and mountainous areas well south of their normal range, thereby adding to the mosaic effect.

In upper tropical latitudes, the arid or semiarid lands of northern Africa, Asia, and Latin America are covered by savanna woodlands in which trees are widely scattered over grassy plains. Thousands of years of cutting and burning, especially in Africa, have so transformed the vegetation that it bears little resemblance to its former state in which tree cover was probably denser than it is today, but still had a relatively open canopy. These open woodlands contrast with closed forests in which trees are so close together that their crowns form a continuous canopy over the ground. The two types of woody cover are referred to here as woodlands and forests respectively.

Tropical rain forests flourish in the high temperature and humidity of the low latitudes on either side of the equator. Their evergreen broadleaved trees do not shed their leaves seasonally. On the fringes of the tropical rain forests grow the tropical moist deciduous forests, also called monsoon forests, which lose their leaves in the dry season. The tropical rain forests and moist deciduous forests, the two main forest types in the humid tropics, are referred to collectively as tropical moist forests.

Extent of the World's Forests

Closed forests cover 2.8 billion hectares or 21 percent of the Earth's land surface. Other wooded areas include tropical open woodlands and tropical forest fallow—the regrowth that occurs after forestland cleared for shifting cultivation has been abandoned. Including these raises the planet's total woody cover to 4.5 billion hectares, or 34 percent, but this figure should be treated with caution because estimates of open woodland areas are highly uncertain and the actual density of trees in such areas is often very low. (See Table 5.1.)

Of the closed forests, 43 percent are found in the tropics and 57 percent are in the temperate zone. Sixty-two percent of all closed forests are broadleaved and 38 percent are coniferous. Developed nations contain over 90 percent of all coniferous forests and developing nations 75 percent of all broadleaved forests. (See *World Resources 1987*, Table 5.1, p. 59.) Four countries account for more than half of the world's closed forests: the USSR has 792 million hectares, Brazil 357 million hectares, Canada 264 million hectares, and the United States 195 million hectares. This compares with only 43 million hectares in the countries of the European Community and 145 million hectares for all of Europe [1].

The tropical moist forests occupy just under 1.1 billion hectares and account for 90 percent of all tropical closed forests, the remainder being various types of deciduous and semideciduous forests. About half of the area of tropical moist forests is in Latin America with the other half shared about equally between Africa and the Asia-Pacific region. Brazil has the largest area of tropical moist forest, 331 million hectares, three times the forest area of Indonesia or Zaire [2]. Tropical rain forests account for about 66 percent of all tropical moist forests [3].

A large proportion of the remaining forests in Europe and other developed nations has either been artificially planted or substantially modified for commercial timber production. In 1975, plantations covered an estimated 13 million hectares in Western Europe, 17 million hectares in Eastern Europe and the USSR, and 11 million hectares in North America [4].

Forest plantations in the tropics cover a relatively small area. Out of a total of 11.5 million hectares, 4.4 million hectares (39 percent) are nonindustrial plantations for fuelwood production or environmental protection and 7.1 million hectares (61 percent) are industrial plantations for the production of commercial timber, pulpwood, or charcoal [5].

Table 5.1 Distribution of the World's Forest Lands
(millions of hectares)

Region	Land Area	Closed Forest		Other Wooded Areas			Total Forest and Wooded Lands[b]	
		Area	Percent of Land Area	Total Area	Open Woodland	Forest Fallow[a]	Area	Percent
Temperate	6,417	1,590	25	563	X	NA	2,153	34
North America[c]	1,835	459	25	275	X	NA	734	40
Europe	472	145	31	35	X	NA	181	38
USSR	2,227	792	36	138	X	NA	930	42
Other Countries[d]	1,883	194	10	115	X	NA	309	16
Tropical	4,815	1,202	25	1,144	734	410	2,346	49
Africa	2,190	217	10	652	486	166	869	40
Asia and Pacific	945	306	32	104	31	73	410	43
Latin America	1,680	679	40	388	217	170	1,067	64
World[e]	**13,077**	**2,792**	**21**	**1,707**	**734**	**410**	**4,499**	**34**

Sources:
1. For temperate forest areas in North America, Europe, and USSR: United Nations Food and Agriculture Organization (FAO) and United Nations Economic Commission for Europe (ECE), *The Forest Resources of the ECE Region* (FAO/ECE, Geneva, 1985), Table 1, p. 8.
2. For temperate forest areas in "Other Countries": *World Resources 1987*, Table 5.1, p. 59.
3. For tropical forest areas: Jean Paul Lanly, Tropical Forest Resources, United Nations Food and Agriculture Organization (FAO), FAO Forestry Paper No. 30 (FAO, Rome, 1982), p. 34, and Table 1f, p. 50.
4. For Land Area: United Nations Food and Agriculture Organization (FAO), *FAO Production Yearbook 1983* (FAO, Rome, 1984).

Notes:
a. Includes wooded areas with forest regrowth following clearing for shifting cultivation within past 20 years. b. Includes forest areas and other wooded land.
c. Canada and the United States. d. Australia, China, Israel, Japan, New Zealand, and South Africa. e. World land area excludes Antarctica.
X = not available; NA = not applicable.

Trends in world forest cover in recent decades have been influenced by a decline in tropical forests and woodlands and a slow net increase in temperate forest area because of plantation establishment.

The Causes of Tropical Deforestation

Concern is rising about the rapid rate of tropical deforestation—the temporary or permanent clearance of forest for agriculture or other purposes (6). The main cause of deforestation in tropical closed forests is clearing for agriculture to feed growing numbers of people or (to a lesser degree) to earn foreign exchange from exports of cash crops like rubber and beef. Often the only way to increase the agricultural area in densely forested countries is to clear forest or woodland. In all countries some deforestation is planned or promoted by governments, but a substantial proportion takes place spontaneously and without control.

A contributing cause of deforestation is the impact of intensive land use on the poor soils that cover about two thirds of the humid tropics. Permanent field cropping and cattle grazing deplete soil fertility or cause soil erosion if they are too intensive. As soil fertility declines, crop yields fall and more forest must be cleared to maintain the level of food production. When yields drop too low the land is abandoned.

Logging in the tropical rain forests is not usually a direct cause of deforestation because it is mainly selective and clearcutting is rare. Only a few of the thousands of tropical tree species are commercially acceptable. (By contrast, in temperate forests much logging is done by clearcutting all the trees in an area of forest.) Selective logging usually removes 2–10 trees per hectare or 3–30 percent of the total timber volume. However, selective logging does disturb the forest canopy, some of the remaining trees are damaged during felling and log extraction, and the composition and functioning of the forest ecosystem are modified to varying degrees. The extent and duration of these disturbances are not currently known. At the very least, logging degrades the forest ecosystem and can also lead to subsequent deforestation. After loggers have left the area, farmers may use logging roads to gain access to clear the forest for growing crops.

Deforestation of open woodlands in dry areas also occurs because of the need to expand the area under cultivation, but other causes of deforestation dominate in dry areas and montane areas like the Himalayas. The first is the cutting of fuelwood, which is generally in short supply in these areas. The second cause is the heavy lopping of foliage for fodder or direct browsing by goats and other animals.

Rates of Tropical Deforestation

Every year about 11.1 million hectares of tropical forests and woodlands are destroyed. About 7.3 million hectares of tropical closed forests are cleared annually for agriculture, according to estimates made by the United Nations Food and Agriculture Organization (FAO) and the United Nations Environment Program (UNEP) in 1981 (7). The vast majority of this area (6.1 million hectares per

year) is tropical moist forest (8). Another 3.8 million hectares per year of open woodlands in the drier tropics are removed either for agriculture or the harvesting of fuelwood (9). (See Table 5.2.) In addition to this deforestation, about 4.4 million hectares of tropical forests are selectively logged every year (10). Most of the area logged (about 3.7 million hectares per year (11)) is tropical moist forest.

Estimates of the deforestation rate of *tropical moist* forests have varied widely. In the 1970s the commonly accepted figure was between 11 and 15 million hectares per year (12). The current estimate of 6.1 million hectares per year is somewhat more rigorous than previous estimates, but it still relies heavily on estimates by FAO and government forestry departments rather than measurements by satellites and other forms of remote sensing (13). FAO and UNEP are currently preparing a new assessment of tropical forest resources, to be published in 1990. Box 5.1 gives an overview of methods used in assessing the extent of and changes in forests and rangelands.

Trends in Deforestation

Figure 5.1 juxtaposes estimates of original tropical forest cover with estimates of current forest cover to show the areas that have been deforested in Latin America, Africa, and Southeast Asia. (See also Chapter 16, "Land Cover and Settlements," Table 16.1.)

If the present deforestation rate of 6.1 million hectares per year were to continue indefinitely the tropical moist forests would be completely cleared in 177 years. At the moment 0.6 percent of the total area of tropical moist forests is cleared each year, with similar figures for the three tropical regions. (See Table 5.2.) However, in some countries the deforestation problem is much more acute. Cote d'Ivoire and Nigeria annually lose about 5.2 percent of their forests, while in Costa Rica, Sri Lanka, and El Salvador the rates are 3.6 percent, 3.5 percent, and 3.2 percent respectively. Depending on its rate of loss, each of these countries could lose all its forests between 2007 and 2017 (14). (See Chapter 18, "Forests and Rangelands," Table 18.1.)

Until now most forecasts of future trends in tropical

Table 5.2 Annual Rates of Tropical Deforestation 1976–80

(millions of hectares per annum)

| | Closed Forests | | | | Open Woodlands[a] | |
| | All Tropical | | Moist Tropical | | | |
	Area	Percent of Total	Area	Percent of Total	Area	Percent of Total
Africa	1.33	0.61	1.20	0.59	2.34	0.48
Asia-Pacific	1.82	0.59	1.61	0.61	0.19	0.61
Latin America	4.12	0.61	3.30	0.54	1.27	0.59
Total	**7.27**	**0.61**	**6.11**	**0.57**	**3.81**	**0.52**

Sources:
1. For All Tropical Closed Forests and Open Woodlands: Jean Paul Lanly, Tropical Forest Resources, *FAO Forestry Paper No. 30* (United Nations Food and Agriculture Organization, Rome, 1982), Table 6d, p. 80 and Table 6e, p. 84.
2. For Tropical Moist Forests: Alan Grainger, "Quantifying Changes in Forest Cover in the Humid Tropics: Overcoming Current Limitations," *Journal of World Forest Resource Management*, Vol. 1 (1984), Table 8, p. 21.
Note: a. Projections for 1981-85.

5 Forests and Rangelands

Resource managers—including local herdsmen, timber company foresters, ministers of planning, and ecologists interested in global biodiversity—use a variety of tools to inventory and monitor forests and rangelands. Some of these tools have been used since antiquity (see "Traditional Methods of Range Management," below); others are among the most beneficial achievements of the Space Age. However, both ancient and modern methods involve tradeoffs among detail, cost, and sampling frequency. Because no single method can meet all the requirements, several techniques are often used in concert. To date, forests have been more extensively monitored than rangelands, mainly because the forest industry has pushed for monitoring.

MONITORING METHODS

Ground-level Methods

Ground-level sampling is the least technically sophisticated but, in principle, the most accurate method of collecting information on forests and rangelands. One ambitious ground-level program was launched in 1986 to monitor the extent of and trends in forest damage in Europe. (See Chapter 18, "Forests and Rangelands," Table 18.3.) It used almost 60,000 sample plots and evaluated the condition of 1.25 million trees to produce the first internationally comparable data on forest damage. Future surveys will allow government and forestry enterprises to assess trends in forest damage and its ecological and economic costs (1).

Unfortunately, ground-level methods are expensive in labor, money, and time, and are rarely sustained for more than three to five continuous years. Although detailed information can be collected with ground-level methods for small areas, extrapolating these results to other areas is difficult. Thus ground-level monitoring is often done in conjunction with one or more remote methods, either to provide supplementary information or to provide "ground truth" for remotely-sensed observations (2) (3).

Aerial Photography

Aerial photography is used to monitor and create inventories of both forests and rangelands. Foresters have used aerial photographs for many years to measure the area and condition of forests and to estimate the volumes of timber they contain. Aerial photographs can provide data on tree height and canopy cover, soils, vegetation community types, land-use patterns, erosion, and (depending on the scale and the vegetation) botanical composition of vegetation types (4) (5). Aerial photos of Sahelian Africa from the mid-1940s have been compared to photos of the same areas in the 1980s, providing insight into the effects of drought and long-term overgrazing on rangelands. But aerial photography is expensive—a single aerial coverage of a 10,000 square kilometer area

(not including analysis and mapping) can cost $300,000 to $600,000 (6)—so it is most often used for baseline studies and inventories, rather than for long-term monitoring. Even the wealthiest countries cannot afford to use aerial photography more often than once every 10 years for national forest inventories.

Raw remotely-sensed products, including aerial photographs and satellite images, require human interpretation. Experts develop classifications for the remotely-sensed data by comparing some of the data to known ground features (the expensive, all-important process of "ground truthing"). This is not a rigid science, as shown by a recent study that reviewed two aerial photographic assessments undertaken in 1954 and 1980 of the forest resources of Jamaica. Both assessments covered the entire island on the same scale and were conducted by specialists trained in interpreting photographic surveys of tropical vegetation. Comparing the two assessments would indicate that Jamaica experienced a net increase in pristine forest cover of 59 percent in 26 years. However, the early study was much more prone to classify an area as human-influenced "scrub" than the later study was, thus the later study found much more pristine forest. In fact, there is evidence that Jamaica's pristine forest area is now being rapidly reduced (7).

Low-Altitude Flights

A third method of vegetation assessment, low altitude systematic reconnaissance flights using small airplanes, was developed in East Africa in the 1960s. Used primarily for counting game and livestock (8), it can also be used for monitoring changes in vegetation, hydrology, and other natural systems. It is less costly than conventional aerial photography because only about 5 percent of the area is surveyed, and can be repeated at regular intervals. However, it requires sophisticated sampling procedures and considerable ground validation of natural features. The Kenya Rangeland Ecological Monitoring Unit (see Case Study below) has used this method to monitor a variety of range condition indicators.

Satellite Systems

Since the 1960s, satellite-based remote sensing has promised to revolutionize the assessment of forests and rangelands, but large-scale results thus far have been disappointingly few. On paper, the potential of satellite sensing is almost dazzling. Contemporary high resolution land-resources satellites (such as the French SPOT satellite and the U.S. LANDSAT series) can scan large areas in a matter of seconds and collect vast amounts of data in digital form, a real advantage over conventional aerial photography if computer analysis is anticipated (see "Geographic Information Systems," below). For example, a sensor on the LANDSATs can scan an area equivalent to 5,000 aerial photographs taken at a scale of 1:20,000—every 25 seconds (9). In addition,

these satellites overfly the same area about every 2-4 weeks, allowing fairly continuous monitoring of change (10). Although satellite images are expensive (a 34,000 square kilometer LANDSAT image costs about $3,500), they cost much less than aerial photographs for the same area. Analyzing digital satellite data typically costs 60-90 percent less than interpreting aerial photographs covering the same area (11).

Satellite sensing also has a number of disadvantages. In the humid tropics, satellite sensors are frequently "blinded" by clouds; satellites can overfly large areas of the Brazilian Amazon twice a month for years and never get a cloud-free image (12). This constraint applies to aerial photography as well, but another aerial method—side-looking airborne radar (SLAR)—can "see" through dense cloud cover, at a higher resolution (and cost) than satellite sensing. Satellite sensors cannot be used for detailed ecological studies, such as identifying the kinds of trees found in a specific area of forest or the flora of a rangeland tract (13). Satellite-based methods also require substantial investments in supplementary hardware and software, such as receiving stations, computers, display devices, training, and "ground truthing."

USING SATELLITES TO MONITOR THE WORLD'S FORESTS

Satellite technology allows tropical deforestation to be monitored on a global scale, but no system has yet been developed to take on the task of collecting and interpreting such a large amount of data. The United Nations Conference on the Human Environment in Stockholm called for the establishment of a continuous satellite-based monitoring system for world forest resources in 1972, the year in which the first LANDSAT satellite was launched. UNEP and FAO collaborated to implement this resolution and produced a detailed report on tropical forest resources in 1981 (14).

Most of the data compiled by FAO for this assessment were supplied by government forestry departments. Unfortunately, many tropical countries lack sufficient personnel, funds, and equipment to undertake sophisticated monitoring. Less than 60 percent of the total area of the tropical moist forests had been surveyed since 1970 using any form of remote sensing. Half of this area was accounted for by an SLAR survey of Brazilian Amazonia. Similarly, estimates of national deforestation rates were based on remote sensing measurements for just six out of more than 60 countries in the humid tropics, while FAO used national figures from another seven countries and made its own estimates for the remaining countries (15).

A new assessment of tropical forest resources is currently being prepared by FAO and UNEP for publication in 1990. For this assessment, FAO will collate data gathered by agencies in each country, many of which have made significant advances in forest inventory and monitoring since the 1981 assessment. Representatives of seven countries with moist tropical forests (Brazil, Burma, Colombia, Malaysia, Mexico, Nigeria and Zaire) attended a 1987 planning meeting for the 1990 assessment. All seven indicated that their countries plan to complete detailed forest inventories—based on aerial photography, SLAR, or satellite imagery—in time for the 1990 Assessment (16).

Geographic Information Systems

A new computer technology—the Geographical Information System (GIS)—promises to multiply the benefits of all kinds of renewable resource monitoring. Basically a series of computerized "maps," a GIS has three main advantages over traditional hand-drawn maps. First, they are excellent data storage and display tools. Second, they can produce a variety of formats such as maps, tables, and statistical graphics. Third, they are powerful modelling tools, giving resource managers the ability to analyze causes and effects, track resource changes, and test the likely outcomes of policy alternatives. The case study of the Kenya Rangeland Ecological Monitoring Unit program below shows how the power of GIS technology can enhance the utility of monitoring information.

Case Study 1: Brazil Monitors Deforestation and Reforestation

With 357 million hectares of forests, Brazil has probably made more extensive use of remote sensing than any other tropical country. In the early 1970s the Brazilian government obtained the first estimates of the forest area in Amazonia from a specially commissioned comprehensive SLAR survey. SLAR, however, is too expensive for regular monitoring. (This survey cost about $5 million.) Thus in 1979 Brazil established a National Remote Sensing Program to monitor the country's forest resources using satellite technology.

The program monitors the annual rate of deforestation throughout Brazil and particularly in the Amazon region, where change is most rapid. The total deforested area in the state of Rondonia almost tripled between 1982 and 1985 from 1 million hectares to 2.7 million hectares (17). The remote sensing images clearly linked the pace of deforestation to the construction of a road network in the forest. Obtaining better estimates of deforestation rates does not guarantee that Brazil will be able to control deforestation. However, by showing the scale of the problem and identifying likely causes, remote sensing adds a sense of urgency to the policy debate.

Case Study 2: Kenya Monitors its Rangelands

A severe drought in 1973–74 triggered concerns that Kenya's rangelands were threatened by desertification. In 1975 the Kenya

Rangeland Ecological Monitoring Unit (KREMU) was established to monitor range conditions. In the subsequent decade, KREMU has developed an integrated monitoring program serving many users. Using ground and aerial photography and LANDSAT imagery, KREMU monitors rangeland conditions as indicated by the condition and botanical composition of rangeland vegetation. By tracking changes in the conditions of specific vegetation communities, range managers have been able to identify areas of heavy grazing pressure and the animal species (wild and domestic) that are responsible (18).

Low altitude flights are used to monitor Kenya's elephant and black rhinoceros populations. Small aircraft fly across the country along east-west transects and observers count all the animals (both live and dead) found within 100–200 meters of the airplane's path. Three survey rounds (1977–81) revealed precipitous drops in elephant and rhino populations, and increasing ratios of dead to live animals. KREMU called for increased antipoaching efforts and better land use management over the range of the two animals to prevent their extermination (19).

As KREMU evolved into a nationwide ecological monitoring program, its data storage, analysis, and display systems evolved as well. A GIS system was added recently that will allow KREMU to combine satellite, aerial, and ground-collected data into one storage and display system. The GIS will simplify KREMU's data storage requirements, permit more sophisticated analyses of rangeland processes, and produce outputs (such as maps) that are easily understood by nontechnical audiences (20).

References and Notes

1. Programme Co-ordinating Centres, *Forest Damage and Air Pollution: Report on the 1986 Forest Damage Survey in Europe* (United Nations Economic Commission for Europe, Geneva, 1987), Table 1, p. 25.
2. Government of India, "Desertification in the Luni Development Block, Rajasthan, India," in *Case Studies on Desertification*, J.A. Mabbutt and C. Floret, eds. (United Nations Commission for Europe, United Nations Environment Programme and United Nations Development Programme, Paris, 1980), p. 160.
3. H.N. Le Houerou, *Pilot Project on the Inventory and Monitoring of Sahelian Pastoral Ecosystems (Senegal)* (United Nations Food and Agriculture Organization, Rome, 1986).
4. B. Toutain, *et al.*, *Paturages de l'ORD du Sahel et de la Zone de Delestage au Nord est de Fada-N'Gourma* (Haute Volta) (Insitut Medecine Veterinaire Tropicale, Burkina Faso, 1977).
5. H. Barral, *et al.*, *Systemes de Production d'Elevage au Senegal dans la Region du Ferlo* (ISRA/GERDAT-ORSTOM, Paris, 1983).
6. Victor Odenyo, Officer, AGRT, Research and Technical Development Division, United Nations Food and Agriculture Organization, Rome, 1987 (personal communication).
7. Lawrence Alan Eyre, "Jamaica: Test Case for Tropical Deforestation?" *Ambio*, Vol. 16, No. 6 (1987), pp. 338–343.
8. M.D. Gwynne and H. Croze, "East African Habitat Monitoring Practices," presented at Seminar on Evaluation and Mapping of Tropical African Rangelands, International Livestock Center for Africa, Bamako, March 3–8, 1975, pp. 95–136.
9. Alan Grainger, "Quantifying Changes in Forest Cover in the Humid Tropics: Overcoming Current Limitations," *Journal of World Forest Resource Management*, Vol. 1, No. 1 (1984), p. 29.
10. U.S. National Oceanic and Atmospheric Administration (NOAA) and U.S. National Aeronautics and Space Administration (NASA), *Space-Based Remote Sensing of the Earth* (NOAA/NASA, Washington, D.C., September 1987), p. 97 and p. 108.
11. *Op. cit.* 9, pp. 23–27.
12. Jean-Paul Malingreau and Compton J. Tucker, "Large-Scale Deforestation in the Southeastern Amazon Basin of Brazil," *Ambio*, Vol. 17, No. 1, p. 49.
13. For example, Zhao Ji *et al.*, "Remote Sensing Analysis of the Grassland Degradation in Hailar Area (Inner Mongolia)," paper presented at the Fifteenth International Grassland Congress, Kyoto, Japan, 1985, pp. 717–718.
14. Tropical Forest Resources Assessment Project, Forest Resources of Tropical Africa, Tropical Asia, and Tropical America, 4 vols., Jean Paul Lanly, ed. (United Nations Food and Agriculture Organization and United Nations Environment Program Rome, 1981).
15. *Op. cit.* 9, pp. 3–63.
16. Finnish Forest Research Institute, *Proceedings of Ad Hoc FAO/ECE/FINNIDA Meeting of Experts on Forest Resource Assessment: Kotka, Finland, October 26–30, 1987* (FINNIDA, Helsinki, 1987), pp. 144–152, pp. 164–174, pp. 207–227, pp. 239–244, and pp. 294–299.
17. *Op. cit.* 12, p. 54.
18. D.K. Andere, "Rangeland Monitoring in Kenya–The Mara Ecosystem Case Study," *Proceedings of the Twentieth International Symposium on Remote Sensing of Environment* (Environmental Research Institute of Michigan, Nairobi, December 1986) pp. 325–334.
19. J.G. Stelfox, J.W. Kufwafwa and W. Otichilo, *Distributions and Population Trend of Elephants and Rhinoceros in Kenya: 1977–1981* (Kenya Rangeland Ecological Monitoring Unit, Nairobi, 1981), pp. 5–7 and pp. 33–37.
20. *Op. cit.* 18, pp. 325–343.

Figure 5.1 Extent of Tropical Deforestation

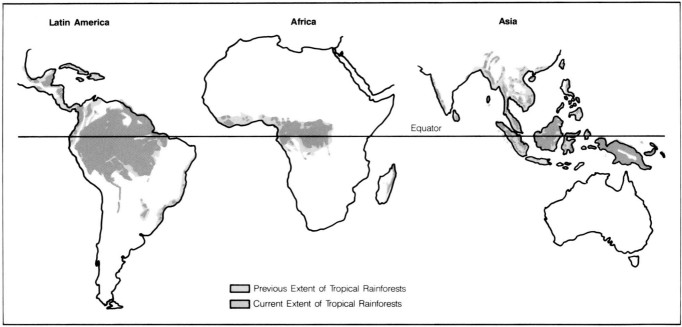

Latin America   Africa   Asia

Equator

☐ Previous Extent of Tropical Rainforests
▨ Current Extent of Tropical Rainforests

Source: *Tropical Rainforests: A Disappearing Treasure* (Smithsonian Institution, Washington, D.C., Traveling Exhibition Service, 1988).

moist areas have simply projected current rates into the future. However, deforestation rates may change because population and economic activity are growing rapidly in many countries, and both market forces and government policies can either promote or restrain deforestation. Growing populations could lead to more deforestation because of the need to grow more food. Economic development is frequently accompanied by an increase in the amount of food each person consumes, possibly requiring the clearance of even more land. On the other hand, economic development also permits greater investment in agriculture. With higher yields per hectare the same amount of food could be grown on a smaller area of land, thereby reducing deforestation rates and offsetting the effects of growing populations. Deforestation may also be curtailed if governments take action to protect remaining forests for long-term timber production or conservation purposes.

A forecast of deforestation rates for 43 tropical countries was made with a mathematical model using likely rates of increase in population, food consumption per capita, and average yield per hectare. The model assumed that once the forest area in a particular country fell to a critical level, governments would take action to prevent further deforestation. The results predicted that deforestation rates could decrease to between 0.9 and 3.7 million hectares per year in 2020. This would lead to corresponding decreases in total forest area of 10 percent and 20 percent respectively, compared with a loss of 23 percent if the rate remained at the present 6.1 million

hectares per year. Although deforestation rates would decline in the long run, they would rise initially in about half of the 43 countries modelled (15).

INDUSTRIAL WOOD PRODUCTION AND TRADE

Increasing attention has been paid in recent years to the vital role forests play in maintaining environmental stability and in storing plant and animal genetic resources. Nevertheless, the most important commercial product obtained from the forest is still wood. In 1985, the world's total wood removals were 3.2 billion cubic meters of which 1.5 billion cubic meters were harvested for industrial purposes and a slightly larger volume (1.7 billion cubic meters) was burned as fuel. (See Table 5.3.) In the developed nations 20 percent of all removals are used as

Table 5.3 World Wood Production 1985
(billions of cubic meters)

	Roundwood Removals			Wood Products[a]	
	Total	Industrial	Fuelwood	Sawnwood	Wood Panels
World	**3,165**	**1,502**	**1,663**	**465**	**109**
Developed Nations	1,405	1,151	255	360	89
Developing Nations	1,760	351	1,408	105	19

Source: United Nations Food and Agriculture Organization (FAO), *Yearbook of Forest Products 1985* (FAO, Rome, 1986), pp. 2-3, pp. 16-17, pp. 36-37, pp. 110-111, pp. 140-141.
Note: a. Volumes shown are product volumes not roundwood equivalent volumes.

fuelwood and 80 percent as industrial wood for conversion into wood products like sawnwood, wood panels, or paper. In developing nations, where fuelwood is still the major energy source, the proportions are exactly the reverse. Softwoods from the great coniferous forests of the northern hemisphere dominate the removals of developed nations and provide the raw material for the pulp and paper industries of North America and Scandinavia, while hardwoods from the tropical rain forests dominate industrial wood removals in tropical regions (16).

Because forests are so widespread over the planet and wood is a low value commodity relative to its bulk, most wood is consumed locally and only a small proportion (3–18 percent) is traded internationally (17). Nevertheless, world trade in wood products was worth about $50 billion in 1985 (18) and wood is the third most valuable primary commodity in world trade after petroleum and natural gas (19). Developed nations dominate world trade in wood products, accounting for 81 percent of imports and 87 percent of exports by value (20).

Trade occurs for a number of reasons. Primarily, it occurs to exchange different types of wood or products not grown or manufactured in respective trading countries. The demand for wood of some developed nations, including Japan and the countries in Western Europe, far exceeds supplies from their own forests. Similarly, some developing nations, like those in West Africa and the Middle East, have few forest resources and import most of their wood needs. And finally, most tree species in natural tropical forests are not suited to being converted into pulp and paper. The production of pulp and paper is thus concentrated in developed nations, and the earnings developing nations receive from timber exports are nearly offset by their imports of pulp and paper (21).

Less developed societies consume a large proportion of wood as fuel and sawnwood, but with economic development they consume more wood panels (like plywood) and paper. Technological advances allow more efficient use of wood in the form of composite panels like particle board and wafer board. Paper consumption rises as literacy increases in developing countries.

FUTURE TRENDS IN INDUSTRIAL WOOD PRODUCTION AND TRADE

World wood consumption has grown consistently since 1945. Total industrial roundwood removals increased from 981 million cubic meters in 1959 to 1.5 billion cubic meters in 1985 (22), a rise of 53 percent. A detailed forecast in 1982 by an FAO Industry Working Party (23) predicted that industrial roundwood removals would increase by 39 percent between 1980 and the year 2000 to reach 1.8 billion cubic meters. Another forecast published simultaneously by FAO was even more optimistic, projecting industrial roundwood removals of between 2.3 and 2.6 billion cubic meters by the year 2000 (24), although this has since been downgraded to 2 billion cubic meters (25).

A major problem with such forecasts is that until now they have been made in a comparatively crude manner that relies heavily on subjective assessments by experts of likely trends in wood supply and demand. Recently,

simulation models of national, regional, and global industrial wood production, processing, and trade have been developed to assess possible future trends more rigorously. Some models treat all types of forest products traded in a specific region (e.g., North America). Others focus on a particular product (e.g., paper) but have a global coverage. A few are ambitious enough to treat all products traded throughout the world.

With such models forest economists are no longer restricted to producing supposedly definitive forecasts at long, irregular intervals. Instead, they can run a model to test a range of different scenarios, (i.e., what happens when the basic assumptions about the future are changed.) Policymakers value these models because they show a variety of possible futures.

Trends in World Trade in Forest Products

The Forest Sector Project at the International Institute for Applied Systems Analysis (IIASA), based in Laxenburg, Austria, produced its Global Trade Model (GTM) after five years of collaboration among forest economists from around the world (26). The GTM projected future demand, supply, and trade for the period 1980–2030 for 16 types of forest products, including logs, fuelwood, sawnwood, wood panels, and pulp and paper. GTM was used to simulate a Base Scenario that contained a moderate set of assumptions about the future, and eight alternative scenarios.

In the Base Scenario, which assumed that the world economy would grow at a slightly lower rate than in the 1960s and 1970s, world industrial roundwood removals would increase from about 1.3 billion cubic meters in 1980 to 1.7 billion cubic meters by the year 2000 and to 2.6 billion cubic meters in 2030—double the 1980 figure. Changing the assumptions about the growth rate of the world economy changes the estimates of industrial roundwood removals. Under low growth and high growth assumptions, removals by the end of the century would be about 1.6 and 1.9 billion cubic meters respectively.

Two of the most interesting scenarios tested the effects of environmental change on forestry. The Acid Rain Scenario looked at the effects of air pollution on forest degradation in Western Europe and assumed that salvage harvests of dead trees would increase potential timber supply by 20 percent between 1985 and 1995 but reduce forest growth by one third. The resulting simulation suggested regional timber removals would be 6 percent higher in 1990 (not 20 percent because salvage harvests would substitute for ordinary removals), but would be about 12 percent lower than the Base Scenario in 2000 and 23 percent lower in 2030. (See Box 5.2.)

Another scenario simulated the effect of an increase in global temperature caused by the greenhouse effect resulting from higher levels of atmospheric carbon dioxide and certain trace gases. (See Chapter 10, "Atmosphere and Climate.") The impact of global warming is expected to be particularly pronounced in higher latitudes covered by coniferous forests where it would lead to more rapid tree growth and an expanded forest area. According to this scenario, by 2030 timber removals would be 33 percent higher in Canada and 50 percent higher in Finland

Box 5.2 Air Pollution Affects European Timber Production

Forest damage from multiple air pollutants is likely to have a major effect on future European timber production. Many dead and severely affected trees will have to be felled soon and forest managers may also decide to remove unaffected trees before they reach the age when they become most vulnerable to damage. As a result, the International Institute for Applied Systems Analysis Forest Sector Project estimated that the potential European timber supply could increase by as much as 20 percent over the next 10 years, although the actual increase will probably be much less because healthy trees that would otherwise have been felled will be left standing (1). In the longer term, however, reduced growth rates caused by pollution stress will likely lead to lower timber production. The effects on the environment as a whole are uncertain but if widespread sanitary fellings in the mountains of Central Europe are not carefully scheduled there could be significant increases in river flows from these watersheds and a greater risk of floods and landslides.

The extent of forest damage from multiple air pollutants and other stresses for the whole of Europe was assessed in 1987 by researchers who collated data on forest area damage from 17 European countries. They estimated that the total volume of trees in forests subject to "moderate or severe damage" is 1,808 million cubic meters: almost 15 percent of the timber volume in these countries and more than six times their total annual timber removals. Damage is particularly severe in Switzerland (25 percent of national timber volume affected), West Germany (21 percent), the Netherlands (20 percent), and Sweden (20 percent) (2). (An earlier assessment measured damage by area rather than volume. See *World Resources 1986*, pp. 203–226 and *World Resources 1987*, p. 155.)

References and Notes

1. Dennis P. Dykstra and Markku Kallio, "Scenario Variations," in *The Global Forest Sector: An Analytical Perspective*, Markku Kallio, Dennis P. Dykstra, and Clark S. Binkley, eds. (John Wiley, New York, 1987), p. 664.
2. Sten Nilsson and Peter Duinker, "The Extent of Forest Decline in Europe," *Environment*, Vol. 29, No. 9 (1987), pp. 7–8.

and the USSR, compared with the Base Scenario (27).

Studies have suggested that world demand for timber could eventually exceed the maximum level of supplies available from forests on a sustainable basis (28) (29). A good indication of the increasing scarcity of wood, or any other commodity, is a rise in its real price. Since 1965 the average real price of wood products in the world has, according to FAO, stayed roughly constant. However, simulations with the GTM suggested that wood will become much scarcer in the future. The simulations predicted steep increases in log prices, with the price of hardwood sawlogs rising faster than the price of softwood sawlogs and pulpwood prices rising more slowly. For example, in the Base Scenario over the period 1980–2010, hardwood and softwood log prices would rise by over 100 percent and 67 percent respectively in Japan and by 67 percent and 40 percent in Europe (30).

Such projections are contradicted by those emerging from another model specifically designed to look at long-term trends in average world timber prices. The global timber supply model built by Roger Sedjo of Resources for the Future and Kenneth Lyon of Utah State University assumed that by the year 2000 world industrial wood removals would increase to 1.8 billion cubic meters per year in the Base Scenario (slightly higher than the 1.7 cubic meters of removals in the Base Scenario of the GTM). Yet, according to Sedjo and Lyon, real timber prices would rise at only 0.2 percent per year (31). The Sedjo and Lyon projection accords with the expectations of many forest economists that real prices will remain essentially constant.

Trends in World Trade in Tropical Hardwoods

Whether or not timber becomes increasingly scarce at a world level, logging and deforestation threaten to deplete the timber reserves in the tropical rain forests. The tropical rain forests account for about 40 percent of all closed forests in the world and 60 percent of all closed broadleaved forests. They are the source of about 30 percent of all log exports, about 10 percent of all sawnwood exports and about 60 percent of all plywood and veneer

exports (32). What happens to this resource is therefore extremely important to the future of world industrial wood production and trade, irrespective of any ecological effects resulting from deforestation.

The TROPFORM model focuses on tropical hardwoods extracted from the tropical rain forests. TROPFORM, built by Alan Grainger at the Oxford Forestry Institute of the University of Oxford, was used to project trends in tropical hardwood supply, demand, and trade flows over the period 1980–2020 (33).

A variety of scenarios were simulated to test the effect of varying the trends in export demand, the rate of deforestation, the rate of regeneration of logged forests, and the increase in commercial timber reserves because

Figure 5.2 Trends in Tropical Hardwood Exports 1980–2020

(millions of cubic meters per annum)

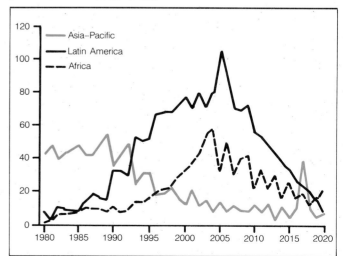

Source: Alan Grainger, "TROPFORM: A Model of Future Tropical Hardwood Supplies," in *Proceedings of CINTRAFOR Symposium of Forest Sector and Trade Models*, (College of Forest Resources, University of Washington, Seattle), Figure 2, p. 210.

of the discovery of new reserves and use of secondary species.

The simulations showed that future supplies of wood from the tropical rain forests are likely to be more limited than assumed by some previous forecasts. According to TROPFORM's Base Scenario, tropical hardwood exports would double by the year 2000, peak shortly afterwards, and then fall to 72 percent of their 1980 level by 2020. Removals would also double between 1980 and 2000, peaking in the first decade of the next century, but by 2020 they would still be more than 20 percent higher than in 1980. Future levels of tropical hardwood exports and removals would be significantly influenced by the rate of deforestation for agriculture.

The model also predicted a major shift in the sources of tropical hardwood exports from Asia-Pacific countries to Latin America. Asia-Pacific countries currently supply 80 percent of all exports, but depleted timber reserves and rising domestic consumption in Asia would reduce this share to only 10 percent by the year 2000. By the end of the century, Asian exports would be only one quarter of their 1980 level. TROPFORM predicted that Latin America would take over from Asia-Pacific as the leading exporter with a 63 percent share of the market by the end of the century. African exports would rise gradually to account for 27 percent share of all exports at that time. (See Figure 5.2.) Because Latin American tropical hardwoods are different from those in Asia-Pacific and the costs of logging and transport are much higher, this transition may not be a smooth one. (See Box 5.3.)

Can the general decline in removals and exports be prevented, while maintaining the resource base? The trends described above include the contribution of wood produced by intensive forest plantations, which have been considered a major potential source of industrial timber. However, by the year 2000 plantation removals will probably account for less than 2 percent of all tropical hardwood removals. Although plantation removals will rise in the next 10 years, they will decline sharply between 2011 and 2020. Because the minimum rotation for plantations producing high quality hardwoods is 30 years, a plantation established now will not affect the supply situation

Box 5.3 Trade in Tropical Hardwoods: Implications for Asian Countries

Asia has dominated the tropical hardwood trade since the early 1960s, supplying about 80 percent of world exports. Indonesia, Malaysia, and the Philippines had the advantage of extensive reserves of high-quality tropical hardwoods that could be extracted at a low cost and shipped to the nearby Japanese market. Until recently, Asian countries mainly exported logs to Japan and large quantities of sawnwood and plywood to Europe and the United States. Logs from the region's forests were converted into sawnwood and plywood in mills situated both in the Southeast Asian producing nations and in the newly industrialized East Asian countries of Hong Kong, South Korea, Singapore, and Taiwan. Since 1980, the East Asian countries have been eclipsed by the massive expansion of plywood capacity in Indonesia.

Asia's preeminence in world trade in tropical hardwoods is likely to decline before the end of the century, according to simulations with the TROPFORM model, because of the depletion of timber reserves by logging and deforestation for agriculture and because of rising domestic consumption [1]. (See also Figure 5.2.) The simulations show that wood for domestic needs could also be in short supply. Remaining reserves of tropical hardwoods in Asia are now only sufficient for current rates of removals to continue for about 40 years, much lower than in Africa and Latin America (85 years and 156 years respectively). Forty years is the accepted harvest cycle for selective logging in Asia [2].

Southeast Asian producing countries therefore should carefully reassess their forestry and land use policies to ensure that future timber removals will be adequate to supply the needs of both export and domestic markets in a sustainable way. Policy priorities might include:
■ *Bringing unplanned deforestation under*

control. Deforestation for agriculture exacts a heavy toll on the region's remaining timber reserves and every year destroys a volume of timber between 20 and 50 percent of that logged for commercial purposes. Controlling deforestation would have a significant effect on future levels of removals and exports over the next 30 years. Achieving this goal will require better land use planning to prevent forest from being cleared for agriculture on poor soils, the promotion of more productive agriculture on better soils, and close cooperation with local people who are more likely to protect forests if their own economic needs and dependence on the forests are taken into account.
■ *Protecting the 54 million hectares of previously logged forests so that regeneration can proceed unhindered by log poaching or agricultural clearing.* If protected, the forests can be logged again 30–40 years after their first logging. Simple protection is an interim measure until better management systems are developed and is vital if export and domestic supplies are to be kept as high as possible without seriously depleting the forest resource. This immediate priority will require a major increase in the number of forestry personnel.
■ *Improving the legal and physical protection of forests in national parks and biosphere reserves.* The status of these forests will probably become more precarious as pressures grow for timber production and agricultural expansion. Preserving areas of pristine forest is important for ecological reasons and to ensure sustained commercial forestry in the region. Forest researchers must have access to untouched forest to study the natural regeneration processes on which new forest management systems will depend. These reserves would also maintain the full genetic diversity of key timber species, which may be replanted in natural forests and grown

in intensive plantations.
■ *Developing and introducing more sustainable systems of forest management than the present selective logging systems.* This goal will require pure research into regeneration processes, applied research to find ways of promoting the growth of favored commercial species, and the training of forestry personnel in the new techniques subsequently developed.
■ *Continuing to establish intensive high-quality hardwood plantations, with an emphasis on medium-rotation (30–40 years) species instead of long-rotation teak.* Currently about 79,000 hectares of high-grade hardwood plantations are established in Southeast Asia each year, more than 80 percent of the total for the whole humid tropics [3]. Because of the anticipated pressures on supplies to the domestic market, more fast-growing plantations should also be established that can produce both hardwoods and softwoods to substitute for high-quality hardwoods for the domestic market.

References and Notes

1. Alan Grainger, "TROPFORM: A Model of Future Tropical Hardwood Supplies," in *Proceedings of CINTRAFOR Symposium on Forest Sector and Trade Models* (College of Forest Resources, University of Washington, Seattle, 1987), pp. 205–212.
2. Alan Grainger, "The Future Role of the Tropical Rain Forests in the World Forest Economy," PhD dissertation, University of Oxford, 1986, pp. 180–221, Table 17.
3. Alan Grainger, "Future Supplies of High Grade Tropical Hardwoods from Tropical Plantations," *Journal of World Forest Resource Management*, Vol. 3 (1988), pp. 15–29.

until 2020. Existing plantations will make only a small contribution to tropical hardwood removals in the foreseeable future because in the past 20–30 years too few high-quality hardwood plantations have been established. Currently, of the 722,000 hectares of plantations established each year in the humid tropics only 95,000 hectares (13 percent) can produce high-grade hardwoods similar to those from the tropical rain forests (34).

Tropical countries have recently established more pulpwood plantations on shorter rotations to reduce their huge paper import bills. Emphasis is also shifting from industrial wood plantations toward tree planting for environmental protection and establishing small woodlots for fuelwood production. Industrial plantations increased from 39 percent of the total planting rate in the 1950s to 85 percent in the 1960s, but by the late 1970s the share had fallen to only 58 percent. High-quality hardwood plantations accounted for 29 percent of the industrial plantations established in the 1950s. This rose to 49 percent in the 1960s, but fell back to only 23 percent by the late 1970s (35).

Because in the immediate future supplies of tropical hardwoods will come largely from natural forests rather than plantations, it would make sense to increase new investment in the management and protection of natural forests. The focus on intensive plantations has led to the neglect of natural forest management in the tropics for the past 20–30 years. Only 1 percent of natural productive tropical moist forests (9 million hectares) was under management in 1980 (36) (37) (38).

Emphasizing natural forest management does not mean that plantation establishment should slow down. Increased planting rates are essential, especially in the Asia-Pacific region, but more medium-rotation (30–40 years) plantations could be encouraged over teak, which takes 60–70 years to mature (39).

RANGELAND RESOURCES

Rangelands are extensive tracts of arid and semiarid lands that are essentially unsuited to rainfed crop cultivation, industrial forestry, protected forests, or urbanization. Without the addition of irrigation systems or other expensive technological inputs, the best use of rangelands is for livestock and wildlife production. Rangelands are a renewable resource that requires little or no commercial energy input to produce meat, milk, wool, hides, and other animal products (40). More than 200 million people use rangelands worldwide for some form of pastoral production, and 30 to 40 million of these people are wholly dependent on livestock. The majority of the world's pastoralists, about 55 percent, are in Africa, 29 percent in Asia, 15 percent in the Americas, and the remaining 1 percent in Australia (41). In northern tropical African countries, pastoral populations make up 10 to 25 percent of the national population, with even higher figures for Sudan, Somalia, and Chad (42). Their economic contribution is great; for example, exports of live animals and meat from Somalia accounted for 82 percent of the country's total export of agricultural products in 1985 (43).

Although no comprehensive global assessment of the

Table 5.4 Distribution of the World's Pastures and Rangelands, 1955–85

(in millions of hectares)

Region	Area of Permanent Pasture[a]				Area of Estimated Wooded and Other Land 1985[b]	Total Estimated Pasture and Range	
	1955	1985	Percent Change 1955–85	Percent of Total Range- land		1985[c]	Percent of Total Land Area
North America	277	272	−2	30	644	916	47
Europe	83	84	+1	55	69	153	31
USSR	124	375	+202	44	480	855	38
Central America	79	95	+20	66	50	145	47
South America	330	458	+39	56	367	825	46
Africa	615	789	+28	41	1,155	1,944	64
Asia	473	645	+36	51	615	1,260	46
Oceania	377	453	+20	73	166	619	73
World	**2,358**	**3,171**	**+35**	**47**	**3,546**	**6,717**	**50**

Sources:
1. United Nations Food and Agriculture Organization (FAO), *Production Yearbook 1955* (FAO, Rome, 1958), Table 1.
2. United Nations Food and Agriculture Organization (FAO), *Production Yearbook 1986* (FAO, Rome, 1987), Table 1.

Notes:
a. Includes permanent meadows and pastures and land that has been used for five years or more for the production of herbaceous forage crops, whether cultivated or wild.
b. Sum of open forests in 1980 (see *World Resources 1987*) and 50 percent of "other land" in 1985.
c. Sum of areas of permanent pasture (1985) and wooded and other land (1985).

extent of rangelands exists, the best estimates are from the United Nations Food and Agriculture Organization (FAO). (See Table 5.4.) About half the land area in the world can be classified as rangeland. This includes permanent meadows and pastures (either wild or cultivated), open forests and woodlands—also claimed as "forestland"—savannas and steppes, and lands not suited to other uses. This figure underestimates the total available forage for livestock because it excludes the considerable biomass from crop by-products, fallow lands and sylvo-pastoral systems such as livestock grazing under coconut plantations. The figures in Table 5.4 are the best available. However, the estimates for developing countries are rarely based on recent surveys.

Rangelands provide more than half the area for livestock production on a worldwide basis, but regional differences are considerable. Livestock production in much of the Far East (with the notable exceptions of China, Mongolia and Indonesia) is almost entirely intensive and depends on "backyard" operations with crop by-products and supplemental feed (44) (45). By contrast, such South American countries as Argentina, Uruguay, and Paraguay rely primarily on rangelands, which can comprise up to 80 percent of their total land area (46). The intensity of use of available rangelands varies significantly from one country to another. For example, 23 million hectares of grass savanna in Indonesia are currently underutilized, while almost all vegetation types accessible to livestock in India are heavily grazed to overgrazed (47).

Loss of Rangelands

In recent years, pastoralists in much of the world have had to contend with the gradual loss of rangelands, which are converted to cropland. In Asia, the total area of arable and permanent cropland increased by 3.3 percent between 1970 and 1985, whereas the total area of permanent pastures decreased by 2.8 percent (48). In Portugal, lands better suited to permanent pasture are being converted to wheat and other crops resulting in problems of erosion and decreasing fertility (49). The conversion of rangeland into cropland is also occurring in South America, especially in northern Argentina and southern Brazil (50), although this trend is offset on a regional basis with the conversion of tropical forests (such as in the Amazon Basin) to extensive ranches (51).

The highest loss of grazing lands is probably occurring in the semiarid zones of sub-Saharan Africa because of increasing populations, expansion of cultivators into rangelands (52), development of government-sponsored irrigation schemes, such as the Bura and Hola Schemes in Kenya (53), and in some cases, transfer of land from smallholders and pastoralists to large-scale private agribusinesses (54). For example, the Il Chamus pastoralists in Baringo District of Kenya have lost an estimated 75 percent of their dry season grazing areas to cultivators (55).

The expansion of cultivation at the expense of rangelands has resulted in fragmented land use patterns. As a result, grazing livestock no longer have clear access paths through the fields to pastures and fallow land. Most of the woody species on which they browse have been cleared from fallow land for fuelwood and cultivation purposes (56). In the more humid zones where less land is available for crop expansion, farmers are forced to shorten fallow cycles, thus reducing the availability of fallow grazing.

RANGELAND CONDITIONS IN ASIA

Asia encompasses a multitude of developed and developing countries, widely differing geographic settings, and extremes in bioclimatic regions. Rangeland types include arctic tundras, temperate grasslands, annual desert grasslands, semiarid shrublands, grazing areas carved from monsoon forests, and even swamplands. Asia contains about 645 million hectares of permanent pasture, the richest type of rangeland. Sixty-three percent of Asia's permanent pasture occurs in China and Mongolia, 42 percent in Near Eastern countries, and less than 1 percent in the Far East and Indochina region (57).

World Resources 1987 presented tabular summaries of rangeland conditions and trends for the Western Asian countries of Syria, Yemen Arab Republic, People's Democratic Republic of Yemen, Iraq, Oman, Jordan, Saudi Arabia, and Iran. (See *World Resources 1987*, Table 5.8, pp. 68–69.) This section focuses on the rest of Asia, excluding the Asian parts of the USSR, for which little current information is available. Far Eastern countries are also excluded, because they generally have small areas of rangeland and little current information is available. Table 5.5 presents information on range conditions for selected countries in Asia. The area of permanent pasture, rather than the area of rangeland, is given because data on permanent pasture area is available for all Asian countries. Rangelands generally include permanent pasture plus other lands.

The Indian Subcontinent

Within the Indian subcontinent, permanent pastures account for 12 million hectares—only about 4 percent of the total land area for the countries of India, Nepal, Sri Lanka, Bangladesh, and Bhutan. In India, the area of permanent pasture declined by 8 percent between 1975 and 1985 (58). For the subcontinent, the FAO classified 49 million hectares (four times the amount of permanent pasture) as "other land"; much of this can be considered rangeland (59).

With the exception of Sri Lanka, where degradation was not reported, most rangelands on the subcontinent are described as overgrazed, with the extensive removal of both herbaceous and woody plant cover, compaction and erosion of the soil, a general loss of carrying capacity, and destabilization of sand dunes. The principal causes noted are overstocking of livestock, drought, improper management, and expansion of agriculture into rangeland areas.

India has long been engaged in rangeland development programs through privatization of land, introduction of improved forage plants, and application of fertilizers (60). India has done considerable research on strategies for common property resource management and has achieved favorable results with experiments on reclaiming degraded arid rangelands by reseeding with improved plant species, fertilizing, establishing proper stocking rates, fencing, and improving management practices (61).

China and Mongolia

The permanent pasture in the People's Republic of China (PRC) is about 290 million hectares and the rangeland is estimated at 340 million hectares (62) (63). It is the third largest grazing area in the world, after Australia and the USSR (64). A World Bank report classifies approximately 55 percent of the total agricultural land in China as range and pasture (65). The FAO estimates that Mongolia contains 123 million hectares of permanent pasture (66), but no information is available on the condition of rangelands in Mongolia (67).

China's grazing lands can be divided into two broad regions: the northern "pastoral" and the southern "agricultural" zones. The Great Wall of China was constructed to separate the nomads of the northern pasturelands from the sedantarized farmers to the south (68). The majority of China's rangeland occurs in the northern pastoral zone. The Chinese perceive these extensive grazing areas as an underutilized resource that can contribute to their national goal of increased livestock production.

Reports of range condition by Western scientists seem contradictory. A World Bank report states that much of this land is already seriously overgrazed (69). Other scientists present a different analysis. For example, while wind and water erosion appear to be a serious and widespread problem in the northwest, overgrazing was not as ubiquitous and seemed to be more the result of poor livestock distribution (70). Site specific observations on state animal husbandry farms in Inner Mongolia in northeast

Table 5.5 Rangeland Conditions in Selected Asian Countries

Country/Locality Size of Permanent Pasture[a]	Range Condition	Range Trend	Causes	Remedial Activities	Source
India 11,850,000 hectares (ha)	• Highly degraded • Overgrazed	• Soil erosion • Desertification • Reduction in ratio of grazing land per animal • Gradual conversion of forests to savannahs; if savannahs are overgrazed they become steppes	• Overstocking of sheep and goats • Expanded agriculture into marginal areas • Government neglect • No management of fodder production or rangelands	• Rajistan Forest Department: pasture land development through controlled grazing • "Drought-Prone Areas Programme" • National and regional efforts to increase fodder production • Experiments in reclaiming degraded rangelands by reseeding, fertilizing and fencing	1,2,3,4
Sri Lanka 439,000 ha	• Native grasses not of high value for grazing • Area not reported to be degraded	• Gradual increase in livestock numbers	• Livestock grazing areas frequently affected by cyclones, heavy rains, overflowing water tanks • Objections by religious groups limit range animal production	• Man and Biosphere experiment with drought resistant herbage	1,5,6
Nepal 1,978,000 ha Rangelands are concentrated in mountainous areas	• Degraded • Overgrazed	• Soil erosion on steep slopes • Deforestation	• Excess of unproductive livestock • Closing of Tibetan border to livestock from Nepal causes overgrazing		1,7,8,9,10,11
Pakistan 5,000,000 ha Rangelands concentrated in Baluchistan	• Poor: estimated that most of the rangelands are producing 10–15% of their potential • The "former acacia savanna" of the alluvial plains of the Indus River is considered the most important grazing area • Dry • Overgrazed • Majority are completely devastated • Elimination of entire species of edible plants • Quetta Valley and valley floors: completely devastated • Other areas: dry and heavily used	• Soil erosion • Desertification • Extensive damage to vegetation cover	• Overstocking: the country is estimated to be overstocked by three times • Heavy nomadic traffic • Fuelwood gathering by city dwellers		1,3,12,13,14,15
Afghanistan 30,000,000 ha	• Low mountains of the Hindukush north slope are good summer pasture • Southern desert is good winter range • Southern areas around Kandahar and the heart of the region are heavily overgrazed • Some fair to good grazing lands still exist in the heavily grazed southeastern foothills of high mountains of Hazaradiat	• In many areas rangelands have seriously declined, and this trend is evidently continuing	• Uncontrolled stocking, especially along major migration routes • Fuelwood gathering • Steady expansion of dryland cultivation	• Department of animal husbandry is introducing improved pasture forage plants	1,3
Bhutan 218,000 ha	• Poor forage quality in subtropical areas	• Years of heavy grazing • Animal production reduced in recent years	• Improper management • Shortage of trained personnel	• Burning of rangelands to expand grazing land	1,16
People's Republic of China 285,690,000	• 41% of total land used for grazing • 25% of grasslands deteriorated	• Erosion is "dangerously accelerated" • Loss of productivity • Desertification	• Population pressure • 27% of desertification attributed to overgrazing • Government heavily favored agriculture over rangelands during the 1950s • Conversion of remaining thin forest and good grassland into cultivated fields		1,17,18,19

Table 5.5

Country/Locality Size of Permanent Pasture[a]	Range Condition	Range Trend	Causes	Remedial Activities	Source
North China	• Too arid • Unproductive • Poor grazing land • Heavily overgrazed • Badly eroded • Heavily utilized • Low forage production • Poor forage quality	• Soil erosion by wind and water • Plant cover deteriorated • Deterioration occurs at faster pace than rehabilitation • Low production	• Removal of some of the best grasslands from livestock grazing for agriculture and urban development has placed increased pressure on remaining rangeland • Formerly productive grasslands are now sand dunes • Conversion of pastures into grainfields caused serious damage to grass • Communal grazing • Poor management of grasses and fodder crops	• Irrigation and tree planting projects to aid in leveling sand dunes • Limited efforts to rehabilitate badly deteriorated grazing lands, emphasis on management of rehabilitated lands or other presently deteriorating rangelands	17,20,21
South China	• Poor pasture quality • Restricted seasonal grazing time • Low carrying capacity	• Poor cattle growth		• Gaopoling Model Beef Farm: Pasture technology for improving wasteland in Hainan Island preliminary results showed improved range conditions after a program of planting improved legumes	18,19

Sources:
1. United Nations Food and Agriculture Organization (FAO), *Production Yearbook 1986* (FAO, Rome, 1987), Table 1, pp. 8–10.
2. U.S. Man and the Biosphere, *Draft Environmental Report on India* (Library of Congress, Washington, D.C., 1980), p. 44.
3. Center for Science and Environment (CSE), *The State of India's Environment 1984–85: The Second Citizens Report* (CSE, New Delhi, 1985), pp. 3–14.
4. Stephen Sandford, *Management of Pastoral Development in the Third World* (John Wiley and Sons, 1983), p. 99.
5. U.S. Man and the Biosphere, *Draft Environmental Report on Sri Lanka* (Library of Congress, Washington, D.C., 1987), pp. 64–65.
6. Evaluation Technologies, Inc., *Sri Lanka: A Country Profile* (Office of U.S. Foreign Disaster Assistance (United States Agency for International Development, Washington, D.C., 1983), p. 15.
7. U.S. Man and the Biosphere, *Draft Environmental Report on Nepal* (Library of Congress, Washington, D.C., 1979), p. 50.
8. M.B. Karki and E.T. Bartlett, "A Multi-level Planning Model for Natural Resource Management Analyzing Whole Systems of Production in the Hill Region of Nepal," in *Rangelands: A Resource Under Siege*, P.J. Joss, P.W. Lynch, and O.B. Williams, eds. (Cambridge University Press, Cambridge, 1986), p. 487.
9. Daniel J. Miller, "High Elevation Grasslands of Nepal," *Rangelands*, Vol. 8, No. 3 (1986), pp. 112–114.
10. Evaluation Technologies, Inc., *Nepal: A Country Profile* (Office of U.S. Foreign Disaster Assistance, United States Agency for International Development, Washington, D.C., 1983), p. 16.
11. International Union for Conservation of Nature and Natural Resources (IUCN), *National Conservation Strategy for Nepal* (IUCN, Gland, Switzerland, 1983).
12. *Ecological Management of Arid and Semi-Arid Rangelands (EMASAR—PHASE II), Volume VI Middle East*, (FAO-U.N., Rome, 1978).
13. U.S. Man and the Biosphere, *Draft Environmental Profile—The Islamic Republic of Pakistan*" (Arid Lands Information Center, The University of Arizona, Tuscon, 1981), p. 26.
14. Nek M. Buzdar and Donald Jameson, "Range Management and Shepherds in Baluchistan, Pakistan," *Rangelands*, Vol. 6, No. 6 (1984), pp. 243–246.
15. United Nations Economic and Social Commission for Asia and the Pacific (ESCAP) *Environmental Impact Assessment in Pakistan* (ESCAP, Bangkok, 1986), pp. 2–8.
16. Daniel J. Miller, "Rangelands of the Himalayan Kingdom of Bhutan," *Rangelands*, Vol. 9, No. 6 (1987), pp. 258–259.
17. D.H. Gates, "Rangelands Management and Livestock Production in Northeastern China," *Rangelands*, Vol. 8, pp. 230–232.
18. D.L. Michalk, *et al.*, "Improvement of Wasteland in Tropical South China," in *Rangelands: A Resource Under Siege*, P.J. Joss, P.W. Lynch, and O.B. Williams, eds. (Cambridge University Press, Cambridge, 1986), p. 313.
19. Wu Chuan-Chun, "Land Utilization," *Managing the Environment in China*, Qu Geping and Woyen Lee, eds. (Tycooly International Publishing, Dublin, 1984), Table 3.1, p. 68.
20. Ze-jiang Zhou, "Land Use in China," *Land*, Vol. 8, No. 1 (1987), p. 8.
21. B.E. Dahl and C.M. McKell, "Use and Abuse of China's Deserts and Rangelands," *Rangelands*, Vol. 8, pp. 267–270.
Note: a. Size of Rangeland: Figures are those given by the United Nations Food and Agriculture Organization for Permanent Pasture, which underestimates total size of rangeland.

China provide an even more favorable picture: for example on the Zuer Tala Farm, the range was judged to be between high-fair to high-good condition (71).

Although Chinese rangelands are concentrated in the north, southern China contains more than 40 percent of the livestock (72). Overall, range conditions in the south and southwest part of China are ecologically better than in the northern pastoral zone, but animal production tends to be low because of poor soil fertility and the low nutrient value of the native forage (73).

Chinese surveys indicate that 21 percent of their rangelands are not being used to their full potential. In order to increase livestock production, the Chinese are attempting to expand the area of cultivated pastures that produce fodder from 1–2 percent of the total grazing land to 10 percent. Chinese range scientists estimate the cultivated pasture area would have to expand to 20–25 percent of the total rangeland area to fully develop the livestock industry. Parallel to this effort are programs to augment forage seed research and production. Because the 30 existing seed farms cannot meet the demand, the government is now paying farmers 5–10 times the price of grain to produce grass seeds (74).

Most of the world's pastoralists (55 percent) live in Africa. More than 100 million people there make at least part of their living herding livestock. Numerous types of development projects have been undertaken to raise the productivity and standard of living of pastoralists, but most have failed. Between the late 1960s and early 1980s, $625 million of international funds was invested in sub-Saharan Africa for livestock development projects (75). But by 1987 agencies were so disenchanted with the failure of livestock development in Africa that funds for such activities were drastically cut. For example, the United States Agency for International Development (76) stopped funding new rangeland projects after an evaluation report in 1983 and has phased out most of its old ones, leaving only such single-target projects as veterinary care and animal breeding. Most other bilateral agencies have concentrated on the humid zones and decreased their involvement with rangelands. Official commitments from all multilateral and bilateral sources to livestock projects as a share of all agriculture, forestry, and fisheries projects, fell from 3.5 percent in 1977–79 to 2 percent in 1983–84 (77), with most of the cutbacks occurring in rangeland projects. One exception to the rule is the FAO, which in 1986–87 invested $161 million in addition to its regular program for livestock and natural resource projects worldwide (78). In 1985, the FAO had initiated the Agricultural Rehabilitation Programme for Africa (ARPA) that by June 1987 had a total budget of $289 million. Its 273 projects included 52 projects dealing with livestock and rangelands (79).

History of Rangeland Development Projects

Since the early 1950s, livestock and range development projects in sub-Saharan Africa have gone through many changes in concept, design, and implementation. In general, they attempted to replace traditional pastoral systems, which had been used for ages in drylands, with modern concepts of range management derived from experience with ranches and economic systems in the developed countries. However, the lack of continuity between old and new techniques, and the fact that the new technology often had few advantages over the old system, contributed to the failure of the new systems. Now a fresh look is being taken at what can be learned from traditional systems.

Animal Health, Water Development, and Land Tenure

In the early 1960s, Africa was viewed by development agencies as a vast, sparsely populated, arid land suited only to livestock production. It suffered from a lack of adequate water and was beset by bush fires. Herders experienced high animal mortality and used poor breeding practices (80). Thus, funds were mobilized for interventions to provide animal health services and reliable water sources. These included veterinary clinics and vaccination teams supplied with health kits, vaccines and trained veterinarians, and boreholes that could pump water from deep aquifers (81).

These interventions benefited local populations but also created unforeseen problems for rangelands (82). For example, veterinary actions independent of complementary efforts to increase rangeland productivity usually led to overstocking.

Likewise, government-sponsored boreholes in Botswana and Senegal attracted herds from distant lands, and after a few years, the areas around them became virtual deserts. Water development projects shifted toward the construction of catchment ponds that captured surface runoff from rainfall rather than tapping groundwater (83). They hold far less water than boreholes, thus do not attract vast numbers of animals. However, catchment ponds proved to be difficult to repair and maintain because the external donors or government agencies who founded them initially expected the local people to repair them. However, the local people viewed the ponds as public works and did not feel responsible for their maintenance.

In the 1950s the ownership of almost all rangelands was legally transferred to the state. Yet, most governments lacked the financial, technical, and logistical means to supervise and maintain the public rangelands. At the same time, nationalization eliminated rules that traditional societies followed to prevent abuse of rangelands. Thus local users no longer had the incentive, nor the capability, to ensure the long-term sustainability of the rangelands (84) (85).

Commercialization

By the mid-1960s, development agencies, led primarily by the World Bank, sought to reduce the problem of overstocking by attempting to transform subsistence pastoralism into the beginnings of commercial livestock production. Destocking was to be achieved by increasing the offtake rate (the number of livestock sold as a percent of the total herd) (86) (87), but this did not work well. The offtake rate from most herds remained in the traditional range of 5 to 12 percent (88), rather than the expected increase to 25 or 35 percent. Efforts to increase the marketing of animals continue, but interventions have been modified by the realization that large herds of animals constitute a form of savings bank for herders— insurance against losses caused by a harsh and inconsistent environment (89). It is now recognized that, without the provision of such viable alternatives as easy access to credit, banks, and insurance schemes, the marketing strategy of pastoralists cannot be expected to change.

Responses to the 1968–74 Drought

In the late 1960s and early 1970s, one of the worst droughts of the century hit sub-Saharan Africa. This prompted a renewed effort by international aid agencies to fund livestock projects, with greater emphasis on solving the problem of rangeland degradation, which appeared to engulf the entire area (90). Efforts were made to sedentarize the nomads, to organize them into group ranches, and to start range rehabilitation projects. But most sedentarization programs resulted in further degradation of range and farmland because the arid zone's low and irregular rainfall could not support an immobile population (91). As a result, by the early 1980s, most sedentarization programs had lost their funding (92).

Group ranches, which recognized Africa's communally organized societies, attempted to vest land tenure with local people. However, most of them failed (93). In many cases, the land allocated to each family or group was insufficient for their needs (94). In some cases, the pastoralists failed to respect ranch boundaries, which were often drawn by project personnel independent of traditionally recognized boundaries between ethnic groups.

Rehabilitation projects, usually involving tree planting and fenced enclosures to stimulate natural regeneration of degraded lands, were limited in their extent and survival. The costly fencing (usually done with imported barbed wire) required external funding and was feasible for only relatively small enclosures. More emphasis is now being placed on convincing traditional herders to guide their animals away from degraded lands (95). Early afforestation programs had limited success because many used non-native species not adapted to local ecological conditions or peoples' needs. They also hired outside workers to plant the trees. Thus the trees often fell prey to local flocks of sheep and goats, or to clandestine felling for firewood. Rehabilitation projects now emphasize choosing native species recommended by the people and involving the people in the design and implementation phases.

A New Approach

The need for participation by local people in the development process has been the common lesson learned from every failure encountered in the past three decades. However, it has proven difficult to practice (96). Most popular participation efforts are passive: the government informs the people of what it plans to do and asks them for their assistance in terms of labor or other resources. In most cases, assistance is readily given, but because these efforts do not incorporate the local people into the decisionmaking process, they often reflect the objectives of the government rather than the local people. Projects that do not reflect local objectives, especially if there is a lack of continuity between old and new ways, tend to be abandoned after funding is stopped or reduced (97) (98). A new style of development is increasingly being called for—one that allows pastoralists and development workers to interact over a longer period of time (say 10 to 15 years, rather than the usual 3 to 5 years of a project). These projects have less technological input, and more reliance on local knowledge and self-help. They are a cooperative search for appropriate technologies and local organizational structures for development (99).

Traditional Knowledge

Many studies have documented the sophistication of local peoples' traditional knowledge of natural resources (100). Traditional knowledge is descriptive (types, names, and properties of soils, flora, and fauna), analytic (ecological dynamics of environmental adaptation, succession, degradation, competition or complement between parts), spatial (location of useful vegetation and wildlife), and practical (limits of exploitation and reaction to human pressure). It is used in daily herding practices to monitor rangelands for signs of overuse, select the best pastures, and defer the use of other pastures (101) (102) (103).

Traditional knowledge can, however, have its shortcomings. Developed under conditions of relatively limitless land and low human and livestock pressure, its objective was to maintain productivity in the short run. Consequently, if loss of soil potential or long-term degradation did occur, there was enough new land in the vicinity onto which to move, allowing ample time for the former pastures to regenerate naturally. In addition, the level of knowledge depends on the level and type of need: for example, nomadic groups have more detailed knowledge of plants and soils than transhumants or settled agropastoralists (104). Finally, traditional knowledge lacks the detailed specialized scientific understanding of such factors as nutrients, disease vectors, and other microprocesses (105). Much traditional knowledge has been lost or is no longer applicable, given changes such as population growth, commercialization, and nationalization of land. Yet, it should be analyzed to discover what can be modified with modern technologies to meet development needs.

Traditional Institutions

Most pastoral groups had developed traditional political institutions (e.g., vertical hierarchy of nations, tribes, and subtribes) and flexible cooperative units (e.g., "chiefs of grass," herding groups, and range monitors). These institutions were used to regulate the use of rangelands, the scheduling of movements within the group and among tribes, the temporary or permanent closure of certain areas to grazing, the granting of rights to outsiders for use of the pastures, etc. (106) (107) (108).

These institutions depended on political alliances and understandings between groups. Starting in the mid-1930s and earlier in some cases, these alliances began to break down because of government policies aimed at breaking tribal political power. Tribal power was further reduced because of land tenure changes, decreasing range resources and competition for more scarce resources, population increase, recurrent droughts, migration to new lands, and settlement in villages and urban areas (109).

Combining the Old and New

One common attribute of the development technologies described in the previous section is that they have *not been any better* over the long term than traditional management strategies in meeting the peoples' needs (110). On the other hand, many of the traditional systems no longer survive, and it is unrealistic to attempt to revive them. However, some traditional systems, or parts thereof, remain viable and can be enhanced with modern scientific knowledge to deal with rangeland degradation. An idea borrowed from the people, developed by the agronomist or range manager, and returned to the people again is much more likely to be adopted than something totally alien to the culture (111). For example, plans for grazing rotation and deferment can be developed with local herders, couched in their language, and based on their knowledge of rangelands (112).

Vocational training in such modern concepts as range condition analysis and range reseeding could be combined with local knowledge of native plants to develop a new class of professional herder (113). To stem the tide of outmigration of the young, the new/old nature of pastoralism could be emphasized in school curricula. A network of field monitors could be based on traditional range supervisors for an early warning system of range degradation. Areas that appear to be managed well by local people with no serious environmental problems could be classified as research stations in order to grant the people and development workers time to study and modernize the traditional systems (114).

Most higher level traditional institutions no longer exist. However, the lower level groups (the cooperative units for managing herds, water, pasture, and markets), remain viable and could provide the nucleus to develop herders' associations (115).

Some rangeland projects are incorporating traditional systems into their grazing management plans. For example, the plans drawn up by the Leo Ranch in Burkina Faso are based on traditional use patterns and on a system of range supervisors (116). Each herders' association is allocated a grazing area based on the traditional boundaries between communally owned lands. The associations are given legal title to the land to check the expansion of cultivators. Each association elects a herder who, as range supervisor, is responsible for monitoring the movements of herds and reporting violations of the grazing plans to a central committee composed of leaders of each association.

The World Bank's livestock and range project in eastern Senegal has helped organize and allocate grazing lands to about 50 herders' associations. A few of these associations have already instituted seasonal grazing plans aimed at avoiding degraded lands in the wet season to allow them to regenerate. Such a seasonal deferment schedule is traditional, but fell out of use when land was nationalized. The herders' associations meet regularly to review grazing plans (117). Although it is too soon to give a final judgment on all of these efforts, the initial signs are promising.

RECENT DEVELOPMENTS

TROPICAL FORESTRY ACTION PLAN PUSHES NATIONAL FORESTRY REVIEWS

Top representatives from government, development agencies, industry, and nongovernmental organizations (NGOs) met in Bellagio, Italy, in July 1987 to move the Tropical Forestry Action Plan (TFAP) toward influencing national forestry policies.

The TFAP is an ongoing process initiated in 1985 by the United Nations Food and Agriculture Organization (FAO), the World Resources Institute, the United Nations Development Programme, and the World Bank to coor-

dinate human needs, environmental management, and sustainable forest development.

The Bellagio statement listed several steps to alleviate tropical deforestation and promote the sustainable use of the world's forests (118). One step suggests that nations put a price tag on deforestation and figure these costs into national economic and development plans. Once the true costs of deforestation are known, both national governments and international development agencies may follow a more rational path to protect tropical forest ecosystems.

National forestry reviews assess the extent of a country's deforestation and target areas for remedial action. National forestry specialists, often with the assistance of FAO consultants, are conducting reviews in 50 countries throughout Africa, Latin America, and Asia. The information will be integrated into long-range development plans that can lead to policy reforms, such as providing farmers with incentives to revive degraded forest land for farming rather than clearing more trees. The country assessments have already influenced international development projects and national programs in Ghana, Sudan, and Kenya (119).

Community and private involvement is crucial for the action plan to succeed, the Bellagio statement said. Government policies cannot combat the deforestation crisis without the support of local groups. The statement calls for incentives to entice private investment in reforestation projects, especially those involving small farmers and women.

The TFAP also encourages the participation of NGOs and local citizens' groups. The World Resources Institute and the Environment Liaison Centre cosponsored workshops in Nairobi, Panama City, and Bangkok in 1987 to explore expanding the roles of citizens' groups in tropical forest protection. In working with international and national agencies, NGOs provide a grassroots perspective on local needs, policies, and projects. A separate NGO statement to the Bellagio meeting said stemming tropical deforestation is the mutual responsibility of all nations and NGOs must become "full players" in determining national forestry policies (120). Despite these efforts, the TFAP has been criticized for neglecting the needs and ideas of forest dwellers (121). A recent set of FAO guidelines for the national forestry reviews stress the need to consider the roles of indigenous peoples, women, and NGOs in these national assessments.

A 13-member international task force, established by the Bellagio group, identified forestry research as a weak link in the conservation process. The task force outlined broad research priorities and listed roadblocks, such as inadequate funding and political support, to forestry research programs in tropical countries. A second Bellagio meeting, scheduled for late 1988, will look at research strategies to implement the TFAP (122).

INTERNATIONAL TROPICAL TIMBER ORGANIZATION STARTS WORK

The new International Tropical Timber Organization (ITTO), in which producers and consumers of tropical timber cooperate to support the growth of the industry through improved forest management, timber processing, and marketing, established its headquarters at Yokohama, Japan in 1987. ITTO coordinates action to implement the International Tropical Timber Agreement, which came into force in 1985 under the auspices of the United Nations Conference on Trade and Development (UNCTAD). (See *World Resources 1986*, p. 79.)

Forty-two countries have now signed the Agreement and become members of ITTO. These include 24 consuming countries, and 18 producing countries, which account for 70 percent of all tropical forests and 95 percent of tropical timber exports.

The main aims of ITTO are to improve market intelligence, assist producing countries to develop better techniques for reforestation and forest management, encourage increased timber processing in producing countries, and support research and development programs to achieve these goals. Unlike other intergovernmental commodity organizations, ITTO does not attempt to intervene in world markets to ensure stable prices and supplies.

ITTO's first projects are getting under way. Sixteen projects were approved in 1987 and by the spring of 1988, 12 of these projects were being implemented.

Several projects focus on improving reforestation and forest management. One is looking at the management of tropical forests for multiple purposes, so management systems may be devised that include both the production of timber and various minor forest products such as oils and rattans (used in furniture manufacture). Another project is investigating ways to rehabilitate the 3.5 million hectares of tropical rain forest in the Indonesian province of East Kalimantan, on the island of Borneo, that was damaged by fire and drought in 1982–83. A project in Brazil will study ways of developing improved techniques for forest management in the Amazon Basin.

One of the most encouraging aspects of ITTO is that producing and consuming countries are working together towards sustainable management of tropical forests. Environmental conservation is also in the forefront of their concerns. Thus among future projects is one that will suggest ways to modify logging systems to reduce their environmental impact.

RADIOACTIVE RANGELAND

Vast areas of rangelands, forests, and water supplies were contaminated as a result of the nuclear accident at the Chernobyl plant in April 1986. By the summer of 1988, lingering radioactivity in most forests and grasslands had dropped below levels of concern, but the long-lived cesium 137 continued to be a problem on lichen-covered rangelands in northern Sweden, Norway, and Finland, and on some grasslands in northern England.

As in other areas, radionuclides fell unevenly on grasslands in the county of Cumbria in northwest England. There, 1,600 farms were restricted from marketing sheep grazed in irradiated pasture; the British government required farmers to submit their flocks for radiation testing. Animals registering above Britain's maximum allowable radiation limit of 1,000 bequerels per kilogram were color-coded as unsafe for consumption and sent back to pasture, where they remained for a month or two until their radiation levels had dropped to acceptable levels [123]. By May of 1988, sheep from only 150 farms in Cumbria (with animals at other locations in northern Wales, Scotland, and Ireland) were still being monitored. Although this decrease in high levels of contamination is a positive sign, the British Landowner's Association has warned that restrictions on U.K. sheep exports will likely remain in force in some of these northern pastures for 30 years [124].

This 30-year waiting period reflects the half life of cesium 137, a primary pollutant among those released with the Chernobyl fallout. Cesium causes the greatest concern in the fragile and slow-growing lichen pastures in northern Sweden, Norway, and Finland, where nearly half a million reindeer graze [125]. The presence of cesium here is significant because lichens take their nutrients from the air and cannot break down contaminants as quickly as grasses or other plants with roots can [126]. Because of these high radiation levels, some of the region's approximately 7,000 reindeer herders have been forced to move the deer to less productive forests where overgrazing is already a problem. Bringing in alternate feed for the reindeer would be too expensive for the farmers in the long run [127]. Reindeer herding remains the foundation of the approximately 70,000 member Scandinavian Sami culture, and long-term contamination of these arctic pastures could threaten the Sami way of life [128] [129].

At the end of 1986, 85 percent of Sweden's reindeer meat registered above the government's 300 bequerels per kilogram limit. Some animals showed radiation levels up to 30,000 bequerels per kilogram. To help farmers, the government bought the contaminated meat and fed it to minks, which are raised for their fur, or buried it in pits in uninhabited areas [130]. Sweden's cost for this solution was estimated at $20 million for just one year [131].

Although it is almost impossible to decontaminate grasslands and pastures, efforts are underway to find low-cost ways to clean meat, milk, and other livestock products. Researchers in Germany are attempting to extract cesium by curing contaminated meat with salt [132]. In Finland, scientists are working on a high-potassium and mineral food for reindeer that would prevent cesium from being taken up in the animals' gut [133].

References and Notes

1. United Nations Economic Commission for Europe (ECE), *The Forest Resources of the ECE Region* (United Nations Food and Agriculture Organization/ECE, Geneva, 1985), Table 1.
2. Alan Grainger, "Quantifying Changes in Forest Cover in the Humid Tropics: Overcoming Current Limitations," *Journal of World Forest Resource Management*, Vol. 1, No. 1 (1984), Table 2, pp. 10–12.
3. Reider Person, *World Forest Resources* (Royal College of Forest Resources, Stockholm, 1974).
4. United Nations Food and Agriculture Organization (FAO), "Development and Investment in the Forestry Sector" (FAO, Rome, 1978), quoted in Roger A. Sedjo, "Forest Resources of the World: Forests in

5 Forests and Rangelands

Transition," in *The Global Forest Sector. An Analytical Perspective*, Markku Kallio, Dennis P. Dykstra, and Clark S. Binkley, eds. (John Wiley, New York, 1987), Table 1.3, p. 10.

5. Jean Paul Lanly, *Tropical Forest Resources* (United Nations Food and Agriculture Organization, Rome, 1982), Tables 5a–5c, pp. 69–72.

6. Alan Grainger, "The Future Role of the Tropical Rain Forests in the World Forest Economy," PhD dissertation, Department of Plant Sciences, University of Oxford, 1986.

7. *Op. cit.* 5, Table 6d, pp. 80–81.

8. *Op. cit.* 2, Table 8, p. 21.

9. *Op. cit.* 5, pp. 84–85.

10. *Op. cit.* 5, Table 3, p. 62.

11. Compiled from published and unpublished data from the United Nations Food and Agriculture Organization (FAO), Rome, 1988.

12. Adrian Sommer, "Attempts at an Assessment of the Tropical Moist Forests," *Unasylva*, Vol. 28, Nos. 112–113 (United Nations Food and Agriculture Organization, Rome, 1976), p. 20.

13. *Op. cit.* 2, pp. 21–22. The 1981 United Nations Food and Agriculture Organization estimates of deforestation rates were based on remote sensing measurements by aerial photography, satellite monitoring and side-looking airborne radar for only six of the 63 countries in the humid tropics. For six other countries government estimates of deforestation rates were used, and for the remaining 51 countries the rates were estimated by FAO itself.

14. These calculations are based on annual area losses due to deforestation given in Chapter 18, "Forests and Rangelands," Table 18.1.

15. Alan Grainger, "A Land Use Simulation Model for the Humid Tropics," in *Proceedings of International Conference on Land and Resource Evaluation for National Planning in the Tropics, Chetumal, Mexico, January 25–31* (USDA Forest Service, Washington D.C., 1987), Table 4, p. 436.

16. United Nations Food and Agriculture Organization (FAO), *Yearbook of Forest Products 1985* (FAO, Rome, 1986), p. 159 and p. 546.

17. United Nations Food and Agriculture Organization (FAO), *Yearbook of Forest Products 1986* (FAO, Rome, 1986). This calculation is for sawnwood and sleepers, roundwood, and wood pulp.

18. *Op. cit.* 16, p. 292 and p. 295.

19. *Op. cit.* 6, pp. 180–221.

20. *Op. cit.* 16, pp. 292–296.

21. *Op. cit.* 16.

22. United Nations Food and Agriculture Organization (FAO), *Yearbook of Forest Products 1960*, Table 1, p. 4; *1985*, p. 36 (FAO, Rome, 1960, 1986).

23. United Nations Food and Agriculture Organization (FAO), *World Forest Products: Demand and Supply 1990 and 2000* (FAO, Rome, 1982), Table 2, p. 25.

24. Forecast by the United Nations Food and Agriculture Organization (FAO), appended to *World Forest Products: Demand and Supply 1990 and 2000* (FAO, Rome, 1982), pp. vii–xx.

25. United Nations Food and Agriculture Organization (FAO), *Agriculture: Toward 2000* (FAO, Rome, 1987), p. 165.

26. Dennis P. Dykstra and Markku Kallio, "Base Scenario," "Scenario Variations," in *The Global Forest Sector: An Analytical Perspective*, Markku Kallio, Dennis P. Dykstra, and Clark S. Binkley, eds. (John Wiley, New York, 1987), Table 29.16 and Table 29.17, pp. 669–670.

27. *Ibid.*

28. United Nations Food and Agriculture Organization (FAO), "Forest Products Prices 1961–1980" (FAO, Rome, 1981).

29. *Op. cit.* 23.

30. *Op. cit.* 28, p. 8.

31. Roger A. Sedjo and Kenneth S. Lyon, "The Adequacy of Long Term Timber Supply: A World Assessment," in *Forest Sector and Trade Models: Theory and Applications: Proceedings of an International Symposium, November 3–4, 1987*, Peter A. Cardellichio, Darus M. Adams, Richard W. Haynes, eds. (Center for International Trade in Forest Products, University of Washington, Seattle, 1987), p. 18 and p. 19.

32. Alan Grainger, "TROPFORM: A Model of Future Tropical Hardwood Supplies," in *Proceedings of CINTRAFOR Symposium of Forest Sector and Trade Models* (College of Forest Resources, University of Washington, Seattle).

33. *Ibid.*

34. *Op. cit.* 6.

35. Alan Grainger, "Future Supplies of High Grade Tropical Hardwoods from Tropical Plantations," *Journal of World Forest Resource Management*, Vol. 3 (1988).

36. United Nations Food and Agriculture Organization (FAO), *Forest Resources of Tropical Asia* (FAO, Rome, 1981), Table 1a, p. 35. India contains almost three quarters of all managed forests in the tropics (29.4 million hectares) but as most of these are moist deciduous or dry tropical forests or temperate montane forests they are not typical of the humid tropics. Added to the countries of Africa and Latin America they raise the proportion of all tropical forests under management to just over 3 percent.

37. United Nations Food and Agriculture Organization (FAO), *Forest Resources of Tropical Africa, Part I: Regional Synthesis* (FAO, Rome, 1981), Table 12, p. 40.

38. United Nations Food and Agriculture Organization (FAO), *Los Recursos Forestales de la America Tropical* (FAO, Rome, 1981), Table 1b, p. 40.

39. *Op. cit.* 6.

40. R. Dennis Child *et al.*, *Arid and Semi-Arid Lands: Sustainable Use and Management in Developing Countries* (Winrock International, Morrilton, Arkansas, 1984), p. 6.

41. *Ibid.*, p. 51.

42. J. Swift, "Major Issues in African Pastoral Rehabilitation and Development," presented at the Informal Seminar on Socio-economic Aspects of Pastoral Development, United Nations Food and Agriculture Organization, Rome, November 25–27, 1987, p. 3.

43. United Nations Food and Agriculture Organization (FAO), *Trade Yearbook 1986* (FAO, Rome, 1987), Table 145, p. 323.

44. Pravee Vijchulata, Tuan Ariffeen Bongso and Mohamed Mahyuddin Dahan, eds., *Animal Production in Malaysia* (Faculty of Veterinary Medicine and Animal Science, University Pertanian Malaysia, 1984), p. 1.

45. Kustiah Kristanto, "Livestock Raising in Indonesia: with Reference to South Sulawesi," presented at the Workshop on Monitoring Change in Pastoral Livestock Systems, University Pertanian Malaysia, Kuala Lumpur, Malaysia, November 1985.

46. United Nations Food and Agriculture Organization (FAO), *Report on Natural Resources for Food and Agriculture in Latin America and the Caribbean* (FAO, Rome, 1986), p. 90.

47. United Nations Food and Agriculture Organization (FAO), *Report on Natural Resources for Food and Agriculture in Asia and Pacific Regions* (FAO, Rome, 1986), p. 48.

48. United Nations Food and Agriculture Organization (FAO), *Production Yearbook* (FAO, Rome, 1986), Table 1, p. 8.

49. G. Van Dijk and N. Hogervorst, "The Demand for Grassland in Europe Towards 2000: Some Implications of a Possible Scenario," paper presented at the Ninth General Meeting of the European Grassland Federation, Lisbon, 1982, pp. 21–31.

50. F. Riveros, Grassland and Pasture Crops Group, United Nations Food and Agriculture Organization, Rome, 1987 (personal communication).

51. S.B. Hecht, ed., "Amazon: Agriculture and Land use Research," Proceedings of International Conference, Rockefeller Foundation, cited in United Nations Food and Agriculture Organization (FAO), *Report on Natural Resources for Food and Agriculture in Latin America and the Caribbean* (FAO, Rome, 1986), p. 37.

52. Peter D. Little, "Land Use Conflicts in the Agricultural/Pastoral Borderlands: the Case of Kenya," in *Lands at Risk in the Third World: Local-level Perspectives*, P.D. Little, Michael M. Horowitz and A. Endre Nyerges, eds. (Westview, Boulder, Colorado 1987), pp. 197–198, and p. 203.

53. D.J. Campbell, "Land Use Competition at the Margins of the Rangelands: an issue in Development Strategies for Semi-arid Areas," in *Planning African Development*, Glen Norcliffe and Tom Pinfold, eds. (Westview, Boulder, 1981), p. 40.

54. P. Koehn, "African Approaches to Environmental Stress: a Focus on Ethiopia and Nigeria," in *International Dimensions of the Environmental Crisis*, Richard N. Barrett, ed. (Westview, Boulder, 1982), p. 256.

55. *Op. cit.* 52, p. 203.

56. G.C. Boudet and B. Toutain, "The Integration of Browse Plants within Pastoral and Agropastoral Systems in Africa," in *Browse in Africa*, H.N. Le Houerou, ed. (ILCA, Mali, 1980), pp. 427–432.

57. United Nations Food and Agriculture Organization (FAO), *Production Yearbook 1986* (FAO, Rome, 1987), Table 1, pp. 8–10.

58. *Ibid.*, p. 9.

59. *Ibid.*, pp. 8–10.

60. J. Venkateswarlyu, Project Director, Central Research Institute for Dryland Agriculture, Hyderabad, India, 1985 (personal communication).

61. R. S. Paroda and H.S. Mann, "Rangeland Management for Increased Primary and Secondary Productivity in Indian Arid Zones," in *Arid Land Plant Resources*, J.R. Goodin and D.K. Northington, eds. (International Center for Arid and Semi-Arid Lands Studies, Texas Tech University, Lubbock, 1976), pp. 661–676.

62. *Op. cit.* 57, Table 1, p. 8.

63. World Bank, *Annex: China—Agriculture to the Year 2000—Prospects and Options* (The World Bank, Washington, D.C., 1984), pp. 72–73.

64. *Op. cit.* 57, Table 1, pp. 8–13.

65. *Op. cit.* 63, p. 73.

66. United Nations Food and Agriculture Organization (FAO), *1986 FAO Production Yearbook*, Vol. 40 (FAO, Rome, 1987), Table 1, p. 10.

67. *Op. cit.* 63, pp. 72–73.

68. D. H. Gates, "Rangeland Management and Livestock Production in Northeastern China," in *Rangelands*, Vol. 8, No. 5, pp. 229–233.

69. *Op. cit.* 63, p. 76.

70. New Mexico State University (NMSU), *Range Livestock Production in the People's Republic of China, Proceedings of the International Symposium* (NMSU, Las Cruces, 1983), pp. 32–32.

71. L. Rittenhouse, *USDA/OICD Agricultural Scientific and Technical Exchange with China—Management of Arid Grazing Lands* (Department of Range Science, Colorado State University, Fort Collins, 1982), p. 76.

72. *Op. cit.* 63, p. 77.

73. *Op. cit.* 63, p. 76 and p. 78.

74. R. Jizhou, in *Range Livestock Production in the People's Republic of China, Proceedings of the International Symposium* (New Mexico State University, Las Cruces, 1983), pp. 23–26.

75. Neville Dyson-Hudson, "Pastoral Production Systems and Livestock Development Projects: an East African Perspective," in *Putting People First: Sociological Variables in Rural Development*, M.M. Cernea, ed. (World Bank, Washington, 1985), p. 158.

76. John Lewis, Head of Sahel Desk, U.S. Agency for International Development, State Department, Washington D.C., 1987 (personal communication).

77. United Nations Food and Agriculture Organization (FAO), *The State of Food and Agriculture 1985: A Mid-Decade Review of Food and Agriculture* (FAO, Rome, 1986), p. 188.

78. United Nations Food and Agriculture Organization (FAO), *Review of Field Programmes 1986–87* (FAO, Rome, 1987), Table 1.4, p. 14. The $161 million comes from extra-budgetary expenditures, including FAO/United Nations Development Programme and Trust Funds. Because of the multi-disciplinary nature of its projects, it is difficult to give a precise figure for the total investment in range projects.

79. *Ibid.*, p. 30.

80. *Op. cit.* 75, p. 157.

81. *Op. cit.* 40.

82. W. Goldschmidt, "The Failure of Pastoral Economic Development Programs in Africa," in *The Future of Pastoral Peoples*, J.G. Galaty, *et al.*, eds. (International Development Research Center, Ottawa, 1981), p. 106.

83. See for example, Consortium for International Development (CID), *Final Design Report: Bakel Range and Livestock Project, Eastern Senegal* (CID, Utah State University, Logan, 1976).

84. J. Gilles and K. Jamtgaard, "The Commons Reconsidered," in *Rangelands*, Vol. 4, No. 2 (1982), pp. 51–54.

85. Neal E. Artz, "Must Communal Grazing Lead to Tragedy?" in *Proceedings of the International Rangelands Resources Development Symposium, Salt Lake City, Utah, February, 1985*, Larry D. White and James A. Tiedman, eds. (Society for Range Management, Utah, 1985), pp. 146–156.

86. *Op. cit.* 75, pp. 157–158.

87. P. Horst and K.J. Peters, "Utilization of Natural Production Potentials in Dry Regions of the Tropics," *Quarterly Journal of International Agriculture*, Vol. 22, No. 2 (1983), pp. 130–148.

88. H. Josserand and P. Thomas, *Eastern Senegal Range and Livestock Development Project: Socio-Economic Study* (Center for Research and Economic Development, University of Michigan, Ann Arbor, 1985).

89. H.K. Schneider, "Livestock as Food and Money," in *The Future of Pastoral Peoples*, J.G. Galaty *et al.*, eds. (International Development Research Center, Ottawa, 1981), pp. 211–213.

90. Some recent studies also suggest that arid rangelands are very resilient, and not as fragile as commonly thought. However, long-term range ecological studies that could resolve the issue are lacking.

91. T.M. Farvar and J.P. Milton, eds., *The Careless Technology: Ecology and International Development, Proceedings of the Conference on the Ecological Impacts of International Development* (Conservation Foundation, Natural History Press, 1972).

92. BOSTID Ad Hoc Panel, "The Improvement of Tropical and Subtropical Rangelands" (National Research Council, unpublished draft, 1985).

93. P. Evangelou, *Livestock development in Kenya's Maasailand* (Westview, Boulder, 1984), p. 120.

94. Clare Oxby, "Settlement Schemes for Herders in the Subhumid Tropics of West Africa: Issues of Land Rights and Ethnicity," *Pastoral Development Network*, Paper No. 19f (February 1985), p. 225.

95. For example, the World Bank project in Eastern Senegal (Project Development Sengal Orientale), where herders agree to avoid the fragile areas close to settlements during the rainy season.

96. P. Richards, *Indigenous Agricultural Revolution: Ecology and Food Production in West Africa* (Hutchinson, London, 1985), p. 17.

97. C. Bryant and L.G. White, *Managing Development in the Third World*

98. N. Uphoff, "Fitting Projects to People," in *Putting People First: Sociological Variables in Rural Development*, Michael M. Cernea, ed. (World Bank, Washington, D.C., 1985), p. 364.

99. *Op. cit.* 75, p. 177.

100. See for example H. Barral, *Le Ferlo des Forages: Gestion Ancienne et Actuelle de l'Espace Pastorale* (ORSTOM, Paris, 1982), and M. Niamir, *Senegal Range and Livestock Project: Range Management Report* (Center for Research on Economic Development, University of Michigan, Ann Arbor, 1985).

101. P.H. Gulliver, *The Family Herds: a Study of Two Pastoral Tribes in East Africa: the Jie and Turkana* (Negro University Press, Connecticut, 1955).

102. Gufu Oba, "Local Participation in Guiding Extension Programs: a Practical Proposal," *Nomadic Peoples*, Vol. 18, pp. 27–45.

103. A. Khan, "Ekwars, Ere and Ewoi: Browse and Fodder Trials in a Traditional Sylvopastoral system (The Turkana)" (Oxfam draft memorandum, 1987).

104. C. Toupet, "La Sedentarization des Nomades en Mauritanie Central Sahelienne," PhD dissertation, Universite de Lille III, Paris, 1977.

105. C.M. McCorkle, "An Introduction to Ethnoveterinary Research and Development," *Journal of Ethnobiology*, Vol. 6, No. 1 (1986), p. 133.

106. Neal E. Artz, "The Fusion of Islamic and Berber Culture," paper presented at the International Rangeland Development Symposium, Society for Range Management, Idaho, 1987, pp. 37–44.

107. J. Gallais and G. Boudet, *Projet de Code Pastoral Concernant plus Specialement la Region du Delta Central du Niger au Mali* (Institute Medecine Veterinaire Tropicale, Paris, 1980).

108. J. Lewis, "Range Use and the Fulbe Social Organizations," in *Studies of Third World Societies*, No. 3 (William and Mary College, Virginia, 1981).

109. M.M. Horowitz, *The Sociology of Pastoralism and African Livestock Development* (Institute for Development Anthropology, New York, 1979).

110. P. Nowicki, "Culture, Ecology and Management of Natural Resources, or Knowing when not to Meddle," in *Culture and Conservation: the Human Dimension in Environmental Planning*, J.A. McNeely and D. Pitt, eds. (Croom Helm, London, 1985), p. 280.

111. P. Richards, "'Alternative' Strategies for the African Environment: 'Folk ecology' as a basis for community oriented agricultural development," in *African Environments: Problems and Perspectives*, P. Richards, ed. (International African Institute, Special Report No. 1, London, 1975), p. 110.

112. Maryam Niamir, *Senegal Range and Livestock Project: Range Management Report* (Center for Research on Economic Development, University of Michigan, Ann Arbor, 1985).

113. Dr. I. Toure, Director, Cours Post-Universitaire, United Nations Sahel Office, Dakar, 1985 (personal communication).

114. L.A. Brownrigg, "Native Cultures and Protected Areas: Management Options," in *Culture and Conservation: the Human Dimension of Environmental Planning*, J.A. McNeely and D. Pitt, eds. (Croom Helm, London, 1985), p. 41.

115. Jeremy Swift, and Angelo Maliki, "A Cooperative Development Experiment among Nomadic Herders in Niger," *Pastoral Development Network*, Paper No. 18c (Overseas Development Institute, London, 1984).

116. Project reports, Dutch Cooperation, Government of Burkina Faso, Ministry of Livestock Development, 1983–87.

117. Project reports, Project Development Senegal Orientale, World Bank, Washington, D.C., 1976–85.

118. "Statement of the Bellagio Strategy Meeting on Tropical Forests," paper presented at the Bellagio Strategy Meeting on Tropical Forests, Bellagio, Italy, July 1987.

119. Peter Hazelwood, Project Associate, Program in Forests and Biological Diversity, World Resources Institute, Washington, D.C., 1988 (personal communication).

120. "A Statement by Nongovernmental Organizations to the Bellagio Strategy Meeting on Tropical Forests," paper presented at the Bellagio Strategy Meeting on Tropical Forests, Bellagio, Italy, July 1987.

121. Catherine Caufield, "Conservationists Scorn Plans to Save Tropical Forests," *New Scientist* (June 25, 1987).

122. "Bellagio Forestry II: Research Strategies to Implement the Tropical Forestry Action Plan," minutes to the first meeting of the Bellagio task force, Rockefeller Foundation, New York, March 1988.

123. Brian Harding, Agricultural Attache, Embassy of the United Kingdom of Great Britain, Washington, D.C., 1988 (personal communication).

124. British Broadcasting Corporation World Services Radio Program, "Science in Action," January 22, 1988.

125. Sharon Stephens, "Lapp Life after Chernobyl," *Natural History*, Vol. 12 (December 1987), p. 34.

126. Deborah MacKenzie, "The Rad-Dosed Reindeer," *New Scientist*, December 18, 1986, p. 39.

127. *Ibid.*

128. *Ibid.*, p. 40.

129. *Op. cit.* 125, p. 34.

130. *Op. cit.* 126, pp. 37–38.

131. Robin Knight and David Bartal, "The Legacy of Chernobyl: Disaster for the Lapps," *U.S. News & World Report*, March 23, 1987, p. 36.

132. G.S. Child, Senior Forestry Officer, Wildlife and Protected Area Management Forest Resources Division, United Nations Food and Agricultural Organization, Rome, 1987 (personal communication).

133. *Op. cit.* 126, p. 40.

6. Wildlife and Habitat

All the world's civilizations have used products derived from wild plants and animals. Farming and pastoralism, which still dominate the Third World economy, are based on domesticating wild species—historically, a long, arduous process that relied on selection traits from a wide variety of plant and animal species. Today, genetic engineering, which could be considered an ultramodern, speeded-up form of domestication, depends on the continued diversity of wild species.

Concern is growing over the future of biodiversity. However, measuring the decline in biodiversity is not easy. Because we don't know exactly how many species exist, we don't know how many are lost when a habitat is destroyed. Counting species extinctions and calculating habitat losses are two widely used indicators of the global condition of wildlife, but they are not without flaws, the most glaring of which is a lack of baseline information. More attention has been paid to the plight of some special wildlife populations, such as island-dwelling and migratory species or those whose products have become so valuable that restrictions have been placed on their trade. Even here, though, there are often large gaps in our knowledge about numbers and survival requirements of these species. Still less is known about how many species are threatened when their habitats are fragmented by development.

To fight the erosion of biodiversity, conservationists have fashioned many tools, including designating wildlife preserves, setting aside wilderness areas, and passing international treaties regulating or banning certain forms of commerce in wild species and their products. Recently, conservationists have become more sensitive to the needs of local people, who may be threatening the existence of species by farming or poaching. The practice of sustainable development attempts to address the needs of local people while putting less pressure on natural resources. Sustainable development projects can help reduce development pressure on wildlife areas and can show local people how they can benefit from maintaining a diverse biota.

Past volumes of *World Resources* have touched on parts of these questions. The 1986 volume looked at trends for threatened species and at the world's systems of protected areas. In 1987, the economic value of wildlife was examined. This volume examines in detail how conditions and trends in biodiversity relate to the conventional economic thinking that dominates global policymaking today.

CONDITIONS AND TRENDS

LOSS OF BIOLOGICAL DIVERSITY

Diversity among wildlife continues to erode steadily throughout the world, and populations of many individual species are decreasing as well. Habitat loss is the main cause. Almost 40 percent of the net productivity of all plants is appropriated for human use (1). The result is usually extreme simplification of ecosystems. When wildland is destroyed for agricultural, industrial, and domestic purposes, a complex ecosystem capable of supporting many plants and animals is often turned into one that can sustain far fewer wildlife forms, as when tropical forests are cut down so crops can be grown and when wetlands are filled for housing.

Until recently, the human population was distributed sparsely enough that it had little effect on the prevailing background rate of extinction—an average of about 90 species disappeared each century (2). But between 1950 and 1987, the human population doubled (3). The demand for food and material goods has increased commensurately, to the detriment of wildlife habitat; today's extinction rate is far higher than ever before (4). Because it takes between 2,000 and 100,000 generations for new species to evolve, this loss cannot possibly be balanced (5).

Why Maintain Diversity?

What does it matter if wildlife is becoming less diverse? Many people believe that we owe nothing less than our entire civilization to the vast diversity of life found on Earth and that our future depends on its continuation. Given the importance of agriculture (which began with wild species) and fossil fuels (which are formed from the remains of plants), their contention may be near the mark. Yet this reasoning is not universally shared, so conservationists are campaigning to justify the importance of maintaining biodiversity.

Three general arguments are made. The most all-encompassing is that biodiversity is the foundation of the "ecosystem services" upon which society depends. Diverse natural ecosystems serve people by helping to keep air clean, lessening extremes of weather, disposing of wastes, recycling nutrients essential for agriculture, creating soils, and controlling disease, among other contributions (6). Individual species often play key roles in providing ecosystem services, and successful substitutes are hard to find (7). If biodiversity is lost, it is contended, so too are these services.

A related but more politically potent argument is that biodiversity is worth a lot of money. Over the past decade, several books have been written about the economic value of wildlife. In at least one industry—genetic engineering—maintaining biodiversity is already a lucrative business. Advocates of the economic argument regard every species as the embodiment of unique solutions to a series of biological problems. In other words, species are knowledge, knowledge that can be used in genetic engineering (as well as in traditional endeavors) to solve human problems (8).

For many, the least practical argument is the most compelling: that, as a matter of ethics, all forms of life should be respected (and therefore not squandered). Adherents to this point of view contend that even species with no foreseeable economic use are intrinsically valuable (9) (10). They caution that economic worth and worthlessness are transitory notions, so current monetary valuations may not be the most stable justifications for

protecting biodiversity. Further, they point out that emphasizing the economic value of wildlife can actually endanger it; once prices are set, paying compensation justifies its destruction.

Conservation Biology

As these differing views suggest, biodiversity issues cut across many disciplines. One of the newest, called conservation biology, is trying to provide policymakers with principles and tools for preserving biodiversity. Conservation biology proceeds from the basic assumptions that biodiversity has inherent value and that mass extinction can be averted (11) (12). It aims to combine evolutionary science (drawn mainly from island biogeography, population biology, and genetics) with human needs (as identified by environmental ethics, social science, and politics) and incorporate the mix into policymaking (13) (14).

Practitioners of conservation biology are sometimes willing to sacrifice neat scientific certainty when immediate action is required. For example, conservation biologists successfully urged Indonesia to create a reserve in the Kumawa Mountains of Irian Jaya even though no endangered species of animal was definitely known to occur there. The recommendation was based entirely on an informed guess that these isolated mountains contain a moderate number of endemic species (i.e., those found nowhere else)—a guess that was confirmed when the reserve was surveyed in 1983 (15).

Through its emphasis on maintaining biodiversity, conservation biology seeks to correct some of the past imbalances in scientific endeavor. Research and popularized accounts of natural history have largely concentrated on the fauna and flora of northern temperate zones. Only a few botanists work in the tropics, and just a handful of scientists are expert on tropical invertebrates, which are by far the largest part of the Earth's organisms (16). Scientists are beginning to make progress, with efforts like Project Wallace, in which 160 researchers from 17 countries went to Dumoga-Bone National Park on the Indonesian island of Sulawesi to catalog insects (17). At the same time, other scientists set out to document the ecology of the entire island (18). But even knowledge of well-studied areas is sparse; only in the past few years has a concerted effort been made to study rare plants or assess the diversity of ecosystems in the United States (19) (20).

Advocates of biodiversity must decide whether they want to preserve species as they are now or preserve their capacity to survive and evolve. The first two choices may require strict, almost farm-like wildlife management; they are also the easiest to enlist support for because people seem to prefer life forms over life processes (21). In the public mind, wildlife conservation has always been a freeze-frame, working to save *the* tiger, not the tiger's potential for change. The third choice, more difficult for nonscientists to grasp, gives species room to evolve responses to the ever increasing challenges of living in a changing world—or even, if they fail, to become extinct (22).

Table 6.1 Range Loss for Primates in Southeast Asia[a], 1986

Species	Original Range (square kilometers)	Remaining Range (square kilometers)	Percent Lost
Orangutan	553,000	207,000	63
Siamang	465,110	169,800	63
Agile- and dark-handed gibbons	532,270	184,345	65
White-handed gibbon	185,700	73,340	61
Bornean gibbon	395,000	253,000	36
Kloss gibbon	6,500	4,500	31
Javan and grey gibbons	43,274	1,608	96
Concolor gibbon	349,330	87,532	75
Lar gibbon	95,000	26,900	72
Hoolock gibbon	168,353	56,378	67
Pileated gibbon	70,000	11,200	84
Long-tailed macaque	383,181	123,315	68
Mentawai macaque	6,500	4,500	31
Crested macaque	12,000	4,800	60
Celebes macaque	67,000	38,500	33
Moor macaque	23,000	2,800	88
Pig-tailed macaque	1,568,623	481,685	69
Stump-tailed macaque	1,546,964	556,466	64
Assam macaque	802,193	335,002	59
Formosan macaque	37,281	11,556	69
Rhesus macaque	1,732,270	568,638	67
Ochreate black ape	29,500	18,500	37
Proboscis monkey	29,496	17,750	40
Pig-tailed (snub-nosed) langur[b]	6,500	4,500	31
Tonkin snub-nosed langur[c]	29,688	9,060	70
Douc langur	296,000	72,270	76
Javan leaf monkey	43,274	1,608	96
Silvered leaf monkey	412,170	169,970	59
Javan lutong	46,890	6,898	86
White-fronted leaf monkey	125,000	61,500	51
Bornean or grey leaf monkey	104,000	54,000	48
Banded leaf monkey[d]	450,834	168,227	63
Dusky leaf monkey	155,494	56,767	64
Mentawai langur	6,500	4,500	31
Maroon leaf monkey	415,000	266,000	36
Thomas's leaf monkey	68,000	30,800	55
Francois leaf monkey	97,400	14,106	86
Phayre's leaf monkey	708,572	193,172	73
Capped langur	65,868	34,622	48
Western tarsier	609,000	305,000	50
Eastern or spectral tarsier	154,400	70,730	54
Philippine tarsier	60,248	13,050	79
Slow loris	2,109,712	653,545	69
Pygmy loris	296,000	72,720	76

Source: John MacKinnon and Kathy MacKinnon, *Review of the Protected Areas System in the Indo-Malayan Realm* (International Union for Conservation of Nature and Natural Resources and United Nations Environment Programme, Gland, Switzerland, 1986), Tables 4.4-4.6, pp. 220-225.
Notes:
a. Includes Indonesia, North Borneo, the Malay Peninsula, the Philippines, and Indochina.
b. *Simias concolor*.
c. *Pygathrix avunculus*.
d. Includes both *Presbytis melalophos* and *P. femoralis*.

Table 6.2 Loss of and Protection for the Range of African Elephants, 1979

	Original Range (thousand square kilometers)	Percent of Original Range Remaining	Percent of Original Range Now in Protected Areas
Forest	26,512	72	< 5
Forest/Grassland	27,726	35	5–10
Woodland	62,672	38	21–30
Woodland/Grassland	8,161	62	5–10
Bushland	29,447	21	21–30
Bushland/Grassland	4,126	29	31–40
Grassland	5,219	44	5–10
Montane	6,086	14	11–20
Arid and Semi-Arid	22,584	4	< 5
Aquatic	2,396	54	11–20
Halophytic	501	74	11–20
Mangrove Swamps	855	20	< 5
Total	**196,285**	**36**	**13–19[a]**

Source: Anne Burrill, Iain Douglas-Hamilton, and John MacKinnon, "Protected Areas as Refuges for Elephants," in *Review of the Protected Areas System in the Afrotropical Realm*, John MacKinnon and Kathy MacKinnon, eds. (International Union for Conservation of Nature and Natural Resources and United Nations Environment Programme, Gland, Switzerland, 1986), Table 4.13, p. 179.
Note: a. Values of < 5 percent were computed into the total as 5 percent.

INDICATORS OF THE CONDITION OF THE WORLD'S WILDLIFE

Most scientists and resource managers agree that prospects for the survival of wildlife, and hence biodiversity, are continually worsening (23) (24). Although there is no single method of measuring conditions, several indicators are widely used. The two most common are species and habitat loss.

Species loss is the most graphic indicator of the plight of wildlife. Yet extinction is not a flawless measure of global wildlife conditions. One reason is that the definition of species is a human and therefore somewhat subjective judgment (25). Focusing solely on species loss also undermines the importance of the decline in numbers of individuals within a species. Many wildlife species are not in immediate danger of extinction, but their populations have been severely reduced. Some are on the verge of disappearing locally or regionally. Because such population reductions are occurring far faster and more frequently than extinctions (26), numbers losses may be a better sign of the global condition of wildlife, and even of the well-being of entire ecosystems.

Habitat loss is the most comprehensive indicator of all, for the reasons given at the beginning of the chapter. But the idea of habitat loss has its own difficulties. Strictly speaking, loss is a misnomer because habitat is rarely destroyed; it is converted from one kind to another—a change that often benefits opportunistic plants and animals. Certainly, the number of raccoons, blue jays, and water hyacinths has increased following human settlement of their ranges (27) (28). Most wildlife, though, is less adaptable to habitat disturbance. Moreover, it is difficult to separate severe habitat degradation from complete habitat loss. The former is nearly as serious as the latter—species have been shown to be reduced by as much as 50–67 percent without outright conversion of land use (29).

Range loss—shrinking of the geographical area in which a given species is found—is often the beginning of a downward spiral toward extinction. It may be the trend for primates in Southeast Asia. (See Table 6.1.) Of 44 species, 33 have lost at least half their range in the region. The populations of most Southeast Asian primates are declining, mostly because their ranges are being reduced by habitat conversion. Range loss resulting from habitat conversion is not always the cause of declining populations; hunting and capture are also factors (30). In the mid-15th Century, the earliest European explorers of Africa reported elephants throughout the continent except the Sahara and Namib-Kalahari Deserts; the range of the elephant is now about one third its former size (31). (See Table 6.2.) Yet in many localities, the number of elephants is decreasing more because of poaching than habitat loss (32). Nonetheless, losses in both range and numbers can obviously lead to species loss.

Species Loss

Understanding species loss is impeded by a glaring lack of information. How many species exist and how many have been identified? For some classes of organisms, both conservative and liberal estimates of the total number agree. At least 87 percent of all mammals, reptiles, amphibians, birds, and fishes are believed to have been identified. Plants are less well known. At least 69 percent of plants and vertebrates have been identified. Unfortunately, over 90 percent of the estimated total number of species belong to classes that have been studied the least. Invertebrates and microorganisms are the great unknown. At best, only 29 percent of these species have been identified; the figure is quite likely much lower.

Until the mid-1960s, scientists believed that there were about 3 million species on Earth (33). Now it is thought that there are at least 5 million, and many experts give 10 million as a moderately conservative estimate (34). A liberal estimate of more than 30 million is based on a recent survey of insect life in the canopy of a tropical forest in Peru. By fogging the treetops with insecticides, scientists were able to gather specimens from the previously inaccessible interlocking tangle of vegetation high above the forest floor. The diversity there was remarkable. One tree yielded as many species of ants as have been identified in the entire British Isles (35). If initial estimates from this study hold, there may be as many as 30 million insect species in tropical forests alone (36). Surveys of other remote habitats suspected to be biotically rich,

such as coral reefs, may well raise the estimate again (37); indeed, one researcher ventures a total of 37 million (38). Experts may disagree about the totals, but no one is disputing the fact that the number of species is far higher than was thought just a few years ago.

The validity of species loss estimates depends on the accuracy of the estimated number of species. Some widely quoted estimates published between 1979 and 1987 projected a 15–33 percent loss of wildlife worldwide by 2000 (39) (40). Not all scientists agree with these projections (41) (42). Similarly, speculations on the rate of loss— such as one species becoming extinct every minute— have been called impossible (43). But whatever the vagaries of these numbers, all recent estimates and projections of species losses are high, implying a consensus that extinction is becoming a critical problem (44).

How do these projections compare with mass extinctions in the geological past, such as the one that spelled the end of the dinosaurs? Six such episodes occurred; in the most dramatic, 52 percent of marine animal families, 78 percent of amphibian families, and 81 percent of reptile families disappeared (45). A recent study of extinctions in the tropical moist forests of Amazonia helps put these numbers in perspective. Limited to birds and flowering plants (for which extensive data exist), the study found no immediate threat of a mass extinction in Amazonia.

Box 6.1 Terrestrial Islands

Human activities that destroy or radically change wildlife habitat rarely proceed in an orderly fashion. For example, a large tract of virgin forest will probably not be cut down all at once, beginning on only one side. More likely, a dozen small farms eat away at the outside edges of a tract. Roads are built to move goods to and from the farms. Once the roads are in place, more farmers—not to mention loggers, miners, and settlers—are enticed to enter the newly accessible forest and to begin clearing it from within; soon more roads are needed, and so on. Studies of Amazonia, deciduous forests, prairies, marshes, and the mountains of North America confirm this pattern of degrading the world's species richness— habitat is divided and subdivided, in fits and starts (1).

For many plants and animals, these fragments of the original habitat act as terrestrial islands isolated from each other, not by expanses of water but by inhospitable landscapes. Sometimes wildlife cannot cross to another remnant of its former habitat. For the pika, a small North American mammal, a distance of just 300 meters between rock outcrops can be an insurmountable barrier to movement. Large carnivorous animals, which typically require vast contiguous ranges, are quickly affected by habitat fragmentation; so are other specialized feeders (2). Habitat loss through fragmentation is the greatest threat to the survival of species in temperate areas (3).

When continental wildlife species are forced to live in smaller areas, their populations usually decline, in turn making them more vulnerable to environmental disturbances (4) (5).

Fragmentation puts them into a double jeopardy of extinction: both the total size of their habitat and their ability to move from portion to portion within it are reduced (6).

Unlike species of real islands, those whose habitats are now fragmented have not had the benefit of thousands of years of unmolested isolation to evolve strategies for surviving in an insular environment. Newly isolated species may be more liable to extinction than those with long histories of island life. A further threat is that, in contrast to real oceans, the ocean of human-altered landscapes around terrestrial islands can help cause the extinction of island dwellers. The number of songbirds that breed in small wood lots in the eastern United States has been decreasing for the past 40 years, their nests victimized by the growing numbers of predators—cowbirds, blue jays, raccoons, and squirrels—now abundant in the suburban and agricultural habitats commonly surrounding these forest islands (7).

Since the mid–1970s, scientists have used the equilibrium theory of island biogeography to theorize about the optimal design of nature reserves. An extensive exchange of scientific papers has developed around this topic. Some contend that a single nature reserve, made as large as possible, is likely to contain the most species; this point of view obtained wide currency and was incorporated into the *World Conservation Strategy* (8). Others assert that several smaller reserves would contain as many species (9). And there are those who altogether discount the validity of applying species-area relationships to conservation (10). Recently, it was argued that the debate should

not focus on how many species are there when a reserve is established, but on how large the reserve should be to maintain minimum viable populations of the species that are present (11).

A long-term study in Brazil is beginning to answer some questions about how habitat area, fragmentation, and species survival are related. Because Brazilian law requires half the land in any development project to remain forested, cattle growers in the state of Amazonas have agreed to let the National Institute for Amazon Research and the World Wildlife Fund create 25 research reserves among new ranch lands. These reserves, which will eventually comprise forest fragments of 1, 10, 100, and 1,000 hectares, are marked off and studied both before and after they are isolated by the surrounding land's being cut over or burned to turn it into pasture. A 10,000-hectare tract will represent the intact original forest (12).

Among the findings of this minimum critical size of ecosystems (MCSE) study is the fact that more trees are dying in small fragments of 1 and 10 hectares than in the larger fragments (13). Certain primates with specialized diets have left the smaller fragments, as have birds that eat army ants—even before the ants themselves disappeared (14) (15).

The MCSE project was set up specifically to look at how reducing habitat area affects wildlife. But as the study nears its halfway point, the researchers are focusing on the edge between the altered landscapes and the original habitat of the reserves. Within days after a forest is cleared, changes in humidity, air temperature, and exposure to wind and

Table 6.3 Estimated Number of Species Worldwide

	Identified	Conservative Estimate of Total	Liberal Estimate of Total	Percent Identified
Mammals, reptiles, and amphibians	12,410–12,962	13,644	13,800	90–95
Birds	8,715–9,040	9,000	9,224	94–100
Fishes	19,056–21,000	21,000	23,000	83–100
Subtotal	40,181–43,002	43,644	46,024	87–99
Plants[a]	322,300–400,000	400,000	480,000	67–100
Subtotal	362,481–443,002	443,644	526,024	69–99.9
Invertebrates and microorganisms	1,027,634–1,300,000	4,400,000	33,000,000	3–27
Total	**1,390,115–1,743,002**	**4,443,644**	**33,526,024**	**4–39**

Sources:
1. World Resources Institute and International Institute for Environment and Development, *World Resources 1986* (Basic Books, New York, 1986), Table 6.1, p. 86.
2. Edward C. Wolf, *On the Brink of Extinction: Conserving the Diversity of Life* (Worldwatch Institute, Washington, D.C., 1987), Table 1, p. 7.
Note: a. Includes higher (vascular) and lower (nonvascular) plants.

But if current trends continue, 12 percent of the bird and 15 percent of the plant species will be gone by 2000. Furthermore, if deforestation were to continue unabated throughout the 21st Century, the percentage of species lost in the Amazon would eventually approach that of almost every episode of mass extinction. At worst (if wildlands were reduced to an area equal to that currently included in protected areas), species loss for birds and plants would reach 69 percent and 66 percent, respectively [46].

Adding to the concern over the potentially high rate of species loss is the fact that removing a single plant or animal from a natural community can profoundly affect other wildlife. Certain species are vital to the workings of their ecosystems. Among them are large carnivores that regulate predator-prey relationships, large herbivores that significantly change vegetation, plants that bear fruit at times when few others do, and organisms that pollinate plants [47]. For example, when coyotes were removed from some canyons in the western United States, the number of bird extinctions there went up, not down, because foxes, house cats, and other small predators—all of them preyed on or chased out by coyotes and all of them better than coyotes at catching birds—thrived [48].

Habitat Loss

Attempts to calculate habitat loss usually involve single ecosystems rather than entire regions, let alone the world. Far and away the most attention has been given to a particular means of habitat loss—deforestation, the total clearing of a natural forest formation [49]. Deforestation in the tropics is widely considered the worst threat

Box 6.1

sunlight affect vegetation along the margins. Refugee birds from surrounding cutover areas crowd into the understory of the reserves. Butterflies that thrive in the deep forest suddenly have to compete for space with other butterflies, normally found only in second-growth habitats, that invade the reserves from the new ranch land [16].

To ease the effects of fragmentation, setting aside corridors of habitat to connect terrestrial islands has been suggested. Such corridors already exist unintentionally; many trees are situated along the edges of farm fields, for example, because animals that carry tree seeds tend to travel along the fences. Barring connections made up of closed-canopy forests, habitat along streams has been suggested as the ideal corridor [17]. Planners envision corridors as only one part of a larger land management strategy. In the United States, managers have put together a plan to preserve the few remaining Florida panthers, whose habitat is now restricted to a small part of one of the country's fastest-growing states. Streamside and terrestrial corridors would connect wilderness-like landscapes recreated by closing roads and limiting public access [18] [19]. One drawback of corridors is that they may also serve as pathways for disease and fires. It is also suggested that funds for corridors intended to save a single species might be better spent on broader conservation projects [20].

References and Notes

1. David S. Wilcove, "From Fragmentation to Extinction," *Natural Areas Journal*, Vol. 7, No. 1 (1987), p. 23.
2. Larry D. Harris, *The Fragmented Forest: Island Biogeography Theory and the Preservation of Biotic Diversity* (University of Chicago Press, Chicago, 1984), p. 83 and pp. 86–87.
3. David S. Wilcove, Charles H. McLellan, and Andrew P. Dobson, "Habitat Fragmentation in the Temperate Zone," in *Conservation Biology: The Science of Scarcity and Diversity*, Michael E. Soulé, ed. (Sinauer, Sunderland, Massachusetts, 1986), p. 240.
4. *Op. cit.* 1, pp. 24–27.
5. *Op. cit.* 2, pp. 82–83.
6. *Op. cit.* 3, p. 238.
7. *Op. cit.* 3, pp. 248–249.
8. Jared M. Diamond, "The Island Dilemma: Lessons of Modern Biogeographic Studies for the Design of Natural Reserves," *Biological Conservation*, Vol. 7, No. 2 (1975), pp. 129–146.
9. Daniel Simberloff and Lawrence G. Abele, "Refuge Design and Island Biogeographic Theory: Effects of Fragmentation," *The American Naturalist*, Vol. 120, No. 1 (1982), pp. 41–50. The supporters of this theory work from the assumption that the cumulative area of the smaller reserves would equal that of the hypothetical single large reserve.
10. William J. Boecklen and Nicholas J. Gotelli, "Island Biogeographic Theory and Conservation Practice: Species-Area or Specious-Area Relationships?" *Biological Conservation*, Vol. 29, No. 1 (1984), pp. 63–79.
11. Michael E. Soule and Daniel Simberloff, "What Do Genetics and Ecology Tell Us about the Design of Nature Reserves?" *Biological Conservation*, Vol. 35, No. 1 (1986), pp. 23–26.
12. The Conservation Foundation (CF), *State of the Environment: A View toward the Nineties* (CF, Washington, D.C., 1987), pp. 562–563.
13. Thomas E. Lovejoy, *et al.*, "Ecosystem Decay of Amazon Forest Remnants," in *Extinctions*, Matthew H. Nitecki, ed. (University of Chicago Press, Chicago, 1984), p. 316.
14. *Op. cit.* 12, p. 562.
15. T.E. Lovejoy, *et al.*, "Edge and Other Effects of Isolation on Amazon Forest Fragments," in *Conservation Biology: The Science of Scarcity and Diversity*, Michael E. Soulé, ed. (Sinauer, Sunderland, Massachusetts, 1986), pp. 277–280.
16. *Ibid.*, pp. 258–259, pp. 262–264, and p. 270.
17. *Op. cit.* 2, pp. 141–144.
18. Reed F. Noss, "Corridors in Real Landscapes: A Reply to Simberloff and Cox," *Conservation Biology*, Vol. 1, No. 2 (1987), p. 161.
19. Keith Henderson, "Letting Florida's Wildlife Roam," *Christian Science Monitor* (April 8, 1986), p. 29 and p. 32.
20. Daniel Simberloff and James Cox, "Consequences and Costs of Conservation Corridors," *Conservation Biology*, Vol. 1, No. 1 (1987), pp. 63–71.

Table 6.4 Wildlife Habitat Loss in Indomalayan Nations, 1986[a]

	Original Wildlife Habitat (square kilometers)	Amount Remaining (square kilometers)	Habitat Loss (percent)
Bangladesh	142,77	68,567	94
Bhutan	34,500	22,770	34
Brunei	5,764	4,381	24
Burma	774,817	225,981	71
China[b]	423,066	164,996	61
Hong Kong	1,066	32	97
India	3,017,009	615,095	80
Indonesia	1,446,433	746,861	49
Japan[c]	320	138	57
Kampuchea	180,879	43,411	76
Laos	236,746	68,656	71
Malaysia[d]	356,254	210,190	41
Nepal	117,075	53,855	54
Pakistan	165,900	39,816	76
Philippines	308,211	64,724	79
Sri Lanka	64,700	10,999	83
Taiwan	36,961	10,719	71
Thailand	507,267	130,039	74
Vietnam	332,116	66,423	80
Total	**8,169,860**	**2,487,683**	**68**

Source: John MacKinnon and Kathy MacKinnon, *Review of the Protected Areas System in the Indo-Malayan Realm* (International Union for Conservation of Nature and Natural Resources and United Nations Environment Programme, Gland, Switzerland, 1986), pp. 18-19 and pp. 247-274.

Notes:
a. Excludes Christmas and Cocos Islands (Australia), the Maldives, and the Chagos archipelago (U.K. protection).
b. Tropical portion only (i.e., area south of Yunnan high hills, including the southern coastal strip and the island of Hainan).
c. Tropical portion only (i.e., southern Ryukyu archipelago).
d. Includes Singapore.

to the world's wildlife because even though tropical forests make up only 6 percent of the Earth's land surface, they are home to an estimated 50–90 percent of all species (50).

Tropical forests are roughly classified as "moist" or "dry." In prehistory, moist forests covered some 1.6 billion hectares. At least 28 percent of them, or 448 million hectares, have been destroyed. Over 90 percent of the moist Brazilian coastal forest is gone. So is 98 percent of the dry tropical forest on the Pacific coast of Central America and Mexico (51). For the world as a whole, tropical deforestation is most extensive in Southeast Asia and Central America (52). (See Chapter 5, "Forests and Rangelands," Figure 5.1.)

Some other terrestrial habitats are all but lost. The tallgrass prairies of the United States, for example, have been reduced 98 percent (53). Wetlands and other habitats have suffered less drastic but serious losses; 25–50 percent of the world's swamps and marshes have been destroyed (54). None of these figures indicates the condition of the habitat that ostensibly remains intact. In reality, it may be severely impoverished, having been invaded by exotic species, degraded by pollution, or cut off from other wildlands by development. National studies suggest the disruption of a great deal of habitat. The U.S. Agency for International Development's environmental profiles of 67 developing nations describe some ecosystem degradation in nearly all the countries (55).

There is no worldwide reckoning of terrestrial habitat loss. Estimates have recently been made for two regions exceptionally rich in wildlife—Indomalaysia (the area of Southeast Asia running from India east through the Philippines and from extreme southern China south

through Indonesia) and tropical (sub-Saharan) Africa. The studies were commissioned by the International Union for Conservation of Nature and Natural Resources (IUCN) and the United Nations Environment Programme (UNEP). For the Indomalayan report, vegetation maps and satellite imagery were used to measure the loss for all forms of habitat (56). For the Afrotropical report, United Nations Food and Agriculture Organization statistics, satellite imagery, and vegetation maps were used; nonforested area estimates were extrapolated from figures on land converted to agriculture (57). The IUCN-UNEP study found that 68 percent of the original wildlife habitat in Indomalayan countries and 65 percent in tropical Africa has been lost. (See Tables 6.4 and 6.5.) In these regions, only Brunei and Zambia have lost less than 30 percent of their original habitat. In contrast, Bangladesh, the most densely populated large country in the world, has suffered a 94 percent loss.

Within these regions, certain areas have sustained particularly high losses. The nine West African coastal nations stretching from Mauritania through Ghana have

Table 6.5 Wildlife Habitat Loss in Afrotropical Nations[a], 1986

Country	Original Wildlife Habitat (square kilometers)	Amount Remaining (square kilometers)	Habitat Loss (percent)
Angola	1,246,700	760,847	39
Benin	115,800	46,320	60
Botswana	585,400	257,576	56
Burkina Faso	273,800	54,760	80
Burundi	25,700	3,598	86
Cameroon	469,400	192,454	59
Central African Rep.	623,000	274,120	56
Chad	720,800	172,992	76
Congo	342,000	174,420	49
Cote d'Ivoire	318,000	66,780	79
Djibouti	21,800	11,118	49
Equatorial Guinea	26,000	12,740	51
Ethiopia	1,101,003	30,300	70
Gabon	267,000	173,550	35
Gambia	11,300	1,243	89
Ghana	230,000	46,000	80
Guinea	245,900	73,770	70
Guinea Bissau	36,100	7,942	78
Kenya	569,500	296,140	48
Lesotho	30,400	9,728	68
Liberia	111,400	14,482	87
Madagascar	595,211	148,803	75
Malawi	94,100	40,463	57
Mali	754,100	158,361	79
Mauritania	388,600	73,834	81
Mozambique	783,203	36,776	57
Namibia	823,200	444,528	46
Niger	566,000	127,880	77
Nigeria	919,800	229,950	75
Rwanda	25,100	3,263	87
Senegal	196,200	35,316	82
Sierra Leone	71,700	10,755	85
Somalia	637,700	376,243	41
South Africa	1,236,500	531,695	57
Sudan	1,703,000	510,900	70
Swaziland	17,400	7,656	56
Tanzania	886,200	505,134	43
Togo	56,000	19,040	66
Uganda	193,700	42,614	78
Zaire	2,335,900	1,051,155	55
Zambia	752,600	534,346	29
Zimbabwe	390,200	171,688	56
Total	**20,797,441**	**8,340,920**	**65**

Source: John MacKinnon and Kathy MacKinnon, *Review of the Protected Areas System in the Afrotropical Realm* (International Union for Conservation of Nature and Natural Resources and United Nations Environment Programme, Gland, Switzerland, 1986), p. vii, pp. 16-17, and pp. 188-253.

Note: a. The Afrotropical realm is defined as all the continent south of the Sahara Desert, including the island of Madagascar. Therefore, data for Mauritania, Mali, Niger, Chad, and Sudan cover only part of those countries. Comoros, Seychelles, São Tomé and Principe, Mauritius, Rodrigues, Reunion, and the extreme southeastern corner of Egypt are not included.

each lost at least 78 percent of their wildlife habitat except for Guinea (70 percent). This subregion includes the Gambia, which has tropical Africa's highest rate of loss (89 percent). These figures help explain why wildlife conservation in West Africa has lagged behind that in the eastern and southern parts of the continent (58).

The largest absolute losses of habitat in both regions are in their largest countries. India has lost about 2.4 million square kilometers of habitat and Zaire about 1.3 million square kilometers. Sudan is not far behind, with a loss of nearly 1.2 million square kilometers. Nevertheless, considerable amounts of undisturbed habitat exist in all three countries. Others that still have the capacity to conserve large amounts of original habitat include Indonesia, Burma, and Malaysia in Indomalaysia and Angola, Zambia, South Africa, Tanzania, and Namibia in tropical Africa.

ISLAND HABITATS

The direct connection between the size of an area and the number of species it contains has been known to science for some 150 years (59). Nowhere is the species-area relationship more apparent than on islands. The unique makeup of island wildlife communities has given rise to one of the most influential ecological theories of this century. In island biogeography (first propounded in the 1960s), the species-area relationship is a basis for predicting that, over the years, the number of species of plants and animals on an island tends to approach a dynamic equilibrium. This equilibrium is reached when the number of species immigrating to a given island equals the number becoming extinct on it. Immigration and extinction depend on the size of the island and its proximity to the nearest source of colonists (usually another island or a continent) (60). The smaller and more isolated the island, the lower is the equilibrium number of species. Island biogeography is also used to study isolated habitats on mainlands. (See Box 6.1.)

What makes island biogeography useful is that it provides insights into how isolation affects the formation and extinction of species. Isolation cuts both ways. It can help create species; if two populations of the same species are separated long enough, their characteristics may diverge so much that they no longer interbreed. But prolonged isolation in a confined area may eventually predispose some species to extinction because they become so specialized that they cannot adapt quickly enough to environmental changes.

Endemic Species: Specialized and Vulnerable

Endemic species—those found in restricted locales and nowhere else—are central to the world's biological diversity, and they best illustrate how speciation is aided by isolation. Many island species are endemic on islands, particularly in the tropics. Large islands with sharp topographical relief and ample rainfall tend to have high percentages of endemic plants because separate vegetation communities are formed at different elevations. Smaller, flatter, drier islands—such as Puerto Rico and the Galápagos—have relatively little floral endemism (61). Yet,

once established on an island, even the most mobile animals can become endemic. Almost 900 species of birds—over 10 percent of the world's total—have ranges that are limited to one island (62).

On the other hand, species that have taken generations to adapt to isolated surroundings may eventually become victims of their own success. For example, a species that has evolved highly specialized characteristics to take advantage of an ecosystem on a remote island, only to have the island's ecological conditions changed by the coming of human settlers, may not be able to adapt to these changes fast enough to survive. The most famous extinction in history, that of the dodo, is an example. Living on the remote island of Mauritius in the Indian Ocean, the dodo had no natural enemies. Over centuries of evolution in isolation, the dodo lost its power of flight and any fear it may have had of humans. The first Europeans came to Mauritius in 1497; by about 1662, the last dodos were dead, most of them easily killed for their meat (63).

This process is being played out today on many islands. About 75 percent of the mammals and birds that have become extinct in recent history were island-dwelling species (64). On many islands, a high percentage of endemic plants currently faces extinction. (See Table 6.6.) For all forms of wildlife, Oceania has the world's highest proportion of endangered species (65).

Some islands face imminently severe problems. Madagascar, separated from the southeast African coast by the Mozambique Channel, has flora and fauna that evolved in partial isolation from the continent for at least 30 million years. More than 6,000 flowering plants are unique to the island, as are 106 birds, 142 frogs, and half the world's chameleon species. Since humans first arrived 1,500 years ago, several of Madagascar's endemic species have been extinguished, including 14 lemurs, a pygmy hippopotamus, and the largest bird known to have existed, the 3-meter-tall, 450-kilogram elephant bird. Today, much of the island's wildlife is threatened by slash-and-burn agriculture, which, along with other human activities, has destroyed 80 percent of the natural vegetation. Madagascar has been given a high priority by two international conservation organizations, particularly

Table 6.6 Status of Endemic Vascular Plant Taxa on Selected Oceanic Islands, 1986

Island	Total	Not Threatened	Insufficiently Known	Rare, Threatened, or Extinct
Ascension Island	11	0	1	10 (91 %)
Azores	55	14	11	30 (55 %)
Canary Islands	569	160	26	383 (67 %)
Galapagos	229	77	2	150 (66 %)
Juan Fernandez	118	6	17	95 (81 %)
Lord Howe Island	75	2	0	73 (97 %)
Madeira	131	23	22	86 (66 %)
Mauritius	280	39	69	172 (61 %)
Norfolk Island	48	0	2	46 (96 %)
Rodrigues	48	2	0	46 (96 %)
St. Helena	49	0	2	47 (96 %)
Seychelles	90	0	17	73 (81 %)
Socotra	215	81	2	132 (61 %)

Source: Stephen H. Davis, *et al., Plants in Danger: What Do We Know?* (International Union for Conservation of Nature and Natural Resources, Gland, Switzerland, 1986), Tables 3 and 4, pp. xxviii-xxix.

because just 1.5 percent of the country is within protected areas (66) (67).

But even the best-planned protected areas cannot ensure the integrity of sensitive island ecosystems if the resolve of the authorities is not sustained. Outside scientific reserves, few protected areas in the world have restrictions on humans more stringent than those for Ecuador's Galápagos National Park. Since 1969, 88 percent of the land area of the archipelago—located in the Pacific Ocean about 1,000 kilometers west of South America— has been managed by the National Park Service. The endemic wildlife of the Galápagos is famous for helping form the idea of evolution by natural selection in the mind of the young Charles Darwin. In recent years, this wildlife has made the islands an increasingly favored international tourist destination. Elaborate supervision of the numbers and movement of visitors began in 1970. But in 1983, the Ecuadoran Park Service increased the annual visitor limit from 12,000 to 25,000 and is considering raising it again. In reality, the number of visitors has exceeded these limits for some time. Over the past few years, accounts have been published about other ways in which visitor controls are breaking down, jeopardizing the park's unique wildlife and its habitat (68) (69) (70).

Island Habitat Disturbances

All animals and plants, not only endemics, are at risk when an island's environment is disturbed. Islands are exposed to more biological invasion now than ever before. Regular ship runs, fast plane service to remote areas, and the emergence of worldwide trade make it far easier for all kinds of plants and animals to become established far from their original ranges (71).

Few other places have had as much trouble with biological invasions as the Hawaiian Islands, where 28 percent of the insects and 65 percent of the plants are now nonnative (72) (73). Several indigenous plant species have been lost to browsing by feral goats and pigs; thousands of these animals have been shot in Hawaiian national parks without eliminating them. Introduced black rats feed on the fruit of rare species such as the Haleakala sandalwood, and mongooses feed on the endangered nene (Hawaiian goose) and dark-rumped petrel. On average, 16 insect species are introduced to Hawaii every year; one of them, the voracious ant *Pheidole megacephala*, has eliminated most endemic insects near sea level (74).

These sorts of problems are all the more acute on small islands that are less than 10,000 square kilometers (75). The risks posed by natural hazards are particularly magnified on a small island. In a drought or tidal wave, the animals cannot migrate to escape (76). On Rodrigues in the Indian Ocean, a hurricane-force wind that blew for just eight hours damaged three quarters of the island's forest (77).

Indiscriminate clearing of forest cover is common on the small islands of the Pacific and Indian Oceans and the Mediterranean Sea and at lower elevations on the Caribbean islands (78). Unrestricted fuelwood cutting and overgrazing by introduced goats, cattle, and rabbits have

caused the loss of vegetation (79) (80). Without its vegetation cover the land is degraded. Soil on small islands typically erodes quickly and is lost immediately to the sea, rather than building up as it does (at least temporarily) in the deltas of the mainland (81). On small low-lying Pacific islands, wood (including coconut shell) is the primary source of energy, and shifting subsistence agriculture still prevails. Where fertilizers and herbicides are used, their residues tend to contaminate the groundwater and build up to toxic levels faster than they would on the mainland (82).

For a variety of reasons, many island nations are persuaded to concentrate their agriculture on a single export. A few of these plantation islands are producing cash crops at the expense of their rich indigenous flora and fauna. Much of Mauritius is now swathed in sugar, tea, and pine plantations; one of the world's most interesting native forests has been virtually destroyed, along with over half the island's bird, mammal, and reptile species that are found nowhere else (83).

MIGRATORY SPECIES

Migratory animals, as opposed to more sedentary creatures, travel established routes between their separate breeding and nonbreeding grounds. For many terrestrial and avian species, migration involves long distances, even thousands of kilometers. For others, migration is based on elevation—perhaps only a short move from high country in warm weather to lowlands in cold. Many migrants cross political jurisdictions in their annual movements. This situation poses problems for their conservation. It highlights the limitations of protected areas and the difficulty of achieving international cooperation.

A major shortcoming of protected areas in this regard is that they are static, and wildlife is dynamic. Survival for an animal may be a matter of a few meters, depending on whether it is inside or outside a protected area. For almost all migrants (and indeed for most large mammal species), existing protected areas are too small to cover their ranges completely.

Pointing out this defect is not to say protected areas have no place in the conservation of migratory species. On the contrary, if a migrant's breeding and nonbreeding grounds are both safeguarded, its chances of surviving are much better. But even double-ended security leaves species vulnerable while on the move. Shorebirds migrating between North and South America funnel into food bottlenecks—that is, huge numbers gather at a handful of sites (for which there are few, if any, alternatives) to feed. At times, more than 80 percent of a bird's breeding population may be found at one of these bottlenecks, which are generally along coasts or in wetlands—two habitats undergoing intense development pressure. Not only are the sites being encroached upon, but they are also acutely vulnerable to such catastrophes as spills from oil tankers. A single severe disruption at one bottleneck during a migration could conceivably threaten whole continental populations of shorebirds (84).

Legal and managerial protection at all key points along a migration route would go a long way toward ameliorating problems caused by different jurisdictions and quirks of biology. It would also help assuage cultural differences in the treatment of wildlife. European songbirds, for example, are not eaten in the northern countries where they breed, but they are commonly trapped or shot for food when passing through the Mediterranean region (85).

For some species, the problem is that their destination is an area of just a few hectares. The nonbreeding habitats of monarch butterflies are confined to a few small sites along the Pacific coast in the United States and in the mountains of central Mexico. These grounds are jeopardized by housing developments and farming; their loss could cause the North American population of monarchs to become extinct (86).

The Bonn Convention Could Protect Migratory Species

Comprehensive protection for migrants can be gained only through worldwide legal agreements. There is a long history of bilateral, regional, and even international treaties concerned with or bearing on migratory wildlife, but only one is devoted specifically to the state of these species globally—the Convention on Conservation of Migratory Species of Wild Animals (87). The treaty was concluded in Bonn in 1979. As of April 1987, it had 23 parties. (See Chapter 24, "Policies and Institutions," Table 24.1.) The Secretariat is provided by UNEP.

The Bonn Convention uses a double appendix system to pursue its objectives. Animals listed in Appendix I are those in danger of extinction in all or a significant part of their ranges, including migratory routes. They are to receive the strictest protection from those parties to the Convention whose nations form part of their ranges (the "range states"). Because the language governing Appendix I is extraordinarily broad for an international treaty, its terms of enforcement are unusually rigorous. In essence, range states are obligated to remedy every possible threat to an Appendix I animal, even if it is endangered in only part of its range (88).

Appendix II lists migratory animals whose situations could greatly benefit from international cooperation; it has nothing to do with whether they face extinction. Range states of Appendix II animals must try to conclude agreements among themselves (and with nonparties, if possible) to benefit these species (89).

Because of its strict requirements, the Bonn Convention is potentially a powerful tool for conserving migratory wildlife. However, few countries have acceded to it. Some have not acceded because of enforcement costs; the United States and others have declined because of problems they have had with international conservation treaties (90) (91).

ILLEGAL TRADE

Worldwide, the estimated minimum value for wildlife and wildlife products reported in trade is $5 billion annually. Some 25–33 percent of this trade is estimated to be illegal (92). Concern about the unlawful buying and selling of wildlife and its products centers on rare and endangered species.

The CITES Regulations

The foremost control on trafficking in restricted animals and plants is the Convention on International Trade in Endangered Species of Wild Fauna and Flora (CITES), concluded in Washington in 1973. CITES currently has 96 parties. (See Chapter 19, "Wildlife and Habitat," Table 19.3 and Chapter 24, "Policies and Institutions," Table 24.1.) UNEP provides its Secretariat.

Like the Bonn Convention, CITES uses a tier of lists to prohibit or control trade in various species. CITES Appendix I lists imminently endangered species and forbids (with a few exceptions) commerce in them. Appendix I also allows "split listings" of subspecies and distinct populations of plants and animals. Appendix II species are not yet in jeopardy of extinction, but they may soon be. CITES limits their export so the Secretariat can monitor the effects of continued trade on their survival. Appendix III, which so far has been little used, provides for countries to make their unilateral domestic endangered species laws known. The Secretariat administers a central system of import, export, and reexport permits to enforce the Convention (93).

Illegal trade is monitored worldwide by the TRAFFIC (Trade Records Analysis of Flora and Fauna in Commerce) network, which now has 11 branches. TRAFFIC is affiliated with the World Wildlife Fund (WWF) and IUCN and works closely with the CITES-UNEP Secretariat (94).

CITES controls trade not only in live specimens but also in wildlife products, which account for most of the illegal market. It defines "specimen" to include "any readily recognizable part or derivative" of a listed species. Although this definition gives CITES far more power to regulate illegal trade, the Convention does not further define what is "readily recognizable" (95). This omission has proven to be a loophole because it allows parties to suit their definitions to their purposes. Hong Kong, for example, does not consider worked ivory a readily recognizable derivative of an elephant tusk—an interpretation used to justify continued trade there (96). Similar abuses are possible with the CITES exemption for trade in wildlife products considered "personal or household effects" (97).

The biggest CITES loopholes are the "reservations" that parties can take at the time of signing. Reservations are nothing more than exemptions from CITES that countries can arrogate to themselves with regard to individual species. Parties can declare a reservation for any species, even one listed in Appendix I, and so continue its trade (98). As of March 1987, 56 reservations were held for Appendix I species and 45 for Appendix II species (99). If not checked, use of these loopholes can circumvent CITES's intent, as has happened recently in countries of the European Community (EC). The existence of free ports with few or no import controls (e.g., Hamburg), along with lax enforcement in overseas departments (e.g., French Guiana), allows legal entrance of restricted wildlife products into the EC from around the world (100). Despite these drawbacks, CITES has been called one of the most successful international wildlife conservation treaties because it is so vigorously administered (101).

Some believe that the species nominations have

become unwieldy and politicized, particularly for Appendix I, the banned list (102). In recent years, alternatives to outright bans have been widely discussed. National governments are interested in co-opting illegal markets so they can derive income from wildlife assets that now benefit only criminals. Others believe that bans cannot succeed in closing established industries that depend on restricted wildlife products; rather, the bans will only drive illegal trade underground where it cannot be monitored (103). Restrictions on wildlife trade tend to work best when local people are given a stake in the efforts. This is the principle behind the new CITES quotas for African elephant ivory (104). (See Box 6.2.)

Another way to co-opt the illegal market is to allow big game hunting, but only after charging a high license fee. Rather than pay similar sums to poacher-guides, trophy hunters in Zimbabwe can spend about $5,000 for an elephant license and pursue their sport legally. Some of the profits from the fees revert to farming communities in the elephants' range as compensation for crop damage; a community can make as much as $15,000 a year in this

way (105). The profits to be made from licensing are considerable; African governments are missing out on an estimated $29 million in annual revenue by not allowing more sport hunting of and trade in leopards (106).

Parties to CITES are also looking at ways that endangered species can be exploited without killing individuals. At the biennial CITES conference held in Canada in July 1987, the parties decided to reopen trade in the wool of Peruvian and Chilean vicuña, but only if it is taken from live animals (107).

The Asian Markets

Asia continues to be the leading consumer of four valuable restricted wildlife products: ivory, tortoise shell, musk, and rhinoceros horn. Most ivory is taken from African elephants, and 85 percent ends up in Hong Kong and Japan, where it is carved into jewelry and figurines or is used for scrimshaw (108). Japan consumes more tortoise shell taken from the endangered hawksbill sea turtle than any other nation, using it to support a segment of the

---

Box 6.2 The African Ivory Quota System

Illegal trade in the tusks of African elephants is worth at least $50 million per year. The high price ivory commands (in 1986, more than $100 per kilogram) has led to widespread poaching in Africa, often by organized gangs with sophisticated automatic weapons. As a result, elephant numbers have dropped sharply since 1981. Faced with the prospect of uncontrollable poaching, in 1986 the CITES-UNEP Secretariat created a parallel legal market by sponsoring a system of quotas and certifications for African ivory exports (1) (2).

In this system, African governments are responsible for the internal control of the trade. Each year they submit to the Secretariat proposed quotas, which include poached tusks. All shipping documents are referred to the Secretariat, whose export permits for legal ivory have been made harder to forge. Each tusk is indelibly marked. The keystone of the whole system is the agreement by Hong Kong and Japan to refuse ivory unless it is certified as legal under CITES. If all these conditions are met, the Secretariat believes, the price of illegal ivory will be forced down enough to make poaching unprofitable (3). In effect, the illegal market will have been appropriated.

In 1986, the first year of the system, the 19 African exporting nations filled about 55 percent of their combined quota of 108,441 tusks. Their total exports of 59,433 tusks represent 278,583 kilograms of ivory, worth about $28 million (4). Sudan and Somalia were the only large exporters able to fill their quotas, although it is believed illegal traders in Tanzania and Zaire shipped at least the equivalent of these nations' quotas. Another reason why the first-year quotas were not met is that many countries held large stockpiles of ivory. Nonproducing nations (e.g., Belgium, Burundi, and Singapore) have now joined the system and registered 653,000 kilograms of stockpiled

tusks (5). Forty-five nations were in the system by 1987, and the export quota was set at 216,670 tusks (6). Certified ivory is already selling at several times the price of ivory that is not accompanied by legitimate paperwork (7). Yet the 1986 and 1987 quotas will account for less than half of all African ivory production; in 1986, the tusks of some 89,000 elephants entered the trade illegally (8).

Although it is too early to judge the success of the quota system, it has forced the hand of at least two governments that had disregarded CITES. Burundi and the United Arab Emirates (UAE) have long been important entrepôts for illegal ivory moving from Africa to Asia (9). Burundi recently assured the Secretariat that it will abide by the quota network (10). This news was offset, however, when the UAE withdrew from CITES in January 1988—the first party ever to do so (11). Even before the UAE renounced the Convention, CITES members had been urged to ban trade with this country because of its lack of cooperation with the Secretariat.

At the 1987 CITES Conference of the Parties, delegates were alarmed by a report of the IUCN African Elephant and Rhino Specialist Group, which estimated a 36 percent decline in the elephant population on the continent since 1981 (from 1.2 million to 764,000) (12). Some predicted that if the downward trend is not arrested soon, there will be calls for replacing quotas with drastic restrictions on illegal trading (13). A few African wildlife officials have already pressed for banning elephant hunting and ivory trade within their countries until they can set up the strong internal controls needed to make quotas work (14).

References and Notes

1. Keith Lindsay, "Trading Elephants for Ivory," New Scientist, Vol. 122, No. 1533 (1986), p. 49 and p. 51.
2. Erik Eckholm, "New Tactics Transform Wildlife Conservation," New York Times (November 18, 1986), p. C4.
3. Op. cit. 1, p. 51.
4. J.R. Caldwell, "The Effect of Recent Legislative Changes on the Pattern of the World Trade in Raw Ivory," Traffic Bulletin, Vol. 9, No. 1 (IUCN Wildlife Trade Monitoring Unit, Cambridge, U.K., 1987), Table 1, p. 7 and p. 10. The figure for total value assumes a price of $100 per kilogram for raw ivory.
5. Ibid., p. 8.
6. "Ivory Quotas Set for 1987," TRAFFIC (U.S.A.), Vol. 7, No. 4 (1987), Table 2, p. 15.
7. Op. cit. 4, p. 10.
8. International Union for Conservation of Nature and Natural Resources, African Elephant and Rhino Specialist Group, "Elephant Population Estimates, Trends, Ivory Quotas and Harvests," report to the Sixth Meeting of the Conference of the Parties (CITES), Ottawa, Canada, July 1987, pp. 3–4.
9. Simon Lyster, "Setting CITES to Work," BBC Wildlife (October 1987), n.p.
10. "Ivory Market Back Door Closed?" TRAFFIC(U.S.A.), Vol. 7, No. 4 (1987), p. 15.
11. "UAE to Withdraw from CITES," TRAFFIC (U.S.A.), Vol. 7, No. 4 (1987), p. 13.
12. Op. cit. 8, p. 7.
13. Erik Eckholm, "Despite Setbacks, World Control of Trade in Wildlife Expands Influence," New York Times (July 28, 1987), p. C3.
14. Op. cit. 1, p. 52.

Table 6.7 Average Rhino Horn Retail Prices in Selected Asian Markets, 1979–86[a]

Market	1979–81	\$US Per Kilogram 1982–84	1985–86
Seoul, South Korea	1,436	1,797	1,771
Hong Kong	11,103	15,700	14,282
Macao	4,127	7,797	8,644
Kaohsiung, Taiwan	X	X	21,365
Taipei, Taiwan[b]	17,090	X	23,929
Tainan, Taiwan[b]	X	X	29,910
Singapore	11,615	11,804	14,464
Bangkok, Thailand	3,654	X	11,629
Tokyo, Japan	1,620	X	3,417
Osaka, Japan	2,230	2,516	3,771
Bandar Seri Begawan, Brunei	X	6,895	3,797
Djakarta, Indonesia	12,634	X	9,448
Kota Kinabalu, Malaysia	X	X	14,697
Kuala Lumpur, Malaysia	19,801	17,280	11,636

Source: Lili Sheeline, "Is There a Future in the Wild for Rhinos?" *TRAFFIC(U.S.A.)*, Vol. 7, No. 4 (1987), Table 1, p. 6, based on Esmond Bradley Martin, "The Rhino Horn Trade 1985-1986," *World Wildlife Fund Monthly Report* (July 1986), Table III.
Notes:
a. One survey was taken during each time span; the figures given are one-time prices only, not an average.
b. Prices from Taiwanese cities are for horn taken from Asian species. Prices for African horn were at least 90 percent lower.
X = not available.

jewelry and ornament industry. Even though the hawksbill is on CITES Appendix I, Japan continues to accept imports because it took a reservation on this turtle when it joined the Convention in 1980 (109). Oil from the pods of musk deer brings as much as \$60,000 per liter in Asia, where it is a medicinal ingredient (110). In the first four months of 1987, about 54,400 Himalayan musk deer—a protected species native to Nepal, Bhutan, and India—were killed to supply musk oil to Japan (111).

Asian demand for rhinoceros products is probably the most serious illegal trade problem today. Eighty-four percent of the world's population of rhinos (there are five species, three Asian and two African) has disappeared since 1970. About 2,400 Asian rhinos and only 55 of the Javan species are left. About 8,400 African rhinos remain, but only a few years ago, there were many more; the population of the black rhino has dropped 95 percent since 1970 (112). Since 1975, poaching has been the main cause of these declines (113). Rhinos are killed for their horn, hide, hooves, and other body parts.

Horn is the most valuable part. Some Indians use powdered rhino horn as an aphrodisiac, but, contrary to popular belief, most Asians do not. In traditional Asian pharmacology, rhino horn is used to reduce fevers (114). The only large market outside Asia is North Yemen, where jambias (decoratively carved dagger handles) are made of rhino horn. Over the past couple years, North Yemeni imports of horn have decreased considerably because of an economic slump, but demand for horn remains strong (115). By contrast, Asian demand is declining somewhat because youths do not believe so strongly in traditional medicine (116).

In some countries, rhino horn use is still ubiquitous, even though astronomical prices are routinely charged by local pharmacists. (See Table 6.7.) *Chung sim hwan* balls are used in South Korea to treat everything from paralysis to "contaminated blood"; doctors there are reluctant to replace rhino horn as an ingredient in their formulas (117). Similar medicines, whose makers show varying degrees of resistance to substitution, are sold in China, Taiwan,

and elsewhere in East Asia (118). In contrast to ivory, for which there is no acceptable substitute (119), other types of horn will work in traditional Asian medicines—if people can be persuaded to accept them. Conservationists have been pressing for alternatives throughout Asia and have had some success. In Japan, especially around cosmopolitan Tokyo, much of the public has accepted saiga antelope horn as a replacement (120).

FOCUS ON: SUSTAINABLE DEVELOPMENT, BIOLOGICAL DIVERSITY, AND WILDLIFE

Ultimately, all economic development depends on natural resources. Any development that depletes the world's resource base without providing for its replenishment cannot be sustained for long. Many people believe that the world is entering a critical time when demands of the rapidly growing population of the Third World, combined with disproportionately heavy use of energy and other resources in affluent countries, are straining the world's natural resources to the breaking point.

Sustainable development seeks to avert such a catastrophe by promoting forms of growth that are designed to meet current basic human needs without compromising the ability of our descendants to meet theirs. It seeks a more equitable distribution of resources between the wealthy and the poor (121).

Sustainable development differs radically from environmental preservation by virtue of its emphasis on meeting human needs. Preservationists minimize human needs in their deliberations; their ideal is to protect, intact, as much of the world's remaining natural resources as possible. Sustainable development is closer to, but still different from, environmental conservation. Conservationists are concerned with slowing the depletion rate of resources so that future generations can also enjoy their benefits. Proponents of sustainable development are too, but they explicitly link the continual economic betterment of humans with the success of environmental conservation. This distinguishing characteristic of sustainable development promises to be a particularly powerful approach to the problems of the Third World, with its confluence of extreme poverty, rapid population growth, and relatively abundant natural resources. As the World Commission on Environment and Development recently put it, "sustainable development requires meeting the basic needs of all and extending to all the opportunity to fulfill their aspirations for a better life. A world in which poverty is endemic will always be prone to ecological and other catastrophes" (122).

Sustainable development also differs sharply from conventional economic development. Sustainable development aims at keeping resource depletion, environmental degradation, cultural disruption, and social instability to a minimum—all of which are marginal concerns in conventional development theories (123).

Strict environmental preservation and economic development are frequently portrayed as mutually exclusive; they often are. More pointedly, the conflict in the Third World is increasingly between preservation and simple human subsistence. Many protected areas in developing nations exist primarily to preserve wildlife and its habitat. To be successful, they must be spared human encroachment. As a result local people in the Third World often view protected areas as repositories of richness (in terms of their capacity to provide basic needs, e.g., food from game meat) and potential income (e.g., from poaching) set in a gulf of poverty. In a recent survey of threats to the world's protected areas, people problems—unlawful entry, harassment of wildlife, poaching, and illegal removal of vegetation—were often reported by Third World reserve managers. Two thirds of the respondents from the least developed parts of the world considered local attitudes a threat to the protected areas they manage (124) (125).

Some of these attitudes are the residue of conservation efforts in the Third World, which have relied on preservationist models adopted intact from affluent countries (126) (127). The consensus is that these models now often fail developing nations (128).

Third World Conservation Attitudes

No comprehensive study of Third World attitudes toward conservation has been done. However, recent national surveys indicate that there may be potential for building a conservation ethic in developing nations. In a 1983 study of schoolchildren in Tanzania, 45 percent agreed with the following statement: "If food were scarce, national parks should be used for farming," but nearly as many—39 percent—disagreed (129). This study contradicts an earlier one that found universal antagonism toward parks by Tanzanians (130). The 1983 survey also found significantly more support for national parks among pupils who knew more about them (131).

In Rwanda, when farmers living next to a protected area were surveyed in the first and fifth years of a national conservation awareness campaign, a similar relationship was seen. Over the period, the proportion who saw some use in conserving the forest rose from 49 to 81 percent, the proportion who acknowledged wildlife protection benefits rose from 41 to 63 percent, and the proportion who recognized the forest as beneficial to their water supply grew from 49 percent to 86 percent. At the same time, the proportion who thought the protected area should be converted to agriculture fell from 51 to 18 percent (132).

Local people in the Third World occasionally take the initiative for conservation projects. The Kuna Indians of Panama's Atlantic coast recently asked for and received international help in creating a 2,000-hectare tropical forest reserve. The Kunas' objectives—which they unanimously supported—were to protect important religious and cultural areas and to create income from scientists and naturalists, who would be drawn to the new protected areas. Management responsibilities are vested in the Kunas rather than in outside advisory groups (133).

Whatever the conservation attitudes of the Third World public, the reality of the international debt crisis is forcing many governments to draw down their natural resource bases rapidly. They urgently need funds to pay the interest on huge debts to developed countries. Their response can be tantamount to spending irreplaceable national economic capital.

Many Third World countries are willing to sacrifice a part of their environment to economic development, just as the industrialized world did earlier in its history. Some theorists assert that if developed nations want to preserve more environmental amenities than are available at home (e.g., the biological diversity found only in tropical forests), they should be willing to pay the owners for them. In short, the developed world should directly pay developing nations to conserve natural resources (134). To some extent this theory is beginning to be practiced through debt-for-nature swaps and other innovative financing arrangements.

Combining Conservation and Development: Some Initial Attempts

Debt-for-Nature Swaps

The debt crisis is most acute in Latin America and tropical Africa, where total foreign debt and interest are approaching $1 trillion. To reduce this burden, the International Monetary Fund and other lenders favor export-led solutions that require debtor nations to redouble their efforts to increase exports, particularly monoculture cash crops. As a result, developing countries have little choice but to allow marginal wildlands and forests to go under the plow. In the process, not only is biologically diverse habitat lost, but production of foods needed locally is discouraged in favor of cash crops for export (135) (136) (137). Latin America's debt to developed nations was incurred piecemeal over the years. (See Chapter 14, "Basic Economic Indicators," Table 14.2.) Much of the debt is devalued as prospects for its full repayment grow dimmer, and a secondary market has sprung up in which debt obligations are bought and sold at less than face value. Given the slim likelihood of fully repaying these loans in cash, some debtor nations set up debt exchange programs; they offer creditors something—say, equity in a public or private entity or a commodity—in exchange for voluntary cancellation of the dollar amount of the debt. Such transactions are popularly called debt-for-equity swaps.

For example, if a bank wants to sell $100,000 worth of a country's debt and that debt has been devalued to 60 cents on the dollar in the current secondary market (a 40 percent discount), an investor may buy the debt obligation for $60,000. The buyer may then take that obligation to the borrowing country and, under debt exchange clauses, convert it into a local investment worth $100,000 in the debtor's currency. In essence, foreign investors in the secondary market can use debt-for-equity to obtain local currency interests at an attractive discount (138) (139).

Debt-for-nature swaps are a variation of debt-for-equity. The first such swap was made in July 1987. Conservation International used a foundation grant of $100,000 to buy $650,000 worth of Bolivia's $4 billion debt—an 85 percent discount. In exchange for cancellation of this debt, Bolivia agreed to establish three protected areas (totaling nearly 1 million hectares) around the Beni Biosphere Reserve in the Andean foothills. Timber had been cleared in these areas for cattle ranching and lumbering. As part of the agreement, the Bolivian Government will manage the forests for sustainable development. Some economic activity is allowed in the reserves, but parts are set aside for wildlife protection or hunting by indigenous people (the nomadic Chimane Indians live in one of the new reserves) (140). The three new protected areas are also buffer zones for Beni, where 13 of Bolivia's 18 endangered mammal species live. Several are also continentally endangered: the four-eyed opossum, giant armadillo, giant otter, jaguar, maned wolf, and ocelot (141). As part of the agreement, Bolivia will also endow management of the biosphere reserve with the equivalent of $250,000 (142).

Ecuador and Costa Rica completed a different kind of debt-for-nature swap. They exchanged debt for local currency government bonds that are turned over to private conservation groups within the debtor nation. Here, conservationists and government officials in the debtor country, rather than the banks or environmental organizations, set the terms (143).

In the Ecuadoran swap, the nation's leading conservation group, Fundacion Natura, made an agreement with the government to buy up to $10 million in external debt. Because Ecuador's debt sells for about 30 cents on the dollar, if Fundacion Natura raises $3 million, it can buy $10 million in bonds that pay a market-indexed rate of interest. The principal of the bonds would endow Fundacion Natura, with the interest paying for land purchases, management of protected areas, and training for park personnel (144).

Despite the fact that it has attracted a great deal of attention, the usefulness of debt-for-nature is limited. The secondary market for devalued debt is quite small, worth only $7 billion in 1986, or less than 1 percent of the Third World's external debt (145). Further, debt-for-nature swaps may provide opportunities for conservation or sustainable development projects, but they do not guarantee project success. The chances are enhanced in countries that have a conservation track record on which to base long-term expectations and that have well-organized private organizations operating independently of the government, as in Ecuador and Costa Rica. In any case, the signing of a debt-for-nature swap should be seen as only the first step down a long road of commitment.

Conservation Banking

Proponents of conservation and sustainable development are coming to realize that many of their goals cannot be achieved if they ignore orthodox economics—and vice versa. First of all, the philosophical barriers that have been erected between the world of conservation and that of international finance must be overcome. The recent professions of environmental concern by the World Bank may be a sign that major lenders are beginning to entertain conservationist ideas (146) (147).

Several innovative conservation financing plans have been proposed; any of them could be used to promote sustainable development projects. Some multinational companies operating in the Third World hold considerable amounts of local currency as blocked funds (i.e.,

money that the companies are legally prohibited from converting to foreign exchange). These funds could be invested in conservation or sustainable development projects (148). Other techniques include requiring developing nations to publish a national land use policy before they can apply for bilateral aid and multilateral loans, setting up debt exchange programs based on giving special discounts to corporations that devote funds to protected area management, and arranging joint financing of environmentally sound businesses by the World Bank and commercial lenders (149).

Perhaps the most comprehensive proposal is one that would institutionalize environmental concerns within the conventional financial world. The World Commission on Environment and Development endorsed the creation of an international conservation banking program allied with the World Bank. The program would supplement multilateral development banks, aid agencies, and commercial lenders by advising developing nations (both official and nongovernmental organizations) on financing protection of critical habitats and ecosystems. It would also help negotiate environmentally sound transactions between debtor nations and their creditors (150) (151).

National Conservation Strategies

Should an international conservation banking program materialize, its advisory work would often be done in the context of National Conservation Strategies (NCSs) (152). NCSs are nation-by-nation plans for carrying out the World Conservation Strategy, a 1980 policy statement (prepared by IUCN, WWF, and UNEP) that is a manifesto of sustainable development (153).

The aim of an NCS is to enable a country to find its way to sustainable development. Specifically, an NCS reviews all activities affecting the nation's natural resources. Then it identifies any barriers to sustainable use of the natural resource endowment. Typically, a major obstacle is the lack of long-term development planning. The NCS tries to supply a long-term strategy by assessing the urgency of environmental problems, making them known to the public and policymakers, evaluating the supply and demand of natural resources involved, laying out possible approaches, and assigning responsibility for the necessary tasks (154).

Two nations—Zambia and Vietnam—illustrate the range of approaches taken with NCSs. Both are nations in transition. Zambia is trying to move from reliance on copper exports to a more diversified agriculture-based economy (155). Vietnam is still coming to terms with the consequences of the recent war, not the least of which are environmental.

Zambia has a long record of wildlife exploitation, conservation, and tourism (156), and its NCS emphasizes the economic value of wildlife and how it will fit into the country's new agricultural plans. Poaching is seen as the biggest problem because it robs the nation of much-needed income that could be gained through wildlife-based tourism and legal hunting. Zambia considers poaching symptomatic of a failure to distribute the benefits of wildlife conservation to local people. Its NCS proposes controlled hunting in protected areas to provide more protein for local diets and distributing income from safari operations more equitably. It also suggests that Zambia lead the way in forming an ivory cartel so that not all the profits go into the illegal market (157).

Vietnam's NCS, by contrast, treats wildlife more abstractly, emphasizing its potential value as a genetic resource. But the immediate future is dire for wildlife in Vietnam: there are lists of protected species and areas but no control over hunting, and almost all the people have access to guns. Since the war, many animals have been hunted almost to extinction, and their habitats have not yet recovered from the spraying of herbicides, bombing, and other military activities that devastated large tracts of wildlands, including the topsoil. Vietnam's NCS ventures no solutions as detailed as Zambia's, for none of the institutional prerequisites is in place. Vietnam must first create a viable protected area system, enforce existing regulations, control hunting, join CITES, and so on, all in the absence of an environmental ministry and as part of a national reconstruction plan slated to be carried out in just 20 years (158).

Biosphere Reserves

Biosphere reserves are a special kind of protected area that relies upon zoning to safeguard genetic diversity. They form an international protected area system, overseen by the Man and the Biosphere Programme bureau of the United Nations Educational, Scientific and Cultural Organization. As of early 1988, there were 267 biosphere reserves worldwide. (See Chapter 19, "Wildlife and Habitat," Table 19.1.)

Ideally, a biosphere reserve encompasses a core zone that represents one of the earth's major ecosystems, large enough to permit in-situ conservation of its genetic material and mostly undisturbed by human activity, except for scientific research. Multiple-use buffer zones adjoin the core and are managed for the economic benefit of the local population by means of sustainable development projects. (See Figure 6.1.) Although zoning is not new, the biosphere reserve's avowed emphasis on safeguarding genetic diversity, managing problems on surrounding lands, and involving the local populace in the search for solutions is unique (159).

This emphasis is ideal; in most cases, what is achieved is something less. In industrialized countries, biosphere reserves are usually superimposed on existing protected areas, and the managing agency's adherence to the goals of the biosphere reserve is voluntary (160). This situation causes confusion over what biosphere reserves are all about. In countries with preservationist national park systems, the fact that biosphere reserves emphasize the needs of adjacent human populations runs counter to the ingrained idea that protected areas should be kept inviolate (161). Biosphere reserves have reached their greatest potential when they were created from scratch in developing nations. In a few notable instances, the ideal has been approached.

Figure 6.1 Biosphere Reserves

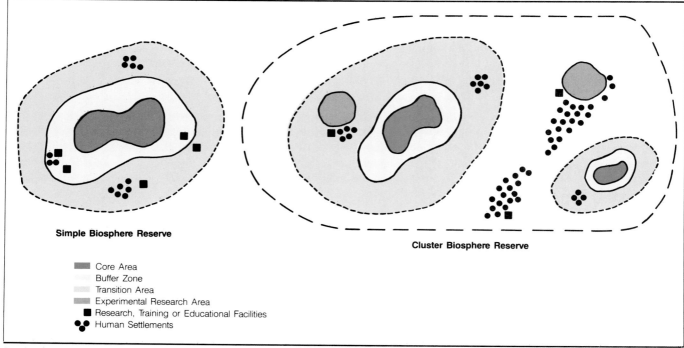

Simple Biosphere Reserve

Cluster Biosphere Reserve

Core Area
Buffer Zone
Transition Area
Experimental Research Area
■ Research, Training or Educational Facilities
● Human Settlements

Source: Michel Batisse, "Developing and Focusing the Biosphere Reserve Concept," *Nature and Resources*, Vol. 22, No. 3 (UNESCO, Man and the Biosphere, Paris, 1986).

Some of the best examples are in Mexico. When Mapim Biosphere Reserve was created in 1977, the whole spectrum of nearby residents, from cattle ranchers to members of local *ejidos* (a communal system of peasant land tenure), helped lay out the boundaries. Ranches and *ejidos* continue to exist in buffer zones surrounding a core that protects the habitat of the endangered desert tortoise *Gopherus flavomarginatus*. Reserve authorities gained solid local support by sponsoring nearly as much practical research in the buffer zone as scientific research in the core. For example, studies were done to improve varieties of prickly pear cactus and sabaneta grass for better livestock feed. The reward came when a public information campaign virtually stopped local hunting of the desert tortoise for its meat (162). The nearby La Michilia Biosphere Reserve also relies on sponsoring sustainable development projects—such as beekeeping and fruit nurseries—to gain local support for protecting its core (163) (164).

It is a new Mexican biosphere reserve, though, that promises to make the most tangible connection yet between preserving genetic diversity and promoting sustainable development. Designated in March 1987, the Sierra de Manantlán Biosphere Reserve, in southwestern Jalisco, includes the site where a wild species of corn, *Zea diploperennis*, was first described in 1979. *Zea diploperennis* is something of a showpiece for advocates of preserving biodiversity. It is resistant or immune to seven major corn viral diseases, is adapted to wet conditions at high altitudes, is a perennial, and can be crossed with commercial corn. A disease-resistant corn crop that would not have to be sown every year has the promise of saving farmers huge sums of money (165) (166).

The University of Guadalajara is coordinating the Sierra de Manantlán project and has created a special project laboratory. The initial socioeconomic and ecological analyses are being done in workshops with local people. Because no land in Sierra de Manantlán will be bought or taken by the government, the entire project is an experiment in self-imposed zoning. The biosphere reserve will be administered by a body that encompasses local communities, the university, and federal, state, and municipal governments (167).

Sierra de Manantlán's fauna is quite diverse, with 452 species—295 bird, 76 mammal, 65 reptile and amphibian, and 16 fish, many of which are migratory. Their habitat is threatened by slash-and-burn agriculture, overgrazing, and fuelwood gathering. Commercial logging had a long history in the region, but few of the profits were ever seen by local residents (5,000 within the reserve itself), almost all of whom are poor.

To solve these social and ecological problems, Sierra de Manantlán's organizers developed an operating plan based on 14 areas of coordination with local people. They include ethnoecology, environmental education, forestry, sustainable development, and *Zea diploperennis* research. The sustainable development section is devoted to raising the area's standard of living through small-scale programs in aquaculture, fruit and vegetable farming, and agroforestry (168).

RECENT DEVELOPMENTS

NEW WORLD CONSERVATION STRATEGY PLANNED

Until recently, the belief that the goals of conservation and development are not only incompatible, but antithetical, went widely unquestioned. This assumption was challenged by the publication of the *World Conservation Strategy* (WCS) in 1980. Not only did the WCS show conservation and development to be compatible, but it also argued that neither can succeed in the long run without the other. The WCS has encouraged more than 35 countries to prepare national conservation strategies and has been instrumental in convincing international development donors' to make their assistance more environmentally sound. The 1987 publication of *Our Common Future*, the final report of the World Commission on Environment and Development, affirmed the tenets of sustainable development—which were first championed in the WCS—and gave them wider currency (169).

Building on this new broader support, a new global conservation strategy is now being prepared. Its working title is the *World Conservation Strategy II* (WCS-II). It is intended as an action plan for international conservation in the 1990s (170).

WCS-II is more than a mere sequel or companion to WCS. At the first meeting of the WCS-II Technical Advisory Committee in October 1987, it was recommended that the new document be addressed to a wider audience: not just conservationists, but government officials whose decisions affect natural resources and those who advise or influence them. This group includes ministers of finance and planning, international development assistance agencies, and national planning commissions, for example. All of them, as well as environmental groups and other interested nongovernmental organizations, will be consulted in preparation of the WCS-II (171).

In early 1988, the International Union for Conservation of Nature and Natural Resources was presented with a proposed table of contents for the WCS-II. It includes the following topics:
■ Redefining sustainable development in terms of ecology, the economy, and equity
■ Building sustainability into the social and economic development process
■ Incorporating women and indigenous people into natural resource management and development
■ Overcoming the weaknesses of traditional economic analysis in evaluating sustainable development
■ Monitoring the sustainability of development
■ Promoting the acceptance of an ethic that embraces plants and animals as well as people
■ Minimizing the adverse effects of population growth, urbanization, industrial development, and energy production
■ Encouraging the recognition of the environmental effects of economic insecurity and armed conflict
■ Reversing the severity and extent of degraded ecosystems upon which humans depend for food and fiber.

As a plan of action, WCS-II will be more prescriptive than WCS. One section of WCS-II will identify priorities (which take into account political and financial limitations) for managing sustainable development: environmental assessment, policy, and planning; involving communities in local conservation action; managing biomes; managing human impacts on nature; managing human impacts on the global commons (e.g., the open oceans and Antarctica); managing information; developing human potential to manage resources; and building institutions to support sustainable development (172).

Preparing WCS-II will take two years. As was the case for the *World Conservation Strategy*, the effort is cosponsored by IUCN, the UNEP and the World Wildlife Fund (173).

WORLD WILDERNESS INVENTORY SPURS AFRICA STUDY

In a world of 5 billion people, it takes a stretch of the imagination to envision vast areas of land that remain untouched by human development. But a recent global wilderness inventory prepared by the Sierra Club in Washington, D.C., discovered that over a third of the Earth is devoid of human settlements, roads, and other signs of modern civilization. The inventory was presented at the 4th World Wilderness Congress in Denver, Colorado in the fall of 1987.

The unprecedented study provided insight into one of the few remaining frontiers on Earth. More than 50 million square kilometers—34 percent of the total land mass—remains wild. Not surprisingly, though, about 42 percent of the wilderness is found in antarctic and high arctic tundra and another 20 percent is mainly desert. Most of the remainder is located along mountain ranges, within tropical forests, and near other imposing landscapes. Few large wilderness areas remain in the continental United States, Mexico, Europe, the eastern Soviet Union, Southeast Asia, or nondesert Australia (174). (See Chapter 16, "Land Cover and Settlements," Table 16.1.)

Antarctica accounts for nearly a quarter of the total wilderness area on the planet. North America retains 36 percent of its wilderness, mostly due to the contributions of Greenland (99 percent) and Canada (65 percent). Only

7 percent of Europe's wildlands remain, the report found. The other continents are between a quarter and a third wild: Africa (30 percent), Australia and Oceania (30 percent), Asia (27 percent), and South America (24 percent).

The Sierra Club group gathered data from space-based photographs used by the U.S. Department of Defense for commercial and military flight navigation. They searched the remotely-sensed maps for "empty quarters," areas without visible evidence of human development. Only wilderness tracts of at least 4,000 square kilometers were included to be consistent with the level of detail from the maps. The inventory did not consider biological value as a criterion for wilderness designation.

The world wilderness inventory was only a broad first step in what is expected to be a more fine-tuned assessment of the balance between human expansion and wild areas. The Sierra Club study sought to provide data that are "accurate in the aggregate," but need to be ground checked to fill in the gaps and relate the findings to specific regional characteristics.

Such an analysis, which focused specifically on African wildlands, was prepared in conjunction with the IUCN. This report compares the total wilderness area in Africa with wildlands that are protected in nature preserves, national parks, and wildlife sanctuaries. Data on the protected lands were culled from the Protected Areas Data Unit at IUCN's Conservation Monitoring Centre. The two sets of data were then integrated by a geographical information system at the World Bank's Center for Earth Resource Analysis to determine the extent to which wilderness lands are protected.

Of the almost 10 million square kilometers of African wilderness, less than 7 percent is protected. Vast stretches of unprotected wilderness run through the uninhabitable Saharan region, but a considerable amount of unprotected land lies to the south where the threat of human encroachment is greater. The Africa study noted that many protected lands are not strictly wilderness areas and that many small areas are free from development (175). The inventory provides a vantage point from which to analyze the world's wilderness areas and to develop strategies to protect some of those areas that still remain wild.

References and Notes

1. Peter M. Vitousek, *et al.*, "Human Appropriation of the Products of Photosynthesis," *BioScience*, Vol. 36, No. 6 (1986), p. 372.
2. D.D. Raup, "Biological Extinction in Earth History," *Science*, Vol. 231, No. 4745 (1986), pp. 1528–1533, cited in World Commission on Environment and Development, *Our Common Future* (Oxford University Press, New York, 1987), p. 150.
3. Robert Repetto, "Population, Resources, Environment: An Uncertain Future," *Population Bulletin*, Vol. 42, No. 2 (1987), p. 3.
4. Steven M. Stanley, "Extinction as Part of the Natural Evolutionary Process: A Paleobiological Perspective," in *Animal Extinc-*

tions: What Everyone Should Know, R.J. Hoage, ed. (Smithsonian Institution Press, Washington, D.C., 1985), p. 31.
5. J. Turk and A. Turk, *Environmental Science* (Saunders College Publishing, New York 1984).
6. Paul R. Ehrlich, "Human Carrying Capacity, Extinctions, and Nature Reserves," *BioScience*, Vol. 32, No. 5 (1982), p. 331.
7. Paul R. Ehrlich and Harold A. Mooney, "Extinction, Substitution, and Ecosystem Services," *BioScience*, Vol. 33, No. 4 (1983), pp. 251–252.
8. Thomas E. Lovejoy, "Species Leave the Ark One by One," in *The Preservation of Species: The Value of Biological Diversity*,

Bryan G. Norton, ed. (Princeton University Press, Princeton, New Jersey, 1986), pp. 16–17.
9. Arne Naess, "Intrinsic Value: Will the Defenders of Nature Please Rise?" in *Conservation Biology: The Science of Scarcity and Diversity*, Michael E. Soulé, ed. (Sinauer, Sunderland, Massachusetts, 1986), pp. 504–515.
10. Holmes Rolston III, "Duties to Endangered Species," *BioScience*, Vol. 35, No. 11 (1985), p. 720, pp. 718–726.
11. Michael E. Soulé, "What is Conservation Biology?" *BioScience*, Vol. 35, No. 11 (1985), pp. 727–734.
12. Michael E. Soulé, "History of the Society

for Conservation Biology: How and Why We Got Here," *Conservation Biology*, Vol. 1, No. 1 (1987), p. 4.

13. *Op. cit.* 11, p. 728.

14. Michael E. Soulé, "Conservation Biology and the Real World," in *Conservation Biology: The Science of Scarcity and Diversity*, Michael E. Soulé, ed. (Sinauer, Sunderland, Massachusetts, 1986), pp. 1–12.

15. Jared Diamond, "The Design of a Nature Reserve System for Indonesian New Guinea," in *Conservation Biology: The Science of Scarcity and Diversity*, Michael E. Soulé, ed. (Sinauer, Sunderland, Massachusetts, 1986), p. 501.

16. Edward O. Wilson, "The Biological Diversity Crisis," *BioScience*, Vol. 35, No. 11 (1985), p. 700, pp. 703–704.

17. Edward C. Wolf, *On the Brink of Extinction: Conserving the Diversity of Life*, (Worldwatch Institute, Washington, D.C., 1987), p. 20.

18. Anthony J. Whitten, *et al.*, "One or More Extinctions from Sulawesi, Indonesia?" *Conservation Biology*, Vol. 1, No. 1 (1987), pp. 42–43.

19. Mary E. Palmer, "A Critical Look at Rare Plant Monitoring in the United States," *Biological Conservation*, Vol. 39, No. 2 (1987), p. 114.

20. Robert E. Jenkins, Jr., "The Identification, Acquisition, and Preservation of Land as a Species Conservation Strategy," in *Animal Extinctions: What Everyone Should Know*, R.J. Hoage, ed. (Smithsonian Institution Press, Washington, D.C., 1985), pp. 131–140.

21. Alan Randall, "Human Preferences, Economics, and the Preservation of Species," in *The Preservation of Species: The Value of Biological Diversity*, Bryan G. Norton, ed. (Princeton University Press, Princeton, New Jersey, 1986), pp. 87–88.

22. Gene Namkoong, "Preserving Natural Diversity," in *Genetics and Conservation: A Reference for Managing Wild Animal and Plant Populations*, Christine M. Schonewald-Cox, *et al.*, eds. (Benjamin/Cummings, Menlo Park, California, 1983), pp. 317–318.

23. Michael J. Bean, "International Wildlife Conservation," in *Audubon Wildlife Report 1987*, Roger Di Silvestro, ed. (Academic Press, Orlando, Florida, 1987), p. 308.

24. U.S. Congress, Office of Technology Assessment, *Technologies to Maintain Biological Diversity* (U.S. Government Printing Office, Washington, D.C., 1987), p. 63.

25. *Op. cit.* 10, pp. 720–721.

26. Paul R. Ehrlich, "Extinctions and Ecosystem Functions: Implications for Humankind," in *Animal Extinctions: What Everyone Should Know*, R.J. Hoage, ed. (Smithsonian Institution Press, 1985), p. 162.

27. David S. Wilcove, "From Fragmentation to Extinction," *Natural Areas Journal*, Vol. 7, No. 1 (1987), p. 26.

28. John MacKinnon and Kathy MacKinnon, *Review of the Protected Areas System in the Indo-Malayan Realm* (International Union for Conservation of Nature and

Natural Resources and United Nations Environment Programme, Gland, Switzerland, 1986), pp. 51–52.

29. G. Nabhan, Assistant Director, Desert Botanical Gardens, Phoenix, Arizona, quoted in U.S. Congress, Office of Technology Assessment, *Technologies to Maintain Biological Diversity* (U.S. Government Printing Office, Washington, D.C., 1987), p. 78.

30. *Op. cit.* 28, p. 212 and pp. 220–225.

31. Anne Burrill, Iain Douglas-Hamilton, and John MacKinnon, "Protected Areas as Refuges for Elephants," in John MacKinnon and Kathy MacKinnon, *Review of the Protected Areas System in the Afrotropical Realm* (International Union for Conservation of Nature and Natural Resources and United Nations Environment Programme, Gland, Switzerland, 1986), p. 177.

32. I. Douglas-Hamilton, "African Elephants: Population Trends and Their Causes," *Oryx*, Vol. 21, No. 1 (1987), pp. 11–24.

33. Norman Myers, *The Sinking Ark: A New Look at the Problem of Disappearing Species* (Pergamon Press, Oxford, U.K., 1979), p. 15.

34. *Op. cit.* 24.

35. Richard Conniff, "Inventorying Life in a Biotic Frontier before It Disappears," *Smithsonian*, Vol. 17, No. 6 (1986), p. 82.

36. Terry L. Erwin, "Tropical Forest Canopies: The Last Biotic Frontier," *Bulletin of the Entomological Society of America* (spring 1983), pp. 14–19.

37. The Conservation Foundation (CF), *State of the Environment: A View toward the Nineties* (CF, Washington, D.C., 1987), p. 544.

38. Norman Myers, "The Extinction Spasm Impending: Synergisms at Work," *Conservation Biology*, Vol. 1, No. 1 (1987), p. 14.

39. *The Global 2000 Report to the President of the U.S.*, Vol. II, *The Technical Report* (Pergamon Press, New York, 1980), p. 328 and p. 331.

40. *Op. cit.* 38.

41. Julian L. Simon and Aaron Wildavsky, "On Species Loss, the Absence of Data, and Risks to Humanity," in *The Resourceful Earth*, Julian L. Simon and Herman Kahn, eds. (Basil Blackwell, New York, 1984), pp. 172–176.

42. Julian L. Simon, "Disappearing Species, Deforestation, and Data," *New Scientist*, Vol. 110, No. 1508 (1986), pp. 60–63.

43. *Op. cit.* 8, p. 14.

44. *Op. cit.* 8, p. 14.

45. Daniel Simberloff, "Are We on the Verge of a Mass Extinction in Tropical Rain Forests?" in *Dynamics of Extinction*, David K. Elliott, ed. (John Wiley & Sons, New York, 1986), pp. 166–167.

46. *Ibid.*, pp. 165–180.

47. *Op. cit.* 38, p. 16.

48. Nini Bloch, "Too Small an Ark: Extinction Is a Way of Life in Our National Parks," *Expedition News*, Vol. 8, No. 3 (1987), p. 41.

49. John Spears and Edward K. Ayensu, "Resources, Development, and the New Century," in *The Global Possible: Resources, Development, and the New

Century*, Robert Repetto, ed. (Yale University Press, New Haven, Connecticut, 1985), p. 302.

50. World Commission on Environment and Development, *Our Common Future* (Oxford University Press, New York, 1987), p. 151.

51. *Op. cit.* 17, p. 19.

52. Robert J. Buschbacher, "Tropical Deforestation and Pasture Development," *BioScience*, Vol. 36, No. 1 (1986), p. 22.

53. *Op. cit.* 33, p. 5.

54. International Institute for Environment and Development and World Resources Institute, *World Resources 1987* (Basic Books, New York, 1987), p. 87.

55. *Op. cit.* 24, pp. 67–68.

56. *Op. cit.* 28, p. 12.

57. *Op. cit.* 28, p. 12.

58. Yaa Ntiamoa-Baidu, "West African Wildlife: A Resource in Jeopardy," *Unasylva*, Vol. 39, No. 2 (1987), pp. 27–28.

59. Thomas E. Lovejoy, "Strategies for Preserving Species in the Wild," in *Animal Extinctions: What Everyone Should Know*, R.J. Hoage, ed. (Smithsonian Institution Press, Washington, D.C., 1985), p. 105.

60. R.H. MacArthur and E.O. Wilson, *The Theory of Island Biogeography* (Princeton University Press, Princeton, New Jersey, 1967).

61. Alwyn H. Gentry, "Endemism in Tropical versus Temperate Plant Communities," in *Conservation Biology: The Science of Scarcity and Diversity*, Michael E. Soulé, ed. (Sinauer, Sunderland, Massachusetts, 1986), pp. 158–159.

62. Barry Phillips, *The ICBP Oceanic Islands Data Base: A Preliminary Demonstration* (International Council for Bird Preservation, Cambridge, U.K., 1985), p. 1.

63. John Parnell, Peter Wyse Jackson, and Quentin Cronk, "A Paradise about to Be Lost," *New Scientist*, Vol. 112, No. 1528 (1986), p. 46.

64. O.H. Frankel and Michael E. Soule, *Conservation and Evolution* (Cambridge University Press, New York, 1981), p. 19.

65. International Union for Conservation of Nature and Natural Resources (IUCN) and United Nations Environment Programme, *Review of the Protected Areas System in Oceania* (IUCN, Gland, Switzerland, 1986), p. 2.

66. Erik Eckholm, "International Effort Aims to Safeguard Wildlife Treasures of Madagascar," *New York Times* (June 16, 1987), p. C1.

67. *Op. cit.* 28, p. viii and pp. 218–219.

68. Peter Kramer, "The Galápagos: Islands under Siege," *Ambio*, Vol. 12, No. 3–4 (1983), pp. 188–189.

69. R.S. de Groot, "Tourism and Conservation in the Galápagos Islands," *Biological Conservation*, Vol. 26, No. 4 (1983), pp. 294–300.

70. Bradley Graham, "Tourism, Immigration Put Strain on Galápagos," *Washington Post* (March 19, 1987), pp. A25–A26.

71. H.A. Mooney and J.A. Drake, "The Ecology of Biological Invasions," *Environment*, Vol. 29, No. 5 (1987), pp. 13–14.

72. Lloyd L. Loope and Charles P. Stone,

"Introduced vs. Native Species in Hawaii: A Search for Solutions to Problems of Island Biosphere Reserves," in *Conservation, Science, and Society* (United Nations Educational, Scientific and Cultural Organization, Paris, 1984), p. 283.

73. *Op. cit.* 71, p. 10.

74. *Op. cit.* 72, pp. 284–287.

75. U.S. Department of State, *Proceedings of the Interoceanic Workshop on Sustainable Development and Environmental Management of Small Islands*, William S. Beller, ed. (U.S. Government Printing Office, Washington, D.C., 1987), p. 9.

76. *Op. cit.* 64, p. 29.

77. Daniel W. Gade, "Man and Nature on Rodrigues: Tragedy of an Island Common," *Environmental Conservation*, Vol. 12, No. 3 (1985), p. 214.

78. *Op. cit.* 75, p. 45, p. 47, and p. 52.

79. *Op. cit.* 77, p. 211.

80. Steven G. North and David J. Bullock, "Changes in the Vegetation and Populations of Introduced Mammals of Round Island and Gunner's Quoin, Mauritius," *Biological Conservation*, Vol. 37, No. 2 (1986), p. 112.

81. Alison L. Hess, "Research Opportunities for Sustainable Development and Environmental Management on Small Islands," in U.S. Department of State, *Proceedings of the Interoceanic Workshop on Sustainable Development and Environmental Management of Small Islands*, William S. Beller, ed. (U.S. Government Printing Office, Washington, D.C., 1987), p. 70.

82. *Op. cit.* 75, p. 24, p. 28, and p. 29.

83. Anthony Cheke, "The Legacy of the Dodo—Conservation in Mauritius," *Oryx*, Vol. 21, No. 1 (1987), p. 29.

84. J.P. Myers, *et al.*, "Conservation Strategy for Migratory Species," *American Scientist*, Vol. 75, No. 1 (1987), pp. 19–26.

85. S.K. Eltringham, *Wildlife Resources and Economic Development* (John Wiley & Sons, New York, 1984).

86. Christopher Nagano and Curtis Freese, "A World Safe for Monarchs," *New Scientist*, Vol. 114, No. 1554 (1987), pp. 43–47.

87. Cyrille de Klemm, "A Review of Existing International Instruments Relating to Migratory Species," in *Migratory Species: An International Overview* (International Union for Conservation of Nature and Natural Resources, Gland, Switzerland, 1986), pp. 9–25.

88. Simon Lyster, *International Wildlife Law: An Analysis of International Treaties Concerned with the Conservation of Wildlife* (Grotius, Cambridge, U.K., 1985), pp. 278–284 and p. 297.

89. *Ibid.*, pp. 288–291.

90. *Ibid.*, p. 279, pp. 297–298.

91. *Op. cit.* 23, pp. 570–571. Note: An important reason for the Reagan administration's recent decision not to join the Bonn Convention was the reluctance of state fish and game agencies. They had become skeptical of international treaties after engaging the government in a controversy over the practice of group-listing species for CITES.

92. TRAFFIC(U.S.A.), *World Trade in Wildlife* (World Wildlife Fund, Washington, D.C.,

1988), p. 1.

93. *Op. cit.* 88, pp. 240–248.

94. TRAFFIC(U.S.A.), "Monitoring Wildlife Trade—The Traffic Network", Factsheet (World Wildlife Fund, Washington, D.C., 1987).

95. *Op. cit.* 88, p. 242.

96. J.R. Caldwell, "The Effect of Recent Legislative Changes on the Pattern of the World Trade in Raw Ivory," *Traffic Bulletin*, Vol. 9, No. 1 (IUCN Wildlife Trade Monitoring Unit, Cambridge, U.K., 1987), p. 9.

97. *Op. cit.* 88, pp. 258–259.

98. *Op. cit.* 88, pp. 262–264.

99. *TRAFFIC(U.S.A.)*, "Reservations of CITES Parties," Vol. 7, No. 4 (1987), Tables 3 and 4, pp. 17–20.

100. *Op. cit* 23, p. 310.

101. *Op. cit.* 88, p. 240 and p. 277.

102. R.B. Martin and T. De Meulenaer, "Survey of the Status of the Leopard (*Panthera pardus*) in Sub-Saharan Africa" (abbreviated version), report to the Sixth Meeting of the Conference of the Parties (CITES), Ottawa, Canada, July 1987, section 4.1, n.p.

103. International Union for Conservation of Nature and Natural Resources, African Elephant and Rhino Specialist Group, "Elephant Population Estimates, Trends, Ivory Quotas and Harvests," report to the Sixth Meeting of the Conference of the Parties (CITES), Ottawa, Canada, July 1987, p. 6.

104. Erik Eckholm, "New Tactics Transform Wildlife Conservation," *New York Times* (November 18, 1986), pp. C1, C4.

105. David Spurgeon, "The Ivory Merchants, Wildlife Terrorists," *South*, No. 84 (1987), p. 83.

106. *Op. cit.* 102, Table 4, n.p.

107. Erik Eckholm, "Despite Setbacks, World Control of Trade in Wildlife Expands Influence," *New York Times* (July 28, 1987), p. C3.

108. TRAFFIC(U.S.A.), "Elephant Ivory Trade," Factsheet (World Wildlife Fund, Washington, D.C., December 1986), pp. 1–2.

109. Amanda Jorgenson, "Central American Hawksbills Exploited for Japanese Market," *TRAFFIC(U.S.A.)*, Vol. 6, No. 3 (1985), p. 12.

110. Maria Elena Hurtado and David Spurgeon, "Policing the Wildlife Terrorists," *South* (October 1987), p. 83.

111. Daniel Sneider, "Japan Accused of Flouting Wildlife Protection Accords," *Christian Science Monitor* (June 30, 1987), p. 9.

112. TRAFFIC(U.S.A), "Rhinoceros Trade," Factsheet (World Wildlife Fund, Washington, D.C., December 1986), p. 1.

113. Esmond Bradley Martin, "The Rhino Horn Trade 1985–1986," *World Wildlife Fund Monthly Report* (July 1986), p. 178.

114. *Op. cit.* 85, p. 15.

115. Daniel Martin Varisco, "Horns and Hilts: Wildlife in North Yemen (YAR)," report prepared for the Asia/Near East Bureau of the U.S. Agency for International Development and World Wildlife Fund U.S., 1987, p. 14 and p. 32.

116. *Op. cit.* 113, pp. 183–184.

117. *Op. cit.* 113, p. 180.

118. *Op. cit.* 113, pp. 180–181.

119. *Op. cit.* 85, p. 58.

120. *Op. cit.* 113, pp. 180–181.

121. *Op. cit.* 50, pp. 8–9.

122. *Op. cit.* 50, p. 8.

123. Edward B. Barbier, "The Concept of Sustainable Economic Development," *Environmental Conservation*, Vol. 14, No. 2 (1987), pp. 101–103.

124. Gary E. Machlis and David L. Tichnell, "Economic Development and Threats to National Parks: A Preliminary Analysis," *Environmental Conservation*, Vol. 14, No. 2 (1987), Tables III and IV, p. 154.

125. *Op. cit.* 54, Table 6.1, p. 79. Note: All seven African reserves, added in 1986 to the International Union for Conservation of Nature and Natural Resources' list of the world's most threatened protected areas, were included at least partly because of the threat of uncontrolled poaching.

126. Gary E. Machlis and David L. Tichnell, *The State of the World's Parks: An International Assessment for Resource Management, Policy, and Research* (Westview, Boulder, Colorado, 1985), pp. 17–19.

127. David Harmon, "Cultural Diversity, Human Subsistence, and the National Park Ideal," *Environmental Ethics*, Vol. 9, No. 2 (1987), pp. 147–158.

128. Many papers given at the Third World Congress on National Parks in 1982 called for new directions in protected area management. See Jeffrey A. McNeely and Kenton R. Miller, eds., *National Parks, Conservation, and Development: The Role of Protected Areas in Sustaining Society* (Smithsonian Institution Press, Washington, D.C., 1984).

129. A.H. Harcourt, H. Pennington, and A.W. Weber, "Public Attitudes to Wildlife and Conservation in the Third World," *Oryx*, Vol. 20, No. 3 (1986), p. 152.

130. F. Jurji, *Conservation Areas and Their Demographic Settings in Tanzania*, Research Report No. 18 (Bureau of Land Use Practice, University of Dar es Salaam, Tanzania, 1979).

131. *Op. cit.* 129, p. 153.

132. *Op. cit.* 129, pp. 153–154.

133. B. Rich and S. Schwartzman, "The Role of Development Assistance in Maintaining Biological Diversity *In-Situ* in Developing Countries," U.S. Congress, Office of Technology Assistance (OTA), 1985, cited in OTA, *Technologies to Maintain Biological Diversity* (U.S. Government Printing Office, Washington, D.C., 1987), p. 297.

134. Theodore Panayotou, "Economics, Environment, and Development," presented at the Fourth World Wilderness Congress, Estes Park, Colorado, September 1987, pp. 26–27.

135. Barbara J. Bramble, *Third World Debt and Natural Resources Conservation* (National Wildlife Federation, Washington, D.C., n.d.), pp. 1–2.

136. *Op. cit.* 134, pp. 23–24.

137. Peter H. Raven, "We're Killing Our World," presented at the American Association for the Advancement of Science, Chicago, February 1987, pp. 5–6.

138. Michael Chamberlin, "Debt Exchanges—Some Nuts and Bolts" (unpublished, October 1987), p. 2 and p. 9.

139. The World Bank, *World Development Report 1987* (Oxford University Press, New York, 1987), Box 2.2, p. 22.

140. Philip Shabecoff, "Bolivia to Protect Lands in Swap for Lower Debt," *New York Times* (July 14, 1987).

141. "Blueprint for Conservation and Development: Swapping Debt for Nature," *Tropicus*, Vol. 1, No. 1 (Conservation International, Washington, D.C., 1987), p. 3.

142. Joseph Palca, "High-Finance Approach to Protecting Tropical Forests," *Nature*, Vol. 328, No. 6192 (1987), p. 373.

143. Roque Sevilla, President, Fundacion Natura, letter to *Los Angeles Times* (January 14, 1988), editorial page.

144. Diana Page, International Institute for Environment and Development, March 3, 1988 (personal communication).

145. *Op. cit.* 139, Box 2.2, p. 22.

146. The World Bank, *The World Bank's Operational Policy on Wildlands: Their Protection and Management in Economic Development* (The World Bank, Washington, D.C., 1986), pp. 1–6.

147. For a cautionary response, see Edward Goldsmith, "Open Letter to Mr. Conable, President of The World Bank: You Can Only Be Judged on Your Record," *The Ecologist*, Vol. 17, No. 2–3 (1987), pp. 58–61.

148. John Walsh, "Bolivia Swaps Debt for Conservation," *Science*, Vol. 237, No. 4815 (1987), pp. 596–597.

149. National Wildlife Federation (NWF), "Environmental Management and Debt Adjustment," in *Environmental Management & Developing World Debt Adjustments: A New Strategy* (NWF, Washington, D.C., 1987), pp. 10–12.

150. *Op. cit.* 50, pp. 338–339.

151. I. Michael Sweatman, "The International Conservation Banking Program, or Facility" (unpublished, June 1987), pp. 2–6.

152. *Ibid.*, p. 4.

153. International Union for Conservation of Nature and Natural Resources (IUCN), World Wildlife Fund, and United Nations Environment Programme, *World Conservation Strategy: Living Resource Conservation for Sustainable Development* (IUCN, Gland, Switzerland, 1980), pp. 1–2.

154. *Ibid.*, pp. 19–20.

155. Government of Zambia and International Union for Conservation of Nature and Natural Resources (IUCN), *The National Conservation Strategy for Zambia* (IUCN, Gland, Switzerland, 1985), p. 7 and p. 22.

156. Stuart A. Marks, *The Imperial Lion: Human Dimensions of Wildlife Management in Central Africa* (Westview, Boulder, Colorado, 1984), pp. 105–117.

157. *Op. cit.* 155, p. 45.

158. Committee for the Rational Utilisation of Natural Resources and Environmental Protection and International Union for Conservation of Nature and Natural Resources (IUCN), *Vietnam: National Conservation Strategy* (IUCN, New Delhi, 1985), pp. 13–18, p. 25, pp. 36–40, p. 44, p. 47, and p. 61.

159. Michel Batisse, "The Biosphere Reserve: A Tool for Environmental Conservation and Management," *Environmental Conservation*, Vol. 9, No. 2 (1982), pp. 101–103.

160. Monica Goigel Turner and William P. Gregg, Jr., "The Status of Scientific Activities in United States Biosphere Reserves," *Environmental Conservation*, Vol. 10, No. 3 (1983), p. 234.

161. Stephen R. Kellert, "Public Understanding and Appreciation of the Biosphere Reserve Concept," *Environmental Conservation*, Vol. 13, No. 2 (1986), pp. 101–102.

162. Gonzalo Halffter, "The Mapimi Biosphere Reserve: Local Participation in Conservation and Development," *AMBIO*, Vol. 10, Nos. 2–3 (1981), pp. 93–96.

163. Christina Barbin, "Durango: Where Progress and Conservation Go Hand in Hand," in *Ecology in Practice: Insights from the Programme on Man and the Biosphere (MAB)* (United Nations Educational, Scientific and Cultural Organization, Paris, 1981), pp. 75–80.

164. Gonzalo Halffter and Exequiel Ezcurra, "Evolution of the Biosphere Reserve Concept," presented at the Fourth World Wilderness Congress, Estes Park, Colorado, September 1987, pp. 11–15.

165. Eduardo Santana, Rafael Guzman, and Enrique Jardel, "The Sierra de Manantlan Biosphere Reserve: The Difficult Task of Becoming a Catalyst for Regional Sustained Development," presented at the Fourth World Wilderness Congress, Estes Park, Colorado, September 1987, p. 3.

166. A.C. Fisher, "Economic Analysis and the Extinction of Species," University of California, Berkeley, Department of Energy and Resources, 1982, cited in World Commission on Environment and Development, *Our Common Future* (Oxford University Press, New York, 1987), p. 155.

167. *Op. cit.* 165, p. 5 and p. 10.

168. *Op. cit.* 165, pp. 1–12.

169. International Union for Conservation of Nature and Natural Resources, United Nations Environment Programme, and World Wildlife Fund, "Report of the First Meeting of the Technical Advisory Committee, World Conservation Strategy II," Washington, D.C., October 29–30, 1987, p. 3.

170. International Union for Conservation of Nature and Natural Resources, "Preparation of World Conservation Strategy II: Proposed Framework for WCS-II," discussion paper, February 3, 1988.

171. *Op. cit.* 169, p. 2.

172. International Union for Conservation of Nature and Natural Resources, "Preparation of World Conservation Strategy II: Annotated Table of Contents," discussion paper, February 3, 1988, pp. 1–6.

173. *Op. cit.* 170.

174. J. Michael McCloskey and Heather Spaulding, Sierra Club, "A Reconnaissance-Level Inventory of the Wilderness Remaining in the World," presented at the 4th World Wilderness Congress, Denver, Colorado, September 1987.

175. "Protected African Wilderness Areas: A Preview to a World Wilderness Inventory," paper presented at the 4th World Wilderness Congress, Estes Park, Colorado, September 1987.

7. Energy

The demand for commercially traded energy continued to grow during 1986, but more slowly than in previous years. At 1986 production rates, coal reserves should last more than 220 years, much longer than natural gas (59 years) and oil (33 years) (1). Serious shortages of fuelwood—the sole source of energy for half the world—continue in many developing countries. (For a discussion of the fuelwood crisis, see *World Resources 1986*, pp. 110–113.)

The relative amounts and types of energy used for transportation, industry, agriculture, and residential-commercial applications around the world are discussed below. Examining these consumption patterns reveals such trends as the overreliance of one of these economic sectors on a single source of energy. Understanding these consumption patterns is basic to promoting energy efficiency and addressing energy-related environmental problems.

Energy in the USSR and Eastern Europe—including the importance of energy to security and economic growth—is highlighted in this edition of *World Resources*. The vast wealth of Soviet energy resources afforded the USSR and Eastern Europe protection from international price fluctuations experienced during the energy crises of the 1970s (2). As export commodities, oil, gas, and coal are significant in the balance of trade of the Soviet Union and to a lesser extent, in Eastern Europe. However, slow economic growth during the 1980s, compounded by dwindling domestic resources, may force Eastern Europe to rely more heavily on Soviet energy supplies (3).

Problems of acidic deposition, climate change, stratospheric ozone depletion, Third World debt, global economic development, and national security are all exacerbated by wasteful energy use. Finding more efficient ways of using energy must, therefore, be a part of any comprehensive approach to dealing with these issues. Improvements in energy efficiency are constrained by the characteristics of energy use in individual economic sectors. Over the past decade, per capita energy consumption in Organisation for Economic Co-operation and Development (OECD) countries has either declined or remained constant while their economies continued to grow (4). However, per capita energy consumption is still increasing in countries with centrally planned economies and in developing countries. The potential for continuing improvements in energy efficiency and conservation are examined by sector in Focus On: Energy Conservation, below.

CONDITIONS AND TRENDS

PRODUCTION AND CONSUMPTION BY FUEL TYPE

Oil is the main commercial fuel in Western Europe, Australia, North America, and the developing countries; consumption in the USSR is led by natural gas; and in China, coal is the primary fuel. More than half the developing countries rely on imported oil for over 75 percent of their commercial energy needs (5). Renewable energy sources are unlikely to become a major alternative to fossil fuels in the next few decades.

Nonrenewable Energy

Oil

Gasoline prices on the Rotterdam Spot Market remained approximately 30 percent lower in spring 1988 than before their collapse in spring 1986 (6)—the result of OPEC's high oil production levels. Some higher-cost non-OPEC production fell in response to low market prices; for example, U.S. oil production fell 3 percent in 1986 (7). Excluding Alaskan oil, U.S. production has been declining since 1970 (8).

Falling oil prices on world markets did not necessarily mean lower consumer prices in some developing countries. For example, gasoline and kerosene cost more in India, Tanzania, Brazil, and Ecuador in 1986 than in 1985. National oil companies sometimes kept the prices high to recover losses sustained when they subsidized more expensive oil. Other factors that may have kept developing countries' retail prices at 1985 levels include government precautions against a possible world price rebound and a lag in price adjustments often common in regulated markets (9). In Ghana, prices for a range of imported goods rose when the government brought the official exchange rate in line with the actual (black market) exchange rate (10).

Global oil production grew 4.5 percent in 1986, led by OPEC's 13.1 percent increase; production outside OPEC grew less than 1 percent. Output from the world's largest single producer, the USSR, grew 3 percent in 1986 after declining in 1984 and 1985. During 1986, oil accounted for the largest share (38 percent) of global commercial energy (11). (See Table 7.1.) Global production in 1987 (60.2 million barrels per day) was approximately the same as in 1986 (12).

After growing throughout the 1960s and 1970s, world oil consumption declined during the first part of the 1980s. But in 1986, consumption increased again, mainly in response to low prices. Global oil consumption increased 2.5 percent that year (13); in 1987, it rose another 2.1 percent. The United States continued to lead the world in oil consumption, followed by the USSR and Japan (14).

The Middle East is the world's largest net oil exporter by a substantial margin, followed by Latin America and the USSR. The three main oil importers are the United States, Japan (with the highest ratio of consumption to production), and Western Europe (excluding the United Kingdom and Norway, which are net exporters) (15).

After rising for six years, the world ratio of oil reserves to production rates fell in 1986. (The previous rise was due in part to lower demand, the subsequent fall to the fact that lower oil prices discouraged exploration.) At the end of 1986, total proven world oil reserves were sufficient to last a little over three decades at 1986 production levels. (See Table 7.2.) Middle East oil reserves are about 58 percent of the total.

Natural Gas

Worldwide production of natural gas increased 1.8 percent in 1986 and another 5.9 percent in 1987. Over the past decade, global production has risen every year but one (1982). The bulk of this growth occurred during 1986 in the Soviet Union, where natural gas production exceeded oil production (in energy-equivalent terms) for the first time (16). The USSR and the United States are the world's leading producers by a wide margin (17).

World gas consumption grew moderately in 1986, primarily because natural gas prices responded slowly to drops in oil prices. The Soviet economy was more dependent on natural gas in 1986 than any other country in the world.

The USSR and the Middle East have far more natural gas reserves than any other regions—about two thirds of the world total. (See Table 7.2.)

Coal

China produced 23 percent of the world's coal in 1986 (see Table 7.1), followed by North America with 23 percent and the USSR with 16 percent. More than half (54 percent) the coal was produced in Asian and European countries with centrally planned economies.

Table 7.1 Commercial Energy Production and Consumption by Region and Fuel, 1986

(petajoules)[a]

Region	Oil Production	Oil Consumption	Natural Gas Production	Natural Gas Consumption	Coal Production	Coal Consumption	Nuclear Power Production and Consumption	Hydropower Production and Consumption	Total Production	Total Consumption
North America	23,845	34,078	19,654	19,239	22,174	19,725	5,431	6,582	77,686	85,055
Latin America	13,834	9,019	2,835	2,981	758	925	63	3,442	20,932	16,430
Western Europe	8,299	24,582	6,511	8,060	8,332	10,468	5,803	4,233	33,178	53,062
Middle East	26,772	4,535	2,010	2,010	29	92	X	109	28,920	6,745
Africa	10,501	3,421	1,792	1,193	4,149	2,772	42	674	17,158	8,102
Asia and Australasia	7,449	17,137	3,894	3,772	9,693	10,957	2,290	2,378	225,704	36,537
Centrally Planned Economies										
USSR	25,666	18,632	25,851	21,157	15,818	15,751	1,474	2,198	71,007	59,213
China	5,468	4,154	494	507	22,568	22,241	X	1,181	29,711	28,082
Other[b]	963	5,070	2,629	4,183	14,793	13,746	502	950	19,837	24,452
World Total[c]	**122,796**	**120,627**	**65,669**	**63,102**	**98,315**	**96,682**	**15,605**	**21,747**	**324,132**	**317,764**

Source: British Petroleum (BP), BP Statistical Review of World Energy (BP, London, 1987), p. 4, p. 8, p. 22, p. 24, pp. 26-28, and pp. 30-32.
Notes:
a. Conversion factors: 1 million metric tons of oil equivalent = 41.87 petajoules.
b. Albania, Bulgaria, Czechoslovakia, German Democratic Republic, Hungary, Kampuchea, Laos, Mongolia, Democratic People's Republic of Korea, Poland, Romania, Viet Nam and Yugoslavia.
c. Figures may not total due to rounding.
X = not available.

Table 7.2 Proven Commercial Energy Resources at the End of 1986
(petajoules)[a]

	Oil		Natural Gas		Coal			
Region	Reserves	R/P[b] (years)	Reserves	R/P[b] (years)	Hard Coal Reserves	Soft Coal Reserves	R/P[b] (years)	Total Reserves
North America	213,537	9.0	310,720	15.5	3,782,335	1,886,973	313	6,193,565
Latin America	519,188	37.7	213,620	71.6	75,552	59,874	241	868,234
Western Europe	100,488	12.2	240,808	35.9	970,291	846,018	212	2,157,605
Middle East	2,294,476	85.5	1,013,724	100+	X	X	X	3,308,200
Africa	305,651	29.3	221,388	100+	1,833,213	3,127	362	2,363,379
Asia and Australasia	104,675	14.3	217,504	54.4	1,186,733	603,519	211	2,112,431
Centrally Planned Economies								
USSR	334,960	13.1	1,705,076	64.0	3,036,608	1,897,164	X	6,973,808
China	100,488	18.5	31,072	64.8	4,365,124	189,856	X	4,686,540
Others[c]	12,561	11.0	15,536	6.4	897,083	643,905	X	1,569,085
World	**3,986,024**	**32.5**	**3,969,448**	**58.7**	**16,146,939**	**6,130,436**	**226**	**30,232,847**

Source: British Petroleum (BP), *BP Statistical Review of World Energy* (BP, London, 1987), p. 2, p. 21, and p. 25.
Notes:
a. Conversion factors: 1 mtoe = 41.87 PJ, 1 bcm natural gas = 38.84 PJ, 1 mtce (hard coal) = 27.91 PJ, 1 mtce (soft coal) = 13.96 PJ.
b. R/P is the ratio of proven reserves to 1986 production rate.
c. Albania, Bulgaria, Czechoslovakia, Cuba, German Democratic Republic, Hungary, Kampuchea, Laos, Mongolia, Democratic People's Republic of Korea, Poland, Romania, Viet Nam, and Yugoslavia.
X = not available.

Coal consumption rose 1.6 percent in 1986, well below the 4.5 percent growth experienced just one year earlier. The drop was due largely to low oil prices. China and the USSR were responsible for most of the growth in demand, while the demand for coal in OECD countries declined slightly (18). In 1987, coal consumption grew 3.4 percent (19).

Unlike oil and natural gas, coal reserves are distributed fairly evenly around the world. North America has the largest reserves, followed closely by China and the USSR. (See Table 7.2.) Between now and the end of the century, it is unlikely that serious coal shortages will occur anywhere (20).

Nuclear Power

Despite the accident at the Soviet Union's Chernobyl nuclear power station in April 1986, consumption of nuclear power continued to grow, but its 7.1 percent growth rate was the lowest since 1979. In the USSR and West Germany, a decade-long growth pattern was broken in 1986, with reduced production of electricity from nuclear power stations (21).

It is early to assess the long-term implications of the Chernobyl accident for the nuclear power industry. (See Recent Developments, New Studies of the Chernobyl Accident Health Impacts, below.) Most nuclear programs showed signs of weakness even before the accident. Plant construction in 1986 had fallen to half its peak in 1980, and it is likely to fall further by 1990. Nuclear power's share of global electricity production may well be lower in the year 2000 than it was in 1987 (22).

The United States continues to be the largest user of nuclear power in absolute terms; however, relative to its total energy consumption, France uses nuclear energy most extensively (23).

Renewable Energy

Low oil prices limit the economic competitiveness of wind turbines, photovoltaics, solar thermal collectors, and other renewable sources of energy. Biomass and hydropower provide 21 percent of the total energy consumed worldwide (15 percent and 6 percent, respectively).

Fuelwood

Wood is the primary source of energy for almost one half the world population (24). According to the United Nations, the largest fuelwood producer is India, followed by Brazil, China, Indonesia, the United States, and Nigeria (25). Most fuelwood is collected on a noncommercial basis for domestic heating and cooking, so it is not usually included in official energy statistics.

In many areas, fuelwood can no longer be thought of as a renewable resource because consumption rates exceed sustainable yields (26). In certain locations, chiefly around cities, fuelwood gathering can damage forests. In the developing countries of sub-Saharan Africa, fuelwood accounts for 80 percent of total energy consumed, and increased consumption could contribute to severe environmental deterioration in some areas. The situation in parts of the Sudan-Saharan and southeastern regions is already serious and it could become critical (27).

Hydropower

Hydropower supplied 21 percent of electricity worldwide in 1986—less than coal or oil but more than nuclear power (28). North America produces more hydropower than any other region in the world—the United States and Canada accounted for 30 percent of global production in 1986. Latin America produces almost 16 percent of the world's hydroelectricity, followed by the USSR with just over 10 percent (29).

The developing world has by far the largest share of unexploited hydropower capacity. By 1980, Asia had tapped just 9 percent, Latin America 8 percent, and Africa 5 percent of their potential resource (30). Although the debt crisis is slowing the availability of funds for expanding capacity, the World Bank projects that 223.5 gigawatts of large hydropower project capacity will be installed in developing countries between 1981 and 1995, more than half of them in Brazil, India, and China. Thirteen developing countries added almost 41 gigawatts of capacity between 1980 and 1985 (31).

In 1986, Venezuela completed its Guri Dam; with a 10-gigawatt capacity, it is the largest hydropower project in the world. Brazil is building a hydroelectric plant with a 12-gigawatt capacity, and China is considering moving ahead with its 13-gigawatt Three Gorges project (32). (See Box 7.1.)

According to the World Bank, 31 developing countries doubled their hydropower capacity between 1980 and 1985, much of it with small-scale projects. Small-scale hydropower generation provided almost 10 gigawatts worldwide by 1983. China is the world leader, with about 90,000 small hydropower stations supplying electricity to rural areas (33).

Ocean energy captured from waves and tides is being exploited on a limited basis. In 1986, Norway began operating the world's first wave-power plants (two proto-type plants with a combined capacity of 0.85 megawatts). For two decades, France has operated the world's largest tidal power plant, a 240-megawatt unit. China and Canada have 10-megawatt and 18-megawatt tidal-power facilities, respectively (34).

Windpower

The international market for wind generators increased seventeenfold between 1981 (34 megawatts sold) and

---

Box 7.1 Energy in China

Like the Soviet Union, China relies on domestic reserves to meet its energy demand. Energy self-sufficiency insulated China from the market fluctuations experienced by the rest of the world during the past 15 years, and this policy will likely continue. However, regional imbalances in energy resource distribution hamper efforts to supply sufficient energy to all of China's economic sectors (1).

Energy is becoming a key limiting component in the growth of China's economy: an estimated 20 percent of potential industrial output is lost because of a shortage of electricity (2). China plans to quadruple industrial and agricultural output by the turn of the century, but the absence of infrastructures for exploiting the resources, distributing the energy, and using it efficiently is a principal obstacle to modernization (3). Joint ventures with foreign energy firms are now common, providing access to needed technology, expertise, and capital.

ENERGY PRODUCTION

Chinese energy development efforts are dominated by coal (see Table 1); the country boasts the world's largest hard coal reserves—27 percent of the world total. China's combined reserves of hard and soft coal at the end of 1986 were third, behind the United States and the USSR. (See Table 7.2.) Proven reserves are sufficient to last 1,000 years at 1984 production levels. One quarter of the coal is produced at small local mines; between 1980 and 1984, the number of small mines tripled and their output increased 80 percent (4).

Over 75 percent of the coal is mined in the northeastern provinces (5), requiring a significant transportation system. As the Chinese economy expands, the ability of this transportation system will be strained (6).

China's oil industry has developed almost entirely since the People's Republic was founded in 1949. The industry went into a production slump in 1979, largely because it was suffering from two decades of rapid growth (7). With the help of foreign technology and expertise, production began to rise steadily again in 1982. At 4.4 percent of the world total in 1986, China's oil production was comparable to the United Kingdom or Mex-

Table 1 Commercial Energy Production, Consumption, and Exports in the People's Republic of China
(petajoules)[a]

Energy Source	1965	1975	1986
Oil[b]			
Production	473	3,228	5,485
Consumption	461	2,726	4,053
Exports	13	502	1,432
Coal			
Production	6,794	14,133	25,500
Consumption	6,692	14,034	25,198
Exports	103	100	302
Natural Gas			
Production and Consumption	43	346	486
Hydro Electricity			
Production and Consumption	37	171	336
Total Electricity			
Production	243	705	1,602

Sources: The World Bank, *Report on PR China* (The World Bank, Washington, D.C., 1985), cited in Michele Ledic, "Energy Key to Economic Growth," *Petroleum Economist* (November 1987), p. 406.
Notes:
a. Conversion factors: 1 million metric tons of oil = 41.87 petajoules (PJ); 1 million metric tons of coal = 29.31 PJ; 1 billion cubic meters of natural gas = 38.84 PJ; 1 terawatt hour of electricity = 3.6 PJ.
b. Crude oil and products.

ico (8). Oil reserves, estimated at 24 billion barrels, are considered sufficient through 2030 (9). China is Asia's second largest oil exporter after Indonesia, with shipments principally to Japan and the United States. Oil accounted for 17.5 percent of 1986 export earnings (10).

Natural gas production has grown over the past two decades, but in 1986 it remained a minor component of the Chinese energy balance.

In addition to hard coal, China also has the world's largest hydropower resources, but like coal, they are not located near population centers. Seventy percent are in the remote southwest portion of the country (11) and therefore electricity transmission must cover long distances. Both insufficient funds and the lack of workers in western China hamper hydropower development.

Over the past decade, large- and small-scale hydropower capacity has been added steadily. In 1986, hydropower delivered 4.2 percent of the country's primary energy consumption (12) and about 30 percent of China's electricity. Plans call for doubling hydropower over the next 15 years (13). The target is considered optimistic, although less than one quarter of the exploitable hydropower potential (379 gigawatts) had been developed by 1985 (14).

After years of planning to build 10,000 megawatts of nuclear power capacity by the year 2000, it appears that because of nuclear power's high cost in foreign exchange, the Chinese will develop their hydroelectric potential instead (15). If built, the 13-gigawatt Three Gorges Dam, on the Chang Jiang (Yangtze) in southeast China, would be the largest hydropower project in the world (16).

ENERGY CONSUMPTION

Although over 20 percent of the world's people live in China, they accounted for less than 9 percent of total energy consumption in 1986 (17). In 1985, per capita energy consumption was less than one fifth that in the USSR and Eastern Europe and one third the global average (18). Table 2 shows China's energy consumption in 1980. In 1986, coal accounted for 79 percent of China's energy consumption, oil 15 percent, hydropower 4 percent, and natural gas 2 percent (19).

Rural and urban energy consumption differ vastly. The 80 percent of China's 1 billion people who live in rural areas consume only 40 percent of total energy, and 90 percent of that is either biomass or locally produced commercial energy. The rural areas rely little on nationally distributed

1985 (567 megawatts sold). Much of this growth occurred in California, where capacity grew from 7 megawatts in 1981 to almost 1.5 gigawatts in 1987 (35).

China plans to build wind farms with a total capacity of 100 megawatts between 1990 and 1996, the Netherlands 150 megawatts by 1992 and 1 gigawatt by 2000, Spain 45 megawatts by 1993, and Greece 80 megawatts by the year 2000. Smaller wind farms are either in place or planned in Australia, Belgium, Israel, Italy, the USSR, the United Kingdom, and West Germany. The most ambitious windpower project by far is planned for India, where the government hopes to have 5 gigawatts of windpower generating capacity by the year 2000 (36).

Solar Power

Solar thermal collectors are used worldwide for tasks ranging from heating water to generating electricity. With low oil prices, the market for these devices has dropped substantially from peak years in the early 1980s. Lower oil and gas prices, coupled with elimination of tax credits, caused U.S. sales to fall 70 percent between 1984 and 1986 (37).

Photovoltaic modules convert sunlight directly into electricity. From 1976 to 1986, the market price fell 88 percent, to just over $5 (1986 constant dollars) per peak watt (38). Correspondingly, the market grew at an average

---

Box 7.1

commercial energy, and that policy will continue. Urban areas today consume 85 percent of commercial energy. Industry is the largest consumer of commercial energy (63 percent in 1980) (20). (See Table 2.) Consumption by the transportation, domestic, and agricultural sectors is low relative to the rest of the world.

China is still an inefficient energy user. (See Table 7.3.) If China can modernize industrial boilers, furnaces, power plants, and processes, then growth in energy consumption is expected to be only 3.5 percent, while the economy grows at 4.5 percent per year over the next 15 years (21). In addition, plans call for coal and petroleum prices to be adjusted from their abnormally low value to make them comparable to other forms of energy. Currently, China's energy prices are determined by two mechanisms: government-planned prices, and market prices for energy produced above the output quota. The planned prices will rise gradually to the level of market prices, in order to provide incentives for energy conservation, promote development of energy resources, and keep pace with plans for opening the economy to foreign operators (22).

Much coal is used in small-scale industry and in the residential and commercial sectors (23). As a result, winter air quality of northern Chinese cities ranks among the worst in the world (24).

RURAL ENERGY DEVELOPMENT

Eighty-five percent of rural energy needs are met using some form of biomass. For example, 4.5 million anaerobic digesters produce gas from animal wastes for cooking and lighting while retaining fertilizer components for the fields (25). In the country as a whole, the rate of wood use continues to cause soil erosion problems (26). Problems of fuelwood overuse are being remedied by replanting programs, increased coal production, energy-saving domestic ovens, and a major rural electrification effort involving small-scale hydropower.

After the 1949 revolution, China's hydropower plans for rural electrification followed the Soviet model, emphasizing large-scale dams. But during the Cultural Revolu-

Table 2 Energy Consumption in China by Sectors, 1980
(percent)

	Industry	Agriculture	Domestic	Transport	Total
Total Share of Energy Consumption	**63.0**	**7.0**	**22.0**	**8.0**	**100**
Breakdown of energy consumption					
Coal	51.5	45.5	91.3	43.9	59.2
Coke and Derivatives	15.5	X	X	X	9.8
Crude Oil and Derivatives	16.5	42.7	1.9	55.0	18.2
Natural Gas	4.1	X	2.9	X	3.2
Coking Gas	1.4	X	0.6	X	1.0
Electric Power	7.5	11.8	2.9	1.1	6.3
Heating from Cogeneration Plants	3.5	X	0.4	X	2.3
Total	**100**	**100**	**100**	**100**	**100**

Source: World Energy Conference (WEC), *Energy: Needs and Expectations,* 13th Congress, Cannes, October 5-11, 1986 (WEC, London, 1987), Table 5, p. 149.
X = not available.

tion, thousands of small-scale dams were constructed. China is the only developing nation today that places a high priority on developing small-scale (less than 6 megawatts per unit) hydropower. Between 1968 and 1983, about 90,000 small-scale hydro plants were built to provide 6,330 megawatts of generating capacity (27). At the end of 1984, 74,000 units with a 9,000-megawatt capacity accounted for 40 percent of China's rural electricity consumption. By the year 2000, total small-scale hydropower capacity is expected to reach 25,000 megawatts (28).

References and Notes

1. Michele Ledic, "China: Energy Key to Economic Growth," *Petroleum Economist* (November 1987), pp. 406–07.
2. "Potentially Serious Energy Woes Seen for China," *Oil Gas Journal* (October 26, 1987), p. 26.
3. Zhuang Qian, "China's Energy Policy and Its Problems," *Technology in Society,* Vol. 8 (1986), pp. 329–334.
4. *Op. cit.* 1, pp. 405–407.
5. *Op. cit.* 1, p. 405.
6. Fereidun Fesharaki and David Fridley, *China's Petroleum Industry in the International Context* (Westview Press, Boulder, Colorado, 1986), p. 60.
7. *Op. cit.* 1, pp. 405–406.
8. British Petroleum (BP), *BP Statistical Review of World Energy* (BP, London,

9. *Op. cit.* 2.
10. *Op. cit.* 1.
11. World Energy Conference (WEC), *Energy: Needs and Expectations,* 13th Congress, Cannes, October 5–11, 1986 (WEC, London, 1987), p. 149.
12. *Op. cit.* 8, p. 30 and p. 33.
13. Christopher Flavin, "The Saudis of Coal," *The Sun* (March 31, 1986, Baltimore) p. 1.
14. *Op. cit.* 1.
15. Jasper Becker, "China Switches from Nuclear Power to Hydroelectricity," *New Scientist* (April 3, 1986), p. 21.
16. Kenneth Lieberthal and Michael Oksenberg, *Bureaucratic Politics and Chinese Energy Development* (U.S. Department of Commerce, Washington D.C., 1986), p. 379 and p. 383.
17. *Op. cit.* 8, p. 32.
18. *Op. cit.* 11, p. 45 and p. 149.
19. *Op. cit.* 8, p. 33.
20. *Op. cit.* 1, p. 407.
21. *Op. cit.* 6, p. 56 and p. 58.
22. *Op. cit.* 11, pp. 245–246.
23. *Op. cit.* 1, p. 405.
24. *Op. cit.* 13.
25. *Op. cit.* 11, p. 15.
26. *Op. cit.* 11, p. 69, p. 148, and p. 298.
27. Christopher Flavin and Daniel Deudney, *Renewable Energy: The Power to Choose* (W.W. Norton, New York, 1983), p. 181.
28. *Op. cit.* 11, p. 299.

annual rate of 44 percent from 1980 to 1985 (39). The largest installation as of May 1988 was a 6.3-megawatt (peak) facility at Carissa Plains, California (40).

Half the photovoltaic modules sold in 1986 provide power to villages or equipment without access to power grids; the communications industry is the largest user. In the Third World, photovoltaic modules supply electricity for refrigerators, irrigation pumps, and lighting; worldwide, they supply electricity to more than 15,000 homes (41).

Geothermal Energy

The geothermal energy in the upper 5 kilometers of the Earth's crust is equal to about 40 million times the energy contained in world crude oil and natural gas liquid reserves. However, because it is dispersed, only a tiny fraction is economically exploitable. Intense, shallow concentrations of geothermal energy are found along the western edge of North America, in the Caribbean, on the islands of the mid-Atlantic Ridge, in the Himalayan range, in East Africa, western Arabia, in Central Asia, and along the eastern Pacific belt (42).

By 1985, more than 4,700 megawatts of geothermal electric power capacity had been installed throughout the world, and direct use of geothermal energy for heating was estimated at an additional 12,000 megawatts. Electricity produced from geothermal sources grew 14.5 percent annually between 1970 and 1980 and 17.5 percent annually between 1980 and 1985 (43).

ENERGY INTENSITY AND CONSUMPTION BY ECONOMIC SECTOR

Overall Energy Intensity

A country's energy intensity—the energy required to produce each unit of gross domestic product (GDP)—reflects the economic structure of the country (e.g., whether it is based on agriculture, industry, or services) as well as the efficiency with which the energy is used within that economic structure. Table 7.3 shows energy consumption per unit of GDP for 39 countries in 1984–85.

The Table 7.3 energy intensity data are only an imperfect measure for comparing the energy efficiencies of different national economies, especially when comparing developed with developing countries. In addition to the fact that energy use depends on the structure of the economy, two other influences must be considered. First, when GDP is converted into U.S. dollars, as in the table, the resulting energy intensity depends on the exchange rate. For example, Tanzania's energy intensity figure has roughly tripled in the past two years because of the devaluation of the U.S. dollar. Second, developing countries calculate GDP differently, especially for nonmarketed (subsistence) production; these differences skew GDP numbers for lower-income countries (44).

Between 1973 and 1985, the total primary energy requirements of OECD countries increased 5 percent while GDP increased 32 percent. The result was a 20 percent decline in energy intensity. About half the change occurred in 1979–82; since then, energy intensity

Table 7.3 Primary Energy Consumption per Unit Gross Domestic Product[a]

Country/Region	1984–85	Average Annual Growth Rate (percent)
North America[b,c]		
Canada	0.80	−0.5
United States	0.61	−2.2
Average	0.62	−2.1
Oceania[b,c]		
Australia	0.45	−0.5
Japan	0.29	−3.1
New Zealand	0.50	+1.8
Average	0.32	−2.5
Europe[b,c]		
Austria	0.33	−1.2
Belgium	0.36	−2.2
Denmark	0.27	−1.7
Germany	0.31	−1.7
Greece	0.44	+1.2
Ireland	0.44	−1.4
Italy	0.33	−1.8
Luxembourg	0.65	−4.9
Netherlands	0.36	−1.7
Norway	0.40	−1.4
Portugal	0.49	+1.5
Spain	0.32	+0.3
Sweden	0.40	−0.6
Switzerland	0.25	+0.3
Turkey	0.56	−1.0
United Kingdom	0.35	−2.0
Average	0.34	−1.4
Asia[d,e]		
Bangladesh	0.27	X
People's Republic of China	1.40	−1.3
India	0.79	+1.4
Indonesia	0.35	+3.3
Republic of Korea	0.63	+0.4
Malaysia	0.36	+0.3
Pakistan	0.64	+4.2
Philippines	0.35	−2.7
Taiwan	0.62	+0.2
Thailand	0.38	−0.8
Average	0.97	+0.5
Latin America[d,e]		
Argentina	0.29	+1.8
Brazil	0.68	+2.1
Mexico	0.56	+2.2
Venezuela	1.40	+4.6
Average	0.57	+2.7
West Africa[d,f]		
Cote d'Ivoire	0.13	+2.8
Morocco	0.27	0.0
Nigeria	0.18	+9.4
Senegal	0.49	+3.6
Average	0.20	+6.5

Sources:
1. Jayant Sathaye, Andre Ghirardi, and Lee Schipper, "Energy Demand in Developing Countries: A Sectoral Analysis of Recent Trends," in *Annual Review of Energy 1987*, Vol. 12 (1987), Table 3, p. 259.
2. Organisation for Economic Co-operation and Development and International Energy Agency (OECD/IEA), *Energy Conservation in IEA Countries* (OECD/IEA, Paris, 1987), Table 1, p. 43.
Notes: a. Gross domestic product metric tons of oil equivalent per $1,000 U.S. (constant 1980 dollars). b. 1985 data. c. Average annual growth rate for 1973–85. d. 1984 data. e. Average annual growth rate for 1973–84. f. Average annual growth rate for 1977–84.
X = not available.

has declined more slowly. These trends reflect improved energy efficiency encouraged primarily by high energy prices, plus the movement of energy-intensive industries to developing countries as OECD countries' economies become more service-based. During the past 10 years, improved energy efficiency in OECD countries has had a larger overall effect than shifts to less energy intensive industries (45).

Among the developed countries of North America, the Pacific, and Europe listed in Table 7.3, Canada, Luxembourg, and the United States are the most energy intensive; Denmark, West Germany, Japan, and Switzerland are the least energy intensive. OECD countries with the least decrease or with increases in annual energy consumption are generally those with the most rapidly expanding industrial sectors or with plentiful supplies of cheap electricity. Elsewhere, higher energy prices have lowered overall energy intensity by boosting the demand for less energy intensive products and services (46).

Relative energy intensity in the developing countries of Asia, Latin America, and West Africa has changed since 1973. In China, the Philippines, and Thailand, GDP grew faster than energy demand, but in most developing countries, energy demand grew faster than GDP. The average rise in energy required per unit of GDP was least in Asia, much more in Latin America, and still more in West Africa. Total regional GDP in West Africa was lower in 1984 than in 1977 but energy consumption grew steadily through 1982 (47). Nigeria, with the highest energy consumption growth rate shown in Table 7.3, has rapidly expanding industry and plentiful domestic energy resources.

In addition to comparing the energy intensities of national economies, it is also valuable to examine the energy consumption patterns of various economic sectors—industry, agriculture, transportation, residential,

commercial, and public—on a global or regional scale. (See Figure 7.1.) In the industrial sector, energy intensity can be assessed as the amount of energy consumed per dollar value of production. In other sectors, energy intensity can often be more easily assessed as energy efficiency.

Industrial Sector

Oil is the main energy source for OECD countries' industry, followed roughly equally by coal and natural gas. (See Table 7.4.) In the USSR and Eastern Europe, both coal and natural gas are more important than oil. (See Energy in the USSR and Eastern Europe, below.) In China (see Box 7.1) and to a lesser extent India, coal and other solid fuels supply industry's energy; Brazil's industry depends mostly on hydroelectricity. The large contribution of solid fuel in Brazil is due less to coal, which is under 30 percent of the solid fuel used in Brazil's industry, than to fuelwood, sugar cane bagasse, and other biomass. Other Latin American countries use more natural gas and oil than solid fuel. Both Indonesia and the West African nations rely primarily on oil, but Indonesia also has large natural gas reserves. South Korea relies on oil, most of it imported, for over 50 percent of its industrial needs.

Among the OECD countries, industry uses more energy than any other sector, 37 percent of total consumption in 1985. (See Table 7.4.) Industrial energy demand fell 1.3 percent annually from 1973 to 1984 while industrial output increased about 2 percent. As a result, the industrial energy intensity declined 30 percent. Improved efficiency was the major reason for the decrease in industrial energy use, but a shift to less energy intensive industries was also important (48).

Among the developing countries listed in Table 7.4, industry varies from old, heavy industry to new, light manufacturing to relatively undeveloped industrial sectors. Industrial energy intensity increased the most in Indonesia, Nigeria, and Venezuela, and it fell in most oil-importing developing countries (49).

China and India have a great deal of coal-fueled heavy industry and the most energy-intensive industry in Asia. Venezuela's industrial sector is also highly energy intensive because of the type of industry involved and the low energy prices, both supported by plentiful energy resources. On the other hand, oil conservation efforts and the introduction of more energy-efficient equipment have helped lower industrial energy intensity in the Philippines, South Korea, Taiwan, and Thailand (50).

Agricultural Sector

The United Nations Food and Agriculture Organization (FAO) estimates that in 1982, the latest year for which global figures are available, agriculture consumed 287 million metric tons of oil equivalent. This figure represents only about 4 percent of total energy consumption and it includes energy accounted for in the industrial sector—namely, energy used in manufacturing farm equipment, pesticides, fertilizers, and fertilizer feedstocks. If this "embodied" energy were excluded, agricultural

Figure 7.1 Fuel Consumption by Economic Sector for Selected Countries
(percent)

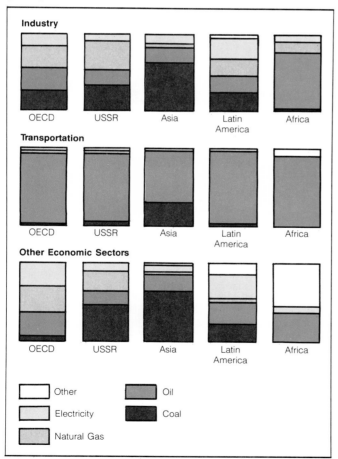

Source: Table 7.4
Notes:
a. Includes the People's Republic of China, India, Indonesia, and the Republic of Korea.
b. Includes Argentina, Brazil, Mexico, Paraguay, and Venezuela.
c. Includes the Ivory Coast, Morocco, Nigeria, and Senegal.
d. Includes the agricultural, residential, commercial, public, and other sectors.

Table 7.4 Sectoral Energy Consumption for Selected Countries and Regions
(petajoules)[a]

	OECD[b] (1985)	USSR (1987)	Eastern Europe[c] (1983)	China (1980)	India (1984)	West Africa[d] (1984)	Latin America[e] (1984)	Brazil (1983)	Indonesia (1984)	Republic of Korea (1985)
Total Energy Consumption[f]	106,972	46,509[g]	11,301	17,667	7,517	863	5,462	5,117	1,179	1,954
Energy Demand by Sector										
Agriculture[h]	1,748	934	X[i]	1,237	251	X	X[i]	274	X	X
Coal/solid fuels	32	84	X	563	X	X	X	136	X	X
Oil/liquid fuels	1,443	641	X	528	174	X	X	99	X	X
Natural gas/gaseous fuels	120	209	X	X	X	X	X	X	X	X
Electricity and heat	153	X	X	146	77	X	X	39	X	X
Other energy	X	X	X	X	X	X	X	X	X	X
Industry[h]	37,878	15,295	5,920	11,130	1,667	172	2,066	2,309[j]	516	801
Coal/solid fuels	9,666	4,275	1,144	7,457	1,201	4	149	808	5	271
Oil/liquid fuels	11,390	4,262	791	1,837	160	126	639	397	259	411
Natural gas/gaseous fuels	9,320	6,758	1,195	612	39	21	914	82	207	1
Electricity and heat	7,502	X	2,790	1,224	267	267	276	946	45	118
Other energy	X	X	X	X	X	X	88	76	X	X
Transportation[h]	32,750	6,045	870	1,413	746	381	2,071	1,067	328	281
Coal/solid fuels	9	301	98	620	190	X	X	1	1	X
Oil/liquid fuels	32,491	5,673	693	777	546	343	2,068	1,054[k]	327	278
Natural gas/gaseous fuels	17	71	5	X	X	X	X	X	X	X
Electricity and heat	233	X	74	16	10	X	3	13	X	3
Other energy	X	X	X	X	X	38	X	X	X	X
Residential/Commercial/Public[h]	33,260	6,729	X[i]	3,887	489	109	X[i]	1,467	335	787
Coal/solid fuels	2,825	3,685	X	1,706	105	X	X	564	5	467
Oil/liquid fuels	8,629	574	X	2,138	288	84	X	174	266	255
Natural gas/gaseous fuels	11,707	2,470	X	X	1	X	X	8	30	3
Electricity and heat	10,099	X	X	43	95	25	X	721	34	62
Other energy	X	X	X	X	X	X	X	X	X	X
Other[h]	1,336	X	4,511[l]	X	4,364[m]	201[n]	1,325[o]	X	X	85
Coal/solid fuels	187	X	2,107	X	X	17	13	X	X	X
Oil/liquid fuels	647	X	721	X	X	100	557	X	X	X
Natural gas/gaseous fuels	329	X	553	X	X	84	235	X	X	X
Electricity and heat	173	X	1,125	X	X	X	157	X	X	X
Other energy	X	X	5	X	4,364[m]	X	363	X	X	85

Sources:
1. For OECD: Organisation for Economic Co-operation and Development and International Energy Agency, (OECD/IEA), *Energy Balances of OECD Countries, 1970-1985* (OECD/IEA, Paris, 1987), Table 1, p. 19.
2. For USSR: International Energy Agency, Paris, estimates, 1988.
3. For Eastern Europe: The Vienna Institute for Comparative Economic Studies, ed., *COMECON Data 1985* (Greenwood Press, New York, 1986), Table 0/1, p. 33, and Table V/1.3, p. 426.
4. For the People's Republic of China: World Energy Conference (WEC), *Energy: Needs and Expectations,* 13th Congress, Cannes, October 5-11, 1986 (WEC, London, 1987), p. 149.
5. For India: WEC, *13th Congress National Energy Data Profile: India 1970-84* (WEC, Indian National Committee, 1986), Tables 5 and 6.
6. For West Africa: Jayant Sathaye, Andre Ghirardi, and Lee Schipper, "Energy Demand in Developing Countries: A Sectoral Analysis of Recent Trends," *Annual Review of Energy,* Vol. 12 (1987), Table 4, p. 260; Table 7, p. 265; Table 9, p. 270; and Table 12, p. 276.
7. For Latin America: WEC, 13th Congress, *National Energy Data Profile: Argentina Republic* (WEC, Member, Committee of the Argentina Republic, Buenos Aires), Table 5.1, p. 5; *National Energy Data Profile: Mexico* (WEC, Mexican National Committee, Mexico, D.F.), Table 5.1, p. 5; *National Energy Data Profile: Paraguay* (WEC, Paraguayan Committee), Table 5.1, p. 5; *National Energy Data Report: Republic of Venezuela 1986* (WEC, Venezuelan National Committee, Caracas), Table 5.1, p. 5.
8. For Brazil: Ministry of Mines and Energy (Brazil), *National Energy Balance 1984* (Ministry of Mines and Energy, Brasilia), Table E-11, pp. 122-123.
9. For Indonesia: WEC, *13th Congress 1986 National Energy Data Profile for the Republic of Indonesia,* (WEC, Indonesian National Committee, Jakarta), Table 5.1, p. 5.
10. For Republic of Korea: WEC, 13th Congress, *National Data Profile: The Republic of Korea* (WEC, Korean National Committee, Seoul), Table 5.1, p. 5.
Notes: a. Conversion factors: 1 mtoe = 41.87 PJ, 1 mtcc = 29.31 PJ. b. Includes Australia, Austria, Belgium, Canada, Denmark, Finland, France, the Federal Republic of Germany, Greece, Iceland, Italy, Japan, Luxembourg, the Netherlands, New Zealand, Norway, Portugal, Spain, Sweden, Switzerland, Turkey, the United Kingdom, the United States, and Yugoslavia. c. Includes Bulgaria, Czechoslovakia, German Democratic Republic, Hungary, Poland, and Romania. d. Includes Senegal, Morocco, Nigeria, and Cote d'Ivoire. e. Includes Argentina, Mexico, Paraguay, and Venezuela. f. Data are not from sources, but are a summation of sectoral energy consumption. g. Primary electricity and heat are included in total energy consumption, but are not presented on a sectoral basis. h. Data are not from sources, but are a summation of individual fuel consumptions from sources. i. Data for the Agriculture and Residential/Commercial/Public sectors are combined and reported in the "Other" sector. j. Includes the energy sector. k. Includes 149 PJ (petajoules) of ethanol. l. Combination of the residential, agricultural, trade, and other sectors. m. Estimated 1984 consumption of noncommercial energy: fuelwood, agricultural waste, and animal dung. n. Undefined use; balance of total consumption unaccounted for in sectoral data. o. Combination of agriculture, commercial, residential, and public sectors.
X = not available.

consumption was probably much lower than 4 percent of the global energy total for 1982.

Oil, used in many agricultural inputs as well as for machine fuel, is the main energy source (83 percent) in the OECD countries, the USSR, and India. Fuelwood is a major energy source in Brazil's agriculture, as are coal and other solid fuels in China's agricultural sector. Rural China receives little or no commercial energy. (See Box 7.1.)

Mineral fertilizer is the fastest growing user of commercial energy in agriculture; in 1982, it accounted for 70 percent of agricultural energy consumption in developing countries and 44 percent of world agricultural energy use. Eighty-five percent of the energy used in mineral fertilizer was used to produce nitrogenous fertilizer. The manufacture and operation of farm machinery is the largest, albeit declining, share of commercial energy use

in agriculture—52 percent in 1982, largely because of its importance in the developed countries. Pesticides and irrigation each consumed 2 percent of agricultural energy consumption worldwide in 1982. Estimates of annual fuel requirements for irrigation are 160 kilograms of oil equivalent per hectare for developed countries and 200 kilograms per hectare in Africa and the Near East (51).

Transportation Sector

In all the areas shown in Table 7.4, energy consumption in transportation is dominated by liquid fuel, especially oil. China and India, with fewer personal vehicles and more trains, use a larger proportion of coal and other solid fuels. Brazil's ethanol program, which substitutes ethanol for gasoline and diesel fuel, decreased reliance on petroleum for transportation between 1970 and 1984;

in 1986, ethanol accounted for 19 percent of transportation fuel (52).

Among the OECD countries, oil accounts for almost 99 percent of energy consumption for transportation and road transport is responsible for 80 percent of it. Although transportation energy efficiency has improved since 1973, overall energy use has not been consistent— the demand rose between 1973 and 1979, fell from 1979 to 1982, and has risen slowly since then (53).

Improvements in the energy efficiency of passenger cars are partially offset by lower oil prices and better economic conditions that encourage consumption, especially in commercial transportation. Automobiles accounted for 67 percent of energy consumption in road transport in OECD countries during 1973 and 61 percent in 1983; commercial vehicles accounted for 33 percent in 1973 and 39 percent in 1983. Of the overall 20 percent reduction in energy consumption per passenger and commercial vehicle between 1973 and 1983, 65 percent of the decrease was due to improved efficiency and 35 percent to reduced average distance traveled per vehicle (54).

Most other modes of transportation have not experienced the efficiency improvements of automobiles; one notable exception is a new commercial aircraft, which consumes an average of 20 percent less fuel per passenger mile than existing planes (55). Maritime, air, and rail transport in OECD countries depend on petroleum; they accounted for 17 percent of oil consumption by the transportation sector in 1973 and 1984 (56).

The key influence on energy consumption by transportation in most developing countries is the growing number of vehicles. Since 1978, the growth rate in the number of vehicles in Asia, excluding China, has doubled or tripled the growth rate in GDP. Growth in the number of vehicles has also exceeded GDP growth in Latin America and West Africa. Air travel is also a growing industry in many developing countries; railroads are important for transporting passengers and commodities only in India and China (57).

The number of vehicles is certain to grow in India and South Korea, where automobile manufacturing is already expanding. In the mid-1980s, about 3 of every 1,000 Asians owned a car (5 per 1,000 if China were excluded); in Latin America, the figure was about 70 per 1,000. In the higher-income nations of South Korea, Taiwan, and Malaysia, the number of autos has been increasing at rates of over 10 percent per year (58).

Residential, Commercial, and Public Sectors

The predominant fuel varies in the residential, commercial, and public sectors for the countries shown in Table 7.4. In OECD countries, natural gas and primary electricity lead, followed closely by oil and then by coal. In the USSR, coal and natural gas are the most important energy sources. Solid fuel predominates in South Korea and coal-rich China; in Brazil, hydroelectricity is abundant. In these sectors, oil is the most important fuel for the four West African countries, Indonesia, India, and virtually all low-income countries, where kerosene is often used for lighting.

Among the OECD countries, the residential and commercial sectors are the second largest and fastest-growing energy users; their per capita energy use grew 2.5 percent between 1973 and 1979, declined about 12 percent between 1979 and 1984, and then rose again 2.1 percent in 1985 (59). Major energy efficiency improvements in the commercial sector, especially in buildings and lighting, have aided energy performance; for example, energy use per employee in the United States dropped 24 percent between 1970 and 1982 (60).

Average consumption in the residential and commercial sectors of the developing countries listed in Table 7.3 grew between 1978 and 1984—an 18 percent average increase in the Asian countries (excluding China), 21 percent in the four Latin American countries, and 36 percent in the four West African countries (61).

Energy use in these sectors rises with per capita GDP. The increased introduction of appliances in developing countries during the early 1980s and construction of an increasing number of high-rise buildings raised electricity's share of energy use there. Between 1978 and 1984, overall energy use in Asian countries listed in Table 7.3 (excluding China) rose 37 percent—electricity was up 80 percent and oil 29 percent. In the four Latin American countries, the overall increase was 39 percent— electricity was up 51 percent and oil 27 percent. And in the four West African countries, the overall increase was 86 percent from a much smaller base—electricity rose 50 percent and oil 100 percent (62).

ENERGY IN THE USSR AND EASTERN EUROPE

Energy is important to the regional security and economic growth of the USSR and its Eastern European allies, Poland, Hungary, East Germany, Bulgaria, Czechoslovakia, and Romania. These seven nations are members of the Council for Mutual Economic Assistance (CMEA) (63), through which they coordinate energy trade. In essence, the energy requirements of these Eastern European countries are met by combining domestic resources with imports from the USSR. Tables 7.5 and 7.6 show commercial energy production and consumption for the USSR and Eastern Europe (hereafter the six CMEA members only).

Although the latest five-year plans of the USSR and Eastern Europe call for increased emphasis on reducing demand through energy-efficient technologies and conservation, increasing supplies seems to be the key to meeting increased energy demand. At the same time, there are signs that the Soviet and Eastern European governments are beginning to feel the same domestic pressure as the West regarding energy-related environmental problems, particularly related to coal burning.

The USSR

Perhaps no other country has more energy resources than those of the Soviet Union, but nearly 75 percent of known reserves are in Siberia. Still relatively untapped, Siberia's resources may contain half the world's accessible coal. Two of its 50,000 rivers, the Yenisei and the Lena, have more energy potential than all the rivers in the United States put together (64).

7   Energy

Table 7.5 Primary Energy Production in the USSR and Eastern Europe, by Fuel Type, 1970–85
(petajoules)[a]

	Oil 1970	Oil 1980	Oil 1985	Solid Fuels[b] 1970	Solid Fuels[b] 1980	Solid Fuels[b] 1985	Natural Gas 1970	Natural Gas 1980	Natural Gas 1985	Hydropower 1970	Hydropower 1980	Hydropower 1985	Nuclear Power 1970	Nuclear Power 1980	Nuclear Power 1985	Total 1970	Total 1980	Total 1985
Eastern Europe																		
Bulgaria	14	12	13	434	446	456	17	7	5	8	13	8	NA	22	47	473	500	529
Czechoslovakia	9	4	5	1,809	1,888	1,871	37	21	23	13	17	16	NA	16	42	1,868	1,947	1,958
German Democratic Republic	4	2	46	2,342	2,294	2,756	20	106	100	5	6	6	2	43	46	2,373	2,451	2,955
Hungary	88	118	121	402	289	264	114	237	274	0.3	0.6	0.6	NA	NA	23	605	644	682
Poland	19	15	10	3,614	4,909	4,953	186	193	162	7	12	14	NA	NA	NA	3,826	5,129	5,139
Romania	87	513	471	324	498	620	979	1,455	1,522	10	45	43	NA	NA	NA	1,900	2,512	2,657
Subtotal[c]	721	664	666	8,925	10,324	10,920	1,353	2,019	2,086	43.3	93.6	87.6	2	81	158	11,044	13,181.6	13,917.6
USSR	15,063	25,749	24,960	13,456	15,017	15,072	6,670	15,149	22,149	448	662	742	13	216	612	35,651	56,795	63,536
Total[c]	**15,784**	**26,413**	**25,626**	**22,381**	**25,341**	**25,992**	**8,023**	**17,168**	**24,235**	**491.3**	**755.6**	**829.6**	**15**	**297**	**770**	**46,694.3**	**69,974.6**	**77,452.6**

Sources:
1. United Nations (U.N.), *Energy Statistics Yearbook 1982* (U.N., New York, 1984), Table 3, pp. 132-142, and Table 38, pp. 679-683.
2. United Nations (U.N.), *Energy Statistics Yearbook 1985* (U.N., New York, 1987), Table 3, pp. 78-84, and Table 43, pp. 400-406.
Notes:
a. Conversion factors: 1 Terawatt hour (elecricity) = 3.6 petajoules.
b. Mainly coal (all forms) but includes wood, peat, and other solid fuels.
c. Figures may not total due to rounding.
NA = not applicable.

At 1986 production levels, proven Soviet oil resources could last until around the year 2000; natural gas could last for more than 50 years and coal for more than 350 years (65). Undiscovered reserves of oil, gas, and coal may well be substantial, but they will be difficult to recover and transport from Siberia.

Although precise data on USSR energy resources are a state secret (66), it is known that the Soviets lead the world in producing petroleum and natural gas. In 1986, the USSR produced 613 million metric tons of oil, compared to the United States' 486 million metric tons and Saudi Arabia's 251 million metric tons. Soviet gas production in 1986 was the highest in the world, at 665 billion cubic meters followed by the United States with 437 billion cubic meters. Coal production was third highest in the world, after China and the United States (67).

Growth in Soviet oil production slowed substantially between 1975 and 1983, temporarily peaked at around 616 million metric tons in 1983, and then declined in 1984–85. In 1986, Soviet oil production turned around, when it almost equaled the total production of all Middle Eastern countries combined (68). This growth continued into 1987, when the USSR produced 624 million metric tons of oil (69).

With about 40 percent of the world's natural gas, the Soviet Union has the largest proven recoverable reserves (70). But most of the reserves are in the Arctic regions of western Siberia, where exploration and production are difficult (71). Gas production more than doubled between 1975 and 1985, from 284 to 643 billion cubic meters; forecast production for 1987 was up to 727 billion cubic meters (72).

Coal production between 1975 and 1985 increased only 25 million metric tons—3.4 percent. But, in 1986, production abruptly rose another 25 million metric tons, to 751 million metric tons. The 1986 expansion was led by the large strip mines in Siberia and Kazakhstan, which offset a net decline in production from mines in European Russia and the Urals (73).

After a decade of steady growth, output from both hydro and nuclear power plants dropped slightly in 1986. The loss of primary electricity capacity at the Chernobyl plant in April 1986 was the principal reason for the decline in nuclear power output, and the relatively dry year led to hydropower shortages. Increased output at thermal power plants made up the difference, keeping electricity production at targeted goals (74).

Soviet oil consumption peaked in 1982 at 450 million

Table 7.6 Energy Consumption in the USSR and Eastern Europe, by Fuel Type, 1970–85
(petajoules)

	Liquid Fuels[a] 1970	Liquid Fuels[a] 1980	Liquid Fuels[a] 1985	Solid Fuels 1970	Solid Fuels 1980	Solid Fuels 1985	Gaseous Fuels[b] 1970	Gaseous Fuels[b] 1980	Gaseous Fuels[b] 1985	Electricity[c] 1970	Electricity[c] 1980	Electricity[c] 1985	Total 1970	Total 1980	Total 1985
Eastern Europe															
Bulgaria	346	575	562	570	615	672	17	148	216	7	49	71	940	1,387	1,521
Czechoslovakia	371	668	567	1,792	1,861	1,878	79	298	330	25	40	71	2,267	2,867	2,846
East Germany	433	690	632	2,602	2,523	2,856	22	302	288	8	54	53	3,065	3,569	3,829
Hungary	223	424	392	496	374	373	121	364	393	13	27	63	853	1,189	1,221
Poland	301	610	512	2,878	4,230	4,170	222	363	363	7	11	6	3,408	5,214	5,051
Romania	406	688	760	410	689	813	971	1,507	1,599	1	47	51	1,788	2,931	3,223
Subtotal	2,080	3,655	3,425	8,748	10,292	10,762	1,432	2,982	3,189	61	228	315	12,321	17,157	17,691
USSR	9,283	14,770	14,450	12,933	14,440	14,596	6,611	13,209	19,761	442	811	1,257	29,270	43,229	50,065
Total	**11,363**	**18,425**	**17,875**	**21,681**	**24,732**	**25,358**	**8,043**	**16,191**	**22,950**	**503**	**1,039**	**1,572**	**41,591**	**60,386**	**67,756**

Sources:
1. United Nations (U.N.), *Energy Statistics Yearbook 1982* (U.N., New York, 1984), Table 3, pp. 133-143.
2. U.N., *Energy Statistics Yearbook 1985* (U.N., New York, 1987), Table 3, pp. 79-85.
Notes:
a. All petroleum products and natural gas as wood and peat.
b. Natural gas, manufactured gas, coke-oven gas, and blast-furnace gas.
c. Hydro, nuclear, and geothermal power.

metric tons and then declined from 1983 to 1985 (75). In 1985, natural gas surpassed oil for the first time in its share of domestic energy consumption; it accounted for over 34 percent and oil less than 32 percent. In 1986, gas rose to 35 percent of domestic Soviet energy demand, while oil dropped to about 31 percent (76). Coal consumption increased 12 percent between 1976 and 1986, from 336 to 376 million metric tons of oil equivalent (mtoe) (77). Soviet oil, natural gas, and solid fuel consumption in different economic sectors is shown in Table 7.7.

Information on energy intensity in the USSR is not available on a basis comparable with the rest of the world because it does not produce data on GDP. Alternative estimates of the Soviet economic performance yield conflicting estimates of recent changes in energy intensity.

Coal was the mainstay energy resource until the late 1950s, long after most other industrialized nations switched to oil and gas (78). As new oil fields opened up, the Soviets changed to liquid fuel relatively swiftly. A decade later, in 1966, coal contributed less than 50 percent to Soviet energy consumption. With oil, gas, and eventually nuclear power increasingly supplanting coal, its relative share dropped below 30 percent by 1977. Replacing coal with natural gas in industry and households helped reduce urban air pollution, which was blamed for serious health problems (79).

Oil is a valuable export commodity for the USSR. The Soviet long-term energy program calls for fundamental changes in the mix of fuels—natural gas will replace oil as the main fuel, coal will supply more domestic requirements than it has, and nuclear power will be developed further (80).

Once again, coal will dominate the energy balance when gas production stagnates about the year 2000. To minimize both urban smog and coal transport costs, the Soviets are building coal-burning power plants in energy complexes near newly discovered vast coal basins east of the Ural Mountains. Electricity will be transmitted to cit-

ies thousands of kilometers away (81). Another effort to alleviate the strained rail system is the use of coal-slurry pipelines. Construction began in 1986 on a 250-kilometer coal slurry line between the Kuzbas and Novosibirsk, a project to test the feasibility of a proposed transcontinental line (82).

Nuclear power will become increasingly important in the USSR. In 1985, nuclear power supplied only 170 terawatt hours, a little more than 10 percent of Soviet electricity. By 1990, the figure is expected to reach 360 terawatt hours (83).

Eastern Europe

Poland is the fourth largest producer of coal in the world. Hard (anthracite and bituminous) coal is the main indigenous energy resource, meeting about 80 percent of domestic energy needs as well as generating a large portion of trade revenue (84). Indigenous and Soviet natural gas meet 7 percent of domestic energy demand; most of the remaining energy supply is oil imported from the USSR (85). Nuclear power is in the planning and construction stages; the first plant is scheduled to start up in the early 1990s, but delays are expected (86).

Czechoslovakia's energy economy is primarily coal based and, at 1986 production levels, its plentiful hard and soft (subbituminous and lignite) coal supplies could last for 100 years and 30 years, respectively (87). The country has virtually no oil or gas reserves. As a result, oil and gas use has been minimized (oil consumption dropped 15 percent between 1979 and 1985), with essentially all coming from the USSR (88). To pay for the gas, the Czechs contribute labor to build and maintain Soviet gas pipelines and charge transit fees for pipelines that cross their borders.

In response to rising oil prices, decreasing coal production rates, and concerns over air pollution, Czechoslovakia is emphasizing large-scale substitution by nuclear power (89).

Romania is richly endowed with oil, gas, and coal reserves, a fact that has allowed it in the past to be less

Table 7.7 Oil, Natural Gas, and Coal Consumption in the USSR, by Sector, 1970–87
(petajoules)

	Production and Transport Losses	Electricity and Heat Generation	Direct Consumption			
			Industry	Transport	Agriculture	Residential/ Municipal
Oil						
1970	X	X	2,485	2,383	1,937	149
1975	X	X	3,397	3,400	2,201	422
1980	X	X	4,464	3,886	2,609	404
1987	1,717	3,496	4,262	5,673	641	574
Gas						
1970	X	X	3,939	53	23	613
1975	X	X	5,539	67	73	1,249
1980	X	X	6,624	91	100	1,679
1987	2,550	7,658	6,758	71	209	2,470
Coal						
1970	X	X	4,585	407	293	2,430
1975	X	X	4,997	384	270	2,638
1980	X	X	5,396	311	211	2,855
1987	800	6,352	4,275	301	84	3,685

Sources:
1. Matthew J. Sagers and Albina Tretyakova, USSR: *Trends in Fuel and Energy Consumption by Sector and Fuel, 1970-1980* (U.S. Bureau of the Census, Center for International Research, Washington, D.C., 1988), Table I-A, pp. 72-73; Table I-B, pp. 74-75; and Table I-C, pp. 76-77.
2. International Energy Agency, Paris, estimates, 1988.

dependent on Soviet energy imports than any of the other Eastern European countries. Because oil was easily traded on international markets, Romania was able to pursue a course of economic development after World War II that did not require adherence to Soviet plans for Eastern European specialization within the CMEA. In the 1960s, however, oil production began to level off; in the 1970s, growing economic problems were compounded when world oil prices rose and Romania was denied the favorable terms of trade for Soviet oil enjoyed by the other Eastern Europeans (90).

In 1982, Romania met 82 percent of its solid fuel, 72 percent of its oil, and 100 percent of natural gas demand through domestic production (91). However, production of all three fuels failed to meet output targets in 1986, causing Romania to suffer perhaps the most severe energy shortages in the region and compounding already severe economic problems. As a result, Romania is apparently forging closer economic ties with the USSR (92).

East Germany has enough indigenous resources of soft coal to supply almost three quarters of its energy (93), but the USSR supplies all its oil and two thirds of its gas (94). Nuclear power generated 11 percent of electricity in 1985, and the country is considering expansion of its nuclear power as a response to environmental concerns over coal (95).

Hungary meets just over half its energy needs with indigenous resources—20 percent of the oil, 60 percent of the natural gas and hard coal, and 100 percent of the soft coal consumed (96). The Soviet Union exports oil, natural gas, and electricity to Hungary. Nuclear power is considered an important future source of energy, and it could supply 40 percent of the country's electricity requirements by 2000, compared with 17 percent in 1986 (97).

Bulgaria imports approximately 65 percent of its energy, most of it from the USSR, in the form of oil, coal, gas, and nuclear reactors. Bulgaria is self-sufficient in soft coal production and has a well-developed but limited hydroelectric system (98). To compensate for its limited resource base, Bulgaria is maximizing use of domestic coal and increasing its nuclear power capacity. In 1987, 31 percent of Bulgarian electricity was generated by nuclear plants, and four other plants are planned to be operating before the year 2000 (99).

Energy Trade between the USSR and Eastern Europe

Oil and natural gas are the major energy commodities exported from the USSR to Eastern Europe. To reserve as much oil as possible for earnings of hard currency, the Soviets limited oil exports to Eastern Europe and instead increased natural gas deliveries and transfers of nuclear reactor technology. In perhaps the most important current Soviet-CMEA joint venture, a new 4,605-kilometer gas pipeline is being built from giant natural gas fields in western Siberia to several Eastern European countries (100).

Since World War II, the USSR has helped sustain the economic programs of its allies by exporting energy on favorable economic terms, sometimes incorporating barter trade and often in exchange for Eastern European labor, technical assistance, and equipment used on Soviet oil and gas projects. Such terms of trade increase Eastern European dependency on the Soviet Union because often their manufactured goods cannot compete on world markets to earn foreign exchange for purchasing energy supplies (101).

During the energy crises of the last decade, a 1975 agreement allowed the Eastern Europeans to purchase Soviet oil at a price equal to the average world price for Soviet oil exports of the previous five years. Initially, the so-called Bucharest Formula resulted in subsidized oil prices. But today the Eastern Europeans are paying approximately $25 per barrel for Soviet oil compared to an average world price of $18 per barrel (102).

Energy Trade between the USSR and the West

In 1970, energy comprised approximately 15 percent of the value of all Soviet exports; by 1986, the figure was about 52 percent. Low world oil prices required the USSR to increase exports of oil, natural gas, and other commodities in order to maintain the balance of trade. The USSR is a major non-OPEC producer, with a 10 percent share of the global crude oil market and a 12 percent share if all oil products are included (103). In 1985, Soviet oil exports (crude and products) were about 166.7 million metric tons, with approximately 45 percent of that going to Eastern Europe (104). Soviet natural gas exports had risen to 15 percent of Western Europe's natural gas supply by late 1987, and, despite strategic concerns, its relatively low cost may well increase the percentage into the 1990s (105).

Petroleum is the most important commodity in the economy of the USSR, and exports to the West account for about 60 percent of all Soviet hard-currency earnings. Because economic modernization programs have increased the demand for goods from the West, Soviet oil exports are expected to continue growing despite the rising costs of domestic production and lower world prices (106).

Energy and the Environment: A New Call to Action

Until recently, the Soviet Union tended to minimize concern over the environmental effects of energy development. The country's size and natural resource wealth led to general complacency over environmental damage (107). But lately, the message from Soviet leaders is that attitudes toward the environment must "radically change" and top government officials will be held responsible for preventing pollution in their areas of oversight (108).

The deteriorating environment in Eastern Europe has created citizen organizations critical of environmentally damaging projects (109) (110) (111). A joint Hungarian-Czechoslovakian hydroelectric project on the Danube River met internal opposition for environmental reasons, and the government agreed to a Hungarian Academy of Sciences recommendation to add $75 million for environmental safeguards (112).

Most environmental damage is due to coal, high-sulfur brown coal in particular, which is a major energy source in the most heavily polluted countries of East Germany, Poland, Czechoslovakia, and Hungary (113).

When Soviet oil exports declined slightly in the early 1980s, the East Germans stepped up brown coal production. Today, with the highest per capita sulfur dioxide emissions in the world (114), East Germany is attempting to control sulfur dioxide emissions technologically, and by increased use of low-sulfur coal (115).

Czechoslovakia emits 3.5 million metric tons of sulfur dioxide per year, twice that of West Germany, which has more than four times the population. The Czech government calls Prague a disaster zone because of its heavy pollution from coal combustion (116).

In Northern Bohemia, where six power stations produce 60 percent of Czechoslovakia's electric power, the situation is even worse. Open-pit mining for brown coal has given rise to a local tag, "the lunar country." The forests of Czechoslovakia are affected; a recent survey found Czech forest damage on a scale comparable to the much-publicized *Waldsterben* in West Germany (117). (See *World Resources 1986*, pp. 203–226). To control the problem, the Czechs are installing desulfurization equipment, promoting nuclear power as a clean energy source, and converting from coal to natural gas for residential heating where possible (118).

Environmental concerns seem to be an issue that Eastern and Western European governments can agree upon, and bilateral environmental pacts are common. West Germany, Austria, and Hungary all have agreements with both East Germany and Czechoslovakia. Within Europe, 21 countries have signed a protocol to reduce sulfur emissions 30 percent. (See Chapter 11, "Atmosphere and Climate," Thirty Percent Club Comes of Age.) Before the East Europeans will sign a similar treaty on nitrogen emissions, however, they want the West to make its superior filters for coal-burning power plants available. So far, the West has refused (119).

FOCUS ON: ENERGY CONSERVATION

Energy conservation should be a central part of all national strategies for meeting energy requirements. The recent experience of the OECD countries in the face of rising oil prices demonstrated that economic growth does not have to depend on increased consumption of energy. (See also Box 7.2.) Between 1973 and 1985, conservation measures in OECD countries reduced per capita energy use 5 percent while per capita GDP grew 32 percent. This trend shattered the widely held belief that an increased energy supply is basic to economic growth (120). At the same time, the environmental consequences of burning fossil fuels make energy conservation an attractive means of addressing a variety of critical problems ranging from local air pollution to global climate change. (See Chapter 10, "Atmosphere and Climate.")

In the developing world the need to meet long-term energy requirements of future economic development in the face of limited and uncertain supplies makes energy efficiency and conservation an essential element of development efforts.

Strategies to improve energy efficiency and promote energy conservation must take into account the specific fuel mix and technologies being employed in each economic sector.

Industrial Sector

Most of the electricity consumed by industry is used to drive motors. Larger motors (above 100 horsepower) are generally more efficient than smaller ones. However, larger motors are inefficient if they are run below optimal speed, and users often buy oversized motors because they expect their load needs to expand. Substantial energy savings can be realized with speed controls that match motor output to load demand. If industrial motors in the United States were equipped with available speed control technology, the nation's total electricity consumption would decrease 7 percent (121).

Industrial processes such as the production of aluminum, steel, cement, and fertilizer are important energy consumers in many countries, and advanced technologies allow energy savings. Aluminum producers in India, for example, reduced the electricity use of their processes 15 percent between 1975 and 1980 (122). Swedish steel producers reduced the energy demand of their already efficient processes 27 percent between 1976 and 1983, and new technologies could decrease demand another 50 percent (123).

A far greater advantage can be obtained simply by recycling processed materials. When recycled aluminum is used, producing a die-cast part requires 95 percent less energy than when it is fabricated from primary metal (124). In the United States use of recycled aluminum grew from 25 percent to 50 percent of total aluminum production between 1970 and 1983 (125).

The industrial base of an economy strongly influences energy demand, especially for electricity. In Brazil, the seven most electricity-intensive industries account for 52 percent of industrial electricity used but only 13 percent of the value added by industrial processing. A significant contributor to lower industrial energy intensity in many developed countries is the move away from basic materials processing toward fabrication, finishing, and service activities (126).

Agricultural Sector

Agricultural modernization in the developing world is essential to feed rapidly growing populations. (See Chapter 4, "Food and Agriculture.") To meet this demand, FAO called for a modernization effort to double agricultural production by 2000—energy use for agriculture in developing countries will have to increase 8 percent annually between 1980 and 2000 (127). However, because agriculture accounts for only about 4 percent of total global energy use, this involves only a small absolute increase in energy consumption.

Water pumps are a principal energy consumer in agriculture. During 1981–82, irrigation pumps in India used almost 20 percent of the country's total electricity. However, a demonstration project involving efficiency retrofits of electrical pumps showed an average savings of 26 percent in India (128). Energy consumption for irrigation can also be reduced through better water management. In Pakistan, water requirements were reduced 42

Box 7.2 Conservation Incentives Pay Off, but Unmanaged Growth Is Costly: California and Texas

Between 1977 and 1984, California and Texas pursued two different energy growth strategies. California developed strict conservation standards for all sectors of the economy, but Texas allowed energy demand to grow without governmental incentives to conserve. The two states are somewhat comparable in terms of population, economic growth, land area, climate, and technological sophistication. The results of their different policies toward energy conservation are revealing.

In 1984, the average Californian used 267 kilowatt hours less than in 1977, while the average Texan used 1,424 kilowatt hours more. (See Figure 1.) Conservation and cogeneration efforts in California industry resulted in energy's accounting for only 3.5 percent of every dollar of value added in 1982. Comparable values were 7.1 percent and 4.5 percent in Texas and the United States, respectively [1].

California, which had 11 percent of the U.S. population and 12 percent of the national income, consumed only 8 percent of U.S. electricity in 1984; Texas, with only 7 percent of both the national population and income, consumed 9 percent of the U.S. total. Further, Californians used less than half as much electricity per dollar of gross state product than did Texans.

California set mandatory building and appliance efficiency standards reinforced by massive utility conservation programs. By 1993, refrigerator efficiency standards alone will lead to improvements over 1977 models that annually save 1,200 kilowatt hours for each household and 15 billion kilowatt hours for the state—the equivalent of three 1,000-megawatt baseload power plants. Similar standards and conservation programs were established for all economic sectors. Texas, on the other hand, left matters entirely to the marketplace. As a result, California added new capacity or acquired outside electricity equivalent to only three new power plants during 1977–84, while Texas required 11.

Texas is now following in California's footsteps, advancing conservation and load-management initiatives. Although it is not possible to tell precisely how much of the difference was due to regulation, it is clear that California's conservation initiatives, both public and private, effected substantial economic and social savings.

In the early 1970s, U.S. electricity demand

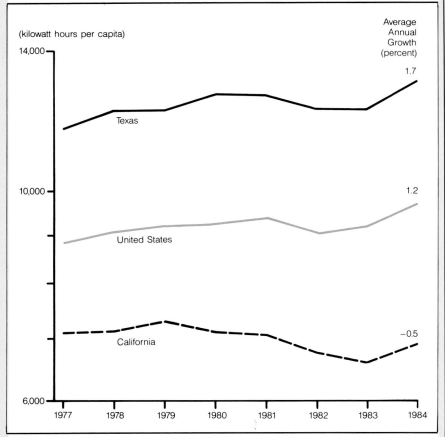

Figure 1 Per Capita Energy Consumption in California, Texas, and the United States, 1977–84[a]

(kilowatt hours per capita)

Average Annual Growth (percent)

Texas — 1.7

United States — 1.2

California — –0.5

Source: Evan Mills and Arthur H. Rosenfeld, "Managed versus Unmanaged 7-Year Electric Growth: Californians Needed 3 New Plants, Texans Needed 11," *Physics and Society,* Vol. 16, No. 2 (1987), p. 3.
Note: a. The y-axis is logarithmic.

was expected to continue to double every 10 years. Planners, largely ignorant of the potential for conservation, were focusing only on supply expansion. Since then, conservation has proven to be three to five times cheaper than new power plants. Energy efficiency standards like California's have stretched the national "demand doubling" time from one decade to three, saving the country billions of dollars each year.

References and Notes

1. Evan Mills and Arthur H. Rosenfeld, "Managed Versus Unmanaged 7-year Electric Growth: Californians Needed 3 New Plants, Texans Needed 11," *Physics and Society,* Vol. 16, No. 2 (1987), pp. 3–4.

percent by canal renovation and more precise land leveling, with a corresponding reduction in the demand for energy by water pumps (129).

Transportation Sector

Automobiles and light trucks, a major source of urban air pollution, used about 17 percent of all oil used worldwide in 1982. In the OECD countries, with 80 percent of all cars in the world, autos burned one fourth of all oil used. In the developing countries, the number of automobiles is expected to increase 150–200 percent by the year 2000 (130). Increased automotive fuel efficiency in both the

industrialized and the developing countries could be a major factor in slowing oil price rises as well as in reducing air pollution emissions. (See Chapter 10, "Atmosphere and Climate.")

As of 1987, the most fuel-efficient automobile on the U.S. market carried four passengers and averaged 4.1 liters of gasoline per 100 kilometers (lhk) (57 miles per gallon (mpg)) on the highway. Further improvements are technically feasible; for example, a Japanese prototype used lightweight materials, a direct-injection diesel engine, a continuously variable transmission, and other special features to attain 2.4 lhk (98 mpg). A Swedish prototype met stricter safety standards than cars sold in the United States, accelerated from 0 to 96 kilometers per hour in 11 seconds, and averaged 3.6 lhk (65 mpg) (131).

If new cars in the mid-1990s attain the fuel efficiencies of 3.9–3.6 lhk (60 to 65 mpg) that are possible with today's technology, the average for all automobiles operating in the year 2000 would be approximately 4.9 lhk (48 mpg). With an estimated 533 million autos in 2000 achieving an average 4.9 lhk, cars would use 2.9 million barrels of oil per day *less* than did the 319 million cars on the road in 1982. Coincidentally, 2.8 million barrels per day is what FAO estimates is needed to double agricultural production in developing countries by 2000 (132).

Housing and Municipal Sectors

Energy-efficient fluorescent light bulbs offer large energy savings over traditional incandescent bulbs, but the improved bulbs do cost more initially. A demonstration project in the Netherlands reduced electricity consumption in an office building 63–84 percent with readily available technologies. Individual light switches replaced single switches for banks of lights, daylight sensors and dimmers were installed, and more efficient lamps were used. The payback period in energy savings from the extra investment ranged from two to nearly five years (133). A Brazilian study showed that the capital investment required to install increased hydroelectric capacity was 2.5–5 times the cost of simply replacing incandescent with fluorescent light bulbs (134).

Air conditioning is a major consumer of electricity, especially in higher-income countries in hotter climates. In Kuwait, cooling accounts for an estimated 45 percent of power consumption, and this fraction is rising (135). Design features and technologies to cool buildings include insulation, reflective window glass, and dehumidifiers.

Refrigerators use about 25 percent of residential electricity in the United States and Sweden (136). Refrigerators produced in industrialized countries during the past 15 years have added insulation and more efficient motors and require 30–70 percent less electricity than older models. Shifting to these more efficient refrigerators could save Brazil an estimated 3,500 megawatts of baseload capacity (15 terawatt hours per year) by the year 2000, for 25–50 percent of what it would cost to increase hydroelectric capacity (137).

Energy Conservation in the Third World: Crucial to Sustainable Development

A few years ago, the World Bank expected electricity production in developing countries to triple by 1995, an annual growth rate of 7.7 percent (138). But the power sources necessary for this increase would exact a heavy toll on the environment. Hydropower projects inundate large areas of land, often in the most agriculturally productive areas, and thermal power plants release a range of atmospheric pollutants. (See Chapter 10, "Atmosphere and Climate.")

Increasing the efficiency of electricity use in developing countries instead of expanding capacity offers two major advantages. In Brazil, for example, investing $10 billion over the next 15 years in more efficient refrigerators, lighting for streets and commercial buildings, motors, and

variable speed industrial motor drives would eliminate the need for new generating capacity of 22 gigawatts that would cost approximately $44 billion (139). Lessening the demand also avoids the negative environmental effects of increasing supply.

Even when developing countries import sophisticated energy-efficient technologies, reductions in net foreign exchange requirements for energy are possible. Importing more efficient technologies often costs less than importing both the conventional less efficient technologies and the extra energy to power them (140).

The more advanced developing countries could manufacture many efficient end-use devices if manufacturers saw a market for these products. India's automobile industry, for example, manufactures cars with fuel efficiencies of around 5.9 lhk (40 mpg). In Brazil, a survey showed that manufacturers could produce a wide range of energy-efficient refrigerators, lights, heat pumps, motors, and other electrically powered technologies, given sufficient markets. Ironically, the most efficient U.S.-made refrigerator uses a Brazilian compressor to gain its efficiency advantage, but the Brazilian manufacturer markets a less-efficient compressor domestically (141).

RECENT DEVELOPMENTS

NEW STUDIES OF THE CHERNOBYL ACCIDENT HEALTH IMPACTS

On April 26, 1986, the world's worst nuclear power accident occurred during an explosion and fire at the Soviet Union's Chernobyl plant, located in the Ukraine. In the months following the mishap, 31 workers and emergency personnel exposed on the reactor site died, and more than 200 other persons were hospitalized (142).

Although most of the radioactive materials escaped on the first day, the release continued for 10 days after the initial explosion (143). About 1–3 million curies (144) of cesium 137 (a fission byproduct with a 30-year radioactive half life) (145) were released—one third was deposited in the USSR, one third in other European countries, and one third over the rest of the Northern Hemisphere (146). Large amounts of released iodine 131 (with an eight-day half life) caused measurable thyroid uptake in humans, especially through the grass-cow-milk pathway (147).

In the Soviet Union, long-term monitoring and research of health effects from Chernobyl are being coordinated at a special new medical center at Kiev. Soviet scientists project the collective dose (average dose times number of people) to the entire population of the USSR over the next 50 years at approximately 2 percent of the natural background exposure during that time, resulting in excess cancer deaths equal to about 0.1 percent of expected cancer deaths (148).

Fallout from the accident outside the USSR affected Scandinavia more than the rest of Europe; wind movements and local spring rains carried the heaviest fallout to central Sweden and Norway. Radioactive contamination of plants and the animals that fed upon them pose serious public health problems as a result of contamination of milk, berries, sheep, cows, fish, and reindeer (149). (See Chapter 5, "Forests and Rangelands," Recent Developments.)

Most long-term health effects of the Chernobyl accident will be statistically undetectable because they will be spread anonymously through a population of hundreds of millions and over decades (150). A preliminary assessment of the health impacts on Europe by the United Kingdom's National Radiological Protection Board found that extra cancers in European Community countries (151) over the next 50 years will be on the order of 1,000. About 30 million will die from "natural" cancers during that time (152).

The U.S. Department of Energy (DOE) projects additional fatal cancers in the Northern Hemisphere at 28,000, a 0.005 percent increase in risk, over the next 50 years. Among the approximately 100,000 people living within 30 kilometers of Chernobyl, the effects are expected to be more severe—400 additional cancer deaths, a 2 percent risk increase. For the European population, the dose received from Chernobyl is expected to be about the same as a few years of exposure to natural background radiation (153).

The projections from both the U.K. and the U.S. studies are much less serious than was feared at first. However, the U.S. scientific community does not agree completely with DOE's analysis. There are widely diverging views on two sensitive parameters used in the calculations. First is the uptake of cesium 137 by plants and by humans via the food chain in the Ukraine and other parts of the Soviet Union. The second concerns the cancer-risk coefficient, a calculation used to project the number of cancer deaths associated with a given amount of radiation exposure. The DOE report uses the lower values of the coefficients (154). Scientists using higher values project thousands to tens of thousands of additional cancer deaths resulting from Chernobyl (155).

THE IRAN-IRAQ WAR AND THE FLOW OF PERSIAN GULF OIL

Since its beginning, the war between Iran and Iraq has threatened commercial vessels passing through the Persian Gulf, many carrying oil to global markets. Between 1981, when merchant shipping was first threatened, and late 1987, more than 300 ships were attacked and more than 200 sailors killed (156). A major U.S. naval force, dispatched in 1987 to protect the shipping lanes of the Gulf, was still there in July 1988.

As much as 6.4 million barrels per day—25 percent of oil traded by market-economy countries (157)—passes through the Gulf. Shipping disruptions would affect exports from Kuwait, Saudi Arabia, Iran, and Iraq (158)—all important sources of oil for Europe, Japan, and Southeast Asia (159).

Most concern focuses on passage through the Strait of Hormuz, a strategically vulnerable, narrow stretch of the Gulf. All oil-consuming nations, not just those most dependent on Gulf oil, would be affected by a closing of the strait. Countries not heavily reliant on Gulf oil would feel the effect because those hurt by the supply disruption would bid up oil prices until they obtained their supplies. World demand could just barely be met by combining unused Persian Gulf pipeline capacity, spare productive capacity throughout the world, and private and government storage (160).

The war has significantly decreased production from both Iran and Iraq because oil facilities are a common military target. In the year before the war, Iran produced more than 3 million barrels per day and Iraq almost 3.5 million. Their combined output in 1986 had fallen to 3.6 million barrels per day. Even if the war continues, oil exports are expected to rise somewhat during 1988, when an expanded pipeline network becomes operational, allowing Iran and Iraq to export oil to ports beyond the Persian Gulf (161).

ADVANCES IN SUPERCONDUCTIVITY AND POSSIBLE ENERGY APPLICATIONS

More than 75 years ago, a Dutch physicist discovered that at temperatures approaching absolute zero, (–273°C), some materials conducted electricity without heat dissipation or energy loss (162). However, because cooling the materials to those low temperatures required costly liquid helium, potential applications were economically impractical.

The situation changed dramatically in September 1986, when higher-temperature (–238°C) superconductivity was achieved with ceramic rather than metallic material. Shortly thereafter, a U.S. scientist developed a ceramic material that overcame the liquid helium cooling barrier when it became a superconductor at –175°C, well within the cooling range of less expensive liquid nitrogen (163).

Today, the search for higher temperature superconductors is underway around the world, in hopes of eventually developing materials that will conduct electricity at room temperature without heat or energy loss. As of March 1988, the world record was held by a material that superconducts at –148°C (164).

Superconductors offer a range of potential energy applications that are primarily a result of their ultraefficient electricity transmission. Compared to ordinary copper wire, which loses the vast majority of electricity passing through it as dissipated heat, superconductors transmit direct current electricity without resistance, and therefore without loss. Geographically remote electricity sources (e.g., certain hydropower sites, deep-water ocean-thermal energy conversion facilities) would become more practical. Superconductors would cut electricity losses substantially, resulting in less depletion of natural resources and less pollution.

Superconductors would significantly reduce the large fraction of electricity lost in the transmission grid, which would provide more economical electricity.

The energy storage density of superconducting ceramics is about 100 times that of alkaline cell batteries (165), another result of their resistance-free electricity transmissions. Superconductor storage is best understood by imagining a superconductor ring into which electricity has been fed. After the ring is detached from the power source, the electric current would continue to flow around the ring indefinitely. Experiments with metallic superconductors have shown that the current would persist for 100,000 years; in ordinary copper wire, the current would be consumed by resistance and disappear in less than one second. Reconnect wires to the superconductor ring, and electricity would flow back out, ready for use.

A giant version of such a device using older lower-temperature costly superconductors is in use at a utility in the state of Washington. The device is used to level out fluctuations in a conventional powerline by storing up to 5 megawatts during peaks of supply, and releasing it during peak demand hours (166). In the future such devices, made more practical with high-temperature superconductors, could allow power plants to charge up superconducting coils at night to help meet daytime power demand.

Electric vehicles could be improved by more efficient electric motors and storage. High-speed trains levitated by efficient superconductor magnets might be developed. A Japanese prototype using liquid-helium-cooled superconductors reaches speeds of 300 miles per hour. Nuclear fusion development would benefit if powerful superconductor magnets could solve a major hurdle: containment

of the plasma fuel (167).

Before any of these uses are realized, major obstacles must be overcome. Temperature requirements are too low for most applications. In addition, superconductors are made from brittle ceramic materials that are not as malleable as the copper wire now used. And although the most advanced superconducting wires carry hundreds of amps at liquid-nitrogen temperatures, they must carry hundreds of thousands of amps for use in energy transmission. Another major challenge is fabricating reliable and consistent superconductor materials in the quantities required by the electric power industry. Further, questions remain about the health effects of the powerful magnetic fields that would be associated with superconducting transmission lines.

If these problems can be solved in the international race to develop practical superconductors, their potential applications promise to play a major role in future global energy.

References and Notes

1. British Petroleum Company (BP), *BP Statistical Review of World Energy* (BP, London, 1987), p. 2, p. 21, and p. 25.
2. World Energy Conference (WEC), *Energy: Needs and Expectations*, 13th Congress, Cannes, October 5-11, 1986 (WEC, London, 1987), p. 25.
3. W.G. Davey, "Energy Issues and Policies in Eastern Europe," *Energy Policy* (February 1987), pp. 68-70.
4. OECD countries are Australia, Austria, Belgium, Canada, Denmark, the Federal Republic of Germany, Greece, Ireland, Italy, Japan, Luxembourg, the Netherlands, New Zealand, Norway, Portugal, Spain, Sweden, Switzerland, Turkey, the United Kingdom, and the United States.
5. Cynthia Pollock Shea, *Renewable Energy: Today's Contribution, Tomorrow's Promise* (Worldwatch Institute, Washington, D.C., 1988), p. 8.
6. U.S. Department of Energy, Energy Information Administration, *Weekly Petroleum Status Report*, November 29, 1985, Table 3; May 20, 1988, Table 3.
7. *Op. cit.* 1, p. 4.
8. Ian Davison, "BP Statistical Review of World Energy 1988," (preliminary) (British Petroleum Company, London, April 1988).
9. Russell de Lucia, "Lower Oil Prices: Implications for Household Fuel Strategies," (draft), The World Bank Energy Department Paper, Washington, D.C., December 1986.
10. Matthew Mendis, The World Bank, Washington, D.C., June 1988 (personal communication).
11. Ian Davison, *BP Statistical Review of World Energy 1988* (British Petroleum Company, London, 1987), p. 4.
12. *Op. cit.* 8.
13. *Op. cit.* 1, p. 8.
14. *Op. cit.* 8.
15. *Op. cit.* 1, p. 19.
16. *Op. cit.* 1, p. 22.
17. *Op. cit.* 8.
18. *Op. cit.* 1, p. 27.
19. *Op. cit.* 8.
20. World Energy Conference, *1986 Survey of Energy Resources* (Holywell Press, London,

1986), p. v.
21. *Op. cit.* 1, p. 28.
22. Christopher Flavin, *Reassessing Nuclear Power: The Fallout from Chernobyl* (Worldwatch Institute, Washington, D.C., 1987), p. 7.
23. *Op. cit.* 1, p. 29.
24. *Op. cit.* 20, p. 129.
25. *Op. cit.* 5, p. 19.
26. World Commission on Environment and Development, *Our Common Future* (Oxford University Press, Oxford, U.K., 1987), p. 192.
27. *Op. cit.* 2, p. 239.
28. *Op. cit.* 5, p. 9.
29. *Op. cit.* 1, p. 30.
30. World Energy Conference, *Survey of Energy Resources 1980*, cited in *Op. cit.* 5, p. 9.
31. The World Bank, *A Survey of the Future Role of Hydroelectric Power in 100 Developing Countries* (The World Bank, Washington, D.C., 1984), cited in *Op. cit.* 5, p. 10.
32. *Op. cit.* 5, p. 9.
33. *Op. cit.* 5, p. 14.
34. *Op. cit.* 5, pp. 15-17.
35. *Op. cit.* 5, p. 37.
36. *Op. cit.* 5, p. 40.
37. *Op. cit.* 5, p. 28.
38. *Op. cit.* 5, p. 31.
39. *Op. cit.* 5, p. 31.
40. James Caldwell, President, ARCO Solar, Inc., Camarillo, California, 1988 (personal communication).
41. *Op. cit.* 5, pp. 32-33.
42. *Op. cit.* 20, p. 183.
43. *Op. cit.* 20, Table I, p. 184, and Table II, p. 185.
44. Gerald Leach, Director of Energy, International Institute for Environment and Development, London, 1988 (personal communication).
45. Organisation for Economic Co-operation and Development and International Energy Agency (OECD/IEA), *Energy Conservation in IEA Countries* (OECD/IEA, Paris, 1987), pp. 39-41.
46. *Ibid.*, p. 42.
47. Jayant Sathaye, Andre Ghirardi, and Lee Schipper, "Energy Demand in Developing Countries: A Sectoral Analysis of Recent

Trends," *Annual Review of Energy*, Vol. 12 (Annual Reviews, Palo Alto, California, 1987), p. 256.
48. *Op. cit.* 45, pp. 47-49.
49. *Op. cit.* 47, pp. 262-263.
50. *Op. cit.* 47, pp. 263-264.
51. United Nations Food and Agriculture Organization (FAO) *The State of Food and Agriculture 1985* (FAO, Rome, 1986), p. 71.
52. "Avaliagao do Programa Nacional do Alcool," Comissao Nacional de Energia, Assessoria Technica, Brasilia, Brasil, May 1988.
53. *Op. cit.* 45, p. 51 and p. 53.
54. *Op. cit.* 45, p. 53.
55. *Op. cit.* 45, p. 77.
56. *Op. cit.* 45, p. 53.
57. *Op. cit.* 47, p. 267.
58. *Op. cit.* 47, p. 271.
59. *Op. cit.* 45, p. 49.
60. *Op. cit.* 45, p. 51.
61. *Op. cit.* 47, pp. 272-273.
62. *Op. cit.* 47, pp. 272-273.
63. CMEA (Council for Mutual Economic Assistance, also known as COMECON) countries are the USSR, East Germany, Poland, Czechoslovakia, Romania, Bulgaria, Hungary, Cuba, Viet Nam, Mongolia, and North Korea.
64. Andrei Trofimuk, "Siberia Unfreezes Its Assets," *New Scientist* (June 25, 1987), p. 52.
65. *Op. cit.* 1, p. 2, p. 21, and pp. 25-26.
66. "Export Prospects for Soviet Oil," *Energy in Europe: Energy Policies and Trends in the European Community*, No. 8 (October 1987), p. 11.
67. *Op. cit.* 1, p. 4, p. 22, and p. 26.
68. *Op. cit.* 1, p. 4.
69. Matthew J. Sagers, Chief, Soviet Branch, Center for International Research, U.S. Bureau of the Census, Washington, D.C., 1988 (personal communication).
70. *Op. cit.* 1, p. 21.
71. Isabel Gorst, "Soviet Union: New Developments to Boost Gas Supply," *Petroleum Economist* (February 1987), pp. 70-71.
72. *Op. cit.* 69.
73. Theodore Shabad and Matthew J. Sagers,

"News Notes," *Soviet Geography*, Vol. 28, No. 4 (1987), pp. 269–271.

74. *Ibid.*, p. 276.

75. *Op. cit.* 1, p. 8.

76. Matthew J. Sagers, "The Soviet Push for Oil Exports," *The World & I* (October 1987), p. 120.

77. *Op. cit.* 1, p. 27.

78. Marshall I. Goldman, *The Enigma of Soviet Petroleum* (George Allen & Unwin, Boston, 1980), pp. 10–11.

79. *Ibid.*, pp. 51–52.

80. Isabel Gorst, "Soviet Union: Big Increase in Energy Investment," *Petroleum Economist* (August 1986), p. 287.

81. Isabel Gorst, "Soviet Union: Growing Importance of Coals," *Petroleum Economist* (August 1987), p. 299.

82. *Op. cit.* 73, p. 272.

83. A. Petrosyants, "The Soviet Union and the Development of Nuclear Power," *IAEA Bulletin* (autumn 1986), pp. 5–6.

84. Isabel Gorst, "East Europe: Gas and Nuclear Fuel Replacing Oil," *Petroleum Economist* (May 1987), p. 192.

85. PlanEcon Inc., *PlanEcon Energy Service Soviet and Eastern European Data Bank*, Vol. II (PlanEcon, Washington, D.C., 1987).

86. *Op. cit.* 84.

87. Isabel Gorst, "East Europe: Looking for Alternatives to Oil," *Petroleum Economist* (May 1987), p. 216.

88. *Op. cit.* 85.

89. *Op. cit.* 3, p. 62.

90. *Op. cit.* 3, p. 66.

91. *Op. cit.* 3, p. 60.

92. *Op. cit.* 84.

93. *Op. cit.* 84, p. 191.

94. *Op. cit.* 3, p. 60.

95. *Op. cit.* 87, pp. 216–217 and Table I, p. 216.

96. *Op. cit.* 3, p. 64.

97. *Op. cit.* 84.

98. *Op. cit.* 3, p. 65.

99. *Op. cit.* 87, Table I, p. 216.

100. *Op. cit.* 84, p. 174.

101. *Op. cit.* 3, pp. 69–71.

102. William Echikson, "Energy Crunch Hits the East Bloc," *Christian Science Monitor* (February 2, 1987), p. 9.

103. *Op. cit.* 66.

104. USSR, Financy i Statistika, *Narodone Khoziaistvo, SSSR za 70 Lct.* (Moscow, 1987), p. 641.

105. *Oil & Gas Journal* (December 7, 1987), p. 89.

106. *Op. cit.* 76, pp. 121–122.

107. Charles E. Ziegler, "The Bear's View: Soviet Environmentalism," *Technology Review* (April 1987), p. 45.

108. William H. Mahoney, "Soviet Brass Call for Action to Repair Environmental Harm," *World Environment Report* (August 6, 1987), p. 123.

109. William Echikson, "Environmental Problems Are Explosive Issues for East Bloc," *Christian Science Monitor* (November 16, 1987), p. 9.

110. William Echikson, "Hungarians Blue over Fate of Danube," *Christian Science Monitor* (November 17, 1987), p. 9.

111. William Echikson, "Hostile Neighbors Find Common Ground in Fighting Pollution," *Christian Science Monitor* (November 18, 1987), p. 8.

112. *Op. cit.* 110, p. 9.

113. *Op. cit.* 109.

114. Misha Glenny, "Living in a Socialist Smog," *New Scientist* (September 1987), p. 41.

115. *Op. cit.* 3, p. 61.

116. *Op. cit.* 114, pp. 41–42.

117. *Op. cit.* 114, pp. 41–44.

118. *Op. cit.* 114, p. 44.

119. *Op. cit.* 111.

120. *Op. cit.* 45, p. 39.

121. Howard S. Geller, *Improving End-Use Electrical Efficiency: Options for Developing Countries* (The World Bank, Washington, D.C., 1986), p. 10 and p. 14.

122. National Productivity Council (NPC), *Report on Utilisation and Conservation of Energy: Sectoral Reports—Energy Audit Studies* (NPC, New Delhi, 1983), cited in *Ibid.*, p. 15.

123. Jose Goldemberg, *et al.*, *Energy for a Sustainable World* (World Resources Institute, Washington, D.C., 1987), p. 5 and Table 11, p. 68.

124. C.N. Cochran, R.H.G. McClure, and J.J. Tribendis, *Recycling of Automotive Aluminum—Present and Future*, Report No. 830099 (Society of Automotive Engineers, Warrendale, Pennsylvania, 1983), cited in *Op. cit.* 121, p. 16.

125. M. Ross, E.D. Larson, and R.H. Williams, "Energy Demand and Materials Flows in the Economy," in *Energy, The International Journal*, cited in *Op. cit.* 121, p. 16.

126. *Op. cit.* 121, p. 19.

127. United Nations Food and Agriculture Organization, "Agriculture toward 2000," cited in *Op. cit.* 123, pp. 48–49.

128. National Productivity Council (NPC), *Report on Utilisation and Conservation of Energy, Sectoral Reports—Energy Audit Studies* (NPC, New Delhi, 1983), cited in *Op. cit.* 121, pp. 29–30.

129. E.T. Smerdon and E.A. Hiler, "Energy in Irrigation in Developing Countries," paper prepared for the U.S. Agency for International Development, Washington, D.C., 1980, cited in *Op. cit.* 121, p. 30.

130. *Op. cit.* 123, pp. 59–61.

131. Deborah Lynn Bleviss, "Preparing for the 1990's: The World Automotive Industry and Prospects for Future Fuel Economy Innovation in Light Vehicles," Federation of American Scientists, Washington, D.C., draft, January 1987, Table 3-1, p. 156.

132. *Op. cit.* 123, Table 9, p. 62 and pp. 65–67.

133. Commission of the European Communities (CEC), *Energy Saving from Optimum Design and Control of Lighting in Office Buildings*, EUR 9537 EN (CEC Luxembourg, 1985), cited in *Op. cit.* 121, p. 22.

134. *Op. cit.* 121, p. 34.

135. S. Ayyash, "Power Needs of Cooling Systems in Kuwait and their Effects on the Utility," *Applied Energy*, Vol. 13 (1983), pp. 109–120, cited in *Op. cit.* 121, p. 24.

136. *Op. cit.* 123, p. 55.

137. Howard S. Geller, *The Potential for Electricity Conservation in Brazil* (Companhia Energetica de São Paulo, São Paulo, 1984), cited in *Op. cit.* 121, p. 37.

138. The World Bank, *The Energy Transition in Developing Countries* (The World Bank, Washington, D.C., 1983), cited in

Op. cit. 121, p. 16.

139. *Op. cit.* 137, p. 58.

140. *Op. cit.* 123, pp. 33–34.

141. *Op. cit.* 139, p. 33.

142. U.S. Department of Energy (DOE), *Health and Environmental Consequences of the Chernobyl Nuclear Power Plant Accident* (DOE, Washington, D.C., 1987), p. vii.

143. *Ibid.*

144. One curie is the amount of a material that undergoes 37 billion radioactive disintegrations per second.

145. Radioactive half life is the time required for a substance to lose 50 percent of its radioactivity by decay.

146. *Op. cit.* 142, p. viii.

147. *Op. cit.* 142, p. ix.

148. International Atomic Energy Agency (IAEA), *IAEA News Features*, No. 1 (IAEA, Vienna, April 15, 1988), p. 5.

149. Sharon Stephens, "Lapp Life after Chernobyl," *Natural History*, Vol. 96, No. 12 (1987), pp. 37–38.

150. Frank von Hippel and Thomas B. Cochran, "Chernobyl: The Emerging Story: Estimating Long-Term Health Effects," *Bulletin of the Atomic Scientists* (August/September 1986), p. 18.

151. The European Community comprises Belgium, Denmark, France, Germany, Greece, Ireland, Italy, Luxembourg, the Netherlands, Portugal, Spain, and the United Kingdom.

152. M. Morrey, *et al.*, *A Preliminary Assessment of the Radiological Impact of the Chernobyl Reactor Accident on the Population of the European Community* (National Radiological Protection Board, Dicot, U.K., 1987), cited in "Chernobyl—Limited Health Impacts," *The Environmentalist*, Vol. 7, No. 2 (1987), p. 144.

153. *Op. cit.* 142, p. x.

154. Cheryl Sullivan, "Nuclear Reactor Accident Will Have Slight Long-Term Impact, Researchers Say," *Christian Science Monitor* (August 31, 1987), p. 3.

155. *Op. cit.* 150, p. 24.

156. "Foundering in the Gulf," *South* (October 1987), p. 75.

157. "Oil Importers Seen Surviving Closure of Strait," *Oil & Gas Journal* (August 31, 1987), p. 20.

158. "A Question of Crude Realities," *South* (January 1988), p. 11.

159. "The Real Spoils of War," *South* (January 1988), p. 46.

160. *Op. cit.* 157.

161. *Op. cit.* 158.

162. Peter Krause, "Superconductors," *Environmental Action* (November/December 1987), p. 18.

163. *Ibid.*

164. James Gleick, "Superconductors: Scientists Hail Latest Materials," *New York Times* (March 8, 1988), p. C1.

165. "New Age of Electricity," *South* (September 1987), pp. 91–92.

166. Boyce Rensberg, "Superchallenge: The Race to Exploit Superconductors. A Current of Change for Motors, Computers," *The Washington Post* (May 18, 1987), p. A1.

167. *Op. cit.* 162, pp. 18–20.

8. Freshwater

Earth is the water planet; over 70 percent of its surface is covered by water, most of it the saltwater of the oceans. Freshwater, upon which land-based animals and most plants depend, is only a small fraction (3 percent) of the water on the planet. Nevertheless, the total amount of freshwater (36 million cubic kilometers) is more than enough to sustain all life forms on Earth. The supply is continuously renewed by the endless cycling of water, driven by sun energy. Freshwater falls as precipitation. When it infiltrates the soil, it aids plant production and recharges groundwater, or it may run off the surface into lakes, streams, and rivers. Freshwater returns to the atmosphere by transpiration from plants or by evaporation, either from land and inland water bodies or after flowing to the sea.

This global abundance, however, is not distributed evenly. In many areas of the world limited precipitation, high population density, or both make available freshwater barely adequate for—or present substantial limits to—human uses. The "availability" of water for human use, even in a relatively small area, is difficult to define and measure. It depends not only upon climate and precipitation but also on the timing of precipitation, river flows, availability of groundwater, and human interventions either to increase the total supply (e.g., by importing water from another area) or to use the existing water supply more efficiently.

There is no international consensus on defining and measuring water availability. National statistics are misleading because countries are inconsistent regarding river flow from and to other countries and the inclusion or exclusion of groundwater. In addition, simple annual averages mask substantial seasonal and interannual differences in precipitation, streamflow, and groundwater storage. To be fully meaningful, water availability data must be applied to specific locations at specific times.

Rapidly increasing populations in many parts of the world place growing demands on water for irrigation, domestic use, and industrialization. Responses to these increased demands include not only such traditional steps as well drilling and dam construction, but also improved management of available freshwater. These nonengineering approaches include more effective allocation of freshwater and more efficient use through water conservation.

The quality of water strongly affects its usefulness. Although human activities have long polluted freshwater, governments have made significant efforts to control specific "point sources" of pollution such as industrial facilities and urban sewage systems. However, many major sources of pollution remain largely uncontrolled because they are "scattered." Important categories of these "nonpoint sources" are agricultural runoff and urban surface runoff.

CONDITIONS AND TRENDS

GLOBAL FRESHWATER AVAILABILITY

Water is an essential ingredient of all life [1]. For land-based forms of life, however, about 97 percent of the

Figure 8.1 Distribution of the World's Water

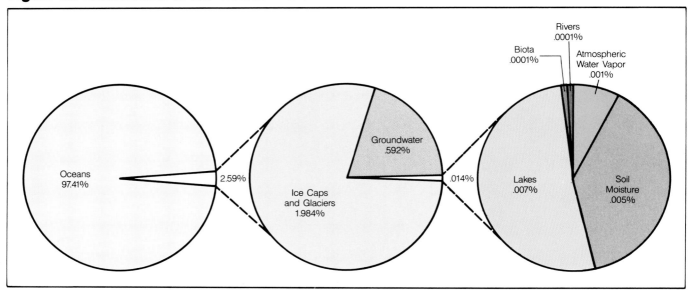

Source: David H. Speidel and Allen F. Agnew, "The World Water Budget," in *Perspectives on Water Uses and Abuses*, David H. Speidel, Lon C. Ruedisili, and Allen F. Agnew, eds. (Oxford University Press, New York, 1988), Table 3.1, p. 28.

water is not available for consumption because of its salinity. Even the 3 percent that is fresh is not all readily available; much of it is either locked in glacial ice or stored underground. (See Figure 8.1.)

The primary source of freshwater to support human and other land-based life is the precipitation that falls on land. Although it is a relatively small fraction of the water on Earth, the precipitation that falls on land is still an enormous resource—more than 110,000 cubic kilometers annually. (See Table 8.1.) Sixty-five percent of it eventually returns to the atmosphere via evapotranspiration from the land, and the remainder recharges aquifers, streams, and lakes as it flows to the sea. (See Chapter 11, "Global Systems and Cycles," for a discussion of the global hydrological cycle.)

The total annual river runoff shown in Table 8.1 takes into account human withdrawals and use. In the United States, for example, about 467 square kilometers of freshwater are withdrawn from surface and groundwater each year, an amount equal to 19 percent of the domestic renewable supply. About 27 percent of withdrawals are

actually consumed—lost to evaporation or incorporated into products—and are not returned to streamflows (2). Countries with large, consumptive withdrawals of water, especially for irrigation, can have even larger relative impacts on their water budgets. (See Chapter 21, "Freshwater," Table 21.1.)

The abundance of freshwater masks its uneven global distribution and the frequent mismatch between the locations of people and water. Table 8.2 classifies 24 countries as water-rich or water-poor based upon the annual per capita availability of freshwater runoff resulting from precipitation falling within a country's borders. Table 8.2 shows three measures of available freshwater: total annual runoff from domestic precipitation, annual runoff per hectare, and annual runoff per capita. The countries are listed in the order of available freshwater per capita. (See Chapter 21, "Freshwater," Table 21.1.) Much of the variation in freshwater availability is based on climatic differences. Many North African and Middle Eastern countries, such as Egypt, have low precipitation levels and high evaporation rates, resulting in low levels of runoff per

Table 8.1 Total Annual Water Availability and Use
(square kilometers per year)

			Runoff		
	Precipitation	Evapotranspiration	Total River Runoff	Surface (Flood) Runoff	Stable (Base) Flow
Europe	7,165	4,055	3,110	2,045	1,065
Asia	32,690	19,500	13,190	9,780	3,410
Africa	20,780	16,555	4,225	2,760	1,465
North America	13,910	7,950	5,960	4,220	1,740
South America	29,355	18,975	10,380	6,640	3,740
Australia & Oceana	6,405	4,440	1,965	1,500	465
All Inhabited Continents	**110,305**	**71,475**	**38,830**	**26,945**	**11,885**

Source: Mark I. L'vovich, *World Water Resources and Their Future* (translated from Russian) (American Geophysical Union, Chelsea, Michigan, 1979), Table 20, p. 201.

Table 8.2 Annual Runoff from Endogenous Precipitation in Selected Countries, 1987

	Total (cubic kilometers)	By Area (thousand cubic kilometers per hectare)	Per Capita (thousand cubic meters per person)
Water-Rich Countries			
Iceland	170	16.96	685.48
New Zealand	397	14.78	117.53
Canada	2,901	3.15	111.74
Norway	405	13.16	97.40
Nicaragua	175	14.74	49.97
Brazil	5,190	6.14	36.69
Ecuador	314	11.34	31.64
Australia	343	0.45	21.30
Cameroon	208	4.43	19.93
USSR	4,384	1.97	15.44
Indonesia	2,530	13.97	14.67
United States	2,478	2.70	10.23
Water-Poor Countries			
Egypt	1.00	0.01	0.02
Saudi Arabia	2.20	0.01	0.18
Barbados	0.05	1.16	0.21
Singapore	0.60	10.53	0.23
Kenya	14.80	0.26	0.66
Netherlands	10.00	2.95	0.68
Poland	49.40	1.62	1.31
South Africa	50.00	0.41	1.47
Haiti	11.00	3.99	1.59
Peru	40.00	0.31	1.93
India	1,850.00	6.22	2.35
China	2,800.00	3.00	2.58

Source: International Institute for Environment and Development and World Resources Institute, *World Resources 1987* (Basic Books, New York, 1987), Table 81.1, pp. 268–269, and Table 23.1, pp. 314–315.

hectare. By contrast, such diverse countries as Iceland, Ecuador, and Indonesia have well over 1,000 times as much freshwater per hectare because of their climates.

In terms of availability for human use, however, the location and density of the population are equally important. Canada and China, for example, annually receive roughly equal amounts of precipitation, both in total and on a per hectare basis. But because China's population is about 40 times that of Canada (see Chapter 15, "Population and Health," Table 15.1), the average Chinese has 2.3 percent of the freshwater resources of the average Canadian. Although much of Australia is dry, it is sparsely populated except in the coastal areas, where rainfall is relatively abundant and per capita water availability is relatively high. Conversely, despite Central Europe's moderate precipitation per hectare, Poland's relatively high population density lowers its per capita water availability.

DEFINING FRESHWATER AVAILABILITY ON A NATIONAL LEVEL

National statistics on freshwater are inconsistent because there are no international standards. Table 8.2 points up some of the difficulties in determining water availability. Although classifying Saudi Arabia as a water-poor country seems obvious, including the Netherlands in this category is not so clear. Part of the explanation is population. The Netherlands is densely populated and its water resources must be widely shared. However, its low per capita figure also results from including only runoff originating from precipitation falling within the borders of the country. The Netherlands is a coastal country at the mouth of the Rhine River, which receives 80 cubic kilometers of water each year from countries upstream. This

inflow is an eightfold increase in the amount of freshwater available for use within the country, and including it would certainly change the per capita figure. (See Chapter 21, "Freshwater," Table 21.1.) Some countries include river inflow in their water data and others do not. Groundwater resources are also treated inconsistently.

Availability of freshwater also depends on the location and timing of precipitation. Average annual precipitation can mask large variations within a country. For example, the U.S. Southwest is dry and some parts are desert. Other sections of the United States have abundant water—significant parts of the Olympic Peninsula in the Pacific Northwest are covered by rainforest. Overall U.S. water availability figures mask these differences. Similarly, rainfall and runoff vary widely over time. The annual monsoon pattern of rainfall in South Asia can result in alternating flood and dry periods. Most flood waters that pass through India and Bangladesh during the monsoon are no more "available" for use during the floods than they are during the dry seasons.

A realistic assessment of freshwater availability for human use must consider climate, location, timing, population, political boundaries, and human intervention. Figure 8.2 shows the many factors affecting the availability of water for human use within a country.

The first source is precipitation (line 1). Most of it returns directly to the atmosphere by evaporation from the land and inland waters or by transpiration from plants (line 2). Much of the rainwater absorbed by vegetation is used indirectly by humans when they use natural vegetation and rainfed crops. However, this is water that is not available for direct withdrawal and use. How much runs off the land into lakes, streams, and rivers depends on temperature, soil type, and vegetation. As shown in Table 8.1, total river runoff in Africa is only about 20 percent of the rainfall. By contrast, over 40 percent of Europe's precipitation ends up as river flow. Human activities increase surface runoff significantly at a local level by removal of vegetative cover or construction of roads and cities.

A country's total river flow is fed by surface runoff from endogenous precipitation, groundwater, and river water entering from countries upstream (line 3). River water inflow can be significant. In Egypt, river inflow provides over 50 times more water than domestic rainfall does. (See Table 8.2 and Chapter 21, "Freshwater," Table 21.1.) However, river inflow is subject to upstream nations' actions and therefore is less secure than domestic supplies. Egypt and Sudan have a formal agreement on the fraction of Nile water that Sudan may divert. However, Ethiopia, from which 86 percent of the Nile's water enters Sudan, is not a party to any such agreement. Even a small diversion of water by Ethiopia would cause significant problems for both Sudan and Egypt. Diversion of the Ganges River by India, a major problem for Bangladesh, is a potential source of friction between the two countries. (See *World Resources 1987*, pp. 184–187.)

Roughly two thirds of total river runoff is flood runoff, which is not generally available for human use. Availability of freshwater for human use depends largely on the remaining one third of river runoff, referred to as stable

Figure 8.2 Freshwater Availability for a Country

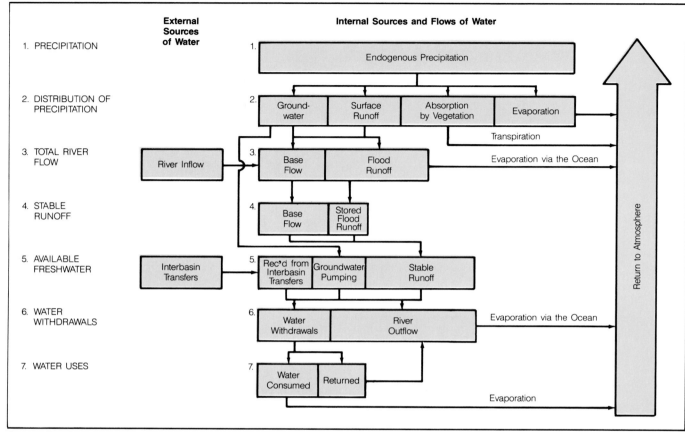

Source: Compiled by *World Resources 1988–89.*

runoff or base flow (line 4). Stable runoff is the sustained low flow of streams and rivers, which results primarily from groundwater inflow in most parts of the world. The capture and storage of flood runoff in reservoirs—and subsequent release of stored water during periods of low river flow—add to this stable runoff. They can be a significant factor in increasing water availability. It is estimated that on a worldwide basis, the natural base flow has been augmented by about 15 percent by capturing flood runoff behind dams (3).

Available freshwater from rivers can be supplemented by groundwater. If the freshwater withdrawn from an aquifer does not exceed what is recharged in a year, the aquifer serves as a reservoir. During dry periods, availability is increased by drawing down groundwater that is replenished during the next wet season. But, if pumping groundwater exceeds recharge rates (mining), available freshwater is depleted. Mining groundwater is not uncommon; it is a significant source of freshwater in Bangkok, Beijing, and parts of the midwestern United States. (See *World Resources 1987*, pp. 119–121.)

Within a country where the abundance of water varies widely, areas with surplus (unused) water can transfer water to areas of scarcity (line 5). Transfers from one river basin to another are common in the western United States. While technically feasible, international interbasin water transfers have rarely, if ever, occurred. The high costs of these transfers limit their use even within a country. (See Focus On: Managing an Increasingly Scarce Resource, below.)

Water has both instream and offstream uses. Instream uses (e.g., fishing, recreation, sewage disposal) do not affect the physical availability of freshwater, although they can degrade water quality. Offstream uses (line 6) involve withdrawing surface and groundwater for irrigation, industry, power plant cooling, and domestic supplies. Most surface and underground water withdrawals lower total river flow. These consumptive uses, primarily for agriculture, directly reduce availability of water downstream. However, some water that has been withdrawn is returned to streams or rivers for possible reuse downstream (line 7). On the other hand, this returned water is frequently polluted physically, chemically, or thermally, thereby limiting its subsequent uses.

FOCUS ON: MANAGING AN INCREASINGLY SCARCE RESOURCE

Many freshwater problems of the 21st Century will arise from an increasing demand for water generated by population growth, urbanization, industrialization, and irrigation (4). In the face of this growing demand, countries have three basic options when freshwater availability is limited: they can reallocate available water to accommodate new, competing demands, they can stretch the limited supply by improved efficiency of use through conservation and reuse, and they can increase the available supply of freshwater through traditional engineering solutions such as building dams to capture and store more flood runoff, drilling wells to tap additional groundwater, and transferring water from areas of surplus to areas of scarcity. Constructing dams and drilling wells continues to be a major answer to increased demands, especially in developing countries, where the technical potential for such solutions is only beginning to be used.

Rather than depending solely upon ways to increase freshwater availability, countries are recognizing the need for better management of existing freshwater supplies. The result is that management strategies are changing. With a few notable exceptions, countries have turned away from large-scale interbasin water transfers because of their high costs and frequent environmental damages. Nations are beginning to find ways to reallocate water use and make more efficient use of the water they have (5).

Many countries are constantly faced with trying to implement programs and technologies within an institutional framework long antiquated and resistant to change, an international expert recently reported (6). In most countries, comprehensive water policies and laws either do not exist or are inadequate for managing an increasingly scarce resource. This situation costs millions of dollars in wasted freshwater and crop production, and it continues to contribute to the mismanagement of national and donor funds (7).

These problems led the 13th International Congress on Irrigation and Drainage to focus on improving water management in developing countries. When the 81 member countries met in 1987, they examined ways to integrate irrigation, drainage, and flood control projects under a single national planning structure (8). Following the conference, India adopted a national water policy that will use the river basin as the basic unit for water development planning (9). Cote d'Ivoire will adopt a national policy of integrated river basin management by the end of 1989. Under a national water authority, the country's basin agencies will police and coordinate all water uses in each river system (10). The United Kingdom had reorganized its water management under 10 river basin authorities in 1973. In 1987, however, the government stripped the river basin authorities of responsibility for water resources planning, pollution control, land drainage, fisheries, navigation, and conservation. Although these responsibilities were transferred to a new National Rivers Authority, some water resources experts considered the move a step backward in integrated water management. The privatized basin authorities are now only utilities: they supply water, sewerage, and waste disposal services (11).

As the objective of water management becomes the efficient and equitable allocation of water among competing uses, management will be guided more strongly by economic and ecological realities. Trends now becoming apparent include applying the user-pays principle instead of public subsidies, overcoming the legal and bureaucratic restraints to water reallocation, recognizing the interrelationships of water and land use, and reorganizing into national water authorities the institutions that govern water supply and quality. Even water engineers are now often calling for these measures (12).

Reallocation

One response to growing demands for a limited amount of water is reallocation, either by direct government regulation or through water markets. In semiarid regions where populations are increasing rapidly, the call for more water is forcing reevaluation of current allocations. In Africa, for example, the goal of self-sufficiency in food production may be revised as governments and world lending institutions face the economic reality that it is often cheaper to transport food rather than water during a sustained drought (13).

China is trying to reallocate water from low- to high-value uses in its semiarid north. In 1988, its State Science and Technology Commission, in conjunction with the East-West Center in Honolulu, recommended measures to reduce demand by charging more for water, eradicating leaks, and promoting conservation (14).

Reallocating water is not easy. Who owns the water? How is it distributed? And how does the law avoid or resolve disputes? International aspects add complications because 40 percent of the world population lives in international river basins (15). A basic requirement for countries, therefore, is to know how much of their water is endogenous (originates within the country) and how much is exogenous (flows from other countries). Water availability data, as discussed earlier in the chapter, are essential to compute water balances if workable water policies are to be developed and wise management decisions made (16).

Under the mounting pressure of population growth in the United States' arid Southwest, scarce water is increasingly subject to reallocation by water marketing or water rights sales. The shift in the use of freshwater from agriculture to municipalities and industry so far has mostly affected groundwater, ownership of which is tied to the land. Arizona, with its pioneering 1980 groundwater law restricting mining or withdrawals that exceed replenishment, is witnessing a historic reallocation as cities buy or lease farms for their well-water rights. In 1987, Phoenix bought 14,000 acres of farmland 100 miles to its west for $29 million to prepare for a population that is expected to reach 2.1 million by 1990. With a 1986 population of 1.7 million (a 26 percent rise from 1980), Phoenix is the fastest-growing metropolitan area in the United States (17) (18).

Water marketing as a way of reallocating water use, however, has its drawbacks. It does not take account of instream values (water needed for animal and aquatic life). Further, water quality values are not always adequately represented, as in five water markets assessed in the western United States (19). Some water resource experts argue that water cannot be treated like a commodity and therefore should not be "given over to free market forces" (20). Selling surface water rights across state boundaries in the United States poses legal as well as political problems. A proposal to market Yampa River water in Colorado to San Diego, California, has gone nowhere, largely because Colorado would not permit it (21).

Whether water marketing will become a useful device in other parts of the world with differing legal and institutional systems is uncertain. Whatever the form, however, the trend in water management to reallocate usage is underway, as in the semiarid north area of China. As countries that share water resources deal increasingly with water scarcity, they will be forced to resolve upstream-downstream water allocation conflicts such as the current quarrel over the Ganges-Brahmaputra River Basin between India and Bangladesh. (See *World Resources 1987*, pp. 186–187.)

Increasing Efficiency

The greatest potential for using freshwater more efficiently is with irrigated agriculture, which accounts for about 70 percent of total world use. Since 1950, irrigated land area has nearly tripled to about 270 million hectares. One third the world's food is grown on irrigated lands, which comprise only 18 percent of total cropland. But most irrigation methods are grossly inefficient. Worldwide, only 37 percent of irrigation water contributes to the growth of crops; the other 63 percent is wasted. Overwatering with inadequate drainage causes waterlogging and salinization, thus degrading the land (22).

Water use efficiency can be increased through both technological improvements and economic incentives. If irrigation water losses were cut 10 percent in the Indus region of Pakistan, the savings could irrigate an additional 2 million hectares (23). The surge technique that coats the ground in gravity supply irrigation systems, for example, can significantly reduce seepage. In this technique, a water valve is timed to open and close at intervals, thus creating surges of water. Drip or trickle microirrigation also saves water through its direct application to plant roots, greatly reducing evaporation.

A technological approach being tested in more than 100 countries is a biointensive agriculture program called Common Ground, which is both simple and inexpensive. Using an organic gardening technique that can outperform commercial farms in terms of yields per hectare, it requires only one quarter of the water and fertilizer that commercial farms use. Common Ground has major research and development programs in Mexico, India, China, and the Philippines. The program is called biointensive because one person's "complete, balanced, vegetarian diet" can be grown on one hundredth of a hectare—just one thirtieth of the land required to produce a complete diet in many developing countries (24). Although this is a small-scale manual labor program, it could significantly conserve freshwater while increasing local food production.

Improved economic incentives can also help conserve irrigation water. Historically, government subsidies have underpriced water relative to its costs. Options for changing water prices were put forward in 1987 by the Organisation for Economic Co-operation and Development (OECD), reflecting a 4-year study of practices and trends

among its 24 member countries. The report recommended marginal cost pricing, in which the price is set at or near what it costs a water utility to provide or buy its most recent additional water; this figure is usually higher than earlier acquisition costs. Cost pricing would discourage water demand by significantly increasing the price of water to customers. Even charging customers the average cost would increase prices substantially. The OECD study urged countries to end subsidies by taxpayers and cross-subsidies among users of different services, except for special "social" reasons (25).

In developing nations, public irrigation is heavily subsidized, and farmers in most countries pay only 10–20 percent of the costs of building and operating the systems. Further, charges in many countries are levied not by the unit of water applied but by the unit of land irrigated. This practice removes any incentive to conserve water. The result is wasted water and inefficient and inequitable irrigating systems (26). (See Chapter 12, "Policies and Institutions.")

In the United States, where western farmers paid only 16 percent of government costs to provide the irrigation water (27), political support to curtail these enormous government subsidies is growing. Since late 1986, when the Congress enacted cost-sharing requirements for new water projects, agriculture water beneficiaries must pay 35 percent of construction costs. Other cost-sharing ratios vary from a minimum of 25 percent for flood control projects to 100 percent for hydroelectric power, municipal, and industrial uses (28).

Another management trend in increasing efficiency is recycling or reuse of wastewater. In Tokyo, where recycling is common, wastewater is used to flush toilets in high-rise buildings. The city's Water Recycling Center takes wastewater from a slow-sand filtration tertiary treatment plant, chlorinates it, and pumps it to 11 high-rise office buildings. The center plans to double its capacity of 4,000 cubic meters a day. In Japan, recycled water costs the user less than freshwater (29).

The Chinese State Science and Technology Commission has recommended reusing wastewater and recycling industrial water as one of several methods to meet predicted water shortages in Beijing and in Tianjin, a nearby seaport and industrial center. Both cities face a projected water deficit of 4 billion cubic meters by 2000 (30).

In the water-short Middle East, Israel reused 35 percent of its wastewater in 1986, primarily for irrigation and, by the year 2000, plans to recycle 80 percent of its wastewater. Israel expects wastewater reuse to increase its renewable water supply 25 percent (31).

Israel's pioneering work in wastewater reuse was conceived to motivate towns and cities to build treatment facilities. A coalition formed by the Health Ministry, sanitary engineers, and farmers created the country's first major sewage irrigation project in the early 1950s, a high-rate trickling filter plant in Jerusalem. By 1956, wastewater reuse was part of the National Water Plan. To help the fledgling program, liberal health guidelines were adopted. They allowed sewage water that had undergone primary treatment (mechanical cleansing) to be used for

Figure 8.3 Israel's Water Gap

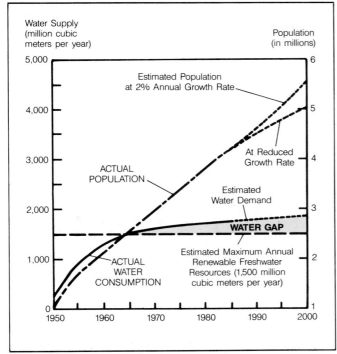

Source: Hillel I. Shuval, "The Development of Water Reuse in Israel," *Ambio*, Vol. 16, No. 4 (1987), Figure 4, p. 188.

fodder crops and for fruit trees cultivated by the ridge-and-furrow method.

In 1965, the guidelines were upgraded to require oxidation pond treatment before reuse. Then, in 1970, a cholera outbreak in Jerusalem was traced to the illegal irrigation of salad crops with raw (untreated) wastewater. This episode spurred efforts to develop a national sewerage program, which laid the foundation for the country's water reuse success by treating more wastewater. It was also evident that the country was outgrowing its freshwater supply—by 1990, a water gap would grow to 200–300 million cubic meters a year. (See Figure 8.3.) With the costs of desalination prohibitively high, wastewater recycling became a part of national water policy (32).

Interbasin Water Transfers—A Costly Way to Increase Supply

A recent study of water projects in China, India, Bangladesh, Pakistan, Mexico, and the United States concluded that publicly financed water transfer systems based on irrigation demands lead to poor use of water and capital (33). The study underscored the continuing controversy over the efficacy of costly government-subsidized schemes to transfer water long distances. In the United States, the era of building huge federal dams and long aqueducts and canals appears to have ended. The scarcity of good dam sites, high costs, food surpluses, and environmental opposition explain why (34). (See Small Dams as a Development Tool, below.) A U.S. congres-

sional study found that highly subsidized water projects waste both water and money. The study said that "artificially inexpensive irrigation water" gave little incentive to farmers to use it efficiently, and it promoted water-intensive crops that would not have been grown if water were priced at the cost of providing it (35). Further, those regions with surplus water in the northern United States and Canada are increasingly unwilling to agree to any water removals, although they currently have abundant supplies (36).

The Soviet Union appears to be moving in the same direction, despite the continuing demand for irrigation water in the semiarid southern regions of the USSR. In August 1986, the Communist Party's Central Committee officially abandoned the "project of the century," a grandiose scheme 15 years in the planning. It would have diverted the flow of rivers emptying into the Arctic and Pacific Oceans and pumped the water southward into the Central Asian republics and Kazakhstan (37). The complicated multistage project, which would not have been completed until the middle of the 21st Century, would have diverted a total of 120 cubic kilometers of water a year—one fifth of the Mississippi River's annual flow at its mouth (38).

Why did the Soviets give up on their unprecedented water transfer plan? (See Box 8.1.) A major reason given by Alexander Yanshin, vice president of the USSR Academy of Scientists, is the reversal of conditions at the Caspian Sea. Prior to 1979, the Caspian had been drying up, but since then, the sea has been rising, undermining port facilities and threatening the Buzachi Peninsula's oil fields. Diversions from the north would have made matters worse (39).

One major interbasin water transfer that is going forward will divert about 5 percent of the mean flow of the Chang Jiang (Yangtze River) to China's semiarid northern provinces. The primary conduit will be a 1,000-kilometer canal using the still navigable Grand Canal (rebuilt by Kublai Khan in 1291), which runs from Hangzhou west of Shanghai to Beijing (40). Almost a quarter of China's cultivable land goes out of production each year because of drought or flood. The full-scale Chang Jiang diversion will cross under the sluggish Huang He (Yellow River). Two proposed water routes to the west would create more irrigable acreage. One environmental drawback is possible harm to fisheries in the estuary because of changed salinity levels (41). Work to widen and deepen the Grand Canal, begun in 1987, should take five years to complete and will cost more than $700 million (42). The project's first stage, which will pump 600 cubic meters of water per second, will stop just south of the Huang He. The completed project will divert 1,500 cubic meters per second (43).

NONPOINT SOURCE POLLUTION

In the industrialized world, nonpoint source pollution means all the pollutants that enter the water from sources other than municipal sewage treatment plants and industrial waste. In developing countries, the distinc-

Figure 8.4 Sources and Types of Nonpoint Pollution in Impacted U.S. Rivers and Lakes

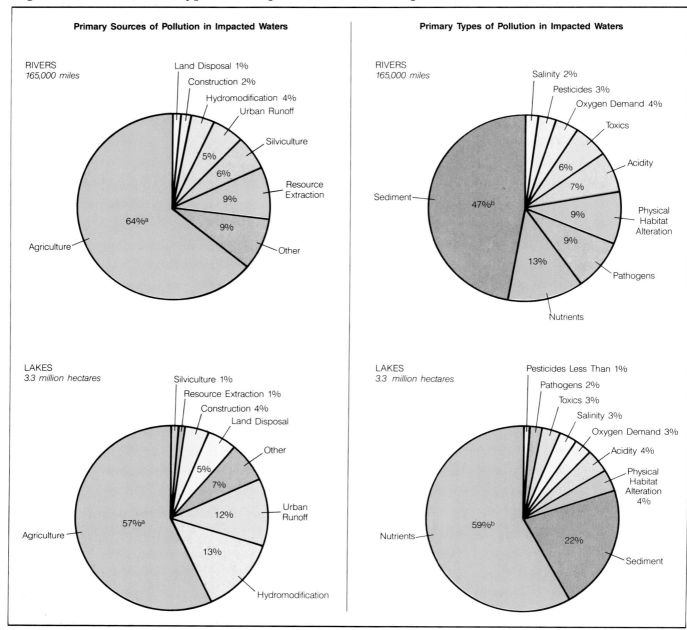

Source: Association of State and Interstate Water Pollution and Control Administrators (ASIWPCA), *America's Clean Water: The States' Nonpoint Source Assessment 1985* (ASIWPCA, Washington, D.C., 1985), p. 7 and p. 10.
Notes:
a. Percent of impacted river miles (or hectares of lakes) for which agriculture is the primary source of nonpoint pollution.
b. Percent of impacted river miles (or hectares of lakes) for which sediment is the primary type of nonpoint pollutant.

tion between point and nonpoint sources has less meaning because so much of their sewage and industrial waste remains untreated. However, as the less developed countries develop economically through industrial growth, urbanization, and chemical-dependent agriculture, they will face the same nonpoint pollution problems that plague industrialized nations (44).

Put another way, nonpoint source pollution simply refers to the diffuse sources of water pollution that result from human activity on the land. They include agricul-

ture, mining and oil production, silviculture, urbanization, dams and stream channelization, and construction. Some are directly related to soil loss and sedimentation.

Pollutants are anthropogenic or natural (45). The nondegradable toxic chemicals used in pesticides are synthetic pollutants. The arsenic found in China's Huang He is a natural pollutant that comes from the highly eroded Loess Plateau (46). Nitrates, which are a public health threat, originate from both natural (soil nitrogen) and anthropogenic (fertilizer) sources (47). Whether a nonpoint pollutant causes a problem depends on the assimilative capacity of the receiving water body and whether the water can still be used as desired (48).

Although the global severity of nonpoint pollution is not known, in the United States, 6 of 10 Environmental Protection Agency regions report that nonpoint source pollution is now "the principal cause of inadequate water quality" (49).

Rural Nonpoint Pollutants

A major source of nonpoint pollution worldwide is agriculture. In the United States, where nonpoint sources of pollutants have been identified and measured, farm runoff is the principal source of pollution in 64 percent of the country's impacted rivers and 57 percent of its impacted lakes. (See Figure 8.4.) Impacted waters are those in which uses are severely or moderately impaired by nonpoint sources or in which nonpoint sources threaten to impair a designated use. In the United States, 165,000 out of a total of 1.8 million miles of rivers are impacted, and 8.1 million acres out of a total of 39.4 million acres of lakes are impacted (50).

Nutrients from both fertilizers and animal wastes were the primary pollutants in 13 percent of the miles of impacted U.S. rivers and in 59 percent of impacted lakes. (See Figure 8.4.) Pesticides were the primary pollutant in only 3 percent of the river miles and less than 1 percent of the lakes. The principal nutrients are nitrates, considered a growing public health problem, and phosphorus, which depletes oxygen, speeds eutrophication, and triggers fish kills.

The use of pesticides in the United States has more than doubled since 1962 (51); they are now a contamination problem in the groundwater of 40 of the 50 U.S. states (52). The world pesticide market reached an estimated $18 billion in 1987, with Brazil, India, and Mexico the leading consumers. Where regulation of the use of pesticides is lax or nonexistent, the threat to public health may be significant. Where pesticides are better regulated, a few have been banned (DDT, EDB, and aldicarb in the United States), and scientific debate continues about the health significance of trace amounts of many others. (See Chapter 2, "Population and Health.")

Information on pesticide and fertilizer use is inadequate. Pesticide data for Europe and North America compiled by OECD in 1987 indicated a general increase over the past decade of from 1 percent for Sweden (1976–84) to 127 percent for France (1975–82). However, OECD omitted 8 of its 25 member countries and included data beyond 1982 for only 8 (53).

The OECD 1987 fertilizer data were more complete. (See Tables 8.3 and 8.4.) Between 1970 and 1985, use of nitrogenous fertilizer in OECD countries increased 32 percent, but phosphate fertilizer consumption dropped 2 percent. In individual countries, these increases were large. Increased use of nitrogen fertilizers was sharpest in Canada (323 percent), New Zealand (300 percent), Turkey (277 percent), and Ireland (271 percent). World figures showed a 120 percent increase in nitrogenous fertilizers and a 32 percent increase in phosphates, but no regional or national breakdowns were given.

Table 8.3 Nitrogen Fertilizer Use in OECD Countries, 1970–85
(thousand metric tons)

	1970	1975	1980	1985
Europe	6,779	8,202	10,241	11,239
North America	7,655	10,001	11,755	10,910
Australia-New Zealand	152	177	258	360
Japan	688	653	614	680
OECD Total	**15,274**	**19,033**	**22,868**	**23,189**
World Total	**31,750**	**43,241**	**60,727**	**69,895**

Source: Organisation for Economic Co-operation and Development (OECD), *OECD Environmental Data Compendium 1987* (OECD, Paris, 1987), Table 15.6A, p. 279.

Table 8.4 Phosphate Fertilizer Use in OECD Countries, 1970–85
(thousand metric tons)

	1970	1975	1980	1985
Europe	5,633	5,343	6,027	5,426
North America	4,672	5,245	5,565	4,600
Australia-New Zealand	1,066	876	1,135	985
Japan	653	623	690	741
OECD Total	**12,024**	**12,087**	**13,417**	**11,752**
World Total	**25,262**	**25,181**	**31,607**	**33,431**

Source: Organisation for Economic Co-operation and Development (OECD), *OECD Environmental Data Compendium 1987* (OECD, Paris, 1987), Table 15.6B, p. 281.

Although commercial fertilizers are the primary source of anthropogenic nitrogen and phosphorous entering the environment, other sources include manure, sewage sludge, septic tanks, atmospheric deposition, and urban runoff. The resultant eutrophication of waters is one of the most pervasive water pollution problems globally. The complexity of this growing nonpoint source is well-illustrated by a long-term study of several drainage basins in Sweden's Scania region. Although more than 70 percent of nitrate pollution came from agricultural activities, the atmosphere was also a significant source. Commercial fertilizer and manure accounted for 95 percent of the Scania region's phosphorous pollution. Contributions of phosphorous from the atmosphere, sewage treatment plant sludge, and septic tank infiltration were slight (54).

Excessive nitrates in drinking water may cause methemoglobinemia (blood poisoning) in infants, hypertension in children, gastric cancers in adults, and fetal malformations. The combination of high nitrates and pesticides, a common phenomenon, may form nitrosamines, which are both carcinogenic and mutagenic. These synergistic possibilities may involve such other drinking water pollutants as microbial pathogens in untreated rural supplies and heavy metals (cadmium, mercury, and lead). A reevaluation of risk assessment procedures is needed (55).

Nitrate concentrations in some European rivers have been increasing since 1960 at an average annual rate of 0.15 milligrams per liter (56). They are approaching the World Health Organization's recommended limit of 11.3 milligrams per liter, occasionally surpassing the acceptable limit of 22.6 milligrams per liter. During the past decade, one third the surface water monitoring sites in the United Kingdom exceeded the 11.3 milligrams per liter standard. These levels are associated with low rain-

Figure 8.5 Hydrologic Changes in Ontario, Canada, Caused by Urbanization

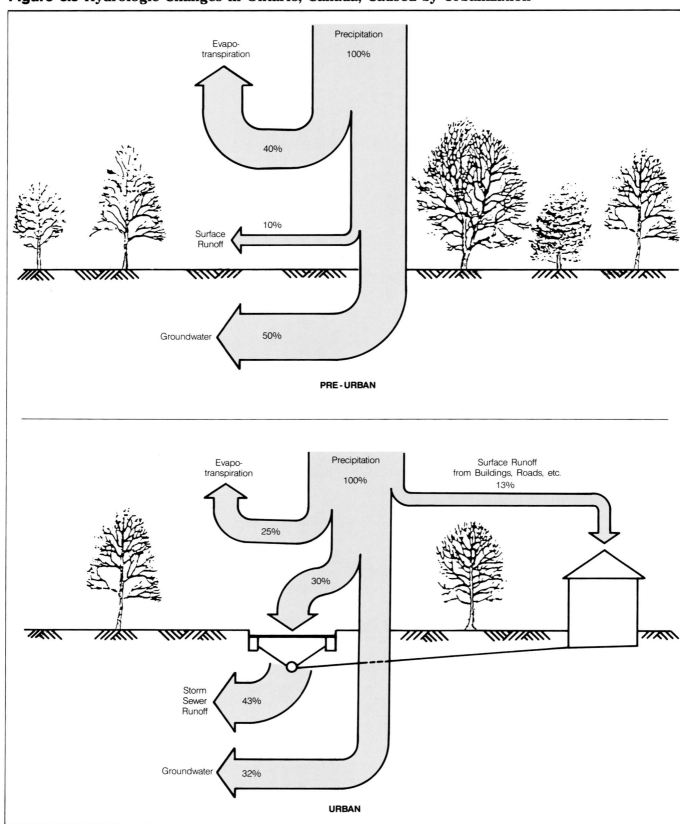

Source: Organisation for Economic Co-operation and Development (OECD), *Control of Water Pollution from Urban Runoff* (OECD, Paris, 1986), Figure A-2, p. 43.

fall and intensive farming. Nitrate levels vary with climate, season, and land practices that cause widely fluctuating leaching patterns. Groundwater supplies appear to be more at risk, with 7 percent consistently exceeding the 11.3 milligrams per liter level in Britain and 8 percent in Denmark. A European Economic Community directive to tighten nitrate standards 50 percent is being debated by member countries (57). In the United States, 6 percent of 124,000 wells tested exceeded the drinking water limit of 10 milligrams per liter (58).

Quantifying the farm runoff problem in the developing world is difficult because of the lack of national fertilizer use data, pesticide registration, and manufacturers' unwillingness to provide sales information (59). However, there is little reported evidence of damage to aquatic ecosystems from current levels of pesticide use (60). Developing countries accounted for 22 percent of pesticide use in 1978, a world share that was expected to change little in the 15 years after that except for Africa, where use is expected to triple or quadruple by 1993 (61). DDT is still used in some countries, and endosulfan, lindane, and other persistent compounds extremely toxic to fish are still being applied to rice in Southeast Asia (62).

Mining is a major pollutant source in Asia and the Pacific. Copper, zinc, lead, and cadmium pollute many of Australia's rivers. In Malaysia, sediments from mining and construction pollute 31 rivers. Sediment from mining also pollutes rivers and irrigation canals in the Philippines. In Thailand mining wastes pollute surface waters, along with farm runoff full of agricultural chemicals and animal manure. But nonpoint source information from this region is anecdotal and non-comprehensive (63).

Urban Nonpoint Pollutants

No one used to worry about stormwater runoff from cities and towns. However, research shows that the water quality of urban runoff is often worse than that of treated sewage. Traffic emissions, construction, road de-icing, street refuse, organic residues from vegetation and animals, and atmospheric deposition are producing growing amounts of sulfuric and nitric acid, copper, zinc, vanadium, hydrocarbons, phosphates, asbestos, particulates, lead, chlorides, chromates, complex cyanides, dirt, organics, and untreated garbage (64). Further, the hydrologic changes resulting from urbanization are only now beginning to be understood in terms of surface and groundwater pollution. (For an example, see Figure 8.5.) Urbanization heightens the relationship between water quantity and quality by increasing peak flow in receiving streams, decreasing base flow, and lessening groundwater replenishment (65). As more watersheds are urbanized, widespread use of impervious surfaces and storm or combined sewer systems will facilitate the introduction of pollutants. The result is that urban nonpoint pollution may equal or surpass the impact of rural nonpoint pollution on freshwater supplies (66).

This situation is particularly common where climate and topography combine to create high storm water volumes in low-slope terrains. In the United States, Florida's experiences with urban nonpoint pollution are an example. In 1980, stormwater discharges accounted

for more than half of Florida's freshwater pollution. Urban runoff caused 80–85 percent of heavy metal pollution, and virtually all its sediment deposits. It raised the levels of suspended solids and biochemical oxygen demand (BOD) to 450 times and 9 times, respectively, those of secondarily treated sewage effluent. And it caused nutrient loads comparable to treated sewage discharges (67).

Sediment

Sediment is a major nonpoint source pollutant associated with both rural and urban runoff. In the United States, sediment accounts for 47 percent of river pollutants and 22 percent of lake pollutants. (See Figure 8.4.) Sediments cause turbidity, and they may transport pollutants: nutrients, pathogens, and toxic chemicals.

Historically, sedimentation has contributed to the demise of civilizations, such as the Harrappan that flourished more than 4,000 years ago on the alluvial plains of the Indus River. Recurring floods eventually covered its cities with silt (68). Deforestation, industrialization, and urbanization are now making sedimentation a matter of global concern, particularly in Asia. China's Huang He (Yellow River), named for its constantly high sediment load, carries the most eroded soil of any large river in the world. (See Table 8.5.) Silt is a water quality problem, especially in China, Malaysia, and Indonesia (69).

Most sediment drops out of the water and is stored at the base of steep hills when a river slows. This sediment can be picked up again by the river if its velocity changes. Ironically, land use practices to curtail erosion may not always result in less suspended sediment at first because the "cleaner" upstream water is able to take some of the deposited sediment out of storage (70).

This concept of sediment storage modifies the assumption that soil conservation practices always improve water quality by reducing the number and levels of chemicals and nutrients that are transported as particulates or are attached to suspended matter. Although generally true,

Table 8.5 Sediment Loads in Selected Rivers of the World

River	Country	Catchment Area (square kilometers)	Mean Water Discharge (square meters per second)	Annual Sediment Load (million metric tons per year)
Rhine	Netherlands	160,000	2,200	2.8
Po	Italy	54,300	1,550	15
Wisla	Poland	193,900	950	1.4
Danube	Romania	816,000	6,200	65
Don	USSR	378,000	830	4.2
Ob	USSR	2,430,000	12,200	15
Niger	Nigeria	1,081,000	4,900	21
Congo	Zaire	4,014,000	39,600	72
Mississippi	United States	3,269,000	24,000	300
Amazon	Brazil	6,100,000	172,000	850
Parana	Argentina	2,305,100	X	90
Indus	Pakistan	969,000	5,500	435
Ganga	India Bangladesh	955,000	11,800	1450
Brahmaputra	India Bangladesh	666,000	12,200	730
Irrawaddy	Burma	430,000	13,500	300
Red	Socialist Republic of Viet Nam	120,000	3,900	130
Zhu Jiang	China	355,000	8,000	70
Chang Jiang	China	1,807,000	29,200	480
Huang He	China	752,000	1,370	1640

Source: A. Sundborg, "Sedimentation Problems in River Basins," *Nature: Resources* (April-June 1983), Table 1, p. 17.
X = not available.

the soil storage phenomenon can sometimes exacerbate water quality problems as well as skew the monitoring of nonpoint source pollution control efforts. An example is the practice of conservation tillage to reduce soil loss where the phosphorus in fertilizers is promoting lake eutrophication. Where conservation tillage is practiced, most fertilizers are applied to the surface. Because soil chemicals then stratify, the concentration of soluble phosphorus may increase. Thus, although conservation tillage reduces soil loss and therefore the amount of phosphorus in the runoff, initially the chemical's higher concentration can cause an increase in eutrophication (71).

Pollution Control Strategies

Regulating how the land is used lies at the heart of rural nonpoint pollution control and bears heavily on reducing urban pollution. Regulation, in turn, depends on the environmental institutions and policies of national governments and regional organizations. Governments generally employ either command-and-control water quality rules to restrict pollution, with penalties for overpolluting (as in the United States), or they employ the polluter-pays principle, taxing polluters according to how much they pollute (as in Japan). These strategies work best with point sources—such as municipal sewage treatment plants and industries that discharge into rivers and lakes. To control nonpoint pollution, governments must affect agricultural practices and a myriad of other activities on the land. Ideally, a country would establish a national policy or program to assure comprehensive planning and institutional coordination (72). Few countries, however, have done so.

The Comprehensive Water Quality Management Project in the Philippines shows the challenges and difficulties involved in pollution control (73). The project was created in the early 1970s to deal with Laguna de Bay, the largest freshwater lake in Southeast Asia. The lake—used for crop irrigation, commercial fishing, and municipal water supply—was suffering from acute eutrophication caused primarily by nitrogen loadings from farm and urban runoffs. Crop irrigation and industrial discharges were also polluting the lake with heavy metals, toxic wastes, and various organic materials. Laguna de Bay is fed by 21 tributaries that drain a catchment basin of 3,822 square kilometers. The land supports some 50 towns, several industrial areas, and intensive farming. Further, projected municipal needs for the growing Manila metropolitan area include the withdrawal of raw water from the lake by 1990.

The Laguna Lake Development Authority (LLDA), which had river basin jurisdiction, measured the water quality, set interim standards, and determined goals to support lake use. The authority inventoried all the pollution sources, monitored the pollutant loadings, and projected future loadings. LLDA concluded that about 80 percent of the lake's nitrogen pollution came from farm runoff and domestic wastes. If the basin's growth continued, nitrogen pollution was expected to double by the year 2000. The lake authority then developed pollution control plans that included low-cost sewage treatment technologies and changes in farming practices to reduce nitrogen losses into irrigation drainages. Environmental impact statements were prepared for all the pollution control methods, and the benefit-cost analysis included a hydraulic control structure to prevent further saltwater intrusion. It yielded a favorable ratio of 1.2 to 1.

LLDA has experienced major difficulties in its program implementation because of competing interests and a

---

Box 8.1 An Interbasin Project Hits *Glasnost*

The Soviet Union is water blessed; enough water flows down its rivers to meet current freshwater demands at least 15 times over. The problem, however, is that three quarters of its people live where only 16 percent of the water is available. Most of the water flows northward and eastward into the Arctic and Pacific Oceans. Most of the people live in the southern European, Kazakhstan, and Central Asian parts of the country. For this reason, a multistaged diversion scheme to reverse river flow southward looked promising. Fifteen years in the planning, the "project of the century" would shift 120 cubic kilometers a year to where the water is needed most (1).

Construction was underway when, in August 1986, the Communist Party's Central Committee and the USSR's Council of Ministers stopped work for "further study of ecological and economic aspects." Why? According to Soviet documents, "broad sections of the public" criticized the plan. Opposition first surfaced in February 1983, when the USSR's Academy of Sciences' Council for Optimum Planning and Management met with the project's chief engineers. "They heard a serious and well-argued criticism of the project,

but the Academy of Sciences does not have the power to solve economic matters," recalled Prof. Mikhail Lemeshev, head of the council. "This is why the work went on. We, for our part, formed a commission under a vice president of the Academy, prepared substantial objections, and passed them on to the Politburo and the government." The Academy was split, with its president, Anatoli Alexandrov, in support of the project (2).

In late 1985, the newspaper *Sovetskaya Rossiya* ran pro and con stories, as did the ecological magazine *Priroda I Chelovek*. The weekly *Ekonomicheskaya Gazeta* published an article by a staff member of the Council for the Investigation of Productive Forces of the USSR's State Planning Institute. It noted that one reason for the diversion—the dropping water level of the Caspian Sea—no longer existed. Readers began writing to the editor supporting the project's critics. A resident of Krivoi Rog in the southern Ukraine wrote that the money would be better spent cleaning up the region's "heavily polluted" rivers. That letter was included in the mail review for the Presidium of the Supreme Soviet, which receives more than 90,000 letters a year on environmental issues (3).

Ten years ago the situation would have been quite different. *Izvestia's* Leningrad correspondent said of the controversy surrounding a flood control barrage being built on the Gulf of Finland: "Opponents—hydrologists, biologists, geologists, even some naval experts—came to me 10 years ago and gave me objections. Unfortunately, at the time it was not possible to make their remarks known in the newspaper"(4).

References and Notes

1. G.V. Voropaev and A.L. Velikanov, "Partial Southward Diversion of Northern and Siberian Rivers," in *Large Scale Water Transfers: Emerging Environmental and Social Experiences*, Genady N. Golubev and Asit K. Biswas, eds. (Tycooly Publishing Ltd., Oxford, U.K., 1985), pp. 67–83.
2. Yevgeny Novikov, "The USSR Shelves a Water Diversion Plan," *WorldPaper* (November 1986, Boston), p. 6.
3. *Ibid.*
4. Bill Keller, "Storm of Protest Rages Over Dam Near Leningrad," *New York Times* (September 27, 1987), p. 9, sec. I.

lack of authority for the entire river basin. So far it has not managed to reduce lake pollution as planned.

SMALL DAMS AS A DEVELOPMENT TOOL

Dam technology is centuries old. Impoundments were developed for a variety of uses—for the distribution of water by Roman aqueducts, as irrigation tanks in India more than 2,000 years ago, for subsurface dams in North Africa and the islands of Sardinia, and to power water-wheels to lift water and grind grain worldwide. More recently, in addition to irrigation and water supply, dams were built for flood control, power, and other purposes.

By today's standards, most dams constructed before the middle of the 20th Century were small. But as developed countries centralized their water and power services, the scale of dams increased considerably. All but 7 of the 100 largest dams in the world were completed after World War II (74) (75). Beginning in the 1960s, developing countries undertook large dam projects. Two thirds the dams that are more than 150 meters high and that will be completed in the 1980s are in developing countries (76). For industrialized countries, the number of new large dams decreased significantly in the 1970s. Sites were not available, development costs were increasing while available funds were decreasing, concern for environmental damage was growing, and the public objected.

In developed countries, the construction of large dams has declined recently and there has been a resurgence in the construction of small dams. By 1980, private land-holders in the United States built more than 2.1 million ponds for livestock, irrigation, fish production, fire protection, wildlife habitat, recreation, and landscape improvement (77). In addition, legislation in the late 1970s and generous tax subsidies encouraged both retrofitting of existing dams and new construction of dams for small-scale hydropower. The result is an increase in small-scale hydropower facilities of almost 300 megawatts in the past few years. Several hundred megawatts of additional capacity are also being built in the United States (78).

No comprehensive data exist to document the extent of small dam construction and use globally. Although 4.5 percent of the total volume of reservoir storage is estimated to be contained in small impoundments, the number of these small reservoirs has not been estimated (79). A recent literature review concluded that interest in small-scale irrigation has grown, although little has been published about it (80). In developing countries, the small dam picture is mixed. China and India, with 54 percent of the world's irrigated land, have many years experience with small dam technology, in contrast with other countries.

China constructed 6 million small ponds (with a capacity of less than 100,000 cubic meters each) for irrigation and other purposes between 1950 and 1980 (81). The number of small dams built for hydropower plants at the same time is equally impressive—89,000 plants supplying 6,300 megawatts of power (82). Approximately 40 percent of China's rural townships and one third of its 2,200 counties now receive most of their power from small hydropower dams (83). From the 1950s to the 1970s, irrigated land in Central and Southern China increased 53

percent. By 1978, 84,000 reservoirs had been developed (most used small dams), with a combined capacity of 400 billion cubic meters; by 1982, 36 percent of cultivated land was irrigated (84). The Meichuan Irrigation District in Hubei Province is an example of combining small dams and large reservoirs. Using this "two legs" strategy, the Chinese expanded their traditional ponds and connected them to larger reservoirs by canals so that the ponds can be refilled several times a year. This additional diversion and storage capacity for the district allows two rice crops during the growing season (85). Small dams have helped China achieve multiple development objectives with strong local participation by brigades and communes. In Enping County, Guangdong Province, the Jin Jiang cascades were dammed and 130 small hydropower plants constructed to produce 36 megawatts of power. All 18,670 hectares of farmland along both banks were irrigated, and 8,000 hectares of low-lying farmland previously threatened by waterlogging became stable high-yielding farmland (86).

In India, the use of tanks—small reservoirs formed by earthen dams—is among the oldest ways to obtain water for irrigation through systematic storage of runoff or water diverted from streams. This technique dates back more than 2,000 years. In 1856, the British found 53,000 tanks in one district of the Madras Presidency but did not maintain them. The feudal princes, who had strong local authority, were more successful. For example, the tank-irrigated area increased from 4,000 hectares in 1896 to 364,000 hectares by the late 1940s in the Hyderabad State. Except for the first decade following India's independence in 1950, India has largely neglected construction and maintenance of tanks. The tank-irrigated area, which peaked in 1958–59 at 4.8 million hectares, fell to 3.9 million hectares 20 years later. Tanks are beneficial not only in providing supplemental irrigation but also in stabilizing soils, increasing crop yields, and reducing the waterlogging and salinity problems often associated with large-scale irrigation projects. Although rehabilitating tanks and constructing new ones is not a national program, progress is being made in selected areas. In Gujarat, a voluntary organization mobilized villagers to build 100 dams; the result was a rise in the water table. Bank loans then helped subsistence farmers dig wells and buy diesel pump sets and pipes for irrigation.

In Himachal Pradesh, Punjab, and Haryana Provinces, the Indian government is committed to building 3,000 tanks with earthen dams less than 10 meters high to arrest gully erosion, trap water to irrigate a second crop of wheat, and recharge groundwater. Planning or construction is in progress in each province (87).

A project in the village of Sukhomajri demonstrates how small dams can aid development. Water from a small dam built at the foot of a highly eroded ravine was used to irrigate 80 acres of village land. Farm production improved and the farmers leveled and built check dams on their own lands. Increased crop yields added to the fodder from residue, which lessened grazing pressure on nonagricultural land. Trees, bushes, and grasses began to grow again in the watershed. Three rainfed reservoirs were then built nearby with small earthen dams. Concomitantly, the grass yield increased from 40 kilograms to

Table 8.6 Existing and Potential Small Hydropower Project Sites in Selected Countries[a]

Country	Existing Sites	Potential Sites
Bangladesh	0	21
Burma	7	10
India	120	340
Indonesia	36	14
Malaysia	10	100
Peru	185	80
Bolivia	183	40
Ecuador	31	10
Burundi	4	100
Madagascar	4	120
Zaire	1	50
Cote d'Ivoire	0	50

Sources:
1. *Small Hydropower for Asian Rural Development*, Colin R. Elliot, ed., proceedings of a workshop on small-scale hydropower technology applications in Asian rural settings, The Asian Institute of Technology, Bangkok, Thailand, June 1981, pp. 8-19.
2. *Small-Scale Hydropower in Africa*, workshop proceedings, African Development Bank, Union of Producers, Conveyors and Distributors of Electrical Energy in Africa, National Rural Electric Cooperative Association, U.S. Agency for International Development, Abidjan, Ivory Coast, March 1982, pp. 19-31.
3. *Small Hydropower in Africa*, workshop proceedings, National Rural Electric Cooperative Association, Mbabane, Swaziland, June, 1983, pp. 169-175 and pp. 181-185.
4. *Small Hydroelectric Power Plants: An Information Exchange on Problems, Methodologies, and Development*, workshop proceedings, National Rural Electric Cooperative Association, Quito, Ecuador, 1980.

Notes:
a. These figures are for public project sites. Although based on field assessments, they tend to be conservative. The number of private sites often exceeds the number of existing public sites by several factors.
b. Several numbers have been updated by the author through unpublished data and personal communications.

2,000 kilograms and the sale of milk alone significantly increased income. The village society is planning to establish village industries based on local products as a source of productive and remunerative employment (88).

Although the first small hydropower plant was installed in Darjeeling in 1887, India has almost totally neglected the development of small hydropower plants. In 1980, India had an installed capacity of 220 megawatts from small hydropower plants that ranged in size from 5 kilowatts to 6,800 kilowatts. A potential 2,000 megawatt capacity exists in the hilly regions, and another 3,000 megawatts could be gained from irrigation drop structures (89).

Other developing countries have some experience with small dams for water supply, irrigation, and power development. But, until recently, this experience was often gained with the use of technical assistance and equipment from other countries. Largely because of the two sharp oil price increases in the 1970s, many developing countries began to consider small-scale hydropower plants, particularly for isolated rural sites. Table 8.6 shows existing and potential small hydropower sites for selected countries from data collected in the late 1970s and early 1980s. As population growth and development increase demands for power and water, interest in small dams is likely to grow.

RECENT DEVELOPMENTS

MORE SMALL DAMS: OLD AND NEW

Japan has built more than 1,000 inflatable dams for irrigation, flood control, and groundwater recharge. They are made of a rubber treated to withstand the sun's ultraviolet rays. A major advantage is the elimination of silt when a dam is collapsed during periods of low water. Other advantages over traditional gated dams are lower costs, more design flexibility, and less maintenance.

The dams are filled with air or water. They are bolted to foundations on the river floor containing flexible materials that act as shock absorbers when the dams are deflated. The broadest span erected so far is 135 meters. Several generate electricity, for example, such as the 40-meter span on the Mikata River that is 2 meters high. The two Japanese companies that make the dams—Sumitomo of Osaka and Bridgestone of Tokyo—are exporting the process to South Korea and Southeast Asia and are planning sales to western Europe (90).

Another type of low-cost small dam—first used in Sardinia at the time of the Roman Empire—is enjoying a renaissance in developing countries. It is the groundwater dam. They are built in riverbeds either below or above the ground—often both—to store groundwater when the rivers and aquifers beneath them dry up. The advantages of groundwater dams are their relatively low construction costs; lack of evaporative losses; reduced risk of pollution; and elimination of common problems, such as the loss of valuable land, siltation, and the spread of disease by mosquitoes that breed in surface reservoirs.

Subsurface dams are built in riverbeds to arrest the flow of groundwater in the alluvial sediments below. Sand dams across streambeds collect sediments that then become an artificial aquifer. In both cases, the object is to maintain water in shallow wells year-round. Sub-Saharan African nations, India, and Brazil are showing increasing interest in building these small dams, primarily for drinking water in rural areas (91).

CONVERTING THE SEA: A BREAKTHROUGH?

Tropical oceans can generate electricity and produce freshwater. But can they do so on a commercial scale? Two U.S. research facilities, the Argonne National Laboratory in Argonne, Illinois, and the Solar Energy Research Institute in Golden, Colorado, have demonstrated the feasibility of using the heat in tropical oceans to generate power, which is then used to desalinate water without consuming energy from outside sources. Researchers estimate that a full-size version could produce 10 megawatts of electricity and 5 million gallons of freshwater per day—enough power and potable water for a city of up to 20,000 people.

The top layer of tropical ocean water provides the energy. This water, at a temperature of about 26°C, is pumped into a vacuum chamber where about 1 percent of the water is immediately converted into steam. The steam drives conventional turbines to produce electricity and the condensation from the spent steam provides freshwater. The turbine heat exchanger that produces the condensate is cooled by 6°C water pumped from half a mile below the ocean surface. The generated power is more than enough to run the system, called ocean thermal energy conversion (OTEC). In addition to providing electricity, future OTEC plants could provide freshwater to islands and coastal cities (92).

NEW YORK CITY PONDERS WATERSHED MANAGEMENT

Recent droughts are combining with the population growth in the eastern United States to spur new interest in river basin water management. In recent years, the United States has moved further away from the river basin concept, dropping six river basin commissions created by a 1965 law. The country now manages only three rivers as river basin units: the Tennessee, the Delaware, and the Susquehanna.

Counties in the upper basin of the Hudson River are agitating for another river basin commission because of New York City's growing needs. The city, which currently uses about 1.4 billion gallons a day, could require as much as 250 million to 1 billion gallons more by 2025 unless its current wasteful water use practices change. None of the city's current needs are met by using the Hudson River, which has an average annual streamflow of about 12 billion gallons a day.

New York City draws half its water from three reservoirs in the upper Delaware River. The water is transported by a system of aqueducts and a tunnel under the Hudson River. The rest of its water comes from the Catskill and Croton watersheds in the Hudson River basin. However, a new watershed planning group for the city recommended taking Hudson River water on a non-emergency basis. It is also considering tying its system to the aquifers of adjacent Long Island and is calling for installation of domestic water meters and a leakage abatement program.

A half-dozen upriver communities rely on the Hudson for their drinking water, and the city's future water needs have alarmed these communities. For brief periods in past droughts, the river's "salt front," or unacceptable salinity level, has reached Poughkeepsie, a town more than 100 kilometers upriver. Large withdrawals to meet the needs of New York City would greatly exacerbate the salinity problem, and they could lead to water shortages for the upstream communities. A Hudson River Basin Commission would give the communities a voice in managing the river (93).

References and Notes

1. *New Century World Atlas* (Rand McNally, Chicago, 1986), p. 16.
2. Wayne B. Solley, Robert R. Pierce, and Charles F. Merk, *Preliminary Water-Use Estimates in the United States in 1985* (U.S. Geological Survey, Reston, Virginia, 1985), Table 1.
3. Mark I. L'vovich, *World Water Resources and Their Future* (translated from Russian) (American Geophysical Union, Washington, D.C., 1979), Table 26, p. 264.
4. Malin Falkenmark, L. da Cunha, and L. David, "New Water Management Strategies Needed for the 21st Century," *Water International*, Vol. 12, No. 3 (1987), p. 94.
5. H. Fish and Chen Shenyi, "Water Resources Management," in *World Water '86: Water Technology for the Developing World* (Thomas Telford, London, 1987), p. 19.
6. George E. Radosevich, "National Water Goals, Policies, and Laws: The Institutional Framework," paper presented at the Regional Symposium on Water Resources Policy, Dhaka, Bangladesh, August 1985, p. 20.
7. *Ibid.*
8. "Morocco Venue Ideal for ICID," *World Water*, Vol. 10, No. 8 (1987), p. 20.
9. "India Adopts River Basin Plan," *World Water*, Vol. 10, No. 10 (1987), p. 9.
10. "Ivory Coast Adopts Basin Integration," *World Water*, Vol. 10, No. 10 (1987), p. 13.
11. "UK to Abandon River Basin Management?" *World Water*, Vol. 10, No. 8 (1987), p. 11.
12. *Op. cit.* 5, p. 23.
13. Malin Falkenmark, Asit K. Biswas, *et al.*, "Water-Related Limitations to Local Development," *Ambio*, Vol. 16, No. 4 (1987), pp. 191–200.
14. East-West Center and State Science and Technology Commission, China, *Water Resources Policy and Management for Deijing-Tranjin Region* (East-West Center, Honolulu, Hawaii, 1988).
15. *Op. cit.* 4, p. 95.
16. *Op. cit.* 13, p. 200.
17. Robert Lindsey, "Booming Cities Buy Up 'Water Ranches' in Southwest," *New York Times* (August 16, 1987), p. E5.
18. Mary A.M. Gindhart, "Retirees Are More Profitable than Cotton," *WorldPaper* (Boston, November 1986), p. 7.
19. Bonnie Colby Saliba, "Do Water Markets 'Work'? Market Transfers and Trade-Offs in the Southwestern States," *Water Resources Research*, Vol. 23, No. 7 (1987), p. 1113.
20. Freshwater Foundation, *Water Values and Markets: Emerging Management Tools* (Freshwater Foundation, Navarre, Minnesota, 1986), p. 8.
21. Mohamed T. El-Ashry and Diana C. Gibbons, *Troubled Waters: New Policies for Managing Water in the American West* (World Resources Institute, Washington, D.C., 1986), p. 33.
22. Sandra Postel, "Effective Water Use for Food Production," *Water International*, Vol. 11, No. 1 (1986), p. 23.
23. W.R. Rangeley, "Irrigation and Drainage in the World," paper presented at the International Conference on Food and Water, College Station, Texas, May 26–30, 1985, p. 8.
24. "Circle of Plenty," television transcript, KCTS Association, Seattle, May 13, 1987.
25. Organisation for Economic Co-operation and Development (OECD), *Pricing of Water Services* (OECD, Paris, 1987).
26. Robert Repetto, *Skimming the Water: Rent-Seeking and the Performance of Public Irrigation Systems* (World Resources Institute, Washington, D.C., 1986), p. 11 and p. 24.
27. U.S. Department of the Interior, Bureau of Reclamation, "Westwide Report on Acreage Limitation," draft environmental impact statement, Appendix G, Washington, D.C., January 1985, cited in Robert Repetto, *Skimming the Water: Rent-Seeking and the Performance of Public Irrigation Systems* (World Resources Institute, Washington, D.C. 1986), Table 4, p. 16.
28. William Goldfarb, "An Analysis of the Water Resources Development Act," *The Water Reporter*, Vol. 11, No. 5 (1987), p. 37.
29. "High-Rise Toilets Flushed by Treated Waste," *World Water*, Vol. 10, No. 7 (1987), p. 32.
30. *Op. cit.* 14.
31. Hillel I. Shwal, "The Development of Water Reuse in Israel," *Ambio*, Vol. 16, No. 4 (1987), p. 186.
32. *Ibid.*, pp. 187–188.
33. *Op. cit.* 26, p. 37.
34. "BuRec Moves: HQ to Denver and 50% Staff Cut in Dams to Conservation Role Shift," *The Water Reporter*, Vol. 11, No. 12 (1987), pp. 85–86.
35. U.S. Congressional Budget Office (CBO), *Efficient Investments in Water Resources: Issues and Options* (CBO, Washington, D.C., 1983), p. 32.
36. Henry P. Caulfield, Jr., "Viability of Inter-basin, Interstate/International Transfers of Water," *Water International*, Vol. 11, No. 1 (1986), p. 33.
37. Yevgeny Novikov, "The USSR Shelves a Water Diversion Plan," *WorldPaper* (Boston, November 1986), p. 6.
38. Philip P. Micklin, "The Vast Diversion of Soviet Rivers," *Environment*, Vol. 27, No. 2 (1985), p. 13.
39. "Why USSR Abandoned Diversion Scheme," *World Water*, Vol. 9, No. 10 (1986), pp. 44–45.
40. Zhao Qinghua, "Diverting the Yangtze," *WorldPaper* (Boston, November 1986), p. 4.

41. *Op. cit.* 36, p. 35.
42. *Op. cit.* 40, p. 4.
43. Malcolm M. Hufschmidt, Senior Consultant, Environment & Policy Institute, East-West Institute, Honolulu, Hawaii, 1988 (personal communication).
44. Enzo Fano, Marcia Brewster, and Terrence Thompson, "Water Quality Management in Developing Countries," paper presented at the Fifth World Congress on Water Resources, International Water Resources Association, Brussels, June 9–15, 1985.
45. *Ibid.,* p. 642.
46. United Nations Economic and Social Commission for Asia and the Pacific (UNESCAP), *State of the Environment in Asia and the Pacific,* Vol. 2 (UNESCAP, Bangkok, [1983]), pp. 163–164.
47. George R. Hallberg, "Agrichemicals and Water Quality," paper presented at the Colloquium on Agrichemical Management to Protect Water Quality, National Research Council, Board on Agriculture, Washington, D.C., March 21, 1986, p. 7.
48. *Op. cit.,* 44, p. 642.
49. Lee M. Thomas, speech to the 58th Annual Conference of the Water Pollution Control Federation, Kansas City, Missouri, October 7, 1985, quoted in George R. Hallberg, "Agrichemicals and Water Quality," background paper prepared for the Colloquium on Agrichemical Management to Protect Water Quality, National Research Council, Board on Agriculture, Washington, D.C., March 21, 1986, p. 1.
50. Association of State and Interstate Water Pollution Control Administrators (ASIWPCA), *America's Clean Water: The States' Nonpoint Source Assessment 1985* (ASIWPCA, Washington, D.C., 1985), p. 4.
51. Timothy Aeppel, "'Safe' Pesticides Polluting Environment," *Christian Science Monitor* (July 20, 1987), pp. 6–7.
52. Margaret O'Hare, *et al.,* "Contamination of Ground Water in the Contiguous United States from Usage of Agriculture Chemicals," Vol. IV (University of Oklahoma, Environmental and Ground Water Institute, Norman, Oklahoma, 1985), p. 144.
53. Organisation for Economic Co-operation and Development (OECD), *OECD Environmental Data Compendium 1987* (OECD, Paris, 1987), Table 15.7B, p. 287.
54. Sven Olof Ryding, "The Need of Multidisciplinary and Selective Approaches to Combat Water Pollution Problems in Agricultural Areas," paper presented at the Water for Mankind in the Years 2000 Symposium, Sciences et Devenir de L'Homme, Paris, April 1987.
55. *Op. cit.,* 47, pp. 53–54.
56. U.K. Department of Environment/National Water Council. *Fourth Biennial Report of the Standing Advisory Committee on Water Quality* (Her Majesty's Stationary Office, London, 1983), cited in Gareth Roberts, "Trends in Nitrate Concentration in the Countries of Western Europe in Relation to Agricultural Practices with Particular Emphasis on the Situation in the United Kingdom," paper presented at the Water for Mankind in the Year 2000 Symposium, Sciences et Devenir de L'Homme, Paris, April 1987.
57. Gareth Roberts, "Trends in Nitrate Concentration in the Countries of Western Europe in Relation to Agricultural Practices with Particular Emphasis on the Situation in the United Kingdom," paper presented at the Water for Mankind in the Year 2000 Symposium, Sciences et Devenir de L'Homme, Paris, April 1987.
58. United States Geological Survey (USGS), *National Water Summary 1984: Hydrologic Events, Selected Water-Quality Trends, and Ground-Water Resources* (USGS, Washington, D.C., 1985), p. 3.
59. Deborah V. Chapman, *Pesticides in the Aquatic Environment: A Global Assessment of Use and Effects* (Monitoring and Assessment Research Centre, King's College London, University of London, 1987), p. 1.
60. *Ibid.*
61. Deborah V. Chapman, C.A. Edwards, "Agrochemicals as Environmental Pollutants," in *Control of Pesticide Applications and Residues in Food,* B. Hofsten and G. Ekstrom, eds. (Swedish Science Press, Uppsala 1986), pp. 1–19, cited in *Pesticides in the Aquatic Environment: A Global Assessment of Use and Effects* (Monitoring and Assessment Research Centre, King's College London, University of London, 1987), p. 2.
62. Deborah V. Chapman, Sahabat Alam Malaysia (SAM), *Pesticide Dilemma in the Third World—A Case Study of Malaysia,* 2d ed. (SAM, Pulau Pinang, Malaysia, 1984), cited in *Pesticides in the Aquatic Environment: A Global Assessment of Use and Effects* (Monitoring and Assessment Research Centre, King's College London, University of London, 1987), p. 46.
63. United Nations Economic and Social Commission for Asia and the Pacific (UNESCAP), *State of the Environment in Asia and the Pacific* (UNESCAP, Bangkok, Thailand, [1983]), p. 172, p. 177, and p. 182.
64. J. Margat, Charge de Mission Eau, Direction du Service Geologique National, Orleans, France, 1987 (personal communication).
65. Organisation for Economic Co-operation and Development (OECD), *Control of Water Pollution from Urban Run-Off,* OECD Environment Monographs No. 3 (OECD, Paris, 1986), p. 15.
66. V. Novotny, "Urbanization and Nonpoint Pollution," paper presented at the Fifth World Congress on Water Resources, International Water Resources Association, Brussels, June 9–15, 1985, p. 40.
67. Eric H. Livingston and John H. Cox, "Urban Stormwater Quality Management: The Florida Experience," paper presented at the National Conference on Nonpoint Source Pollution, U.S. Environmental Protection Agency, Kansas City, Missouri, May 1985, p. 289.
68. Ake Sundborg, "Sedimentation Problems in River Basins," *Nature: Resources* (April-June, 1983), p. 15.
69. *Op. cit.* 63, p. 165, p. 169, and p. 172.
70. *Op. cit.* 47, p. 4.
71. *Op. cit.* 47, p. 5.
72. *Op. cit.* 44, pp. 656–659.
73. *Op. cit.* 44, pp. 659–660.
74. Frits van der Leeden, ed. *Water Resources of the World: Selected Statistics* (Port Washington, New York, Water Information Center, Inc., 1975), Table 7.15, pp. 466–468.
75. *Ibid.*
76. Philip Williams, "Damming the World," *Not Man Apart,* Vol. 13, No. 1, (1983), p. 10.
77. U.S. Department of Agriculture, Soil Conservation Service, *Ponds-Planning Design, Construction,* Agriculture Handbook No. 590 (1982), p. 1.
78. Raymond J. O'Connor, (former) Chairman of the Federal Energy Regulatory Commission, response to inquiry by the Subcommittee on Energy Conservation and Power, House Committee on Energy and Commerce, February 17, 1984.
79. *Op. cit.* 3, p. 263.
80. G. Le Moigne, "Trends in Irrigation," in World Water '86: Water Technology for the Developing World, Proceedings of an International Conference, London, July 14–16, 1986.
81. Jan-Erik Gustafsson, *Water Resources Development in the People's Republic of China* (Royal Institute of Technology, Stockholm, 1984), Table 10, p. 48.
82. Ministry of Water Conservation (China), *Chinese Experiences in Mini-Hydropower Generation* (United Nations, 1985), New York, p. 7.
83. Worldwatch Institute, *State of the World, 1987* (W.W. Norton & Company, New York, 1987), p. 96.
84. Peter P. Rogers, "Fresh Water," in *The Global Possible: Resources, Development and the New Century,* Robert Repetto, ed. (Yale University Press, New Haven, 1985), p. 275.
85. *Op. cit.* 81, p. 114 and p. 146.
86. *Op. cit.* 82, p. 9.
87. Sudhirendar Sharma, "Mini-Dams to Save Shiwaliks," *World Water,* Vol. 10, No. 7 (1987), p. 21 and p. 24.
88. Centre for Science and Environment, New Delhi, *The State of India's Environment: 1984–85, The Second Citizens' Report* (Ravi Chopra, New Delhi, 1985), p. 114.
89. *Op. cit.* 88, p. 110.
90. "Inflatable Dams Furnish Flexibility," *World Water,* Vol. 10, No. 7 (1987), pp. 21–23.
91. Ake Nilsson, *Ground-Water Dams for Rural Water Supply in Developing Countries* (Royal Institute of Technology, Stockholm, 1984), pp. 1–4.
92. Boyce Rensberger, "From Sea: Power and Potable Water," *Washington Post* (October 26, 1987).
93. Lawrence Mosher, "Towards a New National Water Policy: Eastern Droughts and Seaboard Growth Are Changing the Nation's Water Politics; New York City's Growing Thirst Raises Anew the Issue of River Basin Planning," *The Water Reporter,* Vol. 12, No. 1 (1988), pp. 1–8.

9. Oceans and Coasts

Far from being homogeneous bodies of water, oceans are a dynamic system that interacts closely with the atmosphere. Their major wind-driven surface currents affect navigation, climate, and the distribution of marine organisms. Deep currents play a major but little understood role in the global carbon cycle, which may influence the extent of climate warming caused by the greenhouse effect.

Until recently, most fisheries scientists did not pay much attention to the influence of the ocean's circulation and chemistry on the growth of fish. The two El Niño events of the 1970s and 1980s, which seriously disrupted the Peruvian anchovy fishery and changed fisheries elsewhere, convinced some fisheries scientists that understanding ocean circulation is important to predicting fish abundance. Overfishing and pollution are the major causes of the decline of many regional fisheries. The world is now approaching the annual fish catch estimated by the United Nations Food and Agriculture Organization as the largest that can be taken sustainably over the long term.

Marine protected areas are receiving attention as a useful management tool for preserving underwater habitats as fish nurseries or as tourist attractions. Marine protected areas range from Japan's tiny, intensely used tourist parks to Australia's Great Barrier Reef, an expansive 350,000 square kilometers of water, reefs, and islands. Like terrestrial protected areas, marine protected areas must have adequate funding and management. A study of 112 protected areas in the Caribbean found that only 25 percent had both a budget and a staff and 26 percent had neither.

In each edition, *World Resources* discusses one of the world's regional seas. The East Asian seas—including the Andaman Sea, the South China Sea, and the Celebes Sea—have some of the most intense and diverse uses of all the regional seas. Fishing, oil drilling, shipping, turtle nesting, and tourism are activities that often overlap. Oil—from both local offshore wells and tankers following an ancient trade route through the Strait of Malacca—is the most significant of a number of environmental threats to East Asian Seas. Five nations have joined to study the possible damage from oil spills and to discuss plans for emergency clean-up and other coordinated actions to protect these seas.

After centuries of being hunted, marine mammals now have increasing protection through international agreements and national laws. Whaling countries have agreed to a temporary moratorium on commercially hunting large whales. However, marine mammals continue to be threatened by coastal development, habitat destruction, oil and pesticide pollution, interactions with fisheries, and entanglement in marine debris and fishing nets. The latter threat may be lessened as an international agreement prohibiting the dumping of plastic materials at sea takes effect in December 1988.

CONDITIONS AND TRENDS

OCEAN CURRENTS AND CIRCULATION

Data on physical ocean phenomena are of more than academic interest. The major currents, described below, create areas of high productivity where the world's great fisheries are found. Variations in the physical characteristics of these currents affect productivity of the fisheries.

The mixing of ocean waters by both surface currents and the slower, deep currents is of interest in planning for disposal of waste material. Pollutants can be diluted in the sea, but currents also disperse them over large areas. The sea bottom of the continental shelves, once thought of as a tranquil area suitable for waste disposal, is now known to experience violent underwater storms that last from days to weeks (1). All the water in the oceans—even the deepest waters—mix over centuries. Thus, although safe disposal sites may be found for many waste materials, finding a stable resting place for long-lived radioactive isotopes in the sea may not be possible. (For a discussion of Marine Pollution and ocean dumping, see *World Resources 1987*, pp. 126–132.)

Atmospheric scientists studying the mechanisms of global climate change and ozone depletion recently began examining the interactions between the atmosphere and the ocean, especially deep ocean currents. For example, the oceans are important to the absorption of carbon dioxide, a major greenhouse gas. An estimated 30–40 percent of the carbon dioxide emitted by human activities is absorbed by the ocean, and much of it is stored in deep bottom waters. Because the ocean contains 53 times more carbon than the atmosphere, how oceanic carbon behaves and how it returns to the atmosphere are key to determining the rate of global warming (2). (See Chapter 10, "Atmosphere and Climate," Climate Change.)

Surface Currents

Surface currents and upwellings influence the location and productivity of ocean fisheries. Currents and upwellings often bring nutrient-rich subsurface waters that support the growth of phytoplankton and other marine organisms, thus forming biologically productive areas. (See Figure 9.1.) Variations in currents and upwellings cause major fluctuations in biological productivity.

Major ocean surface currents generally circulate in huge loops or gyres that correspond roughly to wind patterns at five latitudes: the equator, 30ºN and S, and 60ºN and S (3). The strongest gyres are at about 30ºN and S in the North and South Atlantic and in the North and South Pacific. The most powerful ocean currents are those on the western boundaries of oceans; they flow northward in the Northern Hemisphere and southward in the Southern Hemisphere. The relatively narrow Gulf Stream in the Atlantic and the Kuroshio Current in the Pacific are the most rapid, with water moving at 40–120 kilometers per day (4). Their flow extends to 1,000 meters or more below the surface. These fast-moving currents carry warm water north to produce more moderate climates than would otherwise be expected in Northern Europe and along the southern shore of Alaska. The western boundary currents of the Southern Hemisphere —the Brazil Current and the East Australian Current—are not as prominent (5).

Eastern boundary currents, which carry cold water from the poles to the equator, are weaker and broader than their western counterparts (6). However, many eastern boundary areas experience upwellings, in which wind forces surface water offshore and allows cold, nutrient-rich bottom water to rise to the surface. Especially rich upwelling areas are found off the coasts of Peru, California, and southwest Africa.

Perhaps the most well-known upwelling is off the coast of Peru. It supports one of the world's most productive fisheries; but every three or four years the upwelling disappears. Known as "El Niño" or "the Child" because it happens near Christmas, this event occurs when the winds that normally blow the warm surface water westward across the Pacific slacken and the warm waters roll back eastward to cover the cold upwelling water. Originally thought to be a local event, El Niño was seen to have far-reaching impacts during a particularly severe event in 1982–83. The change in surface water temperatures affected weather patterns throughout the tropical Pacific. Locally, the failure of the upwelling decimated the anchovy fishery, causing serious hardship for Peruvian fishing communities. (See Chapter 11, "Global Systems and Cycles," Environmental History, and *World Resources 1987*, pp. 169–173.) Some upwellings occur only seasonally. The upwelling off the coast of central Viet Nam occurs only during the winter monsoon season. In the summer, south winds produce a sinking of surface water in the same area (7).

Another phenomenon that creates biologically rich ocean areas is movement of a strong current across a relatively shallow bank or continental shelf. Turbulence of the current stirs up bottom sediments and releases nutrients that would otherwise be unavailable to marine organisms. Two examples of this phenomenon are Georges Bank in the North Atlantic, historically a rich fishing area and the waters off the northeast coast of Japan where the Oyashio and Kuroshio Currents converge over the continental shelf. (See Box 9.1.)

Deep Ocean Circulation

The general circulation pattern of deep ocean water involves cold water sinking near the poles and flowing slowly and erratically along the ocean bottom toward the equator. Water near the poles is denser than warmer water at lower latitudes, because it is colder and saltier (since ice contains no sea salt, polar waters are left with a higher salt content when ice forms) (8). The two most prominent "sinks" for ocean water are an area off the southeastern tip of Greenland, where the East Greenland and Irminger Currents converge, and the area around Antarctica, especially the Weddell Sea, where the world's densest water is formed (9). After leaving the sea surface, these dense waters may be isolated from the atmosphere for 500–2,000 years (10). They can be detected by their chemical composition, which changes little.

Antarctic water can cover the ocean bottom as far as 40ºN in the Atlantic (11). North Atlantic bottom water flows southward over this layer as far as 60ºS, where it is transported by the Antarctic circumpolar current around Africa to the Pacific Ocean. There it flows northward and surfaces near Alaska. In the Atlantic, bottom water exiting the Mediterranean forms a distinct layer of salty wa-

Figure 9.1 Major Ocean Currents and Areas of Highest Biological Productivity

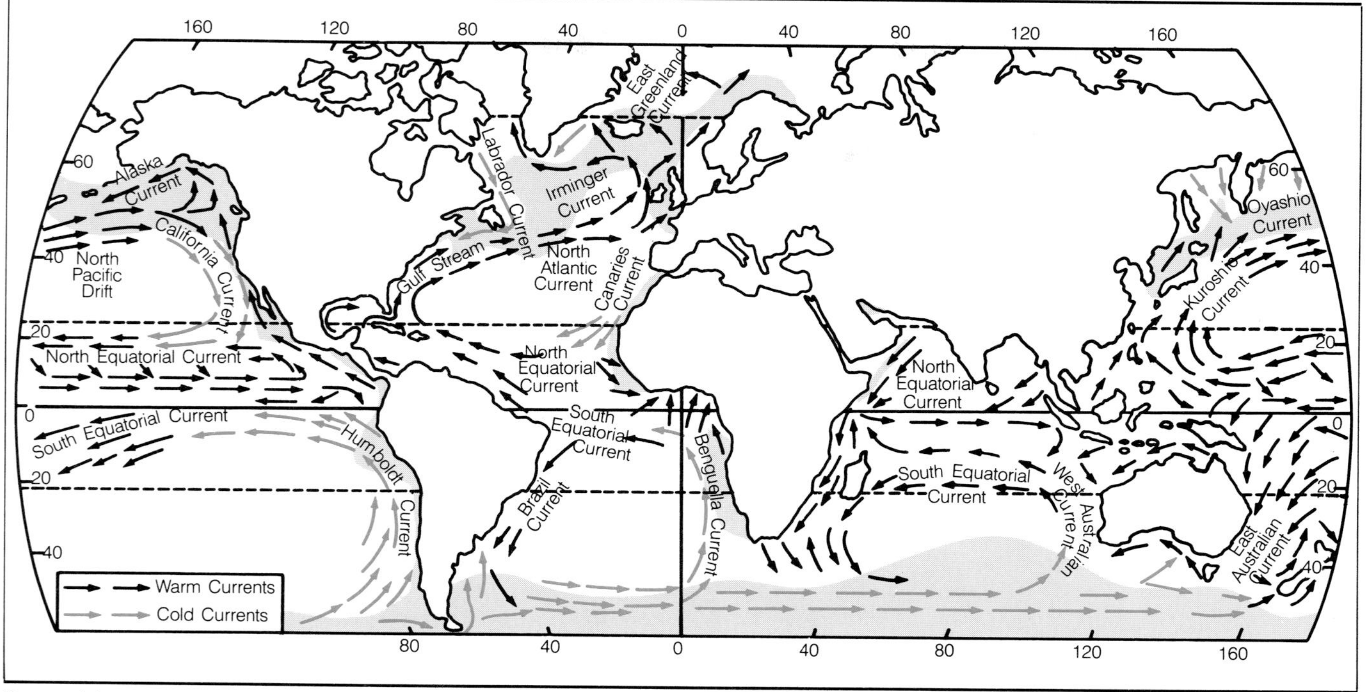

Source: Adapted from I.W. Duedall et al., "Energy Waste and the Ocean: Choices for the Future," *Wastes in the Ocean*, Vol. 4, (Wiley-Interscience, New York, 1985) p. 33.7.
Note: Shaded areas are areas of highest biological productivity.

ter that retains its identity as far as 2,400 kilometers from its source (12).

The slow circulation of deep ocean waters is of extreme interest to atmospheric scientists investigating global climate warming caused in part by a buildup of carbon dioxide in the atmosphere. The deep oceans contain most of the world's carbon—36,700 billion metric tons compared with 728 billion metric tons in the surface waters and plankton, 2,130 million metric tons in land vegetation and soil, and 725 million metric tons in the atmosphere. While the surface water, vegetation, and atmosphere cycle carbon in equilibrium, the deep ocean is a "sink" for carbon: each year 3 billion metric tons enter the deep ocean and do not return to the surface. This carbon comes both from the diffusion of atmospheric carbon dioxide in sea water and the constant rain of decaying matter from sea life (13).

A combination of biological and physical processes act as a pump to maintain a high level of carbon in the deep abyss. Some scientists fear that a warming climate may alter the pump's processes, causing it to fail. If the pump fails, atmospheric carbon dioxide could increase severalfold, perhaps causing a sudden and severe climate change (14). Even if the pump remains operative, the oceans' ability to store heat absorbed from the atmosphere is one of the major uncertainties in predicting global warming (15).

To learn more about the workings of the deep currents and other physical aspects of the ocean, an extensive international interdisciplinary investigation was launched in 1983. Called the World Ocean Circulation Experiment (WOCE), it is coordinated by the World Climate Research Programme. Its plans include the first comprehensive global survey of the physical properties of oceans and the creation of a four-dimensional model of world ocean circulation (three spatial dimensions plus time) that will help atmospheric scientists understand how oceans affect climate change (16).

WORLD FISHERIES: APPROACHING MAXIMUM SUSTAINABLE YIELD?

World fisheries appear to be approaching a catch size that the United Nations Food and Agriculture Organization (FAO) believes may be the maximum sustainable harvest from the oceans. The FAO estimates the maximum sustainable yield of all conventional fish at about 100 million metric tons. Maximum sustainable yield refers to the amount of fish that can be harvested year after year without depleting the natural breeding stock. "Conventional" fish are those species for which large markets now exist. The term does not include squid and octopus, which are plentiful but have limited markets. In 1986, the world fish harvest was estimated at almost 91 million metric tons, or 84 millon metric tons if one subtracts the 7 million metric tons of production from aquaculture (17)— about 16 million metric tons shy of the maximum sustainable yield. If the annual catch continues to climb at the 1986 rate, the 100 million metric tons maximum sustainable yield figure would be surpassed by 1991.

Figure 9.2 Global Fish Catch and Use, 1950–86

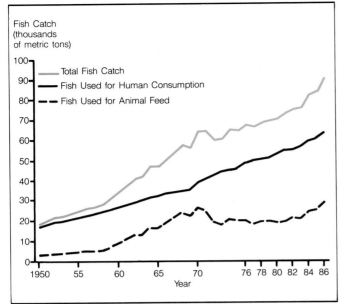

Fish Catch (thousands of metric tons)

— Total Fish Catch
— Fish Used for Human Consumption
--- Fish Used for Animal Feed

Source: United Nations Food and Agriculture Organization (FAO) Fisheries Department, unpublished data (FAO, Rome, 1988).

A major omission from FAO figures is the catch by artisanal fisheries around the world. Local fishermen who catch fish for their families or for sale in their communities do not report catch data (18). The fish and shellfish catch by artisanal fishermen is estimated at about 24 million metric tons per year (19). If this estimate is correct, we have surpassed the maximum sustainable yield figure.

Theoretically, if the maximum sustainable yield is exceeded, a fishery will begin to decline, and the same amount of fishing effort should produce smaller catches. Eventually a lower maximum sustainable yield could be set, based on the smaller population. But if a fish population is reduced too much, it may take some time to recover to a commercially exploitable level. A decline in fish populations has been observed regionally, but the annual fish catch continues to climb globally. It is also possible that the maximum sustainable yield figure, calculated in the 1970s, should be revised. More likely, the effects of overfishing would be felt regionally in areas where overfishing and pollution combine to reduce the catch. Hardest hit by any reduction in fish catches would be artisanal fishermen and others in coastal areas of developing countries who depend heavily on fish for protein and on fishing for employment.

Worldwide, the long-term trends in fish catches show steady increases between 1958 and 1971 (through

Box 9.1 Large Marine Ecosystems

The concept of defining a management unit by natural physical boundaries and of managing for all marine species—not just certain commercially important fish—within that unit is slowly being integrated into U.S. fisheries policy. It has been the subject of a number of fisheries conferences over the past few years.

Kenneth Sherman of the U.S. National Marine Fisheries Service Narragansett Laboratory in Rhode Island, and Lewis Alexander of the University of Rhode Island pioneered this concept. Sherman has identified 20 areas in the world's oceans, which he calls "large marine ecosystems" (LMEs). (See Figure 1.) LMEs are generally larger than 200,000 square kilometers, and they have unique currents, bottom topography, and populations of organisms that are linked in a food web (1) (2). Most LMEs are near coastal currents or upwellings or are seas enclosed by land—the Baltic and the Mediterranean, for example.

Sherman cites the failure of traditional fisheries management either to understand what causes changes in most fish populations or to predict accurately the number of fish that will be "recruited" into a given "year class" of fish, especially fish of an age and size that are eligible to be taken by fishermen. The ability to predict the number of fish in a given year class is essential to setting catch limits. Sherman argues that predicting how many fish will survive to a catchable size can be done only by considering many physical and biological aspects of the ecosystem.

TYPES OF LMEs

In categorizing LMEs, Sherman makes a major distinction between LMEs whose recruitment cycles are driven chiefly by environmental forces and those driven chiefly by predation—either by natural predators or human fishing pressure. LMEs driven by predation are easier to manage because predation, especially fishing, is easier to control than environmental forces. Knowing an LME category is necessary for making sound management decisions. For example, reducing fishing pressure in an LME driven by environmental factors may not result in a large increase in the fished species.

Twenty LMEs have been studied in some detail. (See Figure 1.) For four—the Yellow Sea, the Gulf of Thailand, the Great Barrier Reef, and the Northeast Continental Shelf—predation is the controlling variable. In the Great Barrier Reef, the predator is the crown of thorns starfish; in the other three, it is the fisherman. Environmental change is the predominant variable in six other LMEs: the Oyashio Current, the Kuroshio Current, the California Current, the Humbolt Current, the Iberian Coastal Current, and the Benguela Current. In the Baltic LME, the dominant influence is pollution. Insufficient information is available to make a determination for the remaining nine LMEs (3).

A recent example of a change in biomass resulting from environmental factors is the dramatic increase in the number of sardines off the coasts of Japan and Chile. Between

1974 and 1984, the total world fish catch rose 10 million metric tons, 4 million of which came from the increase in the sardine catch in these areas (4). The increased yields are attributed to a vast increase in plankton, which sardines feed upon, because of shifts in the mixing areas of the Oyashio and Kuroshio Currents off Japan and the Humbolt Current off the coast of Chile. When the Oyashio and Kuroshio converge over the shallow continental shelf, they stir up more nutrients from the bottom, which trigger the growth of more phytoplankton, than they would when they converge farther offshore in deeper water (5).

Sherman argues that fisheries managers must pay attention to all species within an LME, not just the target species. Many LMEs have experienced "biomass flips," in which a previously dominant species declines and the population of another species rises dramatically. Fisheries managers may or may not be able to control or even affect these conditions, but they should at least understand the implications for target species.

An example of a predator-driven system that experienced a biomass flip is the northeast continental shelf ecosystem, which includes the Georges Bank, where the commercially important Atlantic herring was replaced in numbers by the sand eel, for which no fishery exists. Herring prey on sand eels, and sand eels prey on herring larvae. A third species, mackerel, prey on the larvae of both. Heavy fishing of herring and mackerel in the mid-1970s released the predation pressure on sand eels and allowed their

technical advances in fishery gear), a dip during 1972–73 because of the El Niño and its effects on the Peruvian anchovy fishery, and then a continuing increase to 1986. (See Figure 9.2.) The fairly steep increase in fish catches between 1983 and 1986 is due partly to the recovery of the Peruvian anchovy fishery and to the expansion of the U.S. pollack fishery in the Northeast Pacific. Preliminary FAO data for 1987 indicate the possibility of no growth over 1986 because of a mild El Niño event in 1986 (20).

Harvests of cod, hake, haddock, and other demersal or bottom-dwelling fishes that are normally marketed for human consumption have increased steadily over the past 36 years. These fish are of relatively high value, and most populations have been under heavy fishing pressure for several decades. Their numbers seem to be influenced mostly by fishing pressure rather than environmental factors.

A group of smaller fish called coastal pelagics— sardines, anchovies, and other fish most commonly used for animal feed—show fluctuations in numbers that cannot be explained entirely by fishing pressure or management. Although fishing pressure certainly affects the health of their populations, the large fluctuations may be caused by change in a current, failure of an upwelling, or other environmental factors. A combination of overfishing and climate changes is thought to have caused the col-

lapse of the Peruvian anchovy fishery during the El Niño events of 1972–73 and 1982–83.

Despite the steady growth in world catch, the FAO is pessimistic about the chances of sustaining large annual catch increases. In its 1987 report on world fisheries, the FAO stated that "the time of spectacular and sustained increases in fisheries catches is over.... Almost all important stocks of demersal species are either fully exploited or overfished. Many of the stocks of more highly-valued species are depleted. Reef stocks and those of estuarine/littoral zones are under special threat from illegal fishing and environmental pollution" (21).

Figure 9.2 shows annual total world fish catches from 1950 to 1986 by use for human consumption and animal feed. In 1950, only 15 percent of the total catch was used for animal feed. With the expansion of fishing fleets and improvements in gear, much of it designed to catch coastal pelagics, the proportion climbed to 32 percent in 1960 and 40 percent in 1970. With the decline of the Peruvian anchovy fishery, it fell to 36 percent in 1980 but rose to 45 percent in 1986. Fish catch data by country are shown in Chapter 22, "Oceans and Coasts," Table 22.1.

Regional Fisheries

The FAO divides the world into 19 fishery areas, with boundaries based roughly on geographical and political

Box 9.1

population to skyrocket (6). Now, with a lessening of fishing pressure, mackerel are beginning to recover. Biologists expect that mackerel will "graze down" the sand eel population, thus aiding the recovery of both mackerel and herring (7).

References and Notes

1. Kenneth Sherman, "Large Marine Ecosystems as Global Units for Recruitment Experiments," paper presented at the North Atlantic Treaty Organization advanced research workshop, Toulouse, France, June 1–5, 1987.
2. Kenneth Sherman, "Introduction to Parts One and Two: Large Marine Ecosystems as Tractable Entities for Measurement and Management," in *Variability and Management of Large Marine Ecosystems*, Kenneth Sherman and Lewis M. Alexander, eds. (Westview Press, Boulder, Colorado, 1986), p. 3.
3. *Op. cit.* 1, pp. 5–6.
4. *Op. cit.* 1, p. 6.
5. Kenneth Sherman, Chief, Ecosystem Dynamics Branch, National Marine Fisheries Service, Northeast Fisheries Center Narragansett Laboratory, Narragansett, Rhode Island, 1987 (personal communication).
6. *Op. cit.* 1, p. 9.
7. *Op. cit.* 5.

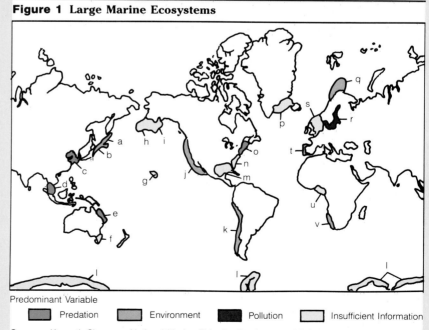

Figure 1 Large Marine Ecosystems

Predominant Variable — Predation, Environment, Pollution, Insufficient Information

Source: Kenneth Sherman, National Marine Fisheries Service, unpublished photograph (Narragansett, Rhode Island, 1988).
Notes: a. Oyashio Current. b. Kuroshio Current. c. Yellow Sea. d. Gulf of Thailand. e. Great Barrier Reef. f. Tasman Sea. g. Insular Pacific. h. East Bering Sea. i. Gulf of Alaska. j. California Current. k. Humboldt Current. l. Antarctic. m. Gulf of Mexico. n. Southeast Continental Shelf. o. Northeast Continental Shelf. p. East Greenland Sea. q. Barents Sea. r. Baltic Sea. s. North Sea. t. Iberian Coastal. u. Gulf of Guinea. v. Benguela Current.

considerations. (For fish catches and maximum sustainable yields, see Chapter 22, "Oceans and Coasts," Table 22.2.) Two regions, the Mediterranean and Black Seas and the Northwest Pacific, have exceeded their estimated sustainable yields. Two other regions, the Northeast and Northwest Atlantic, are near their sustainable yield estimates. Some fish catches continue to exceed maximum sustainable yield estimates. Others, as in the Northwest Atlantic, declined substantially.

Most world fisheries are moderately to heavily exploited. Of the roughly 280 fish stocks on which the FAO keeps records, only 25 are categorized as underexploited to moderately exploited (22). Possibly the only area with increased large-scale fisheries potential is the Southwest Atlantic, especially off the coast of Argentina (23). Smaller stocks are underexploited elsewhere including the Pacific off New Zealand and the western Indian Ocean (24). Three species regarded as "underutilized" in several areas are octopus, squid, and krill. Although vast amounts of krill exist off Antarctica, it is not well established how much can be harvested without upsetting the food web of marine mammals in the area.

Meeting Demand

In a 1987 report using calculations made in 1980, the FAO projected that the demand for fish in the year 2000 would exceed 100 million metric tons (coincidentally, the same as the sustainable yield estimate) (25). Trends in catch data between 1980 and 1986 indicate that this demand level may be reached even sooner.

The major increase in demand for fish is expected to come from developing countries, mainly because of increasing populations. The FAO projects the need in developing countries for an additional 22.5 million metric tons of fish over 1980 levels compared to an additional 5.9 million metric tons in developed countries (26). Annual fish consumption varies greatly, ranging from more than 40 kilograms per capita in Japan, Iceland, Denmark, Norway, Hong Kong, Malaysia, the Democratic People's Republic of Korea, and the Republic of Korea to less than 1 kilogram in Guatemala and Ethiopia (27). Fish is an important source of protein in a number of developing countries—especially in Asia and western Africa—even where per capita consumption may be low or moderate.

The FAO estimates that only half the increase in demand can be met by expanding existing fisheries (28). Five options were recommended for increasing the supply of fish used as human food: 1) expanding aquaculture; 2) expanding the market for squid, octopus, and other "nonconventional species"; 3) expanding the catch of coastal pelagics for use as human food rather than animal feed; 4) switching some of the fish sold as animal feed into the market for human consumption, rather than expanding the total catch; and 5) landing and marketing fish usually discarded at sea. Trawlers, especially shrimpers, now throw overboard an estimated 5–16 million metric tons of finfish incidentally caught in their nets. Many of these fish do not survive. The FAO estimates that 20–70 percent of these finfish could be marketed.

The FAO believes that higher market prices will effect several of these recommendations; they will shift some of the fish sold as animal feed into the food market, expand the market for increased catches of shoaling pelagics, and provide an incentive for fishermen to land and sell previously discarded fish. FAO analysts predict that higher prices for table fish and shellfish will create a market for lower-priced fish. As luxury fish become too expensive for most people, a market may be created for herring, sardines, anchovies, and other lower-priced fish. Fishermen should be able to fetch a higher price for these species by selling them for human consumption rather than for feed. Less expensive substitutes such as soybean meal could replace fishmeal in the feed category. Nonconventional species may also become more widely marketable.

Fisheries Management

Prominent in almost every FAO report on fishery projections is a call for more effective management. Yet there is little sign of progress. From the 1950s through the mid-1970s, the major international fishing grounds were "managed" by a network of international agreements among coastal and fishing nations. Agreements involved geographic areas or a single species. In no case could one country claim jurisdiction over an entire fishing area. For example, in the Northeast Atlantic there were dozens of multilateral and bilateral agreements among fishing nations. The major multilateral agreements were administered by regional fisheries authorities that allocated catch limits to each country, based on information provided by their fishery scientists. It was up to each country to enforce these limits on its own fishermen. This system did not prevent overexploitation of fish stocks. An evaluation of 33 Northeast Atlantic stocks in 1975–76 classified 2 stocks as underexploited, 1 as fully exploited, 28 as overexploited, and 2 as depleted (29).

In the mid-1970s, coastal nations began to extend their jurisdiction 200 miles offshore under an agreement in the Law of the Sea Treaty, thus taking control of the fisheries along their continental shelves. This action was seen as a step that might lead to more effective management: at least a fishery would be under the jurisdiction of no more than a few coastal states rather than the management of a dozen fishing nations. However, fishery scientists found only slight recovery of fish stocks attributable to better management by coastal nations, and they concluded that recovery would most likely be slow. An analysis of 20 Northeast Atlantic fish stocks in 1981–82, five years after jurisdictions were extended, found little improvement. About three years later, at least four important stocks were found recovering following strong management controls (30). The establishment of 200-mile jurisdictions by most coastal nations has at least made a number of developing countries aware of the need for management in local and regional waters. In fact, regional organizations are now responsible for fisheries policy in Southeast Asia, the South Pacific, and the Caribbean (31).

FOCUS ON: MARINE PROTECTED AREAS

The most common approach to managing marine resources is regulating commercial or sport fishing, shipping, or oil drilling and other individual activities. A newer approach is designating a coastal or marine area for special management as a marine protected area. This management may involve strict protection, development for tourism, or a zoning approach that allows different activites in different zones. Marine protected areas vary in size from less than a hectare to hundreds of thousands of square kilometers, and they may include coastal areas and small islands, coral reefs, estuaries, seagrass beds, historic shipwrecks, and open water areas. (See Table 9.1.)

Several surveys of marine protected areas produced different results because they used different definitions—some counted only protected areas with a substantial marine component, others included all protected areas with shorelines. By 1985, 430 marine protected areas had been legally established in 69 nations, and 298 proposals

were under consideration (32). A 1988 International Union for Conservation of Nature and Natural Resources (IUCN) survey lists 820 marine and coastal protected areas, about 400 of which have a significant marine component (33). (See Chapter 19, "Wildlife and Habitat," Table 19.1.) A 1986 literature survey showed approximately 1,000 coastal and marine protected areas in 87 countries (34).

Benefits of Marine Protected Areas

Marine protected areas can provide relatively safe places for fish and other marine organisms to feed, grow, and reproduce, thus enhancing the variety and abundance of life both in the protected area and around it. Marine protected areas can enhance artisanal fisheries, ensure safe breeding grounds for whales and other large marine mammals, and preserve marine invertebrates that may someday be a source of ingredients for important medicines.

Marine protected areas, like other protected areas, also offer the benefits of ecosystem services. For example, salt marshes, mangroves, and seagrass beds can filter out pollutants from land. Marshes, mangroves, coral reefs, and barrier islands protect the shore from damaging storm surges, and marshes provide feeding grounds for migrating waterfowl. Marine protected areas can offer valuable scientific and educational laboratories. And they can allow for the regeneration of ecosystems damaged by pollution, blast fishing, and mining.

Three Approaches to Marine Protected Areas

In the summer of 1988, IUCN was drafting policy guidelines for nations to use in setting up marine protected areas. It had a variety of models upon which to draw. Programs in Japan, Australia, and the United States illustrate the different approaches that are possible. Japan has formed many small marine protected areas exclusively for recreation and education. Australia created the world's largest marine protected area—the Great Barrier Reef Marine Park—and set up a sophisticated system of zoning to regulate activities. The U.S. marine sanctuaries program's management approaches range from strict protection to multiple use management (35).

In 1985 Japan had 57 marine park areas throughout the country; these are parks, not reserves. Their goal is "preserving beautiful underseascapes," and the criteria for selection include interesting topography, clear water, abundant flora and fauna, slow currents, a depth of less than 20 meters, and space on nearby land to construct visitor facilities. Most are small—17 are less than 10 hectares and the largest is 233 hectares—and many have aquaria, scuba trails, boat tours, and other recreational facilities. In 1980, the marine parks received 18 million visitors, an indication of their popularity.

Australia's Great Barrier Reef Marine Park is often cited as the world's best marine protected area. It is the world's largest, covering 350,000 square kilometers, and perhaps the most spectacular, encompassing 2,600 reefs, shoals, islands, and other formations along the continental shelf off the northeast coast of Australia. In addition to numerous species of coral and fish, the reef is the habitat of six species of turtles and the dugong, a marine mammal rare in most of its range but fairly common on

Table 9.1 Types of Marine Protected Areas

Habitat	Importance	Threats	Number of Protected Sites	Area in Protected Sites[a] (million hectares)
Estuaries	• Nursery for fish and other marine organisms • Protection of coast from storm surges by fringing mangroves and marshes	• Landfills, development, clear-cutting of mangroves, diversion of freshwater	50	5.6
Coral Reefs	• Species-rich habitat • Sustainable development of some reefs for tourism	• Sediment disposal from dredging, sewage discharge, or siltation • Dynamite fishing or trawling • Coral mining • Pollution	72	5.8
Marine	• Preservation of underwater habitats such as seagrass beds or rocky areas as fish conservation areas • Historic and cultural sites (e.g., shipwrecks)		134	98.6
Islands	• Many harbor species found nowhere else • Possible inclusion of a coral reef or fish sanctuary in underwater component of an island • Possible inclusion of a bird rookery, sea turtle nesting area, or area needed by marine mammals in terrestrial component	• Development • Pollution • Overfishing	138	4.1
Littoral	• Provision of bird and sea turtle nesting areas, recreation, and storm protection along shores of larger terrestrial protected areas	• Development • Pollution	441	83.4

Source: Derived from unpublished data provided by the International Union for the Conservation of Nature and Natural Resources, Conservation Monitoring Centre, Cambridge, U.K., 1988).
Notes:
a. Includes the terrestrial components of the protected areas.

the reef. Whales and dolphins frequent the area, and 240 species of birds nest on islands there (36).

The Great Barrier Reef Park was established in 1975 following a public outcry over the prospect of offshore oil drilling and mining on the reef. The park is administered by the Great Barrier Reef Marine Park Authority, which has broad authority to regulate and prohibit activities in the park. The Authority may also be given the power to regulate activities outside the park that pollute or harm the plants or animals within it. The management plan for the park uses the concept of zoning, as does the design of terrestrial biosphere reserves. (See Chapter 6, "Wildlife and Habitat," Biosphere Reserves.) The Great Barrier Reef Park's six zones range from "general use," where all activities except mining are allowed (although some require a permit), to a highly restricted "scientific and preservation" zone. (See Table 9.2.) The park's objective is to promote human enjoyment and use of the area consistent with conservation of the ecosystem (37).

The United States began its National Marine Sanctuaries Program under the National Marine Sanctuaries Act of 1972. It provides a means of managing marine areas as ecosystems rather than single marine resources such as fish or minerals. The Secretary of Commerce can designate National Marine Sanctuaries to protect natural resources and historic sites, such as shipwrecks, in coastal waters and the Great Lakes. By 1985, seven sites had been designated, including six in U.S. waters and one in American Samoa. The sanctuaries range in size from the 0.06-hectare Fagatele Bay Sanctuary in American Samoa to the 342-hectare Channel Islands National Marine Sanctuary off Santa Barbara, California (38).

The National Marine Sanctuaries Program stirred controversy when many areas were nominated for sanctuary status without a clear process for selection. Oil drilling and fishing interests feared that large areas of ocean on the continental shelf would be heavily restricted. Thus, in 1984, Congress amended the act to require more environmental studies, wider consultation, and more attention to economic impacts (39). No new sanctuaries have been added since 1985. As of summer 1988, 26 areas were listed as potential marine sanctuaries and 4 were scheduled to be designated by 1990 (40).

Managing Caribbean Marine Protected Areas

Designation of a marine area as protected is the first step in the management process; giving protected areas full protection—staff, budget, and programs—may be more difficult. For example, the Greater Caribbean Basin, which includes the Gulf of Mexico, has 112 legally established marine protected areas—perhaps a quarter of the marine protected areas in the world. Most were established in the past 20 years (41). These protected areas are recognized by country governments, IUCN, and the Regional Seas Programme of the United Nations Environment Programme (UNEP). But, most are "paper parks" without management or enforcement; only 28—just 25 percent—have a budget and staff, a management plan, and institutional support, according to an Organization of American

Table 9.2 Activities in Zones of the Great Barrier Reef Marine Park

	General Use 'A' Zone	General Use 'B' Zone	Marine National Park 'A' Zone	Marine National Park Buffer Zone	Marine National Park 'B' Zone	Scientific Zone Research	Preservation Zone
Boating, Diving	Yes	Yes	Yes	Yes	Yes	No	No
Collecting (e.g. beach-de-mer, shells corals, aquarium fish)	Permit	Permit	No	No	No	No	No
Line Fishing	Yes	Yes	Yes	No	No	No	No
Gill Netting	Yes	Yes	No	No	No	No	No
Bait Netting	Yes	Yes	Yes	No	No	No	No
Trolling (for pelagic species)	Yes	Yes	Yes	Yes	No	No	No
Spearfishing	Yes	Yes	No	No	No	No	No
Pole and Line Tuna Fishing	Permit	Permit	No	No	No	No	No
Trawling	Yes	No	No	No	No	No	No
Traditional Fishing	Yes	Yes	Permit	Permit	Permit	Permit	No
Traditional Hunting	Permit	Permit	Permit	Permit	Permit	Permit	No
Cruise Ships	Yes	Permit	Permit	Permit	Pemit	No	No
General Shipping (other than shipping area)	Yes	No	No	No	No	No	No
Crayfishing	Yes	Yes	No	No	No	No	No
Scientific Research	Permit	Permit	Permit	Permit	Permit	Permit	Permit

Source: Graeme Kelleher and Richard Kenchington, "Policy for Marine Conservation and the Establishment of Marine Protected Areas" (Great Barrier Reef Marine Park Authority, 1980).

Table 9.3 Carribbean Marine and Coastal Protected Areas, 1988

Degree of Protection

Region/Country	Total No.	Total Hectares	Park-Like[a] No.	Park-Like[a] Hectares	Reserve-Like[b] No.	Reserve-Like[b] Hectares	Degree of Protection[c] Legal	Partial	Full
U.S. and Bahamas	23	1,009,468	14	889,627	9	119,841	3	4	16
Central America	21	1,603,278	11	493,886	10	1,109,382	1	20	0
South America	20	1,334,126	16	1,090,902	4	243,224	6	12	2
Greater Antilles	22	1,597,687	10	132,117	12	1,465,570	11	8	3
Lesser Antilles	26	20,633	11	15,924	15	4,709	9	11	6
Total	**112**	**5,565,192**	**62**	**2,689,285**	**50**	**2,884,655**	**30**	**55**	**28**

Uses of Marine Protected Areas

Region/Country	Recreation[d]	Fishing[e]	Research	Important Wildlife Habitat[f]	Important Ecosystems Coral Reef	Important Ecosystems Man-grove	Important Ecosystems Seagrass Bed	Endangered and Threatened Species	Cultural[g]
U.S. and Bahamas	17	10	13	13	12	9	7	7	3
Central America	14	13	12	14	12	6	0	3	7
South America	9	10	11	16	6	14	2	3	3
Greater Antilles	9	11	7	14	6	10	1	2	6
Lesser Antilles	18	9	10	21	10	9	3	1	5
Total	**67**	**53**	**53**	**78**	**46**	**48**	**13**	**16**	**24**

Problems of Marine Protected Areas

Region/Country	Over-fishing[h]	Hunting[i]	Chemical Pollu-tion[j]	Physical Damage and Sediment Loading[k]	Nutrient Loading[l]	Solid Waste[m]	Damage by Tourists[n]	Other Development Stresses[o]	Introduction of Exotic Species	Natural Stresses[p]
U.S. and Bahamas	4	4	8	9	0	5	8	8	2	1
Central America	8	6	3	7	1	2	9	10	0	3
South America	8	5	6	9	1	5	4	12	0	0
Greater Antilles	6	6	5	6	0	2	4	6	0	2
Lesser Antilles	4	4	3	6	9	1	9	9	0	0
Total	**30**	**25**	**25**	**37**	**11**	**15**	**34**	**45**	**2**	**6**

Source: M. Wilson and A. Heyman, *Caribbean Marine and Coastal Protected Areas: Inventory and Analysis* (Organization of American States, Washington, D.C., in press.)
Notes: a. Wildlife protection and sustainable public use for tourism and recreation are both major management objectives. b. Management objectives emphasize wildlife protection and limit public use. c. Legal means protected area exists in legal sense only; partial means partially protected; and full means fully protected. d. Foreign and domestic tourism and watersports. e. Recreational and commercial. f. Breeding area for turtles, birds, fish, and invertebrates; important area in the life cycle of wildlife. g. Archaeological or anthropological attraction, lighthouse, and shipwreck. h. Fishing exceeding sustainable yield, and violation of fishing regulations; includes only sea fauna (e.g., fish, turtles, lobster, conch, marine mammals). i. Includes only terrestrial animals and birds. j. Pollution from petroleum extraction, and transportation and processing from industrial, domestic, and agricultural sources (pesticides and herbicides). k. Physical damage from boat grounding and anchoring, beach erosion, and sedimentation and dredging. l. Fertilizer runoff sewage. m. Litter and garbage. n. Overuse and abuse from tourism: shell and coral collecting and trampling reefs. o. Damage from human settlements; loss of species and habitat; and agricultural, industrial, and urbanization pressure. p. El Niño, forest fires, and hurricanes.

States (OAS) assessment in 1988 (42).

Establishing these protected areas was an admirable first step by the governments involved. Still, the degradation of coral reefs in the Caribbean, including those in protected areas, continues. Virtually no pristine reefs remain in the Caribbean, and the shallow-water fisheries—the only fisheries accessible to artisanal fishermen—are seriously depleted in almost all Caribbean countries (43). Coral reefs are especially important to the economies of Caribbean island nations, many of which depend on tourism for a large portion of their gross national product, employment, foreign exchange, and government revenue (44).

The major uses and problems of Caribbean marine protected areas are shown in Table 9.3. The two major uses are recreation (67 areas) and wildlife habitat (78 areas), and they often conflict. The most significant problems stem from development stresses such as urban, agricultural, and industrial pressure (45 areas) and direct physical damage from boat anchoring and sediment loading caused by dredging and runoff (37 areas). Direct damage by tourists is a problem in 34 areas, overfishing in 30, and hunting in 25. Of concern in fewer areas are solid waste disposal (15 areas), nutrient loading (11 areas),

natural stresses such as hurricanes (6 areas), and introduction of exotic species (2 areas). Most protected areas suffer from development pressure, which stems from both growing local populations and development of tourist facilities.

Lack of funding is a major obstacle to effective management of marine protected areas. Can protected areas generate enough income through tourism and fishing to be self-sustaining? Or should protected areas depend on government and conservation organization funds? Marine protected areas may be envisioned on a spectrum from "park-like" areas to "reserve-like" areas. In the former, management of resources can be coordinated with tourism to generate income. But the latter, which should be preserved for scientific study or as breeding sites for marine organisms, usually have little potential for generating income in the short term though they may be a valuable long-term asset. The OAS study recommended that feasibility studies of 30–40 promising park-like areas be made and the results presented to banks and international lending agencies. Reserve-like areas would depend on foundations and international conservation organizations (45). Table 9.3 shows the 62 park-like and 50 reserve-like marine protected areas in the Caribbean.

Figure 9.3 East Asian Regional Seas

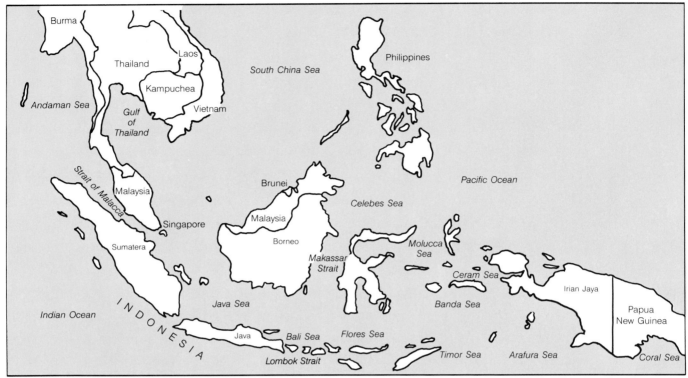

Source: East-West Environment and Policy Institute, *Atlas for Marine Policy in Southeast Asian Seas,* Joseph R. Morgan and Mark J. Valencia, eds. (University of California Press, Berkeley, 1983.)

Marine parks can be good investments, according to several feasibility studies conducted by the OAS. Brief studies by teams that included an economist, a biologist, and a park management specialist resulted in funding proposals for parks in the Caribbean islands of St. Vincent and the Grenadines, Jamaica, and St. Lucia.

Artisanal fisheries can be enhanced by both park-like and reserve-like protected areas that preserve a breeding ground for fish. Unchecked fishing pressure on many reefs has caused severe depletion of a fishery. For example, in the Tobago Cays area of St. Vincent and the Grenadines, the fish catch dropped from 83 metric tons in 1974 to 25 metric tons in 1987 because of overfishing (46). (See Box 9.2.)

REGIONAL SEAS: EAST ASIA

The East Asian seas, one of 10 regions in UNEP's Regional Seas Programme, is an area of intense economic activity—trade, shipping, oil production, offshore mining, and commercial fishing—combined with tropical beauty and a diverse marine life. In many areas, fishing grounds have been polluted, coral reefs mined, and mangroves destroyed without regard to the potential loss to the region. Five nations are making an effort, which may sometimes seem halting, to improve both the monitoring and the management of marine resources in East Asia. In the Regional Seas Programme, UNEP is a catalyst in bringing nations together to set goals, conduct studies,

and adopt protocols for reducing pollution.

The East Asian seas cover a large area—but as a regional seas program, they are one of the smallest in the number of countries participating and in budget. Members of the East Asian Regional Seas Programme are the five countries in the Association of Southeast Asian Nations (ASEAN): Indonesia, Malaysia, Philippines, Singapore, and Thailand. Other countries bordering East Asian seas are Viet Nam, Kampuchea, Burma, the People's Republic of China, Taiwan, and Brunei. (See Figure 9.3.)

Physical and Natural Resources

East Asian seas are tropical waters with little change in surface temperature and medium tidal variation. They have relatively strong currents, which reverse directions in some areas with seasonal monsoons and thus do not effectively flush pollutants out to the ocean (47). Many of the islands are fringed by mangroves and coral reefs, both of which are being destroyed at a rate that concerns area scientists. Migratory sea turtles nest on several beaches in Indonesia and Malaysia. Both eggs and turtles are harvested for local consumption and the tourist trade (48). The only documented fishing for whales and dolphins is conducted in southern Indonesia by local people and perhaps by pirate whalers. Dolphins are also incidentally killed in the nets of tuna fishermen. Another marine mammal of note is the rare dugong, found in Indonesia (49).

Box 9.2 Marine Protected Areas: Success and Failure in the Philippines

Two programs—both sponsored by the same university on small islands in the Philippines—illustrate the extremes of marine reserve management. In the successful case described first, islanders set up and now routinely protect a marine reserve with a clear understanding that it is a fish nursery that enhances the local fishery. In the second case, which must be described at least currently as a failure, an established marine reserve was invaded by the mayor and local fishermen. They perceived no benefit from it and felt that they were being denied access to a traditional fishing ground by the university.

APO, BALICASAG, AND PAMILACAN RESERVES

The first case involves a two-year project that could be a model of how local communities can define, patrol, and profit from marine protected areas. In three tiny islands in the Philippines—Apo, Balicasag, and Pamilacan (see Figure 1)—marine protected areas produced an increase in both the numbers and variety of reef fish within the reserves (1). Of even more interest to the islanders, protection often increased the number of fish available outside the reserves, as well (2).

The Marine Conservation and Development Program of Silliman University in the Philippines undertook the project to help local island communities manage their marine resources. Although all three islands were sparsely populated, the surrounding reefs had suffered degradation from overfishing, both by locals and nonislanders but especially from destructive blast fishing (3).

Although the project goal was to improve local marine management, it did not start with marine scientists nor with marine issues. Five full-time community organizers were stationed on the islands three weeks out of four. Marine scientists on the project staff trained both the community organizers and the islanders in marine matters. The organizers assisted the islanders in making decisions about the location and construction of a community center, which was part of the project. From this construction project grew an organized community group that would later manage the marine reserve (4).

Local fishermen decided on the size and locations of the reserves. The areas they chose were ecologically sound but were small and not popular for fishing (5). Although larger reserves may have been preferable to conservationists, the fact that these small reserves were accepted and patrolled by the local fishermen made them successful.

In an informal survey, respondents on Apo and Pamilacan Islands said they saw no decrease in fish catch or personal income since establishment of the reserves, and most believed a sanctuary would improve fishing because sanctuaries serve as a "semilyahan" (breeding place) for fish (6). Fish yield studies in fishing areas outside the reserves indicate that yields were at least stable and probably increasing at Apo Island and were higher

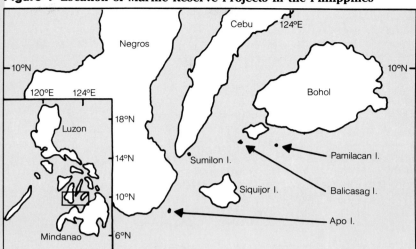

Figure 1 Location of Marine Reserve Projects in the Philippines

Source: Alan T. White and Gail C. Savina, "Community-Based Marine Reserves, A Philippine First," in *Coastal Zone '87*, conference proceedings, Seattle, May 1987 (American Society of Civil Engineers, New York, 1987), p. 2023.

than expected at Pamilacan Island. None of the islanders opposed creation of the reserves. Although enforcement was sometimes spotty because of lack of manpower—it was conducted by island volunteers—25 violations (mostly by outsiders) were recorded in one year (7).

SUMILON ISLAND RESERVE

By contrast, a thriving marine protected area on the Philippine island of Sumilon was rendered inoperable by a lack of community support and the antagonism of a local mayor and fishermen. Established in 1974, the Sumilon island reserve was the first nationally protected marine park in the Philippines. It was a traditional fishing ground for residents of Cebu, a nearby larger island in the central Philippines. The reserve was jointly managed by Silliman University and the Cebu municipality of Oslob.

Oslob elected a new mayor in 1980. His family owned the largest *muro-ami* fishing operation in the Philippines (8). During the campaign, he had promised to "take back" Sumilon Island from the university and open the protected reef to fishing. Within a month of his election, the mayor personally led a fishing party to the reserve. After four more fishing expeditions, the university filed a complaint with the national police in Manila and the fishing stopped. Silliman University turned again to the national government and had the reserve declared a national fish sanctuary. In 1982 in a series of radio speeches, the governor of Cebu condemned the university for displacing local fishermen. Fishing expeditions and verbal exchanges continued. When the Silliman University caretaker of the reserve was physically threatened in 1984, he left the island, ending effective enforcement of reserve

rules. Intensive fishing began in the reserve, and as of June 1988, the reserve was no longer managed or protected (9).

The Sumilon island reserve failed largely because of the lack of rapport between the university and the local community, particularly the mayor. Cebu fishermen acknowledged a higher fish yield and perceived the benefits of maintaining a fish nursery, but they were also tempted by the sizable standing stock of fish in the sanctuary. Although the university surveyed fishermen's attitudes and conducted an education campaign when the reserve opened, the campaign did not outweigh the impassioned speeches of the mayor and governor (10).

References and Notes

1. Alan T. White and Gail C. Savina, "Community-Based Marine Reserves, A Philippine First," in *Coastal Zone '87*, conference proceedings, Seattle, May 1987 (American Society of Civil Engineers, New York, 1987), p. 2022.
2. *Ibid*, pp. 2032–2033.
3. *Ibid.*, p. 2023.
4. *Ibid.*, pp. 2024–2025.
5. *Ibid.*, p. 2035.
6. *Ibid.*, p. 2035.
7. *Ibid.*, pp. 2023–2033, p. 2027, and p. 2034.
8. Muro-ami fishing is a technique that employs a large stationary net into which many swimmers herd fish by making noise with weighted lines. It can be very destructive to coral reefs.
9. Alan T. White, "Philippine Marine Park Pilot Site: Benefits and Management Conflicts," *Environmental Conservation*, Vol. 14, No. 1 (1987), p. 358.
10. *Ibid.*

The area supports an extremely productive fishery consisting of 2,500 species of fish and many invertebrates. Eleven percent of the world marine catch comes from these waters. In East Asia, 5 million people depend directly on fishing for their livelihood, and 25 million are affected by decisions regarding the fishing industry in that region (50). In some areas, the fishery has potential for further expansion, but two of the major nearshore fishing areas—the Gulf of Thailand and the Strait of Malacca—have been overfished and polluted by municipal and industrial discharge.

The location of the East Asian countries is a major influence on their economic development. Historically, the seasonal winds made it possible for both the Chinese and Arabs to sail their coastal junks and dhows to the area to trade. European traders followed and changed the centers of trade to meet the requirements of their deeper-draft vessels. East Asian countries are major suppliers of tin—dredged from shallow offshore waters, spices, rice, coffee, tea, sugar, palm oil, rubber, and oil from offshore drilling (51).

East Asian seas are also the trade route for oil tankers traveling from the Middle East to Japan. Most tankers pass through the Strait of Malacca, a tricky navigational area and also a major fishing ground, then head northeast through the South China Sea and pass southeast of Taiwan. Ships classed as very large crude carriers must take a deeper-water route through the Lombok Channel in southern Indonesia, north through the Makassar Strait and the Celebes Sea, and into the Pacific (52).

Pollution

Oil pollution from shipping and offshore oil rigs is a prime concern in the East Asian seas. Because of the proximity of the countries, an oil spill off the coast of one would likely foul the coasts of others (53). Oil pollution is worse in harbors and along shipping lanes. The highest hydrocarbon concentrations are in the South China Sea off southern Viet Nam and in the Makassar Strait, both shipping areas (54). Dumai, Indonesia's largest port, has a relatively low oil pollution level (1.2–1.5 parts per million), perhaps because it has a deballasting facility for ships (55).

Oil pollution and fishing conflict in several areas; the most obvious is the Strait of Malacca which annually produces more than 1,000 kilograms of fish per square kilometer. Others include the northern Gulf of Thailand and the archepelagic waters of the Philippines (56).

Land-based pollution is also a serious problem, especially in harbors near Bangkok, Kuala Lumpur, Jakarta, Manila, and other major cities. Sewage from these densely populated cities is a source of marine pollution. By contrast, Singapore treats 80 percent of its domestic sewage and consequently has less water pollution (57). Land-based pollution affects major fishery areas in the Strait of Malacca, the west coast of peninsular Malaysia, Thailand's Andaman Sea coast, the bight of Bangkok, and Manila Bay (58).

Another major source of pollution is sedimentation from agriculture, logging, mining, and construction. Sedimentation in the marine environment causes tur-

bidity that blocks light to aquatic plants and thus reduces primary productivity. It also smothers coral reefs and shellfish beds. Offshore mining and dredging for tin also increase turbidity. Heavy metals such as lead, mercury, cadmium, and zinc are becoming a problem near industrial areas. These metals become concentrated in fish and shellfish, posing a hazard to humans who eat them.

Many East Asian countries have passed laws relative to land-based pollution, but the laws are not always followed by regulations and enforcement. The Philippines, Singapore, Malaysia, and China have strong laws and regulations; Indonesia and Thailand have some laws; but all have little enforcement (59).

The Regional Seas Action Plan

UNEP dates the development of an action plan for East Asian seas to a 1976 UNEP-initiated workshop on marine pollution in Penang, where regional scientists discussed major problems. The following year, at the request of East Asian governments, UNEP's Governing Council agreed to help develop an action plan for East Asia. A first draft was prepared by UNEP in 1979, and a revised draft was adopted in Manila in 1981 by representatives of Indonesia, Malaysia, the Philippines, Singapore, and Thailand. The nations refrained from adopting a legally binding protocol along with the plan. They agreed on the objective of "development and protection of the marine environment and the coastal areas for the promotion of the health and well-being of present and future generations." At a separate meeting, they adopted priorities for the action plan, established a coordinating body—the Coordinating Body on the Seas of East Asia (COBSEA) to set policy and direct activities—and set up a trust fund through which member countries' contributions would finance the action plan. The governments asked UNEP to continue as secretariat of the action plan (60).

The East Asian Seas Action Plan (61), like other Regional Seas action plans, has three major objectives: to assess the state of the marine environment, to promote the management of coastal activities that affect the marine environment and sustainable use of marine resources, and to coordinate nations to implement specific plans (62). The East Asian plan set ambitious monitoring and management goals. Monitoring goals included assessment of: pollution dispersion patterns; the impacts of oil pollution on marine organisms; the effects of nonoil pollutants, especially metals, organics, nutrients, and sediments; the impacts of pollution on mangrove and coral ecosystems; the impacts of offshore petroleum exploration, mining, and dredging; thermal pollution in coastal waters, and atmospheric pollution reaching the marine environment.

To encourage environmental management, the action plan proposed establishing regional advisory services for oil spill control, setting guidelines for discharge of wastes into coastal waters, and selecting marine dumping sites for hazardous waste disposal. It did not cover coastal development or marine conservation, which it said could be addressed under other regional environmental programs (63).

With the exception of controlling oil spilled accidentally, most projects relate to environmental assessment (research and monitoring) rather than to environmental management (64). As of 1987, six projects, three of them dealing with oil pollution, were funded by COBSEA. After the 1987 meeting of COBSEA, UNEP reported that "the implementation of the projects has progressed with various degrees of success" (65). Some projects experienced staff changes, equipment failures, and funding delays; others were proceeding in stages. One successful project, a study on cleaning up urban rivers, was completed in 1986 (66). COBSEA members expressed concern about the lack of progress and the piecemeal nature of the projects regarding oil pollution, the priority issue. They proposed that a group of experts meet with oil industry representatives to determine what scientific work, funding, and regulations are needed (67).

As recommended, an experts' meeting was held in Bali in 1987, and participants agreed on necessary scientific work, including a regional network of monitoring stations (68). Their recommendations, along with comments from a second experts' meeting, were to be discussed by COBSEA in 1988.

A major weakness of the action plan, as evaluated by UNEP in 1987, is its uncertain financial footing. Each member nation made a pledge to the trust fund, which totaled $94,600 in 1986 (69). But the plan has not mobilized larger commitments from governments; nor has it attracted other donors. The resources of the trust fund are inadequate for any significant environmental action in the region, according to UNEP (70).

There are several other environmental initiatives outside the action plan. ASEAN is working to develop a regional approach to managing oil spills, including oil company assistance. With assistance from the International Maritime Organization and UNEP, Indonesia, Malaysia, and the Philippines developed an action plan for oil spills in the Celebes Sea (71). In addition, marine protected areas have been established to protect sea turtle nesting grounds, mangroves, coral reefs, beaches, and shore bird habitat. (See Box 9.2.)

MARINE MAMMALS

Marine mammals are divided into three main groups: cetaceans, which include whales and dolphins; pinnipeds, which include seals, sea lions, and walruses; and sirenians, which include manatees and dugongs. Other sea-dependent mammals are sea otters and polar bears.

Cetaceans are the farthest ranging of the marine mammals, living in the open seas with no dependence on land. There are at least 80 species, some of which are known only by skeletal remains found on beaches. Baleen whales—gray, blue, humpback, bowhead, fin, sei, Bryde's, minke, and right whales—feed on plankton, krill, invertebrates, or fish by straining a huge volume of sea water through baleen (whalebone) plates. The toothed whales—including the huge sperm whale, a number of smaller whales, and all dolphins—feed primarily on fish and squid.

Pinnipeds live mainly in the far north and extreme south, where they congregate on remote shores. One subgroup, Otarids, which have bear-like ancestors, evolved mainly in the North Pacific into fur seals, sea lions, and walruses. All have external ears and hind flippers that can be turned forward for walking. Another subgroup, Phocids, probably evolved from otter-like creatures in the North Atlantic. They include the elephant, monk, and other true seals (72).

Sirenians are large, slow-moving creatures that live in sheltered coastal areas and rivers and feed on aquatic plants, mangrove leaves, and algae (73). Living sirenians include three manatee and one dugong species; all are threatened with extinction. Manatees, reputed to have inspired the legend of the mermaid among sea-weary sailors, include the Amazonian manatee, the Caribbean manatee, and the West African manatee. The single species of dugong is found in scattered areas throughout the South Pacific and Indian Oceans (74).

Sea otters, the smallest of marine mammals, inhabit the North Pacific shoreline from the Bering Sea to southern California. Another small population lives near Chile and Peru. In shallow water, sea otters feed on clams, urchins, and other benthic animals (75). Polar bears live on land and ice in the Arctic and are excellent swimmers. They feed mainly on fish.

Table 9.4 shows the population levels and major threats to the most endangered marine mammals.

Hunting of Marine Mammals

In the 18th and 19th Centuries, whaling concentrated on the large slow-moving species. Sperm whales were hunted for their oil, which was used in lamps, and right, bowhead, and gray whales were hunted for oil, ingredients for perfumes, and whalebone for corset stays. In the last half of the 19th Century, the use of petroleum products in lamps drove down the price of whale oil, but high whalebone prices kept whalers active (76). By 1872, a Norwegian-designed cannon-fired harpoon allowed whalers to catch faster species such as the blue, fin, sei, Bryde's, and minke whales (77). They were used for pet food and, in Japan and elsewhere, for human consumption. Figure 9.4 shows catch statistics for five species. Each in turn was hunted until it was no longer economically exploitable and sometimes to levels that threatened extinction. (For a list of marine mammals, estimates of their original and current population sizes, and catch data from 1920 to 1985, see *World Resources 1987*, Table 24.2, pp. 328–330.)

Regulation of Whaling and Sealing

Prior to the 1940s, few international agreements regulated the capture of marine mammals. In 1946, the International Convention for the Regulation of Whaling established the International Whaling Commission (IWC), which regulates the hunting of 12 species of great whales and the minke whale. The IWC, whose membership now numbers 38 nations, sets catch and size limits and gear specifications and disseminates information on whale biology. The IWC objective is to regulate whale harvests for the benefit of the whaling industry—an approach similar to fisheries management.

Table 9.4 Endangered and Vulnerable Marine Mammals

Species	Distribution	Prewhaling Population	Present Population	IUCN Category[a]	Threats	Protection
CETACEANS						
Baleen Whales						
Gray whale	NE Pacific NW Pacific	15,000–20,000	Nearly extinct in NW Pacific; NE Pacific: 13,450–19,210	N. Pacific – recovering; Atlantic – extinct	19th Century whaling	IWC[b]
Blue whale	N Atlantic N Pacific N Indian Antarctic, Subarctic Indian	166,000–226,400	7,500–15,000	Endangered	20th Century whaling	IWC
Humpback whale	Worldwide NW Atlantic	>119,400	8,957–10,489	Endangered	20th Century whaling	IWC
Bowhead whale	NE Atlantic NW Atlantic N Pacific Okhotsk	54,680	3,500–4,417	Endangered	19th–20th Century whaling	IWC
Black right whale	Originally worldwide, increasing in southern oceans only	X	3,000	Endangered	15th–19th Century whaling	
Fin whale	Southern Hemisphere N Atlantic N Pacific	>443,000	96,000–121,714	Vulnerable	Whaling	IWC (partial)
Toothed Whales						
Northern bottlenose whale	Boreal, Arctic, and N Atlantic	X	X	Vulnerable	19th Century whaling	IWC
Dolphins						
Indus dolphin	Originally Indus River system and main tributaries, now Indus in Sind and Punjab Provinces of Pakistan	X	300—600	Endangered	Hunting, habitat destruction by impoundment & water diversion	Pakistan law
PINNIPEDS						
Otaroids (fur seals, sea lions, and walruses)						
Japanese sea lion		X	X	Possibly extinct	Persecution by fishermen and coastal development	
Galapagos fur seal	Galapagos Islands	X	1,000–40,000	Vulnerable	19th Century sealing, hunting predation, and tourism	
Juan Fernandez fur seal	Once ranged from Strait of Magellan to Peru, now on a few islands off Chile	Several million	705–2,416	Vulnerable	19th Century sealing	Chilean law, CITES App. I[c]
Guadalupe fur seal	Once ranged from South California to Baja, California, now on several islands	200,000	1,300–1,600	Vulnerable	20th Century sealing, habitat loss, and human disturbance	U.S.–Mexican law, CITES App. I
Phocoids (Northern seals, elephant seals, and monk seals)						
Caribbean monk seal	Originally from Caribbean and Gulf of Mexico	X	X	Possibly extinct	18th Century sealing, persecution by fishermen, and human disturbance	IUCN/UNEP, CITES App. I draft action plan
Mediterranean monk seal	Mediterranean, NW Africa	X	500–800	Endangered	Persecution by fishermen	Draft action plan, CITES App. I
Hawaiian monk seal	Hawaiian Islands	X	500–1,500	Endangered	19th Century sealing, human disturbance	U.S. laws, CITES App. I
SIRENIANS						
Manatees and Dugongs						
Amazonian manatee	Throughout Amazonian system (Brazil, Colombia, Peru) and headwaters of the Orinoco	X	>10,000	Endangered	Commercial/subsistence hunting (now illegal hunting)	CITES App. I
West African manatee	Formerly from Senegal to Angola, now much reduced	X	X	Vulnerable	Subsistence hunting	National laws incompletely enforced
West Indian (Caribbean) manatee	Originally Florida to Guyana now Belize, Guyana, and Suriname, declining elsewhere	X	5,000–10,000	Vulnerable	Hunting, entanglement in fishing nets, marine pollution, boat traffic, incidental catch, shrinking habitat, herbicides	CITES App. I national laws incompletely enforced
Dugong	Tropical and subtropical Indo-Pacific	X	Australia: several thousand; entire range: <30,000	Vulnerable	Hunting (now illegal hunting), incidental catch, pollution of seagrass beds	CITES App. I, except for Australian population, national laws incompletely enforced

Sources:
1. International Union for Conservation of Nature and Natural Resources (IUCN), the *IUCN Mammal Red Data Book*, Part 1, *Threatened Mammalian Taxa of the Americas and the Australasian Zoogeographic Region (Excluding Cetacea)* (IUCN, Gland, Switzerland, 1982).
2. United Nations Environment Programme (UNEP), *Marine Mammals: Draft Global Plan of Action and Financial Plan* (UNEP, Nairobi, 1984), Appendix 1, pp. 72-76.
3. World Resources Institute and International Institute for Environment and Development, *World Resources 1987* (1987), Table 24.2, p. 328.

Notes:
a. Status as classified by the International Union for Conservation of Nature and Natural Resources (IUCN). See Source 1.
b. International Whaling Commission (IWC).
c. Convention of International Trade in Endangered Species of Wild Fauna and Flora (CITES).
X = not available.

At the 1972 United Nations Conference on the Human Environment in Stockholm, however, a total moratorium on whaling was proposed, and in succeeding years, public sentiment in western countries pressed for the preservation of cetaceans as intelligent animals rather than as commodities to be harvested. Greenpeace, the International Fund for Animal Welfare, and other international groups publicized the effects of whaling and sealing. This "save the whales" movement drew considerable public support in the United States and Europe. The popularity of whale watching, films about whales, and aquaria shows by whales and other marine mammals reveals a favorable sentiment for whales in a number of countries.

In 1979, the IWC established a sanctuary in the Indian Ocean where whaling was prohibited for 10 years. In 1982, in response to the mounting public pressure to stop whaling and to the declining economics of whaling, the IWC voted to halt commercial whaling beginning in 1986 and to assess whale stocks in 1990 in order to reconsider the moratorium. Japan, Norway, and the Soviet Union objected to the moratorium and continued commercial whaling until 1988. During 1986 and 1987, the three countries took 6,981 whales (78). A controversial provision of the moratorium allows killing whales for scientific purposes. In 1986–87, Japan, South Korea, Iceland, and Norway killed an additional 933 whales for scientific research (79). In response to criticisms about this research, the IWC passed a resolution tightening criteria for scientific permits issued by member countries and recommended against approval of all research proposals presented at its June 1987 meeting (80). However, the IWC has no authority to prevent countries from proceeding with their "research" plans. National policies and international public opinion are now the only enforcement mechanisms. The IWC concerns itself only with commercially important whales, not with smaller whales and dolphins.

Unlike whales, seals and walruses are protected by a number of regional treaties, not by a single global convention. Because about half the world's pinniped population consists of crabeater seals in Antarctica, the 1972 Antarctic seal convention is especially important. Some populations are gradually recovering from uncontrolled exploitation (81), but nowhere are they near their former size. In greatest danger presently are various monk seals, whose habitat requirements make them susceptible to coastal development and pollution, and some fur seals and sea lions (82). The Caribbean monk seal, reported as abundant by Spanish explorers, has not been seen since 1952 and is presumed extinct (83).

Current Threats to Marine Mammals

Although commercial hunting has taken a huge toll on certain marine mammal populations, present threats are mainly coastal development, habitat destruction, marine pollution, interactions with fisheries, and entanglement in marine debris and fishing nets. (See Table 9.4 and Recent Developments, Preventing Pollution from Plastics.)

Coastal Development, Habitat Destruction, and Pollution

Coastal development and increasing recreational use of

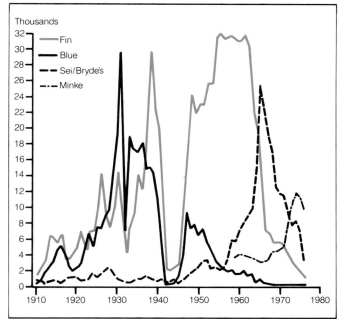

Figure 9.4 World Catches of Five Whale Species, 1910–76

Source: Bureau of International Whaling Statistics as cited in Sir Sydney Frost. *Whales and Whaling,* Vol. 1 (Australian Government Publishing Service, Canberra, 1978), pp. 32–33.

waters threaten marine mammals, such as the sireniens and freshwater dolphins that live in rivers, and the pinnipeds, which breed onshore. For example, in Florida, most manatees are scarred by boat propellers and about 27 manatees are killed each year in collisions with boats or barges (84). In Venezuela, pollution of Lake Maricaibo could be harmful to the few remaining manatees, and extensive land reclamation in the Orinoco Delta is reducing their feeding grounds (85).

All five species of river dolphin are threatened by habitat destruction and by subsistence hunting and incidental take by fishermen. Dam construction and other riparian development being undertaken or planned in Brazil, Nepal, and China are potentially serious threats to these species (86). The remaining Mediterranean monk seals withdrew to remote islands as tourism and industry expanded along the coast (87).

Several types of marine mammals are affected by oil pollution and accumulated pesticides and heavy metals. Oil pollution stresses fur seals, sea otters, and polar bears, whose thermoregulation or buoyancy depends on their fur. A large oil spill in the Arctic or Antarctic, where low temperatures slow the degradation of oil and surface ice makes cleanup almost impossible, would be especially harmful to these mammals (88).

Research indicates that no marine mammal anywhere in the world is without a body burden of a variety of synthetic organic compounds (89). An accumulation of DDT, PCBs, dieldrin, or other halogenated hydrocarbons has been shown to cause reproductive failure in ringed seals, sea lions in the Baltic and California, harbor seals in Puget Sound in the northwestern United States, and seals in the Netherlands' Wadden Sea (90) (91). These chemicals accumulate in fatty tissue, which most marine mammals have in abundance for insulation. Especially at risk are toothed whales, dolphins, and pinnipeds.

Fishing and Hunting

Fishermen often catch marine mammals incidentally along with fish in their nets. Gillnets and other nets that are set and left unattended cause significant damage (92). Incidental netting is the second biggest cause of mortality of sirenians (93).

Fishermen in the eastern tropical Pacific set purse seines around schools of spinner dolphins, which often associate with schools of yellowfin tuna. In this manner, they captured large numbers of tuna but also killed 200,000–500,000 dolphins annually between 1959 and 1972, reducing the spinner dolphin population substantially. When this practice became known outside the fishing community, public pressure forced regulations on fishermen to modify the nets to allow dolphins to escape. The dolphin kill dropped to 25,000–56,000 annually between 1973 and 1986 but rose again to 129,000 in 1987 (94). (The higher 1987 figure may be the result of observers being placed on more boats that year (95).)

Discarded and lost monofilament nets and plastic debris are also a problem. Formerly made of natural fibers, most fishing nets are now a synthetic monofilament, which is invisible to fish and marine mammals and is not biodegradable. Nets discarded or lost at sea are called "ghost nets" that can continue to "fish" for years, often entangling and drowning mammals and birds as well. (See Recent Developments, Preventing Plastic Pollution.)

In establishing its moratorium on commercial whaling, the IWC exempted subsistence hunting of the bowhead and several other species of great whales by indigenous people. In Alaska and Canada, subsistence hunting of marine mammals is managed jointly by local committees and government conservation officials. Research is needed to determine whether this hunting is further endangering the species. Manatees and dugongs continue to be hunted with little management control in the Amazon, West Africa, East Asia, and the South Pacific for both their meat and their sturdy hides (96).

Protection of Marine Mammals

Although 92 countries have enacted laws regarding marine mammals, only New Zealand, Seychelles, and the United States had comprehensive marine mammal protection legislation as of 1986. The others relate only to some types of mammals, or their laws are fragmented among fishery, wildlife, and import-export control agencies. Methods of control among countries with comprehensive legislation vary. Seychelles has simply declared itself a marine mammal sanctuary and can impose a sentence of up to five years in prison on anyone who kills or harasses a marine mammal. With the U.S. Marine Mammal Protection Act of 1972, the United States set up a system of permits and review of permit applications for

the taking of marine mammals. The number of countries with laws related to each of the major types of marine mammals is as follows: cetaceans, 69 countries; pinnipeds, 51 countries; and sirenians and sea otters, 69 countries (97). Among the marine mammals whose populations have begun to recover are the northern elephant seal, the Antarctic fur seal, the gray whale, and the California and Alaska sea otters (98). Some recovery has occurred in the Galapagos fur seal and the Guadalupe fur seal (99).

Global Action Plan for Marine Mammals

In 1984, UNEP issued a Global Plan of Action for Marine Mammals to stimulate and coordinate conservation efforts. The plan recommends increasing research by individual scientists and international organizations, establishing marine protected areas, and encouraging public education on marine mammals. It set up a committee to identify situations in which species or populations are especially endangered and bring these to the attention of the national governments. Coordinated through the UNEP Oceans and Coastal Areas Programme Activity Center in Nairobi, the plan addresses national governments, international agencies, and nongovernmental organizations (100).

RECENT DEVELOPMENTS

PREVENTING POLLUTION FROM PLASTICS

An international agreement that takes effect in December 1988 makes it illegal for ships registered in the 31 ratifying nations to dump plastic debris in the ocean. A growing body of evidence suggests that this debris poses a significant threat not only to individual marine organisms but to some populations as well (101).

Oceangoing merchant vessels, fishing vessels, military ships, and recreational boats discard plastic sheeting, packing strands and pellets, fishing nets, plastic cups, and other consumer items in large enough quantities to endanger marine mammals, sea birds, and turtles by entanglement or ingestion and to strew popular beaches with litter.

Estimates of the amount of plastics released in the oceans are sketchy because plastics come from so many sources and are so widely distributed. One study estimates that 639,000 plastic containers, including plastic bags, are dumped each day by the world merchant fleet (102). Estimates of worldwide losses and discards of commercial fishing nets, which can entrap marine mammals and turtles, range from 1,224–122,472 metric tons per year (103).

Ocean currents concentrate the debris around islands, foraging grounds, areas where currents converge, upwelling areas, and other places of importance to marine species. Certain species are actually attracted to the debris (104). For example, at least 50 species of sea birds are known to ingest small plastic pellets that float on the surface, probably mistaking them for fish eggs or larvae. Although small quantities of plastics may not present a health risk to adult birds, adults often feed plastic pellets to their chicks, which may die if fed too many of them

(105). Turtles may mistake plastic bags for jellyfish, their natural prey (106). Some marine mammals, such as northern fur seals, may be attracted to discarded fishing nets that contain entrapped fish. While trying to pluck out the fish, the seals may become entangled themselves. There is evidence that juvenile seals become entangled by playing with these nets or the debris trapped in them (107).

The northern fur seal is the best-studied example of the interaction of a marine species with plastic debris. Since the mid- to late 1970s, the population of fur seals on the Pribilof Islands has declined at a rate of 4–8 percent per year. This decline parallels the rapid growth of the trawl and driftnet fisheries in the North Pacific (108). Recent analyses suggest that the population decline is largely caused by the entanglement of young seals in lost or discarded nets or packing bands (109).

The international agreement that will end disposal of plastics from ships is Annex V of the International Convention for the Prevention of Pollution from Ships (MARPOL). Two other annexes governing oil and chemicals are in force. Annex V prohibits "the disposal into the sea of all plastics, including but not limited to synthetic ropes, synthetic fishing nets, and plastic garbage bags" (110). The new agreement is expected to make a significant contribution to reducing the amount of plastics in the sea (111). Ratifying nations will be expected to provide port disposal facilities for plastics from ships.

Two land-based sources of plastics contribute as much, if not more than ships, to the problem of plastics in the sea. The first is manufacturing sites of the tiny pellets of raw plastic that are among the most common plastic litter on beaches and are mistaken for fish eggs by many sea birds and turtles. These spill out of waste pipes into rivers or coastal waters. The second source is the diffuse solid waste generated by cities and industries, some of which finds its way to the sea (112).

Long-range solutions are to develop biodegradable plastics that will serve their purpose, but then decay when discarded and to cut back on the use of disposable plastics.

THE RISING SEAS

One aspect of the impending global warming from the greenhouse effect has already moved from the realm of computer models to the realm of engineering conferences. The U.S. Army Corps of Engineers and others are working on plans to protect coastal areas from a sea level rise. If average temperatures rise 1.5°–4.5°C by 2030, the global sea level is expected to rise 20–140 cen-

timeters over the following several decades (113) (114). This rise would be caused by the expansion of sea water as it is warmed, and by the melting of glaciers and ice caps.

Such a rise in sea level would have noticeable effects on shorelines around the world. In the past 100 years, the sea level has risen only 10–15 centimeters (115).

The major effects of a rising sea level include: the narrowing or destruction of recreational sandy beaches; loss of mangrove and wetland areas; and destruction or costly fortification of shoreline property. Higher water levels increase storm damage and salinity in groundwater as saltwater intrudes on the freshwater table (116).

Several studies discuss how specific areas would be affected by a sea level rise.

■ In Bangladesh, the situation would be severe. It would lose 12–28 percent of its area, which houses 9–27 percent of its population. Floods could penetrate further inland, leaving the nation vulnerable to the type of storm that killed 300,000 people in the early 1970s (117). (See Chapter 10, "Atmosphere and Climate," Figure 10.4.)

■ Maldives, a nation of 1,190 small islands that rises barely 2 meters above sea level in the Indian Ocean, would be entirely submerged by a 2-meter sea level rise and severely damaged by storm surges with a 1-meter rise (118).

■ In Asia, brackish-water fishponds constructed along coastal areas would be submerged, and rice paddies farther inland might be converted to fish ponds (119).

■ In Charleston, South Carolina, sea walls would probably have to be constructed around the historic downtown area, and residential areas on nearby marshy islands might have to be abandoned (120).

■ The world-famous beaches of Copacabana and Ipanema in Brazil would disappear unless they are constantly replenished at public expense (121).

■ Along the coast of Brazil and elsewhere, mangrove areas would disappear as the sea level lapped against developed land further inland (122).

In 1987, research moved from predicting the effects of sea level rise to evaluating engineering and management responses. The Dutch, to whom many are turning for advice, are making plans to strengthen their dikes. The U.S. Army Corps of Engineers is considering how to integrate rising sea levels into its plans for waterway development, and the U.S. National Academy of Sciences published a report on engineering responses to changes in sea level (123). The state of Maine, on the other hand, has proposed regulations putting property owners on notice that if their lands are flooded, they will be expected to move their dwellings inland.

References and Notes

1. Richard Lipkin, "Bedlam at the Bottom of the Sea," *Insight*, March 28, 1988, pp. 54–55.
2. Roger Revelle, "The Oceans and the Carbon Dioxide Problem," *Oceanus*, Vol. 26, No. 2 (1983), p. 6.
3. Jerome Williams, John J. Higginson, and John D. Rohrbough, "Oceanic Surface Currents," in *Sea and Air: The Naval Experiment* (Naval Institute Press, Annapolis, Maryland, 1968), pp. 171–184, reprinted in *Oceanography: Contemporary Readings in Ocean Science*, R. Gordon Pirie, ed. (Oxford University Press, Oxford, U.K., 1973), pp. 100–101.
4. M. Grant Gross, *Oceanography* (Charles E. Merrill, Columbus, Ohio, 1971), p. 88.
5. *Ibid.*
6. *Ibid.*
7. K. Wyrtki, *Physical Oceanography of the Southeast Asian Waters*, NAGA Report, Vol. 2 (Scripps Institution of Oceanography, La Jolla, California, 1961), pp. 13–14, cited in Joseph R. Morgan and Donald W. Fryer, "The Marine Geography of Southeast Asia," in George Kent and Mark J. Valencia, *Marine Policy in Southeast Asia*

(University of California Press, Los Angeles, 1985), p. 14.

8. *Op. cit.* 4, pp. 97–99.

9. *Op. cit.* 3, pp. 120–121.

10. *Op. cit.* 4, p. 99.

11. *Op. cit.* 3, p. 120.

12. *Op. cit.* 3, p. 122.

13. B. Bolin, "How Much CO$_2$ Will Remain in the Atmosphere?" in *The Greenhouse Effect: Climate Change and Ecosystems*, Bolin Warrick and Doos Jager, eds. (John Wiley & Sons, New York, 1986), p. 94.

14. *Op. cit.* 2.

15. Kirk Bryan, "Man's Great Geophysical Experiment: Can We Model the Consequences?" *Oceanus*, Vol. 29, No. 4 (winter 1986–87), pp. 37–38.

16. Melborne G. Briscoe, *A Primer on the U.S. Contribution to the World Ocean Circulation Experiment* (U.S. Planning Office for World Ocean Circulation Experiment, College Station, Texas, 1986), pp. 1–5.

17. Michael Robinson, Senior Fisheries Statistician, United Nations Food and Agriculture Organization, Fisheries Division, Rome, 1988 (personal communication).

18. A. Crisboldi, Statistician, United Nations Food and Agriculture Organization, Rome, July, 1988 (personal communication).

19. D. Thompson, "Conflict within the Fishing Industry," *International Center for Living Aquatic Resource Management Newsletter*, Vol. 3, No. 3 (1980), p. 4.

20. United Nations Food and Agriculture Organization (FAO), unpublished data (FAO, Rome, 1988).

21. United Nations Food and Agriculture Organization (FAO), *World Fisheries Situation and Outlook* (FAO, Rome, 1987), p. 6.

22. United Nations Food and Agriculture Organization (FAO), *Review of the State of the World Fishery Resources* (FAO, Rome, 1987), Tables 3–19, pp. 41–64.

23. Michael A. Robinson, "Trends and Prospects in World Fisheries" (United Nations Food and Agriculture Organization, Rome, 1984), p. 9.

24. *Op. cit.* 22, p. 18 and p. 28.

25. *Op. cit.* 21, pp. 5–7.

26. *Op. cit.* 22.

27. United Nations Food and Agriculture Organization, Rome, cited in National Fishery Statistics Program, *Fisheries of the United States 1986* (U.S. Department of Commerce, Washington, D.C., 1987), pp. 84–85.

28. *Op. cit.* 21, pp. 7–8.

29. Gerald Moore and Gunnar Saetersdal, "Managing Extended Fisheries: A Decade's Modest Progress," *Ceres*, Vol. 20, No. 5 (1987), p. 40.

30. *Ibid.*

31. *Ibid.*

32. Graeme Kelleher and Richard Kenchington, *Policy for Marine Conservation and the Establishment of Marine Protected Areas* (Great Barrier Reef Marine Park Authority, Canberra, Australia, 1987).

33. International Union for Conservation of Nature and Natural Resources, Conservation Monitoring Centre (IUCN/CMC), unpublished data, IUCN/CMC, Cambridge, U.K., 1988.

34. Maynard E. Silva, Ellen M. Gately, and Ingrid Desilvestre, *A Bibliographic Listing of Coastal and Marine Protected Areas: A Global Survey* (Woods Hole Oceanographic Institution, Woods Hole, Massachusetts, 1986), p. 1.

35. *Op. cit.* 32.

36. Aquatic Resources Conservation Group, "Working Paper on Marine Protected Areas and the U.S. National Marine Sanctuary Program," draft, Center for Environmental Education, Washington, D.C., 1987, pp. 18–19.

37. *Ibid.*, pp. 19–23.

38. Nancy M. Foster and Jack H. Archer, "The National Marine Sanctuary Program—Policy, Education, and Research," *Oceanus*, Vol. 31, No. 1 (1988), pp. 5–13.

39. *Ibid.*

40. Art Jeffes, Sanctuary Projects Manager, Marine and Estuarine Management Division, Office of Ocean and Coastal Resource Management, National Ocean Service, National Oceanic and Atmospheric Administration, U.S. Department of Commerce, July 1988 (personal communication).

41. M. Wilson and Arthur M. Heyman, *Caribbean Marine and Coastal Protected Areas: Inventory and Analysis* (Organization of American States, Washington, D.C., in press).

42. *Ibid.*

43. Arthur M. Heyman, "Making Caribbean Marine Parks Work for Economic Development" (Organization of American States, Washington, D.C., 1988), p. 1.

44. Arthur M. Heyman, "Natural Tourism Attractions: It Pays to Protect Them," unpublished paper, Organization of American States [1988], Table 2, p. 5.

45. Arthur M. Heyman, Advisor for Planning and Natural Resource Management, Organization of American States, Washington, D.C., 1988 (personal communication).

46. Arthur M. Heyman, *Self-Financed Resource Management: A Direct Approach to Maintaining Marine Biological Diversity* (Organization of American States, Washington, D.C., in press).

47. Joseph R. Morgan and Donald W. Fryer, "The Marine Geography of Southeast Asia," in *Marine Policy in Southeast Asia*, George Kent and Mark J. Valencia, eds. (University of California Press, Los Angeles, 1985), p. 15.

48. Alan T. White, "Conservation of the Marine Environment," in *Marine Policy in Southeast Asia*, George Kent and Mark J. Valencia, eds. (University of California Press, Los Angeles, 1985), p. 328.

49. *Ibid.*, p. 329.

50. Elizabeth D. Samson, "Fisheries," in *Marine Policy in Southeast Asia*, George Kent and Mark J. Valencia, eds. (University of California Press, Los Angeles, 1985), p. 101.

51. George Kent and Mark J. Valencia, "Introduction," in *Marine Policy in Southeast Asia*, George Kent and Mark J. Valencia, eds. (University of California Press, Los Angeles, 1985), p. 1.

52. *Ibid.*

53. Abu Baker Jaafar and Mark J. Valencia, "Marine Pollution: National Responses and Transnational Issues," in George Kent and Mark J. Valencia, *Marine Policy in Southeast Asia* (University of California Press, Los Angeles, 1985), p. 274.

54. *Ibid.*

55. *Ibid.*, p. 272.

56. East-West Environment and Policy Institute, *Atlas for Marine Policy in Southeast Asian Seas*, Joseph R. Morgan and Mark J. Valencia, eds. (University of California Press, Berkeley, 1983), p. 134 and p. 138.

57. *Op. cit.* 53, p. 270.

58. *Op. cit.* 56, p. 134.

59. *Op. cit.* 53, pp. 274–296.

60. United Nations Environment Programme (UNEP), *The East Asian Seas Action Plan: Evaluation of Its Development and Achievements* (UNEP, Nairobi, 1987), pp. 1–2.

61. United Nations Environment Programme (UNEP), *Action Plan for the Protection and Development of the Marine and Coastal Areas of the East Asian Region* (UNEP, Nairobi, 1983).

62. *Ibid.*

63. *Ibid.*, p. 7.

64. United Nations Environment Programme (UNEP), *Report of the Executive Director of UNEP on the Implementation of the East Asian Seas Action Plan in 1986–87* (UNEP, Nairobi, 1987), p. 3.

65. *Ibid.*, p. 2.

66. *Ibid.*, p. 3.

67. *Ibid.*, p. 5.

68. *Op. cit.* 60.

69. *Op. cit.* 60, Table 2, p. 10.

70. *Op. cit.* 60, p. 7.

71. *Op. cit.* 53, p. 298.

72. S. Holt, "Mammals in the Sea," *Ambio*, Vol. 15, No. 3 (1986), p. 127.

73. United Nations Environment Programme (UNEP), *Marine Mammals* (UNEP, Nairobi, 1985), p. 8.

74. *Ibid.*

75. *Op. cit.* 72, p. 128.

76. Sir Sidney Frost, *Whales and Whaling* (Australian Government Publishing Service, Canberra, 1978), p. 25.

77. *Ibid.*, p. 27.

78. Dean Wilkinson, Legislative Director for Ocean Ecology, Greenpeace, Washington, D.C., July 1988 (personal communication).

79. *Ibid.*

80. *Marine Mammal News* (Nautilus Press, Washington, D.C., June/July 1987), pp. 3–4.

81. United Nations Environment Programme (UNEP), *Marine Mammals: Draft Global Plan of Action and Financial Plan* (UNEP, Nairobi, 1984), p. 3 and p. 13.

82. *Ibid.*, p. 3

83. International Union for the Conservation of Nature and Natural Resources (IUCN), *The IUCN Mammal Red Data Book*, Part 1, *Threatened Mammalian Taxa of the Americas and the Australian Zoogeographic Region (Excluding Cetacea)* (IUCN, Gland, Switzerland, 1982), p. 411.

84. Marine Mammal Commission, *Annual Report of the Marine Mammal Commission, Calendar Year 1986: A Report to Congress* (Marine Mammal Commission, Washington, D.C., 1987), p. 99.

85. *Op. cit.* 83, p. 434.
86. *Op. cit.* 84, pp. 134–135.
87. *Op. cit.* 73, p. 24.
88. *Op. cit.* 73, p. 25.
89. Robert W. Risebrough, "Pollutants in Marine Mammals: A Literature Review and Recommendations for Research," paper prepared for the U.S. Marine Mammal Commission, Washington, D.C., 1978, p. 1.
90. *Ibid.*, p. 3.
91. W.N. Bonner, "Seals in the Human Environment," *Ambio*, Vol. 15, No. 3 (1986), p. 174.
92. Robert J. Hofman, "Conservation and Protection of Marine Mammals: Past, Present, and Future," *Marine Mammal Science*, Vol. 1, No. 2 (1985), p. 116.
93. United Nations Food and Agriculture Organization (FAO), *Mammals in the Seas*, Vol. I (FAO, Rome, 1978), p. 144.
94. Lesley Scheele, "Background Paper on the Eastern Tropical Pacific Tuna/Dolphin Issue," Greenpeace, Washington, D.C., 1988, Table 1, p. 58.
95. *Op. cit.* 78.
96. *Op. cit.* 83, pp. 417–441.
97. United Nations Food and Agriculture Organization (FAO), *Compendium of National Legislation on the Conservation of Marine Mammals*, Vol. 1 (FAO, Rome, 1986), pp. 1–107.
98. Robert J. Hofman, Scientific Program Director, Marine Mammal Commission, Washington, D.C., 1988 (personal communication).
99. *Op. cit.* 83, p. 401 and p. 407.
100. *Op. cit.* 81, p. 8.
101. Douglas A. Wolfe, "Persistent Plastics and Debris in the Ocean: an International Problem of Ocean Disposal," *Marine Pollution Bulletin*, Vol. 18, No. 6B (1987), p. 303.
102. P.V. Horsman, "The Amount of Garbage from Merchant Ships," *Marine Pollution Bulletin*, Vol. 13 (1982), pp. 167–169.
103. A.T. Pruter, "Sources, Quantities and Distribution of Persistent Plastics in the Marine Environment," *Marine Pollution Bulletin*, Vol. 18, No. 6B (1987), p. 306.
104. David Laist, "Overview of the Biological Effects of Lost and Discarded Plastic Debris in the Marine Environment," *Marine Pollution Bulletin*, Vol. 18, No. 6B (June 1987), p. 324.
105. *Ibid.*, p. 321.
106. *Ibid.*, p. 321.
107. Charles W. Fowler, "Interactions of Northern Fur Seals and Commercial Fisheries," published in *Transactions of the 47th North American Wildlife and Natural Resources Conference* (The Wildlife Management Institute, Washington, D.C., 1982), pp. 278–292, as cited in David Laist, "Overview of the Biological Effects of Lost and Discarded Plastic Debris in the Marine Environment," *Marine Pollution Bulletin*, Vol. 18, No. 6B (1987), pp. 323–324.
108. *Op. cit.* 104.
109. Charles W. Fowler, "Marine Debris and Northern Fur Seals: A Case Study," *Marine Pollution Bulletin*, Vol. 18, No. 6B, p 326.
110. Sally Ann Lentz, "Plastics in the Marine Environment: Legal Approaches for International Action," *Marine Pollution Bulletin*, Vol. 18, No. 6B, p. 362.
111. *Ibid.*
112. Michael J. Bean "Legal Strategies for Reducing Persistent Plastics in the Marine Environment," *Marine Pollution Journal*, Vol. 18, No. 6B, p. 359.
113. Robert Thomas, "Future Sea Level Rise and Its Early Detection by Satellite Remote Sensing," in *Effects of Changes in Stratospheric Ozone and Global Climate*. Vol. 4, *Sea Level Rise*, James G. Titus, ed. (United Nations Environment Programme and U.S. Environmental Protection Agency, October 1986), p. 28.
114. United Nations Environment Programme (UNEP), *The Changing Atmosphere*, UNEP Environment Brief No. 1 (UNEP, Nairobi, n.d.).
115. *Op. cit.* 113, p. 20.
116. Eric C.F. Bird, "Potential Effects of Sea Level Rise on the Coasts of Australia, Africa, and Asia," in *Effects of Changes in Stratospheric Ozone and Global Climate Change*. Vol. 4, *Sea Level Rise*, James G. Titus, ed. (United Nations Environment Programme and U.S. Environmental Protection Agency, Washington, D.C., 1986), p. 84.
117. James Broadus, *et al.*, "Rising Sea Level and Damming of Rivers: Possible Effects in Egypt and Bangladesh," in *Effects of Changes in Stratospheric Ozone and Global Climate*. Vol. 4, *Sea Level Rise*, James G. Titus, ed. (United Nations Environment Programme and U.S. Environmental Protection Agency, Washington, D.C., 1986), pp. 175–186.
118. Maumoon Abdul Gayoom, President, Maldives, speech before the United Nations General Assembly, New York, October 19, 1987.
119. *Op. cit.* 116, p. 90.
120. Michael Gibbs, "Planning for Sea Level Rise Under Uncertainty: A Case Study of Charleston, South Carolina," in *Effects of Changes in Stratospheric Ozone and Global Climate*. Vol. 4, *Sea Level Rise*, James G. Titus, ed. (United Nations Environment Programme and U.S. Environmental Protection Agency, Washington, D.C., 1986), pp. 59–60.
121. Stephen P. Leatherman, "Impacts of Sea Level Rise on the Coasts of South America," *Effects of Changes in Stratospheric Ozone and Global Climate*. Vol. 4, *Sea Level Rise*, James G. Titus, ed. (United Nations Environment Programme and U.S. Environmental Protection Agency, Washington, D.C., 1986), p. 78.
122. *Ibid.*, p. 76.
123. U.S. National Academy of Sciences, *Responding to Changes in Sea Level: Engineering Implications* (National Academy Press, Washington, D.C., 1987).

10. Atmosphere and Climate

The campaign against atmospheric pollution will look back on 1987–88 as a biennium of both failure and success. Emissions of traditional air pollutants continued their seemingly inexorable upward march in many countries, and ambient air quality in many cities worsened, threatening the health of millions of people. Acidic rain continued to fall over much of the industrialized world, bringing to Earth industrial emissions from hundreds of kilometers away. The Antarctic ozone hole was larger and lasted longer in the austral spring of 1987 than in any previous year. And the scientific community, in its first comprehensive assessment of ozone depletion trends, determined that 1987 global ozone levels had already been depleted to the point that models had predicted for the 2020s.

Progress, however, was also widely evident. In September 1987, the landmark Montreal Protocol to Protect the Ozone Layer was opened for signature, the first step in limiting chlorofluorocarbon damage to the stratospheric ozone layer. An important regional agreement—the Thirty Percent Club—entered into force in the same month, binding member countries to reduce sulfur dioxide emissions, an important contributor to urban air pollution and acidic deposition. A separate regional agreement capping emissions of nitrogen oxides was being negotiated through 1987–88.

Simple cause-and-effect relationships are the exception rather than the rule with air pollutants. The impacts of individual pollutants are identifiable in the laboratory, but damage is usually the result of several pollutants interact-

ing. This chapter presents current data on emissions and ambient levels of individual pollutants: sulfur dioxide, nitrogen oxides, lead, carbon dioxide, and others. Their impacts—individual and collective—are then discussed. A third section examines our emerging understanding of the complexity of air pollution—how individual pollutants have different impacts in different places, and how different pollutants interact in synergistic and antagonistic ways. Clearly, comprehensive pollution control strategies are needed, and some options are suggested to help policymakers take an integrated approach to atmospheric pollution.

CONDITIONS AND TRENDS

EMISSIONS AND AMBIENT AIR QUALITY

Sulfur Dioxide

Sources and Emissions

Sulfur dioxide (SO_2) is a corrosive gas that is hazardous to human health and has several deleterious impacts on the environment. SO_2 is emitted by both natural and anthropogenic processes; natural sources include volcanoes, decaying organic matter, and sea spray. Anthropogenic sources of SO_2 include combustion of sulfur-containing fuels (e.g., coal and petroleum products) and smelting of nonferrous ores [1]. Electricity generation using fossil fuels is the largest single source of SO_2 emis-

Table 10.1 Anthropogenic Emissions of Air Pollutants in Selected Countries, 1970–85[a]

(thousand metric tons)

		Australia[b,c]	Canada	France[d]	Fed. Rep. Germany	Czechoslovakia	Hungary	Ireland[e]	Japan[f]	United Kingdom	United States
Sulfur Dioxide											
Total	1970	X	6,678	3,743	3,640	X	X	180	X	6,120[g]	28,200
Emissions	1980	1,479[h]	4,612	3,460	3,200	3,100	1,633	217	1,259	4,670[g]	23,200
	1985	X	3,727[f]	2,185	2,640[i]	3,150	1,400	140	1,079	3,580[g]	20,700
Electricity	1970	X	8	27	46	X	X	X	X	45[g]	56
Generation (%)	1980	X	17	36	58[i]	X	X	X	X	61[g]	67
	1985	X	X	31	X	X	X	X	31	71[g]	69
Nitrogen Oxides											
Total	1970	X	1,329	1,699	2,400	X	X	56	X	1,832[k]	18,100
Emissions	1980	242	1,716	1,847	3,090	1,204	370	68	1,339	1,932	20,300
	1985	X	X	1,674	3,030[i]	1,120	400	57	1,416	1,837	20,000
Transport	1970	X	60	51	42[l]	X	X	X	X	34[k]	42
Sector (%)	1980	59	63	56	55[l]	X	X	X	40	37	45
	1985	X	X	65	57[l]	5[l]	30	33	49	42	45
Particulates											
Total	1970	X	2,028	310	1,300	X	X	88	X	720[m]	18,100
Emissions	1980	271[h]	1,873	278	725[n]	X	547	91	X	290[m]	8,400
	1985	X	X	187	X	1,370	492	100	X	260[m]	7,300
Industry (%)	1970	X	70	37	58	X	X	X	X	11[m]	56
	1980	X	64	26	61[n]	X	X	X	X	10[m]	38
	1985	X	X	27	X	X	X	3	X	12[m]	37
Carbon Monoxide											
Total	1970	X	11,584	X	13,470	X	X	399	X	4,690[k]	98,700
Emissions	1980	2,416	10,256	5,200[h]	8,960	X	1,730	497	X	5,127	76,000
	1985	X	X	X	7,410[i]	X	1,800	472	X	5,394	67,500
Transport	1970	X	81	X	44[l]	X	X	X	X	77[k]	73
Sector (%)	1980	86[o]	76	X	59[l]	X	X	X	X	82	69
	1985	X	X	X	59[l]	X	60[l]	81	X	84	70
Lead (metric tons)											
Total	1970	X	X	X	X	X	X	700	X	6,500	203,800
Emissions	1980	4,011	13,000[n]	X	X	X	600[p]	900	X	7,500	70,600
	1985	X	X	X	X	X	530[p]	500[o]	X	6,500	21,000
Motor	1970	X	X	X	X	X	X	X	X	X	77
Vehicles (%)	1980	93	62[n]	X	X	X	X	X	X	X	80
	1985	X	X	X	X	X	X	X	X	X	69
Hydrocarbons											
Total	1970	X	1,876	X	1,840	X	X	54	X	1,838[k]	27,200
Emissions	1980	659	1,838	2,185	1,860	350	X	62	X	1,954	22,800
	1985	X	X	X	1,830[i]	350	X	62	X	2,059	21,300
Motor	1970	X	50	X	36[l]	X	X	X	X	24[k]	41
Vehicles (%)	1980	47	36	X	45[l]	X	X	X	X	26	30
	1985	X	X	X	45[l]	X	X	X	X	26	28

Source: Compiled by the staff of *World Resources* from published national and international sources.
Notes:
a. Emission estimation methods differ, so country data are not strictly comparable. b. 1980 data refer to 1976. c. Seven capital cities, except for SO_2 and particulates, which are national estimates. d. 1970 data are for 1973; 1985 data are for 1983. e. 1970 data refer to 1972; 1985 data refer to 1983. f. 1985 data refer to 1983. g. Data refer to fuel combustion only; non-combustion sources are excluded. h. Refers to 1978. i. 1984. k. 1975. l. Mobile sources. m. Suspended particulate matter (SPM) data are for coal combustion only. In the United Kingdom, coal combustion was estimated to have contributed approximately 70 percent of total SPM emissions. n. Calculated from weighted average of 1978 and 1982 data. o. Motor vehicles only. p. Transport only.

sions in many industrialized countries. Countries with large hydro and nuclear electricity capacities have relatively smaller contributions from power generation. (See Tables 10.1 and 10.2.)

Globally, natural and anthropogenic sources add roughly equal amounts of sulfur compounds to the atmosphere. However, over land—and especially in industrialized regions—the fraction generated by people is much larger (2). For example, less than 2 percent of all sulfur emissions in the United States in 1980 were caused by decaying organic matter. The average annual emission of sulfur from Mount St. Helens, a U.S. volcano that erupted in the early 1980s, was equal to about 1 percent of U.S. anthropogenic emissions (3).

Global SO_2 emissions have been rising for more than a century. (See Figure 10.1.) Several countries, however, substantially reduced SO_2 emissions in 1970–85. (See Table 10.1.) Many developed countries experienced a pronounced shift away from heavy industries during that period. In addition, several countries imposed progressively stricter emission standards on pollution sources,

Table 10.2 Sulfur Dioxide Emissions and Electricity Generation in Selected Countries 1970–85

(grams per kilowatt hour)

		Fed. Rep. Germany	United Kingdom	France	United States	Canada
Percent of Total	1970	10	13	43	17	77
Electricity Generation from Nonfossil Fuels	1985	35	22	84	27	79
Electricity Generation Growth (percent)	1970–85	68	18	122	54	125
Sulfur Dioxide	1970	6.8	11.1	6.2[a]	9.6	2.5
Emissions from Electricity Generation per Unit of Electricity Generated from All Fuel Sources	1985	5.1[b]	8.6	2.4[c]	5.6	1.7[c]

Sources: Electricity: United Nations (U.N.), *Energy Statistics Yearbook, 1982* and *1985* (U.N., New York, 1984 and 1987); for 1982: Table 34, p. 388, p. 392, p. 402, and p. 404; for 1982: Table 38, p. 671, p. 673, p. 680, and p. 681. Sulfur Dioxide Emissions: refer to Table 10.1.
Notes:
a. 1973 data used in numerator and denominator; 1973 electricity generation calculated as the simple average of 1970 and 1975 data.
b. 1982 data used in numerator and denominator.
c. 1983 data used in numerator and denominator.

Figure 10.1 Global Sulfur Dioxide Emissions, 1860–1980

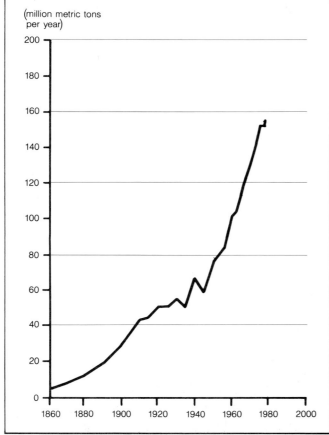

Source: D. Möller, "Estimation of the Global Man-Made Sulphur Emission," *Atmospheric Environment*, Vol. 18, No. 1 (1984), Figure 2, p. 24.

many cities exceeded the WHO-recommended levels, and 625 million people lived in urban areas where SO_2 pollution exceeded the WHO guideline (6).

Sulfur dioxide pollution in urban areas has declined substantially in several countries in the last decade. Most industrialized countries reduced SO_2 pollution by 20–60 percent in 1975–84. (See Table 10.3.) Box 10.1 discusses trends in SO_2 pollution in urban areas of developing countries.

Nitrogen Oxides

Sources and Emissions

Nitric oxide (NO) is emitted by several natural and anthropogenic processes; NO is then rapidly converted to nitrogen dioxide (NO_2) in the atmosphere. (NO_x is used to denote these two nitrogen oxides.) Nitrogen oxides damage human health and the natural environment.

NO is formed naturally when lightning causes molecular nitrogen and oxygen in the atmosphere to combine. NO is also emitted by microorganisms involved in the breakdown of organic matter. Anthropogenic NO_x emissions result from high–temperature combustion (e.g., that found in automobile engines) that provides sufficient energy for nitrogen and oxygen in the air to combine. Transportation and the generation of electricity are the most important anthropogenic sources. In the European Community, about 50 percent of anthropogenic emissions are from motor vehicles and 25–33 percent are from electricity generation (7). The transport sector emitted about 45 percent of the U.S. total in 1985, and 34 percent was emitted by electric utilities (8). Other industrialized countries showed similar patterns. (See Table 10.1.)

In temperate industrialized regions, it is likely that anthropogenic sources far outweigh natural sources. One estimate holds that 90 percent of all NO_x emissions in North America are anthropogenic (9). In the less industrialized tropics, however, anthropogenic emission rates are lower (although they may well rise as the use of automobiles and electricity increases), and about 60 percent of all lightning occurs in the tropics (10).

Trends in national NO_x emissions vary. Emissions rose in several countries from 1970 to 1980 and then stabilized or declined to roughly 1970 levels. In no country, however, was the decline in NO_x emissions as striking as that for SO_2 because NO_x emissions are more difficult to control than SO_2 emissions. The major SO_2 sources (coal-burning electricity plants) are large, and there are only a few of them, whereas the principal NO_x sources (vehicles) are small and numerous. As a result, NO_x sources are less easy to identify and regulate.

In the United States, for example, just 200 large coal-fired electricity plants were responsible for 57 percent of all SO_2 emissions in 1986 (11). Controlling NO_x emissions from U.S. vehicles, however, requires that each category of vehicle have its own emission standards and control technologies. Engine recalibration and catalysts to treat engine exhaust can reduce NO_x emissions from gasoline-powered automobiles more than two thirds per kilometer traveled. Standards were phased in between 1973 and 1981, and NO_x emissions from this class of vehicles

and some mandated the installation of flue gas desulfurization equipment (scrubbers) or other pollution control devices on new and/or existing facilities. The most important reduction of SO_2 emissions, however, came from switching to cleaner fuels. Many electric power plants have switched to lower-sulfur grades of coal; for example, the coal used by U.S. generating facilities in 1985 caused 44 percent less SO_2 to be emitted per unit of electricity generated than in 1975 (4). Other countries switched large fractions of their electricity-generating capacity away from coal altogether. (See Table 10.2.)

Ambient Levels

Most SO_2 monitoring is motivated by health concerns and is therefore conducted in urban and suburban areas. Thus "national" monitoring programs do not necessarily represent rural regions (5).

Figure 10.2 shows SO_2 pollution levels in 54 cities during the early 1980s. The five-year average SO_2 level in most cities was below or within the range of annual standards recommended by the World Health Organization (WHO) to protect human health. However, specific sites in

Figure 10.2 Sulfur Dioxide Levels in Selected Cities, 1980–84

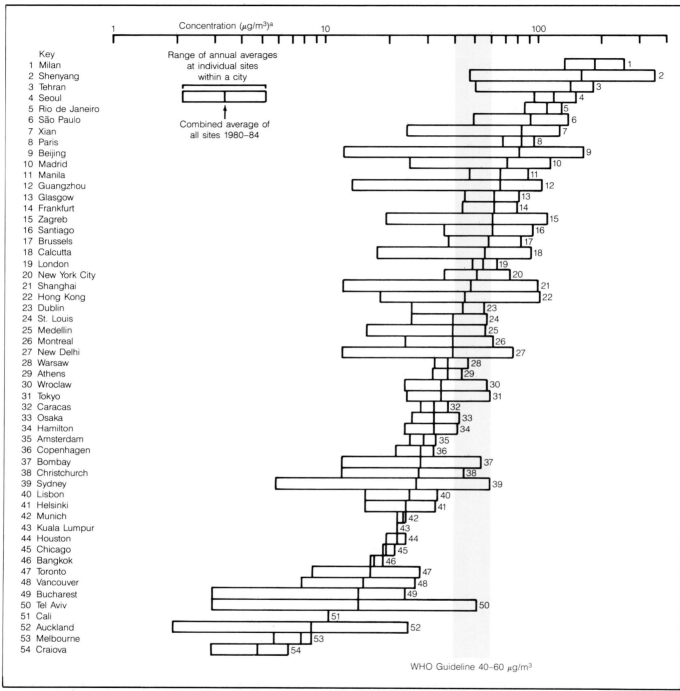

Source: World Health Organization and United Nations Environment Programme, *Global Pollution and Health* (Yale University Press, London, 1987), Figure 2, p. 5.
Note: a. Note logarithmic scale.

declined 21 percent between 1975 and 1985. Large diesel-powered trucks, however, require extensive engine modifications just to halve NO_x emissions. The emission standards for these trucks only began to be phased in in 1985; and NO_x emissions from these vehicles increased by 33 percent between 1975 and 1985 (12) (13).

Ambient Levels

Countries have had varying success controlling NO_x in urban air. All five countries that reported "national samples" to the Organisation for Economic Co-operation and Development (OECD) reported a decline in NO_x levels in

Table 10.3 Trends in Ambient Levels of Urban Air Pollution, 1975–84[a]

	Sulfur Dioxide		Nitrogen Oxides		Particulates	
	Percentage Change	Number of Monitoring Stations Used	Percentage Change	Number of Monitoring Stations Used	Percentage Change	Number of Monitoring Stations Used
National Samples[b]						
Canada	−53	46	−7[c]	27	−26	74
United States	−33	229	−10	119	−20	1344
Japan	−51	38	−11	31	X	X
Luxembourg	−64	12	X	X	−65	12
Norway	−40[d]	35	X	X	−24[c]	35
United Kingdom	−39[e]	X	X	X	X	X
Belgium	−19[f]	5	−18[f]	5	−19[f]	5
Netherlands	−33[f]	9	−6[f]	9	X	X
Developed World Cities[g]						
Australia (Sydney)	−19[h]	3	344[h]	2	−33[e]	5
Austria (Vienna)	−61[d]	1	74[f]	1	X	X
France (Paris)	−53[d]	13	X	X	−20[e]	13
Ireland (Dublin)	−40[e]	12	X	X	X	X
Italy (Rome)	22[i]	2	X	X	X	X
Portugal (Lisbon)	−1[d]	11	X	X	−13[i]	11
Sweden (Stockholm)	−54	5	29[k]	2	16[c]	3
Yugoslavia (Belgrade)	−17[l]	1	X	X	0[l]	1
Greece (Athens)	−38[m]	2	X	X	X	X
Poland (Warsaw)	17[m]	2	X	X	58[m]	2
United Kingdom (London)	X	X	−27	1	−53[d]	35
Japan (Tokyo)	X	X	X	X	−34	7

Sources:
1. Greece and Poland: Economic Commission for Europe (ECE), *Environmental Statistics in Europe and North America* (ECE, Geneva, 1987), Table I-23, p. I-60, Table I-35, p. I-62, and Table I-37, p. I-63.
2. All others: Organisation for Economic Co-operation and Development (OECD), *OECD Environmental Data Compendium 1987* (OECD, Paris, 1987), Tables 2.2A-2.2 C, pp. 30-37.
Notes:
a. All changes are from one date to the other, i.e., these changes do not reflect fitted regression lines. Country and city trends are determined from the simple average of trends in the mean values for all sites. City trends based on 1-5 sites are questionable, because conditions and trends may vary in different parts of a city.
b. Most national samples are biased towards urban areas. c. 1979-84. d. 1975-85. e. 1975-83. f. 1979-85. g. Trends in major cities do not necessarily reflect trends in other urban areas. h. 1975-82. i. 1979-82. j. 1981-85. k. 1981-84 l. 1979-83. m. 1980-85.
X=not available.

1975–84, but no decline in national NO$_x$ levels (with the exception of Belgium's) was as striking as the decline in national SO$_2$ levels. (See Table 10.3.)

Particulates

Particulates—solid and liquid materials suspended in the air—range from fine suspended aerosols to larger grit. The impact of particulate matter varies with its size and composition; larger particulates reduce visibility but have relatively minor health impacts. Finer particulates cause eye and lung damage and aggravate existing respiratory diseases.

Sources and Emissions

Particulates arise from both natural and anthropogenic sources. Dust, sea spray, forest fires, and volcanic emissions are among the natural sources. Most of these particulates are relatively large (14). Anthropogenic sources vary by country; in the Federal Republic of Germany and the United States, industry is the largest single source. (See Table 10.1.) In Ireland, domestic fuel combustion accounted for 80 percent of all particulate emissions in 1983 (15).

Several countries have reduced particulate emissions. The most important contributors to this reduction are installation of emission control equipment and switching to fuels that produce fewer particulates. In the United States, for example, the 1985 emission of particulates would have been 21.6 million metric tons rather than the 7.3 million metric tons that were emitted if emission

levels allowable in 1970 had not been tightened. U.S. emissions had already fallen 26 percent between 1950 and 1970 (16). Emission restrictions in the United Kingdom caused households to burn coal smokelessly or switch to smokeless fuels; particulate emissions from coal combustion declined 59 percent from 1960 to 1970, followed by an additional 63 percent decline between 1970 and 1986 (17).

Ambient Levels

The levels of particulate matter in the air of 41 urban areas are shown in Figure 10.3. The five-year average concentrations in about half the cities exceeded WHO guidelines, some by a substantial margin. Many other cities fell within the guideline values, and only a few cities met the guideline. The 10 cities with the highest levels are all in Asian developing countries, and 9 of the 10 cities with the lowest concentrations are in developed countries. This difference may reflect natural conditions in developing world cities (i.e., some cities have high levels of naturally occurring dust) as well as the stricter emission controls in force in developed world cities (18).

Reflecting the decrease in particulate emissions, ambient levels of particulates also declined in most countries and cities for which trend data were available. (See Table 10.3.) Only a few of these cities registered increasing particulate levels over the past 15 years. For example, Warsaw's particulate pollution worsened by 58 percent (1980–85) and Stockholm's by 16 percent (1979–84). Particulate pollution in urban areas of developing countries is discussed in Box 10.1.

Carbon Monoxide

Carbon monoxide (CO) is an odorless, colorless gas that, when inhaled, inhibits blood's absorption of oxygen. Oxygen deficiency can lead to angina, impaired vision, and poor physical and mental coordination (19). CO has no direct impacts on the natural environment (20), but it is critical to processes affecting the levels of tropospheric oxidants, greenhouse gases, and stratospheric ozone.

Sources and Emissions

Natural sources of carbon monoxide, chiefly decomposition of organic matter, account for 60–90 percent of global emissions (21) (22). However, anthropogenic sources far outweigh natural sources in certain urban areas and regions. The main anthropogenic source of CO is incomplete combustion of fossil fuels, especially in the transport sector. In 1985, the transport sector contributed 59–84 percent of anthropogenic emissions in the five countries for which data were available. (See Table 10.1.) Between 1970 and 1985, CO emissions declined 32 percent in the United States and 45 percent in the Federal Republic of Germany. Emissions increased 15 percent in the United Kingdom between 1975 and 1985.

Ambient Levels

Only a few countries regularly monitor ambient CO levels (23). In Japan, a network of monitoring stations located along roadways has recorded a steady decline in ambient CO levels, amounting to a 58 percent decrease between 1971 and 1984. In 1984, a larger network of 192 monitoring stations found ambient air in full compliance with Japan's daily (10 parts per million (ppm)) and eight-hour (20 ppm) CO standards (24). In the United States, ambient levels of CO decreased 36 percent between 1976 and 1985 as measured by a network of 163 monitoring stations. Over this same period, the number of exceedances of the U.S. eight-hour CO standard (9 ppm) declined 92 percent (25).

Lead

High levels of lead compounds have deleterious impacts on the natural environment and on human health. In natural ecosystems, lead is toxic to microorganisms, inhibiting the decomposition of organic matter. High concentrations of lead inhibit photosynthesis and plant respiration under laboratory conditions. Because lead is not removed from natural ecosystems in any significant degree, elevated lead levels and their impacts are essentially permanent. In animals, including humans, lead contamination has toxic impacts on the neurological system (especially in children) and causes kidney disease. It may also affect fetal development and the immune system (26).

Sources and Emissions

Most lead in the living environment is from anthropogenic sources (27). Lead has been used for millennia in coins, piping, and roofing. However, most lead emissions (70–90 percent) come from the use of leaded gasoline. (See Table 10.1.) Several countries have recently taken significant steps to eliminate lead additives from gasoline. The result is a dramatic decline in lead emissions and ambient levels since the 1970s—a major environmental success. The European Community gradually tightened restrictions on lead additives, with allowable levels dropping from 0.4 grams per liter (g/l) in 1978 to 0.15 g/l in 1985. Member countries were directed to make unleaded gasoline (with less than 0.013 g/l of lead) available by October 1989 (28).

The Japanese Government directed refineries to reduce the lead content of gasoline in 1970, and lead-free gasoline was introduced in 1975. Currently, 99 percent of all gasoline sold in Japan is lead free (29). The United Kingdom reduced allowable lead levels in gasoline from 0.84 g/l in 1972 to 0.40 g/l in 1981 and to 0.15 g/l in December 1985. Unleaded gasoline was introduced in 1985. Emissions declined 12 percent from 1975 to 1985 (while gasoline sales increased 27 percent) and 55 percent between 1985 and 1986 (30).

Beginning in the early 1970s, the U.S. Environmental Protection Agency (U.S. EPA) gradually restricted the level of lead allowed in gasoline; the most recent cut reduced gasoline lead levels from 0.26 g/l in early 1985 to 0.026 g/l in January 1986. Additionally, the U.S. EPA mandated the availability of unleaded gasoline in 1975 to prevent "poisoning" of catalytic converters then being installed on automobiles to control NO_x, CO, and hydrocarbon emissions (31). These measures produced a 90 percent reduction in lead emissions between 1970 and 1985. Had 1970 emissions standards remained in effect, 1985 emissions would have been 10 percent *higher* than they were in 1970 (32).

Ambient Levels

Several countries monitor the ambient levels of lead in the air. Lead concentrations have generally declined over the past 15 years. One monitoring site (with the highest pollutant levels) in Paris reported a 50 percent decline in lead levels between 1978 and 1983 (33). A 21-site network in the United Kingdom reported a 50 percent decline in lead levels between the first quarters of 1985 and 1986 (34). More than 50 urban monitoring sites in the United States reported a 79 percent drop in lead levels between 1976 and 1985 and an additional 35 percent drop between 1985 and 1986 (35) (36). Sampling stations in 53 Canadian cities reported a 55 percent decline in the annual mean lead level between 1975 and 1983 (37).

Hydrocarbons, Tropospheric Ozone, and Photochemical Oxidants

Ozone (O_3) is formed in the lower atmosphere (troposphere) by reactions among NO_2, CO, oxygen, and hydrocarbons other than methane. These reactions are triggered by sunlight, and they may also produce hydrogen peroxide (H_2O_2), peroxyacetyl nitrate (PAN), and other compounds (38). O_3, PAN, H_2O_2, and a few other chemicals are called photochemical oxidants: *photochemical* because of the essential role that sunlight plays in their formation and *oxidant* because they react strongly with other materials. Photochemical oxidants damage vegetation, human health, and materials.

Sources and Emissions of Hydrocarbons

The two primary ozone-forming chemicals are NO_x and hydrocarbons. (See Table 10.1.) This section focuses on hydrocarbons, which not only contribute to ozone formation but are pollutants in their own right. Several hydrocarbon compounds are known or suspected carcinogens, mutagens, or teratogens [39].

Anthropogenic hydrocarbon emissions result mainly from incomplete combustion of fossil fuels, although storage and transportation of fossil fuels, industrial processes, and solvent evaporation also contribute. Natural sources of hydrocarbon emissions include: vegetation, microbial decomposition, forest fires, and natural gas seeps. The relative importance of anthropogenic and natural hydrocarbon sources on a global scale is unknown. In the United States, they are apparently of the same order of magnitude on an annual basis. Because most natural emissions occur in the sunny months, they are more important in oxidant formation than they would be if the emissions were spread evenly over the year [40].

Trend data on anthropogenic hydrocarbon emissions are available for several countries. (See Table 10.1.) Most countries experienced little change in emissions from 1970 to 1985; the largest changes were in the United Kingdom (up 12 percent between 1975 and 1985) and the United States (down 22 percent between 1970 and 1985).

Figure 10.3 Suspended Particulate Matter Levels in Selected Cities, 1980–84

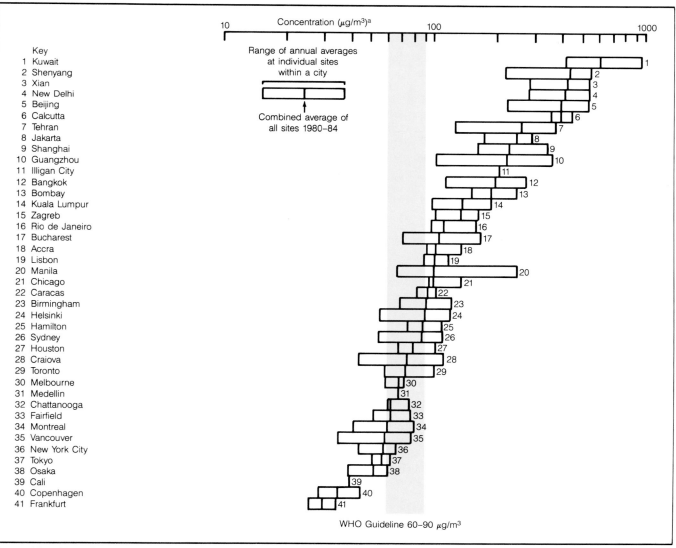

Source: World Health Organization and United Nations Environment Programme, *Global Pollution and Health* (Yale University Press, London, 1987), Figure 3, p. 6.
Note: a. Note logarithmic scale.

Ambient Tropospheric Ozone Levels

Tropospheric ozone pollution is monitored by a few countries. Canada's ozone monitoring network of more than 40 stations has reported no significant trend between 1979 and 1985. More than half the stations have reported annual mean ozone concentrations in excess of the Canadian standard (15 parts per billion (ppb)) throughout the period. In the United States, a 242-site network reported a 13 percent decline in peak ozone levels between 1979 and 1986; however, 5–10 sites per day had ozone levels that exceeded the U.S. ozone standard (41). More than 75 million people live in U.S. counties that exceeded the national ozone standard in 1986 (42). In Japan, 171 photochemical oxidant warnings were issued in 1985 (43), the fourth annual increase in the number of warnings since the record low of 59 in 1981. Before then, the number of warnings had declined steadily from a peak of more than 300 in 1973 (44).

Acidic Deposition

In addition to their direct health and ecological impacts, SO_2 and NO_x also contribute to acidic deposition. A variety of other compounds in the atmosphere (e.g., tropospheric ozone) reacts with SO_2 and NO_x to form gaseous, particulate, and aqueous acids. These acids are removed from the atmosphere in wet (rain, hail, and snow) and dry deposition, damaging vegetation, lakes, streams, and structures. Because wet deposition is better understood and more easily measured than dry deposition, the discussion here treats wet deposition only. Dry deposition, however, is an important contributor to acidification, especially near large pollution sources (45).

Natural Levels of Wet Acidic Deposition

Precipitation is naturally somewhat acidic because atmospheric carbon dioxide dissolves in water, forming carbonic acid. It gives rainwater a pH of about 5.6 (46). This natural pH varies according to local natural influences. In the arid western United States, for example, the natural pH is believed to be 5.3—6.0; in the moister eastern United States, it is about 5.0 (47).

Current Levels of Wet Acidic Deposition

The pattern of wet acidic deposition in North America and Europe is shown in Chapter 23, "Atmosphere and Climate," Figures 23.2 and 23.3. It is clear that wide areas of both continents are currently receiving anthropogenically acidified precipitation. Most of the developing world (with the exception of China) appears to have no serious acidic deposition problem, although increases in SO_2 and NO_x emissions may bring one about (48). Acidic deposition monitoring in developing countries is limited compared with North America and Europe. (See *World Resources 1986*, Table 11.7, p. 325.)

The long-term trends in acidification in Europe and North America are uncertain; spatially and temporally comparable acidic deposition data have been collected only since 1978. Trends in urban SO_2 and NO_x concentrations cannot be used to predict acidic deposition trends because part of the decline in urban pollution levels results from a diversion of emissions to other areas. In the United States and United Kingdom, for example, electricity generation facilities installed tall smokestacks to reduce local SO_2 pollution (49) and many new facilities were sited in nonurban areas (50). The effect of these trends has been to disperse pollutant emissions and to inject them higher into the atmosphere, making long-range transport and acidic deposition more likely.

An analysis of 44 monitoring stations in eastern North America found that sulfate concentrations in precipitation declined significantly at 15 stations (no change at 29), and nitrate concentrations declined significantly at 5 (1 increase and 38 unchanged) between 1978 and 1984 (51). The acidity of precipitation declined at 5 of 30 stations (most in eastern North America) in 1979–85 and remained unchanged at the other 25 (52). No similar analysis has been done for Europe (53).

Important Trace Gases

Several trace gases directly influence climate through the greenhouse effect. In addition, some directly and indirectly influence stratospheric ozone depletion. Trends in emissions of these gases are shown in Chapter 23, "Atmosphere and Climate," Table 23.2. Figure 23.1 shows long-term trends in atmospheric concentrations.

Sources, Emissions, and Ambient Levels

Carbon dioxide (CO_2) is emitted from natural and anthropogenic sources. Natural sources include volcanic emissions and decaying organic matter. Anthropogenic sources are dominated by fossil fuel combustion; they also include natural gas flaring and cement production. Annual emissions from these sources more than tripled between 1950 and 1986. Clearing land for agriculture and grazing is an additional source because carbon stored in vegetation is released to the atmosphere when the total biomass of an area is reduced. The level of CO_2 in the atmosphere fluctuated between 190 and 290 ppm for the 160,000 years before the Industrial Revolution (54). Since 1750, the level has been rising and the rate of increase accelerating (55). The atmospheric concentration in 1987 was 349 ppm, up from 316 in 1959. (See Table 23.1.)

Chlorofluorocarbons (CFCs) are a group of synthetic industrial chemicals used as aerosol propellants, refrigerant working fluids, solvents, and foam blowing agents. Emissions of these gases increased from 100 to 35,000 metric tons between 1931 and 1950 and to 649,000 metric tons by 1985. Measurements taken at Cape Meares, Oregon, in the United States, showed that the concentration of CFC-12 in the atmosphere increased from 200 parts per trillion (ppt) in 1975 to 384 ppt in 1985; at the same time, CFC-11 increased from 120 to 223 ppt.

Methane (CH_4) is emitted by a variety of sources, both natural and anthropogenic. Natural sources include wetlands and wild ruminants. Human-influenced sources include extensive rice cultivation, livestock management, natural gas venting, and biomass combustion. Emission trends cannot be determined because other sources may

Box 10.1 Urban Air Pollution in Developing Countries

With the exception of Milan, all of the worst-polluted cities that report data to the Global Environmental Monitoring System (GEMS) are in developing countries. (See Figures 10.2 and 10.3.)

The data in Table 1 are from GEMS urban air quality monitoring stations operated by national institutions that have adopted GEMS-designed siting guidelines, monitoring methods, and quality control programs to ensure that data are comparable among countries [1]. Thus GEMS data are essential for worldwide analysis of urban air quality. Although many nations have sophisticated national air monitoring systems, because they use different designs and operations their data are not comparable, thus are not shown here.

There are several dozen GEMS stations in the developing countries of Latin America and Asia, including 20 stations in China that commenced operations in 1981. Only a few stations have been sited in Africa, and most of these are moribund.

Average and peak concentrations of suspended particulate matter (SPM) exceeded the air quality standards recommended by the World Health Organization (WHO) at 62 of the 73 monitoring sites in developing countries; only eight South American monitoring sites, and no Asian sites, had SPM levels that fully complied with WHO standards. (By comparison, about half the GEMS stations in developed countries are in compliance with WHO standards.) SPM levels in a few South American cities exceeded the standards by a factor of two and SPM levels in some Asian cities exceeded the standards by factors of three to five. The trend in SPM pollution is ambiguous; more stations showed declines than increases in average SPM levels, but the opposite was true for peak values.

Sulfur dioxide (SO_2) pollution levels in developing-country cities were not as bad as SPM pollution: about half the stations recorded SO_2 levels that exceeded WHO standards. (About 15 percent of the GEMS stations in developed countries also exceeded the standards.) Trend data indicate neither a broad improvement nor a worsening of SO_2 pollution: approximately equal numbers of stations reported increases and decreases in SO_2 pollution over the 1979–85 period.

The causes of urban air pollution vary. In Beijing, for example, household coal burning bears much of the blame. Seventy-seven percent of the fuel consumed in Beijing in 1980 was coal, much of which was not washed or pretreated to reduce its ash and sulfur content. In winter, 1.5 million small coal-fired furnaces and household stoves are used for

space heating and cooking, emitting 22 tons of particulates per day from low chimneys, and causing SPM levels to increase by 300–500 micrograms per cubic meter over summer values [2]. These heaters and stoves may also contribute up to 72 percent of the city's SO_2 concentration [3].

Industrial emissions are responsible for the majority of Sao Paulo's air pollution. More than 45,000 industrial enterprises are located in the greater Sao Paulo region, making it the most densely industrialized region of South America. In 1976, the State of Sao Paulo's environmental protection agency—the Companhia de Saneamento Ambiental (CETESB)—was given authority to control industrial pollution and embarked on a program to cap SPM emissions and cut SO_2 emissions 80 percent by the end of 1985 [4]. CETESB set standards for emissions and for facility design (such as chimney height), licensed facilities in compliance with the standards, fined or closed violators, and forbade the establishment of new industrial pollution sources in pollution-saturated areas [5]. By 1985, CETESB's efforts produced some tangible results: three GEMS stations in Sao Paulo each monitored six annual reductions in SO_2 levels from 1980 to 1985, yielding a 56–62 percent drop in mean levels. Particulate pollution, however, neither

increased nor decreased over the same period.

References and Notes

1. See, for example, World Health Organization (WHO) and World Meteorological Organization (WMO), *Air Monitoring Programme Design for Urban and Industrial Areas* (WHO, Geneva, 1977), and WHO, *Selected Methods of Measuring Air Pollutants* (WHO, Geneva, 1976).
2. Su Ge, "A Critical Review of Air Pollution Research in China over the Last Decade," Master's Thesis, Oregon Graduate Center, Beaverton, Oregon, 1986, pp. 31–33.
3. Dianwu Zhao and Bozen Sun, "Air Pollution and Acid Rain in China," *Ambio*, Vol. 15, No. 1 (1986), pp. 3–4.
4. L.M. Moreira-Nordemann *et al.*, "Some Aspects of Environmental Problems in Sao Paulo State (Brazil)," paper presented at Symposium on Acidification in Tropical Countries, Caracas, Venezuela, April 6–11, 1986, pp. 58–59, and p. 67.
5. Vinod Thomas, *Pollution Control in Sao Paulo, Brazil: Costs, Benefits and Effects on Industrial Locations* (The World Bank, Washington, D.C., 1981), pp. 32–35.

Table 1 Conditions and Trends in Urban Air Pollution in Developing Countries, 1979–85[a]

| | | Number of Monitoring Stations[b] | | | |
| | | Sulfur Dioxide | | Suspended Particulate Matter | |
		Average Levels[c]	Peak Levels[c]	Average Levels[c]	Peak Levels[c]
South America					
Conditions[d]	Below WHO Standard[e]	8	9	8	7
	Within WHO Standard	4	4	1	1
	Above WHO Standard	6	5	11	12
Trends[f]	Downward	4	8	3	3
	None	3	1	2	2
	Upward	6	4	2	2
Asia					
Conditions	Below WHO Standard	15	12	0	0
	Within WHO Standard	6	4	2	3
	Above WHO Standard	26	31	51	50
Trends	Downward	4	4	14	7
	None	3	1	2	1
	Upward	5	7	3	11

Source: World Health Organization (WHO) and United Nations Environment Programme (UNEP), unpublished data (WHO/UNEP, February 1988).

Notes: a. No African monitoring site had data that met the criteria discussed in notes d and f. b. Data were largely drawn from Chapter 23, "Atmosphere and Climate," Tables 23.4 and 23.5 c. Average levels refer to the annual mean of daily values; peak levels refer to the 98th percentile of daily values. d. Condition data refer to 1982-85 or 1979-81 period averages, which had at least 2 years of data. e. WHO's air quality standards are discussed in the Technical Notes for Chapter 23, "Atmosphere and Climate," Tables 23.4 and 23.5. f. Trends were calculated if there were at least 2 years of data in the 1982-85 period and at least two years of data in the 1979-81 period. Upward and downward trends in the average required a change of at least six ug/m³ between periods. Trends in peak values required a change of at least 11 ug/m³.

---

be discovered, and the emission rates of the known sources are uncertain. The atmospheric concentration of methane was steady at a level of 700 ppb between about 1500 BC and 1700 AD, when it began to increase. The rate of increase has grown from about 1.5 ppb per year during the period 1700–1900 to the current rate of 17 ppb per year. The current atmospheric concentration of methane is 1,711 ppb [56].

Nitrous oxide (N_2O) is emitted by the decomposition of organic matter and the combustion of fossil fuels and biomass. Its emissions may be enhanced by the use of artificial fertilizers. As with methane, the total emission rate is unknown because several of the emission sources probably remain to be discovered. (See Chapter 11, "Global Systems and Cycles," The Global Nitrogen Cycle.) The atmospheric concentration of N_2O was steady at a level of 285 ppb between 3,000 and 150 years ago. The level in 1984 was 307 ppb and increasing at a rate of about 0.8 ppb per year. The increase is probably due to the increased use of fossil fuels and, to a lesser extent, to nitrogen fertilizers (57).

IMPACTS ON THE BIOSPHERE FROM TROPOSPHERIC POLLUTION, GREENHOUSE WARMING, AND OZONE LAYER DEPLETION

Each of the pollutants discussed above has a direct damaging effect on human health or the environment. Many of these also interact with other pollutants to indirectly add to the problems of tropospheric pollution, climate change, and depletion of stratospheric ozone. Impacts in each of these areas are examined in this section.

Tropospheric Pollution

Tropospheric pollution damages agricultural crops, forests, aquatic systems, structural materials, and human health. Primary tropospheric pollutants (SO_2, NO_x, hydrocarbons, and CO) often react in the atmosphere to form secondary pollutants (e.g., acidic compounds and photochemical oxidants). Environmental damage frequently results from several primary and secondary pollutants acting in concert rather than from a single pollutant.

Impacts on Agricultural Crops

Both ozone and PAN damage crops and natural vegetation; PAN primarily affects herbaceous crops. Ozone injures plant tissues, inhibits photosynthesis, and increases the susceptibility of crops to other pollutants, disease, and drought (58). Average ozone concentrations in the eastern United States are high enough to cause yield reductions ranging from 1 percent or less for sorghum and corn, to around 7 percent for cotton and soybeans, to over 30 percent for alfalfa (59). Overall, United States crop yields are probably depressed by 5–10 percent (60), representing an estimated economic loss of $1–2 billion annually (61).

The co-occurrence of ozone with sulfur dioxide and nitrogen dioxide can increase the susceptibility of vegetation to damage. U.S. studies indicate that sulfur dioxide may increase the sensitivity of plants to leaf injury by ozone (62); research in West Germany and the Netherlands indicates that combinations of ozone, sulfur dioxide, and nitrogen dioxide may reduce dry matter production more than ozone alone or a combination of two pollutants (63).

Highly acidic rain lowers agricultural crop yields under laboratory conditions, but the impact of ambient acidic deposition on crop production is negligible (64). Nevertheless, it is possible that certain local conditions, such as those in the immediate vicinity of a pollution source, may raise acidic concentrations to damaging levels.

Impacts on Forests

Acidic deposition and oxidant pollutants are contributing to the destruction of forests, especially in Europe and North America. (See Chapter 18, "Forests and Rangelands," Table 18.3 and *World Resources 1986*, Chapter 12, "Multiple Pollutants and Forest Decline.") Forest decline may be triggered by leaf damage caused by acidic compounds, soil acidification, the combined stresses of multiple pollutants, and direct exposure to oxidants.

Oxidants such as ozone can make trees more vulnerable to disease, interfere with photosynthesis, and damage leaf cells, increasing the loss of nutrients that are leached by acidic rain and mists (65). Oxidant damage on forests looks like the crown dieback seen in European forests, where the foliage yellows from the top down and drops off (66).

Peak ozone concentrations experienced in the United States are toxic to tree seedlings, and they are suspected of inducing stress and reducing growth in some regional forests (e.g., Jeffrey and Ponderosa pine trees in the San Bernardino National Forest in California) (67). Repeated ozone peaks have damaged white pine in the eastern United States and Canada and have reduced growth rates for red spruce at high elevations in the Appalachian Mountains.

Damage to forests from acidic deposition occurs both above and below ground. Foliar damage and mortality are common symptoms of acidic deposition in certain high-elevation forests of Europe and North America, perhaps because clouds, mist, and fog are considerably more acidic than acid rain (68). Soil acidification displaces nutrients and leaches aluminum, a metal that is toxic to plants, out of the soil minerals and into organic matter. The loss of nutrients retards plant growth, and the aluminum inhibits root absorption of water and the remaining nutrients. Once depleted, the soil will take decades to rejuvenate. Over the long term, soil acidification may be the greatest threat to forests (69).

Impacts on Aquatic Systems

Because of acidic deposition, some susceptible lakes in North America and Europe can no longer support aquatic life. The most sensitive lakes in these areas now lack a natural ability to neutralize acids after decades of absorbing acidic compounds, so that additional acidic deposition simply increases their acidity. Half the 700,000 lakes in the six eastern provinces of Canada are extremely acid sensitive, as are many in the northern United States. The Netherlands, Belgium, Denmark, Switzerland, Italy, West Germany, Ireland, and Scandinavia all have acid-sensitive areas. Vast areas in Asia, Africa, and South America are also acid sensitive (70).

Most early records of damage to fish populations focused on adult game fish instead of on the more sensitive juveniles and organisms lower in the food chain (71). The early disappearance of this part of the food chain may starve larger predatory fish well before the direct toxic action of increased acidity kills them. The few case studies focused on streams indicate that their biota may be even more sensitive to acidification than that of lakes. Aluminum released to lakes and streams from acidified soils and sediments is also toxic to fish. For these reasons, estimates of damage to aquatic communities caused by acidic deposition may be too low (72).

If acidic deposition is reduced, the natural chemistry of damaged lakes may be restored; however, it may take many years for them to return to their original conditions because soils are slow to recover.

Impacts on Structures and Materials

All materials suffer degradation from natural weathering processes, but air pollution has accelerated degradation rates since the mid-19th Century (73). Wet and dry acidic deposition and tropospheric oxidants are the principal agents of this destruction.

Ozone damages natural and synthetic rubber and fades certain dyes (74); SO_2 corrodes metals, building materials, and paint (75); NO_x also damages materials (76). Acidic deposition causes corrosion and tarnishing of metals; erosion and soiling of surface stone, brick, and concrete; and erosion, discoloration, and peeling of paint (77). Limestone and marble, which were commonly used in historic buildings and monuments, are also highly susceptible to damage by gaseous sulfur oxides (78).

Impacts on Human Health

Tropospheric pollutants have significant effects on human health. Ozone damages lung and respiratory tract tissue (79). Sulfuric acid aerosols damage the lungs' interior protective linings, and exposure to sulfur dioxide and nitrogen dioxide may affect respiratory functions (80). Nitrogen oxides, hydrocarbons, and carbon monoxide react in sunlight to form photochemical smog, which causes health problems (81).

Some population groups are especially sensitive to tropospheric pollutants. For example, asthmatics are particularly sensitive—exposure increases airway resistance and bronchoconstriction following exercise (82). For all groups, the level of physical activity may be a factor in the health effects of pollution, just as pollution levels are (83).

Acidic deposition may indirectly affect human health by leaching toxic metals and asbestos into drinking water from watersheds, sediments, and plumbing (84) (85). In addition, mercury levels in food fish increase as the acidity of water increases (86).

The London smog of 1952 is believed to have caused 4,000 premature deaths from heart and lung ailments. During the 1970s, pollution-related health problems in the United States alone cost billions annually. Today, evidence from Katowice, Poland, one of the most polluted cities in the world, shows that pollution is causing circulatory and respiratory disease, cancers, and deformation in children (87).

Climate Change

Concern over probable changes in climate arises from the buildup of greenhouse gases in the troposphere. These gases—carbon dioxide, methane, ozone, CFCs, nitrous oxide, and other trace gases—essentially form a partial energy shield around the Earth. They allow solar energy in but slow the loss of reradiated heat from the Earth's surface and lower atmosphere.

Although many uncertainties remain about the expected extent and timing of climate change, the consensus of recent studies is that the greenhouse effect will result in a warmer planet (88). The global average temperature could rise anywhere from 1–7°C by 2030, with the most likely increase being between 1.5–4.5°C based upon a projected greenhouse effect equivalent to a doubling of atmospheric CO_2 over preindustrial levels (89). To judge the severity of such a change, one must realize that the coldest global average surface temperature during the Ice Age was only 5°C lower than it is today (90). A 5°C rise in temperature would make the planet warmer than at any time in the last 2 million years (91).

Under these circumstances, the average air temperature would increase about 4°C over much of Europe and North America, about 5°C over much of the Sahara, and even more at latitudes above 60° (92). The number of days per year on which the temperature in New York exceeds 32°C would triple from the present 15 to 48. In Chicago, the number would rise from 16 to 56 and, in Los Angeles, from 5 to 27 (93).

Until recently, carbon dioxide released from fuel combustion and deforestation was considered the chief contributor to the greenhouse effect. During the past decade, however, it was discovered that other trace gases collectively contribute to greenhouse warming on a scale comparable to that of carbon dioxide. These gases may account for nearly 50 percent of the incremental greenhouse effect by the 1990s (94).

The effects of rising global temperatures will be felt in regional climate changes and precipitation, rising sea levels, and agriculture.

Impacts on Regional Climate and Precipitation

No one really knows how regional climates will respond to greenhouse warming. Computer models can simulate large-scale climate responses but cannot accurately simulate all the detailed factors affecting regional climates. For example, contemporary models assume that ocean currents, which are important in shaping regional climate, will remain relatively stable. However, geological evidence indicates that sudden shifts in ocean currents coincided with major changes in the global climate (95). Secondary climate feedback mechanisms may also affect regional climate. For example, warmer temperatures may increase the evaporation rate, thereby increasing the amount of atmospheric water vapor and cloud cover, which in turn may affect regional rainfall patterns.

A warmer climate will probably shift the middle-latitude rainbelt poleward, as moisture-laden air from the tropical oceans travels farther toward the poles before the moisture condenses as precipitation. In winter, soil wetness may increase in these areas because of increased precipitation and because more of the precipitation would fall as rain rather than as snow. In summer, the shift of precipitation patterns may cause soil in Southern Europe, North America, and Siberia to be drier than it now is (96).

Compounding this effect over Siberia and the Great Plains of North America is the probability of an earlier snow melt in a warmer climate. An early melt would cause the soil to absorb more solar energy, in turn caus-

Figure 10.4 Coastal Impacts of Sea-Level Rise in Bangladesh

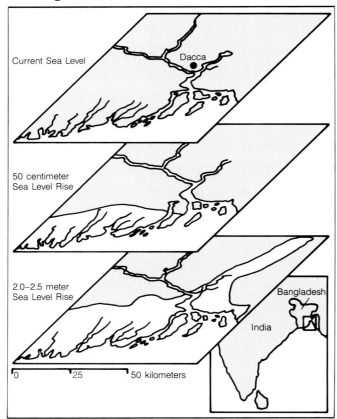

Current Sea Level

Dacca

50 centimeter
Sea Level Rise

2.0–2.5 meter
Sea Level Rise

Bangladesh

India

0   25   50 kilometers

Source: United Nations Environment Programme (UNEP), *The Greenhouse Gases,* UNEP/Global Environment Monitoring System Environment Library No. 1 (UNEP, Nairobi, 1987), p. 31.

ing more moisture to evaporate from the soil in those regions. These increased evaporation rates could reduce total runoff even in areas where rainfall increases. As a result soil could become dryer than normal in the summer. With less water in the soil, evaporation rates would probably decrease, which in turn may reduce cloud cover, and increase the amount of solar energy striking the Earth's surface. This increase might further enhance soil drying (97). (See Chapter 11, "Global Systems and Cycles," The Global Water Cycle.)

Potential for Rising Sea Levels

A rise in sea level is probably the most widely recognized consequence of global warming. In a warmer climate, the oceans would expand when heated, and polar ice packs in Greenland and Antarctica may partially melt (98). Scientists calculate that the expansion effect alone could raise sea levels 20–140 centimeters if the average temperature rises 1.5–4.5°C. A temperature rise in the middle of this range might increase sea levels 80 centimeters, more than enough to flood vast unprotected coastal lands (99).

Such a rise in sea level could inundate low-lying areas,

destroy coastal marshes and swamps, erode shorelines, worsen coastal flooding, and increase the salinity of rivers, bays, and aquifers. Nearly one third the human population lives within 60 kilometers of a coast (100), and many reside on land that would be lost. In Egypt, a 50-centimeter rise in sea level would displace 16 percent of the population. The situation in Bangladesh might be even worse—a 50-centimeter rise would flood large areas of the country, and a 2-meter rise would claim 28 percent of the land, where 27 percent of its people live (101). (See Figure 10.4.) A 2-meter rise could cost the Dutch $8.8 billion more to hold back the sea (102).

Low-lying coastal areas may also be more vulnerable to storms and their floods, especially if warmer water increases storm frequency (103). If coastal areas suffer more erosion, funds may be spent on saving developed coastal areas rather than undeveloped coastal ecosystems, and those ecosystems would be lost. (See Chapter 9, "Oceans and Coasts," Recent Developments.)

Impacts on Agriculture and Vegetation

Changes in climate and the composition of the atmosphere may bring significant changes to regions traditionally rich in agriculture and alter the global distribution of natural vegetation. Climate has frequently changed in the past (see Chapter 11, "Global Systems and Cycles," Environmental History), but anthropogenic change is likely to occur much more rapidly. During past climate changes, vegetation communities have "migrated" to favorable areas, but this climate change may occur too rapidly and some species may be lost. Eventually, forests could be replaced by shrubby woodland that is adapted to a wider variety of environmental conditions (104).

A small absolute increase in temperature could create a larger response in cool climate ecosystems than in warm climate ecosystems. Similarly, a small absolute increase in moisture could more profoundly affect arid regions. The environmental changes required for a change in vegetation of comparable magnitude in a wet, warm region would have to be much greater than in a cool, dry region. Thus, one would expect the boreal forests to be most sensitive to a climate warming (105).

As noted earlier, climate changes may lead to drier summer soil over extensive mid-continental regions of North America, Southern Europe, and Siberia (106). As a result, global warming may damage some of the world's most agriculturally productive regions—the core wheat-growing areas of North America and Europe, for example. However, other regions may become more favorable for agricultural production (107).

Indirect factors, such as changing soil chemistries, insect populations, and disease, may be equally significant. Outbreaks of many plant diseases, including potato blight and wheat rust, are triggered by specific weather conditions. Climate changes may affect the frequency or incidence of such outbreaks (108). On the other hand, studies on individual trees under controlled conditions have shown that elevated CO_2 levels promote growth, at least in the short term. However, whether such effects would be sustained over the long term in natural forest environments is uncertain (109).

Depletion of the Stratospheric Ozone Layer

Ozone in the stratosphere is a shield that reduces the amount of harmful ultraviolet (UV-B) radiation reaching the Earth's surface. Increased levels of UV-B radiation are expected to affect not only humans, but also vegetation, wildlife, and aquatic organisms.

Impacts on Human Health

Direct exposure to UV-B radiation damages both skin and eyes. Added exposure could increase the incidence of skin cancers and cataracts, suppress the immune system response, and, as a result, increase the occurrence of some infectious diseases. Overall, sun induces over 50 percent of all skin diseases among fair-skinned people in areas with prolonged sun exposure. Fair-skinned individuals are more prone than others to all types of sun-induced skin cancers. Ultraviolet radiation also ages the skin prematurely (110).

Worldwide, some 100,000 people die from skin cancers each year, and UV-B is implicated in most cases. For each 1 percent depletion of the ozone layer in the stratosphere, the incidence of skin cancers would rise an estimated 2 percent (111).

Impacts on Vegetation

Virtually nothing was known about the effects of UV radiation on plants 15 years ago (112). Today, more than 200 plant species and varieties have been tested under increased exposure to UV radiation, and two thirds showed sensitivity (113). Most (90 percent) of the studies involved crop species; members of the pea and bean, squash and melon, and cabbage families are especially sensitive (114).

Plant response to UV radiation varies. In general, UV radiation reduces leaf size and thus the area available to capture sunlight for photosynthesis. Stunted growth is often typical of UV-irradiated plants. In addition, seed quality sometimes suffers; preliminary studies on soybeans suggest increased susceptibility to weeds, pests, and disease. Little is known about UV radiation effects on natural plant communities. The distribution of plant species could well be quite different in a UV-enriched future—if UV-tolerant plants proliferate at the expense of UV-sensitive ones (115).

Impacts on Aquatic Systems

Not enough is yet known to quantify the risks of ozone depletion to aquatic ecosystems. However, the sensitivity of aquatic organisms in laboratory studies to relatively small increases in UV-B indicates a potentially great risk (116).

Aquatic plants, most of which grow near the surface, are likely to suffer from depletion of stratospheric ozone (117). For phytoplankton, the small plants at the bottom of the aquatic food web, a change in species composition rather than a decrease in net production may result (118). This reduction in species diversity may increase susceptibility of phytoplankton communities to changes in water temperature, nutrient availability, disease, and pollution (119).

Because aquatic plants provide food for almost all fish, changes in plant productivity affect fish populations. Further, increased UV-B radiation causes direct damage to zooplankton, fish larvae and juveniles, shrimp larvae, crab larvae, and other organisms essential to the aquatic food web (120). Some species cannot tolerate additional UV-B radiation exposure (121). For example, the number of abnormal anchovy larvae could increase as much as 18 percent from a 10 percent reduction in the stratospheric ozone (122). A 15-day exposure to UV-B levels 20 percent higher than normal can kill off anchovy larvae to a water depth of 10 meters (123).

FOCUS ON: THE INTERACTIONS AMONG POLLUTANTS AND ATMOSPHERIC PROCESSES

The intricate interactions of pollutants and their effects in various levels of atmosphere are only partially understood. Although some pollutants may exacerbate a problem, others may ameliorate it, and the effects of still others are not known. Scientists use elaborate computer models to evaluate the impacts of perturbations of the atmosphere, and, in the end, the results may reflect our lack of basic understanding. Because many processes and interactions are incompletely known (after all, the Antarctic ozone hole was discovered only in 1985), decades of research may be required to refine the models so that predictions can be made with confidence. Given the complex interactions, we may never be able to predict the outcome with certainty.

Tropospheric Pollution

Tropospheric oxidants illustrate the complexity of atmospheric chemistry and processes. They help form acidic compounds, contribute to greenhouse warming, and individually damage human health, plant life, and materials. NO_x, hydrocarbons, and CO interact to form oxidants in the troposphere.

Even changes in stratospheric ozone, high above the troposphere, can affect tropospheric oxidant levels. As Figure 10.5 illustrates, if increased UV-B radiation penetrates a depleted ozone shield, the photochemical formation of ground level oxidants may be enhanced. Greenhouse warming could amplify this effect; a preliminary study of conditions in three U.S. cities—Nashville, Philadelphia, and Los Angeles—showed that a large depletion of stratospheric ozone, coupled with the greenhouse warming, could increase smog formation as much as 50 percent (124). The study also showed that hydrogen peroxide concentrations might increase more than tenfold.

Stratospheric Pollution

CFCs are extremely stable pollutants that migrate easily through the troposphere without being destroyed. When they reach the stratosphere, chlorine atoms are split off from CFC molecules by intense solar radiation. A single chlorine atom can then catalyze the destruction of thousands of stratospheric ozone molecules over an extended period. Other pollutants, halons, also reach the stratosphere and help destroy ozone.

Figure 10.5 The Complex Interactions of Atmospheric Pollutants

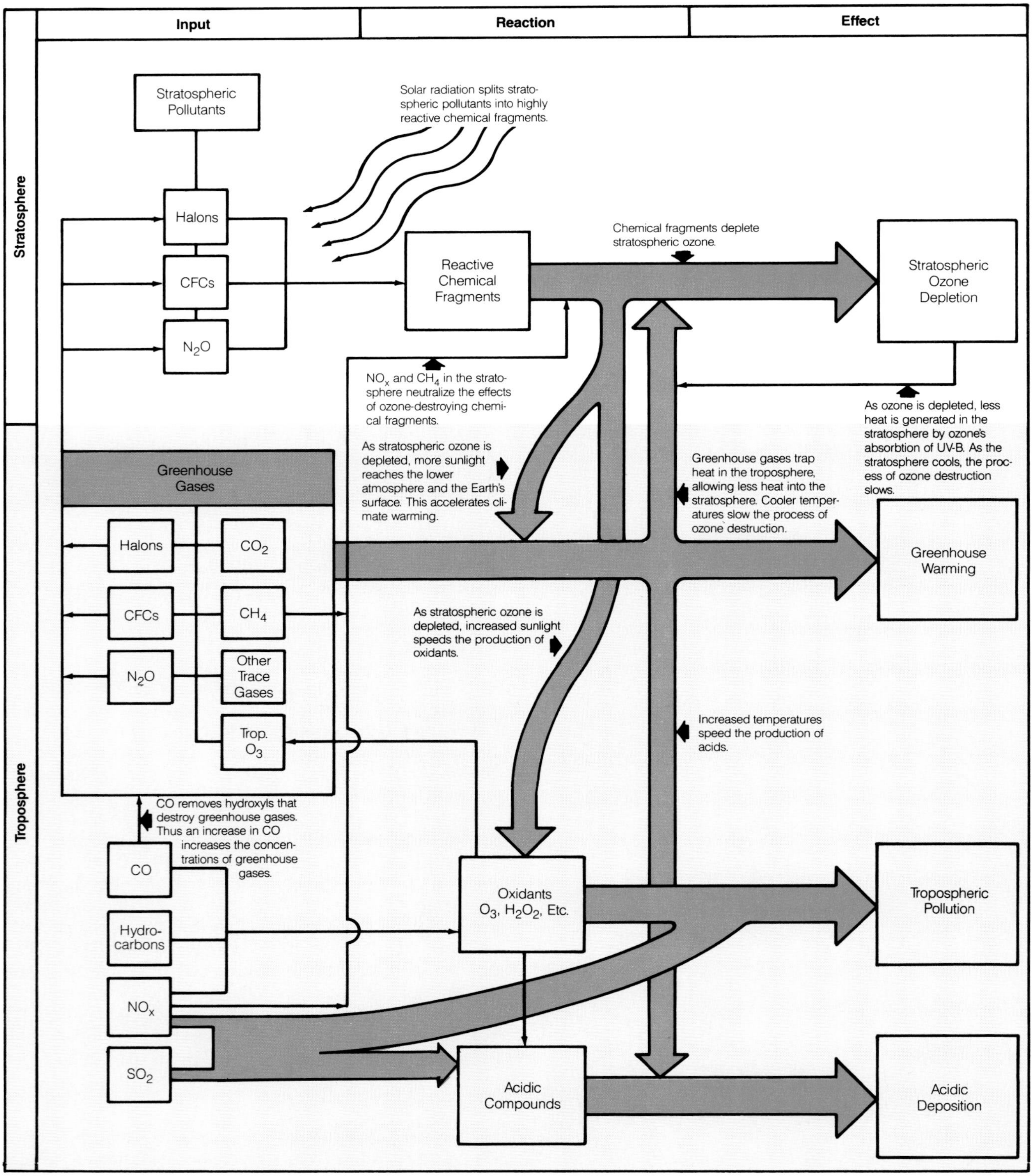

Input	Reaction	Effect

Stratospheric Pollutants

Solar radiation splits strato-spheric pollutants into highly reactive chemical fragments.

Stratosphere

Halons

CFCs

N_2O

Reactive Chemical Fragments

Chemical fragments deplete stratospheric ozone.

Stratospheric Ozone Depletion

NO_x and CH_4 in the strato-sphere neutralize the effects of ozone-destroying chemical fragments.

As stratospheric ozone is depleted, more sunlight reaches the lower atmosphere and the Earth's surface. This accelerates climate warming.

As ozone is depleted, less heat is generated in the stratosphere by ozone's absorbtion of UV-B. As the stratosphere cools, the process of ozone destruction slows.

Greenhouse Gases

Halons CO_2

CFCs CH_4

N_2O Other Trace Gases

Trop. O_3

Greenhouse gases trap heat in the troposphere, allowing less heat into the stratosphere. Cooler temperatures slow the process of ozone destruction.

Greenhouse Warming

As stratospheric ozone is depleted, increased sunlight speeds the production of oxidants.

Increased temperatures speed the production of acids.

Troposphere

CO removes hydroxyls that destroy greenhouse gases. Thus an increase in CO increases the concentrations of greenhouse gases.

CO

Hydro-carbons

NO_x

SO_2

Oxidants O_3, H_2O_2, Etc.

Tropospheric Pollution

Acidic Compounds

Acidic Deposition

Source: Compiled by *World Resources 1988-89.*

Key

CFCs — chlorofluorocarbons
N_2O — nitrous oxide
CH_4 — methane

CO_2 — carbon dioxide
Trop. O_3 — tropospheric ozone (a pollutant, as opposed to stratospheric ozone, which is beneficial)

CO — carbon monoxide
NO_x — nitrogen oxides (NO and NO_2)
SO_2 — sulfur dioxide

H_2O_2 — hydrogen peroxide
UV-B — ultraviolet B radiation

Three other greenhouse gases—nitrous oxide, methane, and carbon dioxide—are also important to ozone levels. When chlorine levels are high, increased concentrations of these gases are thought to counter ozone depletion. Ozone depletion estimates (See Emissions and Ambient Air Quality, above) assume that these greenhouse gases will increase at historical rates, enhancing the greenhouse effect and countering ozone depletion. If greenhouse gas emissions do not increase at historical rates, however, ozone depletion will exceed current projections (125). According to a recent study, although methane could slow overall depletion of the stratospheric ozone layer by neutralizing free chlorine atoms, ozone depletion over Antarctica may increase when methane combines with a hydroxyl to form water (the Antarctic ozone hole is promoted by the presence of atmospheric ice crystals) (126).

Depletion of the stratospheric ozone layer could have opposing effects on greenhouse warming. As more UV radiation reaches the Earth's surface, the planet should warm. However, if less UV radiation is absorbed in the stratosphere, the stratosphere itself could cool, contributing to a cooling of the Earth (127). The relative importance of these effects depends on the vertical distribution of stratospheric ozone depletion and other factors. The stratospheric ozone depletion-stratospheric cooling link could be complicated if greenhouse gases capture reradiated heat in the troposphere and reduce the amount of heat returned to the stratosphere. This cooling could potentially slow the rate at which stratospheric ozone is destroyed.

Effective Management of a Complex Problem

Acidic deposition and stratospheric ozone depletion are directly measurable, and evidence of their damage has led to national and international corrective measures. (See Recent Developments, below.) Analyses of climate change scenarios, on the other hand, are confined to computer models whose resolutions are not detailed enough for regional impact predictions. This situation creates a policy dilemma: although the scientific community is virtually unanimous in projecting a climate change, uncertainty about its degree, timing, and consequences leaves policymakers without a clear perception of what action to take. Another dilemma is created by the tradeoffs implicit in emission control strategies: reducing emissions of one pollutant may enhance emissions of another.

The energy-atmospheric pollution link is integral to any solution strategy. (See Chapter 7, "Energy.") Although pollution is exacerbated by agricultural and industrial nonenergy emissions as well as deforestation, the net emissions from those sources are generally less than those from fuel combustion.

Emission control technologies (e.g., power plant scrubbers) are applicable to acidic deposition problems, but they generally reduce efficiency and thus increase the amount of carbon dioxide generated per unit of energy produced. On the other hand, when the biomass is harvested on a sustainable basis, carbon dioxide emitted from combustion of biomass-based fuels is recycled from the atmosphere into the growing biomass feedstock. In the longer term, energy efficiency and conservation and a shift away from pollution-intensive fuels are the most effective solutions to energy-based atmospheric pollution.

For heat and electricity production, increased use of coal and synthetic fuels aggravates almost every major atmospheric pollution problem. Natural gas causes less pollution (per unit of energy produced) than other fossil fuels, but its combustion nevertheless generates greenhouse gases (albeit at a lower rate than coal or petroleum products). Nuclear power produces no air pollution, but nuclear wastes are a major environmental problem. Hydropower, solar energy, and biofuels (produced on a renewable basis) generally minimize or eliminate environmentally damaging emissions.

Among possible transportation fuels, gasoline and synfuels exacerbate most atmospheric pollution problems. Use of compressed natural gas would reduce greenhouse gas emissions relative to petroleum- and coal-based fuels but would still produce greenhouse gases. Biomass-based ethanol and methanol fuels would reduce net carbon dioxide emissions, but methanol produced from coal and natural gas results in a net increase in emissions of greenhouse gases. Electric vehicles are emissionless, but production of the fuel used to generate the electricity is a relevant factor.

Our growing understanding of the links among these atmospheric processes demonstrates the important point that a solution to one problem must avoid exacerbating another problem. The challenge is to devise comprehensive policies based on an imperfect understanding of chemical interactions and processes.

RECENT DEVELOPMENTS

THIRTY PERCENT CLUB COMES OF AGE

A milestone in air pollution control was reached in September 1987 when the Protocol to the 1979 Convention on Long-Range Transboundary Air Pollution (LRTAP) on the Reduction of Sulphur Emissions or Their Transboundary Fluxes by at Least 30 Percent entered into force upon being ratified by the necessary 16 countries (128). In ratifying the Protocol, these countries agreed that, by 1993 at the latest, they would reduce national sulfur emissions or their transboundary flows at least 30 percent from 1980 levels (129). Seventeen European countries and Canada had ratified the Protocol as of June 1988 (130). Twenty-one have signed, but some of the largest sulfur emitters have not—including the United States, the United Kingdom, and Poland (131). Ratifying countries hoped that a coordinated reduction in sulfur emissions would reduce transboundary air pollution (e.g., acidic deposition) and ease international tensions.

While the sulfur protocol was entering into force, a new LRTAP protocol to limit nitrogen oxide emissions was being negotiated. The draft agreement under discussion in April 1988 called on member nations to freeze NO_x emissions at 1987 levels by 1994 using the best available technology on new stationary and mobile sources of NO_x. However, the United States, arguing that it had already cut NO_x emissions, wanted to amend the

10 Atmosphere and Climate

agreement so that countries could select any year (presumably the year of maximum emissions) as the base for establishing an emission freeze. A compromise was then suggested—countries could use any year as the base for an emission freeze, but only if annual levels of transboundary flows of NO$_x$ are capped at 1987 levels by the end of 10 years. The formula is under discussion as this report goes to press. The negotiating parties hope to have a final protocol available for signature on October 31, 1988, but substantial hurdles remain (132) (133) (134).

MONTREAL PROTOCOL TO PROTECT THE OZONE LAYER

In a major step toward international cooperation on global environmental threats, delegates from 30 countries and the European Community signed a historic agreement to cut CFC consumption in half by the end of the century. The agreement, signed in Montreal on September 16, 1987, will come into force in 1989, when CFC production will be frozen at 1986 levels. Consumption will be gradually reduced to 20 percent below 1986 levels by 1994 and to 50 percent below 1986 levels by 1999.

The Montreal Protocol must be ratified by at least 11 of the signatory countries before it enters into force, but the United Nations Environment Programme expects many more countries to agree to ratification.

The agreement also has other benefits. Because tropospheric CFCs are greenhouse gases, reduced emissions will help slow the greenhouse effect. The Montreal Protocol is also a precedent for international agreements on other global environmental problems.

NEW GLOBAL AND ANTARCTIC STRATOSPHERIC OZONE MEASUREMENTS

In March 1988, a study showed that stratospheric ozone had decreased as much as 3 percent over the Northern Hemisphere during the past two decades, revealing a larger ozone loss than had been predicted. The study, considered the most authoritative to date, was a collaborative effort of more than 100 scientists from many countries, who reanalyzed and reinterpreted nearly all ground-based and satellite data for total column and vertical profiles of ozone (135) (136).

After discounting for natural causes of stratospheric ozone depletion the study found that the ozone layer over most of the heavily populated regions of China, Japan, the Soviet Union, Western Europe, the United States, and Canada had decreased 1.7–3 percent between 1969 and 1986. Even greater ozone losses were reported during the winter and at high northern latitudes, including wintertime drops of more than 6 percent in the Scandinavian countries and Alaska (137).

The dramatic springtime ozone loss over Antarctica now affects much of the Southern Hemisphere; year-round ozone levels south of 60° have been reduced 5 percent or more since 1979 (138).

In light of these findings, some scientists called for invoking a provision of the Montreal Protocol that allows member nations to reconvene if scientific evidence demonstrates that the agreement is insufficient to protect the ozone layer. As of mid-March 1988, however, only two (the United States and Mexico) of 31 signatory countries had ratified the Protocol, and no reconvening was planned (139).

After the study was released, E.I. DuPont Company (the largest manufacturer of CFCs in the world), announced that it would phase out production of ozone-depleting CFC formulations.

References and Notes

1. Detlev Möller, "Estimation of the Global Man-Made Sulphur Emission," *Atmospheric Environment*, Vol. 18, No. 1 (1984), pp. 19–23.
2. J.R. Freney, M.V. Ivanov, and H. Rodhe, "The Sulphur Cycle," in *The Major Biogeochemical Cycles and Their Interaction*, Bert Bolin and Robert B. Cook, eds. (John Wiley and Sons, Chichester, 1983), p. 60.
3. National Acid Precipitation Assessment Program (NAPAP), *Interim Assessment: The Causes and Effects of Acidic Deposition*, Vol. II, *Emissions and Controls* (NAPAP, Washington, D.C., 1987), Table 1-13, p. 1.43.
4. *Ibid.*, p. 1.31.
5. Organisation for Economic Co-operation and Development (OECD), *OECD Environmental Data Compendium 1987* (OECD, Paris, 1987), p. 28.
6. World Health Organization and United Nations Environment Programme, *Global Pollution and Health* (Yale University Press, London, 1987), Table 2, p. 7.
7. Commission of the European Communi-

ties (CEC), *The State of the Environment in the European Community 1986* (CEC, Luxembourg, 1987), p. 151.
8. U.S. Environmental Protection Agency (U.S. EPA), *National Air Pollutant Emission Estimates, 1940–1985* (U.S. EPA, Research Triangle Park, North Carolina, 1987), Table 9, p. 19.
9. *Op. cit.* 3, pp. 1.43–1.45.
10. *Op. cit.* 3, p. 1.55.
11. U.S. Environmental Protection Agency (U.S. EPA), *National Air Quality and Emissions Trends Report 1986* (U.S. EPA, Research Triangle Park, North Carolina, 1988), p. 3.17.
12. *Op. cit.* 3, p. 2.81 and p. 2.86.
13. *Op. cit.* 8, Table 15, p. 25.
14. U.S. Environmental Protection Agency (U.S. EPA), *Air Quality Criteria for Particulate Matter and Sulfur Oxides*, Vol. 1 (U.S. EPA, Research Triangle Park, North Carolina, 1982), p. 1.4, p. 1.7, and p. 1.15.
15. David Cabot, ed., *The State of the Environment: A Report Prepared for the Minister for the Environment* (An Foras Forbartha, Dublin, 1985), Figure 18, p.

134.
16. *Op. cit.* 8, Table 2, p. 12, and Table 29, p. 53.
17. United Kingdom Department of the Environment, *Digest of Environmental Protection and Water Statistics* (Her Majesty's Stationery Office, London, 1988), Table 2.3, p. 12.
18. *Op. cit.* 6, p. 6.
19. *Op. cit.* 7, p. 142.
20. U.S. Environmental Protection Agency (U.S. EPA), *National Air Quality and Emissions Trends Report 1985* (U.S. EPA, Research Triangle Park, North Carolina, 1987), Table 2-1, pp. 2.2–2.3.
21. World Meteorological Organization (WMO), *et al.*, *Atmospheric Ozone 1985: Assessment of Our Understanding of the Processes Controlling Its Present Distribution and Change*, Vol. 1 (WMO, Geneva, 1986), p. 105.
22. *Op. cit.* 7, pp. 141–142.
23. *Op. cit.* 19, p. 143.
24. Environment Agency (Japan) (JEA), *Quality of the Environment in Japan 1986* (JEA, Tokyo, 1986), pp. 84–85; Fig-

ure 2.5 and Table 2-4, p. 85; and p. 248.
25. *Op. cit.* 20, pp. 2.3 and 3.19.
26. U.S. Environmental Protection Agency (U.S. EPA), *Air Quality Criteria for Lead*, Vol. 1 (U.S. EPA, Research Triangle Park, North Carolina, 1986), p. 1.53, and pp. 1.116–1.124.
27. *Ibid.*, p. 1.12.
28. *Op. cit.* 7, p. 154.
29. Environment Agency (Japan) (JEA), *Motor Vehicle Pollution Control* (JEA, 1984), pp. 27–30.
30. *Op. cit.* 17, p. 18.
31. *Op. cit.* 20, p. 3.38.
32. *Op. cit.* 8, Table 29, p. 53.
33. Ministry of the Environment (France), *The State of the Environment 1985* (Ministry of the Environment, Neuilly-sur-Seine, 1986), Figure 3314, p. 63.
34. *Op. cit.* 17, p. 18.
35. *Op. cit.* 20, p. 3.38.
36. *Op. cit.* 11, p. 3.38.
37. Environment Canada, *Ambient Air Particulate Lead Concentrations in Canada 1975–1983* (Minister of Supply and Services, Ottawa, Canada, 1985), p. 1 and p. 5.
38. U.S. Environmental Protection Agency (U.S. EPA), *Air Quality Criteria for Ozone and Other Photochemical Oxidants*, Vol. 1 (U.S. EPA, Research Triangle Park, North Carolina, 1986), pp. 1.4–1.6.
39. *Op. cit.* 7, p. 156.
40. *Op. cit.* 3, pp. 1.65–1.66.
41. In contrast to Canada's annual standard, the U.S. standard is for peak events; hourly average ozone levels may exceed 120 parts per billion on no more than one day per year.
42. *Op. cit.* 11, p. 2.3, pp. 3.31–3.34, and p. 4.1.
43. Warnings are issued in individual prefectures when the hourly average ozone level exceeds 120 parts per billion. All the 1985 warnings were issued in 16 prefectures; 107 (84 percent) were issued in the Tokyo and Osaka regions.
44. *Op. cit.* 24, pp. 103–104.
45. National Acid Precipitation Assessment Program (NAPAP), *Interim Assessment: The Causes and Effects of Acidic Deposition*, Vol. III, *Atmospheric Processes and Deposition* (NAPAP, Washington, D.C., 1987), pp. 4.15–4.16, pp. 4.30–4.32, pp. 4.37–4.38, p. 4.53, and pp. 4.55–4.59.
46. The pH scale measures acidity and alkalinity; pH 7 is neutral, less than 7 is acidic, and above 7 is alkaline. Each whole-unit decline (e.g., from 7 to 6) in pH represents a 10-fold increase in acidity. Each decimal decline (e.g., from 5.6 to 5.5) represents a 26 percent increase in acidity.
47. *Op. cit.* 45, p. 5.96.
48. Su Ge, "A Critical Review of Air Pollution Research in China over the Last Decade," Master's Thesis, Oregon Graduate Center, Beaverton, Oregon, 1986.
49. *Op. cit.* 3, pp. 1.25–1.27.
50. *Op. cit.* 3, p. 5.106.
51. *Op. cit.* 3, p. 5.79.
52. Anthony R. Olsen, Staff Scientist, Battelle Pacific Northwest Laboratories, Richland, Washington, United States, 1988 (personal

communication).
53. Jan Schaug, Research Scientist, Norwegian Institute for Air Research, Lillestrom, Norway, 1987 (personal communication).
54. J.M. Barnola, *et al.*, "Vostok Ice Core Provides 160,000-year Record of Atmospheric CO_2," *Nature*, Vol. 329, No. 6138 (1987), p. 410.
55. A. Neftel, *et al.*, "Evidence from Polar Ice Cores for the Increase in Atmospheric CO_2 in the Past Two Centuries," *Nature*, Vol. 315 (1985), pp. 45–47.
56. M.A.K. Khalil and R.A. Rasmussen, "Atmospheric Methane: Trends over the Last 10,000 Years," *Atmospheric Environment*, Vol. 21, No. 11 (1987), pp. 2447–2450.
57. M.A.K. Khalil and R.A. Rasmussen, "Nitrous Oxide: Trends and Global Mass Balance over the Last 3,000 Years," *Annals of Glaciology* (in press).
58. *Op. cit.* 38, p. 1.55 and p. 1.76.
59. National Acid Precipitation Assessment Program (NAPAP), *Interim Assessment: The Causes and Effects of Acidic Deposition*, Vol. I, *Executive Summary* (NAPAP, Washington, D.C., 1987), p. 1.26.
60. *Op. cit.* 59, p. 1.26.
61. D.J. Dudek and M. Oppenheimer, "The Implications of Health and Environmental Effects for Policy," in *Effects of Changes in Stratospheric Ozone and Global Climate*, Vol. I, *Overview*, James G. Titus, ed. (U.S. Environmental Protection Agency, Washington, D.C., 1986), p. 371.
62. *Op. cit.* 38, p. 1–78.
63. World Health Organization (WHO), *Air Quality Guidelines for Europe*, European Series No. 23 (WHO Regional Publications, 1987), p. 391.
64. *Op. cit.* 59, p. 1–25.
65. Gordon J. MacDonald, *Climate Change and Acid Rain* (MITRE Corporation, McLean, Virginia, 1985), pp. 33–35.
66. *Op. cit.* 38, pp. 1.90–1.91.
67. *EPA Journal*, Vol. 13, No. 8 (1987), p. 11.
68. National Acid Precipitation Assessment Program (NAPAP), *Interim Assessment: The Causes and Effects of Acidic Deposition*, Vol. IV, *Effects of Acidic Deposition* (NAPAP, Washington, D.C., 1987), p. 7-i.
69. *Op. cit.* 65, p. 36.
70. D.W. Schindler, "Effects of Acid Rain on Freshwater Ecosystems," *Science*, Vol. 239 (January 8, 1988), pp. 149–157.
71. Sport fishing records from Norway, Sweden, the United Kingdom, and eastern Canada were the earliest indicators of changes that resulted from acidification, and early scientific surveys concentrated on these same species of fish. Recent general reviews of pH tolerance of organisms are given in D.W. Schindler, "Effects of Acid Rain on Freshwater Ecosystems," *Science*, Vol. 239 (January 8, 1988), p. 151.
72. *Ibid*, pp. 151–153.
73. *Op. cit.* 68, p. 9-1.
74. *Op. cit.* 38, p. 1.98–1.100.
75. *Op. cit.* 14, p. 1.45.
76. U.S. Environmental Protection Agency (U.S. EPA), *Air Quality Criteria for Oxides of Nitrogen* (U.S. EPA, Research Triangle Park, North Carolina, 1982), p.

1.37.
77. *Op. cit.* 68, p. 9-4.
78. *Op. cit.* 68, pp. 9.3–9.4.
79. *Op. cit.* 38, pp. 1.107–1.109.
80. *Op. cit.* 68, p. 10.38.
81. *Op. cit.* 68, pp. 10.69–10.71.
82. *Op. cit.* 68, pp. 10.38–10.39.
83. *Op. cit.* 68, p. 10.2.
84. *Op. cit.* 68, p. 10.46.
85. *Op. cit.* 68, p. 10.1.
86. *Op. cit.* 68, p. 10.74.
87. J.H.W. Karas and P.M. Kelly, "Global Implications of Air Pollution," in *Proceedings of the SAM/APPEN International Conference on Global Development and Environmental Crisis—Has Man a Future?* (in press).
88. United Nations Environment Programme (UNEP), World Meteorological Organization (WMO), and International Council of Scientific Unions, *An Assessment of the Role of Carbon Dioxide and of Other Greenhouse Gases in Climate Variations and Associated Impacts* (WMO, Geneva, 1985).
89. United Nations Environment Programme (UNEP), *The Greenhouse Gases*, UNEP/Global Environment Monitoring System Environment Library No. 1 (UNEP, Nairobi, 1987), p. 23.
90. Stephen H. Schneider, "The Greenhouse Effect: What We Can or Should Do About It," paper presented at the First North American Conference on Preparing for Climate Change: A Cooperative Approach, Washington, D.C., October 27–29, 1987.
91. James G. Titus and Stephen R. Siedel, "Overview of the Effects of Changing the Atmosphere," in *Effects of Changes in Stratospheric Ozone and Global Change*, Vol. 1, *Overview*, James G. Titus, ed. (U.S. Environmental Protection Agency, Washington, D.C., 1986), p. 8.
92. *Op. cit* 89, p. 22.
93. J. Hansen *et al.*, "The Greenhouse Effect: Projection of Global Climate Change," in *Effects of Changes in Stratospheric Ozone and Global Change*, Vol. 1, *Overview*, James G. Titus, ed. (U.S. Environmental Protection Agency, Washington, D.C., 1986), p. 214.
94. World Meteorological Organization (WMO), *et al.*, *Atmospheric Ozone 1985: Assessment of Our Understanding of the Processes Controlling its Present Distribution and Change*, Vol. III (WMO, Geneva, 1986), Figure 15-22, p. 874.
95. Wallace S. Broecker, Dorothy M. Peteet, and David Rind, "Does the Ocean-Atmosphere System Have More than One Stable Mode of Operation?" *Nature*, Vol. 315 (1985), pp. 21–26.
96. Syukuro Manabe, statement before the U.S. Senate Committee on Energy and Natural Resources, November 9, 1987.
97. *Ibid*.
98. *Op. cit.* 91, pp. 12–13.
99. United Nations Environment Programme (UNEP), *The Changing Atmosphere*, UNEP Environment Brief No. 1 (UNEP, Nairobi, n.d.).
100. *Ibid*.
101. *Op. cit.* 91, pp. 12–15.

102. Tom Goemans, "The Sea Also Rises: The Ongoing Dialogue of the Dutch with the Sea," in *Effects of Changes in Stratospheric Ozone and Global Climate*, Vol. 4, *Sea Level Rise*, James G. Titus, ed. (U.S. Environmental Protection Agency, Washington, D.C., 1986), p. 55.

103. *Op. cit.* 91, p. 14.

104. John Firor, statement before the U.S. Senate Committee on Energy and Natural Resources, November 9, 1987.

105. Bert Bolin *et al.*, *The Greenhouse Effect, Climatic Change, and Ecosystems (SCOPE 29)* (John Wiley and Sons, New York and Chichester, 1986), pp. 510–511.

106. *Op. cit.* 96.

107. Martin L. Parry and Timothy R. Carter, "Effects of Climatic Changes on Agriculture and Forestry," in *Effects of Changes in Stratospheric Ozone and Global Change*," Vol. 1, *Overview*, James G. Titus, ed. (U.S. Environmental Protection Agency, Washington, D.C., 1986), p. 270.

108. *Ibid.*, p. 293.

109. *Op. cit.* 105, p. 510.

110. Edward A. Emmett, "Health Effects of Ultraviolet Radiation," in *Effects of Changes in Stratospheric Ozone and Global Change*, Vol. 1, *Overview*, James G. Titus, ed. (U.S. Environmental Protection Agency, Washington, D.C., 1986), pp. 129–130.

111. *Op. cit.* 99.

112. D.S. Nachtwey, M.M. Caldwell, and R.H. Biggs, *Climate Impact Assessment Program (CIAP)*, Monograph No. 5 (U.S. Department of Transportation, Washington, D.C., 1975), cited in Alan H. Termura, "Overview of Our Current State of Knowledge of UV Effects on Plants," in *Effects of Changes in Stratospheric Ozone and Global Change*, Vol. 1, *Overview*, James G. Titus, ed. (U.S. Environmental Protection Agency, Washington, D.C., 1986), p. 165.

113. Alan H. Teramura, "Overview of Our Current State of Knowledge of UV Effects on Plants," in *Effects of Changes in Stratospheric Ozone and Global Change*, Vol. 1, *Overview*, James G. Titus, ed. (U.S. Environmental Protection Agency, Washington, D.C., 1986), p. 165.

114. *Ibid.*, p. 165–168.

115. *Ibid.*, pp. 167–168.

116. John Hoffman, Director, Stratospheric Protection Program, U.S. Environmental Protection Agency, Washington, D.C., 1988 (personal communication).

117. *Op. cit.* 91, p. 7.

118. R.C. Worrest, "The Effect of Solar UV-B Radiation on Aquatic Systems: An Overview," in *Effects of Changes in Stratospheric Ozone and Global Change*, Vol. 1, *Overview*, James G. Titus, ed. (U.S. Environmental Protection Agency, Washington, D.C., 1986), p. 175.

119. *Op. cit.* 91, p. 7.

120. *Op. cit.* 118, p. 175.

121. John Calkins and Mary Blakefield, "An Estimate of the Role of Current Levels of Solar Ultraviolet Radiation in Aquatic Ecosystems: An Overview," in *Effects of Changes in Stratospheric Ozone and Global Climate*, Vol. 2, *Stratospheric Ozone* (U.S. Environmental Protection Agency, Washington, D.C., 1986), pp. 213–215.

122. B. Thomson, "Is the Impact of UV-B Radiation on Marine Zooplankton of Any Significance?" in *Effects of Changes in Stratospheric Ozone and Global Climate*, Vol. 2, *Stratospheric Ozone* (U.S. Environmental Protection Agency, Washington, D.C., 1986), Table 1, p. 205.

123. *Op. cit.* 99.

124. Gary Z. Whitten and Michael W. Gery, "The Interaction of Photochemical Processes in the Stratosphere and Troposphere," in *Effects of Changes in Stratospheric Ozone and the Global Climate*, Vol. 2, *Stratospheric Ozone* (U.S. Environmental Protection Agency, Washington, D.C., 1986) pp. 300–302.

125. *Op. cit.* 116.

126. Donald R. Blake and F. Sherwood Rowland, "Continuing Worldwide Increase in Tropospheric Methane, 1978–1987," *Science*, Vol. 239, pp. 1129–1131.

127. United Nations Environment Programme (UNEP), *The Ozone Layer*, UNEP/Global Environment Monitoring System Environment Library No. 2 (UNEP, Nairobi, 1987), p. 10.

128. *Acid Rain Digest* (November 1987), p. 93.

129. United Nations Environment Programme (UNEP), *Register of International Treaties and Other Agreements in the Field of the Environment*, Supplement 1 (UNEP, Nairobi, 1987), p. 34.

130. John Zylman, Office of the Assistant Legal Advisor for Treaty Affairs, U.S. Department of State, June 1988 (personal communication).

131. Economic Commission for Europe (ECE), *National Strategies and Policies for Air Pollution Abatement* (United Nations, New York, 1987), p. 55.

132. Michael Weisskopf, "Nations Fail to Agree on Acid-Rain Controls," *Washington Post* (April 30, 1988), p. A15.

133. Edward Williams, Director, Environmental Analysis, U.S. Department of Energy, 1988 (personal communication).

134. Jamison Koehler, U.S. Environmental Protection Agency, International Activities Office, 1988 (personal communication).

135. Ozone Trends Panel, *Executive Summary of the Ozone Trends Panel* (National Aeronautics and Space Administration, Washington, D.C., 1988).

136. Scientists measure ozone profiles in terms of the total column content (the amount of ozone in a vertical column of atmosphere) and vertical distribution (the concentrations of ozone at various elevations above the Earth's surface).

137. Philip Shabecoff, "Study Shows Significant Decline in Ozone Layer," *New York Times* (March 16, 1988), p. A25.

138. *Op. cit.* 135.

139. *Op. cit.* 137, p. A25.

11. Global Systems and Cycles

Close proximity to an environmental process or problem enriches our understanding of specific issues. However, by stepping back, we can connect local effects with distant causes and learn the true dimensions of a phenomenon that seemed neatly framed. Stepping back is a lesson that can be applied in both space and time. A *global* view enriches the understanding of the intricate web of life and nonlife that unifies the planet. A *historical* view places humans alongside the natural forces that have shaped and continue to shape the world we inhabit.

Each year the Global Systems and Cycles chapter focuses on a biogeochemical cycle. *World Resources 1987* described the carbon cycle. This year the nitrogen and water cycles are examined. These two biogeochemical cycles demonstrate humanity's ever-increasing impact on planetary-scale phenomena. People, who had a fairly trivial impact on the global flows of nitrogen as recently as 40 years ago, are now a global agent in the nitrogen cycle, as important as rain, riverflow, or the rest of the world's biota. Today, industrial fertilizer factories remove nitrogen from the atmosphere to supply nutrients for agricultural crops as rapidly as the planet's vegetation does for itself. People have also changed the natural flow of the water cycle by clearing forests, building dams, and irrigating crops.

Because water is a critical component of most global systems such as climate, vegetation, and erosion, human disturbances of one part of the water cycle inevitably have impacts in other, frequently unexpected places. For example, global-scale alterations in the water cycle may be brought about by human tampering with the global climate through the greenhouse effect.

The prism of history places humanity in the context of the planet's other sculpting forces. Only by looking into the past do we realize the true scale of the environmental damage we are causing today. The atmosphere's carbon dioxide level, now at 350 parts per million never rose above 280 ppm in the past 160,000 years, a period covering three glacial and interglacial intervals. The modern rate of extinction, driven in large part by humanity's ever-increasing appropriation of the planet's resources, is now approaching the rates seen in the geological record when the dinosaurs died. Historical records can help separate human impacts on the environment from natural ones and identify where human activities are causing rapid (and often accelerating) change. Natural and written historical records truly tell the stories of their times, providing us with an abundance of material from which to learn about the processes of global change and humanity's increasing ability to influence and supersede them.

CONDITIONS AND TRENDS

THE GLOBAL NITROGEN CYCLE

Carbon provides the basic matrix of life, but nitrogen is also a key ingredient. Although nitrogen is a relatively rare element in the biosphere—carbon is about 100 times more abundant—its critical presence in proteins (of which enzymes, hormones, chlorophyll, and genes are made) makes it indispensable for all living creatures (1). Together with carbon and sulfur, it is one of the three elements with a truly global biogeochemical cycle (2). Preindustrial civilizations caused insignificant modifications of nitrogen's global flows, but humans now affect the nitrogen cycle on a massive scale.

Human interference in the nitrogen cycle began with large-scale alteration of natural vegetation (see *World Resources 1987*, Table 18.3, p. 272) and exploded with the rapid expansion of synthetic nitrogen fertilizer production after 1950. The worldwide production of nitrogen fertilizers may currently be as large as the rate of natural nitrogen fixation. Widespread use of artificial fertilizers started in Europe and North America and is now increasingly common in developing countries, especially for high-value cash crops.

Heavy use of fertilizers produces a number of undesira-

ble side effects ranging from the global impacts of nitrous oxide on stratospheric ozone and climate to the local impact of water pollution by nitrates. People also impinge on the natural cycle with concentrated discharge of organic nitrogen compounds from urban populations and confined livestock, and with the emission of nitrogen oxides during fossil fuel combustion. Although these discharges are controllable (at considerable cost), large, uncontrolled releases are still common, even in countries where pollution control is standard. However, new agricultural and fuel combustion technologies offer the hope that human interferences in the nitrogen cycle can be reduced in the future (3).

Stocks and Flows

Nitrogen cycling is vigorous, relatively rapid, and extraordinarily complicated, because it cycles both through air

Figure 11.1 The Global Nitrogen Cycle

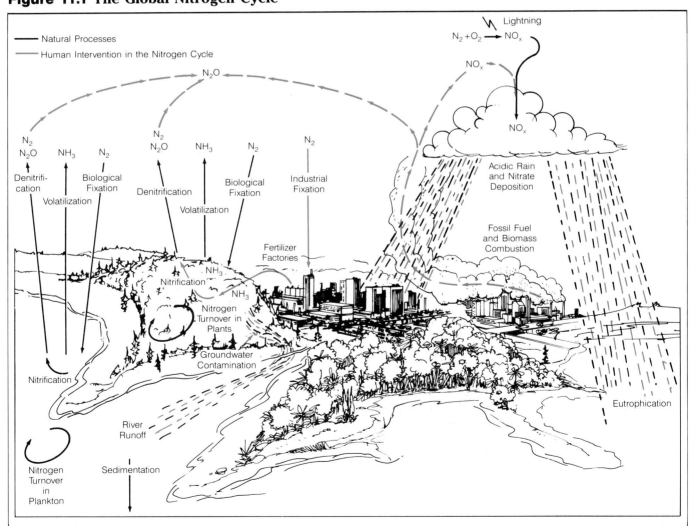

Sources:
1. Thomas Rosswall, "The Nitrogen Cycle," in *The Major Biogeochemical Cycles and Their Interactions*, B. Bolin and R.B. Cook, eds. (John Wiley & Sons, Chichester, 1983), pp. 47–49.
2. National Academy of Sciences/National Research Council, *Global Change in the Geosphere-Biosphere: Initial Priorities for an IGBP* (National Academy Press, Washington, D.C., 1986), p. 73.

and water. (See Figure 11.1.) If this movement were to stop for an instant, the global inventory of nitrogen would appear to be gathered in a few, discrete *stocks*. Transfers between the stocks are called *flows*. (See Table

Table 11.1 Stocks and Flows of the Global Nitrogen Cycle

Stocks[1]	Billion Metric Tons of Nitrogen	Percent of Total
Atmosphere		
Molecular nitrogen (N_2)	3,900,000	>99.999
Nitrous oxide (N_2O)	1.4	<0.0001
Ammonia (NH_3)	0.0017	<0.0001
Ammonium (NH_4)	0.00004	<0.0001
Nitric oxide + Nitrogen dioxide (NO_x)	0.0006	<0.0001
Nitrate (NO_3)	0.0001	<0.0001
Organic nitrogen	0.001	<0.0001
Ocean		
Plant biomass	0.30	0.001
Animal biomass	0.17	0.0007
Microbial biomass	0.02	0.00006
Dead organic matter (dissolved)	530	2.3
Dead organic matter (particulate)	3–240	0.01–1.0
Molecular nitrogen (dissolved)	22,000	95.2
Nitrous oxide	0.2	0.009
Nitrate	570	2.5
Nitrite	0.5	0.002
Ammonium	7	0.03
Terrestrial Biosphere		
Plant biomass	11–14	2.6
Animal biomass	0.2	0.04
Microbial biomass	0.5	0.1
Litter	1.9–3.3	0.5
Soil: organic matter	300	63
inorganic	160	34
Lithosphere		
Rocks	190,000,000	99.8
Sediments	400,000	0.2
Coal Deposits	120	0.00006

Selected Flows	Estimated Range (million metric tons of nitrogen per year)	Source
Fixation		
Biological		
Land	44–200	1
Oceans	1–130	1
Industrial[a]	90	2
Formation of NO_x		
Lightning	<10	3
Soil Releases	10–15	3
Fossil Fuel Combustion[b]	22	4
Biomass Burning	7–12	3
Formation of N_2O		
Oceans	1–3	3
Tropical and subtropical forests and woodlands	3.4–11.4	3
Fertilized agricultural land	0.4–1.2	3
Combustion: fossil fuel	3–5	3
biomass	0.5–0.9	3
Deposition		
NO_x (wet and dry)	40–116	1
NH_3/NH_4 (wet and dry)	110–240	1
River Runoff to the Oceans	26	5

Sources:
1. Thomas Rosswall, "The Nitrogen Cycle," in *The Major Biogeochemical Cycles and Their Interactions*, B. Bolin and R.B. Cook, eds. (John Wiley & Sons, Chichester, 1983), pp. 47–50.
2. William F. Sheldrick, *World Nitrogen Survey* (The World Bank, Washington, D.C., 1987), p. 16.
3. World Meteorological Organization (WMO), *et al.*, *Atmospheric Ozone 1985, Assessment of Our Understanding of the Processes Controlling Its Present Distribution and Change* (WMO, Geneva, 1986), p. 81 and p. 86.
4. Sultan Hameed and Jane Dignon, "Changes in the Geographical Distributions of Global Emissions of NO_x and SO_x from Fossil-Fuel Combustion Between 1966 and 1980," *Atmospheric Environment*, Vol. 22, No. 3 (1988), p. 447.
5. Michel Meybeck, "How to Establish and Use World Budgets of Riverine Materials," in *Physical and Chemical Weathering in Geochemical Cycles*, A. Lerman and M. Meybeck, eds. (D. Reidel, Dordrecht, in press 1988), p. 14.
Notes:
a. Datum is for 1985.
b. Datum is for 1980.

11.1.) The largest nitrogen stock is in igneous rocks, beyond the reach of biospheric flows. The oceans store very little nitrogen while the large atmospheric stock is dominated by stable molecular nitrogen gas (N_2). The concentrations of other nitrogen-containing gases in the atmosphere—nitric oxide (NO), nitrogen dioxide (NO_2), nitrous oxide (N_2O), and ammonia (NH_3)—are measured in parts per billion or trillion. Nitrogen compounds and nitrogen cycle processes are described in Table 11.2. Soil stores most of the nitrogen found within the terrestrial part of the biosphere, largely in organic matter [4]. Plants, animals, and humans contain only a small fraction of the nitrogen stock. Although there is little doubt about the relative sizes of the major global stocks, only two of the many flows can be quantified with confidence—industrial nitrogen fixation and NO emissions from fossil fuel combustion. Similar uncertainties prevail on regional and local scales.

One major process in nitrogen cycling and the dominant source of nitrogen for plant growth is *nitrogen fixation*, the conversion of atmospheric molecular nitrogen (N_2) to ammonia (NH_3) by a small number of bacteria and algae. Of these, the best known is the symbiotic bacterium *Rhizobium*, which lives in the root nodules of leguminous plants. Unfortunately, despite enormous research effort devoted to the study of symbiotic fixation [5], precise estimates of annual fixation rates do not exist for even one crop species because of the wide variability of field conditions in which leguminous plants grow [6]. Almost all published values for crops have at least a

Table 11.2 Guide to the Nitrogen Cycle

The nitrogen cycle is a complex process. This guide identifies the key players and processes.

Major Chemical Forms of Nitrogen		
Ammonia/Ammonium	NH_3/NH_4	A major nutrient, ammonia is a gas and is highly soluble in water
Nitrogen gas (molecular nitrogen)	N_2	Principal constituent of the atmosphere, unusable except by a few nitrogen-fixing bacteria and algae
Nitrous oxide (laughing gas)	N_2O	Important role in ozone cycle and greenhouse effect, product of denitrifying bacteria
Nitric oxide	NO NO_x	Combustion product, natural regulator of stratospheric ozone
Nitrogen dioxide	NO_2	Formed by the reaction of NO with oxygen in the air, NO_2 is an urban air pollutant, a precursor of acidic deposition, and aids the formation of tropospheric ozone
Nitrite ion	NO_2	Intermediate product in the conversion of ammonia to nitrate
Nitrate ion	NO_3	Principal nutrient form, component of acid rain, contributes to methemoglobinemia

Principal Chemical Processes	
Fixation	Conversion of N_2 to NH_3 by nitrogen-fixing bacteria and algae.
Nitrification	Subsequent oxidation of ammonia to nitrate. The key early steps are performed only by a few types of bacteria.
Denitrification	A chain of reactions by a few types of bacteria that ultimately returns nitrogen to the atmosphere as N_2O and N_2.
Volatilization	Direct loss of soil nitrogen to the atmosphere as NH_3.

Source: Compiled by *World Resources 1988–89*.

threefold range, and we know even less about the fixation rates of rhizobia associated with tropical trees and other wild vegetation. Thus, given the uncertainties in plant-specific fixation rates and in global vegetation cover, the magnitude of global nitrogen fixation can only be approximated.

Nitrogen fixation is followed by bacterial *nitrification*, which converts ammonium (NH_4) to nitrites (NO_2), nitrates (NO_3), and the amino form (NH_2) used in protein synthesis. Nitrogen can be recycled to the atmosphere through the process of *denitrification*. This series of chemical reactions carried out by bacteria converts nitrates to nitrous oxide and molecular nitrogen [7]. Our knowledge of denitrification is highly uncertain. Volatilization of ammonia is the other, less important, route of airborne loss of soil nitrogen. Waterborne losses of soil nitrogen by leaching and soil erosion differ regionally with the soil nitrogen content, precipitation, and agronomic practices (see below) [8].

Artificially-Fixed Nitrogen

Traditional farmers intervene in the nitrogen cycle by cultivating legumes interspersed with other crops, or in rotation with them, plowing legumes under as green manure, and by recycling biomass such as crop residues and animal and human wastes. Modern agriculture retains some of these practices, but the total mass of recycled organic nitrogen is now dwarfed by industrial production of nitrogen fertilizers from atmospheric nitrogen. Synthetic ammonia production has grown exponentially since its commercialization in the early 1920s. Worldwide output is now 90 million metric tons of nitrogen, with 80 percent used as fertilizer [9].

Synthetic ammonia is used directly as a cheap, highly concentrated fertilizer or converted to urea, nitrates, or compound fertilizers (combinations of nitrogen with phosphate, potassium, and micronutrient elements). Fertilizer use in 1985–86 averaged 51 kilograms of nitrogen per hectare of arable land on a worldwide basis, with Africa using an average of 12 kilograms of nitrogen per hectare and Europe using an average of 123 kilograms of nitrogen per hectare [10]. More than one third of all synthetic nitrogen is now produced in developing countries [11].

When excess nitrogen fertilizer is applied to a field the levels of nitrate in the runoff and nitrous oxide in the atmosphere increase. Nitrous oxide levels are enhanced because nitrification and denitrification, which convert nitrogen fertilizers and biomass to nitrous oxide and then to nitrogen gas, sometimes stops with the production of nitrous oxide. When farmers fertilize or over-fertilize crops with synthetic nitrogen fertilizers produced from nitrogen gas, they essentially withdraw nitrogen from the atmosphere in its stable molecular form and return some of it as nitrous oxide, a compound that has important environmental impacts. (See Atmospheric Issues, below.)

Water Pollution Issues

Nitrogen compounds are associated with two major water pollution problems: contamination of drinking water and eutrophication of aquatic ecosystems. These issues generated a wave of public concern in the late 1960s and early 1970s, but further research initially downplayed

nitrogen's role in water pollution. However, both issues have recently been rekindled as further evidence of nitrate pollution accumulates.

Discharge of urban sewer systems and runoff from fertilized cropland, irrigation, and livestock have been identified as contributors to nitrate and ammonia levels in water. Nitrate levels have been rising in surface and groundwater supplies in Europe and North America as more fertilizer is applied to cropland. Urban areas amplify nitrogen pollution because they concentrate the consumption and disposal of nitrogen-containing foodstuffs, often crops raised with the aid of nitrogen fertilizers. (See Chapter 8, "Freshwater," Nonpoint Source Pollution.)

Nitrates in drinking water and food pose a particular threat to infants. Nitrates can be converted in the human body to nitrites; nitrites, in turn, combine with hemoglobin (the blood's carrier of oxygen) to form methemoglobin, a compound that is incapable of carrying oxygen. One to two percent of the body's hemoglobin is normally found in the methemoglobin form, but when nitrate-polluted drinking water and food induce higher levels, respiratory distress (at 10 percent conversion) or even death (at 30–40 percent conversion) may occur. Infants are at much greater risk of methemoglobinemia because their stomach and blood chemistry are more favorable for the formation of methemoglobin than those of adults. This natural susceptibility is aggravated where nitrate-polluted water is used to prepare baby formula and food, especially when the water is boiled to kill pathogens because boiling concentrates the nitrates [12] [13]. In the United States, only one death has been attributed to methemoglobinemia since 1960, and four other severe cases have been reported in agricultural areas [14]. Numerous infant deaths from methemoglobinemia caused by contaminated drinking water have been reported in other countries [15].

Nitrogen in surface waters appears to pose fewer, and less acute, dangers of eutrophication than was thought in the 1960s [16]. (Eutrophication is a natural process of nutrient enrichment that stimulates plant and algae growth. Normally occurring over thousands of years, eutrophication is greatly accelerated by anthropogenic nutrient loading. Rapid eutrophication can lead to algae blooms, depletion of dissolved oxygen, and fish kills.) Phosphorus, rather than nitrogen, has been repeatedly identified as the principal cause of eutrophication in most lakes. However, nitrogen is responsible for blooms in shallower eutrophic lakes that receive heavy nitrogen loading. Nitrogen may also be a major factor in eutrophication of the Atlantic coastal waters of the United States. A recent report found that fertilizer runoff was the largest single contributor of nitrogen to these areas, but it also announced the surprising finding that atmospheric deposition of nitrates may contribute significantly to the loading of nitrogen compounds—as much as one quarter of all loading in the Chesapeake Bay, for example [17].

Atmospheric Issues

Nitrogen in its stable molecular form (N_2) accounts for over 75 percent of the volume of the atmosphere. Several

Box 11.1 Biotechnological Research on Nitrogen Fixation

Scientists have long known that nitrogen fixation in leguminous plants takes place within root nodules populated by bacteria known as *Rhizobia*. A series of genes on *Rhizobia's* chromosomes, or on plasmids, governs the process.

Researchers at the genetic engineering company Biotechnica have succeeded in "amplifying" the genetic activity of these nitrogen-fixing genes under laboratory conditions. *Rhizobia's* nitrogen-fixing genes are transferred into the genetic apparatus of *E. coli* bacteria, which makes extra, repetitive, copies of these same genes. The extra genes are then transferred back into *Rhizobia*. *Rhizobia's* nitrogen-fixing capability is thus "amplified" and the result is a sharp increase in the rate and volume of ammonia production. This enhancement of crops' supply of nitrogen would obviate the need for heavy use of sup-

plemental fertilizer. And, because the nitrogen would be delivered at the roots, nitrogen runoff and volatilization would be less than is commonly found when artificial nitrogen fertilizers are used (1).

A second development involves clarifying the structure of the nitrogenase enzyme from the nitrogen-fixing organism *Klebsiella*. Nitrogenase is an extremely complex enzyme that actually performs the catalysis that converts atmospheric nitrogen to ammonia.

Researchers are trying to separate this active portion from the enzyme with the hope of using it as an industrial catalyst for producing ammonia. Such a natural catalysis allows ammonia production to be performed more speedily and at lower temperatures than is possible with current industrial processes. Success is by no means imminent, but research is moving swiftly (2).

Another major area of research involves breeding nitrogen-fixing capability on non-leguminous plants such as corn. This research, however, is not advancing as much as had been hoped because *Rhizobia*, so far, cannot be made to adapt from one plant to another. Researchers hope to develop a more widely adaptable nodulating gene so that non-leguminous plants could be "leguminated." But so far, no successes have been reported (3).

References and Notes

1. Donald L. Keister, Research Leader, Nitrogen Fixation and Soybean Genetics Laboratory, Agricultural Research Service, U.S. Department of Agriculture, Washington, D.C., 1988 (personal communication).
2. *Ibid.*
3. *Ibid.*

other nitrogen compounds, although found only in trace quantities in the atmosphere, can have profound environmental impacts. Human activities have increased the concentrations of these gases, leading to local, regional, and global environmental damage.

When fuel combustion takes place at such high temperatures as those found in automobile engines and electric power plants, atmospheric oxygen and nitrogen can react in the combustion chamber, producing nitric oxide (NO). Fuel combustion worldwide emits over 20 million metric tons of nitrogen in the form of nitric oxide per year, a flow comparable in magnitude to the natural formation of this compound (18). Nitric oxide reacts in the atmosphere to form nitrogen dioxide (NO and NO_2 are denoted as NO_x); NO_x pollutes urban air, contributes to the formation of acidic precipitation and tropospheric oxidants, and increases the loading of nutrient nitrogen to aquatic ecosystems. (For additional information on sources, emissions, and impacts of NO_x, see Chapter 10, "Atmosphere and Climate," Emissions and Ambient Air Quality.) NO_x emissions, which roughly doubled on a global basis between 1960 and 1980, are now increasing slowly in many developed countries. But in developing countries, NO_x emissions may rise rapidly if use of fossil fuels increases (19).

Another gaseous nitrogen compound, nitrous oxide (N_2O), plays an important role in regulating the stratospheric ozone layer and in the greenhouse effect. Nitrous oxide is emitted naturally during nitrification and denitrification, but the advent of industrial nitrogen fertilizer use may have accelerated the flow of N_2O to the atmosphere (see above). N_2O is also emitted during fossil fuel combustion. N_2O levels in the atmosphere have increased recently over preindustrial levels (see Chapter 23, "Atmosphere and Climate," Figure 23.1), and may be contributing to the recent loss of stratospheric ozone observed over much of the Northern Hemisphere as well as the 1.5–4.5°C greenhouse warming that may occur as soon as 2030. (For additional information on these effects, refer to Chapter 10, "Atmosphere and Climate.")

Reducing Human Impacts

Technical and economic tools are available to mitigate some of the worst damage people cause by their interference in the nitrogen cycle. Implementation of some mitigation measures, however, is stymied by high cost, occasionally uncertain benefits, and political barriers. The numerous and elusive pathways followed by nitrogen compounds through the biosphere confuse the identification and quantification of cause-and-effect relationships, so the full benefits of controlling a specific source of nitrogen pollution are rarely known with confidence. Nevertheless, many governments recognize that uncontrolled releases of nitrogen compounds can seriously damage human health and the natural environment, and have begun to restrict them. Using new, low-pollution production techniques, farmers, automobile manufacturers, industries, and other emitters of nitrogen compounds have begun to comply with pollution restrictions.

Managing nitrogen pollution of surface and ground water demands a multidisciplinary approach. The effluent nitrogen compounds from point sources such as urban sewage systems can be controlled using sedimentation and biological treatment techniques (20), but these systems are extensively applied only in wealthier countries. Advanced sewage treatment, which often includes a nitrogen-removal process, covers over 70 percent of the population of some OECD countries (New Zealand, Denmark, Sweden, Switzerland, the United Kingdom, and the Federal Republic of Germany) but covers less than 20 percent in some other OECD countries (Spain, Portugal and Turkey) (21).

Nitrate runoff from fertilized cropland can be minimized by reducing excess applications of nitrogenous fertilizers and by reducing runoff from the field. Supplemental fertilizer is not always essential. Substituting leguminous crops for synthetic fertilizer and incorporating organic matter into the soil can maintain adequate soil nitrogen to promote crop growth without promoting excessive leaching. Delaying fertilizer applications, using ammonia fertilizer rather than nitrate fertilizer, and instituting anti-erosion measures can also reduce nitrate runoff (22). Box 11.1 discusses some advances in biotechnology that may reduce the need for heavy applications of supplemental fertilizers. (For a discussion of how government policies can affect fertilizer use, see Chapter 12, "Policies and Institutions," Agricultural Policies.)

Reducing NO_x emissions from automobiles and power plants can be accomplished through a variety of technical modifications. For example, in automobiles, passing the engine exhaust gases over certain catalysts converts NO back to inert nitrogen gas and oxygen. Newer engines with fuel injection systems (as opposed to carburetors) can also be finely calibrated to minimize NO_x emissions. Using these two general approaches (increasingly in combination), manufacturers have been able to produce automobiles in compliance with ever-stricter emission standards. Vehicles without any emission controls emit NO_x at the rate of 2.2 grams of NO_x per kilometer travelled (g/km). In the United States, emissions standards for automobiles were tightened from 1.9 g/km in 1973 to 0.6 g/km in 1981, and to 0.4 g/km for cars sold in California (23).

THE GLOBAL WATER CYCLE

Water is one of nature's remarkable inventions, differing from other liquids in almost every respect. The chemistry of life takes place in liquid water because of water's unusual ability to dissolve a wide variety of materials. Earth is home to the only life we know in the solar system because liquid water is common here and nowhere else. Water circulates through the biosphere it helps create, connecting and driving processes occurring on land, in the sea, and in the air. Water moderates the planet's temperature, molds the land surface, and sustains the profusion of living things that gave rise to and now feed humanity. It is one of the fundamental systems that makes life on Earth possible.

In the past few centuries humans have gained the power to interfere with this cycle, and may now be altering it to the point that environmental impacts can be expected on a planetary scale. The water cycle connects many of today's most intractable environmental problems: deforestation, climate change, desertification, soil erosion, water pollution, and others. By tracing water's role in each of these problems, one can see that they are

Figure 11.2 The Global Water Cycle

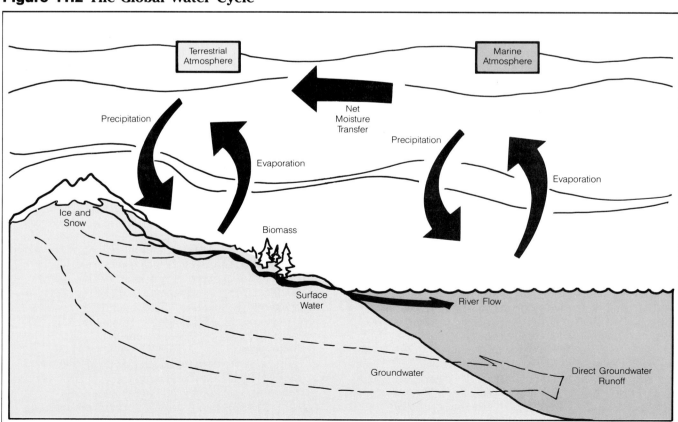

Source: Based on U.S. Committee for an International Geosphere—Biosphere Program, Commission on Physical Science, Mathematics, and Resources, Natural Resources Council, *Global Changes in the Geosphere—Biosphere: Initial Priorities for an IGBP* (National Academy Press, Washington, D.C., 1986), Figure 6.1, p. 73.

Table 11.3 Stocks and Flows of the Global Water Cycle

	Best Estimate[a]	Range of Published Estimates	Residence Time[b]
Stocks (cubic kilometers)			
Oceans	1.35 billion	1.32–1.37 billion	2,500 years
Atmosphere	13,000	10,500–15,500	8 days
Land			
Rivers	1,700	1020–2120	16 days
Lakes	100,000	30,000–177,000	17 years
Inland seas	105,000	85,400–125,000	X
Soil moisture	70,000	16,500–150,000	1 year
Groundwater	8.2 million	7–330 million	1,400 years
Glaciers and icecaps	27.5 million	16.5–48.02 million	c
Biota	1,100	600–50,000	hours
Flows (cubic kilometers per year)			
Evaporation from Land	71,000	63,000–73,000	
Precipitation on Land	111,000	99,000–119,000	
Evaporation from the Ocean	425,000	383,000–505,000	
Precipitation on the Ocean	385,000	320,000–458,000	
Runoff from Land to Oceans	39,700	33,500–47,000	
Rivers	27,000	27,000–45,000	
Direct groundwater runoff	12,000	0–12,000	
Glacier runoff (water and ice)	2,500	1,700–4,500	
Net Moisture Transfer from Marine to Terrestrial Atmospheres	39,700	X	

Sources:
1. D.H. Speidel and A.F. Agnew, "The World Water Budget," in *Perspectives on Water: Uses and Abuses*, D.H. Speidel, L. Ruedisili, and A.F. Agnew, eds. (Oxford University Press, New York, 1988), p. 28. (This source summarizes several other primary references.)
2. NAS/NRC, *Global Change in the Geosphere–Biosphere: Initial Priorities for an IGBP* (National Academy Press, Washington, D.C., 1986), p. 73.
3. R. K. Klige, "Trends in Variation of Surface Waters of the Hydrosphere," *Vodnye Resursy*, Vol. 3, No. 9 (May/June 1982), pp. 272–83.
4. E.K. Berner and R.A. Berner, *The Global Water Cycle: Geochemistry and Environment* (Prentice-Hall, Englewood Cliffs, 1987), p. 14.
5. M.I. Budyko, "Water Cycle on the Earth," *Studies and Reports in Hydrology*, Vol. 25, 1982, pp. 57–117.

Notes:
a. Estimated by source 1.
b. Estimated by source 5.
c. Water in montane glaciers and polar icecaps have residence times of 1,600 and 9,700 years, respectively.
X = not available.

related, that they can have unexpected impacts far from their immediate surroundings, and that they have the potential to damage the water cycle itself.

Stocks and Flows

Water is constantly in motion, at paces that range from the imperceptible creep of glaciers to the relatively rapid downpour of rainfall. Oceans, lakes, and water contained in living things are all water *stocks*. Water *flows* between the stocks as rainfall, evaporation, and riverflow.

Figure 11.2 presents a simplified model of the stocks and flows of the global water cycle; their magnitudes are summarized in Table 11.3. The oceans are the dominant component of the water cycle, containing over 97 percent of the total stock. The remainder is freshwater, the majority of which is found as ice, snow, and groundwater. The surface water that nurtures terrestrial life accounts for only one or two ten-thousandths of the global water stock. The Earth's biota contain far less water; according to the best estimate, the water contained in the Earth's biota would not fill Africa's Lake Victoria. (See Chapter 21, "Freshwater," Table 21.4.)

Although the volumes of some of the water stocks are known within 20 percent, the rates of many of the flows are only estimated within a factor of two. Precipitation and evaporation over the oceans, for example, are poorly

measured. A better understanding of the water cycle is a priority for the World Climate Research Programme and the International Geosphere-Biosphere Programme, so it is likely that knowledge of stocks, flows, and water-cycle processes will increase substantially over the next 15 years. (See Box 11.2 and Recent Developments.)

Human Impacts on the Water Cycle

As human populations and economic activity have increased, the global water cycle has been significantly modified from its natural state. Flows have been altered substantially by the withdrawal of water from rivers and aquifers, evaporation from reservoirs, destruction of natural ecosystems, and the construction of cities. However, it is not yet clear whether these modifications will produce major feedbacks such as altered rainfall patterns.

The most important human impact on the water cycle is consumptive use. Water is withdrawn from rivers and aquifers for domestic, industrial, and agricultural purposes. Although some water is returned to the stream after use (such as water used to cool industrial facilities), much evaporates or is incorporated into products (such as crops). This loss reduces riverflow. Irrigation, which loses large quantities of water to evaporation during conveyance and on the field, is a heavy consumer of water.

Other modifications, although smaller, also have important impacts. Reservoirs created by dams are rich sources of evaporation and help to create a larger supply of stable runoff. (See Box 11.3.) The impermeable asphalt and concrete in cities allow less water to soak into the ground and cause more to be diverted to flood runoff. The water quality of urban runoff is frequently degraded as well. Cutting down forests and draining wetlands modify evaporation and runoff regimes, although the specific impacts depend on the location and the nature of what replaces these natural ecosystems.

Many of humanity's past interventions in the water cycle have had clear benefits. The 18 percent of the world's cropland that is irrigated produces about one third the world's food supply (24). Dams have increased the reliability of water supplies, reduced the incidence and severity of floods, and provided hydroelectric power. The availability of water for industrial uses has allowed many regions to achieve high levels of economic development. Alterations of the water cycle have caused hydrological and other environmental problems in some river basins, but human interference with the water cycle has not yet caused planetary-scale problems.

If water use grows, however, this could change. The area under irrigation more than doubled between 1900 and 1950 from 40 million to 90 million hectares and is estimated to have tripled between 1950 and 1985 (25). Land under irrigation in 93 developing countries, excluding China, is projected to grow 50 percent between 1983 and 2000 (26). Continuing growth in industrial and domestic water demand is also possible. (For a further discussion of efficient water use see Chapter 8, "Freshwater," and *World Resources 1987*, Chapter 8, "Freshwater.") The hydroelectric potentials of Asia, South America, and Africa are still largely untapped and invite expanded hydroelectric power development. (See Chapter 20, "Energy, Materials, and Wastes," Table 20.2.)

Box 11.2 Global Research on the Water Cycle

Very little about the global water cycle is well known. Some of the stocks and flows have been measured with reasonable accuracy, but most have not. Estimates of the total volume of soil moisture vary by a factor of 10, and for glacial runoff by a factor of three. (See Table 11.3.) No one knows if the Greenland and Antarctic ice sheets are presently gaining or losing mass. The net impact of clouds on climate is uncertain and their future role in climate change cannot be predicted without better understanding of their current role. Much of the rain that falls on continents is transpired through plants, but not enough is known about how plants and ecosystems respond to changes in precipitation, radiation and temperature.

Several international research programs have been launched in the last decade that will help overcome some of this ignorance. The majority are concerned with such issues as climate and climate change, in which the water cycle plays an important role. The two largest—the World Climate Research Programme and the International Geosphere-Biosphere Programme—involve scientists from over a hundred countries working in laboratories, in the field, on ocean-going ships, and with data gathered by remote sensing satellites.

The World Climate Research Programme (WCRP), jointly managed by the World Meteorological Organization and the International Council of Scientific Unions (ICSU), has numerous components that will add to our knowledge of the water cycle. The International Satellite Cloud Climatology Project (ISCCP), the first of these to be launched, entered its operational phase in 1983. Clouds are known to play key roles in regulating the natural greenhouse effect and in determining the Earth's albedo (the percentage of incoming solar radiation reflected back to space by air, clouds and the Earth's surface). They are also expected to be a critical factor in amplifying or moderating future climate change processes. ISCCP will collect and analyze satellite-observed cloud data and quantify the impact of clouds on the Earth's radiation budget and climate processes (1).

A second effort under the WCRP, the Global Precipitation Climatology Project (GPCP), is motivated by the lack of reliable long-term precipitation data over the oceans and much of the continental land surface. Land-based rain gauges are often unreliable or are too scattered, and ocean precipitation conditions are modelled based on rainfall over a few islands. The GPCP will develop methods of using satellite data (verified by reliable rain gauges) to produce accurate, large-scale, global rainfall estimates (2).

The International Satellite Land-Surface Climatology Project (ISLSCP), organized by ICSU's Committee on Space Research and the International Association of Meteorology and Atmospheric Physics, will investigate the impact of land-surface conditions on climate. Vegetation, for example, affects the albedo, evapotranspiration, and the planet's surface temperature and radiation budget. ISLSCP will use satellite remote sensing data to quantify the relationships between land-surface conditions and climate processes, and will attempt to document the impacts of climate and people on the land surface (3).

The Global Energy and Water Cycle Experiment (GEWEX), another major WCRP program, may produce the richest flow of data on the water cycle. GEWEX will attempt to unify global models of the energy and water cycles by developing improved data (derived in some cases from the projects discussed above) on precipitation, evapotranspiration, latent heat flows, atmospheric and oceanic circulation, radiation budgets and clouds, and surface processes. This ambitious program is in an exploratory phase, and will not become operational before 1995 (4).

The International Geosphere-Biosphere Programme (IGBP) is an international effort to "describe and understand the interactive physical, chemical, and biological processes that regulate the total Earth system, the unique environment that it provides for life, the changes that are occurring in this system, and the manner in which they are influenced by human actions" (5). Coordinated by ICSU, the IGBP established four program panels in 1987 to identify and develop research objectives to be pursued in the 1990s. One panel—on Biospheric Aspects of the Hydrological

Cycle—has direct relevance to water cycle research, and has already outlined a few research themes. These include: developing improved hydrological models to couple with atmospheric models; studying the influence of vegetation on the heat and moisture budget of the land surface; and, investigating the biological and physiological characteristics of plants that affect energy and water cycles (6). For additional details on the IGBP, see *World Resources 1987*, pp. 177–78.

References and Notes

1. Committee on Space Research (COSPAR), International Council of Scientific Unions, *Report of the COSPAR Ad-hoc Group on Remote Sensing for Global Change* (National Aeronautics and Space Administration, Goddard Space Flight Center, Greenbelt, Maryland, October 1986), pp. 23–24.
2. World Climate Research Programme, *Report of the Workshop on Global Large-Scale Precipitation Data Sets for the World Climate Research Programme* (World Meteorological Organization, Geneva, January 1986), p. 1.
3. Thomas Schmugge and Piers Sellers, eds., *Experiment Plan for the First ISLSCP Field Experiment: FIFE* (National Aeronautics and Space Administration, Goddard Space Flight Center, Greenbelt, Maryland, May 1986), p. 4.
4. World Climate Research Programme, *Report of the Workshop on Space Systems Possibilities for a Global Energy and Water Cycle Experiment* (World Meteorological Organization, Geneva, 1987), pp. 1–3.
5. International Council of Scientific Unions (ICSU), Ad Hoc Planning Group on Global Change, *The International Geosphere-Biosphere Programme: A Study of Global Change* (ICSU, Paris, August 1986), p. 3.
6. Coordinating Panel on Biospheric Aspects of the Hydrological Cycle, International Geosphere-Biosphere Programme, *A Study of Global Change, Selected Research Objectives* (draft, 1987), pp. 12–16.

The Water Cycle and the Atmosphere

Water is a minor constituent of the atmosphere, and the atmosphere contains only one one-thousandth of 1 percent of the global stock of water. Yet the interactions between the atmosphere and water cycle are critical. They create a life-sustaining climate and set the water cycle in motion. Disturbance of this interaction, through human-induced climatic change for example, could cause profound alterations in the water cycle. Similarly, disturbance of the water cycle could have direct impacts on local, regional, and global climate.

Global Interactions

Only about half the solar radiation arriving at the edge of the atmosphere is absorbed by the ground. (See Figure 11.3.) About 31 percent of the incoming solar radiation is reflected back to space by air, clouds, and the Earth's surface. (This fraction is known as the planet's *albedo*.) Some of the rest is absorbed by the atmosphere and clouds.

The energy that actually reaches the ground must eventually be removed if the Earth's surface is to remain in energy equilibrium. This is accomplished in three ways. First, a small percentage of this energy directly warms the air. Second, a larger percentage is released as *latent heat*, the energy that evaporates water from oceans and land surfaces. Finally, the remaining energy is released as long-wave radiation. Certain gases in the atmosphere (e.g., carbon dioxide and water vapor) absorb and re-emit this long-wave radiation, forming a partially closed cycle of energy flow. This trapping action, the nat-

Figure 11.3 The Water Cycle and Global Climate[a] [b]

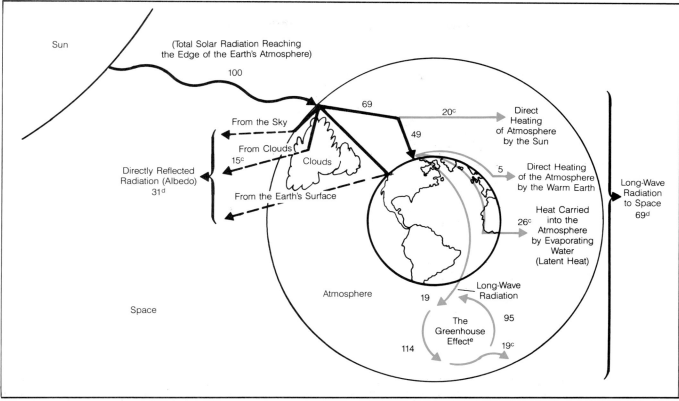

Source: Adapted from: V. Ramanathan, "The Role of Earth Radiation Budget Studies in Climate and General Circulation Research," *Journal of Geophysical Research*, Vol. 92, No. D4, p. 4076 (1987).
Notes:
a. Each unit is 3.43 watts per square meter.
b. Numbers may not total due to independent rounding.
c. Processes involving the water cycle.
d. Measured by satellite instruments. Other data are modelled or derived from other measurements.
e. Caused by water vapor, clouds, and carbon dioxide and other gases.

ural *greenhouse effect*, warms the atmosphere and makes life on Earth possible.

Water also plays an important role in moderating climate fluctuations between day and night and among the seasons. For example, the top 3 meters of the ocean store as much heat energy as the entire atmosphere. The oceans can thus absorb and give up great quantities of heat without a substantial change in temperature; this moderates the climate near coasts. In continental interiors at middle latitudes, the temperature difference between the summer maximum and winter minimum can reach 80°C. Over the ocean, the range in air temperature rarely exceeds 10°C (27).

Water is clearly a component of the global climate system. Atmospheric water helps regulate the global energy budget. Water in the form of clouds, oceans, snow, and ice helps define the albedo; without clouds, for example, the Earth's surface and atmosphere would receive 21 percent more radiation than they do now. Atmospheric water vapor absorbs both incoming solar radiation and outgoing longwave radiation emitted by the Earth's surface. Evaporating water is a major means of releasing heat from the Earth's surface. Without clouds, carbon dioxide, and atmospheric water vapor, the Earth's average

surface temperature would be 22°C colder than it is now and the planet would be covered with ice (28).

Continental Scale Interactions

The preceding section assumes that all parts of the globe experience the same energy balance. In reality, different regions receive different inputs of solar radiation; this causes a natural flow of energy from areas of surplus to areas of deficit, and the water cycle is the principal means of transporting this energy. The most important movement of energy is from the equator towards the poles; equatorial regions receive over four times as much solar radiation as polar regions do. Three mechanisms transport the surplus: flows of warm air, warm ocean currents, and the transport of water vapor containing its latent heat of vaporization. Ocean currents, for example, account for about 40 percent of the heat flow in the northern hemisphere (29) (30).

Climate Change and the Water Cycle

The natural greenhouse effect helps make the planet habitable. However, the atmospheric concentrations of natural and synthetic greenhouse gases (carbon dioxide, methane, chlorofluorocarbons, etc.) have been increasing rapidly over the past few centuries because of human combustion of fossil fuels, deforestation, and widespread industrialization. As a result, the planet could be committed to a 1.5–4.5°C temperature increase by 2030. (See Chapter 10, "Atmosphere and Climate," Climate Change.)

The water cycle is so intimately linked to climate that global warming would affect every stock and flow, with incalculable consequences for humanity. Unfortunately, existing climate models are unable to identify exactly *where* changes will occur, or how large they will be. Our knowledge of the water cycle is sketchy (see Table 11.3),

and the computing power available to modelers allows only coarse geographic resolution, which prevents realistic representation of many features of the water cycle, such as soil moisture, evapotranspiration, and runoff (31). Thus, a discussion of climate change's future impact on the water cycle remains largely qualitative (32).

Evaporation and precipitation are expected to increase in a warmer world. Global average precipitation would probably be enhanced by 5–10 percent because of greater evaporation from oceans and land surfaces and more rapid transpiration through plants (33). *Soil moisture* will probably change in many regions because of

---

Box 11.3 The Water Cycle in Miniature

The basins of the world's two longest rivers—the Amazon and the Nile—demonstrate the intimate linkages between the water cycle, vegetation, the atmosphere, and sediment transport. Humans have altered, and may have broken, some of these linkages, raising the possibility of disastrous repercussions within these river basins and possibly worldwide.

THE NILE

The Nile basin has been home to a settled agricultural civilization for millennia. For most of that period the valley and delta supported one crop per year, usually planted after the summer flood receded.

For the past 150 years, the government of Egypt has built engineering works to permit year-round cultivation in most of the country. Egypt's population grew rapidly from 2.5 million in 1800 to 50 million in 1988, and with limited new area to cultivate, intensifying agriculture was the only way to grow more food (1) (2). Cash crops, especially cotton, have made additional demands on the limited land and water resources.

Against a backdrop of steadily rising water demands in Egypt and in Sudan, along with the need to control the Nile floods, the Egyptian government decided to build the largest engineering work on the Nile and one of the greatest in the world: the High Dam at Aswan. Constructed over the period 1960–70, the dam rises 111 meters above the river channel, and is 3,820 meters long, 980 meters thick at the base and 40 meters thick at the top (3). Lake Nasser, the reservoir formed by the dam, has a surface area of over 5,000 square kilometers and a volume of 164 cubic kilometers, of which 30 cubic kilometers are set aside for sedimentation over the next 300 years (4).

The dam has produced undisputed benefits but has also created large costs, some unexpected. On the positive side, the large annual flood of the Nile is now completely controlled, and the dam moderates year-to-year fluctuations in the Nile's flow. (See Figure 1.) As a result, Egypt and Sudan are now assured of a supply of 74 cubic kilometers of water each year, compared with their pre-dam combined withdrawal of 52.5 cubic kilometers per year. An additional 10–15 cubic kilometers per year are lost from the reservoir by evaporation (5).

The benefits to Egypt alone are more

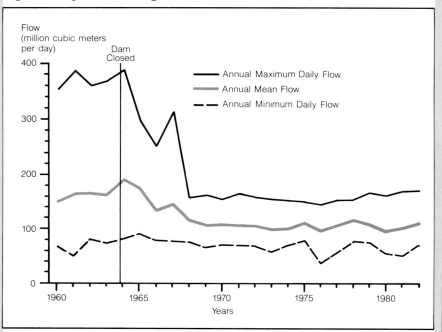

Figure 1 Impact of the High Dam at Aswan on the Nile's Flow Downstream

Flow (million cubic meters per day)

Dam Closed

— Annual Maximum Daily Flow
— Annual Mean Flow
- - - Annual Minimum Daily Flow

Years

Source: Stephan Kempe, "Impact of Aswan High Dam on Water Chemistry of the Nile," in *Transport of Carbon and Minerals in Major World Rivers,* Egon T. Degens, Stephan Kempe and Hassan Soliman, eds. (University of Hamburg, Hamburg, 1983), Part 2, p. 411.

ambiguous. Of the 21.5 cubic kilometers of water per year made available by the dam, Egypt can claim 7.5 cubic kilometers, with Sudan receiving the balance. However, this apportionment was predicated on an estimated loss of 15 cubic kilometers per year from Lake Nasser from both evaporation and seepage. Some recent estimates, however, place evaporative losses alone in that range, and seepage losses may be an additional 5 cubic kilometers per year. Over the long term, more than half of Egypt's share of the new water may be lost during storage (6).

The dam has also changed the Nile's sediment budget, almost certainly in a detrimental manner. Formerly, about 125 million metric tons of suspended sediment passed Aswan each year, 98 percent during the flood season. Lake Nasser is now the final destination of most of this sediment; the sediment load

below the dam averages 2.5 million metric tons per year, 2 percent of its former mass (7). The valley and delta lands downstream of the dam no longer receive a layer of silt with each flood, and are thus deprived of nutrients and soil bulk. The loss of some nutrients can be replaced by expensive artificial fertilizers. However, the loss of new soil mass has created several problems. The brickmaking industry, which formerly used silt cleared from irrigation canals, now buys topsoil from farmers to supply its kilns. This further depletes topsoil, which is already being depleted by intensive cropping (8). The shoreline of the Nile Delta, deprived of much of its annual sediment deposit, is now retreating under the Mediterranean's erosive action (9). The loss of nutrients flowing into the Eastern Mediterranean has been at least partially responsible for the reduction in Egypt's sar-

changes in precipitation, evaporation, and the composition of vegetation. Because the amount and timing of soil moisture is a critical factor in plant growth, changes could have profound impact on global cropping patterns and the viability of natural ecosystems. *Runoff*, and its partition into surface and groundwater flow, would be altered by any changes in precipitation, evapotranspiration, soil moisture, and vegetation cover. Changes in the amount and timing of runoff would affect dams, levees, irrigation projects, and even cities. For example, such water control structures as dams and levees are designed based on a river's historical behavior, but climate-change induced alterations of runoff regimes (coupled with direct human modification of river hydrology) could result in peak flows for which the control systems are inadequate (34).

Several water stocks would also be affected by climate change. Polar ice caps and montane glaciers would retreat in response to a warmer temperature, transferring water to the oceans and raising the sea level. The oceans themselves would expand because water becomes less dense as it warms. A 10–15 centimeter rise in the global sea level has been observed over the last 100 years; researchers believe that 2–5 centimeters of this rise have

---

Box 11.3

dine catch from 18,000 metric tons in 1962 to essentially zero in 1978 (10).

THE AMAZON

The Amazon drains a 5.8 million square kilometer basin and discharges 5,500 cubic kilometers of water per year, one fifth of the world's riverflow (11). Sixty percent of the basin is covered by lowland tropical rainforest, harboring a fantastic diversity of plants and animals (12). About 12,700 cubic kilometers of rain falls on the basin each year, half of which (7,200 cubic kilometers per year) derives from evapotranspiration within the basin. The forest has its own water cycle. Plants, as with most biomass, are largely water, and the air trapped under the tropical forest canopy often has a relative humidity of 100 percent. Water circulates within this area, carrying nutrients from the canopy—where an active community of herbivores and carnivores consumes and excretes biomass—to the forest floor where they are taken up again by plants. Some elements, such as phosphorus and magnesium, are essentially locked in the internal nutrient cycle of the forest; they are not added to the forest from rainfall in any appreciable quantity and do not leave the forest in streamflow (13).

The past few decades have witnessed accelerating deforestation in the Amazon Basin. All of the basin countries have built roads into the sparsely populated rainforest to encourage agricultural colonization, timber production, mineral exploitation, and cattle raising. Brazil built several highways transecting the forest. Millions of colonists have followed the roads, clearing virgin forest land and raising crops and cattle on the fragile soil. Many colonists were fleeing the drought-stricken northeast region of the country, but an even greater number were compelled to leave small holdings or sharecropping arrangements in the southern part of the country when large-scale farming enterprises centralized and mechanized their operations (14).

In one Brazilian state, Rondonia, the construction of a highway through the rainforest brought in nearly half a million colonists between 1960 and 1980. The deforested area increased from 121,700 hectares in 1975 to 2,610,000 hectares in 1985. Rondonia had about 21 million hectares of forest cover prior to colonization, but by 1985 11 percent of the

forest area had been deforested and another 24 percent disturbed (15) (16). About 2–3 million hectares are cleared annually in all of Brazilian Amazonia (17).

The ongoing deforestation of the Amazon Basin could alter the regional water balance through several linked mechanisms. As forests are cleared, more water will be lost from the basin as flood flow because less will be retained in plants or in soil moisture. Because a large fraction of Amazonian rainfall derives from evapotranspiration within the basin, less transpiration could well mean less rainfall. A lower rate of evapotranspiration may also cause the temperature to rise because evapotranspiration removes heat as well as water (18). A decrease in evapotranspiration might also reduce the formation of clouds, increasing the amount of sunlight reaching the surface. Although the net effect of these interactive processes is a matter of considerable dispute, it is possible that deforestation in Amazonia could trigger a self-reinforcing process of desiccation.

Impacts could also be felt far from the Amazon Basin. Evapotranspiration from Amazonia contributes to the poleward flow of heat and moisture in the atmosphere, and Amazonian deforestation could alter these flows on a global scale. These developments could have major effects on cloud formation and rainfall patterns in the temperate zones (19). At present these fears are entirely speculative; current models are not sophisticated enough to simulate the atmospheric consequences of deforestation.

References and Notes

1. Stephan Kempe, "Impact of Aswan High Dam on Water Chemistry of the Nile," in *Transport of Carbon and Minerals in Major World Rivers*, Egon T. Degens and Hassan Soliman, eds. (University of Hamburg, 1983), Part 2, p. 402.
2. United Nations (U.N.), Department of International Economic and Social Affairs, *World Population Prospects: Estimates and Projections as Assessed in 1984* (U.N., New York, 1986), p. 194.
3. S.D. Wahby and N.F. Bishara, "The Effect of the River Nile on Mediterranean Water Before and After the Construction of the High Dam at Aswan," in *River Inputs to Ocean Systems* (United Nations, New York, 1981), p. 311.
4. *Op. cit.* 1, Part 2, p. 406.
5. John Waterbury, *Hydropolitics of the Nile Valley* (Syracuse University Press, Syracuse, New York, 1979), p. 72.
6. *Ibid.*, pp. 124–125.
7. Mamdouh Shahin, *Hydrology of the Nile Basin* (Elsevier, Amsterdam, 1985), pp. 459–460.
8. *Op. cit.* 5, pp. 129–131.
9. Scot E. Smith and Adel Abdel-Kader, "Coastal Erosion Along the Egyptian Delta," *Journal of Coastal Research*, Vol. 4, No. 2 (1988), p. 253.
10. Arid Lands Information Center, University of Arizona, *Draft Environmental Report on Arab Republic of Egypt* (U.S. Agency for International Development, Washington, D.C., 1980), p. 46.
11. P.R. Leopoldo, *et al.*, "Towards a Water Balance in the Central Amazonian Region," *Experientia*, Vol. 43 (1987), pp. 223–224.
12. Michael Williams, University Lecturer in Geography and Fellow of Oriel College Oxford, "Forest Change," paper presented at Earth as Transformed by Human Activity Conference, Clark University, Worcester, Massachusetts, October 1987, p. 49.
13. *Op. cit.* 11, p. 231.
14. *Op. cit.* 12, pp. 49–50.
15. Jean-Paul Malingreau and Compton J. Tucker, "Large-Scale Deforestation in the Southeastern Amazon Basin of Brazil," *Ambio*, Vol. 17, No. 1 (1988), pp. 53–54.
16. George M. Woodwell, Richard A. Houghton, and Thomas A. Stone, "Deforestation in the Brazilian Amazon Basin Measured by Satellite Imagery," in *Tropical Rain Forests and the World Atmosphere*, Ghillean T. Prance, ed. (Westview Press, Boulder, Colorado, 1986), p. 25.
17. Eneas Salati, "The Forest and the Hydrological Cycle," in *The Geophysiology of Amazonia: Vegetation and Climate Interactions*, Robert E. Dickinson, ed. (John Wiley & Sons, New York, 1987), p. 291.
18. *Ibid.*, pp. 291–293.
19. Eneas Salati and Peter B. Vose, "Amazon Basin: A System in Equilibrium," *Science*, Vol. 225, No. 4658 (1984), pp. 136–137.

been caused by thermal expansion of water and the remainder by melting of glaciers and ice caps (35). A rise of 80 centimeters over the level in the 1880s is possible by 2030, which could inundate densely populated coastal lowlands, contaminate coastal aquifers, and increase the risk of devastating storm surges. (See Chapter 9, "Oceans and Coasts," Recent Developments, and Chapter 10, "Atmosphere and Climate," Climate Change.)

The water cycle will also play a key role in climate change processes. For example, a rise in the global temperature is expected to increase evaporation. Increased evaporation would introduce more water vapor into the atmosphere. But water vapor is a greenhouse gas, so this may accelerate the warming process. Clouds present another problem. Clouds are the single largest determinant of the planetary albedo; they reduce the amount of radiation striking the Earth's surface and cool it by at least 12°C. Clouds also play an important role in the natural greenhouse effect, which warms the Earth (36). The net effect of clouds on climate is still unclear, and clouds' impact on climate change (and vice versa) is one of the largest unknowns facing researchers.

The Water Cycle and the Solid Earth

Flowing water shapes the surface of the Earth, creating soils, rearranging the landscape, and moving materials and nutrients to the sea. The water cycle levels mountains, carves river channels, deposits nutrient-rich silt in river valleys, builds deltas, and nourishes the productivity of near-shore ecosystems.

Water is a key factor in the formation of soils. Many of the chemical compounds found in rocks dissolve in water, especially when the water is acidic. Anthropogenically acidified rainwater is increasingly common (see Chapter 10, "Atmosphere and Climate," Impacts on the Biosphere from Tropospheric Pollution), and water in contact with rocks has an even larger input of acids produced by plants and microbial metabolism. Water also plays a role in the physical weathering of rocks; when water freezes in rock cracks it expands, breaking apart the rock and exposing more surface area to chemical weathering. Soil forms as water and other agents weather rock, and the relationship between soil type and climate is so strong that major soil classes can initially be mapped based on climate patterns (37).

Materials Transport

Water transports materials in two forms: as dissolved minerals and as bulk material, such as soil, sand, and pebbles. Water's movement of rock and soil gradually erodes the global land surface at a rate of about 6.5 centimeters per thousand years (38).

Water erodes soil and rock, carrying dissolved minerals and sediment with it. The movement of material by rivers is impressive; overall, rivers discharge about 13 billion metric tons of sediment each year to the sea. (See Figure 11.4.)

People interfere with sediment transport in a number of ways. Such large-scale vegetation alteration as clearing forests for cropland is believed to accelerate erosion and sediment transport (see below, The Water Cycle and the Biosphere). Humans also modify sediment budgets by building dams, levees, and dikes, and by dredging ports and navigation channels. On a global scale, 2–5 billion metric tons of sediment are trapped behind dams each year, about one quarter the amount that actually reaches the oceans (39). The impact of the Aswan Dam on the sediment budget of the Nile is discussed in Box 11.3.

Rivers also transport material in dissolved form, principally soluble ions such as chloride, sulfate, calcium, sodium, magnesium, bicarbonate, silica, and potassium (40). Most of these dissolved materials derive from weathered rock, so rivers bear the chemical "fingerprints" of the lands they flow through.

The atmosphere also influences dissolved material transport by depositing such soluble materials as sea salts and mineral dust into rivers. These materials are then transported downstream (41). Water pollution is the third major factor in river chemistry. Industrial effluents, domestic sewage, and agricultural runoff contain a variety of soluble ions; in addition, human activity adds polluting pesticides and industrial chemicals, such as DDT and PCBs that have no natural counterparts. Anthropogenic pollution may increase river loading of some ions by over 30 percent on a global basis (42).

The Water Cycle and the Biosphere

The water cycle and biosphere interact in a variety of ways. At the most fundamental level, water is essential for life; living things are mostly water, and water is the medium in which the chemistry of life takes place.

On a regional scale, water and energy are the principal determinants of large-scale vegetation communities and their productivity. Forests dominate when rainfall is plentiful enough throughout most of the year to create a water surplus after evaporation. When there is sufficient solar energy to fully evaporate precipitation and produce an extended dry season, different vegetation groups dominate: first savannas, steppes, and prairies, and then semi-deserts and deserts as the energy surplus desiccates the environment.

Vegetation, in turn, has two potent impacts on the water cycle. About 70 percent of the precipitation falling on land returns to the atmosphere by evapotranspiration through plants. This can be multiplied by a recycling effect: water transpired from one region often falls as precipitation in another, where it is transpired again. Loss of vegetation can disrupt this process. Large-scale deforestation in the Amazon Basin, for example, could have devastating impacts on that region's hydrology. (See Box 11.3.)

Vegetation also helps determine how much of the net precipitation (precipitation minus evapotranspiration) soaks into the ground or flows over the surface as flood runoff. Dense vegetation prevents soil from being compacted by raindrops and promotes biological activity that aerates it. Densely vegetated land can usually absorb a substantial portion of the rainfall from any rainstorm, but reduced vegetation cover impairs the soil's ability to absorb rainfall and increases flooding and soil erosion (43).

Large-scale removal of vegetation can change the

Figure 11.4 Annual Discharge of Suspended Sediment from Various Drainage Basins of the World

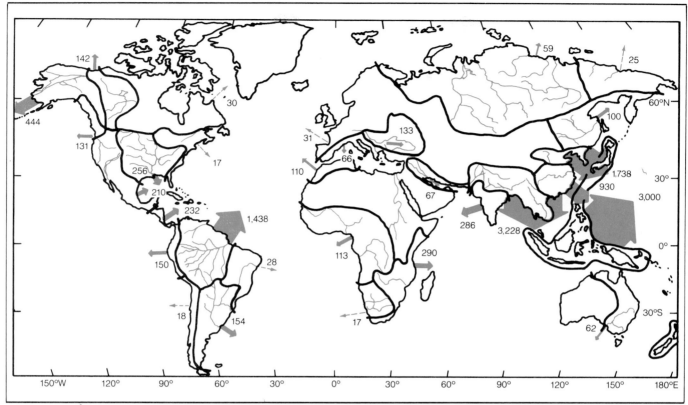

Source: J.D. Milliman and R.H. Meade, "Worldwide Delivery of River Sediment to the Ocean," *Journal of Geology,* vol. 91 (January 1983), p. 16.
Note: Width of arrows corresponds to relative discharge of sediment. Numbers refer to average annual input in millions of metric tons. Direction of arrows does not indicate direction of sediment movement.

hydrology and sediment budget of whole countries. Seventy-five percent of Haiti, for example, was probably covered by forests prior to European colonization. By 1954, only 8–9 percent of the original forest remained; the balance was lost to commercial timber exploitation, fuelwood demand, and expanding agriculture. By 1978, 12 of the 30 major watersheds in Haiti were completely deforested, with 8 more expected to be denuded by 1990. Deforestation has had a disastrous impact on water availability; the rivers and streams of Haiti now flow in torrential bursts after each rainfall and less water flows in the stable runoff of the dry season. The hydroelectric installation at the Peligre dam, the main electricity source for the capital city, has had to operate below design capacity because the reservoir lost 30 percent of its volume to siltation over the last 25 years (44).

ENVIRONMENTAL HISTORY

During the 1930s, the United States Department of Agriculture sent Dr. W.C. Lowdermilk, then head of the Soil Conservation Service, to survey the damage done by soil erosion on lands around the globe that had been under cultivation for thousands of years. His mission was to learn how the experience of these older civilizations might help the United States face the problem of massive soil erosion in the Dust Bowl area and the South. His research led to a call for increased commitment to soil conservation techniques in the United States. After visiting over a dozen countries, Lowdermilk observed that "the land does not lie; it bears a record of what men write on it," a statement that is also true of the environment as a whole (45). Researchers are now beginning to learn how to read this record, and to understand the importance of the information it provides for decisions about the future. (See Boxes 11.4 and 11.5 for descriptions of the most common methods of reading natural and written environmental records.)

Environmental history is one of the most important tools available for understanding how the Earth's systems work. It can be broadly defined as the sum of all those techniques that are used to reconstruct the Earth's environmental past. This reconstruction enables us to see how the Earth has evolved over billions of years, and to place recent trends and events in their historical context. More importantly, by describing the natural variability of the Earth's systems, environmental history allows us to evaluate the magnitude of impacts from past human activities, and to judge possible consequences from present ones. Finally, environmental history provides data against which predictive scientific models can be tested; whether models can accurately reconstruct the past is

11 Global Systems and Cycles

Pollen grains on the ocean floor and coral reefs found on mountaintops are two examples of the many materials that reveal information about the Earth's past. Most natural archives describe global change less dramatically, but all hold a wealth of information for those who know what to look for. Moreover, because these sources capture data over various timespans and require different dating methods, it is possible to answer many questions by examining the natural historical record.

Perhaps the most important and widely used technique in environmental history is isotopic analysis. All elements occur in a variety of isotopes: versions of an element that have slightly different masses. Some of these isotopes undergo radioactive decay and others are stable. By measuring the ratio of one isotope to another, scientists are able to date samples, trace the movement of materials through the environment, and obtain clues to past environmental conditions. Radiocarbon dating, the most common method of dating organic materials, measures the amount of radioactivity being produced by carbon 14, an unstable isotope of carbon. Carbon-14 is absorbed by vegetation, along with more common carbon-12, and comprises about 1 percent of the carbon in living wood. When a plant dies, it stops absorbing carbon 14, and the existing carbon-14 in its tissue begins to decay. Since carbon-14's level of radioactivity falls by half every 5,568 years, a measurement of the fraction of carbon-14 remaining can permit dating of organic materials up to 50,000 years old (1) (2). Other radioisotopes, such as those for lead and beryllium, with half lives of 22.3 years and 1.5 million years respectively, can be used to date materials on shorter or longer timescales (3) (4).

Substances formed in layers, such as sediments, polar ice, peat deposits, and tree rings, can also be dated stratigraphically—by counting the layers of growth or accumulation and

investigating their contents. These layers often correspond to a regular cycle, which may be seasonal, annual, or longer. Trees, for example, add annual growth rings. In ice cores, variations in stable isotope ratios reveal seasonal differences, and in areas with high snow accumulation and little melting, fairly precise chronologies can be established (5). Sediment layers, called varves, are formed annually in many lakes.

Natural records of the Earth's history are contained in the items below.

Sediment Cores. Cores from the seabed and lake bottoms provide records of a variety of environmental conditions, such as the contents of the effluents and atmospheric deposition received by that body of water. Lake sediments capture pollutants on a local or regional scale, while the more isolated deep ocean sediments indicate the global distribution of a pollutant. Nondegradable pollutants such as metals that are immobilized in fine particles of sediment are the best candidates for sediment core analysis.

The biotic (fossil and pollen) and isotopic records embedded in lake and ocean bottoms can provide information on water temperature, acidity, salinity, and species diversity. For example, the isotopic ratio of heavy oxygen 18 to more common oxygen 16 in fossilized plankton is an indicator of the historical global ice volume, because more light oxygen isotopes evaporate and are stored in the ice caps during ice ages, leaving behind a disproportionately large amount of heavy oxygen in seawater. Marine fossils are particularly valuable because ocean sedimentation occurs very slowly, and undisturbed regions can yield records going back millions of years (6).

On a more recent timescale, historic events, either natural or anthropogenic, may create "markers" in the core. For example, a layer of seashell fragments in marine cores can be correlated with a specific hurricane. Several radionuclides have entered the environment

since the advent of nuclear testing, and their appearance can often pinpoint a specific year (7).

Ice cores and snow. As sediment cores capture information on past aquatic conditions, ice cores from the polar regions provide a long-term record of the contents of the atmosphere that may extend back 500,000 years (8). Particulates from natural and anthropogenic sources are deposited in the ice, allowing trend analysis of atmospheric pollutant deposition, as well as aerosols from volcanic explosions. In addition, air bubbles trapped in the ice contain samples of gas concentrations from previous eras. These tiny samples of ancient air have enabled scientists to determine that carbon dioxide concentrations have risen 25 percent (9) and that methane concentrations have doubled in the past century (10).

Data collected from the northern and southern polar regions differ. Since air masses generally do not cross the equator, northern polar areas capture pollutants generated in the industrialized northern hemisphere, and the Antarctic provides less data on pollutant aerosols and more on gas concentrations (11).

Coral Reefs. Corals, like trees, reflect the environmental conditions in which they grow. They can therefore serve as indicators of marine pollution, sea-surface temperature, and other aquatic conditions. Perhaps most importantly, corals can indicate past sea levels. Raised 125,000-year-old reefs off Bermuda, Australia, the Bahamas, and Hawaii indicate that sea level stood about 6 meters higher during the warmest part of the last interglacial than it does today because the West Antarctic ice sheet had melted (12).

Coral from the Galápagos Islands is being used to trace the occurrences of El Niños for periods before reliable instrumental records. Usually, the cold current off the islands is rich in nutrients and cadmium. During El Niños, however, the cold water is replaced by warm

one test of how reliably they can predict the future.

Human impacts on the environment, like natural changes, occur on all scales. Many are minor, and do not exceed the limits of natural variability. Yet even human impacts that are dwarfed by natural fluctuations can have important environmental consequences. Many oceanic pelagic fish species, for example, like the anchovy and the sardine, are subject to natural changes that can cause population levels to rapidly rise and fall. When these fish populations are subject to the additional stress of overfishing, a naturally caused decline could become a collapse.

Just as the impacts of human activities can add to natural stresses, the cumulative effect of many small-scale anthropogenic changes can disrupt global systems. Centuries of burning fossil fuels, deforestation, and other industrial activities have caused atmospheric carbon dioxide levels to climb by nearly 25 percent since the industrial revolution, surpassing even the peak levels before the last

ice age. Responding to and planning for these and other environmental changes requires an understanding of the processes governing these changes, and an ability to distinguish natural and human causes at all scales.

Natural Variability

Global change is natural, and occurs on many different time scales. Severe weather events may occur abruptly and last only a few hours; continental drift occurs gradually over millions of years. Some forms of natural variability, like the seasons, are predictable. Others are not, and can have huge social and economic impacts. A large degree of variability in rainfall, for example, can mean the difference between a successful harvest and famine. In Africa, outside the humid zones, rainfall may deviate from the mean by 20–40 percent each year (46). Even when average total rainfall is realized, an extended dry spell can damage crops during vulnerable periods in

Box 11.4

waters low in cadmium. These changes are recorded in the coral and should help illuminate long-term trends in El Niño occurrences (13).

Tree Rings. Trees are natural archives, each annual ring reflecting the environmental conditions of the past year. Five thousand-year-old bristlecone pine trees found in California's White Mountains, with even older dead trees, provide a record extending back nearly 9,000 years (14). About 20 years ago, a ring analysis from one of these trees showed that atmospheric levels of carbon 14 varied with changes in solar activity, rather than remaining constant as had been assumed. Many dates that had been determined by radiocarbon dating were inaccurate. A revised scale for radiocarbon dating based on the bristlecone pine record was created and is the standard today (15).

The width of tree rings measures the past year's growth, and thus reflects such environmental factors as pollution and precipitation. For example, in the western United States a recent large-scale study of conifer growth trends revealed a systematic increase in tree-ring width since the mid-19th Century consistent with the increased growth of vegetation expected from rising atmospheric carbon dioxide concentrations (16). Stunted growth and the chemical composition of trees can also pinpoint the impacts of pollutants on vegetation. For example, many trees along roadsides in industrialized countries showed increased concentrations of lead following its introduction as a gasoline additive (17).

Museum Specimens. Museum specimens are used less often for historical analysis than the materials mentioned above because they do not usually provide data over an unbroken succession of years. However, when trend data are unavailable from other sources, historical specimens are useful for comparison with current ones. For example, the discovery that DDT and its metabolites caused the thinning

of eggshells of certain bird species was made during the 1960s by comparing current eggshells with museum specimens from the 1920s and 1930s (18). Atmospheric scientists are examining antique buttons, telescopes, clocks, and other objects that might contain air trapped from an earlier period to determine the concentrations of greenhouse gases in pre-industrial air.

Human Remains. Human remains are valuable from an ecological as well as an anthropological standpoint. The remains of hair, teeth, bones, and organs can provide data on diets, living conditions, and pollutant exposure. Scientists have analyzed hundreds of hair samples from the past three centuries in an attempt to compare historical exposure to lead and other metals with present levels found in humans (19). Although many of these experiments have proven inconclusive, one resulted in a surprising discovery. Chemists who analyzed a sample of Napoleon Bonaparte's hair found high levels of arsenic, suggesting that contrary to most historical accounts, he may have died from deliberate poisoning rather than natural causes (20).

References and Notes

1. H.H. Lamb, *Climate, History, and the Modern World* (Methuen, New York, 1982), p. 86.
2. Monitoring and Assessment Research Centre (MARC), *Historical Monitoring* (MARC, London, 1985), p. 6.
3. Herbert Friedman, "The Science of Global Change—An Overview," Keynote Address presented to the Symposium on Global Change of the 20th General Assembly of the International Council of Scientific Unions, September 25, 1984, Ottawa, Canada, p. 4.
4. D.H.M. Alderton, "Sediments," in *Historical Monitoring* (Monitoring and Assessment Research Centre, London, 1985), p. 4.
5. *Op. cit.* 2, pp. ix–x.
6. *Op. cit.* 1, p. 84 and pp. 99–100.
7. *Op. cit.* 4, p. 3.
8. Eric W. Wolff and David A. Peel, "The Record of Global Pollution in Polar Snow and Ice," *Nature*, Vol. 313 (February 14, 1985).
9. World Resources Institute and International Institute for Environment and Development, *World Resources 1986* (Basic Books, New York, 1986), p. 174.
10. B. Stauffer, *et al.*, "Increase in Atmosphere Methane Recorded in Antarctic Ice Core," *Science*, Vol. 229, p. 1386.
11. D.H.M. Alderton and D.O. Coleman, "Ice Cores and Snow," in *Historical Monitoring* (Monitoring and Assessment Research Centre, London, 1985), pp. 100–101.
12. U.S. Committee for an International Geosphere-Biosphere Program, *Global Change in the Geosphere-Biosphere* (National Academy Press, Washington, D.C., 1986), p. 18.
13. Staff, "Historical Coral," *Science News*, Vol. 132, No. 11, p. 168.
14. Scott Thybony, "Dead Trees Tell Tales," *National Wildlife*, August-September 1987, p. 40.
15. *Ibid.*
16. *Op. cit.* 12, p. 16.
17. M.A.S. Burton, "Tree Rings," *Historical Monitoring* (Monitoring and Assessment Research Centre, London, 1985), pp. 181–182.
18. D.O. Coleman and M. Hutton, "Museum Specimens," in *Historical Monitoring* (Monitoring and Assessment Research Centre, London, 1985), p. 214.
19. D.O. Coleman, "Human Remains," in *Historical Monitoring* (Monitoring and Assessment Research Centre, London, 1985), p. 281.
20. *Ibid.*, p. 282.

growth cycles. The human and economic costs of this lost agricultural production are enormous.

Changing weather is perhaps the most ubiquitous reminder of natural climatic variability, but other important climatic events occur over years, centuries, and longer. For example, the El Niño phenomenon, which occurs every few years, has global climatic and economic impacts. El Niño involves the movement of warm surface water from the western equatorial Pacific to the eastern equatorial region off the coasts of Peru, Ecuador, and Chile. The warm water displaces the cold, nutrient-rich water that sustains an important fishery. El Niño is closely linked to the Southern Oscillation, a large-scale exchange of tropical air masses between the eastern and western hemispheres, with impacts on sea surface temperature and atmospheric pressure. An El Niño Southern Oscillation (ENSO) is the result of interactions between the Pacific tropical ocean, the atmosphere, and the seasonal cycle, but it is not yet fully understood (47). (For an

expanded discussion of the El Niño see *World Resources 1987*, Figures 11.2, 11.3, and 11.4, pp. 170–172.)

El Niño impacts on the Peruvian anchoveta fishery are well known, but strong ENSOs have impacts in many other parts of the world. During the 1982–83 ENSO, the most severe on record, Indonesia experienced its worst drought in a decade, causing per capita rice production to fall for the first time since 1974. The drought also contributed to the damage of 3.5 million hectares of tropical forest in Kalimantan, most of it lost to fire. Indonesia's lost revenues in terms of damaged logs and reduced forest growth have been estimated at more than $6 billion (48). During the same period, the monsoons failed on the Indian subcontinent, causing drought over 37 percent of India, and a 4 percent drop in agricultural production (49).

In an attempt to anticipate these events and predict their impacts, scientists are studying past El Niños in order to identify early warning signals and probable impacts. El Niños can be identified from records of sea

Box 11.5 Written Environmental Records

During the summer of 1588, a series of violent storms occurred in the English Channel. Through various climate records of the 16th Century, we now know that these storms were part of a pattern of severe weather events and climatic anomalies that characterized the Little Ice Age. At the time, the storms were recorded because they sank most of the Spanish Armada and prevented the probable invasion of England (1). Then, as now, environmental events and trends were most often recorded because of their economic or political importance.

Fortunately, many types of records kept for other purposes can be used to reconstruct environmental histories: records of celestial and weather events, diaries and letters, and government documents such as censuses. And, with the rapid advancement of scientific inquiry beginning in the 17th Century, measurements from scientific instruments—the most straightforward sources of environmental data—gradually became available. However, since environmental monitoring is a very recent development in most parts of the world and early instrumental data are unreliable, it is necessary to rely on alternative sources for earlier periods (2).

Many documents are impressionistic, fragmented, and indirect indicators of environmental conditions, but when examined carefully they can provide an accurate and detailed picture of many environmental variables. Climatic events, for example, were often well-recorded because of their impacts on agriculture and their religious significance to early peoples. Other records now used for environmental analysis were related originally to economic activities, such as harvest dates or industrial output. For example, U.S. sulfur and carbon emissions from the mid-19th Century to the present have been estimated from records of coal production and use by region (3) (4). Toxic waste dumps created before protective legislation have been located by surveying local industrial records to identify those activities known to produce dangerous, long-lived wastes.

Government records, because they are often well preserved and cover a wide range of activities, can be excellent sources of environmental information. In South and Southeast Asia, several countries that were part of the British empire, for example, kept detailed accounts of land use through administrative offices. Through these records, historians have been able to reconstruct information on changes in vegetative cover (and, by implication, on species diversity) (5). This work also feeds into research on the role of vegetation in changes in the global carbon budget. (See Chapter 16, "Land Cover and Settlements," Table 16.3, for data on long-term land use change.)

Ships' logs can also be valuable because they are among the few sources describing open ocean conditions before monitoring began. Although these descriptions are usually qualitative and early instrumental records are suspect, records of sailing times, storms, winds, and fishing conditions provide valuable clues about atmospheric and oceanic cycles.

By surveying hundreds of ships' logs and other navigation and trade documents for South America, a 400-year history of El Niño occurrences was constructed, revealing that El Niños have occurred about every 3–4 years, and that the interval between strong El Niños is about 6–7 years (6). (See *World Resources 1987*, Figures 11.2–11.4, pp. 170–172).

References and Notes

1. Captain Alan Villers, *Men, Ships and the Sea* (National Geographic Society, Washington, D.C., 1962), p. 117.
2. T.M.L. Wigley, *et al.*, eds., *Climate and History* (Cambridge University Press, Cambridge, 1981), p. 182.
3. R.M. Rotty, "Anthropogenic Sources of CO_2," in *Carbon Dioxide Review*, W.C. Clark, ed. (Oxford University Press, Oxford, 1982.)
4. Gerhard Gschwandter, *et al.*, *Historic Emissions of Sulfur and Nitrogen Oxides in the United States from 1900 to 1980* (U.S. Environmental Protection Agency, Washington D.C., April 1985).
5. John F. Richards, *et al.*, "Changing Land Use in Bihar, Punjab and Haryana 1850–1970," *Modern Asian Studies*, Vol. 19, No. 3 (1985), p. 702–704.
6. William H. Quinn and Victor T. Neal, "El Nino Occurrences Over the Past Four and a Half Centuries," *Journal of Geophysical Research*, Vol. 92 (December 15, 1987), p. 14,453–14,455.

surface temperature and atmospheric pressure, which go back over a century at some sites. (See Box 11.5.) At the U.S. National Center for Atmospheric Research, newspaper and journal accounts of climatic anomalies during El Niños have been compared to identify the climatic events that occurred during most El Niños. For example, during 1957–58, 1972–73, and 1982–83, the three most recent strong El Niños, droughts occurred in eastern Australia, northeastern Brazil, and southeastern Africa (50). Of the last 26 El Niños, 21 have been associated with monsoon failure in India (51). Events that occur during most El Niños are thought to be teleconnections—relationships between climatic and/or oceanic anomalies in widely separated areas that are being used to check the predictions of El Niño models (52).

Policymakers tend to focus on environmental changes that occur over relatively short time spans because their impacts are felt immediately. But short-term changes need to be understood within a larger historical context because they are often part of longer, more complex changes. The Earth's systems may take decades or centuries to respond to environmental changes, and trends may not be noticed until they are well underway. For example, temperature records show that the global surface temperature rose by 0.5°C over the past century, and by 1.5°C in the Northern Hemisphere. Yet during the 1940s and 1950s, temperatures in the Northern Hemisphere dropped so rapidly that scientists wondered if the world was heading into an ice age. Around 1960 the trend reversed, and the slight increase in temperature has spurred speculation about the beginnings of the expected greenhouse warming. These short-term trends must be superimposed on the century-long warming trend, which in turn is part of an interglacial period that began 10,000 years ago (53).

The impacts of long-term environmental changes, though gradual or delayed, can be far reaching. Human responses to such major shifts in the Earth's system like climate change are largely a matter of adaptation, and it is useful to look at past changes that have required large scale adaptations. The "Little Ice Age," which occurred in Europe from the 16th to the 19th Centuries, was a brief divergence from the warming trend that began 10,000 years ago at the end of the last ice age. It is one of the best documented examples of long-term environmental change.

Although there were great temperature variations from year to year, the average global temperature was about 1°C colder than now, and temperatures in Northern and Central Europe were probably even colder (54). Throughout Northern Europe, people had to contend with harsher winters, poor fishing years, and crop failures during this period. In many northern areas agriculture had to be abandoned altogether (55).

In Scotland, which suffered acutely during this period, thousands of farmers relocated to milder Northern Ireland

(56). And in Greenland, where Vikings had established three colonies during the warmer 10th Century, the growing sea ice during the 14th and 15th Centuries isolated the settlers, cutting off all contact with Iceland and Scandinavia, and pushing fish stocks further south and out of reach. All three settlements died out during this period. When a Danish expedition sailed to Greenland in 1921 to examine the history of the Viking settlements, they found evidence that the grazing land had been buried under advancing glacial ice and that most farmland had been rendered useless by permafrost. Skeletons of the settlers were found to be deformed and diseased from famine (57) (58).

In addition to harsh winters, people also suffered from drought, floods, and heat waves in the summers (59). The increased number of climatic extremes, not the lower average temperature, was probably the most damaging climatic impact of the period. As these examples illustrate, the impacts of even slight changes in climate can be severe, and worse, unpredictable.

Natural Baselines and Human Impacts

Given the range of variability, natural changes need to be understood so that human beings can adapt accordingly. The boundaries of natural variability can also serve as a baseline from which to measure human impacts on the environment. Establishing a baseline enables policymakers to see more clearly what the impacts of industrialization, land conversion, and other human activities have been.

For example, how does the current carbon dioxide increase and potential warming compare to similar events in the Earth's past? Although carbon dioxide concentrations have been monitored continuously only since 1957, it is possible to determine carbon dioxide levels and estimate temperatures from much earlier periods by analyzing air bubbles trapped in glacial ice cores from Antarctica and Greenland. (See Box 11.4.)

Glacial cores reveal that the Earth's environment has changed dramatically between the glacial and interglacial periods that have occurred in cycles averaging 100,000 years. Typically, the atmosphere fluctuated by 6°C in temperature, by fivefold in atmospheric dust, and by 20 percent in carbon dioxide concentrations (60). The cycles governing ice ages are thought to be caused by periodic eccentricities in the Earth's orbit due to the gravitational pull of the sun and moon.

In 1987, French and Soviet scientists published the first analyses of the Vostok, Antarctica, ice core. At Vostok an ice core was drilled that revealed an environmental record dating back 160,000 years. The core provides the longest temperature and carbon dioxide record yet examined, and the first to extend through the last ice age and previous interglacial period. By measuring the proportion of deuterium, a heavy form of hydrogen, in the ice, scientists were able to estimate past atmospheric temperatures. Levels of deuterium in rain and snow increase with increasing temperature (61). (See Figure 11.5.)

Showing clear links between carbon dioxide levels and temperature, the Vostok ice core has been recognized as irrefutable evidence for a fundamental link between the

global climate system and the carbon cycle (62). However, it is still not clear whether rising carbon dioxide levels caused or followed rising temperatures. Historical carbon dioxide levels have ranged from 190–200 parts per million during glacial periods to 260–280 ppm during interglacials (63). Today, carbon dioxide levels have risen to nearly 350 ppm (64). Vostok data also confirmed that the warmest part of the last interglacial was only about 2°C warmer than today (65).

Reconstructing the Earth's climatic history and varying levels of carbon dioxide concentrations has enabled scientists to determine that current levels of carbon dioxide are outside the range of its natural fluctuations. And, if the expected 1.5° – 4.5°C temperature increase occurs over the next 50 years, global surface temperature may also be higher than any time within the past 160,000 years. The data from the Vostok ice core are not detailed enough to verify data from Greenland ice cores and ocean sediments that suggest that shifts in climate have often been abrupt, perhaps because rapid changes in temperature disrupted the ocean currents that regulate regional climates (66). If this is true, we may have less time to adapt to the impacts of climate change than is currently assumed. (See Chapter 9, "Oceans and Coasts.")

A natural baseline not only highlights changes that fall outside the range of natural variability, but also those that occur at increased rates. For example, natural or background extinction rates are on the order of a few species per million years (67). According to fossil records, however, North American mammals became extinct at a rate 1,000 times faster than the natural extinction rate

Figure 11.5 Long-Term Variations of Global Temperature and Atmospheric Carbon Dioxide

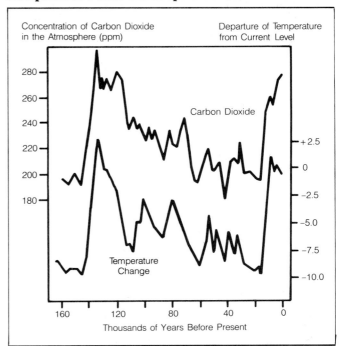

Source: J.M. Barnola, *et al.*, "Vostok Ice Core Provides 160,000-year Record of Atmospheric CO$_2$," *Nature*, Vol. 329, No. 6138 (1–7 October 1987), p. 410.

after the arrival of humans on the continent (68). Today, the loss of large areas of tropical forest and other habitat worldwide has led some biologists to estimate that the extinction rate for bird and mammal species is more than 50 times the natural rate (69).

Current extinction rates, which are accelerating, are now thought to be causing a mass extinction approaching the scale of those in the Earth's geologic past (70). Mass extinctions have been defined as those events that double the background rate of extinction among many different kinds of plant and animal groups (71). Although the causes of mass extinctions are hotly debated, it is known that they have occurred in 26 million year cycles. Five major extinction events have occurred in the past 600 million years. The largest mass extinction in the marine fossil record occurred about 200 million years ago, when an estimated 91–96 percent of then-living species became extinct (72) (73). Despite uncertainty about current rates of species loss (estimates range from 100 a year to 100 a day), scientists believe that the current anthropogenic mass extinction is the most severe since the disappearance of the dinosaurs (74). (For a discussion of extinctions and other species loss indicators, see Chapter 6, "Wildlife and Habitat," Indicators of the Condition of the World's Wildlife.)

Soil is another resource that is being lost at rates much higher than it is formed in many areas, because of deforestation, nonsustainable agriculture, and other human activities. Today, an estimated 6–7 million hectares of agriculturally productive land are irreversibly lost each year. This rate is 30 to 35 times higher than the average loss of productive land since agriculture began, and 2.5 times higher than the average annual loss over the past 300 years (75).

The pace of global change has been accelerating since the start of the industrial revolution 300 years ago, and today, few places on the Earth have been left untouched. Over the past 120 years, roughly 850 million hectares of land have been converted to cropland. Although the growth in agricultural land was evenly distributed over the period, the greatest land conversion between 1860 and 1920 occurred in the United States and the Soviet Union. Between 1920 and 1978, the greatest land conversion occurred in the developing world, especially Africa (76).

Most new agricultural land was created by deforestation, draining of wetlands, or irrigation. In the United States, more than 50 million hectares of wetlands have been drained for agriculture, and in Europe and the USSR, nearly 21 million hectares have been drained (77). Currently, 220 million hectares of land are irrigated (78). And over the past 10,000 years, an estimated 900 million hectares of forests and woodlands, 18 percent of the original global forested area, has been converted to agriculture (79).

Major environmental changes can be attributed to industrial activities as well. For example, the presence of many toxic chemicals, including PCBs and DDT, and ozone-depleting chloroflorocarbons in the environment can be attributed solely to human activities. Most cases are not so clear cut. Sulfur and nitrogen are produced in large quantities by natural and anthropogenic sources.

Isotopic tracing is one way of determining the current source of these pollutants, but pollution histories are needed to see both long-term trends and the impact of these pollutants over time. Documenting historical trends for many pollutants is difficult because extensive monitoring did not begin until after they were recognized as a problem. But, through various techniques, including analysis of tree rings and ice and sediment cores, some trends can be traced.

An ice core drilled in Greenland in 1984, for example, provides a representative sample of the content of the Northern Hemisphere's atmosphere over the past century. Greenland is remote enough to reflect regional rather than local pollution sources, and because most air masses do not cross the equator, the more polluted northern air is recorded in the arctic snow (80) (81). Researchers found that sulfate concentrations in the Greenland ice have tripled over natural background levels since 1900, and that nitrate concentrations have doubled since around 1955. Both dates are consistent with the rise in industrial activities producing these pollutants (82).

Increasing amounts of heavy metals in the environment have also been documented through environmental history techniques. Metals can have serious health effects at low levels. They occur naturally in the environment, but concentrations have increased rapidly over the past century because of their use in industrial activities. Current annual anthropogenic emissions of lead, for example, exceed the natural rate by well over an order of magnitude. In many lakes, such as Clearwater Lake in Missouri, the heavy metals lodged in bottom sediments correspond directly with the onset of mining and industrialization in the region (83). Other lake sediments reflect pollution from such diffuse sources as atmospheric deposition. Over the past few thousand years, lead concentrations in Greenland ice cores have increased about 140-fold (84). (See also Chapter 10, "Atmosphere and Climate," Impacts on the Biosphere from Tropospheric Pollution.)

Environmental History and Policy

What lessons do these natural and recorded histories have for policymakers? After all, they only describe events in the past and sometimes events over which human beings have no control. Yet environmental history makes two contributions essential to sensible policy: the scientific data and the historical perspective necessary to make informed decisions.

Historical examples cannot serve as prescriptions for current problems, but they can provide information relevant to policy decisions. For example, in 1986, the U.S. National Research Council (NRC) conducted an analysis of long-term trends in acid precipitation in the Northeastern United States to provide some answers to the many policy questions raised by the issue. Lake sediments containing the skeletons of diatoms, tiny algae that can indicate a lake's acidity, were analyzed for 10 New York lakes that were naturally vulnerable to acid pollution. The NRC found that 6 out of the 10 lakes had become increasingly acidic between 1930 and 1970. Noting the high levels of industrial sulfur emissions during this period (extrapolated from records of coal production and use) and the small quantities of sulfur produced from other sources, the NRC concluded that acid deposition was the most probable cause of lake acidification. This conclusion was supported by data recording reductions in fish populations in 9 of the 10 lakes over the same period (85).

Diatom analysis has also been used to survey the history of lakes in southwest Scotland. The composition of diatom skeletons in sediment cores taken from several lakes showed that acid-sensitive species in earlier periods gave way to new species more typical of acidic waters. Based on these trends, researchers estimated that the pH of the lakes declined from 5.5 in 1950 to 4.6 today. The changes in pH corresponded precisely with the appearance of heavy metals and soot from industrial sources that also lodged in the sediment.

These findings challenge the conventional wisdom that many Scottish lakes became acid over 5,000 years ago when the upland forests were cleared, triggering an acidification of the soils. The results also undermine claims that acidification in Scandinavia was caused by changes in land use over the past century rather than by air pollution (86).

Even when environmental changes are natural rather than anthropogenic, the human and economic costs of a severe El Niño or a Little Ice Age amply demonstrate the enormous impacts natural shifts can have on human affairs. Human activities did not trigger these changes, but people had to adapt to them nonetheless, and successful policy must take these changes into account. Examining the historical record for natural cycles, feedback mechanisms, and early warning signals of global change are essential for understanding and responding to natural change. Today, through the use of models based on contemporary and historical data, we are beginning to move past adaptation toward the ability to anticipate environmental events and trends.

History also provides the opportunity to learn from experience by recording the impacts of human activities. Environmental records make clear that damage to the environment has not been limited to modern times. Through analysis of pollen grains, scientists have found that Easter Island off the coast of Chile, now treeless, was covered by palm forests when the first Polynesians arrived in 400 A.D. By 1500, the island's population had grown to about 7,000, and the forest had been completely destroyed. Today, its tree species are extinct. The loss of the island's forests had three harmful consequences: soil erosion, leading to lower crop yields; lack of trees to build canoes for fishing and a consequent loss of fish as a major protein source; and an inability to erect the enormous stone statues that dominate the island, which required the use of logs as levers. The human population exceeded the carrying capacity of the island, and warfare, cannibalism, and slavery became chronic (87).

Historical changes in land use and land degradation have direct and long lasting impacts on people's ability to feed themselves. Many societies have suffered serious consequences because they were unable to maintain agricultural production because of soil erosion. Obviously, such changes in land cover as the conversion of forests

to agricultural lands are not always negative. Growth in fertile agricultural land may enable societies to grow and prosper. But a recognition of how much the global landscape has been altered is valuable because it makes us conscious of past and present human impacts on the land. Looking at remaining wildlands from a historical perspective may encourage countries to preserve their natural heritage for their ecosystem benefits, species diversity, and benefit to future generations. For example, rapid population growth has left nine sub-Saharan countries with only 20 percent or less of the original vegetation remaining (88). One of these countries, Ghana, has recently adapted a conservation plan to protect representative samples of all the flora and fauna in the country (89).

Perhaps the most important point raised by environmental history is that human impacts on the Earth, like natural impacts, take time to manifest themselves. The impacts of a decision to burn coal, manufacture DDT or to clear the Amazon for agriculture may not be felt for decades, but they will be felt. And while the past cannot foretell the future of these decisions, it may teach us to approach them with care.

RECENT DEVELOPMENTS

THE ROLE OF THE OCEANS IN BIOGEOCHEMICAL CYCLES

The oceans, which are key actors in the global nitrogen cycle (see Table 11.1), are of equal if not greater importance in the geochemical cycles of other biologically active elements: carbon, sulfur, oxygen, and others. To date, however, scientists have only a crude understanding of how the oceans affect these critical cycles.

An international scientific program—the Joint Global Ocean Flux Study (JGOFS)—was launched in 1987 to address some of these interactions. JGOFS is an umbrella program that coordinates several national projects. For example, the United States has a Global Ocean Flux Study; the Federal Republic of Germany has a Coastal and Ocean Flux Study; and the United Kingdom has a Biogeochemical Ocean Flux Study. The objectives of these projects contribute to the JGOFS goal: to elucidate and quantify, on a global scale, the processes affecting the flows of biologically active elements within the oceans, and between the oceans and the atmosphere, sea floor, and continental boundaries.

The goal will be difficult to achieve; the wanderings of some elements in the ocean can be extraordinarily complex. Carbon, for example, bridges life and nonlife (when carbon dioxide is used by oceanic plants and animals), air and water (when atmospheric carbon dioxide dissolves in the oceans), water and sediment (particulate carbon compounds settling to the bottom), and particulate and dissolved forms. Scientists will attempt to enumerate and understand all of these flows, quantify their rates, determine the oceanic area in which they occur, and learn about their variability. Their tools will range from the primitive to the exotic—buckets and buoys, isotope tracing, and satellite remote sensing devices will all be used (90).

Studying the global ocean flux is highly relevant to many current and prospective environmental concerns. For example, it is known that the carbon dioxide (CO_2) level in the atmosphere has varied through geological history (see Figure 11.5); the oceans are the only place where enough CO_2 could have been sequestered from and released to the atmosphere to cause such marked variations in the atmospheric concentration (91). Now people are emitting CO_2 to the atmosphere in ever-increasing amounts (see Chapter 23, "Atmosphere and Climate," Table 23.1), and it appears that the oceans are removing about half of all anthropogenic emissions (92). How the oceans do it, and how the human perturbation of the global carbon cycle may affect those processes, will be among the subjects of study in the JGOFs. Given the prominent role that carbon dioxide is expected to play in a future climate warming, studying the oceans' role in the carbon cycle becomes relevant indeed. (See also Chapter 9, "Ocean and Coasts," Deep Ocean Circulation.)

UGANDA INSTALLS A GEOGRAPHICAL INFORMATION SYSTEM

Uganda, seeking to improve its collection and management of information on natural resources, completed the pilot phase of a new Geographical Information System (GIS) in 1987. Although basic data on natural resources had been collected previously, much of it was scattered, stored in incompatible formats, or quietly gathered dust, unknown to public and private resource managers (93).

GIS technology promises to solve some of these problems, and thus increase the usefulness of natural resource data. GISs are a family of specialized computer software that allow geographically-oriented data (such as political boundaries, forest locations, or population centers) to be housed together on a set of computerized maps. GISs represent a quantum leap in cost-effective data management and analysis; they combine data from diverse sources and can analyze and display the relationships among many environmental parameters. (For additional information, see World Resources 1987, Chapter 11, "Global Systems and Cycles.")

The United Nations Environment Programme (UNEP), through its Global Resource Information Database (a global GIS), helped the Uganda project acquire data and computer software, and provided training to Ugandan nationals, who conducted the pilot project. UNEP also helped the project request bilateral assistance for ongoing operation. Uganda plans to use the GIS system to rebuild its natural resource data base (data collection and analysis had been seriously disrupted by civil strife). This data base will be important for land use planning and natural resource management (94).

In the pilot phase, Uganda's GIS drew raw geographical data from a variety of Ugandan government publications and from the data bases of international organizations such as the United National Food and Agriculture Organization and UNEP. For example, the 1967 Atlas of Uganda provided data on precipitation patterns, soil classes, and topography. Two sets of satellite imagery (from 1973 and 1986) were analyzed for land cover and land use information (95).

Because these data (and others) were entered into the GIS in digital form, computer models in the GIS could combine and analyze several sets of data simultaneously, creating new analytical products. Prior to the use of a GIS, the raw data were locked in their original forms and could not be further manipulated or quantitatively analyzed.

For example, maps of Ugandan soil types, topography, population density, and land use were combined to produce an entirely new map indicating areas at high risk of soil erosion. Doing this job by hand, using conventional cartography with overlaying maps, would have been a far more onerous job. Furthermore, a hand-drawn product would not have been flexible; GIS output can be used as input to other models and can be processed to display data in a wide variety of forms.

In a novel application, the suitability of Ugandan lands for growing Robusta coffee, the country's most important cash crop, was assessed under two scenarios. One scenario used present-day climate patterns; the other assumed that the average temperature would rise 2°C as a result of the greenhouse effect. The results: wide areas of the country are suitable for Robusta cultivation under current conditions, but a 2°C warming would drastically reduce the suitable area (96).

The potential utility of GISs has been recognized at the highest levels of the Ugandan government. The Prime Minister personally endorsed the installation of the technology in the Ministry of Environmental Protection, which will establish a data collection and analysis office as a central data base for the entire government. The GIS will allow resource managers to examine the possible effects of development proposals on various sectors. Proposals could be fine-tuned to bring the greatest benefit to the whole country, rather than to a particular sector (97).

References and Notes

1. Needham summed up the element's importance by noting that "every vital phenomenon is due to some change in nitrogen compound and indeed in the nitrogen atom of that compound". Arthur Edwin Needham, The Uniqueness of Biological Materials (Pergamon Press, Elmsford, New York, 1965).
2. Vaclav Smil, Carbon Nitrogen Sulfur Human Interferences in Grand Biospheric Cycles (Plenum Press, New York, 1985).
3. United Nations Food and Agriculture Organization (FAO), Agriculture: Toward 2000 (FAO, Rome, 1987), pp. 134–137.
4. F.J. Stevenson, ed., Nitrogen in Agricultural Soils (American Society of Agronomy, Madison, Wisconsin, 1982).
5. Fixation literature is vast. Excellent summaries are found in J.M. Vincent, ed., Nitrogen Fixation in Legumes (Academic Press, New York, 1982) and R.C. Burns and R.W.F. Hardy, Nitrogen Fixation in Bacteria and Higher Plants (Springer-Verlag, Berlin, 1975).
6. Thomas A. La Rue and Thomas G. Patterson, "How Much Nitrogen Do Legumes Fix?," Advances in Agronomy, Vol. 34 (1981), pp. 15–38.
7. R. Knowles, "Denitrification," Ecological Bulletin, Vol. 33 (1981), pp. 315–329.

8. The best account for the United States is W.E. Larson, F.J. Pierce, and R. H. Dowdy, "The Threat of Soil Erosion to Long-Term Crop Production," *Science*, Vol. 219 (1983), pp. 458–465.
9. William F. Sheldrick, *World Nitrogen Survey* (World Bank, Washington, D.C., 1987), p. 6.
10. United Nations Food & Agriculture Organization (FAO), *FAO Fertilizer Yearbook 1986* (FAO, Rome, 1987), Table 20, pp. 52–56.
11. *Ibid.*, Table 2, p. 2.
12. World Health Organization (WHO), *Guidelines for Drinking-Water Quality.* Vol. 2, *Health Criteria and Other Supporting Information* (WHO, Geneva, 1984), p. 132.
13. Ruth Patrick, Emily Ford and John Quarles, *Groundwater Contamination in the United States* (University of Pennsylvania Press, Philadelphia, 1987), p. 139.
14. *Ibid.*
15. *Op. cit.* 12, p. 132.
16. Organisation for Economic Co-operation and Development (OECD), *Eutrophication of Waters: Monitoring, Assessment and Control* (OECD, Paris, 1982).
17. Diane Fisher *et al.*, *Polluted Coastal Waters: The Role of Acid Rain* (Environmental Defense Fund, New York, 1988), p. 1.
18. Sultan Hameed and Jane Dignon, "Changes in the Geographical Distributions of Global Emissions of NO_x and SO_x from Fossil Fuel Combustion Between 1966 and 1980," *Atmospheric Environment*, Vol. 22, No. 3, p. 447.
19. *Ibid.*, pp. 443–444, and p. 447.
20. E.D. Schroeder, "Denitrification in Wastewater Management," in *Denitrification, Nitrification, and Atmospheric Nitrous Oxide*, C.C. Delwiche, ed. (John Wiley & Sons, New York, 1981), pp. 105–125.
21. Organisation for Economic Co-operation and Development (OECD), *OECD Environmental Data Compendium 1987* (OECD, Paris, 1987), p. 53.
22. *Op. cit.* 4, p. 5.
23. National Acidic Precipitation Assessment Program (NAPAP), *Interim Assessment: The Causes and Effects of Acidic Deposition.* Vol. 2, *Emissions and Controls* (NAPAP, Washington, D.C., 1987), pp. 2–80, 2–81, 2–82, 2–98.
24. W. Robert Rangeley, "Irrigation and Drainage in the World," paper presented at the International Conference on Food and Water, College Station, Texas, May 26–30, 1985, p. 10.
25. *Ibid.*, pp. 8–9.
26. *Op. cit.* 3, p. 127.
27. International Institute for Environment and Development, World Resources Institute, *World Resources 1987* (Basic Books, New York, 1987), p. 168.
28. Bruce R. Barkstrom, "Earth's Radiation Budget: A Current Perspective," in *Report of the Workshop on Space Systems Possibilities for a Global Energy and Water Cycle Experiment* (World Climate Research Programme, Geneva, 1987), Appendix J, p. 2.
29. Elizabeth Kay Berner and Robert A. Berner, *The Global Water Cycle: Geochemistry and Environment* (Prentice-Hall, Englewood Cliffs, New Jersey, 1987), pp. 24–28.
30. V. Ramanathan, "The Role of Earth Radiation Budget Studies in Climate and General Circulation Research," *Journal of Geophysical Research*, Vol. 92, No. D4 (April 20, 1987), p. 4079.
31. World Climate Applications Programme, *Water Resources and Climate Change: Sensitivity of Water-Resource Systems to Climate Change and Variability* (World Meteorological Organization, Geneva, in press 1988), p. 18.
32. See, for example, D. Rind, "The Doubled CO_2 Climate and the Sensitivity of the Modeled Hydrologic Cycle," *Journal of Geophysical Research*, Vol. 93, No. D5 (May 20, 1988), pp. 5385–5412.
33. Peter H. Gleick, "Regional Water Resources and Global Climatic Change," in *Effects of Changes in Stratospheric Ozone and Global Climate.* Vol. 3, *Climate Change*, James G. Titus, ed. (United Nations Environment Programme and U.S. Environmental Protection Agency, Washington, D.C., October 1986), p. 222.
34. *Op. cit.* 31, pp. 26–27.
35. T.M.L. Wigley and S.C.B. Raper, "Thermal expansion of sea water associated with global warming," *Nature*, Vol. 330 (November 12, 1987), p. 131.
36. *Op. cit.* 28.
37. *Op. cit.* 29, p. 161.
38. *Op. cit.* 29, p. 226.
39. Michel Meybeck, Ecole Normale Superieur, Paris, 1988 (personal communication).
40. Michel Meybeck, "Pathways of Major Element from Land to Ocean through Rivers," in *River Inputs to Ocean Systems* (United Nations, New York, 1981), p. 18.
41. *Ibid.*, p. 20.
42. *Op. cit.* 29, p. 208.
43. Thomas Dunne, "Description of Runoff Processes," in *Perspectives on Water: Uses and Abuses*, David H. Speidel, Lon C. Ruedisili, and Allen F. Agnew, eds. (Oxford University Press, New York, 1988), p. 68.
44. Marko Ehrlich, *et al.*, *Haiti: Country Environmental Profile: A Field Study* (U.S. Agency for International Development, Washington, D.C., n.d.), pp. 24–31, and p. 38.
45. W.C. Lowdermilk, "Conquest of the Land Through 7,000 Years," *Agriculture Information Bulletin No. 99* (U.S. Government Printing Office, Washington D.C., August 1986).
46. *Op. cit.* 27, p. 223.
47. Neville Nicholls, "The El Niño/Southern Oscillation Phenomenon," in *The Societal Impacts Associated with the 1982–83 Worldwide Climate Anomalies*, Michael Glantz, *et al.*, eds. (National Center for Atmospheric Research, Boulder, 1987) pp. 5–7.
48. Jean-Paul Malingreau, "The 1982–83 Drought in Indonesia: Assessment and Monitoring," in *The Societal Impacts Associated with the 1982–83 Worldwide Climate Anomalies*, Michael Glantz, *et al.*, eds. (National Center for Atmospheric Research, Boulder, 1987) p. 12 and p. 16.
49. S.K. Sinha, "The 1982–83 Drought in India: Magnitude and Impact," in *The Societal Impacts Associated with the 1982–83 Worldwide Climate Anomalies*, Michael Glantz, *et al.*, eds. (National Center for Atmospheric Research, Boulder, 1987), p. 12 and p. 16.
50. *Op. cit.* 47, pp. 8–9.
51. "The Seeds of Disaster," *South* (November 1987), p. 81.
52. *Op. cit.* 47, p. 8.
53. U.S. Committee for an International Geosphere-Biosphere Programme, *Global Change in the Geosphere-Biosphere* (National Academy Press, Washington, D.C., 1986), p. 7.
54. John Imbrie and Katherine Palmer Imbrie, *Ice Ages, Solving the Mystery* (Harvard University Press, Cambridge, Massachusetts, 1986), pp. 182–183.
55. H.H. Lamb, *Climate, History, and the Modern World* (Methuen, New York, 1982) pp. 206–207.
56. *Ibid.*, pp. 209–213.
57. Reid A. Bryson, *Cultural Sensitivity to Environmental Change: Some Cultural and Economic Consequences of Climatic Change* (Center for Climate Research, University of Wisconsin-Madison, Madison, 1975), p. 11.
58. Joseph M. Morgan, *et al.*, eds., *Introduction to Environmental Science* (W.H. Freeman and Company, New York, 1986), p. 318–319.
59. *Op. cit.* 55, p. 208, pp. 219–220, and p. 224.
60. Wallace S. Broeker, "Unpleasant Surprises in the Greenhouse?" *Nature*, Vol. 328 (July 9, 1987), p. 124–125.
61. J. Jouzel, *et al.*, "Vostok Ice Core: A Continuous Isotope Temperature Record over the Last Climate Cycle (160,000 years)," *Nature*, Vol. 329 (October 1, 1987), p. 403.
62. Eric T. Sundquist, "Ice Core Links CO_2 to Climate," *Nature*, Vol. 329 (October 1, 1987), p. 389.
63. J. M. Barnola, *et al.*, "Vostok Ice Core Provides 160,000-year Record of Atmospheric CO_2," *Nature*, Vol. 329 (October 1, 1987), p. 410.
64. World Resources Institute and International Institute for Environment and Development, *World Resources 1987* (Basic Books, New York, 1987), p. 334.
65. *Op. cit.* 62.
66. *Op. cit.* 60.
67. David Jablowski, "Mass Extinctions: New Answers, New Questions," in *The Last Extinction*, Les Kaufmann and Kenneth Mallory, eds. (Massachusetts Institute of Technology Press, Cambridge, 1986), p. 44.
68. Working Group on Geological Processes Past and Present, "Global Change, the Lithosphere and Soils—Geological Processes Past and Present," unpublished paper from National Academy of Science Workshop held February 20–21, 1986, following the International Union of Geological Sciences' symposium on geology and problems of global change, p. 3.
69. Paul Erlich and Anne Erlich, *Extinction* (Random House, New York, 1981) p. 8.
70. Les Kaufmann, "Why the Ark is Sinking," in *The Last Extinction*, Les Kaufmann and Kenneth Mallory, eds. (Massachusetts Institute of Technology, Cambridge, 1986), p. 14.

71. *Op. cit.* 67.

72. Colin Patterson and Andrew B. Smith, "Is the Periodicity of Extinctions a Taxonomic Artifact?" *Nature*, Vol. 330 (November 19, 1987), p. 248.

73. *Op. cit.* 67, p. 46.

74. *Op. cit.* 70, p. 1.

75. B.G. Rozanov and V.O. Targulian, "Man-Induced Global Soil Change," unpublished paper presented at the Earth as Transformed by Human Activities Conference, Clark University, Worchester, Massachusetts, October 1987.

76. John F. Richards, "Global Patterns of Land Conversion," *Environment*, Vol. 26, No. 9, p. 8.

77. *Ibid.*, p. 12.

78. United Nations Food and Agriculture Organization (FAO), *1985 FAO Production Yearbook* (FAO, Rome, 1986) p. 59.

79. E. Mathews, "Global Inventory of Pre-Agricultural and Present Biomass," *Progress in Biometeorology 1984*, Vol. 3, pp. 237–246.

80. D.H.M. Alderton and D.O. Coleman, "Ice Cores and Snow," in *Historical Monitoring* (Monitoring and Assessment Research Centre, London, 1985), p. 117.

81. Eric W. Wolff and David A. Peel, "The Record of Global Pollution in Polar Snow and Ice," *Nature*, Vol. 313 (February 14, 1985).

82. P.A. Mayewski, *et al.*, "Sulfate and Nitrate Concentrations from a South Greenland Ice Core," *Science*, Vol. 232, p. 975.

83. Ian D.C. Foster and John A. Dearing, "Quantification of Long-Term Trends in Atmospheric Pollution and Agricultural Eutrophication: a Lake-Watershed Approach," in *The Influence of Climate Change and Climate Variability on the Hydrologic Regime and Water Resources* (Proceedings of the Vancouver Symposium, August 1987), pp. 183–184.

84. *Op. cit.* 81.

85. Committee on Monitoring and Assessment of Trends in Acidic Deposition, *Acid Deposition: Long-Term Trends* (National Academy Press, Washington, D.C., 1986), pp. 6–9.

86. "Acid Secrets Beneath the Lochs of Galloway," *New Scientist*, January 23, 1986, p. 35.

87. Jared Diamond, "The Environmentalist Myth," *Nature*, Vol. 324 (November 6, 1986), pp. 19–20.

88. International Union for Conservation of Nature and Natural Resources (IUCN), *Coverage of Protected Areas in the Afrotropical Realm* (IUCN, Gland, Switzerland, 1987) pp. 188–254.

89. *Ibid.*, p. 209.

90. Scientific Committee on Oceanic Research (SCOR), *The Joint Global Ocean Flux Study—JGOFS—Background, Goals, Organization, and Next Steps* (SCOR, Paris, 1987), pp. 2–9 and pp. 21–31.

91. Peter G. Brewer, *et al.*, "The Global Ocean Flux Study (GOFS): Status of the U.S. GOFS Program," *Eos*, Vol. 67, No. 44 (November 4, 1986), p. 828.

92. James J. McCarthy, Peter G. Brewer, and Gene Feldman, "Global Ocean Flux," *Oceanus*, Vol. 29, No. 4 (1986), p. 20.

93. Harvey Croze, GRID Coordinator, United Nations Environment Programs, 1988 (personal communication).

94. *Ibid.*

95. United Nations Environment Programme (UNEP), *Uganda Case Study: A Sampler Atlas of Environmental Resource Datasets within GRID* (UNEP, Nairobi, June 1987), n.p.

96. *Ibid.*

97. *Op. cit.* 1.

12. Policies and Institutions

Economic Policies and Natural Resource Management in Developing Countries

Natural resources are critical to the economies of many developing countries. In their efforts to promote economic development, raise living standards, earn foreign exchange, and accomplish other public objectives, the governments of developing nations frequently seek to increase production in agriculture, forestry, and other sectors dependent upon natural resources. Yet many of the economic policies adopted by developing countries to promote this increased production (or for other purposes) lead to inefficient or destructive use of natural resources with negative long-term impacts both on the environment and on economic development.

This chapter focuses on economic policies that alter the economic costs or benefits faced by farmers, logging companies, and others. These policies include public subsidies, tax credits, concessionary leases, price controls, and tariffs. The chapter examines how failure to fully recognize both the incentive effects of these policies on producers and the implications of these policies for natural resource use and for the environment often leads to unsustainable use of natural resources and environmental degradation. Further, these policies often promote inefficient use of natural resources, thus do not fully attain even the short-term economic benefits they are designed to achieve.

No attempt is made here to examine all the economic issues related to the environment and natural resources. Several important issues are not included: the effects of the large foreign debts of many developing countries on the exploitation of their natural resources, the long-term economic effects of the loss of biological diversity, the economic and social costs of pollution from industrial activities, and the restructuring of national economic indicators to reflect depletion of natural resource assets.

The chapter focuses more narrowly on economic policies that, in the name of economic development, alter the economic incentives for producers. It examines economic incentives and pricing policies affecting agriculture, economic policies designed to promote forestry and livestock production, and their impacts on natural resources.

AGRICULTURAL POLICIES

Stimulating agricultural output is a common objective of many developing countries, especially those whose economies depend heavily on agriculture. Increased agricultural output contributes to economic development, generates foreign exchange earnings, increases domestic food supplies, and improves farmers' incomes.

Although various policies can be used to increase agricultural output (e.g., investing in agricultural research and improving agricultural extension services), governments often adopt policies that increase output by altering incentives for farmers. Subsidizing agricultural inputs and granting tax exemptions for targeted investments are examples.

At the same time, many developing countries have adopted other policies designed to capture the economic benefits of increased agricultural output—to increase government revenues or foreign exchange earnings, or to hold down domestic food prices—all of which have the opposite effect of diminishing the incentives for production. The effects of these frequently conflicting policies on farmers often lead to unintended economic and environmental results. (It should be noted that industrialized countries may also have agricultural policies that are environmentally and economically unsound. See *World Resources 1987*, pp. 47–50.)

On the whole, agricultural policies in the developing world have increased output. Total cereal food production in the developing countries increased more than 55 percent between 1970 and 1985. At the same time, non-cereal food production rose about 40 percent, and non-food agricultural production (e.g., cocoa, coffee, tea, vegetable fibers, tobacco, and rubber) increased about 45 percent (1). (See Chapter 4, "Food and Agriculture," and Chapter 17, "Food and Agriculture," Table 17.1.) However, these increases in production were frequently achieved at a high cost to the long-term productivity of the land, used resources inefficiently, and resulted in unnecessarily high budgetary costs to the government.

Input Subsidies

Given the relatively low level of agricultural technology in many developing countries, especially in the 1950s and early 1960s, one obvious way to increase agricultural output was to use additional fertilizers, pesticides, water, and machinery. Many countries promoted increased use by subsidizing their costs to the farmer. Subsidies were frequently applied to a package of inputs including fertilizers, pesticides, water, and high-yielding seed varieties, and they were often targeted to one or two favored crops. The use of subsidies is generally justified on the grounds that:

■ farmers would be reluctant to spend their own limited financial resources on untried new technologies;

■ even if farmers were convinced that they should use the new inputs, their lack of money and restricted access to credit would initially make it impossible to purchase them;

■ subsidies were necessary to compensate farmers for adverse agricultural pricing and tax policies (2).

The first two justifications are economically valid in the short term assuming that increased use of these inputs continues to make economic sense over the long term after subsidies are removed. But many input subsidies have become permanent, with unintended results. The appropriateness of the third argument for subsidies also needs to be examined.

Pesticide Subsidies

Chemical pesticides can significantly improve agricultural output by killing insects, weeds, and other pests that destroy or slow the growth of crops. Their use is widespread in both developed and developing countries. Given their poisonous ingredients, inappropriate or excessive use of pesticides can be hazardous to human health and the environment. (See Chapter 2, "Population and Health," Focus On: Pesticide Use and Health.) In particular, excessive use facilitates the emergence of resistant pests, thereby reducing pesticide effectiveness and putting farmers on a treadmill of increased chemical use that does not advance their interests.

Subsidies for pesticides in developing countries can be either direct price subsidies or the indirect result of governments waiving taxes on imported pesticides, providing farmers low-interest credit for their purchases, or granting local manufacturers production incentives. The costs of pesticide subsidies to government treasuries, in terms of both foregone revenue and direct budgetary costs, can be large. Table 12.1 shows the annual costs of these subsidies in several developing countries in the early 1980s. For all of them, the annual costs ran into the millions of dollars. Egypt and China each spent more than $200 million per year, and Indonesia's annual costs exceeded $100 million. The effect of the subsidies on pesticide prices was also large. In Senegal, Egypt, and Indonesia, subsidies covered more than 80 percent of the full retail cost.

Large reductions in pesticide prices can seriously distort the farmers' choices. The use of pesticides is inefficient if they cost more than the value of the increased harvest that results from pest control. Agricultural economists at the International Rice Research Institute found that although pesticides are effective in reducing pests and increasing output in Philippine rice field experiments, heavier pesticide applications often cost more (unsubsidized) than the value of the additional yields that resulted (3). At heavily subsidized prices, however, even small increases in crop yields seem to justify the use of more pesticides, resulting in substantial overuse.

Overuse of pesticides can only exacerbate their already serious health and environmental effects. Although data are limited, worldwide estimates of acute pesticide poisonings range from more than 800,000 to more than 1 million each year; 3,000–20,000 result in death (4). No worldwide estimates have been made of the chronic health impacts on the general population of land and water contamination by pesticides. Given the persistence of many pesticides and their accumulation throughout the food chain, this health risk may also be substantial. (See Chapter 2, "Population and Health," Focus On: Pesticide Use and Health.)

Table 12.1 Pesticide Subsidies in Selected Countries, Early 1980s

Region and Country	Annual Value of Subsidy (million U.S. dollars)	Size of Subsidy (percentage of full retail cost)
Africa		
Senegal	4	89
Egypt	207	83
Ghana	20	67
Latin America		
Honduras	12	29
Colombia	69	44
Ecuador	14	41
Asia		
Indonesia	128	82
China	285	19

Source: Robert Repetto, *Paying the Price: Pesticide Subsidies in Developing Countries* (World Resources Institute, Washington, D.C., 1985), Table 1, p. 5 and Table 2, p. 6.

Beyond their effects on human health, pesticides are known to kill nonpest species of animals and plants, contribute to the emergence of new pests whose natural predators have been destroyed, and encourage the development of pesticide resistance in target populations. More than 400 insect, tick, and mite pests are known to have developed resistance to pesticides since their use became widespread, and other pests are developing resistance as well (5). (See Figure 12.1.) Resistant pests lead to reduced effectiveness of pesticides and renewed crop losses that, in turn, often lead to further increases in use as well as to the need for new, more effective and often more toxic pesticides.

In Indonesia, 50,000–60,000 hectares of irrigated rice were destroyed in 1986–87 because of an outbreak of a pesticide-resistant strain of the brown planthopper. The resulting loss of 1 million metric tons of rice was worth about $180 million at world market prices. In addition, 35 percent of the total harvested area had to be converted to a more pest-resistant but less productive rice variety. The result was a 10–15 percent fall in rice yields (1 million metric tons) worth another $120 million (6). These impacts prompted the government of Indonesia to consider alternative pest controls with the assistance of the World Bank and the United Nations Food and Agriculture Organization. The government has already prohibited the use of 57 pesticide formulations (7).

Alternative pest control methods that rely less on chemical pesticides are available and effective. Integrated pest management (IPM) programs (often incorporating traditional pest management practices) reduce the use of chemicals through careful monitoring of pests to determine whether and when to apply pesticides, using pest-resistant crop varieties, and introducing natural enemies of the pests (8). IPM often requires increased labor, which may make it most appropriate in developing countries where farm labor costs are lower. An IPM program for cotton in Egypt, for example, included avoiding peak pest infestation by planting late, hand picking egg masses from young plants, monitoring pest breeding patterns to determine optimal spraying periods, and burning infested cotton bolls at the end of the growing season (9). Far fewer chemicals—and much more labor—were used.

Integrated pest management has not received the financial, research, and extension service commitment that it needs to become a viable alternative in many areas. The use of IPM techniques requires a level of sophistication and training that may be difficult to achieve in some parts of the developing world. Yet, devoting limited resources to improved agricultural extension services, for example, may be far more cost effective than subsidizing excessive use of pesticides (10).

The costs of subsidies and the environmental problems of excessive pesticide use have led some developing countries to begin reducing their subsidy programs. Indonesia's budget for pesticide subsidies dropped to $25 million in 1986–87, covering only 40 percent of the full retail price compared to 80 percent just three years earlier (11). However, the price effects have not yet reached the farmers, and it is too early to see how the lower subsidy affects pesticide use.

Figure 12.1 Growth in Resistant Species of Pests 1900–80

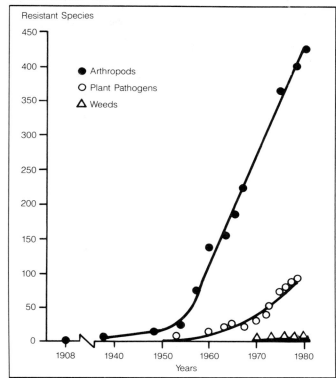

Source: Georghiou and Mellon, "Pesticide Resistance in Time and Space," in Dover, *Getting Tough: Public Policy and the Management of Pesticide Resistance* (World Resources Institute, Washington, D.C., 1985).

Pakistan has eliminated pesticide subsidies. Pesticides were first used in Pakistan on a large scale in the 1950s, when they were donated by the U.S. Agency for International Development and other organizations and were distributed free or at low prices. Cotton, sugar cane, and rice crops were sprayed aerially (12). Subsequently, the government subsidized 50 percent or more of the procurement costs of private distributors. Several evaluations found the system highly inefficient and pesticide use excessive (13).

In 1980, the Pakistani Government ended its spraying program, removed price subsidies on pesticides, and turned all distribution over to private firms without price regulation. Substantial reductions in pesticide sales occurred initially, but pest control was apparently not affected (14). Farmers began to exercise more discretion by choosing only effective and less expensive chemicals and by significantly reducing wastage (15).

Irrigation Subsidies

Irrigation is a key factor in the success of the Green Revolution. The high-yielding varieties of rice and wheat, which have turned many Asian countries from food importers to surplus producers, depend highly on readily available water supplies (16). Worldwide, in 1985, the 270 million hectares of irrigated land—which accounted for about 18 percent of all land under cultivation—produced one third the world harvest (17). In developing countries, the investment in irrigation systems is estimated at $250 billion. By the year 2000, another $100 billion is expected to be invested (18). Most irrigation facilities have been and will continue to be built with public funds to promote expansion in agricultural productivity. However, project costs are usually greater and agricultural benefits smaller than were expected initially (19).

The costs of developing and operating public irrigation facilities are high, and farmers' fees for irrigation services are usually relatively low. Table 12.2 compares the costs of providing irrigation water with the fees recipients pay for it in six Asian nations. Only in the Philippines did user charges for irrigation cover the costs of operating and maintaining the systems and defray a fraction of the capital costs. In no other country did the charges for irrigation water even fully cover operation and maintenance costs, much less the capital costs.

At the same time, the market value of the increased output that results from using irrigation is usually much higher than the cost of the water to the farmer. This difference between the market value of the additional output due to the use of a production factor (e.g., water or land) and the cost of obtaining the use of that factor is referred to as economic rent. Economic rent accrues to the producer because of ownership or control of a factor that is fixed in supply and not allocated on the basis of competitive bidding.

In most countries, entitlements to water in public irrigation systems are attached to specific plots of land, frequently because the land is favorably located near the water source. Because farmers on other land cannot bid up the price of the water, benefits accrue to the farmers whose land has water entitlements, thus yielding economic rents. To have access to such rents, farmers' groups, communities, and individual owners of large farms lobby policymakers for extension of existing irrigation services or construction of new irrigation works to serve their farms, knowing that they will not bear the capital costs. Table 12.3 indicates the magnitude of these

rents in several developing countries. These rents and the political and bureaucratic benefits of more water projects are shared among farmers who use irrigation water, irrigation officials who determine water allocations, and elected representatives who promote irrigation investment projects for their constituencies. They all profit, even when the irrigation project becomes a public loss.

The low water costs and the substantial benefits for the privileged farmers reduce their incentives to use the water efficiently. Wasteful water use by farmers and inefficient operation and maintenance by irrigation agencies (partly because low water charges provide insufficient funds) combine to damage the environment. Poorly maintained and unlined canals plus the waste of water from flooding fields for longer times than necessary cause waterlogging and salinization. Through 1984, India and Pakistan, for example, lost more than 17 million hectares of cultivable land through waterlogging, with approximately 16.8 million additional hectares of irrigated land subject to salinization (20) (21). (See *World Resources 1987*, Table 19.3, p. 280.) Loss of productive land, in turn, leads to pressure to irrigate new areas and to cultivate marginal lands, resulting in still further land degradation.

Policymakers have long debated whether higher water prices would induce farmers to use water more efficiently. Empirical evidence is limited because few public irrigation systems have increased user charges to levels approaching the marginal value of water (22). However, some evidence supports the conclusion that higher pricing of water would improve on-farm water management efficiency (23). In Mexico, water use efficiency was substantially greater where charges varied with the amount of water consumed than where farmers paid fixed rates regardless how much they use (24). In China, farmers used water more efficiently where volumetric irrigation fees were introduced, and the higher revenues collected enabled government agencies to maintain the systems better (25).

Politically and institutionally, higher prices for water and pricing systems based upon water use are difficult to put in place in both developing and developed countries.

Table 12.2 Irrigation Service Fees Paid by Farmers Compared to Public Irrigation System Costs, Selected Asian Countries[a]

Country	Actual Revenue from Service Fees (dollars per hectare)	Operating and Maintenance Costs (dollars per hectare)	Revenue as a Proportion of Operating and Maintenance Costs (percent)	Total Capital and Operating Costs — Moderate Estimate (dollars per hectare)	Total Capital and Operating Costs — High Estimate (dollars per hectare)	Revenue as a Proportion of Total Costs — Moderate Estimate (percent)	Revenue as a Proportion of Total Costs — High Estimate (percent)
Indonesia	25.90	33.00	78.5	191	387	13.6	6.7
South Korea	192.00	210.00	91.4	1057	1523	18.2	12.6
Nepal	9.10	16.00	56.9	126	207	7.2	4.4
Philippines	16.85	14.00	120.4	75	166	22.5	10.2
Thailand	8.31	30.00	27.7	151	272	5.5	3.1
Bangladesh (major surface systems)	3.75	21.00	17.9	375	X	1.0	X

Sources: For Bangladesh: Q. Shahabuddin, "Irrigation Water Charges, Subsidies, and Cost Recovery in Bangladesh, paper prepared for the World Resources Institute, September 1985; for all other countries: Leslie E. Small, Marietta S. Adriano, and Edward D. Martin, "Regional Study on Irrigation Service Fees: Final Report," International Irrigation Management Institute, Kandy, Sri Lanka, January 1986, as adapted from R. Repetto, *Skimming the Water: Rent-Seeking and the Performance of Public Irrigation Systems* (World Resources Institute, Washington, D.C., 1986), Table 1, p. 5.
Note: a. Figures obtained by converting local currency values at official exchange rates prevailing in June 1985.
X = not available.

Table 12.3 Economic Rents in Public Irrigation Systems

Country	Charges as a Percentage of Farmer Benefits
Indonesia	8–21
Korea	26–33
Nepal	5
Philippines	10
Thailand	9
Pakistan[a]	6
Mexico	11–26

Sources: Based on Leslie E. Small, Marietta S. Adriano, and Edward D. Martin, "Regional Study on Irrigation Service Fees: Final Report," International Irrigation Management Institute, Kandy, Sri Lanka, January 1986, Table 5, p. 37; Muhammed A. Chaudry, "Water Charges, Cost Recovery, and Irrigation Subsidies in Pakistan," prepared for the World Resources Institute, Washington, D.C., 1985; and Ronald Cummings and Victor Brajer, "Water Subsidies in Mexico's Irrigated Agricultural Sector," paper prepared for the World Resources Institute, Washington, D.C., 1985, cited in Robert Repetto, *Skimming the Water: Rent-Seeking and the Performance of Public Irrigation Systems* (World Resources Institute, Washington, D.C., 1986), Table 3, p. 13.
Note: a. Punjab Province, major irrigated crops, surface irrigation.

In the United States, for example, the political forces supporting continued subsidies of water in the West are renowned (26). The same situation has existed in other parts of the world. However, some developing countries are attempting to recover a higher fraction of the costs for providing irrigation water. In both the Republic of Korea and the Philippines, national policy requires that water prices recover both the full costs of operating and maintaining irrigation facilities and some capital costs. In fact, the pricing structure in both countries remains a flat rate per hectare, and actual water charges recovered are still somewhat below the full costs of operation and maintenance of the irrigation systems. In the Philippines, the official charges are about 20 percent higher than the average cost of operations and maintenance, but actual collections are far below the cost of the service (27).

Other Input Subsidies

Pesticides and water are but two of the many agricultural inputs that developing countries' governments subsidize to increase agricultural production. Other key inputs that are subsidized are fertilizers, farm machinery, high-yielding varieties of seeds, and farm credit.

Chemical fertilizers are a key ingredient in the productivity gains of the Green Revolution. Fertilizer consumption per hectare of arable land rose almost fourfold in low-income countries and doubled in middle-income countries between 1970 and 1985. Increases were especially rapid in South Asia and in China, Egypt, Indonesia, and other heavily populated farming societies (28).

Subsidies were important to expanding the use of chemical fertilizers. Although the economic benefits of increased fertilizer use have now been realized by farmers, subsidies are still common in developing countries, and they are frequently large and costly (29).

In the early 1980s, many subsidies exceeded 30 percent of the imported or factory price. In Nigeria, subsidies were as high as 80–90 percent (30). The result was significant government costs. In 1981, Nigeria, Pakistan, and Turkey spent $250 million, $210 million, and $620 million, respectively, to subsidize fertilizer; in 1982, Iran spent $340 million, and in 1983–84, India spent more than $1 billion (31).

Like the pesticide and water subsidies, the low price of chemical fertilizers especially relative to organic fertilizers, tends to encourage overuse. Chemical fertilizers then substitute for, rather than complement, organic manuring and other soil conservation practices. Although the immediate effects of overreliance on chemical fertilizers are less apparent than those of overuse of pesticides, they have long-term impacts on soil fertility. Chemical fertilizers provide specific plant nutrients, but they cannot compensate for organic manures in improving soil structures. In sandy soils, organic fertilizers improve water retention and prevent the loss of nutrients associated with leaching; they also moderate the tendency of soils to become excessively acidic or alkaline. In clay soils, organic matter increases porosity, making it easier for water to filter through the soil, and thereby reduces run-off and erosion. It also prevents baking and hardening of the soil. Further, because organic matter significantly increases biological activity in the soil, it promotes the growth of soil microorganisms necessary for healthy plant growth (32). Overreliance on chemical fertilizers can, therefore, lead to the long-term decline of soil productivity (33).

Chemical fertilizers can also lead to water pollution. Agricultural runoff containing high levels of nitrogen and phosphorous can result in eutrophication of lakes and rivers. Although primarily a problem in developed countries, it is also a growing concern in the developing world. (See Chapter 8, "Freshwater," Rural Nonpoint Pollutants.)

Subsidies for farm machinery similarly encourage the use of tractors, irrigation pumps, and other equipment, sometimes even where their use is inappropriate to the type of land. For example, plowing in tropical areas leads to increased soil erosion and related problems (34) (35).

Subsidies on high-yielding varieties of seeds and farm credit tend to have less direct impacts on natural resource use. The environmental effects of promoting a single crop over others are complex. However, both environmental and economic risks are associated with exclusive reliance on one or two major crops, and such focused subsidies frequently overlook the many people who depend upon less favorable lands. (See Chapter 4, "Food and Agriculture," Focus On: Building on the Green Revolution.)

Phasing Out Subsidies

Substantial benefits could be gained from reform of agricultural input subsidies in many developing countries. Phasing out these subsidies could save money, encourage prudent and efficient use of inputs, and lessen natural resource degradation.

The initial economic arguments for subsidies (i.e., encouraging the use of new technologies and providing the means to acquire new inputs in the face of limited access to financial resources) are generally no longer appropriate. In areas where use of these technologies and materials is appropriate, they have demonstrated their economic benefits. But further subsidies can lead—and in many cases have led—to increased costs that are not offset by revenues and to unintended adverse effects on natural resources from misuse or overuse of the subsidized input(s).

Removing subsidies is always a difficult political step, because those who benefit most from the subsidies are often among the most powerful segments of society. However, the potential advantages of reducing or removing subsidies are becoming apparent. Pakistan is the most prominent example of a country dropping subsidies of pesticides, but Indonesia is also moving in this direction.

Many East Asian countries have abandoned fertilizer subsidies, and they are declining in Bangladesh and Pakistan as well as in Senegal, Mali, Burkina Faso, Benin, and Togo (36). Elimination of all irrigation subsidies is probably unlikely given the large capital investments in irrigation facilities, but shifting to higher user fees based upon the value of water used may be more feasible. As China and Mexico show, these policy reforms may significantly affect water management.

Product Pricing Policies

In most industrial countries, agricultural pricing policies are designed to guarantee some minimum price floor in order to protect farmers' income. Governments in developing countries, on the other hand, often try to control the farm prices of food crops, including such staples as maize, rice, and wheat, to hold down food prices, especially in urban areas. For export crops, the economic policies of developing countries also frequently hold down farm prices. To raise government revenues and foreign exchange earnings, governments levy export taxes or sometimes establish state-run export monopolies, which pay farmers low prices for their crops while receiving higher prices from foreign sales. Very often, too, foreign exchange rates are overvalued to protect domestic industries that depend heavily on imported inputs, further depressing the local currency proceeds of agricultural exports.

The effect of all these policies is to reduce the prices farmers receive for their crops and the profitability of farming relative to other activities. The lower prices and profits tend to discourage agricultural production, ironically the opposite of what most developing countries are trying to accomplish with their agricultural policies. Table 12.4 shows estimates of the effect of a 10 percent increase in the farm prices of various crops. Conversely, lowering farm prices reduces agricultural output. The lower ends of the estimates shown represent the likely short-term responses to the price changes, and the higher estimates reflect the long-term responses (37).

Low prices for crops also reduce incentives to invest in agriculture, including investments necessary to maintain the resource base through soil conservation, water management, and other activities. Further, if agricultural pricing policies affect crops differentially, they also tend to distort farmers' decisions about which crops to grow, because it is relatively easy to convert farmland from one crop to another. These points are illustrated by the

Table 12.4 The Effect of Price Changes on Crop Production

Crop	Percentage Increase in Production With a 10 Percent Increase in Price	
	Africa	Other Developing Countries
Wheat	3.1–6.5	1.0–10.0
Maize	2.3–24.3	1.0–3.0
Sorghum	1.0–7.0	1.0–3.6
Groundnuts	2.4–16.2	1.0–40.5
Cotton	2.3–6.7	1.0–16.2
Tobacco	4.8–8.2	0.5–10.0
Cocoa	1.5–18.0	1.2–9.5
Coffee	1.4–15.5	0.8–10.0
Rubber	1.4–9.4	0.4–4.0
Palm Oil	2.0–8.1	

Sources: Hossein Askari and J.T. Cummings, *Agricultural Supply Responses: A Survey of Econometric Evidence* (Praeger, New York, 1976); and Pasquale L. Scandizzo and Colin Bruce, *Methodologies for Measuring Agricultural Price Intervention Effects* (The World Bank, Washington, D.C., 1980), cited in The World Bank, *World Development Report 1986* (The World Bank, Washington, D.C., 1986), Table 4.4, p. 68.

experience of three developing countries: Ghana, Sudan, and Thailand.

Ghana's cocoa pricing policy in the 1970s is a clear example of the production effects of holding down agricultural prices. Ghana's Cocoa Marketing Board (CMB) was established in 1947 with the sole right to purchase and export cocoa. It organized and financed the purchasing, transportation, and shipment of cocoa. This institutional arrangement initially operated economically and was socially beneficial. Over time, however, CMB profits became a major source of government revenues and foreign exchange. Recently, cocoa has accounted for about 10 percent of the gross domestic product and 60 percent of export earnings (38). In spite of a rising world market price for cocoa, the government held down the price it paid to farmers in order to capture increased revenues. While the world market price for cocoa nearly tripled (in constant dollars) between 1964–65 and 1978–79 (39), the effective export duty on cocoa rose from 8.5 percent to 60 percent (40). Further, because the local currency is deliberately overvalued, the implicit export duty on cocoa in 1979 reached 88.5 percent and real prices to farmers actually fell (41). This policy virtually removed all incentives to produce cocoa. Sales to CMB fell from 538,000 metric tons in 1964–65 to only 220,000 metric tons in 1981–82 (42). Because of low and declining real prices to farmers, some cocoa farmers left their farms uncared for, shifted into cultivating staples like cassava and maize that were relatively more profitable, and smuggled some of their declining harvests into neighboring Cote d'Ivoire and Togo.

Similar policies led to similar results in Sudan where low and declining farm prices for cotton—resulting from direct and indirect export taxes—led to a precipitous drop in cotton production from 659,000 metric tons in 1974–75 to 259,000 metric tons in 1980–81. The attendant drop in export earnings due to low production led to significant policy reform. With higher prices and other reforms, cotton production rebounded to 625,000 metric tons by 1984–85 (43).

Although depressing agricultural product prices reduces incentives for soil conservation and land improvements, unequal agricultural taxation rates also affect soil productivity through induced changes in cropping patterns and land use (44). The distorting effects of differential policies affecting agricultural product prices are seen in Thailand. Thailand accounts for 20–30 percent of the world rice market. Successive Thai governments consistently taxed rice in an effort to encourage diversification (45). Against this background, cultivating cassava, which was not taxed, was relatively more attractive. In addition, the emphasis in Thai agriculture shifted from subsistence crops to commercial crops, especially for export. With a significant international market for cassava (through a loophole in the European Economic Community's common agricultural policy), the area planted with cassava in Thailand increased about 50 percent from 1976–77 to 1985–86 (46), and Thailand came to dominate the world market for cassava (47).

The significant increases in the amount of land used for cassava and the quantities produced were achieved at a heavy environmental cost. Clearing of upland forests for cassava production resulted in considerable soil erosion. When land use changed from forest to row crops, as in eastern Thailand where land was converted from evergreen forests to cultivation of cassava, soil losses increased 6–10 times unless soil and water conservation measures were employed. Some areas may have soil losses at least 20 times the recommended tolerable levels (48).

FORESTRY AND LIVESTOCK POLICIES

Forests are a highly valuable economic resource in many developing countries, particularly in the tropics. In addition to their value as raw timber for domestic use and export, forest resources are a base for the development of wood processing industries. Forests provide important goods and services beyond the commercial value of the wood: nuts, berries, game, and other food, resins, essential oils, rattan, and medicinal substances; protection of watersheds; and habitat for diverse plant and animal species with unmeasured economic potential (49).

Many developing countries concentrate on short-term development and economic benefits by leasing concessions to private logging firms, taxing exports, and promoting domestic wood processing industries through import and export controls and tax incentives. By adopting such policies, many governments fail to recognize the economic and environmental benefits of standing forests, the need to sustain timber harvests over the long term, and even the full revenue potential of current timber harvests. The result is rapid and unsustainable exploitation of forests and extensive forest degradation. The long-term impacts of this degradation include: loss of habitat and biodiversity, and loss of watershed protection, soil erosion prevention, and other environmental services. More immediately, governments suffer budgetary losses through foregone revenues, which are needed to protect inefficient and noncompetitive wood products industries.

Timber Concessions

Many nations with abundant forest resources promote increased wood production to generate government revenues, earn foreign exchange, promote wood-based industry, provide job opportunities, and further regional development (50).

Although most large forested areas in developing countries are publicly owned, governments often lease timber rights. Timber concessions involve the assignment of exclusive rights to loggers to harvest timber from specified forest areas over a fixed period. In their desire to boost private sector logging, most governments negotiate contracts with concessionaires on the basis of standard terms instead of through competitive bidding. Given the fixed supply of timber in the short term, negotiating concessions creates the potential for loggers to obtain substantial economic rents (51). As noted above, economic rent is the difference between the market value of the added output that results from use of a production factor (in this case, timber) and the actual cost of obtaining that factor.

Theoretically, governments could extract the value of this rent from the loggers by increasing lease costs. But most forest resource-rich countries do not recognize the presence of these rents and therefore have not tried to appropriate them. Policies are often aimed at deriving the maximum short-term financial value from timber harvesting (52). Instead of capturing the rents accruing to concessionaires, many governments increase concessionaire profits even further by bearing some costs of marketing the timber harvested—the costs of building access roads, port facilities, and other infrastructure and of surveying, marking, and grading saleable timber (53). This statement applies equally to industrial countries. For example, at a cost to taxpayers of more than $100 million per year, the U.S. Forest Service subsidizes timber harvesting on more than 40 million hectares of national forests that are economically unfit for sustained timber production. Further, Forest Service timber prices do not cover costs (54).

The value of economic rents from timber activities can be large. In the following examples, rent is measured as the difference between the logs' average export value and the total costs (excluding taxes and fees) of harvesting and transporting them to the ports. The government's actual rent capture is the portion of this difference recovered through timber royalties, land taxes, reforestation fees, and other user charges.

Between 1979 and 1982, timber exported from Kalimantan and Sumatra, two major concession areas in Indonesia, produced an average $61 of potential rent per cubic meter of wood. The Indonesian Government captured only $30 per cubic meter (55). At the same time, total exports of raw and processed timber generated $4.9 billion in rents. The government's rent capture was only $1.6 billion. Of the $3.3 billion in potential revenues lost, $500 million was lost through higher costs associated with inefficient domestic timber processing (56). (See Wood Processing Industries, below.) The remaining $2.8 billion went to the concessionaires as profits.

Table 12.5 compares government rent capture in three Asian countries. It shows that government fees captured

**Table 12.5 Government Rent Capture in
Tropical Timber Production, 1979–82**
(million U.S. dollars)

Country	Potential Rent from Log Harvest[a]	Actual Rent from Log Harvest[b]	Official Government Rent Capture[c]	Percentage of Actual Rent Captured by Government
Indonesia	4,958	4,409	1,654	37.5
Sabah, Malaysia	2,065	2,064	1,703	82.5
Philippines	1,504	1,001	141	14.0

Source: Robert Repetto, "Overview," in *Public Policy and the Misuse of Forest Resources*, Robert Repetto and Malcolm Gillis, eds. (Cambridge University Press, Cambridge, U.K., in press), Table 1.7, p. 20.
Notes:
a. *Potential rent* assumes that all harvested logs are allocated to uses (direct export, sawmills, plymills) that yield the largest net economic rent.
b. *Actual rent* is the actual difference between the market value and the costs at the time of sale.
c. *Government rent capture* includes timber royalties, export taxes, and other official fees and charges.

between 14 percent and 82.5 percent of the actual rents generated in 1979–82 by logging concessions in these countries. Even in Sabah, where the Malaysian Government captured the largest proportion of rent, the difference between actual rent from the harvest and government rent capture was over $350 million.

These enormous rents made timber exploitation so lucrative to timber companies that applications for and allocations of logging concessions led to the "timber booms" experienced by many countries during the 1970s. For example, in Sabah, Malaysia, total timber export value increased more than fourfold from 1971 to 1984 (57), and Indonesia's annual log harvests rose from 10 million cubic meters in 1970 to about 26 million cubic meters in 1987 (58). The result was accelerated rates of forest disturbance and deforestation (59). Malaysia estimates that the undisturbed forest area of Sabah fell from 55 percent to about 25 percent of total land area between 1973 and 1983 (60). In the Philippines, timber concession areas rose from 4.5 million hectares in 1960 to 10.5 million hectares in 1970. Logging peaked in the mid-1970s, and by mid-decade, virtually all major production forests were logged out (61).

Logging in tropical areas does not usually cause deforestation directly because logging companies tend to harvest only the most valuable logs. In the process of taking the valuable tree species, little or no attention is paid to the remaining trees, which are frequently damaged, leaving a highly disturbed forest area that has extensive logging roads cut through it. Given other pressures to expand the land under cultivation, logged-over forests are often prime targets. In the Sabah region of Malaysia, 40–45 percent of deforestation since 1976 can be attributed to logging, followed by agricultural conversion (62). (See Chapter 5, "Forests and Rangelands," the Causes of Tropical Deforestation.)

The central problem of concessionary leases is that they significantly undervalue forests. The low prices of the user fees leads logging firms to cut more timber than they would if the prices were higher. At the same time, the foregone revenues to developing country governments reduce the countries' incentives and budgets to invest in reforestation and management of forests for sus-

tained timber production. In addition, these leases place no value on watershed protection, biological diversity, and other nonwood benefits, the loss of which is a real cost to society that should be recovered through higher user fees (63).

The counterproductive incentives that low user charges create are often exacerbated by the duration and other terms of the timber leases and the structure of the royalties, taxes, and fees imposed on the logging firms.

Because of the long growing cycles of commercial tropical hardwoods, the interval between harvests in a given woodlot should be a minimum of 25–35 years for sustainable timber production. The 20-year average duration of concession leases reduces concessionaires' incentives to minimize damage to residual trees in order to maximize a second cut, and the lease length may even encourage them to reenter the stands in 5–10 years, as many have done in Indonesia (64). In Sabah, Malaysia, one-year leases, which apply to small concessions averaging 2,000 hectares, accounted for 55 percent of all leases in 1985 (65). In Cote d'Ivoire, contracts were for only five years, except for 1965–68, when forest-based industries were permitted 15-year contracts (66).

The lease fee structure also affects depletion rates and degradation of forest resources. Flat annual license fees per hectare and uniform royalty and export taxes that fail to recognize different values for different log species encourage selective logging ("high grading") of trees with the highest value. For a target volume of logs, then, the concessionaire tends to harvest a wider area, thereby opening it up to other uses and damaging more residual trees (67).

Although royalties and export taxes are currently the most important sources of government revenues from logging, reforestation fees have great potential both to increase the proportion of rents captured by the government and to promote more sustainable forest production. A special reforestation fee in Sabah, Malaysia, accounted for 6–11 percent of forest revenue between 1973 and 1983 (68); the fee does not cover the full costs of reforestation. It is estimated that the revenues collected could finance the reforesting of 32 percent of the total area deforested annually at 1981 extraction levels (69). Similarly, a reforestation deposit fee in Indonesia introduced in late 1980 is refundable to loggers upon presentation of evidence of adequate replanting programs. In practice, it has not encouraged replanting and is regarded simply as another tax (70). The cost of replanting is estimated at two to three times the refundable amount; with relatively short-term leases, logging firms have no incentive to invest in long-term reforestation. Nevertheless, the government of Indonesia plans to tap this funding source to begin substantial reforestation (71).

It is clear that substantial economic and environmental benefits could be realized by increasing the user fees, taxes, and other charges to firms with logging concessions. Most important, the higher costs of extracting the wood would reduce the environmentally damaging and economically inefficient rates of forest exploitation. At the same time, the higher revenues would ease the budgetary constraints faced by many developing nations and could be used to improve long-term management of the natural forests for sustained use.

Wood Processing Industries

In addition to promoting logging concessions, many developing countries with substantial forest resources sought to promote economic development by encouraging wood processing industries to produce sawnwood and plywood for export and domestic consumption. This economic strategy was initially attractive for two reasons. First, processed wood products should have a higher value per unit of wood cut, resulting in higher foreign exchange earnings for a given level of timber harvest. Alternatively, this higher volume could enable countries to reduce their rates of logging (and forest degradation) without sacrificing export value and foreign exchange earnings. Second, the sawmills and plymills would generate substantial job opportunities and income (72).

This development strategy is made more attractive by the fact that shipping costs for raw timber are high, and substantial savings could be achieved in reduced shipping costs per dollar of exports. However, developed countries generally have erected much higher tariff barriers to imports of processed wood than to logs to protect their own wood processing industries (73). As a result, fostering wood processing industries has required substantial incentives, among them: reduced export taxes on processed wood, generous investment incentives, including income tax exemptions and subsidized credit, and banned export of raw logs (74).

The effects of these economic policies and incentives are large. For example, in Ghana in 1982, the wood processing industry consisted of 95 sawmills, 10 veneer and plywood plants, and 30 furniture and other wood processing firms (75). In Indonesia, where incentives for local processing began in 1978 with an increased export tax on logs, the number of sawmills and plymills rose from 16 in 1977 to 182 by 1983 (76). By 1985, wood export industries employed over 660,000 workers (77).

The economic costs of this growing industrial activity and employment are high and their impacts on forest degradation significant. Many new wood processing plants in developing countries are small and relatively inefficient. In the Philippines, the average conversion rate (the fraction of the raw timber that becomes finished plywood) of plymills was only 43 percent in 1980, compared to 55 percent in Japan (78). This inefficiency adds to logging pressure.

With these low conversion factors, the value of exported plywood, as measured by the value of the logs used to produce it, is also low. In Indonesia, the value was $109 per cubic meter of wood, but because the export value of the raw log was $100 per cubic meter, domestic processing into plywood added only $9 per cubic meter to the value of the wood. However, the loss of revenues to the Indonesian Government from waiving export taxes for plywood amounted to $20 per cubic meter. The government, therefore, gave up more than twice as much in revenue as it gained in foreign exchange earnings. In 1988, the annual revenue loss is expected to reach $400 million (79).

These inefficient wood processing operations also contribute to continuing rapid exploitation of forests. For a given level of finished wood products, the protected domestic sawmills and plymills require a higher level of logging. In addition, the growing wood processing industries and the jobs they generate create a political imperative to keep industry supplied with new logs, regardless of the economic and environmental reasons for reducing the harvest (80).

As a result, the rapid development of domestic wood processing industries in developing countries through the incentives, credit subsidies, and other protective measures has often led to significant revenue losses for these countries' governments and to inefficient use of forest resources. It has also contributed to long-term forest decline.

Forest Conversion for Cattle Ranching

Most deforestation results from clearing forest land for other uses, particularly expansion of agriculture. (See Chapter 5, "Forests and Rangelands," The Causes of Tropical Deforestation.) Conversion of forest land to other uses is appropriate when the alternative use is sustainable and is economically more valuable than keeping the land in forests.

Too often, however, governments underestimate the value of forests and overestimate the economic and environmental viability of alternative uses. As a result, many developing countries have adopted costly economic policies that create large incentives for private development of forest lands; after the forests have been destroyed, the policies turn out to be environmentally and economically unsound.

In Latin America, development of the cattle industry in many countries has led to large-scale conversion of forests to pastures (81). The soil characteristics of cleared forest areas were often unsuitable to sustained use, and the areas were abandoned after a few years of intensive use (82).

Brazil is a clear example. Government incentives led to massive deforestation in the tropical forests of the Amazon. In the mid-1960s, the government adopted broad policies designed to foster private sector development of the Amazon. At the heart of these policies were tax-based subsidies for investment in approved projects.

Program emphasis was on the livestock sector because of presumed advantages of expanded cattle production over other sectors. Given the low level of infrastructure development in the Amazon, ranching was seen as requiring relatively little new investment in infrastructure (because cattle can walk to the market, if necessary). Abundant labor (underemployed cowboys) was available in the region, and export prospects looked good. Pasture-fed cattle from Latin America were viewed as an economical alternative to the more expensive grain-fed cattle of North America, where the demand for cheap beef for fast foods was rising rapidly by the early 1960s. Brazil viewed the enticement of corporate investment in the Amazon's land-intensive livestock sector as a necessary step toward gaining a competitive edge in the foreign market for beef (83). Presumably, the incentive program was a short-term measure that in the long-run would lead to a self-sustaining beef industry capable of generating export earnings, stimulating the domestic economy and employment, and increasing tax revenues.

Brazil's fiscal incentives included three mechanisms. First, an investment tax credit of up to 50 percent of federal income tax liabilities was available to corporations investing in approved development projects. Second, income from approved projects could be exempted from federal taxes for up to 15 years (in practice, exemptions were limited to 10 years), and losses could be deducted from corporate taxable income from other activities. Third, individuals and corporations could deduct from taxable income stock investments in the investment fund established to support development projects (84). In addition, corporations often received subsidized loans to cover remaining capital and operating expenses at interest rates 15 percent below inflation rates in the late 1970s (85).

These subsidies created strong incentives to invest in cattle ranching. Between 1965 and 1983, 469 large cattle ranches were established in Amazonia, averaging 23,000 hectares each. Even though less than 25 percent of this land had been cleared for new pasture by 1983, the ranches were responsible for 30 percent of the total deforestation detected by the Landsat monitoring program between 1973 and 1983 (86).

Initially, the newly created pastures can support an average of one animal per hectare. But without further investment to combat weeds and maintain soil fertility, productivity falls after about five years so that it takes 4 hectares to support one animal (87). Under these circumstances, the subsidies create incentives to clear more forests rather than to maintain soil productivity (88). The result is abandonment of the degraded land and more deforestation.

The cattle subsidy program is an enormous fiscal burden on the government. Between 1965 and 1983, $1.4 billion in tax credit subsidies were disbursed to private investment projects; nearly $600 million went to the 469 beef cattle projects (58 percent of all projects) (89). For individual investors, these projects were highly profitable because of the heavy government subsidies. From the standpoint of the national economy, however, they are huge economic losses.

An assessment of the profitability of a typical (20,000-hectare) cattle ranch operating under the Brazilian subsidy program is shown in Table 12.6. Based on a study of 24 large-scale government-approved cattle ranches, the assessment calculated the total profits and losses of a 15-year project; assuming all assets, including cattle and land, would be sold at the end of the project. If land value increased at 2 percent per year above the rate of inflation and the real annual discount rate was 5 percent, the total investment over the life of the project would be $5.1 million and the project would yield a net loss of $2.8 million. Only if cattle prices doubled would the project become marginally profitable (90).

From the perspective of the private investor, however, the project would be highly profitable. With all the subsidies, an investment of just $744,000 would reap a profit

Table 12.6 Winners and Losers: Government-Assisted Cattle Ranch Development in the Brazilian Amazon

	Total Investment Outlay[a] (U.S. dollars)	Cumulative Profits (Losses)[a] (U.S. dollars)	Return on Investment (percent)
Society	$5,143,700	($2,824,000)	−55
Private Investors	$ 743,650	$1,875,400	+249

Source: John O. Browder, "Public Policy and Deforestation in the Brazilian Amazon," in *Public Policy and the Misuse of Forest Resources*, Robert Repetto and Malcolm Gillis, eds. (Cambridge University Press, Cambridge, U.K., in press), Table 6.11, p. 276.
Note: a. Net present value.

of about $1.9 million in 15 years. Thus, an intrinsically uneconomic venture would be highly profitable to the private investor (91).

Overall, the Brazilian program of subsidizing cattle ranch development in the Amazon was a failure both economically and environmentally. For a total cost of $2.5 billion through 1983, the government subsidized substantial deforestation and land degradation to create 469 large-scale cattle ranches that would not be economically viable in the absence of the subsidies (92).

CONCLUSION

This chapter examines economic policies adopted by governments in the developing world. However well-meant, they have led to unintended and often counter-productive financial, economic, and ecological results. They were caused by faulty assumptions underlying the policies and misreadings of individual responses to the incentives that these policies created.

In all the cases discussed above, these incentive policies induced excessive use of or reduced incentives to conserve the affected resources by artificially cheapening their prices, absolutely or relative to other resources. Agricultural subsidies lowered the costs of pesticides and chemical fertilizers, leading to their overuse. Subsidized low charges for irrigation water led to waste of the water and disincentives for reducing water losses. Low taxes and fees on timber concessions led to rapid exploitation of forests and disincentives for sustainable management of forest resources.

The impacts of these policies are uniformly negative with respect to sustained use of natural resources. They have led to soil degradation and loss of agricultural productivity. They have contributed to high rates of deforestation.

Even judged solely on economic grounds, these policies are not successful. They have necessitated huge government budget costs, generated enormous economic losses, sacrificed net foreign exchange earnings, and created unearned windfalls for a few firms and individuals.

There are growing indications that some developing countries recognize the damage that these policies cause and are moving to rectify them. In the past decade, a few countries have initiated policy reforms to reduce or remove inappropriate subsidies and incentives.

References and Notes

1. United Nations Food and Agriculture Organization (FAO), *1948–1985 World Crop and Livestock Statistics* (FAO, Rome, 1987), Tables 1, 10, 14, 42, 52, 74–81, 84–93; pp. 7–26, 129–150, 195–216, 393–398, 494–499, 573–608, 617–691.
2. Elliot Berg, "Fertilizer Subsidies," background paper prepared for The World Bank, Washington, D.C., draft, December 1985, p. 3.
   Robert Repetto, *Paying the Price: Pesticide Subsidies in Developing Countries* (World Resources Institute, Washington, D.C., 1985), p. 12.
4. Marcello Lotti, "Production and Use of Pesticides," in *Toxicology of Pesticides: Experimental, Clinical, and Regulatory Perspectives*, Lucio Costa, Corrado L. Galli, and Sheldon D. Murphy, eds. (Springer-Verlag, Berlin and New York, 1987).
5. Michael Dover and Brian Croft, *Getting Tough: Public Policy and the Management of Pesticide Resistance* (World Resources Institute, Washington, D.C., 1984), p. 5.
6. Edward B. Barbier, "Cash Crops, Food Crops and Sustainability: The Case of Indonesia" (International Institute for Environment and Development, London, n.d.), pp. 26–27.
7. Edward B. Barbier, "Natural Resources and Environmental Management Review: Indonesia," Annex 1, "Natural Resources Policy and Economic Framework," draft, U.S. Agency for International Development, Jakarta, Indonesia, 1987, pp. 1–16.
8. *Op. cit.* 3, p. 15.
9. L. Brader, "Integrated Pest Management in the Developing World," *Annual Review of Entomology*, Vol. 24 (1979), pp. 237–238.
10. *Op. cit.* 3, p. 16.
11. *Op. cit.* 7.
12. *Op. cit.* 3, p. 25.
13. *Op. cit.* 3, p. 26.
14. *Op. cit.* 3, p. 26.
15. *Op. cit.* 3, p. 26.
16. Robert Repetto, *Skimming the Water: Rent-Seeking and the Performance of Public Irrigation Systems* (World Resources Institute, Washington, D.C., 1986), p. 3.
17. Robert Repetto, *Economic Policy Reform for Natural Resource Conservation*, World Resources Institute, Washington, D.C., 1986, p. 17.
18. Jeremy J. Warford, "Environment, Growth, and Development," paper prepared for The World Bank, Washington, D.C., March 1987, p. 14.
19. Paul Faeth, *Determinants of Irrigation Performance in Developing Countries* (U.S. Department of Agriculture, Washington, D.C., 1984), p. 6.
20. B.B. Vohra, *Land and Water: Towards a Policy for Life Support Systems* (The Indian National Trust for Art and Cultural Heritage, New Delhi, 1985), p. 4.
21. Pakistan Federal Bureau of Statistics, *Pakistan Statistical Yearbook 1985* (Pakistan Federal Bureau of Statistics, Karachi, 1985), pp. 140–141.
22. *Op. cit.* 16, pp. 11–14 and pp. 29–32.
23. See, for example, B. Delworth Gardner, "Water Pricing and Rent Seeking in California Agriculture," in *Water Rights: Scarce Resource Allocation, Bureaucracy, and the Environment*, T. Anderson, ed. (Pacific Institute for Public Policy Research, San Francisco, 1983), pp. 83–113.
24. Gunter Schramm and Fernando Gonzales V., "Pricing Irrigation Water in Mexico: Efficiency, Equity, and Revenue Considerations," *The Annals of Regional Science*, Vol. 11, No. 1 (March 1977), p. 24.
25. Lester Ross, "Environmental Policy in China, Department of Political Science, Purdue University, cited in *Op. cit.* 16, p. 14.
26. See, for example, Alfred G. Cuzán, "Appropriators versus Expropriators," in *Water Rights: Scarce Resource Allocation, Bureaucracy, and the Environment*, T. Anderson, ed. (Pacific Institute for Public Policy Research, San Francisco, 1983), pp. 13–43.
27. Leslie E. Small, Marietta S. Adriano, and Edward D. Martin, "Regional Study on Irrigation Service Fees: Final Report," paper prepared for the Asian Development Bank (1986), Annex 4 and Annex 6.
28. *Op. cit.* 17, p. 40.
29. *Op. cit.* 2, p. 1.
30. The World Bank, *World Development Report 1986* (The World Bank, Washington, D.C., 1986), p. 95.
31. *Op. cit.* 17, pp. 43–44.
32. Robert Repetto, "Economic Incentives for Sustainable Production," *The Annals of Regional Science*, Vol. 21, No. 3 (1987), p. 50.
33. *Op. cit.* 30, p. 96.
34. *Op. cit.* 32, p. 52.
35. *Op. cit.* 30, pp. 97–98.
36. *Op. cit.* 30, pp. 106–109.
37. *Op. cit.* 30, p. 68.
38. Ernesto May, "Farmer's Incentives and Government Controls: The Case of Cocoa in Ghana," notes prepared for The World Bank, Washington, D.C., September 1985, p. 1.
39. The World Bank, *Commodity Trade and Price Trends* (The Johns Hopkins University Press, Baltimore, 1986), p. 49.
40. *Op. cit.* 38, p. 2.
41. *Op. cit.* 38, p. 2.
42. *Op. cit.* 38, p. 2.
43. *Op. cit.* 30, p. 108.
44. *Op. cit.* 17, p. 16.
45. Theodore Panayotou, "Economics, Environment and Development," paper prepared for the 4th World Wilderness Congress, Estes Park, Colorado (Harvard Institute for International Development, Cambridge, Massachusetts, 1987), pp. 13–14.
46. Thailand Development Research Institute (TDRI), *Thailand: Natural Resources Profile* (TDRI, Bangkok, 1987), p. 30.
47. *Op. cit.* 45.
48. *Op. cit.* 46.
49. Robert Repetto, *The Forest for the Trees? Government Policies and the Issue of Forest Resources* (World Resources Institute, Washington, D.C., 1988), pp. 10–11.
50. Malcolm Gillis, "Indonesia: Public Policies, Resources Management and the Tropical Forest," in *Public Policy and the Misuse of Forest Resources*, Robert Repetto and Malcolm Gillis, eds. (Cambridge University Press, Cambridge, U.K., in press), p. 56.
51. Robert Repetto, "Creating Incentives for Sustainable Forest Development," *Ambio*, Vol. 16, Nos. 2–3 (1987), p. 94.
52. *Op. cit.* 50, p. 56.
53. *Op. cit.* 51, p. 95.
54. *Op. cit.* 51, p. 95.
55. *Op. cit.* 51, p. 95.
56. *Op. cit.* 51, p. 95.
57. Malcolm Gillis, "Malaysia: Public Policies and the Tropical Forest," in *Public Policy and the Misuse of Forest Resources*, Robert Repetto and Malcolm Gillis, eds. (Cambridge University Press, Cambridge, U.K., in press), Table 3.7, p. 125.
58. *Op. cit.* 50, Table 2.3, p. 54.
59. *Op. cit.* 51.
60. *Op. cit.* 57, p. 141.
61. *Op. cit.* 49, p. 20.
62. *Op. cit.* 49, p. 53.
63. *Op. cit.* 45, pp. 8–10.
64. *Op. cit.* 50, p. 63.
65. *Op. cit.* 51, p. 95.
66. Malcolm Gillis, "West Africa: Resource Management Policies and the Tropical Forest," in *Public Policy and the Misuse of Forest Resources*, Robert Repetto and Malcolm Gillis, eds. (Cambridge University Press, Cambridge, U.K., in press), p. 337.
67. *Op. cit.* 57, pp. 130–131.
68. *Op. cit.* 57, p. 129.
69. *Op. cit.* 57, p. 131.
70. *Op. cit.* 50, p. 62.
71. *Op. cit.* 7, pp. 1–21.
72. Robert Repetto, "Overview," in *Public Policy and the Misuse of Forest Resources*, Robert Repetto and Malcolm Gillis, eds. (Cambridge University Press, Cambridge, U.K., in press), pp. 26–32.
73. *Op. cit.* 49, pp. 23–24.
74. *Op. cit.* 17, p. 70.
75. *Op. cit.* 66, p. 338.
76. *Op. cit.* 49, p. 25.
77. *Op. cit.* 7, pp. 1–20.
78. *Op. cit.* 49, p. 26.
79. *Op. cit.* 49, p. 25.
80. *Op. cit.* 49, p. 25.
81. Susanna Hecht, "Cattle Ranching in the Eastern Amazon: Environmental and Social Implications," in *The Dilemma of Amazonian Development*, Emilio F. Moran, ed. (Westview Press, Boulder, Colorado, 1983), pp. 156–157.
82. *Ibid.*, p. 175.
83. John O. Browder, "Public Policy and Deforestation in the Brazilian Amazon," in *Public Policy and the Misuse of Forest Resources*, Robert Repetto and Malcolm Gillis, eds. (Cambridge University Press, Cambridge, U.K., in press), p. 256.
84. *Ibid.*, pp. 257–261.
85. *Op. cit.* 51, p. 99.
86. *Op. cit.* 83, pp. 265–266.
87. *Op. cit.* 81, p. 173.
88. *Op. cit.* 49, p. 30.
89. *Op. cit.* 83, pp. 257–259.
90. *Op. cit.* 49, pp. 30–31.
91. *Op. cit.* 49, p. 31.
92. *Op. cit.* 49, p. 32.

13. Rehabilitating and Restoring Degraded Lands

ENVIRONMENTAL DEGRADATION IN PERSPECTIVE

THE COSTS OF DEGRADATION AND RECOVERY

Environmental degradation is not a recent phenomenon. Six thousand years ago, poor irrigation practices in Mesopotamia caused huge tracts to become salinized. Food production declined and, partly in consequence, so did Sumerian culture (1). Around the Mediterranean, areas covered today by maquis vegetation (scrub oak, heath, and so on) were once productive forests (2). Even the remote Easter Islands lost their native palm forests by the year 1500 (3).

Much of the historical degradation of the land went unrepaired. Population densities were low enough—and productive, accessible lands abundant enough—for people to move away from newly degraded areas until the land recovered on its own, or they simply abandoned severely degraded land. Second, the destructiveness of modern technology was realized far earlier than its recuperative potential. For example, efficient coal mining is much older than the science of growing plants on denuded land around an abandoned mine.

Environmental degradation has intensified during the worldwide population boom—just since 1950, the population has doubled (4). The concomitant demands for living space and for higher food and energy production have resulted in some lands being converted to intrinsically unsuitable uses. Slash-and-burn farm plots cut out of rainforests, which at best will support only a few years of crops, are one example of land use practices that were nearly harmless in an era of low population densities and resource demand but that are fast becoming unsustainable.

Despite the acceleration of degradation worldwide, most nations are able to downplay or even to ignore the problem with impunity because they still have some excess land available to meet the demand. But if projections of population growth are accurate, this extra land will soon be in use. By 2025, an additional 3 billion people are projected; over 90 percent of them will live in developing countries, many of which seem to be approaching the limits of their land's productive capacity at current input levels (5). The number of people at risk from environmental degradation can only grow larger. In India and some other regions, it is likely that degraded lands will have to be restored to productivity if human needs are to be met in the next century.

Attempting such a recovery is necessarily expensive, but the costs of doing nothing are much higher. In 1980, the United Nations estimated an annual loss of $26 billion in agricultural productivity from desertification (6). This figure does not even begin to reckon indirect costs. The experience of the Sahel during its recent prolonged drought, which was worsened by anthropogenic desertification, shows that the social costs of severe environmental degradation—famine, disease, civil unrest, and massive dislocation—may initially affect only the rural poor who live on marginal lands but will eventually affect other economic classes.

Recovery programs, to repair and reverse the effects of degradation, are expensive because they entail remedial intervention in biological, geophysical, and social systems—a complicated undertaking. Good management—that is, preventing and arresting environmental degradation—is always cheaper (7). Combining the two is a capital investment in the Earth's most basic production systems.

Large initial outlays are often required. Between 1985 and 1987, for example, the United Nations Food and Agriculture Organization (FAO) spent $289 million on degraded African agricultural lands (8). FAO believes even larger amounts will have to be spent over the next few years. (See Table 13.1.) Yet some recovery projects with low start-up costs have been effective; overall, they are often the most effective remedy.

Besides capital, another large investment is labor. Recovery projects are usually labor intensive (9). Here, some developing nations are at an advantage because of their large supply of labor, China, for example. On the other hand, the degradation of North Yemen's dry highlands is attributable to a labor shortage; rock terraces essential to agriculture cannot be kept up because so much of the work force has gone to oil-rich neighbors (10). Other sparsely populated rural areas experience similar degradation from the seasonal exodus to off-farm employment (11).

The backdrop is natural degradation. How is anthropogenic degradation distinguished from the effects of natural processes that tend to lower productivity? Some erosion will always take place in mountains, even when the topography is altered by terracing. Similarly, no catchment can contain all the rain that falls during the most torrential monsoon. With no comprehensive baseline data for distinguishing natural and human causes of degradation, official policy runs the risk of being ill-informed. Land use studies of a given area, each purporting to be scientific, can come to widely divergent conclusions about what needs to be done (12).

The study of recovering degraded land is so new that important terms are used in widely different ways. Simply stated, *degradation* is the diminution of the biological productivity expected of a given tract of land. Degradation is keyed to human expectations, which vary by land use. Indeed, each type of land—farmland, wildland, or rangeland, for example—is nothing more than a set of expectations about the form its biota should take. The concept of degraded lands, therefore, is somewhat subjective, and a condition that constitutes degradation on a particular type of land may be considered normal elsewhere.

Typically, however, on degraded land soil is impoverished or eroded, less usable water is available due to increased surface runoff or contamination, vegetation is diminished, reproduction of biomass is lowered, and the diversity of wildlife is reduced. The diminution that degradation embodies is expressed in many ways, depending on the type of land. On a farm, it may be reflected in lower crop yields, on a ranch in a drop in

Table 13.1 Investments Needed to Rehabilitate Upland Watersheds and Semiarid Lowlands in Selected Countries, 1987–91

Country	Recommended Program	Investment Needed (million U.S. dollars)
Colombia	Technical assistance, primarily training of management and extension staff, for watershed rehabilitation to protect hydropower investments.	$50
Ethiopia	Technical assistance in preparation, training, and organization of watershed rehabilitation projects in the Central Highlands Plateau region; soil conservation and provision of inputs to improve agricultural yields; and shelterbelts and on farm tree planting on denuded areas.	$100
India	Watershed rehabilitation treatment of 45 million hectares to protect the 18 out of 31 flood control reservoirs considered most urgently in danger of destruction by sedimentation; and tree planting and rehabilitation of agricultural land at a cost of $250 per hectare.	$500
Indonesia	Technical assistance in support of the government watershed management program to: improve agricultural productivity emphasizing tree crops; replant denuded areas of protective forest on steep slopes; and develop productive agricultural settlement on Sumatra, Kalimantan, and other islands. Expand watershed rehabilitation program 50,000 hectares per year at $4 per hectare.	$100
Kenya	Rehabilitation of 200,000 hectares of upland areas in the upper Tana River watershed through soil conservation, agricultural improvement, and tree planting activities. Sediment control in semiarid areas of the lower Tana River watershed through improved grazing and tree planting.	$35
Madagascar	Technical assistance for rehabilitation of degraded watersheds, including reforestation, soil conservation, and agricultural improvement, at $2 million per year.	$10
Nepal	Technical assistance for panchayat forest development on 75 watersheds in the Middle Mountains covering 375,000 hectares.	$15
Pakistan	Land use reorganization, control, and rehabilitation of the lower watersheds above the Mangla and Tarbella dams, including reforestation of critical slopes with forage and fuel-wood trees, terracing and improvement of permanent agriculture, and protection of forests.	$45
Philippines	Rehabilitation and protection of the 200,000 hectares of annually logged virgin forest to ensure regeneration of forest cover at $120 per hectare.	$120
Zimbabwe	Land use reorganization and improvement in communal areas (grazing management, tree planting, and irrigation schemes with watershed protection).	$46
Total		**$1,021**

Source: Adapted from United Nations Food and Agriculture Organization (FAO), *Tropical Forestry Action Plan* (FAO, Rome, 1985), pp. 139–140.

the number of animal units, and in a nature reserve in fewer plant and animal species.

Degradation on drylands (arid, semiarid, and subhumid lands) is called *desertification* because desert-like conditions appear where none existed before (13). Desertified drylands are characterized by low primary productivity (less than 400 kilograms of dry matter per hectare per year) and poor rain-use efficiency (usually less than 1 kilogram of dry matter produced per hectare per year for each millimeter of rainfall) (14).

In the United Nations Plan of Action to Combat Desertification, the term desertification is not restricted to the degradation of drylands. However, most papers on desertification discuss drylands alone (15). Understandably enough, desertification conjures up images of arid land. It therefore seems useful to treat desertification as a subset of land degradation rather than to consider the terms synonymous (16).

THE PLAN OF ACTION TO COMBAT DESERTIFICATION

The 1977 U.N. Conference on Desertification (UNCOD) represented a new look at the problem of degraded lands. Organizers of this first worldwide meeting on environmental degradation believed that enough was known about how to fight it and the next step was to mobilize the technology to rehabilitate these lands. Most delegates agreed, but many also felt that social and political inequities are at the heart of degradation; thus the solution demands nothing less than restructuring the world's economic order. Not surprisingly, UNCOD's unanimous assent for a Plan of Action to Combat Desertification (PACD) came only after much political compromise on its contents (17).

The PACD has three objectives: to stop and then reverse the environmental processes of desertification; to put in place ecologically appropriate, productive, and sustainable land uses; and to secure the social and economic advancement of the people affected. The plan spells out recovery measures for rangelands, rainfed and irrigated croplands, and woodlands. It also contains several institutional recommendations, including a call for nations to create high-ranking bodies devoted to overcoming desertification.

So far, the PACD is an almost unqualified failure. During the first general assessment of the PACD in 1984, the United Nations Environment Programme (UNEP) tried to obtain information on progress in developing countries affected by desertification. To UNEP's dismay, none of the countries could supply the necessary data. Despite workshops, conferences, and desertification studies, five years after UNCOD, only two national plans and nine draft plans had been developed with the assistance of the UNEP Desertification Branch (18). In 1983, UNEP Executive Director Mostafa Tolba characterized the responses of both developed and developing countries as "totally inadequate" (19).

Combating desertification has no immediate payoff; it is a long-term process. Both potential donors and recipient countries tend to favor projects with more immediate economic development goals. In fact, some countries reject long-term planning to reverse desertification as conflicting with immediate development needs (20).

Lack of attention to the PACD may also reflect the fact that frequently desertification most directly affects the poorest and least politically powerful people in a country. Unless environmental degradation precipitates a transna-

tional crisis—as it did in the Sahel—governments will not commit large amounts of money to programs that stand to benefit only the least powerful people in society and that have a high risk of failure.

THE EXTENT OF THE PROBLEM

For those who contend that land productivity around the world has deteriorated, anecdotal evidence is compelling. But there are few hard data to buttress the case. And despite the impetus of UNCOD in the last decade, little progress has been made toward an accurate worldwide assessment of how much degraded land exists (21). Notable improvements have been made in the use of satellite imagery to monitor global degradation, but remote sensing has not been applied to a comprehensive inventory of degraded lands (22).

Even the extent of desertified drylands—which has received more attention than other forms of degradation (except, perhaps, deforestation)—is not known. For certain types of arid land, subjective assessments of trends in desertification in individual countries are abundant, but, again, they lack corroborative data. For example, the condition of grazing land in every nation on the Indian subcontinent (except in Sri Lanka) is considered to be degraded to some degree, but distinctions among heavily degraded, overgrazed, and other classifications are rough. (See Chapter 5, "Forests and Rangelands," Table 5.3.)

So too, the estimates for soil erosion worldwide are rough, although rates and extents have been calculated for many countries and river basins (23). Clearly, far more topsoil is lost from cropland each year than is replaced naturally. An estimated six to seven million hectares of agricultural land are now rendered unproductive each year because of erosion—more than twice the rate in the past three centuries (24). Three other soil problems— waterlogging, salinization, and alkalinization (also called sodication)—reduce the productivity of up to 1.5 million hectares of cropland each year (25).

Knowledge of the extent of degraded soils should be considerably enhanced by the new Global Assessment of Soil Degradation, undertaken in late 1987 by UNEP and the International Soil Reference and Information Centre in the Netherlands. An important result of the project will be a detailed world map showing the distribution of lands affected by wind and water erosion, loss of nutrients, salinization, acidification, and structural changes (e.g., compacting and waterlogging). Causes, severity, and degradation rate will be indicated (26).

In addition to drylands, forests are also being seriously degraded. Although the problem of deforestation is more widely recognized, far more of the world's forests are being degraded than destroyed. For example, clearing forest land for agriculture, rather than logging, is the main cause of tropical deforestation. In logging of tropical forests, stands are usually cut selectively, rather than clearcut, but logging does damage adjacent trees significantly, and overall forest productivity deteriorates. In some logged forests of Malaysia and Indonesia, 45–75 percent of the trees left standing were damaged (27). A new remote sensing study of Brazil's southeastern Amazon basin found that while about 90,000 square kilometers had been cleared by September 1985, nearly three times that amount—266,000 square kilometers—had been damaged (28).

Chemical pollution can cause vast land degradation, especially in industrialized countries, where pollutants and impaired biological productivity are clearly connected. For example, Europe's widespread *Waldsterben* (forest death) is linked to airborne pollution. (See *World Resources 1986*, pp. 203–226.) The forests of several countries have suffered greatly: at least one fifth of the timber volume of Poland, Czechoslovakia, Switzerland, West Germany, the Netherlands, and Sweden has been damaged. Air pollution now adversely affects some 1.8 billion cubic meters (15 percent) of Europe's total timber volume. Sanitary fellings have been carried out in Central Europe to clear the forests of damaged trees. (See Chapter 18, "Forests and Rangelands," Table 18.3.)

REHABILITATION VERSUS RESTORATION

When environmental degradation can no longer be tolerated, the response to the problem is either abandonment or assisted recovery.

Abandonment is more prevalent and, until recently, was a viable response for many people. Short periods of abandonment of temporarily degraded land are the basis for various types of agriculture, particularly shifting cultivation, nomadic pastoralism, and transhumance (seasonal migration). Their success depends entirely upon a simple principle: the fallow period must exceed the time needed for the land to recover from the tree felling, farming, grazing, or other disturbance. The recovery time can be reduced, but only to a certain extent, by adding plant nutrients to a field, for example. Sometimes, out of sheer necessity, people shorten or eliminate the fallow period until there is no chance for recovery. Eventually all utility is exhausted, and the land must be more-or-less permanently abandoned, whereupon those who depended upon it seek out other lands on which to subsist.

The only alternative to this cycle of abandonment is to recover sustainable productivity. *Assisted recovery* encompasses two possible courses of action, depending on the type of land involved. Lands intended for economically productive use can be rehabilitated. Degraded wildlands—those that are suffering a diminution of their potential biodiversity—can be restored (29).

Rehabilitation, as the word suggests, entails making the degraded land useful to humans again. It seeks to optimize the usable biomass of a site, and so has an avowedly utilitarian purpose. *Restoration* is much more ambitious, for it aims to reinstate entire communities of organisms closely modeled on those occurring naturally (30). Because it strives to optimize the biodiversity of a given site, restoration does not emphasize resource utility.

Both rehabilitation and restoration imply that stable land use practices will be established on the site in perpetuity (31). Both involve returning to some earlier point in time in conformity with a plan. In theory, restoration is by far the more complicated concept because it seeks to recreate the former conditions (the total community of

native plants and animals) rather than a single condition (the productivity of a usable resource) sought by rehabilitation. In practice, however, restoration projects often have to settle for an approximation, rather than a duplication of original conditions, and some exotic species may be allowed. (See Box 13.1, "Native or Exotic Species?") Rehabilitation makes no pretensions about authenticity and admits of no philosophical preconditions favoring native over exotic species. In fact, the choice may be economic. Conceivably, rehabilitation programs could convert degraded land to a completely new use, if that best served human needs (32).

The distinctions between rehabilitation and restoration gain meaning when the terms relate to populous developing countries. There, abandoning degraded lands in the hope that they will restore themselves to their former state is not practical because the time needed is far too long. Experiments in Brazil's caatinga forests indicate that natural growback of cutover and slash-and-burn sites will take more than a century. If a site were cleared with a bulldozer, unassisted recovery would take at least 1,000 years (33). These times are far too long where resource demand is intense. Rehabilitation is then more relevant to the immediate needs of the people because it emphasizes the fact that production can ameliorate hunger, fuel shortages, and poverty.

This discussion does not suggest that restoring degraded wildlands is not desirable in the developing world—quite the contrary. In fact, by maintaining vital "ecosystem services," existing wildlands provide substantial (although largely unacknowledged) benefits to developing countries. (See Chapter 6, "Wildlife and Habitat.") Moreover, the functions of rehabilitation and restoration are not set in stone; rehabilitation could eventually find wider use, not as an end in itself but as an interim step to restoring selected sites. Once enough rehabilitated land satisfies resource demand, the productivity of some part of this land could be diversified in a second stage of full restoration. In developing countries whose population situations are not so dire, restoration may even today be a valid initial response to the problem of degraded lands. (See Box 13.2, "Guanacaste: Restoring a Dry Tropical Forest and the Culture of Its People.")

THREE TYPES OF LAND AT RISK

REVITALIZING DEGRADED MOUNTAINOUS AREAS

The Causes of Degradation in Mountains

Mountainous areas are fragile. The key factor is often population density. In the mountains of the Indonesian island of Java, for example, the connection between population density and environmental degradation is unmistakable. Agricultural tracts typically support 700–900 people per square kilometer, and the density reaches 2,000 in some subdistricts. At least one third of Java's cultivated mountainous areas are eroding seriously (34). More than 1 million hectares of these holdings are now useless for farming, depriving people of their only means of support (35). Excessive erosion directly threatens

Box 13.1 Native or Exotic Species?

One consequence of degradation is that plants and animals vital to the land's productivity have often died out or left a site. These missing species, or substitutes for them, must be reintroduced if the site's productive capacity is to be realized. Under favorable conditions, desirable plants and animals (as opposed to unwanted species, e.g., noxious weeds) may be able to colonize degraded lands on their own. But many will need help if recovery goals are to be met within a reasonable period. It is up to planners to decide whether native (indigenous) species or exotic species will better serve the recovery.

For restorations, the choice between native and exotic species is relatively clear cut: natives are always preferred, all things being equal. Yet the cost of using natives (some of which may be quite rare) plus the need for practicality may tip the scale toward exotic. The U.S. Government recently undertook a huge (and costly—$33 million over 10–15 years) restoration of a redwood and Douglas fir forest that had been partly logged. Even though the use of exotic species was avoided whenever possible, the government found that the exigencies of repairing the damage resulted in a flora that was only about one-half native (1).

By contrast, rehabilitation projects are not tied to using natives over exotics. It would appear, therefore, that choosing appropriate species for rehabilitation is simply a matter of determining which will optimize the land's utility to humans.

In reality, the choice is not so simple. For example, a fast-growing exotic plant may thrive on a degraded site, and it may even initially produce a larger volume of usable biomass than the native vegetation. But will this output be sustainable in the long run? Or will it fall a few years hence because some unsuspected ecological threshold was passed, leaving the land even more degraded than before?

Aside from the considerations of sustainability and the environmental consequences of failure, there is the larger question of the status of global biodiversity, which is already at risk because of the proliferation of aggressive exotic species. Intentional establishment of exotics on sites that are habitat for rare species may well add to this risk. On the other hand, plantations of exotic trees have been suggested as "foster ecosystems" for endangered species and the rehabilitation of highly damaged sites. In parts of the tropics, native forest understories develop abundantly in plantations of pine and mahogany, two important commercial species. After the foster plantation has prepared the site, the native tree cover can be quickly reestablished by thinning the exotics (2).

Carefully chosen exotics may have the capacity to enhance natural succession and thus speed the recovery of a degraded site. In a recent experiment in the American tropics,

researchers compared the number of species in an area undergoing natural plant succession with the number found in a multispecies agroecosystem they created by enriching succession with introduced exotics. After the first year, the natural succession plot had more species than the enriched plot had, but after 47 months, the enriched succession had produced about 13 percent more species (3).

Exotics can find a rightful place within a well-considered mix of species used to rehabilitate degraded lands. If they are relied upon exclusively as a quick fix, however, they may present serious problems.

No exotic species used for rehabilitation are more controversial than the hundreds that compose the genus *Eucalyptus*. Eucalypts generally produce at least twice as much biomass per hectare as other tree species, using less water per unit of biomass produced, although their overall consumption of water is high (4). They mature within a decade of planting and readily coppice (i.e., sprout new shoots from old growth). Much favored by industrial foresters, eucalypts—which are native to the southeast Pacific region—have been introduced all over the world. Some species now form a significant part of the global timber industry. Some countries have adopted eucalypts wholeheartedly: in Portugal, plantations on former vineyards, olive groves, and pasturelands form the basis for a large cellulose trade (5). There are about 5 million hectares of eucalyptus and pine plantations in southern Brazil, covering wide areas seemingly at the expense of native forests. Yet charcoal from the plantations provides about 40 percent of the energy needed for the Brazilian steel industry—energy formerly obtained by making charcoal from native trees (6).

Eucalypts are often reviled by farmers because their leaves are useless as fodder and they are believed to be water-sucking menaces that rob nearby vegetation of moisture (7). Farmers in Malawi avoid potential water-availability problems by segregating eucalypts into community woodlots solely for timber and fuelwood. The woodlots are placed well away from cropland (8).

It has been suggested that the profits to be made from planting groves of eucalypts have enticed people to convert food cropland to tree farms and so have dampened participation in social forestry programs. The result is a delay in needed rehabilitation efforts on other degraded land (9). Because they are often planted in monocultural stands, eucalypts are also criticized for maximizing wood production to the detriment of biodiversity. Planners who favor them point out that this criticism could be applied equally well to any number of cash crops (10). Others point out that each eucalypt has properties that vary under different conditions, and the challenge is to match the species to the site (11).

Any time degraded lands are to be rehabilitated by planting large monocultural stands of exotic species, no matter how useful they appear to be, there is reason for caution. This attitude was forcefully expressed recently when the president of Kenya decreed that 90 percent of all trees grown in the country's nurseries must be native species because of the problems posed by large single-species stands of exotics. The restrictions caused consternation among many foresters working in Kenya who think eucalypts and other exotics should not be eliminated without viable alternatives. In response, research has begun on planting fast-growing African tree species that may not have harmful effects (12).

References and Notes

1. Robert Belous, "Restoration among the Redwoods," *Restoration & Management Notes*, Vol. 2, No. 2 (1984), p. 57 and pp. 62–63.
2. Ariel E. Lugo, "Ecosystem Rehabilitation in the Tropics," paper presented at the International Conference on Ecosystem Redevelopment, Budapest, April 1987, pp. 12–13.
3. B.J. Brown and J.J. Ewel, "Herbivory in Complex and Simple Tropical Successional Ecosystems," *Ecology*, Vol. 68 (1987), pp. 108–116, cited in *Ibid.*, p. 10.
4. Peter S. Ashton, "Current Research on Forest Biology in India and Its Implications for Social Forestry and Agroforestry Practices," in *Perspectives in Environmental Management: Addresses Delivered at the 73rd Session of the Indian Science Congress*, T.N. Khoshoo, ed. (Oxford & Ibh, New Delhi, 1987), p. 190.
5. Lars Kardell, Eliel Steen, and Antonio Fabiao, "Eucalyptus in Portugal—A Threat or a Promise?" *Ambio*, Vol. 15, No. 1 (1986), p. 7.
6. Doug Fuller, "Eucalyptus Fuel the Furnaces of Brazil's Steelworks," *New Scientist* (February 18, 1988), p. 57.
7. Christopher Joyce, "The Tree That Caused a Riot," *New Scientist* (February 18, 1988), pp. 54–55.
8. Hans Gregersen, Sydney Draper, and Dieter Elz, eds., "People and Trees: Social Forestry Contributions to Development," review draft, The World Bank, Washington, D.C., 1986, p. 109.
9. Vandana Shiva, J. Bandyopadhyay, and N.D. Jayal, "Afforestation in India: Problems and Strategies," *Ambio*, Vol. 14, No. 6 (1985), pp. 331–332.
10. Gerald Foley and Geoffrey Barnard, *Farm and Community Forestry* (International Institute for Environment and Development, London, 1984), pp. 157–158.
11. *Op. cit.* 7, p. 57.
12. Debora MacKenzie, "Kenya's President Causes Panic among Foresters," *New Scientist* (February 18, 1988), p. 59.

Box 13.2 Guanacaste: Restoring a Dry Tropical Forest and the Culture of Its People

When the Spanish conquistadors arrived in Central America in the 16th Century, there were more than 550,000 square kilometers of dry tropical forest on the Pacific side of the isthmus. Like moist tropical rainforests, undisturbed dry tropical forests are diverse ecosystems, habitat for a large number of wildlife species. Today, less than 2 percent of this area is free of degradation (1). In Central America, cutting dry forests has been even more far-reaching than the better-publicized deforestation of moist forests, partly because lands once covered with dry forests are easier to convert to farms and ranches (2).

In 1986, scientists and the general public joined in an ambitious attempt to restore part of Costa Rica's dry forest. A new protected area, Guanacaste National Park, is being created out of private lands, part of an existing national park, and other public holdings with diminished productivity. By mid-1987, about half the proposed park was officially established, with the rest given intermediate protected status (3).

Guanacaste is perhaps the most comprehensive effort to restore, rather than just rehabilitate, a large area of degraded land in a developing country, possibly anywhere in the world (4). The project has three objectives:
■ To use leftover fragments of intact dry forest to restore about 700 square kilometers to a condition able to support all the flora and fauna found in Costa Rica when the conquistadors arrived,
■ To be economically useful to the people of the surrounding area, and
■ To reestablish the cultural ties of the local people to their land (5).

Fire management is central to the ecological restoration. Much of the land in the proposed park is taken up with exotic grassland species perpetuated by fires intentionally set by local ranchers. For the dry forest to take hold again, burning within the park will have to be stopped. Strip forests made up of native tree species will be planted on the downwind side of existing firebreaks along the park's boundaries to help slow fire entry. Some cattle grazing will be allowed to keep grass down while the woody dry forest vegetation is being established. Otherwise, enough grass would build up to fuel a catastrophe should a fire start (6) (7).

As budgets permit, native trees will be reestablished either by direct seeding or transplanting them as seedlings. The first areas to be replanted are those suspected of acting as "wicks" that conduct fire from adjacent lands (8). To further this end, hunting will be banned in Guanacaste because game species are natural seed dispersers. So too are cattle, which also eat *jaragua*, a dense exotic grass (native to Africa) that impedes the growth of tree seedlings (9).

Anywhere from 10 to 50 years may pass before a closed-canopy forest and substantial portions of its characteristic fauna reappear in Guanacaste. Another 50 or so years will pass before the park is free of grass. In 300 years, an intact forest may be expected, but a complete restoration of truly pristine flora and fauna may take millennia (10) (11).

One of the most powerful aspects of the project is its cultural foundation. The park is intended to affirm the principle that the culture of nearby residents will be disfigured if it is severed from its basis in the natural world. Guanacaste's planners hope the park will help restore to local people the understanding of the area's natural history that was common among their grandparents. An educational program begun in March 1987 includes field trips for local students and school presentations by Costa Rican biologists. Adult education is also planned. It is hoped that the classes will enrich local sensitivity to park biology—for now and when today's schoolchildren are in positions of power. This emphasis may also draw tourists and thus provide immediate economic benefits, as will hiring local people to work in the park (12).

The Guanacaste restoration is being coordinated by Daniel H. Janzen, a scientist from the University of Pennsylvania in the United States. He cautions that the project particulars should not be taken as the only model for similar undertakings in the developing world. Guanacaste has been carefully tailored (based on long years of experience) to the lands and the society in which the restoration is taking place. Janzen believes, however, that the philosophy and technology behind Guanacaste's design can serve well in other developing countries (13).

The scope of the restoration at Guanacaste and its avowed emphasis on the cultural value of wildlands could be a landmark in the newly joined struggle to preserve wildlife biodiversity. (See Chapter 6, "Wildlife and Habitat.") Janzen maintains that "the natural world is by far the most diverse and evocative intellectual stimulation known to humans". Having seen the near-obliteration of Central America's dry forest and other tropical land degradation, he contends that "tropical humans are experiencing nearly total loss of this integral part of their mental lives". In this sense, rehabilitation in developing countries will not be enough if it is seen as an end in itself, for "ten thousand acres of rice is one of the dullest habitats on Earth". In Janzen's view, the wholesale degradation and destruction of tropical wildlands in the face of agricultural expansion may feed the mouths of those in developing countries, but their minds would starve instead. Loss of wildlife "strands the schoolchildren of a tropical town without either their predecessors' contact with the natural world or the cultural offerings of the large cities that are supported by their parents' agriculture" (14).

References and Notes

1. Daniel H. Janzen, *Guanacaste National Park: Tropical Ecological and Cultural Restoration* (Editorial Universidad Estatal a Distancia, San José, Costa Rica, 1986), p. 11.
2. Marjorie Sun, "Costa Rica's Campaign for Conservation," *Science*, Vol. 239 (March 18, 1988), p. 1368.
3. William H. Allen, "Biocultural Restoration of a Tropical Forest," *BioScience*, Vol. 38, No. 3 (1988), p. 158.
4. William R. Jordan III, "Making a User-Friendly National Park for Costa Rica—A Visit with Daniel Janzen," *Restoration & Management Notes*, Vol. 5, No. 2 (1987), p. 72.
5. *Op. cit.* 1, pp. 11–12.
6. *Op. cit.* 4, pp. 74–75.
7. *Op. cit.* 1, pp. 69–70 and p. 73.
8. *Op. cit.* 4, p. 75.
9. *Op. Cit.* 3.
10. *Op. cit.* 3.
11. Daniel H. Janzen, "Tropical Ecological and Biocultural Restoration," *Science*, Vol. 239 (January 15, 1988), p. 243.
12. *Op. cit.* 3, pp. 156–161.
13. *Op. cit.* 1, pp. 12–13.
14. *Op. cit.* 11, p. 244.

the livelihood of about 12 million poor in Java (36).

Historically, officials have paid less attention to resource problems in mountains than lowlands. Degradation in sparsely populated mountainous districts has been less visible to policymakers or was considered less pressing than other problems because fewer people were affected. As a result, governments are ill-prepared to handle the environmental problems that built up over the centuries. They are even less prepared for the recent influxes of displaced land-seekers onto marginal steep lands.

So long as their populations were sparse, mountain communities could tolerate the problems of slope and elevation. Throughout history, mountain people consistently demonstrated how well they could manage with steep slopes and less fertile soils. In the face of rapid population growth, their resilience may collapse.

Principles of Mountain Rehabilitation

The usefulness of steep lands is governed almost entirely by gravity. Rain falling on slopes must be caught quickly if humans are to use it. If it cannot be caught, its force must be directed away from valuable crops and forage. Engineering interventions are central to mountain rehabilitation. They need not be elaborate. Check dams (small walls of stone built across gullies), bench terraces arrayed lengthwise across a slope, trenches cut along the land's contours, and channels dug to prevent erosive sheets of water from forming can all be built fairly cheaply and independently by local people. Unfortunately, recurring maintenance and rebuilding are necessary. Check dams, for example, typically last only 10 or 15 years (37).

Upgrading ground cover is another vital part of mountain rehabilitation. Reforestation, afforestation, reseeding grassy slopes and high-country pastures, planting the lips of terraces, and introducing perennial crops may be required. Fruit trees exemplify how perennials help rehabilitate degraded steep lands. Seventy percent of Jordan's rainfed cropland has a slope of 9 percent or more. The government has successfully persuaded farmers to replace traditional cereal crops—ground preparation for which greatly contributes to erosion—with olives, peaches, almonds, pomegranates, and other fruit trees. At the same time, farms were stone- or earth-terraced to reduce erosion. The key to the program's success was the World Food Programme's providing supplemental food and paid employment until the newly planted fruit trees provided an economic return. The program has helped keep young farmers from joining the tide of migrants to Jordan's cities; it has even encouraged older ones who had left to come back to the land (38).

Reducing the number of livestock may seem like an obvious way to alleviate an important source of erosion in mountains, but only if it does not deprive people of their livelihood. Concentrating pastoral impacts in less critical areas by stall feeding livestock is one solution. Better still is the simultaneous planting of high-yielding leguminous forage grasses, shrubs, and trees on heavily used sites. Not only do these plants check soil erosion by providing continuous ground cover, but they allow even more grazing animals to be stocked (39).

All three—engineering, changes in vegetation, and sustainable resource use—came together in the Phewa Tal watershed management project in Nepal. Begun in 1975 by the United Nations Development Programme (UNDP) and FAO, the project sought to control free-ranging grazing on the unterraced slopes draining into Phewa Tal, a small natural lake. The planners recognized a seemingly obvious but all-too-elusive fact: although farmers are willing to carry fodder uphill to their livestock, when the water is downhill, they have little choice but to drive their animals down to it, thereby adding to soil compaction and erosion. To supply water to the steep lands, stone-walled stock tanks were built around high hillside springs, and more water was drawn down from even higher sources through plastic piping. Beyond these engineered improvements, the people were encouraged to plant gullies with elephant grass, which produced enough extra forage to sell some to neighboring wards. Rather than trying to ban grazing, which would have rankled a society in which the number of animals owned is a measure of wealth, the planners persuaded the people to stall-feed their livestock. This innovation was particularly popular with the women, who had a much easier time

gathering manure for fertilizer and fuel. In fact, the increased efficiency of manure-gathering for fertilizer was successful enough to allow a second crop, winter wheat, to be alternated with the main crop, rainfed rice (40).

Watershed Management and Equity

Environmental degradation in mountainous districts has significant effects downstream. Soil washed from mountains forms deltas or islands at the mouths of major rivers, lowland floods may become more severe, and reservoirs accumulate silt faster. Indeed, far from responding to the plight of highlanders, many governments may ultimately rehabilitate degraded mountainous areas because of political pressure from the more populous lowlands. If so, watershed management will be aimed at protecting lowland investments from environmental hazards originating upslope.

Whatever the motivations, any rehabilitation will fail if equity is not established in the distribution of costs and benefits between upstream and downstream land users. Often, highlanders bear the disruptive burdens of the rehabilitation while lowlanders realize both the financial and nonmonetary benefits. Unless mountain rehabilitation directly produces goods and services that people in the local area want, they will have no interest in the project (41).

Instituting upstream-downstream equity requires three successive incentives for the mountain residents. First, they must have an *initial inducement* to join in the rehabilitation. In the Phewa Tal project, the farmers received funds to plant forage grasses as a prelude to stall feeding. Second, until the rehabilitation is profitable, short-term *subsidies* must be provided. This interim changeover period is when a rehabilitation program is most vulnerable. Indonesia's Upland Agricultural and Conservation Project managed by giving farmers grants-in-kind to help with terracing and planting tree crops, by extending commercial credit to those who adopted improved cropping practices, and by compensating the people for their loss of production during the changeover. Third, *cost-sharing* measures must be instituted to maintain upland-lowland equity. In Colombia's Upper Magdalena watershed project, 4 percent of the revenues from hydropower companies (who themselves and whose lowland customers benefit from soil conservation in the mountains) are required by law to be reinvested in upstream watershed management. These funds are used to subsidize part of the debt undertaken by the mountain farmers who borrowed to change over to more sustainable land uses, for example, planting perennial instead of annual crops (42).

The Himalaya: A Regional Perspective on Degradation

The Himalaya is a complex system of mountains spanning several countries on the northern edge of the Indian subcontinent. Conditions in the Hindu Kush, at the far western end, differ markedly from those in Arunachal Pradesh, other areas of the eastern Himalaya, and the central sectors. Himalaya is a term of convenience, and extrapolating the situation in one small area of the region—say, a Nepalese district near Mount Everest—is misleading (43).

Over the past decade or so, many popular and scientific publications have contended that environmental degradation in the Himalaya has worsened rapidly since about 1950. It is argued that the population explosion in the region (especially in Nepal) led to huge resource-demand pressure, causing massive deforestation and expansion onto marginal lands. In turn, soil erosion and downstream sediment loads increased catastrophically, with attendant floods, silted reservoirs, and sand and gravel deposition on low-lying agricultural land. As more and more mountain dwellers are forced to live on degraded land, the situation has progressively deteriorated. A prescription is massive environmental and social interventions to rehabilitate the Himalaya.

Significant dissent from this view has developed in the past couple years. Some scientists argue that, at the very least, many of the above assumptions can be proved untenable in certain instances and specific areas (44). For example, a recent study found that deforestation and reforestation in humid sections of the Himalaya do not influence major flooding (45). These criticisms raise legitimate doubts about how much of the Himalaya has been deforested since 1950, how population growth is affecting regional change, and the extent to which mountain dwellers (as opposed to natural causes) are to blame for the huge floods that struck lowland India and Bangladesh and for other recent downstream disasters.

The most detailed recent study of historical patterns of deforestation in the Middle Mountains of Nepal concluded that the amount of forest area has changed little since 1950, but the quality of the forest has deteriorated significantly (46). This finding is certainly true for the Naini Tal and Almora Districts of Nepal (an area just over 200,000 hectares), where only 6.2 percent of the forests have more than 60 percent crown cover (47). A new overview of Himalayan vegetation concludes that most forests in accessible areas have been destroyed and good quality forests now cover only 4.4 percent of the region (48). Himalayans themselves are beginning to perceive environmental deterioration as a drastic problem (49), and even the most ardent of the dissenters readily acknowledges that severe environmental degradation has taken place lately in certain quarters of the region (50).

A recent review of Nepal's population growth concluded that, quite apart from questions about degradation, Nepal is fast approaching its physical limit of arable land. Perhaps only 730,000 hectares remain that could reasonably be converted to crop production—an amount roughly equal to what was brought into cultivation in the past 20 years (51). This point suggests that not only must Nepal's present agricultural practices become more efficient, but its degraded farms will have to be rehabilitated.

The issues dominating the debate over Himalayan degradation, although not irrelevant to successful rehabilitation, largely miss the point: no matter how localized the mountain degradation is, or who caused it, or when, it will eventually have to be faced. The welfare of the ever-increasing population demands it. This statement does not deny the practical value of the debate. A valuable insight of the dissenting criticism for planners of the Himalayan rehabilitation programs is that the very real magnitude of the problem has been disguised by its oversimplification and exacerbated by the generalized and bureaucratic approach to its solution (52). Rehabilitation programs created for one area of the Himalaya will likely fail if they are forced to fit into another.

Specificity is not the only determinant of success in rehabilitation of the Himalayas. The form of intervention is also important. At one extreme, the Indian Government confiscated private lands for rehabilitation under the Kandi watershed project in Punjab (53). Phewa Tal's top-down approach, in which officials informed local farmers of project plans in order to obtain their agreement to government rehabilitation activities, is somewhere in the middle of the spectrum. It has worked well as far as it goes. But farmers there were given little information on conservation practices they can carry out on their own (54).

Educating Himalayans about the need for rehabilitation is vital, and the education would be all the more effective if it were initiated by local land users. The evidence is seen in the achievements of the Chipko movement, a grassroots phenomenon that began in Garwhal Himalaya but has since spread over most of mountainous India. Chipko arose in the early 1970s as a direct response to environmental degradation in the highland districts. It focused on maintaining the ecosystem services of forests (e.g., their role in protecting soil and water supplies) rather than on their value as producers of timber. Through noncooperation, a spirited public awareness campaign, and other nonviolent methods, Chipko has achieved a 15-year ban on commercial forestry in the hills of Uttar Pradesh (55).

There are other reasons for optimism. A recent study by the International Centre for Integrated Mountain Development in Nepal concluded that at least some of the Himalayan countries exhibit the following trends: the amount of irrigated land with bench terracing and drain channels is increasing; slash-and-burn agriculture is decreasing in most places; the amount of sloping agricultural land being terraced is increasing and old terraces are being allowed to revegetate; the per capita population of livestock is falling and the percentage being stall fed is rising; and the number of trees per hectare of farmland is increasing, as is the percentage of farmers planting trees. Many of these advances were initiated locally (56).

REGAINING THE PRODUCTIVITY OF DEGRADED DRYLANDS

Earth's ever-growing population is putting pressure on available arable land, especially in parts of the developing world. By 2000, it is projected that there will be only 0.19 hectares of cropland for each person in the developing countries, compared with 0.46 hectares in developed countries (57). Inevitably, rural people in the Third World are being compelled to cultivate less-suitable land. They often do so at the expense of the millions of traditional pastoralists who depend on arid or semiarid rangelands

Table 13.2 Drylands in Developing Regions

(million hectares)

Growth Days	Africa[a]	Southwest Asia	Southeast Asia	Central America	South America	East Asia	Total
1–74	488.0 (17%)[b]	72.6 (11%)	47.4 (5%)	62.3 (23%)	114.6 (6%)	27.7 (3%)	812.6 (11%)
75–119	231.8 (8%)	61.8 (9%)	54.9 (6%)	14.5 (5%)	142.8 (8%)	70.4 (7%)	586.2 (7%)
Total Drylands	719.8 (25%)	134.4 (20%)	102.3 (11%)	76.8 (28%)	257.4 (14%)	98.1 (10%)	1388.8 (18%)
Total Area	**2,878.1**	**677.4**	**897.6**	**271.6**	**1,770.2**	**954.6**	**7,449.5**

Source: United Nations Food and Agriculture Organization (FAO), *Improving Productivity of Dryland Areas* (FAO, Rome, 1987), p. 2.
Notes:
a. Excludes South Africa.
b. Parentheses indicate percentage of total land areas for each region, e.g., Africa.

for their living.

Drylands cover 18 percent of the land area in developing countries. (See Table 13.2.) Central America and Africa have the highest proportions of dryland, with 28 percent and 25 percent, respectively. Although population densities tend to be lower in arid and semiarid areas, more than 300 million people in developing countries live in drylands (58). (See Table 13.3.)

As densities continue to increase in arid districts, lands less suited to farming are being cultivated. The result is lower and lower yields, forcing farmers to sow even more land. To meet the higher consumption demands of the burgeoning population, fallow periods are shortened. Because crops planted more frequently use up more soil nutrients, yields drop still further. Farmers impinge on the least arid—that is, the best—rangelands first. Thus, when livestock numbers increase along with the human population, pressure on the remaining suboptimal pasture climbs exponentially (59).

The result is that both crop- and rangeland become marginal, leaving farmer and herder vulnerable to environmental extremes. It has been estimated that 80 percent of the rangelands and 60 percent of the croplands in the developing countries' dryland regions are declining in productivity because of resource degradation (60).

Agriculturalists who live on drylands commonly strive to protect themselves from crop failure or livestock die-off during drought years (e.g., by building up herds during good years). This food security is often as important as cash from selling their crops or livestock. The margin of safety in the face of drought is reduced whenever productive land is being degraded.

Fuelwood in the Drylands

Besides food, the other facet of the relationship between subsistence and environmental degradation is energy. Throughout much of the developing world, energy means fuelwood. Developing nations do not have the means to distribute natural gas, electricity, and petroleum even if people could afford them. Burning wood is the only alternative for most households, and gathering it is a major cause of degradation. In the Sahel and Sudan, the situation is worst around cities, where demand has driven woodcutters to denude forest cover over wide areas (61). For the foreseeable future, rehabilitation in the developing world will be strongly tied to fuelwood production.

For this situation to be changed, it has been suggested that countries need a mix of many forms of energy (e.g., biomass, solar, coal, petroleum, natural gas, hydro, and nuclear), none of which would supply over 20 percent of national energy needs (62). In Africa, firewood commonly accounts for at least 80 percent of energy consumption; most is burned at an efficiency of only 8–10 percent. Such dependence on a single energy source, especially when exploited at a low efficiency, aggravates environmental degradation because it continually requires excessive amounts of fuelwood. Of course, diversifying energy sources will not, by itself, stop degradation as long as the energy produced is used inefficiently (63). Here, better cooking stoves and other technological improvements are sorely needed. (See *World Resources 1987*, pp. 232–233.)

Dryland Rehabilitation Techniques

The standard way to rehabilitate degraded rangelands is to reseed them and then prohibit grazing until they are

Table 13.3 Human Populations in Drylands in Developing Regions, 1975

(millions)

Growth Days	Africa[a]	Southwest Asia	Southeast Asia	Central America	South America	East Asia	Total
1–74	33.1 (9%)[b]	15.9 (12%)	46.1 (4%)	8.5 (8%)	9.3 (4%)	X	112.9 (6%)
75–119	37.8 (10%)	24.3 (18%)	101.1 (9%)	3.7 (3%)	20.4 (9%)	X	187.3 (10%)
Total Drylands	70.9 (19%)	40.2 (29%)	147.2 (13%)	12.2 (11%)	29.7 (14%)	X	300.2 (15%)
Total (All Lands)	**380.2**	**136.3**	**1,117.7**	**106.6**	**215.8**	**X**	**1,956.6**

Source: United Nations Food and Agriculture Organization (FAO), *Improving Productivity of Dryland Areas* (FAO, Rome, 1987), p. 2.
Notes:
a. Excludes South Africa.
b. Parentheses indicate percentage of total population for each region.
X = not available.

productive. In Iran, revegetation of overgrazed and cultivated rangelands began as early as 1957. At least 50,000 hectares of degraded rangelands have since been revegetated using standard farm machinery. Perennial grasses, legumes, and other plants were selected to maximize herbage production under given soil and climate conditions. In addition to the reseeding, the ranges were restructured to conserve water. Contour furrows 10–30 centimeters deep were made on some sloping land, with the earth thrown downhill to create a soil berm below the furrow. Cross dikes were added at intervals to control excess runoff. On broad, uniform slopes, cross-cut furrows help hold down surface runoff. Pits dug along the contour of these restructured lands act as microcatchments for rainfall. After being fenced off for three years, these lands showed a 300–500 percent improvement in productivity. The outlay was $212 per hectare. When the cost of stabilizing encroaching sand dunes is included (conventional methods are fencing off fragile areas, planting windbreaks, and reseeding), the total was $279 per hectare (64) (65).

Because the net productivity of drylands is so low, rehabilitation techniques must be inexpensive or they will not be adopted widely. Two promising methods are land imprinting and using livestock and game animals to disperse seeds.

One of the first steps in rejuvenating vegetation is reseeding. Modern seedbed preparation conventionally involves plowing and discing, which violates the structural integrity of the soil. Although discing has many advantages, it renders the destabilized soil more vulnerable to wind and water erosion. An alternative is land imprinting, which shapes and firms the seedbed rather than cutting it apart. Land imprinting mimics the role that hoof prints of browsing and grazing livestock play in unassisted seedbed preparation. Hoof prints act as microcatchments for rainfall, operating collectively as a natural irrigation system. In these indentations, water penetrates the soil more readily, giving seeds a better chance to germinate.

Under conditions of increasing livestock density, hoof prints tend to be concentrated along trails, around watering holes, and in resting areas, often leading to soil compaction rather than optimal indentation. Mechanical land imprinters, on the other hand, create indentations in an orderly and evenly spaced pattern. Further, imprinting can be scheduled to penetrate dry soil for seeding. The method also makes mulch out of unwanted plant cover, thus helping to shade the seedlings.

Land imprinters are simply rolling cylinders with angle-iron teeth welded onto them. Once mounted on a towing frame, the machine is pulled by a tractor across the range. Aside from the daily lubrication of two bearings, the imprinter requires no maintenance and is almost indestructible. In 1981, making one cost about $7,000. Even without the tractor, this is far too expensive for most developing country agriculturalists to finance. Yet donor agencies could provide efficient seedbed preparation over a wide area of rangeland, all at a moderate per hectare cost, by making several tractor-and-imprinter rigs available as part of a large rehabilitation program.

Mechanical land imprinting is in use in the United States, Israel, and Australia (66).

In India, the degradation of commonly held drylands may be due more to underinvestment than overexploitation. One way to rehabilitate these areas is to encourage pastoralists to make small investments. In the arid state of Rajasthan, for example, the well-established exotic tree *Prosopis cineraria* spreads readily on its own; no costly planting is required. The seeds of *P. cineraria* are contained in edible pods. Either the government or an outside development agency could supply pods to pastoralists to feed their roaming herds; the seeds would be spread over a wide area in the dung. The propagation success rate would probably be low, but so too is the cost to donor and herder. Many other valuable rangeland trees and legumes that produce palatable pods could be propagated by livestock (67). If a large enough area were involved, the overall results might be more cost effective than conventional tree-planting schemes. The Guanacaste National Park restoration in Costa Rica may prove to be the test of this. (See Box 13.2.)

For rainfed cropland in semiarid areas, the simple expedient of planting windbreaks and shelterbelts has made many tracts productive again. Windbreaks keep soil, seeds, and seedlings from being blown away or sandblasted. They also provide shade and absorb incoming wind energy, thus lowering evaporation from surrounding fields and leaving more water available to the plants. Higher retention of water by the soil leads to slight, yet beneficial, increases in local atmospheric humidity, which in turn aids plant growth. Even after allowing for the loss of planting area to the trees, fields protected by windbreaks usually gain in overall crop production (68). Windbreaks are an integral part of China's agricultural program. They protect 17.6 million hectares of farmland in the central, western, and northern plains, and increases in yields have been dramatic: 43 percent for sorghum and millet, 36 percent for soybeans, 25 percent for rice, 20 percent for wheat, and 16 percent for maize (69). Similar gains have been made in other countries. (See Table 13.4.)

The Future of Dryland Recovery

One of the most encouraging signs is the emergence of regional self-directed cooperation in fighting desertification. In December 1985, the First African Ministerial Conference on the Environment, held in Cairo, was cosponsored by UNEP, the Organization of African Unity, and the Economic Commission for Africa. The conference formulated an environmental strategy for the continent. Called the Cairo Programme, it includes a regional pilot project for sustainable development of semiarid rangelands in 30 African countries. The goal is to regain the productivity of large areas (100,000–400,000 hectares) that are vulnerable to desertification (70). In northern Kenya, rehabilitation will be coordinated with the Integrated Project in Arid Lands, which began in 1976 and has somewhat similar goals. A network of strategically placed shallow wells will be fitted with hand pumps. It is hoped that this arrangement will redistribute the livestock

Table 13.4 Net Increase in Crop Yields Attributable to Shelterbelts in Selected Countries

Crop	Country	Average Increase in Crop Yield (percent)
Cereals	United States	5–18
Cotton	USSR	10–20
	Egypt	35
	United States	23–27
Hay	USSR	10–100
Maize	Romania	165
	Egypt	13–74
Melons and vegetables	USSR	50–70
Millet	Niger	23
Potatoes	USSR	71
Rice	Egypt	10
Wheat	USSR	17–25
	Egypt	38
	Turkey	25
	Romania	20–50

Source: Adapted from The World Bank, *Sudan Forestry Sector Review*, Annex IV (The World Bank, Washington, D.C., 1986), cited in Hans Gregersen, Sydney Draper, and Dieter Elz, eds., "People and Trees: Social Forestry Contributions to Development," review draft, (The World Bank, Washington, D.C., 1986), Table 3.1, p. 106.

away from the present few watering points, allowing the denuded areas around them to recover (71) (72).

Nowhere is the dividing line between good management and rehabilitation less clear than on drylands. Attempts to regrow natural bush cover on degraded sites within Niger's Guesselbodi forest reserve have been pursued since 1981. They strongly suggest that components of both management and rehabilitation are needed. Vegetative cover has been improved through antierosion and water harvesting measures along with replanting and timely harvesting of woody species, but it improved only when the sites were protected against overuse and fire (73).

REJUVENATING DEGRADED IRRIGATED CROPLAND

Irrigation, an important component of food production for centuries, is now vital to human well-being. In 1985, about 30 percent of the world harvest came from the 270 million hectares of irrigated cropland (74). Many countries would be left with acute food shortages if their irrigated lands were damaged. Indonesia, India, Chile, and Peru derive 50–55 percent of their total food production from these lands; in China, the figure is 70 percent; in Pakistan 80 percent (75). Egypt's dependence is almost total—98.6 percent of its croplands are irrigated (76).

Waterlogging, salinization, and alkalinization are the major problems with irrigated land. All three are associated with poor water management. Most prevalent in arid and semiarid regions, they are also found in humid climates, especially along coasts. (Some lands, it should be noted, are naturally saline, alkaline, or subject to waterlogging. In these cases, it is probably more economical to try to raise the productivity of better land than to attempt reclamation.) About 30 percent of the world's potentially arable land is affected by salt. Nations where these problems are severe pay a high cost; in the

Euphrates Valley of Syria alone, the annual crop loss caused by salinity problems is valued at $300 million (77).

Waterlogging

Cropland becomes waterlogged when excess water on the surface forms a pond or when it collects in the root zone of the soil. Below-ground waterlogging occurs when percolation is impaired by poor drainage or a rising water table. The roots of most crops absorb oxygen from the soil and release carbon dioxide into it; this respiration is stifled in waterlogged soils (rice is a notable exception).

If respiration is crippled, so too is crop growth. When the pores of the soil in the root zone do not have enough air because they are full of water, toxic concentrations of carbon dioxide can build up, stunting the roots' growth and ability to absorb nutrients. The timing of the water buildup in relation to the crop's stage of development is also important; just two or three days of waterlogging can kill seedlings when the entire root zone is affected (78).

Unless remedial measures are taken, plants "drown" in waterlogged soils. If a water-tolerant paddy crop cannot be introduced into a field, the only way to solve the problem is to drain or pump out the excess water. Poorly drained or low-lying lands prone to waterlogging may require permanent drainage works to keep them productive.

The problem of waterlogging is substantially complicated on irrigated lands by the fact that it often occurs in concert with salinization. The high surface evaporation rates and upward movement of water and dissolved salts that typify waterlogged soils can cause high levels of salt to accumulate in the root zone and on the surface of the land. This condition can develop even when the salt content of the irrigation water is low (79).

Salinization

Two processes contribute to salinization: salt concentration and salt loading. Salts begin to accumulate in and on soils whenever large amounts of water are lost through evaporation and transpiration. Because salt does not dissipate, its concentration increases in whatever water is left. Salt loading takes place when salts are added to water. In irrigated areas, water not used by crops—mostly seepage and runoff—often picks up salts from the soil and carries them into groundwater or rivers. Concentration and loading can cause salt to build up in the upper layers of the soil, where it inhibits plant growth by impairing the root zone (80). In extreme cases, salt appears on the surface. Such accretions tend to be patchy, but areas affected become virtually sterile.

Poor water management in the field (and, to a lesser extent, badly drained water delivery systems) causes the twin problems of waterlogging and salinization on irrigated lands. The need for tight water management is universally acknowledged by planners, but this goal is hard to achieve in practice. There are numerous instances in which the water table rose from 20 or 30 meters to less than 2 meters from the surface within a decade after irrigation was begun. This change occurred in many

13 Degraded Lands

areas of Egypt after the Aswan High Dam was built (81) (82). Further, almost all canals are unlined earth trenches, so seepage losses in conveyance are as high as 50–60 percent of the water intake (83). Pricing systems that do not charge farmers for the water they use encourage excessive applications to fields, aggravating the problem even more (84).

Salinization occurs in the absence of waterlogging as well. Throughout much of Tunisia and in parts of Algeria and the Middle East, soils become salinized because the irrigation water has a high salt content to begin with. Salinization is also brought on by shoddy field leveling that doesn't allow proper drainage (85).

Alkalinization

By contrast to salinized soils, which are affected by neutral sodium salts, alkaline soils are generally affected by sodium salts that are capable of alkaline hydrolysis (86). Widely known as alkalinization, the process is more properly known as sodication. In alkalinized soils, adsorbed sodium accumulates on clay particles. When the level of adsorbed sodium in the soil is high and soil salinity is low, the clay particles become unstable and are easily dispersed. A sodic soil forms whose permeability is reduced because the dispersed clay plugs the soil's pores. Low permeability (which also promotes waterlogging), poor aeration, and high alkalinity (which upsets the nutritional balance in plants) combine to inhibit or prevent crop growth (87) (88).

Rehabilitation Techniques

Waterlogged and salinized soils can be rehabilitated only by pumping or draining away the excess water or by leaching the soluble salts (89). Installation of water control equipment and subsurface drains would be a multimillion-dollar effort. Therefore, the farmers intended to be served by such a system must first be convinced of the value of good drainage, then learn the technical skills to maintain the equipment (90).

The choice of drainage methods depends on local conditions; horizontal tile drains or vertical tube wells may be chosen. Tube wells are likely to have a short working life. Screens and pump parts, easily corroded by saline groundwater and clogged by calcium carbonate crusts, must be replaced frequently. Further, tube wells can be used only where the land is underlain by an aquifer that conducts water to the well and that is hydrologically connected with the water table above. Otherwise, horizontal tile drains should be used (91).

A novel drainage method is being tried in the Indian state of Uttar Pradesh, where tracts of salinized land are being rehabilitated by planting *Terminalia arjuna*. This saline-tolerant tree lowers the water table by taking up water through its roots. The water is then transpired out the foliage, which is used to feed silkworms. This ancillary, short-term economic benefit is vital to the success of the plantings because it may take 25 years for the salinity level of even part of the surrounding land to be low enough for crops (92).

A slight change in cultivation practices can help lessen the effects of salinization. Because salt tends to gather on

Figure 13.1 Barren Site With Alkalinized Soil, Banthra, India, 1956

the tops of furrows, reshaping the seedbed or planting further down the sides of the furrows may be all that is needed on some fields. Adopting the border method of irrigation also minimizes salts around the seeds and in the root zone (93).

Alkalinized soils can also be rehabilitated by pumping excess water up through tube wells. To lower or neutralize the high pH of alkalinized soil, various chemicals can be applied. The most commonly used is gypsum, although several byproducts of mining and industry (e.g., the phosphogypsum produced by fertilizer factories) also work (94) (95).

On heavily alkalinized tracts in poor countries, introducing tolerant crops promises to be the most cost-effective answer. Rice is the ideal choice because it directly enhances the rehabilitation process; it mobilizes the insoluble calcium carbonate layer that lies below the surface of some sodic soils. Forage grasses that tolerate high alkalinity, such as karnal, rhodes, para, and bermuda, can be planted at little expense—a particular boon to subsistence pastoralists (96).

India led the way in rehabilitating alkalinized lands. From 1982 to 1986, nearly 200,000 hectares were brought under cultivation in Haryana, Punjab, and Uttar Pradesh (97). The National Botanical Research Institute's test facility at Banthra (near Lucknow) is a pioneer in this endeavor. Until the research station was founded in 1956, the Banthra area had long been a barren alkalinized wasteland. (See Figure 13.1.) In consultation with local

Figure 13.2 Same Site After Rehabilitation, 1976

Source: T.N. Khoshoo, *Ecodevelopment of Alkaline Lands: Banthra—A Case Study* (National Botanical Research Institute, CSIR, Lucknow, Uttar Pradesh, 1987), pp. xxii–xxiii.

residents, scientists began rehabilitation using low-cost methods and much hand labor. Tube wells were sunk and drainage canals and holding ponds constructed. Instead of bringing in costly chemical additives, the researchers used any easily available source of organic matter (e.g., the green manure *dhaincha*) to amend the soil. Vegetation succession was designed, and once alkaline-tolerant species were established, they improved the soil for less-tolerant ones. By 1973, the site was thriving. (See Figure 13.2.)

Today, part of it is cropland, with a mix of food, oil, and aromatic plants. Another part is grassland, where fodder species are grown. Yet another part is woodland, which supports a variety of wildlife. Even the drainage waterways support fish and geese. The village of Banthra has also been transformed. Three crops per year are possible on some fields, and farm production and incomes have risen so much that the people can afford electricity and modern conveniences (98) (99).

LESSONS FOR POLICYMAKERS

THE SOCIAL COSTS OF DEGRADATION

Rehabilitating and restoring degraded lands is at least as much a social, economic, and political problem as an ecological one (100). Government officials and other

policymakers must be made to recognize how high the indirect costs of degradation are. People who are compelled to abandon degraded lands not only suffer tremendous hardships themselves, but they also impose high social costs on others. The displaced frequently crowd into cities, creating squatter settlements that tax available city services to the limit. Such shantytowns are ripe breeding grounds for crime and civil unrest (101).

Intentionally resettling people away from degraded lands, which is often put forward as a solution, has the potential for many unintended effects. In fact, it may simply spread the degradation. (See Box 13.3.)

MATCHING ECONOMIC POLICIES AND TECHNOLOGIES TO NEEDS

Global environmental degradation is not occurring *en masse*. The productive capacity of the world's lands is being whittled away, tract by tract, in a succession of thousands upon thousands of small losses. It is clear, too, that global recovery cannot be accomplished by financing a few sweeping programs. Vast sums of money must be spent, but not in great chunks.

The Banthra rehabilitation of alkalinized land, discussed above, is a good example of a project whose formula for success could be adapted to other degraded areas. Banthra succeeded, first of all, because of its scale: all organization was at the village level. The people were more comfortable with this arrangement and so were willing to work with the research scientists when asked to help plan the rehabilitation—the second ingredient of success. Rather than impose their plans on the populace, the scientists consulted the people from the beginning. Third, Banthra followed the rule of thumb—"cheaper is better." Because heavy machinery, chemical additives, and other expensive technology were eschewed at the outset, the initial capital investment was kept low. This decision made sense given the riskiness of the program. Equally important, the hand labor rehabilitation methods introduced were likely to be adopted, whereas technically more sophisticated methods might have been too unfamiliar for adoption (102) (103).

This participatory approach to rehabilitation (it applies equally well to restoration) does not preclude using advanced recovery methods, but sophistication has its costs. For example, if high-output agriculture is to be part of a recovery, it must be supported by requisite inputs. Fast-growing cultivars and high-yielding crop varieties remove more nutrients from the soil than traditional crops, the former because they allow double- and even triple-cropping and the latter because of their higher yields. When such plants are to be grown on recovering lands, they require more fertilizer to ensure the continuing fertility of the soil. Organic manures and mineral fertilizers should be used wherever possible. Not only does their effectiveness compare favorably with chemical fertilizers, but they help prevent and repair soil degradation. In sandy soils, organic manures raise water retention levels, lower nutrient leaching, and moderate any tendencies toward excessive acidity or alkalinity. In clay soils, organic manures make the soil more porous, so water filters through it better and erosion from runoff is

Box 13.3 The Resettlement Question

For any rehabilitation or restoration program to work, human demands on the degraded area must be reduced or relieved, at least temporarily. This period of forbearance is when the support of the people affected by the recovery program is most likely to be lost because they are being deprived of income or resource use. If they are subsistence farmers or pastoralists, calling on them to refrain from using even a small part of their land is to ask a great sacrifice indeed. Before any lands are taken out of service, program planners (which should include representatives of the people affected) must find answers to two interrelated questions: What is the best way to relieve pressure on the degraded area while minimizing disruption to the lives of the people? and, How long must the period of forbearance last?

There are three possible strategies for relieving human pressure on degraded ecosystems. The most desirable is to persuade the people to make continued but less intense use of the area. This change is possible, however, only where the degradation is not yet too severe and the ecosystem is resilient enough to recover its productivity gradually while it is being used. Another tactic is to convince the people to stop using part of the area but allow them to remain on the rest. This strategy is practica-ble only when the land being fenced off is not vital to their livelihood. When it is, the most disruptive strategy—planned resettlement—may be necessary.

The choice is partly influenced by how long the recovery is expected to take. Although the reversibility of environmental degradation has not been well enough studied to know how long it will take in a particular case, most degraded areas can regain some degree of productivity if left alone long enough (1).

It matters little to subsistence farmers and herders whether recovery takes one year, five years, or a thousand years—if the land they need to survive from day to day is not available to them. For this reason, people who can no longer earn a living from degraded land often resettle on their own. The term environmental refugees was coined to describe those who flee from land whose productivity has deteriorated to a point at which it can no longer support them (2). No one has reckoned the number of environmental refugees worldwide, but hundreds of thousands of people were displaced from the Sahel alone during the recent prolonged drought (3). Many headed for nearby cities, some of which are growing 10–20 percent each year (4). Similarly, thousands of Haitians fled the severely degraded countryside for Port-au-Prince, the capital, doubling its population between 1975 and 1985 (5).

Most environmental refugees end up in substandard shantytowns on the edges of cities, in "transit" camps that become permanent fixtures on the landscape (and that depend on regular outside relief), or in other rural areas, where the newly increased level of demand leads to further degradation (6).

Nomads respond to degradation in a different way. By contrast to environmental refugees, who leave the land with no firm expectation of returning, nomads follow a cycle of planned temporary abandonments within a rural area. Nomadism is a rational strategy that has evolved in response to the fragility of arid and semiarid lands. Some governments, however, tend to view these pastoralists as aberrants—no doubt because mass movements of people are difficult to control—and have tried to settle them and bring them into the mainstream of society. International funding for almost all plans to settle mobile pastoralists has been withdrawn because they failed to improve the lot of pastoralists. (See Chapter 5, "Forests and Rangelands.")

When people living on degraded lands were unwilling or unable to move on their own, some governments and international agencies stepped in to organize sponsored

---

reduced (104). Further, the increased use of mineral fertilizers can help stop the "mining" of nutrients from the soil—one of the chief causes of cropland degradation.

IUCN GUIDELINES FOR RECOVERING DEGRADED LANDS

International conservation bodies and development agencies have begun to take notice of the extent of degraded lands. At its most recent general assembly in January 1988, the International Union for Conservation of Nature and Natural Resources (IUCN) adopted guidelines for rehabilitating or restoring degraded lands. The recommendations were developed at a workshop on restoration ecology held in Varanasi, India, in December 1987 (105).

The guidelines call for international conservation programs to pay more attention to the extent and condition of degraded lands, for multilateral development banks to fund pilot recovery projects, and for ecologists to study more thoroughly the effects of stress and disturbance on ecosystems. The heart of the guidelines is the following general recommendations on how recovery projects should be carried out:

■ Critical sites—such as those especially liable to erosion, sources of saline water in the upper reaches of a watershed, or habitats of threatened and endangered species—should be rehabilitated or restored first.

■ For the initial revegetation, plants should come from different successional stages to lessen the chances of natural succession being thwarted and to let slow-dispersing species be included.

■ Plants that facilitate succession or maintain nutrient and water cycles should be included. Nitrogen-fixers are an important example, as are plants whose roots can penetrate beyond infertile upper soil layers.

■ Because socioeconomic issues may well decide the success or failure of recovery projects, social scientists should help plan them from the beginning. Local people should also be involved, some of whom may be able to contribute traditional knowledge about local plants and soils.

■ Rehabilitation programs should provide economic benefits to the participants. Incentives are better than sanctions, but if new laws regulating land use are passed, they must be enforced consistently.

■ Laws and customs affecting the area under recovery should be reviewed periodically. If they are serving to degrade the environment, the people should be encouraged to change them.

■ Tree plantations should be established on degraded lands rather than on undisturbed or otherwise productive tracts.

■ As a corollary to recovery projects, protected areas should be set aside to conserve plant and animal wildlife species that may be needed for future rehabilitations or restorations.

Any number of criteria may be used to evaluate a recovery program. A checklist of possibilities is given in Table 13.5.

Box 13.3

resettlement projects. Although they may relieve human demands in degraded areas, they may also be unjust. For one thing, resettlement almost always involves the least-empowered people in the society. As such, resettlement projects are potentially a convenient vehicle for controlling or ending land use behavior that, apart from its environmental consequences, is incompatible with the sponsor's goals. The projects thereby are open to the suggestion of an ulterior motive. For example, the Ethiopian Government has been accused of using mass resettlement, ostensibly to relieve pressure on degraded lands, as a counterinsurgency technique in its long civil war against rebellious provinces (7).

Resettlement projects may fail to reverse degradation; in fact, they can even make it worse. Indonesia's transmigration program is the world's largest voluntary government-assisted resettlement effort. Since 1905, at least 2.5 million people have been moved to sparsely populated outer islands from overcrowded, environmentally degraded areas on the central islands, particularly the uplands of Java. Nonetheless, the annual population increment on Java more than offsets the number of migrants departing, and the poor condition of Java's uplands has not been alleviated. Indeed, in some areas of Indonesia the effect of transmigration has been to

disperse the degradation rather than lessen it. Unofficial migrants, drawn to move by the experience of friends and relatives, are encroaching on many of Indonesia's protected areas. In Lampung, a province in Sumatra that has received many transmigrants, some have had to be resettled a second time, away from newly degraded hillsides and forests there. Other transmigrants have been relocated onto tracts of tropical forest, which they cleared at the expense of an exceptionally rich natural flora and fauna. This has caused a furor among many conservation groups. However, since 1986, transmigration has been at a virtual standstill because of a government-wide budget cut (8).

References and Notes

1. An exception might be certain heavily desertified soils (those that are shallow and receive less than 100–150 millimeters of rain per year), but deeper, sandier soils, even those receiving as little as 60 millimeters annual rainfall, can regenerate—if they are completely protected for five years or more. Henri Noel Houerou and Hubert Gillet, "Conservation versus Desertization in African Arid Lands," in *Conservation Biology: The Science of Scarcity and Diversity*, Michael E. Soulé, ed. (Sinauer, Sunderland, Massachusetts, 1986), p. 456.
2. Environmental refugees also include those whose homes were destroyed either temporarily or permanently by natural disasters, construction, or the effects of war. Essam El-Hinnawi, *Environmental Refugees* (United Nations Environment Programme, Nairobi, 1985), pp. 4–5, pp. 33–34, and pp. 38–40.
3. Essam El-Hinnawi, *Environmental Refugees* (United Nations Environment Programme, Nairobi, 1985), pp. 10–11.
4. Henri Noel Houerou and Hubert Gillet, "Conservation versus Desertization in African Arid Lands," in *Conservation Biology: The Science of Scarcity and Diversity*, Michael E. Soulé, ed. (Sinauer, Sunderland, Massachusetts, 1986), p. 460.
5. *Op. cit.* 3, pp. 23–24.
6. *Op. cit.* 3, pp. 11–12.
7. Virginia Luling, "Resettlement, Villagisation and the Ethiopian Peoples," *Development: Seeds of Change*, No. 1 (1987), pp. 32–35.
8. Anthony J. Whitten, "Indonesia's Transmigration Program and Its Role in the Loss of Tropical Rain Forests," *Conservation Biology*, Vol. 1, No. 3 (1987), pp. 239–240, p. 242, and p. 245.

THE FUTURE OF RESTORATION

Although this chapter focuses primarily on rehabilitation in the developing world, it does not imply that restoration has no future there. Most wildlife species live in the tropics and, therefore, in developing countries. Thus, efforts to preserve biodiversity *in situ* will necessarily be concentrated there. Restoration programs could potentially be a vital contributor. There is already ample evidence that the world's protected areas are far too small to support most biological communities intact. As pristine habitat becomes scarcer, "recycling" disturbed ecosystems may be the only way to make additions to protected-area systems (106).

Ecological restoration is certainly a fledgling discipline. So far, most of the work has taken place in developed countries, and efforts are only just beginning. In North America, a few prairies, shrub-grasslands, savannas, freshwater wetlands, and rivers have been or are being restored with the goal of maximizing biodiversity (107). Restoration in much of the developing world will likely be even more difficult because tropical ecosystems are far more fragile and take longer to recover than temperate ones (108).

Further into the future, one of the most promising uses of restoration could be to create new ecosystems designed to enhance biodiversity. Some lands might even be restored specifically to increase the chances of survival for particular endangered species; computer data bases could be used to match species habitat requirements with the potential characteristics of ecosystem sites where recovery is contemplated. Such areas would act as outdoor zoos in which species recruitment occurred naturally (109). Similarly, restoration may one day figure in

Table 13.5 Preliminary Checklist for a Successful Rehabilitation Program

Biological and Geophysical Indicators of Site Stability
Is the soil surface secure?
Are plant cover and (if applicable) crop yields adequate?
Are the numbers and diversity of plant and animal species appropriate?
Is the vegetation regenerating satisfactorily?
Is the quality of ground- and surface water acceptable?
Is the albedo (the fraction of light being reflected by the Earth's surface) near normal?

Sociocultural Indicators of Program Stability
Is the local population neither rising nor falling sharply?
Are market prices for commodities produced on the site relatively steady?
Are adequate food and fuel energy available?
Are changes in land use and tenure gradual?
Has a balance been struck between subsistence and cash crops?
Is consumption of fuelwood and water sustainable?
Are the economic benefits from the rehabilitation accruing equitably?

Indicators of Program Efficiency
Are soil amendments (seed, fertilizer, pesticides) needed?
Are weed control and irrigation needed?
Is the public actively involved with the program?

Indicators of Program Flexibility
To what extent can alternative or multiple use be made of the land?

Source: Adapted from D. Lamb, "IUCN Guidelines for Restoration of Degraded Ecosystems," prepared for the General Assembly of the International Union for Conservation of Nature and Natural Resources, San José, Costa Rica, January 1988, Table 1, p. 34.

Box 13.4 The Promise and Pitfalls of Traditional Rehabilitation Strategies

Problems of scale loom large in the rehabilitation of degraded ecosystems. Some examples of deterioration seem beyond hope unless vast sums of money and modern technology are devoted to them. But even in these situations, cheap, simple, time-honored methods promise to work best, particularly in developing countries. Traditional rehabilitation strategies, which are usually site specific, are increasingly being revived and adopted by outside planners.

Traditional knowledge should not be accepted uncritically, however. Most pastoral techniques, for example, developed during an era of low human population densities and light livestock pressure. The accent was on short-run productivity because herders had plenty of other good land when pastures became exhausted. These conditions are now gone and, short of some catastrophic plunge in the world population, are never to return. So the same techniques, if presumed infallible and allowed to operate without modification, may be useless or even detrimental to recovery efforts today.

Moreover, the social conditions under which traditional strategies developed are no longer the same. The *dina* grazing system of inland Mali, which dates from the 1820s, was an efficient, equitable communal strategy that regulated the use of seasonally flooded rangelands and reduced conflicts between farmers and pastoralists. Each year, large areas of the Masina region are temporarily inundated; when they dry out, livestock are grazed there despite regular infestations of parasites and other insects. These areas are also used to grow rice. Under the *dina* system, land use was regulated by allocating grazing zones for the exclusive use of local villages; larger zones were reserved for herds driven in from surrounding areas. Transhumance was also practiced to move livestock out during the worst of the insect season.

With better disease control, livestock populations can now withstand infestations thus no longer migrate. The reduced need for the migration, coupled with development projects that encourage rice cultivation, have increased tensions between farmers and herders. Further, the government abolished rights of exclusivity to the grazing zones, and outside pastoralists now bring their herds in and overgraze the land. Under these changed conditions, the *dina* system is not nearly so effective (1).

Some social and religious taboos can actually hinder an ecosystem's recovery from degradation. In the Kakamega District of Kenya, men own all the trees, and women are strongly discouraged from planting trees because it is believed that they will become infertile if they do. Although the women get around this restriction by a variety of ruses, it is plain that any reforestation attempt in such an area would be quite complicated (2). As another example, a successful part of India's Himalayan Watershed Management Project was discontinued because of a religious ban on slaughtering cows. The government had to cancel the program under which it traded one milking buffalo to farmers in exchange for three or four cattle—thereby reducing grazing pressure considerably in Uttar Pradesh while maintaining or increasing milk production—because it could no longer afford to run the *goshalla*, the cow homes needed to care for all the cattle it received in exchange (3).

Nonetheless, before traditional practices are condemned as environmentally unsound by outside observers, all the nuances should be fully understood. A recent report on Nepal, written by representatives from a multilateral development bank, criticized the terraces built there on rainfed cropland. They are "poorly constructed," the report said, because they slope outward rather than inward and do not have a grassed bund at the edge to catch rainwater. It has since been pointed out that there are two distinct kinds of terrace in Nepal. *Bari* terraces on rainfed land are intentionally built sloping outward with no bund so the crops of maize, millet, and buckwheat cannot be damaged by waterlogging. *Khet* terraces, by contrast, are built on irrigated land (usually to support paddy rice) and are designed to slope inward. Further, it may be a mistake to take instances of badly maintained *bari* terraces as a sign of environmental degradation. Instead, they may reflect a conscious decision of Nepal's farmers to concentrate their energy on repairing the higher-yielding *khet* terraces because the rice grown on them is more important to the immediate survival of a subsistence family (4).

References and Notes

1. M.L. Ba, "A Summary of the Herima System in Masina, Mali," (1984), a revised version to be published in National Research Council, "The Improvement of Tropical and Subtropical Rangelands," Washington, D.C.
2. J.B. Raintree, "Agroforestry Pathways: Land Tenure, Shifting Cultivation and Sustainable Agriculture," *Unasylva*, Vol. 38, No. 4 (1986), p. 11.
3. Anis D. Dani and J. Gabriel Campbell, *Sustaining Upland Resources: People's Participation in Watershed Management* (International Centre for Integrated Mountain Development, Kathmandu, Nepal, 1986), p. 72.
4. Jack D. Ives, "The Theory of Himalayan Environmental Degradation: Its Validity and Application Challenged by Recent Research," *Mountain Research and Development*, Vol. 7, No. 3 (1987), p. 193.

relocating entire biological communities to more favorable environments to save them from disruptions wrought by changes in the Earth's climate (110). (See Chapter 10, "Atmosphere and Climate.")

THE FUTURE OF REHABILITATION

Two of the most important elements of a successful rehabilitation program are giving the people affected a secure interest in the benefits to be gained and compensating them for any disruptions to their livelihood caused by the rehabilitation. Often, a lack of legally recognized land or resource-usage tenure contributes to continued environmental degradation. In many developing countries, the record of land ownership shown on the deed books bears no resemblance to what is practiced. People who depend on degraded lands to support themselves are quite likely to be there on an illegal or quasi-legal basis or, at best, as tenants. In any case, as nonowners, they have little incentive to worry about long-term productivity (111). An international Centre for Integrated Mountain Development study of watersheds in the Himalaya supports this point. Deforestation, overgrazing, and erosion show less evidence of being countered on public than on private lands (112).

Providing recognized tenure is not enough if the short-term livelihood of the people affected is not also guaranteed. All recovery projects could benefit by adopting the three-step incentive approach—inducements, subsidies, and cost-sharing—described above for mountain watersheds. If changes in land use behavior are called for as part of a rehabilitation program—and they often will be—those risking the change must be compensated for any loss of production or income during the critical initial period. If the people think the changes are too much of a gamble, they are not likely to cooperate. Local support for the project may then flag or even collapse—and with it the recovery effort.

Local perceptions of the environment must be fully understood before outside experts tackle a problem whose solution might only bring on more hardship. For example, scientists and conservationists assume that gullied land is undesirable. From their point of view, the slopes of southern Mexico's Nochixtlan Valley should be some of the most unwanted in the world. They are riven by active gullies, with an average of 5 meters of soil stripped away each year. But for the Mixtec farmers of the valley floor, these gullies are a means to better crop yields. By using them to direct the flow of eroded material, the farmers feed their fields with fertile soil. Over the past 1,000 years, the Mixtecs have used gullying to increase the agricultural productivity of the Nochixtlan substantially (113). This example is instructive on how difficult it is for outsiders to evaluate local rehabilitation knowledge. (See Box 13.4.)

The problem of degraded lands cannot be solved until it is also seen as fundamentally a social question, one whose answer must take into account social welfare and economics as well as strictly environmental concerns (114). Such a culturally integrated approach to development is being attempted in Thailand, where shifting cultivators have been settled in "forest villages." There, they are given salaries, land and resource-usage tenure, medical care, and schools in exchange for rehabilitating nearby degraded lands by planting teak on them (115) (116) (117). A slightly different approach is being taken in Africa as part of the Cairo Programme. One hundred fifty villages (three in each country) that, taken together represent the full spectrum of African environmental and social conditions, will participate in an integrated development scheme emphasizing local traditional skills in food and energy self-sufficiency. The goal is to find "economically feasible, environmentally sound, and socially acceptable methods" to reinstate the cultural and economic self-reliance that once typified rural Africa and to stop drift migration from the countryside to cities (118) (119). The Cairo Programme's goal is not simply to assist these villages, but to demonstrate local techniques that other governments can adapt to their own circumstances (120).

A related issue is the role of women in rural development. In many societies women are the most important land use decisionmakers. Gender also often determines on whose shoulders the costs and benefits of specific rehabilitation procedures will fall. Women should be involved in planning every recovery program, and their participation is essential in societies where they play an important role in resource decisionmaking.

A signal finding of the 1985 Cairo conference was that Africa is in the midst of an environmental crisis—namely, a continentwide deterioration in the quality of the land—that is directly related to overpopulation (121). The same could be said for other regions of the world. To be sure, degradation proceeds most rapidly where human densities are high, so any global solution to the problem will have to consider the sensitive matter of population planning. If no significant progress is made in stemming population growth, it is far from certain whether even the rehabilitation of a large percentage of the world's degraded resource-production lands can satisfy the need for food and fuel. Mounting such a massive effort may seem a distant prospect now, but priorities could change once the effects of degradation spread beyond the rural poor.

There is some truth to the view, first discussed seriously at UNCOD, that nothing short of a reordering of society will have to take place before land degradation can be reversed. This idea may seem like wishful thinking, but an outline for an enduring egalitarian world global community has already been sketched by the World Commission on Environment and Development (122). The challenge of recovering from environmental degradation, it would seem, is threefold: to regain and maintain the *productivity* of the land, to ensure *sustainability* of land use so that its products are not squandered, and to establish *equity* in the distribution of the benefits. Meeting this challenge may be the key to the well-being of millions of people in the decades ahead.

References and Notes

1. Mohamed T. El-Ashry, Jan van Schilfgaarde, and Susan Schiffman, "Salinity Pollution from Irrigated Agriculture," *Journal of Soil and Water Conservation*, Vol. 40, No. 1 (1985), p. 48.
2. Ruggero Tomaselli, "The Degradation of the Mediterranean Maquis," *Ambio*, Vol. 6 (1977), pp. 356–362.
3. Jared Diamond, "The Environmentalist Myth," *Nature*, Vol. 24, No. 6092 (1986), pp. 19–20.
4. Robert Repetto, "Population, Resources, Environment: An Uncertain Future," *Population Bulletin*, Vol. 42, No. 2 (1987), p. 3.
5. Population Reference Bureau (PRB), *Human Needs and Nature's Balance: Population, Resources, and the Environment* (PRB, Washington, D.C., 1987), p. 2.
6. Martin W. Holdgate, Mohammed Kassas, and Gilbert F. White, eds., *The World Environment, 1972–1982: A Report by the United Nations Environment Programme* (Tycooly International, Dublin, 1982), p. 273.
7. The distinction between recovery methods and good management practices is difficult to make in the field, because they tend to coalesce. William R. Jordan III, Robert L. Peters II, and Edith B. Allen, "Ecological Restoration as a Strategy for Conserving Biological Diversity," *Environmental Management*, Vol. 12, No. 1 (1988), p. 56.
8. United Nations Food and Agriculture Organization (FAO), *Review of Field Programmes 1986–87* (FAO, Rome, 1987), p. 30.
9. John Todd, "Restoring Diversity: The Search for a Social and Economic Context," in *Biodiversity*, E.O. Wilson, ed. (National Academy Press, Washington, D.C., 1988), p. 346.
10. Mohammed Kassas, "Seven Paths to Desertification," *Desertification Control Bulletin*, No. 15 (1987), p. 25.
11. Jane L. Collins, "Labor Scarcity and Ecological Change," in *Lands at Risk in the Third World: Local-Level Perspectives*, Peter D. Little, Michael M. Horowitz, and A. Endre Nyerges, eds. (Westview Press, Boulder, Colorado, 1987), pp. 19–37.
12. Peter D. Little and Michael M. Horowitz, "Social Science Perspectives on Land, Ecology, and Development," in *Lands at Risk in the Third World: Local-Level Perspectives*, Peter D. Little, Michael M. Horowitz, and A. Endre Nyerges, eds. (Westview Press, Boulder, Colorado, 1987), pp. 1–3.
13. World Resources Institute and International Institute for Environment and Development, *World Resources 1986* (Basic Books, New York, 1986), pp. 278–279.
14. Henri Noel Houérou and Hubert Gillet, "Conservation versus Desertization in African Arid Lands," in *Conservation Biology: The Science of Scarcity and Diversity*, Michael E. Soulé, ed. (Sinauer, Sunderland, Massachusetts, 1986), p. 446.

15. See, for example, Anders Rapp, "Reflections on Desertification 1977–1987: Problems and Prospects," *Desertification Control Bulletin*, No. 15 (1987), p. 27.

16. One of the leading authorities on desertification, Harold E. Dregne, argues forcefully for the PACD definition. See his "Reflections on the PACD," *Desertification Control Bulletin*, No. 15 (1987), pp. 8–9.

17. B. Spooner, "The Significance of Desertification," in *Global Aspects of Food Production*, M.S. Swaminathan and S.K. Sinha, eds. (Tycooly International, Oxford, U.K., 1986), pp. 339–341.

18. United Nations Environment Programme (UNEP), Desertification Control Programme Activity Centre, *Rolling Back the Desert, Ten Years After UNCOD* (UNEP, Nairobi, 1987), pp. 3–5.

19. James Walls, "Back to the War," *Desertification Control Bulletin*, Supplement to No. 10 (1984), p. 6.

20. *Ibid.*, p. 8.

21. *Op. cit.* 16, p. 11.

22. J.A. Mabbutt, "A Review of Progress since the U.N. Conference on Desertification," *Desertification Control Bulletin*, No. 15 (1987), p. 13.

23. See *World Resources 1987*, Table 19.4, p. 281 and p. 282; and *World Resources 1986*, Table 4.11, p. 53, and Part IV, Table 5.5, p. 270 and pp. 271–272.

24. B.G. Rozanov *et al.*, "Man-Induced Global Soil Change," paper presented at the Earth as Transformed by Human Activities conference, Worcester, Massachusetts, October 1987.

25. V.A. Kovda, "Loss of Productive Land due to Salinization," *Ambio*, Vol. 12, No. 2 (1983), p. 92.

26. W.G. Sombroek, Director, International Soil Reference and Information Centre, Wageningen, The Netherlands, 1988 (personal communication).

27. Malcolm Gillis, "Malaysia: Public Policies and the Tropical Forest," in *Public Policy and the Misuse of Forest Resources*, Robert Repetto and Malcolm Gillis, eds. (Cambridge University Press, Cambridge, U.K., in press).

28. Jean-Paul Malingreau and Compton J. Tucker, "Large-Scale Deforestation in the Southeastern Amazon Basin of Brazil," *Ambio*, Vol. 17, No. 1 (1988), Table 1, p. 53.

29. A third term, *reclamation*, is used in several distinct senses, often in connection with repairing drastically disturbed land around mines. It can also mean imputing an economic utility to lands where such utility is not natural; converting swamp to farmland is an example. Because the extent of such areas is relatively small, reclamation is not treated at any length here.

30. William R. Jordan III, Robert L. Peters II, and Edith B. Allen, "Ecological Restoration as a Strategy for Conserving Biological Diversity," *Environmental Management*, Vol. 12, No. 1 (1988), p. 55.

31. National Research Council, *Rehabilitation Potential of Western Coal Lands* (Ballinger, Cambridge, Massachusetts, 1974).

32. John Cairns, Jr., "Restoration, Reclamation, and Regeneration of Degraded or Destroyed Ecosystems," in *Conservation Biology: The Science of Scarcity and Diversity*, Michael E. Soulé, ed. (Sinauer, Sunderland, Massachusetts, 1986), pp. 467–468.

33. Christopher Uhl, *et al.*, "Ecosystem Recovery in Amazon Caatinga Forest after Cutting, Cutting and Burning, and Bulldozer Clearing Treatments," *OIKOS*, Vol. 38, No. 3 (1982), p. 313.

34. U.S. Agency for International Development (U.S. AID), "*Republic of Indonesia; Upland Agriculture and Conservation Project* (U.S. AID, Washington, D.C., 1984), cited in Robert Repetto, "Soil Loss and Population Pressure on Java," *Ambio*, Vol. 15, No. 1 (1986), p. 14.

35. Government of Indonesia and U.S. Agency for International Development (U.S. AID), *Composite Report of the Watershed Assessment Team* (U.S. AID, Indonesia, 1983), cited in Robert Repetto, "Soil Loss and Population Pressure on Java," *Ambio*, Vol. 15, No. 1 (1986), p. 14.

36. Robert Repetto, "Soil Loss and Population Pressure on Java," *Ambio*, Vol. 15, No. 1 (1986), p. 14.

37. K.G. Tejwani, "Watershed Management in the Indian Himalaya," in *Perspectives in Environmental Management: Addresses Delivered at the 73rd Session of the Indian Science Congress*, T.N. Khoshoo, ed. (Oxford & Ibh, New Delhi, 1987), p. 217.

38. Hans Gregersen, Sydney Draper, and Dieter Elz, eds., "*People and Trees: Social Forestry Contributions to Development*," review draft, The World Bank, Washington, D.C., 1986, p. 61.

39. *Op. cit.* 36, p. 18.

40. *Op. cit.* 38, pp. 63–65.

41. *Op. cit.* 38, pp. 61–62.

42. *Op. cit.* 38, p. 65, pp. 70–71, and p. 72.

43. Much the same can be said for the Andes. See Stephen B. Brush, "Diversity and Change in Andean Agriculture," in *Lands at Risk in the Third World: Local-Level Perspectives*, Peter D. Little, Michael M. Horowitz, and A. Endre Nyerges, eds. (Westview Press, Boulder, Colorado, 1987), p. 271.

44. Jack D. Ives, "The Theory of Himalayan Environmental Degradation: Its Validity and Application Challenged by Recent Research," *Mountain Research and Development*, Vol. 7, No. 3 (1987), pp. 192–193.

45. D.A. Gilmour, M. Bonell, and D.S. Cassells, "The Effects of Forestation on Soil Hydraulic Properties in the Middle Hills of Nepal: A Preliminary Assessment," *Mountain Research and Development*, Vol. 7, No. 3 (1987), p. 239 and pp. 247–248.

46. T.B.S. Mahat, D.M. Griffin, and K.R. Shepard, "Human Impact on Some Forests of the Middle Hills of Nepal," *Mountain Research and Development*, Vol. 6, Nos. 3 and 4 (1986), and Vol. 7, Nos. 1 and 2 (1987), cited in Jack D. Ives, "The Theory of Himalayan Environmental Degradation: Its Validity and Application Challenged by Recent Research," *Mountain Research and Development*, Vol. 7, No. 3 (1987), p. 196.

47. A.K. Tiwari and J.S. Singh, "Analysis of Land-Use and Vegetation in a Part of Central Himalaya, Using Aerial Photographs," *Environmental Conservation*, Vol. 14, No. 3 (1987), p. 240.

48. J.S. Singh and S.P. Singh, "Forest Vegetation of the Himalaya," *Botanical Review*, Vol. 53 (1987), pp. 80–192.

49. Donald A. Messerschmidt, "Conservation and Society in Nepal: Traditional Forest Management and Innovative Development," in *Lands at Risk in the Third World: Local-Level Perspectives*, Peter D. Little, Michael M. Horowitz, and A. Endre Nyerges, eds. (Westview Press, Boulder, Colorado, 1987), p. 374.

50. *Op. cit.* 44, p. 196.

51. Jaños P. Hrabovsky and K. Miyan, "Population Growth and Land Use in Nepal: The Great Turnabout," *Mountain Research and Development*, Vol. 7, No. 3 (1987), p. 265.

52. *Op. cit.* 44, p. 198.

53. Anis D. Dani and J. Gabriel Campbell, *Sustaining Upland Resources: People's Participation in Watershed Management* (International Centre for Integrated Mountain Development, Kathmandu, Nepal, 1986), p. 4 and p. 75.

54. *Ibid.* pp. 81–83.

55. Vandana Shiva and J. Bandyopadhyay, "The Evolution, Structure, and Impact of the Chipko Movement," *Mountain Research and Development*, Vol. 6, No. 2 (1986), p. 133 and p. 140.

56. *Op. cit.* 53, pp. 10–12.

57. *Op. cit.* 13, Table 4.2, p. 47.

58. United Nations Food and Agriculture Organization (FAO), *Improving Productivity of Dryland Areas* (FAO, Rome, 1987), p. 3.

59. *Op. cit.* 14, p. 447.

60. *Op. cit.* 58.

61. Willem Floor and Jean Gorse, "Household Energy Issues in West Africa," in *Desertification Control and Renewable Resource Management in the Sahelian and Sudanian Zones of West Africa*, Francois Falloux and Aleki Mukendi, eds. (The World Bank, Washington, D.C., 1988), p. 73.

62. T.N. Khoshoo, "Environmental Priorities in India and Sustainable Development," in *Perspectives in Environmental Management: Addresses Delivered at the 73rd Session of the Indian Science Congress*, T.N. Khoshoo, ed. (Oxford & Ibh, New Delhi, 1987), p. 17.

63. See Mohan K. Wali, "The Structure, Dynamics, and Rehabilitation of Drastically Disturbed Ecosystems," in *Perspectives in Environmental Management: Addresses Delivered at the 73rd Session of the Indian Science Congress*, T.N. Khoshoo, ed. (Oxford & Ibh, New Delhi, 1987), p. 165.

64. Nasser Nemati, "Pasture Improvement and Management in Arid Zones of Iran," *Journal of Arid Environments*, Vol. 11 (1986), pp. 30–31 and p. 35.

65. Identical costs for sand dune stabilization were incurred in a rehabilitation project covering part of the Thar desert in northwestern India. There, it was found that increases in rangeland productivity repaid this investment of $67 per hectare after 13 years. H.S. Mann, "Revegetation of the Indian Desert," *Desertification Control*

Bulletin, No. 6 (April 1982), p. 6.

66. Ray Anderson, "Grassland Revegetation by Land Imprinting: A New Option in Desertification Control," *Desertification Control Bulletin*, No. 14 (1987), pp. 40–41, p. 43.

67. J.B. Raintree, "Agroforestry Pathways: Land Tenure, Shifting Cultivation and Sustainable Agriculture," *Unasylva*, Vol. 38, No. 4 (1986), p. 13.

68. *Op. cit.* 38, p. 102.

69. *Op. cit.* 38, p. 104.

70. African Ministerial Conference on the Environment, "A Report on the Pilot Project Programme Submitted to the Donor's Meeting," paper presented at Geneva, September 1986, p. 5.

71. Walter J. Lusigi, "Combatting Desertification and Rehabilitating Degraded Production Systems in Northern Kenya: The IPAL Project," *Desertification Control Bulletin*, No. 10 (May 1984), pp. 29–36.

72. *Op. cit.* 70, p. 1.

73. *Op. cit.* 61, p. 76.

74. Robert Repetto, *Economic Policy Reform for Natural Resource Conservation* (World Resources Institute, Washington, D.C., 1986), p. 17.

75. W.R. Rangeley, "Irrigation and Drainage in the World," presented at the Conference on Water and Water Policy in World Food Supplies, Lubbock, Texas, May 1985, p. 24, *Op. cit.* 13, Table 4.6, p. 48.

76. United Nations Food and Agriculture Organization, "State of Irrigation—Facts and Figures," paper presented at the Consultation on Irrigation in Africa, Lome, Togo (April 1986), Table 9, p. 16.

77. I.P. Abrol, "Salt-Affected Soils: Problems and Prospects in Developing Countries," in *Global Aspects of Food Production*, M.S. Swaminathan and S.K. Sinha, eds. (Tycooly International, Oxford, U.K., 1986), Table 13.1, pp. 284–285.

78. Lambert K. Smedema and David W. Rycroft, *Land Drainage: Planning and Design of Agricultural Drainage Systems* (Cornell University Press, Ithaca, New York, 1983), p. 39.

79. Harold E. Dregne, *Desertification of Arid Lands* (Harwood, Chur, Switzerland, 1983), pp. 46–47.

80. *Op. cit.* 1, pp. 48–49.

81. *Op. cit.* 77, pp. 286–288.

82. M.A. Kishk, "Land Degradation in the Nile Valley," *Ambio*, Vol. 15, No. 4 (1986), p. 228.

83. *Op. cit.* 25.

84. *Op. cit.* 77, pp. 290–291.

85. *Op. cit.* 77, pp. 289–290.

86. I. Szabolcs, "Salt-Affected Soils: Problems and Prospects in Developed Countries," in *Global Aspects of Food Production*, M.S. Swaminathan and S.K. Sinha, eds. (Tycooly International, Oxford, U.K., 1986), p. 310.

87. *Op. cit.* 79, p. 49.

88. T.N. Khoshoo, "Banthra—Then and Now," in *Ecodevelopment of Alkaline Land: Banthra—A Case Study*, T.N. Khoshoo, ed. (National Botanical Research Institute, Lucknow, Uttar Pradesh, 1987), p. xxv.

89. *Op. cit.* 86, p. 319.

90. *Op. cit.* 77, p. 291.

91. Mostafa M. Elgabaly, "Salinity and Water-logging in the Near-East Region," *Ambio*, Vol. 6, No. 1 (1977), p. 38.

92. *Op. cit.* 38, p. 130 and p. 132.

93. *Op. cit.* 77, p. 290.

94. *Op. cit.* 77, pp. 294–296.

95. *Op. cit.* 86, p. 330.

96. *Op. cit.* 77, pp. 296–297 and pp. 300–302.

97. *Op. cit.* 77, p. 300.

98. *Op. cit.* 88, pp. xxix–xxx, pp. xl–xliii, p. xlvii, and p. xlix.

99. V. Chandra, "Historical," in *Ecodevelopment of Alkaline Land: Banthra—A Case Study*, T.N. Khoshoo, ed. (National Botanical Research Institute, Lucknow, Uttar Pradesh, 1987), pp. 2–8.

100. D. Lamb, "IUCN Guidelines for Restoration of Degraded Ecosystems," prepared for the General Assembly of the International Union for Conservation of Nature and Natural Resources, San José, Costa Rica, January 1988, p. 26.

101. Essam El-Hinnawi, *Environmental Refugees* (United Nations Environment Programme, Nairobi, 1985), p. 24.

102. Thomas M. Catterson, "Mechanisms to Enhance Effective Popular Participation," in *Desertification Control and Renewable Resource Management in the Sahelian and Sudanian Zones of West Africa*, Francois Falloux and Aleki Mukendi, eds. (The World Bank, Washington, D.C., 1988), pp. 28–29.

103. *Op. cit.* 61, pp. 87–88.

104. Robert Repetto, "Economic Incentives for Sustainable Production," *The Annals of Regional Science*, Vol. 21, No. 3 (1987), p. 50.

105. *Op. cit.* 100, pp. 35–41.

106. *Op. cit.* 30.

107. *Op. cit.* 30, pp. 56–64.

108. John Cairns, Jr., "Increasing Diversity by Restoring Damaged Ecosystems," in *Biodiversity*, E.O. Wilson, ed. (National Academy Press, Washington, D.C., 1988), p. 337.

109. *Op. cit.* 32, pp. 481–482.

110. Robert L. Peters II, "Global Climate Change: A Challenge for Restoration Ecology," *Restoration & Management Notes*, Vol. 3, No. 2 (1985), pp. 62–67.

111. Gerald Foley and Geoffrey Barnard, *Farm and Community Forestry* (International Institute for Environment and Development, London, 1984), pp. 63–64.

112. *Op. cit.* 53, p. 12.

113. Anne Whyte, *Guidelines for the Field Study of Environmental Perception* (United Nations Educational, Scientific and Cultural Organization, Paris, 1977), *Op. cit.* 17, pp. 352–353.

114. *Op. cit.* 17, p. 355.

115. *Op. cit.* 67, p. 4.

116. S-A. Boonkird, E.C.M. Fernandes, and P.K.R. Nair, "Forest Villages: An Agroforestry Approach to Rehabilitating Forest Land Degraded by Shifting Cultivation in Thailand," *Agroforestry Systems*, Vol. 2 (1984), p. 87.

117. *Op. cit.* 100, pp. 20–21.

118. United Nations Environment Programme (UNEP), *African Environmental Conference: Report of the Conference*, Annex I (UNEP, Nairobi, 1985), p. 15.

119. Mostafa K. Tolba, "The Tenth Anniversary of UNCOD," *Desertification Control Bulletin*, No. 15 (1987), pp. 7–8.

120. African Ministerial Conference on the Environment (AMCE), "Report on the Inter-Agency Working Group (IAWG) Meeting (Geneva, July 10–11 1986)," paper presented at the First Meeting of the AMCE Conference Bureau, Nairobi, October 1986, p. 4.

121. United Nations Environment Programme (UNEP), *African Environmental Conference: Report of the Executive Director of the United Nations Environment Programme* (UNEP, Nairobi, 1985), p. 2 and p. 7.

122. World Commission on Environment and Development, *Our Common Future* (Oxford University Press, Oxford, U.K., 1987).

14. Basic Economic Indicators

A country's economic status and growth can be measured by data on gross national product (GNP) and GNP growth, GNP per capita, debt, and income distribution. Commodity price trends give a global picture of trends in the value of major agricultural and mineral products.

GNP—the economic value of a country's output of goods and services for a given year—is an indicator of economic activity. (See Table 14.1.) In 1986, Switzerland and the United States had the highest per capita GNPs; Ethiopia had the lowest. Although GNP per capita grew in most countries between 1973 and 1986, in 1986 it was still below $500 in 40 countries, 28 of them in Africa. All nine countries whose economies shrank during this period had a GNP per capita under $900.

Many developing countries rely heavily on loans and aid from the developed world for investment capital. (See Tables 14.1 and 14.2.) Six African countries receive over 25 percent of their GNP from official development assistance (ODA), grants and concessional loans made to governments. One country, Cape Verde, receives 58 percent. Although several Asian countries have reduced their reliance on ODA over the past decade, ODA as a percentage of countries' GNP has increased in most African and Latin American countries since the mid-1970s.

The amount of money given in bilateral and multilateral aid reflects countries' commitments toward alleviating poverty and stimulating economic growth, but is also influenced by political, military, and economic interests. Most donor countries have increased ODA payments over the past decade, although ODA as a percentage of GNP has usually remained steady or declined. In the mid-1970s, members of the Organization of Petroleum Exporting Countries (OPEC) were the largest donors in terms of GNP. With the fall in oil prices, most OPEC countries significantly reduced their development assistance, but between 1984 and 1986, Saudi Arabia and Kuwait gave more development assistance as a percentage of their GNP than any other country. The United States was the largest donor in absolute terms, spending over $9 billion annually between 1984 and 1986, but one of the smallest in relation to its GNP. (See Chapter 24, "Policies and Institutions," Table 24.3 for data on sectoral allocation of ODA.)

Between 1980 and 1986, the total external debt of 109 developing countries nearly doubled to over $1 trillion. (See Table 14.2.) Nearly 40 percent of this total is owed by Latin American countries. Many Latin American and African countries are in arrears on their debt or have stopped repayments, triggering debate in lending coun-

tries about their relationship with delinquent debtors and the wisdom of lending new funds.

Debt as a percentage of GNP and debt service as a percentage of exports indicate a country's ability to finance its debts over the long and short term, respectively. In sub-Saharan Africa, public long-term debt was 58 percent of the region's GNP in 1986, and debt service consumed 21 percent of the region's export income. In Latin America, the region's 1986 long-term debt was 46 percent of its GNP; debt service was 30 percent of exports.

Reduced earnings from commodity exports is one important reason why many developing countries are unable to finance their debts. Table 14.3 shows price trends in constant 1980 dollars for many agricultural and mineral commodities. Commodity prices peaked in the mid-1970s and have been falling ever since. Cocoa, tea, rice, and sugar prices have fallen to less than half their 1977 level.

Data on the distribution of household income, although problematic, are among the few available indicators of economic inequality within a country. (See Table 14.4.) In Brazil, for example, the richest 20 percent of the population receives 30 times the income of the poorest 20 percent. By comparison, in the German Democratic Republic, the richest 20 percent receives only 2½ times the income of the poorest quintile. Income distribution data add perspective to the GNP indicators, which are *averages* of national conditions but do not reflect the wide disparities in income and wealth within a country. (Although income and wealth are distinct concepts, they are clearly related. Data on agricultural land distribution, an indicator of wealth in most developing countries, are shown in Chapter 17, "Food and Agriculture," Table 17.3.) Poverty is linked to high mortality; it also affects many environmental issues, since people who lack alternatives often crowd into city slums or marginal lands, adding pressure to these fragile or overstressed environments.

The data in Table 14.4 should be interpreted with care, as they are limited by several factors. First, the data were often taken from surveys designed for other purposes, and the available information on income is often rudimentary. Households were ranked by their total income, which tends to mask the poverty of large households (often the poorest on a per capita basis). In addition, the poorest people may not be represented in household surveys. Finally, definitions of income varied among different surveys, so data for different countries may not be comparable.

Table 14.1 Gross National Product and Official Development

	Gross National Product 1986		Average Annual Change in Real GNP (percent)		Distribution of Gross Domestic Product 1986 (percent)			Average Annual Official Development Assistance (ODA)a (million $US)			ODA as a Percentage of GNPa		
	Total (million $US)	Per Capita ($US)	1965-73	1973-86	Agriculture	Industry	Services	1974-76	1979-81	1984-86	1974-76	1979-81	1984-86
WORLD													
AFRICA													
Algeria	58,040	2,570	7.9	5.6	12	44	44	120	9	102	1	0	0
Angola	X	X	X	X	X	X	X	15	54	106	X	X	X
Benin	1,140	270	2.7	3.7	49	13	37	49	86	104	10	8	9
Botswana	930	840	13.0	10.8	4	58	38b	45	101	101	17	14	12
Burkina Faso	1,240	150	3.2	3.5	45	22	33	90	209	223	14	16	19
Burundi	1,140	240	5.0	3.5	58	17	25	43	112	157	11	12	15
Cameroon	9,580	910	2.5	9.4	22	35	43	107	245	190	4	4	2
Cape Verde	150	460	X	6.5	19	20	61b	X	49	81	X	41	58
Central African Rep	770	290	3.1	0.1	41	12	47	44	99	119	12	13	16
Chad	X	X	X	X	46	18	36b	69	60	154	15	X	X
Comoros	130	280	X	X	37	13	50	25	36	45	44	33	35
Congo	2,020	1,040	6.7	7.1	8	54	38b	56	88	93	8	6	5
Cote d'Ivoire	7,730	740	8.4	3.8	36	24	40	95	165	146	3	2	2
Djibouti	X	X	X	X	X	X	X	31	54	100	X	X	X
Egypt	37,700	760	3.3	7.0	20	29	51	1,746	1,376	1,734	15	7	5
Equatorial Guinea	X	X	X	X	X	X	X	X	7	18	X	X	X
Ethiopia	5,400	120	3.9	2.0	48	15	36	132	216	573	5	5	11
Gabon	3,150	3,020	6.9	1.0	10	35	55	41	45	72	2	1	2
Gambia	180	230	4.5	1.8	33	16	52b	10	53	68	8	24	39
Ghana	5,130	390	3.4	-0.2	45	17	39b	75	170	264	3	4	5
Guinea	X	X	X	X	40	22	38	19	84	139	2	X	X
Guinea-Bissau	150	170	X	1.6	45	12	43	X	59	61	X	47	41
Kenya	6,470	300	8.2	4.3	30	20	50	136	399	436	4	6	7
Lesotho	660	410	X	6.7	21	27	52	27	88	94	10	14	15
Liberia	1,030	450	5.4	-0.4	37	28	35	21	96	107	4	9	11
Libya	X	X	8.5	1.3	X	X	X	-164	-259	-69	-1.30	-0.84	X
Madagascar	2,390	230	3.4	-0.3	43	16	41	70	201	219	4	7	9
Malawi	1,180	160	7.1	2.5	37	18	45	56	141	158	9	13	14
Mali	1,330	170	3.0	2.8	50	13	37b	117	230	357	20	15	28
Mauritania	760	440	3.4	1.9	34	24	42	110	192	187	25	29	26
Mauritius	1,240	1,200	2.4	3.7	15	32	53	24	41	40	4	4	4
Morocco	13,160	590	5.5	3.6	21	30	49	200	800	509	2	5	4
Mozambique	3,030	210	X	X	35	12	53	31	153	327	X	X	10
Niger	1,690	260	-1.6	2.2	46	16	39	136	179	258	21	8	16
Nigeria	66,210	640	9.6	0.1	41	29	30	34	-29	-7	0	0	0
Rwanda	1,820	290	6.4	4.9	40	23	37	72	152	186	13	13	11
Senegal	2,840	420	1.5	2.2	22	27	51	133	322	410	8	12	15
Sierra Leone	1,170	310	4.0	2.1	45	22	33	14	68	71	2	6	6
Somalia	1,560	280	2.9	2.5	58	9	34b	113	329	409	17	21	16
South Africa	59,910	1,800	4.8	1.7	6	46	49	X	X	X	X	X	X
Sudan	7,290	320	0.8	2.0	35	15	50	268	629	897	6	8	13
Swaziland	470	600	8.6	4.2	X	X	X	17	46	30	6	8	7
Tanzania, United Rep	5,370	240	5.6	1.4	59	10	31	242	657	575	9	13	11
Togo	780	250	5.9	1.3	32	20	48	41	88	133	7	9	18
Tunisia	8,340	1,140	7.1	5.1	16	33	52	192	227	180	5	3	2
Uganda	X	X	X	X	76	6	18	31	99	181	1	X	X
Zaire	5,070	160	3.6	-0.7	29	36	35	193	413	362	3	4	8
Zambia	2,060	300	2.4	0.6	11	48	41	69	276	344	3	8	16
Zimbabwe	5,410	620	6.2	3.1	11	46	43	X	130	253	X	2	5
NORTH & CENTRAL AMERICA													
Barbados	1,310	5,140	6.4	1.9	6	20	74	6	14	7	1	2	1
Canada	361,720	14,100	5.6	2.9	X	X	X	-821	-1,106	-1,650	-0.49	-0.43	-0.48
Costa Rica	3,790	1,420	7.0	2.0	21	29	50	26	58	231	1	2	6
Cuba	X	X	X	X	X	X	X	24	32	16	X	X	X
Dominican Rep	4,680	710	7.1	3.2	17	30	53	28	103	175	1	2	4
El Salvador	4,000	820	4.3	-0.7	20	21	59	34	108	321	2	3	8
Guatemala	7,640	930	6.0	2.3	X	X	X	44	72	94	1	1	1
Haiti	1,990	330	1.7	2.2	X	X	X	48	102	154	6	8	8
Honduras	3,360	740	4.5	3.1	27	25	48b	41	103	285	4	4	9
Jamaica	1,980	880	5.6	-2.6	6	40	54	26	138	172	1	6	9
Mexico	149,110	1,850	7.8	3.8	9	39	52b	59	77	160	0	0	0
Nicaragua	2,670	790	3.6	-1.7	23	33	44b	43	170	122	3	9	5
Panama	5,190	2,330	7.5	4.1	9	18	73	33	40	65	2	1	1
Trinidad and Tobago	6,170	5,120	3.5	2.1	5	35	59	5	2	10	0	0	0
United States	4,221,750	17,500	3.1	2.6	2	31	67	-4,065	-5,868	-9,226	-0.26	-0.21	-0.23
SOUTH AMERICA													
Argentina	72,920	2,350	4.4	0.1	13	44	44	30	35	59	X	0	0
Bolivia	3,540	540	4.2	-0.4	24	23	52	63	166	232	4	6	5
Brazil	250,520	1,810	9.9	4.0	11	39	50b	148	142	154	0	0	0
Chile	16,200	1,320	3.7	1.8	X	X	X	54	-15	13	1	-0.06	0
Colombia	35,530	1,230	6.5	3.6	20	25	56	90	82	71	1	0	0
Ecuador	11,200	1,160	7.3	3.9	14	42	45b	64	58	140	1	1	1
Guyana	400	500	4.2	-2.5	26	28	47	18	47	27	4	9	7
Paraguay	3,360	880	4.3	6.7	27	26	47	38	39	56	3	1	2
Peru	21,540	1,130	4.1	1.4	11	38	51b	77	212	299	1	1	2
Suriname	1,010	2,510	6.4	1.9	10	28	62	68	91	6	15	10	1
Uruguay	5,630	1,860	2.4	0.9	12	33	56	12	11	12	0	0	0
Venezuela	51,940	2,930	5.8	1.3	9	37	54	-57	-100	-55	-0.20	-0.17	-0.12

Assistance, 1965–86

Table 14.1

	Gross National Product 1986		Average Annual Change in Real GNP (percent)		Distribution of Gross Domestic Product 1986 (percent)			Average Annual Official Development Assistance (ODA)[a] (million $US)			ODA as a Percentage of GNP[a]		
	Total (million $US)	Per Capita ($US)	1965–73	1973–86	Agriculture	Industry	Services	1974–76	1979–81	1984–86	1974–76	1979–81	1984–86
ASIA													
Afghanistan	X	X	1.1	2.6	X	X	X	71	54	9	3	1	X
Bahrain	3,670	8,530	X	2.6	1	38	61	63	134	124	X	5	3
Bangladesh	16,070	160	0.0	4.4	47	14	39	691	1,184	1,269	7	9	8
Bhutan	200	160	X	X	X	X	X	X	8	27	X	X	14
Burma	7,450	200	2.8	5.7	48	13	39	66	319	349	2	6	5
China	314,800	300	7.8	7.6	31	46	23	X	187	957	X	0	0
Cyprus	2,920	4,360	X	X	8	30	62	36	43	30	5	X	X
India	213,440	270	4.1	4.5	32	29	39	1,629	1,802	1,732	2	1	1
Indonesia	82,110	500	8.0	6.1	26	32	42	675	882	662	2	1	1
Iran	X	X	X	X	X	X	X	-603	97	31	-1.10	X	X
Iraq	X	X	X	X	X	X	X	-240	-565	21	-1.80	X	X
Israel	26,730	6,210	9.6	3.1	X	X	X	409	950	1,724	3	5	7
Japan	1,559,720	12,850	9.4	4.1	3	41	56[b]	-1,126	-3,070	-4,583	-0.22	-0.28	-0.30
Jordan	4,220	1,540	X	8.6	8	28	63	385	1,213	588	37	38	14
Kampuchea, Dem	X	X	X	X	X	X	X	130	173	14	22	X	X
Korea, Dem People's Rep	X	X	X	X	X	X	X	X	X	X	X	X	X
Korea, Rep	98,370	2,370	6.1	7.2	12	42	45	240	201	X	1	0	X
Kuwait	24,650	13,890	4.7	5.2	X	X	X	-771	-1,084	-831	-5.86	-3.55	-3.28
Lao People's Dem Rep	X	X	X	X	X	X	X	42	43	40	X	X	X
Lebanon	X	X	X	X	X	X	X	58	264	78	X	X	X
Malaysia	29,500	1,850	6.9	6.3	X	X	X	77	134	250	1	1	1
Mongolia	X	X	X	X	X	X	X	X	X	3	X	X	X
Nepal	2,640	160	X	X	X	X	X	43	160	245	3	8	10
Oman	6,440	4,990	18.6	7.0	X	X	X	129	188	76	8	4	1
Pakistan	34,690	350	5.5	6.3	24	28	47	955	859	790	8	4	3
Philippines	31,820	570	5.5	3.1	26	32	42	175	314	613	1	1	2
Qatar	4,180	12,520	X	X	X	X	X	-221	-267	-5	-8.82	-4.33	-0.10
Saudi Arabia	83,270	6,930	12.0	3.4	4	50	46	-2,543	-5,027	-3,101	-7.23	-4.14	-3.53
Singapore	19,160	7,410	12.8	7.8	1	38	62	15	14	32	0	0	0
Sri Lanka	6,460	400	4.5	4.9	26	27	47	140	363	507	5	9	8
Syrian Arab Rep	16,980	1,560	6.2	5.5	22	21	58[b]	561	1,667	773	8	13	5
Thailand	42,440	810	7.7	6.0	17	30	53	110	406	484	1	1	1
Turkey	57,120	1,110	6.4	3.8	18	36	46	90	757	255	0	1	0
United Arab Emirates	20,590	14,410	X	7.5	X	X	X	-857	-960	-63	-9.28	-3.71	-0.27
Viet Nam	X	X	X	X	X	X	X	414	269	123	X	X	X
Yemen	4,510	550	X	6.0	34	16	50	186	383	278	19	13	6
Yemen, Dem	1,030	480	X	4.3	X	X	X	88	88	91	25	11	8
EUROPE													
Albania	X	X	X	X	X	X	X	X	X	X	X	X	X
Austria	75,540	10,000	5.4	2.3	3	38	59[b]	-63	-176	-209	-0.17	-0.25	-0.28
Belgium	91,010	9,230	5.0	1.5	2	33	65	-330	-604	-478	-0.53	-0.56	-0.54
Bulgaria	X	X	X	X	X	X	X	X	X	X	X	X	X
Czechoslovakia	X	X	X	X	X	X	X	X	X	X	X	X	X
Denmark	64,610	12,640	3.9	1.6	5	24	71[b]	-196	-448	-528	-0.53	-0.73	-0.85
Finland	60,040	12,180	5.1	2.9	8	37	55	-46	-112	-234	-0.17	-0.23	-0.41
France	595,180	10,740	5.5	2.1	X	X	X	-1,951	-3,929	-4,296	-0.61	-0.64	-0.74
German Dem Rep	X	X	X	X	X	X	X	X	X	X	X	X	X
Germany, Fed Rep	735,940	12,080	4.4	2.0	2	X	X	-1,572	-3,380	-3,185	-0.38	-0.45	-0.45
Greece	36,690	3,680	7.5	2.3	17	29	54	-18	32	15	-0.08	0.08	0.04
Hungary	21,440	2,010	5.9	2.6	17	41	43	X	X	X	X	X	X
Iceland	3,260	13,370	3.6	3.3	X	X	X	X	X	X	X	X	X
Ireland	18,190	5,080	X	X	X	X	X	X	-10	-45	X	-0.06	-0.25
Italy	489,880	8,570	5.2	2.1	5	39	56[b]	-208	-541	-1,545	-0.11	-0.13	-0.33
Luxembourg	5,830	15,920	4.6	4.3	X	X	X	X	X	X	X	X	X
Malta	1,240	3,470	7.7	7.2	5	40	56[b]	28	28	12	6	2	1
Netherlands	X	X	4.7	1.5	4	34	62[b]	-591	-1,538	-1,381	-0.69	-0.99	-0.97
Norway	64,440	15,480	4.0	3.8	3	42	55	-178	-461	-637	-0.65	-0.88	-1.06
Poland	77,730	2,070	X	X	X	X	X	X	X	X	X	X	X
Portugal	22,880	2,230	6.5	2.0	10	40	51[b]	X	111	113	X	0	1
Romania	X	X	X	X	X	X	X	X	X	X	X	X	X
Spain	188,030	4,840	6.2	1.9	6	37	57	X	X	X	X	X	X
Sweden	109,950	13,170	3.1	1.3	3	36	61	-525	-956	-890	-0.76	-0.84	-0.84
Switzerland	115,360	17,840	4.4	1.2	X	X	X	-95	-234	-336	-0.17	-0.23	-0.30
United Kingdom	504,850	8,920	2.5	1.4	2	42	56	-859	-2,067	-1,570	-0.40	-0.42	-0.33
Yugoslavia	53,590	2,300	6.1	3.3	12	42	46	X	-20	11	X	-0.03	0.02
USSR	X	X	X	X	X	X	X	-1312	-2127	-3286	X	X	X
OCEANIA													
Australia	190,470	11,910	5.5	2.4	4	34	62	-454	-649	-759	-0.55	-0.42	-0.42
Fiji	1,280	1,810	8.1	2.7	19	21	60	19	36	35	3	3	3
New Zealand	23,300	7,110	3.0	1.8	X	X	X	-53	-69	-61	-0.39	-0.30	-0.26
Papua New Guinea	2,470	690	X	X	34	26	40	270	315	281	20	13	12
Solomon Islands	150	530	X	7.1	X	X	X	18	34	23	X	30	18

Sources: The World Bank; and Organisation for Economic Co-operation and Development.
Notes:
a. For ODA, flows to recipients are shown as positive numbers; flows from donors are shown as negative numbers.
b. 1985.
0 = zero or less than half the unit of measure; X = not available.
For additional information, see Sources and Technical Notes.

Table 14.2 External Debt Indicators, 1975–86

	Total External Debt (million $US)			Disbursed Long-Term Public Debt (million $US)				Long-Term Public Debt as Percentage of GNP				Debt Service as a Percentage of Exports of Goods and Services			
	1980	1983	1986	1975	1980	1983	1986	1975	1980	1983	1986	1975	1980	1983	1986
TOTAL 109 COUNTRIES	579,399	807,831	1,021,166	126,161	359,103	528,041	780,435	12	18	26	37	9	13	17	21
SUB-SAHARAN AFRICA	55,620	77,955	102,030	13,929	41,318	58,440	84,079	16	22	34	58	6	7	17	19
Benin	411	696	890	89	343	626	781	16	30	65	54	4	4	13	X
Botswana	156	234	358	147	152	230	355	58	18	28	36	3	2	3	4
Burkina Faso	334	422	665	63	299	395	616	10	21	36	42	6	8	10	15
Burundi	165	307	551	18	141	292	528	4	15	28	44	6	7	7	19
Cameroon	2,511	2,703	3,533	372	2,049	1,854	2,267	15	30	26	21	5	9	11	11
Cape Verde	20	71	113	1	20	71	107	1	15	55	69	X	X	X	X
Central African Rep	181	252	453	71	160	215	393	19	20	35	40	7	1	11	9
Chad	199	154	187	87	187	144	172	14	26	25	21	6	4	0	X
Comoros	44	86	161	5	43	84	156	8	36	75	96	X	2	7	6
Congo	1,676	1,965	3,534	401	1,427	1,799	2,861	54	90	93	144	13	9	27	44
Cote d'Ivoire	5,916	7,732	10,865	943	4,328	4,915	6,500	26	48	78	73	9	24	32	21
Djibouti	32	46	125	X	26	34	119	X	X	X	X	X	X	X	X
Equatorial Guinea	75	119	152	25	58	94	141	X	X	X	X	X	X	X	X
Ethiopia	803	1,393	2,139	344	701	1,225	1,989	13	17	25	36	7	6	12	22
Gabon	1,550	908	1,568	772	1,308	674	1,095	18	34	21	37	5	17	10	17
Gambia	137	209	273	13	106	158	228	10	45	77	132	1	1	9	11
Ghana	1,269	1,497	2,385	682	1,099	1,132	1,413	24	25	28	25	6	8	21	11
Guinea	1,088	1,319	1,516	759	1,032	1,249	1,421	X	X	X	X	X	X	X	X
Guinea-Bissau	130	190	307	7	125	153	294	6	119	95	182	X	X	13	54
Kenya	3,484	3,751	4,504	608	2,214	2,435	3,438	19	32	44	52	4	12	20	23
Lesotho	71	135	186	14	63	131	182	5	10	18	29	0	1	5	4
Liberia	706	992	1,303	179	574	740	1,002	25	53	76	99	8	6	7	6
Madagascar	1,247	2,068	2,899	167	955	1,783	2,635	9	30	66	106	3	11	13	X
Malawi	816	888	1,114	257	644	713	910	41	56	62	X	8	20	23	40
Mali	719	1,008	1,716	343	685	943	1,566	43	41	86	96	3	4	7	14
Mauritania	823	1,284	1,761	189	734	1,159	1,637	42	109	157	218	21	11	11	17
Mauritius	457	563	644	46	296	328	427	7	26	31	32	2	6	16	7
Niger	863	914	1,459	112	399	635	1,026	11	16	37	51	5	6	18	25
Nigeria	8,888	18,586	21,876	1,053	4,238	12,237	21,496	3	5	16	45	3	2	18	23
Rwanda	190	242	439	24	164	226	412	4	14	16	22	1	2	5	8
Sao Tome and Principe	23	48	75	X	23	47	74	X	51	131	172	X	5	24	X
Senegal	1,284	1,894	2,990	293	958	1,495	2,456	16	33	64	69	6	20	9	X
Seychelles	84	50	106	X	25	42	67	X	18	28	X	X	0	3	7
Sierra Leone	420	521	590	149	346	388	459	23	32	27	40	10	14	7	8
Somalia	756	1,388	1,580	230	712	1,236	1,415	32	49	57	75	3	4	14	44
Sudan	4,670	6,748	8,272	1,235	3,793	5,684	7,057	29	57	78	97	22	13	10	8
Swaziland	181	223	232	34	166	175	208	12	28	30	46	1	3	4	7
Tanzania, United Rep	2,544	3,226	3,955	817	2,042	2,671	3,650	32	40	44	85	6	11	12	15
Togo	1,032	926	1,050	120	914	821	882	20	82	121	93	10	8	13	32
Uganda	708	1,009	1,193	212	603	637	929	X	X	X	X	5	7	20	7
Zaire	X	X	X	1,718	4,286	4,373	5,430	25	43	61	97	15	17	11	18
Zambia	3,247	3,781	5,300	1,143	2,187	2,661	3,575	50	61	85	241	11	18	12	8
Zimbabwe	X	2,306	2,480	190	697	1,539	1,712	6	13	27	32	1	3	32	20
LATIN AMERICA & CARIBBEAN	242,176	359,650	399,424	45,285	129,325	221,692	301,270	13	19	37	46	14	21	25	30
Argentina	27,157	45,087	48,908	3,124	10,181	25,445	38,453	8	18	43	52	22	18	25	50
Bahamas	151	264	249	95	90	237	199	X	X	X	X	2	2	4	3
Barbados	166	565	601	27	98	279	454	7	12	27	35	2	3	4	8
Belize	63	100	119	5	47	76	97	4	27	45	51	X	X	X	9
Bolivia	2,701	3,775	4,619	824	2,229	3,076	3,523	49	77	112	91	15	28	32	24
Brazil	70,300	98,175	110,675	14,144	40,168	59,815	82,523	12	17	31	31	18	35	29	33
Chile	12,116	18,202	20,741	3,733	4,740	6,872	15,109	54	18	38	101	27	22	18	31
Colombia	6,936	11,409	14,619	2,377	4,084	6,871	11,437	19	12	18	37	11	9	22	28
Costa Rica	2,736	4,246	4,453	421	1,692	3,226	3,582	22	37	115	96	11	17	52	26
Dominican Rep	1,966	2,891	3,301	411	1,191	2,186	2,609	13	20	36	53	5	12	18	21
Ecuador	5,997	7,543	8,954	435	3,300	5,494	7,919	10	30	56	74	4	19	20	32
El Salvador	915	1,682	1,680	196	527	1,348	1,463	11	15	38	38	9	3	17	18
Grenada	17	50	54	8	15	43	53	23	22	46	42	X	4	10	9
Guatemala	1,166	1,799	2,601	143	549	1,386	2,187	4	7	16	30	2	2	12	23
Guyana	758	954	1,131	296	562	698	772	60	102	164	187	5	17	23	X
Haiti	302	569	698	57	267	448	585	8	18	28	27	7	7	5	6
Honduras	1,467	2,085	2,863	264	989	1,612	2,342	24	42	58	69	5	10	15	19
Jamaica	1,906	3,317	3,882	695	1,423	2,365	2,993	32	59	77	152	7	15	20	32
Mexico	57,450	92,965	101,722	11,414	33,987	66,765	74,962	13	19	50	62	25	32	40	37
Nicaragua	2,171	4,016	6,370	593	1,662	3,383	5,343	39	81	144	198	12	16	18	13
Panama	2,974	4,388	4,802	771	2,271	3,145	3,439	42	68	76	72	6	6	7	8
Paraguay	958	1,407	1,960	189	633	1,145	1,752	13	14	36	48	9	12	15	19
Peru	9,987	12,286	15,303	3,021	6,167	8,569	11,049	19	31	46	45	26	31	20	14
Saint Vincent & Grenadines	11	24	32	3	10	22	29	11	18	24	25	X	1	2	X
Trinidad and Tobago	739	1,298	1,427	159	623	886	1,154	7	10	12	25	2	6	9	16
Uruguay	1,660	3,292	3,770	618	1,127	2,510	2,759	18	11	50	46	41	12	21	21
Venezuela	29,410	37,260	33,891	1,262	10,694	13,791	24,485	5	18	21	51	5	13	15	29

Table 14.2

	Total External Debt (million $US)			Disbursed Long-Term Public Debt (million $US)				Long-Term Public Debt as Percentage of GNP				Debt Service as a Percentage of Exports of Goods and Services			
	1980	1983	1986	1975	1980	1983	1986	1975	1980	1983	1986	1975	1980	1983	1986
EAST ASIA & PACIFIC	**93,959**	**141,724**	**184,970**	**18,006**	**52,583**	**82,137**	**129,514**	**7**	**10**	**15**	**24**	**4**	**6**	**9**	**13**
China	7,973	9,607	22,724	X	4,781	5,607	17,193	X	2	2	7	X	5	7	8
Fiji	281	437	422	56	180	292	293	8	15	27	23	2	3	7	10
Indonesia	20,888	30,138	42,090	7,994	14,971	21,654	31,901	26	20	28	44	8	8	13	29
Korea, Rep	29,750	40,900	45,108	5,709	16,203	22,657	29,108	28	27	30	31	12	12	14	17
Malaysia	X	X	X	1,342	3,948	11,826	16,759	14	17	42	65	3	3	6	14
Papua New Guinea	719	1,861	2,304	275	510	927	1,147	21	21	41	48	4	6	11	12
Philippines	17,387	24,057	28,173	1,449	6,523	10,586	19,828	9	19	31	66	7	7	16	18
Singapore	X	X	X	550	1,320	1,495	2,120	10	12	9	12	1	1	1	1
Solomon Islands	19	35	75	X	17	29	69	X	15	23	59	X	0	0	X
Thailand	8,258	13,868	17,959	616	4,070	7,000	11,023	4	12	18	27	2	5	10	17
Vanuatu	4	29	120	X	4	4	9	X	X	X	X	X	X	1	2
Western Samoa	59	74	75	16	55	61	65	X	X	58	59	7	18	14	24
SOUTH ASIA	**36,934**	**51,488**	**71,278**	**19,840**	**33,062**	**40,904**	**58,843**	**17**	**16**	**17**	**21**	**15**	**11**	**15**	**21**
Bangladesh	4,030	5,494	7,868	1,605	3,549	4,883	7,282	15	28	41	47	15	8	13	25
Burma	1,493	2,325	3,766	281	1,452	2,225	3,665	8	25	37	44	17	20	33	55
India	19,334	28,449	41,088	12,224	17,733	21,410	31,913	14	11	11	15	13	9	11	18
Maldives	26	77	70	X	25	48	60	X	104	120	104	X	0	6	X
Nepal	205	453	747	34	173	364	711	2	9	15	28	1	2	3	9
Pakistan	9,923	11,653	13,620	5,099	8,785	9,753	11,765	45	34	31	34	20	20	31	27
Sri Lanka	1,923	3,037	4,120	597	1,345	2,220	3,448	20	34	44	54	22	6	12	X
NORTH AFRICA & MIDDLE EAST	**56,105**	**65,604**	**86,672**	**13,856**	**46,246**	**53,479**	**70,007**	**27**	**41**	**42**	**45**	**11**	**20**	**24**	**33**
Algeria	18,685	14,902	17,929	4,477	16,360	12,945	14,777	29	40	27	25	9	27	33	52
Egypt	17,972	23,167	28,556	4,983	13,885	18,134	22,788	45	64	67	59	30	18	23	21
Jordan	1,759	2,813	4,134	340	1,279	2,230	3,079	33	39	58	71	5	8	11	29
Lebanon	491	610	451	46	197	214	211	X	X	X	X	X	X	X	X
Morocco	X	X	X	1,668	7,354	10,260	14,610	19	43	81	104	7	36	41	41
Oman	603	1,489	2,997	287	440	1,132	2,501	17	8	16	38	2	5	3	11
Syrian Arab Rep	2,738	3,039	4,350	685	2,107	2,288	3,060	10	16	14	18	8	12	11	16
Tunisia	3,684	4,279	5,987	1,029	3,224	3,800	5,001	24	38	49	59	8	13	19	29
Yemen	986	1,739	2,308	244	900	1,574	2,052	26	30	36	41	9	6	14	45
Yemen, Dem	583	987	2,059	97	499	901	1,927	31	62	85	190	0	8	38	45
EUROPE & MEDITERRANEAN	**94,604**	**111,410**	**176,793**	**15,245**	**56,570**	**71,389**	**136,723**	**9**	**17**	**22**	**39**	**5**	**9**	**14**	**22**
Cyprus	545	856	1,591	76	398	651	1,170	11	19	31	40	3	5	11	12
Greece	9,447	13,157	20,862	2,633	4,788	8,203	15,015	12	12	23	38	13	11	18	28
Hungary	10,314	9,624	17,218	X	6,409	6,548	13,567	X	29	32	59	X	14	18	36
Israel	17,530	23,270	23,775	5,915	11,500	14,985	15,938	46	53	55	56	19	14	19	19
Malta	150	178	241	32	128	136	114	7	10	12	8	1	0	1	2
Poland	X	X	36,638	X	X	X	35,200	X	X	X	49	X	X	X	19
Portugal	9,358	14,481	16,658	1,097	6,703	10,056	13,929	7	28	51	50	4	15	27	32
Romania	9,762	9,129	6,639	X	7,131	7,585	5,309	X	X	X	X	X	10	13	12
Turkey	19,012	20,256	31,808	3,167	14,933	16,009	23,309	9	27	32	41	13	28	30	31
Yugoslavia	18,486	20,458	21,364	2,325	4,581	7,215	13,174	8	6	15	20	7	5	6	11

Source: The World Bank.
0 = zero or less than half the unit of measure; X = not available.
For additional information, see Sources and Technical Notes.

Table 14.3 World Commodity Indexes and Prices, 1960–87

Commodity Indexes (index numbers based on constant prices with 1979–81 = 100)

	1960	1961	1962	1963	1964	1965	1966	1967	1968	1969	1970	1971	1972	1973
33 Nonfuel Commodities	116	109	107	110	117	119	119	110	112	112	111	98	94	124
Total Agriculture	117	108	107	113	114	109	107	104	105	104	103	93	92	124
Total Food	106	102	101	110	112	107	104	103	102	101	103	93	93	124
Beverages	105	97	91	92	103	98	93	89	89	88	96	80	80	88
Cereals	109	115	125	127	124	120	131	137	134	127	109	100	97	170
Fats and Oils	119	118	114	122	123	135	126	120	115	108	121	115	104	185
Other Foods	96	89	91	122	111	91	89	92	93	98	97	94	103	107
Nonfood Agriculturals	157	131	129	121	121	117	115	108	113	115	101	97	91	124
Timber	57	58	62	62	52	59	60	64	66	60	60	58	53	79
Metals and Minerals	124	120	115	114	137	155	160	134	138	144	142	117	106	133

Commodity Prices (in constant 1980 $US per unit measure)

	1972	1973	1974	1975	1976	1977	1978	1979	1980	1981	1982	1983	1984	1985	1986
Cocoa (kg)	1.61	2.44	2.76	1.98	3.21	5.41	4.23	3.61	2.60	2.07	1.75	2.20	2.53	2.35	1.83
Coffee (kg)	2.81	3.29	2.86	2.94	5.17	9.70	3.97	4.26	4.58	3.85	3.20	3.26	3.48	3.49	4.50
Tea (kg)	2.63	2.28	2.48	2.21	2.41	3.84	2.72	2.36	2.23	2.01	1.95	2.41	3.64	2.07	1.70
Rice (metric ton)	367.5	754.3	959.3	578.2	399.5	388.9	456.5	363.3	433.9	480.4	295.6	286.6	265.6	225.1	185.6
Grain Sorghum (metric ton)	140.0	200.4	214.2	178.2	165.2	126.3	116.5	118.8	128.9	125.8	109.5	133.3	124.6	107.4	72.8
Maize (metric ton)	140.0	211.2	233.6	190.5	176.5	136.1	125.1	126.6	125.3	130.2	110.3	140.8	143.2	117.0	77.2
Wheat (metric ton)	178.3	317.2	369.4	288.7	234.1	165.4	167.5	189.0	190.8	195.4	168.0	175.5	174.3	180.7	141.6
Sugar (kg)	0.40	0.45	1.16	0.72	0.40	0.26	0.21	0.23	0.63	0.37	0.19	0.19	0.12	0.09	0.12
Beef (kg)	3.70	4.33	2.80	2.11	2.48	2.15	2.66	3.16	2.76	2.46	2.41	2.53	2.40	2.25	1.85
Lamb (kg)	2.46	2.98	2.32	2.27	2.42	2.36	2.70	2.60	2.89	2.73	2.40	2.00	2.02	1.92	1.90
Bananas (kg)	0.41	0.36	0.33	0.39	0.40	0.39	0.36	0.36	0.38	0.40	0.38	0.44	0.39	0.40	0.34
Black Pepper (kg)	2.55	2.76	3.31	3.19	3.08	3.59	2.91	2.32	1.99	1.58	1.57	1.75	2.40	4.0	4.26
Copra (metric ton)	352.3	761.0	1,171.7	408.1	431.7	574.7	584.4	737.6	453.8	377.0	317.1	513.5	748.2	402.5	174.6
Coconut Oil (metric ton)	585.5	1,105.6	1,766.4	626.6	656.2	826.0	848.7	1,079.5	673.8	567.1	468.6	755.6	1,216.7	615.2	261.9
Groundnut Meal (metric ton)	305.0	573.3	308.0	222.9	276.3	311.4	254.7	231.4	240.3	236.7	190.8	207.0	187.6	153.3	145.5
Groundnut Oil (metric ton)	1,064.8	1,177.2	1,905.8	1,364.7	1,163.3	1,217.6	1,340.6	974.5	858.8	1,037.8	590.2	735.9	1,071.3	943.7	501.8
Linseed (metric ton)	362.5	689.4	923.4	538.2	478.8	388.4	310.1	366.0	350.9	352.5	300.7	287.1	314.0	285.7	183.4
Linseed Oil (metric ton)	516.0	1,212.1	1,998.6	1,116.2	857.1	659.9	539.4	700.7	697.1	656.7	523.3	501.7	602.7	654.8	369.5
Palm Kernels (metric ton)	290.3	557.3	822.7	329.3	361.1	466.1	451.9	548.3	345.1	315.7	267.4	378.2	556.4	303.4	125.2
Palm Oil (metric ton)	543.3	813.6	1,184.1	691.4	638.2	757.1	745.6	716.9	583.5	567.9	449.1	519.0	768.2	522.4	226.6
Soybeans (metric ton)	350	625	490	350	363	400	333	327	296	287	247	292	297	234	183
Soybean Oil (metric ton)	675	1,002	1,407	986	688	823	754	726	597	504	451	545	763	596	302
Soybean Meal (metric ton)	323	651	326	247	311	329	265	267	262	251	220	246	208	164	163
Fish Meal (metric ton)	598	1,168	658	390	590	649	509	433	504	466	356	469	393	292	283
Cotton (kg)	1.98	2.92	2.50	1.85	2.66	2.22	1.95	1.85	2.05	1.84	1.61	1.92	1.88	1.37	0.93
Burlap (meter)	0.56	0.46	0.52	0.35	0.30	0.31	0.27	0.33	0.40	0.27	0.27	0.30	0.39	0.36	0.22
Jute (metric ton)	747.5	622.8	624.8	590.8	464.1	458.4	540.0	424.8	308.0	274.6	288.4	312.8	559.3	607.8	238.2
Sisal (metric ton)	600	1,136	1,869	924	736	733	609	775	765	642	598	583	615	548	453

Table 14.3

Commodity Indexes (index numbers based on constant prices with 1979–81 = 100)

1974	1975	1976	1977	1978	1979	1980	1981	1982	1983	1984	1985	1986	1987
134	101	112	123	101	105	105	91	82	89	92	81	69	62
135	100	116	134	108	106	104	91	81	89	94	81	71	59
140	103	117	143	111	106	104	90	81	88	95	83	75	57
83	71	134	205	132	121	99	82	85	88	104	95	98	58
202	142	115	96	100	92	101	107	79	87	85	74	54	46
172	104	110	124	112	114	96	92	76	92	110	76	50	52
173	129	95	78	79	86	121	92	79	85	77	74	67	65
114	89	111	102	97	102	106	92	82	95	90	76	58	66
78	53	70	74	68	104	110	87	88	84	99	80	73	99
144	113	110	103	92	103	105	92	83	88	85	79	62	64

Commodity Prices (in constant 1980 $US per unit measure)

	1972	1973	1974	1975	1976	1977	1978	1979	1980	1981	1982	1983	1984	1985	1986
Wool (kg)	6.00	11.07	6.50	4.37	5.35	5.11	4.66	4.86	4.60	4.25	3.96	3.77	3.87	3.71	2.92
Natural Rubber (kg)	10.03	16.92	15.38	10.49	13.71	13.10	13.75	15.61	16.24	12.46	101.10	128.20	115.50	96.40	83.30
Logs (cubic meter)	94.0	141.4	139.1	94.4	125.0	128.3	114.0	175.7	192.9	143.9	146.5	140.0	159.1	137.6	X
Plywood (sheet)	2.39	4.07	2.70	1.94	2.32	2.36	2.35	2.88	2.74	2.44	2.35	2.38	2.39	2.20	2.41
Sawnwood (cubic meter)	265.0	336.4	253.3	265.0	263.9	220.1	255.2	371.8	365.1	312.6	304.7	315.0	323.3	288.1	234.7
Tobacco (metric ton)	2,405	2,073	2,266	2,416	2,215	2,386	2,099	2,336	2,300	2,338	2,432	2,324	2,097	2,140	1,787
Coal (metric ton)	47.9	45.0	78.8	86.4	84.1	77.5	69.2	62.0	55.7	57.8	56.9	59.5	60.9	58.0	46.6
Petroleum (barrel)	4.8	5.8	19.8	17.4	18.4	18.3	16.0	20.4	30.5	34.2	33.5	30.1	30.0	29.0	X
Gasoline (metric ton)	76.0	189.2	232.0	191.6	216.5	188.0	198.8	367.3	358.0	352.3	326.5	293.2	271.2	266.1	128.7
Jet Fuel (metric ton)	78.3	195.5	188.9	180.3	187.8	185.0	181.6	384.1	349.3	333.7	325.3	287.4	275.7	276.1	142.3
Gas Oil (metric ton)	67.0	180.2	182.8	159.2	168.6	168.3	159.8	340.9	307.1	297.2	292.3	256.9	251.1	250.1	125.5
Fuel Oil (metric ton)	35.3	61.9	123.0	98.9	107.5	108.9	94.0	146.5	170.2	182.6	165.5	168.7	187.8	158.2	64.7
Aluminum (metric ton)	1,080	1,429	1,671	1,099	1,353	1,416	1,298	1,667	1,730	1,331	1,071	1,548	1,445	1,160	1,112
Bauxite (metric ton)	30.00	26.94	41.06	40.29	42.70	44.00	42.61	40.13	41.20	39.80	36.33	35.92	34.77	31.28	24.69
Copper (metric ton)	2,678	3,849	3,644	1,970	2,199	1,870	1,696	2,177	2,183	1,733	1,493	1,648	1,453	1,478	1,212
Lead (metric ton)	755	927	1,050	664	699	883	822	1,325	906	723	551	440	468	408	358
Tin (metric ton)	9,425	10,405	14,515	10,940	11,903	15,374	16,035	16,950	16,775	14,089	12,943	13,445	12,933	12,456	X
Zinc (metric ton)	978	981	1,404	1,368	1,292	1,083	849	901	825	977	856	944	1,130	928	739
Iron Ore (metric ton)	32.0	36.9	33.6	36.0	34.4	30.9	24.1	25.6	26.7	24.2	26.1	24.8	24.3	23.7	19.4
Manganese Ore (10 kg Mn)	1.59	1.61	1.99	2.19	2.28	2.11	1.78	1.51	1.57	1.67	1.66	1.57	1.51	1.47	1.22
Nickel (metric ton)	7,700	7,270	6,770	7,277	7,808	7,433	5,729	6,563	6,519	5,924	4,881	4,837	5,008	5,108	3,422
Steel (metric ton)	449.3	403.5	452.2	461.9	464.2	460.9	452.1	444.4	452.8	505.4	539.5	565.3	569.1	563.2	354.8
Phosphate Rock (metric ton)	28.8	29.7	96.5	106.7	56.5	43.6	36.0	36.2	46.7	49.3	42.8	38.2	40.4	35.3	30.2
Diammonium Phosphate (metric ton)	227.5	256.0	588.7	386.9	188.4	190.0	173.7	212.0	222.2	194.0	184.5	190.0	199.3	176.2	136
Potassium Chloride (metric ton)	83.8	91.6	107.1	129.5	86.3	72.9	70.1	84.1	115.7	111.8	82.3	78.0	88.2	87.6	60.7
Triple Superphosphate (metric ton)	170	216	538	322	143	139	122	161	180	160	139	140	138	126	107
Urea (metric ton)	148.3	204.3	558.9	315.3	175.8	182.0	179.9	189.6	222.1	214.9	160.2	140.2	180.5	142.1	94.4

Source: The World Bank.
X = not available.
For additional information, see Sources and Technical Notes.

Table 14.4 Income Distribution, 1970–86

	Survey Year	Distribution of Household Income by Percentile Group						Income of Highest Quintile Divided by Income of Lowest Quintile
		Lowest Quintile	Second Quintile	Third Quintile	Fourth Quintile	Highest Quintile	Highest 10 Percent	
AFRICA								
Botswana	1974–75	4.3	7.7	12.0	18.4	57.6	42.0	13.4
Cote d'Ivoire	1985–86	2.4	6.2	10.9	19.1	61.4	43.7	25.6
Egypt	1975	5.8	10.7	14.7	20.8	48.0	33.2	8.3
Kenya	1976	2.6	6.3	11.5	19.2	60.4	45.8	23.2
Mauritius	1980–81	4.0	7.5	11.0	17.0	60.5	46.7	15.1
Reunion	1976–77	3.1	6.1	9.6	16.0	65.2	51.4	21.0
Seychelles	1978	4.1	9.0	14.0	21.3	51.6	35.6	12.6
Zambia	1976	3.4	7.4	11.2	16.9	61.1	46.4	18.0
AMERICAS								
Argentina	1970	4.4	9.7	14.1	21.5	50.3	35.2	11.4
Bahamas	1979	3.6	9.6	15.7	23.0	48.1	32.1	13.4
Bermuda	1982	7.2	13.0	17.6	22.8	39.4	24.7	5.5
Brazil	1972	2.0	5.0	9.4	17.0	66.6	50.6	33.3
	1982	2.3	5.9	10.3	17.8	63.7	48.3	27.7
Canada	1981	4.6	11.0	17.7	25.2	41.6	25.0	9.0
Costa Rica	1971	3.3	8.7	13.3	19.8	54.8	39.5	16.6
Dominican Rep	1976–77	4.5	8.2	12.1	18.7	56.5	41.7	12.6
El Salvador	1976–77	5.5	10.0	14.8	22.4	47.3	29.5	8.6
Guatemala	1979–81	5.3	8.4	11.9	18.0	56.4	42.1	10.6
Mexico	1977	3.5	7.9	13.2	21.6	53.8	36.3	15.4
Panama	1973	2.0	5.2	11.0	20.0	61.8	44.2	30.9
Peru	1972	1.9	5.1	11.0	21.0	61.0	42.9	32.1
	1977–78	5.9	10.6	15.4	23.0	45.2	28.4	7.7
Trinidad and Tobago	1975–76	2.6	8.3	14.7	23.4	51.0	33.6	19.6
United States	1980	4.2	10.1	16.4	24.4	44.9	28.2	10.7
	1980	5.0	11.4	17.3	24.3	41.9	25.8	8.4
	1985	4.6	10.9	16.9	24.2	43.5	X	9.5
Uruguay	1983	6.0	10.9	15.5	22.3	45.3	29.3	7.6
Venezuela	1970	3.0	7.3	12.9	22.8	54.0	35.7	18.0
ASIA								
Bangladesh	1973–74	6.6	11.0	15.1	21.1	46.3	31.2	7.0
	1976–77	6.2	10.9	15.0	21.0	46.9	32.0	7.6
	1981–82	6.6	10.7	15.3	22.1	45.3	29.5	6.9
China	1984[a]	11.8	16.1	18.9	22.4	30.7	X	2.6
	1984[b]	10.6	15.6	19.0	22.9	31.7	X	3.0
Hong Kong	1980	5.4	10.8	15.2	21.6	47.0	31.3	8.7
	1981	4.3	9.5	14.1	20.1	52.0	37.3	12.1
India	1975–76	5.0	9.6	14.1	20.9	50.4	34.9	10.1
Indonesia	1976	6.6	7.8	12.6	23.6	49.4	34.0	7.5
Israel	1979–80	6.1	12.2	17.6	24.1	40.0	24.4	6.6
Japan	1979	9.1	14.0	17.7	22.3	36.9	22.7	4.1
Korea, Rep	1976	5.7	11.2	15.4	22.4	45.3	27.5	7.9
	1981	8.0	13.0	17.0	22.4	39.6	24.5	5.0
	1981	8.1	13.1	17.1	22.4	39.3	24.2	4.9
Malaysia	1973	3.5	7.7	12.4	20.3	56.1	39.8	16.0
Nepal	1976–77	3.1	6.3	9.7	16.4	64.5	50.7	20.8
Philippines	1971	3.5	7.8	12.4	19.8	56.5	40.9	16.1
	1985	5.2	8.9	13.2	20.2	52.5	37.0	10.1
Singapore	1977–78	6.5	10.3	14.0	20.0	49.2	34.4	7.6
Sri Lanka	1980–81	5.9	10.3	14.1	19.9	49.8	35.2	8.4
Thailand	1975–76	5.1	8.2	11.7	17.9	57.1	42.8	11.2
Turkey	1973	3.5	7.9	12.5	19.4	56.7	41.5	16.2
EUROPE								
Austria	1976	4.0	10.2	16.5	24.2	45.1	28.7	11.3
Belgium	1978–79	7.9	13.7	18.6	23.8	36.0	21.5	4.6
Bulgaria	1982	9.7	14.6	17.9	21.8	36.0	22.5	3.7
Czechoslovakia	1981	10.0	14.4	17.7	22.1	35.8	21.8	3.6
Denmark	1981	4.3	11.6	18.3	25.6	40.2	24.0	9.3
	1981	5.4	12.0	18.4	25.6	38.6	22.3	7.1
Finland	1981	6.3	12.1	18.4	25.5	37.6	21.7	6.0
France	1975	4.0	9.6	14.9	21.6	49.9	34.5	12.5
German Dem. Rep.	1980	12.2	17.1	19.3	21.6	29.8	17.5	2.4
Germany, Fed Rep	1978	6.0	12.0	17.9	24.5	39.6	24.0	6.6
	1978	7.2	12.8	18.0	23.9	38.1	22.8	5.3
Hungary	1982	6.9	13.6	19.2	24.5	35.8	20.5	5.2
Ireland	1973	7.2	13.1	16.6	23.7	39.4	25.1	5.5
	1980	4.6	10.8	16.9	24.4	43.3	26.5	9.4
	1980	5.2	11.6	17.2	24.0	42.0	25.8	8.1
Italy	1977	6.2	11.3	15.9	22.7	43.9	28.1	7.1
Netherlands	1981	7.1	13.1	17.7	23.1	38.9	23.9	5.5
	1981	8.3	14.1	18.2	23.2	36.2	21.5	4.4
Norway	1982	5.0	12.0	17.9	25.1	40.0	23.7	8.0
	1982	6.0	12.9	18.3	24.6	38.2	22.8	6.4
Poland	1983	10.1	14.5	18.1	22.6	34.7	20.6	3.4

Table 14.4

	Survey Year	Lowest Qintile	Second Quintile	Third Quintile	Fourth Quintile	Highest Quintile	Highest 10 Percent	Income of Highest Quintile Divided by Income of Lowest Quintile
				Distribution of Household Income by Percentile Group				
Portugal	1973–74	5.2	10.0	14.4	21.3	49.1	33.4	9.4
Spain	1980–81	6.9	12.5	17.3	23.2	40.0	24.5	5.8
Sweden	1981	5.6	11.7	17.3	24.4	41.0	24.6	7.3
	1981	7.4	13.2	17.9	23.6	37.9	22.7	5.1
Switzerland	1978	6.0	12.6	17.4	22.6	41.4	27.0	6.9
	1978	6.6	13.5	18.4	23.4	38.0	23.7	5.8
United Kingdom	1979	7.0	11.5	17.0	24.8	39.7	23.4	5.7
	1982	5.8	11.0	17.6	24.7	41.0	24.8	7.1
	1982	6.8	11.9	17.6	24.2	39.5	23.9	5.8
Yugoslavia	1978	7.2	12.7	17.3	23.0	39.8	24.7	5.5
OCEANIA								
Australia	1975–76	5.4	10.0	15.0	22.5	47.1	30.5	8.7
	1978–79	6.4	12.7	18.1	24.2	38.6	23.2	6.0
New Zealand	1981–82	5.1	10.8	16.2	23.2	44.7	28.7	8.8

Sources: United Nations; and The World Bank.
Notes:
a. Refers to cities only.
b. Refers to county towns only.
For additional information, see Sources and Technical Notes.

Sources and Technical Notes

Table 14.1 Gross National Product and Official Development Assistance, 1965–86

Sources: GNP: The World Bank, *The 1988 Update of the 1987 World Bank Atlas* (The World Bank, Washington, D.C., in press 1988). Change in GNP and distribution of gross domestic product: The World Bank, *World Development Report 1988* (The World Bank, Washington, D.C., 1988). Official Development Assistance: Organisation for Economic Co-operation and Development (OECD), *Development Co-operation* (OECD, Paris, 1988); OECD, *Geographical Distribution of Financial Flows to Developing Countries 1971/77* and *1983/86* (OECD, Paris, 1978, 1988); OECD, *Twenty-Five Years of Development Assistance* (OECD, Paris, 1985).

Gross National Product is the sum of two components: the *Gross Domestic Product* (the final output of goods and services produced by the domestic economy, including net exports of goods and nonfactor services) and net factor income from abroad. Net factor income from abroad is income in the form of overseas workers' remittances, interest on loans, profits, and other factor payments that residents receive from abroad less payments made for factor services (labor and capital). Most countries estimate Gross Domestic Product by the production method. This method sums the final outputs of the various sectors of the economy (agriculture, manufacturing, government services, etc.) from which the value of the inputs to production have been subtracted.

Gross National Product in domestic currency was converted to U.S. dollars using a three-year average exchange rate, adjusted for domestic and U.S. inflation. However, the strong appreciation of the U.S. dollar through 1985 affects the conversion factor and may mask real growth in GNP and GNP per capita in some countries.

The average annual percentage change of GNP was calculated by fitting a least-square regression line to the logarithmic values for GNP in constant prices.

Net *Official Development Assistance* (ODA) is the net amount of disbursed grants and concessional loans given or received by a country. Grants include gifts, in money, goods, or services, for which no repayment is required. A concessional loan has a grant element of 25 percent or more. The grant element is the amount by which the face value of the loan exceeds its present market value because of below-market interest rates, favorable maturity schedules, and repayment grace periods. Nonconcessional loans are not a component of ODA.

ODA contributions are shown as negative numbers; receipts are shown as positive numbers. Data for donor countries include contributions directly to developing countries and through multilateral institutions. The GNP data used to determine *ODA as a Percentage of GNP* were derived by using single year exchange rates, not the three-year exchange rates discussed above.

Sources of ODA include the development assistance agencies of members of the Organisation for Economic Co-operation and Development (OECD), of members of the Council for Mutual Economic Assistance (CMEA), and of members of the Organization of Petroleum Exporting Countries (OPEC). Grants and concessional loans to and from multilateral development agencies are also included in contributions and receipts.

OECD gathers ODA data through questionnaires and reports from countries and multilateral agencies. Only limited data are available on ODA flows among developing countries.

Data for OPEC countries, many of which both contribute to and receive ODA, were determined by subtracting ODA contributions from ODA receipts for each country. 1974-76 and 1979-81 figures for the USSR are total donations made by all members of CMEA; USSR donations comprise 85–90 percent of the CMEA total.

Table 14.2 External Debt Indicators, 1975–86

Source: The World Bank, *World Debt Tables* (The World Bank, Washington, D.C., January 1988).

The World Bank operates the Debtor Reporting System (DRS), which compiles reports supplied by 109 of the Bank's member countries. Countries submit detailed reports on the annual status, transactions, and terms of the long-term external debt of public agencies and of publicly guaranteed private debt. Additional data are drawn from the World Bank, the International Monetary Fund (IMF), regional development banks, government lending agencies, and the Creditor Reporting System (CRS). The CRS is operated by the Organisation for Economic Co-operation and Development to compile reports from the members of its Development Assistance Committee.

The *total external debt* figures include long-term debt, use of IMF credit, and short-term debt. Long-term debt is described below. Use of IMF credit refers to all drawings on the Fund's General Resources Account. Use of IMF credit is converted to dollars by using the average Special Drawing Right exchange rate in effect for the year being calculated. Short-term debt is public or private debt that has a maturity of one year or less. This class of debt is especially difficult for countries to monitor. Only a few countries supply these data through the DRS; the World Bank supplements these data with creditor-country reports and information from international clearinghouse banks and other sources to derive rough estimates of short-term debt.

Long-term debt is an obligation with a maturity of at least one year that is owed to nonresidents and is repayable in foreign currency, goods, or services. Long-term debt is divided into long-term public and publicly guaranteed debt and long-term private debt.

Private debt is an external obligation of a private debtor that is not guaranteed by a public entity. Data for this class of debt are less extensive than those for public debt; many countries do not report these data through the DRS. Reporting has improved recently, however, with complete or partial data currently available from 39 countries and World Bank estimates available for nine others. These 48 countries account for the majority of the private nonguaranteed debt of developing countries. In 1986, the private nonguaranteed debt of the 109 members of the DRS was about 10 percent of all long-term debt.

The data described as *disbursed long-term public debt* are outstanding public and publicly guaranteed long-term debt. Public debt is an obligation of a national or subnational government or of their agencies and autonomous bodies. Publicly guaranteed debt is an external obligation of a private debtor that is guaranteed for repayment by a public entity.

Debt as a percentage of GNP is calculated using the disbursed long-term public debt described above. Gross National Product is defined in the Technical Note for Table 14.1. The GNP data used to derive debt-to-GNP ratios were converted from local currencies at a single year exchange rate, rather than the three-year average exchange rate used to determine GNP data in Table 14.1. Total debt service comprises actual interest payments and repayments of principal made on the disbursed long-term public debt in foreign currencies, goods, and services in the year specified. Exports of goods and services are the total value of goods and all services sold to the rest of the world. These data are from IMF files.

Debt data are reported to the World Bank in the units of currency in which they are payable. The World Bank converts these data to U.S. dollar figures using the IMF par values or central rates or, where appropriate, the current market rates. Debt service data are converted to U.S. dollar figures at the average exchange rate for the given year. Comparability of data among countries and years is limited by variations in methods, definitions, and comprehensiveness of data collection and reporting. Refer to the source for details.

Table 14.3 World Commodity Indexes and Prices, 1960–87

Source: The World Bank, *Commodity Trade and Price Trends* (The World Bank, Washington, D.C., in press 1988).

Price data are compiled from major international market places for standard grades of each commodity. For example, the gasoline series refers to 91/92 octane regular gasoline, in barges, f.o.b. (free on board) Rotterdam. Recent data are provisional.

The 1980 U.S. constant dollar figures were derived by converting current average monthly prices in local currencies to U.S. dollars using the monthly average exchange rate. These monthly average U.S. dollar figures were then averaged to produce an annual average dollar figure, which was adjusted to 1980 constant dollars using the Manufacturing Unit Value (MUV) index. The MUV index is a composite price index of all manufactured goods traded internationally.

The aggregate price indexes have the following components:

1. 33 Nonfuel commodities: individual items listed under 4–10 below;
2. Total agriculture: total food and nonfood agricultural products;
3. Total food: beverages, cereals, fats and oils, other foods;
4. Beverages: coffee, cocoa, tea;
5. Cereals: maize, rice, wheat, grain sorghum;
6. Fats and oils: palm oil, coconut oil, groundnut oil, soybeans, copra, groundnut meal, soybean meal;
7. Other food: sugar, beef, bananas, oranges;
8. Nonfood agricultural products: cotton, jute, rubber, tobacco;
9. Timber: logs;
10. Metals and Minerals: copper, tin, nickel, bauxite, aluminum, iron ore, manganese ore, lead, zinc, phosphate rock.

Table 14.4 Income Distribution, 1970–86

Sources: United Nations (U.N.), *National Accounts Statistics: Compendium of Income Distribution Statistics* (U.N., New York, 1985). Data for Cote d'Ivoire, Egypt, Kenya, Argentina, Brazil (1972), Costa Rica, Panama, Peru (1972), Venezuela, Bangladesh (1981–82), Hong Kong (1980), Indonesia, Republic of Korea (1976), Malaysia, Philippines (1985), Ireland (1973), Italy, Portugal, United Kingdom (1979), and Australia (1975–76): The World Bank, *World Development Report 1987* (The World Bank, Washington, D.C., 1987). United States (1985): U.S. Department of Commerce, *Statistical Abstract of the United States 1987* (U.S. Department of Commerce, Washington, D.C., 1987). China: State Statistical Bureau, PRC, *A Survey of Income and Household Conditions in China* (New World Press and China Statistical Information and Consultancy Service Centre, Beijing, 1985).

The United Nations Department of International Economic and Social Affairs compiles data on income distribution from questionnaires sent to national statistical authorities and from the published reports of national agencies. The World Bank collects income distribution data from various national, regional, and international agencies.

Most countries gathered income distribution data from household surveys that included

questions about income. Income was usually defined as the total pretax household income received from wages or salary; own business or farm; government social security and welfare benefits; superannuation; interest, dividends, and rents; and other sources such as a trust or will, alimony, or maintenance. Households are defined as a group of related or unrelated persons living together. Institutional and collective households were generally excluded.

The methods and concepts used to determine income distribution vary among countries, and data are not strictly comparable. Definitions of income usually did not include employers' contributions to social security and similar schemes. Definitions of income varied among countries regarding the inclusion of: the rental value of owner-occupied dwellings, the value of income in kind from various sources (including unpaid family workers), casualty insurance benefits, inheritances, and the income of domestic servants and boarders. The data are also limited because most countries rank households by *total* household income rather than by *per capita* household income. As a result, large households with low per capita income but large total income are ranked in a higher percentile than they would be if ranked by per capita income.

The quintile distribution shows the proportion of all household income obtained by five groups of households, each containing 20 percent of all households. For example, the first quintile refers to the 20 percent of all households with the lowest income, and the fifth quintile refers to the 20 percent of all households with the highest income. Income distribution by quintile is supplemented with data on the proportion of all household income obtained by the 10 percent of households with the highest income, a subset of the fifth quintile. For countries where quintile breakdowns of income distribution were not provided by the countries themselves, the United Nations determined figures by fitting probability distribution functions to the data supplied.

The income of the highest quintile divided by the income of the lowest quintile is a measure of income inequality in a country. In a country with complete equality, the ratio would be one.

Most of the data are nationally representative. Data for Botswana refer to rural areas only; data for Malawi, Peru, Uruguay, China, Israel, and the Republic of Korea refer to urban areas only.

For additional information, refer to the sources.

15. Population and Health

Population and health data, including those on rates of population growth, total fertility, and infant, child, and maternal mortality reflect a gulf between industrialized and developing countries. In addition, trends in these indicators and in access to safe drinking water, sanitation, child immunization, contraceptives, and education show the progress many countries have made in pursuing health and population policies.

Although most countries' population growth rates have fallen in the past decade, many countries are still growing rapidly because a large portion of the population is in its reproductive years. (See Table 15.1.) Asia's population growth rates have declined by a third in the past 20 years, but the region's population still grows by nearly 50 million each year, just as it did 20 years ago. Population growth rates rose in 34 African countries over the past decade. Africa's population grows by 18 million each year, compared with 4 million in Europe and the USSR combined. Data on births, deaths, fertility, and age structure are shown in Table 15.2; basic health and nutrition indicators are shown in Table 15.3. For an analysis of recent population trends, see Chapter 2, "Population and Health."

Child deaths, the principal component of high mortality in developing countries, have fallen dramatically since the 1960s. (See Table 15.3.) However, rates remain high in Africa and parts of Asia. In 20 developing countries, 20 percent or more of the children born will probably die before their fifth birthday. Globally, over 14 million children under the age of five die each year, most of them from infections complicated by malnutrition. About 20–25 percent of all childhood deaths are caused by diarrheal diseases. Most of these deaths could be prevented by oral rehydration therapy (a simple and inexpensive procedure to restore body fluids) and by ensuring access to safe drinking water and adequate sanitation. (See Table 15.4.) Another 25 percent of childhood deaths could be prevented by immunizing children against infectious diseases, such as tetanus, measles, polio, diphtheria, pertussis (whooping cough), and tuberculosis. (See Table 15.5.) The World Health Organization (WHO) and the United Nations Children's Fund have begun a global campaign to immunize all children against these six diseases by 1990; half of the world's children were immunized by 1987, up from only 5 percent a decade before.

About half a million women (99 percent of them in developing countries) die each year from causes related to pregnancy and childbirth. (See Table 15.5.) High maternal mortality rates reflect lack of access to health services and high-risk patterns of childbearing (women under 15 and over 40 giving birth and lack of spacing between births). In developing countries, maternal deaths account for one quarter to one third of the deaths of women in their childbearing years and contribute to high infant and child mortality rates.

Education is a necessary prerequisite for economic development, but also has important impacts on health and population issues. (See Table 15.5.) The percentage of children in primary school is increasing in most countries, as are adult literacy rates. However, education of females lags behind that of males in many developing countries. Female education is an important force in improving women's status and in the survival of their children. It helps women gain the knowledge and confidence to make use of available health services for their children and themselves and is an important factor in reducing fertility rates.

Contraceptives are used increasingly throughout most parts of the world. In the developing world, contraceptive use is highest in eastern Asia and parts of Latin America, where 50 to 74 percent of women report using some method. (See Table 15.6.) China, the world's most populous country, reports the highest contraceptive use of any developing country. By contrast, in Africa, less than 10 percent of women in the 12 countries surveyed used contraceptives. Over the past decade, use has grown most rapidly in Thailand, Sri Lanka, Hong Kong, and the Republic of Korea, largely because of government and private family planning programs. Many governments promote contraceptive programs as one means of reducing population growth and its demands on social and environmental resources.

Contraceptive use allows women greater control over their fertility and, by enabling child spacing and preventing unwanted births, can reduce both maternal and child mortality rates. According to the World Fertility Survey, if all the women who wanted no more children were able to stop childbearing, births would drop by 35 percent in Latin America, by 33 percent in Asia, and by 17 percent in Africa. WHO estimates that maternal mortality would fall by equivalent amounts because high-risk childbearing and abortions would be reduced. Unmet need figures in Table 15.6 are *minimum* estimates because they do not include women who need contraceptives to space births.

Table 15.1 Size and Growth of Population and Labor Force,

	Population (millions)			Average Annual Population Change (percent)			Average Annual Increment to the Population (thousands)			Average Annual Growth of the Labor Force (percent)		
	1960	1989	2025	1965–70	1975–80	1985–90	1965–70	1975–80	1985–90	1960–70	1970–80	1980–90
WORLD	3,018.9	5,162.4	8,205.8	2.04	1.75	1.63	71,746	74,680	81,913	1.7	2.1	1.9
AFRICA	280.1	626.0	1,616.5	2.62	2.97	3.02	8,848	13,223	18,071	2.2	2.5	2.5
Algeria	10.8	24.7	50.6	2.85	3.06	3.21	365	530	755	0.3	3.2	3.7
Angola	4.8	9.7	24.5	1.52	3.39	2.67	82	241	250	1.2	2.8	1.8
Benin	2.3	4.6	12.7	2.06	2.77	3.12	53	90	137	1.5	2.0	2.1
Botswana	0.5	1.3	4.2	2.54	3.84	3.70	15	32	45	1.2	3.0	3.3
Burkina Faso	4.3	7.7	20.1	1.76	2.02	2.65	86	118	196	1.4	1.8	2.0
Burundi	2.9	5.3	11.8	1.45	1.80	2.84	48	71	144	1.3	1.3	2.2
Cameroon	5.5	11.0	27.8	2.13	2.57	2.80	136	208	297	1.8	1.6	1.9
Cape Verde	0.2	0.4	0.7	3.04	0.87	2.36	8	3	8	3.2	1.0	3.3
Central African Rep	1.6	2.8	6.3	1.63	2.22	2.42	29	48	66	0.9	1.2	1.4
Chad	3.1	5.5	12.4	1.82	2.10	2.44	64	89	130	1.4	1.7	1.9
Comoros	0.2	0.5	1.0	2.43	3.40	3.08	6	12	15	2.1	3.1	2.5
Congo	1.0	1.9	4.7	2.18	2.46	2.73	25	35	51	1.9	2.1	1.9
Cote d'Ivoire	3.7	11.3	30.0	4.15	3.77	3.45	208	281	370	2.9	2.6	2.6
Djibouti	0.1	0.4	1.2	2.42	7.41	3.32	18	96	66	X	X	X
Egypt	25.9	51.4	90.4	2.35	2.69	2.27	733	1,046	1,125	2.0	2.1	2.6
Equatorial Guinea	0.3	0.4	0.9	1.56	1.99	2.31	4	7	10	0.9	1.1	1.4
Ethiopia	24.2	48.7	122.3	2.41	2.32	2.79	695	842	1,306	2.3	2.0	1.9
Gabon	0.9	1.2	2.6	0.97	1.19	2.01	9	12	24	0.5	0.8	0.7
Gambia	0.4	0.7	1.5	2.24	2.15	2.13	10	12	14	1.9	2.0	1.3
Ghana	6.8	15.5	47.0	2.02	3.30	3.36	166	352	497	1.5	2.4	2.7
Guinea	3.7	6.7	15.6	1.95	2.17	2.48	81	111	160	1.5	1.8	1.7
Guinea-Bissau	0.5	1.0	2.0	0.06	5.04	2.08	0	36	20	-0.6	3.9	1.3
Kenya	7.9	24.4	82.9	3.66	4.03	4.20	377	613	963	3.3	3.6	3.5
Lesotho	0.9	1.7	3.9	2.01	2.41	2.61	20	30	42	1.4	2.0	2.0
Liberia	1.0	2.5	7.5	2.73	3.36	3.25	35	58	77	2.4	2.6	2.3
Libya	1.3	4.2	11.1	4.04	4.03	3.67	73	109	145	3.3	3.8	3.6
Madagascar	5.4	11.2	28.1	2.32	2.70	2.90	147	220	313	1.9	2.2	2.0
Malawi	3.5	7.9	21.9	2.56	2.82	3.32	109	157	251	2.1	2.3	2.6
Mali	4.6	9.1	24.1	2.15	2.19	2.94	116	146	256	1.6	1.7	2.6
Mauritania	1.0	2.1	5.8	2.45	2.75	3.08	29	42	63	1.9	1.8	2.8
Mauritius	0.7	1.1	1.6	1.82	1.91	1.65	15	17	18	2.8	2.5	2.9
Morocco	11.6	24.1	40.1	2.78	2.27	2.30	397	415	535	1.9	3.5	3.2
Mozambique	6.5	15.5	37.2	2.28	4.42	2.69	175	481	402	1.8	3.8	2.0
Niger	3.2	6.9	18.9	2.08	2.59	3.01	82	129	199	2.2	1.9	2.4
Nigeria	42.3	109.4	338.1	3.23	3.49	3.49	1,709	2,577	3,629	2.7	3.1	2.7
Rwanda	2.8	6.9	20.2	3.05	3.31	3.36	105	157	222	2.5	3.1	2.8
Senegal	3.0	7.2	17.9	2.89	3.46	2.71	108	180	187	2.6	3.3	1.9
Sierra Leone	2.5	3.9	7.4	1.38	1.59	1.93	38	50	73	0.8	1.0	1.2
Somalia	2.1	5.1	12.2	2.14	4.23	2.11	53	153	103	1.7	3.7	1.7
South Africa	18.3	35.8	76.4	2.27	2.30	2.53	488	622	872	2.8	1.3	2.8
Sudan	11.2	24.2	55.4	2.29	3.08	2.89	300	534	669	1.8	2.7	2.9
Swaziland	0.3	0.7	2.1	2.39	2.90	3.14	10	15	22	1.8	2.1	2.3
Tanzania, United Rep	10.0	26.0	83.8	3.08	3.42	3.65	385	593	900	2.7	2.9	2.9
Togo	1.5	3.3	8.9	4.33	2.52	3.06	79	60	98	2.6	2.1	2.3
Tunisia	4.2	7.7	12.9	2.04	2.61	2.17	99	156	163	1.2	3.7	3.1
Uganda	6.6	17.8	55.2	3.95	3.19	3.49	352	387	590	3.9	2.6	2.8
Zaire	15.9	33.8	90.1	2.11	2.86	3.04	390	690	983	1.3	1.9	2.3
Zambia	3.1	7.6	23.8	2.96	3.08	3.43	115	161	249	2.6	2.7	3.3
Zimbabwe	3.6	10.1	32.7	3.61	3.39	3.61	175	230	347	3.5	2.9	2.8
NORTH & CENTRAL AMERICA	268.6	423.5	625.8	1.60	1.53	1.38	4,954	5,513	5,729	2.0	2.7	1.6
Barbados	0.2	0.3	0.3	0.30	0.28	0.60	1	1	2	-0.1	2.7	1.5
Canada	17.9	26.5	33.3	1.72	1.16	1.01	352	273	264	2.7	3.1	1.2
Costa Rica	1.2	2.9	5.1	3.11	2.96	2.44	50	63	67	3.4	3.9	2.8
Cuba	7.0	10.4	13.6	1.87	0.84	0.98	153	80	100	1.0	3.1	2.3
Dominican Rep	3.2	6.8	12.2	2.80	2.34	2.21	112	123	146	2.2	3.1	3.4
El Salvador	2.6	6.3	15.0	3.52	2.93	3.10	116	131	186	3.5	3.0	3.1
Guatemala	4.0	8.9	21.7	2.77	2.77	2.88	136	179	247	2.5	2.2	2.9
Haiti	3.7	7.3	18.3	2.14	2.38	2.62	94	130	185	1.3	0.9	2.0
Honduras	1.9	5.0	13.3	2.72	3.53	3.10	67	120	147	2.5	3.2	3.9
Jamaica	1.6	2.5	3.7	1.20	1.24	1.52	22	26	37	0.7	2.9	2.8
Mexico	37.1	87.0	154.1	3.25	2.86	2.39	1,535	1,848	2,003	2.7	4.4	3.2
Nicaragua	1.5	3.7	9.2	3.18	2.81	3.36	60	73	120	2.8	2.9	3.8
Panama	1.1	2.4	3.9	2.88	2.26	2.07	41	42	47	3.0	2.5	2.9
Trinidad and Tobago	0.8	1.3	1.9	1.27	1.64	1.59	12	17	20	1.2	2.3	2.4
United States	180.7	246.3	311.9	1.08	1.06	0.86	2,150	2,353	2,082	1.8	2.3	1.1
SOUTH AMERICA	146.8	291.2	498.2	2.45	2.27	2.08	4,408	5,151	5,873	2.5	2.9	2.3
Argentina	20.6	32.4	47.4	1.45	1.61	1.46	336	437	463	1.4	1.0	1.1
Bolivia	3.4	7.1	18.3	2.37	2.59	2.76	97	135	189	1.8	2.1	2.8
Brazil	72.6	147.4	245.8	2.57	2.31	2.07	2,311	2,651	2,961	3.1	3.4	2.2
Chile	7.6	12.8	18.3	1.97	1.47	1.52	177	158	190	1.7	2.5	2.4
Colombia	15.5	31.2	51.7	2.77	2.14	2.05	538	523	621	2.7	2.5	2.7
Ecuador	4.4	10.5	22.9	3.17	2.88	2.79	178	218	281	2.6	2.7	3.0
Guyana	0.6	1.0	1.6	1.90	2.07	1.74	13	17	17	2.1	3.8	2.8
Paraguay	1.8	4.1	8.6	2.52	3.30	2.78	54	96	110	2.4	3.5	3.0
Peru	9.9	21.8	41.0	2.80	2.63	2.51	345	427	527	2.0	3.4	2.9
Suriname	0.3	0.4	0.6	2.28	-0.54	1.46	8	-1	6	2.1	0.5	2.6
Uruguay	2.5	3.1	3.9	0.84	0.56	0.76	23	16	23	0.8	0.2	0.7
Venezuela	7.5	19.2	38.0	3.35	3.42	2.61	327	472	484	2.8	4.9	3.3

1960–2025

Table 15.1

	Population (millions)			Average Annual Population Change (percent)			Average Annual Increment to the Population (thousands)			Average Annual Growth of the Labor Force (percent)		
	1960	1989	2025	1965–70	1975–80	1985–90	1965–70	1975–80	1985–90	1960–70	1970–80	1980–90
ASIA	**1,668.2**	**3,009.1**	**4,535.1**	**2.43**	**1.86**	**1.63**	**48,128**	**46,001**	**47,887**	**2.0**	**2.2**	**2.2**
Afghanistan	10.8	20.2	37.9	2.42	0.87	4.83	310	137	903	2.1	1.5	2.7
Bahrain	0.2	0.5	1.1	2.79	4.87	3.72	6	15	18	2.8	8.6	4.7
Bangladesh	51.6	112.3	219.4	2.66	2.83	2.61	1,659	2,328	2,819	1.5	2.1	2.9
Bhutan	0.9	1.5	2.7	1.90	2.02	2.03	19	25	30	1.6	1.8	1.9
Burma	21.7	40.1	66.0	2.29	2.04	1.89	587	654	738	2.0	2.3	1.9
China	657.5	1,110.8	1,475.2	2.61	1.43	1.18	20,297	13,773	12,859	2.2	2.5	2.2
Cyprus	0.6	0.7	0.9	1.09	0.65	1.01	7	4	7	0.9	1.3	1.1
India	442.3	813.4	1,228.8	2.28	2.08	1.72	11,951	13,631	13,645	1.5	1.7	2.0
Indonesia	96.2	178.5	272.7	2.33	2.14	1.74	2,648	3,058	3,020	2.0	2.1	2.4
Iran	20.3	49.9	97.0	3.30	2.95	2.77	864	1,058	1,325	3.1	3.2	3.3
Iraq	6.8	18.2	43.5	3.19	3.75	3.31	276	454	572	2.7	4.0	3.7
Israel	2.1	4.5	6.9	2.98	2.31	1.65	82	85	73	3.7	2.8	2.3
Japan	94.1	123.3	132.1	1.07	0.93	0.51	1,090	1,057	625	1.8	0.7	0.9
Jordan	1.7	4.1	13.6	3.17	2.34	3.99	67	65	155	2.9	1.0	4.4
Kampuchea, Dem	5.4	8.1	12.3	2.44	-2.07	2.48	159	-139	192	2.2	0.7	1.3
Korea, Dem People's Rep	10.5	22.4	39.6	2.76	2.57	2.36	358	435	511	2.3	2.9	2.9
Korea, Rep	25.0	44.1	61.6	2.40	1.87	1.89	679	569	714	3.2	2.6	2.4
Kuwait	0.3	2.1	4.8	9.17	6.24	4.15	55	74	84	7.8	7.4	5.2
Lao People's Dem Rep	2.4	4.5	8.6	2.60	1.44	2.43	74	51	106	2.0	1.3	2.0
Lebanon	1.9	2.9	5.2	2.75	-0.72	2.13	64	-19	60	2.4	1.2	2.1
Malaysia	8.2	17.0	26.8	2.62	2.24	2.12	266	291	348	2.7	3.8	2.9
Mongolia	0.9	2.1	4.5	3.09	2.82	2.74	36	44	56	2.5	2.9	2.9
Nepal	9.4	18.1	33.9	2.10	2.41	2.28	229	333	397	1.1	1.8	2.3
Oman	0.5	1.4	3.5	2.71	5.01	3.18	17	44	43	2.2	4.6	3.8
Pakistan	50.1	109.7	210.0	2.77	2.84	2.23	1,699	2,282	2,369	2.1	2.8	2.9
Philippines	27.9	59.7	102.8	2.89	2.53	2.25	1,010	1,150	1,295	2.6	2.5	2.5
Qatar	0.0	0.4	0.9	9.28	5.42	5.44	8	11	20	12.0	8.1	5.7
Saudi Arabia	4.1	13.5	36.2	3.62	5.13	3.84	190	424	489	3.3	5.7	4.0
Singapore	1.6	2.7	3.3	1.97	1.30	1.09	39	30	29	3.0	4.4	1.5
Sri Lanka	9.9	17.2	24.4	2.28	1.71	1.48	270	243	249	2.1	2.3	1.6
Syrian Arab Rep	4.6	12.2	31.8	3.23	3.36	3.69	187	272	426	2.2	3.4	3.6
Thailand	26.9	54.8	85.9	3.04	2.34	1.61	1,026	1,026	860	2.9	2.8	2.3
Turkey	27.5	53.6	91.9	2.51	2.11	2.06	834	889	1,071	1.4	1.7	2.2
United Arab Emirates	0.1	1.5	2.7	8.70	13.27	3.46	16	95	50	14.5	18.8	4.0
Viet Nam	34.7	64.8	108.5	2.17	2.41	2.05	878	1,229	1,288	0.9	2.1	2.8
Yemen	4.0	7.7	20.8	1.47	2.49	2.92	69	140	215	1.2	1.0	2.9
Yemen, Dem	1.2	2.4	5.9	2.05	2.36	3.01	29	41	69	1.7	1.7	2.9
EUROPE	**425.1**	**497.2**	**524.0**	**0.64**	**0.42**	**0.27**	**2,894**	**2,029**	**1,348**	**0.6**	**0.7**	**0.6**
Albania	1.6	3.3	5.8	2.68	2.39	2.10	54	61	68	2.3	3.0	2.8
Austria	7.0	7.5	7.3	0.52	-0.04	0.01	38	-2	1	-0.8	0.8	0.6
Belgium	9.2	9.9	10.1	0.36	0.11	0.09	35	11	9	0.3	0.9	0.5
Bulgaria	7.9	9.2	10.1	0.75	0.32	0.38	63	28	35	0.4	0.2	0.0
Czechoslovakia	13.7	15.8	18.2	0.28	0.68	0.32	41	102	50	1.2	0.8	0.4
Denmark	4.6	5.1	4.7	0.71	0.25	-0.01	34	13	0	1.3	1.3	0.5
Finland	4.4	5.0	5.0	0.18	0.29	0.30	8	14	15	0.8	0.8	0.7
France	45.7	55.3	58.4	0.77	0.38	0.31	382	201	171	0.9	0.9	0.8
German Dem Rep	17.2	16.9	17.6	0.06	-0.13	0.15	9	-22	25	-0.4	0.6	0.6
Germany, Fed Rep	55.4	60.4	53.5	0.56	-0.09	-0.18	338	-52	-108	0.3	0.5	0.3
Greece	8.3	10.0	10.8	0.56	1.28	0.41	48	119	41	0.1	0.7	0.5
Hungary	10.0	10.7	10.6	0.40	0.32	-0.07	41	34	-7	1.3	-0.5	0.1
Iceland	0.2	0.3	0.3	1.22	0.91	0.95	2	2	2	2.5	2.9	1.5
Ireland	2.8	3.8	5.3	0.53	1.18	1.26	16	39	47	0.1	1.1	1.6
Italy	50.2	57.5	57.2	0.61	0.44	0.09	324	248	52	0.1	0.5	0.6
Luxembourg	0.3	0.4	0.3	0.43	0.09	-0.10	1	0	0	-0.2	1.6	0.2
Malta	0.3	0.4	0.5	0.35	1.32	0.66	1	5	3	1.2	2.1	1.0
Netherlands	11.5	14.7	14.7	1.17	0.51	0.34	148	71	50	1.5	1.5	1.2
Norway	3.6	4.2	4.3	0.81	0.39	0.17	31	16	7	1.3	2.0	0.8
Poland	29.6	38.3	45.3	0.72	0.89	0.70	232	310	265	2.0	0.7	0.6
Portugal	8.8	10.5	12.3	-1.36	0.95	0.64	-120	92	66	0.0	2.5	0.9
Romania	18.4	23.7	29.2	1.35	0.88	0.68	266	101	160	0.6	0.0	0.7
Spain	30.3	39.5	46.0	1.14	1.00	0.62	373	367	241	0.3	0.8	1.1
Sweden	7.5	8.3	7.7	0.78	0.29	-0.11	62	24	-8	1.3	1.1	0.4
Switzerland	5.4	6.4	5.8	1.35	-0.25	0.04	82	-15	3	1.8	0.3	0.5
United Kingdom	52.6	56.2	55.9	0.35	-0.03	0.02	192	-17	13	0.5	0.5	0.4
Yugoslavia	18.4	23.8	26.8	0.94	0.87	0.63	187	189	148	0.9	0.8	0.9
USSR	**214.3**	**289.3**	**368.2**	**0.91**	**0.93**	**0.93**	**2,152**	**2,420**	**2,641**	**0.6**	**1.6**	**0.7**
OCEANIA	**15.8**	**26.1**	**37.8**	**1.97**	**1.56**	**1.43**	**363**	**343**	**364**	**2.4**	**2.2**	**1.8**
Australia	10.3	16.5	22.6	1.95	1.51	1.25	233	214	202	2.5	2.3	1.7
Fiji	0.4	0.7	1.0	2.29	1.77	1.59	11	11	11	3.5	3.0	2.1
New Zealand	2.4	3.4	4.2	1.41	0.52	0.86	38	16	29	2.2	2.0	1.6
Papua New Guinea	1.9	3.9	7.5	2.40	2.70	2.38	55	78	89	1.8	1.9	2.1
Solomon Islands	0.1	0.3	0.6	2.79	3.01	3.96	22	31	59	X	X	X

Source: United Nations Population Division; and International Labour Organization.
0 = zero or less than half the unit of measure; X = not available.
For additional information, see Sources and Technical Notes.

Table 15.2 Births, Deaths, Fertility, and Age Structure, 1960–90

	Crude Birth Rate (births per thousand population)		Crude Death Rate (deaths per thousand population)		Total Fertility Rate		Percentage of the Population In Specific Age Groups					
							1960			1990		
	1965–70	1985–90	1965–70	1985–90	1965–70	1985–90	0–14	15–64	65+	0–14	15–64	65+
WORLD	**33.9**	**26.0**	**13.3**	**9.9**	**4.86**	**3.28**	**37.0**	**57.7**	**5.3**	**31.9**	**61.9**	**6.2**
AFRICA	**47.7**	**45.2**	**21.5**	**15.1**	**6.60**	**6.22**	**43.6**	**53.3**	**3.1**	**45.3**	**51.7**	**3.0**
Algeria	49.8	41.1	17.4	9.1	7.48	6.15	43.8	52.3	3.9	44.6	52.0	3.4
Angola	49.1	47.2	28.1	20.6	6.38	6.39	41.8	55.4	2.8	44.8	52.2	3.0
Benin	49.5	50.5	28.9	19.4	6.86	7.00	40.7	52.1	7.2	47.5	49.7	2.8
Botswana	53.7	48.8	18.1	11.3	6.48	6.50	47.5	49.1	3.4	49.4	48.5	2.1
Burkina Faso	49.9	47.7	28.1	18.6	6.51	6.50	42.3	54.8	2.9	44.1	53.0	2.9
Burundi	46.5	45.7	25.0	17.4	5.83	6.31	40.4	56.6	3.0	45.6	51.1	3.3
Cameroon	41.9	42.5	20.6	14.5	5.68	5.79	40.5	56.5	3.0	44.0	52.1	3.9
Cape Verde	39.5	33.4	11.1	9.9	5.99	4.41	43.2	52.2	4.6	39.6	56.3	4.1
Central African Rep	43.2	44.3	27.0	20.1	5.69	5.89	38.5	57.4	4.1	43.2	53.0	3.8
Chad	45.2	44.2	27.0	19.9	6.05	5.89	39.6	56.7	3.7	42.8	53.6	3.6
Comoros	47.2	45.2	19.8	14.5	6.29	6.13	44.2	52.8	3.0	46.0	51.1	2.9
Congo	45.1	44.4	23.4	17.2	5.93	5.99	40.9	55.9	3.2	44.0	52.6	3.4
Cote d'Ivoire	43.9	45.2	22.7	14.3	6.63	6.60	40.9	54.4	4.7	46.1	51.0	2.9
Djibouti	X	X	X	X	X	X	X	X	X	X	X	X
Egypt	41.8	32.8	18.3	9.8	6.56	4.30	42.5	54.2	3.3	39.2	56.8	4.0
Equatorial Guinea	41.9	42.4	26.4	19.4	5.66	5.66	37.5	57.6	4.9	42.0	53.9	4.1
Ethiopia	48.7	49.3	24.6	22.3	6.70	6.70	44.5	53.0	2.5	45.3	52.1	2.6
Gabon	31.3	37.3	21.6	17.2	4.07	5.12	32.4	61.7	5.9	36.9	57.1	6.0
Gambia	47.2	48.2	32.5	26.9	6.40	6.39	39.7	56.7	3.6	43.1	53.9	3.0
Ghana	49.3	46.9	19.3	13.4	6.57	6.50	44.6	52.9	2.5	47.1	50.1	2.8
Guinea	48.5	46.6	29.1	21.9	6.41	6.19	41.5	54.2	4.3	43.6	53.4	3.0
Guinea-Bissau	41.2	40.8	26.2	20.0	5.19	5.38	37.4	59.1	3.5	41.3	54.4	4.3
Kenya	56.7	54.2	20.3	12.4	8.10	8.00	49.7	47.7	2.6	52.6	45.6	1.8
Lesotho	42.4	41.2	20.9	15.2	5.71	5.79	40.5	55.6	3.9	42.6	53.8	3.6
Liberia	45.6	48.1	21.2	15.6	6.27	6.90	42.4	54.4	3.2	47.7	49.3	3.0
Libya	49.5	43.9	16.8	9.4	7.48	6.87	43.3	52.7	4.0	45.8	51.8	2.4
Madagascar	43.6	44.1	20.4	15.2	5.83	6.09	41.1	55.9	3.0	44.8	51.8	3.4
Malawi	53.6	53.1	25.5	20.0	6.92	7.00	45.7	51.7	2.6	46.1	51.2	2.7
Mali	51.6	50.1	27.3	20.8	6.58	6.70	43.4	54.0	2.6	46.6	50.7	2.7
Mauritania	49.6	50.0	25.1	19.2	6.87	6.90	43.6	53.7	2.7	47.0	50.2	2.8
Mauritius	32.2	22.8	7.8	5.8	4.25	2.45	46.6	50.9	2.5	30.9	65.1	4.0
Morocco	48.2	32.5	17.4	9.5	7.09	4.31	44.8	52.6	2.6	38.3	58.0	3.7
Mozambique	45.1	45.2	24.1	18.4	5.87	6.09	40.8	56.2	3.0	43.3	53.4	3.3
Niger	49.4	50.9	28.6	20.9	7.10	7.10	41.5	52.8	5.7	47.3	49.9	2.8
Nigeria	52.3	50.5	22.0	15.7	7.10	7.10	45.4	52.3	2.3	48.6	49.0	2.4
Rwanda	50.6	50.7	20.2	17.2	7.00	7.31	44.6	52.9	2.5	48.3	49.2	2.5
Senegal	46.7	46.4	24.6	19.4	6.66	6.50	42.6	54.4	3.0	44.6	52.4	3.0
Sierra Leone	48.0	46.9	34.2	27.6	6.12	6.13	40.2	56.6	3.2	41.9	55.1	3.0
Somalia	46.0	47.7	24.7	22.6	6.60	6.60	41.6	55.4	3.0	45.3	51.7	3.0
South Africa	41.2	37.9	18.6	12.7	5.61	4.94	40.1	55.0	4.9	41.0	55.0	4.0
Sudan	47.0	44.2	23.0	15.4	6.68	6.38	44.3	52.8	2.9	45.1	52.0	2.9
Swaziland	47.4	47.1	20.9	15.8	6.33	6.50	43.3	54.0	2.7	46.5	50.5	3.0
Tanzania, United Rep	51.4	50.3	20.7	13.9	6.87	7.10	46.0	51.1	2.9	49.2	48.5	2.3
Togo	44.2	44.9	20.8	14.4	6.17	6.09	42.4	54.0	3.6	45.3	51.5	3.2
Tunisia	41.8	30.4	15.5	8.7	6.83	4.10	43.4	52.4	4.2	37.4	58.2	4.4
Uganda	49.1	50.1	18.7	15.4	6.91	6.90	46.6	50.8	2.6	48.5	49.0	2.5
Zaire	47.0	44.8	20.5	14.5	5.98	6.09	44.2	52.9	2.9	45.3	51.8	2.9
Zambia	48.9	47.9	19.3	13.7	6.65	6.76	45.2	52.4	2.4	47.7	49.6	2.7
Zimbabwe	47.1	47.0	16.5	11.0	6.61	6.60	45.5	51.8	2.7	48.0	49.3	2.7
NORTH & CENTRAL AMERICA	**24.8**	**21.1**	**9.8**	**8.2**	**3.53**	**2.62**	**34.6**	**57.7**	**7.7**	**27.9**	**62.8**	**9.2**
Barbados	23.8	18.6	8.5	8.6	3.44	2.00	38.1	55.2	6.7	25.3	64.6	10.1
Canada	18.8	14.9	7.5	7.6	2.51	1.75	33.5	59.0	7.5	21.3	67.4	11.3
Costa Rica	38.3	28.5	7.2	4.2	5.80	3.26	47.5	49.5	3.0	36.3	59.6	4.1
Cuba	32.0	18.2	7.4	6.7	4.30	1.97	34.4	60.8	4.8	23.5	68.3	8.2
Dominican Rep	45.5	30.9	13.1	7.1	7.01	3.63	46.8	48.9	4.3	37.8	59.0	3.2
El Salvador	44.9	37.9	12.8	7.0	6.62	5.10	45.1	52.0	2.9	43.4	53.1	3.5
Guatemala	45.6	40.8	15.9	8.9	6.60	5.77	46.0	51.4	2.6	45.4	51.4	3.2
Haiti	43.7	40.8	19.3	12.8	6.15	5.56	40.9	55.2	3.9	43.6	53.1	3.3
Honduras	50.0	39.4	15.9	8.4	7.42	5.59	45.6	52.3	2.1	45.2	51.7	3.1
Jamaica	37.3	26.0	8.0	5.5	5.43	2.86	41.7	54.0	4.3	34.3	59.6	6.1
Mexico	44.2	31.2	10.3	6.5	6.70	3.98	45.6	51.0	3.4	39.1	57.2	3.7
Nicaragua	48.4	41.8	14.7	8.0	7.09	5.50	48.0	49.7	2.3	45.8	51.5	2.7
Panama	39.3	26.7	8.4	5.2	5.62	3.14	43.5	52.5	4.0	35.0	60.2	4.8
Trinidad and Tobago	30.3	24.0	7.5	6.5	3.89	2.68	43.0	53.0	4.0	32.0	62.6	5.4
United States	18.3	15.7	9.5	9.0	2.55	1.91	31.0	59.8	9.2	22.1	65.7	12.2
SOUTH AMERICA	**35.6**	**28.8**	**10.9**	**8.0**	**5.17**	**3.60**	**46.0**	**50.5**	**3.5**	**38.6**	**56.4**	**5.0**
Argentina	22.6	23.2	9.1	8.6	3.04	3.26	30.8	63.7	5.5	31.1	59.9	9.0
Bolivia	45.6	42.8	20.2	14.1	6.56	6.06	42.9	53.9	3.2	43.9	52.9	3.2
Brazil	36.4	28.6	10.8	7.9	5.31	3.46	43.6	53.5	2.9	35.2	60.1	4.7
Chile	30.4	22.0	10.0	6.6	4.12	2.50	39.4	56.3	4.3	28.8	65.3	5.9
Colombia	39.6	29.2	10.4	7.4	5.94	3.58	46.3	50.6	3.1	36.2	59.8	4.0
Ecuador	44.5	35.4	12.8	7.6	6.70	4.65	44.8	51.2	4.0	40.6	55.7	3.7
Guyana	35.4	24.8	7.7	5.4	5.30	2.75	48.5	48.2	3.3	34.6	61.2	4.2
Paraguay	40.4	34.3	10.1	6.8	6.40	4.48	46.0	50.7	3.3	40.9	55.5	3.6
Peru	43.6	34.3	15.6	9.2	6.56	4.49	43.3	53.3	3.4	39.2	57.1	3.7
Suriname	40.0	25.9	8.8	6.1	5.94	2.97	47.6	48.3	4.1	34.4	61.1	4.5
Uruguay	20.5	18.9	9.6	10.2	2.81	2.61	27.9	64.0	8.1	26.2	62.6	11.2
Venezuela	40.6	30.7	7.7	5.4	5.90	3.77	46.1	51.5	2.4	38.3	58.0	3.7

World Resources 1988–89

Table 15.2

	Crude Birth Rate (births per thousand population)		Crude Death Rate (deaths per thousand population)		Total Fertility Rate		Percentage of the Population In Specific Age Groups					
							1960			1990		
	1965–70	1985–90	1965–70	1985–90	1965–70	1985–90	0–14	15–64	65+	0–14	15–64	65+
ASIA	**38.4**	**25.4**	**14.1**	**9.1**	**5.69**	**3.14**	**39.6**	**56.3**	**4.1**	**31.8**	**63.2**	**5.0**
Afghanistan	53.2	47.5	29.1	23.9	7.13	6.65	42.4	55.5	2.1	41.9	55.4	2.7
Bahrain	43.4	29.0	10.1	4.0	6.97	4.14	43.1	54.2	2.7	33.3	64.8	1.9
Bangladesh	47.5	41.7	21.0	15.6	6.91	5.53	40.8	55.2	4.0	44.5	52.6	2.9
Bhutan	41.8	37.0	22.7	16.7	5.89	5.33	40.2	56.6	3.2	39.3	57.3	3.4
Burma	39.1	28.8	16.2	9.9	5.74	3.69	41.1	55.5	3.4	35.4	60.2	4.4
China	36.9	18.4	10.9	6.6	5.97	2.11	38.9	56.3	4.8	25.4	68.7	5.9
Cyprus	21.0	18.3	9.9	8.2	2.78	2.31	36.7	57.4	5.9	26.5	63.9	9.6
India	40.2	28.1	17.5	10.9	5.69	3.69	39.8	56.8	3.4	34.5	60.9	4.6
Indonesia	42.6	28.6	19.3	11.3	5.57	3.48	40.2	56.5	3.3	35.7	60.5	3.8
Iran	48.5	38.5	15.6	10.8	7.55	5.21	47.1	50.8	2.1	41.3	55.4	3.3
Iraq	48.8	40.8	16.9	7.7	7.17	6.05	46.1	51.5	2.4	46.0	51.2	2.8
Israel	25.5	21.3	6.7	7.1	3.79	2.84	36.1	59.0	4.9	29.9	61.3	8.8
Japan	17.8	12.3	6.9	7.2	2.02	1.83	30.2	64.1	5.7	19.2	69.4	11.4
Jordan	48.0	46.4	16.3	6.6	7.17	7.28	44.4	51.5	4.1	48.1	49.4	2.5
Kampuchea, Dem	43.9	41.4	19.4	16.6	6.22	4.71	42.5	54.8	2.7	34.9	62.2	2.9
Korea, Dem People's Rep	38.8	28.9	11.2	5.4	5.64	3.60	43.7	53.0	3.3	37.0	59.2	3.8
Korea, Rep	31.9	23.2	10.4	5.9	4.49	2.50	41.9	54.8	3.3	30.0	65.6	4.4
Kuwait	49.6	34.6	6.3	3.1	7.48	5.74	34.8	63.0	2.2	39.9	58.5	1.6
Lao People's Dem Rep	44.8	38.1	18.9	13.9	6.13	5.41	41.3	56.4	2.3	41.6	55.2	3.2
Lebanon	38.8	28.9	11.8	7.7	6.05	3.38	40.8	53.4	5.8	35.3	59.6	5.1
Malaysia	38.5	27.1	10.4	5.9	5.91	3.30	44.9	50.9	4.2	35.7	60.4	3.9
Mongolia	41.9	34.7	11.2	7.4	5.89	4.82	41.6	54.4	4.0	40.7	55.9	3.4
Nepal	45.5	39.4	23.5	16.7	6.17	5.84	38.4	57.7	3.9	41.9	55.0	3.1
Oman	50.0	44.3	22.7	12.5	7.17	6.87	43.3	54.0	2.7	45.4	52.0	2.6
Pakistan	47.8	40.4	20.2	13.8	7.21	5.33	43.7	51.9	4.4	43.0	54.2	2.8
Philippines	40.2	30.8	10.7	7.6	6.01	3.91	46.9	49.5	3.6	38.7	57.8	3.5
Qatar	37.0	33.6	14.1	4.3	6.97	6.56	39.0	58.3	2.7	36.2	62.0	1.8
Saudi Arabia	48.1	40.6	19.2	7.4	7.26	6.87	43.3	53.4	3.3	44.8	52.6	2.6
Singapore	24.9	16.5	5.6	5.6	3.42	1.65	43.2	54.7	2.1	22.8	71.6	5.6
Sri Lanka	31.5	24.2	8.3	6.1	4.65	2.87	42.1	54.3	3.6	33.6	61.3	5.1
Syrian Arab Rep	47.6	45.4	15.3	7.0	7.79	6.83	44.4	51.8	3.8	48.6	48.8	2.6
Thailand	41.8	23.5	11.4	7.4	6.14	2.73	45.6	51.1	3.3	32.6	63.5	3.9
Turkey	39.6	29.2	13.6	8.4	5.80	3.65	41.2	55.3	3.5	34.6	61.2	4.2
United Arab Emirates	38.6	24.9	12.3	4.2	6.76	5.43	43.7	52.9	3.4	32.6	65.7	1.7
Viet Nam	38.3	29.6	16.6	9.2	6.70	3.69	38.7	57.1	4.2	37.5	58.4	4.1
Yemen	48.8	47.4	26.6	16.4	6.97	6.76	42.4	54.4	3.2	46.7	49.9	3.4
Yemen, Dem	49.0	46.6	25.3	15.7	6.97	6.56	44.8	52.3	2.9	44.5	52.7	2.8
EUROPE	**17.7**	**13.5**	**10.3**	**10.8**	**2.47**	**1.83**	**25.8**	**64.5**	**9.7**	**20.1**	**66.8**	**13.1**
Albania	34.8	26.5	8.0	5.4	5.09	3.32	41.1	53.7	5.2	34.0	61.1	4.9
Austria	17.3	12.4	13.0	12.3	2.53	1.61	22.1	65.9	12.0	18.1	67.2	14.7
Belgium	15.5	12.2	12.4	11.7	2.34	1.60	23.5	64.5	12.0	18.3	67.4	14.3
Bulgaria	15.8	14.9	8.7	11.0	2.16	2.21	26.1	66.4	7.5	22.0	65.3	12.7
Czechoslovakia	15.5	14.6	10.4	11.4	2.09	2.09	27.4	64.0	8.6	23.1	65.3	11.6
Denmark	16.6	10.9	10.0	11.5	2.24	1.47	25.2	64.2	10.6	17.1	67.5	15.4
Finland	16.3	12.6	9.7	10.2	2.06	1.64	30.4	62.4	7.2	19.2	67.8	13.0
France	17.1	13.7	11.1	10.6	2.61	1.83	26.4	62.0	11.6	20.3	66.7	13.0
German Dem Rep	15.1	14.2	13.7	12.8	2.30	1.90	21.1	65.2	13.7	20.4	66.9	12.7
Germany, Fed Rep	16.6	10.6	11.8	12.4	2.34	1.40	21.3	67.9	10.8	15.2	69.7	15.1
Greece	18.0	14.4	8.1	10.3	2.37	2.06	26.5	65.2	8.3	21.1	65.5	13.4
Hungary	14.3	12.1	10.8	12.8	1.99	1.84	25.3	65.7	9.0	20.2	66.3	13.5
Iceland	22.5	16.7	7.0	7.2	3.16	2.04	34.7	57.3	8.0	25.2	64.5	10.3
Ireland	21.5	21.4	11.5	8.8	3.85	2.93	31.1	57.7	11.2	28.8	61.1	10.1
Italy	18.3	11.6	9.7	10.7	2.49	1.60	24.9	65.8	9.3	17.5	68.4	14.1
Luxembourg	14.7	11.0	11.2	12.6	2.22	1.44	21.3	67.9	10.8	17.0	70.0	13.0
Malta	16.6	16.1	9.2	9.4	2.18	1.97	36.8	55.9	7.3	23.8	66.4	9.8
Netherlands	19.2	11.7	8.1	8.8	2.75	1.43	30.0	61.0	9.0	17.9	69.5	12.6
Norway	17.7	11.7	9.7	11.0	2.72	1.57	25.9	63.0	11.1	18.4	65.4	16.2
Poland	16.6	16.4	7.6	9.4	2.28	2.20	33.5	60.7	5.8	24.9	65.1	10.0
Portugal	21.4	16.6	8.1	9.4	2.84	2.09	29.2	62.8	8.0	23.8	65.1	11.1
Romania	21.3	16.9	9.2	10.1	3.06	2.37	28.2	65.1	6.7	24.4	65.4	10.2
Spain	20.5	15.1	8.7	8.9	2.91	2.05	27.4	64.4	8.2	22.6	65.7	11.7
Sweden	15.0	10.1	10.2	11.9	2.12	1.47	22.0	66.0	12.0	16.7	65.6	17.7
Switzerland	17.7	10.8	9.3	10.4	2.28	1.45	23.6	66.3	10.1	16.6	68.6	14.8
United Kingdom	17.6	13.1	11.7	12.3	2.53	1.78	23.3	65.0	11.7	19.0	65.4	15.6
Yugoslavia	19.8	15.2	8.8	8.9	2.49	1.99	30.5	63.2	6.3	22.8	68.0	9.2
USSR	**17.6**	**18.3**	**7.6**	**9.1**	**2.42**	**2.37**	**30.7**	**62.5**	**6.8**	**25.1**	**65.5**	**9.4**
OCEANIA	**24.5**	**20.0**	**10.3**	**8.2**	**3.49**	**2.56**	**32.9**	**59.7**	**7.4**	**26.7**	**64.3**	**9.0**
Australia	19.8	15.6	8.9	7.7	2.88	1.93	30.1	61.4	8.5	22.5	66.7	10.8
Fiji	32.0	27.3	7.6	5.0	4.57	3.19	48.0	49.5	2.5	36.7	59.4	3.9
New Zealand	22.6	15.6	8.7	8.4	3.22	1.86	32.9	58.5	8.6	22.4	66.8	10.8
Papua New Guinea	42.4	35.9	19.1	12.1	6.18	5.25	40.5	56.6	2.9	40.1	56.8	3.1
Solomon Islands	X	X	X	X	X	X	X	X	X	X	X	X

Source: United Nations Population Division.
X = not available.
For additional information, see Sources and Technical Notes.

Table 15.3 Health and Nutrition, 1960–90

	Life Expectancy at Birth (years)		Infant Mortality (infant deaths per thousand live births)		Child Mortality (deaths of children under 5 per thousand live births)		Minimum Daily Calorie Requirement	Daily Calorie Supply as Percentage of Requirement		
	1965–70	1985–90	1965–70	1985–90	1965–70	1985–90		1964–66	1974–76	1983–85
WORLD	**54.8**	**61.1**	**103**	**71**	**161**	**105**				
AFRICA	**43.9**	**51.3**	**158**	**101**	**261**	**163**				
Algeria	51.4	62.5	150	74	230	105	2,400	72	90	113
Angola	36.0	44.0	186	137	312	232	2,350	81	84	X
Benin	38.0	46.0	160	110	270	184	2,300	88	88	93
Botswana	48.5	56.5	110	67	160	92	2,320	88	91	93
Burkina Faso	38.9	47.2	183	139	320	235	2,370	91	91	83
Burundi	44.1	48.5	140	114	237	191	2,330	103	98	95
Cameroon	43.4	52.9	136	94	230	153	2,320	89	100	89
Cape Verde	50.1	61.5	120	63	176	86	2,350	75	93	111
Central African Rep	40.0	45.0	160	132	270	223	2,260	91	99	90
Chad	37.0	45.0	179	132	302	223	2,380	99	73	X
Comoros	45.0	52.0	115	80	193	127	2,340	94	89	89
Congo	40.5	48.5	110	73	184	115	2,220	101	102	114
Cote d'Ivoire	43.0	52.5	164	100	260	148	2,310	102	101	106
Djibouti	X	X	X	X	X	X	X	X	X	X
Egypt	49.7	60.6	170	85	280	124	2,510	97	107	130
Equatorial Guinea	38.0	46.0	173	127	291	214	X	X	X	X
Ethiopia	38.9	41.9	162	149	273	252	2,330	77	68	X
Gabon	43.0	51.0	147	103	250	169	2,340	81	86	X
Gambia	31.6	37.0	199	164	350	281	2,380	90	90	94
Ghana	48.0	54.0	118	90	197	145	2,300	87	96	73
Guinea	35.2	42.2	192	147	321	249	2,310	81	84	75
Guinea-Bissau	38.0	45.0	173	132	291	223	2,310	80	77	X
Kenya	45.4	55.3	108	72	179	113	2,320	98	97	93
Lesotho	43.3	51.3	140	100	194	135	2,280	89	91	103
Liberia	43.0	51.0	167	122	282	206	2,310	94	99	101
Libya	50.4	60.8	130	82	205	118	2,360	83	147	153
Madagascar	43.7	51.5	94	59	153	90	2,270	108	112	109
Malawi	39.5	47.0	197	150	347	263	2,320	91	107	105
Mali	37.0	44.0	206	169	363	291	2,350	83	79	76
Mauritania	39.0	46.0	166	127	281	214	2,310	88	78	90
Mauritius	61.6	68.2	67	23	93	28	2,270	103	113	120
Morocco	50.4	60.8	138	82	220	118	2,420	92	106	111
Mozambique	43.1	47.3	170	141	294	241	2,340	86	83	71
Niger	37.5	44.5	176	135	296	228	2,350	85	83	96
Nigeria	42.5	50.5	172	105	290	173	2,360	95	91	87
Rwanda	44.1	48.5	140	122	237	205	2,320	73	83	87
Senegal	38.7	45.3	168	131	290	222	2,380	104	96	98
Sierra Leone	30.2	36.0	218	169	385	291	2,300	79	84	80
Somalia	38.9	41.9	162	149	273	252	2,310	92	85	89
South Africa	47.5	55.5	120	72	168	96	2,450	107	119	120
Sudan	40.9	50.3	156	106	263	175	2,350	79	91	85
Swaziland	43.5	50.5	147	118	220	173	2,320	89	106	110
Tanzania, United Rep	44.1	53.0	135	106	228	174	2,320	85	97	100
Togo	43.0	52.5	141	93	238	152	2,300	101	91	96
Tunisia	52.1	63.1	138	71	210	99	2,390	94	109	118
Uganda	46.0	51.0	118	103	197	169	2,330	96	100	98
Zaire	44.0	52.0	137	98	232	161	2,220	98	103	97
Zambia	45.3	53.3	115	80	192	127	2,310	91	100	92
Zimbabwe	49.0	57.8	101	72	165	113	2,390	87	89	88
NORTH & CENTRAL AMERICA	**67.5**	**72.0**	**39**	**24**	**55**	**34**				
Barbados	67.6	73.5	46	11	55	14	2,420	108	122	129
Canada	72.0	76.3	21	8	25	9	2,660	122	128	129
Costa Rica	65.6	73.7	66	18	88	22	2,240	104	114	124
Cuba	68.5	74.0	49	15	61	18	2,310	102	115	134
Dominican Rep	55.4	64.6	105	65	158	82	2,260	85	99	109
El Salvador	55.9	67.1	112	59	161	84	2,290	80	90	X
Guatemala	50.1	62.0	108	59	193	99	2,190	93	98	105
Haiti	46.2	54.7	172	117	257	170	2,260	88	86	82
Honduras	50.9	62.6	123	69	195	106	2,260	87	93	98
Jamaica	66.3	73.8	45	18	62	23	2,240	100	119	115
Mexico	60.3	67.2	79	47	113	68	2,330	111	116	135
Nicaragua	51.6	63.3	115	62	173	93	2,250	107	105	X
Panama	64.3	72.1	52	23	82	33	2,310	98	103	105
Trinidad and Tobago	65.7	70.2	41	20	50	23	2,420	103	110	123
United States	70.4	75.0	22	10	26	12	2,640	126	133	138
SOUTH AMERICA	**58.7**	**65.5**	**91**	**57**	**130**	**78**				
Argentina	66.0	70.6	56	32	68	38	2,650	119	124	121
Bolivia	45.1	53.1	157	110	259	171	2,390	77	84	88
Brazil	57.9	64.9	100	63	139	86	2,390	100	104	110
Chile	60.6	70.7	95	20	112	24	2,440	108	107	106
Colombia	58.4	64.8	74	46	119	68	2,320	94	100	111
Ecuador	56.8	65.4	107	63	156	87	2,290	83	89	89
Guyana	62.5	69.8	56	30	74	37	2,270	101	103	110
Paraguay	59.5	66.1	67	42	105	61	2,310	112	118	122
Peru	51.5	61.4	126	88	200	122	2,350	98	97	91
Suriname	63.5	69.6	55	30	72	37	2,260	99	101	118
Uruguay	68.6	71.0	48	27	54	30	2,670	106	110	102
Venezuela	63.7	69.7	60	36	84	43	2,470	94	99	103

Table 15.3

	Life Expectancy at Birth (years)		Infant Mortality (infant deaths per thousand live births)		Child Mortality (deaths of children under 5 per thousand live births)		Minimum Daily Calorie Requirement	Daily Calorie Supply as Percentage of Requirement		
	1965–70	1985–90	1965–70	1985–90	1965–70	1985–90		1964–66	1974–76	1983–85
ASIA	**53.3**	**61.1**	**110**	**74**	**171**	**108**				
Afghanistan	35.4	39.0	203	183	357	318	2,440	90	90	X
Bahrain	60.0	70.6	78	27	109	32	X	X	X	X
Bangladesh	43.3	49.6	140	119	228	188	2,210	91	83	84
Bhutan	40.6	47.9	164	128	260	196	2,310	X	X	X
Burma	49.5	60.0	110	63	160	85	2,160	89	99	117
China	59.6	69.4	81	32	113	44	2,360	86	94	109
Cyprus	70.3	74.6	29	15	34	16	2,480	108	122	X
India	48.0	57.9	145	99	239	148	2,210	89	87	98
Indonesia	45.1	56.0	120	74	201	117	2,160	81	95	116
Iran	53.2	59.0	150	107	224	155	2,410	87	115	X
Iraq	53.0	63.9	111	69	168	94	2,410	89	98	X
Israel	70.8	75.1	25	14	30	16	2,570	109	119	119
Japan	71.1	77.2	16	6	20	8	2,340	112	119	120
Jordan	51.7	66.0	102	44	150	57	2,460	93	96	X
Kampuchea, Dem	45.4	48.4	130	130	193	192	2,220	98	85	X
Korea, Dem People's Rep	57.6	69.4	58	24	76	31	2,340	99	118	134
Korea, Rep	57.6	69.4	58	24	76	31	2,350	96	117	120
Kuwait	64.4	72.7	55	20	73	23	X	X	X	X
Lao People's Dem Rep	45.4	52.0	147	110	221	160	2,220	86	82	X
Lebanon	62.9	67.2	52	39	69	49	2,480	99	103	X
Malaysia	59.4	68.6	50	26	72	35	2,240	101	111	118
Mongolia	58.0	64.5	82	45	116	58	2,430	106	103	116
Nepal	40.6	47.9	164	128	260	196	2,200	87	86	93
Oman	43.8	55.4	186	100	325	157	X	X	X	X
Pakistan	45.5	52.1	145	109	239	165	2,310	76	91	95
Philippines	56.2	63.5	70	45	114	72	2,260	82	94	102
Qatar	59.0	69.2	85	32	120	38	X	X	X	X
Saudi Arabia	49.9	63.7	140	71	228	98	2,420	79	83	128
Singapore	67.9	72.8	24	9	31	11	2,300	97	114	119
Sri Lanka	64.2	70.0	61	33	87	43	2,220	100	93	109
Syrian Arab Rep	54.0	65.0	107	48	160	63	2,480	89	101	129
Thailand	56.7	64.2	84	39	118	49	2,220	95	102	110
Turkey	54.4	64.1	153	76	206	92	2,520	105	118	126
United Arab Emirates	59.0	69.2	85	32	120	38	X	X	X	X
Viet Nam	47.9	60.8	133	67	197	91	2,160	97	94	X
Yemen	40.9	50.9	186	120	325	196	2,420	80	84	93
Yemen, Dem	40.9	50.9	186	120	325	196	2,410	84	79	95
EUROPE	**70.6**	**74.0**	**30**	**13**	**35**	**15**				
Albania	66.2	72.1	77	40	107	48	2,410	102	107	X
Austria	69.9	73.9	27	10	31	12	2,630	126	126	132
Belgium	70.9	74.3	23	10	26	12	2,640	128	134	140
Bulgaria	70.8	72.6	31	15	36	19	2,500	137	141	145
Czechoslovakia	70.1	72.0	23	14	27	16	2,470	139	139	141
Denmark	72.9	75.1	16	7	19	9	2,690	127	125	131
Finland	69.6	74.6	15	6	18	7	2,710	116	116	111
France	71.5	75.2	21	8	24	10	2,520	135	137	132
German Dem Rep	71.3	73.1	21	10	26	12	2,620	122	133	144
Germany, Fed Rep	70.3	74.5	23	9	27	11	2,670	118	123	130
Greece	71.0	74.8	42	15	50	16	2,500	124	139	146
Hungary	69.2	71.3	37	17	41	19	2,630	122	130	134
Iceland	73.4	77.1	13	6	17	7	2,660	118	112	114
Ireland	71.1	73.8	23	9	26	11	2,510	138	139	151
Italy	71.0	75.2	33	11	37	12	2,520	124	137	138
Luxembourg	69.9	71.9	21	8	27	10	X	X	X	X
Malta	69.4	72.7	28	11	31	13	2,480	118	116	104
Netherlands	73.6	76.5	14	7	17	9	2,690	123	128	125
Norway	73.8	76.4	14	7	18	9	2,680	115	116	120
Poland	69.9	72.4	36	17	41	19	2,620	123	132	124
Portugal	66.1	73.0	61	17	80	20	2,450	107	123	128
Romania	68.4	71.1	52	23	60	28	2,650	114	125	128
Spain	71.6	75.0	33	9	37	11	2,460	117	133	136
Sweden	74.1	76.8	13	6	15	7	2,690	117	117	113
Switzerland	72.2	76.5	17	7	20	8	2,690	127	124	128
United Kingdom	71.4	74.5	19	9	22	11	2,520	133	129	124
Yugoslavia	66.6	71.7	61	25	72	28	2,540	128	138	142
USSR	**69.6**	**72.1**	**26**	**22**	**36**	**27**	**2,560**	**126**	**132**	**133**
OCEANIA	**64.2**	**69.1**	**48**	**26**	**67**	**33**				
Australia	70.9	75.7	18	8	22	10	2,660	120	124	126
Fiji	62.7	70.4	55	26	73	31	2,660	93	99	110
New Zealand	71.3	74.5	18	11	22	12	2,640	127	131	129
Papua New Guinea	45.1	54.0	130	62	193	84	2,660	72	78	X
Solomon Islands	X	X	X	X	X	X	2,660	84	77	78

Sources: United Nations Population Division; United Nations Children's Fund; and United Nations Food and Agriculture Organization.
X = not available.
For additional information, see Sources and Technical Notes.

Table 15.4 Drinking Water and Sanitation, 1980–85

	Percentage of Population with Access to Safe Drinking Water						Percentage of Population with Access to Sanitation Services					
	Total		Urban		Rural		Total		Urban		Rural	
	1980	1985	1980	1985	1980	1985	1980	1985	1980	1985	1980	1985
WORLD												
AFRICA												
Algeria	X	68	X	85	X	55	X	57	X	80	X	40
Angola	26	33	85	87	10	15	20	19	40	29	15	16
Benin	18	50	26	80	15	34	16	33	48	58	4	20
Botswana	X	53	X	84	X	46	X	40	X	93	X	28
Burkina Faso	31	67	27	43	31	69	7	9	38	44	5	6
Burundi	23	25	90	98	20	21	35	58	40	84	35	56
Cameroon	X	32	X	43	X	24	X	43	X	100	X	1
Cape Verde	25	52	100	83	21	50	11	10	34	32	10	9
Central African Rep	X	X	X	13	X	X	X	X	X	X	X	X
Congo	20	X	42	X	7	X	X	X	X	X	X	X
Djibouti	45	43	50	50	20	20	39	64	43	78	20	17
Egypt	75	X	88	X	64	X	X	X	X	X	X	10
Equatorial Guinea	X	X	47	X	X	X	X	X	99	X	X	X
Ethiopia	X	16	X	69	X	9	X	X	X	96	X	X
Gambia	X	59	85	97	X	50	X	X	X	X	X	X
Ghana	45	56	72	93	33	39	26	30	47	61	17	16
Guinea	15	18	69	41	2	12	11	X	54	X	1	X
Guinea-Bissau	10	21	18	17	8	22	15	21	21	29	13	18
Kenya	26	X	85	X	15	X	30	X	89	X	19	X
Lesotho	15	36	37	65	11	30	14	15	13	22	14	14
Liberia	X	53	X	100	X	23	X	X	X	6[a]	X	2
Libya	96	X	100	X	90	X	88	X	100	X	72	X
Madagascar	21	31	80	81	7	17	X	X	9	55[a]	X	X
Malawi	41	56	77	97	37	50	83	X	100	X	81	X
Mali	X	16	37	46	X	10	X	19	79	90	X	3
Mauritania	84	X	80	73	85	X	X	X	5	8	X	X
Mauritius	99	100	100	100	98	100	94	92	100	100	90	86
Morocco	X	59	X	100	X	25	X	X	X	62[a]	X	16
Mozambique	X	15	X	38	X	9	X	20	X	53	X	12
Niger	33	47	41	35	32	49	7	X	36	X	3	X
Nigeria	X	38	X	100	X	20	X	X	X	X	X	5
Rwanda	55	50	48	79	55	48	51	56	60	77	50	55
Sao Tome and Principe	X	45	NA	NA	X	45	X	15	NA	NA	X	15
Senegal	43	53	77	79	25	38	36	X	100	87	2	X
Seychelles	X	95	NA	NA	X	95	X	X	NA	NA	X	X
Sierra Leone	14	24	50	68	2	7	12	24	31	60	6	10
Somalia	X	34	X	58	X	22	X	18	X	44	X	5
Sudan	51	X	100	X	31	X	X	X	73	X	X	X
Swaziland	X	31	X	100	X	7	X	45	X	100	X	25
Tanzania, United Rep	X	53	X	90	X	42	X	66	X	93	X	58
Togo	38	54	70	100	31	41	13	14	24	31	10	9
Tunisia	60	70	100	100	17	31	X	55	100	84	X	16
Uganda	X	20	X	37	X	18	X	30	X	32	X	30
Zaire	X	32	X	52	X	21	X	X	X	X	X	9
Zambia	X	58	X	76	X	41	X	55	X	76	X	34
Zimbabwe	X	X	X	X	X	32	X	X	X	X	X	15
NORTH & CENTRAL AMERICA												
Bahamas	100	100	100	100	NA	NA	88	100	88	100	NA	NA
Barbados	99	99	99	100	98	99	X	X	X	100	X	X
Belize	68	64	99	100	36	26	69	66	62	87	75	45
Cayman Islands	X	X	100	98	X	X	X	X	94	96	X	X
Costa Rica	90	91	100	100	82	83	91	95	99	99	84	89
Dominican Rep	60	62	85	85	34	33	15	23	25	41	4	10
El Salvador	50	51	67	68	40	40	35	58	48	82	26	43
Guatemala	46	37	90	72	18	14	30	24	45	41	20	12
Haiti	19	38	51	59	8	30	19	21	42	42	10	13
Honduras	59	49	93	56	40	45	35	30	49	24	26	34
Jamaica	51	96	50	99	46	93	7	91	12	92	2	90
Mexico	73	83	90	99	40	47	55	58	77	77	12	13
Nicaragua	39	48	67	76	6	11	X	27	34	35	X	16
Panama	81	82	100	100	62	64	71	81	83	99	59	61
Trinidad and Tobago	97	98	100	100	93	95	93	98	96	100	88	95
Turks and Caicos Islands	X	77	X	87	X	68	X	X	X	X	X	X
SOUTH AMERICA												
Argentina	54	56	61	63	17	17	X	69	80	75	35	35
Bolivia	36	43	69	82	10	27	18	21	37	33	4	10
Brazil	72	77	83	85	51	56	X	63	X	86	1	1
Chile	84	87	100	98	17	29	83	84	100	100	10	4
Colombia	86	X	93	100	73	76	61	X	93	96	4	13
Ecuador	50	57	79	81	20	31	43	65	73	98	17	29
Guyana	72	76	100	100	60	65	78	86	73	100	80	79
Paraguay	21	28	39	53	9	8	86	85	95	89	80	83
Peru	50	55	68	73	18	17	36	49	57	67	0	12
Suriname	88	83	100	71	79	94	88	62	100	78	79	48
Uruguay	81	85	96	95	2	27	51	59	59	59	6	59
Venezuela	86	89	93	93	53	65	52	50	60	57	12	5

Table 15.4

	Percentage of Population with Access to Safe Drinking Water						Percentage of Population with Access to Sanitation Services					
	Total		Urban		Rural		Total		Urban		Rural	
	1980	1985	1980	1985	1980	1985	1980	1985	1980	1985	1980	1985
ASIA												
Afghanistan	11	21	28	38	8	17	X	X	X	5	X	X
Bahrain	X	100	X	100	X	100	X	100	X	100	X	100
Bangladesh	39	46	26	24	40	49	3	5	21	24	1	3
Bhutan	7	X	50	X	5	19	X	X	X	X	X	X
Burma	21	27	38	36	15	24	20	24	38	33	15	21
Cyprus	X	100	X	100	X	100	X	100	X	100	X	100
India	42	57	77	76	31	50	7	9	27	31	1	2
Indonesia	23	38	35	43	19	36	23	37	29	33	21	38
Iran	66	X	82	X	50	X	69	X	96	X	43	X
Iraq	X	86	X	100	X	54	X	74	X	100	X	11
Jordan	86	96	100	100	65	88	70	X	94	92	34	X
Korea, Rep	75	75	86	90	61	48	100	100	100	100	100	100
Kuwait	87	X	86	97	100	X	100	X	100	100	100	X
Lao People's Dem Rep	21	X	28	X	20	X	5	X	13	X	4	X
Malaysia	63	84	90	96	49	76	70	75	100	100	55	60
Maldives	2	21	11	58	3	12	13	22	60	100	1	2
Nepal	11	28	83	70	7	25	1	X	16	17	1	1
Oman	X	53	X	90	X	49	X	31	X	88	X	25
Pakistan	35	44	72	83	20	27	13	19	42	51	2	6
Philippines	45	52	49	49	43	54	72	67	81	83	67	56
Qatar	71	X	76	X	43	X	X	X	X	X	X	X
Saudi Arabia	90	94	92	100	87	88	70	82	81	100	50	33
Singapore	100	100	100	100	NA	NA	80	99	80	99	NA	NA
Sri Lanka	28	40	65	82	18	29	67	44	80	65	63	39
Syrian Arab Rep	74	X	98	X	54	X	50	X	74	X	28	X
Thailand	63	64	65	56	63	66	45	52	64	78	41	46
Turkey	76	X	95	X	62	X	X	X	56	X	X	X
United Arab Emirates	92	X	95	X	81	X	80	X	93	X	22	X
Viet Nam	X	45	X	70	32	39	X	X	X	X	55	X
Yemen	31	40	100	100	18	25	X	X	60	83	X	X
Yemen, Dem	52	X	85	X	25	X	35	X	70	X	15	X
EUROPE												
Belgium	X	94	X	94	X	91	X	99	X	100	X	80
Czechoslovakia	X	100	X	100	X	100	X	100	X	100	X	100
Finland	X	100	X	100	X	99	X	99	X	99	X	99
France	X	100	X	100	X	100	X	X	X	X	X	X
German Dem Rep	X	100	X	100	X	100	X	71	X	71	X	71
Hungary	X	99	X	100	X	98	X	99	X	100	X	98
Monaco	X	X	X	100	X	X	X	X	X	X	X	X
Netherlands	X	100	X	100	X	99	X	100	X	100	X	100
Poland	X	89	X	100	X	73	X	77	X	100	X	42
Portugal	X	46	X	100	X	22	X	39	X	100	X	11
Spain	X	95	X	100	X	81	X	72	X	73	X	69
Switzerland	X	X	X	100	X	X	X	X	X	100	X	X
United Kingdom	X	100	X	100	X	100	X	100	X	100	X	100
Yugoslavia	X	74	X	91	X	60	X	X	X	X	X	X
OCEANIA												
Cook Islands	X	92	100	99	X	88	X	99	100	100	76	99
Fiji	77	X	94	X	66	X	70	X	85	X	60	X
Niue	X	X	X	X	X	100	X	X	X	X	X	100
Papua New Guinea	16	26	55	95	10	15	15	44	96	99	3	35
Solomon Islands	X	X	96	X	45	X	X	X	80	X	21	X
Tokelau	X	X	X	X	X	100	X	X	X	X	41	
Tonga	17	99	86	99	70	99	19	52	97	99	94	40
Tuvalu	X	X	X	100	X	100	X	X	100	81	80	73
Vanuatu	X	64	65	95	53	54	X	40	95	86	68	25
Western Samoa	X	69	97	75	94	67	X	84	86	88	83	83

Sources: World Health Organization; and United Nations Population Division.
Note: a. Data refer to sewerage only.
0 = zero or less than half of one percent; X = not available; NA = not applicable.
For additional information, see Sources and Technical Notes.

Table 15.5 Maternal and Child Health, 1980–86

	Maternal Mortality 1980–84 (annual deaths from pregnancy-related causes per 100,000 live births)	Percentage of Births Attended by Trained Health Personnel 1984	Percentage of Infants with Low Birth Weight 1982–85	Percentage of Children under 5 Suffering from Malnutrition 1980–86		Percentage of Children Aged 12–23 Months Suffering from Wasting 1980–86	Percentage of One-Year Olds Fully Immunized Against							
				Mild to Moderate	Severe		TB[a] 1981	TB[a] 1986	DPT[b] 1981	DPT[b] 1986	Polio 1981	Polio 1986	Measles 1981	Measles 1986
WORLD														
AFRICA														
Algeria	129	X	9	X	X	X	59	88	33	68	30	68	17	67
Angola	X	15	19	X	X	X	X	59	X	20	X	58	X	44
Benin	1,680	34	10	X	X	14	X	44	X	19	X	19	X	22
Botswana	300	52	8	31	X	19	80	67	64	64	71	60	68	62
Burkina Faso	1,500	X	21	X	X	17	16	67	2	36	2	36	23	68
Burundi	X	12	14	30	5	36	65	80	38	60	6	61	30	57
Cameroon	141	X	13	X	X	X	8	83	5	45	5	42	16	44
Cape Verde	X	X	X	X	X	X	X	X	X	X	X	X	X	X
Central African Rep	600	X	23	X	X	X	26	59	12	24	12	24	16	30
Chad	X	X	11	X	X	X	X	15	X	3	X	3	X	7
Comoros	X	X	X	X	X	X	X	X	X	X	X	X	X	X
Congo	X	X	15	30	X	X	92	91	42	65	42	71	49	86
Cote d'Ivoire	X	X	14	X	X	21	70	16	42	11	34	11	28	31
Djibouti	X	X	X	X	X	X	X	X	X	X	X	X	X	X
Egypt	80	24	7	46	X	X	71	84	82	87	84	86	65	85
Equatorial Guinea	X	X	X	X	X	X	X	X	X	X	X	X	X	X
Ethiopia	X	58	13	60	10	36	10	12	6	6	7	6	7	9
Gabon	124	X	16	X	X	X	X	79	X	48	X	48	X	55
Gambia	X	X	X	X	X	X	X	X	X	X	X	X	X	X
Ghana	1,074	73	17	23	7	28	67	37	22	14	25	13	23	45
Guinea	X	X	18	X	X	X	4	46	X	10	X	8	15	41
Guinea-Bissau	400	X	15	X	X	X	X	47	X	11	X	11	X	34
Kenya	168	X	13	30	2	8	X	80	X	72	X	72	X	65
Lesotho	X	28	10	X	X	7	81	91	56	82	54	80	49	73
Liberia	X	89	X	31	4	7	87	50	39	25	26	25	X	50
Libya	80	76	5	X	X	X	55	77	55	62	55	62	57	50
Madagascar	300	62	11	X	X	X	25	10	40	30	8	30	X	10
Malawi	250	59	10	30	X	28	86	79	66	54	68	55	65	42
Mali	X	X	13	X	X	26	19	15	X	3	X	3	X	5
Mauritania	X	23	10	30	10	X	57	74	18	21	18	21	45	59
Mauritius	52	84	9	17	7	20	87	86	82	84	82	84	X	70
Morocco	327	X	9	40	5	X	X	71	43	53	45	53	X	48
Mozambique	300	28	15	X	X	X	46	45	56	32	32	32	32	39
Niger	420	47	20	17	9	21	28	27	6	4	6	23	19	49
Nigeria	1,500	X	25	24	X	16	23	30	24	14	24	14	55	16
Rwanda	210	X	17	29	8	23	51	86	17	67	15	72	42	55
Senegal	530	X	10	20	X	20	X	32	X	54	X	54	X	40
Sierra Leone	450	25	14	24	3	36	35	80	15	21	13	21	28	66
Somalia	1,100	2	X	16	X	X	3	29	2	18	2	18	3	26
South Africa	X	X	12	X	X	X	X	X	X	X	X	X	X	X
Sudan	X	20	15	33	8	X	3	23	1	14	1	14	1	11
Swaziland	X	X	X	X	X	X	X	X	X	X	X	X	X	X
Tanzania, United Rep	370	74	14	43	7	17	78	82	58	62	49	62	76	67
Togo	84	X	20	X	X	9	44	66	9	41	9	40	47	48
Tunisia	X	60	7	60	4	X	65	80	36	70	37	70	65	65
Uganda	300	X	10	15	4	X	18	51	9	21	8	21	22	33
Zaire	800	X	20	15	5	X	34	45	18	30	18	30	17	30
Zambia	109	X	X	X	X	X	72	82	44	46	77	46	21	55
Zimbabwe	145	69	15	X	X	X	64	76	39	63	38	63	56	53
NORTH & CENTRAL AMERICA														
Barbados	X	X	X	X	X	X	X	X	X	X	X	X	X	X
Canada	2	99	6	X	X	X	X	X	X	X	X	X	X	X
Costa Rica	26	93	9	46	X	X	81	92	83	90	85	90	71	95
Cuba	31	98	9	X	X	X	97	98	67	91	82	88	49	85
Dominican Rep	56	98	15	39	2	X	34	51	27	93	42	82	17	89
El Salvador	74	35	13	52	6	X	47	50	42	70	38	70	44	24
Guatemala	105	X	18	X	X	X	29	30	42	31	42	32	8	42
Haiti	156	20	17	65	5	18	60	57	14	19	3	19	X	21
Honduras	82	50	9	29	2	X	46	67	38	62	37	62	38	55
Jamaica	102	89	8	39	1	14	X	73	39	74	37	74	X	36
Mexico	92	X	15	X	X	X	41	16	41	40	85	92	33	74
Nicaragua	65	X	15	X	X	X	65	95	23	45	52	80	20	51
Panama	90	83	8	48	3	8	77	94	49	73	50	71	53	83
Trinidad and Tobago	81	90	X	48	X	X	X	X	52	70	55	71	X	45
United States	9	100	7	X	X	X	X	X	X	37	X	24	96	82
SOUTH AMERICA														
Argentina	85	X	6	X	X	X	63	89	46	63	38	69	73	67
Bolivia	480	X	13	49	3	X	30	15	13	38	15	31	17	65
Brazil	154	73	8	55	X	X	62	58	47	62	99	86	73	63
Chile	55	95	6	9	X	11	93	100	91	91	93	85	63	91
Colombia	126	51	10	43	8	10	57	77	20	61	22	62	26	51
Ecuador	220	27	X	40	X	X	82	93	26	44	19	44	31	50
Guyana	104	93	20	54	X	X	X	76	45	64	37	67	X	42
Paraguay	469	22	6	X	X	X	42	99	28	54	26	97	16	46
Peru	314	44	9	38	X	X	63	53	18	50	18	50	24	41
Suriname	X	X	X	X	X	X	X	X	X	X	X	X	X	X
Uruguay	56	X	8	X	X	X	76	92	57	70	58	84	95	76
Venezuela	65	82	9	X	X	X	77	92	54	49	75	59	43	56

Table 15.5

	Maternal Mortality 1980–84 (annual deaths from pregnancy-related causes per 100,000 live births)	Percentage of Births Attended by Trained Health Personnel 1984	Percentage of Infants with Low Birth Weight 1982–85	Percentage of Children under 5 Suffering from Malnutrition 1980–86		Percentage of Children Aged 12–23 Months Suffering from Wasting 1980–86	Percentage of One-Year Olds Fully Immunized Against							
				Mild to Moderate	Severe		TB[a] 1981	TB 1986	DPT[b] 1981	DPT 1986	Polio 1981	Polio 1986	Measles 1981	Measles 1986
ASIA														
Afghanistan	640	X	17	20	X	X	8	16	3	9	3	9	6	12
Bahrain	X	X	X	X	X	X	X	X	X	X	X	X	X	X
Bangladesh	600	X	50	63	21	21	1	5	1	5	1	4	X	3
Bhutan	X	3	X	33	6	X	36	32	8	16	7	16	9	15
Burma	135	97	20	50	X	48	15	32	5	20	X	4	X	3
China	44	X	6	X	X	X	X	70	X	62	X	68	X	63
Cyprus	X	X	X	X	X	X	X	X	X	X	X	X	X	X
India	500	33	30	33	5	37	12	29	31	53	7	45	X	1
Indonesia	800	43	14	27	3	17	55	67	X	48	X	46	X	47
Iran	X	X	10	X	X	X	6	75	29	69	47	72	48	73
Iraq	X	60	9	X	X	X	76	78	13	91	16	91	33	75
Israel	5	99	7	X	X	X	70	X	84	85	91	87	69	85
Japan	15	X	5	X	X	X	85	85	X	98	X	98	X	73
Jordan	X	75	7	X	X	9	0	2	81	53	87	54	40	39
Kampuchea, Dem	X	X	X	32	5	X	X	54	X	37	X	35	X	54
Korea, Dem People's R	41	99	X	X	X	X	52	53	52	61	51	62	31	44
Korea, Rep	34	X	9	X	X	X	42	47	61	76	62	80	5	88
Kuwait	18	99	7	X	X	3	X	4	54	90	76	90	66	5
Lao People's Dem Rep	X	X	15	38	X	X	4	11	7	8	7	8	7	4
Lebanon	X	45	10	X	X	X	X	4	X	30	X	30	X	30
Malaysia	59	82	10	X	X	6	91	99	59	68	61	68	X	48
Mongolia	140	99	10	X	X	X	53	52	99	81	99	86	X	10
Nepal	850	10	X	50	7	27	32	67	16	38	1	34	2	66
Oman	X	60	14	X	X	X	49	90	9	84	9	84	6	76
Pakistan	600	24	27	60	10	14	11	68	3	55	3	55	2	40
Philippines	80	X	18	18	4	14	61	72	51	55	44	55	X	53
Qatar	X	X	X	X	X	X	X	X	X	X	X	X	X	X
Saudi Arabia	X	78	6	X	X	9	49	88	53	84	52	84	12	79
Singapore	11	100	8	X	X	9	83	72	87	78	88	81	57	73
Sri Lanka	90	87	25	X	X	22	58	76	45	77	46	77	X	47
Syrian Arab Rep	280	37	9	23	2	X	36	82	14	73	14	73	14	70
Thailand	270	33	12	27	X	18	71	83	52	62	31	62	X	39
Turkey	207	78	7	X	X	X	42	24	64	45	69	45	52	36
United Arab Emirates	X	96	7	X	X	X	18	88	45	72	45	73	42	66
Viet Nam	110	99	18	39	13	12	X	57	X	43	X	44	X	37
Yemen	X	12	9	54	4	17	15	28	25	16	25	16	40	19
Yemen, Dem	100	10	12	32	8	36	9	12	5	6	5	5	6	6
EUROPE														
Albania	X	X	7	X	X	X	93	92	94	96	92	94	90	96
Austria	11	X	6	X	X	X	90	90	90	90	90	90	90	25
Belgium	10	100	5	X	X	X	X	X	95	95	99	95	50	X
Bulgaria	22	100	6	X	X	X	97	99	97	99	98	99	98	99
Czechoslovakia	8	100	6	X	X	X	95	99	95	99	95	99	95	98
Denmark	4	X	6	X	X	X	95	85	85	94	97	94	X	X
Finland	5	X	4	X	X	X	90	90	92	94	90	78	70	81
France	13	X	5	X	X	X	80	96	79	97	80	97	X	55
German Dem Rep	17	X	6	X	X	X	95	99	80	94	90	94	95	99
Germany, Fed Rep	11	X	5	X	X	X	40	30	50	30	80	80	35	25
Greece	12	X	6	X	X	X	95	56	95	54	95	96	X	77
Hungary	28	99	10	X	X	X	99	99	99	99	98	99	99	99
Iceland	X	X	X	X	X	X	X	X	X	X	X	X	X	X
Ireland	7	X	4	X	X	X	X	80	36	45	76	90	X	63
Italy	13	X	7	X	X	X	X	50	X	12	X	90	X	12
Luxembourg	X	X	X	X	X	X	X	X	X	X	X	X	X	X
Malta	X	X	X	X	X	X	X	X	X	X	X	X	X	X
Netherlands	5	X	4	X	X	X	X	X	97	97	97	97	93	93
Norway	4	100	4	X	X	X	X	90	X	85	X	90	X	90
Poland	12	X	8	X	X	X	95	95	95	96	95	97	65	95
Portugal	15	X	8	X	X	X	74	82	75	76	16	77	70	66
Romania	175	99	6	X	X	X	X	X	X	95	X	92	X	88
Spain	10	96	X	X	X	X	X	X	X	87	X	87	X	79
Sweden	4	100	4	X	X	X	X	14	99	99	99	98	56	92
Switzerland	5	X	5	X	X	X	X	X	X	X	X	X	X	X
United Kingdom	7	98	7	X	X	X	X	5	44	60	71	78	52	62
Yugoslavia	27	X	7	X	X	X	99	85	90	89	95	90	95	91
USSR	X	100	6	X	X	X	X	93	95	85	95	99	95	95
OCEANIA														
Australia	11	99	6	X	X	X	X	X	X	X	X	X	X	68
Fiji	X	X	X	X	X	X	X	X	X	X	X	X	X	X
New Zealand	20	99	5	X	X	X	X	20	72	72	X	83	X	71
Papua New Guinea	1,000	34	25	38	X	X	64	78	31	43	31	37	X	29
Solomon Island	X	X	X	X	X	X	X	X	X	X	X	X	X	X

Source: United Nations Children's Fund.
Notes:
a. TB = tuberculosis.
b. DPT = diphtheria, pertussis (whooping cough), and tetanus.
0 = zero or less than half the unit of measure; X = not available.
For additional information, see Sources and Technical Notes.

Table 15.6 Education, 1970–86

	Adult Literacy Rate				Secondary School Enrollment as a Percentage of Age Group 1983–86		Primary School Enrollment as a Percentage of Age Group				Percentage of First Grade Enrollment Completing Primary School 1980–86
	Female		Male				Female		Male		
	1970	1985	1970	1985	Female	Male	1960	1986	1960	1986	
WORLD											
AFRICA											
Algeria	11	37	39	63	X	X	37	83	55	104	83
Angola	7	X	16	49	X	X	X	121	X	146	24
Benin	8	16	23	37	12	29	15	43	38	87	15
Botswana	44	69	37	73	31	27	48	109	35	98	80
Burkina Faso	3	6	13	21	3	7	5	24	12	41	75
Burundi	10	26	29	43	3	5	9	44	27	61	94
Cameroon	19	55	47	68	18	29	43	97	87	116	70
Cape Verde	X	X	X	X	X	X	X	X	X	X	X
Central African Rep	6	29	26	53	8	24	12	51	53	98	53
Chad	2	11	20	40	2	11	4	21	29	55	29
Comoros	X	X	X	X	X	X	X	X	X	X	X
Congo	19	55	50	71	X	X	53	X	103	X	74
Cote d'Ivoire	10	31	26	53	12	27	24	65	68	92	89
Djibouti	X	X	X	X	X	X	X	X	X	X	X
Egypt	20	30	50	59	52	73	52	76	80	94	64
Equatorial Guinea	X	X	X	X	X	X	X	X	X	X	X
Ethiopia	1	X	8	X	9	14	3	28	11	44	41
Gabon	22	53	43	70	20	30	X	121	X	124	59
Gambia	X	X	X	X	X	X	X	X	X	X	X
Ghana	18	43	43	64	27	45	25	59	52	75	75
Guinea	7	17	21	40	6	18	16	19	44	42	37
Guinea-Bissau	6	17	13	46	4	18	15	40	35	81	18
Kenya	19	49	44	70	16	25	30	91	64	97	62
Lesotho	74	84	49	62	26	18	102	127	63	102	27
Liberia	8	23	27	47	13	33	18	50	45	82	X
Libya	13	50	60	81	X	X	24	X	92	X	82
Madagascar	43	62	56	74	30	43	45	118	58	125	30
Malawi	18	31	42	52	2	6	45	53	X	71	28
Mali	4	11	11	23	4	10	6	17	14	29	25
Mauritania	X	X	X	X	6	19	3	29	13	45	80
Mauritius	59	77	77	89	49	53	93	106	103	105	X
Morocco	10	22	34	45	25	38	27	63	67	98	70
Mozambique	14	22	29	55	4	9	36	74	60	94	26
Niger	2	9	6	19	3	9	3	20	7	37	67
Nigeria	14	31	35	54	X	X	27	81	46	103	31
Rwanda	21	33	43	61	2	3	30	63	68	66	47
Senegal	5	19	18	37	9	18	17	45	36	66	86
Sierra Leone	8	21	18	38	11	23	15	48	30	68	48
Somalia	1	6	5	18	12	23	5	18	13	32	33
South Africa	X	X	X	X	X	X	85	X	94	X	X
Sudan	6	14	28	33	13	19	14	49	35	57	61
Swaziland	X	X	X	X	X	X	X	X	X	X	X
Tanzania, United Rep	18	88	48	93	3	5	18	81	33	79	76
Togo	7	28	27	53	10	33	24	73	63	118	43
Tunisia	17	41	44	68	33	46	43	108	88	127	78
Uganda	30	45	52	70	5	11	32	50	X	66	58
Zaire	22	45	61	79	33	81	32	84	88	112	65
Zambia	37	67	66	84	13	23	34	96	51	106	85
Zimbabwe	47	67	63	81	38	56	X	126	X	132	79
NORTH & CENTRAL AMERICA											
Barbados	X	X	X	X	X	X	X	X	X	X	X
Canada	X	X	X	X	103	102	105	104	108	106	X
Costa Rica	87	93	88	94	43	39	95	100	97	101	75
Cuba	87	96	86	96	88	82	109	101	109	108	86
Dominican Rep	65	77	69	78	X	X	98	X	99	X	88
El Salvador	53	69	61	75	X	X	77	X	82	X	68
Guatemala	37	47	51	63	X	X	39	X	50	X	38
Haiti	17	35	26	40	17	19	42	72	50	83	45
Honduras	50	58	55	61	X	X	67	102	68	103	27
Jamaica	97	93	96	90	60	56	93	107	92	106	80
Mexico	69	88	78	92	54	56	77	114	82	116	66
Nicaragua	57	X	58	X	X	X	66	X	65	X	27
Panama	81	88	81	89	63	56	94	102	98	107	73
Trinidad and Tobago	89	95	95	97	79	74	87	96	89	93	78
United States	99	X	99	X	98	99	X	101	X	101	X
SOUTH AMERICA											
Argentina	92	95	94	96	75	66	99	108	98	107	66
Bolivia	46	65	68	84	34	40	50	85	78	96	32
Brazil	63	76	69	79	X	X	93	99	97	108	20
Chile	88	96	90	97	69	63	107	106	111	108	33
Colombia	76	87	79	89	51	50	77	119	77	116	37
Ecuador	68	80	75	85	53	51	79	117	87	117	50
Guyana	89	95	94	97	X	X	106	X	107	X	84
Paraguay	75	85	84	91	30	31	90	98	105	104	48
Peru	60	78	81	91	61	68	71	120	95	125	51
Suriname	X	X	X	X	X	X	X	X	X	X	X
Uruguay	93	94	93	93	X	X	111	109	111	111	88
Venezuela	71	85	79	88	50	41	100	108	100	109	68

World Resources 1988–89

Table 15.6

	Adult Literacy Rate				Secondary School Enrollment as a Percentage of Age Group 1983–86		Primary School Enrollment as a Percentage of Age Group				Percentage of First Grade Enrollment Completing Primary School 1980–86
	Female		Male		Female	Male	Female		Male		
	1970	1985	1970	1985			1960	1986	1960	1986	
ASIA											
Afghanistan	2	8	13	39	5	11	2	11	15	24	54
Bahrain	X	X	X	X	X	X	X	X	X	X	X
Bangladesh	12	22	36	43	10	26	26	50	66	70	20
Bhutan	X	X	X	X	1	6	X	18	5	32	25
Burma	57	X	85	X	X	X	52	X	61	X	27
China	X	56	X	82	32	45	X	114	X	132	66
Cyprus	X	X	X	X	X	X	X	X	X	X	X
India	20	29	47	57	24	45	40	76	80	107	38
Indonesia	42	65	66	83	34	45	58	116	86	121	80
Iran	17	39	40	62	37	54	27	101	56	122	70
Iraq	18	87	50	90	39	69	36	92	94	108	65
Israel	83	93	93	97	80	73	97	101	99	98	X
Japan	99	X	99	X	97	95	102	102	103	101	100
Jordan	29	63	64	87	78	80	59	99	94	98	97
Kampuchea, Dem	23	65	X	85	20	45	X	80	X	100	50
Korea, Dem People's Rep	X	X	X	X	X	X	X	X	X	X	X
Korea, Rep	81	88	94	96	93	98	89	94	99	94	94
Kuwait	42	63	65	76	80	85	102	99	131	102	98
Lao People's Dem Rep	28	76	37	92	15	23	16	79	34	101	14
Lebanon	58	69	79	86	56	57	99	95	105	105	66
Malaysia	48	66	71	81	53	52	83	99	108	100	97
Mongolia	74	86	87	93	92	84	78	106	79	104	95
Nepal	3	12	23	39	19	51	1	44	19	80	27
Oman	X	12	X	47	21	43	X	80	X	97	60
Pakistan	11	19	30	40	8	21	13	33	46	66	34
Philippines	80	85	83	86	66	63	93	106	98	105	64
Qatar	X	X	X	X	X	X	X	X	X	X	X
Saudi Arabia	2	12	15	35	33	51	2	61	22	77	79
Singapore	55	79	82	93	73	70	101	113	121	118	90
Sri Lanka	69	83	85	91	67	60	90	102	100	105	91
Syrian Arab Rep	20	43	60	76	49	72	39	101	89	116	67
Thailand	72	88	86	94	35	35	79	93	88	93	64
Turkey	35	62	69	86	31	53	58	112	90	119	85
United Arab Emirates	7	38	24	58	65	53	X	99	X	99	97
Viet Nam	X	80	X	88	41	44	X	94	X	107	50
Yemen	1	3	9	27	3	17	X	22	14	112	15
Yemen, Dem	9	25	31	59	11	26	5	35	20	96	40
EUROPE											
Albania	X	X	X	X	64	74	86	95	102	99	X
Austria	X	X	X	X	81	77	104	98	106	100	95
Belgium	99	X	99	X	97	94	108	96	111	94	75
Bulgaria	89	X	94	X	91	90	92	101	94	102	87
Czechoslovakia	X	X	X	X	X	X	93	98	93	97	94
Denmark	X	X	X	X	103	104	103	99	103	98	99
Finland	X	X	X	X	110	95	95	103	100	104	X
France	98	X	99	X	87	80	143	106	144	108	95
German Dem Rep	X	X	X	X	77	80	113	100	111	102	X
Germany, Fed Rep	X	X	X	X	75	73	X	96	X	96	96
Greece	76	88	93	97	84	87	101	106	104	106	93
Hungary	98	X	98	X	72	71	100	99	103	98	93
Iceland	X	X	X	X	X	X	X	X	X	X	X
Ireland	X	X	X	X	101	91	112	100	107	100	X
Italy	93	96	95	98	73	74	109	99	112	99	100
Luxembourg	X	X	X	X	X	X	X	X	X	X	X
Malta	X	X	X	X	X	X	X	X	X	X	X
Netherlands	X	X	X	X	100	103	104	96	105	94	95
Norway	X	X	X	X	100	95	100	97	100	97	100
Poland	97	X	98	X	79	73	107	100	110	102	94
Portugal	65	80	78	89	51	43	129	119	132	120	88
Romania	91	X	96	X	76	74	95	97	101	98	X
Spain	87	92	93	97	91	88	116	107	106	108	95
Sweden	X	X	X	X	88	79	96	99	95	97	98
Switzerland	X	X	X	X	X	X	118	X	118	X	99
United Kingdom	X	X	X	X	87	83	92	103	92	103	X
Yugoslavia	76	86	92	97	80	84	108	96	113	96	98
USSR	**97**	**X**	**98**	**X**	**X**	**X**	**100**	**X**	**100**	**X**	**X**
OCEANIA											
Australia	X	X	X	X	97	94	103	105	103	106	X
Fiji	X	X	X	X	X	X	X	X	X	X	X
New Zealand	X	X	X	X	86	84	106	106	110	107	X
Papua New Guinea	24	35	39	55	8	15	7	55	59	68	67
Solomon Island	X	X	X	X	X	X	X	X	X	X	X

Source: United Nations Children's Fund.
X = not available.
For additional information, see Sources and Technical Notes.

Table 15.7 Contraceptive Prevalence and Unmet Need, 1961–87

	Date of Survey	Any Method	Sterilization	Pill	Injectable	IUD	Condom	Vaginal Barriers	Traditional Methods[b]	Unmet Need for Contraception[a] (percent) Low Estimate	High Estimate	Desired Number of Children
AFRICA												
Benin	1981/82	9.2	0.0	0.2	0.0	0.1	0.1	0.1	8.7	3	X	X
Botswana	1984	27.8	1.5	10.0	1.0	4.8	1.2	0.1	9.2	5	X	X
Burundi	1987[c]	8.7	0.1	0.2	0.5	0.3	0.1	0.0	7.6	X	X	X
Cameroon	1978	2.4	X	0.2	X	0.2	0.2	0.0	1.8	1	1	X
Cote d'Ivoire	1980/81	2.9	0.0	0.4	0.0	0.1	0.0	0.0	2.4	2	3	X
Egypt	1974/75	24.9	X	19.9	0.0	2.5	X	X	2.4[d]	X	21	4.1
	1980	24.2	0.8	16.5	0.1	4.0	1.1	0.2	1.4	X	X	X
	1984	29.7	1.5	16.5	0.3	8.4	1.3	0.7	1.0	X	X	X
Ghana	1979/80	9.5	0.5	2.4	0.1	0.3	0.6	1.6	4.0	5	8	6.1
Kenya	1977/78	6.7	0.8	2.0	0.6	0.7	0.1	0.0	2.5	6	10	7.2
	1984	17.0	2.6	3.1	0.5	3.0	0.3	0.1	7.3	X	X	X
Lesotho	1977	5.3	0.8	1.2	0.2	0.1	0.1	0.0	2.8	5	9	5.9
Liberia	1986[c]	6.5	1.1	3.4	0.3	0.6	0.1	0.2	0.9	X	X	X
Mauritania	1981	0.8	0.2	0.0	0.0	0.0	0.0	0.1	0.5[i]	6	X	9.2
Mauritius	1975	45.7[e]	X	21.0	1.6	1.5	5.1	X	16.4[f]	X	X	X
	1985	75.4	4.7	21.0	6.2	2.3	10.8	0.6	29.8	3	X	X
Morocco	1980	19.7	0.8	13.9	0.0	1.6	0.3	0.0	3.0	11	X	X
	1983/84	25.5	1.7	16.8	X	2.0	0.4	0.3	4.3	X	X	X
	1987[c]	35.9	2.2	22.9	0.3	2.9	0.5	0.1	6.9	X	X	X
Nigeria	1981	4.8	0.1	0.2	0.2	0.1	0.0	X	4.1	2	X	X
Rwanda	1983	10.1	0.0	0.2	0.4	0.3	0.0	0.0	9.3	X	X	X
Senegal	1978	3.8	0.0	0.3	0.0	0.2	0.1	0.0	3.2	X	X	X
	1986[c]	11.7	0.2	1.4	0.1	0.8	0.1	0.1	9.0	X	X	X
South Africa	1981	48.0	8.0	15.0	14.0	6.0	3.0[f]	X	3.0	X	X	X
Sudan	1978/79	4.6	0.3	3.1	0.0	0.1	0.1	0.1	0.9	6	9	6.3
Tunisia	1978	31.4	7.5	6.6	0.3	8.8	1.3	0.6	6.3	X	X	X
	1983	41.1	12.5	5.3	0.4	13.2	1.3	1.5	6.9	10	19	X
Zimbabwe	1984	38.4	1.7	22.6	0.8	0.7	0.7	0.1	11.8	X	X	X
NORTH & CENTRAL AMERICA												
Barbados	1980/81	46.5	14.6	15.8	2.2	4.0	5.4	2.6	1.9	X	19	2.4
Canada	1984	73.1	43.5	11.0	X	5.8	7.9	1.5	3.6	X	X	X
Costa Rica	1976	64.4	13.3	22.5	2.0	5.2	8.8	1.7	10.9	X	X	X
	1981	65.2	17.8	20.6	2.2	5.7	8.4	1.2	0.0	6	11	4.7
	1986	69.5	14.4	20.7	1.0	8.0	13.4	0.7	11.3	X	X	X
Cuba	1982	60.0	0.0	7.0	0.0	37.0	7.0	0.0	9.0	X	X	X
Dominican Rep	1975	31.7	12.0	7.9	0.2	2.8	1.5	1.6	5.8	12	21	4.6
	1986	50.0	33.0	8.8	0.1	3.0	1.4	0.4	3.3	X	X	X
El Salvador	1975	19.3	8.6	6.5	0.4	2.0	0.5	X	1.3	X	X	X
	1985	47.3	32.5	6.6	0.7	3.3	1.2	0.2	2.8	X	X	X
Guatemala	1978	18.1[g]	6.3	5.4	1.1	1.3	0.7	0.4	2.9	X	X	X
	1983	25.0[g]	11.1	4.7	0.0	2.6	1.2	1.0	4.4	21	X	X
Haiti	1977	18.9	0.3	3.5	X	0.4	1.1	0.1	13.5	13	30	3.5
	1987	23.2	11.3	4	0.5	1.8	1.1	0.4	4.1	X	X	X
	1983	6.9	0.8	2.2	0.2	0.2	0.5	0.0	3.0	X	X	X
Honduras	1981	26.9	8.2	11.7	0.3	2.4	0.3	0.6	3.2	9	21	X
	1984	34.9	12.3	12.7	0.3	3.8	0.9	0.4	4.6	X	X	X
Jamaica	1975/76	38.3	13.4	11.8	6.2	2.0	6.6	1.5	2.1	X	X	X
	1983	51.4[g]	10.9	19.3	7.6	2.0	7.6	1.0	3.0	18	X	4.3
Mexico	1976	30.3	2.9	10.8	1.7	5.7	0.8	1.4	7.1	X	X	X
	1979	38.9	9.2	13.1	2.6	6.1	0.9	1.1	5.9	14	22	4.5
	1982	47.7	13.7	14.2	5.1	6.6	0.9	1.0	6.1	X	X	X
Nicaragua	1981	27.0	7.2	10.5	1.4	2.3	0.8	0.6	4.4	X	X	X
Panama	1976	54.1	21.6	17.2	0.7	3.7	1.2	1.8	8.1	X	X	X
	1984	58.2[g]	32.8	11.8	0.8	6.0	1.6	1.2	4.0	13	X	4.2
Trinidad and Tobago	1970/71	43.6[h]	2.1	17.1	X	3.0	9.8	4.5	9.2	X	X	X
	1977	51.6	4.5	18.0	1.0	2.2	15.0	5.0	5.9	14	19	3.8
United States	1965	63.2	7.9	15.1	0.0	0.8	13.9	8.3	17.3	X	X	X
	1976	67.8	18.5	22.5	0.0	6.3	7.3	5.9	7.1	X	X	X
	1982	68.0	27.8	13.5	0.0	4.8	9.8	6.5	5.5	X	X	X
SOUTH AMERICA												
Bolivia	1983	26.0	3.0	3.0	1.0	4.0	0.0	1.0	15.0	X	X	X
Brazil	1986[c]	65.3	28.2	25.0	0.0	0.9	1.6	0.5	9.3	X	X	X
Colombia	1969	20.5	1.4	4.8	0.0	2.7	X	X	11.5[i]	X	X	X
	1976	42.5	4.2	13.3	0.4	8.5	1.7	2.3	12.0	X	X	X
	1980	48.5	10.9	17.4	X	8.1	4.6[f]	X	0.0	7	24	4.1
	1986[c]	63.2	17.8	16.5	2.4	10.3	1.5	2.3	12.3	X	X	X
Ecuador	1979	33.6	8.0	9.5	0.8	4.8	1.0	1.6	7.9	13	26	X
	1982	39.9	12.4	10.3	0.7	6.4	1.1	2.0	7.0	X	X	X
	1987[c]	44.2	15.0	8.4	0.7	9.8	0.6	1.2	8.4	X	X	X
Guyana	1975	31.4	8.6	9.0	0.3	5.6	2.9	1.9	3.1	23	29	4.6
Paraguay	1977	28.6[g]	3.2	11.8	0.9	4.0	2.6	0.8	5.2	X	X	X
	1979	36.4	2.2	11.9	1.7	5.4	1.5	0.8	0.0	9	17	X
	1987[c]	44.8	4.0	13.5	3.6	5.1	2.3	0.5	15.8	X	X	X
Peru	1969/70	26.0	2.0	3.0	X	1.0	3.0	1.0	16.0	X	X	X
	1981	41.0	4.0	5.0	2.0	4.0	1.0	1.0	24.0	13	41	3.8
	1986[c]	45.8	6.2	6.5	1.4	7.4	0.7	0.9	22.8	X	X	X
Venezuela	1977	49.3	7.7	15.3	0.2	8.6	4.8	1.1	11.5	10	22	4.2
ASIA												
Afghanistan	1972/73	1.6	0.0	1.0	0.0	0.4	0.2	X	0.2[f]	X	X	X
Bangladesh	1976	7.7	0.8	2.8	0.0	0.4	0.8	0.0	2.9	X	X	X
	1983	19.1	7.4	3.3	0.2	1.0	1.5	0.3	5.5	25	28	4.1
	1985	25.2	9.3	5.1	0.5	1.4	1.8	0.2	6.9	X	X	X

Table 15.7

	Date of Survey	Percentage of Married Couples Currently Using								Unmet Need for Contraception[a] (percent)		Desired Number of Children
		Any Method	Sterilization	Pill	Injectable	IUD	Condom	Vaginal Barriers	Traditional Methods[b]	Low Estimate	High Estimate	
China	1982	70.6	25.0	6.0	X	35.4	1.4	X	2.8[f]	X	X	X
	1985	74.0	36.0	5.0	X	30.0	2.0	1.0	1.0	X	X	X
Hong Kong	1967	42.0	X	X	X	X	X	X	0.0	X	X	X
	1972	49.6	11.4	17.9	1.5	5.0	3.5	4.0	3.5	X	X	X
	1977	71.9	18.7	23.0	2.2	2.9	12.9	4.3	0.7	X	X	X
India	1970	13.6	6.3	0.3	X	0.7	2.6	0.1	4.1	X	X	X
	1980	34.1	21.4	0.9	X	0.4	4.2	X	7.1[f]	X	X	X
	1982	34.0	22.0	1.0	0.0	1.0	5.0	0.0	6.0	X	X	X
Indonesia	1976	18.3[h]	0.1	11.6	X	4.1	1.5	X	2.1[j]	10	15	4.1
	1980	26.8	0.0	14.3	X	6.7	0.9	X	4.9[f,j]	X	X	X
	1985	38.5	1.6	15.4	7.4	11.9	0.6	X	1.6[f]	X	X	X
Iraq	1974	14.5	0.6	8.7	0.6	0.6	1.4	1.0	1.7	X	X	X
Japan	1961	42.3	X	X	0.0	X	X	X	X	X	X	X
	1971	52.6[h]	2.1	0.8	0.0	4.3	38.9	2.9	20.7	X	X	X
	1979	62.2[h]	2.5	2.0	0.0	5.2	50.4	1.4	18.6	X	X	X
	1986	64.3	9.9	1.0	0.0	3.5	44.6	0.7	18.2	X	X	X
Jordan	1972	22.3[h]	1.0	14.1	0.0	1.0	1.1	0.4	8.5	X	X	X
	1983	26.0[g]	3.8	7.8	0.2	8.3	0.6	0.1	5.3	20	X	6.3
	1985	26.5	4.9	6.0	0.1	10.8	0.4	0.1	4.2	X	X	X
Korea, Rep	1974	34.9	5.0	8.4	0.2	8.0	5.1	0.3	8.0	X	X	X
	1979	54.5	20.4	7.2	X	9.6	5.2	0.7[i]	11.4[f]	X	23	3.2
	1985	70.4[h]	40.5	4.3	X	7.4	7.2	X	11.0	X	X	X
Lebanon	1971	53.0	1.0	14.0	X	1.0	7.0	X	35.0	X	X	X
Malaysia	1966/67	8.7	1.0	4.0	0.0	0.2	0.8	0.2	2.5[k]	X	X	X
	1974	32.6	3.6	16.0	0.3	0.7	2.6	0.0	9.2	15	23	4.4
	1984	51.4[h]	7.7	11.6	0.5	2.2	7.7	0.2	31.3	X	X	X
Nepal	1976	2.5	1.8	0.4	0.0	0.1	0.2	X	0.1	X	X	X
	1981	7.0	5.3	1.1	0.1	0.1	0.4	X	0.0	22	27	3.9
	1986	13.8	12.0	0.8	0.8	0.1	0.6	X	0.0	X	X	X
Pakistan	1975	5.2	1.0	1.0	X	0.6	1.0	0.2	1.5	17	27	4.2
	1984/85	7.6	2.2	1.2	0.5	0.7	1.7	0.1	1.2	X	X	X
Philippines	1968	15.5	0.2	1.3	0.0	0.9	0.5	0.3	12.3	X	X	X
	1978	38.5	5.6	5.0	0.2	2.5	3.9	0.1	21.2	11	29	4.4
	1986	43.9	10.6	6.2	0.3	2.4	1.1	0.0	23.2	X	X	X
Singapore	1973	60.1	10.8	21.7	X	3.3	17.0	X	7.3[f]	X	X	X
	1982	74.2	22.9	11.6	X	X	24.3	14.2[l]	1.2[j]	X	X	X
Sri Lanka	1975	31.9	9.9	1.5	0.3	4.7	2.3	0.0	13.0	X	X	X
	1982	54.9	20.7	2.6	1.4[f]	2.5	3.2	X	24.3	18	31	X
	1987[c]	62.0	29.7	4.1	2.7	2.1	1.9	0.0	21.5	X	X	X
Syrian Arab Rep	1978	19.8	0.4	11.8	0.3	0.6	0.6	1.3	4.8	7	15	6.1
Thailand	1969/70	14.4	7.1	3.8	0.4	2.1	0.1	X	0.7[f]	X	X	X
	1981	59.0	22.9	20.2	7.1	4.2	1.9	X	2.7[f]	13	17	3.7
	1984	64.6	27.9	19.8	7.6	4.9	1.8	X	2.6[f]	X	X	X
	1987	67.5	27.9	20.0	9.2	7.2	1.2	0.0	2.0	X	X	X
Turkey	1968	32.0	X	2.2	X	1.6	4.4	1.1	29.8	X	X	X
	1978	38.0	0.7	6.1	0.3	3.0	3.1	0.3	24.7	13	X	3
	1983	51.0	1.1	7.5	0.2	7.4	4.1	2.4	28.5	X	X	X
Viet Nam	1979	1.1	0.2	0.7	0.0	0.1	0.1	0.0	0.0	X	X	X
	1982	20	X	X	X	X	X	X	X	X	X	X

EUROPE

	Date of Survey	Any Method	Sterilization	Pill	Injectable	IUD	Condom	Vaginal Barriers	Traditional Methods[b]	Low Estimate	High Estimate	Desired Number of Children
Austria	1981/82	71.4	1.3	40.0	0.0	8.4	4.0	2.6	15.2	X	X	X
Belgium	1966	72.0	2.0	5.0	0.0	0.0	3.0	1.0	62.0	X	X	X
	1975	87.0	6.0	30.0	0.0	3.0	8.0	0.0	39.0	X	X	X
	1982/83	81.0	7.0	32.0	0.0	8.0	6.0	0.0	17.0	X	X	X
Bulgaria	1976	76.0	2.0	2.0	0.0	2.0	2.0	X	69.0	X	X	X
Czechoslovakia	1970	66.0[n]	0.0	3.0	0.0	9.0	13.0	X	41.0	X	X	X
	1977	95.0[n]	3.0	14.0	0.0	18.0	13.0	1.0	46.0	X	X	X
Denmark	1970	67.0	X	25.0	0.0	3.0	20.0	6.0	13.0	X	X	X
	1975	63.0	X	22.0	0.0	9.0	25.0	4.0	4.0	X	X	X
Finland	1971	77.0	0.0	20.0	0.0	3.0	31.0	0.0	23.0	X	X	X
	1977	80.0	5.0	11.0	0.0	29.0	32.0	1.0	3.0	X	X	X
France	1972	64.0	0.0	11.0	0.0	1.0	8.0	1.0	43.0	X	X	X
	1978	78.7	4.6	26.6	0.0	10.3	6.1	X	31.1	X	X	X
Germany, Fed Rep	1985	77.9	12.4	33.7	0.0	14.6	5.7	1.2	10.1[k]	X	X	X
Hungary	1958	58.0	X	X	0.0	X	12.0	6.0	40.0	X	X	X
	1966	66.6	X	0.1	0.0	0.1	11.6	6.4	48.4	X	X	X
	1977	73.1	X	36.1	0.0	9.6	4.3	1.8	21.3	X	X	X
	1986	73.1	X	39.3	0.0	18.6	3.5	0.9	10.7	X	X	X
Italy	1979	78.0	1.0	14.0	0.0	2.0	13.0	2.0	46.0	X	X	X
Netherlands	1969	59.0	X	27.0	0.0	1.0	14.0	1.0	17.0	X	X	X
	1975	75.0	4.0	50.0	0.0	4.0	10.0	1.0	6.0	X	X	X
	1985	76.0	25.0	30.0	X	9.0	8.0	X	4.0	X	X	X
Norway	1977	71.0	6.0	13.0	0.0	28.0	16.0	2.0	7.0	X	X	X
Poland	1972	60.0	X	2.0	0.0	1.0	10.0	X	48.0	X	X	X
	1977	75.0	X	7.0	0.0	2.0	14.0	3.0	49.0	X	X	X
Portugal	1979/80	66.3	1.0	19.1	1.5	3.6	5.6	2.0	33.6	6	X	X
Romania	1978	58.0	X	1.0	0.0	0.0	4.0	1.0	53.0	X	X	X
Spain	1977	51.0	0.0	13.0	0.0	1.0	5.0	1.0	31.0	X	X	X
	1985	59.4	4.6	15.5	X	5.7	12.2	X	21.5[f,j]	X	X	X
Sweden	1981	78.1	2.8	23.4	0.0	20.3	25.0[f]	X	7.0	X	X	X
Switzerland	1980	71.2	15.8	28.0	0.0	10.6	8.4	2.1	6.4	X	X	X
United Kingdom	1970	75.0[h]	4.0	19.0	0.0	4.0	28.0	4.0	22.0	X	X	X
	1975	76.0[h]	13.0	30.0	0.0	6.0	18.0	2.0	10.0	X	X	X
	1983	83.0[h]	28.0	24.0	0.0	7.0	17.0	3.0	8.0	X	X	X
Yugoslavia	1970	59.0[e]	X	5.0	0.0	1.0	4.0	X	50.0	X	X	X
	1976	55.0[e]	X	5.0	0.0	2.0	2.0	3.0	43.0	X	X	X

Table 15.7 Contraceptive Prevalence and Unmet Need, 1961–87
(continued)

		Percentage of Married Couples Currently Using								Unmet Need for Contraception[a] (percent)		Desired Number of Children
	Date of Survey	Any Method	Sterilization	Pill	Injectable	IUD	Condom	Vaginal Barriers	Traditional Methods[b]	Low Estimate	High Estimate	
OCEANIA												
Fiji	1974	41.0	15.9	8.2	0.3	4.7	6.0	0.0	5.8	10	15	4.2
New Zealand	1976	69.5	20.5	28.6	X	4.4	8.0	X	9.8	X	X	X

Sources: United Nations Population Division; The World Bank; World Fertility Survey; Contraceptive Prevalence Surveys; Population Reference Bureau; Center for Population and Family Health, Columbia University; and U.S. Centers for Disease Control.
Notes: a. Among women wanting no more children; does not include unmet need for purposes of birth spacing only. b. Traditional methods include rhythm, withdrawal, abstinence, douche, and other non-supply methods. c. Preliminary. d. Includes sterilization, condom, and vaginal barrier methods. e. Excludes sterilization. f. Includes vaginal barrier methods. g. Excludes some traditional methods (abstinence, douche, and folk methods). h. Women using a combination of methods are shown under each method. i. Includes condom and barrier methods. j. Includes injectables. k. Includes those using a combination of methods. l. Includes injectables, IUD, and rhythm. m. Excludes rhythm. n. Couples reporting ever having used any method.
X = not available. For additional information, see Sources and Technical Notes.

Sources and Technical Notes

Table 15.1 Size and Growth of Population and Labor Force, 1960–2025

Sources: United Nations Population Division (U.N.), *World Population Prospects: Estimates and Projections as Assessed in 1984* (U.N., New York, 1986). International Labour Office (ILO), *Economically Active Population: Estimates 1950–1980, Projections 1985–2025* (ILO, Geneva, 1986).

Population refers to the midyear population. Most data are estimates based on population censuses and surveys. All projections are for the medium-case scenario (see below). The average annual growth rate of population takes into account the effects of international migration. The average annual increment refers to the number of people added to the population each year during the specified period.

Many of the pre-1980 data in Tables 15.1–15.3 are estimated using models. Several kinds of demographic information are required to estimate the growth and composition of a country's population: the size of the population, age and sex distribution, fertility and mortality rates by age and sex groups, the growth rates of both the urban and rural population, and the levels of internal and international migration.

Recent population censuses and surveys have collected information needed to calculate or estimate the above indicators, although the degree of accuracy varies. The Population Division of the United Nations Department of International Economic and Social Affairs compiles and evaluates national census and survey reports from all countries. When necessary, the data are adjusted for over- and under-enumeration of certain age and sex groups (infants, female children, young males), misreporting of age and sex distributions, changes in definitions, etc. These adjustments incorporate data from civil registrations, population surveys, earlier censuses, and, when necessary, population models based on information from socioeconomically similar countries. (Because the figures have been adjusted, they are not strictly comparable to the official statistics compiled by the United Nations Statistical Office and published in the *Demographic Yearbook*.)

After the figures for size and age/sex composition of the population have been adjusted, the data are scaled to 1980. Because most countries conducted a population census or large-scale population survey in the 1970s or early 1980s, the scaling is usually minor. Similar estimates are made for each five-year period between 1950 and 1980. Historical data are used when deemed accurate, with adjustments and scaling similar to those described above. For many developing countries, however, accurate historical data do not exist. The Population Division estimates the main demographic parameters for these countries using available information and demographic models.

Projections are based on estimates of the 1980 base year population. Age- and sex-specific mortality rates are applied to the base year population to determine the number of survivors at the end of each five-year period. Births are projected by applying age-specific fertility rates to the projected female population. The births are distributed by an assumed sex ratio, and the appropriate age- and sex-specific survival rates are applied. Future migration rates are also estimated on an age- and sex-specific basis. Combining future fertility, mortality, and migration rates yields the projected size and composition of the population.

Assumptions about future mortality, fertility, and migration rates–the three components of population growth–are made on a country-by-country basis and, when possible, are based on historical trends. Four scenarios of population growth (high, medium, low, and constant) are created using different assumptions about these rates. The medium-case scenario, for example, assumes medium levels of fertility, mortality, and migration, assumptions that may vary widely among the countries. The medium mortality assumption includes a five-year gain of 2.5 years in life expectancy at birth until it reaches 62.5 years. Life expectancy is assumed to increase

more slowly thereafter. For countries that have had little or no reduction in mortality recently (some sub-Saharan African and South Asian countries), the five-year gain in life expectancy was assumed to be two years or less. Refer to the source for further details.

The *labor force* is made up of all people who work or are seeking work to produce economic goods and services. It includes all employed people (employers, the self-employed, salaried employees, wage earners, unpaid family workers, members of producer cooperatives, and members of the armed forces) and the unemployed, both experienced workers and those looking for work for the first time.

The International Labour Organisation (ILO) determines the growth of the labor force by multiplying the activity rates of age/sex groups (the fraction of an age/sex group that is economically active) by the number of people in those groups. Estimates of activity rates are based on information from national censuses and labor force surveys. ILO adjusts national labor force statistics when necessary to conform to international definitions. The growth of age/sex groups is provided to ILO by the United Nations Population Division.

Table 15.2 Births, Deaths, Fertility, and Age Structure, 1960–90

Source: United Nations Population Division, *World Population Prospects: Estimates and Projections as Assessed in 1984* (U.N., New York, 1986).

The *crude birth rate* is derived by dividing the number of live births in a given year by the midyear population. This ratio is then multiplied by 1,000.

The *crude death* rate is derived by dividing the number of deaths in a given year by the midyear population. This ratio is then multiplied by 1,000.

The *total fertility rate* is an estimate of the number of children that an average woman would have if current age-specific fertility rates remain constant during her reproductive years.

The age structure shows the percentage

of the population aged 0–14, 15–65 and over 65.

For details on data collection, estimation, and projection methods, refer to the sources or to the Technical Note for Table 15.1.

Table 15.3 Health and Nutrition, 1960–90

Sources: Life expectancy and infant mortality data: United Nations Population Division (U.N.), *World Population Prospects: Estimates and Projections as Assessed in 1984* (U.N., New York, 1986). Child mortality: United Nations Children's Fund (UNICEF), *State of the World's Children* (UNICEF, New York, 1988) and UNICEF, unpublished data (UNICEF, New York, April 1988). Minimum daily requirement of calories and calorie supply as percentage of requirements: United Nations Food and Agriculture Organization (FAO), unpublished data, September 1986, and *FAO Production Yearbook* (FAO, Rome, 1987).

Life expectancy at birth is the average number of years that a newborn baby is expected to live if the age-specific mortality rates effective at the year of birth apply throughout his or her lifetime.

The *infant mortality* rate is derived by dividing the number of babies who die before their first birthday in a given year by the number of live births in that year. This ratio is then multiplied by 1,000.

Child mortality rates are derived by dividing the number of children under five years of age who die in a given year by the number of live births in that year. This ratio is then multiplied by 1,000. These data are provided to UNICEF by the United Nations Population Division and the United Nations Statistical Office.

The *minimum daily calorie requirement* is the energy intake necessary to meet the energy needs of an average healthy person. It is calculated for each country by the World Health Organization, which takes into account body size, age and sex distribution, physical activity level of the population, climate, and other factors.

The calorie supply as a percentage of requirements includes calories from all food sources: domestic production, international trade, stock drawdowns, and foreign aid. The quantity of food available for human consumption, as estimated by FAO, is the food that reaches the consumer. The amount of food actually consumed may be lower than the figures shown, depending on how much is lost in home storage, preparation, and cooking in addition to what is fed to pets and domestic animals or is discarded.

For more information on access to food and on malnutrition, see Chapter 4, "Food and Agriculture."

Table 15.4 Drinking Water and Sanitation, 1980–85

Sources: Drinking water and sanitation: World Health Organization (WHO), *The International Drinking Water Supply and Sanitation Decade: Review of Mid-Decade*

Progress (as at December 1985) (WHO, Geneva, September 1987); WHO, *The International Drinking Water Supply and Sanitation Decade: Review of National Baseline Data: December 1980* (WHO, Geneva, 1984); and unpublished data (WHO, Geneva, September 1986). Urban and rural fractions of total population: United Nations Population Division, *The Prospects of World Urbanization, Revised as of 1984–85* (U.N., New York, 1987).

WHO used questionnaires to collect data from national governments in 1980, 1983, and 1985. The questionnaires were completed by public health officials, WHO experts, and Resident Representatives of the United Nations Development Programme. From the data collected, a baseline of information was developed for assessing progress toward meeting global goals set for the International Drinking Water Supply and Sanitation Decade. One hundred fourteen developing countries responded to at least one of the questionnaires. These countries represent about 70 percent of the population of the developing world. Most of the remaining 30 percent of the people in developing countries live in China, which does not supply data on access to drinking water and sanitation. The total includes 46 African countries; 27 North and South American countries; 31 Asian countries; and 10 Oceanian countries.

Data for 14 developed countries are shown; many others routinely report comprehensive provision of drinking water and sanitation services.

The definitions of urban and rural population were supplied by national governments. Service levels in these categories were weighted by the 1980 and 1985 urban and rural populations for the national total service levels. Refer to the Technical Note for Table 16.2 for details.

WHO defines reasonable access to safe drinking water in an urban area as access to piped water or a public standpipe within 200 meters of a dwelling or housing unit. In rural areas, reasonable access implies that a family member need not spend a disproportionate part of the day fetching water. "Safe" drinking water includes treated surface water and untreated water from protected springs, boreholes, and sanitary wells. Other sources are considered unsafe.

Urban areas with access to sanitation services are defined as urban populations served by connections to public sewers or household systems such as pit privies, pour-flush latrines, septic tanks, communal toilets, etc. Rural populations with access were defined as those with adequate disposal such as pit privies, pour-flush latrines, etc.

Application of these definitions is clearly open to subjective judgment. Comparisons among countries may therefore be misleading because of varied interpretations of definitions as well as incomplete responses.

Table 15.5 Maternal and Child Health, 1980–86

Source: United Nations Children's Fund (UNICEF), *State of the World's Children 1988*

(UNICEF, New York, 1988).

The *maternal mortality* rate refers to the annual number of deaths from pregnancy or childbirth related causes per 100,000 live births. A maternal death is defined by the World Health Organization (WHO) as the death of a woman while pregnant or within 42 days of termination of pregnancy from any cause related to or aggravated by the pregnancy, but not from accidental or incidental causes. Deaths from abortion are included. Most official maternal mortality rates are underestimated because classifications of cause of death are often incorrect or unavailable. In some countries, over 60 percent of women's deaths are registered without a specified cause. Maternal mortality is highest in very young women (aged 10–15), women over 40, and in women with five or more children. Data are provided to UNICEF by WHO, and refer to a single year between 1980 and 1984.

The *percentage of births attended by trained health personnel* includes all health personnel accepted by national authorities as part of the health system. Personnel included in this definition vary by country; in some countries traditional birthing assistants and midwives are included; in others, only doctors are included. Data are provided to UNICEF by WHO.

The *percentage of infants with low birth weight* refers to all babies weighing 2,500 grams or less at birth. WHO has determined that healthy babies, regardless of race, should weigh more than 2,500 grams at birth. These data are provided to UNICEF by WHO, and refer to a single year between 1982 and 1985.

The *percentage of children suffering from mild to moderate malnutrition* refers to all children under the age of five who weigh 60 to 80 percent of the desired weight-for-age standard determined by the United States National Center for Health Statistics (NCHS). *Severe malnutrition* refers to children who are less than 60 percent of the desired weight-for-age. Weight-for-age values reflect growth, both linear and of soft tissue, and can be considered a combination of weight-for-height and height-for-age measurements. Weight-for-height, an indicator of wasting, is discussed below. Height-for-age is an indicator of stunting, or long-term undernutrition. NCHS has determined that healthy children under the age of five do not differ appreciably in weight or height (regardless of race). Children with low weight-for-age are at a higher risk of mortality.

Wasting is an indicator of current acute malnutrition, and refers to the percentage of children between the ages of 12 and 23 months whose weight-for-height is less than 77 percent of the median weight-for-height of the NCHS reference population. Malnutrition and wasting data are provided to UNICEF by WHO, and refer to a single year between 1980 and 1986.

Immunization data show the percentage of one-year old children fully immunized against: TB (tuberculosis); DPT (diphtheria, pertussis [whooping cough], and tetanus); polio; and measles. Immunization data are compiled from data supplied by WHO and

15 Population and Health

UNICEF field offices.

Data for some countries are outside the range of years indicated. For additional information, refer to the source.

Table 15.6 Education, 1970–86

Source: United Nations Children's Fund (UNICEF), *State of the World's Children 1988* (UNICEF, New York, 1988).

Educational data are supplied to UNICEF by the United Nations Educational, Scientific and Cultural Organization (UNESCO), which compiles educational information provided by the countries themselves.

Adult literacy rates refer to the percentage of persons over the age of 15 who can read and write. UNESCO recommends defining a person as illiterate when she or he cannot, with understanding, both read and write a short simple statement on her or his everyday life. This concept is widely accepted, but its interpretation and application varies among countries, and does not include persons who might still be considered functionally illiterate.

The *primary and secondary school enrollment* ratios refer to the total number of children enrolled in primary or secondary school (regardless of age) as a percentage of the total number of children in the relevant age group for that level. Age-specific population estimates are provided by the United Nations Population Division. The ratio may overstate the actual percentage of the population of primary and secondary-age children enrolled because the numerator may include students who are older or younger than the age group defined in the denominator.

The *percentage of first grade enrollment completing primary school* includes all the children entering the first grade who eventually complete primary school.

Definitions of adult literacy and the criteria applied to primary and secondary levels of education vary and are not strictly comparable among countries.

Table 15.7 Contraceptive Prevalence and Unmet Need, 1961–87

Sources: Contraceptive prevalence: United Nations Population Division, *Recent Levels and Trends of Contraceptive Use As Assessed in 1987* (U.N., New York, in press 1988). 1982 contraceptive prevalence data for Cuba, India, and Viet Nam: National Family Planning and Child Survival Study Project, unpublished data (Center for Population and Family Health, Columbia University, New York, March 1988). Unmet need for contraception: The World Bank, *World Development Report 1984* (The World Bank, Washington, D.C., 1984); International Statistical Institute, World Fertility Survey (WFS), *The World Fertility Survey, Major Findings and Implications* (International Statistical Institute, Beatrixlaan, the Netherlands, 1984); Westinghouse Public Applied Systems (WPAS), *Botswana Family Health Survey 1984* (WPAS, Columbia, Maryland,

December 1985); WPAS, *Fertility and Family Planning in Egypt 1984* (WPAS, Columbia, Maryland, July 1985); U.S. Centers for Disease Control (CDC), *1983 Jordan Fertility and Family Health Survey* (CDC, Atlanta, Georgia, 1983); CDC, *1983 Guatemala Family Planning/Maternal-Child Health Survey* (CDC, Atlanta, Georgia, 1983); CDC, *1984 Panama Maternal-Child Health/Family Planning Survey* (CDC, Atlanta, Georgia, 1984); CDC, *1985 Mauritius Contraceptive Prevalence Survey* (CDC, Atlanta, Georgia, 1985). Desired number of children: The World Bank, *World Development Report 1984* (The World Bank, Washington, D.C., 1984); and Mary M. Kent and Ann Larson, *Family Size Preferences: Evidence from the World Fertility Survey* (Population Reference Bureau, Washington, D.C., April 1982).

Contraceptive prevalence is the level of current contraceptive use among couples in which the woman is of childbearing age. *Unmet need for contraception* is defined as the percentage of married women of childbearing age who are fecund, do not want more children, and are not pregnant or protected from the risk of pregnancy.

The data were obtained from nationally representative sample surveys of women between the ages of 15 and 49 who are married or cohabitating. The ages of women interviewed for some surveys varied slightly from this range. Most of these surveys were conducted as part of the WFS or contraceptive prevalence surveys (CPSs). The table also includes data from independent national surveys on fertility and family planning, such as those conducted by China and India.

Surveys provided a comprehensive picture of contraceptive use, as they cover use of all methods, including those which do not require supplies or medical assistance. The procedure of determining use of a method varied: most surveys named and described each contraceptive method, while some only named each method.

Sterilization includes both female and male voluntary sterilization. Female sterilization is significantly more prevalent than male sterilization; the Netherlands is the only country where male sterilization exceeds female. *Pill* refers to oral contraceptives. *Injectable* refers to injectable hormonal contraceptives; this method is a relatively new technology and is not widely available in many countries. *Condom* use may be slightly underreported, as studies have shown that prevalence of condom use is higher when men, rather than women, are surveyed. *Vaginal barrier* methods include the diaphragm, cervical cap and spermicides (foam, jelly, and cream). *Traditional* (also known as non-supply) *methods* include rhythm, withdrawal, abstinence, douche, and methods categorized as "other." Users of folk remedies, and contraceptive users who do not identify their method, are included in "other."

Unmet need for contraception refers to the percentage of all married women who want no more children and are not using contraception. Because estimates do not

include women who need contraception to space births, all figures presented here should be considered minimum estimates.

A range of estimates of unmet need is given for some countries. *Low estimates* treat women who are breastfeeding during the first year after a birth as protected from pregnancy, and include in the unmet need category only those women who are not using any form of contraception. *High estimates* do not treat breastfeeding as protection from pregnancy; they also consider women using inefficient methods of family planning as having an unmet need for contraception. Efficient methods of contraception include male and female sterilization, oral contraceptives, IUDs, injectables, diaphragms, and condoms. Inefficient methods include withdrawal, rhythm, and traditional methods.

Desired number of children is based on ever-married women's answers to the question, "If you could choose exactly the number of children to have in your whole life, how many would that be?" The data shown are the mean for respondents who gave numerical answers. However, these data can provide only a general indication of desired family size. Many women did not give numerical answers. Of those who did, the answers of a significant percentage were inconsistent with their answers to the same question in follow-up surveys. Further, the question is hypothetical for women with large families, because many would not wish for fewer children than they already have.

Both the WFS and CPSs provide information on fertility, contraceptive use, and attitudes toward fertility, but their purposes and methods differ. First, the WFS conducted surveys in both developing and developed countries, and CPSs were limited to developing countries. (Because developed countries conducted their own surveys for the WFS and modified the standard WFS survey, results are not strictly comparable to developing-country data. No estimates of unmet need have been compiled for developed countries.) Second, in assessing unmet need, the WFS addressed only married women's demands for contraception—and only for the purpose of limiting births. Several CPSs surveyed unmarried and married women, and they included questions on the use of contraception for spacing births, thus permitting identification of categories of unmet need that the WFS does not.

Unmet need data for Benin, Nigeria, Mauritania, Morocco, Turkey, and Portugal were taken from the WFS. Estimates for Mauritius, Jordan, Panama, and Guatemala were provided by CDC.

Surveys are nationally representative, but many did not include remote areas with a small percentage of the population. Surveys with more restricted coverage were: Sudan (northern population only), Mauritania (sedentary population only), and Malaysia (Peninsular Malaysia only).

16. Land Cover and Settlements

Data on a basic environmental relationship—that between people and land—are presented here. Information on country size, recent and long-term trends in land use, and the rural and urban distribution of populations are included.

Table 16.1 shows land area, population density, and changes in land use. Trends in types of land cover can be traced through data gathered by the United Nations Food and Agriculture Organization (FAO). According to FAO, the global area devoted to cropland has increased more than 9 percent in the past 20 years. Most of the 123 million hectares of new cropland created during this period was in Latin America, where nearly 90 million hectares of forests were cleared. Over the past two decades, deforestation has occurred most extensively in Brazil, where more forested area was cleared than in all of Asia.

FAO updates its land use database frequently, adjusting the definitions of land use categories and sometimes substantially revising earlier data. For example, in 1985, FAO began excluding from the cropland category land used for shifting cultivation but currently lying fallow. In addition, FAO's newly released 1986 data (not shown) on the area of permanent pasture in Africa were 19 percent lower than the 1983–85 average. Because these changes reflect data reporting procedures in addition to actual land use changes, apparent trends should be interpreted with caution.

In the first global survey of wilderness areas, the Sierra Club found that about one third of the Earth's land surface (51 million square kilometers in 78 countries, plus Antarctica) appears to be wilderness. Wilderness is defined as any area lacking signs of human habitation (such as buildings and roads), although it may not have high biological or recreational value. Most of the world's wilderness area is in polar or desert regions. Antarctica contains 26 percent of the world wilderness area, followed by the USSR (17 percent), Canada (13 percent), and Australia (5 percent). This inventory will provide a baseline measurement of wilderness area so that future trends can be tracked. The Sierra Club also plans a follow-up inventory to identify wilderness units smaller than 4,000 square kilometers, the minimum area counted in the first survey. (See also Chapter 6, "Wildlife and Habitat," Recent Developments.)

The distribution of a country's population between rural and urban areas can cause different types of environmental and social problems. (See Table 16.2.) As

developing countries urbanize, they face increasing pollution, congestion, and waste disposal problems. Areas where population growth is rapid, whether urban or rural, often have problems meeting people's needs for food, housing, and basic human services.

Countries adopt definitions of urban and rural to suit national needs. As a result, what constitutes an urban area varies country by country. Despite these variations, it is clear that urban areas in most developing countries are growing rapidly. In 68 developing countries (42 of them in Africa), urban growth rates were expected to reach 4 percent or more a year between 1985 and 1990. Though still high throughout the developing world, urban growth rates have begun to decline in recent years, falling in 56 developing countries over the past decade.

Urbanization usually accompanies economic development. The populations of most of the developed countries were over 60 percent urban in 1985. By contrast, of the nine countries with less than 10 percent of their population living in urban areas, seven had a GNP per capita of less than $600. (See Chapter 14, "Basic Economic Indicators," Table 14.1.) Similarly, within developing countries, rural dwellers tend to be poorer than their urban counterparts and are more likely to lack access to drinking water, sanitation, and other services. These services are also often unavailable in the rapidly growing urban slums, where many people who migrate from rural areas to the cities in search of work may settle. (See Chapter 15, "Population and Health," Table 15.4 for data on urban and rural access to drinking water and sanitation.)

Data on land use over the long term can be used to identify trends that may not be apparent, or may seem insignificant, on a shorter time scale. Long-term land use data also help place current trends in a broader context. (See Table 16.3.) Analysis of long-term land use trends provides information on the cumulative impact and increasing rates of change in land cover. Six south Asian countries, for example, have lost 48 percent of their total wetlands area during the past century. Average decadal losses increased from 5,000 square kilometers early in this century to 12,000 square kilometers in the 1970s.

Table 16.3 is the beginning of an effort to present comprehensive global data on land use trends over the past several centuries. Additional information on long-term land use trends will be included in future editions of *World Resources*.

Table 16.1 Land Area and Use, 1964–89

	Land Area (thousand hectares)	Population Density 1989 (people per thousand hectares)	Land Use (thousand hectares)								Wilderness Area[a]	
			Cropland		Permanent Pasture		Forests and Woodland		Other Land		Total (thousand hectares)	as Percentage of Total Land Area
			1983–85	Percentage Change Over 1964–66	1983–85	Percentage Change Over 1964–66	1983–85	Percentage Change Over 1964–66	1983–85	Percentage Change Over 1964–66		
WORLD	**13,078,873**	**395**	**1,474,992**	**9.1**	**3,159,846**	**-0.1**	**4,081,900**	**-2.8**	**4,363,578**	**0.0**	**5,088,731**	**39**
AFRICA	**2,964,595**	**211**	**184,037**	**14.0**	**782,039**	**-0.5**	**695,388**	**-8.6**	**1,304,346**	**3.6**	**917,767**	**31**
Algeria	238,174	104	7,518	11.0	31,733	-15.1	4,384	37.0	194,539	2.0	152,641	64
Angola	124,670	78	3,500	5.6	29,000	0.0	53,400	-3.1	38,770	4.1	32,674	26
Benin	11,062	414	1,821	26.5	442	0.0	3,770	-23.4	5,029	18.0	1,697	15
Botswana	56,673	23	1,360	32.4	44,000	5.3	962	0.4	11,593	-22.8	35,963	63
Burkina Faso	27,380	282	2,633	20.8	10,000	0.0	6,960	-14.1	7,767	9.4	928	3
Burundi	2,565	2,062	1,313	32.9	910	44.7	63	31.9	279	-69.0	0	0
Cameroon	46,944	235	6,963	21.3	8,300	-6.4	25,200	-7.6	6,481	28.1	1,432	3
Cape Verde	403	888	40	0.0	25	0.0	1	0.0	337	0.0	0	0
Central African Rep	62,298	46	1,918	7.8	3,000	0.0	37,123	3.0	20,196	-6.0	24,559	39
Chad	125,920	44	3,152	8.7	45,000	0.0	15,533	4.3	62,235	-2.3	64,951	52
Comoros	217	2,313	94	11.0	15	0.0	35	0.0	73	-11.4	NM	NM
Congo	34,150	57	675	8.2	10,000	0.0	21,280	-1.9	2,195	19.6	14,481	42
Cote d'Ivoire	31,800	355	4,033	51.1	3,000	0.0	7,880	-58.9	16,887	143.3	5,039	16
Djibouti	2,198	189	0	0.0	200	0.0	6	-14.3	1,992	0.1	0	0
Egypt	99,545	516	2,477	-6.6	0	0.0	1	-33.3	97,066	0.2	47,182	47
Equatorial Guinea	2,805	153	230	3.6	104	0.0	1,430	10.4	1,041	-12.1	0	0
Ethiopia	110,100	442	13,930	12.0	45,200	-2.1	27,223	-8.0	23,747	8.4	24,479	22
Gabon	25,767	48	452	120.5	4,700	-6.9	20,000	0.0	615	20.1	9,097	35
Gambia	1,000	700	163	30.7	90	0.0	192	-36.8	555	15.3	0	0
Ghana	23,002	675	2,803	6.7	3,430	-5.2	8,490	-13.5	8,279	19.4	0	0
Guinea	24,586	273	1,576	0.4	3,000	0.0	10,260	-14.1	9,750	20.7	0	0
Guinea–Bissau	2,812	344	299	13.7	1,213	-5.2	1,070	-2.7	222	41.2	0	0
Kenya	56,925	428	2,338	23.7	3,747	-3.8	3,297	-23.5	47,543	1.5	14,321	25
Lesotho	3,035	556	299	-16.3	2,000	-9.9	0	0.0	736	60.8	2,440	80
Liberia	9,632	259	371	-0.3	240	0.0	3,760	-2.6	5,261	2.0	1,618	17
Libya	175,954	24	2,113	5.8	13,300	33.0	640	27.7	159,901	-2.2	71,847	41
Madagascar	58,154	193	3,024	34.7	34,000	0.0	14,423	-19.8	6,707	70.6	965	2
Malawi	9,408	843	2,355	18.5	1,840	0.0	4,430	-12.8	783	56.3	928	10
Mali	122,000	74	2,060	22.0	30,000	0.0	8,640	-8.1	81,300	0.5	59,541	49
Mauritania	103,040	21	195	-28.6	39,250	0.0	15,045	-0.6	48,550	2.3	76,116	74
Mauritius	185	6,070	107	15.1	7	0.0	58	-4.9	13	-45.8	NM	NM
Morocco	44,630	540	8,375	16.0	15,300	22.4	5,198	-0.4	15,756	-20.0	0	0
Mozambique	78,409	198	3,083	14.8	44,000	0.0	15,133	-12.8	16,192	12.7	6,869	9
Niger	126,670	54	3,687	63.1	9,213	-12.1	2,660	-30.0	111,110	0.9	67,497	53
Nigeria	91,077	1,201	30,852	5.7	20,950	8.5	14,700	-29.7	24,575	13.4	2,042	2
Rwanda	2,495	2,781	1,011	54.3	430	-50.0	424	-24.9	630	51.8	0	0
Senegal	19,200	374	5,225	16.1	5,700	0.0	5,942	-12.0	2,333	3.7	2,122	11
Sierra Leone	7,162	543	1,774	23.6	2,204	0.0	2,077	-3.0	1,107	-20.0	0	0
Somalia	62,734	81	1,068	8.8	28,850	0.0	8,853	-10.6	23,963	4.2	14,879	24
South Africa	122,104	294	13,473	3.2	80,299	-5.0	4,422	7.0	23,910	17.3	0	0
Sudan	237,600	102	12,458	11.2	56,000	0.0	47,700	-17.5	121,442	7.9	93,966	40
Swaziland	1,720	428	153	7.2	1,130	-15.8	102	-21.2	335	216.0	0	0
Tanzania, United Rep	88,604	294	5,190	36.7	35,000	0.0	42,410	-5.8	6,004	25.7	8,593	10
Togo	5,439	615	1,427	27.1	200	0.0	1,500	-38.8	2,312	38.8	0	0
Tunisia	15,536	497	4,768	10.0	3,020	20.8	556	27.7	7,192	-13.0	2,069	13
Uganda	19,971	891	6,467	32.6	5,000	0.0	5,860	-7.4	2,644	-29.7	822	4
Zaire	226,760	149	6,523	15.0	9,221	0.0	176,290	-3.4	34,726	17.9	14,666	6
Zambia	74,072	103	5,168	6.3	35,000	0.0	26,343	-15.8	7,561	158.7	17,424	24
Zimbabwe	38,667	262	2,699	27.4	4,856	0.0	23,810	0.0	7,302	-7.4	0	0
NORTH & CENTRAL AMERICA	**2,139,185**	**198**	**274,011**	**7.7**	**362,056**	**-2.4**	**660,074**	**-5.9**	**843,044**	**1.5**	**900,665**	**42**
Barbados	43	6,023	33	0.0	4	0.0	0	0.0	6	0.0	NM	NM
Canada	922,097	29	46,547	12.0	26,233	27.7	326,129	1.2	523,188	-6.3	642,179	70
Costa Rica	5,066	566	626	29.0	2,205	105.5	1,599	-45.6	636	12.0	0	0
Cuba	11,086	940	3,229	74.9	2,541	-7.9	2,200	43.8	3,115	-37.1	0	0
Dominican Rep	4,838	1,411	982	-6.4	1,395	-33.3	428	-35.6	444	-56.9	0	0
El Salvador	2,072	3,034	727	10.5	610	0.3	116	-41.1	619	-0.5	0	0
Guatemala	10,843	824	1,822	18.0	1,334	5.9	4,230	-19.4	3,457	24.0	0	0
Haiti	2,756	2,653	903	23.7	500	-17.8	69	-5.9	1,285	-4.5	0	0
Honduras	11,189	443	1,775	17.8	3,400	0.0	3,740	-29.3	2,274	129.2	1,485	13
Jamaica	1,083	2,294	269	-6.3	198	-20.7	228	8.4	388	1.0	0	0
Mexico	192,304	452	24,350	3.7	74,499	0.0	45,923	-18.6	47,531	25.5	3,633	2
Nicaragua	11,875	315	1,267	6.3	5,100	24.4	4,040	-34.7	1,468	271.6	1,777	15
Panama	7,599	312	572	2.5	1,161	12.7	4,050	-12.3	1,816	30.6	0	0
Trinidad and Tobago	513	2,462	145	4.6	11	57.1	226	-7.8	131	7.1	0	0
United States	916,660	269	189,915	6.2	241,467	-6.4	265,188	-9.7	220,090	20.1	36,008	4
SOUTH AMERICA	**1,753,454**	**166**	**139,507**	**35.2**	**457,412**	**9.4**	**922,734**	**-7.3**	**233,801**	**-1.4**	**422,270**	**24**
Argentina	273,669	118	35,783	22.2	142,800	-2.2	59,800	-1.8	35,286	-5.8	17,000	6
Bolivia	108,439	66	3,386	106.4	26,900	-4.3	55,950	-5.9	22,203	15.3	21,624	20
Brazil	845,651	174	75,243	46.4	165,000	28.7	565,280	-5.9	40,128	-38.6	237,297	28
Chile	74,880	171	5,528	24.9	11,900	17.2	15,400	-0.1	41,972	-6.3	25,540	34
Colombia	103,870	300	5,693	12.7	30,000	0.0	49,900	-23.2	18,277	374.7	14,773	14
Ecuador	27,684	379	2,511	-0.6	4,700	113.6	13,600	-21.2	6,873	20.8	0	0
Guyana	19,685	52	495	36.7	1,230	23.1	16,369	-10.0	1,591	1,225.6	13,128	67
Paraguay	39,730	104	2,019	123.6	15,500	10.7	20,400	-4.4	1,811	-47.9	6,763	17
Peru	128,000	170	2,521	-4.8	27,120	-1.3	69,900	-6.4	27,402	18.0	38,634	30
Suriname	16,147	25	58	53.5	24	200.0	15,572	-0.4	493	5.7	11,167	69
Uruguay	17,362	179	1,446	2.8	13,632	-0.6	630	5.5	1,654	0.6	0	0
Venezuela	88,205	218	3,762	8.0	17,400	8.5	32,553	-13.0	34,490	10.3	28,776	33

Table 16.1

	Land Area (thousand hectares)	Population Density 1989 (people per thousand hectares)	Cropland (thousand hectares) 1983–85	Percentage Change Over 1964–66	Permanent Pasture 1983–85	Percentage Change Over 1964–66	Forests and Woodland 1983–85	Percentage Change Over 1964–66	Other Land 1983–85	Percentage Change Over 1964–66	Wilderness Area[a] Total (thousand hectares)	as Percentage of Total Land Area
ASIA	2,678,827	1,123	455,629	4.2	644,419	–3.0	528,416	–4.6	1,017,191	–0.7	372,454	14
Afghanistan	64,750	311	8,054	2.1	30,000	0.0	1,900	–5.0	24,796	–0.3	11,404	18
Bahrain	62	8,113	2	0.0	4	0.0	0	0.0	56	0.0	NM	NM
Bangladesh	13,391	8,389	9,127	1.4	600	0.0	2,131	–4.2	1,533	–2.0	0	0
Bhutan	4,700	327	100	44.9	218	5.2	3,285	6.0	1,097	–17.1	1,273	27
Burma	65,774	610	10,068	–2.2	361	2.4	32,165	0.0	23,178	–0.2	3,209	5
China	932,641	1,191	100,890	–3.4	285,690	0.0	134,532	24.7	411,530	–5.3	182,247	20
Cyprus	924	754	432	0.0	93	0.0	171	0.0	228	0.0	0	0
India	297,319	2,736	168,550	3.8	11,900	–19.4	67,327	10.7	49,542	–16.5	1,538	1
Indonesia	181,157	985	20,680	19.0	11,867	–5.1	121,698	–1.5	26,912	–2.1	14,536	8
Iran	163,600	305	14,453	–6.5	44,000	0.0	18,013	0.1	87,133	1.1	14,799	9
Iraq	43,397	419	5,450	11.2	4,000	0.0	1,767	–9.4	32,180	–1.1	8,620	20
Israel	2,033	2,236	431	5.8	818	–0.5	114	15.2	670	–4.9	0	0
Japan	37,643	3,275	4,781	–18.5	614	332.4	25,198	–1.2	6,690	19.7	0	0
Jordan	9,718	424	416	19.3	330	230.3	50	67.8	8,921	–3.4	0	0
Kampuchea, Dem	17,652	457	3,049	5.1	580	0.0	13,372	0.0	651	–18.7	0	0
Korea, Dem People's Rep	12,041	1,862	2,321	20.2	50	0.0	8,970	0.0	700	–35.8	0	0
Korea, Rep	9,819	4,494	2,159	–3.6	75	257.1	6,544	–1.3	1,041	12.1	0	0
Kuwait	1,782	1,205	2	133.3	134	0.0	2	0.0	1,644	–0.1	0	0
Lao People's Dem Rep	23,080	197	893	7.2	800	0.0	13,067	–14.0	8,320	33.2	716	3
Lebanon	1,023	2,833	299	2.6	10	11.1	77	–18.6	637	1.4	0	0
Malaysia	32,855	516	4,353	17.7	27	12.5	20,677	–16.8	7,798	82.6	3,063	9
Mongolia	156,500	14	1,334	60.0	123,389	–11.7	15,178	1.2	16,599	1,754.6	29,015	19
Nepal	13,680	1,320	2,323	26.9	1,850	8.8	3,022	25.9	6,485	–16.3	0	0
Oman	21,246	67	44	70.5	1,000	0.0	2,013	0.0	20,202	–0.1	5,463	26
Pakistan	77,088	1,424	20,423	6.2	5,000	0.0	3,033	48.1	49,154	–4.7	3,156	4
Philippines	29,817	2,001	10,150	10.2	1,140	39.4	11,783	–30.5	6,744	136.8	0	0
Qatar	1,100	359	3	233.3	50	0.0	0	0.0	1,047	–0.2	0	0
Saudi Arabia	214,969	63	1,155	50.6	85,000	0.0	1,334	–20.6	127,480	0.0	72,382	34
Singapore	57	46,895	6	–56.4	0	0.0	3	–25.0	48	20.8	NM	NM
Sri Lanka	6,474	2,659	2,198	17.2	439	56.8	2,383	–28.3	1,454	14.2	0	0
Syrian Arab Rep	18,406	662	5,628	–12.9	8,344	7.0	504	6.4	3,930	5.6	0	0
Thailand	51,177	1,071	19,553	55.1	308	0.0	15,267	–41.4	16,049	31.4	3,793	7
Turkey	77,076	695	27,114	3.5	9,033	–19.0	20,199	0.1	20,730	6.0	0	0
United Arab Emirates	8,360	183	16	74.1	200	0.0	3	NM	8,142	–0.1	2,281	27
Viet Nam	32,536	1,992	7,040	17.6	272	0.0	13,100	–6.8	12,124	–0.9	0	0
Yemen	19,500	394	1,831	43.0	7,000	0.0	1,600	0.0	9,069	–5.7	5,278	27
Yemen, Dem	33,297	72	182	49.2	9,065	0.0	1,843	5.3	22,207	–0.7	9,681	29
EUROPE	472,695	1,052	140,133	–5.0	85,067	–4.9	155,260	7.1	92,298	3.9	18,941	4
Albania	2,740	1,211	712	36.7	447	–37.5	1,107	–11.6	475	87.6	0	0
Austria	8,273	907	1,522	–11.2	1,997	–11.4	3,213	0.9	1,541	37.6	0	0
Belgium	3,282	3,029	819	–18.1	681	–14.9	700	1.8	1,083	36.0	0	0
Bulgaria	11,055	833	4,137	–9.4	2,036	66.6	3,863	7.0	1,019	–38.4	0	0
Czechoslovakia	12,540	1,258	5,163	–1.9	1,656	–6.8	4,583	3.1	1,142	5.9	0	0
Denmark	4,237	1,209	2,629	–3.2	230	–29.4	493	9.8	885	18.8	0	0
Finland	30,547	162	2,367	–6.3	131	9.2	23,288	6.6	4,761	–21.4	2,922	10
France	54,563	1,014	18,820	–8.3	12,401	–7.8	14,604	18.3	8,738	6.0	0	0
German Dem Rep	10,557	1,597	4,988	–0.4	1,250	–13.1	2,969	0.6	1,374	12.3	0	0
Germany, Fed Rep	24,428	2,473	7,446	–2.5	4,601	–15.1	7,328	0.7	5,053	23.3	0	0
Greece	13,080	768	3,963	2.9	5,260	3.8	2,620	0.6	1,237	–20.5	0	0
Hungary	9,234	1,155	5,293	–6.2	1,257	–4.0	1,643	15.5	1,041	21.2	0	0
Iceland	10,025	25	8	33.3	2,274	–0.2	120	0.0	7,623	0.0	2,997	30
Ireland	6,889	551	915	–26.9	4,878	10.9	335	67.5	762	–26.6	0	0
Italy	29,402	1,955	12,218	–20.2	4,999	–2.4	6,402	5.1	5,783	100.8	0	0
Luxembourg	X	X	X	X	X	X	X	X	X	X	NM	NM
Malta	32	12,281	13	–4.8	X	X	X	X	19	3.7	NM	NM
Netherlands	3,392	4,335	877	–9.0	1,137	–12.0	297	2.3	1,082	35.3	0	0
Norway	30,786	135	855	0.7	95	–41.7	8,330	16.3	21,506	–4.9	10,211	33
Poland	30,449	1,257	14,815	–6.1	4,075	–3.9	8,721	8.3	2,840	17.9	0	0
Portugal	9,164	1,143	3,285	–21.2	530	0.0	3,641	10.3	1,708	46.7	0	0
Romania	23,034	1,027	10,584	0.9	4,414	2.7	6,338	–0.6	1,698	–9.0	0	0
Spain	49,941	791	20,488	0.3	10,437	–13.7	15,620	16.3	3,396	–15.2	0	0
Sweden	41,162	202	2,994	–5.8	631	–7.8	26,424	0.4	11,113	1.3	2,811	7
Switzerland	3,977	1,606	412	2.2	1,609	–9.4	1,052	7.2	904	8.4	0	0
United Kingdom	24,155	2,326	7,018	28.8	11,641	–4.3	2,224	23.1	3,308	20.2	0	0
Yugoslavia	25,540	930	7,784	–6.3	6,370	–1.1	9,333	6.4	2,053	1.6	0	0
USSR	2,227,200	130	232,264	1.3	373,600	0.2	929,000	8.4	692,336	–9.9	875,390	39
OCEANIA	842,917	31	49,411	26.6	455,251	–1.2	157,694	–16.4	180,562	16.8	260,346	31
Australia	761,793	22	47,760	27.3	440,684	–1.5	106,000	–23.0	167,349	20.2	251,643	33
Fiji	1,827	404	238	15.5	60	–14.3	1,185	0.4	344	–7.3	0	0
New Zealand	26,867	128	479	–1.6	14,023	9.0	10,567	44.0	1,798	–70.9	4,035	15
Papua New Guinea	45,171	86	378	21.8	96	37.1	36,247	–6.3	8,451	38.5	4,668	10
Solomon Islands	2,754	115	54	8.0	39	0.0	2,560	0.0	101	–3.8	0	0

Sources: United Nations Food and Agriculture Organization; Sierra Club; and United Nations Population Division.
Note: a. Refers only to areas larger than 4,000 square kilometers.
0 = zero or less than half the unit of measure; X = not available; NM = not meaningful.
For additional information, see Sources and Technical Notes.

Table 16.2 Urban and Rural Populations, 1960–90

| | Urban Population as Percentage of Total Population | | | | | Average Annual Change in Population (percent) | | | | | |
| | | | | | | Urban | | | Rural | | |
	1960	1970	1980	1985	1990	1965–70	1975–80	1985–90	1965–70	1975–80	1985–90
WORLD	**34.2**	**37.1**	**39.6**	**41.0**	**42.6**	**2.8**	**2.4**	**2.4**	**1.6**	**1.3**	**1.1**
AFRICA	**18.8**	**22.5**	**27.0**	**29.7**	**32.6**	**4.4**	**4.9**	**4.9**	**2.1**	**2.3**	**2.2**
Algeria	30.4	39.5	41.2	42.6	44.7	3.8	3.5	4.2	2.2	2.8	2.5
Angola	10.4	15.0	21.0	24.5	28.3	5.1	6.7	5.5	1.0	2.6	1.6
Benin	9.5	16.0	28.2	35.2	42.0	8.9	8.2	6.6	1.0	1.0	0.9
Botswana	1.8	8.4	15.3	19.2	23.6	18.0	8.6	7.8	1.6	3.1	2.6
Burkina Faso	4.7	5.7	7.0	7.9	9.0	3.8	4.0	5.4	1.7	1.9	2.4
Burundi	2.2	2.2	4.1	5.6	7.3	1.5	8.4	8.3	1.5	1.6	2.5
Cameroon	13.9	20.3	34.7	42.4	49.4	6.4	7.7	5.9	1.2	0.3	0.2
Cape Verde	6.7	5.6	5.1	5.3	5.7	1.3	0.9	4.1	3.2	0.9	2.3
Central African Rep	22.7	30.4	38.2	42.4	46.6	4.2	4.5	4.3	0.6	1.0	0.9
Chad	7.0	11.4	20.8	27.0	33.3	6.7	8.4	6.7	1.3	0.7	0.6
Comoros	4.1	11.3	23.2	25.2	27.6	20.4	5.1	4.9	1.0	2.9	2.4
Congo	33.0	34.8	37.3	39.5	42.2	2.7	3.3	4.1	1.9	2.0	1.8
Cote d'Ivoire	19.3	27.4	37.1	42.0	46.6	7.6	6.6	5.6	3.0	2.3	1.8
Djibouti	49.6	62.0	73.7	77.7	80.7	4.8	8.9	4.1	−0.9	3.8	0.5
Egypt	43.2	43.5	44.7	46.4	48.8	2.4	3.1	3.3	2.3	2.4	1.4
Equatorial Guinea	25.5	39.0	53.7	59.7	64.5	5.6	4.8	3.9	−0.7	−0.8	−0.3
Ethiopia	6.4	8.6	10.5	11.6	12.9	4.9	4.3	5.1	2.2	2.1	2.5
Gabon	17.4	25.6	35.8	40.9	45.7	4.7	4.3	4.2	−0.2	−0.4	0.3
Gambia	12.4	15.0	18.1	20.1	22.5	4.3	4.0	4.4	1.9	1.8	1.5
Ghana	23.3	29.0	30.7	31.5	33.0	4.1	3.9	4.3	1.2	3.1	2.9
Guinea	9.9	13.8	19.1	22.2	25.6	5.3	5.3	5.4	1.5	1.5	1.6
Guinea–Bissau	13.6	18.1	23.8	27.1	30.8	2.9	7.8	4.6	−0.5	4.3	1.1
Kenya	7.4	10.3	16.1	19.7	23.6	7.2	8.4	7.8	3.3	3.3	3.2
Lesotho	3.4	8.6	13.6	16.7	20.3	8.0	7.0	6.4	1.5	1.8	1.7
Liberia	18.6	26.0	34.9	39.5	44.0	6.0	6.2	5.4	1.7	2.0	1.7
Libya	22.7	35.8	56.6	64.5	70.2	10.3	7.8	5.4	1.2	−0.1	0.2
Madagascar	10.6	14.1	18.9	21.8	25.0	5.1	5.6	5.7	1.9	2.1	2.1
Malawi	4.4	6.0	9.7	12.0	14.8	6.8	7.5	7.4	2.3	2.4	2.7
Mali	11.1	14.3	17.3	18.0	19.2	4.7	3.5	4.2	1.8	1.9	2.7
Mauritania	6.7	13.9	26.9	34.6	42.1	9.7	9.1	7.0	1.5	0.9	0.7
Mauritius	33.2	42.0	42.9	42.2	42.3	4.4	1.6	1.7	0.2	2.2	1.6
Morocco	29.3	34.6	41.3	44.8	48.5	4.4	4.0	3.9	2.0	1.1	0.9
Mozambique	3.7	5.7	13.1	19.4	24.8	6.7	12.8	7.5	2.0	3.4	1.3
Niger	5.8	8.5	13.2	16.2	19.5	6.6	6.9	6.7	1.7	2.0	2.2
Nigeria	13.1	16.4	20.4	23.0	26.1	5.4	5.8	6.0	2.8	2.9	2.7
Rwanda	2.4	3.2	5.0	6.2	7.7	5.9	7.8	7.6	3.0	3.1	3.0
Senegal	31.9	33.4	34.9	36.4	38.4	3.3	3.9	3.8	2.7	3.2	2.1
Sierra Leone	13.0	18.1	24.5	28.3	32.2	4.6	4.6	4.5	0.7	0.7	0.8
Somalia	17.3	23.1	30.2	34.1	38.1	5.0	6.8	4.4	1.4	3.2	0.8
South Africa	46.7	47.9	53.2	55.9	58.5	2.5	3.3	3.5	2.0	1.2	1.3
Sudan	10.3	16.4	19.7	20.6	22.0	6.9	4.0	4.2	1.5	2.9	2.5
Swaziland	3.9	9.7	19.8	26.3	33.1	10.4	9.8	7.7	1.7	1.5	1.2
Tanzania, United Rep	4.8	6.9	16.5	22.3	29.3	7.5	13.3	9.2	2.8	1.9	1.7
Togo	9.8	13.1	18.8	22.1	25.7	7.3	6.0	6.1	3.9	1.8	2.1
Tunisia	36.0	43.5	52.3	56.8	60.8	4.0	4.5	3.6	0.7	0.7	0.2
Uganda	5.2	7.8	8.7	9.5	10.6	7.6	4.4	5.7	3.7	3.1	3.2
Zaire	22.3	30.3	34.2	36.6	39.5	5.1	4.1	4.5	0.9	2.3	2.1
Zambia	17.2	30.4	42.8	49.5	55.6	8.2	6.3	5.8	1.0	1.0	0.9
Zimbabwe	12.6	16.9	21.9	24.6	27.6	6.8	5.8	5.9	3.0	2.8	2.8
NORTH & CENTRAL AMERICA	**63.2**	**67.4**	**68.9**	**70.0**	**70.8**	**2.4**	**1.9**	**1.7**	**0.3**	**1.0**	**0.8**
Barbados	35.4	37.1	40.1	42.2	44.7	0.8	1.1	1.8	0.0	−0.2	−0.3
Canada	68.9	75.7	75.7	75.9	76.2	2.5	1.2	1.1	−0.4	1.1	0.8
Costa Rica	36.6	39.7	46.0	49.8	53.6	3.9	4.7	3.9	2.6	1.6	0.9
Cuba	54.9	60.2	68.1	71.8	74.9	2.8	2.0	1.8	0.6	−1.5	−1.4
Dominican Rep	30.2	40.3	50.5	55.7	60.4	5.6	4.5	3.8	1.1	0.4	−0.1
El Salvador	38.3	39.4	39.3	39.1	39.8	3.8	2.9	3.5	3.4	3.0	2.9
Guatemala	33.0	35.7	38.5	40.0	42.0	3.5	3.5	3.9	2.4	2.3	2.2
Haiti	15.6	19.8	24.6	27.2	30.3	4.5	4.5	4.7	1.6	1.7	1.8
Honduras	22.7	28.9	36.1	40.0	44.0	5.1	5.7	5.0	1.8	2.4	1.7
Jamaica	33.8	41.6	49.8	53.8	57.6	3.2	3.0	2.9	−0.1	−0.3	−0.2
Mexico	50.8	59.0	66.4	69.6	72.6	4.7	4.0	3.2	1.4	0.8	0.4
Nicaragua	39.6	47.0	53.4	56.6	59.8	5.1	4.0	4.5	1.6	1.5	1.8
Panama	41.2	47.6	50.5	52.4	54.8	4.3	2.8	2.9	1.7	1.7	1.1
Trinidad and Tobago	22.5	38.8	56.9	63.9	69.1	6.4	4.9	3.2	−1.4	−2.0	−1.5
United States	70.0	73.6	73.7	73.9	74.1	1.6	1.1	0.9	−0.2	1.0	0.7
SOUTH AMERICA	**51.7**	**60.2**	**68.9**	**72.8**	**76.0**	**4.1**	**3.6**	**3.0**	**0.4**	**−0.3**	**−0.5**
Argentina	73.6	78.4	82.7	84.6	86.2	2.0	2.1	1.8	−0.6	−0.6	−0.8
Bolivia	39.3	40.8	44.3	47.8	51.4	2.7	3.9	4.2	2.1	1.6	1.3
Brazil	44.9	55.8	67.5	72.7	76.9	4.6	4.1	3.2	0.2	−0.9	−1.3
Chile	67.8	75.2	81.1	83.6	85.6	2.9	2.2	2.0	−0.7	−1.3	−1.2
Colombia	48.2	57.2	64.2	67.4	70.3	4.1	3.2	2.9	1.1	0.3	0.2
Ecuador	34.4	39.5	47.3	52.3	56.9	4.4	5.1	4.5	2.4	1.1	0.7
Guyana	29.0	29.4	30.5	32.2	34.6	2.0	2.7	3.2	1.9	1.8	1.0
Paraguay	35.6	37.1	41.7	44.4	47.5	3.0	4.6	4.1	2.3	2.4	1.7
Peru	46.3	57.4	64.5	67.4	70.2	4.8	3.6	3.3	0.4	1.0	0.7
Suriname	47.3	45.9	44.8	45.7	47.5	1.8	−0.5	2.3	2.7	−0.5	0.8
Uruguay	80.1	82.1	83.8	84.6	85.5	1.1	0.8	1.0	−0.2	−0.4	−0.4
Venezuela	66.6	76.2	83.7	86.6	88.4	4.6	4.3	3.0	−0.1	−0.4	−0.3

Table 16.2

	Urban Population as Percentage of Total Population					Average Annual Change in Population (percent)					
						Urban			Rural		
	1960	1970	1980	1985	1990	1965–70	1975–80	1985–90	1965–70	1975–80	1985–90
ASIA	**21.5**	**23.9**	**26.6**	**28.1**	**29.9**	**3.3**	**2.9**	**2.9**	**2.2**	**1.5**	**1.1**
Afghanistan	8.0	11.0	15.6	18.5	21.7	5.7	4.4	8.1	2.0	0.3	4.0
Bahrain	78.6	78.2	80.5	81.7	82.9	2.7	5.2	4.0	3.1	3.7	2.4
Bangladesh	5.1	7.6	10.4	11.9	13.6	6.7	5.5	5.4	2.4	2.5	2.2
Bhutan	2.5	3.1	3.9	4.5	5.3	4.1	4.6	5.3	1.8	1.9	1.9
Burma	19.3	22.8	23.9	23.9	24.6	4.0	2.0	2.5	1.8	2.0	1.7
China	19.0	20.1	20.4	20.6	21.4	2.8	1.6	2.0	2.6	1.4	1.0
Cyprus	35.6	40.8	46.3	49.5	52.8	2.4	2.0	2.3	0.2	−0.4	−0.4
India	18.0	19.8	23.4	25.5	28.0	3.3	3.8	3.6	2.0	1.6	1.0
Indonesia	14.6	17.1	22.2	25.3	28.8	3.9	4.9	4.3	2.0	1.4	0.8
Iran	33.6	41.0	49.1	51.9	54.9	5.5	4.4	3.9	1.9	1.7	1.5
Iraq	42.9	56.2	66.4	70.6	74.2	5.3	5.3	4.3	0.8	1.0	0.7
Israel	77.0	84.2	88.6	90.3	91.5	3.8	2.8	1.9	−0.8	−0.8	−1.0
Japan	62.5	71.2	76.2	76.5	76.9	2.2	1.1	0.6	−1.5	0.5	0.2
Jordan	42.7	50.6	60.1	64.4	68.1	4.9	4.0	5.1	1.5	0.1	1.8
Kampuchea, Dem	10.3	11.7	10.3	10.8	11.6	4.0	−2.1	4.0	2.2	−2.1	2.3
Korea, Dem People's Rep	40.2	50.1	59.7	63.8	67.4	4.9	4.2	3.5	0.9	0.4	0.3
Korea, Rep	27.7	40.7	56.9	65.3	71.1	6.8	4.9	3.4	−0.4	−2.2	−2.0
Kuwait	72.3	77.8	90.2	93.5	95.8	9.2	7.7	4.6	9.1	−3.8	−4.4
Lao People's Dem Rep	7.9	9.6	13.4	15.9	18.6	5.5	4.8	5.6	2.3	1.0	1.8
Lebanon	39.6	59.4	74.8	80.1	83.4	6.4	1.0	2.9	−1.6	−5.1	−1.5
Malaysia	25.2	27.0	34.2	38.2	42.3	3.3	4.6	4.2	2.4	1.1	0.8
Mongolia	35.7	45.1	51.1	50.8	51.2	4.4	3.8	2.9	2.0	1.8	2.5
Nepal	3.1	3.9	6.1	7.7	9.6	4.3	7.1	6.7	2.0	2.1	1.9
Oman	3.5	5.1	7.3	8.8	10.6	6.4	8.7	6.8	2.5	4.7	2.8
Pakistan	22.1	24.9	28.1	29.8	32.0	3.9	4.1	3.7	2.4	2.4	1.6
Philippines	30.3	33.0	37.4	39.6	42.4	3.7	3.5	3.6	2.5	2.0	1.3
Qatar	72.4	80.3	86.0	88.0	89.6	10.2	6.0	5.8	5.8	2.3	2.7
Saudi Arabia	29.7	48.7	65.9	72.4	76.7	8.2	7.5	5.0	0.1	1.3	0.5
Singapore	100.0	100.0	100.0	100.0	100.0	2.0	1.3	1.1	0.0	0.0	0.0
Sri Lanka	17.9	21.9	21.6	21.1	21.4	4.2	1.3	1.7	1.8	1.8	1.4
Syrian Arab Rep	36.8	43.3	47.4	49.5	51.8	4.8	4.2	4.6	2.1	2.6	2.7
Thailand	12.5	13.3	17.3	19.8	22.6	3.7	5.0	4.3	2.9	1.8	0.9
Turkey	29.7	38.4	43.8	45.9	48.4	4.9	3.1	3.1	1.2	1.3	1.1
United Arab Emirates	40.0	42.3	81.2	77.8	74.9	9.3	13.6	2.7	8.3	11.8	5.9
Viet Nam	14.7	18.3	19.3	20.3	21.9	4.3	2.9	3.6	1.7	2.3	1.6
Yemen	3.4	7.5	15.3	20.0	25.0	9.3	9.0	7.3	1.0	1.5	1.7
Yemen, Dem	28.0	32.1	36.9	39.9	43.3	3.4	3.8	4.6	1.4	1.6	1.9
EUROPE	**60.9**	**66.7**	**70.2**	**71.6**	**72.8**	**1.5**	**0.8**	**0.6**	**−1.0**	**−0.5**	**−0.6**
Albania	30.6	33.5	33.4	34.0	35.3	3.5	2.8	2.8	2.3	2.2	1.7
Austria	49.9	51.7	54.6	56.1	57.7	0.9	0.5	0.6	0.1	−0.7	−0.7
Belgium	92.5	94.3	95.4	96.3	96.8	0.6	0.3	0.2	−2.7	−3.1	−3.0
Bulgaria	38.6	52.3	62.5	66.5	70.3	3.4	2.0	1.5	−1.8	−2.2	−2.0
Czechoslovakia	46.9	55.2	62.3	65.3	67.7	1.8	1.7	1.0	−1.4	−0.9	−1.1
Denmark	73.7	79.7	84.3	85.9	87.4	1.4	0.8	0.3	−1.8	−2.4	−2.2
Finland	38.1	50.3	59.6	64.0	67.9	2.9	1.9	1.5	−2.2	−1.8	−2.0
France	62.4	71.0	73.2	73.4	73.8	1.9	0.4	0.4	−1.8	0.2	0.1
German Dem Rep	72.3	73.7	76.2	77.0	77.8	0.3	0.1	0.4	−0.5	−0.9	−0.6
Germany, Fed Rep	77.4	81.3	84.4	85.5	86.4	1.0	0.2	0.0	−1.4	−1.6	−1.3
Greece	42.9	52.5	57.7	60.1	62.6	2.6	2.1	1.2	−1.4	0.2	−0.9
Hungary	40.0	45.6	53.5	56.2	58.9	1.7	1.7	0.9	−0.7	−1.1	−1.3
Iceland	80.3	84.9	88.2	89.4	90.3	1.8	1.2	1.2	−1.5	−1.3	−0.8
Ireland	45.8	51.7	55.3	57.0	59.1	1.7	1.8	2.0	−0.7	0.4	0.3
Italy	59.4	64.3	66.5	67.4	68.3	1.4	0.7	0.4	−0.7	−0.1	−0.5
Luxembourg	62.1	67.8	77.6	81.0	83.1	1.9	1.1	0.4	−2.4	−3.1	−2.4
Malta	70.0	77.5	83.1	85.3	86.9	1.3	1.9	1.0	−2.6	−1.3	−1.6
Netherlands	85.0	86.1	88.4	88.4	88.5	1.3	0.5	0.4	0.4	0.5	0.2
Norway	32.1	64.8	70.5	72.8	74.4	7.0	1.1	0.6	−7.2	−1.2	−1.1
Poland	47.9	52.3	58.2	61.0	63.2	1.6	1.9	1.4	−0.2	−0.5	−0.4
Portugal	22.5	26.2	29.5	31.2	33.3	0.1	2.1	2.0	−1.9	0.5	0.0
Romania	34.2	41.8	48.1	49.0	50.4	3.4	1.7	1.2	0.0	0.1	0.2
Spain	56.6	66.0	72.8	75.8	78.0	2.6	1.9	1.2	−1.5	−1.2	−1.3
Sweden	72.6	81.1	83.1	83.4	83.9	1.8	0.4	0.0	−3.1	−0.1	−0.6
Switzerland	51.0	54.5	57.0	58.2	59.6	2.0	0.2	0.5	0.6	−0.8	−0.6
United Kingdom	85.7	88.5	90.7	91.5	92.1	0.7	0.2	0.2	−2.0	−1.9	−1.4
Yugoslavia	27.9	34.8	42.3	46.3	50.2	3.1	2.8	2.3	−0.1	−0.4	−0.9
USSR	**48.8**	**56.7**	**63.1**	**65.6**	**67.5**	**2.5**	**1.9**	**1.5**	**−1.0**	**−0.7**	**−0.2**
OCEANIA	**66.3**	**70.8**	**71.5**	**71.1**	**71.0**	**2.6**	**1.5**	**1.4**	**0.5**	**1.8**	**1.5**
Australia	80.6	85.2	85.8	85.5	85.5	2.5	1.5	1.3	−0.9	1.7	1.2
Fiji	29.7	34.8	38.7	41.2	44.0	3.6	2.8	2.9	1.6	1.1	0.6
New Zealand	76.0	81.1	83.3	83.7	84.2	2.0	0.7	1.0	−0.8	−0.2	0.3
Papua New Guinea	2.7	9.8	13.0	14.3	15.8	15.1	4.5	4.5	1.4	2.5	2.0
Solomon Island	8.6	8.9	9.2	9.7	10.6	3.2	3.4	5.7	2.8	3.0	3.8

Source: United Nations Population Division.
0 = zero or less than .05 of one percent.
For additional information, see Sources and Technical Notes.

Table 16.3 Long-Term Land Use Change, 1700–1980

	1700	1880	1890	1900	1910	1920	1930	1940	1950	1960	1970	1980
					(area in square kilometers; population in thousands)							
Canada												
Built Up/Settled	X	X	X	X	X	X	X	X	33,703	41,027	48,786	57,779
Population	X	X	X	X	X	X	X	X	13,737	17,909	21,406	24,090
United States												
Cropland	X	760,836	1,003,656	1,290,993	1,404,309	1,626,894	1,671,411	1,614,753	1,655,223	1,586,424	1,554,048	1,634,988
Pasture	X	4,334,337	3,893,214	3,367,104	3,148,566	2,958,357	2,909,793	2,909,793	2,836,947	2,828,853	2,800,524	2,679,114
Forests	X	2,161,098	2,258,226	2,909,793	2,917,887	2,917,887	2,921,934	2,942,169	2,917,887	2,946,216	2,925,981	2,650,785
Other	X	445,170	546,345	1,618,800	1,715,928	1,683,552	1,683,552	1,724,022	1,788,774	1,829,244	1,881,855	2,201,568
Total Land Area[a]	X	7,701,441	7,701,441	9,186,690	9,186,690	9,186,690	9,186,690	9,186,690	9,194,784	9,198,831	9,190,737	9,162,408	9,166,455
Population	X	50,156	62,948	75,995	91,972	105,711	122,775	131,669	150,697	177,846	205,052	227,738
Brunei												
Arable Land	X	15	18	23	31	53	75	96	175	163	138	105
Built Up/Settled	X	2	2	2	3	3	4	4	5	10	16	23
Closed Forests	X	3,546	3,535	3,514	3,474	3,389	3,304	3,220	3,104	2,879	2,659	2,440
Open Forests	X	428	445	480	550	688	825	961	1,084	1,362	1,644	1,929
Grasslands	X	80	85	95	112	152	189	222	243	290	338	389
Desert/Unvegetated	X	14	14	14	15	15	15	14	14	14	15	15
Major Wetlands	X	1,507	1,493	1,464	1,409	1,292	1,181	1,074	968	875	783	692
Population	X	16	18	20	22	26	30	36	41	85	136	226
Malaysia												
Arable Land	X	3,360	4,040	5,640	8,170	15,220	23,520	25,260	28,050	25,530	40,490	48,060
Built Up/Settled	X	380	470	870	1,160	1,220	1,480	1,630	1,770	2,150	3,140	3,760
Closed Forests	X	248,880	245,840	241,050	236,220	227,180	217,580	212,820	206,340	202,250	179,750	154,200
Open Forests	X	19,010	20,930	22,940	25,350	27,540	29,760	32,410	35,670	41,690	47,170	55,960
Grasslands	X	5,480	6,830	8,350	8,980	10,410	11,280	14,100	15,960	20,660	26,430	41,570
Desert/Unvegetated	X	1,030	1,050	1,070	1,090	1,110	1,120	1,150	1,190	1,240	1,280	1,270
Major Wetlands	X	48,390	47,370	46,620	45,560	43,850	41,780	39,070	37,290	33,020	28,290	21,710
Population	X	1,458	1,752	2,191	2,971	3,614	4,533	5,341	5,805	7,415	10,078	13,195
Burma												
Arable Land	X	37,470	43,520	60,090	76,030	83,020	90,360	92,660	92,820	95,340	100,020	102,610
Built Up/Settled	X	1,840	2,160	2,580	3,050	3,420	3,830	4,510	4,080	5,850	7,650	9,060
Closed Forests	X	274,150	265,280	253,080	240,610	231,520	222,320	215,000	208,800	201,730	193,320	182,040
Open Forests	X	222,560	219,820	213,020	206,620	203,750	200,880	199,550	198,780	197,230	194,580	189,480
Grasslands	X	88,930	95,970	100,730	105,340	111,440	117,380	124,060	130,950	137,040	142,580	156,380
Desert/Unvegetated	X	8,240	8,420	8,380	8,340	8,440	8,560	8,740	8,980	9,130	9,260	9,400
Major Wetlands	X	27,830	25,850	23,140	21,040	19,440	17,680	16,500	15,620	14,690	13,600	12,050
Population	X	7,591	8,872	10,579	12,115	13,198	14,611	16,759	18,785	21,717	28,237	35,037
Bangladesh												
Arable Land	X	7,738	7,884	8,356	8,267	8,438	8,456	8,523	9,006	8,784	9,099	9,147
Built Up/Settled	X	348	380	408	451	473	504	567	569	699	971	1,158
Closed Forests	X	1,135	1,118	1,098	1,061	993	1,001	986	950	950	925	900
Open Forests	X	1,477	1,386	1,149	1,218	1,266	1,275	1,201	1,010	1,052	928	875
Grasslands	X	1,663	1,604	1,483	1,519	1,337	1,309	1,329	1,139	1,147	793	694
Desert/Unvegetated	X	139	139	139	139	139	139	139	139	139	139	139
Major Wetlands	X	1,134	1,123	1,001	980	988	952	889	823	863	780	722
Population	X	24,895	26,915	29,210	31,753	33,439	36,232	41,953	41,883	50,842	71,342	86,940
Northern India[b]												
Arable Land	X	534,470	564,960	579,890	609,590	626,240	647,910	669,750	718,180	792,820	815,450	814,530
Built Up/Settled	X	24,340	26,240	26,820	26,780	26,660	28,780	33,520	37,510	46,380	56,970	70,770
Closed Forests	X	306,850	292,430	280,300	267,790	257,980	246,420	232,510	217,000	198,580	184,630	170,810
Open Forests	X	228,080	224,830	224,430	223,020	220,950	218,420	214,890	205,060	197,020	189,860	186,050
Grasslands	X	262,130	250,840	253,610	246,290	247,150	248,480	243,130	227,690	199,770	196,250	200,820
Desert/Unvegetated	X	322,740	321,800	318,470	312,740	308,080	297,450	295,050	288,530	261,930	256,090	259,100
Major Wetlands	X	56,900	54,410	51,990	49,290	48,430	48,050	46,580	41,070	38,150	35,760	32,590
Total Area	X	1,793,780	1,793,780	1,793,780	1,793,780	1,793,780	1,793,780	1,793,780	1,793,780	1,793,780	1,793,780	1,793,780
Population	X	132,662	142,846	143,072	146,975	145,999	160,371	185,832	208,607	256,305	319,295	403,146
Pakistan												
Arable Land	X	104,390	98,420	104,670	140,400	141,650	152,050	134,120	162,560	176,830	199,950	196,620
Built Up/Settled	X	6,000	3,560	4,040	4,410	4,810	5,690	6,760	8,020	9,870	13,780	16,280
Closed Forests	X	43,970	42,430	40,790	39,050	37,590	35,520	33,410	30,110	26,610	25,090	23,610
Open Forests	X	97,560	94,450	91,900	86,270	82,330	78,770	74,990	69,060	63,900	53,670	43,700
Grasslands	X	144,500	156,710	154,990	140,370	141,340	137,670	157,280	136,560	130,400	120,970	132,530
Desert/Unvegetated	X	473,150	470,230	470,520	456,450	459,090	456,860	459,940	460,130	458,900	453,240	454,130
Major Wetlands	X	1,980	2,660	2,850	2,680	2,660	2,610	2,640	2,590	2,500	2,320	2,130
Population	X	21,126	22,724	18,755	20,119	20,720	24,097	29,256	35,028	43,795	66,211	86,647
Thailand												
Forests	X	X	X	X	X	X	X	X	X	271,238[c]	235,414	168,884
Population	X	X	X	X	8,260	9,200	11,500	14,460	17,440	26,250	34,390	46,960
Turkey												
Grasslands	X	X	X	X	X	X	X	X	378,000	X	X	217,000
Population	X	X	X	X	X	X	X	X	20,809	27,509	35,321	44,468
Sweden												
Arable Land	X	X	X	X	X	X	52,170	X	57,580	51,440	X	50,110
Forests	X	X	X	X	X	X	231,840	X	234,490	240,390	X	241,130
Wetlands	X	X	X	X	X	X	58,380	X	51,750	50,540	X	50,310
Other Land	X	X	X	X	X	X	68,190	X	67,140	68,140	X	70,080
Population	X	X	X	X	X	X	X	X	20,809	27,509	X	44,468
Russian Plain[d]												
Arable Land	365,612	X	925,600	X	X	X	X	X	X	X	X	X
Forests	2,438,956	X	1,957,644	X	1,619,800	X	X	X	X	X	1,504,100	X
Grasslands	763,620	X	675,688	X	X	X	X	X	X	X	X	X
Barren Lands	1,059,812	X	1,069,068	X	X	X	X	X	X	X	X	X
Caucasia[e]												
Arable Land	42,604	X	X	X	X	X	X	X	X	X	X	214,375[f]
Forests	146,828	X	X	X	X	X	X	X	X	X	X	94,940[f]
Other Land	280,568	X	X	X	X	X	X	X	X	X	X	160,685[f]

Sources: Conference on Earth As Transformed by Human Action; J.F. Richards; U.S. Census Bureau; and other sources.
Notes: a. Land area data for 1900 through 1980 include Alaska and Hawaii. It was assumed that no change in land cover occurred in these territories between 1900 and 1950. b. Refers to an area of 1,793,780 square kilometers, 60 percent of the national area. c. 1961. d. Refers to an area of 4,628,000 square kilometers, 21 percent of the national area. e. Refers to an area of 470,000 square kilometers. f. 1987.
X = not available.
For additional information, see Sources and Technical Notes.

Sources and Technical Notes

Table 16.1 Land Area and Use, 1964–89

Sources: Land area and use: United Nations Food and Agriculture Organization (FAO), *FAO Production Yearbook 1986* (FAO, Rome, 1987); and unpublished data (FAO, Rome, September 1986). Population data: United Nations Population Division, *World Population Prospects: Estimates and Projections as Assessed in 1984* (United Nations, New York, 1986). Wilderness area: Sierra Club, unpublished data (Sierra Club, Washington, D.C., January 1988).

Data for land area and land use are provided to FAO by national governments in response to annual FAO questionnaires. FAO also compiles data from national agricultural censuses; for further details on these censuses, refer to the Technical Note for Table 17.2 in Chapter 17, "Food and Agriculture." When official information is lacking, FAO prepares its own estimates or relies on unofficial data. Land use data are periodically revised and may change significantly from year to year. For the most recent land use statistics, see the latest *FAO Production Yearbook*.

Land area data are for 1985; they exclude major inland water bodies, national claims to the continental shelf, and Exclusive Economic Zones. (See Chapter 22, "Oceans and Coasts," Table 22.1.) Antarctica is excluded from the world total. The population density and land distribution figures for the world refer to the six inhabited continents.

Cropland includes land under temporary and permanent crops, temporary meadows, market and kitchen gardens, and temporarily fallow land. Permanent cropland is land under crops such as cocoa, coffee, rubber, fruit trees, and vines, that do not need to be replanted after each harvest. (It excludes land used to grow trees for wood or timber.)

Permanent pasture is land used for five or more years for forage, including natural crops and cultivated crops. Grassland not used for forage is included under *other land*. This category is difficult for countries to assess because it includes wild land used for pasture. In addition, few countries regularly report data on permanent pasture. As a result, absence of a trend in permanent pasture area (zero percent change for many African countries) may not reflect actual conditions, but indicates differences in land classification and data reporting.

Forests and woodland includes land under natural or planted stands of trees as well as logged-over areas that will be reforested in the near future.

Other land includes uncultivated land, grassland not used for pasture, built-on areas, wetlands, wasteland, and roads.

Several countries use definitions of total area and land use that differ from those used above. Refer to the sources for details.

Wilderness area refers to lands showing no evidence of development, such as settlements, roads, buildings, airports, railroads, pipelines, powerlines, and reservoirs. The data were derived from 65 detailed aeronautical navigational maps published in the early and mid-1980s by the United States Defense Mapping Agency at scales of 1:2,000,000 and 1:1,000,000. The maps show human constructs in remote areas to provide orienting landmarks for navigators. Although the maps do not always show agricultural development or logging, these activities usually occur near roads and settlements. The minimum unit of wilderness surveyed was 4,000 square kilometers because it was not possible to identify smaller wilderness areas from these maps.

Wilderness areas include areas classified as forest and woodlands or other lands by FAO.

Global and continental totals for wilderness area include countries not shown in the table. Africa includes 18.9 million hectares in Western Sahara and 25 million hectares in Namibia; North America includes 215.6 million hectares in Greenland; and South America includes 7.6 million hectares in French Guiana. The global total includes 1.32 billion hectares in Antarctica.

Table 16.2 Urban and Rural Populations, 1960–90

Source: United Nations Population Division, *The Prospects of World Urbanization Revised as of 1984–85* (United Nations, New York, 1987).

Urban population is defined as the portion of the total population residing in urban areas. The remainder of the population is defined as rural. Definitions of urban area vary from country to country. For a list of individual country definitions, see the source. For additional information on methods of data collection and estimation, refer to the Technical Note for Table 15.1 in Chapter 15, "Population and Health."

Table 16.3 Long-Term Land Use Change, 1700–1985

Sources: Canada (land use): Environment Canada, *State of the Environment Report for Canada* (Environment Canada, Ottawa, 1986). **United States** (land use): U.S. Bureau of the Census, *Historical Statistics of the United States: Colonial Times to 1970* (U.S. Department of Commerce, Washington, D.C., 1975) and U.S. Council on Environmental Quality,

Environmental Quality 1984 (U.S. Government Printing Office [GPO], Washington, D.C., 1986); (population): U.S. Bureau of the Census: *Statistical Abstract of the United States 1986* (U.S. GPO, Washington, D.C., 1986). **Asia:** John F. Richards, *et al.*, "Changing Land Use in Pakistan, Northern India, Bangladesh, Burma, Malaysia, and Brunei, 1880–1980" (unpublished). **Sweden:** Statistics Sweden, *Naturmiljon i Siffror* (Statistics Sweden, Stockholm, 1984). **USSR:** E.B. Alayev, "The Russian Plain. Regional Review," and Y.P. Badenkov, *et al.*, "Caucasia. Regional Review," presented at the Earth As Transformed by Human Action Conference, Clark University, Worcester, Massachusetts, October 25–30, 1987. **Thailand:** Thailand Development Research Institute, *Thailand Natural Resources Profile* (National Environment Board, Bangkok, 1987). **Turkey:** Environmental Problems Foundation of Turkey (EPFT), *Environmental Profile of Turkey 1981* (EPFT, Ankara, 1981). Population: (Canada, Turkey, Sweden): United Nations Population Division, *World Population Prospects: Estimates and Projections As Assessed in 1984* (United Nations, New York, 1986).

Data for Canada were derived from land maps produced by local and provincial governments. Built-on land includes land occupied by residential, commercial, or industrial buildings, roadways (rural and urban), transport terminals, airports, and rail beds.

Land use data for the United States dating back to the last century were compiled by the U.S. Department of Agriculture from U.S. Censuses of Agriculture, forest lands surveys conducted by the U.S. Forest Service, and population censuses.

For Brunei, Malaysia, Burma, Bangladesh, Northern India, and Pakistan, the authors compiled data from the British colonial and post-independence eras from administrative records, agricultural statistics, British land settlement reports, and agricultural censuses. These figures were then compared with contemporary descriptions of land cover in gazettes and other official and unofficial documents to determine overall changes in land use. Figures were calculated so as to approximate the current political boundaries of countries as closely as possible.

Data for Thailand, Turkey, Sweden, the Russian plain and Caucasia were derived from various historical sources. For Sweden, 1930 refers to land use documented between 1923 and 1929; 1950 refers to 1938–52; 1960 refers to 1958–67; and 1980 refers to 1978–82.

Because methods and categories of land use differ, data are not strictly comparable among countries.

17. Food and Agriculture

Agriculture has had a greater impact on the environment than any other human activity. This chapter presents data on world food production, agriculture, and agriculture's relationship to the natural resource base.

World agricultural production has grown significantly over the past 20 years. (See Table 17.1.) Between 1980 and 1985, gross world agricultural production increased 13 percent. Agricultural production outpaced population growth, resulting in a 4 percent increase in agricultural production per person.

While per capita food production indices do not measure a country's ability to feed its people, they do show regional and national trends in the amount of food produced per person. Population growth and production declines eroded per capita food production in many African countries, where it fell 8 percent between 1965 and 1980 and by another 5 percent between 1980 and 1985. In contrast, per capita food production in Asia increased 8 percent between 1965 and 1980, and 12 percent more between 1980 and 1985.

Crop yields are influenced by both environmental and economic conditions. (See Table 17.1.) Low yields may reflect less favorable soil and climate conditions, low crop prices, planting on marginal or eroded land, and lack of access to inputs such as fertilizers, irrigation, improved seed varieties, and pest control. Use of agricultural inputs has increased significantly since the 1960s. (See Table 17.2.) World fertilizer use per unit area of cropland has grown 39 percent over the past decade. However, the national figures shown in Table 17.2 conceal differences in use of inputs within a country. For example, many developing countries concentrate fertilizer application on export crops, yet food crops receive little chemical fertilizer.

The yield increases gained by use of agricultural inputs such as pesticides have serious environmental costs. Pesticide misuse can increase health risks to agricultural workers and consumers, harm wildlife, pollute groundwater, and lead to the evolution of pesticide-resistant agricultural pests. These problems are particularly severe in the developing world, where pesticides are widely distributed and poorly regulated. Unlike data for other agricultural inputs, data on pesticide use are unavailable for most countries, impairing policymakers' ability to evaluate their agricultural benefits or environmental and health costs. (See Chapter 2, "Population and Health.")

In most developing countries, the distribution of agricultural land reflects the distribution of wealth. Table 17.3 shows the distribution of agricultural holdings by size and the percentage of all agricultural land held by farms in each size class. Unequal distribution of land, combined with growing rural populations, exacerbates rural poverty in the developing world. In 1987, FAO's World Conference on Agrarian Reform and Rural Development noted that the number of landless and near-landless is growing in Southeast Asia, Latin America, and Africa, and is highest in South Asia.

Food trade statistics show changing patterns of national food self-sufficiency. (See Table 17.4.) Currently, only 10 developing countries are net exporters of cereals. Since 1975, net imports of cereals have increased substantially in all other developing countries with the sole exception of India. Among developed countries, France, Canada, and Australia have increased their net cereal exports by over 65 percent since 1975. In Europe, the number of cereal-exporting countries was four in 1975; by 1985, the number had increased to 10.

Although the flow of food aid is greatest during periods of severe famine, food aid is also given regularly in nonemergency situations. (See Table 17.4.) In 1985–86, 46 percent of food aid was given to governments for domestic sale, enabling countries to earn revenue for balance-of-payments and budgetary support. Twenty-four percent was given as a component of agricultural, rural development, and nutrition projects, and to establish food security reserves. Egypt, Bangladesh, and Sudan were the largest recipients of food aid; the United States, Canada, and the European Community were the largest donors.

Livestock are important sources of meat, clothing, and fuel and are the primary means of agricultural production on range and pasture lands. Table 17.5 shows livestock populations by country, as well as cattle per capita, highlighting those countries where livestock is an important subsistence activity or industry.

In many regions, soil is eroding far above its natural rate due to poor farm management and the overgrazing or cultivation of land unsuitable for agriculture. The data shown in Table 17.6 were collected in site-specific studies and indicate the severity of the problem in particular areas. They are not comparable because of differences in monitoring periods and methods.

Table 17.1 Food and Agricultural Production, 1964–86

	Index of Agricultural Production (1979–81 = 100)				Index of Food Production (1979–81 = 100)				Crop Yields					
									Cereals			Roots and Tubers		
	Total		Per Capita		Total		Per Capita		Kilograms per Hectare	Percentage Change Over		Kilograms per Hectare	Percentage Change Over	
	1964–66	1984–86	1964–66	1984–86	1964–66	1984–86	1964–66	1984–86	1984–86	1964–66	1974–76	1984–86	1964–66	1974–76
WORLD	**71**	**113**	**95**	**104**	**70**	**113**	**94**	**104**	**2,552**	**65**	**31**	**12,768**	**24**	**12**
AFRICA	**72**	**110**	**109**	**95**	**71**	**110**	**108**	**95**	**1,077**	**28**	**7**	**7,735**	**26**	**17**
Algeria	67	119	104	102	67	118	105	101	867	65	27	7,525	3	3
Angola	118	102	176	89	85	102	127	90	461	-47	-39	14,088	22	7
Benin	66	137	94	118	66	133	94	114	825	54	14	8,241	34	8
Botswana	82	96	135	79	81	96	134	79	178	-52	-70	5,385	35	16
Burkina Faso	83	128	110	114	85	127	113	113	690	33	30	6,568	96	40
Burundi	75	109	94	95	79	109	100	95	1,101	12	-3	7,538	-3	8
Cameroon	63	108	88	94	63	108	89	94	935	18	-2	2,455	10	3
Cape Verde	121	X	162	X	122	X	163	X	551	-11	23	3,007	-27	-29
Central African Rep	72	104	95	93	71	103	94	92	513	-31	-1	3,882	10	20
Chad	94	112	126	100	92	112	124	100	531	-13	-7	5,182	14	28
Comoros	70	X	114	X	70	X	114	X	1,116	-15	1	3,259	-4	-6
Congo	77	106	110	93	78	106	110	93	622	-43	-6	6,457	31	14
Cote d'Ivoire	47	113	85	94	40	122	73	101	981	23	21	6,282	70	38
Djibouti	X	X	X	X	X	X	X	X	X	X	X	X	X	X
Egypt	73	113	102	100	70	117	98	104	4,471	26	14	18,572	7	4
Equatorial Guinea	X	X	X	X	X	X	X	X	X	X	X	2,395	-33	-12
Ethiopia	78	98	111	87	78	97	111	86	1,081	39	12	2,827	-7	-13
Gabon	93	106	110	98	93	106	110	98	1,481	-6	1	6,393	0	9
Gambia	107	127	150	115	109	127	152	116	1,207	15	29	3,000	-32	-8
Ghana	81	130	119	110	82	131	120	111	969	7	11	8,641	5	41
Guinea	78	104	105	93	78	104	106	93	728	-10	-13	7,089	-5	0
Guinea–Bissau	91	138	140	125	91	138	140	125	848	19	16	6,154	0	26
Kenya	60	115	108	93	67	105	119	85	1,611	31	3	8,929	21	14
Lesotho	91	95	127	84	86	94	120	83	683	-12	-12	15,000	3	16
Liberia	61	115	96	98	60	116	95	99	1,302	107	7	4,014	-3	3
Libya	43	162	78	133	43	162	78	133	616	107	37	6,777	48	34
Madagascar	73	112	106	98	72	113	105	98	1,731	1	-4	5,926	-7	-3
Malawi	55	110	83	94	58	105	87	90	1,162	24	7	4,231	-13	-7
Mali	70	115	97	100	73	115	100	100	807	3	4	9,240	12	2
Mauritania	97	101	143	87	97	101	143	87	431	20	4	1,903	-24	70
Mauritius	86	113	106	103	90	110	111	100	3,200	59	24	25,939	108	65
Morocco	73	120	110	106	73	120	110	105	1,145	58	9	5,420	-48	-53
Mozambique	83	98	138	85	80	99	132	85	660	-29	-8	5,783	20	18
Niger	74	98	105	85	74	98	105	85	366	-30	-7	8,877	10	34
Nigeria	76	121	126	102	76	121	125	103	1,121	67	69	11,260	43	12
Rwanda	47	104	76	88	48	102	78	86	1,289	2	24	7,780	42	-6
Senegal	94	116	155	102	95	115	156	101	709	24	-1	4,232	2	39
Sierra Leone	78	104	97	95	79	106	99	97	1,431	8	0	3,425	-6	-20
Somalia	78	105	144	90	78	105	144	90	725	47	14	10,792	8	12
South Africa	61	95	85	84	58	94	82	84	1,398	48	0	13,531	63	12
Sudan	62	113	93	98	59	110	89	96	508	-27	-22	3,408	-1	-5
Swaziland	44	112	65	96	46	112	68	96	1,528	225	3	1,815	-53	-52
Tanzania, United Rep	59	108	96	91	54	111	87	93	1,109	41	13	11,075	109	58
Togo	77	105	119	91	77	104	118	90	865	83	-8	10,498	-12	-19
Tunisia	69	119	96	107	70	119	96	107	808	17	-2	11,262	37	19
Uganda	73	132	119	112	67	131	110	111	949	5	-22	6,432	64	46
Zaire	76	116	110	100	75	115	110	100	851	24	14	7,016	4	2
Zambia	64	113	100	96	63	112	98	95	1,747	106	44	3,687	13	9
Zimbabwe	63	117	105	98	58	112	96	94	1,460	63	3	4,907	22	23
NORTH & CENTRAL AMERICA	**73**	**105**	**92**	**98**	**71**	**106**	**90**	**99**	**3,837**	**57**	**33**	**19,720**	**26**	**9**
Barbados	98	88	106	87	98	88	106	87	2,500	30	-4	8,013	-9	-25
Canada	82	115	100	109	82	115	100	109	2,299	32	13	24,917	35	16
Costa Rica	52	111	80	97	50	105	77	92	2,395	74	38	7,056	-4	-16
Cuba	58	113	72	110	56	113	70	109	2,691	127	32	6,377	18	17
Dominican Rep	65	111	97	99	63	113	94	100	3,229	55	20	6,307	0	4
El Salvador	65	91	104	78	55	102	88	88	1,747	48	13	15,090	95	29
Guatemala	56	103	88	89	53	112	84	97	1,672	81	15	4,528	18	18
Haiti	80	108	112	95	77	108	108	95	1,221	14	4	4,110	-3	-5
Honduras	57	103	91	87	59	102	94	86	1,412	21	29	7,262	36	109
Jamaica	75	110	92	102	74	110	91	102	2,033	73	15	12,102	13	19
Mexico	60	110	96	97	56	111	90	98	2,368	81	39	14,382	68	19
Nicaragua	70	89	111	76	63	90	99	76	1,862	81	78	5,764	39	42
Panama	63	111	93	99	63	108	93	97	1,567	63	31	8,149	-1	-1
Trinidad and Tobago	90	98	99	90	89	99	97	91	2,460	1	-14	12,069	35	2
United States	74	103	86	98	72	105	84	100	4,618	59	38	31,215	45	15
SOUTH AMERICA	**66**	**112**	**94**	**100**	**64**	**113**	**91**	**101**	**2,038**	**44**	**24**	**11,452**	**2**	**4**
Argentina	71	107	90	98	70	107	89	99	2,508	61	27	16,202	61	22
Bolivia	59	105	86	91	60	106	87	93	1,272	34	11	5,100	-7	-27
Brazil	61	117	88	105	56	119	81	107	1,719	28	21	12,072	-8	1
Chile	77	109	100	101	76	109	100	101	3,003	71	79	13,963	52	43
Colombia	57	104	82	94	56	107	79	96	2,608	96	10	11,404	49	23
Ecuador	73	115	113	99	73	114	114	98	1,783	96	32	11,026	34	3
Guyana	81	89	109	81	81	89	109	81	3,471	71	62	7,131	18	8
Paraguay	54	120	85	103	59	115	92	99	1,555	23	11	14,330	6	1
Peru	89	111	135	98	89	114	134	100	2,457	58	34	8,093	21	15
Suriname	83	122	88	116	81	122	86	116	4,007	31	10	6,234	-13	6
Uruguay	91	107	99	104	87	104	94	101	1,951	101	52	5,727	19	9
Venezuela	56	107	95	93	54	106	92	92	2,135	69	38	8,577	-1	12

World Resources 1988–89

Table 17.1

	Index of Agricultural Production (1979–81 = 100)				Index of Food Production (1979–81 = 100)				Crop Yields					
	Total		Per Capita		Total		Per Capita		Cereals			Roots and Tubers		
									Kilograms per Hectare	Percentage Change Over		Kilograms per Hectare	Percentage Change Over	
	1964–66	1984–86	1964–66	1984–86	1964–66	1984–86	1964–66	1984–86	1984–86	1964–66	1974–76	1984–86	1964–66	1974–76
ASIA	**66**	**123**	**92**	**113**	**66**	**122**	**92**	**112**	**2,523**	**80**	**38**	**13,950**	**57**	**16**
Afghanistan	80	101	105	97	79	102	104	98	1,314	23	–1	13,648	36	0
Bahrain	X	X	X	X	X	X	X	X	X	X	X	22,407	12	3
Bangladesh	80	114	121	99	79	114	119	99	2,227	35	26	10,566	29	6
Bhutan	70	112	94	102	70	113	94	102	1,407	–1	–1	6,873	6	4
Burma	66	135	95	123	66	136	95	124	2,925	91	68	9,805	189	74
China	59	133	81	125	59	130	80	122	3,891	122	58	15,614	81	21
Cyprus	67	98	72	92	66	98	71	93	1,610	51	15	21,659	40	9
India	67	122	94	111	66	123	93	111	1,590	76	35	14,268	61	21
Indonesia	57	128	81	117	57	130	80	118	3,458	126	48	10,304	48	23
Iran	54	114	87	98	52	113	83	98	1,185	35	12	14,243	–21	–18
Iraq	64	130	106	108	63	129	104	108	1,020	31	19	16,474	65	83
Israel	53	114	80	103	57	117	87	106	1,679	–1	–21	38,518	66	26
Japan	96	108	113	105	94	110	111	107	5,901	34	5	24,495	33	15
Jordan	128	122	191	102	129	122	193	102	542	–47	–16	19,082	115	62
Kampuchea, Dem	191	162	201	144	182	161	191	143	1,209	8	–5	7,709	–24	–8
Korea, Dem People's Rep	49	120	73	106	49	120	72	106	4,388	53	22	12,954	23	6
Korea, Rep	60	112	80	103	60	113	80	104	5,625	86	36	21,456	27	27
Kuwait	X	X	X	X	X	X	X	X	X	X	X	15,000	X	17
Lao People's Dem Rep	63	138	93	124	63	139	93	125	2,118	159	61	9,901	33	0
Lebanon	74	119	93	118	73	120	90	120	1,225	29	0	20,951	78	200
Malaysia	47	117	68	104	43	123	63	109	2,772	33	2	9,653	3	–8
Mongolia	88	108	136	94	88	110	136	96	1,248	60	38	11,968	51	56
Nepal	82	113	116	101	82	114	116	102	1,651	–10	–6	5,676	–1	0
Oman	X	X	X	X	X	X	X	X	1,787	60	40	4,032	X	X
Pakistan	60	121	91	104	59	118	90	101	1,668	91	20	10,199	10	–5
Philippines	53	106	78	94	53	106	79	94	1,852	77	39	5,895	5	11
Qatar	X	X	X	X	X	X	X	X	2	X	–100	13,430	X	35
Saudi Arabia	41	220	80	176	41	221	80	177	3,356	150	356	18,900	115	274
Singapore	43	101	55	96	42	102	54	96	X	X	X	11,144	10	–4
Sri Lanka	63	97	84	89	51	95	68	87	2,850	60	56	11,141	81	151
Syrian Arab Rep	47	113	78	94	41	111	69	93	899	13	–5	16,840	68	29
Thailand	56	120	83	109	55	120	82	108	2,075	14	10	13,731	5	–4
Turkey	65	110	92	99	64	111	91	100	1,961	67	24	18,715	61	35
United Arab Emirates	X	X	X	X	X	X	X	X	2,190	X	X	10,257	X	–36
Viet Nam	66	128	93	116	66	128	93	116	2,698	41	27	5,603	–4	–13
Yemen	78	124	102	108	78	125	101	109	543	–27	–34	21,312	245	94
Yemen, Dem	74	101	101	88	71	99	98	87	1,655	36	0	13,558	171	19
EUROPE	**75**	**109**	**82**	**107**	**75**	**109**	**82**	**107**	**4,234**	**82**	**33**	**21,412**	**28**	**17**
Albania	61	108	88	97	59	109	85	97	3,050	171	44	8,996	9	28
Austria	79	108	82	108	79	108	82	108	5,060	92	26	27,786	36	17
Belgium	78	104	82	104	78	104	81	104	6,116	70	46	35,667	16	7
Bulgaria	75	102	81	100	72	103	77	102	3,843	57	11	10,533	–3	–6
Czechoslovakia	69	119	74	117	69	119	74	117	4,599	109	29	19,532	31	22
Denmark	89	125	95	126	89	125	95	126	5,184	34	40	36,203	56	61
Finland	87	113	91	110	87	113	91	110	2,975	66	15	18,542	24	28
France	76	109	85	107	76	109	84	107	5,655	92	50	33,788	82	62
German Dem Rep	75	109	73	109	75	108	73	109	4,589	67	28	23,956	34	55
Germany, Fed Rep	80	112	84	113	80	112	84	113	5,293	74	33	34,119	40	26
Greece	64	105	72	101	63	103	71	100	3,391	99	36	18,967	101	26
Hungary	64	111	68	112	64	111	67	112	5,171	127	36	19,445	114	57
Iceland	80	98	96	92	79	98	95	92	X	X	X	12,400	–8	16
Ireland	69	110	81	103	69	110	81	104	5,468	77	39	22,703	–1	–12
Italy	78	101	84	100	78	101	85	99	3,844	64	19	18,255	70	12
Luxembourg	X	X	X	X	X	X	X	X	X	X	X	X	X	X
Malta	68	114	79	109	68	114	79	109	3,786	148	81	6,895	9	–22
Netherlands	58	108	67	106	58	108	67	106	6,934	79	45	41,740	38	19
Norway	84	110	92	109	84	110	92	108	3,910	60	28	24,879	17	8
Poland	85	111	96	106	85	111	96	106	2,960	65	11	17,833	9	–5
Portugal	92	104	98	100	92	104	97	100	1,484	80	33	8,838	–6	1
Romania	55	117	64	114	55	117	64	114	3,821	106	45	23,214	169	83
Spain	63	108	74	105	63	108	73	105	2,557	104	39	17,281	50	23
Sweden	89	107	96	106	89	107	96	106	4,063	36	11	32,592	38	39
Switzerland	77	108	83	106	77	108	83	106	5,721	69	27	38,099	49	7
United Kingdom	79	112	81	111	79	112	81	111	6,081	66	55	36,072	50	41
Yugoslavia	70	103	80	99	69	103	79	99	4,112	79	25	8,892	8	0
USSR	**75**	**111**	**86**	**106**	**75**	**112**	**86**	**107**	**1,625**	**41**	**11**	**12,509**	**18**	**13**
OCEANIA	**74**	**108**	**98**	**100**	**70**	**107**	**92**	**99**	**1,599**	**24**	**13**	**10,906**	**14**	**10**
Australia	75	110	97	103	70	108	90	101	1,548	23	12	25,872	73	31
Fiji	69	110	94	100	70	110	95	101	2,157	24	–1	9,139	2	–3
New Zealand	76	109	91	105	73	111	87	106	4,727	40	36	28,783	39	13
Papua New Guinea	64	111	96	97	71	112	106	99	1,428	–35	–24	6,973	3	1
Solomon Islands	55	128	89	107	55	128	89	107	2,673	27	34	15,702	23	19

Source: United Nations Food and Agriculture Organization.
0 = zero or less than half of 1 percent; X = not available.
For additional information, see Sources and Technical Notes.

Table 17.2 Agricultural Inputs, 1964–86

	Cropland Total (thousand hectares)	Cropland Hectares Per Capita 1985	Fertilizer Use (kilograms per hectare of cropland) 1964–66	1974–76	1983–85	Irrigated Land as a Percentage of Arable and Permanent Cropland 1974–76	1984–86	High Yielding Varieties Rice 1970	1983	High Yielding Varieties Wheat 1970	1984	Improved Varieties Maize 1986	Average Annual Pesticide Use (metric tons of active ingredient) 1970–75	1976–80	1981–85
WORLD	1,476,483	0.31	34	62	86	13	15					71			
AFRICA	184,869	0.33	7	13	19	5	5								
Algeria	7,610	0.35	7	21	27	3	4	X	X	X	20	X	X	X	22a
Angola	3,500	0.40	1	2	4	X	X	X	X	X	X	X	X	X	X
Benin	1,838	0.45	1	2	4	0	0	X	X	X	X	X	X	X	X
Botswana	1,360	1.23	2	2	1	0	0	X	X	X	X	X	X	X	X
Burkina Faso	2,633	0.38	0	1	5	0	0	X	7	X	X	X	X	X	X
Burundi	1,325	0.28	0	1	2	4	5	X	X	X	X	X	X	X	X
Cameroon	6,965	0.71	2	2	6	0	0	X	X	X	X	30	X	X	X
Cape Verde	40	0.12	X	2	X	5	5	X	X	X	X	X	X	X	X
Central African Rep	1,983	0.77	0	1	1	X	X	X	X	X	X	X	X	X	X
Chad	3,155	0.63	0	3	2	0	0	X	X	X	X	X	X	X	X
Comoros	97	0.22	X	X	X	0	0	X	X	X	X	X	X	X	X
Congo	677	0.39	3	5	4	0	1	X	X	X	X	X	X	X	X
Cote d'Ivoire	4,090	0.42	4	10	11	1	1	X	X	X	X	10	X	X	X
Djibouti	0	0.00	X	6	X	X	X	X	X	X	X	X	X	X	X
Egypt	2,486	0.05	117	170	357	100	100	X	X	X	X	64	X	22,073a	17,157a
Equatorial Guinea	230	0.59	3	0	X	X	X	X	X	X	X	X	X	X	X
Ethiopia	13,930	0.32	0	2	4	1	1	X	X	X	X	X	X	X	X
Gabon	452	0.39	X	1	5	X	X	X	X	X	X	X	X	X	X
Gambia	165	0.26	3	8	18	6	7	X	X	X	X	X	X	X	X
Ghana	2,820	0.21	0	7	7	0	0	X	X	X	X	30	X	X	X
Guinea	1,576	0.26	2	1	0	4	4	X	X	X	X	X	X	X	X
Guinea-Bissau	320	0.36	X	1	5	X	X	X	X	X	X	X	X	X	X
Kenya	2,370	0.12	13	23	39	2	2	X	X	X	83	66	X	X	5,774*a
Lesotho	300	0.20	2	3	14	X	X	X	X	X	X	X	X	X	X
Liberia	371	0.17	2	13	8	1	1	X	X	X	X	X	X	X	X
Libya	2,127	0.59	3	16	38	10	11	X	X	X	X	X	X	X	X
Madagascar	3,040	0.30	2	3	4	17	27	X	X	X	X	4	X	X	X
Malawi	2,376	0.34	2	8	15	1	1	X	X	X	X	26	X	X	X
Mali	2,073	0.26	1	4	9	6	9	X	X	X	X	X	X	X	X
Mauritania	195	0.10	0	4	6	6	6	X	8	X	X	X	X	X	X
Mauritius	107	0.10	245	228	256	14	16	X	X	X	X	X	753a	1,085a	981*a
Morocco	8,401	0.38	7	22	31	14	15	X	X	X	30	X	X	X	X
Mozambique	3,090	0.22	2	3	5	1	3	X	X	X	X	X	X	X	X
Niger	3,740	0.61	0	0	1	1	1	X	X	X	X	X	X	X	X
Nigeria	31,085	0.33	0	2	9	3	3	X	X	X	X	40	X	X	X
Rwanda	1,012	0.17	X	0	1	0	0	X	X	X	X	X	X	X	X
Senegal	5,225	0.81	3	8	5	3	3	X	X	X	X	30	X	X	X
Sierra Leone	1,781	0.49	0	1	1	1	2	X	X	X	X	X	X	X	X
Somalia	1,071	0.23	1	2	3	11	17	X	X	X	X	X	X	X	X
South Africa	13,169	0.41	29	57	65	8	9	X	X	X	X	97	X	X	X
Sudan	12,478	0.58	2	6	6	14	15	X	X	X	X	X	X	X	X
Swaziland	180	0.28	35	59	104	34	34	X	X	X	X	X	X	X	X
Tanzania, United Rep	5,190	0.23	2	6	5	1	2	X	X	X	X	12	2,992a	5,733a	X
Togo	1,427	0.48	0	2	4	0	0	X	X	X	X	33	X	X	X
Tunisia	4,923	0.70	5	11	17	3	5	X	X	5	36	X	X	X	X
Uganda	6,600	0.43	1	0	X	0	0	X	X	X	X	36	X	23a	X
Zaire	6,600	0.22	0	2	1	0	0	X	X	X	X	X	X	X	X
Zambia	5,188	0.78	2	12	14	0	0	X	X	X	X	64	X	X	X
Zimbabwe	2,734	0.31	35	56	57	3	6	X	X	X	100	77	X	X	X
NORTH & CENTRAL AMERICA	274,626	0.69	50	80	88	9	10								
Barbados	33	0.13	211	157	202	X	X	X	X	X	X	X	X	X	X
Canada	46,780	1.84	17	30	49	1	2	X	X	X	X	100	X	X	X
Costa Rica	605	0.23	59	128	135	7	18	X	X	X	X	20	X	X	X
Cuba	3,236	0.32	134	107	172	19	26	X	X	X	X	X	X	X	X
Dominican Rep	1,470	0.24	12	65	33	11	13	X	80	X	X	X	X	863*	X
El Salvador	732	0.13	71	150	114	5	15	X	X	X	X	71	1,310*	2,838*	X
Guatemala	1,835	0.23	14	43	46	4	4	X	X	X	100	60	X	4,087*	X
Haiti	905	0.14	0	2	4	8	8	X	36	X	X	1	156a	X	X
Honduras	1,778	0.41	6	13	15	5	5	X	97	X	X	X	193	X	X
Jamaica	269	0.12	62	74	51	12	13	X	X	X	X	X	X	X	X
Mexico	24,750	0.31	15	43	64	20	20	X	92	X	95	42	17,229	24,952	34,390*
Nicaragua	1,268	0.39	17	28	47	5	7	X	X	X	X	17	7,068	X	X
Panama	568	0.26	17	46	42	4	5	X	X	X	X	X	X	X	X
Trinidad and Tobago	118	0.10	56	49	53	12	18	X	X	X	X	X	X	X	X
United States	189,915	0.80	63	97	101	9	10	X	X	X	X	100	X	392,816*	394,629*
SOUTH AMERICA	140,638	0.53	7	24	27	5	6								
Argentina	36,050	1.18	1	2	4	4	5	X	20	X	90	100	X	15,580	10,419*
Bolivia	3,397	0.53	1	1	2	4	5	X	X	X	30–35	X	X	6,186*	X
Brazil	75,780	0.56	5	35	35	2	3	X	X	X	43	70	X	73,832*	50,878
Chile	5,528	0.46	26	25	30	24	23	X	X	X	70	81	X	4,965	X
Colombia	5,695	0.20	28	45	59	6	8	X	X	X	X	15	X	13,868*	X
Ecuador	2,540	0.27	6	20	29	20	21	X	X	X	X	32	7,964	9,376	X
Guyana	495	0.52	23	34	22	31	26	X	X	X	X	X	X	13	X
Paraguay	2,176	0.59	2	1	5	4	3	X	63	X	20	X	X	298*	X
Peru	3,696	0.19	29	39	22	35	33	X	X	X	10	50	X	2,876*	X
Suriname	59	0.16	33	89	207	73	89	X	X	X	X	X	X	974	1,720*
Uruguay	1,446	0.48	29	44	31	4	7	X	X	X	X	X	1,363	2,236	1,017*
Venezuela	3,770	0.22	10	40	63	8	9	X	X	X	X	43	X	6,495*	X

Table 17.2

	Cropland Total (thousand hectares)	Cropland Hectares Per Capita 1985	Fertilizer Use (kilograms per hectare of cropland) 1964–66	1974–76	1983–85	Irrigated Land as a Percentage of Arable and Permanent Cropland 1974–76	1984–86	High Yielding Varieties Rice 1970	1983	Wheat 1970	1984	Improved Varieties Maize 1986	Average Annual Pesticide Use (metric tons of active ingredient) 1970–75	1976–80	1981–85
ASIA	454,253	0.16	17	36	83	27	30								
Afghanistan	8,054	0.49	0	5	7	31	33	X	10–15	X	X	X	X	1,000*	605
Bahrain	2	0.00	X	11	222	50	50	X	X	X	X	X	X	X	X
Bangladesh	9,135	0.09	6	22	60	15	22	3	25	8	96	X	X	X	673
Bhutan	102	0.07	X	1	2	X	X	X	X	X	X	X	X	X	X
Burma	10,067	0.27	1	5	17	10	11	3	51	X	X	34	X	X	X
China	100,883	0.10	24	62	176	42	44	X	X	X	34	72	X	X	X
Cyprus	432	0.65	38	33	45	7	7	X	X	X	X	X	X	4,127*	X
India	168,950	0.22	5	17	43	20	26	12	49	30	76	36	X	57,957*	49,144
Indonesia	20,880	0.13	6	25	81	25	33	10	83	X	X	25	X	4,740*	8,328
Iran	14,830	0.33	3	21	69	36	39	X	X	X	X	X	X	X	X
Iraq	5,450	0.34	1	7	22	30	32	X	X	X	X	X	X	X	X
Israel	418	0.10	96	169	198	43	65	X	X	X	X	X	10,064*	12,089*	X
Japan	4,758	0.04	333	389	435	62	61	X	X	X	X	X	X	X	X
Jordan	418	0.12	12	16	39	9	10	X	X	X	X	X	X	X	X
Kampuchea, Dem	3,056	0.42	1	0	2	3	3	X	X	X	X	X	X	X	X
Korea, Dem People's Rep	2,362	0.12	90	218	349	42	46	X	X	X	X	X	X	X	X
Korea, Rep	2,144	0.05	167	351	352	47	57	X	34	X	X	X	X	29,212*	17,244
Kuwait	3	0.00	X	X	358	100	33	X	X	X	X	X	X	X	X
Lao People's Dem Rep	900	0.22	1	0	1	5	13	X	X	X	X	X	X	X	X
Lebanon	300	0.11	69	87	119	26	29	X	X	X	X	X	X	X	X
Malaysia	4,370	0.28	27	61	119	7	8	19	54	X	X	X	X	X	X
Mongolia	1,354	0.71	X	5	13	3	3	X	X	X	X	X	X	X	X
Nepal	2,319	0.14	1	6	17	10	28	4	36	34	92	X	X	X	X
Oman	47	0.04	X	9	74	92	87	X	X	X	100	X	X	X	X
Pakistan	20,500	0.20	5	28	64	69	77	31	46	43	86	28	X	X	232*
Philippines	7,900	0.14	11	27	33	11	18	44	85	X	X	26	X	3,097*	4,571
Qatar	4	0.01	X	83	224	X	X	X	X	X	X	X	X	X	X
Saudi Arabia	1,175	0.10	8	7	220	34	35	X	X	X	X	X	X	X	X
Singapore	5	0.00	185	361	869	X	X	X	X	X	X	X	X	X	X
Sri Lanka	2,205	0.14	51	44	80	23	26	5	87	X	X	X	X	195*	210
Syrian Arab Rep	5,623	0.54	3	12	35	10	11	X	X	3	50	100	X	X	4,892ª
Thailand	19,620	0.38	3	12	23	14	19	0	13	X	X	70	X	3,081*	2,787
Turkey	27,541	0.56	6	31	58	7	8	X	X	X	40	46	X	956	X
United Arab Emirates	17	0.01	X	78	273	42	29	X	X	X	X	X	X	X	X
Viet Nam	6,795	0.11	12	52	55	17	26	X	X	X	X	38	X	X	X
Yemen	1,351	0.20	0	2	10	8	18	X	X	X	X	X	X	324ª	2,510*ª
Yemen, Dem	167	0.08	X	6	12	29	37	X	X	X	40	X	X	X	X
EUROPE	139,625	0.28	123	200	229	9	11								
Albania	713	0.23	15	99	140	49	55	X	X	X	X	X	X	X	X
Austria	1,525	0.20	180	211	253	0	0	X	X	X	X	X	X	3,995*	4,758
Belgium	806	0.08	466	535	536	0	0	X	X	X	X	X	X	7,207*	9,088*
Bulgaria	4,134	0.46	82	145	232	26	30	X	X	X	X	100	X	3,994*	3,559
Czechoslovakia	5,153	0.33	167	311	341	3	4	X	X	X	X	X	X	19,017*	X
Denmark	2,620	0.51	183	234	257	7	15	X	X	X	X	X	X	6,045	7,414
Finland	2,410	0.49	135	206	218	2	3	X	X	X	X	X	1,947	2,123	2,092
France	18,928	0.35	155	255	308	4	6	X	X	X	X	100	X	82,035*	X
German Dem Rep	4,973	0.30	257	369	303	3	3	X	X	X	X	100	X	18,067*	18,464
Germany, Fed Rep	7,453	0.12	367	430	423	4	4	X	X	X	X	X	X	32,930*	30,374
Greece	3,940	0.40	66	119	165	23	27	X	X	X	X	100	X	31,269*	35,124*
Hungary	5,294	0.49	64	258	284	5	3	X	X	X	X	100	X	33,700	32,500
Iceland	8	0.03	3155	3443	3750	X	X	X	X	X	X	X	X	3	5
Ireland	800	0.22	197	425	727	X	X	X	X	X	X	X	1,166*	1,470*	X
Italy	12,200	0.21	68	114	170	22	25	X	X	X	X	100	X	X	X
Luxembourg	X	X	X	X	X	X	X	X	X	X	X	X	X	X	X
Malta	13	0.03	30	23	62	8	8	X	X	X	X	X	X	X	X
Netherlands	892	0.06	582	756	787	51	59	X	X	X	X	X	X	X	X
Norway	858	0.21	196	288	290	5	10	X	X	X	X	X	X	1,443	1,465
Poland	14,845	0.40	84	237	231	1	1	X	X	X	X	100	X	9,331*	12,727
Portugal	2,760	0.27	40	65	72	17	23	X	X	X	X	18	X	21,945*	11,839*
Romania	10,622	0.46	25	104	153	15	27	X	X	X	X	X	X	X	X
Spain	20,416	0.53	X	74	75	14	16	X	X	X	X	100	X	X	X
Sweden	2,984	0.36	121	171	154	2	2	X	X	X	X	X	X	9,634	13,882
Switzerland	412	0.06	324	374	432	6	6	X	X	X	X	X	X	X	X
United Kingdom	7,077	0.13	288	258	368	1	2	X	X	X	X	X	5,515	5,099	9,968
Yugoslavia	7,780	0.34	57	89	121	2	2	X	X	X	X	75	24,604ª	35,713ª	X
USSR	232,187	0.83	27	71	102	6	9	X	X	X	X	95	X	127,000*	158,500
OCEANIA	50,285	2.04	39	31	35	4	4								
Australia	48,600	3.10	28	20	25	3	3	X	X	X	X	X	X	X	X
Fiji	240	0.35	32	53	43	0	0	X	X	X	X	X	X	X	X
New Zealand	501	0.15	908	1218	1062	36	51	X	X	X	X	X	X	X	X
Papua New Guinea	383	0.11	1	19	20	X	X	X	X	X	X	X	X	X	X
Solomon Islands	55	0.20	X	X	X	X	X	X	X	X	X	X	X	X	X

Sources: United Nations Food and Agriculture Organization; United Nations Population Division; and other sources.
Note: a. May not be active ingredients.
0 = zero or less than half the unit of measure; X or blank = not available or less than half the unit of measure; * = one year of data.
For additional information, see Sources and Technical Notes.

Table 17.3 Agricultural Land Distribution, 1960–80

	Agricultural Holdings: Distribution by Size of Holdings (percent)									Agricultural Area: Distribution by Size of Holdings (percent)								
	1960			1970			1980			1960			1970			1980		
	less than 5 ha	5–50 ha	more than 50 ha	less than 5 ha	5–50 ha	more than 50 ha	less than 5 ha	5–50 ha	more than 50 ha	less than 5 ha	5–50 ha	more than 50 ha	less than 5 ha	5–50 ha	more than 50 ha	less than 5 ha	5–50 ha	more than 50 ha
WORLD																		
AFRICA																		
Algeria	X	X	X	69	30	1	X	X	X	X	X	X	14	63	23	X	X	X
Angola	X	X	X	X	X	X	X	X	X	X	X	X	X	X	X	X	X	X
Benin	X	X	X	X	X	X	X	X	X	X	X	X	X	X	X	X	X	X
Botswana	X	X	X	74	26	0	X	X	X	X	X	X	26	74	0	X	X	X
Burkina Faso	X	X	X	X	X	X	X	X	X	X	X	X	X	X	X	X	X	X
Burundi	X	X	X	X	X	X	X	X	X	X	X	X	X	X	X	X	X	X
Cameroon	X	X	X	97	4	0	X	X	X	X	X	X	84	16	0	X	X	X
Cape Verde	X	X	X	X	X	X	X	X	X	X	X	X	X	X	X	X	X	X
Central African Rep	X	X	X	98	3	0	X	X	X	X	X	X	90	10	0	X	X	X
Chad	X	X	X	89	11	0	X	X	X	X	X	X	72	28	0	X	X	X
Comoros	X	X	X	X	X	X	X	X	X	X	X	X	X	X	X	X	X	X
Congo	X	X	X	99	1	0	X	X	X	X	X	X	98	2	0	X	X	X
Cote d'Ivoire	X	X	X	64	36	0	X	X	X	X	X	X	32	68	1	X	X	X
Djibouti	X	X	X	X	X	X	X	X	X	X	X	X	X	X	X	X	X	X
Egypt	90	10	0	X	X	X	X	X	X	51	34	16	X	X	X	X	X	X
Equatorial Guinea	X	X	X	X	X	X	X	X	X	X	X	X	X	X	X	X	X	X
Ethiopia	X	X	X	X	X	X	96	4	0	X	X	X	X	X	X	82	18	0
Gabon	X	X	X	100	0	0	X	X	X	X	X	X	100	0	0	X	X	X
Gambia	X	X	X	X	X	X	X	X	X	X	X	X	X	X	X	X	X	X
Ghana	X	X	X	86	14	0	X	X	X	X	X	X	47	54	0	X	X	X
Guinea	X	X	X	X	X	X	X	X	X	X	X	X	X	X	X	X	X	X
Guinea-Bissau	85	16	0	X	X	X	X	X	X	61	39	0	X	X	X	X	X	X
Kenya	74	25	1	90	10	0	93	7	0	14	21	65	38	18	43	47	13	40
Lesotho	94	6	0	96	4	0	X	X	X	77	23	0	84	16	0	X	X	X
Liberia	X	X	X	93	7	0	X	X	X	X	X	X	36	35	29	X	X	X
Libya	24	62	14	X	X	X	X	X	X	2	35	63	X	X	X	X	X	X
Madagascar	97	3	0	X	X	X	5	60	35	89	11	0	X	X	X	0	8	92
Malawi	X	X	X	100	0	0	100	0	0	X	X	X	100	0	0	100	0	0
Mali	68	32	0	X	X	X	X	X	X	37	63	0	X	X	X	X	X	X
Mauritania	X	X	X	X	X	X	93	7	0	X	X	X	X	X	X	58	42	0
Mauritius	X	X	X	X	X	X	X	X	X	X	X	X	X	X	X	X	X	X
Morocco	75	25	0	X	X	X	X	X	X	38	62	0	X	X	X	X	X	X
Mozambique	X	X	X	X	X	X	X	X	X	X	X	X	X	X	X	X	X	X
Niger	X	X	X	X	X	X	58	42	0	X	X	X	X	X	X	33	67	0
Nigeria	X	X	X	X	X	X	X	X	X	X	X	X	X	X	X	X	X	X
Rwanda	X	X	X	X	X	X	100	0	0	X	X	X	X	X	X	100	0	0
Senegal	72	28	0	X	X	X	X	X	X	41	59	0	X	X	X	X	X	X
Sierra Leone	X	X	X	94	6	0	X	X	X	X	X	X	80	20	0	X	X	X
Somalia	X	X	X	X	X	X	X	X	X	X	X	X	X	X	X	X	X	X
South Africa	5	19	76	X	X	X	X	X	X	0	0	100	X	X	X	X	X	X
Sudan	X	X	X	X	X	X	X	X	X	X	X	X	X	X	X	X	X	X
Swaziland	X	X	X	87	13	0	X	X	X	X	X	X	8	6	85	X	X	X
Tanzania, United Rep	X	X	X	95	5	0	X	X	X	X	X	X	79	21	0	X	X	X
Togo	87	13	0	97	3	0	100	0	0	57	43	0	74	27	0	100	0	0
Tunisia	41	55	4	X	X	X	X	X	X	6	54	40	X	X	X	X	X	X
Uganda	75	25	0	X	X	X	X	X	X	43	57	0	X	X	X	X	X	X
Zaire	X	X	X	99	1	0	X	X	X	X	X	X	60	5	35	X	X	X
Zambia	0	14	86	94	6	0	X	X	X	0	0	100	34	19	47	X	X	X
Zimbabwe	0	9	91	X	X	X	X	X	X	0	0	100	X	X	X	X	X	X
NORTH & CENTRAL AMERICA																		
Barbados	81	7	13	X	X	X	X	X	X	6	5	89	X	X	X	X	X	X
Canada	4	30	66	5	24	72	6	25	69	0	7	93	0	3	97	0	3	97
Costa Rica	39	48	15	49	37	15	X	X	X	2	22	76	2	18	80	X	X	X
Cuba	X	X	X	X	X	X	X	X	X	X	X	X	X	X	X	X	X	X
Dominican Rep	86	13	1	77	21	2	X	X	X	21	31	48	13	30	57	X	X	X
El Salvador	85	13	2	89	10	1	84	14	2	15	28	57	20	31	49	13	24	63
Guatemala	74	24	3	X	X	X	84	14	2	13	24	63	X	X	X	13	24	63
Haiti	X	X	X	96	4	0	X	X	X	X	X	X	78	23	0	X	X	X
Honduras	X	X	X	64	32	4	X	X	X	X	X	X	9	35	56	X	X	X
Jamaica	90	10	1	94	6	0	94	5	1	23	23	54	29	19	52	28	17	55
Mexico	66	22	12	60	26	14	X	X	X	1	3	96	1	4	96	X	X	X
Nicaragua	40	43	16	X	X	X	X	X	X	2	18	79	X	X	X	X	X	X
Panama	46	47	6	56	37	8	66	27	7	5	37	58	4	33	64	4	30	66
Trinidad and Tobago	72	27	2	X	X	X	X	X	X	20	34	46	X	X	X	X	X	X
United States	8	45	47	7	39	54	10	39	51	0	9	91	0	6	94	0	6	94
SOUTH AMERICA																		
Argentina	15	39	47	X	X	X	X	X	X	0	2	98	X	X	X	X	X	X
Bolivia	X	X	X	X	X	X	X	X	X	X	X	X	X	X	X	X	X	X
Brazil	31	51	19	37	47	16	37	45	18	1	13	86	1	14	85	1	12	87
Chile	38	44	18	X	X	X	X	X	X	1	5	94	X	X	X	X	X	X
Colombia	63	31	7	60	32	8	X	X	X	5	20	76	4	19	78	X	X	X
Ecuador	X	X	X	67	27	7	X	X	X	X	X	X	7	28	65	X	X	X
Guyana	X	X	X	X	X	X	X	X	X	X	X	X	X	X	X	X	X	X
Paraguay	44	51	6	X	X	X	34	59	7	1	7	92	X	X	X	1	9	90
Peru	84	14	2	78	20	2	X	X	X	6	8	86	7	14	79	X	X	X
Suriname	81	19	0	81	19	0	X	X	X	24	27	49	28	28	45	X	X	X
Uruguay	15	50	36	14	48	38	12	46	42	0	5	95	0	4	96	0	4	96
Venezuela	50	40	10	44	43	14	X	X	X	1	7	92	1	7	93	X	X	X

World Resources 1988–89

Table 17.3

	Agricultural Holdings: Distribution by Size of Holdings (percent)									Agricultural Area: Distribution by Size of Holdings (percent)								
	1960			1970			1980			1960			1970			1980		
	less than 5 ha	5–50 ha	more than 50 ha	less than 5 ha	5–50 ha	more than 50 ha	less than 5 ha	5–50 ha	more than 50 ha	less than 5 ha	5–50 ha	more than 50 ha	less than 5 ha	5–50 ha	more than 50 ha	less than 5 ha	5–50 ha	more than 50 ha
ASIA																		
Afghanistan	X	X	X	X	X	X	X	X	X	X	X	X	X	X	X	X	X	X
Bahrain	X	X	X	100	0	0	72	28	0	X	X	X	35	63	3	33	65	1
Bangladesh	X	X	X	X	X	X	100	0	0	X	X	X	X	X	X	100	0	0
Bhutan	X	X	X	X	X	X	X	X	X	X	X	X	X	X	X	X	X	X
Burma	X	X	X	X	X	X	X	X	X	X	X	X	X	X	X	X	X	X
China	X	X	X	X	X	X	X	X	X	X	X	X	X	X	X	X	X	X
Cyprus	X	X	X	X	X	X	76	23	0	X	X	X	X	X	X	31	53	16
India	87	13	0	89	11	0	91	9	0	47	51	3	47	50	4	51	46	3
Indonesia	98	3	0	98	2	0	X	X	X	67	21	12	69	18	14	X	X	X
Iran	53	46	1	X	X	X	X	X	X	17	69	14	X	X	X	X	X	X
Iraq	57	36	7	49	49	2	X	X	X	2	19	79	8	66	26	X	X	X
Israel	X	X	X	68	30	3	84	14	2	84	16	X	12	30	58	14	14	71
Japan	98	2	0	99	2	0	98	2	0	84	16	0	83	17	0	79	21	0
Jordan	X	X	X	X	X	X	70	29	1	X	X	X	X	X	X	19	53	28
Kampuchea, Dem	X	X	X	X	X	X	X	X	X	X	X	X	X	X	X	X	X	X
Korea, Dem People's Rep	X	X	X	X	X	X	X	X	X	X	X	X	X	X	X	X	X	X
Korea, Rep	100	0	0	100	0	0	100	0	0	100	0	0	100	0	0	100	0	0
Kuwait	X	X	X	74	23	3	X	X	X	X	X	X	13	47	37	X	X	X
Lao People's Dem Rep	X	X	X	X	X	X	X	X	X	X	X	X	X	X	X	X	X	X
Lebanon	80	20	1	82	17	1	X	X	X	39	45	17	22	43	35	X	X	X
Malaysia	89	10	1	X	X	X	X	X	X	30	14	56	X	X	X	X	X	X
Mongolia	X	X	X	X	X	X	X	X	X	X	X	X	X	X	X	X	X	X
Nepal	X	X	X	97	3	0	97	3	0	X	X	X	72	27	1	71	29	0
Oman	X	X	X	X	X	X	X	X	X	X	X	X	X	X	X	X	X	X
Pakistan	80	20	0	68	31	1	73	26	1	32	68	0	30	58	11	34	57	9
Philippines	81	19	0	85	15	0	86	14	0	43	45	12	48	38	14	51	37	12
Qatar	X	X	X	X	X	X	X	X	X	X	X	X	X	X	X	X	X	X
Saudi Arabia	X	X	X	77	20	2	72	25	3	X	X	X	15	39	46	10	32	58
Singapore	X	X	X	100	0	0	X	X	X	X	X	X	98	0	0	X	X	X
Sri Lanka	97	3	0	98	2	0	98	2	0	53	20	28	58	42	0	62	38	0
Syrian Arab Rep	X	X	X	62	36	3	X	X	X	X	X	X	11	57	32	X	X	X
Thailand	72	28	0	X	X	X	74	26	0	43	57	0	X	X	X	42	58	0
Turkey	58	41	1	X	X	X	62	37	1	22	65	13	X	X	X	20	68	12
United Arab Emirates	X	X	X	X	X	X	X	X	X	X	X	X	X	X	X	X	X	X
Viet Nam	89	11	0	X	X	X	X	X	X	61	29	11	X	X	X	X	X	X
Yemen	X	X	X	X	X	X	89	11	0	X	X	X	X	X	X	44	52	5
Yemen, Dem	X	X	X	X	X	X	X	X	X	X	X	X	X	X	X	X	X	X
EUROPE																		
Albania	X	X	X	X	X	X	X	X	X	X	X	X	X	X	X	X	X	X
Austria	42	53	5	41	54	5	34	60	6	5	45	51	5	47	49	4	46	50
Belgium	62	37	1	53	46	1	44	53	3	16	73	11	10	77	13	6	74	20
Bulgaria	X	X	X	X	X	X	X	X	X	X	X	X	X	X	X	X	X	X
Czechoslovakia	X	X	X	98	2	1	100	0	0	X	X	X	7	5	88	7	6	87
Denmark	19	78	3	10	84	7	14	77	9	4	78	18	1	73	26	2	63	35
Finland	53	47	0	36	63	1	31	68	1	28	68	4	19	76	4	16	79	5
France	29	65	6	31	61	8	28	60	12	5	67	29	5	62	34	4	54	42
German Dem Rep	X	X	X	X	X	X	X	X	X	X	X	X	X	X	X	X	X	X
Germany, Fed Rep	55	44	1	39	59	2	35	61	4	17	71	12	9	77	14	6	74	20
Greece	X	X	X	80	21	0	X	X	X	X	X	X	45	53	3	X	X	X
Hungary	X	X	X	99	0	0	100	0	0	X	X	X	5	0	95	4	0	96
Iceland	X	X	X	X	X	X	X	X	X	X	X	X	X	X	X	X	X	X
Ireland	17	76	7	20	73	7	X	X	X	3	65	32	3	65	32	X	X	X
Italy	76	23	1	76	23	1	76	23	2	20	43	36	18	40	42	16	39	45
Luxembourg	X	X	X	25	63	13	27	58	15	X	X	X	3	83	14	2	58	40
Malta	91	9	0	91	9	0	97	3	0	77	23	0	77	23	0	83	17	0
Netherlands	54	46	1	35	64	1	31	67	2	12	79	9	6	85	9	4	81	15
Norway	69	31	0	57	43	1	49	50	1	42	56	2	34	64	2	16	55	29
Poland	63	37	0	62	38	0	60	41	0	24	61	15	26	74	0	25	75	0
Portugal	X	X	X	82	17	1	86	12	2	X	X	X	18	31	51	20	24	56
Romania	X	X	X	X	X	X	X	X	X	X	X	X	X	X	X	X	X	X
Spain	50	45	5	X	X	X	63	32	5	6	29	65	X	X	X	6	24	70
Sweden	37	60	3	26	67	7	16	72	12	10	68	22	16	64	21	9	62	29
Switzerland	X	X	X	45	54	1	42	57	1	X	X	X	9	86	5	6	88	6
United Kingdom	32	49	19	22	52	26	17	52	30	2	24	74	1	20	79	1	18	81
Yugoslavia	71	29	0	74	26	0	79	21	0	33	57	11	33	48	19	35	48	17
USSR																		
OCEANIA																		
Australia	7	25	69	8	24	69	X	X	X	0	0	100	0	0	100	X	X	X
Fiji	X	X	X	58	42	0	85	14	1	X	X	X	13	87	0	17	41	42
New Zealand	3	36	61	5	29	67	10	31	59	0	4	96	0	3	98	0	2	98
Papua New Guinea	X	X	X	X	X	X	X	X	X	X	X	X	X	X	X	X	X	X
Solomon Islands	X	X	X	X	X	X	X	X	X	X	X	X	X	X	X	X	X	X

Source: United Nations Food and Agriculture Organization.
Note: Numbers may not add to 100 percent due to rounding.
0 = zero or less than half of 1 percent; X = not available.
For additional information, see Sources and Technical Notes.

Table 17.4 Food Trade and Aid, 1974–86

	Average Annual Net Trade in Food (metric tons)										Average Annual Donations or Receipts of Food Aid (metric tons)			
	Cereals (000 metric tons)		Oils		Pulses		Milk		Meat		Cereals (000 metric tons)		Oils	Milk
	1974–76	1984–86	1974–76	1984–86	1974–76	1984–86	1974–76	1984–86	1974–76	1984–86	1974–76	1983–85	1983–85	1983–85
WORLD														
AFRICA	8,608	27,693	322,572	1,853,975	-181927	223837	511,413	1,053,785	7,302	500,846	1,799	5,781	126,667	149,615
Algeria	2,061	4,681	135,271	330,553	17,721	93,611	112,303	307,606	2,248	36,104	52	3	211	1,029
Angola	132	331	-2182	30,787	-9601	28,333	4,136	39,700	-189	31,707	2	69	2,224	3,931
Benin	13	60	-15342	-7667	48	267	1,716	3,183	305	2,963	7	14	768	992
Botswana	36	153	0	-4528	-600	4,843	-247	13,447	-16433	-25902	5	27	3,983	2,664
Burkina Faso	42	144	118	6,486	-3000	-3960	1,492	13,398	-454	-162	51	75	5,642	5,804
Burundi	9	16	185	2,861	0	0	0	2,626	68	411	3	12	974	1,859
Cameroon	74	136	-6746	-2860	-215	366	5,322	9,676	-1468	11,637	3	6	634	218
Cape Verde	38	67	358	513	4,307	3,279	1,926	1,989	145	233	7	49	1,271	1,534
Central African Rep	14	25	428	4	0	3	809	1,231	-5801	-2030	1	8	276	232
Chad	26	87	312	0	0	0	669	3,043	-5904	41	30	89	3,279	3,284
Comoros	14	30	0	341	0	15	445	797	143	1,160	1	6	174	267
Congo	71	104	7,230		27	77	1,618	6,346	3,649	6,895	2	3	98	59
Cote d'Ivoire	120	531	-101962	-109382	1,399	195	24,614	54,654	7,814	16,383	2	0	10	43
Djibouti	25	45	0	1,736	0	1,034	0	5,603	81	1,192	0	11	293	370
Egypt	3,248	8,726	340,875	623,587	99,197	53,824	22,459	122,526	25,038	264,387	620	1,850	8,477	28,856
Equatorial Guinea	2	8	-3200	0	0	0	0	213	0	750	0	9	155	292
Ethiopia	4	667	1,015	19,194	-102335	-4283	4,706	25,339	-6507	-1429	79	462	22,260	16,076
Gabon	36	58	1,024	1,005	53	33	4,113	6,498	3,751	26,729	0	0	0	2
Gambia	26	70	-16525	-8069	14	0	873	2,565	122	239	7	17	409	987
Ghana	137	194	22,522	5,608	1,214	293	6,777	5,112	3,756	1,070	34	75	4,562	3,166
Guinea	57	160	0	2,003	0	0	1,500	3,327	0	1,917	30	38	287	438
Guinea–Bissau	21	30	16	-31	196	35	689	374	205	127	7	28	333	254
Kenya	-69	272	34,807	92,798	-11599	-10443	-25829	6,999	-8190	-2998	4	209	2,341	3,450
Lesotho	46	137	0	0	362	4,233	1,133	8,103	0	0	19	50	3,171	3,780
Liberia	46	101	-6262	-3835	91	196	2,668	4,656	1,573	3,510	3	41	73	20
Libya	660	1,308	20,546	58,367	7,808	8,367	47,694	84,833	7,820	14,267	0	0	0	0
Madagascar	105	171	6,324	11,035	-20745	-5152	2,371	3,586	-10914	-2128	24	104	1,889	1,704
Malawi	16	-125	4,380	5,301	-3944	-13452	1,988	1,954	383	8	0	4	234	561
Mali	134	274	-3067	733	-150	0	5,327	5,943	-985	667	109	155	803	1,435
Mauritania	128	242	2,100	5,573	0	233	9,300	32,381	100	73	57	112	3,859	5,708
Mauritius	162	175	12,312	20,877	5,626	8,209	6,184	11,570	4,734	8,062	25	15	57	1,012
Morocco	1,182	2,183	134,189	220,229	-160441	-18200	35,429	32,047	-1176	4,698	100	369	6,536	8,724
Mozambique	155	396	-7788	29,143	-11107	6,467	3,833	8,533	185	1,380	31	277	1,794	4,041
Niger	26	117	-4043	9,057	-1834	-353	2,583	6,872	-474	183	118	81	867	2,308
Nigeria	577	1,636	-20771	157,921	10,508	29,832	85,736	75,120	3,435	15,044	8	0	0	0
Rwanda	7	25	0	6,929	0	0	538	4,319	21	43	12	24	2,231	3,528
Senegal	271	567	-168303	-1482	-22	492	9,057	22,373	-58	355	48	124	1,582	5,756
Sierra Leone	47	101	-7386	178	29	3	4,282	2,507	629	347	7	22	784	1,852
Somalia	114	301	4,287	22,640	5	633	1,023	9,933	-3833	0	61	204	16,239	8,554
South Africa	-2601	679	50,867	184,753	8,637	-1621	17,194	-1474	-11109	2,245	0	0	0	0
Sudan	92	752	-6522	36,637	-2549	18,819	3,655	16,647	-4932	-803	50	531	7,966	6,231
Swaziland	12	50	0	180	-130	0	2,616	4,840	-731	1,648	1	5	139	712
Tanzania, United Rep	327	256	8,978	16,433	-13062	-4567	10,050	8,573	-1479	138	89	145	3,150	4,812
Togo	11	73	123	1,878	0	172	832	4,210	546	11,427	7	13	1,040	1,638
Tunisia	331	1,039	-21396	60,341	-4394	4,417	25,988	30,793	364	17,032	73	164	3,242	5,429
Uganda	19	9	1,285	1,133	48	533	23,314	3,247	83	367	0	18	652	2,435
Zaire	391	313	-81611	-23846	1,400	1,567	13,469	13,367	20,456	48,655	8	100	343	327
Zambia	95	190	5,707	14,839	1,681	348	14,118	2,582	5,912	-3	3	91	8,891	1,183
Zimbabwe	15	-18	1,955	19,208	6,700	987	3,060	1,122	-18657	-15866	0	71	2,464	2,058
NORTH & CENTRAL AMERICA	-83353	-93787	-792193	-1143470	-205040	-392874	285,852	45,324	485,259	432,432	-4749	-6158	-278261	-173138
Barbados	36	60	1,664	1,945	1,284	1,054	4,030	4,030	9,648	11,145	0	0	7	39
Canada	-14000	-22723	-16445	-306770	-51466	-199289	-37342	-167005	51598	-235538	-770	-867	-37361	-13413
Costa Rica	108	197	7,611	5,965	14,045	4,630	2,243	2,287	-28787	-27204	1	132	78	93
Cuba	1,676	2,126	80,594	127,492	95,551	117,857	87,721	77,429	47,011	61,760	0	1	690	965
Dominican Rep	254	424	41,192	63,798	-2731	3,589	2,366	14,486	-4353	-5302	18	141	15,587	2,443
El Salvador	78	221	13,287	49,726	2,704	527	6,281	6,476	-3049	1,106	4	222	15,697	8,510
Guatemala	147	187	7,307	43,032	4,546	-598	1,130	13,405	-16100	-12151	10	20	6,185	5,944
Haiti	92	202	17,379	38,067	244	1,300	5,258	9,360	-734	4,700	20	88	6,719	3,534
Honduras	84	104	8,742	-8950	-3305	-435	3,620	7,335	-16443	-8566	16	103	1,919	4,574
Jamaica	369	391	14,315	19,592	1,790	315	18,591	17,689	28,261	29,256	4	135	3,365	2,485
Mexico	2,508	5,279	55,935	279,862	-13913	96,302	79,696	199,586	275	101,835	0	2	4,257	10,899
Nicaragua	38	133	-4881	35,547	-365	11,190	-2182	11,206	-21806	-4437	5	52	2,541	3,954
Panama	58	105	11,157	22,779	2,289	7,229	3,661	6,291	3,264	4,638	3	2	328	1,122
Trinidad and Tobago	211	236	9,812	16,927	8,272	10,703	15,649	33,800	8,676	19,904	0	0	0	0
United States	-73047	-80893	-1044934	-1542241	-270558	-454195	49,708	-259831	357,020	394,669	-4060	-6189	-298271	-204345
SOUTH AMERICA	-3991	-6354	-313956	-1865626	-74473	-83398	124,121	232,513	-510816	-760670	394	366	22,475	23,881
Argentina	-9785	-17110	-202124	-1614077	-109563	-199862	-22999	-4507	-317349	-242503	-10	-38	0	3
Bolivia	186	391	250	7,864	-24	2,048	6,167	8,837	71	322	44	190	4,327	6,977
Brazil	1,422	5,279	-399467	-838805	30,422	54,340	20,997	98,685	-79700	-420724	18	4	22	5,446
Chile	1,216	580	53,554	68,741	-33087	-60292	31,027	10,424	21,953	3,690	236	11	251	3,775
Colombia	283	844	43,916	142,146	219	33,842	4,577	4,426	-20744	-2160	46	3	342	864
Ecuador	244	289	35,728	47,414	101	673	2,642	3,968	-860	142	12	13	625	635
Guyana	-6	-35	3,640	3,450	2,739	3,867	10,504	1,805	644	120	0	1	410	316
Paraguay	45	34	-11010	-14749	0	0	234	1,298	-19138	-18066	11	4	120	786
Peru	1,166	1,308	65,610	53,888	-1784	9,438	39,883	40,569	14,426	36,285	32	178	16,361	4,909
Suriname	-22	-74	2,961	705	430	1,967	2,003	2,357	1,851	1,013	0	0	0	0
Uruguay	-177	-249	-4243	-6135	579	1,186	-744	-14590	-120919	-121094	5	0	17	170
Venezuela	1,430	2,379	94,837	283,101	35,253	68,970	32,315	75,976	6,682	-2101	0	0	0	0

Table 17.4

	Average Annual Net Trade in Food (metric tons)										Average Annual Donations or Receipts of Food Aid (metric tons)			
	Cereals (000 metric tons)		Oils		Pulses		Milk		Meat		Cereals (000 metric tons)		Oils	Milk
	1974–76	1984–86	1974–76	1984–86	1974–76	1984–86	1974–76	1984–86	1974–76	1984–86	1974–76	1983–85	1983–85	1983–85
ASIA	46,491	64,103	-641445	-619488	44,291	-150953	791,923	1,581,331	660,396	1,591,325	4,202	2,678	144,406	89,543
Afghanistan	9	68	1,133	13,667	470	-9800	2,174	600	0	333	10	72	0	50
Bahrain	24	90	252	5,464	1,178	2,065	5,210	9,851	4,634	17313	0	0	0	0
Bangladesh	1,841	1,964	83,236	273,979	8	2,752	12,069	48,220	-218	-1771	1,308	1,305	11,121	91
Bhutan	-15	19	-14000	0	0	0	340	440	0	0	0	5	223	240
Burma	-346	-588	4,967	29.000	-31667	-100733	10,267	6,367	0	0	11	5	0	42
China	3,852	6,676	145,581	212,733	-48630	-150926	28,870	86,454	-113583	-320184	-59	129	3,168	4,369
Cyprus	174	420	7,052	12,900	1,442	877	7,160	6,491	5,023	5,793	8	3	47	195
India	6,400	415	76,629	1,344,610	-3088	271,333	45,882	47,580	-7669	-41162	981	282	66,332	42,120
Indonesia	1,803	1,517	-386364	-607838	-875	14,670	34,443	55,375	381	-275	236	297	188	4,805
Iran	1,938	4,422	266,989	415,816	475	17,292	50,122	163,725	67,086	224,248	0	0	0	153
Iraq	768	3,982	115924	244,385	31,925	77,134	19,052	83,964	28,949	218,545	1	0	56	0
Israel	1,480	1,807	6,850	9,891	6,524	18,345	7,343	6,463	29,922	26,172	146	3	33	125
Japan	19,502	26,564	385,426	357,191	174,649	174,595	155,429	189,900	429,609	711,960	-188	-414	-584	-1225
Jordan	225	715	5,458	27,868	-244	14,516	6,574	37,854	4,587	39,587	83	31	1,223	2,226
Kampuchea, Dem	115	86	126	333	-4373	0	1,643	33	209	0	193	37	2,413	102
Korea, Dem People's Rep	126	150	6,087	12,700	0	0	187	83	0	-15	0	0	0	0
Korea, Rep	2,861	6,797	107572	273,075	-4	19,762	1,405	3,154	0	12,596	261	18	0	0
Kuwait	172	492	1,254	10,732	5,175	8,365	23,370	42,810	26,110	45,156	0	0	0	0
Lao People's Dem Rep	66	41	29	0	17	0	401	0	295	0	11	3	0	0
Lebanon	420	536	13,285	42,997	11,324	22,800	10,733	26,667	16,202	18,967	25	34	784	1,673
Malaysia	912	2,090	-1240106	-4007576	28,179	52,977	52,448	73,623	11,605	49,137	1	0	3	0
Mongolia	54	19	978	1,600	0	0	4,330	3,800	-40638	-39903	0	0	0	20
Nepal	-39	-50	0	8,109	4,490	-10970	-2100	2,533	0	0	4	27	351	1,684
Oman	58	207	14	2,563	1,933	2,384	9,300	27,281	2,867	40,827	0	0	0	0
Pakistan	555	-142	232,118	843,410	131	40,726	18,567	30,915	27	-39	585	391	53,384	10,843
Philippines	847	1,256	-613756	-803256	1,683	7,255	64,759	80,664	7,440	1,985	98	57	1,583	12,624
Qatar	36	93	23	4,639	648	1,575	5,923	11,497	3,440	17,422	0	0	0	0
Saudi Arabia	693	5,852	5,773	149,776	11,585	38,773	53,121	201,139	34,877	244,297	-3	-38	0	0
Singapore	498	646	2,520	68,257	8,580	12,164	32,425	48,581	28,203	70,427	0	0	0	0
Sri Lanka	1,011	893	-41983	-35499	12,706	34,771	9,380	23,215	9	257	175	346	1,110	3,143
Syrian Arab Rep	293	1,386	5,714	24,995	-17815	-26554	19,347	43,772	7,803	6,180	64	25	1,275	3,595
Thailand	-3595	-7789	6,717	7,152	-103744	-230020	26,905	43,435	-952	-51362	1	9	0	1
Turkey	617	561	91,754	264,331	-66985	-469662	2,052	8,842	-9331	-31855	21	-3	133	505
United Arab Emirates	86	424	0	33,500	0	16,683	0	47,250	11,333	64,104	0	0	0	0
Viet Nam	1,967	463	31,861	-6283	-7	-31667	20,407	3,233	1,145	-2097	196	17	306	530
Yemen	237	766	23	43,600	739	433	5,082	32,300	508	29,150	30	23	247	398
Yemen, Dem	115	294	1,492	16,902	2,642	2,765	3,976	18,087	112	9,503	3	17	1,009	1,230
EUROPE	31,021	-10380	1,734,967	1,040,765	515,620	588,289	-1088326	-2239256	88093	-1440254	-738	-1099	-10839	2,061
Albania	65	-2	3,533	6,333	0	-433	0	1,100	0	2,807	0	0	0	0
Austria	119	-794	44,864	72,106	5,137	4,280	-48557	-84408	20,056	-47945	0	-19	0	-1216
Belgium	3,277	2,066	40,421	-80759	31,117	145,802	-57218	-313395	-167383	-274853	-41	-53	0	-47
Bulgaria	308	676	-20676	-11753	1,378	2,340	-9304	-22863	-64245	-128272	0	0	0	0
Czechoslovakia	1,340	397	50,319	40,652	8,052	2,791	-26623	-94178	11,456	-20621	0	0	0	0
Denmark	-318	-1276	-20902	13,730	-2012	-180424	-305737	-397676	-679700	-950945	-15	-20	-567	-2779
Finland	25	-585	8,503	1,569	4,079	816	-63612	-81293	-6458	-33996	-22	-29	-944	-1295
France	-13772	-25101	269,549	202,276	62,669	-429860	-885434	-1083944	123,805	68,613	-164	-254	0	0
German Dem Rep	3,337	2,732	90,703	64,110	13,729	-532	20,476	-27333	-9267	-27400	0	0	0	0
Germany, Fed Rep	5,330	1,935	30,762	-17141	77,085	377,356	-828159	-2109691	730,820	458,724	-175	-227	-3913	-2653
Greece	995	-669	-5811	-85151	-2494	19,542	81,745	203,989	64,379	214,864	0	-6	-10	0
Hungary	-1361	-1867	-25186	-190004	-38324	-76343	-4438	-30987	-196820	-427079	0	0	0	0
Iceland	32	23	803	1,595	354	341	-1068	-1536	-7571	-6313	0	0	0	0
Ireland	586	247	-4929	8,833	7,983	9,940	-138025	-340941	-286939	-328951	-2	-7	-67	-1152
Italy	6,927	4,517	420,127	403,195	105,069	192,866	1,080,320	2,389,477	580,517	805,594	-51	-117	-148	-209
Luxembourg	X	0	X	X	X	X	X	X	X	X	X	X	X	X
Malta	131	114	4,055	5,010	2,291	1,064	10,306	10,696	7,247	9,437	6	0	0	133
Netherlands	3,907	3,704	154884	127,893	84,988	479,857	-588847	-331228	-697031	-1223209	-48	-113	-3936	-4147
Norway	677	348	1,071	8,621	6,306	5,276	-21884	-22601	18,861	1,556	-3	-32	-112	-63
Poland	4,611	2,026	71,466	71,420	7,789	-42571	-34672	-23113	-190939	-36750	0	64	8,424	19,852
Portugal	1,721	2,447	38,142	-83673	7,488	1,926	9,802	7,824	45,724	18,607	47	0	10	21
Romania	552	231	-128385	-54033	-8094	-7167	-14073	-7717	-151241	-171850	1	0	0	0
Spain	4,308	2,784	-15853	-293612	70,302	63,619	272,821	183,840	80,340	56,214	0	-29	-16	0
Sweden	-1023	-1268	31,930	14,917	3,493	4,328	-19810	-37108	-1528	-71189	-143	-86	-9413	-40
Switzerland	1,413	970	43,426	34,545	6,279	9,946	-4237	-15698	50,441	63,313	-32	-33	-6	-4161
United Kingdom	7,505	-3045	520,243	672,589	57,328	10,005	473,746	64,086	875,606	679,587	-96	-139	-141	-183
Yugoslavia	328	-993	101,106	107,325	3,627	-6527	12,044	29,924	-63746	-72776	0	0	0	0
USSR	10,189	35,576	-301378	779,691	-48297	-24452	-11438	259,562	400,132	833,711	0	0	0	0
OCEANIA	-9619	-19948	-257537	-420258	-14397	-112233	-644207	-802403	-1243906	-1264870	-259	-425	-1419	-2389
Australia	-9932	-20165	-136546	-138650	12,316	-66576	-222573	-219940	-676673	-619493	-271	-425	-1446	-2053
Fiji	56	84	-11330	-3487	2,816	4,244	3,822	4,176	5,929	7,279	12	1	27	158
New Zealand	87	-168	-59044	-86058	-30318	-50788	-445917	-613499	-618668	-739238	0	0	0	-494
Papua New Guinea	84	169	-44767	-153831	109	100	5,268	6,826	21,414	39,300	0	0	0	0
Solomon Islands	5	14	0	-18366	7	5	287	200	635	1,151	0	0	0	0

Source: United Nations Food and Agriculture Organization.
Note: Imports and food aid receipts are shown as positive numbers; exports and food aid donations are shown as negative numbers.
0 = zero or less than half of the unit of measure; X = not available.
For additional information, see Sources and Technical Notes.

Table 17.5 Livestock Populations, 1974–86

	Cattle			Sheep and Goats		Chickens (millions)		Pigs		Horses[a]		Buffaloes and Camels	
	1984-86	Percentage Change Since 1974-76	Cattle per Capita 1984-86	1984-86	Percentage Change Since 1974-76	1984-86	Percentage Change Since 1974-76	1984-86	Percentage Change Since 1974-76	1984-86	Percentage Change Since 1974-76	1984-86	Percentage Change Since 1974-76
WORLD	1,264,621	6	0.4	1,621,754	10	8,583	60	804,155	18	119,545	2	153,004	16
AFRICA	174,192	12	0.3	348,663	16	747	56	11,518	40	17,164	3	13,885	-2
Algeria	1,518	55	0.1	17,873	54	22	35	5	25	719	-7	128	-16
Angola	3,363	18	0.4	1,210	10	6	20	465	31	6	0	0	X
Benin	911	29	0.2	2,191	34	20	578	570	57	7	17	0	X
Botswana	2,621	2	2.4	1,201	31	1	0	8	-50	169	213	0	X
Burkina Faso	3,046	22	0.4	5,387	38	20	103	206	50	270	15	6	20
Burundi	413	-47	0.1	1,166	22	4	22	78	123	0	X	0	X
Cameroon	4,059	57	0.4	4,510	6	9	0	1,033	29	60	-9	0	X
Cape Verde	13	18	0.0	66	23	0	X	51	133	9	-10	0	X
Central African Rep	2,082	137	0.8	1,174	47	2	100	347	213	0	X	0	X
Chad	4,900	53	1.0	5,097	9	3	11	11	89	405	-11	534	12
Comoros	85	16	0.2	103	14	0	X	X	X	4	33	0	X
Congo	70	34	0.0	245	76	1	0	43	8	0	X	0	X
Cote d'Ivoire	848	54	0.1	2,899	48	16	129	430	85	2	0	0	X
Djibouti	45	68	0.1	910	15	0	X	X	X	7	47	55	189
Egypt	2,764	32	0.1	5,131	58	51	96	54	258	1,876	20	2,737	19
Equatorial Guinea	4	0	0.0	42	11	0	X	5	25	0	X	0	X
Ethiopia	26,100	0	0.6	40,763	1	56	9	19	12	6,967	3	1,030	7
Gabon	8	156	0.0	141	25	2	100	151	22	0	X	0	X
Gambia	287	1	0.4	377	40	0	X	12	30	4	0	0	X
Ghana	1,133	22	0.1	4,142	20	9	-18	494	35	29	0	0	X
Guinea	1,829	23	0.3	920	19	11	120	47	47	4	0	0	X
Guinea-Bissau	325	110	0.4	397	275	0	X	282	248	4	300	0	X
Kenya	8,000	-17	0.4	15,054	108	20	27	96	58	2	0	665	18
Lesotho	521	4	0.3	2,424	11	1	0	60	-23	214	10	0	X
Liberia	42	25	0.0	477	39	4	83	126	40	0	X	0	X
Libya	200	12	0.1	6,403	14	27	575	X	X	101	44	180	157
Madagascar	10,423	22	1.0	1,837	-5	15	15	1,356	123	1	-33	0	X
Malawi	920	40	0.1	848	8	8	0	230	33	1	-33	0	X
Mali	4,705	21	0.6	10,433	7	14	10	55	120	611	25	230	28
Mauritania	1,000	-11	0.5	6,816	10	4	22	X	X	163	-6	786	14
Mauritius	60	15	0.1	75	8	2	100	11	120	0	X	0	X
Morocco	2,478	-30	0.1	16,415	-24	33	75	8	-27	1,386	-27	57	-72
Mozambique	1,330	-4	0.1	475	-14	20	40	145	1	20	0	0	X
Niger	3,443	38	0.6	11,020	44	13	67	36	38	794	46	414	61
Nigeria	11,875	7	0.1	39,046	15	160	88	1,317	49	950	-1	18	6
Rwanda	645	-5	0.1	1,306	52	1	0	95	34	0	X	0	X
Senegal	2,200	-5	0.3	3,212	28	11	78	199	9	417	5	6	0
Sierra Leone	331	4	0.1	489	43	5	56	43	67	0	X	0	X
Somalia	3,700	1	0.8	25,900	7	3	50	10	25	48	12	5,750	10
South Africa	12,215	-3	0.4	36,111	0	34	36	1,428	8	454	1	0	X
Sudan	22,037	50	1.0	35,712	44	29	33	X	X	670	-3	2,783	1
Swaziland	618	0	1.0	344	22	1	0	19	7	17	0	0	X
Tanzania, United Rep	14,030	24	0.6	10,548	33	27	93	178	30	169	6	0	X
Togo	255	21	0.1	1,521	0	4	100	256	0	3	-17	0	X
Tunisia	632	-28	0.1	6,677	-1	16	21	4	33	343	5	179	0
Uganda	5,030	6	0.3	4,871	67	18	64	238	43	16	2	0	X
Zaire	1,350	19	0.0	3,685	12	18	61	770	14	0	-100	0	X
Zambia	2,685	50	0.4	404	33	13	-28	207	26	1	0	0	X
Zimbabwe	5,000	-17	0.6	2,022	-23	9	13	171	-15	120	14	0	X
NORTH & CENTRAL AMERICA	175,320	-8	0.4	34,213	-6	1,547	124	92,413	14	26,630	7	8	19
Barbados	16	-14	0.1	87	20	1	X	48	27	5	0	0	X
Canada	11,827	-15	0.5	779	45	96	19	10,744	77	389	11	0	X
Costa Rica	2,451	37	0.9	5	67	5	-7	222	1	119	6	0	X
Cuba	6,217	14	0.6	483	15	26	44	2,367	63	773	-8	0	X
Dominican Rep	1,999	5	0.3	545	38	16	133	1,783	155	424	2	0	X
El Salvador	976	-8	0.2	18	20	4	44	392	-11	115	7	0	X
Guatemala	2,254	49	0.3	746	26	15	36	834	37	146	-11	0	X
Haiti	1,367	59	0.2	1,192	1	8	100	567	-66	721	11	0	X
Honduras	2,771	53	0.6	33	33	5	25	537	5	259	4	0	X
Jamaica	287	3	0.1	432	34	5	25	243	6	37	-15	0	X
Mexico	30,864	8	0.4	17,149	4	212	50	18,874	43	12,447	-4	0	X
Nicaragua	2,271	-11	0.7	9	0	5	33	746	17	323	8	0	X
Panama	1,449	8	0.7	7	17	7	67	203	17	174	3	0	X
Trinidad and Tobago	77	6	0.1	61	22	8	33	82	52	5	0	8	19
United States	109,639	-15	0.5	12,194	-24	1,122	187	54,360	-1	10,643	24	0	X
SOUTH AMERICA	250,506	19	0.9	125,820	4	750	54	52,041	2	20,479	1	835	217
Argentina	53,865	-5	1.8	33,927	-13	43	26	3,867	-7	3,245	-13	0	X
Bolivia	5,945	83	0.9	10,660	1	7	17	1,116	-4	985	-13	0	X
Brazil	127,655	39	0.9	28,084	12	481	56	32,551	-7	8,705	1	835	217
Chile	3,517	1	0.3	6,527	2	19	17	1,100	25	528	5	0	X
Colombia	23,100	0	0.8	3,555	37	35	52	2,378	28	3,140	27	0	X
Ecuador	3,587	45	0.4	2,401	3	40	205	4,376	72	645	15	0	X
Guyana	193	-30	0.2	194	18	15	50	170	44	3	-25	0	X
Paraguay	6,967	35	1.9	497	6	14	52	1,263	30	358	-2	0	X
Peru	3,944	-5	0.2	15,046	-13	42	26	2,197	4	1,365	4	0	X
Suriname	60	123	0.2	8	-17	1	0	22	20	0	X	0	X
Uruguay	9,551	-13	3.2	22,488	47	6	0	210	-54	495	3	0	X
Venezuela	12,099	33	0.7	1,741	13	49	83	2,782	65	1,008	-1	0	X

Table 17.5

	Cattle 1984-86	Cattle % Change Since 1974-76	Cattle per Capita 1984-86	Sheep and Goats 1984-86	Sheep/Goats % Change Since 1974-76	Chickens (millions) 1984-86	Chickens % Change Since 1974-76	Pigs 1984-86	Pigs % Change Since 1974-76	Horses[a] 1984-86	Horses % Change Since 1974-76	Buffaloes and Camels 1984-86	B&C % Change Since 1974-76
ASIA	**380,383**	**10**	**0.1**	**596,777**	**13**	**3,164**	**77**	**385,634**	**22**	**42,188**	**7**	**135,548**	**17**
Afghanistan	3,750	4	0.2	23,000	1	7	17	0	X	1,690	3	270	-10
Bahrain	6	20	0.0	22	38	1	X	0	X	0	X	1	0
Bangladesh	22,707	-11	0.2	11,514	32	66	30	0	X	44	-1	1,803	64
Bhutan	320	20	0.2	90	16	0	X	76	26	43	19	29	19
Burma	9,734	31	0.3	1,530	111	34	110	2,926	83	126	24	2,139	25
China	62,885	12	0.1	159,019	-1	1,360	95	321,371	19	25,655	14	20,134	8
Cyprus	41	28	0.1	860	11	4	33	219	74	49	2	0	X
India	197,853	10	0.3	153,383	36	170	21	8,683	20	2,038	0	74,533	22
Indonesia	6,496	5	0.0	17,092	63	338	263	5,375	97	686	10	2,839	19
Iran	8,300	15	0.2	47,933	-3	95	64	0	X	2,239	-3	257	-7
Iraq	1,533	-39	0.1	10,883	-28	65	333	0	X	529	-17	203	-55
Israel	314	8	0.1	383	13	26	39	120	54	11	0	10	3
Japan	4,707	28	0.0	75	-39	333	36	10,734	39	23	-52	0	X
Jordan	36	-11	0.0	1,530	36	33	43	0	X	31	-38	14	-10
Kampuchea, Dem	1,512	32	0.2	2	-44	6	50	1,169	95	12	6	663	12
Korea, Dem People's Rep	1,082	31	0.1	615	37	18	8	2,807	75	45	25	0	X
Korea, Rep	2,577	53	0.1	356	50	49	112	3,153	88	3	-67	0	X
Kuwait	22	175	0.0	583	192	8	33	0	X	0	X	7	17
Lao People's Dem Rep	498	53	0.1	67	116	8	53	1,436	136	40	47	976	57
Lebanon	48	-21	0.0	584	24	10	100	20	5	16	-41	0	X
Malaysia	618	45	0.0	416	5	55	-31	2,093	56	5	0	245	-14
Mongolia	2,385	2	1.3	17,965	-5	0	X	50	255	1,964	-12	568	-7
Nepal	6,427	-2	0.4	5,705	21	9	-53	439	39	0	X	2,910	-25
Oman	129	2	0.1	882	348	0	X	0	X	23	-8	76	663
Pakistan	16,550	12	0.2	54,783	46	113	320	0	X	3,294	28	13,990	25
Philippines	1,816	6	0.0	2,273	67	55	16	7,397	4	300	-3	2,996	10
Qatar	7	-5	0.0	72	-10	1	X	0	X	2	100	9	0
Saudi Arabia	540	90	0.0	6,083	80	34	750	0	X	119	6	165	57
Singapore	0	X	0.0	2	-17	10	-14	767	-31	0	X	0	-100
Sri Lanka	1,768	3	0.1	565	-3	7	17	85	118	1	-50	961	19
Syrian Arab Rep	743	35	0.1	13,127	96	14	105	0	X	270	-21	9	350
Thailand	4,818	15	0.1	117	48	79	46	4,234	18	20	-47	6,284	10
Turkey	16,700	15	0.3	57,477	-3	60	55	12	-22	2,091	-24	619	-41
United Arab Emirates	40	49	0.0	980	181	5	X	0	X	0	X	100	59
Viet Nam	2,360	55	0.0	282	40	65	16	11,989	34	127	-4	2,582	16
Yemen	949	7	0.1	4,087	-60	13	344	0	X	523	-20	57	-44
Yemen, Dem	96	20	0.0	2,317	18	2	100	0	X	170	21	83	-37
EUROPE	**132,309**	**-1**	**0.3**	**148,050**	**8**	**1,223**	**8**	**179,485**	**15**	**6,385**	**-26**	**391**	**-10**
Albania	607	31	0.2	1,920	5	5	67	210	65	116	-1	2	0
Austria	2,652	3	0.4	259	30	15	22	3,943	13	43	7	0	X
Belgium	3,191	4	0.3	140	32	31	-2	5,395	13	32	-43	0	X
Bulgaria	1,745	12	0.2	10,881	7	40	18	3,805	17	495	2	33	-52
Czechoslovakia	5,138	13	0.3	1,125	17	48	22	6,882	5	46	-37	0	X
Denmark	2,606	-16	0.5	75	24	14	-7	9,042	17	31	-46	0	X
Finland	1,603	-14	0.3	114	-12	7	-19	1,283	18	36	-4	0	X
France	23,171	-3	0.4	11,939	3	187	14	11,061	-5	345	-25	0	X
German Dem Rep	5,814	5	0.3	2,514	33	52	10	13,065	16	98	29	0	X
Germany, Fed Rep	15,622	8	0.3	1,308	20	75	-18	23,783	18	365	11	0	X
Greece	757	-38	0.1	14,726	15	30	3	1,092	43	371	-40	1	-83
Hungary	1,858	-5	0.2	2,775	38	58	9	9,120	18	104	-37	0	X
Iceland	64	-2	0.3	770	-10	0	X	12	76	54	23	0	X
Ireland	5,657	-21	1.6	2,724	-27	7	-22	1,022	16	79	-38	0	X
Italy	9,043	8	0.2	10,543	18	111	4	9,132	6	404	-28	103	23
Luxembourg	X	X	0.0	X	X	X	X	X	X	X	X	X	X
Malta	14	17	0.0	10	-46	1	0	90	309	2	-33	0	X
Netherlands	5,280	13	0.4	827	4	88	33	12,146	69	63	-20	0	X
Norway	973	5	0.2	2,523	47	4	0	703	0	16	-30	0	X
Poland	11,057	-15	0.3	4,812	47	61	-29	17,740	-14	1,404	-37	0	X
Portugal	1,125	-6	0.1	5,797	26	17	8	3,223	70	294	-3	0	X
Romania	7,395	28	0.3	19,321	33	119	89	14,481	65	687	12	212	1
Spain	5,032	14	0.1	20,282	10	52	6	11,253	36	544	-37	0	X
Sweden	1,831	-3	0.2	433	12	12	-3	2,561	2	57	4	0	X
Switzerland	1,924	-3	0.3	441	1	6	0	1,988	-1	49	3	0	X
United Kingdom	12,946	-12	0.2	23,982	-16	111	-17	7,835	-2	173	19	0	X
Yugoslavia	5,194	-10	0.2	7,736	-4	72	39	8,610	14	477	-50	40	-39
USSR	**120,500**	**11**	**0.4**	**149,436**	**0**	**1,085**	**49**	**78,136**	**17**	**6,100**	**-15**	**570**	**-15**
OCEANIA	**31,411**	**-25**	**1.3**	**218,795**	**7**	**67**	**26**	**4,928**	**14**	**601**	**-1**	**0**	**X**
Australia	22,803	-30	1.5	148,601	0	50	16	2,531	10	420	-12	0	X
Fiji	158	0	0.2	57	2	2	67	30	85	41	24	0	X
New Zealand	8,030	-13	2.4	70,061	25	9	24	447	2	98	49	0	X
Papua New Guinea	123	-3	0.0	18	18	4	300	1,476	18	1	33	0	X
Solomon Islands	23	0	0.1	0	X	0	X	49	23	0	X	0	X

Source: United Nations Food and Agriculture Organization.
Note: a. Horses includes mules and asses.
0 = zero or less than half the unit of measure; X = not available.
For additional information, see Sources and Technical Notes.

Table 17.6 Soil Erosion in Selected Countries, 1970–86

	Extent and Location	Affected Area as Percentage of National Area	Amount of Erosion (metric tons per year)	Rate of Erosion (metric tons per hectare per year)	Year of Estimate
AFRICA					
Burkina Faso	Central plateau	X	X	5–35	1970s
Ethiopia	Total cropland (12 million ha)	10	500 million	42	1986
	Central highland plateau (47 million ha)	43	1.6 billion	X	1970s
Kenya	Njemps Flats	X	X	138	mid 1980s
	Tugen Plateau	X	X	72	mid 1980s
Lesotho	Grazing and croplands (2.7 million ha)	88	18.5 million	7	X
Madagascar	Mostly cropland (45.9 million ha)	79	X	25–250	1970s
	High central plateau	X	12–40 million	25–250	1980s
Niger	Small watershed (11,700 ha)	0.01	468,000	40	X
Nigeria	State of Imo (900,000 ha)	1	13 million	14.4	1974
	Jos Plateau	X	6 million	X	1975
	Anambra	X	10–15 million	X	1975
Zimbabwe	Area with moderate to severe erosion (304,000 ha)	0.8	15 million	50	1979
NORTH & CENTRAL AMERICA					
Canada	Cultivated land New Bruswick	X	X	40	1980s
	Cultivated land Nova Scotia	X	X	2–26	1980s
	Fraser River valley British Columbia	X	X	up to 30	1985
Dominican Republic	Boa watershed (9,330 ha)	0.2	X	346	1970s
El Salvador	Cultivated land Acelhuate basin (46,300 ha)	2	X	19–190	1970s
Guatemala	Western highlands	X	X	5–35	1979
Jamaica	Total cropland (208,595 ha)	19	7.45 million	36	1980s
	Upper Yalluhs Valley	X	X	90	X
United States	Total cropland (170 million ha)	19	3.1 billion	18	1982

	Extent and Location	Affected Area as Percentage of National Area	Amount of Erosion (metric tons per year)	Rate of Erosion (metric tons per hectare per year)	Year of Estimate
SOUTH AMERICA					
Argentina, Brazil, and Paraguay	La Plata River basin	X	95 million	18.8	X
Peru	Entire country	100	1.9 billion	15	X
ASIA					
Burma	Irrawaddy River basin (43,000 ha)	.07	X	139	1980s
China	Loess Plateau region (60 million ha)	6.4	X	11–251	1980
India	Seriously affected cropland (80 million ha)	27	6 billion	75	1975
	Cultivated land Deccan Black Soil region	X	X	40–100	1980s
Indonesia	Brantas River basin Java	X	X	43	
Nepal	Entire country (13.7 million ha)	100	240 million	35–70	X
Turkey	Entire country	100	5 million	X	1980s
Yemen	Abandoned terraces Serat Mountains (4,900 ha)	0.03	X	150–400	1984
EUROPE					
Belgium	Central Belgium	X	X	10–25	1970s
USSR	Total cropland (232 million ha)	10	2.5 billion	11	1970s

Source: World Resources Institute and International Institute for Environment and Development.
X = not available.
For additional information, see Sources and Technical Notes.

Sources and Technical Notes

Table 17.1 Food and Agricultural Production, 1964–86

Source: United Nations Food and Agriculture Organization (FAO), *FAO Production Yearbook 1986* (FAO, Rome, 1987).

Indexes of agricultural and food production represent the disposable output (after deduction for feed and seed) of a country's agriculture sector relative to the base period 1979–81. The index for a given year is calculated as follows: the disposable output of a commodity in terms of weight or volume is multiplied by the 1979–81 unit value of the commodity according to average national producer prices. The product of this equation is the total value of the crop for that year in terms of 1979–81 prices. The values of all

crop and livestock products are totaled to derive the value of all agricultural production in 1979–81 prices. The aggregate output for other years is then divided by the aggregate output for 1979–81 and multiplied by 100 to obtain the index number.

The continental and world index numbers for a given year are computed by multiplying the disposable output of each agricultural product produced by all relevant countries during that year by the 1979–81 "international price." The resulting number, the total agricultural output value for that region or the world in terms of 1979–81 prices, is then divided by the 1979–81 output value and multiplied by 100. This method avoids distortions caused by the use of international exchange rates.

The agricultural production index includes all crop and livestock products. The food production index covers all edible agricultural products that contain nutrients.

Crop yields are calculated from production and area data. Production data include cereal production for feed and seed. Area data refer to the area harvested. *Cereals* refer to all cereals harvested for dry grain, exclusive of crops cut for hay or harvested green. *Roots and tubers* refer to all root crops grown principally for human consumption; root crops grown principally for feed are excluded.

Most of the data in Tables 17.1–17.5 are supplied by national agriculture ministries in response to annual FAO questionnaires or are derived from agricultural censuses. FAO compiles data from more than 200 countries and many other sources and enters them into a computerized data base. FAO fills gaps in the data by preparing its own estimates. As more information becomes available, FAO corrects its estimates and recalculates the entire time series as necessary.

Table 17.2 Agricultural Inputs, 1964–86

Sources: Cropland area: United Nations Food and Agriculture Organization (FAO), *FAO Production Yearbook 1986* (FAO, Rome, 1987). **Population data:** United Nations Population Division, *World Population Prospects: Estimates and Projections as Assessed in 1984* (United Nations, New York, 1986). **Fertilizer use:** FAO, *Fertilizer Yearbook 1984, 1985,* and *1986* (FAO, Rome, 1985, 1986, and 1987), and unpublished data (FAO, Rome, June 1988). **Irrigation:** FAO, unpublished data (FAO, Rome, June 1988). **High yielding and improved varieties:** Dana G. Dalrymple, *Development and Spread of High-Yielding Rice Varieties in Developing Countries,* U.S. Agency for International Development (U.S. AID), (U.S. AID, Washington, D.C., 1986); Dana G. Dalrymple, *Development and Spread of High-Yielding Wheat Varieties in Developing Countries* (U.S. AID, Washington, D.C., 1986); The International Maize and Wheat Improvement Center (CIMMYT), *1986 CIMMYT World Maize Facts and Trends* (CIMMYT, Mexico, 1987). **Pesticide use: Latin America:** David K. Burton and Bernard J.R. Philogene, *An Overview of Pesticide Usage in Latin America* (Canadian Wildlife Service Latin American Program, Ottawa, undated); **Europe and North America:** United Nations Statistical Commission and Economic Commission for Europe (ECE), *Environment Statistics in Europe and North America* (United Nations Statistical Commission and ECE, New York, 1987); **Asia:** Regional Network for the Production, Marketing, and Control of Pesticides in Asia and the Far East (RENPAF), *RENPAF Gazette: Supply of Pesticides in Nine Countries* (RENPAF, Bangkok, July 1985); **Mauritius, Tanzania, Uganda:** Environment Liaison Centre, *Africa Seminar on the Use and Handling of Agricultural and Other Pest Control Chemicals* (October 30 to November 4, 1983, Nairobi, Kenya); **Algeria:** Office National des Statistique, *Annuiare Statistique de l'Algerie, 1983–84* (Office National des Statistique, Algiers, 1985); **Egypt:** Central Agency for Public Mobilization and Statistics, *Statistical Yearbook* (Central Agency for Public Mobilization and Statistics, Cairo, August 1983); **Kenya:** United Nations Environment Programme (UNEP), *Kenya, National State of the Environment Report* (UNEP, Nairobi, 1987); **Dominican Republic:** U.S. AID, *The Dominican Republic, Country Environmental Profile* (U.S. AID, Washington, D.C., 1981); **Haiti:** U.S. AID, *Draft Environmental Profile of Haiti* (U.S. AID, Washington, D.C., 1979); **Nicaragua:** U.S. AID, *Draft Environmental Profile of Nicaragua* (U.S. AID, Washington, D.C., 1981); **Brazil** (1981–85): Associacao Nacional de Defensivos Agricolas (ANDEF), unpublished data (ANDEF, Brasilia, 1988); **Israel:** Environmental Protection Service, *The Environment in Israel* (Environmental Protection Service, Jerusalem, 1979); **Syria:** L'Office

Arabe de Presse et de Documentation, *Rapport Economique Syrien 1983–84* (L'Office Arabe de Presse et de Documentation, Damascus, 1984); **Turkey:** Environmental Problems Foundation of Turkey (EPFT), *Environmental Profile of Turkey* (EPFT, Ankara, 1981); **Yemen:** U.S. AID, *Draft Environmental Report on Yemen* (U.S. AID, Washington, D.C., 1982); **Denmark, Finland, Iceland, Norway, Sweden:** Nordic Council and the Nordic Statistical Secretariat, *Yearbook of Nordic Statistics 1985* (Nordic Council and Nordic Statistical Secretariat, Oslo, 1986); **France:** Ministere de L'environnement et du Cadre de Vie, *L'Etat de l'Environnement 1982* (Ministere de l'Environnement et du Cadre de Vie, Paris, 1982); **Ireland:** An Foras Forbartha, *The State of the Environment* (An Foras Forbartha, Dublin, 1985); **United Kingdom:** Raymond J. O'Connor and Michael Shrubb, *Farming and Birds* (Cambridge University Press, Cambridge, U.K., 1986); **Yugoslavia:** Federal Statistical Office, *Statistical Pocket Book of Yugoslavia 1985* (Federal Statistical Office, Belgrade, 1985).

Cropland refers to land under temporary and permanent crops, temporary meadows, market and kitchen gardens, and temporarily fallow land. Permanent cropland is land under crops that do not need to be replanted after each harvest, such as cocoa, coffee, rubber, fruit trees, and vines. For trends in cropland area, see Chapter 16, "Land Cover and Settlements," Table 16.1.

Fertilizer use refers to application of nutrients in terms of nitrogen (N), phosphate (P_2O_5) and potash (K_2O). The fertilizer year is July 1–June 30; data refer to the year beginning in July. For 1964–66, fertilizer use refers to the split years ending in 1964, 1965, and 1966.

Irrigated land refers to areas purposely provided with water, including land flooded by river water for crop production or pasture improvement, whether this area is irrigated several times or only once during the year.

High-yielding varieties of rice and wheat are semidwarf or intermediate height varieties developed by international agricultural research centers or national agricultural research programs. They are characterized by short stems, early maturation, and higher tillering capacity, which enable them to better respond to agricultural inputs such as fertilizer and irrigation. *Improved* maize varieties refer to first generation hybrids and open-pollinated varieties resulting from modern plant breeding.

Some data for high-yielding varieties refer to adjacent years. Data for July-to-June crop years are reported for the year ending in June. Data on the use of high-yielding varieties in developed countries are not shown; crops in developed countries are almost exclusively semidwarf varieties or varieties improved by modern plant breeding.

Pesticide statistics were compiled from many different sources. Data may not be comparable among countries because the quality and completeness of data vary. Most data refer to the net weight of active ingredients in the pesticides consumed, but this may not always be the case. The active ingredients in a pesticide are those chemicals with pesticidal properties. Active ingredients are often mixed

with inert ingredients, which dilute or deliver the active ingredients, in a formulated pesticide.

Active ingredients vary widely in potency; information on the ingredients of pesticides is necessary to ensure accurate application and to minimize harmful environmental impacts. For example, one metric ton of the modern synthetic pyrethroid insecticide permethrin is as potent a pesticide as three to five metric tons of a carbamate or organophosphate and 10–30 metric tons of DDT. The data shown in this table do not describe the potency of the active ingredients used. As a result, two countries with similar levels of pesticide consumption may be treating different amounts of land and getting very different results. Increasingly potent pesticides have been developed in recent years, thus a decline in the amount of active ingredients used may not indicate a reduction in the amount of toxic materials introduced into the environment.

When data are given in terms of formulated products rather than active ingredients, as is probably the case with some of the data shown, very little can be assumed about the amounts of chemicals involved or the likely problems resulting from their use.

Data for Europe and North America are based on reports made by countries to the United Nations Food and Agriculture Organization (FAO). FAO compiles data on pesticide use in its *Production Yearbook*, but because of poor reporting by many member countries, FAO pesticide data are often incomplete. Data for Latin American countries were based on FAO data, along with estimates made by the United Nations Industrial Development Organization, agricultural chemical companies, and other experts. Data for Asia were provided by the RENPAF Pesticide Data Collection Project, an ongoing project undertaken by nine Asian countries to gather and report pesticide supply data.

Data for Brazil (1981–85), Denmark, Finland, Iceland, Norway, and Sweden refer to pesticide sales. Data for Mauritius, Tanzania, Haiti, and Yemen refer to pesticide imports.

For additional information on pesticide data, see E.J. Tait and A.B. Lane, "Insecticide Production, Distribution and Use: Analyzing National and International Statistics," in *Management of Pests and Pesticides: Farmers' Perceptions and Practices,* Joyce Tait and Banpot Napompeth, eds. (Westview Press, London, 1987).

Table 17.3 Agricultural Land Distribution, 1960–80

Sources: 1960: United Nations Food and Agriculture Organization (FAO), *Report on the 1960 World Census of Agriculture: Analysis and International Comparison of Results* (FAO, Rome, 1971). 1970: FAO, *1970 World Census of Agriculture: Analysis and International Comparison of Results* (FAO, Rome, 1981). 1980: FAO, *Report on the 1980 World Census of Agriculture,* Census Bulletins 2–25 (FAO, Rome, October 1983–November 1986) and unpublished data (FAO, Rome, June 1988).

The years *1960, 1970,* and *1980* refer to those rounds of the World Censuses of Agriculture organized by FAO. Data for 1960 were compiled from national censuses con-

17 Food and Agriculture

ducted between 1958 and 1964. The 1970 round of censuses covered 1966–74. The 1980 census round includes national censuses conducted between 1977 and 1985. Refer to the sources for dates of country censuses.

Agricultural Holdings, as defined in the *World Census of Agriculture*, are agricultural production units comprising all livestock kept and all land used wholly or partly for agriculture. An agricultural holding may consist of one or more parcels of land, or of livestock without agricultural land. Common grazing land and lands producing only forest products are not considered holdings. Rented land is considered the holding of the operator, not the owner.

Agricultural Area includes all land under temporary or permanent crops and land used as permanent pasture. (See the Technical Note for Table 16.1 in Chapter 16, "Land Cover and Settlements.")

Countries sometimes deviate from the standard FAO definitions and survey techniques, making comparisons among countries (or across years for the same country) difficult. For example, the censuses of many countries exclude holdings below a given size or level of economic importance. In the 1980 census, several countries classified holdings by sizes different from those in the table. These countries' holdings were classified by applying the categories most closely approximating a holding's actual size.

Refer to FAO's census publications for additional information.

Table 17.4 Food Trade and Aid, 1974–86

Sources: Trade data: United Nations Food and Agriculture Organization (FAO), *Trade Yearbook 1976* and *1986* (FAO, Rome, 1977 and 1987); Food Aid data: FAO, *Food Aid in Figures, No. 4* (FAO, Rome, 1986).

Figures shown for food trade are *net* imports or exports: exports were subtracted from imports.

Two definitions of trade are used by coun-tries reporting trade data. "Special trade" reports only imports for domestic consumption and exports of domestic goods. "General trade" records total imports and total exports, including re-exports. Trade figures for Czechoslovakia, German Democratic Republic, Hungary, Poland, Romania, and the USSR include goods purchased by the country that are re-exported to a third country without ever entering the purchasing country. For information on the definition used by a particular country, see the *Trade Yearbook*.

Trade in *cereals* includes wheat and wheat flour, rice, barley, maize, rye, and oats. Trade in *oils* includes oils from soybean, groundnut (peanut), olive, cottonseed, sunflower seed, rapeseed, colza, mustard, linseed, palm, coconut, palm-kernel, castor, and maize; and animal oils, fats, and greases. Trade in *pulses* includes all kinds of dried leguminous vegetables, with the exception of vetches and lupins. Trade in *milk* includes fresh, dry, condensed, and evaporated milk and cream, butter, cheese, and curd. Trade in *meat* includes fresh, chilled, frozen, dried, salted, smoked, and canned meat.

Continental totals include information for small countries not shown in the table.

Food aid refers to the donation or concessional sale of food commodities. *Cereals* include wheat, rice, coarse grains, bulgur wheat, wheat flour, and the cereal component of blended foods. *Oils* include vegetable oil and butter oil. *Milk* includes skimmed milk powder and other dairy products (mainly cheese).

Food aid data are reported by donor countries and international organizations.

Table 17.5 Livestock Populations, 1974–86

Sources: Livestock data: United Nations Food and Agriculture Organization (FAO), *FAO Production Yearbook 1983* and *1986* (FAO, Rome, 1984 and 1987) and unpublished data (FAO, Rome, June 1988). Human population data: United Nations Population Division,

World Population Prospects: Estimates and Projections as Assessed in 1984 (U.N., New York, 1986).

Data on livestock include all livestock in the country, regardless of place or purpose of their breeding. Data on livestock numbers are collected by FAO; estimates are made by FAO for countries that do not or only partially report data. Human population data, used to calculate *cattle per capita*, are for 1985. FAO notes that figures for the number of *chickens* in some countries do not seem accurate. Data on chickens for some countries include all poultry. *Horses* includes mules and asses. For more information on FAO agricultural surveys, see the Technical Note for Table 17.1.

Table 17.6 Soil Erosion in Selected Countries, 1970–86

Sources: Compiled by the World Resources Institute and the International Institute for Environment and Development.

Soil erosion is the removal of soil from the land by the erosive processes of moving wind and water. The natural rate of erosion is determined by climate, topography, soil type, and vegetative cover. It can be exacerbated by poor agricultural practices and by vegetation degradation caused by deforestation and livestock overgrazing.

Erosion rates can be estimated at three locations within a watershed. "Upstream methods" calculate the amount of erosion based on field observations; "midstream methods" are based on the sediment loads carried by rivers; and "downstream methods" are based on the volume of sediment deposited in lakes, in reservoirs, or at the drainage point of a water basin.

Some data in the table are based on a few measurements made at one time and extrapolated to reflect an annual average. Estimates of erosion take into account rainfall and runoff, soil type, slope, land use and cover, and management practices.

18. Forests and Rangelands

Forests and rangelands encompass a variety of ecosystems of great ecological and economic importance. Forests provide habitats for millions of species, protect soil against erosion, and play an important role in biogeochemical cycles. People depend on forests for fuelwood, building materials, and other forest products. Rangelands provide the livelihood for pastoralists and support the herds of the world's major meat producing countries.

Many countries monitor their forest resources. However, different survey procedures and varying definitions of forest resources make it difficult to compare the data compiled in national studies. Table 18.1 presents globally comparable figures on the status of forests and on tropical deforestation. These data are from the 1980 Tropical Forest Resources Assessment, a joint project of the United Nations Food and Agriculture Organization (FAO) and the United Nations Environment Programme (UNEP). FAO and UNEP will complete a second forest resources assessment in 1990.

The Forest Resources Assessments are the most thorough and well-documented surveys of forest resources. Scientists, researchers, and policymakers from many disciplines depend on them for vital information on forest species and biological diversity, on the role of forests and deforestation in the global carbon and water cycles, and on fuelwood production and deficits. The 1980 assessment provided baseline data to address some of these concerns, and the 1990 assessment is expected to provide even more information. For example, the 1980 assessment surveyed only tropical forests and used a narrow definition of deforestation so that deforestation data only included forest lands that had been completely cleared. In the 1990 assessment, FAO and UNEP plan to evaluate the extent of both the tropical and temperate forests of all developing countries and the deforestation of tropical forests in the 1980s. In addition, the 1990 assessment will evaluate the risks to forests from other disturbances (e.g., selective logging) and the environmental implications of forest degradation and deforestation, especially in fragile tropical ecosystems.

Table 18.2 shows production of forest products: roundwood, fuelwood and charcoal, sawnwood, panels, and paper. While developing countries are major producers of roundwood (a raw material) and of fuelwood and charcoal, their contribution to world production of processed forest products is relatively small. See Chapter 14, "Basic Economic Indicators," Table 14.4, for data on wood commodity prices.

A growing body of scientific data indicates that a complex interaction of anthropogenic pollutants and natural stresses is responsible for forest decline *(Waldsterben)* in Europe and to a lesser extent in North America, although the mechanisms remain elusive. Intensive study of permanent forest research plots and extensive surveys of damaged forests are being conducted in Europe and North America to identify the causes of forest damage and gauge its extent. Table 18.3 draws on the first standardized survey of forest decline in Europe, which concluded that the decline of coniferous forests slowed in 1986, but damage to broadleaved trees increased substantially.

Any forest that experiences a hot, dry season is at risk of fire. (See Table 18.4.) While fires can promote nutrient recycling and trigger seed germination, many fires go beyond their beneficial role and destroy large areas of species-rich forest ecosystems. Studies in the Amazon Basin have found that forest fires are significant sources of several air pollutants and contribute to the degradation of global air quality.

Forest fires in the Mediterranean region are a serious concern. During the period 1978–81, Mediterranean countries experienced 82 percent of the total number of fires in Europe, accounting for almost 99 percent of the area burned (excluding the USSR, for which no data are available). Although large areas of forests in developing countries have been lost to fires, statistics on fires in Asia, Africa, and Latin America are not systematically collected. These fires have been attributed to lightning, drought, slash and burn farming, and poor forest management, such as improper treatment of logging slash. In 1982–83, fires burned for several months on the island of Borneo, damaging 3.5 million hectares, including 800,000 hectares of primary lowland rain forest.

Rangelands are not as extensively monitored as forests, so quantitative data on their extent, condition, use, and management are scarcer. In the decade since the 1977 United Nations Conference on Desertification in Nairobi, little progress has been made in assessing the extent or rate of desertification of rangelands. (See Table 18.5.) For qualitative information on rangeland conditions in Asia, the Middle East, and Africa, see Chapter 5, "Forests and Rangelands," in this volume and in *World Resources 1987* and *1986*.

Table 18.1 Forest Resources, 1980s

	Extent of Forest and Woodland, 1980s (thousand hectares)		Deforestation, 1980s Average Annual Extent (thousand hectares per year)	Percent per Year	Reforestation 1980s (thousand hectares per year)	Managed Closed Forest 1980s (thousand hectares)	Protected Closed Forest 1980s (thousand hectares)
	Open	Closed					
WORLD	**1,261,869**	**2,859,535**					
AFRICA	**483,943**	**221,376**	**3,347**	**0.5**	**196**	**2,331**	**9,501**
Algeria	249	1,518	40	2.3	22	X	8
Angola	50,700	2,900	84	0.2	0	X	X
Benin	3,820	47	67	1.7	0	X	X
Botswana	32,560	0	20	0.1	X	X	0
Burkina Faso	4,464	271	80	1.7	2	X	X
Burundi	14	27	1	2.7	1	X	13
Cameroon	7,700	17,920	110	0.4	1	X	X
Cape Verde	X	X	X	X	0	X	X
Central African Rep	32,300	3,590	55	0.2	X	X	X
Chad	13,000	500	80	0.6	0	X	0
Comoros	X	16	0	X	0	X	X
Congo	X	21,340	22	0.1	2	X	130
Cote d'Ivoire	5,376	4,458	510	5.2	3	1	648
Djibouti	100	6	X	X	X	0	0
Egypt	X	X	X	X	2	X	X
Equatorial Guinea	X	1,295	3	0.2	X	X	X
Ethiopia	22,800	4,350	88	0.3	6	X	X
Gabon	75	20,500	15	0.1	X	X	X
Gambia	150	65	5	2.4	0	X	X
Ghana	6,975	1,718	72	0.8	3	1,167	397
Guinea	8,600	2,050	86	0.8	0	X	0
Guinea-Bissau	1,445	660	57	2.7	0	X	X
Kenya	1,255	1,105	39	1.7	0	70	471
Lesotho	X	X	X	X	0	X	X
Liberia	40	2,000	46	2.3	1	X	X
Libya	56	134	X	X	9	X	X
Madagascar	2,900	10,300	156	1.2	12	X	930
Malawi	4,085	186	150	3.5	6	X	146
Mali	6,750	500	36	0.5	0	X	X
Mauritania	525	29	13	2.4	0	X	X
Mauritius	X	3	0	X	1	X	X
Morocco	1,703	1,533	13	0.4	5	421	7
Mozambique	14,500	935	120	0.8	1	X	25
Niger	2,450	100	67	2.6	2	X	X
Nigeria	8,800	5,950	400	2.7	14	0	X
Rwanda	110	120	5	2.3	2	X	12
Senegal	10,825	220	50	0.5	2	0	63
Sierra Leone	1,315	740	6	0.3	0	X	X
Somalia	7,510	1,540	13	0.1	1	X	X
South Africa	X	300	X	X	63	10	290
Sudan	47,000	650	104	0.2	11	50	X
Swaziland	70	4	0	X	5	X	X
Tanzania, United Rep	40,600	1,440	130	0.3	7	0	410
Togo	1,380	304	12	0.7	0	X	X
Tunisia	111	186	5	1.7	4	163	X
Uganda	5,250	765	50	0.8	0	442	58
Zaire	71,840	105,750	347	0.2	0	X	5,700
Zambia	26,500	3,010	80	0.3	3	5	193
Zimbabwe	19,620	200	80	0.4	5	X	X
NORTH & CENTRAL AMERICA	**277,772**	**528,791**	**X**	**X**	**2,528**	**102,884**	**36,849**
Barbados	X	X	X	X	X	X	X
Canada	172,300	264,100	X	X	720	X	4,870
Costa Rica	160	1,638	65	3.6	0	X	320
Cuba	X	1,455	2	0.1	11	200	X
Dominican Rep	X	629	4	0.6	0	X	X
El Salvador	X	141	4	3.2	0	X	X
Guatemala	100	4,442	90	2.0	3	X	62
Haiti	X	48	2	3.8	0	X	X
Honduras	200	3,797	90	2.3	X	58	X
Jamaica	X	67	2	3.0	1	X	2
Mexico	2,100	46,250	615	1.3	17	X	360
Nicaragua	X	4,496	121	2.7	0	250	X
Panama	X	4,165	36	0.9	0	X	X
Trinidad and Tobago	X	208	1	0.4	1	14	X
United States	102,820	195,256	X	X	1,775	102,362	31,198
SOUTH AMERICA	**204,590**	**662,505**	**6,003**	**0.7**	**416**	**X**	**17,022**
Argentina	X	44,500	1550	3.5	40	0	2,594
Bolivia	22,750	44,010	117	0.2	0	X	X
Brazil	157,000	357,480	2,323	0.5	346	0	4,660
Chile	X	7,550	50	0.7	X	X	1,070
Colombia	5,300	46,400	890	1.7	8	X	2,316
Ecuador	480	14,250	340	2.3	4	X	350
Guyana	220	18,475	3	0.0	0	X	12
Paraguay	15,640	4,070	212	1.1	0	X	90
Peru	960	69,680	270	0.4	4	X	850
Suriname	170	14,830	3	0.0	0	X	580
Uruguay	X	490	X	X	X	X	X
Venezuela	2,000	31,870	245	0.7	14	X	4,500

World Resources 1988–89

Table 18.1

| | Extent of Forest and Woodland, 1980s (thousand hectares) | | Deforestation, 1980s | | Reforestation 1980s (thousand hectares per year) | Managed Closed Forest 1980s (thousand hectares) | Protected Closed Forest 1980s (thousand hectares) |
	Open	Closed	Average Annual Extent (thousand hectares per year)	Percent per Year			
ASIA	**65,120**	**431,072**	**X**	**X**	**5,649**	**49,415**	**25,865**
Afghanistan	400	810	0	X	X	100	X
Bahrain	X	X	X	X	X	X	X
Bangladesh	X	927	8	0.9	9	795	25
Bhutan	40	2,100	1	0.1	1	0	X
Burma	X	31,941	105	0.3	2	3,419	299
China	17,200	97,847	0	X	4,552	0	X
Cyprus	24	153	X	X	X	153	25
India	5,393	51,841	147	0.3	120	32,557	6,779
Indonesia	3,000	113,895	620	0.5	187	40	13,620
Iran	1,000	2,750	20	0.5	X	400	X
Iraq	1,160	70	X	X	X	X	X
Israel	20	80	X	X	2	56	7
Japan	1,390	23,890	X	X	240	X	X
Jordan	50	X	0	X	3	X	X
Kampuchea, Dem	5,100	7,548	30	0.2	X	X	X
Korea, Dem People's Rep	X	8,970	X	X	200	X	X
Korea, Rep	240	6,275	X	X	152	X	X
Kuwait	X	X	X	X	X	X	X
Lao People's Dem Rep	5,215	8,410	130	1.0	1	X	X
Lebanon	20	X	0	X	X	X	X
Malaysia	X	20,996	255	1.2	4	2,499	959
Mongolia	5,000	10,000	X	X	X	X	X
Nepal	180	1,941	84	4.0	2	X	330
Oman	X	X	X	X	X	X	X
Pakistan	295	2,185	9	0.4	7	410	15
Philippines	X	9,510	92	1.0	42	X	690
Qatar	X	X	X	X	X	X	X
Saudi Arabia	170	30	0	X	X	X	X
Singapore	X	X	X	X	X	X	X
Sri Lanka	X	1,659	58	3.5	10	X	193
Syrian Arab Rep	90	60	0	X	X	60	X
Thailand	6,440	9,235	379	2.4	13	X	2,220
Turkey	11,343	8,856	X	X	82	8,856	139
United Arab Emirates	X	X	X	X	X	X	X
Viet Nam	1,340	8,770	65	0.6	20	70	560
Yemen	10	X	0	X	X	X	X
Yemen, Dem	X	X	X	X	X	X	X
EUROPE	**21,887**	**137,005**	**X**	**X**	**1,031**	**74,628**	**1,732**
Albania	0	1,280	X	X	X	X	X
Austria	0	3,754	X	X	21	1,489	0
Belgium	80	682	X	X	19	272	0
Bulgaria	400	3,328	X	X	50	3,600	100
Czechoslovakia	145	4,435	X	X	37	4,435	X
Denmark	18	466	X	X	X	330	56
Finland	3,340	19,885	X	X	158	10,578	294
France	1,200	13,875	X	X	51	2,957	92
German Dem Rep	285	2,700	X	X	X	2,697	85
Germany, Fed Rep	218	6,989	X	X	62	3,886	X
Greece	3,242	2,512	X	X	X	1,603	55
Hungary	25	1,612	X	X	19	1,612	41
Iceland	100	X	X	X	X	X	X
Ireland	33	347	X	X	9	298	0
Italy	1,700	6,363	X	X	15	699	162
Luxembourg	X	X	X	X	X	38	0
Malta	X	X	X	X	X	X	X
Netherlands	61	294	X	X	2	225	0
Norway	1,066	7,635	X	X	79	1,130	60
Poland	138	8,588	X	X	106	8,099	103
Portugal	349	2,627	X	X	4	X	7
Romania	410	6,265	X	X	X	5,940	X
Spain	3,905	6,906	X	X	92	2,007	40
Sweden	3,442	24,400	X	X	207	14,301	230
Switzerland	189	935	X	X	7	627	7
United Kingdom	151	2,027	X	X	40	1,505	0
Yugoslavia	1,390	9,100	X	X	53	6,300	400
USSR	**137,000**	**791,600**	**X**	**X**	**4,540**	**791,600**	**20,000**
OCEANIA	**71,557**	**87,186**	**X**	**X**	**114**	**X**	**146**
Australia	65,085	41,658	X	0.0	62	X	X
Fiji	0	811	2	0.2	4	X	X
New Zealand	2,300	7,200	X	0.0	43	X	X
Papua New Guinea	3,945	34,230	23	0.1	2	0	136
Solomon Islands	17	2,423	1	0.0	2	X	X

Sources: U.N. Food and Agriculture Organization; U.N. Economic Commission for Europe; and country data sources.
Notes:
0 = zero or less than half the unit of measure; X = not available.
For additional information, see Sources and Technical Notes.

Table 18.2 Wood Production, 1974–86

| | Average Annual Production (thousand cubic meters) | | | | | | | | | | Paper (1000 metric tons) | |
| | Roundwood | | Fuelwood and Charcoal | | Industrial Roundwood | | Sawnwood | | Panels | | | |
	1984–86	Percentage Change Since 1974–76	1984–86	Percentage Change Since 1974–76	1984–86	Percentage Change Since 1974–76	1984–86	Percentage Change Since 1974–76	1984–86	Percentage Change Since 1974–76	1984–86	Percentage Change Since 1974–76
WORLD	3,180,851	21	1,646,061	28	1,534,791	15	466,979	11	113,332	27	194,596	36
AFRICA	438,081	34	384,694	35	53,386	24	7,823	36	1,793	60	2,233	84
Algeria	1,885	35	1,655	36	230	31	13	–7	X	X	122	307
Angola	4,900	23	3,903	34	997	–8	4	–97	7	–77	X	X
Benin	4,404	33	4,181	33	223	29	8	0	X	X	X	X
Botswana	1,180	47	1,107	46	73	49	X	X	X	X	X	X
Burkina Faso	6,757	25	6,452	25	306	24	X	X	X	X	X	X
Burundi	3,638	26	3,593	26	45	41	X	X	X	X	X	X
Cameroon	11,836	38	9,134	30	2,702	71	646	121	73	0	X	X
Cape Verde	X	X	X	X	X	X	X	X	X	X	X	X
Central African Rep	3,391	25	2,925	32	466	–7	56	–31	X	X	X	X
Chad	3,567	25	3,063	25	505	25	X	X	X	X	X	X
Comoros	X	X	X	X	X	X	X	X	X	X	X	X
Congo	2,434	36	1,585	29	849	49	62	13	64	14	X	X
Cote d'Ivoire	12,000	14	7,970	45	4,030	–19	706	32	206	140	X	X
Djibouti	X	X	X	X	X	X	X	X	X	X	X	X
Egypt	2,010	29	1,917	29	93	29	X	X	44	16	145	33
Equatorial Guinea	587	37	447	16	140	218	38	138	X	X	X	X
Ethiopia	37,945	28	36,132	27	1,813	38	45	–49	15	7	X	X
Gabon	4,009	6	2,525	15	1,484	–6	123	71	221	117	X	X
Gambia	850	10	829	9	21	110	X	X	X	X	X	X
Ghana	9,330	20	8,219	38	1,111	–40	340	–18	63	–7	X	X
Guinea	4,251	24	3,647	25	604	17	90	0	X	X	X	X
Guinea–Bissau	559	11	422	7	137	26	16	0	X	X	X	X
Kenya	32,429	51	30,874	50	1,555	59	181	39	X	X	93	272
Lesotho	525	28	525	28	X	X	X	X	X	X	X	X
Liberia	4,470	34	3,913	43	557	–6	169	21	X	X	X	X
Libya	634	19	536	10	98	109	31	182	X	X	6	20
Madagascar	6,890	39	6,083	32	807	139	234	111	X	X	10	25
Malawi	6,513	33	6,211	34	302	8	16	–56	X	X	X	X
Mali	4,908	29	4,599	29	309	26	5	25	X	X	X	X
Mauritania	12	33	7	40	5	25	X	X	X	X	X	X
Mauritius	18	–55	14	–36	5	–72	X	X	X	X	X	X
Morocco	2,043	58	1,274	63	769	50	149	84	105	184	106	116
Mozambique	15,169	49	14,203	54	966	4	35	–82	37	429	X	X
Niger	3,922	31	3,680	31	242	32	X	X	X	X	X	X
Nigeria	95,421	44	87,656	41	7,765	106	2,645	193	215	169	X	X
Rwanda	5,773	15	5,535	12	237	295	13	550	X	X	X	X
Senegal	4,051	34	3,505	33	546	37	11	120	X	X	X	X
Sierra Leone	7,775	18	7,635	18	140	2	19	–21	X	X	X	X
Somalia	4,425	43	4,358	43	67	29	14	8	X	X	X	X
South Africa	19,022	11	7,078	2	11,944	17	1,552	–11	398	9	1,551	76
Sudan	19,531	34	17,690	35	1,841	32	13	–13	X	X	X	X
Swaziland	2,223	–4	560	20	1,663	–10	136	39	5	25	X	X
Tanzania, United Rep	23,058	42	21,604	41	1,454	51	101	44	6	–50	X	X
Togo	766	30	603	31	163	27	5	0	X	X	X	X
Tunisia	2,791	26	2,672	26	119	35	X	X	X	X	43	139
Uganda	12,501	37	10,868	38	1,633	31	23	–43	6	100	X	X
Zaire	30,490	33	27,989	34	2,501	29	121	3	53	36	X	X
Zambia	9,933	29	9,418	29	515	34	50	43	X	X	X	X
Zimbabwe	7,214	43	5,867	41	1,347	55	141	40	30	400	72	89
NORTH & CENTRAL AMERICA	693,037	37	154,387	169	538,650	20	146,019	25	39,579	25	79,833	27
Barbados	X	X	X	X	X	X	X	X	X	X	X	X
Canada	173,985	33	6,197	66	167,788	32	52,288	64	5,913	46	14,648	25
Costa Rica	3,091	–4	2,553	32	538	–58	412	–25	46	10	13	86
Cuba	3,275	36	2,751	38	524	26	105	0	127	2,017	129	6
Dominican Rep	978	114	972	121	6	–67	X	X	X	X	10	11
El Salvador	4,755	33	4,673	34	82	6	44	33	X	X	X	X
Guatemala	6,832	24	6,677	32	155	–65	106	–58	7	–61	16	–16
Haiti	5,906	26	5,667	28	239	0	14	0	X	X	X	X
Honduras	5,319	28	4,538	41	781	–17	422	–27	8	–27	X	X
Jamaica	93	52	13	86	80	48	31	–6	4	–60	X	X
Mexico	21,074	23	13,842	31	7,233	10	2,107	2	780	212	2,361	87
Nicaragua	3,582	26	2,702	36	880	3	222	–42	14	17	31	X
Panama	2,047	28	1,708	17	339	140	53	–13	12	33	31	121
Trinidad and Tobago	59	–37	22	29	37	–52	18	–49	X	X	X	X
United States	461,738	41	101,922	434	359,816	16	90,168	11	32,669	20	62,590	26
SOUTH AMERICA	308,655	40	216,961	26	91,694	90	24,836	67	3,831	54	6,623	81
Argentina	11,924	28	6,510	19	5,414	41	1,117	132	389	16	906	39
Bolivia	1,315	8	1,167	30	149	–54	97	–33	X	X	X	X
Brazil	234,072	43	168,092	25	65,980	122	17,875	85	2,531	44	4,092	120
Chile	15,667	48	6,076	17	9,591	78	2,115	58	216	279	378	44
Colombia	17,221	17	14,548	24	2,673	–10	721	–23	113	30	436	54
Ecuador	8,497	48	6,040	50	2,458	43	1,228	58	171	362	X	X
Guyana	202	–8	18	80	184	–12	63	–18	X	X	X	X
Paraguay	7,789	61	4,882	29	2,907	178	786	133	X	X	X	X
Peru	7,706	9	6,521	21	1,185	–29	516	–13	39	–44	147	–4
Suriname	202	–25	14	–39	188	–24	65	5	15	–46	X	X
Uruguay	2,630	51	2,362	61	268	–3	58	–43	14	–7	48	55
Venezuela	1,176	3	666	37	510	–22	176	–51	249	219	573	48

Table 18.2

	Average Annual Production (thousand cubic meters)										Paper (1000 metric tons)	
	Roundwood		Fuelwood and Charcoal		Industrial Roundwood		Sawnwood		Panels			
	1984-86	Percentage Change Since 1974-76	1984-86	Percentage Change Since 1974-76	1984-86	Percentage Change Since 1974-76	1984-86	Percentage Change Since 1974-76	1984-86	Percentage Change Since 1974-76	1984-86	Percentage Change Since 1974-76
ASIA	**984,813**	**18**	**739,144**	**17**	**245,670**	**21**	**98,057**	**21**	**22,313**	**56**	**37,582**	**71**
Afghanistan	6,534	8	4,987	10	1,547	4	400	5	X	X	X	X
Bahrain	X	X	X	X	X	X	X	X	X	X	X	X
Bangladesh	27,156	30	26,297	32	859	-15	111	-50	X	X	118	131
Bhutan	3,224	15	2,946	14	278	17	X	X	X	X	8,641	160
Burma	18,714	24	15,852	22	2,861	34	504	25	15	25	X	X
China	262,131	31	170,675	22	91,456	51	26,063	59	1,582	333	X	X
Cyprus	81	-15	23	15	58	-22	60	40	X	X	X	X
India	245,905	24	222,302	22	23,603	45	16,942	148	442	143	1,649	81
Indonesia	155,570	22	127,279	23	28,291	22	6,921	186	4,656	3,914	505	931
Iran	6,745	2	2,369	4	4,376	1	163	16	53	-35	78	15
Iraq	139	21	89	37	50	0	8	0	2	0	X	X
Israel	118	20	11	0	107	23	X	X	145	-1	143	43
Japan	33,062	-11	546	-41	32,516	-10	28,634	-26	8,949	5	20,292	36
Jordan	9	-10	5	25	4	-33	X	X	X	X	X	X
Kampuchea, Dem	5,302	4	4,735	3	567	10	43	0	2	0	X	X
Korea, Dem People's Rep	4,543	17	3,943	20	600	0	280	0	X	X	80	3
Korea, Rep	8,533	-11	6,164	-13	2,369	-6	3,185	49	1,288	-18	2,431	269
Kuwait	X	X	X	X	X	X	X	X	X	X	X	X
Lao People's Dem Rep	4,110	22	3,807	21	303	36	19	-71	X	X	X	X
Lebanon	476	-2	451	-3	25	25	33	0	46	-6	44	29
Malaysia	38,428	30	7,575	26	30,853	30	5,656	27	1,437	95	X	X
Mongolia	2,390	0	1,350	0	1,040	0	470	0	X	X	X	X
Nepal	15,779	25	15,219	27	560	0	220	0	X	X	X	X
Oman	X	X	X	X	X	X	X	X	X	X	X	X
Pakistan	20,833	38	19,564	34	1,269	165	55	-38	61	110	77	64
Philippines	35,527	7	29,398	29	6,129	-41	1,080	-26	565	1	197	-24
Qatar	X	X	X	X	X	X	X	X	X	X	X	X
Saudi Arabia	X	X	X	X	X	X	X	X	X	X	X	X
Singapore	X	X	X	X	X	X	X	X	X	X	X	X
Sri Lanka	8,621	21	7,943	20	679	34	22	-39	14	-44	23	15
Syrian Arab Rep	48	9	15	150	34	-11	X	X	27	108	X	X
Thailand	36,260	17	31,884	24	4,376	-16	1,007	-38	307	169	468	150
Turkey	17,412	-58	11,471	-67	5,941	-13	4,923	86	751	126	452	22
United Arab Emirates	X	X	X	X	X	X	X	X	X	X	X	X
Viet Nam	24,882	26	21,632	24	3,250	38	354	-32	X	X	65	30
Yemen	X	X	X	X	X	X	X	X	X	X	X	X
Yemen, Dem	286	29	286	29	X	X	X	X	X	X	X	X
EUROPE	**348,650**	**9**	**56,508**	**9**	**292,143**	**9**	**86,409**	**5**	**31,772**	**7**	**56,088**	**32**
Albania	2,330	0	1,608	0	722	0	200	0	12	0	8	0
Austria	14,010	16	1,413	41	12,597	14	6,124	10	1,309	27	2,077	53
Belgium	3,247	19	538	148	2,709	8	799	19	1,971	3	841	10
Bulgaria	4,709	1	1,755	70	2,954	-19	1,445	-17	590	23	452	19
Czechoslovakia	18,958	15	1,357	-24	17,601	19	5,233	20	1,411	66	1,250	21
Denmark	2,358	45	380	381	1,978	28	862	13	317	-17	309	40
Finland	40,861	17	3,139	-49	37,722	32	7,580	24	1,346	-11	7,438	59
France	39,008	2	10,426	-3	28,582	3	9,078	-3	2,500	-18	5,355	17
German Dem Rep	X	X	593	26	10,174	32	2,491	14	1,240	42	1,306	9
Germany, Fed Rep	10,767	31	3,795	26	26,775	-5	9,720	-2	6,876	2	9,243	52
Greece	2,810	4	1,915	-4	895	26	311	-7	399	45	286	30
Hungary	6,679	20	2,899	18	3,780	22	1,294	23	384	26	506	45
Iceland	X	X	X	X	X	X	X	X	X	X	X	X
Ireland	1,259	267	46	475	1,213	262	297	519	52	-62	27	-77
Italy	9,433	44	4,905	54	4,528	33	2,251	16	2,260	-8	4,647	14
Luxembourg	X	X	X	X	X	X	X	X	X	X	X	X
Malta	X	X	X	X	X	X	X	X	X	X	X	X
Netherlands	1,036	9	92	197	944	3	391	58	86	-54	1,944	24
Norway	10,407	10	799	55	9,608	8	2,284	7	667	5	1,580	23
Poland	23,866	10	3,724	108	20,143	1	6,683	-20	2,122	27	1,292	0
Portugal	9,080	20	604	11	8,476	21	2,584	47	564	110	575	73
Romania	24,294	14	4,571	-15	19,723	23	4,573	-3	1,594	16	803	25
Spain	15,407	28	2,261	-12	13,146	39	2,319	-7	1,859	36	3,006	51
Sweden	52,146	-11	4,424	75	47,722	-15	11,853	-1	1,381	-30	7,076	42
Switzerland	4,785	22	870	13	3,915	24	1,641	15	648	18	1,029	45
United Kingdom	4,647	33	149	-25	4,499	36	1,681	28	890	36	3,736	-9
Yugoslavia	15,983	14	4,246	9	11,737	16	4,716	30	1,293	41	1,301	96
USSR	**370,500**	**-5**	**85,567**	**3**	**284,933**	**-7**	**98,167**	**-14**	**12,737**	**40**	**9,972**	**16**
OCEANIA	**37,114**	**25**	**8,800**	**33**	**28,314**	**23**	**5,669**	**-4**	**1,308**	**28**	**2,266**	**31**
Australia	19,217	38	2,876	112	16,341	30	3,138	-10	893	27	1,554	35
Fiji	235	42	37	311	198	27	86	4	X	X	X	X
New Zealand	9,205	1	50	-80	9,155	4	2,280	7	384	35	712	23
Papua New Guinea	7,623	30	5,533	16	2,090	85	119	-17	19	-17	X	X
Solomon Islands	649	52	210	12	439	84	16	100	X	X	X	X

Source: United Nations Food and Agriculture Organization.
0 = zero or less than half of 1 percent; X = not available.
For additional information, see Sources and Technical Notes.

Table 18.3 Forest Damage in Europe, 1986

	Total Forest Area (000 ha)	Percent of National Forest Area Surveyed	Number of Trees Assessed	Percent of Trees in Observed Defoliation Classes								
				All Species			Coniferous			Broadleaved		
				Healthy (0–10%)	Slight Damage (11–25%)	Moderate to Severe Damage (26–100%)a	Healthy (0–10%)	Slight Damage (11–25%)	Moderate to Severe Damage (26–100%)a	Healthy (0–10%)	Slight Damage (11–25%)	Moderate to Severe Damage (26–100%)a
Austria	3,754	79	70,638	63	33	5	64	32	5	57	37	6
Belgium	680	X	X	X	X	X	X	X	X	X	X	X
Bulgaria	3,300	29	2,750	66	26	8	75	20	5	38	8	4
Czechoslovakia	4,578	34	5,165	51	33	16	51	33	16	X	X	X
Denmark	466	X	X	X	X	X	X	X	X	X	X	X
Finland	20,059	100	5,431	X	X	X	73	19	9	X	X	X
France	14,440	16	34,000	72	20	8	62	26	13	81	15	5
German Dem Rep	2,955	X	X	X	X	X	X	X	X	X	X	X
Germany, Fed Rep	7,360	100	213,556	46	35	19	47	33	20	45	38	17
Greece	5,754	X	X	X	X	X	X	X	X	X	X	X
Hungary	1,637	11	X	75	13	12	76	15	9	76	12	12
Ireland	380	X	X	X	X	X	X	X	X	X	X	X
Italy	8,675	96	102,500	95	4	1	X	X	X	X	X	X
Liechtenstein	8	100	X	X	X	X	X	X	X	X	X	X
Luxembourg	88	82	4,906	74	21	5	80	16	4	70	25	6
Netherlands	311	90	33,100	45	32	23	41	30	29	53	34	13
Norway	6,660	83	12,792	X	X	X	71	17	12	X	X	X
Poland	8,654	64	700,000	85	10	5	82	12	5	93	4	3
Portugal	2,976	X	X	X	X	X	X	X	X	X	X	X
Spain	11,789	6	10,824	72	15	13	61	21	18	96	2	3
Sweden	23,700	48	18,900	X	X	X	82	16	2	X	X	X
Switzerland	1,186	100	8,059	50	37	13	48	36	16	55	37	8
United Kingdom	2,018	72	3,384	X	X	X	X	X	X	X	X	X
USSR	810,900	X	X	X	X	X	X	X	X	X	X	X
Yugoslavia	9,125	11	24,382	X	X	X	61	16	23	X	X	X

Source: International Co-operative Programme on Assessment and Monitoring of Air Pollution Effects on Forests.
Note: a. Includes dead trees. X = not available. For additional information, see Sources and Technical Notes.

Table 18.4 Forest Fires in Selected Countries, 1975–84

	Fires on Forest and Other Land, 1975–84				Percentage of Area Burned		Average Annual Fire Losses		Average Annual Prevention Expenditures (US$ 000)
	Number		Total Annual Area Burned (hectares)						
	Range	Average	Range	Average	Natural Causes	Human Causes	Total (US$ 000)	Wood (000 m³)	
EUROPE									
Austria	131–547	232	63–474	166	X	X	X	X	28
Belgium	25–652	115	30–2,674	358	X	48	37	X	X
Bulgaria	67–79	74	158–200	183	X	69	46	X	137
Czechoslovakia	225–1,795	478	107–1,300	435	X	100	X	X	X
Denmark	4–200	62	4–2,000	338	0	87	X	X	X
Finland	171–694	441	100–801	505	3	90	X	X	462
France	2,432–9,800	5,458	19,875–88,344	42,646	0	20	X	X	30,264
German Dem Rep	243–2,480	968	144–5,952	1,412	X	X	160	X	X
Germany, Fed Rep	634–5,433	1,510	289–8,768	1,924	0	35	1,752	X	X
Greece	590–1,284	1,018	8,389–81,417	32,931	X	X	X	X	X
Hungary	98–689	234	92–514	264	0	79	241	X	597
Ireland	97–919	341	170–1,248	561	0	9	107	X	X
Italy	5,227–11,052	6,900	50,791–242,218	127,322	0	33	43,931	2,005	X
Luxembourg	1–36	10	0–23	5	0	90	5	X	X
Netherlands	65–443	181	24–1,029	321	0	83	X	X	X
Norway	354–1,769	842	162–2,850	935	X	X	85	X	651
Poland	642–3,827	2,140	680–6,961	3,275	0	62	9,120	X	22,589
Portugal	1,609–6,680	3,427	39,557–97,345	64,184	0	19	X	1,236	X
Romania	20–65	44	40–302	130	0	88	25	X	X
Spain	2,148–10,882	6,310	67,540–434,868	212,195	4	61	294,829	353	X
Sweden	77–5,833	660	417–6,887	1,437	X	X	X	X	X
Switzerland	39–390	134	80–4,834	1,091	0	35	X	X	X
United Kingdom	112–1,655	792	86–2,174	775	0	95	X	X	X
Yugoslavia	633–1,080	814	4,033–20,585	11,537	X	X	3,059	167	X
NORTH AMERICA									
Canada	8,049–11,049	9,389	289,413–5,413,365	2,273,869	95	4	307,888	X	200,342
United States	118,281–189,159	153,367	710,068–1,691,775	1,172,481	15	85	X	X	179,667
MIDDLE EAST/NORTH AFRICA									
Algeria	562–1,584	944	4,668–221,367	67,249	X	X	X	X	X
Cyprus	55–97	80	371–7,512	2,452	0	8	11	X	410
Israel	678–1,128	918	1,740–5,700	3,292	0	14	22	3	1,344
Jordan	41–90	67	38–738	364	X	X	X	X	X
Lebanon	X	X	X	1,200	X	X	X	X	X
Libya	3	3	1–43	16	X	X	X	X	X
Morocco	X	185	1,423–17,730	5,670	X	X	X	X	X
Syrian Arab Rep	X	X	X	1,500	X	X	X	X	X
Tunisia	73–145	108	376–4,139	1,854	X	X	X	X	X
Turkey	702–1,615	1,098	3,554–43,076	14,396	X	X	3,168	103	43,592

Sources: United Nations Economic Commission for Europe and United Nations Food and Agriculture Organization. **Note:** a. 1981–83.
0 = zero or negligible; X = not available. For additional information, see Sources and Technical Notes.

Table 18.5 Extent of Desertification, Early 1980s

| | Total Productive Drylands | | Productive Dryland Types | | | | | |
| | | | Rangelands | | Rainfed Croplands | | Irrigated Lands | |
	Area (million hectares)	Percent Desertified	Area (million hectares)	Percent Desertified	Area (million hectares)	Percent Desertified	Area (million hectares)	Percent Desertified
Total	**3,257**	**61**	**2,556**	**62**	**570**	**60**	**131**	**30**
Sudano–Sahelian Africa	473	88	380	90	90	80	3	30
Southern Africa	304	80	250	80	52	80	2	30
Mediterranean Africa	101	83	80	85	20	75	1	40
Western Asia	142	82	116	85	18	85	8	40
Southern Asia	359	70	150	85	150	70	59	35
USSR in Asia	298	55	250	60	40	30	8	25
China and Mongolia	315	69	300	70	5	60	10	30
Australia	491	23	450	22	39	30	2	19
Mediterranean Europe	76	39	30	30	40	32	6	25
South America and Mexico	293	71	250	72	31	77	12	33
North America	405	40	300	42	85	39	20	20

Source: United Nations Environment Programme.
For additional information, see Sources and Technical Notes.

Sources and Technical Notes

Table 18.1 Forest Resources, 1980s

Sources: Developing countries: U.N. Food and Agriculture Organization (FAO) Forest Resources Division, unpublished data (FAO, Rome, March 1988). Developed countries, Cyprus, Israel, and Turkey: FAO and United Nations Economic Commission for Europe (ECE), *The Forest Resources of the ECE Region* (ECE, Geneva, 1985). Djibouti, Japan, Mongolia, Republic of Korea, and Democratic People's Republic of Korea: FAO, *Forest Resources 1980* (FAO, Rome, 1985). Reforestation data for China: State Statistical Bureau, *China: A Statistics Survey in 1985* (New World Press, Beijing, 1985); Reforestation data for Jordan: Library of Congress, Science and Technology Division, *Draft Environmental Report on Jordan* (Library of Congress, Washington, D.C., August 1979); Reforestation data for Yugoslavia: Socijalisticka Federativna Republika Jugoslavija Savenzi Zavod Za Statistiku, *Statisticki Godisnjak Jugoslavija 1983, 1984, 1985* (Savenzi Zavod Za Statistiku, Belgrade, 1984, 1985, 1986).

Forests and woodlands are natural stands of woody vegetation in which trees predominate. FAO and ECE use slightly different definitions of open and closed forests. FAO defines closed forest as land where trees cover a high portion of the ground and there is not a continuous layer of grass on the forest floor. ECE defines a forest as closed when tree crowns cover more than 20 percent of the area and when the area is used primarily for forestry. Open forests, as defined by FAO, are mixed forest/grasslands with at least 10 percent tree cover and a continuous grass layer. As defined by ECE, open forests are not used for agricultural purposes; have 5–20 percent of their area covered by tree crowns; have no more than half a hectare covered by groups of trees; or have shrubs or stunted trees covering more than 20 percent of their area. In both studies, "natural" means all stands except plantations and includes stands that have been degraded to some degree by catastrophic fire, logging, or agriculture. Trees are distinguished from shrubs on the basis of height: a mature tree has a single well-defined stem and is taller than 7 meters, and a mature shrub is usually less than 7 meters tall.

Deforestation refers to the clearing of forest lands for use in shifting cultivation, permanent agriculture, or settlements. As defined here, deforestation does not include other alterations such as selective logging, which can substantially affect forests, forest soil, wildlife and its habitat, and the global carbon cycle. For an analysis of tropical deforestation based on a broader definition of deforestation, see Norman Myers, *The Primary Source* (Norton, New York, 1984).

Reforestation refers to the establishment of plantations for industrial and nonindustrial uses. Reforestation does not include regeneration of old tree crops (through either natural regeneration or forest management), although some countries may report regeneration as reforestation. Many trees are also planted for nonindustrial uses, such as village wood lots. Reforestation data often exclude this component.

Data for developing countries are based on the 1980 Tropical Forest Resources Assessment, a joint project of FAO and the United Nations Environment Programme (UNEP). The assessment surveyed the moist tropical forests of 76 developing countries, covering 97 percent of the total area of developing countries in the tropics. Data for the study were collected from research institutes; correspondence with national forestry services; visits to national forestry, land use, and survey institutions in some of the major forestry countries, and to FAO regional offices; photographic surveys of all or part of five countries; satellite imagery of all or part of 19 countries; and side-looking airborne radar surveys of four additional countries. Three countries (Burma, India, and Peru) prepared their own national reports. In many cases, FAO adjusted data to fit common definitions and to correspond to a baseline year of 1980. FAO's Forest Resources Division continues to revise and update data collected in the 1980 assessment.

The FAO/ECE survey covered all types of forests in the 32 member countries of the ECE. Data for this study were drawn from four types of sources: official data supplied in response to questionnaires; estimates by experts in some countries; recent ECE and FAO publications, country reports, and official articles; and estimates by the professional staff conducting the study. Most data refer to the period around 1980, but no attempt was made to adjust the data to a baseline year.

For an evaluation and detailed comparison of forest statistics, see Alan Grainger, "Quantifying Changes in Forest Cover in the Humid Tropics: Overcoming Current Limitations," *Journal of World Forest Resource Management* Vol. 1, (1984) pp. 3–23; and J.M. Melillo, *et al.*, "A Comparison of Two Recent Estimates of Disturbance in Tropical Forests," *Environmental Conservation*, Vol. 12, No. 1 (1985).

Table 18.2 Wood Production, 1974–86

Sources: United Nations Food and Agriculture Organization (FAO), *Yearbook of Forest Products 1984* (FAO, Rome, 1986); and unpublished data (FAO, Rome, January 1988).

Roundwood production refers to all wood in the rough, whether destined for industrial uses or for use as fuelwood.

Fuelwood and Charcoal production includes all rough wood used for cooking, heating, and power production. Wood intended for charcoal production, pit kilns, and portable ovens is included.

Industrial roundwood production refers to all roundwood products other than fuelwood and charcoal: sawlogs, veneer logs, sleepers, pitprops, pulpwood, and other industrial products.

Sawnwood includes wood that has been sawn, planed, or shaped into products such as planks, beams, boards, rafters, or railroad ties. Wood flooring is excluded. Sawnwood is usually thicker than 5 millimeters.

Panels include all wood-based panel commodities such as veneer sheets, plywood, particle board, and compressed or noncompressed fiberboard.

Paper includes newsprint, printing and writing paper, and other paper and paperboard.

FAO compiles forest products data from

responses to annual questionnaires sent to national governments. Data from other sources, such as national statistical yearbooks, are also used. In some cases FAO prepares its own estimates. FAO periodically revises its data using new information; the latest figures are subject to revision.

Statistics on the production of fuelwood and charcoal are lacking for many countries. FAO uses population data and country-specific per capita consumption figures to estimate fuelwood and charcoal production for these countries. Consumption of nonconiferous fuelwood ranges from a low of 0.0016 cubic meters per capita per year in Jordan to a high of 0.9783 cubic meters per capita per year in Benin. Consumption was also estimated for coniferous fuelwood. For both coniferous and nonconiferous fuelwood, the per capita consumption estimates were multiplied by the number of people in the country to determine national totals.

Table 18.3 Forest Damage in Europe, 1986

Source: Programme Co-ordinating Centres, International Co-operative Programme on Assessment and Monitoring of Air Pollution Effects on Forests, *Report on the 1986 Forest Damage Survey in Europe* (U.N. Economic Commission for Europe, Geneva, 1987).

In May 1986, European countries adopted a uniform procedure for assessing the impact of air pollution on forests. Published as the *Manual on Methodologies and Criteria for Harmonized Sampling, Assessment, Monitoring, and Analysis of the Effects of Air Pollution on Forests* (Economic Commission for Europe, Geneva, 1986), it was the result of two years of discussion among foresters, plant physiologists, statisticians, biologists, soil scientists, atmospheric scientists, and other experts.

The *Manual* identifies two tree crown condition indicators—foliage discoloration and defoliation—as the primary variables for measuring slowed forest growth and forest death. The 1986 surveys primarily relied on measurements of *defoliation*—foliage loss—as did most previous forest damage surveys. Sample plots were systematically identified throughout each country either in a grid or in proportion to ecotype. National data were extrapolated from measurements done in the sample plots. In the sample plots, the extent of defoliation was estimated by an observer standing on the forest floor. Only Luxembourg measured both defoliation and discoloration in its 1986 survey. Future surveys will measure both foliage loss and discoloration to determine the severity of damage to a tree or stand.

The 25 countries included in Table 18.3 have confirmed their participation in the International Co-operative Programme, and 20 conducted surveys in 1986. Defoliation data are available for the 15 countries that based their surveys on the ECE *Manual*. Some national focal centers received the *Manual* after they had begun planning 1986 surveys; as a result, minor discrepancies in assessment and reporting exist. Liechtenstein conducted an aerial infrared photo survey. Italy, Poland, and Norway reported 1985 data.

The data on total forest area shown in

Table 18.3 may differ slightly from ECE forest area data in Table 18.1 because the former were provided by the participating countries at the time of the forest damage survey, while the latter were collected and standardized by the ECE and FAO.

Using crown condition indicators to measure forest decline is problematic. Climatic extremes, exposure, elevation, soil fertility, and age affect the loss and density of a tree's crown. The relationship between foliage loss and the radial growth of a tree is not precisely known. Scientists believe that a coniferous tree can lose up to 20–25 percent of its needles without reduced growth. However, slowed growth and loss of leaves appear to have a proportional relationship in deciduous trees. For a detailed description of the relationship between crown condition and forest decline, refer to Sten Nilsson and Peter Duinker, "The Extent of Forest Decline in Europe," *Environment* (November 1987), p. 4.

Table 18.4 Forest Fires in Selected Countries, 1975–84

Sources: United Nations Economic Commission for Europe (ECE) and U.N. Food and Agriculture Organization (FAO), *Forest Fire Statistics (Third Edition)* (United Nations, New York, 1986); Algeria, Jordan, Lebanon, Morocco, Syria, and Tunisia: Ricardo Velez, "Forest Fires in Mediterranean Countries" (FAO, unpublished paper, 1986).

The ECE and FAO survey official national sources for forest fire statistics in the ECE region every two years. Data for some countries have been obtained from other sources, such as journals and official publications.

The number of fires and the area they damage vary significantly from year to year. Table 18.4 shows the number of fires that occurred in selected countries, and the area burned each year from 1975 to 1984. The average annual number of fires and hectares burned are also shown. Data on the number of fires and the total area burned are complete for most countries for the years 1975–83, with about half the countries reporting preliminary 1984 estimates. Exceptions include Algeria, Jordan, Lebanon, Morocco, Syria, and Tunisia, which report 1981–84 data; the United States, reporting data for the years 1977–81; and Sweden, which ceased collecting forest fire data in 1980 because of the low number of fires reported in the country.

Some countries' fire statistics are not comprehensive. The United Kingdom includes only fires that occur in state-owned forests. U.S. data for 1981 covers only fires on federally owned land and on land included in the Rural Fire Prevention and Control Program. An estimated additional 60,211 fires, burning 256,465 hectares, occurred in the United States in 1981.

As the causes of many fires are not identified, the percentages of fires attributed to natural and human causes do not add up to 100. The causes of about 45 percent of the fires occurring in Europe in the period 1981–83 were unknown. Human-caused fires include arson and negligence.

Methods used to assess the financial losses caused by forest fires vary by country. If the forest area burned was a mature stand, the

commercial value of the wood burned is usually the basis of the loss estimate. The cost of reestablishment—site preparation, planting, and maintenance—is often used to estimate the lost value of an immature stand. The estimated future value of an immature stand is also used. Fire fighting costs are sometimes included in the loss estimates. Estimates of environmental and nontangible losses, such as the loss of soil protection and recreational value, are usually not included.

Table 18.5 Extent of Desertification, Early 1980s

Source: J.A. Mabbutt, "A New Global Assessment of the Status and Trends of Desertification," *Environmental Conservation*, Vol. 11, No. 2, (1984), p. 106.

Desertification, the diminution or destruction of the biological productivity of the land, can lead ultimately to desertlike conditions. For this table, the definition was applied only to the world's drylands: hyperarid, arid, semiarid, and subhumid zones of low and variable rainfall. These regions are inherently vulnerable to water stress and droughts, and particularly vulnerable to deterioration resulting from unsustainable human use of the land.

Desertification is generally associated with a sequence of interactive processes: impoverishment of and reduction in vegetative cover; exposure of the soil surface to accelerated wind and water erosion; reduction of the soil's organic matter and nutrient content; and deterioration of soil structure, moisture-holding capacity, and fertility.

The principal indicators used to assess desertification include deterioration of rangeland and of rainfed croplands, waterlogging and salinization of irrigated lands, deforestation and destruction of woody vegetation, decline in availability and the quality of surface and groundwater, and encroachment of sand sheets and dunes.

Moderate desertification generally implies a less than 25 percent loss of productivity; severe desertification causes a 25–50 percent loss of productivity; and very severe desertification causes a loss of productivity of more than 50 percent. The *percent desertified* is the fraction of the productive land that is moderately to very severely desertified.

Data for this table were compiled from many sources, which involved extrapolation from partial data. More than 100 countries affected by desertification received questionnaires from the United Nations Environment Programme (UNEP) requesting information on land use patterns, the status and trends of desertification, and actions taken to combat desertification. Twenty-five countries submitted extensive reports updating earlier studies conducted for the United Nations Conference on Desertification (UNCOD, 1977). Regional assessments were prepared by U.N. regional commissions (including the U.N. Sudano-Sahelian office). Other published and unpublished works by organizations such as the United Nations Educational, Scientific and Cultural Organization, the World Meteorological Organization, the United Nations Food and Agriculture Organization, and UNEP were used.

19. Wildlife and Habitat

Countries vary in their biological wealth and their commitment to the conservation of their living resources. Data on species diversity allow assessments of biological wealth and information on protected areas, status of species, and wildlife trade provide insight into the effects of countries' conservation policies.

Parks and protected areas are an important tool for conserving species and natural areas. Table 19.1 includes marine and coastal as well as terrestrial areas. Marine parks, which offer an opportunity to conserve marine and coastal resources such as commercially important fisheries, are discussed in Chapter 9, "Oceans and Coasts."

The area a country devotes to parks and protected areas indicates its commitment to preserving natural areas. In 1988, 15 countries had designated more than 10 percent of their land as protected areas. However, no standards have been established to evaluate the quality of protection that parks provide, and the effectiveness of protection systems varies among countries.

Data on the diversity and status of species accumulate slowly and are still scarce for several regions. (See Table 19.2.) Although the International Union for the Conservation of Nature and Natural Resources (IUCN), the International Council for Bird Preservation (ICBP), and other conservation organizations have gathered data on the status of threatened animals and plants, much of this information has not yet been organized by country. In 1988, the ICBP will complete a country-by-country listing of threatened bird species.

Data on swallowtail butterflies are shown to represent invertebrates since country-level data on most other invertebrates are poor. Swallowtails have worldwide distribution and many are endangered due to habitat loss, pollution, and collecting. Because many species are spectacular, they can be easily seen, identified, and monitored.

In recent years, conservation practice has increasingly emphasized conserving habitats to protect both species and ecosystem services. Habitat conservation allows the protection of areas of high endemicity and diversity, even when little is known about the species residing there. Important habitat types have been identified for many plant and animal species. For example, some 30 percent of the world's bird species depend on tropical forests, and 65 percent of the African bird species shown in Table 19.2 are forest-dependent. (See Chapter 18, "Forests and Rangelands," Table 18.1 for data on deforestation.)

Data on trade in wildlife reported by members of the Convention on International Trade in Endangered Species of Wild Flora and Fauna (CITES) are shown in Table 19.3. Members of CITES agree not to trade in species listed on the Convention's Appendix I, and to record all trade in species being monitored on Appendixes II and III. Since 1975, when CITES entered into force, the populations of several species threatened by trade, such as the American alligator, have rebounded and are out of immediate danger. Table 19.3 lists many major species groups and wildlife products that are traded and could be depleted by trade. Other species threatened by trade are not shown because the volume of trade was low or because the data were poor.

Although CITES is an important conservation tool, it provides only a partial solution to the problems caused by wildlife trade. No estimates of the total volume of illegal trade in wildlife and wildlife products are available, but illegal trade surpasses legal trade in some products. Moreover, only 20 of CITES' 96 members report their wildlife trade transactions annually, as required by the treaty, and many countries active in wildlife trade do not belong to CITES. As a result, the figures shown in Table 19.3 do not reflect the true volume of trade. Although the CITES Secretariat estimates that enforcement of the treaty is 60 to 65 percent effective, violations of the treaty remain common in many member countries.

Plant conservation lags behind that of vertebrate species, largely because plants lack the public support that many animal species enjoy. (See Table 19.4.) In addition, many more species of vascular plants (nearly 250,000 species) than vertebrates (about 41,000 species) are known. Because of the large number of plants, many have not been thoroughly studied. In an effort to integrate plant conservation into conservation and development planning, the IUCN/World Wildlife Fund (WWF) Plant Conservation Programme is preparing several publications on strategies for plant conservation, public education, and the role of botanical gardens in conservation. IUCN and WWF are also working with the United Nations Food and Agriculture Organization and the World Health Organization to promote the conservation of wild agricultural and medicinal plants. A List of Useful Plants for Conservation and Development is also being prepared to protect wild plants with potentially high economic value.

Table 19.1 National and International Protection of Natural Areas, 1988

| | National Protection Systems | | | | | International Protection Systems | | | | |
| | All Protected Areas | | Marine and Coastal Protected Areas | | Percentage of National Land Area Protected | Biosphere Reserves | | Natural World Heritage Sites | Wetlands of International Importance | |
	Number	Area (hectares)	Number	Area (hectares)		Number	Area (hectares)	Number	Number	Area (hectares)
WORLD	**3,948**	**454,130,991**	**820**	**196,732,997**	**2.9**	**269**	**142,983,285**	**78**	**404**	**28,640,031**
AFRICA	**485**	**88,144,813**	**57**	**12,640,733**	**3.0**	**40**	**19,919,999**	**21**	**27**	**2,990,634**
Algeria	15	488,295	3	89,438	0.2	1	7,200,000	1	2	8,400
Angola	5	1,517,700	4	1,502,700	1.2	0	0	0	—	—
Benin	2	843,500	0	0	7.6	1	880,000	—	—	—
Botswana	8	9,934,200	NA	NA	17.0	0	0	—	—	—
Burkina Faso	6	689,000	NA	NA	2.5	1	16,300	0	—	—
Burundi	0	0	NA	NA	0.0	0	0	0	—	—
Cameroon	12	1,702,200	1	160,000	3.6	3	850,000	1	—	—
Cape Verde	0	0	0	0	0.0	0	0	—	—	—
Central African Rep	7	3,904,000	NA	NA	6.3	2	1,640,200	0	—	—
Chad	1	114,000	NA	NA	0.1	0	0	—	—	—
Comoros	0	0	0	0	0.0	0	0	0	—	—
Congo	10	1,353,100	1	300,000	4.0	2	172,500	0	—	—
Cote d'Ivoire	10	1,958,000	1	30,000	6.2	2	1,480,000	3	—	—
Djibouti	0	0	0	0	0.0	0	0	—	—	—
Egypt	5	616,100	5	616,100	0.6	1	1,000	0	—	—
Equatorial Guinea	0	0	0	0	0.0	0	0	—	—	—
Ethiopia	9	1,767,500	0	0	1.6	0	0	1	—	—
Gabon	6	1,753,000	2	1,058,000	6.8	1	15,000	0	3	1,080,000
Gambia	0	0	0	0	0.0	0	0	—	—	—
Ghana	8	1,175,075	0	0	5.1	1	7,770	0	1	7,260
Guinea	1	13,000	0	0	0.1	2	133,300	1	—	—
Guinea-Bissau	0	0	0	0	0.0	0	0	—	—	—
Kenya	29	3,089,402	2	5,500	5.4	4	851,359	—	—	—
Lesotho	1	6,805	NA	NA	0.2	0	0	—	—	—
Liberia	1	130,700	0	0	1.4	0	0	—	—	—
Libya	3	155,000	1	35,000	0.1	0	0	0	—	—
Madagascar	31	1,031,312	1	1,750	1.8	0	0	0	—	—
Malawi	9	1,066,900	NA	NA	11.3	0	0	1	—	—
Mali	6	876,100	NA	NA	0.7	1	771,000	0	3	162,000
Mauritania	2	1,483,000	2	1,483,000	1.4	0	0	0	1	1,173,000
Mauritius	1	3,611	1	3,611	2.0	1	3,594	—	—	—
Morocco	10	294,434	4	22,600	0.7	0	0	0	4	10,580
Mozambique	0	0	0	0	0.0	0	0	—	—	—
Niger	3	372,000	NA	NA	0.3	0	0	0	1	220,000
Nigeria	4	960,082	0	0	1.1	1	460	0	—	—
Rwanda	2	262,000	NA	NA	10.5	1	15,065	—	—	—
Senegal	9	2,177,259	3	80,000	11.3	3	1,093,756	2	4	99,750
Sierra Leone	2	99,500	0	0	1.4	0	0	—	—	—
Somalia	1	334,000	1	334,000	0.5	0	0	—	—	—
South Africa	151	5,766,751	14	231,947	4.7	0	0	—	6	202,044
Sudan	4	2,198,970	0	0	0.9	2	1,900,970	0	—	—
Swaziland	4	40,045	NA	NA	2.3	0	0	—	—	—
Tanzania, United Rep	15	10,601,775	0	0	12.0	2	2,337,600	4	—	—
Togo	6	463,000	0	0	8.5	0	0	—	—	—
Tunisia	7	56,455	3	19,305	0.4	4	32,425	1	1	12,600
Uganda	18	1,332,029	0	0	6.7	1	220,000	0	1	15,000
Zaire	9	8,827,000	0	0	3.9	3	297,700	4	—	—
Zambia	19	6,359,000	NA	NA	8.6	0	0	0	—	—
Zimbabwe	19	2,760,267	NA	NA	7.1	0	0	1	—	—
NORTH & CENTRAL AMERICA	**465**	**165,399,866**	**150**	**122,995,339**	**4.5**	**62**	**88,455,099**	**21**	**55**	**15,215,553**
Barbados	1	2,500	1	2,500	5.8	0	0	—	—	—
Canada	79	22,977,933	19	6,391,543	2.5	4	382,738	6	30	13,153,509
Costa Rica	21	451,400	6	105,806	8.9	2	728,955	1	—	—
Cuba	11	285,005	6	226,813	2.6	4	323,600	0	—	—
Dominican Rep	12	571,624	5	288,144	11.8	0	0	0	—	—
El Salvador	7	20,178	0	0	1.0	0	0	—	—	—
Guatemala	13	99,083	2	12,400	0.9	0	0	1	—	—
Haiti	3	9,900	0	0	0.4	0	0	0	—	—
Honduras	2	357,500	1	350,000	3.2	1	500,000	1	—	—
Jamaica	0	0	0	0	0.0	0	0	0	—	—
Mexico	28	938,254	7	623,541	0.5	6	1,282,877	1	1	47,480
Nicaragua	6	43,300	1	4,000	0.4	0	0	0	—	—
Panama	9	825,979	3	616,364	10.9	1	597,000	1	—	—
Trinidad and Tobago	6	16,088	2	3,388	3.1	0	0	—	—	—
United States	247	67,506,028	84	43,098,780	7.4	43	14,639,929	11	7	968,054
SOUTH AMERICA	**289**	**64,312,209**	**75**	**23,410,812**	**3.7**	**22**	**10,834,241**	**8**	**3**	**216,877**
Argentina	33	4,571,871	1	63,000	1.7	4	2,004,980	2	—	—
Bolivia	12	4,837,143	NA	NA	4.5	3	435,000	0	—	—
Brazil	51	11,929,634	15	1,843,996	1.4	0	0	1	—	—
Chile	65	12,781,114	28	10,760,496	17.1	7	2,406,633	0	1	4,877
Colombia	32	4,932,765	8	561,100	4.7	3	2,514,375	0	—	—
Ecuador	13	10,619,171	5	8,975,200	38.4	1	766,514	2	—	—
Guyana	1	11,655	0	0	0.1	0	0	0	—	—
Paraguay	9	1,120,538	NA	NA	2.8	0	0	—	—	—
Peru	19	5,354,328	1	366,936	4.2	3	2,506,739	3	—	—
Suriname	13	734,800	5	128,400	4.6	0	0	—	1	12,000
Uruguay	7	30,278	1	3,290	0.2	1	200,000	—	1	200,000
Venezuela	34	7,388,912	11	708,394	8.4	0	0	—	—	—

Table 19.1

	National Protection Systems					International Protection Systems				
	All Protected Areas		Marine and Coastal Protected Areas		Percentage of National Land Area Protected	Biosphere Reserves		Natural World Heritage Sites	Wetlands of International Importance	
	Number	Area (hectares)	Number	Area (hectares)		Number	Area (hectares)	Number	Number	Area (hectares)
ASIA	**882**	**52,365,026**	**156**	**11,686,173**	**2.0**	**33**	**5,938,242**	**8**	**33**	**1,468,356**
Afghanistan	4	131,000	NA	NA	0.2	0	0	0	—	—
Bahrain	0	0	0	0	0.0	0	0	—	—	—
Bangladesh	9	94,961	3	32,386	0.7	0	0	0	—	—
Bhutan	5	876,058	NA	NA	18.6	0	0	—	—	—
Burma	1	3,056	0	0	0.0	0	0	—	—	—
China	71	2,278,606	5	11,367	0.2	6	1,602,305	1	—	—
Cyprus	0	0	0	0	0.0	0	0	0	—	—
India	267	12,910,021	14	473,802	4.3	0	0	4	2	119,373
Indonesia	135	13,590,792	66	8,595,298	7.5	6	1,482,400	—	—	—
Iran	23	3,055,536	3	74,889	1.9	9	2,609,731	0	18	1,297,550
Iraq	0	0	0	0	0.0	0	0	0	—	—
Israel	5	33,996	0	0	1.7	0	0	—	—	—
Japan	48	2,245,942	19	569,575	6.1	4	116,000	—	2	5,571
Jordan	2	34,300	0	0	0.4	0	0	0	1	7,372
Kampuchea, Dem	0	0	0	0	0.0	0	0	—	—	—
Korea, Dem People's Rep	0	0	0	0	0.0	0	0	—	—	—
Korea, Rep	17	557,766	3	284,671	5.7	1	37,430	—	—	—
Kuwait	0	0	0	0	0.0	0	0	—	—	—
Lao People's Dem Rep	0	0	NA	NA	0.0	0	0	0	—	—
Lebanon	0	0	0	0	0.0	0	0	0	—	—
Malaysia	38	1,597,144	9	55,840	4.9	0	0	—	—	—
Mongolia	13	317,840	NA	NA	0.2	0	0	—	—	—
Nepal	11	964,887	NA	NA	7.1	0	0	2	1	17,500
Oman	2	54,000	0	0	0.3	0	0	0	—	—
Pakistan	52	7,290,580	1	15,540	9.4	1	31,355	0	9	20,990
Philippines	29	498,947	5	30,722	1.7	1	23,545	0	—	—
Qatar	0	0	0	0	0.0	0	0	0	—	—
Saudi Arabia	1	415,000	1	415,000	0.2	0	0	0	—	—
Singapore	1	2,434	0	0	4.3	0	0	—	—	—
Sri Lanka	37	687,028	6	332,197	10.6	2	9,376	0	—	—
Syrian Arab Rep	0	0	0	0	0.0	0	0	0	—	—
Thailand	65	4,015,912	10	621,904	7.8	3	26,100	0	—	—
Turkey	13	235,150	3	113,785	0.3	0	0	1	—	—
United Arab Emirates	0	0	0	0	0.0	0	0	0	—	—
Viet Nam	13	193,068	0	0	0.6	0	0	0	—	—
Yemen	0	0	0	0	0.8	0	0	0	—	—
Yemen, Dem	0	0	0	0	1.3	0	0	0	—	—
EUROPE	**890**	**26,121,123**	**126**	**6,870,763**	**5.5**	**81**	**3,761,665**	**11**	**243**	**2,441,792**
Albania	13	54,500	5	19,000	2.0	0	0	—	—	—
Austria	34	424,119	NA	NA	5.1	4	27,600	—	5	102,369
Belgium	4	11,720	0	0	0.4	0	0	—	6	9,607
Bulgaria	30	114,126	0	0	1.0	17	25,201	2	4	2,097
Czechoslovakia	40	1,802,986	NA	NA	14.4	4	176,974	—	—	—
Denmark	22	125,329	4	12,670	3.0	0	0	0	27	734,202
Finland	33	803,400	0	0	2.6	0	0	0	11	101,343
France	58	4,719,845	18	811,263	8.7	4	344,527	1	1	85,000
German Dem Rep	20	70,723	2	2,962	0.7	2	18,884	—	8	46,187
Germany, Fed Rep	84	2,753,548	9	724,840	11.3	1	13,100	0	20	313,600
Greece	23	149,251	5	68,300	1.1	2	8,840	0	11	80,500
Hungary	39	438,924	0	0	4.8	5	128,884	0	8	29,450
Iceland	19	789,050	5	509,000	7.9	0	0	—	1	20,000
Ireland	4	22,634	0	0	0.3	2	8,808	—	8	6,516
Italy	42	741,259	8	124,594	2.5	3	3,798	0	41	51,732
Luxembourg	4	114,350	NA	NA	44.2	0	0	0	—	—
Malta	0	0	0	0	0.0	0	0	0	—	—
Netherlands	47	150,914	10	53,521	4.4	1	260,000	—	9	229,775
Norway	60	1,270,838	13	3,513,478	4.1	1	1,555,000	0	14	16,256
Poland	61	1,664,955	4	73,091	5.5	4	25,836	1	5	7,090
Portugal	13	382,216	5	73,968	4.2	1	395	0	2	30,563
Romania	17	148,486	0	0	0.6	3	41,213	—	—	—
Spain	60	1,699,478	6	63,016	3.4	10	614,977	1	3	52,392
Sweden	68	1,715,927	5	10,790	4.2	1	96,500	0	20	271,075
Switzerland	19	120,989	NA	NA	3.0	1	16,870	0	2	1,816
United Kingdom	49	1,548,266	20	776,040	6.4	13	44,258	2	35	162,128
Yugoslavia	21	337,290	7	34,230	1.3	2	350,000	4	2	18,094
USSR	**157**	**18,411,999**	**23**	**4,802,629**	**0.8**	**19**	**9,331,366**	**—**	**12**	**2,987,185**
OCEANIA	**773**	**39,104,026**	**230**	**14,161,656**	**4.6**	**12**	**4,742,673**	**9**	**31**	**3,319,634**
Australia	623	35,690,096	184	12,339,523	4.7	12	4,743,223	7	29	3,304,690
Fiji	2	5,350	1	4,000	0.3	0	0	—	—	—
New Zealand	123	3,059,370	32	1,499,371	11.4	0	0	2	2	14,944
Papua New Guinea	4	201,133	2	197,990	0.4	0	0	0	—	—
Solomon Islands	0	0	0	0	0.0	0	0	—	—	—

Source: International Union for Conservation of Nature and Natural Resources.
0 = zero or less than half the unit of measure; — = country not a full party to the convention; NA = not applicable.
For additional information, see Sources and Technical Notes.

Table 19.2 Globally Threatened Animal Species, Mid-1980s

	Mammals		Birds		Reptiles		Amphibians		Swallowtail Butterflies	
	Number of Species Known	Number Threatened	Number of Species Known	Number Threatened	Number of Species Known	Number Threatened	Number of Species Known	Number Threatened	Number of Species Known	Number Threatened
AFRICA										
Algeria	97	15	X	4	X	2	X	X	X	X
Angola	275	13	X	12	X	7	X	X	27	1
Benin	187	7	X	X	X	5	X	X	X	X
Botswana	154	7	X	6	X	1	X	X	X	X
Burkina Faso	147	6	X	X	X	X	X	X	X	X
Burundi	103	6	X	4	X	1	X	X	15–20	1
Cameroon	297	18	X	16	X	5	X	1	39	2
Cape Verde	9	3	X	4	X	3	X	X	X	X
Central African Rep	208	8	X	1	X	3	X	X	24–29	1
Chad	131	11	X	1	X	3	X	X	7–8	0
Comoros	X	X	X	9	X	1	X	X	3–4	2
Congo	198	12	X	3	X	7	X	X	37–38	1
Cote d'Ivoire	226	15	X	7	X	6	X	1	X	X
Djibouti	22	6	X	1	X	X	X	X	6–7	0
Egypt	105	12	X	2	X	4	X	X	X	X
Equatorial Guinea	182	13	X	3	X	4	X	1	13–21	1
Ethiopia	256	18	X	11	X	2	X	X	15–16	0
Gabon	190	9	X	5	X	7	X	X	25–31	1
Gambia	108	5	X	X	X	5	X	X	X	X
Ghana	222	10	X	7	X	7	X	X	X	X
Guinea	188	13	X	4	X	4	X	1	X	X
Guinea-Bissau	109	8	X	2	X	6	X	X	X	X
Kenya	308	13	X	15	X	5	X	X	30	1
Lesotho	33	2	X	4	X	X	X	X	X	X
Liberia	193	14	X	9	X	6	X	1	X	1
Libya	76	9	X	1	X	3	X	X	X	X
Madagascar	X	X	X	29	X	11	X	X	13	3
Malawi	192	5	X	9	X	1	X	X	22	0
Mali	136	11	X	2	X	2	X	X	X	X
Mauritania	61	10	X	2	X	5	X	X	X	X
Mauritius	X	2	X	8	X	6	X	X	2	1
Morocco	108	13	X	3	X	4	X	X	X	X
Mozambique	183	6	X	16	X	5	X	X	16	0
Namibia	161	12	X	6	X	2	X	X	X	X
Niger	131	9	X	1	X	1	X	X	X	X
Nigeria	274	18	X	7	X	5	X	X	X	1
Reunion	X	X	X	2	X	3	X	X	2	1
Rwanda	147	9	X	6	X	2	X	X	18–21	2
Sao Tome	7	0	X	7	X	1	X	X	X	X
Senegal	166	10	X	2	X	7	X	X	X	X
Seychelles	X	X	X	10	X	2	X	3	X	X
Sierra Leone	178	11	X	7	X	6	X	X	X	1
Somalia	173	14	X	6	X	4	X	X	12	0
South Africa	279	20	X	10	X	X	X	X	X	X
Sudan	266	19	X	5	X	3	X	X	20	0
Swaziland	46	3	X	4	X	1	X	X	X	X
Tanzania, United Rep	310	15	X	27	X	7	X	X	34	1
Togo	196	6	X	0	X	6	X	X	X	X
Tunisia	77	14	X	2	X	2	X	X	X	X
Uganda	311	10	X	14	X	2	X	X	31–32	2
Western Sahara	15	7	X	3	X	2	X	X	X	X
Zaire	409	24	X	27	X	6	X	X	48	3
Zambia	228	6	X	8	X	2	X	X	23	0
Zimbabwe	194	7	X	7	X	1	X	X	X	X
AMERICAS										
Argentina	255	26	927	18	204	7	124	1	36–37	1
Bahamas	17	2	218	8	39	18	6	0	5	0
Belize	121	9	504	1	107	8	26	0	X	X
Bermuda	X	1	X	1	X	X	X	X	1	0
Bolivia	267	24	1177	5	180	10	96	0	43–44	2
Brazil	394	42	1567	35	467	19	487	1	74	8
Canada	163	8	X	7	X	1	X	X	18	0
Cayman Islands	X	X	X	3	X	5	X	X	3	0
Chile	90	10	393	6	82	3	38	0	2–3	0
Colombia	358	25	1665	28	383	24	375	0	59	0
Costa Rica	203	10	796	5	218	8	151	1	X	X
Cuba	39	9	286	14	100	10	40	0	13	1
Ecuador[a]	280	21	1447	17	345	36	350	0	64	0
El Salvador	129	7	432	3	92	7	38	0	X	X
French Guiana	142	11	628	3	136	14	89	0	29–31	3
Greenland (Denmark)	26	7	X	2	X	X	X	X	X	X
Guatemala	174	9	666	8	204	10	99	0	X	X
Guyana	198	12	728	3	137	14	105	0	30–31	1
Hispaniola	23	3	211	2	134	6	53	0	8	2
Honduras	179	8	672	5	161	9	57	0	X	X
Jamaica	29	2	223	5	38	4	20	0	7	2
Lesser Antilles	37	4	193	29	94	14	15	0	3	0
Mexico	439	18	961	16	717	25	284	3	52	2
Netherlands Antilles	9	0	171	0	22	3	2	0	X	X
Nicaragua	177	9	610	4	162	9	59	0	X	X

Table 19.2

	Mammals		Birds		Reptiles		Amphibians		Swallowtail Butterflies	
	Number of Species Known	Number Threatened	Number of Species Known	Number Threatened	Number of Species Known	Number Threatened	Number of Species Known	Number Threatened	Number of Species Known	Number Threatened
Panama	217	13	920	6	212	10	155	2	X	X
Paraguay	157	14	630	8	110	8	69	0	26-32	0
Peru	359	30	1642	10	297	15	235	0	58-59	2
Puerto Rico	17	1	220	11	46	15	26	1	2-3	0
Suriname	200	11	670	3	131	12	99	0	30-31	1
Tobago	29	2b	157	6b	39	8b	8	0b	13-14	0b
Trinidad	85	X	347	X	76	X	15	0	X	X
United States	367	38	X	66	X	17	X	14	30-31	1
Uruguay	77	7	367	3	66	9	37	1	7-8	0
Venezuela	305	18	1295	8	246	20	183	0	35-39	1
ASIA										
Afghanistan	X	10	X	2	X	2	X	X	19	1
Bangladesh	X	5	X	4	X	8	X	X	10-15	X
Bhutan	X	12	X	3	X	1	X	X	22-30	2
Brunei	X	6	X	X	X	3	X	X	35-37	1
Burma	X	15	X	14	X	12	X	X	68	1
China	X	30	X	7	X	X	X	X	131-136	7
India	X	29	X	5	X	12	X	X	91	2
Indonesia	X	22	X	14	X	11	X	X	121	14
Iran	X	9	X	3	X	6	X	X	7-9	0
Iraq	X	8	X	3	X	1	X	X	6-7	0
Japan	186	9	632	19	85	2	58	1	22	0
Korea, Dem Rep	X	8	X	10	X	X	X	X	14	0
Korea, Rep	X	8	X	9	X	X	X	X	14-15	0
Malaysia	X	8	X	7	X	7	X	X	54-56	3
Mongolia	X	6	X	4	X	X	X	X	11	1
Nepal	X	17	X	2	X	4	X	X	37-38	1
Pakistan	X	13	X	6	X	9	X	X	14	0
Philippines	X	X	X	X	X	X	X	X	49	9
Sri Lanka	X	7	X	2	X	34	X	4	15	1
Turkey	31	X	217	X	X	X	X	X	X	1
EUROPE									11	2
Austria	83	X	201	X	X	X	X	X	X	1
Belgium	X	X	X	X	X	X	X	X	X	0
Denmark	49	X	190	X	5	X	14	X	X	0
Finland	62	X	232	X	5	X	5	X	X	1
France	113	X	342	X	36	X	29	X	X	2
Germany, Fed Rep	94	X	305	X	12	X	19	X	X	1
Greece	X	X	X	X	X	X	X	X	X	1
Ireland	31	X	139	X	1	X	3	X	X	0
Italy	97	X	419	X	46	X	28	X	X	2
Luxembourg	60	X	140	X	8	X	16	X	X	0
Netherlands	60	X	257	X	7	X	15	X	X	0
Norway	54	X	220	X	5	X	5	X	X	1
Portugal	56	X	288	X	24	X	17	X	X	0
Spain	100	X	389	X	49	X	23	X	X	1
Sweden	65	X	250	X	6	X	13	X	X	1
Switzerland	86	X	190	X	15	X	20	X	X	1
United Kingdom	77	X	233	X	11	X	14	X	X	0
Yugoslavia	X	X	X	X	X	X	X	X	X	1
USSR	X	X	X	X	X	X	X	X	42-44	3
OCEANIA										
Australia	299	32	700	28	550	5	150	X	19	0
Fiji	X	X	X	5	X	5	X	X	1	0
New Caledonia	X	1	X	4	X	X	X	X	3-4	0
New Zealand	69	X	282	X	39	X	5	X	0	0
Papua New Guinea	X	10	X	1	X	7	X	X	37	9
Solomon Islands	X	1	X	3	X	5	X	X	15	3
Vanuatu	X	1	X	1	X	2	X	X	4	0
Western Samoa	X	X	X	1	X	1	X	X	1	0

Sources: International Union for Conservation of Nature and Natural Resources and Organisation for Economic Co-operation and Development.
Notes:
a. Includes the Galapagos Islands.
b. Refers to both Trinidad and Tobago.
0 = zero; X = not available.
For additional information, see Sources and Technical Notes.

Table 19.3   CITES-Reported Trade in Wildlife and Wildlife

	CITES Reporting Record (percentage of reporting requirements met)	Mammals Live Primates (number)		Mammals Cat Skins (number)		Raw Ivory (kilograms)		Birds Live Parrots (number)		Reptiles Reptile Skins[b] (number)	
		Imports	Exports	Imports	Exports	Imports	Exports	Imports	Exports	Imports	Exports
WORLD		42,400	42,993	175,344	179,543	679,618	720,555	606,539	607,467	8,910,417	8,953,382
AFRICA		17	7,832	6,698	7,663	14,162	303,660	13,162	160,314	3,387	359,678
Algeria	0	0	0	0	0	0	0	0	0	0	0
Angola*	NA	0	0	0	0	0	0	1	4	0	0
Benin	0	0	1	0	0	0	10	2	0	0	7,012
Botswana	67	0	24	1	6,549	2,093	14,705	120	0	0	5
Burkina Faso*	NA	0	0	0	0	0	20	0	0	0	0
Burundi*	NA	0	0	0	0	0	5	0	0	0	0
Cameroon	83	0	57	0	0	0	1,603	0	11,198	0	67,290
Cape Verde*	NA	0	0	0	0	0	0	0	0	0	0
Central African Rep	43	0	6	0	17	0	121,598	0	788	0	0
Chad*	NA	0	0	0	0	0	8	2	0	0	0
Comoros*	NA	0	0	0	0	0	0	0	0	0	0
Congo	100	0	4	8	0	0	14,502	0	41	0	0
Cote d'Ivoire*	NA	0	1	1	X	31	452	1	339	0	5
Djibouti*	NA	0	0	0	0	0	0	12	0	0	0
Egypt	0	3	0	0	0	5	3	3,136	0	65	1
Equatorial Guinea*	NA	0	0	0	0	0	0	0	0	0	0
Ethiopia*	NA	0	1,702	0	10	0	5	0	0	0	1
Gabon*	NA	0	0	61	3	0	372	4	286	0	0
Gambia	30	0	0	0	1	0	0	0	1	0	0
Ghana	45	0	0	0	0	0	0	0	9,775	0	4
Guinea	33	0	6	0	9	0	5	0	159	0	26
Guinea-Bissau*	NA	0	0	0	0	0	0	0	1	0	0
Kenya	25	2	4,187	0	15	15	8,575	3	24	5	1
Lesotho*	NA	0	0	5	0	0	0	0	0	0	0
Liberia	67	0	1	0	6	0	25	0	4,774	0	0
Libya*	NA	6	0	0	0	0	0	19	0	3	0
Madagascar	83	0	21	0	0	0	0	0	11,660	0	5
Malawi	80	0	0	1	8	0	1,355	0	0	0	208
Mali*	NA	0	0	0	0	0	0	0	5,193	22	192,237
Mauritania*	NA	0	0	0	0	0	0	0	0	0	0
Mauritius	75	0	50	1	0	0	0	290	0	3	0
Morocco	9	0	0	0	0	0	0	20	0	92	0
Mozambique	67	0	0	0	0	10	360	0	0	0	8
Niger	33	0	0	0	0	5	29	0	0	0	2
Nigeria	0	0	8	2	32	10	217	1	27	330	2,413
Rwanda	17	0	0	1	2	5	35	18	0	2	2
Senegal	50	1	1,328	0	0	0	55	3	19,880	0	1
Sierra Leone*	NA	0	0	0	0	0	10	0	1	0	3
Somalia	0	0	0	0	0	0	3	1	0	0	0
South Africa	92	2	3	6,607	724	11,960	56,796	8,598	19,148	2,789	4,566
Sudan	25	0	1	0	5	0	18,613	84	0	0	79,235
Swaziland*	NA	0	0	2	0	5	0	760	0	0	0
Tanzania, United Rep	57	0	131	0	124	0	23,658	1	70,419	0	4
Togo	38	2	267	0	0	0	25	46	6,045	5	107
Tunisia	100	0	0	0	0	0	0	6	0	71	0
Uganda*	NA	0	6	X	1	0	5,078	0	4	0	0
Zaire	55	1	28	1	5	0	7,817	2	179	0	158
Zambia	33	0	0	0	37	0	2,110	0	4	0	881
Zimbabwe	67	0	0	7	115	23	25,611	32	364	0	5,503
NORTH & CENTRAL AMERICA		17,861	5,586	43,693	87,114	26,570	2,313	322,620	36,231	2,436,162	930,207
Barbados*	NA	0	459	0	0	0	0	0	0	0	0
Canada	100	1,501	284	23,484	25,983	333	55	10,816	73	211,570	1,662
Costa Rica	58	0	0	0	0	0	0	11	313	0	2
Cuba*	NA	13	0	0	0	2	0	16	0	0	0
Dominican Rep	X	7	0	0	0	0	0	299	46	0	0
El Salvador	X	0	0	0	1	0	0	16	2,065	0	14,755
Guatemala	86	0	30	0	5	0	0	5	10,043	0	343,645
Haiti*	NA	0	0	0	0	0	0	0	0	56	0
Honduras	0	0	0	0	1	0	0	21	17,164	0	4
Jamaica*	NA	0	0	0	0	5	0	2	4	100	0
Mexico*	NA	113	1	10	46	45	0	103	9	64,176	7,077
Nicaragua	80	0	0	0	0	0	0	31	282	0	7
Panama	33	0	0	4	1	0	0	264	50	45,832	235,679
Trinidad and Tobago	0	3	0	0	0	0	0	607	14	0	0
United States	83	16,224	4,812	20,195	61,077	26,185	2,258	310,429	6,168	2,114,428	327,376
SOUTH AMERICA		80	3,841	1,009	3,358	105	4	6,206	265,339	80,740	1,900,259
Argentina	100	0	46	0	0	85	0	360	179,473	33,932	1,250,384
Bolivia	38	0	0	0	3,320	0	0	0	115	0	243,535
Brazil	33	27	4	8	3	20	0	73	16	33,505	195
Chile	33	15	0	0	0	0	0	450	952	0	0
Colombia	50	30	2	0	8	0	4	10	31	0	0
Ecuador	67	0	0	0	8	0	0	77	278	0	0
Guyana	10	4	3,125	0	0	0	0	103	24,718	0	110,418
Paraguay	40	0	0	0	2	0	0	0	5	11,398	17,212
Peru	83	0	585	0	7	0	0	156	33,921	0	41
Suriname	100	0	75	0	0	0	0	4,805	7,322	0	0
Uruguay	58	2	0	1,000	0	0	0	0	18,455	0	0
Venezuela	56	2	4	1	10	0	0	172	53	1,905	278,474

Products, 1985[a]

Table 19.3

	CITES Reporting Record (percentage of reporting requirements met)	Mammals Live Primates (number) Imports	Mammals Live Primates (number) Exports	Cat Skins (number) Imports	Cat Skins (number) Exports	Raw Ivory (kilograms) Imports	Raw Ivory (kilograms) Exports	Birds Live Parrots (number) Imports	Birds Live Parrots (number) Exports	Reptiles Reptile Skins[b] (number) Imports	Reptiles Reptile Skins[b] (number) Exports
ASIA		**7,258**	**22,689**	**7,694**	**60,763**	**505,232**	**280,283**	**67,625**	**89,366**	**2,480,336**	**4,198,455**
Afghanistan	0	8	0	0	1	0	0	0	0	0	0
Bahrain*	NA	0	0	0	0	0	0	778	1	0	0
Bangladesh	80	8	0	0	1	0	0	0	1	0	618,010
Bhutan*	NA	0	0	0	0	0	0	778	1	0	0
Burma*	NA	4	0	0	0	0	0	0	0	0	0
China	100	52	121	2,137	59,629	2,488	5,153	145	28	5,000	0
Cyprus	42	1	1	0	0	5	0	704	0	100	0
Hong Kong	100	30	23	3,486	67	161,846	108,849	2,605	146	71,722	16,297
India	100	12	8	2	1	16,770	1,711	184	22,084	80	7,466
Indonesia	88	12	8,964	0	0	10	0	348	44,339	4,964	868,159
Iran	18	0	0	0	0	0	0	0	2	0	0
Iraq*	NA	0	0	0	0	0	0	1	0	0	0
Israel	0	6	0	1	0	20	0	1,968	0	3,489	10
Japan	86	3,560	48	1,906	0	322,029	81,820	23,022	58	1,545,625	436,417
Jordan	0	0	0	0	0	0	0	483	1	0	0
Kampuchea, Dem*	NA	0	0	0	0	0	0	0	0	0	0
Korea, Dem People's Rep	NA	9	4	0	0	0	0	20	0	0	0
Korea, Rep*	NA	25	2	1	1,060	0	0	309	1	46,018	1,289
Kuwait*	NA	0	0	0	0	0	0	2,916	0	2	0
Lao People's Dem Rep*	NA	0	0	0	0	0	0	0	0	0	0
Lebanon*	NA	0	0	0	1	0	30	121	1	250	0
Malaysia	78	2	2	0	0	10	0	1,252	6,282	268	3,919
Mongolia*	NA	0	0	0	0	0	0	0	0	0	0
Nepal	58	0	0	0	0	0	0	0	0	0	0
Oman*	NA	0	0	0	0	0	0	1,330	2	0	0
Pakistan	100	0	0	1	0	6	0	511	0	0	0
Philippines	83	0	13,494	1	0	0	30	0	1,197	0	86,679
Qatar*	NA	0	0	0	0	0	0	521	2	0	0
Saudi Arabia*	NA	24	0	1	0	9	5	10,693	84	95	0
Singapore	X	20	3	1	0	31	43,370	5,100	5,279	727,530	1,494,364
Sri Lanka	25	0	15	0	1	0	0	409	4	0	0
Syrian Arab Rep*	NA	0	0	0	0	0	0	110	1	0	0
Taiwan*	NA	3,354	0	5	0	265	0	8,020	6,099	22,607	62,303
Thailand	75	71	1	0	0	816	6	405	3,731	9,263	603,541
Turkey*	NA	0	0	152	2	10	0	188	3	43,246	0
United Arab Emirates*	NA	60	1	0	0	917	39,309	4,704	5	76	1
Viet Nam*	NA	0	2	0	0	0	0	0	15	0	0
Yemen*	NA	0	0	0	0	0	0	0	0	1	0
Yemen, Dem*	NA	0	0	0	0	0	0	0	0	0	0
EUROPE		**15,354**	**2,994**	**116,245**	**14,927**	**133,277**	**134,285**	**195,947**	**55,662**	**3,908,928**	**1,539,866**
Albania*	NA	0	0	0	0	0	0	28	0	0	0
Austria	100	77	11	2,175	0	276	160	2,300	126	147,568	12,524
Belgium	100	1,062	139	238	83	70,012	77,144	21,078	13,564	22,257	13,681
Bulgaria*	NA	0	0	0	0	15	0	1	0	0	0
Czechoslovakia*	NA	17	1	0	0	5	0	13	123	0	0
Denmark	70	64	26	3,874	1,661	125	5	5,873	734	6	47
Finland	45	0	5	2,474	338	70	0	1	42	284	0
France	92	2,094	152	4,405	652	18,147	22,581	17,059	961	1,341,131	374,921
German Dem Rep	55	103	9	1,012	842	55	0	24	6,180	100	0
Germany, Fed Rep	100	667	138	73,795	10,351	9,248	223	54,627	385	93,741	305,528
Greece*	NA	3	0	1,036	139	105	44	1,310	0	5,279	0
Hungary	0	49	2	0	0	0	5	757	0	7	0
Iceland*	NA	NA	0	0	0	0	0	0	0	0	0
Ireland*	NA	1	0	1	0	20	0	0	0	0	0
Italy	100	821	14	14,053	138	689	10	7,771	2	1,034,515	196,516
Luxembourg	100	0	0	0	0	0	0	0	0	0	0
Malta*	NA	32	0	0	46	0	0	802	1	320	0
Netherlands	100	2,145	1,704	2	0	51	41	28,775	30,822	366,518	56,290
Norway	91	0	0	13	0	25	0	0	11	37	0
Poland*	NA	97	10	0	0	25	0	51	0	0	0
Portugal	0	7	0	5	0	42	24,093	1,198	0	302	0
Romania*	NA	52	0	0	0	0	0	5	0	0	0
Spain	100	106	2	1,931	1	1,072	1,101	13,100	19	368,906	269,441
Sweden	100	637	35	191	204	76	119	17,259	2,621	62	0
Switzerland	100	97	99	0	0	327	7,958	2,577	22	291,466	54,987
United Kingdom	100	5,223	647	11,040	472	32,887	801	21,336	49	235,874	255,931
Yugoslavia*	NA	2,000	0	0	0	5	0	2	0	555	0
USSR	**73**	**1,744**	**31**	**0**	**5,717**	**0**	**0**	**646**	**24**	**4**	**0**
OCEANIA		**86**	**20**	**5**	**1**	**272**	**10**	**333**	**531**	**860**	**24,917**
Australia	100	77	16	4	1	217	10	0	525	858	684
Fiji*	NA	0	0	0	0	0	0	0	0	0	0
New Zealand*	NA	9	4	1	0	55	0	333	6	0	0
Papua New Guinea	73	0	0	0	0	0	0	0	0	2	24,233
Solomon Islands*	NA	0	0	0	0	0	0	0	0	0	0

Source: International Union for Conservation of Nature and Natural Resources.
Notes:
a. Includes all trade reported by members of the Convention on International Trade in Endangered Species of Wild Flora and Fauna (CITES).
b. Reptile skins include skins of snakes, lizards, and crocodilians.
0 = zero or no trade reported; X = not available; NA = not applicable; * = not a member of CITES as of February 1988.
For additional information, see Sources and Technical Notes.

Table 19.4 Globally Rare and Threatened Plant Species, 1988

	Number of Plant Species	Endemic Flora as Percentage of Total	Number of Rare and Threatened Plant Species	Completeness of Data on Rare and Threatened Plants[a]	Red Data Book or List
WORLD					
AFRICA					
Algeria	3,139–3,150	8	144	3	Yes
Angola	5,000	25	19	3	No
Benin	2,000	1	3	3	Yes
Botswana	X	17[b]	4	3	Yes
Burkina Faso	1,096	X	X	3	No
Burundi	2,500	X	X	3	Yes
Cameroon	8,000	2	74	2	Yes
Cape Verde	659	14	1	3	No
Central African Rep	3,600	4	X	3	No
Chad	1,600	X	13	3	No
Comoros	416	33	3	3	No
Congo	4,000	22	1	3	No
Cote d'Ivoire	3,660	2	69	2	No
Djibouti	534	X	3	3	No
Equatorial Guinea					
Bioko	1,150	4	X	3	No
Pagula	208	8	X	3	No
Egypt	2,085	4	94	2	IP
Ethiopia	6,283	8	44	3	No
Gabon	8,000	22	83	3	No
Gambia	530	1	X	3	No
Ghana	3,600	1	34	3	Yes
Guinea	X	88[c]	36	3	No
Guinea–Bissau	1,000	X	X	3	No
Kenya	6,500	4	132	2	Yes
Lesotho	1,591	X	7	3	No
Liberia	X	59[c]	1	3	Yes
Libya	1,600–1,800	8	56	2	Yes
Madagascar	10,000–12,000	80	191	3	No
Malawi	3,600	2	50	2	No
Mali	1,600	1	15	2	No
Mauritania	1,100	X	3	3	No
Mauritius	800–900	33	226	1	IP
Morocco	3,500–3,600	18	194	2	Yes
Mozambique	5,500	4	82	2	No
Namibia	3,159	11[c]	17	3	No
Niger	1,178	X	1	3	Yes
Nigeria	4,614	5	9	3	Yes
Principe	314	11	X	3	No
Reunion	720	30	87	1	Yes
Rwanda	2,150	X	X	X	No
Sao Tome	601	18	X	X	No
Senegal	2,100	1	32	2	No
Seychelles	274	15	76	3	No
Sierra Leone	2,480	3	12	3	No
Somalia	3,000	17	51	3	No
South Africa	23,000	80	1,144	1	Yes
Sudan	3,200	2	9	3	Yes
Swaziland	2,715	X	25	3	Yes
Tanzania, United Rep	10,000	11	154	2	Yes
Togo	2,302[e]	1	X	3	No
Tunisia	2,120–2,200	X	26	3	Yes
Uganda	5,000	1	11	3	No
Western Sahara	300	X	X	3	No
Zaire	11,000	29	3	3	Yes
Zambia	4,600	5	1	3	No
Zimbabwe	5,428[d]	2	68	2	Yes
NORTH & CENTRAL AMERICA					
Antigua and Barbuda	724[e]	1	1	3	No
Bahamas	1,350	9	22	2	Yes
Bermuda	165	10	14	2	No
Barbados	700	1	1	3	No
Belize	3,240	5	27	1	IP
British Virgin Islands	X	X	1	3	No
Canada	3,220	X	11	3	IP
Costa Rica	8,000	X	455	1	No
Cuba	7,000	50	845	1	Yes
Dominica	1,600	1	62	2	No
El Salvador	2,500	19[c]	33	1	Yes
Grenada	X	X	3	3	No
Guadeloupe	2,800[e]	45	14	3	Yes
Guatemala	8,000	15	289	1	Yes
Hispaniola	5,000	1800[c]	58	2	IP
Honduras	5,000	3	37	1	No
Jamaica	3,582	30	8	2	Yes
Martinique	X	X	12	3	No
Montserrat	X	X	1	3	No
Mexico	20,000	17	795	1	Yes

Table 19.4

	Number of Plant Species	Endemic Flora as Percentage of Total	Number of Rare and Threatened Plant Species	Completeness of Data on Rare and Threatened Plants[a]	Red Data Book or List
Nicaragua	5,000	1	36	1	No
Panama	8,000–9,000	15	332	1	No
Saint Lucia	X	X	3	3	No
Saint Vincent and the Grenadines	X	12[c]	4	3	No
Trinidad and Tobago	2,281	9	4	3	Yes
United States	20,000[f]	X	1,691	1	Yes
Hawaii	1,145	90	1,701	1	Yes
Puerto Rico	3,000	8	85	2	Yes
Virgin Islands	X	X	10	2	Yes
SOUTH AMERICA					
Argentina	9,000	25–30	155	2	No
Bolivia	15,000–18,000	X	14	2	No
Brazil	55,000	X	60	2	No
Chile	5,500	50	191	2	Yes
Juan Fernandez	147	118[c]	96	1	Yes
Colombia	45,000	33	236	2	IP
Ecuador	10,000–20,000	X	76	2	No
Galapagos Islands	543[d]	229[c]	144	1	IP
French Guiana	6,000–8,000	X	41	2	Yes
Guyana	6,000–8,000	X	57	2	No
Paraguay	7,000–8,000	X	5	2	No
Peru	20,000	X	429	2	No
Suriname	4,500	X	71	2	No
Uruguay	X	X	11	2	No
Venezuela	15,000–20,000	29	37	2	No
ASIA					
Afghanistan	3,000	25–30	1	3	No
Bangladesh	5,000[f]	X	4	3	No
Bhutan	5,000	10–15	5	3	No
Borneo	10,000–11,000	34	22	3	No
Brunei	X[i]	X[i]	4	3	No
Burma	7,000[f]	5	10	3	Yes[g]
China	30,000	X	288	2	IP
Cyprus	2,000	116[c]	46	2	No
India	15,000	33	1,103	1	Yes
Andaman and Nicobar Islands	2,270[f]	10	10	3	No
Indonesia					
Irian Jaya	X[h]	X[h]	23	3	X
Java	5,000	X	87	2	No
Kalimantan	X[i]	X[i]	11	3	X
Lesser Sunda Islands	X	12	9	3	No
Moluccas	X	X	11	3	No
Sulawesi	5,000	X	14	3	No
Sumatra	X	12	48	2	No
Iran	7,000	20	1	3	No
Iraq	2,937	7	3	3	No
Israel	2,317	7	41	2	IP
Japan	4,022	34	395	2	IP
Bonin Islands	369	41	81	1	Yes
Jordan	2,200	X	14	3	No
Kampuchea, Dem	X	X	4	3	No
Korea, Rep	2,838[j]	14[j]	33	2	Yes
Kuwait	350	X	1	3	No
Lao People's Dem Rep	X	X	3	3	No
Lebanon[k]	3,000	11	5	3	Yes
Malaysia					
Peninsular Malaysia	8,500	X	254	2	No
Sabah	X[i]	X[i]	34	2	No
Sarawak	X[i]	X[i]	28	2	No
Nepal	6,500[f]	5	15	3	IP
Oman	1,100	5	2	3	No
Pakistan	5,500–6,000	6	6	3	IP
Philippines	9,000	39	73	2	Yes[g]
Saudi Arabia	3,500	23[c]	1	3	IP
Singapore	2,030	X	15	2	No
Sri Lanka	2,900[f]	9	53	2	Yes[g]
Syrian Arab Rep[k]	3,000	11	12	3	No
Taiwan	3,577	25	84	2	IP
Thailand	12,000	X	40	3	No
Turkey	8,000	31	10	3	IP
Viet Nam	8,000	10	24	3	Yes[g]
Yemen	1,000	3	2	2	No
Yemen, Dem	1,700	5–10	1	3	No
Socotra	680	32	132	2	No
EUROPE					
Albania	3,100–3,300	1	76	3	X
Austria	2,900–3,100	1	27	2	IP
Belgium	1,600–1,800	0	10	1	Yes
Bulgaria	3,500–3,650	2	85	2	Yes
Czechoslovakia	2,600–2,750	1	28	1	Yes

(Continued)

Table 19.4 Globally Rare and Threatened Plant Species, 1988 (continued)

	Number of Plant Species	Endemic Flora as Percentage of Total	Number of Rare and Threatened Plant Species	Completeness of Data on Rare and Threatened Plants[a]	Red Data Book or List
EUROPE					
Denmark	1,000	1	7	1	Yes
Finland	1,150–1,450	0	6	1	Yes
France	4,300–4,450	2	113	2	IP
Corsica	2,516[d]	5	28	2	Yes
German Dem Rep	1,842	1	11	1	Yes
Germany, Fed Rep	2,476	1	15	1	Yes
Greece	5,000[c]	20	528	2	No
Hungary	2,400	1	20	2	No
Iceland	470[c]	1	2	1	No
Ireland	1,000–1,150	0	5	2	IP
Italy	4,750–4,900	11	146	2	No
Sardinia	1900–2000	2	31	1	No
Sicily	2250–2450	2	45	1	No
Luxembourg	1,000	0	2	1	IP
Malta	900	0	4	1	IP
Netherlands	1,400	0	6	1	Yes
Norway	1,600–1,800	1	12	1	Yes
Poland	2,250–2,450	1	15	1	Yes
Portugal	2,400–2,600	4–5	88	1	Yes
Azores	600	9	33	2	Yes
Maderia Islands	760	17	111	2	No
Romania	3,300–3,400	1	65	2	Yes
Spain	4,750–4,900	15	442	2	Yes
Balearic Islands	1,250–1,450	6–8	70	1	Yes
Canary Islands	2,000	500[c]	429	1	Yes
Gibraltar	587	1	1	1	No
Sweden	1,600–1,800	1	8	1	Yes
Switzerland	2,600–2,750	1	20	1	Yes
United Kingdom	1,700–1,850	1	20	1	Yes
Ascension Island	25	44	11	1	Yes
Channel Islands	1,800[d]	0	3	1	Yes
Saint Helena	320	16	49	1	Yes
Tristan da Cunha Islands	74	60	18	2	No
Yugoslavia	4,750–4,900	3–4	190	2	No
USSR	**21,000**	**7**	**518**	**2**	**Yes**
OCEANIA					
Australia	18,000	80	1,967	1	Yes
Fiji	1,500[d]	40–50	25	3	No
Marquesas Islands	247[d]	103[c]	62	1	Yes
New Caledonia	3,250	76	169	2	No
New Guinea	11,000	90	X	3	No
New Zealand	2,000	81	223	1	Yes
Papua New Guinea	X[h]	55	61	3	No
Solomon Islands	2,150	X	3	3	No

Source: International Union for Conservation of Nature and Natural Resources.
Notes: a. 1 = conservation data more or less complete; 2 = considerable amount of work completed for a number of selected families or groups; 3 = miscellaneous records and preliminary data. b. Number of endemic vascular plant species. c. Number of endemic taxa (includes species, subspecies, and varieties). d. Number of vascular taxa (includes species, subspecies, and varieties). e. Number of seed plants. f. Number of flowering plants. g. Preliminary. h. See New Guinea. i. See Borneo. j. Refers to entire Korean peninsula. k. Size of flora and species endemicity data refer to both Syria and Lebanon.
Data for mainland countries do not include island states or territories.
0 = zero or less than half the unit of measure; X = not available; IP = in preparation as of March 1988.
For additional information, see Sources and Technical Notes.

Sources and Technical Notes

Table 19.1 National and International Protection of Natural Areas, 1988

Source: Protected Areas: International Union for Conservation of Nature and Natural Resources, Conservation Monitoring Centre (IUCN/CMC), unpublished data (IUCN/CMC, Cambridge, United Kingdom, July 1988).

The protected areas under *National Protection Systems* in Table 19.1 are aggregated from sites classified in five (of the 10) IUCN management categories. Two other IUCN management categories—Biosphere Reserves and World Heritage Sites (natural as opposed to cultural sites)—are shown under the

heading *International Protection Systems*, although they are often included in National Protection Systems as well. Data for the remaining three categories of the IUCN framework—Resource Reserves, Anthropological Reserves, and Multiple Use Management Areas—are less complete and have therefore been omitted.

The categories that are aggregated for this table are:

■ *Scientific Reserves and Strict Nature Reserves.* These areas possess outstanding and representative ecosystems. The reserves are generally closed to public access. Their size is determined by the area required to ensure the integrity of the site. In many of the reserves,

natural perturbations (e.g., insect epidemics, forest fires) are allowed to occur.

■ *National Parks and Provincial Parks.* These are relatively large areas of national or international significance that are not materially altered by humans. Access is controlled, but visitors are encouraged to use the areas for recreation and study.

■ *Natural Monuments and Natural Landmarks.* These areas contain unique geological formations, special animals or plants, or unusual habitat. Areas vary in size. Access is usually restricted.

■ *Managed Nature Reserves and Wildlife Sanctuaries.* These sites are protected for specific purposes such as conservation of a nationally significant plant or animal species. Some areas may require management. For example, a particular grassland or heath community may be best protected and perpetuated by livestock grazing. The size of the areas vary. Public access is restricted to scientific and educational purposes.

■ *Protected Landscapes and Seascapes.* Areas so designated may be entirely natural, with no human artifacts, or they may include cultural landscapes, such as scenically attractive agricultural areas. Protected landscapes may be coastlines, lake shores, hilly or mountainous terrain along scenic highways, etc. Areas vary in size, and public access depends on the use of the area.

The figures in Table 19.1 do not include locally or provincially protected sites, privately owned areas, or sites where local custom permits hunting and other consumptive uses of wildlife. Areas smaller than 1,000 hectares are not included.

Biosphere Reserves are protected areas representative of terrestrial and coastal environments that have been internationally recognized under the United Nations Educational, Scientific, and Cultural Organization's Man and the Biosphere Programme. They were selected for their conservation value and are intended to foster the scientific knowledge, skills, and human values to support sustainable development. Biosphere reserves form a global network to facilitate information sharing on the conservation and management of natural ecosystems. Each reserve must contain an ecosystem typical of a biogeographical province in diversity and naturalness and must be large enough to be an effective conservation unit. A biogeographical province is a geographic area characterized by distinctive groups of plant and animal species. For further details, refer to M. Udvardy, *A Classification of the Biogeographical Provinces of the World* (IUCN, Morges, Switzerland, 1975). Each Biosphere Reserve must include a defined, minimally disturbed core area for conservation and research and must be surrounded by one or more buffer zones. In the buffer zones traditional uses of the land, experimental research on ecosystems, and rehabilitation of modified or degraded ecosystems may be permitted.

Natural World Heritage Sites are structures or natural areas of "outstanding universal value." (Only "natural sites" are included in the table.) Sites are nominated by any of the countries party to the World Heritage Convention and are reviewed for the Convention Committee by IUCN. To be accepted, a natural site must contain an example of a major stage of the Earth's evolutionary history; a significant ongoing geological process; a unique or superlative natural phenomenon, formation, or feature; or a habitat for endangered or rare species of plants and animals.

Wetlands of International Importance are wetlands so designated by any of the 45 countries (as of December 1987) that have signed the Convention on Wetlands of International Importance Especially as Waterfowl Habitat (Ramsar, Iran, 1971). IUCN collects wetlands data with the assistance of the International Waterfowl Research Bureau, the International Council for Bird Preservation, and

the United Nations Environment Programme. These sites may not be legally protected or managed, but countries signing the wetlands convention agree to respect the ecological integrity of the designated site and to establish wetland nature reserves.

Marine and coastal protected areas refer to all protected areas that include littoral, coral, island, marine, or estuarine components. The area given is that of the whole protected area, not just the marine component. Data on marine protected areas are still in review and are not final. For more details on marine protected areas, see Chapter 9, "Oceans and Coasts."

Some sites are listed under more than one of these headings: Biosphere Reserves, World Heritage Sites, Wetlands of International Importance, Protected Areas, and Marine Protected Areas. Because these categories overlap, the total number of protected sites is less than the sum of the totals for all the categories. For example, all Biosphere Reserves are included under National Protection Systems. Computerized data bases for all five of the protection systems are maintained by the Protected Areas Data Unit of the IUCN Conservation Monitoring Centre at Cambridge, United Kingdom.

Continental and world totals include information for countries not included in the table because they have a population of less than 240,000. For example, the Bahamas, which are not listed, have four protected areas totalling 134,730 hectares. Antarctica is not listed, but its seven protected areas established under the Antarctic Treaty System are included in the world total under national protection systems. Under *All Protected Areas* and Biosphere Reserves, Greenland is included in the North American total. The Ukraine and Byelorussia are included in the USSR figures. The United States and Canada share one World Heritage Site, as do Guinea and Cote d'Ivoire. These sites are listed under each country, but are counted only once in continental and world totals. Under Wetlands of International Importance, the Netherlands Antilles' sites are included in the North American total. Data for China do not include Taiwan. Many small islands and countries are included in global and continental totals for marine protected areas. Most significantly, the total for Africa includes two marine protected areas in Namibia with a combined area of 6,615,800 hectares; the total for North America includes two sites in Greenland with a total area of 71,050,000 hectares; and the global total includes three sites in the Antarctic Treaty Territory of 164,592 hectares.

Table 19.2 Globally Threatened Animal Species, Mid-1980s

Sources: International Union for Conservation of Nature and Natural Resources (IUCN), *The IUCN Mammal Red Data Book, Part I* (IUCN, Gland, Switzerland, 1982), International Council for Bird Preservation (ICBP)/IUCN, *Threatened Birds of Africa and Related Islands* (ICBP/IUCN, Cambridge, United Kingdom, 1985), IUCN, *Threatened Swallowtail Butterflies of the World* (IUCN, Gland, Switzerland, 1985), and IUCN Conservation

Monitoring Centre (CMC), unpublished data (IUCN/CMC, Cambridge, United Kingdom, 1988). Madagascar: IUCN, *Madagascar: An Environmental Profile* (IUCN, Cambridge, 1987). Panama (number of bird species known): James R. Karr, Acting Director, Smithsonian Tropical Research Institute, September 25, 1987, (personal communication). Europe, Turkey, Japan, New Zealand (number of species known): Organisation for Economic Co-operation and Development (OECD), *OECD Environmental Data Compendium 1987* (OECD, Paris, 1987); Australia (number of bird, reptile, and amphibian species known): OECD, *OECD Environmental Data Compendium 1987* (OECD, Paris, 1987).

Globally threatened species are vulnerable to extinction throughout their range (see definitions below). Species may also be threatened in only part of their range. (For data on vertebrate species threatened within countries, see *World Resources 1987*, Table 21.3.)

IUCN has established a standard framework for classification of threatened and endangered species:

■ *Endangered.* "Taxa in danger of extinction and whose survival is unlikely if the causal factors continue operating." Included are taxa whose numbers have been reduced to a critical level or whose habitats have been so drastically reduced that they are deemed to be in immediate danger of extinction. Taxa that may already be extinct but that have been seen in the wild in the past 50 years are also included.

■ *Vulnerable.* "Taxa believed likely to move into the Endangered category in the near future if the causal factors continue operating." Included are taxa of which most or all the populations are decreasing because of overexploitation, extensive destruction of habitat, or other environmental disturbance; taxa with populations that have been seriously depleted and whose ultimate security has not yet been assured; and taxa with populations that are still abundant but are under threat from severe adverse factors throughout their range.

■ *Rare.* "Taxa with world populations that are not at present Endangered or Vulnerable, but are at risk." These taxa are usually localized within restricted geographical areas or habitats or are thinly scattered over a more extensive range.

■ *Indeterminate.* "Taxa known to be Endangered, Vulnerable, or Rare but where there is not enough information to say which of the three categories is appropriate."

■ *Out of Danger.* "Taxa formerly included in one of the above categories, but which are now considered relatively secure because effective conservation measures have been taken or the previous threat to their survival has been removed."

■ *Insufficiently Known.* "Taxa that are suspected but not definitely known to belong to any of the above categories."

In practice, the Endangered and Vulnerable categories may include taxa whose populations are beginning to recover as a result of remedial action, but recovery is insufficient to justify their transfer to another category.

The number of threatened species listed for most countries in Table 19.2 includes species that are Endangered, Vulnerable, Rare, Indeterminate, and Insufficiently Known.

The total number of species includes those introduced to a country, but the number of threatened species excludes introduced species. The data on mammals exclude cetaceans (whales and porpoises). (See Chapter 9, "Oceans and Coasts," Table 9.3 for data on marine mammals.)

Although the list of threatened species is based on the judgment of many experts working in the field and has taken years to compile, it is under continual revision as new species are discovered and as more become threatened. In addition, because the identification of species can be a controversial practice, estimates of the number of species known and the number threatened may vary among different sources. See Chapter 6, "Wildlife and Habitat," for a discussion of species loss indicators.

Table 19.3 CITES-Reported Trade in Wildlife and Wildlife Products, 1985

Source: International Union for Conservation of Nature and Natural Resources, Conservation Monitoring Centre (IUCN/CMC), unpublished data (IUCN/CMC, Cambridge, United Kingdom, March 1988).

IUCN's Wildlife Trade Monitoring Unit compiles data on trade in wildlife products from the annual reports of the parties to the Convention in International Trade in Endangered Species of Wild Fauna and Flora (CITES). CITES members agree to prohibit commercial international trade in endangered species, and to closely monitor trade in species that may become depleted by trade. Species are listed in the CITES appendixes based on how rare or threatened they are and the extent to which they are threatened by trade. Trade is prohibited for about 675 species listed on Appendix I and is regulated for at least 27,000 species on Appendix II. Appendix III, which is seldom used, allows countries to prohibit trade in nationally threatened species. Parties are required to submit annual reports, including trade records, to the CITES Secretariat in Switzerland. These data are computerized by IUCN/CMC's Wildlife Trade Monitoring Unit. The data shown are the most recent comprehensive figures available, and are for 1985.

Figures refer to both legal and illegal trade, although most illegal trade is not reported. For a discussion of illegal wildlife trade, see Chapter 6, "Wildlife and Habitat."

Countries are listed as members of CITES if they had joined as of February 1988. The *CITES Reporting Record* (percentage of reporting requirements met) refers to the percentage of years for which a country has submitted an annual report to the CITES Secretariat since it became a party to the

Convention. (This percentage includes years up to and including 1986.)

Live primates are all nonhuman primate species. The data include both captive-bred and wild specimens.

Cat skins include skins of all species of Felidae. A small number of cat skins reported only by weight or length were excluded from the data.

Raw ivory refers to trade in ivory of the African elephant. Much of this trade was reported by the number of tusks, rather than their weight, but was converted to kilograms by assuming an average tusk weight of five kilograms. This trade is probably overestimated because tusks in the same transaction are often recorded by number in one country and by weight in another country.

Live parrots include all psittacines (parrots, macaws, cockatoos, etc.) except the budgerigar and the cockatiel. There are 329 parrot species in the world; 141 species are native to the Neotropics. Both captive-bred and wild birds were included.

Reptile skins include all crocodilians, and many commonly traded lizard and snake species. About 56 percent of the global reptile skins total is lizards, 26 percent is snakes, and 18 percent is crocodilians. Excluded from the table were skins reported only by weight and size because no conversion factor is available. According to IUCN's Wildlife Trade Monitoring Unit, these unlisted quantities may amount to roughly 330,000 crocodilian skins, 57,000 lizard skins, and 320,000 snake skins.

The numbers of live animals traded do not reflect the full impact of wildlife trade on some species because mortality during capture, transit, and quarantine is usually not reported.

This table shows gross trade in wildlife products: the number of CITES-listed specimens reportedly imported and exported by each country. The total of the gross trade figures would in most cases overestimate the actual number of specimens traded because the same specimen could be imported and re-exported by a number of countries in a single year. The volume of world trade in a given group of wildlife or specimens can be determined by calculating the net trade for each country and then adding these totals together.

In some cases, discrepancies occur between the total imports and exports for a group of species because a large amount of trade was recorded to or from unspecified countries.

Data from national customs agencies were not included because customs agencies often record species not listed in the CITES appendixes, or record trade in units not comparable with CITES data. Customs categories often do not relate to a taxonomically defined group.

Table 19.4 Globally Rare and Threatened Plant Species, 1988

Source: International Union for Conservation of Nature and Natural Resources, Conservation Monitoring Centre (IUCN/CMC), unpublished data (IUCN/CMC, Threatened Plants Unit, Kew, United Kingdom, January 1988).

Unless otherwise noted, size of flora refers to the number of native vascular plant species found in the country.

The number of globally rare and threatened plants include all plants classified as Endangered, Vulnerable, Rare, or Indeterminate. See the Technical Note for Table 19.2 for more information on these categories.

Endemic species are plants that occur only in a single country or island group. Table 19.4 shows the percentage of a country's flora that is endemic.

The Red Data Books list the names and status of a country's plant species as well as additional botanical and conservation information. They have been prepared for over 70 countries or islands and are being prepared for about 20 more. Several small islands for which data are available were not shown. IUCN provides guidelines, technical assistance, and some funding for the preparation of Red Data Books. The books follow a variety of formats, but in most cases use the IUCN classification system to indicate the degree of the threats to individual species. Most distinguish between endemic and nonendemic plants.

Data were compiled by the Threatened Plants Unit of the Conservation Monitoring Centre at Kew, United Kingdom, from a variety of sources. Data on the number of plants were based on the floristic literature, including lists of plants in a particular area, Red Data Books, national lists of threatened species, scientific journals and papers. The number of plants listed in Table 19.4 is usually a total of species recorded, but may include estimates of species expected to occur, based on the floristic literature. Figures are not comparable among countries because taxonomic concepts and the extent of knowledge vary.

Data on rare and threatened plants for each country were scored for completeness by the Threatened Plants Unit. In 1986, the IUCN Threatened Plants Unit data base held records on 34,266 plant taxa, 15,870 of which were rare or threatened on a global scale. For additional information see IUCN, *Plants in Danger: What do We Know?* (IUCN, Gland, Switzerland, 1986).

20. Energy, Materials, and Wastes

A country's patterns of energy and materials use and waste production reflect its energy and mineral resources, level of development, economic structure, and commitment to conservation and efficiency. Most industrialized countries consume large amounts of energy and materials to sustain economic growth and high standards of living. However, increasing energy efficiency and reuse of materials have slowed growth in consumption in many countries. Developing countries consume far less of the world's energy and minerals, although many are major producers.

Between 1970 and 1986, total energy production increased most in the USSR (contributing 37 percent of the increase in world energy production), China, and the United Kingdom. (See Table 20.1.) Over the same period, energy consumption leveled off in most developed countries, but grew rapidly in many developing nations. Still, in 1986, sub-Saharan Africa accounted for only 1 percent of global commercial energy consumption, while the United States accounted for 25 percent.

The amount of energy consumed for each dollar of gross national product (GNP) produced is a measure of the intensity of energy use in a country's economy. Declining energy-to-GNP ratios indicate increasing energy efficiency and/or a structural shift toward a less energy-intensive economy. Reflecting both trends, energy intensity declined in 14 European countries, the United States, Canada, and Japan between 1970 and 1986.

The picture of energy use presented in these tables is incomplete because detailed data on the consumption of fuelwood and other biomass are not available. These noncommercial fuels account for the bulk of household energy use in many developing countries. In Africa, for example, about 90 percent of the population uses fuelwood for cooking. (See Chapter 18, "Forests and Rangelands," Table 18.2 for estimates of fuelwood production by country.)

A nation's energy reserves influence its energy policy and planning. (See Table 20.2.) If a country relies on imported oil to meet its energy requirements, it may be vulnerable to the political and economic pressures of exporting countries or suffer balance-of-payments problems. Domestic nuclear or hydroelectric resources can be developed as an alternative, but these are capital intensive and often have far-reaching safety, spent fuel disposal, and land use impacts. Energy choices also affect air pollution at the local, regional, and global level. China, for example, has 35 percent of the world's proven coal reserves, which, if fully exploited, could increase acidic deposition and significantly contribute to the buildup of carbon dioxide in the atmosphere.

Analyzing energy consumption by end use enables countries to plan energy strategies, identify economic sectors with rapidly changing energy consumption, and investigate fuel substitutes and conservation options. (See Table 20.3.) These data should be interpreted with care, as countries use different sectoral definitions. The data show that industry is the primary consumer of commercial energy in most middle- to high-income countries. However, energy use in transportation has grown rapidly. Since 1970, transportation's share of energy consumption increased in 47 of the 71 countries shown. (See Chapter 7, "Energy," for a discussion of energy use by sector.)

Nuclear power is an important energy source in many countries. (See Table 20.4.) In 1986, 398 nuclear power plants were operating in 26 countries; 243 more were planned or under construction. However, in recent years, concerns about costs, safety, and spent fuel disposal have slowed the expansion of nuclear power. Between 1970 and 1987, 149 nuclear power plants that were planned or under construction (116 of them in the United States) were cancelled. Worldwide, 58 formerly operating nuclear power plants have been retired, but most have not yet been decommissioned (dismantled to protect the public and the environment from radioactivity).

Metal production and consumption patterns are similar to those for energy. (See Table 20.5.) Developed countries are large producers and consumers of metals. Developing countries are also important metal producers, both for domestic use and as major foreign exchange earners. Although most of the growing global consumption of metals has been met by increased mine production, many countries have also turned to recycling and reuse of scrap to meet their needs.

A country's material consumption patterns determine the volume and composition of its wastes. (See Table 20.7.) Although data are not strictly comparable among countries, Bulgaria, the United States, and Australia appear to be the largest per capita generators of municipal wastes. Hazardous waste data are particularly problematic because of varying definitions. (See *World Resources 1987*, Chapter 13, "Managing Hazardous Wastes: The Unmet Challenge." For data on materials recovery, see Chapter 22, "Energy," Table 22.6 in the same volume.)

Table 20.1 Production and Consumption of Commercial Energy,

	Production								Consumption					
	Total		Solid		Liquid		Gas		Total		Per Capita		Per Constant 1980 $US of GNP	
	1986 (peta-joules)	Change over 1970 (percent)	1986 (peta-joules)	Change over 1970 (percent)	1986 (peta-joules)	Change over 1970 (percent)	1986 (peta-joules)	Change over 1970 (percent)	1986 (peta-joules)	Change over 1970 (percent)	1986 (giga-joules)	Change over 1970 (percent)	1986 (kilo-joules)	Change over 1970 (percent)
WORLD	288,367	40	90,004	43	123,731	23	61,625	60	273,201	45	56	9		
AFRICA	16,941	19	4,069	160	10,864	–13	1,818	2,261	7,109	139	12	44		
Algeria	3,441	62	0	X	2,097	2	1,341	1,995	836	465	37	244	15,912	133
Angola	593	171	X	X	583	170	5	150	27	4	3	–36	X	X
Benin	15	X	X	X	15	X	X	X	6	50	1	–32	4,248	–7
Botswana	X	X	X	X	X	X	X	X	X	X	X	X	X	X
Burkina Faso	X	X	X	X	X	X	X	X	6	200	1	154	3,672	79
Burundi	0	X	0	X	X	X	X	X	2	100	0	–100	1,778	26
Cameroon	384	9,500	0	X	376	X	X	X	88	577	9	369	8,469	118
Cape Verde	X	X	X	X	X	X	X	X	0	NM	0	NM	X	X
Central African Rep	0	NM	X	X	X	X	X	X	2	–33	1	–38	2,300	–47
Chad	X	X	X	X	X	X	X	X	3	50	1	83	3,129	42
Comoros	X	X	X	X	X	X	X	X	1	NM	2	NM	X	X
Congo	246	24,500	X	X	245	24,400	0	X	23	360	13	212	10,336	84
Cote d'Ivoire	47	4,600	X	X	42	X	X	X	63	97	6	4	6,498	–2
Djibouti	X	X	X	X	X	X	X	X	3	200	8	26		X
Egypt	1,927	168	X	X	1,725	147	163	5,333	988	289	21	172	34,372	59
Equatorial Guinea	0	NM	X	X	X	X	X	X	1	0	2	–42	X	X
Ethiopia	2	100	X	X	X	X	X	X	25	32	1	34	5,601	–9
Gabon	346	49	X	X	335	45	8	700	37	185	32	134	9,349	36
Gambia	X	X	X	X	X	X	X	X	2	100	3	41	8,428	13
Ghana	14	40	X	X	1	X	X	X	39	–7	3	–38	8,521	–15
Guinea	1	NM	X	X	X	X	X	X	14	27	2	–29	7,718	–15
Guinea–Bissau	X	X	X	X	X	X	X	X	1	0	1	–47	7,452	–23
Kenya	7	600	X	X	X	X	X	X	49	44	2	–34	5,937	–43
Lesotho	X	X	X	X	X	X	X	X	X	X	X	X	X	X
Liberia	1	0	X	X	X	X	X	X	10	–47	4	–71	10,487	–50
Libya	2,279	–67	X	X	2,122	–69	157	X	395	913	106	440	X	X
Madagascar	1	NM	X	X	X	X	X	X	11	–15	1	–48	3,795	–17
Malawi	2	NM	X	X	X	X	X	X	9	50	1	–25	7,046	–23
Mali	0	NM	X	X	X	X	X	X	6	100	1	90	3,358	19
Mauritania	X	X	X	X	X	X	X	X	8	33	4	–17	11,042	6
Mauritius	0	NM	X	X	X	X	X	X	13	63	12	27	8,779	–29
Morocco	30	43	23	77	1	–50	3	50	213	154	9	64	10,413	35
Mozambique	0	–100	0	–100	X	X	X	X	13	–61	1	–75	7,133	X
Niger	1	X	1	X	X	X	X	X	10	233	2	176	4,394	204
Nigeria	3,183	37	4	100	3,048	32	123	2,975	495	519	5	258	5,493	252
Rwanda	1	NM	X	X	X	X	0	X	6	500	1	272	4,412	222
Senegal	X	X	X	X	X	X	X	X	26	73	4	7	7,573	23
Sierra Leone	X	X	X	X	X	X	X	X	7	–30	2	–43	6,004	–46
Somalia	X	X	X	X	X	X	X	X	15	400	3	179	8,076	229
South Africa	3,919	176	3,903	174	X	X	X	X	3,111	87	81	11	40,634	34
Sudan	2	NM	X	X	X	X	X	X	44	–28	2	–55	7,004	–47
Swaziland	X	X	X	X	X	X	X	X	X	X	X	X	X	X
Tanzania, United Rep	2	100	0	X	X	X	X	X	26	18	1	–39	4,825	–19
Togo	0	NM	0	X	X	X	X	X	5	25	2	1	4,825	–12
Tunisia	237	34	X	X	220	24	17	X	151	251	21	150	14,974	46
Uganda	2	–33	X	X	X	X	X	X	13	–35	1	–51	X	X
Zaire	74	429	4	33	54	X	X	X	61	42	2	1	5,923	30
Zambia	50	178	14	–7	X	X	X	X	57	21	8	–29	15,803	9
Zimbabwe	130	7	119	16	X	X	X	X	169	31	19	–22	24,954	–35
NORTH & CENTRAL AMERICA	75,097	8	21,181	37	30,084	11	19,720	–23	79,387	8	195	X	X	X
Barbados	4	X	X	X	3	X	1	X	10	67	39	55	11,765	23
Canada	9,234	54	1,382	285	3,507	18	2,970	41	7,300	32	284	10	24,454	–27
Costa Rica	10	233	X	X	X	X	X	X	37	95	14	28	7,559	10
Cuba	40	471	X	X	39	457	0	X	422	69	42	44	X	X
Dominican Rep	3	NM	X	X	X	X	X	X	84	110	13	39	13,520	14
El Salvador	6	200	X	X	X	X	X	X	28	40	5	–10	8,836	14
Guatemala	15	1,400	X	X	12	X	X	X	45	50	5	–11	6,182	–8
Haiti	1	X	X	X	X	X	X	X	10	100	1	–8	7,279	38
Honduras	3	200	X	X	X	X	X	X	27	50	6	–12	10,708	–10
Jamaica	1	NM	X	X	X	X	X	X	76	15	32	–9	32,207	38
Mexico	6,867	335	177	185	5,971	491	614	36	3,806	144	47	54	20,771	29
Nicaragua	2	100	X	X	X	X	X	X	30	58	9	–3	14,925	51
Panama	8	700	X	X	X	X	X	X	42	20	19	–17	10,620	–39
Trinidad and Tobago	481	26	X	X	365	18	116	59	268	103	223	74	56,923	59
United States	58,422	–5	19,622	30	20,185	–11	16,019	–30	66,766	3	278	–12	20,664	–35
SOUTH AMERICA	11,431	0	518	180	8,035	–22	1,845	158	8,109	94	30	X	X	X
Argentina	1,637	50	9	–40	979	13	553	165	1,580	42	51	10	30,394	20
Bolivia	141	171	X	X	50	4	87	8,600	64	121	10	49	26,586	83
Brazil	2,152	293	151	165	1,233	258	110	3,567	3,088	153	22	73	11,369	–4
Chile	203	13	48	20	80	7	34	–29	330	4	27	–20	12,896	–14
Colombia	1,203	88	304	361	663	34	166	202	669	80	23	29	17,951	–8
Ecuador	633	5,655	X	X	613	6,711	4	300	185	278	19	131	14,990	45
Guyana	0	X	X	X	X	X	X	X	19	–14	20	–36	46,948	–4
Paraguay	6	500	X	X	X	X	X	X	28	180	7	60	5,585	9
Peru	433	130	4	–20	370	140	23	44	310	32	15	–16	14,731	–12
Suriname	9	125	X	X	6	NM	X	X	15	–40	39	–42	16,115	–62
Uruguay	26	550	X	X	X	X	X	X	54	–26	18	–31	6,093	–38
Venezuela	4,987	–43	2	100	4,041	–52	867	127	1,763	145	99	X	30,464	60

1970–86[a]

Table 20.1

	Production								Consumption					
	Total		Solid		Liquid		Gas		Total		Per Capita		Per Constant 1980 $US of GNP	
	1986 (peta-joules)	Change over 1970 (percent)	1986 (peta-joules)	Change over 1970 (percent)	1986 (peta-joules)	Change over 1970 (percent)	1986 (peta-joules)	Change over 1970 (percent)	1986 (peta-joules)	Change over 1970 (percent)	1986 (giga-joules)	Change over 1970 (percent)	1986 (kilo-joules)	Change over 1970 (percent)
ASIA	**71,118**	**52**	**25,441**	**120**	**38,630**	**15**	**4,950**	**337**	**58,114**	**120**	**20**	**X**	**X**	**X**
Afghanistan	119	18	5	0	0	NM	111	17	49	172	3	108	X	X
Bahrain	275	55	X	X	107	-34	168	1,100	193	1,035	429	455	56,755	X
Bangladesh	122	X	X	X	4	X	117	X	188	X	2	X	11,737	X
Bhutan	0	X	X	X	X	X	X	X	1	X	1	X	X	X
Burma	108	184	2	X	60	76	42	2,000	95	102	3	75	12,463	-3
China	24,349	173	17,973	143	5,468	319	547	388	21,771	158	21	106	43,394	-14
Cyprus	X	X	X	X	X	X	X	X	42	91	62	73	14,553	-61
India	5,844	194	4,111	161	1,312	352	210	1,005	6,160	175	8	97	26,348	47
Indonesia	4,169	123	51	920	2,973	64	1,120	2,283	1,392	243	8	137	14,270	29
Iran	4,322	-50	23	44	3,941	-52	336	-26	1,548	94	34	21	X	X
Iraq	3,549	8	X	X	3,473	7	74	139	327	96	20	12	X	X
Israel	2	-99	X	X	1	-100	2	-60	323	74	75	X	13,285	-10
Japan	1,446	-3	412	-61	27	-21	83	-19	12,900	32	106	13	9,797	-33
Jordan	1	X	X	X	1	X	X	X	111	517	30	283	26,528	128
Kampuchea, Dem	0	NM	X	X	X	X	X	X	7	-42	1	-42	X	X
Korea, Dem People's Rep	1,482	90	1,377	86	X	X	X	X	1,696	103	81	35	X	X
Korea, Rep	583	109	467	70	X	X	X	X	1,998	226	48	150	20,470	-6
Kuwait	3,339	-49	X	X	3,128	-52	211	164	432	308	228	60	14,997	136
Lao People's Dem Rep	4	NM	0	NM	X	X	X	X	4	-50	1	-62	X	X
Lebanon	2	-33	X	X	X	X	X	X	82	67	30	51	X	X
Malaysia	1,423	3,134	X	X	1,038	2,705	369	12,200	489	175	31	89	16,504	3
Mongolia	68	224	68	224	X	X	X	X	96	200	49	91	X	X
Nepal	2	NM	0	X	X	X	X	X	13	160	1	X	5,323	69
Oman	1,445	104	X	X	1,375	94	70	X	316	10,433	245	5,241	63,124	5,572
Pakistan	495	204	41	11	80	300	322	235	751	133	7	42	21,666	1
Philippines	77	863	25	2,400	14	X	X	X	403	37	7	-11	12,162	-23
Qatar	870	12	X	X	709	-4	161	313	189	340	564	46	X	X
Saudi Arabia	11,258	39	X	X	10,966	35	291	NM	1,459	1,771	122	799	18,453	666
Singapore	X	X	X	X	X	X	X	X	315	309	122	229	19,093	22
Sri Lanka	10	233	X	X	X	X	X	X	56	24	3	-17	10,883	-37
Syrian Arab Rep	404	123	X	X	388	114	7	NM	382	454	35	217	26,228	102
Thailand	304	2,664	60	1,400	94	NM	130	NM	691	253	13	141	15,798	39
Turkey	780	123	620	228	100	-34	17	X	1,437	191	29	108	19,101	32
United Arab Emirates	3,121	93	X	X	2,970	85	151	1,578	284	1,675	205	186	13,900	X
Viet Nam	168	87	161	83	X	X	X	X	214	-42	4	-54	X	X
Yemen	15	X	X	X	15	X	X	X	35	1,650	5	X	9,776	460
Yemen, Dem	X	X	X	X	X	X	X	X	45	309	20	172	57,997	X
EUROPE	**41,969**	**57**	**19,903**	**3**	**9,112**	**458**	**8,883**	**109**	**64,177**	**27**	**130**	**18**	**X**	**X**
Albania	187	140	34	278	126	100	15	275	117	208	38	114	X	X
Austria	237	-28	37	-31	47	-61	40	-48	885	24	118	23	10,544	-21
Belgium	295	-12	151	-55	X	X	1	-50	1,620	2	163	-1	13,093	-29
Bulgaria	590	25	519	20	13	-7	6	-65	1,543	64	169	53	X	X
Czechoslovakia	1,973	6	1,864	3	6	-33	24	-35	2,866	26	183	16	X	X
Denmark	234	23,300	0	-100	152	NM	81	X	800	2	156	-2	10,814	-27
Finland	173	394	64	6,300	X	X	X	X	809	47	165	38	13,677	-11
France	1,915	7	516	-55	146	16	165	-39	6,236	9	114	1	8,719	-29
German Dem Rep	2,936	24	2,745	17	50	1,150	96	380	3,908	28	233	X	X	X
Germany, Fed Rep	4,545	-11	3,354	-21	235	-27	465	1	10,097	10	166	10	11,304	-23
Greece	286	377	214	328	56	X	5	X	714	151	72	122	16,783	54
Hungary	633	5	253	-37	120	36	233	104	1,170	37	109	32	49,655	-19
Iceland	15	200	X	X	X	X	X	X	38	52	155	26	11,143	-26
Ireland	117	129	49	0	X	X	63	X	381	71	104	38	X	X
Italy	849	12	11	-52	107	67	541	9	5,397	30	94	21	10,989	-12
Luxembourg	0	-100	X	X	X	X	X	X	121	-28	333	-33	16,476	-65
Malta	X	X	X	X	X	X	X	X	18	100	47	70	13,285	-33
Netherlands	2,776	110	0	-100	210	156	2,551	129	3,072	75	211	57	17,157	25
Norway	3,234	1,377	17	31	1,781	NM	1,091	NM	805	56	194	X	11,675	-19
Poland	5,218	36	5,039	39	9	-53	157	-16	5,163	52	138	32	88,255	X
Portugal	37	28	6	-25	X	X	X	X	397	112	39	80	15,426	24
Romania	2,638	39	622	92	462	-21	1,510	54	3,045	70	131	49	X	X
Spain	904	118	581	92	78	1,200	15	650	2,499	72	64	49	10,719	5
Sweden	472	213	0	-100	0	NM	X	X	1,197	-12	143	-15	8,871	-33
Switzerland	195	70	X	X	X	X	X	1	749	27	117	24	6,389	0
United Kingdom	10,478	147	3,168	-14	5,335	76,114	1,747	302	8,858	11	157	X	14,591	-14
Yugoslavia	1,035	65	660	60	178	45	76	95	1,667	98	72	74	21,805	7
USSR	**66,197**	**86**	**15,350**	**14**	**25,794**	**71**	**23,698**	**255**	**52,671**	**80**	**187**	**54**	**X**	**X**
OCEANIA	**5,613**	**202**	**3,544**	**162**	**1,212**	**232**	**711**	**1,085**	**3,635**	**75**	**145**	**35**	**X**	**X**
Australia	5,276	202	3,490	169	1,156	218	571	920	3,122	76	196	39	17,875	11
Fiji	1	X	X	X	X	X	X	X	8	14	11	-18	5,883	-41
New Zealand	333	208	54	-5	57	2,750	140	X	384	67	115	41	15,248	17
Papua New Guinea	2	NM	X	X	X	X	X	X	31	182	9	X	X	X
Solomon Islands	X	X	X	X	X	X	X	X	2	100	7	X	10,764	X

Sources: United Nations Statistical Office, United Nations Population Division, and the World Bank.
Note: a. Primary electricity, which accounts for about 5 percent of global commercial energy production, is shown in *World Resources 1987*, Table 22.2.
0 = zero or less than half the unit of measure; X = not available; NM = not meaningful.
For additional information, see Sources and Technical Notes.

Table 20.2 Reserves and Resources of Commercial Energy, 1984

	Bituminous Coal (million metric tons)			Lignite and Sub-bituminous Coal (million metric tons)			Crude Oil (million metric tons)	Natural Gas (billion cubic meters)	Uranium (metric tons)		Hydroelectric (megawatts)	
	Year of Data	Proved Reserves in Place	Proved Recoverable Reserves	Year of Data	Proved Reserves in Place	Proved Recoverable Reserves	Proved Recoverable Reserves (1984)	Proved Recoverable Reserves (1984)	Recoverable at less than $80 per kilogram (1984)	Recoverable at $80–130 per kilogram (1984)	Technical Potential	Installed Capacity (1985)
WORLD[a]	1984	1,340,000	404,000	1984	765,000	434,000	94,000	85,500	1,498,586	713,376		555,463
AFRICA											307,986	16,647
Algeria	1981	X	43	X	X	X	1,437	3,150	25,000	0	287	285
Angola	X	X	X	X	X	X	250	53	X	X	23,000	400
Benin	X	X	X	X	X	X	X	X	X	X	500	0
Botswana	1977	7,000	3,500	X	X	X	X	X	X	X	200	X
Burkina Faso	X	X	X	X	X	X	X	X	X	X		0
Burundi	X	X	X	X	X	X	X	X	X	X	192[b]	2
Cameroon	X	X	X	X	X	X	65	95	X	X	23,000	497
Cape Verde	X	X	X	X	X	X	X	X	X	X	X	0
Central African Rep	X	X	X	1979	4	4	X	X	X	X	2,000	20
Chad	X	X	X	X	X	X	X	X	X	X	30	0
Comoros	X	X	X	X	X	X	X	X	X	X	10	1
Congo	X	X	X	X	X	X	70	70	X	X	11,000	120
Cote d'Ivoire	X	X	X	X	X	X	15	60	X	X	3,000	885
Djibouti	X	X	X	X	X	X	X	X	X	X	X	0
Egypt	1965	25	13	1979	X	40	400	170	X	X	3,210	2,700
Equatorial Guinea	X	X	X	X	X	X	X	X	X	X	2,000	1
Ethiopia	X	X	X	1984	23	11	X	X	X	X	6,849[b]	222
Gabon	X	X	X	X	X	X	70	12	18,700	4,700	18,000	125
Gambia	X	X	X	X	X	X	X	X	X	X	X	0
Ghana	X	X	X	X	X	X	1	X	X	X	2,000	952
Guinea	X	X	X	X	X	X	X	X	X	X	5,000	50
Guinea-Bissau	X	X	X	X	X	X	X	X	X	X	60	0
Kenya	X	X	X	X	X	X	X	X	X	X	6,000	354
Lesotho	X	X	X	X	X	X	X	X	X	X	450	X
Liberia	X	X	X	X	X	X	X	X	X	X	2,000	81
Libya	X	X	X	X	X	X	2,800	600	X	X	X	0
Madagascar	1977	1,000	X	1977	75	X	X	X	X	X	7,800	45
Malawi	1977	25	12	X	X	X	X	X	X	X	900	126
Mali	X	X	X	1979	0	X	X	X	X	X	2,000	20
Mauritania	X	X	X	X	X	X	X	X	X	X	X	0
Mauritius	X	X	X	X	X	X	0	X	X	X	65	54
Morocco	1981	134	45	1981	44	X	X	4	X	X	2,453	612
Mozambique	1976	X	240	X	X	X	X	X	X	X	15,000	1,523
Niger	1979	5	X	X	X	X	X	X	170,400	X	235	0
Nigeria	X	X	X	1979	338	169	2,200	1,400	X	X	12,400	1,900
Rwanda	X	X	X	X	X	X	X	40	X	X	600	55
Senegal	X	X	X	X	X	X	X	X	X	X	500	0
Sierra Leone	X	X	X	X	X	X	X	X	0	X	1,300	4
Somalia	X	X	X	X	X	X	X	X	0	660	50	0
South Africa	1984	115,530	58,404	X	X	X	X	X	191,000	122,000	X	572[c]
Sudan	X	X	X	X	X	X	40	3	X	X	2,700	148
Swaziland	1961	2,020	1,820	X	X	X	X	X	X	X	600	X
Tanzania, United Rep	1979	304	200	X	X	X	X	6	X	X	9,500	260
Togo	X	X	X	X	X	X	X	X	X	X	270	4
Tunisia	X	X	X	X	X	X	200	85	X	X	65	64
Uganda	X	X	X	X	X	X	X	X	X	X	1,200	156
Zaire	1978	600	600	X	X	X	19	2	1,800	X	120,000	2,111
Zambia	1984	X	72	X	X	X	X	X	X	X	12,000	1,538
Zimbabwe	1977	1,535	734	1979	965	0	X	X	X	X	3,800	633
NORTH & CENTRAL AMERICA												151,527
Barbados	X	X	X	X	X	X	0	X	X	X	X	0
Canada	1984	4,903	3,548	1984	4,119	3,298	865	2,600	155,000	59,000	141,409[d]	57,458
Costa Rica	X	X	X	X	X	X	X	X	X	X	9,071	637
Cuba	X	X	X	X	X	X	X	X	X	X	X	45
Dominican Rep	X	X	X	X	X	X	X	X	X	X	287[b]	165
El Salvador	X	X	X	X	X	X	X	X	X	X	1,377	233
Guatemala	X	X	X	X	X	X	7	X	X	X	4,951[b]	442
Haiti	X	X	X	1979	13	X	X	X	X	X	152	50
Honduras	X	X	X	1979	21	X	X	X	X	X	2,740[b]	130
Jamaica	X	X	X	X	X	X	X	X	X	X	100	25
Mexico	1984	1,597	1,274	1984	804	643	8,032	2,172	23,600	X	19,692[b]	6,601
Nicaragua	X	X	X	X	X	X	X	X	X	X	4,106	103
Panama	X	X	X	X	X	X	X	X	X	X	3,031	551
Trinidad and Tobago	X	X	X	X	X	X	85	290	X	X	X	0
United States	1984	237,640	131,971	1984	205,252	131,872	4,616	5,835	131,300	266,800	183,287	87,979
SOUTH AMERICA												57,853
Argentina	X	X	X	1984	195	130	330	621	15,385	3,552	21,237[b]	5,990
Bolivia	X	X	X	X	X	X	20	140	X	X	18,000	304
Brazil	1984	20	20	1984	3,078	2,323	305	93	163,273	1,000	106,495[b]	36,881
Chile	1984	79	31	1984	4,500	1,150	80	120	1,000	X	14,860[b]	1,775
Colombia	1979	2,025	1,010	1979	48	25	85	117	X	X	94,358	3,775
Ecuador	X	X	X	1981	X	18	228	116	X	X	22,733	741
Guyana	X	X	X	X	X	X	X	X	X	X	8,000	2
Paraguay	X	X	X	X	X	X	X	X	X	X	10,965	890
Peru	1981	28	X	X	X	X	105	25	500	X	60,000	1,999
Suriname	X	X	X	X	X	X	X	X	X	X	2,334	189
Uruguay	X	X	X	X	X	X	X	X	X	X	2,248	881
Venezuela	1984	509	372	X	X	X	3,774	1,664	X	X	32,875[d]	4,426

Table 20.2

	Bituminous Coal (million metric tons)			Lignite and Sub-bituminous Coal (million metric tons)			Crude Oil (million metric tons)	Natural Gas (billion cubic meters)	Uranium (metric tons)		Hydroelectric (megawatts)	
	Year of Data	Proved Reserves in Place	Proved Recoverable Reserves	Year of Data	Proved Reserves in Place	Proved Recoverable Reserves	Proved Recoverable Reserves (1984)	Proved Recoverable Reserves (1984)	Recoverable at less than $80 per kilogram (1984)	Recoverable at $80–130 per kilogram (1984)	Technical Potential	Installed Capacity (1985)
ASIA												101,398
Afghanistan	1965	112	66	X	X	X	X	75	X	75	25,000	272
Bahrain	X	X	X	X	X	X	28	220	X	X	X	0
Bangladesh	1981	1,054	X	X	X	X	X	192	X	X	800	130
Bhutan	X	X	X	X	X	X	X	X	X	X	X	3
Burma	1975	5	2	1975	X	X	4	X	X	X	30,000	169
China	1984	610,600	X	1984	126,500	X	2,600	723	X	X	219,555[b]	26,500
Cyprus	X	X	X	X	X	X	X	X	X	X	2,683[b,e]	0
India	1981	26,331	X	1981	1,581	1,581	471	350	31,025	10,772	100,000	15,115
Indonesia	1984	774	X	1984	22,458	X	1,200	1,870	X	X	80,936[b]	534
Iran	1972	385	193	X	X	X	6,600	11,000	X	X	X	1,804
Iraq	X	X	X	X	X	X	6,000	800	X	X	X	100
Israel	X	X	X	X	X	X	2	0	X	X	X	0
Japan	1984	8,479	997	1984	175	18	8	27	7,700	0	81,918[d]	34,337
Jordan	X	X	X	X	X	X	X	X	X	X	12[b]	0
Kampuchea, Dem	X	X	X	X	X	X	X	X	X	X	10,000	20
Korea, Dem People's Rep	1978	2,000	300	X	300	300	X	X	X	X	X	4,500
Korea, Rep	1984	200	132	X	X	X	X	X	X	10,000	2,000	2,223
Kuwait	X	X	X	X	X	X	10,000	1,000	X	X	X	0
Lao People's Dem Rep	X	X	X	X	X	X	X	X	X	X	28,000	200
Lebanon	X	X	X	X	X	X	X	X	X	X	114[b]	246
Malaysia	1984	X	7	X	X	X	407	1,501	X	X	6,761[b,f]	1,229
Mongolia	1984	12,000	X	X	12,000	X	X	X	X	X	X	0
Nepal	X	X	X	X	X	X	X	X	X	X	18,250	129
Oman	X	X	X	X	X	X	480	87	X	X	X	0
Pakistan	X	X	X	1979	145	102	13	450	X	X	19,600	2,997
Philippines	X	X	X	1979	170	82	3	X	X	X	3,766[b]	1,839
Qatar	X	X	X	X	X	X	450	3,150	X	X	X	0
Saudi Arabia	X	X	X	X	X	X	23,000	2,050	X	X	X	0
Singapore	X	X	X	X	X	X	X	X	X	X	X	0
Sri Lanka	X	X	X	X	X	X	X	X	X	X	715[b]	679
Syrian Arab Rep	X	X	X	X	X	X	183	107	X	80,000	1,282	823
Thailand	X	X	X	1984	15	879	12	105	X	X	20,148	1,824
Turkey	1984	135	94	1984	5,292	4,763	38	14	2,500	2,100	24,543[b]	3,875
United Arab Emirates	X	X	X	X	X	X	4,300	900	X	X	X	0
Viet Nam	1965	300	150	1965	12	X	X	X	X	X	18,000	320
Yemen	X	X	X	X	X	X	X	X	X	X	X	0
Yemen, Dem	X	X	X	X	X	X	X	X	X	X	X	0
EUROPE												155,654
Albania	X	X	X	X	15	X	35	8	X	8	1,598[b]	550
Austria	1984	1	3	1984	177	61	13	9	X	300	6,484[b]	10,171
Belgium	1984	715	410	X	X	X	X	X	X	X	X	1,326
Bulgaria	1979	36	30	1979	4,418	3,700	2	7	X	X	3,015[d]	1,975
Czechoslovakia	1984	5,750	2,700	1984	7,220	2,860	3	10	X	X	X	2,875
Denmark	X	X	X	1984	623	X	62	103	X	27,000	5[d]	12
Finland	X	X	X	X	X	X	X	X	X	3,400	3,196[b]	2,505
France	1984	906	332	1984	160	49	42	52	55,953	11,109	7,670[b]	21,800
German Dem Rep	X	X	X	1984	47,000	21,000	X	60	X	X	X	1,845
Germany, Fed Rep	1984	44,000	23,919	1984	55,000	35,150	43	266	850	4,200	2,626[b]	6,668
Greece	X	X	X	1984	5,312	3,000	9	110	400	X	X	2,032
Hungary	1984	1,407	596	1984	8,306	3,865	25	133	X	X	X	46
Iceland	X	X	X	X	X	X	X	X	X	X	7,306[b]	753
Ireland	1984	7	5	1984	12	9	X	35	X	X	X	516
Italy	1984	X	X	1984	75	39	87	250	4,800	0	6,849[b]	17,166
Luxembourg	X	X	X	X	X	X	X	X	X	X	14[b]	1,132
Malta	X	X	X	X	X	X	X	X	X	X	X	0
Netherlands	1984	1,406	497	X	X	X	25	1,515	X	X	X	0
Norway	X	X	X	1984	35	30	742	1,048	X	X	19,635[b]	22,991
Poland	1983	63,000	28,300	1983	13,200	14,400	5	128	X	X	1,370[b]	1,975
Portugal	1984	28	20	1984	38	33	X	X	6,700	1,500	4,100[b]	3,077
Romania	1966	70	X	1966	3,900	X	120	230	X	X	12,300	4,421
Spain	1984	949	415	1984	778	468	11	14	26,700	6,200	7,557[b]	13,790
Sweden	X	X	X	1984	4	1	X	0	2,000	37,000	11,301[b]	15,690
Switzerland	X	X	X	X	X	X	X	X	X	X	X	11,480
United Kingdom	1984	X	4,600	1984	400	X	752	725	X	X	639[b]	4,190
Yugoslavia	1971	80	70	1978	17,760	16,500	41	90	X	X	17,000	6,650
USSR	**1984**	**136,000**	**108,800**	**1984**	**156,800**	**135,900**	**8,600**	**35,000**	**X**	**X**	**437,329[b]**	**61,257**
OCEANIA												11,127
Australia	1984	48,540	27,442	1981	42,286	38,260	344	890	463,000	63,000	6,107[d]	6,557
Fiji	X	X	X	X	X	X	X	X	X	X	400	80
New Zealand	1984	36	33	1984	1,990	210	20	155	X	X	5,479[b]	4,295
Papua New Guinea	X	X	X	X	X	X	X	14	X	X	29,000	100
Solomon Islands	X	X	X	X	X	X	X	X	X	X	X	0

Sources: World Energy Conference; The World Bank; United Nations Statistical Office; and U.S. Federal Energy Regulatory Commission.
Notes: a. Global data include estimates for countries for which data are unavailable. b. Exploitable potential. c. Figure for South Africa includes Botswana, Lesotho, Swaziland and Namibia. e. Potential at small scale sites (under 1 megawatt) only. f. Refers to Peninsular Malaysia only.
0 = zero or less than half the unit of measure; X = not available.
For additional information, see Sources and Technical Notes.

Table 20.3 Commercial Energy Use by Sector, 1970–85

	Percentage of Commercial Energy Used For														
	Industry			Transport			Agriculture			Commercial and Residential			Other[a]		
	1970	1980	1985	1970	1980	1985	1970	1980	1985	1970	1980	1985	1970	1980	1985
AFRICA															
Algeria	43	30	X	27	37	X	X	X	X	X	X	X	30	33	X
Côte d'Ivoire	9	7	X	20	22	X	1	0	X	X	X	X	70	72	X
Egypt	55	55	X	17	22	X	1	0	X	19	15	X	9	8	X
Gabon	11	21	X	25	29	X	X	X	X	X	X	X	63	50	X
Kenya	5	8	X	9	9	X	1	1	X	1	1	X	85	82	X
Libya	3	9	X	50	64	X	X	X	X	X	X	X	47	28	X
Morocco	37	43	X	28	30	X	X	X	X	X	X	X	35	27	X
Nigeria	3	8	X	3	9	X	0	0	X	93	82	X	0	0	X
Tunisia	21	24	X	30	35	X	X	X	X	X	X	X	48	41	X
Zaire	20	20	X	13	13	X	X	X	X	X	X	X	67	67	X
Zambia	34	32	X	12	11	X	X	X	X	X	X	X	54	57	X
Zimbabwe	29	34	X	16	11	X	X	X	X	X	X	X	55	55	X
NORTH & CENTRAL AMERICA															
Canada	32	37	39	14	28	25	0	2	2	37	29	31	17	4	3
Jamaica	59	73	X	33	15	X	X	X	X	X	X	X	7	12	X
Panama	16	26	X	29	25	X	X	X	X	X	X	X	55	49	X
Mexico	44	37	X	29	37	X	1	1	X	13	13	X	13	11	X
United States	37	34	31	29	32	35	1	1	1	30	29	30	3	4	4
SOUTH AMERICA															
Argentina	36	33	X	36	33	X	4	7	X	12	21	X	12	5	X
Bolivia	13	16	X	15	25	X	X	X	X	X	X	X	72	59	X
Brazil	34	39	X	26	25	X	0	6	X	2	22	X	37	8	X
Chile	32	35	X	34	34	X	0	0	X	2	4	X	31	26	X
Colombia	21	22	X	14	16	X	X	X	X	X	X	X	66	63	X
Ecuador	19	16	X	25	40	X	X	X	X	X	X	X	57	43	X
Peru	27	33	X	28	28	X	X	X	X	X	X	X	46	39	X
Uruguay	28	29	X	30	31	X	X	X	X	X	X	X	42	40	X
Venezuela	30	36	X	28	38	X	0	0	X	37	23	X	5	3	X
ASIA															
Bangladesh	X	23	X	X	9	X	X	X	X	X	X	X	X	68	X
Burma	6	7	X	7	7	X	X	X	X	X	X	X	87	86	X
Hong Kong	31	28	X	38	40	X	X	X	X	X	X	X	30	32	X
India	23	27	X	14	13	X	1	2	X	59	57	X	2	2	X
Indonesia	11	14	X	5	10	X	0	0	X	81	71	X	3	4	X
Iran	63	42	X	19	31	X	0	0	X	15	24	X	3	3	X
Iraq	6	7	X	38	56	X	X	X	X	X	X	X	57	37	X
Japan	62	51	48	17	22	23	1	1	2	10	18	20	11	8	8
Korea, Rep	19	24	X	8	9	X	0	0	X	72	66	X	1	1	X
Kuwait	2	2	X	19	54	X	0	0	X	7	29	X	72	15	X
Malaysia	7	11	X	7	10	X	0	0	X	45	36	X	40	44	X
Pakistan	27	31	X	15	18	X	4	3	X	13	12	X	41	37	X
Philippines	27	26	X	16	12	X	X	X	X	X	X	X	57	63	X
Saudi Arabia	70	51	X	22	32	X	X	X	X	X	X	X	9	17	X
Singapore	80	86	X	8	7	X	0	0	X	8	5	X	3	3	X
Taiwan	67	67	X	17	15	X	X	X	X	X	X	X	16	18	X
Thailand	48	20	X	25	21	X	7	5	X	17	54	X	3	1	X
Turkey	27	27	28	34	21	21	7	4	5	28	47	44	3	2	3
EUROPE															
Austria	35	34	34	18	23	23	3	0	1	38	37	38	6	5	5
Belgium	48	43	41	13	17	19	1	1	1	32	36	37	5	3	2
Bulgaria	X	X	53	X	X	13	X	X	0	X	X	34	X	X	0
Denmark	23	21	18	19	24	26	5	8	7	44	44	43	9	4	7
Finland	45	45	45	13	15	17	3	4	4	36	32	30	2	4	4
France	46	38	33	17	24	26	2	2	2	28	33	35	6	3	3
German Dem Rep	50	49	49	8	5	4	0	0	0	42	46	46	0	0	0
Germany, Fed Rep	39	37	35	17	21	22	1	1	1	36	29	37	8	12	5
Greece	34	36	30	18	35	37	7	7	7	25	20	21	16	4	5
Hungary	X	32	31	X	13	12	X	6	6	X	27	30	X	21	21
Iceland	23	42	40	51	36	44	2	1	2	25	17	11	0	4	2
Ireland	32	33	32	24	27	26	0	0	0	39	37	38	5	3	4
Italy	48	41	36	19	24	27	2	2	2	28	30	32	4	3	3
Luxembourg	82	65	59	5	15	20	0	0	0	11	16	18	2	3	3
Netherlands	38	40	40	6	17	18	1	1	5	32	30	26	23	13	12
Norway	45	46	44	20	19	20	0	2	1	18	29	30	17	3	4
Poland	X	X	47	X	X	8	X	X	0	X	X	45	X	X	0
Portugal	43	44	46	28	31	29	5	4	4	18	17	18	5	4	3
Romania	X	X	64	X	X	4	X	X	0	X	X	32	X	X	0
Spain	49	45	42	26	32	32	5	5	5	14	15	17	5	4	3
Sweden	41	38	37	15	18	20	2	2	2	33	32	36	9	10	5
Switzerland	26	23	23	24	25	28	1	1	1	11	46	45	38	5	3
United Kingdom	44	33	30	19	25	26	1	1	1	31	36	37	5	6	5
Yugoslavia	X	50	47	X	23	20	X	2	2	X	14	13	X	12	18
USSR	X	X	60	X	X	13	X	X	0	X	X	27	X	X	0
OCEANIA															
Australia	48	43	40	31	36	38	3	2	2	10	17	18	8	3	3
New Zealand	28	32	41	35	35	31	5	4	3	25	26	21	6	3	3

Sources: Organisation for Economic Co-operation and Development; World Energy Conference; and Vienna Institute for Comparative Economic Studies.
Note: a. Other includes nonenergy uses, military uses, and nonspecified uses. 0 = zero or less than half of one percent; X = not available.
For additional information, see Sources and Technical Notes.

Table 20.4 Nuclear Power and Waste Generation, 1970–87

	Number of Reactors							Net Capacity (Megawatts)					Spent Fuel Inventories (cumulative metric tons of heavy metal)			
	Operable				Planned or under Construction[a]	Cancelled 1970-87	Retired 1951-87	Installed				Planned or under Construction[a]				
	1970	1975	1980	1986				1970	1975	1980	1986		1970	1975	1980	1986
WORLD TOTAL	66	151	234	398	243	149	58	15,471	68,379	132,782	290,585	256,435	X	X	X	X
MARKET ECONOMIES	54	128	197	324	129	148	55	13,963	62,141	117,573	238,961	128,736	6,205	16,714	34,913	76,800
North America	14	57	77	118	35	117	35	6,433	38,553	56,326	96,166	37,254	145	2,494	9,818	24,300
Canada	1	5	9	18	5	1	2	22	2,078	5,150	10,989	4,361	96	989	3,314	8,700
Mexico	0	0	0	0	2	0	0	0	0	0	0	1,308	0	0	0	0
United States	13	52	68	100	28	116	33	6,411	36,475	51,176	85,177	31,585	49	1,505	6,504	14,000
Asia	6	16	31	53	43	10	2	1,658	7,019	17,712	35,407	37,507	X	X	X	X
India	2	3	4	6	4	0	0	400	602	804	1,164	880	X	X	X	X
Iran	0	0	0	0	0	8	0	0	0	0	0	0	0	0	0	0
Japan	4	12	23	34	30	0	2	1,258	6,292	15,011	24,754	28,871	X	X	X	4,300
Korea, Rep	0	0	1	6	5	0	0	0	0	564	4,480	4,636	0	X	X	300
Pakistan	0	1	1	1	1	0	0	0	125	125	125	600	0	X	X	X
Philippines	0	0	0	0	1	1	0	0	0	0	0	620	0	0	0	0
Taiwan	0	0	2	6	2	0	0	0	0	1,208	4,884	1,900	0	0	X	500
Turkey	0	0	0	0	0	0	1	0	0	0	0	0	0	0	0	0
Europe	34	54	86	148	46	21	18	5,872	16,224	42,164	103,987	48,993	6,060	14,220	25,095	47,400
Austria	0	0	0	0	0	1	0	0	0	0	0	0	0	0	0	0
Belgium	0	1	3	7	0	0	0	0	393	1,656	5,450	0	0	X	X	600
Finland	0	0	4	4	0	0	0	0	0	2,266	2,310	0	0	X	X	400
France	3	6	17	49	15	2	6	1,190	2,478	12,468	44,873	18,975	X	X	X	10,800
Germany, Fed Rep	1	4	10	19	9	3	7	328	2,744	8,523	18,944	10,303	X	X	X	2,500
Italy	2	2	3	3	5	2	1	397	397	1,270	1,282	3,924	X	X	X	1,300
Luxembourg	0	0	0	0	0	1	0	0	0	0	0	0	0	0	0	0
Netherlands	1	2	2	2	0	0	0	52	497	497	500	0	X	X	X	200
Spain	1	3	3	8	10	4	0	153	1,073	1,073	5,668	9,731	X	X	X	2,300
Sweden	0	5	8	12	0	1	1	0	3,130	5,515	9,650	0	X	X	X	1,400
Switzerland	1	3	4	5	2	1	1	350	1,020	1,940	2,930	2,140	X	X	X	500
United Kingdom	25	28	32	38	5	6	2	3,402	4,492	6,956	11,748	3,920	X	X	X	27,400
Yugoslavia	0	0	0	1	0	0	0	0	0	0	632	0	0	0	0	0
Other	0	1	3	5	5	0	0	0	345	1,371	3,401	4,982	X	X	X	X
Argentina	0	1	2	2	1	0	0	0	345	945	935	692	0	X	X	X
Brazil	0	0	1	1	2	0	0	0	0	626	626	2,490	0	X	X	X
Egypt	0	0	0	0	2	0	0	0	0	0	0	1,800	0	0	0	0
South Africa	0	0	0	2	0	0	0	0	0	0	1,840	0	0	0	0	X
NONMARKET ECONOMIES	12	23	37	74	114	1	3	1,508	6,238	15,209	51,624	127,699	X	X	X	X
Bulgaria	0	2	3	5	5	0	0	0	810	1,215	2,713	4,793	0	X	X	X
China	0	0	0	0	9	0	0	0	0	0	0	5,950	0	0	0	0
Cuba	0	0	0	0	2	0	0	0	0	0	0	880	0	0	0	0
Czechoslovakia	0	1	3	8	9	0	1	0	104	864	2,874	5,622	0	X	X	X
German Dem Rep	1	3	5	5	10	0	0	70	886	1,702	1,702	4,080	X	X	X	X
Hungary	0	0	0	3	5	0	0	0	0	0	1,230	3,226	0	0	0	X
Poland	0	0	0	0	6	0	0	0	0	0	0	3,736	0	0	0	0
Romania	0	0	0	0	6	1	0	0	0	0	0	3,920	0	0	0	0
USSR	11	17	26	53	62	0	2	1,438	4,438	11,428	43,105	95,492	X	X	X	X

Sources: U.S. Department of Energy; and Commisseriat Energie Atomique. **Note:** a. As of December 31, 1986. 0 = zero; X = not available. For additional information, see Sources and Technical Notes.

Table 20.5 Producers and Consumers of Selected Metals, 1965–86

	Annual Production (thousand metric tons)						Annual Consumption (thousand metric tons)				
	1965	1970	1975	1980	1986		1965	1970	1975	1980	1986
ALUMINUM						**ALUMINUM**					
United States	2,499	3,607	3,519	4,654	3,037	United States	2,852	3,488	3,265	4,454	4,268
USSR	840	1,100	1,530	1,760	2,300	USSR	1,000	1,281	1,580	1,850	1,885
Canada	753	972	887	1,068	1,360	Japan	286	930	1,171	1,639	1,624
Australia	88	206	214	303	882	Germany, Fed Rep	387	670	704	1,042	1,186
Germany, Fed Rep	234	309	678	731	765	China	95	180	300	550	750
Brazil	33	62	121	260	762	France	249	413	399	601	593
Norway	279	522	595	653	712	Italy	128	279	270	458	510
Venezuela	0	25	45	321	424	Brazil	52	84	209	296	424
China	100	130	200	360	410	Canada	182	250	293	312	405
Spain	52	120	210	386	375	United Kingdom	364	404	393	409	389
Ten Countries Total	**4,878**	**7,052**	**7,999**	**10,497**	**11,027**	**Ten Countries Total**	**5,412**	**7,729**	**8,291**	**11,299**	**12,033**
World Total	**6,318**	**9,653**	**12,145**	**15,383**	**15,314**	**World Total**	**6,699**	**9,928**	**11,299**	**15,285**	**16,396**
COPPER						**COPPER**					
Chile	606	711	828	1,068	1,386	United States	1,819	1,854	1,397	1,868	2,102
United States	1,226	1,560	1,282	1,181	1,022	Japan	428	821	827	1,158	1,219
Canada	461	610	734	716	768	USSR	408	841	1,035	990	1,300
USSR	323	451	580	590	620	Germany, Fed Rep	536	698	635	748	771
Zaire	289	387	495	540	563	China	120	200	315	386	471
Zambia	696	684	677	596	450	France	287	331	365	433	401
Poland	15	72	230	346	431	Italy	192	274	299	388	395
Peru	180	220	193	367	397	United Kingdom	650	554	451	409	340
Mexico	55	61	79	175	285	Belgium	99	145	177	304	303
Australia	92	158	219	244	239	Korea, Rep	2	8	28	84	264
Ten Countries Total	**3,943**	**4,914**	**5,317**	**5,822**	**6,161**	**Ten Countries Total**	**4,538**	**5,717**	**5,500**	**6,684**	**7,565**
World Total	**4,690**	**6,262**	**7,000**	**7,394**	**8,156**	**World Total**	**5,750**	**7,172**	**7,260**	**9,086**	**10,073**

(Continued)

Table 20.5 Producers and Consumers of Selected Metals, 1965–86 (continued)

Annual Production (thousand metric tons)

	1965	1970	1975	1980	1986
LEAD					
Australia	368	457	408	397	435
USSR	350	440	480	420	440
United States	273	519	564	550	353
Canada	275	353	349	297	304
Mexico	167	177	179	147	200
Peru	154	157	184	189	194
China	100	100	100	160	160
Yugoslavia	106	127	127	121	110
Korea, Dem Rep	60	70	120	125	110
South Africa	0	0	3	86	98
Ten Countries Total	**1,793**	**2,328**	**2,390**	**2,281**	**2,403**
World Total	**2,753**	**3,471**	**3,581**	**3,577**	**3,239**
NICKEL					
USSR	85	110	152	154	186
Canada	242	277	242	185	181
Australia	0	30	76	74	70
New Caledonia	31	105	133	87	65
Indonesia	4	16	15	53	44
Cuba	X	35	37	37	33
South Africa	3	12	21	26	25
China	X	X	X	X	25
Dominican Rep	0	X	27	16	22
Colombia	X	X	X	15	22
Ten Countries Total	**365**	**585**	**702**	**632**	**672**
World Total	**426**	**628**	**808**	**759**	**784**
TIN					
Malaysia	64	73	64	61	28
Brazil	2	4	5	7	27
USSR	23	27	30	36	24
Indonesia	15	19	25	33	22
Thailand	19	21	16	34	17
China	25	20	22	15	15
Bolivia	23	29	24	22	12
Australia	4	9	10	12	9
Peru	0	0	0	1	5
United Kingdom	1	2	3	3	5
Ten Countries Total	**178**	**204**	**200**	**223**	**163**
World Total	**205**	**217**	**219**	**236**	**180**
ZINC					
Canada	826	1,239	1,229	1,059	1,294
USSR	470	610	690	785	810
Australia	355	487	501	495	662
Peru	254	299	385	488	598
China	100	100	100	160	396
Mexico	225	266	289	236	285
United States	554	485	426	317	216
Spain	39	98	84	183	223
Japan	221	280	254	238	222
Sweden	79	93	111	167	214
Ten Countries Total	**3,024**	**3,857**	**3,970**	**3,968**	**4,920**
World Total	**4,235**	**5,615**	**6,111**	**6,213**	**6,853**
IRON ORE					
USSR	153,432	195,492	232,803	244,713	249,000
Brazil	20,754	40,200	89,894	114,732	132,000
Australia	6,803	51,189	97,651	95,534	90,000
China	39,000	40,400	65,000	68,000	90,000
India	23,830	31,366	41,405	41,936	47,800
United States	88,842	91,201	80,132	70,730	39,448
Canada	36,250	47,459	46,868	48,754	36,070
South Africa	5,816	7,728	12,298	26,312	24,483
Sweden	29,354	31,509	30,867	27,184	20,489
Venezuela	17,510	22,100	24,772	16,102	19,100
Ten Countries Total	**421,592**	**558,643**	**721,691**	**753,999**	**737,546**
World Total	**620,982**	**769,163**	**902,018**	**895,867**	**847,775**
CRUDE STEEL					
USSR	91,000	115,886	141,325	147,941	161,000
Japan	41,161	93,322	102,313	111,395	98,275
United States	118,985	119,305	105,816	101,455	73,001
China	15,000	18,000	25,000	37,120	52,100
Germany, Fed Rep	36,821	45,041	40,415	43,838	37,134
Italy	12,681	17,277	21,836	26,501	22,872
Brazil	3,024	5,390	8,308	15,339	21,234
France	19,604	23,773	21,530	23,176	18,000
Poland	9,088	11,795	15,007	19,485	17,100
Czechoslovakia	X	X	X	X	15,000
Ten Countries Total	**347,364**	**449,790**	**481,549**	**526,249**	**516,231**
World Total	**459,300**	**594,418**	**643,798**	**713,788**	**714,970**

Annual Consumption (thousand metric tons)

	1965	1970	1975	1980	1986
LEAD					
United States	754	894	820	1,094	1,119
USSR	385	486	620	800	760
Japan	147	211	189	393	389
Germany, Fed Rep	271	309	225	333	359
United Kingdom	312	262	238	296	282
Italy	94	168	146	275	232
China	100	160	185	210	225
France	145	193	174	213	205
Yugoslavia	43	45	83	128	145
Bulgaria	X	77	95	110	116
Ten Countries Total	**2,250**	**2,803**	**2,775**	**3,851**	**3,832**
World Total	**3,179**	**3,914**	**4,759**	**5,392**	**5,489**
NICKEL					
USSR	110	130	115	132	146
Japan	27	98	90	122	127
United States	156	141	133	142	125
Germany, Fed Rep	31	41	43	68	77
France	21	36	32	38	32
Italy	9	20	17	27	30
United Kingdom	37	35	21	23	27
China	X	X	18	18	20
Sweden	13	23	22	20	17
India	X	X	3	12	16
Ten Countries Total	**404**	**524**	**494**	**602**	**616**
World Total	**428**	**567**	**570**	**715**	**792**
TIN					
United States	63	57	56	56	44
Japan	18	29	28	31	32
USSR	29	17	23	25	26
Germany, Fed Rep	13	15	13	16	17
China	15	13	14	13	12
United Kingdom	21	19	14	10	10
France	10	11	10	10	8
Brazil	2	3	3	5	6
Netherlands	4	6	4	5	6
Italy	6	7	8	6	6
Ten Countries Total	**175**	**168**	**166**	**171**	**159**
World Total	**223**	**225**	**216**	**224**	**226**
ZINC					
United States	1,221	1,074	839	810	999
USSR	401	510	900	1,030	990
Japan	322	623	547	752	753
Germany, Fed Rep	334	396	297	406	434
China	100	150	220	200	360
France	186	220	223	330	261
Italy	116	178	150	236	232
United Kingdom	282	278	207	181	182
Belgium	123	128	103	155	172
Poland	114	129	152	178	157
Ten Countries Total	**1,949**	**2,592**	**2,797**	**3,423**	**3,335**
World Total	**4,054**	**5,042**	**5,036**	**6,181**	**6,323**
IRON ORE					
USSR	128,895	159,392	189,177	218,417	201,078[a]
Japan	62,286	106,708	140,584	140,899	130,451[b]
China	38,500	44,000	66,400	80,900	94,000[b]
United States	125,132	133,676	115,952	100,461	73,674[a]
Germany, Fed Rep	44,392	54,141	48,216	53,353	50,256[b]
Brazil	5,429	10,476	11,395	19,984	26,424[b]
France	37,735	40,717	34,452	34,483	25,033[b]
Italy	8,606	12,438	17,916	20,695	20,529[b]
Czechoslovakia	10,856	15,780	17,720	18,894	17,919[b]
Poland	11,664	13,918	14,097	20,985	17,218[b]
Ten Countries Total	**473,495**	**591,246**	**655,909**	**709,071**	**656,582[b]**
World Total	**620,982**	**769,163**	**902,018**	**895,867**	**858,817[b]**
CRUDE STEEL					
USSR	91,000	115,873	141,325	147,931	159,945[a]
United States	125,723	124,514	113,945	111,525	103,779[a]
Japan	31,548	75,835	73,469	82,784	76,638[b]
China	X	X	X	37,217	54,351[a]
Germany, Fed Rep	32,851	41,983	32,959	27,690	31,920[b]
Italy	12,296	20,539	18,618	26,808	22,402[a]
Brazil[c]	3,013	5,178	8,280	11,740	9,249[a]
France	16,935	24,175	20,297	16,457	15,945[a]
Poland	8,659	11,739	17,328	15,000	15,352[b]
United Kingdom	24,076	26,416	20,729	14,962	14,667[b]
Ten Countries Total	**346,101**	**446,252**	**446,950**	**492,114**	**504,248[b]**
World Total	**459,300**	**594,418**	**643,798**	**713,788**	**714,970[b]**

Sources: U.S. Bureau of Mines; World Bureau of Metal Statistics (London); and other sources.
Notes:
a. 1984. b. 1985. c. Rolled steel only.
0 = zero or less than half of 1 percent; X = not available.
For additional information, see Sources and Technical Notes.

Table 20.6 Major Reserves of Selected Minerals, 1988

	Bauxite (million metric tons)		Copper (million metric tons)		Iron Ore (million metric tons)		Lead (thousand metric tons)		Manganese (million metric tons)		Nickel (thousand metric tons)		Tin (thousand metric tons)		Zinc (million metric tons)	
	Reserves	Reserve Base	Reserves	Reserve Base	Reserves	Reserve Base	Reserves	Reserve Base	Reserves	Reserve Base	Reserves	Reserve Base	Reserves	Reserve Base	Reserves	Reserve Base
WORLD	2,100	23,200	340	570	153,416	216,408	75,000	125,000	907	3,538	51,710	100,699	4,260	4,280	148	295
AFRICA	7,000	X	X	X	X	X	X	X	X	X	X	X	X	X	9	23
Botswana	X	X	X	X	X	X	X	X	X	X	408	454	X	X	X	X
Cameroon	680	X	X	X	X	X	X	X	X	X	X	X	X	X	X	X
Gabon	X	X	X	X	X	X	X	X	100	172	X	X	X	X	X	X
Ghana	450	X	X	X	X	X	X	X	X	X	X	X	X	X	X	X
Guinea	5,600	5,900	X	X	X	X	X	X	X	X	X	X	X	X	X	X
Liberia	X	X	X	X	508	813	X	X	X	X	X	X	X	X	X	X
Mozambique	2	X	X	X	X	X	X	X	X	X	X	X	X	X	X	X
Namibia	X	X	X	X	X	X	X	X	X	X	X	X	X	X	X	X
Nigeria	X	X	X	X	X	X	X	X	X	X	X	X	20	20	X	X
Sierra Leone	140	X	X	X	X	X	X	X	X	X	X	X	X	X	X	X
South Africa	0	X	X	X	4,064	9,449	4,000	6,000	369	2,631	2,540	2,631	X	X	3	14
Zaire	X	X	26	30	X	X	X	X	X	X	X	X	20	20	5	7
Zambia	X	X	16	34	X	X	X	X	X	X	X	X	X	X	X	X
Zimbabwe	2	X	X	X	X	X	X	X	X	X	181	1,724	X	X	X	X
NORTH & CENTRAL AMERICA	2,120	X	X	X	X	X	X	X	X	X	X	X	X	X	52	114
Canada	X	X	17	23	11,887	25,502	8,000	15,000	X	X	7,258	13,427	60	60	25	56
Costa Rica	78	X	X	X	X	X	X	X	X	X	X	X	X	X	X	X
Cuba	X	X	X	X	X	X	X	X	X	X	18,144	22,680	X	X	X	X
Dominican Rep	30	X	X	X	X	X	X	X	X	X	726	998	X	X	X	X
Haiti	10	X	X	X	X	X	X	X	X	X	X	X	X	X	X	X
Jamaica	2,000	2,000	X	X	X	X	X	X	X	X	X	X	X	X	X	X
Mexico	0	X	X	X	X	X	3,000	4,000	3	8	X	X	X	X	6	8
United States	38	40	57	90	16,053	25,197	11,000	22,000	X	X	272	2,540	20	40	21	50
SOUTH AMERICA	4,000	X	X	X	X	X	X	X	X	X	X	X	X	X	10	16
Bolivia	X	X	X	X	X	X	X	X	X	X	X	X	140	140	X	X
Brazil	2,250	2,900	X	X	15,850	17,577	X	X	19	63	726	13,427	650	650	2	3
Chile	X	X	79	120	X	X	X	X	X	X	X	X	X	X	X	X
Colombia	0	X	X	X	X	X	X	X	X	X	590	635	X	X	X	X
French Guiana	42	X	X	X	X	X	X	X	X	X	X	X	X	X	X	X
Guyana	700	900	X	X	X	X	X	X	X	X	X	X	X	X	X	X
Peru	X	X	12	32	X	X	2,000	3,000	X	X	X	X	X	X	7	12
Suriname	575	600	X	X	X	X	X	X	X	X	X	X	X	X	X	X
Venezuela	235	350	X	X	2,032	2,032	X	X	X	X	X	X	X	X	X	X
ASIA	2,000	X	X	X	X	X	X	X	X	X	X	X	X	X	23	39
Burma	X	X	X	X	X	X	X	X	X	X	X	X	20	20	X	X
China	150	X	X	X	9,144	9,144	X	X	14	29	X	X	400	400	5	9
India	1,000	1,200	X	X	7,214	12,090	X	X	18	27	X	X	X	X	5	7
Indonesia	750	X	X	X	X	X	X	X	X	X	3,901	5,262	680	680	X	6
Iran	0	X	X	X	X	X	X	X	X	X	X	X	X	X	2	6
Japan	X	X	X	X	X	X	X	X	X	X	X	X	X	X	4	6
Korea, Dem Rep	X	X	X	X	X	X	X	X	X	X	X	X	X	X	4	6
Malaysia	15	X	X	X	X	X	X	X	X	X	X	X	1,100	1,100	X	X
Pakistan	20	X	X	X	X	X	X	X	X	X	X	X	X	X	X	X
Philippines	0	X	12	18	X	X	X	X	X	X	1,814	4,627	X	X	X	X
Thailand	X	X	X	X	X	X	X	X	X	X	X	X	270	270	1	1
Turkey	25	X	X	X	X	X	X	X	X	X	X	X	X	X	1	1
EUROPE	1,500	X	X	X	X	X	X	X	X	X	X	X	X	X	36	54
Albania	X	X	X	X	X	X	X	X	X	X	181	181	X	X	X	X
Finland	X	X	X	X	X	X	X	X	X	X	36	45	X	X	1	2
France	30	X	X	X	2,235	2,235	X	X	X	X	X	X	X	X	1	1
Germany, Fed Rep	2	X	X	X	X	X	X	X	X	X	X	X	X	X	1	2
Greece	600	650	X	X	X	X	X	X	X	X	2,359	2,540	X	X	1	1
Hungary	300	300	X	X	X	X	X	X	X	X	X	X	X	X	X	X
Ireland	X	X	X	X	X	X	X	X	X	X	X	X	X	X	5	7
Italy	5	X	X	X	X	X	X	X	X	X	X	X	X	X	2	3
Poland	X	X	10	15	X	X	X	X	X	X	X	X	X	X	3	4
Portugal	X	X	X	X	X	X	X	X	X	X	X	X	X	X	2	3
Romania	50	X	X	X	X	X	X	X	X	X	X	X	X	X	X	X
Spain	5	X	X	X	X	X	X	X	X	X	X	X	X	X	5	6
Sweden	X	X	X	X	3,048	4,674	X	X	X	X	X	X	X	X	1	3
United Kingdom	0	X	X	X	X	X	X	X	X	X	X	X	90	90	X	X
Yugoslavia	350	400	X	X	X	X	2,000	3,000	X	X	1,270	1,633	X	X	2	3
USSR	300	300	37	54	59,944	59,944	X	X	295	454	6,623	7,348	300	300	10	15
OCEANIA	4,500	X	X	X	X	X	X	X	X	X	4,300	23,700	X	X	X	X
Australia	4,440	4,600	8	41	15,240	33,528	16,000	28,000	68	152	2,087	4,808	250	250	18	49
New Caledonia	X	X	X	X	X	X	X	X	X	X	1,814	15,422	X	X	X	X
Solomon Islands	50	X	X	X	X	X	X	X	X	X	X	X	X	X	X	X
Other Market Economies	2,600	2,900	60	100	4,877	12,294	9,000	14,000	X	X	X	7,893	200	200	X	X
Other CPEs[a]	200	200	6	9	914	914	20,000	30,000	X	X	X	907	30	30	X	X

Source: U.S. Bureau of Mines.
Note: a. Centrally Planned Economies.
X = not available.
For additional information, see Sources and Technical Notes.

Table 20.7 Waste Generation in Selected Countries, 1975–86

	Average Annual Municipal Waste Generation						Industrial Waste Generation				Hazardous and Special Waste Generation	
	Total (thousand metric tons per year)				Per Capita[b] (kg)	Per Unit Area (metric tons per km² per year)	Year of Estimate	Total (thousand metric tons per year)	Per Million $US of Industrial Gross Domestic Product[c] (metric tons)	Per Unit Area (metric tons per km² per year)	Total (thousand metric tons per year)	Per Unit Area (metric tons per km² per year)
	1975	1980	1983	1984/85[a]								
AMERICAS												
Canada	X	12,600	16,000	X	642	1.7	1980	61,000	730	6.6	3,290	0.4
Costa Rica	X	X	534	X	211	10.5	X	X	X	X	X	X
Mexico	X	X	X	32	0	0.0	1986	192	3	0.1	X	X
United States	140,000	160,000	178,000	X	744	19.4	1985	613,000	501	66.9	250,000	27.3
ASIA												
Cyprus	X	X	X	X	X	X	1985	56	X	6.2	X	X
Israel	X	X	X	1,400	330	65.1	X	X	X	X	30	1.4
Japan	38,074	41,511	41,095	X	342	110.8	1983	220,548	494	594.5	768	2.1
Korea, Rep	X	X	15,746	X	679	160.7	1981	7,030	274	71.7	180	X
Singapore	X	1,082	X	1,498	X	2,496.7	X	X	X	X	X	X
EUROPE												
Austria	1,407	1,560	1,630	X	216	19.4	1983	5,110	197	60.8	100	1.2
Belgium	2,900	3,082	X	X	X	205.2	1980	8,000	196	242.4	915	27.7
Bulgaria	X	X	X	6,773	757	0.6	X	X	X	X	X	X
Czechoslovakia	X	X	X	X	X	X	1982	80,910	X	647.3	X	X
Denmark	X	2,046	X	X	399	48.7	1980	814	X	19.4	90	2.1
Finland	X	X	1,200	X	247	3.9	1984	14,000	804	45.9	124	0.4
France	X	14,000	X	X	260	25.6	1980	32,200	137	59.0	2,000	3.7
Germany, Fed Rep	20,423	21,417	20,268	27,544	447	112.9	1982	52,464	172	215.0	4,900	20.1
Greece	X	X	2,500	X	259	19.1	X	X	X	X	X	X
Hungary	X	X	X	7,000	658	76.1	1985	21,146	2,509	229.8	7,081	77.0
Iceland	X	X	X	93	388	0.9	1985	105	X	1.1	X	X
Ireland	555	640	1,100	1,270	359	15.9	1984	1,580	346	22.9	20	0.3
Italy	14,095	14,041	X	X	249	47.8	1980	35,000	207	119.0	2,000	6.8
Luxembourg	X	X	X	190	514	76.0	1985	95	X	38.0	15	6.0
Netherlands	X	7,450	7,180	7,242	500	213.0	1984	4,137	97	121.7	280	8.2
Norway	X	2,200	X	1,700	280	7.1	1980	2,186	93	7.1	120	0.4
Poland	X	X	X	7,900	212	25.9	1985	274,885	X	901.3	X	X
Portugal	X	1,300	1,700	2,246	233	24.4	1980	11,200	1,110	121.7	1,049	11.4
Spain	X	8,028	X	10,600	275	21.2	1985	1,500	X	3.0	X	X
Sweden	2,400	2,500	X	X	301	6.1	1980	4,000	102	9.7	550	1.3
Switzerland	1,600	2,146	X	X	336	53.7	X	X	X	X	100	2.5
United Kingdom	16,036	15,816	16,398	X	291	67.8	1984	50,000	327	206.6	1,500	6.2
USSR	X	X	X	X	X	X	1985	306,258	X	13.8	X	X
OCEANIA												
Australia	X	10,000	X	X	681	1.3	1980	20,000	X	2.6	300	0.0
New Zealand	1,150	1,528	2,106	1,160	653	4.3	1982	300	38	1.1	45	0.2

Sources: Organisation for Economic Co-operation and Development; United Nations; and national sources.
Notes:
a. Refers either to 1984 or 1985.
b. Figures are for most recent year available.
c. The portion of Gross Domestic Product contributed by industry.
For additional information, see Sources and Technical Notes.
X = not available.

Sources and Technical Notes

Table 20.1 Production and Consumption of Commercial Energy, 1970–86

Sources: Energy: United Nations Statistical Office, *Energy Statistics Yearbook 1982* and *1986* (United Nations, New York, 1984 and in press, 1988). Population: United Nations Population Division, *World Population Prospects: Estimates and Projections As Assessed in 1984* (United Nations, New York, 1986). Gross National Product: The World Bank, unpublished data (The World Bank, Washington, D.C., April 1988).

Energy data are compiled by the United Nations Statistical Office (UNSO) primarily from responses to questionnaires sent to national governments, supplemented by official national statistical publications and data from intergovernmental organizations. When official data are not available, UNSO prepares estimates based on the professional and commercial literature.

Total production of commercially traded fuels includes the production of solid, liquid, and gaseous fuels and the production of primary electricity. Electricity production data are shown in *World Resources 1987*, Table 22.2, page 302. *Solid* fuels include bituminous coal, lignite, peat, and oil shale burned directly. *Liquid* fuels include crude petroleum and natural gas liquids. *Gaseous* fuel includes natural gas and other petroleum gases. Fuelwood, bagasse, charcoal, and all forms of solar energy are excluded from production figures, even when traded commercially.

Consumption is defined as domestic production plus net imports, minus net stock increases, minus aircraft and marine bunkers. *Total consumption* includes energy from solids, liquids, gases, and primary electricity.

All the production data and the total consumption data are in petajoules (1 quadrillion joules). One petajoule is the same as 0.000948 Quads (quadrillion British Thermal Units) and is the equivalent of 163,400 "U.N. standard" barrels of oil or 34,140 "U.N. standard" metric tons of coal. The heat content of various fuels has been converted to coal-equivalent and then petajoule-equivalent values using country- and year-specific conversion factors. For example, a metric ton of bituminous coal produced in Argentina has an energy value of 0.843 metric tons of standard coal equivalent (7 million kilocalories). A metric ton of bituminous coal produced in Turkey has an energy value of 0.929 metric tons of standard coal equivalent. The original national production data for bituminous coal were multiplied by these conversion factors and the resulting figures in tons of standard coal equivalent were multiplied by 29.3076×10^{-6} to yield petajoule equivalents. Other fuels were converted to coal-equivalent and petajoule-equivalent terms in a similar manner.

South Africa refers to the South Africa Customs Union: South Africa, Botswana, Lesotho, Swaziland, and Namibia.

Table 20.2 Reserves and Resources of Commercial Energy, 1984

Sources: World Energy Conference (WEC), *1986 Survey of Energy Resources* (WEC, London, 1986). Hydroelectric technical potential: The World Bank, *A Survey of the Future Role of Hydroelectric Power in 100 Developing Countries* (The World Bank, Washington, D.C., 1984). Hydroelectric installed capacity: United Nations Statistical Office, *Energy Statistics Yearbook 1985* (United Nations, New York, 1987). United States (hydroelectric potential and installed capacity): U.S. Federal Energy Regulatory Commission (FERC), unpublished data (FERC, Washington, D.C., 1988).

Energy resource estimates are based on geological, economic, and technical criteria. Resources are first graded according to the degree of confidence in the extent and location of the resource, based on available geological information. Judgements on the technical and economic feasibility of exploiting the resource are then incorporated into the assessment.

Proved reserves in place represent the fraction of total resources that is known to exist in specific locations and in specific qualities. *Proved recoverable reserves* are the fraction of proved reserves in place that can be extracted with existing technology under present and expected economic conditions. Additional energy resources, comprising those that are currently subeconomic, are not shown.

Bituminous coal includes anthracite. Anthracite is probably only a small fraction of the total, but it is not possible to calculate the exact amount of anthracite included in the figures.

In the *lignite and sub-bituminous coal* aggregate, lignite accounts for 66 percent of the global proved reserves in place and 63 percent of the global proved recoverable reserves.

Crude oil includes natural gas liquids, reservoir gas recovered in liquid form in surface separators or plant facilities.

Uranium data refer to known uranium deposits of a size and quality that could be recovered within specified production cost ranges (under $80 U.S. per kilogram and $80–130 per kilogram) using currently proven mining and processing technology.

Hydroelectric technical potential refers to the annual energy potential of all sites where it is physically possible to construct dams,

with no consideration of economic return or of adverse impacts of site development. Data for 34 countries refer to *exploitable potential*, the annual energy that could be generated by hydroelectric plants within the limits of current technology and under present and expected local economic conditions. Data for seven countries refer to *theoretical potential*, the annual energy potentially available in the country if all natural water flows were turbined to sea level with 100 percent mechanical efficiency. Theoretical potential is estimated from national precipitation and water runoff data and is not limited by technical or economic criteria. Exploitable potential, the most conservative estimate of a country's hydroelectric resources, is shown when available; theoretical potential is shown when technical and exploitable potential figures are not available. All three types of estimates include sites where hydroelectric generating plants are currently in place.

Installed Capacity refers to the combined generating capacity of the hydroelectric plants installed in the country as of December 31, 1985.

Table 20.3 Commercial Energy Use by Sector, 1970–85

Sources: Organisation for Economic Co-operation and Development (OECD), *Energy Balances of OECD Countries 1970/85* (OECD, Paris, 1987); OECD, *Energy Balances of Developing Countries 1971/82* (OECD, Paris, 1984). Hungary: World Energy Conference (WEC), *National Energy Data Profile: Hungary* (WEC, London, 1985). German Democratic Republic: WEC, *National Energy Data Profile: German Democratic Republic* (WEC, London, 1986). Bulgaria, Poland, Romania, USSR: Vienna Institute for Comparative Economic Studies, *COMECON Data 1985* (Greenwood Press, Westport, Connecticut, 1986).

Commercial energy includes solid, liquid, and gaseous fuels, as well as primary and secondary electricity. Refer to the Technical Note for Table 20.1 for details.

Use by *industry* includes all use of commercial energy by industry: iron and steel, chemical, petrochemical, nonferrous metals, nonmetallic mineral products, paper, pulp and printing, food, textiles, machinery, nonenergy mining, and nonspecified.

The *transport* sector includes transport in the industrial sector and covers road, railway, air, internal navigation, and nonspecified transport. It excludes international marine bunkers.

The *agriculture* sector includes all uses of commercial energy in agriculture.

The *commercial and residential* sectors include all energy for private homes, public, and commercial use.

The *other* category may include energy used in the agricultural and/or commercial and domestic sectors. It also includes non-energy uses, military uses, and nonspecified uses.

Most countries have difficulties giving a realistic breakdown by fuel for industrial and other sectors, and the quality of the data vary among countries.

Not all data are for the years shown. For

developing countries, 1971 data are shown instead of 1970 data. For Bulgaria, Poland, Romania, and the USSR, 1983 data are shown under the 1985 heading. For Hungary and the German Democratic Republic, 1984 data are shown.

For additional information, refer to the sources.

Table 20.4 Nuclear Power and Waste Generation, 1970–87

Sources: Reactor and capacity data: U.S. Department of Energy (DOE), Energy Information Administration (EIA), *Commercial Nuclear Power: Prospects for the United States and the World* (U.S. DOE/EIA, Washington, D.C., 1987). Spent fuel data: U.S. DOE/EIA, *World Nuclear Fuel Cycle Requirements* (U.S. DOE/EIA, Washington, D.C., 1987) and U.S. DOE/EIA unpublished data (U.S. DOE/EIA, Washington, D.C., 1988). Cancelled and retired plants: Commisseriat Energie Atomique, *Nuclear Power Plants in the World* (Commisseriat Energie Atomique, Paris, 1987).

Operable reactors refers to nuclear power reactors that produce electricity for the commercial electricity grid, although not necessarily at full power. Reactors in extended shutdown are included. Data are as of December 31 of the year indicated.

The number of reactors *planned or under construction* refers to those plants for which planning or construction was underway as of December 31, 1986. The number *cancelled* refers to power plants planned or under construction that were permanently halted between 1970 and 1987. The number *retired* refers to active nuclear power plants that were shut down between 1951 and 1987. Data for cancelled and retired plants include research reactors.

Under *net capacity*, the electricity requirements of generating plants (usually about 5–10 percent of gross generation) have been deducted. Capacity planned or under construction refers to the total additional capacity that would be possible if all the reactors planned or under construction were completed.

Spent fuel inventories are expressed as cumulative totals to the years given and are net of reprocessing. Heavy metal refers to the actinide elements (uranium, plutonium, etc.) contained in the spent fuel.

Table 20.5 Producers and Consumers of Selected Metals, 1965–86

Sources: Production data for 1965, 1970, 1975, and 1980: U.S. Bureau of Mines (U.S. BOM), *Minerals Yearbook 1966, 1976,* and *1981* (U.S. Government Printing Office, Washington, D.C., 1967, 1977, and 1983). Production data for 1986: U.S. BOM, *1986 Minerals Yearbook* (U.S. BOM, Washington, D.C., in press 1988). Consumption data for aluminum, copper, lead, nickel, tin, and zinc: World Bureau of Metal Statistics, *World Metal Statistics* (World Bureau of Metal Statistics, London, April 1970, December 1974, February 1979, June 1985, and January 1988). Consumption data for iron and steel: United Nations Economic Commission for Europe (ECE),

Annual Bulletin of Steel Statistics for Europe (ECE, New York, 1966, 1972, 1977, 1981, and 1986); and U.S. BOM, unpublished data (U.S. BOM, Washington, D.C., December 1986). USSR production and consumption data for copper: Vasili V. Strishkov, *The Copper Industry of the USSR: Problems, Issues, and Outlook* (U.S. BOM, Washington, D.C., 1984).

The U.S. Bureau of Mines prepares mineral production statistics based on information from government mineral and statistical agencies, the United Nations, and U.S. and foreign technical and trade literature.

The World Bureau of Metal Statistics publishes consumption data for the metals presented, excluding iron and steel. Data on the metals included were supplied by metal companies, government agencies, trade groups, and statistical bureaus. Obviously incorrect data have been revised, but most data were compiled and reported without adjustment or retrospective revisions.

The countries listed represent the top 10 producers and the top 10 consumers of each material in 1986.

Production refers to the first solid state of mined ore after melting.

Zinc is given in zinc content of mined ore.

Iron ore refers to iron ore, iron ore concentrates, and iron ore agglomerates (sinter and pellets).

Crude steel refers to the first solid state after melting, in the form of steel ingots, continuously cast primary forms, and steel castings. The United Nations definition of crude steel is the equivalent of the term "raw steel" as used by the United States.

Metal consumption refers to the domestic use of primary refined metals. These metals include metals refined from either primary (raw) or secondary (recovered) materials. Metal used in a product that is then exported is considered consumed by the producing country rather than by the importing country.

Consumption of iron ore was calculated by adding net imports to the quantities of iron ore and concentrates reported as delivered to consuming industries. Consumption of crude steel was calculated by adding net imports to the quantities of crude steel reported as delivered to consuming industries. Global consumption figures for iron ore and crude steel are not consistent with the definitions applied to other metals in Table 22.5. Because world consumption of iron ore and crude steel is roughly equal to world production, world production data were used for the world consumption totals. Worldwide stock inventories are assumed to be negligible.

Table 20.6 Major Reserves of Selected Minerals, 1988

Sources: U.S. Bureau of Mines (U.S. BOM), *Mineral Commodity Summaries 1988* (U.S. BOM, Washington, D.C., 1988). Bauxite: Sam H. Patterson, *et al.*, *World Bauxite Resources* (U.S. Geological Survey Paper 10-76-B,

Washington, D.C., 1986). Zinc: U.S. BOM *Minerals Yearbook, 1986* (U.S. BOM, Washington, D.C., in press).

Mineral *reserves* are the part of the reserve base that could be economically extracted or produced at the time of the assessment. Reserves do not signify that extraction facilities are in place and operative.

The *reserve base* is the portion of the mineral resource that meets grade, quality, thickness, and depth criteria defined by current mining and production practices. It includes both measured and indicated reserves and refers to those resources that are currently economic, marginally economic, and some of those that are currently subeconomic.

Reserve and reserve base estimates are supplied to the Bureau of Mines by the U.S. Geological Survey (USGS).

Table 20.7 Waste Generation in Selected Countries, 1975–86

Sources: Municipal waste and per capita generation (1975–1983), industrial waste, and hazardous waste: Organisation for Economic Co-operation and Development (OECD), *Environmental Data Compendium 1987* (OECD, Paris, 1987); Municipal waste and per capita data (1984–1985), industrial waste (Cyprus, Czechoslovakia, Hungary, Iceland, Poland, USSR) and hazardous waste (Hungary, Iceland, Poland, Portugal, USSR): United Nations Statistical Commission and Economic Commission for Europe (ECE), *Environmental Statistics in Europe and North America* (United Nations, New York, 1987); Costa Rica: Gary Hartshorn, *et al.*, *Costa Rica: Country Environmental Profile* (Tropical Science Center and United States Agency for International Development, San Jose, 1982); Mexico: I. Fernando Ortiz Monasterio, *Manejo de los Desechos Industriales Peligrosos en Mexico* (Universo Veintiuno, Mexico, 1987); Israel: Uri Marinov, State of Israel Environmental Protection Service, Jerusalem, Israel, 1988 (personal communication); Korea: Soo-Saeng Han, *The State of the Environment in Korea* (Office of Environment, Republic of Korea, 1983); Singapore: Ministry of the Environment, Singapore, *Annual Report '85* (Ministry of the Environment, Singapore, 1985). Industrial gross domestic product: The World Bank, *World Development Report 1982–1987* (Oxford University Press, New York, 1982–1987). Geographical area: United Nations Food and Agricultural Organization (FAO), *FAO Production Yearbook 1984* (FAO, Rome, 1985).

Waste data were collected by various means, and are not strictly comparable among countries. OECD collects data using questionnaires completed by government representatives. Refer to the Technical Note for Table 14.1 in Chapter 14, "Basic Economic Indicators," for details concerning Gross Domestic Product. Area data exclude inland water bodies.

Some municipal waste data for 1975, 1980, and 1983 may refer to adjacent years. Municipal waste figures in the 1984–85 column refer to 1984 *or* 1985. Hazardous waste generation estimates are undated, but most refer to the early or mid-1980s.

Municipal waste is the trash collected from households, commercial establishments, and small industries. *Industrial waste* contains both chemical and nonchemical materials. Amounts depend on the definition of waste used in a country, the levels of industrial production, and the types of technology used. *Hazardous waste* is waste known to contain potentially harmful substances. Definitions of hazardous waste vary among countries. Nuclear wastes are not included in this table. Refer to Table 20.4 for data on spent fuel from nuclear reactors.

Country-specific information:
1. Australia—industrial waste includes hazardous and special waste.
2. Austria—industrial waste includes hazardous waste.
3. Canada—hazardous waste is measured in wet weight.
4. Czechoslovakia—industrial waste data are obtained from infrequent surveys; coverage is confined to national industrial enterprises.
5. Denmark—includes only hazardous waste that has been legally disposed of.
6. Finland—municipal waste includes only waste originating in households.
7. France—hazardous waste is the amount of toxic or hazardous waste. Special wastes, totalling 18 million tons per year, are not included.
8. Hungary—municipal waste weight estimated from volume data. Hazardous waste figure based on enterprise declarations.
9. Iceland—municipal waste refers to nonindustrial solid waste.
10. Netherlands—industrial waste includes wastes generated only by enterprises employing ten or more people and includes office and canteen wastes; hazardous waste refers to "notifiable" wastes only.
11. New Zealand—industrial waste is nonchemical waste only.
12. Norway—industrial waste includes chemical waste only.
13. United Kingdom—hazardous waste refers to notifiable wastes.
14. United States—1983 municipal waste figure is an OECD estimate. Industrial waste includes wastewaters that meet the United States' definition of solid waste.

For a more detailed discussion of hazardous waste data collection and reports on hazardous waste management in 12 countries, see William S. Forester and John H. Skinner, *International Perspectives on Hazardous Waste Management* (Academic Press, London, 1987).

21. Freshwater

An ample supply of clean freshwater is critical to the functioning of natural systems and human economies. This chapter presents data on national freshwater resources and on the record that countries have established in husbanding and protecting the quality of their endowment.

A country's most dependable source of freshwater is the net precipitation (precipitation minus evapotranspiration) falling within its boundaries. (See Table 21.1.) However, the uneven distribution of precipitation within a country and within and across years makes it difficult to translate net precipitation data into data on the availability of freshwater. Some countries, particularly those in the Middle East and North Africa, do not receive adequate precipitation to meet their freshwater needs and rely on nonrenewable groundwater and on river flows from other countries to supply the difference. In the long term, transnational river flows may not be reliable sources of freshwater, as upstream use and pollution may threaten the downstream country's freshwater supply. For a discussion of freshwater availability and the difficulty of assessing it, see Chapter 8, "Freshwater."

The amount of freshwater that a country withdraws on a per capita basis is not correlated with its economic wealth or the size of its internal water resources. Some arid countries of the Middle East and North Africa withdraw almost all of their available water resources every year, including transnational river flows. Egypt, Sudan, Yemen, and Iraq each withdraws more than 1,000 cubic meters per capita per year, the vast majority of which is used for irrigation.

Water pollution trends in the countries of the Organisation for Economic Co-operation and Development (OECD) have been mixed. (See Table 21.2.) Municipal sewage treatment facilities have begun to reduce the levels of oxygen-demanding organic wastes in many rivers. For instance, the Guadalquiver and the Tiber both saw dissolved oxygen levels double in the last 15 years, while the biochemical oxygen demand level in the Meuse dropped by 60–70 percent at several stations. Nitrate pollution, however, has increased dramatically in most OECD countries. Almost all of the river data reported by the Netherlands, Spain, and the United Kingdom showed steady and substantial increases in nitrate pollution over the 1970–85 period. Heavy metal pollution—lead, cadmium, chromium, and copper—showed mixed trends. For data on river pollution in developing countries, see *World Resources 1987*, Table 23.3.

Table 21.3 shows mineral transport characteristics for 47 major world rivers. These data are used by scientists to estimate the movement of material from the land surface to the oceans. Because rivers are the oceans' major source of minerals, nutrients, and organic carbon, these transport data are critical to global systems science. The rates of mineral transport have been dramatically affected in some rivers by human activity in the drainage basin. Agriculture, overgrazing, and deforestation have accelerated soil erosion in river basins, adding to the sediment load carried by rivers. In naturally flowing rivers, sediment is deposited on the floodplains and river delta; however, by trapping sediments in reservoirs, dams have drastically reduced sediment loads in many rivers. Industrial wastes discharged into riverwater increase the load of dissolved minerals carried by the river. In semiarid countries, salts from irrigation projects have increased the salinity of riverwater. For more information on the importance of rivers in biogeochemical cycles, see Chapter 11, "Global Systems and Cycles."

The nutrient pollutants—nitrates and phosphorous—are a serious threat to the health of the world's lakes. (See Table 21.4.) Heavy metals and organic pollution are also a major concern. Efforts to standardize data collected by limnologists and to measure land use and economic activities that affect water quality in the drainage basin have only recently begun.

Runoff from agricultural and urban land in lake drainage basins accelerates eutrophication, which normally occurs over thousands of years. Eutrophication, the natural process of nutrient enrichment and increased plant and algae growth, has degraded the water quality and transformed the ecosystems of many of the lakes of Europe, industrialized North America, and densely populated Asian countries like Japan. Eutrophication can be prevented or reversed by controlling the sources of nutrients. For example, Lake Washington, which has human settlement covering 60 percent of its drainage basin (the metropolitan area of Seattle, United States), suffered serious eutrophication in the 1960s. Construction of sewage treatment plants and a 180-kilometer pipeline diverting treated water away from the lake has allowed the water quality to recover.

Table 21.1 Freshwater Resources and Withdrawal, 1959-86

	Internal Renewable Water Resources		River Flows from Other Countries (cubic kilometers per year)	River Flows to Other Countries (cubic kilometers per year)	Withdrawal				Sectoral Withdrawal (percent)		
	Total (cubic kilometers per year)	Per Capita 1989 (thousand cubic meters per year)			Year of Data	Total (cubic kilometers per year)	as a percentage of Water Resources[a]	Per Capita (cubic meters per year)	Public Use[b]	Industry (self-supplied)	Agriculture (irrigation)
WORLD											
AFRICA											
Algeria	18.90	0.77	0.20	0.70	1980	3.00	16	161	23	5	72
Angola	X	X	X	X	X	X	X	X	X	X	X
Benin	26.00	5.67	X	X	X	X	X	X	X	X	X
Botswana	1.00	0.78	17.00	X	1980	0.09	1	98	8	17	75
Burkina Faso	X	X	X	X	X	X	X	X	X	X	X
Burundi	X	X	X	X	X	X	X	X	X	X	X
Cameroon	208.00	18.84	X	X	X	X	X	X	X	X	X
Cape Verde	0.20	0.56	0.00	0.00	1972	0.04	20	148	8	0	92
Central African Rep	X	X	X	X	X	X	X	X	X	X	X
Chad	X	X	X	X	X	X	X	X	X	X	X
Comoros	X	X	0.00	0.00	X	X	X	X	X	X	X
Congo	X	X	X	X	X	X	X	X	X	X	X
Cote d'Ivoire	74.00	6.56	X	X	X	X	X	X	X	X	X
Djibouti	0.30	0.72	0.00	X	1973	0.01	2	28	X	X	X
Egypt	1.80	0.04	56.50	0.00	1985	56.40	97	1,202	7	5	88
Equatorial Guinea	X	X	X	X	X	X	X	X	X	X	X
Ethiopia	110.00	2.26	X	X	X	X	X	X	X	X	X
Gabon	X	X	X	X	X	X	X	X	X	X	X
Gambia	3.00	4.29	19.00	X	1982	0.02	0	33	X	X	X
Ghana	53.00	3.41	X	X	1970	0.30	1	35	44	3	54
Guinea	X	X	X	X	X	X	X	X	X	X	X
Guinea-Bissau	X	X	X	X	X	X	X	X	X	X	X
Kenya	14.80	0.61	X	X	X	X	X	X	X	X	X
Lesotho	X	X	X	X	X	X	X	X	X	X	X
Liberia	X	X	X	X	X	X	X	X	X	X	X
Libya	0.70	0.17	0.00	0.00	1985	2.62	374	262	27	0	73
Madagascar	40.00	3.56	0.00	0.00	1984	16.30	41	1,675	1	0	99
Malawi	X	X	X	X	X	X	X	X	X	X	X
Mali	X	X	X	X	X	X	X	X	X	X	X
Mauritania	0.40	0.19	7.00	X	1978	0.73	10	473	2	0	98
Mauritius	2.20	1.96	0.00	0.00	1974	0.36	16	415	X	X	X
Morocco	30.00	1.25	0.00	0.30	1985	11.00	37	501	6	3	91
Mozambique	X	X	X	X	X	X	X	X	X	X	X
Niger	X	X	X	X	X	X	X	X	X	X	X
Nigeria	X	X	X	X	X	X	X	X	X	X	X
Rwanda	X	X	X	X	X	X	X	X	X	X	X
Senegal	X	X	X	X	X	X	X	X	X	X	X
Sierra Leone	X	X	X	X	X	X	X	X	X	X	X
Somalia	11.50	2.27	0.00	X	X	X	X	X	X	X	X
South Africa	50.00	1.40	X	X	1970	9.20	18	404	17	0	83
Sudan	30.00	1.24	100.00	X	1977	18.60	14	1,089	1	0	99
Swaziland	X	X	X	X	X	X	X	X	X	X	X
Tanzania, United Rep	X	X	X	X	1970	0.48	X	36	38	0	63
Togo	11.50	3.44	X	X	X	0.05	0	22	90	0	10
Tunisia	3.75	0.49	0.60	0.00	1985	2.30	53	325	10	0	90
Uganda	X	X	X	X	1970	0.20	X	20	43	0	57
Zaire	X	X	X	X	X	X	X	X	X	X	X
Zambia	X	X	X	X	1970	0.36	X	86	72	0	28
Zimbabwe	X	X	X	X	X	X	X	X	X	X	X
NORTH & CENTRAL AMERICA											
Barbados	0.05	0.20	0.00	0.00	1962	0.03	51	117	45	35	20
Canada	2,901.00	109.51	X	X	1980	36.15	1	1,501	18	70	11
Costa Rica	95.00	33.11	X	X	1970	1.35	1	779	0	8	92
Cuba	34.50	3.31	0.00	0.00	1975	8.10	23	868	14	4	83
Dominican Rep	20.00	2.93	X	X	X	X	X	X	X	X	X
El Salvador	18.95	3.01	X	X	1975	1.00	5	241	17	0	83
Guatemala	116.00	12.98	X	X	1970	0.73	1	139	0	18	82
Haiti	11.00	1.50	X	X	X	X	X	X	X	X	X
Honduras	102.00	20.60	X	X	1970	1.34	1	508	0	4	96
Jamaica	8.30	3.34	0.00	0.00	1975	0.32	4	157	3	6	91
Mexico	357.40	4.11	X	X	1975	54.20	15	901	5	7	88
Nicaragua	175.00	46.73	X	X	1975	0.89	1	370	18	45	37
Panama	144.00	60.76	X	X	1975	1.30	1	744	12	11	77
Trinidad and Tobago	X	X	0.00	0.00	1975	0.15	X	149	0	50	50
United States	2,478.00	10.06	X	X	1985	467.00	19	2,162	12	46	42
SOUTH AMERICA											
Argentina	694.00	21.40	X	X	1976	27.60	4	1,059	9	18	73
Bolivia	X	X	X	X	1959	X	X	X	1	1	97
Brazil	5,190.00	35.21	X	X	X	X	X	X	X	X	X
Chile	X	X	X	X	1975	16.80	X	1,625	5	4	92
Colombia	1,070.00	34.30	X	X	1960	X	X	X	14	0	86
Ecuador	314.00	29.93	X	X	X	X	X	X	X	X	X
Guyana	X	X	X	X	1971	5.40	X	7,616	1	0	99
Paraguay	X	X	X	X	X	X	X	X	X	X	X
Peru	40.00	1.84	X	X	1975	X	X	X	7	0	93
Suriname	X	X	X	X	X	X	X	X	X	X	X
Uruguay	X	X	X	X	1965	0.65	X	241	15	8	77
Venezuela	856.00	44.48	X	X	1970	4.10	0	387	37	4	59

Table 21.1

	Internal Renewable Water Resources		River Flows from Other Countries (cubic kilometers per year)	River Flows to Other Countries (cubic kilometers per year)	Withdrawal				Sectoral Withdrawal (percent)		
	Total (cubic kilometers per year)	Per Capita 1989 (thousand cubic meters per year)			Year of Data	Total (cubic kilometers per year)	as a percentage of Water Resources[a]	Per Capita (cubic meters per year)	Public Use[b]	Industry (self-supplied)	Agriculture (irrigation)
ASIA											
Afghanistan	50.00	2.48	X	X	X	X	X	X	X	X	X
Bahrain	0.00	0.00	0.00	0.00	1975	0.20	X	735	10	6	84
Bangladesh	1,357.00	12.08	X	X	X	X	X	X	X	X	X
Bhutan	X	X	X	X	X	X	X	X	X	X	X
Burma	1,082.00	26.99	X	X	X	X	X	X	X	X	X
China	2,800.00	2.52	0.00	X	1980	460.00	16	462	6	7	87
Cyprus	0.90	1.29	0.00	0.00	1985	0.54	60	807	7	2	91
India	1,850.00	2.27	X	X	1975	380.00	21	612	3	4	93
Indonesia	2,530.00	14.17	X	X	1978	X	X	X	95	5	0
Iran	117.50	2.35	X	X	1975	45.40	39	1,362	3	0	97
Iraq	34.00	1.87	66.00	X	1970	42.80	43	4,575	2	3	95
Israel	1.70	0.37	0.45	0.00	1986	1.90	88	447	16	5	79
Japan	547.00	4.44	0.00	0.00	1980	107.80	20	923	17	33	50
Jordan	0.70	0.17	0.40	X	1975	0.45	41	173	3[c]	0	97
Kampuchea, Dem	88.10	10.93	X	X	X	X	X	X	X	X	X
Korea, Dem People's Rep	X	X	X	X	X	X	X	X	X	X	X
Korea, Rep	63.00	1.43	X	X	1976	10.70	17	298	11	13	75
Kuwait	0.00	0.00	0.00	X	1974	0.01	X	10	35	4	61
Lao People's Dem Rep	270.00	59.51	X	X	X	X	X	X	X	X	X
Lebanon	4.80	1.66	0.00	0.86	1975	0.75	16	271	13	0	87
Malaysia	456.00	26.90	X	X	1975	9.42	2	765	X	X	X
Mongolia	24.60	11.55	X	X	X	X	X	X	X	X	X
Nepal	170.00	9.42	X	X	X	X	X	X	X	X	X
Oman	2.00	1.42	0.00	X	1975	0.43	22	561	2	0	98
Pakistan	298.00	2.72	X	X	1975	153.40	51	2,053	X	X	X
Philippines	323.00	5.41	0.00	0.00	1975	29.50	9	693	X	X	X
Qatar	0.02	0.06	0.00	X	1975	0.04	174	234	33	0	67
Saudi Arabia	2.20	0.16	0.00	0.00	1975	2.33	106	321	36	6	58
Singapore	0.60	0.22	0.00	0.00	1975	0.19	32	84	X	X	X
Sri Lanka	43.20	2.51	0.00	0.00	1970	6.30	15	503	0	2	98
Syrian Arab Rep	7.60	0.62	27.90	30.00	1976	3.34	9	449	6	0	94
Thailand	110.00	2.01	X	X	1975	X	X	X	1	0	99
Turkey	196.00	3.66	7.00	69.00	1985	15.60	8	317	24	19	58
United Arab Emirates	0.30	0.20	0.00	X	1980	0.42	140	429	9	0	91
Viet Nam	X	X	X	X	X	X	X	X	X	X	X
Yemen	1.00	0.13	0.00	X	X	X	X	X	X	X	X
Yemen, Dem	1.50	0.62	0.00	X	1975	1.93	129	1,167	1	0	99
EUROPE											
Albania	10.00	3.01	11.30	X	1970	0.20	1	94	30	60	10
Austria	56.30	7.50	34.00	X	1980	3.13	3	417	20	77	3
Belgium	8.40	0.84	4.10	X	1980	9.03	72	917	11	88	2
Bulgaria	18.00	1.95	187.00	X	1980	14.18	7	1,600	14	15	71
Czechoslovakia	28.00	1.78	62.60	X	1980	5.80	6	379	24	72	5
Denmark	11.00	2.15	2.00	X	1977	1.40	11	277	35	32	32
Finland	110.00	22.21	3.00	X	1980	3.70	3	774	12	86	1
France	170.00	3.07	15.00	20.50	1984	33.30	18	606	17	71	12
German Dem Rep	17.00	1.01	17.00	X	1980	9.13	27	545	14	71	14
Germany, Fed Rep	79.00	1.31	82.00	X	1981	41.40	26	671	12	87	0
Greece	45.15	4.50	13.50	3.00	1980	7.00	12	726	11	6	83
Hungary	6.00	0.56	109.00	X	1980	5.38	5	502	9	58	33
Iceland	170.00	674.60	0.00	0.00	X	X	X	X	X	X	X
Ireland	50.00	13.18	0.00	X	1972	0.40	1	135	11	83	6
Italy	179.40	3.12	7.60	0.00	1981	46.35	25	811	15	16	69
Luxembourg	1.00	2.76	4.00	X	1976	0.06	1	166	47	50	3
Malta	0.03	0.06	0.00	0.00	1978	0.02	92	68	100	0	0
Netherlands	10.00	0.68	80.00	X	1980	14.20	16	1,004	5	64	32
Norway	405.00	97.10	8.00	X	1980	2.00	0	489	21	74	5
Poland	49.40	1.29	6.80	X	1980	16.80	30	472	17	62	21
Portugal	34.00	3.25	31.60	X	1980	10.50	16	1,062	15	37	48
Romania	37.00	1.56	171.00	X	1980	25.40	12	1,144	8	34	58
Spain	110.30	2.79	1.00	17.00	1985	26.30	24	682	20[b]	0	80
Sweden	176.00	21.16	4.00	X	1980	3.98	2	479	24	75	2
Switzerland	42.50	6.65	7.50	X	1985	3.20	6	502	37	57	6
United Kingdom	120.00	2.14	0.00	X	1980	28.35	24	507	21	79	1
Yugoslavia	150.00	6.32	115.00	200.00	1980	8.77	3	393	17	75	8
USSR	4,384.00	15.15	300.00	X	1980	353.00	8	1,330	6	31	64
OCEANIA											
Australia	343.00	20.78	0.00	0.00	1975	17.80	5	1,306	16	6	77
Fiji	X	X	0.00	0.00	X	X	X	X	X	X	X
New Zealand	397.00	115.57	0.00	0.00	1980	1.20	0	379	52	11	14
Papua New Guinea	X	X	X	X	X	X	X	X	X	X	X
Solomon Islands	X	X	0.00	0.00	X	X	X	X	X	X	X

Sources: Bureau of Geological and Mining Research, National Geological Survey, France; and U.S. Geological Survey.
Notes:
a. Water resources includes both internal renewable resources and river flows from other countries.
b. Domestic, commercial, public services, and industry supplied by public facilities.
c. Public and industrial sectors combined.
0 = zero or less than half the unit of measure; X = not available.
For additional information, see Sources and Technical Notes.

Table 21.2 River Water Quality, 1970–85

	Dissolved Oxygen (milligrams per liter)					Biological Oxygen Demand (milligrams per liter)					Nitrate (milligrams per liter)					Phosphorous (milligrams per liter)				
	1970	1975	1980	1985	Latest Three Years of Data (average)	1970	1975	1980	1985	Latest Three Years of Data (average)	1970	1975	1980	1985	Latest Three Years of Data (average)	1970	1975	1980	1985	Latest Three Years of Data (average)
Canada																				
St. Lawrence	8.1	10.0	X	X	X	X	X	X	X	X	0.19	0.23	0.16	0.21	0.21	0.02	0.01	0.02	0.01	0.02
Mackenzie	X	X	X	X	X	X	X	X	X	X	0.08	0.11	0.11	0.09	0.08	X	0.02	0.04	0.04	0.04
Fraser	X	X	X	X	X	X	X	X	X	X	0.05	0.30	0.06	X	0.08	0.00	0.11	X	X	X
Nelson	X	X	X	X	X	X	X	X	X	X	0.04	0.40	0.06	0.09	0.06	X	0.02	0.01	0.02	0.01
Saskatchewan	X	X	10.5	10.9	11.2	X	X	3.0	X	X	X	X	0.05	0.04	0.07	X	X	0.04	0.05	0.05
Slave	X	X	X	X	X	X	X	X	X	X	X	X	0.05	0.09	0.08	X	X	0.08	0.08	0.10
United States																				
Delaware-Trenton[a]	9.6	10.8	11.9	10.8	11.1	1.9	2.0	2.2	2.6	2.8	X	0.88	1.08	X	X	1.70	0.10	0.01	0.13	0.12
Mississippi-St. Francis[a]	8.4	8.5	8.3	8.6	8.9	2.4	2.2	1.7	1.1	1.8	0.36	1.04	1.30	1.23	1.47	X	0.19	0.24	0.14	0.15
Japan																				
Ishikari	8.9	10.7	10.6	10.2	10.5	1.9	1.4	1.4	1.5	1.5	X	X	0.53	X	X	X	0.09	0.09	0.07	0.09
Yodo	8.2	8.9	9.0	8.2	8.0	5.2	3.2	3.5	3.6	4.1	X	X	0.76	X	X	X	0.19	0.22	0.16	0.18
Tone	9.9	10.3	10.2	10.5	10.3	1.7	1.5	1.6	1.5	1.4	X	X	X	X	X	X	X	X	X	X
Shinano	9.8	9.8	9.8	10.6	10.4	2.5	1.8	1.5	1.7	1.6	X	X	X	X	X	X	X	X	X	X
Australia																				
Brisbane estuary	X	5.6	6.4	6.0	6.2	X	1.6	1.0	1.2	1.2	X	X	0.85	1.05	0.93	X	0.20	0.38	0.48	0.43
Belgium																				
Meuse-Heer	8.2	10.8	10.6	10.4	10.7	4.4	6.6	4.2	8.0	5.4	1.80	7.80	2.18	3.12	2.47	X	1.23	0.22	0.35	0.32
Meuse-Lanaye	7.7	8.9	9.5	8.1	8.6	12.5	4.7	3.9	4.3	4.3	3.90	9.40	2.52	2.79	2.67	X	1.41	0.55	0.72	0.75
Schelde-Bleharies	X	4.0	5.9	6.5	6.6	X	24.1	10.7	3.4	5.5	X	X	4.17	5.62	5.19	X	0.70	0.94	1.09	0.88
Schelde-Doel	6.2	1.3	1.9	3.3	3.4	4.0	8.2	5.0	3.0	3.9	3.00	7.35	4.17	3.91	3.91	X	1.06	0.55	0.87	1.13
Denmark																				
Gudena	X	X	9.7	10.7	10.2	X	X	3.4	4.5	4.3	X	1.25	1.70	2.00	1.84	X	0.30	0.16	0.18	0.13
Skjern	X	X	10.5	10.4	X	X	X	7.3	8.0	8.3	X	X	3.00	3.18	2.92	X	X	0.22	0.13	0.17
Susa	X	X	9.8	8.7	X	X	X	X	2.0	2.1	X	5.27	6.73	5.21	6.09	X	0.66	0.26	0.34	0.30
Finland																				
Torn	11.9	11.9	12.0	12.0	12.0	1.6	1.6	X	X	X	X	X	X	0.02	X	0.02	0.02	0.02	0.02	0.02
Kymijoki	9.5	10.8	9.9	9.5	8.9	3.5	2.4	2.3	X	X	X	X	0.58	X	X	0.05	0.03	0.03	0.03	0.03
France																				
Loire	10.7	11.1	11.8	X	11.6	6.7	4.4	6.6	X	6.0	1.58	1.45	1.99	X	2.12	X	X	X	X	X
Seine	X	3.3	4.9	X	5.2	X	10.2	6.6	X	4.9	X	4.18	5.35	X	5.18	X	X	X	X	X
Garonne	9.7	9.9	10.1	X	9.9	2.2	1.5	2.3	X	2.1	1.15	0.93	1.83	X	1.73	X	X	X	X	X
Rhine-Selz	8.2	9.2	10.9	8.6	8.9	X	4.1	4.8	3.0	3.6	X	1.58	2.92	2.94	2.62	X	X	0.47	X	X
Germany, Fed Rep																				
Rhine-Bimmen L.	5.6	6.8	9.0	9.3	9.3	6.1	7.9	4.0	3.8	4.0	1.82	3.02	3.59	4.20	3.90	0.52	0.75	0.36	0.48	0.52
Elbe	X	X	9.0	8.1	8.2	X	X	6.2	8.6	8.7	X	X	3.90	2.99	2.99	X	X	0.36	0.53	0.54
Vesdre	X	9.4	8.6	8.7	8.7	X	X	5.4	4.3	4.5	X	4.30	5.42	5.08	5.18	X	0.67	0.53	0.36	0.36
Danube-Jochenstein	10.5	10.3	10.6	10.5	10.6	4.8	3.1	3.1	3.2	3.4	0.20	0.30	0.50	0.60	0.53	X	X	0.18	0.21	0.22
Italy																				
Po	8.3	X	7.7	8.7	8.5	X	7.3	6.1	4.6	9.1	0.95	1.35	1.63	3.28	2.55	X	0.23	0.28	0.22	0.26
Adige	X	X	X	X	X	X	X	X	X	X	X	0.88	0.94	X	X	X	0.19	0.18	0.00	0.00
Tiber	4.6	X	5.3	9.4	X	8.3	X	9.5	2.0	X	X	1.50	1.37	X	X	X	0.26	0.40	0.00	0.00
Netherlands																				
Meuse-Keizersveer	8.6	9.4	10.0	9.7	9.7	6.2	4.2	2.3	1.6	1.9	3.07	3.69	3.77	4.28	4.01	0.41	0.57	0.50	0.48	0.43
Meuse-Eijsden	9.8	9.5	9.8	8.1	8.5	4.1	3.7	2.8	2.9	3.0	2.45	2.51	2.78	2.92	2.83	0.43	0.73	0.58	0.57	0.53
Scheur-Maasluis	X	7.1	8.1	9.3	9.0	X	3.9	2.2	1.5	1.6	X	3.37	3.84	4.16	4.05	X	0.56	0.65	0.55	0.55
Ijssel-Kampen	6.7	6.7	8.1	8.2	8.4	5.7	6.3	3.9	2.3	2.7	2.76	3.46	4.27	4.33	4.13	0.43	0.62	0.63	0.57	0.57
Rhine-Lobit	X	X	8.0	8.0	8.3	6.7	7.0	3.2	2.3	2.5	2.68	3.27	3.93	4.51	4.31	0.50	0.72	0.66	0.62	0.59
Norway																				
Skienselva	X	X	X	6.0	X	X	2.5	3.5	X	X	X	0.35	0.35	0.34	0.34	X	0.01	0.01	0.01	0.01
Glama	X	X	X	X	X	X	X	X	X	X	X	X	0.33	0.35	0.32	X	X	0.02	0.02	0.02
Dramselva	X	X	X	X	X	X	X	X	X	X	X	X	0.41	0.35	0.35	X	X	0.01	0.01	0.01
Lagen	X	X	X	X	X	X	X	X	X	X	X	X	0.29	0.31	0.37	X	X	0.01	0.02	0.02
Portugal																				
Tagus	9.0	X	9.0	X	X	1.6	X	2.5	X	X	0.52	X	5.60	X	X	X	X	2.00	X	X
Spain																				
Guadalquivir	X	X	3.1	7.6	7.2	X	11.8	8.8	7.5	X	X	7.20	13.50	10.91	X	0.83	0.86	0.61	1.00	
Douro	X	X	7.2	8.1	7.4	X	2.4	2.8	3.1	X	X	8.50	0.19	0.97	X	X	0.69	0.35	0.60	
Tagus	X	X	7.2	7.4	7.3	X	2.4	2.6	3.2	X	X	1.50	1.55	1.44	X	X	0.42	0.23	0.27	
Ebro	X	X	9.9	9.6	9.1	X	3.4	4.6	4.4	X	X	5.30	10.16	8.92	X	X	0.33	0.74	0.53	
Sweden																				
Dal	X	X	X	X	X	X	X	X	X	X	0.12	0.11	0.14	0.11	0.12	0.02	0.02	0.02	0.02	0.02
Ranealv	X	X	X	X	X	X	X	X	X	X	0.05	0.05	0.03	0.05	0.04	0.01	0.02	0.03	0.02	0.02
Morrumsan	X	X	X	X	X	X	X	X	X	X	0.18	0.23	0.17	0.25	0.21	0.02	0.02	0.02	0.02	0.02
Ronnebyan	X	X	X	X	X	X	X	X	X	X	1.29	1.19	1.49	1.31	1.31	0.04	0.04	0.08	0.06	0.06
Switzerland																				
Rhine-Village	11.6	11.2	10.3	10.5	10.4	X	X	X	X	X	X	X	1.39	1.50	1.39	X	0.07	0.17	0.13	0.16
Aare-Brugg	X	10.2	10.2	10.4	X	X	X	X	X	X	X	X	1.43	1.75	1.33	X	0.23	0.11	0.12	0.44
Limmat-Baden	X	X	X	X	X	X	X	X	X	X	X	X	0.91	1.11	0.92	X	X	0.13	0.15	0.12
Rhone-Port du Scex	X	10.7	10.9	11.2	X	X	X	X	X	X	X	X	0.52	0.54	0.46	X	0.12	0.10	0.13	0.10
United Kingdom																				
Thames[b]	X	10.8	9.9	10.0	10.0	X	3.4	2.7	2.4	2.7	X	6.50	6.89	7.52	7.34	X	1.07	1.16	1.32	1.50
Severn[b]	X	10.5	10.3	10.8	11.0	X	2.8	2.6	1.7	2.2	X	5.52	5.80	6.33	6.16	X	0.75	0.54	0.71	0.87
Clyde[b]	X	7.7	9.4	9.1	8.8	X	7.3	5.6	3.2	3.3	X	2.60	1.85	2.16	2.26	X	0.69	0.50	0.32	0.41
Mersey[b]	X	5.1	6.1	6.2	6.0	X	8.6	X	5.0	5.9	X	1.84	2.29	3.12	2.50	X	X	X	1.36	1.47
Tyne	X	10.8	10.8	10.5	10.4	X	1.9	2.0	2.7	2.3	X	0.97	0.83	1.01	0.83	X	0.14	0.12	0.08	0.11
Trent[b]	X	8.8	9.5	9.3	8.9	X	4.3	3.7	2.9	3.0	X	8.96	10.76	9.51	9.17	X	X	X	1.77	1.65
Yugoslavia																				
Danube	9.6	9.1	9.2	X	9.5	3.4	2.5	3.5	X	3.7	X	1.70	5.80	X	X	X	X	X	X	X
Drava	8.8	7.4	10.1	X	10.0	3.4	2.6	3.1	X	3.1	X	5.20	7.70	X	X	X	X	X	X	X

Table 21.2

	Lead (micrograms per liter)					Cadmium (micrograms per liter)					Chromium (micrograms per liter)					Copper (micrograms per liter)				
	1970	1975	1980	1985	Latest Three Years of Data (average)	1970	1975	1980	1985	Latest Three Years of Data (average)	1970	1975	1980	1985	Latest Three Years of Data (average)	1970	1975	1980	1985	Latest Three Years of Data (average)
Canada																				
St. Lawrence	0.00	0.00	1.00	1.00	X	0.00	0.00	1.00	1.00	X	0.00	0.00	X	1.00	X	0.01	0.01	1.00	1.00	1.00
Mackenzie	10.00	5.00	4.00	3.00	3.67	X	1.00	1.00	1.00	1.00	X	0.01c	X	X	X	10.00	7.00	2.00	1.00	7.67
Fraser	10.00	2.00	X	X	X	X	X	X	X	X	X	X	X	X	X	10.00	4.00	X	X	X
Nelson	X	4.00	4.00	7.00	5.00	X	1.00	1.00	1.00	1.00	X	X	X	X	X	X	4.00	5.00	16.00	7.67
Saskatchewan	X	X	4.00	1.00	X	X	X	X	X	X	X	X	X	1.00	X	X	X	6.00	3.00	X
Slave	X	X	X	X	X	X	X	X	X	X	X	X	X	X	X	X	X	X	X	X
United States																				
Delaware-Trenton^d	X	6.00	2.00	3.00	3.20	X	0.90	0.80	0.50	0.50	X	22.80	6.30	0.50	1.50	X	17.60	3.50	4.80	3.70
Mississippi-St. Francis^d	X	2.00	2.00	2.80	3.00	X	0.50	1.30	0.70	0.70	X	0.60	5.00	0.50	3.30	X	4.00	5.00	5.60	6.90
Japan																				
Ishikari	210.00	1.00	5.00	X	X	0.00	X	0.00	X	X	0.00	0.00	0.00	X	X	35.00	3.00	18.00	3.00	3.67
Yodo	X	X	0.00	X	X	0.00	0.00	0.00	X	X	X	0.00	0.00	X	X	X	0.00	8.00	X	X
Tone	X	X	X	X	X	X	X	X	X	X	X	X	X	X	X	X	X	X	X	X
Shinano	X	X	X	X	X	X	X	X	X	X	X	X	X	X	X	X	X	X	X	X
Australia																				
Brisbane est.	X	X	5.30	5.00	X	X	X	2.00	2.00	X	X	X	X	20.00	X	X	9.70	5.60	5.00	5.20
Belgium																				
Meuse-Heer	X	1.40	4.00	9.12	7.94	X	0.80	0.30	0.22	0.18	X	1.20	1.20	0.40	0.77	X	4.70	7.00	19.00	11.03
Meuse-Lanaye	X	5.70	20.00	6.71	10.60	X	2.60	1.20	0.39	0.87	X	4.60	2.70	5.70	6.13	X	4.50	22.60	7.40	9.37
Schelde-Bleharies	X	11.00	18.00	6.72	8.59	X	1.60	2.60	0.46	0.53	X	12.60	9.80	18.80	15.13	X	6.80	15.60	5.10	7.57
Schelde-Doel	X	203.50	25.00	6.22	15.31	X	1.50	5.80	1.22	0.91	X	15.60	26.10	3.60	9.80	X	15.50	24.40	10.90	12.30
Denmark																				
Gudena	X	X	X	X	X	X	X	X	X	X	X	X	X	X	X	X	X	X	X	X
Skjern	X	X	X	X	X	X	X	X	X	X	X	X	X	X	X	X	X	X	X	X
Susa	X	X	X	X	X	X	X	X	X	X	X	X	X	X	X	X	X	X	X	X
Finland																				
Torn	X	X	0.06	0.57	0.66	X	X	0.01	0.02	0.04	X	1.00c	3.00c	X	X	X	2.00	2.80	X	X
Kymijoki	X	X	0.28c	0.49c	0.83c	X	X	0.01c	0.01c	0.04c	X	X	X	X	X	X	X	X	X	X
France																				
Loire	X	10.00c	4.00	X	4.67	X	10.00c	1.00c	X	1.33	X	10.00c	5.00	X	5.00	X	1.00c	8.00	X	7.33
Seine	X	26.00c	8.00	X	9.67	X	1.00c	1.00c	X	X	X	12.00	13.00	X	20.67	X	52.00	11.00	X	14.33
Garonne	X	10.00c	5.00	X	5.67	X	10.00c	1.00c	X	X	X	10.00c	3.00	X	X	X	1.00c	6.00	X	4.33
Rhine-Selz	X	9.30	12.50	3.20	6.03	X	1.00	0.80	0.20	0.53	X	9.00	16.00	7.60	11.50	X	11.30	15.90	5.10	7.80
Germany, Fed Rep																				
Rhine-Bimmen L.	X	24.00	7.00	11.00	10.67	X	2.40	1.40	0.30	0.30	X	40.00	22.30	10.00	8.67	X	24.00	19.90	13.00	15.33
Elbe	X	X	X	X	X	X	X	X	X	X	X	X	X	X	X	X	X	X	X	X
Vesdre	X	X	2.00	2.80	3.97	X	X	0.50	0.50	0.57	X	X	3.00	3.00	2.87	X	X	5.60	9.20	33.07
Danube-Jochenstein	X	X	X	2.60	2.00	X	X	0.20	0.10	0.13	X	X	X	X	X	X	X	X	X	X
Italy																				
Po^d	X	0.40	0.55	X	X	X	0.16	0.05	X	X	X	0.50	0.60	X	X	X	0.60	0.85	X	0.65
Adige	X	X	X	X	X	X	X	X	X	X	X	X	X	X	X	X	X	X	X	X
Tiber	X	X	X	X	X	X	X	X	X	X	X	X	X	X	X	X	X	X	X	X
Netherlands																				
Meuse-Keizersveer	X	12.00	12.00	3.60	4.83	X	0.90	1.50	0.21	0.28	X	7.00	7.00	3.00	3.63	X	9.00	12.00	3.50	5.47
Meuse-Eijsden	X	17.00	23.00	6.20	10.57	X	3.10	3.40	0.35	0.88	X	14.00	10.00	6.40	9.63	X	16.00	11.00	5.50	7.93
Scheur-Maassluis	X	13.00	11.00	1.90	3.17	X	1.00	0.90	0.26	0.33	X	16.00	19.00	5.30	5.33	X	15.00	12.00	4.90	5.63
Ijssel-Kampen	X	17.00	9.00	5.00	5.67	X	1.40	1.30	0.40	0.70	X	25.00	14.00	7.00	8.67	26.00	16.00	9.00	7.00	7.67
Rhine-Lobit	X	22.00	15.00	4.20	5.63	X	2.30	1.60	0.14	0.25	X	35.00	20.00	7.60	8.73	X	20.00	14.00	5.90	7.97
Norway																				
Skienselva	X	X	X	X	X	X	X	X	X	X	X	X	X	X	X	X	X	X	X	X
Glama	X	X	1.70	0.67	X	X	X	0.15	0.10	X	X	X	2.20	1.00	X	X	X	2.00	2.80	X
Dramselva	X	X	X	X	X	X	X	X	X	X	X	X	X	X	X	X	X	X	X	X
Lagen	X	X	X	X	X	X	X	X	X	X	X	X	X	X	X	X	X	X	X	X
Portugal																				
Tagus	X	X	X	X	X	X	X	X	X	X	X	X	X	X	X	X	X	X	X	X
Spain																				
Guadalquivir	X	X	12.10	0.01	0.01	X	X	0.00	0.02	0.02	X	24.00	10.00	X	3.35	X	0.00	2.70	0.03	0.01
Douro	X	X	X	X	X	X	X	X	X	0.00	X	X	0.00	0.00	0.00	X	X	0.80	0.00	0.09
Tagus	X	X	X	X	X	X	X	X	X	X	X	X	0.00	0.50	0.17	X	X	X	0.01	0.01
Ebro	X	X	5.00	0.00	1.67	X	X	0.00	0.00	X	X	X	X	X	X	X	X	X	X	X
Sweden																				
Dal	X	X	X	X	X	X	X	X	X	X	X	X	X	X	X	X	X	17.00	6.30	12.53
Ranealv	X	X	X	X	X	X	X	X	X	X	X	X	X	X	X	X	X	X	X	X
Morrumsan	X	X	X	X	X	X	X	X	X	X	X	X	X	X	X	X	X	X	X	X
Ronnebyan	X	X	X	X	X	X	X	X	X	X	X	X	X	X	X	X	X	X	X	X
Switzerland																				
Rhine-Village	X	1.60	1.40	0.40	1.60		0.08	0.14	0.02	0.09	X	1.30	2.00	0.80	1.70	X	1.80	4.20	2.76	4.63
Aare-Brugg	X	X	X	X	X	X	X	X	X	X	X	X	X	X	X	X	X	X	X	X
Limmat-Baden	X	X	X	X	X	X	X	X	X	X	X	X	X	X	X	X	X	X	X	X
Rhone-Port du Scex	X	X	3.38	3.57	2.68	X	X	X	X	X	X	X	X	X	X	X	X	3.48	3.88	4.62
United Kingdom																				
Thames	X	X	10.00	9.00	10.00	X	X	1.04	X	0.00	X	X	11.00	X	0.00	X	X	10.00	11.00	10.00
Severn	X	X	X	X	X	X	X	X	X	X	X	X	X	11.00	12.00	X	X	21.00	12.00	15.00
Clyde	X	X	18.00	8.00	13.00	X	X	1.08	0.78	0.66	X	X	25.00	21.00	25.00	X	X	10.00	6.00	6.00
Mersey	X	X	15.00	11.00	13.00	X	X	0.79	0.18	0.00	X	X	X	12.00	13.00	X	X	19.00	9.00	9.00
Tyne	X	X	19.00	25.00	16.00	X	X	1.25	X	0.00	X	X	16.00	X	0.00	X	X	24.00	13.00	10.00
Trent	X	X	17.00	15.00	17.00	X	X	X	0.36	0.61	X	X	14.00	9.00	13.00	X	X	27.00	18.00	20.00
Yugoslavia																				
Danube	X	4.41	29.98	X	X	X	0.21	6.00	X	X	X	X	X	X	X	X	1.39	117.90	X	X
Drava	X	X	X	X	X	X	X	X	X	X	X	X	X	X	X	X	X	X	X	X

Source: Organisation for Economic Co-operation and Development.
Notes:
a. Data for nitrate and phosphorous represent total concentrations.
b. Data for phosphorous represent orthophosphate concentrations.
c. Data represent upper limit (actual averages are lower).
d. Data for lead, cadmium, chromium, and copper refer to dissolved concentrations.
0 = zero or negligible; X = not available.
For additional information, see Sources and Technical Notes.

Table 21.3 Characteristics of Major Rivers

River	Countries in River Basin	Basin Area (thousand square kilometers)	Average Discharge (cubic meters per second)	Average Runoff (liters per second per square kilometer)	Concentrations of Dissolved Minerals (milligrams per liter)	Annual Transport of Dissolved Minerals (million metric tons per year)	Transport Relative to Basin Area (metric tons/km²/year) Dissolved	Solid	Human Impact on Transport in Basin[a]
AFRICA									
Chari	Central African Republic, Chad, Cameroon	600	1,320	2.2	64	2.7	4	7	limited
Congo	Zaire, Angola, Congo, Central African Republic	4,000	39,200	9.8	38	47.0	12	13	limited
Niger	Guinea, Nigeria, Niger, Mali	1,125	6,100	5.5	53	10.0	9	60[b]	moderate
Nile	Uganda, Sudan, Egypt, Ethiopia, Tanzania	3,000	2,830[c]	0.9	208	17.4	6	37[b]	severe
Orange	South Africa, Namibia	800	300	0.4	182	12.0	2	150	moderate
Zambezi	Zambia, Angola, Botswana, Zimbabwe, Mozambique	1,340	7,100	5.3	70	15.4	12	75[b]	moderate
NORTH & CENTRAL AMERICA									
Colorado	United States, Mexico	635	640	1.0	700	12.0	23	220[b]	severe
Columbia	Canada, United States	670	7,960	11.9	139	34.8	52	43[b]	moderate
Mackenzie	Canada	1,800	9,600	5.3	230	70.0	39	65	limited
Mississippi	United States	3,267	18,400	5.7	223	131.0	40	150[b]	severe
Nelson	Canada	1,150	3,500	3.1	280	31.0	27	X	limited
Rio Grande	United States, Mexico	670	100	X	482	3.5	X	X	X
St. Lawrence	Canada, United States	1,025	10,700	10.4	161	54.0	53	5	moderate
Yukon	Canada, United States	770	6,200	8.0	174	34.0	44	103	limited
SOUTH AMERICA									
Amazon	Peru, Brazil	6,300	175,000	28.0	52	290.0	46	143	limited
Madeira[d]	Brazil, Bolivia	1,380	32,000	23.0	60	X	42	157	limited
Magdalena	Colombia	240	7,500	31.0	120	28.0	117	1,000	moderate
Maranon[d]	Peru	407	11,000	27.0	105	X	90	250	limited
Negro	Colombia, Venezuela, Brazil	755	45,300	60.0	5	X	10	10	limited
Orinoco	Venezuela, Colombia	950	30,000	31.6	52	50.0	52	91	limited
Parana	Brazil, Paraguay, Argentina	2,800	18,000	6.4	100	56.0	20	40	moderate
Sao Francisco	Brazil	470	2,900	6.2	X	X	X	X	moderate
Tapajos	Brazil	500	7,200	14.4	8	X	4	1	limited
Tocantins[d]	Brazil	900	11,000	12.2	X	X	X	X	limited
Ucayali[d]	Peru	400	9,700	24.0	180	X	136	307	limited
Uruguay	Brazil, Uruguay, Argentina	350	5,000	14.3	50	8.0	23	70	moderate
Xingu[d]	Brazil	540	7,800	14.4	7	X	3	1	limited
ASIA									
Amur	China, USSR	1,850	11,000	6.0	57	20.0	11	14	limited
Amu Darya	Afghanistan, USSR	450	1,450[c]	3.2	600	27.0	60	209	moderate
Brahmaputra	China, India, Bangladesh	580	19,300	33.0	124	75.0	130	1,370	limited
Ganges	India, Bangladesh, Nepal	975	11,600	12.0	208	76.0	78	537	moderate
Hsi	China	1,350	7,800	22.3	140	X	98	X	moderate
Huang He	China	745	1,480	3.4	450	X	45	1,080	moderate
Indus	China, Pakistan, India	950	6,700[c]	7.0	295	68.0	65	260[b]	severe
Irrawaddy	Burma	430	13,400	31.2	215	X	211	700	limited
Kolyma	USSR	645	3,150	5.8	X	X	X	9	limited
Lena	USSR	2,430	16,300	6.7	165	85.0	36	6	limited
Mekong	China, Laos, Burma, Thailand, Kampuchea, Viet Nam	795	18,300	23.0	105	59.0	75	435	limited
Ob	USSR	2,500	12,350	4.9	130	50.0	20	6	limited
Shatt-al-Arab	Iraq, Iran, Turkey, Syrian Arab Rep.	410	1,750	4.3	320	18.0	43	250	severe
Yangtze	China	1,950	28,000	14.4	185	X	85	250[b]	moderate
Yenisei	USSR	2,600	17,200	6.7	135	73.0	28	5	limited
EUROPE									
Danube	F.R. Germany, Austria, Hungary Yugoslavia, Romania, Bulgaria, USSR	805	6,430	8.0	300	60.0	75	84	severe
Dnieper	USSR	500	1,650	3.3	210	11.0	22	2	severe
Don	USSR	420	870	2.1	495	13.8	33	14	severe
Volga	USSR	1,350	8,400	6.2	290	77.0	57	19	severe
OCEANIA									
Murray	Australia	1,070	740	0.7	380	8.8	8	30	moderate

Source: Physical and Chemical Weathering in Geochemical Cycles (Reidel, Dordrecht, Netherlands, in press 1988).
Notes:
a. Limited = limited human impact, watershed largely pristine; moderate = watershed somewhat affected by human activity; severe = watershed significantly affected by human activity.
b. Solid transport prior to construction of dams.
c. Discharge prior to major irrigation schemes.
d. Amazon tributaries.
X = not available.
For additional information, see Sources and Technical Notes.

Table 21.4 Selected Large Lakes, 1980s

Lake	Countries with Shoreline	Surface Area^a (km²)	Volume (km³)	Area of Drainage Basin^b (km²)	Forest	Farm	Settlement	Population in Basin (thousands)	year	Fish Catch (metric tons)	year	Total Nitrogen (mg/l)	Total Phosphorus mg/l
AFRICA													
Victoria	Kenya, Tanzania, Uganda	68,800	2,750	184,000	X	X	X	504	ND	120,000	1980	X	X
Tanganyika	Burundi, Tanzania, Zaire, Zambia	32,000	18,900	263,000	X	X	X	1,463	ND	X	X	X	X
Chad	Cameroon, Chad, Niger, Nigeria	16,600^c	44	2,426,730	X	X	X	403	ND	X	X	X	X
Nyasa	Malawi, Mozambique, Tanzania	22,490	6,140	65,000	X	X	X	X	X	X	X	X	X
Kariba	Zambia, Zimbabwe	5,400	160	663,000	X	X	X	X	X	11,000	1986	X	X
NORTH AND CENTRAL AMERICA													
Michigan	United States	57,750	4,920	118,100	41	44	9	13,970	1980	10,200	1980	X	X
Huron	Canada, United States	59,500	3,537	133,900	68	27	2	2,258	1980^d	2,670	1980	X	0
Erie	Canada, United States	25,657	483	58,800	21	67	10	12,862	1980^d	23,580	1980	X	0
Winnipeg	Canada	24,387	371	984,200	40	50	X	3,859	1970	7,726	1982	X	X
Ontario	Canada, United States	19,000	1,637	70,700	49	39	7	6,125	1980^d	975	1980	X	0
Superior	Canada, United States	82,100	12,230	127,700	91	3	1	705	1980^d	3,630	1980	X	0
Great Slave	Canada	28,568	2,088	971,000	X	X	X	X	X	X	X	X	X
Great Bear	Canada	31,326	2,381	146,000	X	X	X	X	X	X	X	X	X
Athabasca	Canada	7,935	204	158,000	X	X	X	X	X	X	X	X	X
Cedar	Canada	1,353	X	339,000	X	X	X	X	X	X	X	X	X
Washington	United States	88	3	1,274	30	10	60	1,500	ND	X	X	0	0
Nicaragua	Nicaragua	8,150	108	X	X	X	X	X	X	X	X	X	X
SOUTH AMERICA													
Maracaibo	Venezuela	13,010	280	90,200	X	X	X	X	X	X	X	X	X
Titicaca	Bolivia, Peru	8,030	827	60,800	0	6	0	890	1981	6,327	1980	X	X
ASIA													
Caspian	Iran, USSR	374,000	78,200	3,625,000	X	X	X	X	X	X	X	X	X
Aral	USSR	64,100	1,020	1,618,000	X	X	X	X	X	X	X	X	X
Tungting	China	6,000^c	18	259,430	26	29	13	11,754	1982	70,000	1981	X	0
Baikal	USSR	31,500	22,995	560,000	X	X	X	X	X	X	X	X	X
Balkhash	USSR	18,200^c	112	176,500	X	X	X	X	X	X	X	X	X
Tai Hu	China	2,210	4	X	X	X	X	30,000	ND	13,696	1979	X	X
Helmand	Afghanistan, USSR	2,080^c	8	350,000	X	X	X	X	X	X	X	X	X
Biwa	Japan	674	28	3,174	63	5	9	1,117	1983	5,189	1980	0	0
Laguna de Bay	Philippines	890	3	3,820	24	52	7	2,381	1980	120,000	ND	X	X
Songkhla	Thailand	987	2	8,000	26	68	6	1,055	1973	X	X	1	0
Toba	Indonesia	1,100	1,258	3,440	X	X	X	X	X	X	X	X	X
EUROPE													
Malaren	Sweden	1,096	14	22,600	63	20	X	1,131	1975	340	1978^e	1	0
Ladoga	USSR	17,700	908	X	X	X	X	X	X	X	X	X	X
Geneva	France, Switzerland	580	89	7,975	X	X	X	950	1980	348	1982	X	0
Maggiore	Italy, Switzerland	213	38	6,387	20	X	X	670	1971	155	1981	1	0
Vanern	Sweden	5,648	153	X	X	X	X	X	X	X	X	X	X
Vattern	Sweden	1,856	74	4,503	X	X	X	X	X	X	X	X	X
Constance	Switzerland, Austria, Fed. Rep. Germany	476	47.7	10,446	X	X	X	X	X	856	1983	66	X
OCEANIA													
Alexandrina	Australia	580	2	1,072,000	X	X	X	X	X	X	X	X	X
Eyre	Australia	7,690^c	23	1,122,250	X	X	X	X	X	X	X	X	X

Sources: Lake Biwa Research Institute; Ohio Sea Grant; and Michigan Sea Grant.
Notes:
a. Total area enclosed within the shoreline of the lake, including any islands. b. Area of the catchment basin exclusive of the surface area of the lake. c. Subject to large fluctuations in surface area. d. United States population 1980, Canada 1981. e. Average annual catch, 1976-80.
0 = zero or less than half the unit of measure; X = not available; ND = no date.
For additional information, see Sources and Technical Notes.

Sources and Technical Notes

Table 21.1 Freshwater Resources and Withdrawal, 1959–86

Sources: Water resources and withdrawal: J. Forkasiewicz and J. Margat, *Tableau Mondial de Donnees Nationales d'Economie de l'Eau, Ressources et Utilisation* (Departement Hydrogeologie, Orleans, France, 1980). Data for Algeria, Egypt, Libya, Morocco, Tunisia, Cyprus, Israel, Lebanon, Syrian Arab Republic, Turkey, Albania, France, Greece, Italy, Malta, Spain, and Yugoslavia: J. Margat, Bureau de Recherches Geologiques et Minieres, Orleans, France, April 1988 (personal communication). Withdrawal and sectoral use data for the United States: W.B. Solley, C.F. Merk, and R.R.

Pierce, "Estimated Use of Water in the United States in 1985," *U.S. Geological Survey Circular*, No. 1004 (U.S. Geological Survey, Reston, Virginia, 1988). Population: United Nations Population Division, *World Population Prospects: Estimates and Projections as Assessed in 1984* (United Nations, New York, 1986).

Margat compiles water resources and withdrawal data from published documents, including national, United Nations, and professional literature. Data for small countries and countries in arid and semiarid zones are less reliable than those for larger and wetter countries.

Internal renewable water resources refers

to the average annual flow of rivers and aquifers generated from endogenous precipitation. These annual averages disguise large seasonal, interannual and long-term variations. When data for river flows to and from other countries are not shown, the internal renewable water resources figure may include these flows. *Per capita internal renewable water resources* data were created using 1989 population estimates.

Water is withdrawn when it is taken from a surface or underground source and conveyed to the place of use. *Withdrawal as a percentage of water resources* refers to total water withdrawal as a percentage of internal renewable water resources and river flows from other countries. *Per capita withdrawal* figures were calculated using national population data for the year of data shown for withdrawal. When "year of data" figures were not available, 1975 population figures were used.

Sectoral withdrawal is classified in three categories: public (homes, commercial establishments, public services [e.g., hospitals], and publicly supplied industry), self-supplied industry, and agriculture (principally irrigation). Industrial withdrawal includes water withdrawn to cool thermoelectric plants.

Table 21.2 River Water Quality, 1970–85

Source: Organisation for Economic Co-operation and Development (OECD), *OECD Environmental Data Compendium 1987* (OECD, Paris, 1987).

This table includes data for three broad classes of water pollution: industrial effluents, agricultural runoff, and domestic sewage waste.

Trends in the concentration of *dissolved oxygen* and the level of *biological oxygen demand* (BOD) together indicate the level and type of organic pollution in a river. Dissolved oxygen is removed from water as organisms decompose organic material, such as sewage and domestic wastes. Dissolved oxygen may also be depleted by the proliferation of plant life that results from nutrient pollution. Many aquatic organisms cannot survive at low concentrations of dissolved oxygen. BOD measures the amount of dissolved oxygen consumed by microorganisms in oxidizing organic matter over a period of time.

High levels of *nitrates* and *phosphorous* in river water usually indicate agricultural runoff (fertilizer and livestock wastes), and the presence of industrial and domestic wastes (such as detergents). Both nitrogen and phosphorous are nutrients that contribute to eutrophication. High concentrations of nitrates may be a health hazard, especially for infants. The World Health Organization (WHO) recommends that drinking water contain less than 10 milligrams of nitrates per liter.

The presence of four toxic heavy metals— *lead, cadmium, chromium,* and *copper*— indicates industrial pollution. Because heavy metals do not break down to nontoxic forms, they are a persistent threat to human health and ecological stability. WHO recommends that a liter of drinking water contain less than 50 micrograms of lead; less than 5 micrograms of cadmium; less than 50 micrograms of chromium; and less than 1,000 micrograms of copper.

OECD member countries were asked to submit data that could be used to assess trends in water quality in major rivers that drained large watersheds. Ambient concentrations of pollutants were measured at the mouth or a downstream location of each river, in order to obtain a summary measure of pollution loads and pollution abatement efforts in the upstream basin. These data should be used to compare trends within countries rath-

er than among countries because monitoring methods vary.

In a few cases, data shown for 1970, 1975, 1980, and 1985 may represent data for adjacent years.

Table 21.3 Characteristics of Major Rivers

Source: M. Meybeck, "How to Establish and Use World Budgets of Riverine Materials," in A. Lerman and M. Meybeck, eds., *Physical and Chemical Weathering in Geochemical Cycles* (Reidel, Dordrecht, Netherlands, in press 1988) and M. Meybeck, Institut de Biogeochimie Marine, École Normale Supériéure, Montrouge, France, May 1988 (personal communication).

Meybeck collects data on river characteristics from many international and national agencies and the scientific literature.

The *basin area* of a river is the area of land drained by a river and its tributaries. A river's *average discharge* is the average volume of water that passes a measuring station in a fixed period of time. *Average runoff* is the amount of net precipitation (precipitation minus evaporation) for each square kilometer of the river basin. Both discharge and runoff data vary with the location of the measurement station on the river and with long-term climate trends. Discharge and runoff are also affected by human activities, such as dam construction and large scale irrigation.

Concentration of dissolved minerals is the sum of the concentrations of the following major ions: calcium, magnesium, sodium, potassium, chlorine, sulfate, nitrate, bicarbonate, and silica. *Annual transport of dissolved minerals* is the total mass of these minerals carried by the river from its drainage basin to the ocean. Dissolved organic matter, which may contribute up to 20 percent of a river's dissolved content, was excluded from this study.

River water transports minerals either chemically, as dissolved ions, or mechanically, as suspended particles. *Transport relative to basin area* describes the average annual amount of dissolved and solid materials carried by the river to the ocean per square kilometer of river basin at a given station. Although these figures are closely related to rates of erosion in the river basin, they are not measures of erosion.

Solid material includes both particulate minerals and soil, and is estimated from the amount of material suspended in river water. Although a river carries a relatively constant amount of dissolved minerals through the year, the rate of transport of solid minerals and soil is highly variable, reaching its highest levels during flooding. Most solid minerals transported by a river are deposited in the river bed or flood plain. As a result, solid transport rates are highest in the upper basin.

Some of the rates shown reflect the impact of human activities. *Human impact on transport in basin* is a qualitative assessment, made by Meybeck, of the extent to which human activities in the drainage basin have

affected the amount of dissolved and solid material carried by the river water. Human activities, such as industrialization, deforestation, and agriculture generally increase solid material transport. Dam construction decreases solid material transport. The affect of pollution on the total concentration of dissolved minerals is usually within the margin of error of measurement. However, the addition of salts, such as sodium chloride and calcium sulfate, may significantly increase the total dissolved material.

Table 21.4 Selected Large Lakes, 1980s

Sources: Lake Biwa Research Institute, *Data Book of World Lakes* (National Institute for Research Advancement, Tokyo, 1984) and unpublished data (Lake Biwa Research Institute, Otsu, Japan, May 1988. Surface area, volume, and drainage basin area: Charles E. Herdendorf, *Inventory of the Morphometric and Limnologic Characteristics of the Large Lakes of the World* (Ohio Sea Grant Program, Ohio State University, Columbus, Ohio, March 1984). North American Great Lakes: Michigan Sea Grant College Program, *Extension Bulletins E-1866-70* (Cooperative Extension Service, Michigan State University, East Lansing, Michigan, 1985). Lake Constance: R. Vollenweider, Canada Centre for Inland Waters, Burlington, Ontario, Canada, June 1988 (personal communication).

The lakes shown in this table are natural lakes, defined as essentially static bodies of water. They were selected for their size (surface area), the area of their drainage basin, and the population inhabiting the drainage basin. Data on these criteria were not available for all lakes. With the exception of the lakes of Africa's Rift Valley, the Southern Hemisphere has few large lakes; most of the lakes included in the table lie in the Northern Hemisphere.

The *surface area* of a lake includes any islands. Measurements of surface area vary among sources because the area may fluctuate depending on climatic conditions. *Volume* data can also be imprecise, due to changing climate conditions and a lack of detailed information on the depth of a lake.

The *area of drainage basin* excludes the surface area of the lake. The percentage of *land use* attributed to forest, farm, and settlement may not total 100, as other uses (accounting for a small percentage of land use) are not included. "Settlement" includes industrial, commercial, and residential land use. *Population* in the basin may be the total of the populations of large cities lying within the drainage basin, or the population within the political boundaries that most closely correspond to the actual drainage basin.

Reported *annual fish catch* data refer to the estimated fish catch in the year listed.

The figures for *total nitrogen* and *total phosphorous* are annual mean concentrations, measured at the surface of the lake. Total nitrogen includes ammonia and nitrates. Total phosphorous includes phosphates.

22. Oceans and Coasts

Although fish are the best known marine resource, the seas have many other uses. Some of them, such as the use of marine waters for transport, have been exploited for centuries. Others, such as the mining of marine minerals, are relatively new. This chapter presents information on a variety of marine resources, including fisheries, offshore oil and gas production, and the use of oceans as a receptacle for wastes.

Table 22.1 shows countries' primary coastal resources: coastlines, maritime claims, fish catch, and offshore production of oil and gas. Offshore oil accounted for nearly a quarter of global oil production in 1986, up from 20 percent in 1970. While offshore gas production is still a very small part of the global total, it has grown rapidly in recent years, more than doubling since 1970. Oil and gas are often found in the sedimentary deposits that make up the biologically rich continental margin, leading to concerns that offshore drilling could cause serious environmental damage.

Table 22.2 shows fish catches by region and species groups. Ocean pelagic species, such as herrings, sardines, and mackerels, make up the largest portion—about one fourth—of the global catch. The estimated sustainable yield figures shown are based on current scientific research and models, and refer to the maximum catch that can be sustained under average environmental conditions. Yet catches for four regions have been within or above the range of sustainable yield estimates for the past decade, suggesting that either these estimates are low, or that overfishing in these regions will soon have deleterious effects. (See Chapter 9, "Oceans and Coasts," for a discussion of global fishery trends.)

This chapter does not show data on the ambient levels of pollutants in the marine environment. Marine pollutants are difficult to measure because a single pollutant may reside in ocean sediments, biota, or the water column, and many pollutants' fates are unknown. Several countries and regional seas programs monitor pollutants in their coastal waters, but the methods and scopes of these programs vary, and their results are often not comparable. Estimates of the amount of pollutants put into the seas are also sketchy for many areas. Although land-based sources contribute most of the pollutants entering the marine environment, few countries have prepared reliable estimates of their volume or impacts.

Many countries consider dumping wastes at sea an attractive alternative to land-based disposal methods, which are often expensive and politically unpopular. (See Table 22.3.) Some data on ocean dumping are available because many countries have joined regional and global agreements requiring governments to regulate and report their dumping. One such agreement, the London Dumping Convention (LDC) was adopted in 1972 and had nearly 60 member countries worldwide by 1988. However, developing country members rarely report dumping data, and data on the pollutant content of wastes are often poor. As a result, LDC members decided in 1986 to discontinue annual reports on the amounts of wastes dumped. (Country memberships in the LDC and regional seas conventions are shown in Table 24.1.)

Disposing of hazardous wastes at sea by incineration or dumping has caused much debate. (Incineration data are shown in Table 22.3; however, radioactive wastes are not included, since the LDC prohibits dumping of high-level wastes and low-level wastes are no longer dumped.) In 1983, LDC members suspended dumping of all low-level radioactive wastes until a scientific review of the risks is complete. From 1965 to 1983, nearly 100,000 trillion becquerels of radioactive waste were dumped at sea, nearly a third of it by the United Kingdom.

Incinerating chemical wastes at sea is a controversial disposal method that was used by only five countries in 1984. Between 1981 and 1984, Belgium burned nearly half the 624,000 metric tons incinerated, and the Federal Republic of Germany burned another third. In 1987, eight North Sea countries agreed to phase out the use of ocean incineration in the North Sea by 1994 and to reduce waste incineration by at least 65 percent by the end of 1990. In 1988, the United States suspended testing of incineration technologies at sea.

The number of oil spills and the amount of oil lost have declined substantially over the past decade. (See Table 22.4.) According to the International Maritime Organization, improved safety and tank washing procedures have reduced annual oil pollution from spills and ship operations by 8–10 million metric tons since 1980.

In late 1989, an interagency United Nations group will complete its second global assessment of the health of the oceans. This study will be based on diverse marine pollution monitoring programs and on dumping and other emissions data.

Table 22.1 Coastal Areas and Resources, 1970–88

	Length of Marine Coastline (kilometers)	Maritime Zones 1988 (nautical miles unless otherwise indicated) Territorial Sea	Exclusive Economic Zone	Continental Shelf	Average Annual Marine Catch[a] 1983–85 (thousand metric tons)	Percentage Change Over 1974–76	Offshore Production Oil (thousand barrels per day) 1970	1980	1986	Natural Gas (thousand cubic meters per day) 1970	1980	1986
WORLD					72,173	20	7,532	13,687	13,479	401,826	788,374	958,119
AFRICA					2,659	–13						
Algeria	998	12	X	X	66	81						
Angola	1,600	20	X	X	78	–62	96	97	186	2,227		7,675
Benin	121	200	X	X	4	–38						
Cameroon	402	50	X	X	32	–14			125			
Cape Verde	965	12	200	X	11	248						
Comoros	340	12	200	X	5	38						85
Congo	169	200	X	X	20	22		27	115			
Cote d'Ivoire	515	12	200	200	67	–2		6	19			
Djibouti	314	12	200	X	0	32						
Egypt	2,450	12	X	200m/EXP	26	–5	257	390	590		1,638	3,115
Equatorial Guinea	296	12	200	X	3	–24						
Ethiopia	1,094	12	X	X	1	–76						
Gabon	885	12	200	X	49	838	29	178	105			
Gambia	80	12	X	X	9	–13						
Ghana	539	12	200	200	212	8		2			227	
Guinea	320	12	200	X	26	143						
Guinea-Bissau	350	12	200	X	3	30						
Kenya	536	12	200	200m/EXP	6	60						
Liberia	579	200	X	X	10	61						
Libya	1,770	12	X	X	8	82						
Madagascar	4,828	12	200	200m[b]	13	–22						
Mauritania	754	70	200	200/CM	44	97						
Mauritius	177	12	200	200/CM	11	55						
Morocco	1,835	12	200	X	463	75						
Mozambique	2,470	12	200	X	34	39						
Namibia	1,489	6	X	X	211	–71						
Nigeria	853	30	200	200m/EXP	214	–10	275	579	290		14,160	13,452
Reunion	201	12	200	200m/EXP	3	3						
Senegal	531	12	200	200/CM	235	–30						
Seychelles	491	12	200	200/CM	4	11						
Sierra Leone	402	200	X	200m/EXP	36	–42						
Somalia	3,025	200	X	X	16	92						
South Africa	2,881	12	X	200m/EXP	607	2						
Sudan	853	12	X	200m/EXP	2	165						
Tanzania, United Rep	1,424	50	X	X	38	–10						
Togo	56	30	200	X	14	47						
Tunisia	1,148	12	X	X	77	71		44	6			
Zaire	37	12	X	X	1	–91		22	17			
NORTH & CENTRAL AMERICA					7,467	59						
Antigua and Barbuda	153	12	200	X	2	37						
Bahamas	3,542	3	X	200m/EXP	6	115						
Barbados	97	12	200	X	5	34						
Belize	386	3	X	X	1	–12						
Bermuda	103	3	X	200m/EXP	0	–87						
Canada	58,808[c]	12	X	200m/EXP	1,307	33						
Cayman Islands	160	3	X	X	1	NM						
Costa Rica	1,290	12	200	200m/EXP	12	–13						
Cuba	3,735	12	200	X	190	15						
Dominica	148	12	200	X	1	–33						
Dominican Rep	1,288	6	200	200/CM	13	118						
El Salvador	307	200	X	X	9	26						
Greenland	44,087	3	X	200m/EXP	114	139						
Grenada	121	12	200	X	1	–14						
Guadelupe	306	12	200	200m/EXP	9	32						
Guatemala	400	12	200	200m/EXP	3	–24						
Haiti	1,771	12	200	200m/EXP	4	10						
Honduras	820	12	200	200m/EXP	9	114						
Jamaica	1,022	12	X	200m/EXP	9	–11						
Martinique	290	12	200	200m/EXP	5	43						
Mexico	9,330	12	200	200m/EXP	1,021	133	35	500	1,700		708	26,904
Nicaragua	910	200	X	X	4	–55						
Panama	2,490	200	X	X	197	51						
Trinidad and Tobago	362	12	X	200m/EXP	4	–15	76	167	128	310	11,894	18
United States	19,924	3	200	200m/EXP	4,538	60	1,577	1,038	1,257	243,319	416,397	337,489
SOUTH AMERICA					9,627	52						
Argentina	4,989	200	X	200m/EXP	370	54						
Brazil	7,491	200	X	X	718	31	8	73	376		2,832	6,089
Chile	6,435	12	200	200/350	4,427	290			11			
Colombia	3,208	12	200	200m/EXP	20	–19					1,833	3,597
Ecuador	2,237	200	X	200m[b]	684	194						
French Guiana	378	12	200	200m/EXP	3	140						
Guyana	459	12	X	200/CM	33	54						
Peru	2,414	200	X	200	3,001	–24		30	117	1,831		
Suriname	386	12	200	X	4	–40						
Uruguay	660	200	X	200m/EXP	139	454						
Venezuela	2,800	12	200	200m/EXP	229	63	2,460	1,096	900			42,763

Table 22.1

	Length of Marine Coastline (kilometers)	Maritime Zones 1988 (nautical miles unless otherwise indicated) Territorial Sea	Exclusive Economic Zone	Continental Shelf	Average Annual Marine Catch[a] 1983–85 (thousand metric tons)	Percentage Change Over 1974–76	Offshore Production Oil (thousand barrels per day) 1970	1980	1986	Natural Gas (thousand cubic meters per day) 1970	1980	1986
ASIA					29,257	26						
Bahrain	161	3	X	X	6	157						
Bangladesh	580	12	200	CM	169	78						
Brunei	161	12	X	X	3	73		192	99		27,890	23,081
Burma	3,060	12	200	200/CM	469	37						
China	14,500	12	X	X	3,628	14		2	1			
Cyprus	648	12	X	200m/EXP	2	107						
Hong Kong	733	3	X	200m/EXP	189	30						
India	7,000	12	200	200/CM	1,673	16		142	621		76	6,814
Indonesia	54,716	12	200	X	1,732	73		533	392		12,461	18,795
Iran	3,180	12	X	X	54	–13	322	150	505	99,120		
Iraq	58	12	X	X	6	–38						
Israel	273	6	X	200m/EXP	9	–10						
Japan	13,685	12	X	X	11,367	16	3	2	1		1,351	1,558
Jordan	26	3	X	X	0	–71						
Kampuchea, Dem	443	12	200	200m/EXP	6	–49						
Korea, Dem People's Rep	2,495	12	200	X	1,550	55						
Korea, Rep	2,413	12	X	X	2,459	30						
Kuwait	499	12	X	X	5	–2						
Lebanon	225	12	X	X	1	–46						
Macau	40	6	X	X	11	7						
Malaysia	4,675	12	200	200m/EXP	670	33	146	280	21			
Maldives	644	12	X	X	43	33						
Oman	2,092	12	200	X	105	–45						
Pakistan	1,046	12	200	200/CM	306	81						994
Philippines	36,289	X	200	EXP	1,330	14		4	8			
Qatar	563	3	X	X	3	21	172	248	158	3,034		
Saudi Arabia	2,510	12	X	X	40	71	1,251	2,958	1,107	14,013		
Singapore	193	3	X	X	22	31						
Sri Lanka	1,340	12	200	200/CM	155	37						
Syrian Arab Rep	193	35	X	X	1	13						
Thailand	3,219	12	200	200m/EXP	2,012	42			16			9,683
Turkey	7,200	6/12	X	X	524	347						
United Arab Emirates	1,448	3/12	X	X	73	9	339	1,667	615		17,757	8,921
Viet Nam	3,444	12	200	200/CM	540	35						
Yemen	523	12	X	X	17	18						
Yemen, Dem	1,383	12	200	200/CM	81	74						
EUROPE					12,289	–2						
Albania	362	15	X	200m/EXP	4	0						
Belgium	64	12	X	X	47	1						
Bulgaria	354	12	200	200m/EXP	99	–30						
Denmark	3,379	3	X	200m/EXP	1,778	–3		7	55			13,084
Faeroe Islands	764	3	200	200m/EXP	346	19						
Finland	1,126	4	X	200m/EXP	126	40						
France	3,427c	12	200	200m/EXP	791	1						
German Dem Rep	901	12	X	200m/EXP	200	–38						
Germany, Fed Rep	1,488	3	X	200m/EXP	262	–43						
Greece	13,676	6	X	200m/EXP	93	4			27			142
Iceland	4,988	12	200	200/CM	1,351	39						
Ireland	1,448	3	X	X	205	126					3,540	6,514
Italy	4,996	12	X	200m/EXP	452	14	12	6	9		623	11,756
Malta	140	12	X	200m/EXP	2	3						
Netherlands	451	12	X	200m/EXP	477	51			21		33,134	41,914
Norway	3,419	4	200	200m/EXP	2,469	–12		629	781		68,704	85,272
Poland	491	12	X	200m/EXP	681	–5						
Portugal	860c	12	200	200m/EXP	277	–28						
Romania	225	12	200	200m/EXP	182	115						
Spain	4,964	12	200	200m/EXP	1,305	–12		31	36			736
Sweden	3,218	12	X	200m/EXP	256	25						
United Kingdom	12,429	12	X	200m/EXP	835	–19		1,650	2,237	30,764	102,235	158,592
Yugoslavia	1,521	12	X	200m/EXP	50	55						
USSR	60,085c	12	200	200m/EXP	9,430	5	258	200	165		34,692	36,816
OCEANIA					566	102						
Australia	25,760	3	X	200m/EXP	164	40	216	323	384	1,715	10,988	41,024
Cook Islands	120	12	200	200/CM	1	–17						
French Polynesia	2,525	12	200	200m/EXP	2	–13						
Fiji	1,129	12	200	200m/EXP	26	423						
Kiribati	1,143	12	200	X	27	63						
New Caledonia	2,254	12	200	200m/EXP	3	246						
New Zealand	15,134	12	200	200/CM	286	324		3	14		2,380	10,450
Niue	64	12	200	X	0	NM						
Papua New Guinea	5,152	12	X	200m/EXP	5	–90						
Solomon Islands	5,313	12	200	X	47	125						
Tonga	419	12	200	200m/EXP	2	126						
Tuvalu	24	12	200	X	1	NM						
Vanuatu	2,528	12	200	200/CM	3	6						

Sources: U.S. Department of State; U.N. Office for Ocean Affairs and the Law of the Sea; U.N. Food and Agriculture Organization; and *Offshore Magazine.*

Notes:
a. Marine catch includes marine fishes, molluscs, crustaceans, and miscellaneous aquatic animals. Marine mammals and plants are excluded. b. 200 nautical miles or 100 n.m. from the 2,500-meter isobath. c. Coastline figures for Canada, Portugal, and the USSR exclude islands and overseas territories. France includes Corsica.
0 = zero or less than half the unit of measure; X = no claim made or information not available; NM = not meaningful;
m = meters of water (depth); f = fathom (1.83 meters); CM = edge of continental margin; EXP = limits of exploitable resources;
blank = zero or insignificant. For additional information, see Sources and Technical Notes.

Table 22.2 Marine Fishery Production by Species Group, 1973–85

	Average Annual Catch[a] (thousand metric tons)		Share of Catch (percent)		Change in Catch 1983–85 over 1973–75 (percent)	Estimated Sustainable Yield[b] (thousand metric tons per year)
	1973–75	1983–85	1973–75	1983–85		
ALL MARINE FISHERIES	**58,814**	**72,173**			**23**	**62,250-95,950**
Atlantic, Northwest						
Total catch	4,084	2,771	100	100	–32	3,400-4,300
Cods, hakes, haddocks	1,221	895	30	32	–27	
Herrings, sardines, anchovies	719	507	18	18	–30	
Clams, cockles, arkshells	255	383	6	14	50	
All others	1,890	987	46	36	–48	
Atlantic, Northeast						
Total catch	11,751	11,120	100	100	–5	10,100-12,300
Cods, hakes, haddocks	4,387	3,591	37	32	–18	
Jacks, mullets, sauries	2,088	2,609	18	23	25	
Herrings, sardines, anchovies	2,142	1,592	18	14	–26	
Redfishes, basses, congers	873	1,141	7	10	31	
All others	2,261	2,187	19	20	–3	
Atlantic, Western Central						
Total catch	1,496	2,384	100	100	59	3,200-5,100
Herrings, sardines, anchovies	666	1,038	45	44	56	
Oysters	151	231	10	10	52	
Shrimp, prawns	154	175	10	7	13	
Redfishes, basses, congers	206	116	14	5	–44	
All others	319	824	21	35	159	
Atlantic, Eastern Central						
Total catch	3,425	2,869	100	100	–16	2,900-3,700
Herrings, sardines, anchovies	1,179	970	34	34	–18	
Jacks, mullets, sauries	655	406	19	14	–38	
Redfishes, basses, congers	355	337	10	12	–5	
Tunas, bonitos, billfishes	265	278	8	10	5	
All others	971	879	28	31	–10	
Mediterranean and Black Seas						
Total catch	1,268	1,903	100	100	50	1,090-1,410
Herrings, sardines, anchovies	621	920	49	48	48	
Jacks, mullets, sauries	81	203	6	11	151	
All others	567	780	45	41	38	
Atlantic, Southwest						
Total catch	985	1,645	100	100	67	2,600-3,900
Cods, hakes, haddocks	177	517	18	31	193	
Herrings, sardines, anchovies	211	284	21	17	34	
Redfishes, basses, congers	197	255	20	16	30	
Squids, cuttlefishes, octopuses	5	242	1	15	4,389	
All others	394	346	40	21	–12	
Atlantic, Southeast						
Total catch	2,871	2,175	100	100	–24	2,500-3,100
Herrings, sardines, anchovies	1,254	667	44	31	–47	
Jacks, mullets, sauries	439	675	15	31	54	
Cods, hakes, haddocks	766	497	27	23	–35	
All others	412	336	14	15	–18	
Indian Ocean, Western						
Total catch	2,094	2,416	100	100	15	2,700-4,200
Redfishes, basses, congers	395	481	19	20	22	
Herrings, sardines, anchovies	425	450	20	19	6	
Tunas, bonitos, billfishes	194	308	9	13	59	
Jacks, mullets, sauries	92	251	4	10	172	
Shrimps, prawns	248	213	12	9	–14	
All others	741	713	35	30	–4	
Indian Ocean, Eastern						
Total catch	1,008	1,799	100	100	79	1,500-2,200
Redfishes, basses, congers	125	172	12	10	38	
Herrings, sardines, anchovies	103	172	10	10	66	
All others	779	1,455	77	81	87	

Table 22.2

	Average Annual Catch[a] (thousand metric tons)		Share of Catch (percent)		Change in Catch 1983–85 over 1973–75 (percent)	Estimated Sustainable Yield[b] (thousand metric tons per year)
	1973–75	1983–85	1973–75	1983–85		
Pacific, Northwest						
Total catch	16,734	22,925	100	100	37	13,500-16,500
Herrings, sardines, anchovies	1,337	5,466	8	24	309	
Cods, hakes, haddocks	3,996	4,613	24	20	15	
Mackerels, snoeks, cutlassfishes	1,747	1,911	10	8	9	
All others	9,654	10,935	58	48	13	
Pacific, Northeast						
Total catch	2,153	2,661	100	100	24	2,600-3,200
Cods, hakes, haddocks	1,238	1,563	58	59	26	
Salmons, trouts, smelts	155	388	7	15	150	
Flounders, halibuts, soles	196	292	9	11	49	
Redfishes, basses, congers	217	143	10	5	-34	
All others	346	275	16	10	-21	
Pacific, Western Central						
Total catch	5,119	6,379	100	100	25	5,800-7,800
Tunas, bonitos, billfishes	458	1,090	9	17	138	
Jacks, mullets, sauries	725	753	14	12	4	
Herrings, sardines, anchovies	357	759	7	12	113	
Redfishes, basses, congers	538	607	11	10	13	
All others	3,041	3,170	59	50	4	
Pacific, Eastern Central						
Total catch	1,224	2,075	100	100	69	2,200-3,000
Herrings, sardines, anchovies	439	1,082	36	52	147	
Tunas, bonitos, billfishes	363	402	30	19	11	
Mackerels, snoeks, cutlassfishes	1	208	0	10	23,999	
All others	422	383	34	18	-9	
Pacific, Southwest						
Total catch	328	567	100	100	73	1,200-2,000
Redfishes, basses, congers	53	169	16	30	221	
Squids, cuttlefishes, octopuses	20	113	6	20	466	
Cods, hakes, haddocks	57	78	17	14	38	
Jacks, mullets, sauries	33	53	10	9	60	
Tunas, bonitos, billfishes	74	25	22	4	-67	
All others	92	129	28	23	41	
Pacific, Southeast						
Total catch	4,273	8,167	100	100	91	3,700-10,300
Herrings, sardines, anchovies	3,381	5,497	79	67	63	
Jacks, mullets, sauries	287	2,062	7	25	620	
All others	605	607	14	7	0	
Antarctic						
Total catch	1	317	100	100	55,116	X
Krill, planktonic crustaceans	1	183	100	58	31,706	
Redfishes, basses, congers	0	120	0	38	NM	
All others	0	14	0	4	NM	
Arctic						
Total catch	0	0			NM	X

Source: United Nations Food and Agriculture Organization.
Notes:
a. Catch includes all fish, crustaceans, and molluscs harvested in marine fishing areas.
b. Estimated sustainable yield refers to marine fish, crustaceans and cephalopods. It excludes ocean pelagic species (about 3-5 percent of total potential) and molluscs. Figures may not add due to rounding.
0 = zero or less than half the unit of measure; X = not available; NM = not meaningful.
For additional information, see Sources and Technical Notes.

Table 22.3 Ocean Dumping, 1976–85

| | Total Amount Dumped at Sea (thousand metric tons) | | | | | | Total Amount of Chemical Wastes Incinerated at Sea (metric tons) | |
| | Sewage Sludge | | Industrial Waste | | Dredged Materials | | | |
	1976–80	1981–85	1976–80	1981–85	1976–80	1981–85	1976–80	1981–84
NORTH AMERICA								
Canada	0	137[a,b]	130[c]	140[d]	83,020	63,140	0	0
United States	26,936	42,748[e]	11,458	4,034[e]	297,220	296,380	15,967[f]	5,678[a,g]
ASIA								
Hong Kong	1.4[f]	X	X	4,490[c,h]	34,891[c,i]	7,610[c,h]	X	X
Japan	X	X	X	X	X	X	X	2,045
EUROPE								
Austria	X	X	X	X	X	X	318	809
Belgium	0	0	2,103	3,143	153,384	218,500	12,951[j]	294,957
Denmark	0	0	55	10[k]	1,456[c]	2,858	0[c]	0
Finland	0	0	0[j]	0[k]	0[c]	0	2,500	2,750
France	0	0	12,559	9,508	25,669[c,l]	80,925	4,168[j]	30,561
Germany, Fed Rep	1,296	37[k]	4,594	6,945	27,380[m]	10,232	88,000[j]	200,104
Iceland	0	0	0[j]	0[k]	X	X	X	X
Ireland	537	724	3,931	3,090	1,962[n]	1,930	0[j]	40[k]
Italy	X	X	0	1,000	0	1,800	42	6,231
Netherlands	0	0	5,825	39	106,213	140,771	32,678[c,o]	29,511[k]
Norway	0	0	10	0	0	0	10,035	19,672
Portugal	0	0	0[c]	0[k]	5,038[c]	12,550	0[c]	0
Spain	X	X	2,332[c]	2,645	X	X	X	602[k]
Sweden	0	0	0[c]	0[k]	60[c,m]	0[k]	7,903[c]	14,563[k]
Switzerland	X	X	X	X	X	X	1,873[j]	10,067[k]
United Kingdom	40,645	38,907	12,907	9,904	66,348	54,099	0[j]	6,168
OCEANIA								
Australia	X	X	857[p]	X	X	X	X	X
New Zealand	X	X	X	X	17,046[c]	1,213[c,i]	X	X

Sources: Oslo Commission; International Maritime Organization; U.S. Environmental Protection Agency; and Environment Canada.
Notes:
a. Amount given in thousand liters. b. 1985 only. c. Based fully or partially on amounts licensed for dumping. d. 1981 only. e. Includes 1981-86.
f. 1977 only. g. 1981-82 only. h. 1983 only. i. 1977-80 only. j. 1980 only. k. 1981-83 only. l. 1978-80 only. m. 1976-77 and 1980 only. n. 1976-78 and 1980 only.
o. 1976, 1979 and 1980 only. p. 1977-78 only.
0 = zero or less than half the unit of measure; X = not available.
For additional information, see Sources and Technical Notes.

Table 22.4 Accidental Oil Spills, 1973–87

Year	Number of Tankers Afloat	Accidental Oil Spills	Accidental Spills per Thousand Tankers	Volume of Oil Lost (metric tons)
1973	3,750	36	9.6	84,458
1974	3,928	48	12.2	67,115
1975	4,140	45	10.9	188,042
1976	4,237	29	6.8	204,235
1977	4,229	49	11.6	213,080
1978	4,137	35	8.5	260,488
1979	3,945	65	16.5	723,533
1980	3,898	32	8.2	135,635
1981	3,937	33	8.4	45,285
1982	3,950	9	2.3	1,716
1983	3,582	17	4.7	387,773
1984	3,424	15	4.4	24,184
1985	3,285	9	2.7	79,830
1986	3,139	8	2.5	5,035
1987	3,132	12	3.8	8,700

Source: Tanker Advisory Center.
For additional information, see Sources and Technical Notes.

Sources and Technical Notes

Table 22.1 Coastal Areas and Resources, 1970–88

Sources: Length of marine coastline: U.S. Central Intelligence Agency, *The World Factbook 1986* and *1987* (U.S. Government Printing Office, Washington, D.C., 1986 and 1987). Sovereign and jurisdictional claims to maritime zones: United Nations Office of Ocean Affairs and the Law of the Sea, *Law of the Sea Bulletin*, No. 2 (March 1985); and United Nations (U.N.) unpublished data (U.N., New York, March 1988); U.S. Central Intelligence Agency, *The World Factbook 1987* (U.S. Government Printing Office, Washington, D.C. 1987). Fish catch: United Nations Food and Agriculture Organization (FAO), *Yearbook of Fishery Statistics 1978* and *1985* (FAO, Rome, 1980 and 1987). Offshore Oil and Gas Production: *Offshore Magazine* (PennWell Publishing Company, Tulsa, Oklahoma, June 20, 1974; July 20, 1984; and May 1987).

The United Nations Office for Ocean Affairs and the Law of the Sea compiles information concerning coastal claims from: the U.N. Legislative Series; official gazettes; communications to the Secretary General; legal journals; and other publications. National claims to maritime zones fall into five categories: territorial sea, contiguous zone, exclusive economic zone, fishery zone, and continental shelf. (Territorial sea, exclusive economic zone, and continental shelf claims are shown in Table 22.1. Only those countries with marine coastlines are included in the table.)

Relevant legislation, decrees, and treaty commitments for 137 coastal countries are excerpted in the *Law of the Sea Bulletin*. The list is revised as coastal countries seek to secure their claims to maritime resources under the Law of the Sea Convention, which is not yet in force.

Territorial sea commonly refers to an adjacent zone of water, seabed and subsoil, and airspace over which a nation claims sovereignty. The nation's right to enforce its laws and regulations is qualified only by the right of innocent passage of foreign ships. Nations may also claim certain jurisdictional rights in a contiguous zone beyond the territorial sea out to 24 nautical miles; these rights usually pertain to customs, taxation, immigration, and sanitation.

Turkey claims six nautical miles of territorial sea in the Aegean and 12 nautical miles in the Mediterranean and Black Seas. Sharja, one of the United Arab Emirates (UAE), claims a territorial sea limit of 12 nautical miles; the limit for the other members of the UAE is three miles.

An *Exclusive Economic Zone* (EEZ) may be established by a nation out to 200 nautical miles to claim all the resources within the zone, including fish and all other living resources, minerals, and energy from wind, waves, and tides. Nations may also claim rights to regulate scientific exploration, protect the marine environment, and establish marine terminals and artificial islands. The EEZ data shown do not reflect the decisions of some countries, such as those in the European Community, to share EEZs in some areas.

When countries' EEZs overlap—such as those of United States and Cuba, which both have 200-mile EEZs, yet are only 90 miles apart—a halfway point often serves as the EEZ boundary for that area.

Continental shelf claims include the exclusive right to explore for and exploit all mineral ores, energy resources, and benthic plants and animals found on or beneath the shelf. Claims extend to 200 nautical miles and beyond to the outer limit of the continental margin as defined in the 1982 Convention. Limits usually refer to the farthest distance.

International fishery data are continually revised. The *Yearbook of Fishery Statistics 1985*, the latest edition, contains FAO's most up-to-date figures.

Data are provided annually to the FAO Fisheries Department by national fishery offices and regional fishery commissions. Some countries' data are only provisional for the latest year; for other countries, no data are available. If no new data are submitted, FAO uses the previous year's figures or makes estimates based on other information.

Years refer to calendar years except for Antarctic fisheries data, which are for split years (July 1–June 30). Data for Antarctic fisheries are given for the calendar year in which the split year ends.

Catch data shown in Table 22.1 refer to marine fish killed, caught, trapped, collected, bred, or cultivated for commercial, industrial, and subsistence use. Crustaceans, molluscs, and miscellaneous aquatic animals are included. Quantities taken in recreational activities are excluded. Figures are the national totals averaged over a three-year period; they include fish caught by a country's fleet anywhere in the world.

Tables 22.1 and 22.2 present data on nominal catch, which is defined as gross removal (total live weight of fish caught or killed during fishing operations) minus precatch losses (total live weight of fish that are not caught but that die in fishing operations), minus discarded catch both live and dead (undersized, unsalable, or otherwise undesirable whole fish discarded at the time of capture or shortly afterwards), minus utilization and losses prior to landing (consumption by crew, use for bait, spoilage, handling losses), minus unrecorded, rejected, or dumped landings (such as unrecorded dumping at sea, black market landings, and unrecorded quantities landed for home consumption), minus losses from dressing, handling, and processing (dumped viscera, heads, and other parts, loss of fluids), plus gains prior to landing (gain of fluid content, addition of liquids or solids during shipboard processing).

Offshore Magazine annually queries national governments for offshore oil and gas production statistics. These data are supplemented with figures from oil and gas producing companies, expert sources, and published literature. National governments often have difficulty providing offshore gas production figures; the data are more frequently obtained from alternate sources. Figures for offshore oil and gas production in Middle Eastern countries are particularly difficult to

obtain and, as a result, are less reliable.

1970 offshore oil production data for Malaysia include Brunei. Saudi Arabia's 1970 offshore oil production includes production within the Neutral Zone, an area of disputed sovereignty that lies between Saudi Arabia and Kuwait. Profits from production in the Neutral Zone are shared by the two countries. The 1980 and 1986 Neutral Zone offshore oil and gas production data are included only in the regional and world totals.

Table 22.2 Marine Fishery Production by Species Group, 1973–85

Sources: Marine Fishery Production: United Nations Food and Agriculture Organization (FAO), *Yearbook of Fishery Statistics 1976* and *1985* (FAO, Rome, 1977 and 1987). Estimated sustainable yield: M.A. Robinson, *Trends and Prospects in World Fisheries* (FAO, Fisheries Department, Rome, 1984).

FAO divides the world's oceans into 19 marine statistical areas and organizes catch data by 840 "species items:" species groups broken down at either the family, genus, or species level. The species groups shown in Table 22.2 are FAO groupings, which include species similar to those named. For example, the group designated "herrings, sardines, and anchovies" also includes menhadens, pilchards, and bonefish. Groups shown are those that comprised 10 percent or more of the total catch in either 1973–75 or 1983–85. Years shown are three-year averages. (Refer to the Technical Note for Table 22.1 for the definition of nominal fish catch and additional information on FAO's fishery data base.)

Data on estimated sustainable yield are FAO estimates of marine fisheries' biologically realizable potential. These estimates refer to the maximum harvest that can be sustained by a fishery without depleting the resource, given average environmental conditions. An assumed level of incidental take (catching one species while fishing for another) is subtracted from estimates of potential. The figures exclude the potential harvest from culturing marine fish. Maximum sustainable yield estimates are not strictly comparable to the catch data shown because they exclude molluscs. Estimates of ocean pelagic species (about 3–5 percent of the total marine potential) are unavailable at the regional level and are also excluded.

Table 22.3 Ocean Dumping, 1976–85

Sources: United Nations Environment Programme, *Environmental Data Report* (Basil Blackwell, Oxford, 1987). Data for 1984 and 1985: Oslo Commission, *Eleventh Annual Report* and *Twelfth Annual Report* (Oslo Commission, London, 1985 and 1986). United States: (dredged materials) unpublished data (U.S. Army, Corps of Engineers Dredging Division, Washington, D.C., February 1988); (sewage sludge and industrial wastes) U.S. Environmental Protection Agency (EPA), *Report to Congress on Administration of the Marine*

Protection, Research and Sanctuaries Act of 1972 (January 1981–December 1983) and *1984–1986* (EPA, Washington, D.C., 1984 and 1988). Canada: (dredged materials) Environment Canada, *Survey of Permits Issued Under the Ocean Dumping Control Act in 1986* (Environment Canada, Ottawa, September 1987); (sewage sludge and incineration) Environment Canada, *Keeping the Ocean Clean, Ocean Dumping Control Act 1985/86 Annual Report* (Environment Canada, Ottawa, 1987). New Zealand: (dredged materials) International Maritime Organization (IMO), *Report on Permits Issued in 1983* (IMO, London, September 1986). Hong Kong: (dredged materials and industrial wastes) IMO, *Report on Permits Issued in 1983* (IMO, London, September 1986). Japan: (incineration) IMO, *Report on Permits Issued in 1983* (IMO, London, September 1986).

The IMO and the Oslo Commission secretariats record dumping permits for three types of waste: sewage sludge, industrial waste, and dredged materials. They also record permits for incineration of chemical wastes at sea. The two organizations share information, and data can be compared among countries. Five-year aggregates are shown because dumping data fluctuate from year to year and few clear trends emerge.

Sewage sludge contains much of the solid material separated from liquid effluent during the treatment of municipal wastes. It can contain both toxic pollutants, such as metals and organic chemicals, as well as nontoxic pollutants, such as fecal bacteria, viruses, and nutrients.

The content of industrial wastes varies by country and may include both solid and liquid wastes. In 1985, seven countries dumped 5.9 million metric tons of industrial wastes. Of this total, 2.5 million metric tons were solid waste, primarily fly ash, colliery wastes, and phosphogypsum wastes, and 2.4 million metric tons were liquid waste from the titanium dioxide industry. The remaining 1 million metric tons was comprised of a variety of liquid and sludge wastes.

Dredged materials include sediments from harbors, estuaries, and navigation channels that are dumped at sea. Dredged materials do not usually contain high levels of contaminants, but dredge spoils from harbors tend to contain higher levels than dredge spoils from other sources. Data for the United States and Canada were originally given in millions of cubic meters, and were converted to metric tons by multiplying by a factor of 1.4.

Chemical wastes incinerated at sea are comprised largely of organochlorines. This practice produces hydrogen chloride gas and particulate emissions (primarily metals and other inorganics originally present in the waste). The environmental effects of emissions from incineration at sea are thought to be minimal. The primary risk to the marine environment is the potential for a major accidental spill, which could be catastrophic if it occurred in an environmentally fragile area.

Ocean dumping data are reported to the Oslo Commission by 13 western European countries who are contracting parties to the Oslo Convention of 1972. The Oslo Convention applies to dumping in the Atlantic and Arctic Oceans bounded by latitude 36°N, longitude 42°W, and longitude 51°E. The Convention does not apply to the Baltic and Mediterranean Seas or internal waters, such as harbors and estuaries.

Data for Hong Kong, Japan, New Zealand, Canada, and the United States were reported to the London Dumping Convention, which has global coverage. The International Maritime Organization (IMO), a specialized agency of the United Nations, oversees implementation of the London Dumping Convention.

The LDC and the Oslo Convention ban the dumping of certain dangerous substances, except when they occur in wastes in trace quantities, because of their toxicity, persistence, or bioaccumulation. These include crude oil, mercury, cadmium, and high-level radioactive wastes. Other hazardous substances such as arsenic, lead, and copper may be dumped, but require special permits.

Because reporting to the LDC is so poor, it is not known how well countries comply with these regulations. Reporting is better under the Oslo Convention. In 1985, the Oslo Commission estimated that about 29 metric tons of cadmium and 23 metric tons of mercury were contained in wastes dumped by reporting members. For information on dumping of plastic wastes, see Chapter 9, "Oceans and Coasts." For information on marine pollution monitoring methods and programs, see G. Kullenberg, "The IOC Programme on Marine Pollution," *Marine Pollution Bulletin*, Vol. 17, No. 8 (1986).

Data for Hong Kong, Japan, and New Zealand refer to the amounts of waste specified in the dumping permits issued rather than the actual amounts of wastes dumped. (For data on generation of municipal, industrial and hazardous wastes, see Table 20.7 in Chapter 20, "Energy, Materials, and Wastes.")

Table 22.4 Accidental Oil Spills, 1973–87

Source: Tanker Advisory Center, unpublished data (Tanker Advisory Center, New York, January 1988).

The Tanker Advisory Center compiles oil spill accident data from lists of insurance claims and other known accidents maintained by Lloyd's of London and Liverpool Underwriters. Data for the number of tankers afloat are taken from *The Tanker Register*, maintained by H. Clarkson and Co., London.

For 1973–82, data refer to tankers of at least 6,000 metric tons deadweight and for 1983–87, to tankers of at least 10,000 metric tons deadweight. Vessels carrying liquefied gas are not included.

Spills refer to oil lost during accidents. The volume of oil lost during cleaning and ballasting operations is not included, but is thought to be at least as much as the amount lost during accidents.

23. Atmosphere and Climate

The changes in the Earth's atmosphere and climate caused by human activities are among the most far-reaching environmental issues people face. This chapter presents data on the concentrations and emissions of trace gases that are contributing to global warming and/or depleting the stratospheric ozone layer. It also includes information on local and regional pollutants that damage the environment and human health: acidic deposition, sulfur dioxide, and suspended particulate matter.

Atmospheric concentrations of carbon dioxide and other trace gases, such as methane, nitrous oxide, and chlorofluorocarbons (CFCs), have risen rapidly over the past century with the growth in human population and industrial activities. (See Tables 23.1 and 23.2.) These gases allow the sun's radiation to pass through to the Earth's surface, but trap heat re-emitted from the Earth in a process known as the "greenhouse effect." Some of these trace gases—particularly CFCs—also deplete stratospheric ozone, which shields the Earth from the sun's harmful ultraviolet radiation. Atmospheric concentrations of CFC-11 and CFC-12 increased approximately 85 and 90 percent respectively between 1975 and 1985. Over the past 20 years, stratospheric ozone levels have declined by 3 percent over much of the northern hemisphere, according to a recent study.

The correlation between human activities and rising concentrations of these trace gases is evident when current trace gas concentrations are compared to their levels before the Industrial Revolution. (See Figure 23.1.) Atmospheric carbon dioxide concentrations, for example, fluctuated naturally throughout the Earth's history, ranging from 190 to 280 parts per million (ppm) with changes in the Earth's climate during the past 160,000 years. After the Industrial Revolution, the level of carbon dioxide in the atmosphere began to rise rapidly; today it is 349 ppm, 25 percent higher than the highest levels before 1800. Ice core records of methane and nitrous oxide levels show that concentrations of these gases remained constant for thousands of years until about a century ago when they began to rise; concentrations of methane doubled and concentrations of nitrous oxide are 8 percent higher than their preindustrial level.

Industrial carbon dioxide emissions, primarily from burning fossil fuels, have more than doubled since 1960, and have grown by more than 3.5 percent per year for the past decade. (See Table 23.2.) Biotic carbon dioxide emissions, caused by clearing forests for agriculture, are responsible for about one fourth of all carbon dioxide

emissions, and have more than doubled since 1950. Table 23.3 provides a regional breakdown of biotic and industrial carbon dioxide emissions. In 1980, 46 percent of the world's biotic carbon dioxide emissions came from Latin America, which loses over 3 million hectares of forests each year; 25 percent came from South and Southeast Asia. The United States contributed the largest share of the world's industrial carbon dioxide emissions, followed by the USSR and Western Europe.

Acidic deposition occurs after sulfur and nitrogen oxides emitted into the atmosphere by fossil fuel combustion and industrial processes are transformed into acidic compounds. The impacts of acidic deposition depend on the quantity, timing, and acidity of precipitation and on the susceptibility of soils, vegetation, aquatic ecosystems, and synthetic materials. Acidic deposition affects both industrialized and industrializing nations, but is most severe in Western Europe and North America. It is responsible for the decline or elimination of fish populations in several Scandinavian and North American lakes and is thought to contribute to forest damage in Europe and North America. (See Chapter 18, "Forests and Rangelands," Table 18.3 for data on the extent of forest damage in Europe.)

In Europe, acidic deposition is most severe in southern Scandinavia, West Germany, Czechoslovakia, and Poland. In North America, the region around Lakes Erie and Ontario, and the mountains of the eastern United States are the most seriously affected. (See Figures 23.2 and 23.3.) Although acidic deposition has been considered an important environmental problem in Europe and North America for over a decade, monitoring systems have not been in place long enough to determine regional trends. While the level of acidity decreased at five stations in the United States between 1979 and 1985, 25 other stations showed no changes.

Urban air pollution damages human health as well as the environment. (See Tables 23.4 and 23.5.) The air of many cities has unhealthy levels of sulfur dioxide and suspended particulate matter (SPM), both of which can cause respiratory illnesses, particularly in children. Between 1982 and 1985, nearly one third of the stations that reported sulfur dioxide concentrations, and almost half of those that reported SPM concentrations, exceeded the levels considered safe by the World Health Organization (WHO). Box 10.1 in Chapter 10, "Atmosphere and Climate," discusses urban air pollution in developing countries.

Figure 23.1 Long-Term Trends in Concentrations of Greenhouse

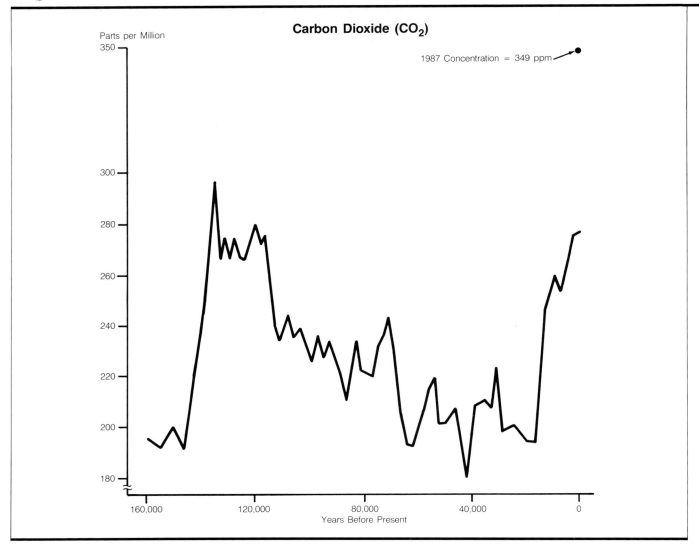

Carbon Dioxide (CO$_2$)

1987 Concentration = 349 ppm

Source: J.M. Barnola, *et al.,* "Vostok Ice Core Provides 160,000-year Record of Atmospheric CO$_2$," *Nature,* Vol. 329, p. 410.
Note: Carbon dioxide (CO$_2$) concentrations fluctuated between 190 and 280 parts per million between 160,000 years ago and 1700 A.D. From 1959 to 1987, CO$_2$ concentrations increased at an average annual rate of 1.2 percent per year.

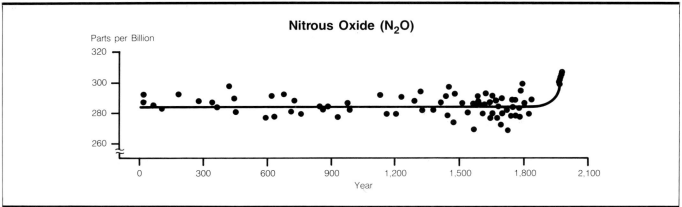

Nitrous Oxide (N$_2$O)

Source: M.A.K. Khalil and R.A. Rasmussen, "Nitrous Oxide: Trends and Global Mass Balance Over the Last 3,000 Years," *Annals of Glaciology,* Vol. 10, 1988.
Note: Nitrous oxide concentrations remained fairly constant between 3,000 years ago and 1850 A.D. at approximately 285 parts per billion. Since 1950, levels of N$_2$O have risen by 8 percent to 307 ppb.

and Ozone-Depleting Gases

Figure 23.1

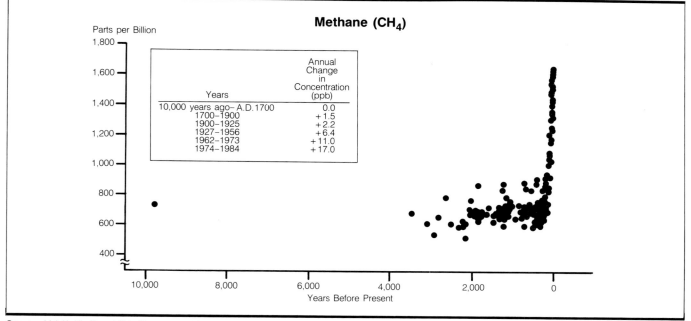

Methane (CH₄)

Years	Annual Change in Concentration (ppb)
10,000 years ago– A.D. 1700	0.0
1700–1900	+1.5
1900–1925	+2.2
1927–1956	+6.4
1962–1973	+11.0
1974–1984	+17.0

Source: M.A.K. Khalil and R.A. Rasmussen, "Atmospheric Methane: Trends Over the Last 10,000 Years," *Atmospheric Environment*, Vol. 21, No. 11.
Note: Present-day concentration = 1653 ppb.
For additional information, see Sources and Technical Notes.

Table 23.1 Atmospheric Concentrations of Greenhouse and Ozone-Depleting Gases, 1959–87

	(parts per million)	(parts per trillion)							(parts per billion)		
	CO₂	CCl₄	CH₃CCl₃	CCl₃F (CFC-11)	CCl₂F₂ (CFC-12)	CHClF₂ (CFC-22)	C₂Cl₃F₃ (CFC-113)	Total Gaseous Chlorine	N₂O	CH₄	CO
1959	316.1	X	X	X	X	X	X	X	X	X	X
1960	317.0	X	X	X	X	X	X	X	X	X	X
1961	317.7	X	X	X	X	X	X	X	X	X	X
1962	318.6	X	X	X	X	X	X	X	X	X	X
1963	319.1	X	X	X	X	X	X	X	X	X	X
1964	X	X	X	X	X	X	X	X	X	X	X
1965	320.4	X	X	X	X	X	X	X	X	X	X
1966	321.1	X	X	X	X	X	X	X	X	X	X
1967	321.9	X	X	X	X	X	X	X	X	X	X
1968	322.7	X	X	X	X	X	X	X	X	X	X
1969	324.2	X	X	X	X	X	X	X	X	X	X
1970	325.5	X	X	X	X	X	X	X	X	X	X
1971	326.5	X	X	X	X	X	X	X	X	X	X
1972	327.6	X	X	X	X	X	X	X	X	X	X
1973	329.8	X	X	X	X	X	X	X	X	X	X
1974	330.4	X	X	X	X	X	X	X	X	X	X
1975	331.0	104	70	120	200	X	X	1,202	291.4	X	X
1976	332.1	106	78	133	217	X	X	1,290	293.3	X	X
1977	333.6	115	86	148	239	X	X	1,416	294.6	X	X
1978	335.2	123	94	159	266	X	X	1,544	296.4	X	X
1979	336.5	116	112	167	283	46	X	1,621	296.3	1,536	X
1980	338.4	121	126	179	307	52	X	1,755	297.6	1,556	X
1981	339.5	122	127	185	315	59	X	1,797	298.5	1,568	72
1982	340.8	121	133	193	330	64	X	1,863	301.0	1,589	72
1983	342.8	126	144	205	350	71	24	1,983	300.9	1,613	70
1984	344.3	130	150	213	366	76	27	2,072	300.4	1,627	73
1985	345.7	130	158	223	384	85	31	2,163	301.5	1,641	75
1986	346.8	X	X	X	X	X	35	X	X	1,653	75
1987	348.6	X	X	X	X	X	X	X	X	X	X

Sources: Scripps Institution of Oceanography; and Oregon Graduate Center.
X = not available.
For additional information, see Sources and Technical Notes.

Table 23.2 Annual Emissions of Greenhouse and Ozone-Depleting Gases, 1925–86

Year	CFC-11 (CCl₃F)	CFC-12 (CCl₂F₂)	Biotic Sources	Fossil Fuel Combustion and Industrial Processes	Year	CFC-11 (CCl₃F)	CFC-12 (CCl₂F₂)	Biotic Sources	Fossil Fuel Combustion and Industrial Processes
1925	0.0	0.0	737	X	1956	28.7	56.1	1,086	2,185
1926	0.0	0.0	746	X	1957	32.2	63.8	1,157	2,278
1927	0.0	0.0	755	X	1958	30.2	66.9	1,222	2,339
1928	0.0	0.0	765	X	1959	30.9	74.8	1,286	2,470
1929	0.0	0.0	774	X	1960	40.5	89.1	1,349	2,586
1930	0.0	0.0	780	X	1961	52.1	99.7	1,408	2,602
1931	0.0	0.1	784	X	1962	65.4	114.5	1,458	2,709
1932	0.0	0.1	789	X	1963	80.0	133.9	1,503	2,855
1933	0.0	0.1	793	X	1964	95.0	155.5	1,545	3,016
1934	0.0	0.2	796	X	1965	108.3	175.4	1,576	3,154
1935	0.0	0.3	797	X	1966	121.3	195.0	1,604	3,313
1936	0.0	0.5	796	X	1967	137.6	219.9	1,624	3,420
1937	0.0	0.8	792	X	1968	156.8	246.5	1,649	3,595
1938	0.1	1.2	788	X	1969	181.9	274.3	1,675	3,808
1939	0.1	1.7	784	X	1970	206.6	299.9	1,700	4,116
1940	0.1	2.3	782	X	1971	226.9	321.8	1,714	4,267
1941	0.1	3.0	778	X	1972	255.8	349.9	1,718	4,435
1942	0.1	3.7	772	X	1973	292.4	387.3	1,714	4,678
1943	0.2	4.5	767	X	1974	321.4	418.6	1,707	4,684
1944	0.2	6.1	764	X	1975	310.9	404.1	1,695	4,660
1945	0.3	8.0	763	X	1976	316.7	390.4	1,688	4,924
1946	0.6	13.9	765	X	1977	303.9	371.2	1,687	5,065
1947	1.3	21.3	769	X	1978	283.6	341.3	1,690	5,108
1948	2.3	24.8	776	X	1979	263.7	337.5	1,691	5,345
1949	3.8	26.6	785	X	1980	250.8	332.5	1,691	5,255
1950	5.5	29.5	796	1,639	1981	248.2	340.7	X	5,115
1951	7.6	32.4	818	1,776	1982	239.5	337.4	X	5,079
1952	11.0	33.7	857	1,803	1983	252.8	343.3	X	5,068
1953	15.0	37.9	904	1,848	1984	271.1	359.4	X	5,236
1954	18.6	42.9	955	1,872	1985	280.8	368.4	X	5,336
1955	23.0	48.2	1,018	2,050	1986	295.1	376.5	X	5,548[a]

CFC columns in thousand metric tons; Carbon Dioxide columns (Biotic Sources, Fossil Fuel Combustion and Industrial Processes) in million metric tons of carbon.

Sources: Chemical Manufacturers Association; Woods Hole Research Center; and University of New Orleans.
Note: a. preliminary.
0 = zero or less than half the unit of measure; X = not available.
For additional information, see Sources and Technical Notes.

Table 23.3 Carbon Dioxide Emissions by Country and Region, 1950–85

	1950 Biotic Total (million metric tons)	1950 Biotic Percentage of World Total	1950 Industrial Total (million metric tons)	1950 Industrial Percentage of World Total	1965 Biotic Total (million metric tons)	1965 Biotic Percentage of World Total	1965 Industrial Total (million metric tons)	1965 Industrial Percentage of World Total	Biotic 1980 Total (million metric tons)	Biotic 1980 Percentage of World Total	Industrial 1985 Total (million metric tons)	Industrial 1985 Percentage of World Total
WORLD	796	100	1,553	100	1,576	100	2,929	100	1,691	100	5,102	100
North America	111	14	723	47	36	2	1,003	34	19	1	1,293	25
United States	X	X	679	44	X	X	935	32	X	X	1,186	23
Canada	X	X	44	3	X	X	68	2	X	X	107	2
Western Europe	35	4	377	24	14	1	643	22	-12	-1	779	15
United Kingdom	X	X	136	9	X	X	169	6	X	X	148	3
France	X	X	55	4	X	X	94	3	X	X	107	2
Germany, Fed Rep	X	X	93	6	X	X	172	6	X	X	182	4
Italy	X	X	11	1	X	X	49	2	X	X	92	2
Other	X	X	81	5	X	X	157	5	X	X	251	5
Eastern Europe	X	X	291	19	X	X	748	26	X	X	1,346	26
USSR	48	6	185	12	200	13	509	17	78	5	958	19
Poland	X	X	30	2	X	X	66	2	X	X	120	2
German Dem Rep	X	X	43	3	X	X	82	3	X	X	89	2
Other	X	X	33	2	X	X	92	3	X	X	178	3
Pacific	35	4	45	3	81	5	138	5	43	3	314	6
Japan	X	X	27	2	X	X	101	3	X	X	244	5
Other	X	X	18	1	X	X	37	1	X	X	70	1
Centrally Planned Asia	X	X	22	1	X	X	146	5	X	X	552	11
China	60	7	21	1	91	6	131	5	83	5	508	10
Other	X	X	X	X	X	X	16	1	X	X	44	1
Developing World	X	X	95	6	X	X	251	9	X	X	818	16
Latin America	191	24	36	2	548	35	87	3	775	46	285	6
Africa	81	10	26	2	220	14	55	2	277	16	144	3
Middle East	27	3	4	0	11	1	29	1	7	0	223	4
South & Southeast Asia	210	26	27	2	375	24	79	3	421	25	166	3

Sources: University of New Orleans and Woods Hole Research Center.
Note: Percentages may not add to 100 due to rounding.
0 = zero or less than half of 1 percent; X = not available.
For additional information, see Sources and Technical Notes.

Figure 23.2 Acidity of European Precipitation, 1985

(pH units)

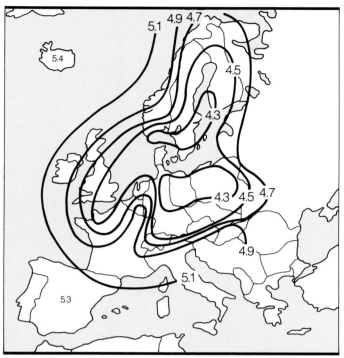

Source: Co-operative Program for Monitoring and Evaluation of the Long-Range Transmission of Air Pollutants in Europe.
For additional information, see Sources and Technical Notes.

Figure 23.3 Acidity of North American Precipitation, 1985

(pH units)

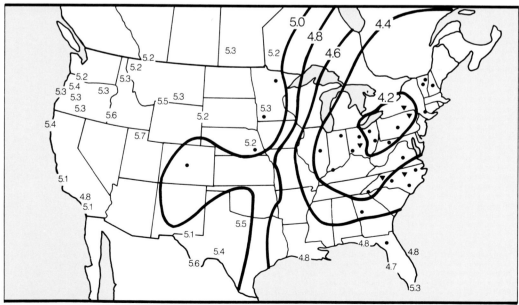

Source: Pacific Northwest Laboratory.
Note: ● = station showing no trend in acidity, 1979–84; ▼ = station showing decreasing acidity, 1979–84.
For additional information, see Sources and Technical Notes.

Table 23.4 Sulfur Dioxide Concentrations in Urban Areas, 1973–85

		Site Type[a]	Average Number of Monitoring Days per Year				Mean of Daily Values (micrograms per cubic meter)				Peak Levels (98th Percentile of Daily Values) (micrograms per cubic meter)			
			1973–75	1976–78	1979–81	1982–85	1973–75	1976–78	1979–81	1982–85	1973–75	1976–78	1979–81	1982–85
AFRICA														
Egypt	Cairo	CCC	340*	294	51*	X	61*	54*	5*	X	163*	150	78*	X
	Cairo	SR	X	79	14*	X	X	26	0*	X	X	130	4*	X
	Cairo	CCR	X	279*	X	X	X	43*	X	X	X	143*	X	X
NORTH & CENTRAL AMERICA														
Canada	Hamilton	SR	X	348	351	321	X	45	33	33	X	149	139	131
	Hamilton	CCC	X	363	363	355	X	52	35	34	X	174	131	105
	Montreal	SR	X	357	281	307	X	23	27	23	X	120	137	93
	Montreal	CCC	X	322	311	250	X	54	44	25	X	192	166	85
	Toronto	SI	X	332	330	337	X	23	17	9	X	96	73	54
	Toronto	SR	X	347	341	347	X	28	21	8	X	131	87	53
	Toronto	CCC	X	X	192*	358	X	X	21*	12	X	X	79*	66
	Vancouver	CCR	300	192	290	298	17	19	18	13	72	74	61	39
	Vancouver	SI	236	161	232	X	6	10	16	X	35	38	39	X
	Vancouver	CCC	X	X	258	219	X	X	9	15	X	X	26	59
Cuba	Havana	CCC	X	319	208*	X	X	58	47*	X	X	130	124*	X
	Havana	CCI	X	320	225*	X	X	25	22*	X	X	99	88*	X
	Havana	CCR	X	327	221*	X	X	38	35*	X	X	121	100*	X
United States	Fairfield (AL)	SI	X	X	X	349	X	X	X	40	X	X	X	86
	Chicago	X	X	X	X	334	X	X	X	30	X	X	X	85
	St. Louis	CCC	X	302	304	X	X	66	34	X	X	318	101	X
	New York City	SR	X	155*	364	358	X	49*	42	35	X	154*	132	77
	New York City	**CCR**	**X**	**169***	**355**	**365**	**X**	**72***	**74**	**65**	**X**	**167***	**203**	**116**
	New York City	CCI	X	59*	363	362	X	88*	52	47	X	204*	148	87
	Harris Co. (TX)	SR	X	41	5*	X	X	3	25*	X	X	22	37*	X
	Houston	CCC	X	49	19*	X	X	9	14*	X	X	87	37*	X
	Houston	SR	X	X	217	280	X	X	17	23	X	X	72	39
SOUTH AMERICA														
Brazil	**Rio de Janeiro**	**CCC**	**X**	**165**	**117***	**133***	**X**	**64**	**115***	**86***	**X**	**161**	**227***	**279***
	Rio de Janeiro	**SR**	**X**	**60***	**31***	**49***	**X**	**125***	**126***	**100***	**X**	**271***	**181***	**383***
	Sao Paulo	**CCR**	**X**	**364**	**364**	**364**	**X**	**121**	**131**	**80**	**X**	**294**	**327**	**173**
	Sao Paulo	**CCM**	**X**	**X**	**362**	**362**	**X**	**X**	**127**	**80**	**X**	**X**	**268**	**165**
Chile	**Santiago**	**CCC**	**X**	**341**	**292**	**330**	**X**	**76**	**63**	**85**	**X**	**221**	**205**	**188**
	Santiago	**CCR**	**X**	**316**	**283**	**346**	**X**	**47**	**43**	**67**	**X**	**148**	**139**	**115**
Colombia	Bogota	CCC	X	246	33	24	X	15	3	14*	X	37	15	70
	Bogota	SR	X	123	X	X	X	23	X	X	X	56	X	X
	Bogota	SI	X	109	63	24	X	69	40	56*	X	142	105	87
	Cali	SI	X	90	22	X	X	15	15	X	X	40	129	X
	Cali	SR	X	147	33	65	X	9	9	11*	X	30	38	78
	Medellin	SR	X	181	58	119	X	21	20	15*	X	46	43	24
	Medellin	CCC	X	237*	22	119	X	27*	9	48*	X	50*	13	81
	Medellin	SI	X	173	X	120	X	30	X	58*	X	53	X	86
Peru	Lima	CCC	X	103*	82	X	X	15*	4	X	X	31*	19	X
	Lima	CCR	X	117	93	X	X	12	4	X	X	29	32	X
	Lima	SR	X	23*	34*	X	X	7*	5*	X	X	51*	38*	X
Venezuela	Caracas	CCC	X	272	211	243	X	21	30	31	X	37	44	49
ASIA														
China	**Beijing**	**SI**	**X**	**X**	**104***	**147**	**X**	**X**	**38***	**100**	**X**	**X**	**146***	**298**
	Beijing	**CCC**	**X**	**X**	**113***	**153**	**X**	**X**	**66***	**167**	**X**	**X**	**290***	**459**
	Beijing	SR	X	X	93*	143	X	X	6*	29	X	X	44*	101
	Beijing	**CCR**	**X**	**X**	**110***	**149**	**X**	**X**	**98***	**228**	**X**	**X**	**397***	**625**
	Guangzhou	**SR**	**X**	**X**	**93***	**163**	**X**	**X**	**140***	**71**	**X**	**X**	**372***	**170**
	Guangzhou	**CCR**	**X**	**X**	**97***	**171**	**X**	**X**	**66***	**90**	**X**	**X**	**270***	**212**
	Guangzhou	**CCC**	**X**	**X**	**76***	**171**	**X**	**X**	**117***	**81**	**X**	**X**	**340***	**206**
	Guangzhou	**CCI**	**X**	**X**	**55***	**163**	**X**	**X**	**12***	**64**	**X**	**X**	**38***	**157**
	Shanghai	**CCI**	**X**	**X**	**88***	**142**	**X**	**X**	**23***	**77**	**X**	**X**	**153***	**200**
	Shanghai	**CCR**	**X**	**X**	**87***	**177**	**X**	**X**	**52***	**77**	**X**	**X**	**176***	**207**
	Shanghai	**CCC**	**X**	**X**	**85***	**178**	**X**	**X**	**65***	**54**	**X**	**X**	**272***	**217**
	Shanghai	SR	X	X	X	178	X	X	X	13	X	X	X	55
	Shenyang	**CCR**	**X**	**X**	**73***	**144**	**X**	**X**	**29***	**133**	**X**	**X**	**390***	**682**
	Shenyang	**CCI**	**X**	**X**	**72***	**144**	**X**	**X**	**136***	**279**	**X**	**X**	**358***	**1119**
	Shenyang	**CCC**	**X**	**X**	**72***	**120**	**X**	**X**	**72***	**160**	**X**	**X**	**320***	**576**
	Shenyang	**SR**	**X**	**X**	**72***	**120**	**X**	**X**	**27***	**55**	**X**	**X**	**299***	**272**
	Xian	**SR**	**X**	**X**	**98***	**174**	**X**	**X**	**22***	**30**	**X**	**X**	**98***	**156**
	Xian	**CCR**	**X**	**X**	**119***	**180**	**X**	**X**	**108***	**109**	**X**	**X**	**349***	**372**
	Xian	**CCC**	**X**	**X**	**120***	**180**	**X**	**X**	**160***	**113**	**X**	**X**	**670***	**398**
	Xian	**SI**	**X**	**X**	**117***	**179**	**X**	**X**	**46***	**59**	**X**	**X**	**256***	**259**
Hong Kong	**Hong Kong**	**CCC**	**357***	**359**	**365**	**308**	**14***	**12**	**37**	**62**	**72***	**87**	**117**	**121**
	Hong Kong	SI	364*	365	365	307	100*	43	76	39	680*	312	415	143
	Hong Kong	SR	362*	364	365	322*	19*	17	27	23*	72*	101	86	84*
India	Bombay	CCC	X	40*	30	17	X	26*	23	8	X	123*	97	38
	Bombay	SR	X	75*	47	31*	X	31*	24	25*	X	121*	81	85*
	Bombay	SC	X	75*	48	28*	X	96*	66	35*	X	253*	188	85*
	Bombay	CCC	X	X	34*	28	X	X	57*	11	X	X	195*	63
	Calcutta	**CCC**	**67**	**46**	**32**	**31**	**46**	**43**	**65**	**68**	**237**	**217**	**288**	**188**
	Calcutta	**SI**	**63**	**48**	**29**	**23**	**51**	**50**	**61**	**70**	**221**	**241**	**244**	**149**
	Calcutta	**SR**	**67**	**48**	**24**	**30**	**34**	**21**	**34**	**39**	**171**	**102**	**123**	**155**
	Delhi	**CCC**	**X**	**44***	**37**	**29**	**X**	**34***	**43**	**68**	**X**	**130***	**111**	**197**
	Delhi	CCR	X	33*	37	29	X	6*	14	28	X	67*	77	97
	Delhi	**CCI**	**X**	**34***	**38**	**29**	**X**	**57***	**37**	**58**	**X**	**474***	**137**	**172**
Indonesia	Jakarta	CCR	X	X	29*	31	X	X	0*	1	X	X	0*	6
	Jakarta	SI	X	X	26*	20*	X	X	0*	0*	X	X	0*	0*
Iran	**Tehran**	**CCC**	**X**	**67**	**81**	**59**	**X**	**65**	**129**	**122**	**X**	**183**	**362**	**467**
	Tehran	**SI**	**X**	**46**	**71**	**57**	**X**	**68**	**106**	**125**	**X**	**138**	**330**	**365**
	Tehran	**SR**	**X**	**46**	**74**	**56**	**X**	**73**	**108**	**79**	**X**	**208**	**376**	**318**

World Resources 1988–89

Table 23.4

		Site Type[a]	Average Number of Monitoring Days per Year				Mean of Daily Values (micrograms per cubic meter)				Peak Levels (98th Percentile of Daily Values) (micrograms per cubic meter)			
			1973–75	1976–78	1979–81	1982–85	1973–75	1976–78	1979–81	1982–85	1973–75	1976–78	1979–81	1982–85
Iraq	Baghdad	SI	X	64	14*	X	X	25	18*	X	X	117	81*	X
Israel	Tel Aviv	CCC	334	X	252	114	28	26	17	24	120	128	85	144
	Tel Aviv	CCI	311	X	X	160*	15	13	X	2*	93	82	X	54*
	Tel Aviv	SR	X	X	196	216	X	X	1	4	X	X	26	52
	Tel Aviv	CCR	X	X	296	202	X	X	3	24	X	X	44	122
Japan	Osaka	CCC	273*	357	359	362	73*	65	39	29	165*	133	80	57
	Osaka	CCI	365*	361	359	364	74*	51	37	30	131*	114	77	62
	Osaka	SR	330*	357	365	365	63*	55	35	27	121*	106	71	53
	Tokyo	CCC	363	363	361	363	68	63	47	25	128	111	91	58
	Tokyo	SR	355	365	362	363	48	49	42	34	102	90	74	62
	Tokyo	CCI	362	365	359	364	78	74	55	31	146	144	107	68
Korea, Rep	**Seoul**	**SI**	**X**	**X**	**X**	**339**	**X**	**X**	**X**	**137**	**X**	**X**	**X**	**474**
	Seoul	**SR**	**X**	**X**	**X**	**276**	**X**	**X**	**X**	**106**	**X**	**X**	**X**	**475**
Malaysia	Kuala Lumpur	SI	X	140*	106	18*	X	43*	14	6*	X	95*	62	20*
	Kuala Lumpur	SR	X	140*	61	13*	X	4*	1	2*	X	19*	9	9*
	Kuala Lumpur	SC	X	X	47*	20*	X	X	6*	4*	X	X	58*	16*
Philippines	Davao	SR	X	X	17*	25	X	X	9*	7	X	X	27*	38
	Davao	SI	X	X	16*	25	X	X	19*	8	X	X	75*	28
	Manila	**SR**	**348***	**355**	**225**	**224***	**68***	**53**	**58**	**61***	**141***	**94**	**147**	**112***
	Manila	**CCC**	**353***	**239**	**156**	**94***	**90***	**67**	**73**	**83***	**183***	**170**	**137**	**161***
	Manila	**SI**	**360***	**273**	**193**	**201**	**130***	**85**	**81**	**41***	**253***	**182**	**189**	**198**
Thailand	Bangkok	SI	X	51*	52*	X	X	15*	10*	X	X	66*	37*	X
	Bangkok	SR	X	X	78	126	X	X	14	18	X	X	46	48
EUROPE														
Belgium	**Brussels**	**CCC**	**328**	**282**	**356**	**328**	**106**	**98**	**77**	**71**	**321**	**305**	**273**	**205**
	Brussels	SR	294	309	340	335	92	74	65	40	263	214	210	122
	Brussels	SI	309	319	339	325	108	78	62	39	281	175	185	121
Czechoslovakia	Prague	CCC	361	284	X	X	137	141	X	X	446	440	X	X
	Prague	SR	344	292	X	X	121	123	X	X	374	386	X	X
	Prague	CCI	251	228	X	X	63	67	X	X	249	216	X	X
Denmark	Copenhagen	CCC	X	350*	362	279	X	30*	28	29	X	83*	82	72
	Copenhagen	SC	X	330*	348	74*	X	20*	19	27*	X	94*	87	135*
	Copenhagen	SI	X	364*	352	271	X	37*	33	28	X	117*	105	83
Finland	Helsinki	CCC	X	353*	349	56*	X	25*	22	28*	X	104*	82	67*
	Helsinki	SI	X	354*	343	262	X	29*	29	38	X	104*	121	103
	Helsinki	CCR	X	348*	319	315*	X	23*	26	19*	X	123*	123	90*
France	**Gourdon**	**SI**	**X**	**364**	**352**	**X**	**X**	**121**	**93**	**X**	**X**	**382**	**327**	**X**
	Gourdon	**CCR**	**X**	**365***	**365**	**X**	**X**	**87***	**76**	**X**	**X**	**304***	**255**	**X**
	Toulouse	CCI	X	213	309*	X	X	3	4*	X	X	41	35*	X
	Toulouse	CCR	X	223	301*	X	X	5	5*	X	X	29	37*	X
Germany, Fed Rep	Frankfurt	SI	303	186	190	245*	83	64	37	40*	242	226	105	95*
	Frankfurt	**CCC**	**321**	**307**	**316**	**306**	**105**	**84**	**73**	**59**	**285**	**231**	**224**	**230**
	Frankfurt	CCC	229	197*	X	X	24	37*	X	X	92	157*	X	X
	Munich	CCC	X	X	335	324*	X	X	23	22*	X	X	93	100*
Greece	Athens	SR	X	307*	126*	X	X	30*	38*	X	X	71*	172*	X
	Athens	SI	X	241*	125	233	X	43*	53	28	X	160*	301	48
	Athens	CCC	X	297*	261	253	X	39*	49	46	X	110*	232	118
Ireland	Dublin	CCR	X	365	362	363	X	50	60	44	X	139	141	118
	Dublin	CCI	X	364	363	314	X	46	38	33	X	98	91	88
	Dublin	SR	X	356	362	350	X	27	33	34	X	78	76	88
Italy	**Milan**	**CCR**	**X**	**241**	**265**	**253**	**X**	**260**	**273**	**166**	**X**	**1053**	**1031**	**798**
	Milan	**CCC**	**X**	**201**	**255**	**257**	**X**	**226**	**171**	**108**	**X**	**686**	**530**	**406**
Netherlands	Amsterdam	CCC	330	318	329	310	44	34	33	24	163	114	123	90
	Amsterdam	SR	339	334	334	325	29	27	35	26	105	89	135	121
	Amsterdam	SI	336	332	311	302	41	32	31	24	147	114	127	93
Poland	**Warsaw**	**CCR**	**X**	**161***	**155**	**182**	**X**	**28***	**32**	**33**	**X**	**142***	**156**	**180**
	Warsaw	**CCI**	**X**	**155***	**190**	**233**	**X**	**38***	**40**	**46**	**X**	**168***	**171**	**205**
	Warsaw	**CCC**	**X**	**158***	**193**	**240**	**X**	**43***	**44**	**39**	**X**	**215***	**198**	**188**
	Wroclaw	**CCC**	**X**	**291***	**291**	**287**	**X**	**45***	**41**	**52**	**X**	**160***	**179**	**199**
	Wroclaw	**CCI**	**X**	**280***	**293**	**278**	**X**	**30***	**30**	**42**	**X**	**114***	**130**	**172**
	Wroclaw	**CCR**	**X**	**263***	**283**	**262**	**X**	**23***	**33**	**38**	**X**	**80***	**140**	**161**
Portugal	Lisbon	CCR	X	X	101	193	X	X	86	37	X	X	282	140
	Lisbon	SR	X	X	X	200	X	X	X	17	X	X	X	89
Spain	**Madrid**	**CCC**	**293**	**120**	**282**	**266**	**156**	**97**	**108**	**64**	**497**	**301**	**333**	**193**
	Madrid	SR	318	275	318	309	65	47	46	31	227	139	152	97
	Madrid	**CCI**	**299**	**214**	**188**	**208***	**168**	**87**	**104**	**91***	**529**	**287**	**314**	**202***
Sweden	**Stockholm**	**CCC**	**X**	**247**	**206**	**X**	**X**	**58**	**62**	**X**	**X**	**149**	**174**	**X**
	Stockholm	SR	X	229	219	X	X	16	15	X	X	56	55	X
	Stockholm	**SI**	**X**	**208**	**187**	**X**	**X**	**37**	**44**	**X**	**X**	**129**	**181**	**X**
	Stockholm	CCI	X	203	194	X	X	24	22	X	X	70	73	X
United Kingdom	Glasgow	CCC	X	365*	363	365	X	94*	78	53	X	326*	208	132
	Glasgow	SR	X	352	290	X	X	73	42	X	X	170	125	X
	Glasgow	CCI	X	361	365	354	X	85	66	43	X	235	200	123
	London	**CCC**	**275**	**364**	**365**	**349**	**147**	**108**	**67**	**49**	**446**	**322**	**216**	**171**
	London	SR	202	234	340*	X	85	79	77*	X	262	228	195*	X
	London	SI	167	203	336	362	118	71	63	34	279	163	133	82
Yugoslavia	**Zagreb**	**CCC**	**338**	**348**	**341**	**361**	**166**	**123**	**85**	**95**	**563**	**443**	**271**	**262**
	Zagreb	**SR**	**336**	**361**	**364**	**352**	**58**	**47**	**38**	**54**	**241**	**216**	**157**	**176**
	Zagreb	**CCI**	**340**	**362**	**365**	**357**	**71**	**61**	**41**	**64**	**266**	**266**	**197**	**224**

Bold = site exceeded the level considered safe by the World Health Organization for the most recent valid monitoring period after 1978. *(continued)*

Table 23.4 Sulfur Dioxide Concentrations in Urban Areas, 1973–85
(continued)

		Site Type[a]	Average Number of Monitoring Days per Year				Mean of Daily Values (micrograms per cubic meter)				Peak Levels (98th Percentile of Daily Values) (micrograms per cubic meter)			
			1973–75	1976–78	1979–81	1983–85	1973–75	1976–78	1979–81	1982–85	1973–75	1976–78	1979–81	1982–85
OCEANIA														
Australia	Melbourne	CCC	292*	293	307	196	16*	14	6	10	50*	39	26	52
	Sydney	CCC	242*	312	343	336	73*	69	52	32	140*	137	127	68
	Sydney	SR	364*	303	256	330	44*	40	22	9	79*	87	56	32
	Sydney	SI	340*	310	338	356	31*	25	33	17	59*	54	86	52
New Zealand	Auckland	SI	78*	269	349	358	20*	22	21	8	57*	55	45	22
	Auckland	CCC	280*	334	347	351	16*	16	12	4	29*	60	29	10
	Auckland	CCR	X	331*	341	323	X	19*	10	3	X	84*	24	9
	Christchurch	SR	X	214	325	330	X	26	21	19	X	83	59	51
	Christchurch	SI	X	259*	326	236	X	23*	34	45	X	77*	89	130
	Christchurch	SC	X	205	327	333	X	22	29	13	X	59	75	48

Source: World Health Organization and United Nations Environment Programme.
Note: a. CCC = center city commercial; CCI = center city industrial; CCR = center city residential; CCM = center city mobile; SI = suburban industrial; SR = suburban residential.
0 = zero or less than half the unit of measure; X = not available; * = one year of data.
For additional information, see Sources and Technical Notes.
Bold = site exceeded the level considered safe by the World Health Organization for the most recent valid monitoring period after 1978.

Table 23.5 Suspended Particulate Matter Concentrations in Urban Areas, 1973–85

		Site Type[a]	Average Number of Monitoring Days per Year				Mean of Daily Values (micrograms per cubic meter)				Peak Levels (98th Percentile of Daily Values) (micrograms per cubic meter)			
			1973–75	1976–78	1979–81	1983–85	1973–75	1976–78	1979–81	1982–85	1973–75	1976–78	1979–81	1982–85
HIGH VOLUME GRAVIMETRIC SAMPLING METHOD														
AFRICA														
Ghana	**Accra**	SI	X	13*	20	3*	X	97*	119	95*	X	175*	303	113*
	Accra	SR	X	16*	19	X	X	75*	108	X	X	162*	198	X
NORTH & CENTRAL AMERICA														
Canada	Montreal	CCC	X	57	59	58	X	66	68	59	X	186	149	151
	Montreal	SR	X	55	59	55	X	76	79	64	X	169	225	147
	Hamilton	SR	X	54	53	55	X	107	104	97	X	234	234	261
	Hamilton	CCC	X	50	53	55	X	116	102	92	X	427	409	253
	Toronto	SI	X	54	60	57	X	76	97	69	X	181	202	178
	Toronto	SR	X	56	56	58	X	68	73	61	X	167	199	166
	Vancouver	CCR	57	51	52	50	65	59	60	40	161	162	166	103
	Vancouver	SI	43	54	50	56	71	86	84	56	194	205	244	163
United States	**Chicago**	CCI	X	107	68	56	X	161	134	100	X	456	267	259
	Chicago	SR	X	110	8*	X	X	74	56*	X	X	203	147*	X
	New York City	SR	X	80	49	57	X	57	51	44	X	130	119	87
	New York City	CCR	X	77	53	58	X	73	64	56	X	142	123	113
	New York City	CCI	X	59	56	56	X	74	65	62	X	139	129	121
	Chattanooga	CCC	X	X	52	60	X	X	79	68	X	X	199	135
	Chattanooga	CCR	X	X	51	61	X	X	59	48	X	X	140	101
	Harris Co. (TX)	SR	X	51	25	57	X	83	65	71	X	436	152	147
	Birmingham	CCI	X	X	237	173	X	X	120	89	X	X	300	213
	Birmingham	CCC	X	327	282	232	X	94	87	75	X	190	166	171
	St. Louis	CCC	93	101	X	X	87	98	X	X	172	399	X	X
	St. Louis	CCI	85	98	X	X	131	120	X	X	333	392	X	X
	Houston	SR	X	57	32	48	X	105	96	79	X	373	172	141
	Houston	CCC	X	43	52	57	X	107	82	75	X	771	149	131
	Fairfield (AL)	SI	X	297	268	231	X	83	76	53	X	169	145	96
SOUTH AMERICA														
Brazil	**Rio de Janeiro**	CCC	X	X	48*	51*	X	X	110	105*	X	X	239*	229*
	Rio de Janeiro	SR	X	X	49*	57*	X	X	97*	105	X	X	226*	230*
	Rio de Janeiro	SI	X	X	31*	41*	X	X	147*	121*	X	X	330*	230*
Colombia	Medellin	SR	X	X	11*	119*	X	X	19*	11*	X	X	27*	16*
	Medellin	CCC	X	X	8*	119*	X	X	43*	67*	X	X	62*	86*
	Cali	SR	X	X	28*	65*	X	X	32*	40*	X	X	115*	113*
ASIA														
China	**Shenyang**	CCR	X	X	72*	144	X	X	465*	491	X	X	971*	1,236
	Shenyang	CCI	X	X	72*	144	X	X	523*	529	X	X	1,410*	1,377
	Shenyang	SR	X	X	72*	120	X	X	225*	258	X	X	589*	663
	Beijing	SI	X	X	75*	132	X	X	479*	462	X	X	1,254*	1,307
	Beijing	SR	X	X	62*	131	X	X	252*	268	X	X	844*	632
	Beijing	CCR	X	X	79*	136	X	X	415*	398	X	X	834*	978
	Guangzhou	CCR	X	X	39*	154	X	X	117*	194	X	X	321*	476
	Guangzhou	SR	X	X	38*	149	X	X	375*	248	X	X	611*	611
	Guangzhou	CCI	X	X	24*	151	X	X	96*	179	X	X	224*	435
	Shanghai	CCI	X	X	89*	148	X	X	330*	285	X	X	770*	738

(Continued)

Table 23.5 Suspended Particulate Matter Concentrations in Urban Areas, 1973–85 (continued)

Country	City	Site Type[a]	Average Number of Monitoring Days per Year 1973–75	1976–78	1979–81	1983–85	Mean of Daily Values (micrograms per cubic meter) 1973–75	1976–78	1979–81	1982–85	Peak Levels (98th Percentile of Daily Values) (micrograms per cubic meter) 1973–75	1976–78	1979–81	1982–85
HIGH VOLUME GRAVIMETRIC SAMPLING METHOD													
	Shanghai	SR	X	X	X	177	X	X	X	152	X	X	X	359
	Shanghai	CCR	X	X	87*	178	X	X	235*	224	X	X	449*	480
	Xian	CCR	X	X	120*	180	X	X	387*	443	X	X	986*	1,269
	Xian	SI	X	X	117*	182	X	X	463*	471	X	X	1,045*	1,389
	Xian	SR	X	X	97*	177	X	X	235*	328	X	X	552*	901
India	Delhi	CCR	X	33*	37	29	X	326*	325	291	X	961*	809	831
	Delhi	CCI	X	34*	38	29	X	432*	445	453	X	972*	878	1,062
	Calcutta	SI	35	37	29	24	438	369	448	426	946	704	1,010	943
	Calcutta	SR	36	37	24	30	353	324	498	333	833	1048	1,227	967
	Calcutta	CCC	38	37	30	31	477	389	428	381	951	739	905	946
	Bombay	SC	X	69*	50	28*	X	234*	243	145*	X	500*	502	261*
	Bombay	SR	X	X	32*	30	X	X	203*	267	X	X	323*	468
	Bombay	SR	X	75*	49	32*	X	166*	184	166*	X	331*	379	374*
	Bombay	CCC	X	40*	29	18	X	136*	154	140	X	381*	302	227
Indonesia	Jakarta	SI	X	10*	54	20*	X	129*	159	18*	X	173*	474	197*
	Jakarta	CCR	X	10*	54	43	X	210*	267	243	X	438*	722	551
Iran	Tehran	SR	X	41	67	51	X	308	233	231	X	574	505	701
	Tehran	CCC	X	57	78	55	X	351	248	238	X	685	548	671
	Tehran	SI	X	41	61	52	X	457	339	326	X	871	636	694
Iraq	Baghdad	SI	X	88	63	X	X	282	518	X	X	1089	1,776	X
Malaysia	Kuala Lumpur	SI	X	114*	116	76	X	153*	166	112	X	258*	454	353
	Kuala Lumpur	SR	X	130*	92	14*	X	90*	92	101*	X	171*	269	259*
	Kuala Lumpur	SC	X	X	41*	50*	X	X	247*	96*	X	X	428*	302*
Philippines	Manila	SI	X	38*	62	52*	X	247*	182	252*	X	592*	380	579*
	Manila	CCC	354*	318	260	255*	77*	84	82	100*	128*	161	158	276*
	Manila	SR	341*	354	209	247*	71*	85	86	66*	164*	177	159	123*
	Davao	SI	X	X	21	23	X	X	170	172	X	X	335	598
Thailand	Bangkok	SR	X	27*	68	106	X	137*	214	198	X	286*	404	386
	Bangkok	SI	X	40	103	106	X	281	195	243	X	429	482	741
EUROPE													
Belgium	Brussels	CCC	X	311	363	353	X	29	25	21	X	87	76	72
Czechoslovakia	Prague	SR	334	293	X	X	137	121	X	X	403	290	X	X
	Prague	CCI	176	168	X	X	156	135	X	X	422	438	X	X
	Prague	CCC	182	182	X	X	251	146	X	X	835	413	X	X
Denmark	Copenhagen	SI	X	132*	352	291	X	43*	48	58	X	96*	125	152
	Copenhagen	SC	X	343	346	77*	X	32	30	54*	X	74	78	383*
	Copenhagen	CCC	X	357	356	114*	X	33	31	44*	X	91	80	159*
Germany, Fed Rep	Frankfurt	CCC	163	254	255	237	46	32	25	36	135	81	70	117
Finland	Helsinki	CCR	X	174*	171	158*	X	144*	136	118*	X	617*	761	516*
	Helsinki	CCC	X	148*	171	172	X	67*	69	80	X	201*	248	314
	Helsinki	SI	X	174*	175	174	X	57*	65	62	X	143*	207	163
Greece	Athens	SR	X	101*	16*	X	X	215*	235*	X	X	453*	462*	X
	Athens	SI	X	95*	34	27	X	206*	211	179	X	392*	440	324
	Athens	CCC	X	101*	68	254	X	259*	233	188	X	438*	439	325
Portugal	Lisbon	CCR	X	X	128*	95	X	X	99*	101	X	X	326*	251
Yugoslavia	Zagreb	CCC	207	177	183	175	175	169	126	133	484	380	359	352
	Zagreb	SR	198	186	195	208	134	134	143	130	356	356	367	341
	Zagreb	CCI	240	232	220	203	163	150	135	120	410	309	363	315
OCEANIA													
Australia	Sydney	SI	50*	54	56	57	156	99	79	63	655*	255	166	149
	Sydney	CCC	42*	58	56	58	98*	93	105	110	200*	197	294	277
	Sydney	SR	53*	58	39	X	76*	76	78	X	344*	148	153	X
	Melbourne	CCC	X	40	45	44	X	85	70	63	X	198	144	139
SMOKE SHADE SAMPLING METHOD													
AFRICA													
Egypt	Cairo	CCC	339*	292	44*	X	64*	59	101*	X	238*	189	291*	X
	Cairo	SR	X	76	17*	X	X	59	83*	X	X	195	172*	X
LATIN AMERICA													
Brazil	Sao Paulo	CCR	X	365	365	364	X	89	86	72	X	283	267	222
	Sao Paulo	CCM	X	X	362	362	X	X	130	106	X	X	367	338
Chile	Santiago	CCR	X	320	281	345	X	43	50	82	X	244	235	293
	Santiago	CCC	X	326	287	332	X	91	106	152	X	307	371	402
Colombia	Medellin	SR	X	184	81	X	X	33	33	X	X	81	244	X
	Medellin	CCC	X	238*	35*	X	X	83*	3*	X	X	159*	5*	X
	Cali	SR	X	154	38	X	X	25	15	X	X	92	76	X
	Cali	SI	X	95	22	X	X	50	22	X	X	103	53	X
	Bogota	SI	X	104	64	X	X	106	146	X	X	278	422	X
	Bogota	CCC	X	238	38	X	X	25	10	X	X	71	35	X
Cuba	Havana	CCR	X	330	221*	X	X	31	49*	X	X	94	188*	X
	Havana	CCC	X	315	207*	X	X	51	43*	X	X	118	128*	X
	Havana	CCI	X	326	225*	X	X	57	101*	X	X	184	382*	X
Peru	Lima	CCC	X	90*	104	X	X	33*	8	X	X	93*	45	X
	Lima	SR	X	80	47	X	X	25	28	X	X	50	53	X
	Lima	CCR	X	126	93	X	X	17	9	X	X	38	41	X
Venezuela	Caracas	CCC	X	302	214	245	X	27	25	30	X	50	41	48

Bold = site exceeded the level considered safe by the World Health Organization for the most recent valid monitoring period after 1978.

(Continued)

World Resources 1988–89

Table 23.5 Suspended Particulate Matter Concentrations in Urban Areas, 1973–85 (continued)

		Site Type[a]	Average Number of Monitoring Days per Year				Mean of Daily Values (micrograms per cubic meter)				Peak Levels (98th Percentile of Daily Values) (micrograms per cubic meter)			
			1973–75	1976–78	1979–81	1983–85	1973–75	1976–78	1979–81	1982–85	1973–75	1976–78	1979–81	1982–85
HIGH VOLUME GRAVIMETRIC SAMPLING METHOD														
ASIA														
Hong Kong	Hong Kong	SI	364*	365	365	309	28*	29	25	21	78*	74	61	51
	Hong Kong	CCC	353*	357	365	309	48*	58	47	48	98*	152	100	111
	Hong Kong	SR	358*	363	365	322*	93*	114	83	43*	178*	252	167	107*
Iran	**Tehran**	**CCC**	X	71	80	61	X	214	168	147	X	539	404	532
	Tehran	**SR**	X	49	77	56	X	110	103	69	X	305	339	343
	Tehran	**SI**	X	48	73	58	X	247	194	168	X	506	439	478
EUROPE														
Belgium	Brussels	SR	294	312	348	338	26	19	18	16	79	57	56	52
	Brussels	CCC	331	287	363	328	35	27	23	31	112	86	71	97
	Brussels	SI	313	324	343	319	27	15	15	23	84	58	54	72
Denmark	Copenhagen	SI	X	363	357	302	X	10	14	22	X	28	48	86
	Copenhagen	**SC**	X	333	348	74*	X	9	12	33*	X	23	42	189*
	Copenhagen	CCC	X	358	362	290	X	15	22	32	X	35	56	85
France	Gourdon	SI	X	365	354	359	X	30	40	36	X	174	134	113
	Gourdon	CCC	X	365*	X	365	X	47*	X	44	X	140*	X	143
	Gourdon	CCR	X	362*	364	363	X	41*	43	38	X	137*	144	117
	Toulouse	CCI	X	254	290*	X	X	23	26*	X	X	88	101*	X
	Toulouse	CCR	X	274	300*	X	X	16	18*	X	X	64	65*	X
Ireland	Dublin	SR	X	357	363	340	X	25	24	31	X	112	116	148
	Dublin	**CCR**	X	365	356	364	X	36	45	52	X	158	203	244
	Dublin	**CCI**	X	364	362	325	X	30	21	33	X	119	101	192
Poland	**Wroclaw**	**CCC**	X	284*	291	292	X	92*	77	91	X	310*	335	374
	Wroclaw	**CCI**	X	280*	291	274	X	64*	54	63	X	198*	190	218
	Wroclaw	**CCR**	X	261*	286	281	X	49*	51	64	X	140*	164	225
	Warsaw	**CCI**	X	158*	189	239	X	51*	48	59	X	161*	203	213
	Warsaw	**CCC**	X	159*	193	256	X	59*	50	67	X	199*	207	244
	Warsaw	**CCR**	X	163*	154	191	X	64*	40	58	X	222*	193	248
Spain	**Madrid**	**CCI**	297	211	188	X	283	175	165	X	903	559	534	X
	Madrid	**CCC**	301	120	275	250	196	191	155	98	629	604	521	318
	Madrid	SR	322	212	315	291	67	51	61	52	266	201	255	148
United Kingdom	London	SI	172	205	343	363	40	35	46	15	151	123	122	57
	London	SR	202	235	340*	X	33	29	25*	X	134	95	101*	X
	London	CCC	276	364	365	351	34	25	18	30	124	74	62	77
	Glasgow	CCI	X	361	365	355	X	32	29	15	X	209	183	81
	Glasgow	SR	X	352	290	X	X	21	20	X	X	152	109	X
	Glasgow	CCC	X	334*	365	365	X	42*	33	19	X	351*	157	94
OCEANIA														
New Zealand	Auckland	CCC	279*	339	343	365	5*	4	5	5	28*	17	19	20
	Auckland	SI	96*	269	343	361	6*	7	6	6	18*	25	24	26
	Auckland	CCR	X	337*	354	364	X	4*	5	5	X	21*	28	29
	Christchurch	**SR**	X	235	339	340	X	42	33	27	X	273	219	167
	Christchurch	SI	X	266*	334	344	X	19*	19	14	X	146*	134	94
	Christchurch	SC	X	206	325	346	X	11	27	19	X	82	198	136
NEPHELOMETER LIGHT SCATTER SAMPLING METHOD														
Japan	Osaka	CCI	344*	365	362	167	85*	75	55	43	225*	174	156	115
	Osaka	SR	343*	363	363	362	70*	70	62	51	170*	176	182	141
	Tokyo	CCC	356	361	361	284	57	61	62	52	178	196	211	143
	Osaka	CCI	365*	361	359	269	61*	61	62	50	151*	152	169	121
	Tokyo	CCI	358	365	363	262	67	64	57	52	193	177	175	142
	Tokyo	SR	357	348	347	287	67	59	54	51	213	181	179	145
	Osaka	CCC	326*	341	362	364	81*	67	52	42	233*	160	140	107
Philippines	Manila	SI	358*	287	209	332*	90*	85	88	95*	178*	155	153	168*
Australia	Melbourne	CCC	348*	327	284*	X	28*	27	21*	X	120*	85	76*	X

Source: World Health Organization and United Nations Environment Programme.
Notes: a. CCC = center city commercial; CCI = center city industrial; CCR = center city residential; CCM = center city mobile; SI = suburban industrial; SR = suburban residential.
X = not available; * = one year of data.
For additional information, see Sources and Technical Notes.
Bold = site exceeded the level considered safe by the World Health Organization for the most recent valid monitoring period after 1978.

Sources and Technical Notes

Figure 23.1 Long-Term Trends in Concentrations of Greenhouse and Ozone-Depleting Gases

Sources: J.M. Barnola, et al., "Vostok Ice Core Provides 160,000-year Record of Atmospheric CO_2," *Nature*, Vol. 329, p. 410;

M.A.K. Khalil and R.A. Rasmussen, "Atmospheric Methane: Trends over the Last 10,000 Years," *Atmospheric Environment*, Vol. 21, No. 11; M.A.K. Khalil and R.A. Rasmussen, "Nitrous Oxide: Trends and Global Mass Balance over the Last 3,000 Years," *Annals of Glaciology*, Vol. 10, 1988.

Figure 23.1 shows long-term trends in atmospheric concentrations of carbon dioxide, nitrous oxide, and methane, respectively. Data for the post-1960 period are from atmospheric monitoring. (See Table 23.1.) Earlier data were created by analyzing the contents of ancient air bubbles trapped in ice near the north and

south poles. These air bubbles provide a record of the atmospheric composition for the
preindustrial period and provide a baseline
from which to determine anthropogenic
impacts.

Ancient air samples are recovered by
drilling cores of ice in polar regions where little melting occurs. At the poles, bubbles of air
are trapped as each year's snowfall turns to
ice and becomes covered with layers of snow
and ice from successive years. These ice cores
are dated and the air bubbles are released by
placing the ice in a vacuum chamber and
melting or crushing the ice. The air's content
is then analyzed by gas chromatographic or
spectrometric methods.

Carbon dioxide. Data were taken from an
ice core drilled at Vostok, Antarctica. The figure shows trends in global carbon dioxide
concentrations for the past 160,000 years,
which encompass the current interglacial
period, the last glaciation, the previous interglacial, and the end of the penultimate glaciation. Carbon dioxide concentrations fluctuated
between approximately 190–280 parts per
million (ppm) until about a century ago. They
were highest during interglacial periods and
lowest during the last ice age.

Nitrous oxide. Nitrous oxide concentrations
were derived from ice cores from both polar
regions. Because only a few measurements
were available for each century, averages
were taken over fifty 400-year periods. Nitrous
oxide concentrations were fairly constant until
about 150 years ago when they began to
increase.

Methane. This 10,000 year record is based
on ice core data from both polar regions, and
represents approximate global average concentrations. Atmospheric methane concentrations remained relatively constant until about
300 years ago when they began to increase.
Increases in methane concentrations have
accelerated over the past century.

Table 23.1 Atmospheric Concentrations of Greenhouse and Ozone-Depleting Gases, 1959–87

Sources: Carbon dioxide: C.D. Keeling,
unpublished data (Carbon Dioxide Information
and Analysis Center, Oak Ridge, Tennessee,
March 1988). CH$_4$ and CFC-113: R.A. Rasmussen and M.A.K. Khalil, unpublished data (Oregon Graduate Center, Beaverton, Oregon,
1987). Other gases: R.A. Rasmussen and
M.A.K. Khalil, "Atmospheric Trace Gases:
Trends and Distributions over the Last
Decade," *Science*, Vol. 232, pp. 1623–1624.

The trace gases listed in Tables 23.1–23.3
affect atmospheric ozone and/or contribute to
the greenhouse effect. For further details concerning these processes, refer to Chapter 10,
"Atmosphere and Climate."

Carbon dioxide (CO$_2$) accounts for about
half the greenhouse effect and is emitted to
the atmosphere by natural and anthropogenic
processes. See the Technical Note for Table
23.2 for further details.

Atmospheric carbon dioxide concentrations
are monitored at many sites worldwide; the
data presented here are from Mauna Loa,
Hawaii (19.53°N, 155.58°W). Trends at Mauna
Loa reflect global trends, although carbon

dioxide concentrations differ significantly
among monitoring sites at any given time.

Annual means disguise large daily and seasonal variations in carbon dioxide concentrations. The seasonal variation is caused by
photosynthetic plants using carbon during the
summer and releasing it in the winter. Some
annual mean figures were derived from inter-
polated data.

Data are revised to correct for drift in
instrument calibration, hardware changes, and
perturbations to "background" conditions.
Data for 1987 are preliminary. The most
recent data may be obtained from the Carbon
Dioxide Information and Analysis Center, Oak
Ridge National Laboratory, Oak Ridge, Tennessee, United States. Details concerning data collection, revisions, and analysis are contained
in C.D. Keeling, *et al.*, "Measurement of the
Concentration of Carbon Dioxide at Mauna
Loa Observatory, Hawaii," in *Carbon Dioxide
Review: 1982*, W.C. Clark, ed. (Oxford University Press, New York, 1982).

Carbon tetrachloride (CCl$_4$) is an intermediate in the production of CFC-11 and CFC-12.
(See the Technical Note for Table 23.2.) A
small amount is used in other chemical and
pharmaceutical applications and for grain
fumigation. Compared with other gases, CCl$_4$
makes a small contribution to the greenhouse
effect and to stratospheric ozone depletion.

Methyl chloroform (CH$_3$CCl$_3$) is used
primarily as an industrial degreasing agent
and as a solvent for paints and adhesives. Its
contribution to the greenhouse effect and to
stratospheric ozone depletion is also small.

*CFC-11 (CCl$_3$F), CFC-12 (CCl$_2$F$_2$), CFC-22
(CHClF$_2$) and CFC-113 (C$_2$Cl$_3$F$_3$)* are potent
depletors of stratospheric ozone. Together they
may also contribute one fourth the greenhouse impact of carbon dioxide. (CFCs are
discussed in the Technical Note for Table
23.2.)

Total Gaseous Chlorine is derived by multiplying the number of chlorine atoms in each
of the chlorine-containing gases (carbon tetrachloride, methyl chloroform, and the CFCs) by
the concentration of that gas.

Nitrous oxide (N$_2$O) is emitted by aerobic
decomposition of organic matter in oceans
and soils, by bacteria, by combustion of fossil
fuels and biomass (fuelwood and cleared
forests), and by the use of nitrogen fertilizers.
N$_2$O is an important depletor of stratospheric
ozone; it may contribute one twelfth the
greenhouse impact of carbon dioxide.

Methane (CH$_4$) is emitted in a variety of
natural anoxic processes, including enteric fer-
mentation in ruminants and anaerobic decomposition in wetlands, bogs, tundra, and lakes.
Emission sources associated with human
activities include livestock management,
anaerobic decomposition in rice paddies, and
combustion of fossil fuels and biomass (fuelwood and cleared forests). Methane acts to
increase ozone in the troposphere and lower
stratosphere; its greenhouse impact is one
third that of carbon dioxide.

Carbon monoxide (CO) is emitted by motor
traffic, other fossil fuel combustion, and slash-
and-burn agriculture. Increasing levels of carbon monoxide can lead to an increase in
tropospheric ozone and a build-up of other
trace gases in the atmosphere.

Data for all gases except carbon monoxide

and CFC-22 are from monitoring at Cape
Meares, Oregon (45°N, 124°W). Although gas
concentrations at any given time vary among
monitoring sites, these data reflect global
trends. Data for carbon monoxide and CFC-22
were taken from several sites and averaged to
reflect global concentrations and trends.

Table 23.2 Annual Emissions of Greenhouse and Ozone-Depleting Gases, 1925–86

Sources: Chlorofluorocarbons: Chemical
Manufacturers Association (CMA), "Production,
Sales, and Calculated Release of CFC-11 and
CFC-12 through 1986" (CMA, Washington, D.C.,
1987). Biotic emissions of carbon dioxide: R.A.
Houghton, unpublished data (Woods Hole
Research Center, Woods Hole, Massachusetts,
March 1988). Carbon dioxide emissions from
fossil fuel combustion and industrial processes:
R.M. Rotty, unpublished data (University of
New Orleans, Louisiana, April 1988).

Emissions of *chlorofluorocarbons* (CFCs) are
estimated based on use-specific release factors
derived from CFC production and sales data.
The CMA contracts with Grant Thornton and
Company, Certified Public Accountants, to collect CFC production and sales data from companies based in countries that are members of
the Organisation for Economic Co-operation
and Development (OECD) and in Argentina,
South Africa, India, Brazil, Venezuela, and
Mexico. The data are examined for reporting
errors and inventory changes. Grant Thornton
and Company has compiled or modeled
annual production data for CFC-11 and CFC-12
from 1931 to the present.

All CFCs used in solvents and aerosols are
assumed to be released within six months of
production; those used in hermetically sealed
refrigeration equipment are assumed to have
an early release peak because of product
defects and filling losses, with the remainder
released over a 12-year period. For details on
the modeling of CFC releases, refer to P.H.
Gamlen, *et al.*, "The Production and Release
to the Atmosphere of CCl$_3$ and CCl$_2$F$_2$ (Chlorofluorocarbons CFC 11 and CFC 12),"
Atmospheric Environment, Vol. 20, No. 6
(1986) pp. 1077–1085.

CFC production and release data are not
available for India (one company has reported
data since 1983), Eastern Europe, China, and
the USSR. The USSR is thought to be the
largest producer of the group, with an estimated production of about 68,000 metric tons
of CFC-11 and 33,000 metric tons of CFC-12 in
1986. These levels of production are equal to
about 19 percent and 8 percent, respectively,
of reported 1986 world production of CFC-11
and CFC-12. Emissions data are not available.

Carbon dioxide emissions are caused by
natural and human factors. Volcanoes emit
carbon dioxide, and major changes in global
vegetation can contribute to, or withdraw
from, the atmospheric carbon reservoir. Combustion of fossil fuels adds carbon to the
atmosphere, as do gas flaring and cement
production. In addition, carbon is released by
the burning or decomposition of the biomass
when forestland is cleared.

Biotic sources: The model used to produce
this data series attempts to account for both

the emission and uptake of carbon dioxide by the biota and soils as a result of changes in land use. Carbon dioxide is released from vegetation and soils when land is cleared for agriculture (emissions from soils and decomposing natural vegetation), and when forests are cut for fuelwood and industrial wood or converted to pasture land. Carbon dioxide is removed from the atmosphere by forest growth on abandoned cropland and pasture and by afforestation. The extent of changes in each land type were determined from historical data.

The 11 types of land cover considered in this model have different stocks of carbon in vegetation and soils, amounts and rates of carbon emissions when disturbed, and extent and rates of recovery. Undisturbed vegetation was assumed to be in carbon equilibrium with the atmosphere.

All fuelwood and industrial wood were assumed to have come from closed forests; it was assumed that no wood was taken from shrublands and grasslands. Fuelwood was assumed to be oxidized in one year, paper and paper products in ten years, and lumber and related products in 100 years.

For developed regions, historical wood harvest data were taken from the literature. For developing regions, pre-1950 fuelwood data were computed using per capita consumption factors. For these regions, industrial wood production was assumed to be one fifth the volume of fuelwood production. For 1950–80, data on wood harvest in developing countries were taken from the four FAO World Forest Inventories and the *FAO Yearbook of Forest Products*. (For additional details, see the Technical Notes for Tables 18.1 and 18.2 in Chapter 18, "Forests and Rangelands.")

Forests were assumed to have been converted to pasture in Latin America only. Afforestation was assumed to have taken place only in China, the USSR, and Europe.

Fossil fuel combustion and industrial processes. Combustion of different fossil fuels releases carbon dioxide at different rates for each unit of heat produced. Burning oil releases about 1.5 times the amount of carbon dioxide released from burning natural gas; coal combustion releases about twice the carbon dioxide of natural gas. Carbon emissions data are derived from the United Nations Statistical Office energy data base.

It was assumed that approximately 1 percent of the coal used by industry and power plants was not burned, and an additional few percent was converted to nonoxidizing uses. Other oxidative reactions of coal are assumed to be of negligible importance in carbon budget modeling. The margin of error in the calculation of carbon emissions using fuel production data was estimated at 6–10 percent.

Carbon emissions from gas flaring and cement production are also included in fossil fuel combustion and industrial processes. These two sources emit about 3 percent of the carbon emitted by fossil fuel combustion.

Table 23.3 Carbon Dioxide Emissions by Country and Region, 1950–85

Sources: Industrial emissions: R.M. Rotty, unpublished data (University of New Orleans,

Louisiana, April 1988). Biotic emissions: C.A. Palm, *et al.*, "Atmospheric Carbon Dioxide from Deforestation in Southeast Asia," *Biotropica*, Vol. 18, pp. 177–188; J.M. Melillo, *et al.*, "Land Use Change in the Soviet Union between 1850 and 1980: Causes of a Net Release of CO_2 to the Atmosphere," *Tellus*, in press; and R.A. Houghton, unpublished data (Woods Hole Research Center, Woods Hole, Massachusetts, February 1988).

For a discussion of the biotic release of carbon dioxide, refer to the Technical Notes for Table 23.2. Negative biotic emissions of carbon dioxide for Europe are probably due to reforestation.

Estimates of industrial carbon emissions differ from those presented in Table 23.2. The basis for the calculations in Table 23.2 is *global fuel production*. Table 23.3 is based on *national fuel consumption*. The author believes that on a global scale the production method is more accurate than the consumption method, but it cannot be used to provide estimates of national carbon emissions. The consumption method makes allowances for international trade, air and sea bunkers, and stock changes. On a global scale, the difference between the two methods is quite small. For example, a 1950 carbon emission estimate based on production data is 3 percent higher than the estimate calculated from consumption data. The difference is approximately 4 percent in 1965 and 5 percent in 1985. The margin of error in the calculation of carbon emissions using fuel production data is 6–10 percent.

Figure 23.2 Acidity of European Precipitation, 1985

Source: Co-operative Programme for Monitoring and Evaluation of the Long-Range Transmission of Air Pollutants in Europe (EMEP), *Summary Report from the Chemical Coordinating Centre for the Third Phase of EMEP* (Norwegian Institute for Air Research, Lillestrom, 1987).

The pH scale is used to measure acidity or alkalinity. Neutral solutions have a pH of 7, acid solutions have a pH less than 7, and alkaline solutions have a pH greater than 7. Each unit change in pH represents a tenfold change in acidity. For example, rainfall with pH 4 is 10 times as acidic as rainfall with pH 5 and 100 times as acidic as rainfall with pH 6. The pH values in this figure are precipitation-weighted annual means.

Typically, rainfall is regularly collected at monitoring sites using techniques established by the monitoring network operating protocol. Depending on the network operating protocol, samples are collected daily, weekly, or monthly. The networks represented on this map use either "wet-only" or "bulk" sampling. Wet-only samplers are exposed to the atmosphere only during precipitation; bulk samplers are exposed to the atmosphere at all times and are influenced by both wet and dry deposition. Precipitation samples are then chemically analyzed and checked for validity.

EMEP is a cooperative air monitoring program undertaken by 23 European countries. National monitoring networks submit air and precipitation chemistry data for selected sites to the central data base supported by EMEP. National analytical laboratories also participate

in interlaboratory comparison programs (including analysis of blind samples) to ensure comparability of the many analytical methods used. Comparability is generally satisfactory, although there are a few national laboratories whose analyses of blind samples deviate from correct values more than 10 percent. All monitoring sites reporting to EMEP collect samples daily. Monitoring stations reporting data to EMEP are regionally representative (i.e., far from local pollution sources).

This map incorporates data from 77 of EMEP's 91 monitoring stations. Data are precipitation-weighted arithmetic means. EMEP monitoring data have not yet been analyzed for temporal trends.

Figure 23.3 Acidity of North American Precipitation, 1985

Source: A.R. Olsen, *1985 Wet Deposition Temporal and Spatial Patterns in North America* (Pacific Northwest Laboratory, Richland, Washington, September 1987). Station trends: A.R. Olsen, Staff Scientist, Pacific Northwest Laboratory, Richland, Washington, March 15, 1988 (personal communication).

This map incorporates data collected at 306 monitoring sites in six North American precipitation monitoring networks: National Atmospheric Deposition Program/National Trends Network, Multi-State Atmospheric Pollution and Power Production Study Precipitation Chemistry Network, Canadian Air and Precipitation Monitoring Network, Acidic Precipitation in Ontario Study (both the cumulative and daily networks), and Utility Acid Precipitation Study Program. All the networks represented on this map use "wet-only" rather than "bulk" sampling. Refer to the Technical Note for Figure 23.2 for a definition of these terms, and of pH.

The monitoring data for 30 stations were analyzed to identify temporal trends in acidity between 1979 and 1984. Five stations showed decreasing acidity; 25 showed no statistically significant change in acidity. The stations showing improvement were: Ithaca, New York; Finley, North Carolina; Charlottesville, Virginia; Scranton, Pennsylvania; and Zanesville, Ohio. Meteorological conditions may have contributed to this trend; longer-term analyses will be required to identify the human contribution to the trend.

The Acid Deposition System (ADS) is a joint data base for nine Canadian and U.S. networks monitoring precipitation chemistry. To join ADS, a network must establish monitoring protocols, screen data, and undertake quality control and quality assurance programs. Analytical laboratories in ADS member networks also participate in interlaboratory comparison studies, which indicate that analyses performed by different laboratories are generally comparable.

For this map, ADS eliminated data that did not meet several selection criteria. The first set of criteria relates to the validity of samples. For example, if a sample has insufficient precipitation for a complete analysis of an ion species, the sample is invalid for that species.

A second set of criteria relates to completeness of the data. One important data completeness criterion is the fraction of precipitation events at a site for which there were valid chemical measurements. (A more relaxed data completeness criterion was used to increase the number of sites available for trend analysis. These relaxed criteria were applied to derive trends for some of the 30 stations shown in Figure 23.3. The stricter criteria were applied to the stations providing data for the base map.)

A third set of criteria addresses site representativeness. Sites that are far from industrial pollution sources, towns, transportation facilities, and other potentially contaminating influences were considered regionally representative. Sites with good data completeness and site representativeness ratings were included in this map.

For details of data and site selection criteria and for data on other monitored ion species, refer to the source.

Table 23.4 Sulfur Dioxide Concentrations in Urban Areas, 1973–85

Source: World Health Organization (WHO)/United Nations Environment Programme (UNEP), Global Environmental Monitoring System (GEMS)/AIR Monitoring Project, unpublished data (Research Triangle Park, North Carolina, April, and June 1988).

Sulfur dioxide is created by both natural and anthropogenic activities. Anthropogenic sources include fossil fuel combustion and industrial activities. High levels of sulfur dioxide and suspended particulate matter (SPM) may cause respiratory problems among adults and children and may also result in lower respiratory tract illness. The World Health Organization (WHO) recommends that annual average sulfur dioxide levels not exceed 40–60 micrograms per cubic meter and that the 98th percentile of daily values not exceed 100–150 micrograms per cubic meter.

The annual mean, the average of all available daily values in a year, represents the overall air quality situation during the year. The 98th percentile represents the level which 98 percent of the daily measurements in a year fall below and 2 percent of the measurements are above. It provides information on air quality during the most polluted days of the year. Both sulfur dioxide and SPM levels can be affected by seasonal patterns in emissions and meteorological conditions. As a result, annual means and 98th percentiles are most meaningful if they include measurements taken during all seasons of the year. Unfortunately, this preliminary analysis did not include seasonality information, so the data shown should be treated with caution. Generally, periods with many monitoring days and more than one year of data are the most reliable.

Data for individual years between 1973 and 1985 were aggregated to show average values for one four-year and three three-year periods. Not shown are stations for which only one period of data was available or stations representing duplicate site types for the same city (e.g., only one site was chosen for cities with more than one center city industrial site).

Monitoring data are submitted by national governments to the Global Environmental Monitoring System (GEMS) maintained by WHO and the United Nations Environment Programme. Monitoring stations are classified by location as center city or suburban, and further classified as industrial, commercial or residential depending on the predominant use of land surrounding the monitoring station. (In addition, Sao Paulo, Brazil has a mobile center city site, which is moved to different locations within the center city.) These classifications, and common site exposure criteria, improve data comparability. Two inter-laboratory comparisons have also been conducted; in each, the majority of the results were well within the statistically acceptable range.

In 1985, about 175 sites in 75 cities (representing approximately 50 countries) were participating in the GEMS program. The coverage of stations and data in the northern hemisphere is better than that in the southern hemisphere.

For additional information on GEMS urban air monitoring, see WHO, *Urban Air Pollution 1973–80* (WHO, Geneva, 1984) or the series *Air Quality in Selected Urban Areas*, published by WHO for the years 1973–1980. UNEP and WHO are currently preparing a review and analysis of the GEMS/AIR monitoring database, which will be published in 1989.

Table 23.5 Suspended Particulate Matter Concentrations in Urban Areas, 1973–85

Source: World Health Organization (WHO)/United Nations Environment Programme (UNEP), Global Environmental Monitoring System (GEMS)/AIR Monitoring Project, unpublished data (Research Triangle Park, North Carolina, April 1988).

Levels of SPM rise both from human and natural activities including combustion of wood and fossil fuels, industrial activities, and dust raised by vehicular traffic or wind. High SPM levels may aggravate respiratory illnesses.

Three methods for measuring SPM concentrations are shown. The two most commonly used methods are high-volume gravimetric and smoke shade. Gravimetric sampling determines the mass of particulates in a given volume of air. Smoke shade methods relate the reflectance of a stain left on filter paper that has had ambient air drawn through it to the concentration of particulates in the air. Smoke shade data cannot be used interchangeably with gravimetrically determined mass measurements because the smoke shade measurement is predominantly an indication of dark material in the air, which may not be proportional to the total weight of suspended matter. High-volume data may be twice as large as concurrent smoke shade results.

WHO recommends that annual average SPM levels not exceed 60–90 micrograms per cubic meter as measured by the high-volume gravimetric method or 50–60 micrograms per cubic meter as measured by smoke shade sampling. The 98th percentile of daily values should not exceed 150–230 or 100–150 micrograms per cubic meter respectively for the two methods.

24. Policies and Institutions

This chapter presents several indicators of a country's commitment to environmental protection: participation in international agreements protecting the environment, the availability of environmental information, and the allocation of official development assistance. Indicators of national environmental policy are difficult to quantify. Laws and regulations controlling pollution and promoting conservation are not listed because they vary widely in scope and enforcement. The increasing activity of nongovernmental environment and development organizations, from the local to international level, reflects growing public concern for natural resources. For information on public opinion on environmental issues, see *World Resources 1987*, Table 26.4.

Table 24.1 shows the countries that participate in critical international treaties protecting the environment. The most recent treaty included in this table is the Protocol on Substances that Deplete the Ozone Layer, which was signed in Montreal by 24 countries and the European Community in September 1987, and now awaits ratification. The terms of the Protocol—a 50 percent reduction in chlorofluorocarbon production by 1999, with allowances for consumption increases in developing countries—appeared stringent at the time of the signing, but more recent evidence of ozone layer depletion indicates that the Protocol may in fact be too lax. Even so, it has been hailed as a model of international cooperation, and could serve as an example for a future treaty addressing greenhouse warming.

The sources of environmental and natural resource information listed in Table 24.2 are comprehensive assessments of natural resources and environmental conditions on the national, regional, and global levels. These reports summarize available information on the condition of the natural resource base, highlight major environmental problems, document trends, and often suggest policies for resource management. Other types of environmental information, such as journals, newsletters, and studies of specific natural resources, are not included in this table.

Most developed countries have produced a state of the environment and/or an environmental statistical report. However, these types of environmental evaluations are available for few developing countries. Many developing countries lack the technical and institutional capacity needed to produce a report addressing all natural resource sectors. Additionally, environmental monitoring is often weak or nonexistent and information about the environment may be politically sensitive. However, these obstacles have been overcome in several developing countries; environmental reports have been produced by governments and by cooperative efforts of nongovernmental organizations, universities, and international organizations.

Provisional figures indicate that $44 billion in Official Development Assistance (ODA)—grants and concessional loans committed by governments to encourage economic development and alleviate poverty—were made available in 1986. Table 24.3 shows the percentages of ODA allocated to different purposes by the countries of the Organisation for Economic Co-operation and Development (OECD) and multilateral development agencies. (See Chapter 14, "Basic Economic Indicators," Table 14.1 for data on ODA donations and receipts by country.)

ODA allocation statistics indicate donors' assistance priorities, although they are usually not detailed enough to allow identification of environmentally-focused expenditures. Most development assistance invested in renewable natural resources and environmental protection is reported under agriculture and under water, sanitation, and other social services. In 1985-86, Denmark and the Netherlands placed the greatest emphasis on these types of projects, each giving about 30 percent of their aid in these two categories. Finland and Norway placed greater priority on health and population projects than other countries did; each gave 14 percent of its total assistance to this area. These types of projects may suffer in the future, as more ODA has recently been shifted from project-oriented assistance to general debt relief and budget support. (See Chapter 14, "Basic Economic Indicators," Table 14.2, for more information on debt.)

Environmental conservation and sustainable development practices may play a greater role in future ODA-sponsored projects. Several bilateral and multilateral development agencies have re-examined the environmental impacts of their projects, and have redirected money to address environmental concerns. The World Bank, for instance, has increased the number of staff members working on environmental and natural resource issues, created an environmental department, and increased funding for environmental assessments in developing countries, tropical forest conservation, forestry projects, and projects to combat desertification and deforestation in Africa.

Table 24.1 Participation in Global Conventions Protecting the

	Wetlands (Ramsar) 1971	World Heritage (Paris) 1972	Endangered Species (CITES) (Washington) 1973	Migratory Species (Bonn) 1979	Ocean Dumping (London, Mexico City, Moscow, Washington) 1972	Pollution from Ships (MARPOL) (London) 1978	Law of the Sea (Montego Bay) 1982	Nuclear Test Ban (Moscow) 1963	Biological and Toxin Weapons (London, Moscow, Washington) 1972	Protection of the Ozone Layer (Vienna) 1985	Protocol on Ozone Depleting Substances (Montreal) 1987	Regional Seas[a] (UNEP)
WORLD												
AFRICA												
Algeria	CP	CP	CP				S	S				M*,ML*,MSP*
Angola							S					
Benin		CP	CP	CP			S	CP	CP			WCA
Botswana			CP				S	S	S			
Burkina Faso							S	S		S		
Burundi		CP					S	S	S			
Cameroon		CP	CP	CP			CP	S	CP			WCA*
Cape Verde					CP		S	CP	CP			
Central African Rep		CP	CP	S			S	CP	S			
Chad				S	S		S	CP				
Comoros							S					
Congo			CP				CP		CP			WCA
Cote d'Ivoire		CP				CP	CP	CP	S			WCA*
Djibouti							S					
Egypt	CP	CP	CP	CP		CP	CP	CP	S	S	S	M*,ML*,MSP*
Equatorial Guinea							S					
Ethiopia		CP					S		CP			
Gabon	CP	CP			CP	CP	S	CP	S			WCA
Gambia			CP				CP	CP	S			WCA*
Ghana		CP	CP				CP	CP	CP		S	WCA
Guinea		CP	CP				CP					WCA*
Guinea-Bissau							CP	CP	CP			
Kenya			CP		CP		S	CP	CP	S		
Lesotho			S		S		S		CP			
Liberia			CP		S	CP	S	CP	S			WCA
Libya		CP			CP		S	CP	CP			M*,ML
Madagascar		CP	CP	S			S	CP	S			EA
Malawi		CP	CP				S	CP	S			
Mali	CP	CP		CP			CP	S	S			
Mauritania	CP	CP					S	CP				WCA
Mauritius			CP				S	CP	CP			
Morocco	CP	CP	CP	S	CP		S	CP	S	S		M*,ML*,MSP
Mozambique		CP	CP				S					
Niger	CP	CP	CP	CP			S	CP	CP			
Nigeria		CP	CP	CP	CP		CP	CP	CP			WCA*
Rwanda			CP				S	CP	CP			
Senegal	CP	CP	CP		S		CP	CP	CP	S		WCA*
Sierra Leone			CP				S	CP	CP			
Somalia			CP	CP	S		S	S	S			EA,R
South Africa	CP		CP		CP	CP	S	CP	CP			
Sudan		CP	CP				CP	CP				R*
Swaziland							S	CP				
Tanzania, United Rep		CP	CP				CP	CP	S			
Togo			CP	S	S		CP	CP	CP		S	WCA*
Tunisia	CP	CP	CP		CP	CP	CP	CP	CP			M*,ML*,MSP*
Uganda				S			S	CP				
Zaire		CP	CP		CP		S	CP	CP			
Zambia		CP	CP				CP	CP				
Zimbabwe		CP	CP				S					
NORTH & CENTRAL AMERICA												
Barbados							S		CP			C*
Canada	CP	CP	CP		CP		S	CP	CP	CP	S	
Costa Rica		CP	CP		CP		S	CP	CP			
Cuba		CP			CP		CP		CP			
Dominican Rep		CP	CP		CP		S	CP	CP			
El Salvador							S	CP	S			
Guatemala		CP	CP		CP		S	CP	CP	CP		C
Haiti		CP			CP		S	S	S			
Honduras		CP	CP		CP		S	CP	CP			C
Jamaica		CP		S			CP	S	CP			C*
Mexico	CP				CP	S	CP	CP	CP	CP	CP	C*
Nicaragua		CP	CP				S	CP	CP			C
Panama		CP	CP		CP	CP	S	CP	CP		S	SEP*, C*
Trinidad and Tobago			CP				CP	CP				C*
United States	CP	CP	CP		CP	CP		CP	CP	CP	CP	C*,SP
SOUTH AMERICA												
Argentina		CP	CP		CP		S	CP	CP	S		
Bolivia		CP	CP		S		S	CP	CP			
Brazil		CP	CP		CP	CP	S	CP	CP			
Chile	CP	CP	CP	CP	CP		S	CP	CP	S		SEP*
Colombia		CP	CP		S	CP	S	CP	CP			SEP*,C
Ecuador		CP	CP					CP	CP			SEP*
Guyana		CP	CP				S		S			
Paraguay			CP	S			CP	S	CP			
Peru		CP	CP		CP		CP	CP	CP	S		SEP
Suriname	CP		CP		CP		S					
Uruguay	CP		CP	S	CP		S	CP	CP			
Venezuela			CP	S				CP	CP		S	C*

Environment, 1988

Table 24.1

	Wetlands (Ramsar) 1971	World Heritage (Paris) 1972	Endangered Species (CITES) (Washington) 1973	Migratory Species (Bonn) 1979	Ocean Dumping (London, Mexico City, Moscow, Washington) 1972	Pollution from Ships (MARPOL) (London) 1978	Law of the Sea (Montego Bay) 1982	Nuclear Test Ban (Moscow) 1963	Biological and Toxin Weapons (London, Moscow, Washington) 1972	Protection of the Ozone Layer (Vienna) 1985	Protocol on Ozone Depleting Substances (Montreal) 1987	Regional Seas^a (UNEP)
ASIA												
Afghanistan		CP	CP		CP		S	CP	CP			
Bahrain							CP					P*
Bangladesh		CP	CP				S	CP	CP			
Bhutan							S	CP	CP			
Burma							S	CP	S			
China		CP	CP		CP	CP	S	CP	CP			
Cyprus		CP	CP				S	CP	CP			M*,ML
India	CP	CP	CP	CP		CP	S	CP	CP			
Indonesia			CP			CP	CP	CP	S			
Iran	CP		CP				S	CP	CP			P*
Iraq		CP					CP	CP	S			P*
Israel			CP	CP		CP	CP	CP	CP		S	M*,ML,MSP*
Japan	CP		CP		CP	CP	S	CP	CP		S	
Jordan	CP	CP	CP		CP			CP	CP			R
Kampuchea, Dem							S		CP			
Korea, Dem People's Rep						CP	S		CP			
Korea, Rep						CP	S	CP	CP			
Kuwait			S		S		CP	CP	CP			P*
Lao People's Dem Rep							S	CP	CP			
Lebanon		CP			S	CP	S	CP	CP			M*,ML
Malaysia			CP				S	CP	S			
Mongolia							S	CP	CP			
Nepal		CP	CP		S		S	CP	S			
Oman		CP			CP	CP	S					P*
Pakistan	CP	CP	CP				S	S	CP			
Philippines		CP	CP	S	CP		CP	CP	CP			
Qatar		CP					S		CP			P*
Saudi Arabia		CP					S		CP			P*,R*
Singapore			CP				S	CP	CP			
Sri Lanka		CP	CP	S			S	CP	CP			
Syrian Arab Rep		CP						CP	S			M*
Thailand			CP				S	CP	CP			
Turkey		CP						CP	CP			M*,ML*,MSP*
United Arab Emirates					CP		S		S			P*
Viet Nam							S		CP			
Yemen		CP					S	S	S			R*
Yemen, Dem		CP					CP	CP	CP			R
EUROPE												
Albania												
Austria	CP		CP				S	CP	CP	CP		
Belgium	CP		CP		CP	CP	S	CP	CP	S	S	
Bulgaria	CP	CP				CP	S	CP	CP			
Czechoslovakia						CP	S	CP	CP			
Denmark	CP	CP	CP	CP	CP	CP	S	CP	CP	S	S	B*
Finland	CP	CP	CP		CP	CP	S	CP	CP	CP	S	B*
France	CP	CP	CP	S	CP	CP	S		CP	CP	S	M*,ML*,MSP*,C*,EA,SP
German Dem Rep	CP		CP		CP	CP	S	CP	CP			B*
Germany, Fed Rep	CP	CP	CP	CP	CP	CP		CP	CP	S	S	B*
Greece	CP	CP		S	CP	CP	S	CP	CP	S	S	M*,ML*,MSP*
Hungary	CP	CP	CP	CP	CP	CP	S	CP	CP			
Iceland	CP				CP	CP	CP	CP	CP			
Ireland	CP		S	CP	CP		S	CP	CP			
Italy	CP	CP	CP	CP	CP	CP	S	CP	CP	S	S	M*,ML*,MSP*
Luxembourg			CP	CP	S		S	CP	CP	S	S	
Malta		CP					S	CP	CP			M*,ML,MSP
Netherlands	CP		CP	CP	CP	CP	S	CP	CP	S	S	C*
Norway	CP	CP	CP	CP	CP	CP	S	CP	CP	CP	S	
Poland	CP	CP	S		CP	CP	S	CP	CP			B*
Portugal	CP	CP	CP	CP	CP	CP	S	S	CP		S	
Romania							CP	CP	CP			
Spain	CP	CP	CP	CP	CP	CP	S	CP	CP			M*,ML*,MSP
Sweden	CP	CP	CP	CP	CP	CP	S	CP	CP	CP	S	B*
Switzerland	CP	CP	CP		CP	CP		CP	CP	CP	S	
United Kingdom	CP	CP	CP	CP	CP	CP		CP	CP	CP	S	C*,SP
Yugoslavia	CP	CP			CP	CP	CP	CP	CP			M*,MSP*
USSR	CP		CP		CP	CP	S	CP	CP	CP	S	B*
OCEANIA												
Australia	CP	CP	CP		CP	CP	S	CP	CP	CP		SP
Fiji							CP	CP	CP			
New Zealand	CP	CP			CP		S	CP	CP	CP	S	SP
Papua New Guinea			CP		CP		S	CP	CP			SP
Solomon Islands					CP		S		CP			

Sources: United Nations Treaties Section; United Nations Environment Programme; and U.S. Department of State.
Note: a. Regional Seas letter codes indicate signature of specific Regional Seas conventions, described in Sources and Technical Notes. The Regional Seas agreement for the Baltic (B) was initiated by the seven bordering countries, not by UNEP.
CP = contracting party (has ratified or taken equivalent action); S = signatory; * = ratification of Regional Seas convention.
For additional information, see Sources and Technical Notes.

Table 24.2 Sources of Environmental and Natural Resource

National Sources of Environmental Information[a]

AFRICA

Algeria
INFOTERRA
Angola
INFOTERRA
Benin
INFOTERRA
Botswana
SOE, 1986*
NCS, in preparation
INFOTERRA
Burkina Faso
AID I, 1980*
AID II, 1982*
INFOTERRA
Burundi
AID I, 1981*
INFOTERRA
Cameroon
AID I, 1981*
INFOTERRA
Cape Verde
AID I, 1980*
INFOTERRA
Central African Rep
INFOTERRA
Chad
INFOTERRA
Comoros
INFOTERRA
Congo
INFOTERRA
Cote d'Ivoire
NCS, in preparation
INFOTERRA
Egypt
AID I, 1980[b]
INFOTERRA
Ethiopia
NCS, in preparation
INFOTERRA
Gabon
INFOTERRA
Gambia
AID I, 1981*
INFOTERRA
Ghana
AID I, 1980*
INFOTERRA
Guinea
AID I, 1983*
INFOTERRA
Guinea-Bissau
NCS, in preparation
INFOTERRA
Kenya
IUCN Expert Profile, 1984
SOE, 1987*
NCS, in preparation
INFOTERRA
Lesotho
AID I, 1982*
NCS, in preparation
INFOTERRA
Liberia
AID I, 1980*
INFOTERRA
Libya
INFOTERRA
Madagascar
NCS, 1984
SOE, 1987*
INFOTERRA
Malawi
AID I, 1982*
NCS, in preparation
INFOTERRA
Mali
AID I, 1980*
NCS, in preparation
INFOTERRA
Mauritania
AID I, 1979*
NCS, in preparation
INFOTERRA
Mauritius
INFOTERRA
Morocco
AID I, 1981*
INFOTERRA
Niger
AID I, 1980*
INFOTERRA

Nigeria
NCS, in preparation
INFOTERRA
Rwanda
AID I, 1981*
AID II, 1987*
INFOTERRA
Sao Tome and Principe
INFOTERRA
Senegal
AID I, 1980*
NCS, in preparation
INFOTERRA
Seychelles
NCS, in preparation
INFOTERRA
Sierra Leone
NCS, in preparation
Somalia
AID I, 1979*
INFOTERRA
South Africa
NCS, 1980
Sudan
AID I, 1982*
AID II, 1983*
INFOTERRA
Swaziland
AID I, 1980*
Tanzania, United Rep
IUCN Expert Profile, 1986
INFOTERRA
Togo
NCS, in preparation
INFOTERRA
Tunisia
AID I, 1980*
INFOTERRA
Uganda
AID I, 1982*
NCS, in preparation
INFOTERRA
Zaire
AID I, 1979*
AID II, 1981*
NCS, in preparation
INFOTERRA
Zambia
AID I, 1982*
IUCN Expert Profile, 1984
NCS, 1985*
INFOTERRA
Zimbabwe
AID I, 1982*
IUCN Expert Profile, 1986
NCS, 1987*
INFOTERRA

NORTH & CENTRAL AMERICA

Barbados
AID I, 1982*
NCS, in preparation
INFOTERRA
Bahamas
INFOTERRA
Belize
AID I, 1982
AID II, 1984*
NCS, in preparation
INFOTERRA
Canada
Env Stats, 1986*
SOE, 1986*
NCS*
INFOTERRA
Costa Rica
AID I, 1981*
AID II, 1982*
INFOTERRA
Dominican Rep
AID II, 1981*
El Salvador
AID I, 1982*
AID II, 1985*[b]
NCS, in preparation
INFOTERRA
Guatemala
AID I, 1981*
AID II, 1984*[b]
NCS, in preparation
INFOTERRA
Haiti
AID I, 1979*
AID II, 1985*
INFOTERRA

Honduras
AID I, 1981*
AID II, 1982*[b]
INFOTERRA
Jamaica
AID I, 1982*
AID II, 1987*
INFOTERRA
Mexico
SOE, 1986*[b]
INFOTERRA
Nicaragua
AID I, 1981*
Panama
AID I, 1980*
AID II, 1980*[b]
Env Stats, 1985
NCS, in preparation
INFOTERRA
St. Lucia
NCS, in preparation
INFOTERRA
United States
Env Stats, 1979*
SOE, 1986*, 1987*
INFOTERRA

SOUTH AMERICA

Argentina
INFOTERRA
Bolivia
AID I, 1979*
AID II, 1980*
INFOTERRA
Brazil
INFOTERRA
Chile
SOE, 1985[b]
INFOTERRA
Colombia
INFOTERRA
Ecuador
AID I, 1979*
AID II, 1983*[b]
SOE, 1981*[b], 1984*[b]
INFOTERRA
Guyana
AID I, 1982*
INFOTERRA
Paraguay
SOE, 1985
AID II, 1985*
INFOTERRA
Peru
AID I, 1979*
INFOTERRA
Uraguay
INFOTERRA
Venezuela
INFOTERRA

ASIA

Bahrain
SOE, 1988
INFOTERRA
Bangladesh
AID I, 1980*
NCS, in preparation
INFOTERRA
Burma
AID I, 1982*
China
SOE, 1984*
INFOTERRA
Cyprus
INFOTERRA
Hong Kong
SOE, 1985
INFOTERRA
India
AID I, 1980*
SOE, 1985*
NCS, in preparation
INFOTERRA
Indonesia
Env Stats, 1983*[b]
NCS, in preparation
INFOTERRA
Iraq
INFOTERRA
Israel
SOE, 1979*
INFOTERRA

Japan
Env Stats, 1980
SOE, 1987*
INFOTERRA
Jordan
AID I, 1979*
NCS, in preparation
INFOTERRA
Korea, Rep
SOE, 1983
INFOTERRA
Kuwait
SOE, 1987
INFOTERRA
Lebanon
INFOTERRA
Malaysia
SOE, 1984*
NCS, in preparation
INFOTERRA
Mongolia
INFOTERRA
Nepal
AID I, 1979*
NCS, 1987*
INFOTERRA
Oman
AID I, 1981*
NCS, in preparation
INFOTERRA
Pakistan
AID I, 1981*
Env Stats, 1984*
NCS, in preparation
INFOTERRA
Philippines
Env Stats, 1979
AID I, 1980*
SOE, 1986*
NCS, in preparation
INFOTERRA
Qatar
SOE, 1987*
INFOTERRA
Saudi Arabia
SOE, 1984
INFOTERRA
Singapore
SOE, 1985*
Sri Lanka
SOE, 1978
AID I, 1978*
IUCN Expert Profile, 1985
NCS, in preparation
INFOTERRA
Syrian Arab Rep
AID I, 1981*
INFOTERRA
Taiwan
NCS published
Thailand
AID I, 1979*
AID II, 1987*
NCS, in preparation
INFOTERRA
Turkey
AID II, 1981*
INFOTERRA
United Arab Emirates
INFOTERRA
Viet Nam
NCS, 1985*
INFOTERRA
Yemen
AID I, 1982*
INFOTERRA
Yemen, Dem
INFOTERRA

EUROPE

Austria
Env Stats, 1985*[b]
INFOTERRA
Belgium
SOE, 1979
INFOTERRA
Bulgaria
INFOTERRA
Czechoslovakia
INFOTERRA
Denmark
SOE, 1982
INFOTERRA

Information, 1988

Table 24.2

Finland
  SOE, 1985
  Env Stats, 1987*[b]
  INFOTERRA
France
  SOE, 1985*
  Env Stats, 1986
  NCS, in preparation
  INFOTERRA
German Dem Rep
  INFOTERRA
Germany, Fed Rep
  Env Stats, 1985*
  INFOTERRA
Greece
  INFOTERRA
Hungary
  Env Stats, 1981
  SOE, 1986*[b]
  INFOTERRA
Ireland
  SOE, 1985*
  INFOTERRA

Italy
  Env Stats, 1984[b]
  SOE, 1987[b]
  NCS completed
  INFOTERRA
Luxembourg
  SOE, 1984[b]
  INFOTERRA
Malta
  INFOTERRA
Netherlands
  SOE, 1985*
  Env Stats, 1987*
  INFOTERRA
Norway
  Env Stats, 1983*[b]
  NCS, in preparation
  INFOTERRA
Poland
  Env Stats, 1985[b]
  INFOTERRA
Portugal
  INFOTERRA
Romania
  INFOTERRA

Spain
  SOE, 1977
  NCS, in preparation
  INFOTERRA
Sweden
  SOE, 1984*
  Env Stats, 1987*[b]
  INFOTERRA
Switzerland
  NCS, in preparation
  INFOTERRA
United Kingdom
  NCS, 1983
  Env Stats, 1986*
  INFOTERRA
Yugoslavia
  SOE, 1983
  Env Stats, 1985[b]
  NCS, in preparation
  INFOTERRA

USSR
  INFOTERRA

OCEANIA

Australia
  NCS, 1983
  Env Stats, 1985*
  SOE, 1987*
  INFOTERRA
Fiji
  NCS, in preparation
  INFOTERRA
New Zealand
  SOE, 1980
  NCS, 1985
  INFOTERRA
Papua New Guinea
  INFOTERRA
Samoa
  INFOTERRA
Vanuatu
  NCS, in preparation
  INFOTERRA

Global and Regional Sources of Environmental Information

World:
Martin W. Holdgate, Mohammed Kassas, and Gilbert F. White, *World Environment 1972-82* (Tycooly, Dublin, 1982).*

United Nations Environment Programme (UNEP), *The State of the Environment 1987* (UNEP, Nairobi, 1987).*

UNEP, *Environmental Data Report* (Basil Blackwell, Oxford, 1987).*

World Commission on Environment and Development, *Our Common Future* (Oxford University Press, Oxford, 1987).*

Lester R. Brown *et al., State of the World 1988* (W.W. Norton, New York, 1988).*

World Resources Institute, International Institute for Environment and Development, *World Resources 1988-89* (Basic Books, New York, 1988).*

Africa:
Bureau for Africa, U.S. Agency for International Development (U.S. AID), *Natural Resources and Environmental Concerns in Sub-Saharan Africa* (U.S. AID, Washington, D.C., 1986).*

International Union for Conservation of Nature and Natural Resources (IUCN), *The IUCN Sahel Report: A Long Term Strategy for Environmental Rehabilitation* (IUCN, Gland, Switzerland, 1986).*

Program for International Development, *Renewable Resource Trends in East Africa* (Program for International Development, Clark University, Worcester, Massachusetts, 1984).*

U.N. Food and Agriculture Organization (FAO), *Natural Resources and the Human Environment for Food and Agriculture in Africa* (FAO, Rome, 1986).*

Latin America:
Eric Cardich, ed., *Conservando el Partimonio Natural de la Region Neotropical* (IUCN, Gland, Switzerland, 1986).*[b]

M.J. Dourojeanni, *Renewable Natural Resources of Latin America and the Caribbean, Situation and Trends* (World Wildlife Fund, Washington, D.C., 1982).*

Inter-American Development Bank (IDB), *Natural Resources in Latin America* (IDB, Washington, D.C., 1983).*

H. Jeffrey Leonard, *Natural Resources and Economic Development in Central America* (International Institute for Environment and Development, Washington, D.C., 1987).*

Jorge Morello, *Perfil Ecologico de Sudamerica* (Instituto de Cooperacion Iberoamericana, Barcelona, 1984).*[b]

Europe and North America:
Commission of the European Communities (CEC), *The State of the Environment in the European Community 1986* (CEC, Luxembourg, 1986).*

U.N. Statistical Commission and Economic Commission for Europe, *Environment Statistics in Europe and North America* (United Nations, New York, 1987).*

Eurostat, *Statistics Related to the Environment* (Eurostat, Luxembourg, 1987).*

Docter-Institute for Environmental Studies-Milan and the Commission of the European Communities, *European Environmental Yearbook 1987* (Docter International U.K., London, 1987).*

OECD:
Organisation for Economic Co-operation and Development (OECD), *OECD Environmental Data Compendium 1987* (OECD, Paris, 1987).*

OECD, *State of the Environment 1985* (OECD, Paris, 1985).*

Asia and Oceania:
A.L. Dahl and L.L Baumgart, *The State of the Environment in the South Pacific* (UNEP, Geneva, 1983).*

U.N. Economic and Social Commission for Asia and the Pacific (ESCAP), *State of the Environment in Asia and the Pacific*, Vols. I and II (ESCAP, Bangkok, 1985).*

Sources: World Resources Institute; International Institute for Environment and Development; International Union for Conservation of Nature and Natural Resources; U.S. Agency for International Development; and United Nations Environment Programme.
Notes:
a. Publication date of most recent edition; multiple dates indicate different reports.
b. Not available in English. Some statistical reports have English table headings.
AID I: U.S. Agency for International Development Phase I Environmental Profile
AID II: U.S. Agency for International Development Phase II Environmental Profile
SOE: National State of the Environment Report
Env Stats: National Environmental Statistical Report
IUCN Expert Profile: IUCN Natural Resources Expertise Profile
NCS: National Conservation Strategy
INFOTERRA: member of INFOTERRA environmental information network
* = Copy held in *World Resources Report* library.
For additional information, see Sources and Technical Notes.

Table 24.3 Allocation of Official Development Assistance by Donors, 1975–86

			Percentage of Official Development Assistance Given[a]									
			Australia	Austria	Belgium	Canada	Denmark	Finland	France	Germany	Ireland	Italy
Social and Administrative	Education	1975-76	8.6	4.1	2.0	3.8	5.3	5.9	34.6	14.4	X	10.6
		1985-86	22.3	38.4	28.6	8.1	2.9	7.7	26.5	19.9	20.3	4.3
	Health and Population	1975-76	3.4	2.1	1.5	1.4	5.1	3.1	10.6	1.3	X	1.3
		1985-86	1.9	2.3	8.8	2.4	5.7	14.3	4.4	2.1	6.6	7.5
	Planning and Public Administration	1975-76	4.0	0.4	0.3	2.8	1.3	0.8	1.3	0.8	X	1.9
		1985-86	2.4	0.2	2.8	1.0	0.2	1.4	5.2	4.0	0.9	3.3
	Water, Sanitation, and Other Social Services	1975-76	1.5	0.4	1.0	8.5	2.4	1.1	7.2	6.9	X	0.3
		1985-86	3.4	2.9	6.0	4.0	15.9	0.5	6.4	7.7	8.5	3.0
Economic Infrastructure	Transport and Communication	1975-76	6.6	0.4	1.2	12.3	0.0	4.6	10.2	9.4	X	2.0
		1985-86	2.0	2.3	9.9	9.5	6.5	0.0	11.1	10.3	0.9	8.7
	Energy	1975-76	0.2	0.0	0.0	2.8	0.0	4.3	2.8	8.3	X	0.0
		1985-86	0.3	27.0	3.4	4.3	9.0	22.6	2.6	9.1	0.0	6.0
	Other Infrastructure	1975-76	0.3	31.1	30.6	4.8	7.5	0.0	4.4	1.5	X	12.7
		1985-86	0.1	1.2	0.6	0.0	10.4	5.1	3.9	0.7	0.0	11.5
Production	Agriculture	1975-76	4.3	3.3	2.7	8.4	11.4	3.6	7.0	7.5	X	2.9
		1985-86	10.1	3.0	11.7	18.8	15.4	19.7	10.1	10.2	18.4	13.8
	Industry, Mining, and Construction	1975-76	1.3	21.2	1.2	3.1	8.4	8.7	5.4	8.5	X	1.7
		1985-86	2.5	9.7	5.2	7.8	15.9	12.5	4.3	6.0	1.9	13.1
	Trade, Banking, and Tourism	1975-76	0.4	4.1	0.5	1.2	1.1	2.5	1.1	6.2	X	1.1
		1985-86	1.0	0.3	2.5	0.5	0.0	1.0	0.1	4.5	2.8	0.5
	Other Production	1975-76	0.3	30.7	30.6	4.8	7.5	0.0	4.4	1.5	X	12.7
		1985-86	0.0	0.8	0.6	0.0	0.0	5.1	1.9	0.6	0.0	0.0
Assistance not Allocated by Sector	Program Assistance	1975-76	43.9	0.0	13.0	9.9	41.7	0.8	6.6	15.7	X	10.7
		1985-86	39.1	0.0	3.5	6.4	0.0	0.0	7.1	5.3	0.0	0.7
	Debt Relief	1975-76	0.0	0.0	0.0	0.0	1.0	0.0	0.8	12.5	X	30.8
		1985-86	0.0	0.2	0.0	0.1	0.0	0.0	6.9	8.7	0.0	0.5
	Food Aid	1975-76	9.2	0.0	2.9	20.6	3.4	7.3	1.1	3.1	X	0.0
		1985-86	6.0	7.0	4.0	12.9	0.0	0.3	1.0	3.2	0.0	7.9
	Emergency Aid	1975-76	0.0	1.2	0.7	0.3	2.6	2.5	0.4	0.4	X	X
		1985-86	1.5	4.5	0.3	3.5	0.0	0.9	0.1	0.7	5.7	7.6
	Miscellaneous	1975-76	16.0	0.4	11.7	15.2	1.4	54.9	2.1	2.1	X	11.3
		1985-86	7.6	0.0	12.0	20.8	18.1	8.8	8.5	7.0	33.9	11.6

			Percentage of Official Development Assistance Given[a]									
			Japan	Nether-lands	New Zealand	Norway	Sweden	Switzer-land	United Kingdom	United States	All Donors	Multi-Laterals[b]
Social and Administrative	Education	1975-76	1.6	11.5	5.5	5.1	9.6	4.7	0.5	1.8	10.1	X
		1985-86	8.1	10.8	9.8	8.3	7.3	7.2	12.8	3.8	10.9	5.0
	Health and Population	1975-76	0.8	11.3	2.3	12.7	6.4	0.3	0.6	3.8	4.6	X
		1985-86	3.7	4.8	2.3	13.8	5.7	3.5	4.3	6.9	5.3	8.9
	Planning and Public Administration	1975-76	0.6	1.1	6.1	0.6	0.2	0.1	0.4	0.4	0.9	X
		1985-86	0.7	1.2	5.3	1.6	1.2	1.8	2.3	1.4	2.2	0.5
	Water, Sanitation, and Other Social Services	1975-76	0.3	10.7	0.6	4.5	6.0	7.2	3.2	2.1	4.3	X
		1985-86	6.0	13.5	4.5	8.4	1.5	7.1	7.4	5.4	6.0	5.8
Economic Infrastructure	Transport and Communication	1975-76	0.0	0.0	1.8	10.4	1.2	5.7	2.4	1.6	4.6	X
		1985-86	22.0	6.9	10.3	16.8	0.9	6.7	4.6	1.6	8.1	15.6
	Energy	1975-76	36.6	12.6	32.1	6.4	1.3	7.5	1.0	0.7	5.9	X
		1985-86	12.3	4.4	9.9	6.1	12.1	1.0	6.1	0.7	5.1	18.7
	Other Infrastructure	1975-76	1.1	1.2	1.3	7.7	0.1	8.2	24.9	0.4	3.9	X
		1985-86	3.0	0.4	0.7	0.4	9.2	4.8	8.5	0.9	3.3	0.0
Production	Agriculture	1975-76	6.0	20.9	23.7	25.9	9.0	17.9	4.3	8.1	8.2	X
		1985-86	14.2	22.2	20.7	14.4	6.0	24.5	10.2	11.2	12.5	22.1
	Industry, Mining, and Construction	1975-76	18.3	7.9	1.9	7.3	13.1	3.3	3.3	3.2	6.0	X
		1985-86	10.9	4.0	2.7	12.0	10.0	9.5	10.4	0.3	5.6	7.5
	Trade, Banking, and Tourism	1975-76	1.2	0.4	1.3	0.1	1.3	1.9	0.6	0.9	1.6	X
		1985-86	0.6	1.1	0.2	1.4	0.6	2.6	1.1	3.9	2.1	3.2
	Other Production	1975-76	1.1	1.2	1.3	7.7	0.2	8.2	24.9	0.4	3.9	X
		1985-86	0.9	0.0	0.0	0.0	3.9	4.8	5.5	0.9	1.1	0.0
Assistance not Allocated by Sector	Program Assistance	1975-76	14.7	2.3	13.7	0.0	11.0	0.0	5.0	35.8	19.8	X
		1985-86	8.3	3.6	27.1	2.1	14.8	6.4	9.4	41.7	18.2	3.4[c]
	Debt Relief	1975-76	12.5	4.8	0.0	0.0	0.6	10.6	4.6	4.7	5.1	X
		1985-86	3.2	1.6	0.0	0.0	3.6	0.0	4.6	0.5	2.8	0.0
	Food Aid	1975-76	0.5	1.6	5.5	0.0	8.4	10.6	0.0	29.5	12.7	X
		1985-86	1.4	2.7	0.1	1.7	0.5	7.7	2.6	12.9	6.4	4.6
	Emergency Aid	1975-76	0.1	1.8	0.2	6.8	2.5	12.2	0.3	1.6	1.1	X
		1985-86	0.1	2.4	2.0	2.8	8.7	11.8	3.9	2.3	2.2	3.2
	Miscellaneous	1975-76	4.6	10.9	2.5	5.0	29.1	1.4	24.0	5.1	7.3	X
		1985-86	4.6	20.5	4.3	10.2	14.1	0.4	6.3	5.6	8.2	1.5[d]

Source: Organisation for Economic Co-operation and Development.
Notes:
a. 1975-76 data includes estimates, and may not be fully comparable with 1985-86 data.
b. 1984-85 figures for allocation of official development finance (ODF).
c. Most program assistance recorded under appropriate sector.
d. Partial figure.
0 = zero or less than five one-hundredths of one percent; X = not available.
For additional information, see Sources and Technical Notes.

Sources and Technical Notes

Table 24.1 Participation in Global Conventions Protecting the Environment, 1988

Sources: United Nations Environment Programme (UNEP), "Environmental Law in the United Nations Environment Programme" (UNEP, Nairobi, 1985); UNEP Governing Council, "Register of International Treaties and Other Agreements in the Field of the Environment, Supplement 1" (UNEP, Nairobi, April 1987); UNEP, "Status of Regional Agreements Negotiated in the Framework of the Regional Seas Programme, Rev. 1" (UNEP, Nairobi, February 1988); U.S. Department of State, *Treaties in Force* (U.S. Department of State, Washington, D.C., 1987); U.S. Department of State, unpublished data (U.S. Department of State, Washington, D.C., March 1988); Treaties Section, United Nations Secretariat, unpublished data (United Nations, New York, March 1988).

A country becomes a *signatory* of a treaty when a person given authority by the national government signs the treaty. A country's signature indicates a commitment to undertake domestic action to ratify the treaty. A country is a *contracting party* when it has ratified the treaty or taken an equivalent action to adopt the provisions of the treaty as national law. A treaty goes into force when a prescribed number of countries have ratified it. Both signatures and ratifications of treaties become official when they are registered with the treaty's depositary, which may be a national government, a United Nations organization, or an international organization. Some treaties have multiple depositaries.

The complete titles of the conventions and treaties summarized in Table 24.1, and their places and dates of adoption, are:
1. Convention on Wetlands of International Importance, Especially as Waterfowl Habitat (Ramsar, 1971);
2. Convention Concerning the Protection of the World Cultural and Natural Heritage (Paris, 1972);
3. Convention on International Trade in Endangered Species of Wild Fauna and Flora (Washington, D.C., 1973);
4. Convention on the Conservation of Migratory Species of Wild Animals (Bonn, 1979);
5. Convention on the Prevention of Marine Pollution by Dumping of Wastes and Other Matter (London, Mexico, Moscow, Washington, D.C., 1972);
6. Protocol of 1978 Relating to the International Convention for the Prevention of Pollution from Ships, 1973 (London, 1978);
7. United Nations Convention on the Law of the Sea (Montego Bay, 1982);
8. Treaty Banning Nuclear Weapon Tests in the Atmosphere, in Outer Space, and under Water (Moscow, 1963);
9. Convention on the Prohibition of the Development, Production, and Stockpiling of Bacteriological (Biological) and Toxin Weapons, and on their Destruction (London, Moscow, Washington, D.C., 1972);
10. Vienna Convention for the Protection of the Ozone Layer (Vienna, 1985);
11. Protocol on Substances that Deplete the Ozone Layer (Montreal, 1987).

The United Nations Convention on the Law of the Sea, the Vienna Convention for the Protection of the Ozone Layer, and the Protocol on Substances that Deplete the Ozone Layer have not yet entered into force. The Vienna Convention for the Protection of the Ozone Layer will enter into force when 20 countries ratify it. The Protocol on Substances that Deplete the Ozone Layer will enter into force January 1, 1989, if at least 11 countries, accounting for at least two thirds of 1986 estimated world chlorofluorocarbon consumption, ratify the treaty in 1988.

The European Community has signed the Convention on the Conservation of Migratory Species of Wild Animals, the United Nations Convention on the Law of the Sea, the Vienna Convention for the Protection of the Ozone Layer, and the Protocol on Substances that Deplete the Ozone Layer.

Some of the symbols used to indicate participation in a Regional Sea convention denote several related conventions and protocols. An asterisk (*) follows the convention abbreviation if a country has ratified at least one of the conventions or protocols. The full titles of Regional Seas conventions, their date of adoption, and the abbreviations used in the table are listed below.

B = Helsinki Convention on the Protection of the Marine Environment of the Baltic Sea (1974).

M = Convention for the Protection of the Mediterranean Sea against Pollution (1976). Protocol for the Prevention of Pollution of the Mediterranean Sea by Dumping from Ships and Aircraft (1976). Protocol Concerning Co-operation in Combating Pollution of the Mediterranean Sea by Oil and Other Harmful Substances in Cases of Emergency (1976).

ML = Protocol for the Protection of the Mediterranean Sea against Pollution from Land-Based Sources (1980).

MSP = Protocol Concerning Mediterranean Specially Protected Areas (1982).

P = Kuwait Regional Convention for Co-operation on the Protection of the Marine Environment from Pollution (1978). Protocol Concerning Regional Co-operation in Combating Pollution by Oil and Other Harmful Substances in Cases of Emergency (1978).

WCA = Convention for Co-operation in the Protection and Development of the Marine and Coastal Environment of the West and Central African Region (1981). Protocol Concerning Co-operation in Combating Pollution in Cases of Emergency (1981).

R = Regional Convention for the Conservation of the Red Sea and Gulf of Aden (1982). Protocol Concerning Regional Co-operation in Combating Pollution by Oil and Other Harmful Substances in Cases of Emergency (1982).

SEP = Convention for the Protection of the Marine Environment and Coastal Area of the Southeast Pacific (1981). Agreement on Regional Co-operation in Combating Pollution of the Southeast Pacific by Oil and Other Harmful Substances in Cases of Emergency (1981). Supplementary Protocol to the Agreement on Regional Co-operation in Combating Pollution of the Southeast Pacific by Oil and Other Harmful Substances in Cases of Emergency (1983). Protocol for the Protection of the Southeast Pacific against Pollution from Land-Based Sources (1983).

C = Convention for the Protection and Development of the Marine Environment of the Wider Caribbean Region (1983). Protocol Concerning Co-operation in Combating Oil Spills in the Wider Caribbean Region (1983).

EA = Convention for the Protection, Management and Development of the Marine and Coastal Environment of the Eastern African Region (1985). Protocol Concerning Protected Areas and Wild Fauna and Flora in the Eastern African Region (1985). Protocol Concerning Co-operation in Combating Marine Pollution in Cases of Emergency in the Eastern African Region (1985).

SP = Convention for the Protection of the Natural Resources and Environment of the South Pacific Region (1986).

The Eastern African and South Pacific Regional Seas conventions and their protocols have not yet entered into force.

Information on the number of Natural World Heritage Sites and Wetlands of International Importance is contained in Chapter 19, "Wildlife and Habitat," Table 19.1. For information on treaty terms, refer to the sources.

Table 24.2 Sources of Environmental and Natural Resource Information, 1988

Source: Compiled by the World Resources Institute and the International Institute for Environment and Development.

The U.S. Agency for International Development (U.S. AID) sponsors the production of two series of environmental profiles. *Phase I* profiles are compiled from published literature. *Phase II* profiles are based on more extensive field studies, often written in collaboration with government institutions or local nongovernmental organizations. Phase II profiles include analyses of the laws, policies, and institutions that affect the environment and natural resource management in the country, and often propose strategies to redress problems. Phase II profiles are comparable to state of the environment reports in scope and detail.

State of the Environment Reports are published by government agencies, multilateral organizations, universities, and nongovernmental organizations. They analyze the condition and management of a country's natural resources and document its progress or failure in sustaining its natural resource base. *National Environmental Statistical Reports* rely on data tables and graphs to present information, and contain little analysis.

National Conservation Strategy reports are prepared by some countries that have adopted a National Conservation Strategy, endorsed by the national government. Some countries that have not officially adopted a National Conservation Strategy may have published a draft document for discussion. For more detailed information on the status of National Conservation Strategies, see past issues of the *IUCN Bulletin Supplement*.

Natural Resources Expertise Profiles are outlines of the major agencies, organizations and individuals working on environmental and natural resources issues in a specific country. The Expertise Profiles are compiled by consultants, under the direction of the International Union for Conservation of Nature and Natural Resources (IUCN).

INFOTERRA, the International Referral System for Sources of Environmental Information, is a network of national information centers established by the United Nations Environment Programme (UNEP) for the exchange of environmental information. Each member country compiles a register of institutions willing to share expertise in environmentally-related areas, such as atmosphere and climate, energy, food and agriculture, plant and animal wildlife, and pollution. An international directory is compiled from the national registers; the directory passes on queries to experts who can answer them. In 1985, the network answered over 10,500 queries, over half of which came from developing countries.

The brief bibliography of Regional Sources of Environmental Information includes both statistical and analytical publications.

Table 24.3 Allocation of Official Development Assistance by Donors, 1975–86

Sources: 1975–76 data: Organisation for Economic Co-operation and Development (OECD), unpublished data (OECD, Paris, March 1988); 1985–86 data: OECD, *Development Co-operation, 1987 Report* (OECD, Paris, 1988).

Official Development Assistance (ODA) is comprised of disbursed grants and concessional loans given by a country. Grants include any gifts, in money, goods, or services. Concessional loans have a grant element of 25 percent or more: the grant element is the amount by which the face value of the loan exceeds its present market value because of below-market interest rates, favorable maturity schedules, and repayment grace periods. Non-concessional loans are not a component of ODA.

OECD gathers ODA data through questionnaires and reports from countries and multilateral agencies.

The countries shown are members of OECD's Development Assistance Committee, and contribute about 80 percent of the world's ODA. Data on major uses of ODA from individual countries describe the allocation of *bilateral* ODA: development assistance given by the donor country directly to the recipient country.

Allocation of aid from multilateral development institutions describes the commitment of *Official Development Finance* (ODA and non-concessional lending to developing countries) by the World Bank, regional development institutions and banks, the International Fund for Agricultural Development, the European Community, World Food Programme, United Nations High Commission on Refugees, United Nations Relief and Works Agency, and includes technical cooperation from other U.N. agencies.

OECD defines four general allocations of development assistance: social and administrative, economic infrastructure, production, and general assistance.

Assistance allocated to *social and administrative* purposes is used to develop human resources. *Education* includes funding for teaching in all fields, from the primary school to university level; funding for building or improving educational establishments; vocational and technical training; scholarships to universities; and training in the donor country. *Health and population* includes assistance to hospitals and clinics, maternal and child care programs, hospital administration, medical insurance programs, family planning services and research, and other health services. Assistance to *planning and public administration* includes funding for administrative buildings and normal government operations, police and fire protection, and aid to governments for development planning. Economic development planning and policy formulation, statistical collection, mapping, and demographic studies are also included in planning and public administration. *Water, sanitation, and other social services* includes assistance given for development and maintenance of water and sanitation facilities (excluding irrigation systems used for agriculture), rural and urban housing projects, community development, assistance to labor organizations, social security and welfare schemes, environmental protection (excluding soil conservation), land settlement programs, and cultural activities.

Economic infrastructure includes many large, capital-intensive projects. *Transport and communication* includes funding for equipment and infrastructure for rail, road, water, and air transport, and assistance to communications development, including radio and television. *Energy* includes funding for power production and distribution, and peaceful uses of nuclear energy. Assistance to petroleum and natural gas production is reported in industry, mining, and construction. *Other infrastructure* includes funding for management, automation, accounting, and business finance and investment programs.

The *production* sector comprises all assistance to directly productive activities. Allocations to *agriculture* include projects assisting agricultural production (direct assistance to raising livestock and crops); services to agriculture such as marketing, co-ops, trade promotion; research; forestry; fishing and hunting; conservation and extension programs; land reclamation; agricultural storage; home economics and nutrition; land and soil surveys; and agricultural development banks. *Industry, mining, and construction* includes assistance to manufacturing and mining industries and their related activities. Only assistance given directly to the construction industry is included in this category: projects involving the construction of specific buildings are classified according to the use of the building. *Trade, banking, and tourism* includes most service industries: trade and export promotion, commerce, banks, and hotels and tourist facilities are included in this category, as well as publishing, journalism, cinema, and photography.

Assistance not allocated by sector includes several types of general assistance, and aid for which a purpose is not reported. *Program assistance* includes all development assistance given to a developing country for general development purposes, such as balance of payments and budget support. *Debt relief* comprises all transactions of debt forgiveness, rescheduling and refinancing. *Food aid* includes any supply of food, whether given in emergencies or not. *Emergency assistance* includes cash and commodity relief (excluding food aid), and aid to refugees. *Miscellaneous* includes funding for projects that straddle multiple sectors, administrative expenses incurred by the donor, aid that cannot be assigned to another category, and aid for which a purpose is not specified.

OECD has recently revised its method of classifying uses of aid. Between 1975–76 and 1985–86, some subsectors were reassigned; as a result, the data are not fully comparable between the two periods.

World Map

World Map

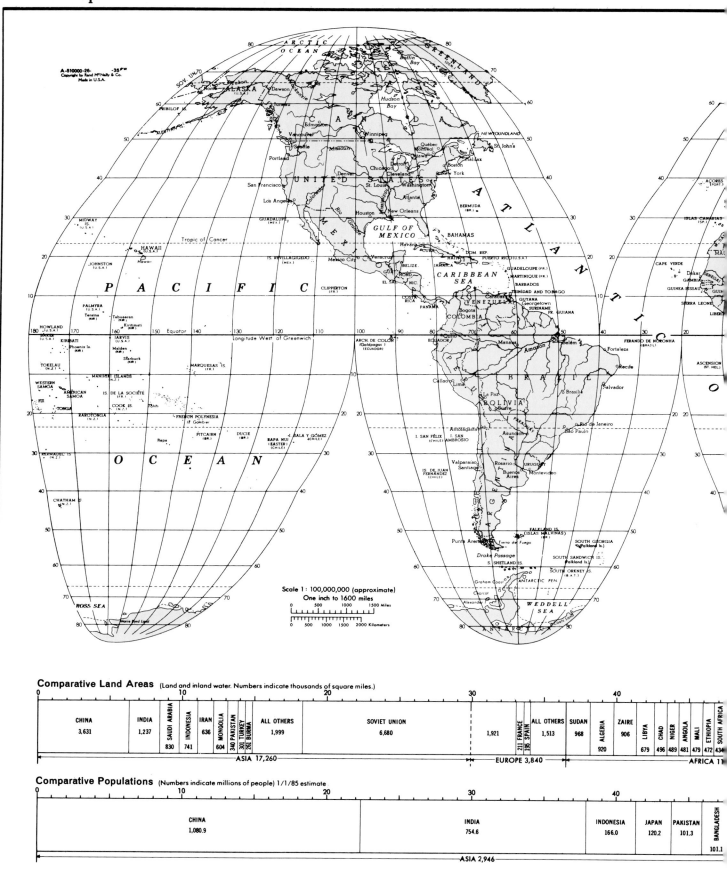

Comparative Land Areas (Land and inland water. Numbers indicate thousands of square miles.)

CHINA 3,631	INDIA 1,237	SAUDI ARABIA 830	INDONESIA 741	IRAN 636	MONGOLIA 604	PAKISTAN 340	TURKEY 301	BURMA 261	ALL OTHERS 1,999	SOVIET UNION 6,680	1,921	FRANCE 211	SPAIN 195	ALL OTHERS 1,513	SUDAN 968	ALGERIA 920	ZAIRE 906	LIBYA 679	CHAD 496	NIGER 489	ANGOLA 481	MALI 479	ETHIOPIA 472	SOUTH AFRICA 434

ASIA 17,260   EUROPE 3,840   AFRICA 1

Comparative Populations (Numbers indicate millions of people) 1/1/85 estimate

CHINA 1,080.9	INDIA 754.6	INDONESIA 166.0	JAPAN 120.2	PAKISTAN 101.3	BANGLADESH 101.1

ASIA 2,946

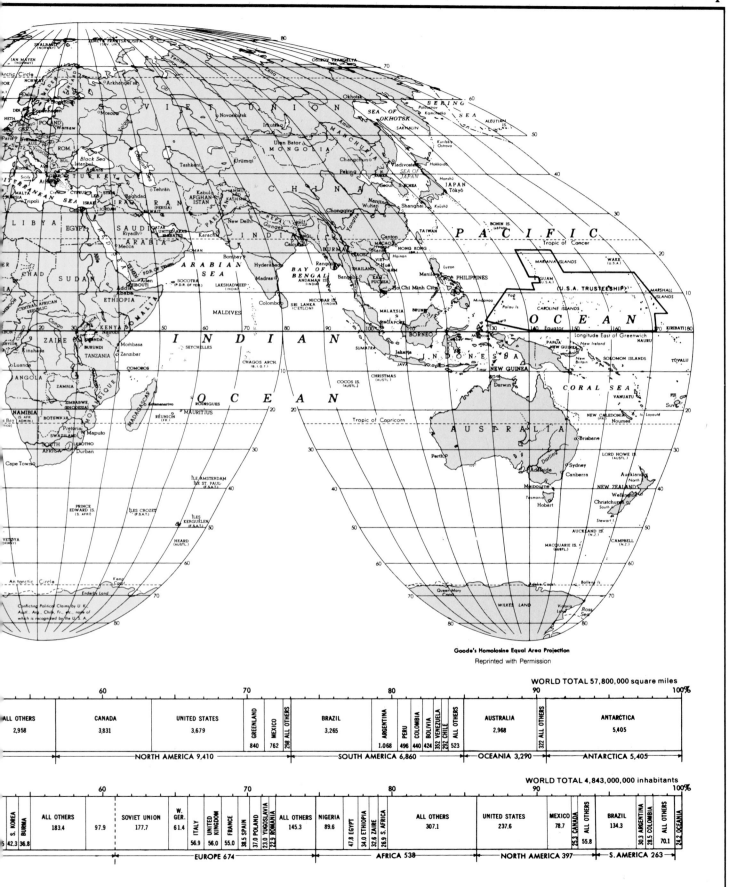

Goode's Homolosine Equal Area Projection
Reprinted with Permission

WORLD TOTAL 57,800,000 square miles

		60		70				80							90		100%

ALL OTHERS	CANADA	UNITED STATES	GREENLAND	MEXICO	ALL OTHERS	BRAZIL	ARGENTINA	PERU	COLOMBIA	BOLIVIA	VENEZUELA	CHILE	ALL OTHERS	AUSTRALIA	ALL OTHERS	ANTARCTICA
2,958	3,831	3,679	840	762	298	3,265	1,068	496	440	424	352	292	523	2,968	322	5,405

NORTH AMERICA 9,410 — SOUTH AMERICA 6,860 — OCEANIA 3,290 — ANTARCTICA 5,405

WORLD TOTAL 4,843,000,000 inhabitants

		60			70							80				90			100%

S. KOREA	BURMA	ALL OTHERS		SOVIET UNION	W. GER.	ITALY	UNITED KINGDOM	FRANCE	SPAIN	POLAND	YUGOSLAVIA	ROMANIA	ALL OTHERS	NIGERIA	EGYPT	ETHIOPIA	ZAIRE	S. AFRICA	ALL OTHERS	UNITED STATES	MEXICO	CANADA	ALL OTHERS	BRAZIL	ARGENTINA	COLOMBIA	ALL OTHERS	OCEANIA
42.3	36.8	183.4	97.9	177.7	61.4	56.9	56.0	55.0	38.5	37.0	23.0	22.9	145.3	89.6	47.8	34.0	32.6	26.9	307.1	237.6	78.7	25.3	55.8	134.3	30.3	28.5	70.1	24.2

EUROPE 674 — AFRICA 538 — NORTH AMERICA 397 — S. AMERICA 263

Index

Numbers in italics refer to pages with tables or figures.

Index

renewable energy in, 111
wilderness area in, 263
Cape Verde, reliance on official development assistance by, 235
Carbon dioxide
affect on climate, 173–177
emissions by country and region (1950–85), 170, *336*
trends in atmospheric concentration of, 305, 333, *334*
Carbon monoxide, sources, emissions, and ambient levels of, 168, *335*
Caribbean Basin
AIDS in, 27–28
marine protected areas in, 7, 143, 150–152
renewable energy in, 114
urbanization in countries of, 36–39
see also individual countries in
Casablanca, Morocco, slum and squatter areas in, 37
Central America
urbanization in, 36–39
see also individual countries in
Chandler, Robert F., 63
Chang Jiang (Yangtze) River (China), 133
Chapin, Harry, 63
Chernobyl, U.S.S.R.
health impact studies on accident at, 123–124
nuclear accident at, 6, 85, 111, 118
Children
health programs for, 2, 26–27
health related statistics concerning, 245, *254–255*
immunization of, 245
China, People's Republic of
agricultural incentives in, 204
agricultural research in, 55–56
biointensive agriculture program, 132
cities' contribution to GNP in, 41
energy consumption in, 109, 112–113, 305
energy exports by, 112
energy reserves and production in, 109, 111–112
family planning program in, 12, 21–22, 245
fertilizer use in, 207
food output per capita in, 53
freshwater availability in, 129
integrated pest management use in, 31
malaria incidence in, 26
per capita food production in, 3
per capita GNP of, 11
rangeland conditions in, 79–81
recovery projects in, 216
recycling waste in, 46–47
reforestation in, 13–14
renewable energy use in, 111–113
rural areas' importance in, 44
small dam construction in, 7, 139–140
total fertility rate rise in, 22, 31
urbanization in, 37
water pricing and use in, 132, 206
Chlorofluorocarbons, 170–172
atmospheric concentrations of, 333, *335*
reduction in production of, 347
Christian Science Monitor, 63
Cities
as agricultural markets, 41–42
effects of changing demographics in developing countries on, 37, 39
encouraging growth in towns and secondary, 43–44
growth of largest (1970–2000), *40*
growth in number and size of, 37–39, *44*
importance of towns and secondary, 42–43

migration from rural areas to, 39, 263
natural resource use and, 13, 41–42
nonpoint pollution in, 137
service availability in, 3, 263
urban population concentrated into countries' largest, 39
waste composition of, *46–47*
waste generation rates in, 3, *46*
see also Settlements, Human; Urbanization
Climate change, 8, 333
deep ocean circulation and, 144–145
environmental impacts of, 159, 173–175
historical, 194–197
water cycle and, 189–192
Coal, 110–111, 118–120
Cocoa Marketing Board (Ghana), 208
Colombia
secondary and intermediate cities in, 43
waste scavenging in, 47
Colorado, water marketing in, 132
Commodities
exports of, 235
indexes of, *240–241*
prices of, 235, *240–241*
research focusing on specific agricultural, 56–57
see also Agriculture; Food
Common Ground, 132
Companhia de Saneamento Ambiental (CETESB)—Brazil, 171
Conservation banking, 101
Conservation biology, 90
Consultative Group on International Agricultural Research (CGIAR), 55, 63
Contraception
prevalence rates for use of, 23, *24, 258–260*
use and category of residence, 39–40, 245
see also Family planning
Convention on International Trade in Endangered Species of Wild Fauna and Flora (CITES), 5, 97–99, 293, *298–299*
Convention on Long-Range Transboundary Air Pollution (LRTAP), 1, 177–178
Coordinating Body on the Seas of East Asia (COBSEA), 154–155
Costa Rica
deforestation in, 71
Guanacaste restoration in, 220, 224
Costs. *See* Expenditures
Côte d'Ivoire, 3
deforestation in, 18, 71
water management in, 131
Council for Mutual Economic Assistance (CMEA), 117, 120
Croplands
conversion of rangelands to, 78–79
population pressure and degradation of, 18–19
rainfed, 61–62, 223
rehabilitating degraded irrigated, 11, 225–227
see also Agriculture; Food; Land use
Czechoslovakia, 119
energy-related pollution in, 121, 333
energy trends in, 117

D

Dams
construction of large, 133, 139
resurgence in construction of small, 7, 139–140

sediment loading and, 317
see also individual dams
Dar es Salaam, Tanzania, countrywide food distribution from, 41–42
Data
on agricultural land distribution, 235
climate change, 333, *334–336*
distribution of household income, 235, *242–243*
on economic indicators, 235, *236–243*
effects of changing reporting procedures for land use, 263
energy use trend, 305, *306–311*
fertilizer use, 135, 137
food and agricultural, 271, *272–281*
forest resources, 285, *286–290*
freshwater resources and use, 127–130, 317, *318–323*
indicators of national environmental policies, 347, *348–349, 352*
materials use trend, 305, *311–313*
on oceans and coasts, 325, *326–330*
plant species that are globally rare and threatened, 293, *300–302*
pollution, 333, *336–342*
population and health, 245, *246–260*
satellite, 64, 71, 72–73, 217
shortage of rangeland, 285
soil erosion, 271, *282*
sources on environmental and natural resources information (1988), *350–351*
waste generation and disposal, 305, *311–314*
wildlife and habitat, 293, *294–299*
Death. *See* Mortality
Debt, external
of developing countries, 235
exchange programs for reducing, 100–101
indicators (by country), *238–239*
official development assistance for relief of, 347
as percentage of GNP, 235
Deforestation, 4
to create cropland, 263
extent of, 4, 285, *286–287*
incentives, 211–212
soil erosion caused by, 317
Tropical Forestry Action Plan strategies for combating, 84
trends in, 1, 14, 71–74
see also Degradation; Forests; Wood
Degradation
abandonment of land suffering from, 218
assisted recovery techniques for land, 218–219
costs of recovery from, 215–217, 219
definition of, 216
future of restoration and rehabilitation of lands suffering, 229–231
guidelines of recovery programs for, 228, *229*
Himalayan Mountains, 221–222
matching economic policies and technologies to needs when rehabilitating land suffering from, 227–228
native versus exotic species use in rehabilitation of areas suffering from, 219
rangeland, 19, 73, 82–83
rehabilitation of drylands suffering from, 222–225
rehabilitation of irrigated cropland suffering from, 225–227
rehabilitation of mountainous areas suffering from, 218–222
social costs of land, 227

E

Index

protected areas management, 151–152
solar power electricity production, 113
solid waste disposal, 45–46
sport hunting, 98
water transfer projects, 133
wildlife and wildlife products trade, 5, 97
see also Incentives; Subsidies
Exports. *See* Trade

Family planning
contraceptives used for (by type and country), *258–260*
effort scores of programs (for 100 countries), *23*
unmet need for devices (by country), 245, *258–260*
see also Contraception
Famine early warning system (FEWS), 64
Farming systems research (FSR), 51, 57
Feinstein, Alan Shawn, 63
Fertility
rates, 12, 21, *22*, *248–249*
reduction effort trends, 21–23, 39–40
Finland
infant mortality rates in, 25
official development assistance projects by, 347
radioactive contamination of rangeland in, 85
Fisheries
demand for products of, *146*, 148
global yields from, *146*
management of, 148
ocean currents and, 7
production of, 7, 325, *328–329*
regional division of, 147–148
sustainable yield of, 145–148
Florida, urban nonpoint pollution in, 137
Food
access to, 51, 53–54
awards for work related to increasing supply of, 63
donations of, 271, *278–279*
index of per capita production of, 53
patterns in self-sufficiency of, 271
population growth implications for production of, 18–19
production, 51–53, 271, *272–273*
trade statistics, 271, *278–279*
see also Agriculture; Croplands
Food aid, 271, *278–279*
Food and Agriculture Organization, United Nations (FAO)
Agricultural Rehabilitation Programme for Africa of, 82
data on land cover trends by, 263
degradation recovery projects of, 216
farming systems research support by, 57
fisheries data by, 145, 146, 147–148
integrated pest management promotion by, 205
land use estimates by, 19, 42, 263
pesticide control study by, 29
plant species conservation work by, 293
rangeland estimates by, 78–79
sustainable fish harvest estimate by, 14, 143, 145, 146
wood production forecasts by, 75
Ford Foundation, 55
Forest Resources Assessment, 285

Forests, 4
acidic deposition effects on, 75–76, 285, *290*, 333
condition of and trends in, 69–74
decline in European, 75–76, 285, *290*
extent and distribution of world, 70–71
fires consuming (in selected countries, 1975–80), 285, *290*
management systems for, 84–85
production of wood products from, 285, *288–289*
status and deforestation of, 285, *286–287*
types of, 69–70
see also Wood
Fossil fuels
carbon dioxide emissions from combustion of, 333
trends in production and consumption of, 109, 305, *306–310*
see also individual fuels
France
cereal exports by, 271, *278–279*
lead levels in, 8
nuclear power in, 111
Freshwater
availability, 6, 127–130, *318–319*
catchment ponds for livestock, 82
factors affecting availability of (for individual countries), 129–130
increasing efficiency in use of, 132–133
interbasin transfers of, 133
pricing, 132, 133, 206
quality of river (1970–85), *320–321*
reallocation, 131–132
total annual availability and use, *128*
see also Drinking water; Groundwater
Fuelwood
deforestation for, 71, 75, 111
restoration of drylands and, 223
shortages of, 109, 111
as source of energy, 5, 111

Ganges River (India), water allocation from, 129, 132
Gapare, Robinson Lysias, 63
General Foods Fund, Inc., 63
Geographical Information System (GIS), 73, 200
German Democratic Republic, 120
energy-related pollution in, 121
energy trends in, 117
income distribution in, 235
Germany, Federal Republic of
acidic deposition in, 75–76, 285, 333
air pollution sources, 167, 168
incinerating hazardous wastes at sea by, 325
migration patterns in, 39
nuclear power in, 111
renewable energy in, 112
Geothermal energy, 114
Ghana
cocoa pricing policy in, 208
national forestry reviews conducted in, 84
Global Assessment of Soil Degradation, 217
Global Energy and Water Cycle Experiment (GEWEX), 188
Global Environmental Monitoring System (GEMS), 14, 171
Global Information and Early Warning Systems (GIEWS), 63–64

Global Precipitation Climatology Project (GPCP), 188
Global Resource Information Database, 200
Global Trade Model (GTM), 75–76
Grainger, Alan, 76
Grasslands. *See* Rangelands
Great Barrier Reef Marine Park (Australia), 7, 143, 149–150
Greece, renewable energy in, 112
Green Revolution, 205, 207
building on, 3–4, 60–63
strategy of, 56
unintended outcomes of, 12, 51, 56–57
Greenhouse effect, 9, 333, *334–336*
causes of, 188–190
impacts, 172, 173–175, 190–192
trends in concentration and emissions of gases causing, 333, *334–336*
Greenpeace, 157
Gross domestic product (GDP), agriculture's contribution to, 41
Gross national product (GNP)
official development assistance and (by country), *236–237*
ratios of energy to, 6, 305
relationship to urbanization of, 263
Groundwater
for livestock production, 82
pollution, 9, 130, 135–137
see also Drinking water; Freshwater
Guadalquiver River (Spain), 317
Guanacaste National Park (Costa Rica), restoration in, 220, 224
Guesselbodi forest reserve (Niger), 225
Guri Dam (Venezuela), 112

Habitats
conservation of, 293
of humans defining wilderness areas, 263
island, 95–96
loss of wildlife, 5, 14, 89
Haiti
AIDS in, 28
deforestation and water availability in 193, 228
Hallet, Jean-Pierre, 63
Harvard Institute for International Development, 28
Hazardous waste
generation data, *314*
ocean disposal of, 325
see also Waste
Health, 2, 15–16
air pollution's effects on, 8, 173, 175
animal, 82
data on population and, 245, *246–260*
impacts of Chernobyl accident, 123–124
impact of safe drinking water and sanitation access on, 245
indicators (by region), *24*
maternal and child, 2, 25, 245, *254–255*
nutrition's impacts on, 245, *250–251*
ozone depletion's impact on human, 175
personnel attending births (percentages by country), *254–255*
pesticide use and, 28–31, 271
trends in world, 24–27
tropospheric pollutants impacts on human, 173
see also Malnutrition
Heavy metal, pollution in OECD countries, 317

Index

Rogers, Marianne, 63
Romania
  energy trends in, 117
  fossil fuel reserves in, 119–120
Rural areas
  energy development in, 113
  migration from, 267
  nonpoint pollution in, 135, 137
  population in, *266–267*
  poverty of people living in, 263
  strategic value of, 44

S

São Paulo, Brazil, commercial and economic
  activity in, 3, 41
Salinization, 225–226, 317
Sanitation, access to, 245, *252–253*
Saudi Arabia
  freshwater availability in, 129
  official development assistance donations
    by, 235
Scandinavia
  acidic deposition in, 333
  health impacts of Chernobyl accident in,
    85, 123
  maternal mortality rates in, 25
  Sami culture of, 85
  see also Europe; Western Europe;
    individual countries in
Sedjo, Roger, 76
Sedimentation
  from drainage basins (annual discharge),
    193
  in rivers and lakes, 137–138
Senegal
  pesticide-use subsidies in, 204
  traditionally based rangeland projects in,
    84
  water development projects in, 82
Settlements, human
  trends in, 2–3, 35–39, 263, *264–268*
  see also Cities; Land use; Rural areas;
    Urbanization
Shanghai, China
  commercial and economic activity in, 41
  waste recycling in, 46–47
Shanghai Resource Recovery and Utilization
  Company (SRRUC), 46–47
Sherman, Kenneth, 146
Singapore
  family planning program in, 12
  fertility reduction efforts in, 22
  marine environment assessment by, 14
Sierra Club, global survey of wilderness areas
  by, 104, 263
Sierra Leone, 24
Smith, Philip L., 63
Soil erosion. *See* Erosion
Solar Energy Research Institute (Colorado),
  140
Solar power, 113–114
South America
  malarial parasite resistance to conventional
    drugs in, 31
  pesticide bans in, 31
  urbanization in, 36–39
  see also individual countries in
South Asia
  biotic carbon dioxide emissions from, 333
  fertilizer use in, 207
  food access in, 53–54
  freshwater availability in, 129

landless people in, 271
per capita food production in, 3
rangeland conditions in, 79, *80*
wetlands loss in, 263
see also Asia; individual countries in
Southeast Asia
  biotic carbon dioxide emissions from, 333
  habitat loss in, 5, 14, 91, 94
  landless people in, 271
  loss of wildlife habitat in, 14
  malaria incidence in, 26, 31
  see also Asia; individual countries in
South Korea. *See* Korea, Republic of
Spain
  AIDS in, 28
  renewable energy in, 112
  water pollution in, 9, 317
Sri Lanka
  deforestation in, 13, 71
  family planning in, 12, 245
  rangeland condition in, 79
State Science and Technology Commission
  (China), 131, 132
Strategies
  government fertility reduction, 21–23
  human settlement conditions improvement
    promotion, 47–48
  pollution control, 138–139
Sub-Saharan Africa
  AIDS in, 27, 28
  energy consumption in, 305
  external debt of countries in, 235
  fuelwood use in, 111
  habitat loss in, 5
  malaria incidence in, 26
  per capita food production in, 3
  rainfed drylands in, 61
  rangeland projects in, 4
  see also Africa; individual countries in
Subsidies
  agricultural input, 6, 9–10, 204–208
  for participation in watershed management
    and mountain rehabilitation, 221
  see also Incentives
Sudan
  food aid given to, 271, *278–279*
  freshwater withdrawal by, 317
  fuelwood use in, 111
  national forestry reviews conducted in, 84
Sulfur dioxide
  ambient levels of, 165
  concentrations in urban areas, *166, 167,*
    338–340
  sources and emissions of, 163–165
Superconductivity, possible energy applications from advances in, 6, 124–125
Suspended particulate matter. *See* Particulates
Sustainable development
  incorporating biological diversity, 99–103
  in forest management, 85
  in world fisheries, 145–148, 325
Swaminathan, M.S., 63
Sweden
  energy conservation in, 123
  health impacts of Chernobyl accident in,
    85, 123
  infant mortality rates in, 25
  radioactive contamination of rangeland in,
    85
Switzerland, 235
Syria, 12

T

Taiwan, 12
Tanzania
  AIDS in, 28
  oil products prices in, 110
  rangeland degradation in, 19
Technologies
  combining traditional and new pastoral
    techniques, 82–84
  Green Revolution, 3–4, 51, 56, 60–63
  matching needs in rehabilitation projects,
    227–228
Teheran, Iran, 14
Thailand
  agricultural subsidies in, 208, 209
  contraceptive use in, 245
  cultivation of cassava in, 209
  cultivation of rice in, 60, 209
  marine environment assessment by, 14
  migration patterns in, 39
Third World. *See* Developing countries
Thirty Percent Club, 163, 177–178
Three Gorges Dam (China), 112
Tiber River, 317
Tolba, Mostafa, 217
Tokyo, Japan
  acceptance of substitute for endangered
    wildlife product in, 99
  wastewater reuse in, 132
Total fertility rates (TFRs), 17, 21, *22,* 31
Trace Gases, sources, emissions, and ambient
  levels of important, 170–172, 333, *335–336*
Trade
  food, 235, 271, *278–279*
  in fossil fuel commodities, 109, 120, 124
  Iran-Iraq war and oil, 124
  in wildlife and wildlife products (CITES-
    reported, 1985), 5, 293, *298–299*
  wood and wood products, 5, 75–78
Transportation
  energy conservation strategies for, 6,
    122–123
  energy intensity in, 116–117
Treaties
  participation in international protection (by
    country, 1988), *348–349*
  see also individual agreements; conven-
    tions; and protocols
TROPFORM, 76–77
Tropical Forest Resources Assessment, 285
Tropical Forestry Action Plan (TFAP), 4, 84

U

Uganda
  AIDS in, 28
  Geographical Information System in, 200
Union of Soviet Socialist Republics (U.S.S.R.)
  energy trends in, 6, 109, 110, 111, 115, 116,
    117–119
  industrial carbon dioxide emissions in, 333
  oil, natural gas, and coal consumption in
    (by sector, 1970–87), 119
  population growth in, 245
  primary energy production in (by fuel type,
    1970–85), *118*
  "project of the century" cancellation in,
    133, 138
  wilderness areas in, 263

World Resources Institute

1735 New York Avenue, N.W.
Washington, D.C. 20006, U.S.A.

The World Resources Institute (WRI) is a research and policy center helping governments, international organizations, the private sector, and others address a fundamental question: How can societies meet human needs and nurture economic growth while preserving the natural resources and environmental integrity on which life, economic vitality, and international security depend?

Through its policy studies, WRI aims to present accurate information about global resources and environmental conditions, analysis of emerging issues, and development of creative yet workable policy responses. In seeking to deepen public understanding, it publishes a variety of reports and papers, undertakes briefings, seminars, and conferences, and offers material for use in the press and on the air.

In developing countries, WRI provides field services and technical support for governments and nongovernmental organizations that are trying to manage natural resources sustainably.

WRI's projects are now directed at two principal concerns:
■ the destructive effects of poor resource management on economic development and the alleviation of poverty in developing countries; and
■ the new generation of globally important environmental and resource problems that threaten the economic and environmental interests of the United States and many other countries.

Independent and nonpartisan, the World Resources Institute has four research programs: Conservation of Forests and Biological Diversity; Climate, Energy and Pollution; Economics and Institutions; and Resource and Environmental Information. Within WRI is the Center for International Development and Environment (CIDE), formerly the International Institute for Environment and Development—North America (IIED-NA), which provides policy advice and technical support for developing countries.

WRI's work is carried out by an 85-member interdisciplinary staff, strong in the sciences and economics, augmented by a network of formal advisors, collaborators, international fellows, and cooperating institutions in more than 50 countries.

WRI is funded by private foundations, United Nations and governmental agencies, corporations, and concerned individuals.

IIED

International Institute for Environment and Development

The International Institute for Environment and Development (IIED) is a global organization, established in 1968 to further the wise use of natural resources as necessary to economic growth that serves basic human needs. Inspired by the renowned British economist and humanitarian Barbara Ward, who became the Institute's President in 1972, IIED has made sustainable development its guiding principle.

IIED's programs include policy research, information and field activities. The Institute draws its staff from around the world and operates from offices in London and Buenos Aires. The work of the Institute reaches from forests and fisheries to the overcrowded living conditions in Third World cities, from the Antarctic to the tropics, finding the means for renewable energy and sustainable agriculture.

All IIED's activities ultimately concern development; the process involves working alongside the people of the developing world in partnership with them. IIED's research is rigorous, scientific, and pioneering. Its origins and applications in the field come from direct interaction with nongovernmental organizations as well as public policymakers in developing countries. The objective of the IIED process is to enable its partners to become self-reliant and to improve their livelihoods on a sustainable basis.

IIED's Earthscan information service publishes books, through Earthscan Publishing Ltd., and articles that reflect the concerns of the developing world. It provides nongovernmental organizations in the Third World with an information network linked to their specific programs and offers them technical assistance.

IIED is funded by private and corporate foundations, international organizations, governments, and concerned individuals.

Europe
3 Endsleigh Street
London, WC1H 0DD, England

Latin America
Corrientes 2835,
Cuerpo A6 Piso
1193 Buenos Aires, Argentina

IIED's Board of Directors:
Robert O. Anderson, *Chairman*
Abdlatif Y. Al-Hamad, *Vice Chairman*
Garret FitzGerald
Katsohiro Kotari
Thomas A. Lambo
Waldemar Nielsen
Arthur Norman
Saburo Okita
Shridath Ramphal
Jack Raymond
Azad Shivdasani
Emil Salim

Officers:
Brian W. Walker, *President*
Richard Sandbrook, *Director*, Europe
Jorge E. Hardoy, *Director*, Latin America

United Nations Environment Programme

P.O. Box 30552
Nairobi, Kenya

Executive Director
Mostafa K. Tolba

Deputy Executive Director
William H. Mansfield III

Regional and Liaison Offices

Latin America and the Caribbean:
UNEP Regional Office for Latin America and Caribbean
Edificio de Naciones Unidas
Presidente Mazaryk 29
Apartado Postal 6-718
Mexico 5, D.F., Mexico

West Asia:
UNEP Regional Office for West Asia
1083 Road No. 425
Jufair 342
P.O. Box 26814
Manama, Bahrain

Asia and the Pacific:
UNEP Regional Office for Asia and the Pacific
United Nations Building
Rajadamnern Avenue
Bangkok 10200, Thailand

Europe:
UNEP Regional Office for Europe
Palais des Nations
CH-1211 Geneva 10, Switzerland

Africa:
UNEP Regional Office for Africa
UNEP Headquarters
P.O. Box 30552
Nairobi, Kenya

New York:
UNEP Liaison Office
UNDC Two Building
Room 0803
Two, United Nations Plaza
New York, New York 10017, U.S.A.

Washington:
UNEP Liaison Office
Ground Floor
1889 F Street, N.W.
Washington, D.C. 20006, U.S.A.

The United Nations Environment Programme (UNEP) was established in 1972 and given by the United Nations General Assembly a broad and challenging mandate to stimulate, coordinate and provide policy guidance for sound environmental action throughout the world. UNEP developed out of the largely nongovernmental and antipollution lobby in industrialized countries. This interest in pollutants remains, but as perceptions of environmental problems broadened to encompass those arising from the misuse and abuse of renewable natural resources, the promotion of environmentally sound or sustainable development also became a main purpose of UNEP.

From the global headquarters in Nairobi, Kenya, and seven regional and liaison offices worldwide, UNEP's staff of some 200 scientists, administrators, and information specialists carry out UNEP's program, which is laid down and revised every two years by a Governing Council of representatives from its 58 member states. These members are elected on a staggered basis for three years by the United Nations General Assembly.

Broadly, this program aims to stimulate research into major environmental problems, promote environmentally sound management at both national and international levels by encouraging the application of the research results, and make such actions and findings known to the public—from scientists and policymakers to industrialists and school children.

By the terms of its mandate UNEP runs its program in cooperation with numerous other United Nations agencies, governments, intergovernmental organizations, and nongovernmental organizations. It focuses on climate change, pollution, water resources, desertification control, forests, oceans, human settlements, renewable sources of energy, environmentally sound management of industry, and international environmental lawmaking.

The essential base for environmentally sound management is provided by UNEP's work on the monitoring and assessment of the state and trends of the global environment. This is carried out in conjunction with agency partners, through the Global Environment Monitoring System (GEMS). The Global Resource Information Database (GRID), an element of GEMS, stores and analyzes geographically referenced environmental and resource data, and provides the essential link between monitoring and assessment and sound environmental management by putting information in forms useful to planners and managers. GEMS, the Geneva based International Register of Potentially Toxic Chemicals, and INFOTERRA provide both the international community and individual countries and organizations with vital environmental information they need to take action.